Handbook of
THE
PSYCHOLOGY
OF AGING

THE HANDBOOKS OF AGING

Consisting of Three Volumes:

Critical comprehensive reviews of
research knowledge, theories,
concepts, and issues

Editor-in-Chief: **James E. Birren**

Handbook of the Biology of Aging

Edited by Caleb E. Finch and Edward L. Schneider

Handbook of the Psychology of Aging

Edited by James E. Birren and K. Warner Schaie

Handbook of Aging and the Social Sciences

Edited by Robert H. Binstock and Ethel Shanas

Handbook of
THE PSYCHOLOGY OF AGING

Second Edition

Editors
James E. Birren
K. Warner Schaie

With the assistance of Associate Editors
Vern Bengtson
Lissy Jarvik
Timothy Salthouse

and Editorial Coordinator
Donna E. Deutchman

VNR VAN NOSTRAND REINHOLD COMPANY
———————————————— New York

105614

Copyright © 1985 by Van Nostrand Reinhold Company Inc.

Library of Congress Catalog Card Number : 84-25598
ISBN: 0–442–21401–4

Manufactured in the United States of America

Published by Van Nostrand Reinhold Company Inc.
135 West 50th Street
New York, New York 10020

Van Nostrand Reinhold Company Limited
Molly Millars Lane
Workingham, Berkshire RG11 2PY, England

Van Nostrand Reinhold
480 Latrobe Street
Melbourne, Victoria 3000, Australia

Macmillan of Canada
Division of Gage Publishing Limited
164 Commander Boulevard
Agincourt, Ontario MIS 3C7, Canada

15 14 13 12 11 10 9 8 7 6 5 4 3 2

Library of Congress Cataloging in Publication Data
Main entry under title:
Handbook of the psychology of aging.
 (The handbooks of aging)
 Includes index.
 1. Aging—Psychological aspects. I. Birren, James E. II. Schaie, K. Warner (Klaus Warner), 1928– . III. Series.
BF724.55.A35H36 1985   155.67   84–25598
ISBN 0–442–21401–4

CONTRIBUTORS

Rhonda Aizenberg, Ph.D.
Head of Traffic Safety Research Group, Public Safety Department, Engineering and Technical Services Division, Automobile Club of Southern California, Los Angeles, California

Martin Albert, M.D.
Professor of Neurology; Director, Behavioral Neurosciences and Geriatric Neurology, Boston University School of Medicine and Veterans Administration Medical Center, Boston, Massachusetts

Ralph A. Alexander, Ph.D.
Fellow, Institute of Life Span Development and Gerontology; Associate Professor, Department of Psychology, The University of Akron, Akron, Ohio

Gene Bammel, Ph.D.
Director, Self-Learning Center; Professor of Leisure Studies, Division of Forestry, West Virginia University, West Virginia

Gerald V. Barret, Ph.D.
Professor and Head, Department of Psychology, The University of Akron, Akron, Ohio

Vern L. Bengtson, Ph.D.
Professor of Sociology; Director, Gerontology Research Institute, University of Southern California, Los Angeles, California

William Bondareff, M.D., Ph.D.
Director, Geriatric Psychiatry, Department of Psychiatry/Medicine, University of Southern California, Los Angeles, California

Lei Lane Burrus-Bammel, Ph.D.
Professor of Leisure Studies, Division of Forestry, West Virginia University, West Virginia

Paul T. Costa, Ph.D.
Chief, Section on Stress and Coping, Laboratory of Behavioral Sciences, Gerontology Research Center, Baltimore, Maryland

Walter R. Cunningham, Ph.D.
Associate Professor, Psychology Department, University of Florida, Gainesville, Florida

Connie Dessonville, Ph.D.
NIMH Postdoctoral Fellow, Department of Psychiatry and Biobehavioral Sciences, University of California, Los Angeles, California

John M. Eiler, Ph.D.
Department of Psychology, Clinical Aging Program, University of Southern California, Los Angeles, California

Terryl T. Foch, Ph.D.
Assistant Professor of Human Development, College of Human Development, Department of Individual and Family Studies, The Pennsylvania State University, University Park, Pennsylvania

Christine L. Fry, Ph.D.
Professor of Anthropology, Department of Sociology and Anthropology, Loyola University of Chicago, Chicago, Illinois

Margaret Gatz, Ph.D.
Associate Professor, Department of Psychology and Senior Staff Associate, Andrus Gerontology Center, University of Southern California, Los Angeles, California

Chad Gordon, Ph.D.
Professor of Sociology, Department of Sociology, Rice University, Houston, Texas

Stephen W. Harkins, Ph.D.
Associate Professor and Director, Gerontology Psychophysiology Laboratory, Gerontology, Psychiatry, and Psychology, Medical College of Virginia, Virginia Commonwealth University, Richmond, Virginia

Marla Hassinger, M.A.
Ph.D. Candidate, Department of Psychology, Clinical Aging Program, University of Southern California, Los Angeles, California

Christopher Hertzog, Ph.D.
Assistant Professor of Human Development, Department of Individual and Family Studies, The Pennsylvania State University, University Park, Pennsylvania

Lissy Jarvik, M.D., Ph.D.
Professor, Department of Psychiatry and Biobehavioral Sciences, Neuropsychiatric Institute/UCLA and Chief, Psychogeriatric Unit, West Los Angeles Veterans Administration Medical Center, Brentwood Division, Los Angeles, California

Robert J. Kastenbaum, Ph.D.
Professor of Gerontology and Director, Adult Development and Aging Program, Arizona State University, Tempe, Arizona

Bryan Kemp, Ph.D.
Co-Chief, Clinical Gerontology Service and Director, Rehabilitation Research and Training Center on Aging, Rancho Los Amigos Hospital; Clinical Associate Professor of Psychology and Assistant Research Professor, Ethel Percy Andrus Gerontology Center, University of Southern California, Los Angeles, California

Donald Kline, Ph.D.
Co-Director, Aging Program and Associate Professor, Department of Psychology, University of Notre Dame, Notre Dame, Indiana

Erich W. Labouvie, Ph.D.
Associate Professor of Psychology, Center of Alcohol Studies and Department of Psychology, Rutgers, The State University, New Brunswick, New Jersey

Gisela Labouvie-Vief, Ph.D.
Professor, Department of Psychology, Wayne State University, Detroit, Michigan

Asenath La Rue, Ph.D.
Assistant Professor, Department of Psychiatry and Biobehavioral Sciences, University of California, Los Angeles; Research Psychologist, West Los Angeles Veterans Administration Medical Center, Los Angeles, California

Sonne Lemke, Ph.D.
Psychologist and Research Associate, Social Ecology Laboratory and Geriatric Research, Education and Clinical Center, Veterans Administration Medical Center, Palo Alto, California

Martin L. Lenhardt, Ph.D.
Director, Bioacoustics Laboratory, Associate Professor of Otolaryngology and Pediatric Dentistry, Virginia Commonwealth University, Richmond, Virginia

Gerald E. McClearn, Ph.D.
Professor of Human Development, College of Human Development, Department of Individual and Family Studies, The Pennsylvania State University, University Park, Pennsylvania

Rudolf H. Moos, Ph.D.
Research Career Scientist and Professor, Veterans Administration and Stanford University Medical Centers, Palo Alto, California

John R. Nesselroade, Ph.D.
Professor of Human Development, College of Human Development, Department of Individual and Family Studies, The Pennsylvania State University, University Park, Pennsylvania

Janice E. Newberry, M.S., P.T.
Director of Physical Therapy, Chesterfield County Nursing Home, Chesterfield, Virginia

Loraine Obler, Ph.D.
Associate Professor, Department of Neurology, Boston University School of Medicine and Boston Veterans Administration Medical Center, Boston, Massachusetts

Alfred L. Ochs, Ph.D.
Assistant Professor of Neurology, Neuro-opthamology Division, Medical College of Virginia, Virginia Commonwealth University, Richmond, Virginia

Lynne Werner Olsho, Ph.D.
Assistant Professor, Department of Psychology, Virginia Commonwealth University, Richmond, Virginia

Christopher D. Pino
Ph.D. Candidate, Yale University, New Haven, Connecticut

Leonard W. Poon, Ph.D.
Director, Mental Performance and Aging Laboratory, Veterans Administration Outpatient Clinic and Harvard Medical School, Boston, Massachusetts

Samuel Popkin, Ph.D.
Geropsychiatry Fellow, Neuropsychiatric Institute, University of California, Los Angeles, California

Margaret Reedy, Ph.D.
Clinical Psychologist, Pacific Coast Psychological Center, Long Beach, California

Hayne W. Reese, Ph.D.
Centennial Professor of Psychology and Coordinator of Graduate Training in Life-Span Developmental Psychology, Department of Psychology, West Virginia University, Morgantown, Virginia

Dean Rodeheaver, Ph.D.
Assistant Professor, Human Development, College of Human Biology, University of Wisconsin–Green Bay, Green Bay, Wisconsin

Leopold Rosenmayr, Ph.D.
Professor, Institute of Sociology, University of Vienna; Director, Ludwig Boltzman Institute for Social Gerontology and Life Span Research, Vienna Austria

Timothy Salthouse, Ph.D.
Associate Professor, Department of Psychology, University of Missouri, Columbia, Missouri

K. Warner Schaie, Ph.D.
Professor of Human Development and Psychology, Department of Individual and Family Studies, The Pennsylvania State University, University Park, Pennsylvania

Rick J. Scheidt, Ph.D.
Associate Professor, Department of Family and Child Development, Kansas State University, Manhattan, Kansas

Frank Schieber, Ph.D.
(Experimental Psychologist) Senior Systems Analyst, Soft-Chip Technology, Inc., South Bend, Indiana

Richard Schulz, Ph.D.
Associate Professor of Psychiatry, Director of Gerontology, University of Pittsburgh, Pittsburgh, Pennsylvania

Ilene C. Siegler, Ph.D.
Associate Professor of Medical Psychology, Department of Psychiatry, Duke University Medical Center;

Senior Fellow, Duke University Center for the Study of Aging and Human Development, Durham, North Carolina

Ross Stagner, Ph.D.
Emeritus Professor of Psychology and Faculty Associate, Institute of Gerontology, Wayne State University, Detroit, Michigan

Harvey L. Sterns, Ph.D.
Associate Professor of Psychology, Director and Fellow, Institute for Life-Span Development and Gerontology, The University of Akron; Research Associate Professor of Gerontology in Community Health Sciences, Northeastern Ohio Universities College of Medicine, Akron, Ohio

Judith Treas, Ph.D.
Associate Professor of Sociology and Research Associate, Andrus Gerontology Center, University of Southern California, Los Angeles, California

Gary R. VandenBos, Ph.D.
Visiting Professor of Clinical Psychology, Institute of Clinical Psychology, University of Bergen, Bergen, Norway

Susan Krauss Whitbourne, Ph.D.
Associate Professor, Education and Psychology, Center for Counseling, Family and Worklife Studies, Graduate School of Education and Human Development, University of Rochester, Rochester, New York

Sherry L. Willis, Ph.D.
Associate Professor of Human Development, College of Human Development, Department of Individual and Family Studies, The Pennsylvania State University, University Park, Pennsylvania

Paul G. Windley, Arch.D.
Professor, Department of Architecture, Kansas State University, Manhattan, Kansas

Diana S. Woodruff, Ph.D.
Professor of Psychology, Department of Psychology, Temple University, Philadelphia, Pennsylvania

Steven H. Zarit, Ph.D.
Associate Professor of Gerontology and Psychology, Ethel Percy Andrus Gerontology Center, University of Southern California, Los Angeles, California

PREFACE

This volume is focused on the psychology of adult development and aging. As a handbook, it is designed to provide the reader with chapters written by experts over the wide range of topics that currently comprise the field.

Since the publication of the first edition of this book, the National Institute on Aging as well as the programs on aging of the National Institute of Mental Health have had a marked influence on the encouragement of research on aging. For this reason, this edition reflects the rapid growth of the psychology of aging as a field of research and practice. Many countries have now established institutes of gerontology within which to conduct research on aging. Also, many new programs of education that focus on aging have been organized during the past decade in institutions of higher learning. Thus, the subject matter is becoming a mainline concern of many disciplines, and the volume of published literature has risen exponentially. Probably by the year 2000 almost all disciplines will have a specialty or subspecialty that relates to organized knowledge and research on the processes of aging. The present publication represents this growth and includes up-to-date research in well established as well as emerging areas of the psychology of aging.

This second edition of *The Handbook of the Psychology of Aging* was designed to meet the same purpose as the first edition: to provide an authoritative review and reference source of the scientific and professional literature on the psychological and behavioral aspects of aging. It has been motivated by the positive response accorded to the first edition and also by the need to take into account the growth of the literature, which might be described as massive. The aging of individuals and the aging of societies are topics that are increasingly occupying the central focus in research. This edition provides chapters on the applications of psychological knowledge to issues affecting both individuals and society as a whole. It has been noted that few attempts have been made in the past to seek out the instructive applications of psychological research. Thus, following the chapters that report on advances in knowledge of basic behavioral processes, this edition takes a look at intervention strategies and the applications of knowledge to specific problems.

Although the growth of published literature continues to be impressive, the growth of research is not uniform. For this reason, chapters of the first edition that are regarded as still representing the current state of knowledge have not been revised. Readers are encouraged, therefore, to use the first edition in concert with the present one to obtain an even more comprehensive coverage of topics. The intention of the *Handbook* is to serve as a definitive reference source for graduate students, researchers, and professionals. For this reason, the basic behavioral processes— from primary sensory phenomena to personality and behavior disorders—are covered. Basically, the task of the various authors is to describe and explain the changes in behavior and capacities that occur with advancing age. Explanation involves causal attributions to generational differences, historical events, and biological and social determinants.

Although the dominant emphasis is on research concerning human behavior, there is material on other animal species. In fact, it is expected that in the coming years more effort will be devoted to obtaining suitable animal models for carrying out research that has relevance to humans but cannot be carried out directly on human subjects.

The Editors for the second edition are Dr. James E. Birren and Dr. K. Warner Schaie; Associate Editors are Dr. Vern Bengtson, Dr. Lissy Jarvik, and Dr. Timothy Salthouse. These individuals plus Dr. Jack Botwinick formed an editorial committee at the onset of planning for the second edition and made recommendations about the areas to be covered and individuals to be asked to submit chapters. After the chapters were received, an Editor and one Associate Editor read each of the chapters, and their responses were given to the chapter authors for consideration in making revisions. Acceptance of material was the responsibility of the two Co-Editors. It was not the responsibility of the Associate Editors to make final decisions concerning the inclusion of the 32 chapters that comprise this volume. When there were differing opinions about subtopics to be covered, emphasis, or order of presentation, the choices, insofar as possible, were left to the authors in accordance with the opinion that their efforts and judgment must be respected since all critical opinion may be heavily influenced by currently dominant, but transient, scientific attitudes.

Grateful acknowledgement is given to Donna E. Deutchman who served as Editorial Coordinator for this volume and carried out the many responsibilities for processing the manuscripts and proofs and for serving as liaison between the editors, authors, and publishers. Acknowledgement is also gratefully expressed to Eleanor James and Sherry Wilson, who provided administrative assistance at many points during the publication process. In addition, Julie Stafford is thanked for her reviews of selected chapter drafts, and Bonnie Hedlund is thanked for her assistance in indexing the volume.

Psychology of aging is one of the areas in which researchers and professionals have much to contribute to advances in knowledge gained through research as well as to applications for enhancing the quality of life for millions of mature persons and for the well-being of our society. Its contributors trust that this edition as well as the previous one will advance the organization of research, the teaching of the subject matter of adult development and aging, and the improvement of human services.

JAMES E. BIRREN
K. WARNER SCHAIE

CONTENTS

PART FOUR

Behavioral Processes

PART SIX

Psychological Applications to Society

Handbook of
THE PSYCHOLOGY OF AGING

PART 1 THEORY AND METHODS IN THE PSYCHOLOGY OF AGING

1
RESEARCH ON THE PSYCHOLOGY OF AGING:
Principles, Concepts and Theory

James E. Birren
University of Southern California
and
Walter R. Cunningham
University of Florida

INTRODUCTION

Time is the messenger of the gods, a messenger who passes through space, matter, energy, and minds. This metaphor is meant to capture the ubiquity of time not only in the process of aging but as a pervasive factor in the organization of all phenomena and their explanations (see Fraser, 1966).

This chapter attempts to provide an orientation and perspective on research in the psychology of adult development and aging as well as to serve as an introduction to the chapters that follow, in which the state of research and knowledge on a wide range of subtopics will be reviewed. Activity and research in this field continues to grow at a rapid pace. This was noted in the 1977 edition of the *Handbook of the Psychology of Aging* (Birren and Renner, 1977), in which it was estimated that there was a doubling of the total volume of published literature over a 15-year period. The period for this rate of doubling has now decreased to 10 years. A 1983 review of the subject for the *Annual Review of Psychology* (Birren, Cunningham, and Yamamoto, 1983) pointed out that it was increasingly difficult to embrace the field as a whole, not only for theoretical reasons, but also because of the practical fact that the volume of published research has increased to the almost unmanageable total of over a thousand articles a year.

Psychology has many scientific traditions: biological, behavioral, and social. In addition, it has traditions of being experimental, descriptive, phenomenological, and clinical. A large volume of information from allied disciplines influences its subject matter as well. Such a range provides a fertile context for the subject but also makes it very difficult to present an integrated picture of the state of knowledge. The scope of the field and, more recently, the degree of its activity and research productivity have resulted in the creation of islands of knowledge with little communication between them. The theory for the most part is no more than microtheory, in areas of cognition, memory, perception, social roles, or selected aspects of emotions and personality. The psychology of the adult portion of the life span is a growth area of research and teaching into which new investigators are carrying the concepts and traditions of the subfields of their own background. Although this has led to a healthy input of new concepts and challenges, it is to be hoped that the field will not become ingrown with barriers to in-

3

formation exchange and transfers of research methods, design, and methods of data analysis.

The traditional question of psychology is, "How is behavior organized?" Increasingly this question is shifting to "How does behavior become organized?" One might also add the question of how behavior becomes disorganized for there is emerging a psychopathology of aging. Psychology for the most part has been attending to the identification of the elements of behavior, but increasingly it will turn to issues of differentiation, development, aging, and the disorganization of behavior.

THE TASK OF PSYCHOLOGY

The task of the psychology of adult development and aging is to explain how behavior becomes organized and, in selected instances, how it becomes disorganized. The organization of behavior from conception to death is the subject matter of ontogenetic psychology. In practice, ontogenetic psychology is divided into an early phase—the developmental psychology of childhood, adolescence, and young adulthood—and a second phase—middle and old age. Developmental psychology usually refers to the increasing differentiation of the organism up to the age of physical maturity. Whereas adult behavior can have antecedents in childhood and any distinctions between development and aging may be somewhat arbitrary, early development appears to be characterized by relatively rapid increases in size, form, and function with increasing age. After adolescence, changes in form and size are slow, though function continues to differentiate as the individual adapts to the environment and personal needs.

The fertilized egg appears to have purpose in systematically increasing its size and capacity for self-regulation. At the time of birth, the child is able to regulate some, if not yet all, of its vital processes without assistance from outside persons. Increasingly with age the child is able to regulate physiological processes as well as environmental interactions. In teleological terms, the purpose of the organism is to establish biological, behavioral, and social regulation so that it may function

through any perturbations of the physical and social environment without reductions that are risks to its survival. Although such a definition implies that the individual ceases to differentiate after adolescence, the basic question for ontogenetic psychology still remains how behavior becomes organized and differentiated over a lifespan.

DEFINITIONS

It is useful at this point to present some of the definitions and concepts that have influenced research on adult development and aging. Many articles and books are written about aging without any reference to the definition of aging that guided the thinking of the authors. It is perhaps more common than not that definitions of aging are avoided with the tacit assumption that most people believe themselves to be considering the same phenomena. An examination of three previous handbooks of aging (Finch and Hayflick, 1977; Birren and Schaie, 1977; Binstock and Shanas, 1976) suggests, however, that there is a hierarchy in which biologists provide definitions of aging most often, psychologists rarely, and social scientists almost never. This leads to the thought that aging and time as variables enjoy a different status among the sciences. Undoubtedly, the lack of formal definitions helps block articulation of knowledge between the various sciences that study aging.

Cowdry (1942, p. 15) gave a statement that represents an informal definition of aging, "Since almost all living organisms pass through a sequence of changes, characterized by growth, development, maturation and finally senescence, ageing presents a broad biological problem." Apparently there is an assumption among biologists that they are studying the length of life of an organism. For example, Cowdry's following quotation of Jenning's definition clearly identifies the length of life as a dependent variable: "There can be no doubt then in all animals from the single-celled protozoa through the invertebrates to man, the length of life is largely determined by inheritance." (Cowdry, 1952, p. 56). Cowdry further distinguished two main points of view not unlike those that exist in psychology: "Two conflicting views are held by students of aging and man. One considers aging as an involuntary process which operates cumulatively with the passage of time and is revealed in different organ systems as inevitable modifications of cells, tissues, and fluids. The other view interprets the changes found in aged organs as structural alterations due to infections, toxins, traumas, and nutritional disturbances or inadequacies giving rise to what are called degenerative changes and impairments." (Cowdry, 1942, p. 16). Thus what we have contrasted here is an endogenous versus an exogenous view of aging that is similar to the nurture versus nature viewpoints in developmental psychology.

Some biologists have offered narrower definitions of aging than did Cowdry. According to Comfort: "Senescence is a change in the behavior of the organism with age, which leads to a decreased power of survival and adjustment" (Comfort, 1956, p. 190). Notice that the word *senescence* was used in place of aging to narrow the implications of the definition. Handler (1960, p. 200) gave a still narrower definition of aging: "Aging is the deterioration of a mature organism resulting from time dependent, essentially irreversible changes intrinsic to all members of a species, such that, with the passage of time, they may become increasingly unable to cope with the stresses of the environment, thereby increasing the probability of death."

Here one sees the implication that the old organism can no longer self-regulate and adjust to the perturbations of the environment. Self-regulation, however, exists at three levels, *biological, behavioral,* and *social.* For this reason, Handler's definition, while precise, is too restrictive for psychologists for whom the organization of behavior over the life span implies outcomes in addition to the probability of dying.

Birren and Renner (1977, p. 4) have offered a general definition of aging for the behavioral sciences that recognizes that there can be incremental functions as well as decremental changes that occur over the adult life span: "Aging refers to the regular changes that occur in mature genetically representative organisms living under representative environ-

mental conditions." By introducing the phrase "genetically representative," one avoids mixing aging with unusual phenomena produced by rare genetic problems or by unusual environmental conditions that do not represent the typical pattern of a species.

Aging implies a representative organism living under representative conditions (see Birren, 1959a, pp. 26–30). The formal properties of definitions of aging involve one or more independent variables whose influence is thought to bring about the changes in the nature of frequency of the dependent variable over the life span of the individual organism.

Psychologists are much less likely than biologists to use length of life as their primary dependent variable. Nevertheless, we should not neglect the fact that ontogenetic psychology has a contribution to make in understanding why there is a characteristic shape to the mortality curve with age. Mortality rates are high for infants, regularly decline to a minimum at about age 10, and then rise progressively throughout the remainder of the life span. Psychologists are more often interested in aspects of behavior only some components of which may be related to length of life. For this reason, definitions of aging usually offered by biologists are too restrictive for psychologists who are interested not only in aspects of behavior that are related to life-limiting biological phenomena or to the probability of dying, but also to other aspects of behavior that may reveal increments in functional capacity or late-life differentiation.

Due to the fact that the quality or quantity of behavioral functions may show increments or decrements with the passage of time, the authors believe that either an exclusively biological or social definition of aging would be too narrow. They take the term "aging" to imply some typicalness of change over time. Consider, for example, the case of Antarctic penguins raised in a tropical environment. The changes in their physiological disease patterns as well as in their behavior with age might be expected to be very different from those exhibited in their "normal" environment. In like manner, a tropical mammal reared over a life span in the Antarctic might also be expected to show different patterns of change.

One of the classical approaches to the study of the behavior changes of animals with age is to keep them in small cages over their life span. Presumably the rat or mouse, both of which are wide-ranging animals when living in natural conditions, would be expected to show a very different pattern of change with age than when housed over a lifetime in such a way that their movements and sensory input are artifically restricted by the usual laboratory conditions. Similarly, germ-free environments created to prevent unusual infectious diseases may not be regarded as fostering "normal aging" in a biological sense since the animals might not show behavior with age that is typical of their species when living under conditions for which they were selected or adapted. Correspondingly, parasitic diseases or infectious diseases of the respiratory tract are not regarded as typical features of aging for the usual laboratory animal. Poor problem-solving ability in rats reared over a lifetime in restricted caging should not be regarded as a typical result of the way the species age. Conversely, experiments that enrich the environments of laboratory rats probably may not be regarded as a means of enhancing the species potential but rather of adding back something that was lost because of artificial laboratory conditions. In this vein, supplying the opportunity for environmental exploration is like supplying a vitamin to an artifically vitamin-restricted group of animals.

Thus typicalness of the genetic background of a species as well as typicalness of environmental circumstances both enter into the psychologist's attempt to identify the usual pattern of change for the species. To some extent there is a conflict of interest between behavioral scientists and biological scientists in controlling the environments in which laboratory animals live. Biologists wish to exclude extraneous pathogens and reduce genetic variability, whereas psychologists are primarily interested in having an organism live under conditions somewhat like those under which it evolved or is commonly found.

Diseases associated with age—such as cancer, cardiovascular disease, cerebrovascular disease, or kidney disease—are not necessarily primary manifestations of aging. They may be secondary manifestations of underlying biological processes that predispose organisms to the expression of any disease. In this sense, a general change in immune processes might be reflected in increased susceptibility to a number of diseases with advancing age. The typicalness of disposition to disease lies in the susceptibility resulting from a universal alteration in the organism.

METATHEORETICAL ISSUES

Throughout recorded history mankind has apparently thought not only about its own relatively limited life span but about immortality. Gruman (1966) reviewed the history of ideas about longevity and earlier beliefs about ways of defeating mortality and extending the life span. Legends about death, immortality, and aging are still a part of our culture today. Found in contemporary writing are echoes of early legends of healing waters and fountains, of people living in remote regions of the world who are very long-lived and possess vital secrets about life. There is also the legend that the people of ancient times not only lived longer than they do now but lost the secret of long life, if not of immortality, when they fell from grace.

It was the middle of the last century that modern experimental science began testing many of the older ideas about aging. Early thoughts about aging emphasized the replacement of lost characteristics. If an old animal became cold in the process of dying, one might rejuvenate it by providing heat. Benjamin Franklin thought that an organism lost some vital process with age that could be rejuvenated by electric shock. A similar focus on the replacement of lost characteristics is manifested by attempts at the rejuvenation of sexual activity. If the male animal shows a reduction in sexual activity in the later years, restitution of the sexual activities might make the animal increasingly long-lived. We know that such attempts at restitution do not necessarily engage an underlying mechanism that paces the human life cycle.

In his excellent book on image, Boulding (1956) notes two opposing forces in history. One of these is the tendency for organizations to run down and eventually become chaotic. Thermodynamically speaking, this tendency would be expressed by the Second Law. The end of the universe, according to this picture, will be a uniformly formless soup. The contrasting view is that there is a tendency for living organisms to differentiate and acquire increasing complexity with the passage of time. Boulding notes that in the course of the history of the universe we observe an increasing complexity of organization culminating at present in man and his societies (1956, p. 19). Whether or not there is a trend in the universe toward increasing organization or disorganization is well beyond the scope of this chapter. However, we should note the relevance of the concept of two opposing trends, one toward an increasing and the other toward a decreasing complexity of function of an organism with age. Perhaps the ultimate disorganization of an organism begins when the complex control mechanisms that exist in its central nervous system lose their effectiveness in maintaining the dynamic equilibrium necessary to adapt and survive changes in the physical and social environments.

If the task for general psychology is to explain how behavior *is* organized, the task for ontogenetic psychology is to explain how behavior *becomes* organized over the course of life. It should be pointed out that answering the question of how behavior is organized does not explain how it becomes less organized or disorganized. A clear illustration of this truth can be found in the conceptual revolution created in biology by Darwin's theory of evolution. Although his predecessors had classified the species and created the discipline of taxonomy, they failed to offer a theory of how the organization of the species had come about. Since evolutionary theory was a dynamic theory (one involving time), it had to wait, in turn, upon the discovery of the chemical structure of the gene before the mechanism of transmission of the controls over size, form, and functions of the members of a species could be identified.

It is suggested that as the various sciences become more mature (gain more facts and theory), their focus shifts from a description of structures to considerations of how structures evolve over time. The physical sciences in particular are not only occupied with explaining the organization of matter, but also how it becomes organized over time. Hierarchically, the behavioral sciences take as given the existence of the universe and its species and are only minimally concerned with theories about their genesis. The theory of evolution, of course, conflicted with the theogenetic interpretation that there was a special and nearly instantaneous creation of all things. However, it is appropriate to point out the hierarchical implications of the establishment of order in the following list.

1. *Theogenesis:* How did God, the gods, or the ultimate force come into being? Theological differences arise as a result of the way in which the God force is considered, whether as static or living and/or evolving.

2. *Cosmogenesis:* How did material things come into being? How was the universe established? Here physical science wrestles with theoretical issues of material origin as a result of a "big bang" or some other circumstance. An understanding of the evolving nature of the universe is also a goal of cosmogenesis.

3. *Phylogenesis:* How did the many species come to exist? This raises the question of the evolution and history of animal species.

4. *Coenogenesis:* How did mankind's institutions of social life come into being? What is their course over time? This relatively new term, *coenogenesis,* was introduced by Schroots (1983) to refer to the history of social institutions. The prefix *coeno* refers to things held in common. A corollary word would be *coenobium,* which refers to life in a community.

5. *Ontogenesis:* How did the individual come to be and what is the course of the individual existence? Ontogenesis implies the existence of previous structures and functions. Thus, the individual would not exist unless there was an antecedent phylum of which he was an individual representative, as well as of the institutions that had been created by previous members of the same phylum. The individual grows up and grows old under the control of his phylogenetic history, of his unique heredity, and of the particu-

lar culture into which he is born and lives. In a sense, the content of culture is in large part the equivalent of DNA; that is, culture is the DNA of society and contributes to the differentiated forms of behavior. The course of behavior over the life of an individual would appear to have three influences: the phylogenetic (or heredity), the cultural, and individual choice and adaptation. Thus, aging can also be viewed as resulting from these three forces, which supply the dynamic quality or direction to the entire course of life.

To emphasize the difference in the sets of variables, Schroots and Birren (1980) proposed that aging be viewed as consisting of three components. The process of biological aging, which resulted in increasing vulnerability and a higher probability of dying, was identified as *senescing*. Concurrent with senescing, individuals show *eldering* social roles appropriate to the expectations of society; that is, there are roles that are age-graded and that are typical of this part of the life span. Patterns of dress and speech are expected of persons of different ages in a society, and the social status accorded to individuals also differs at different ages. To these two processes, one should add psychological aging, called *geronting*. This is defined by the self-regulation the individual exercises, in a field of forces, by making decisions and choices in adapting to the processes of senescing and eldering. How we grow up and grow old is never an exclusive product of any single set of determinants. It is a consequence of our phylogenetic background, our unique individual heredity, the physical and social environments in which these genetic predispositions are expressed, and, for complex mammals like man, the effects of thinking and choice.

TYPES OF AGE

It is relevant to quote the Oxford English Dictionary's (1970) definition of "age," as follows: "The whole duration of the life or existence of any being or thing; the ordinary duration of life." Likewise, "aged" is defined as "having lived or existed long; of advanced age; old."

The definition of "aging" is simply "becoming old" or "becoming aged, showing signs of advancing age." However, in keeping with the previous differentiation of three types of aging, biological (senescence), sociological (eldering), and behavioral (geronting), it is useful to refer to three types of age rather than to one.

If one is aging, then one is moving from an earlier point in time to some later point in time. The *biological age* of an individual can be defined as the individual's present position with respect to his potential life span. Thus, an individual's biological age may be younger or older than his chronological age. The assessment of biological age would encompass measures of the functional capacities of vital or life-limiting organ systems. Presumably the vital organ systems lose their capacity for self-regulation and adaptive change with age so that the probability of dying increases with age.

The *social age* of an individual refers to his roles and habits with respect to other members of the society of which he is a part. An individual may be older or younger depending on the extent to which he shows the age-graded behavior expected of him by his particular society or culture. The measurement of social age would involve such aspects as the individual's type of dress, language habits, and social deference to other persons in leadership positions. Social age here is presumed to result from the dynamic process of eldering, which is the individual's course of life through the social institutions of which the individual is a member.

Psychological age refers to the behavioral capacities of individuals to adapt to changing environmental demands. Thus, just as one may be older or younger than one's chronological age, in both a biological and a social sense, one may also be older or younger psychologically. Clearly psychological age is influenced by the biological and social factors, but the concept goes further in that it involves the use of adaptive capacities of memory, learning, intelligence, skills, feelings, motivations, and emotions for exercising behavioral control or self-regulation. Survival and appropriate functioning in an environment requires a dynamic equilibrium in which the individual must continually adapt to the physical and social environments and also to his own physical state.

Botwinick has discussed the question of just which individuals in our society are to be considered aged. Definitions of aging and age will continue to change as we gain knowledge. He quotes Havighurst's suggestion that as retirement changes and the nature of work changes, old age will be defined less and less in relation to work than to a broad concept of social competence (see Havighurst, 1957). Social competence is thought to be relatively independent of biological functioning although not at the extremes of disability.

Over a broad range of environmental and physiological conditions, it may be expected that there will be a high degree of independence of the three ages of man—biological age, psychological age, and social age. It is probably only at the extreme boundary conditions of the relevant variables that these ages are highly related.

In the nineteen-forties Cowdry wrote: "A general theory of aging is very difficult, if not impossible, to formulate at the present time since the rate and expression of age vary widely in different organisms; some plants, protozoa and insects, for example, do not exhibit the usual sequence of changes nor undergo what is called senescence." (Cowdry, 1942, p. xv.) There is still no general theory of aging, and certainly none that would be acceptable to psychologists. One almost senses that there has been little pressure to stimulate the intellectual endeavor required to produce a unifying theory that would explain how behavior becomes organized or changes over time. Thus, the psychology of aging appears to be a collection of concepts and hypotheses that do no more than explain limited aspects of behavior. No matter how broad or narrow the theoretical issues, however, it will always be true that the use of the term aging or age implies relationships with time. For this reason, some discussion of the nature of time as a variable is in order.

THE NATURE OF TIME

What makes a theory dynamic in its relationship to time? Development and aging clearly refer to changes over time. Theoretical statements about development, like the big bang theory of the origin of the universe or the theory of evolution, clearly imply a pattern of change with time.

The basic subject matter of any science is the recurrence of phenomena. Another way of saying this is that science consists of the observation and explanation of regularly occurring events. In the case of astronomy, observers over the centuries became sensitive to the daily recurrence of patterns in the position of stars and planets as well as the annual cycles of patterns. As the observations of the regularities became communicated, observers began to detect recurring phenomena that had cycle times of longer than one year as well as slower drifts. Clearly to be separated are the observed data and regularities of recurring phenomena in the solar system and the explanations that have been offered to account for the regularities. These range from the early attribution of events to demonic forces to more recent explanations offered in the traditions of natural science that implicate atoms and molecules and forces of attraction.

Time is always involved in any explanation, an explanation being a statement about how things come about. Explanations deal in causal sequences; a cause can occur only before an outcome. Without a notion of time, explanation in a contemporary or scientific sense could not take place. However, it might be pointed out that most explanations of psychologists deal with events over short periods of time. Some experimental psychologists may even object to the use of the term aging, since they believe that time cannot cause anything and, therefore, one cannot have a science based on the organization of events in terms of time. This would seem to be an unduly restrictive idea if only for the fact that there are many time-related events in the nervous system. It seems to be excessively limiting of scientific inquiry and behavior to adhere blindly to a belief that since time does not cause anything there cannot be a science of aging.

The individual human life is a phenomenon of one cycle. Since the length of life of the observer, the course of the individual life, is not the same as that of the phenomenon, as in the case of astronomy, it is necessary to build up observations of many cycles and pass them on to succeeding generations of observers. One may observe in the human life cycle slow drifts in secular changes in the length of life or in the age of puberty. Shorter cycles may also be observed, e.g., annual cycles, monthly cycles, daily cycles, and recurrent cycles within a single day. Recorded history suggests that while certain general characteristics of the course of the individual human life remain the same, there have been drifts toward an average longer life as well as a drift in the development of boys and girls such that they mature and become taller and heavier at an earlier age.

In some inorganic systems, the regularity of molecular change is so great that it can be used as a measure of time and as a standard for other time determinations. Explanations of evolution and the development of culture heavily involve the ordering of events in time. The dating of a piece of charcoal from the remains of a fire of a prehistoric human community, for example, or the dating of a bone, is a very fundamental piece of evidence for scientists. The development of the universe, the formation of our planetary system, the evolution of different forms of life on earth, the development and diffusion of culture, and the life cycles of individuals require a common basis in relation to time regarded as a variable.

Atomic changes can occur with such regularity that their appearance may be used to measure a time lapse. Changes occur in an organic body with time that result in the aging of tissues and the possibility of dating them after the organism has died. Much effort has been spent by anthropologists in dating bits of pottery, carvings, and skeletal remains to test the adequacies of explanations of the development of culture, in North America, for example. How the North American continent was settled, by whom and when, requires detailed measurements of the age of objects. Were there not regular shifts in the amino-acid composition of bone with time, it would be difficult to establish the dating of a skull, say. Concepts of the Stone Age, Bronze Age and Iron Age require the ability to measure time and establish sequence.

One of the most fundamental features of systems is that they possess directions in time. Individually, we appear to move unidirectionally forward in time from our origins. Our age as individuals is marked by our memories and by our "flesh and bones." Expressed in other words, our age is marked by changes in our hardware as well as in our software—both being involved in the organization of thought, emotions, and actions. Schinnar and Stewman have pointed out (1978) that psychological and social duration may not be the same even with the same elapsed chronological duration.

The concept of aging in the general sense implies that if the organism moves forward in time, it has an average time in terms of the system as a whole. Presumably the age of subsystems can differ from the average of the whole. Reichenbach and Mathers (1959) pointed out that time direction in a large system can be different from that in its subsystems; that is, a large system may be moving forward in time, but there may be a subsystem which may be growing "younger" at the same time that other subsystems are growing "older." Thus one might attempt to describe an individual in terms of the mean biological age of the organs, e.g., the nervous system, heart, skin, endocrine glands, etc. Some cells of the body can regenerate without regard to age, such as the liver. During a period of regeneration the average age of the cell population of an organ might, in fact, be younger than it was at some earlier time. As a consequence, the functional capacity of the organ might also be greater at a later date than it was earlier.

Here the picture is one of a complex system moving forward in time that has a mean age that can be applied to the organism as a whole, yet with subsystem variation. Failure of a critical subsystem of the organism would limit the survival of the whole organism, but up to that moment the ages of the subsystems may not be in lockstep. Thus, knowing the average age of the subsystem or organism does not necessarily permit prediction of the probability of the organism's survival since the failure of only one system can limit the life of the whole. The life limiting organs of the body, the ones that seem to be potentially more important in the survival of the whole, are those that are primarily composed of cells fixed at their present level of differentiation and whose tissues may no longer contain primitive precursor cells.

FIXED CELLS

Some organs are made up of fixed, postmitotic cells, which include neurons and the heart muscle cells. These cells lose their capacity early in life for further mitotic division and remain with the individual "from birth to death," unless as individual cells they die earlier. The fact that the nervous system is composed in part of fixed cells makes it the major archival system of the body and thereby of great significance in aging.

Along with the nervous system, the immune system has a memory. It remembers organisms and molecules to which the organism has previously been exposed and which proved to be deleterious. The immune system, having recognized that it has met a certain foreign body before, mobilizes antibodies and cells to destroy it. Time is required to establish the immune defenses of the body, as shown by the high susceptibility of the newborn to infectious diseases. Late in life, the organism again becomes highly susceptible to disease. Burnet (1970a,b) has pointed out that aging of the organism is influenced by a progressive weakening of the immunological surveillance. Others have also pointed out the significance of aging to the immune system (Makinodan, 1977).

Since the nervous system is not only essential to the organization of behavior but also to the regulation of vital physiological functions, it is one of the key organ systems for the study of aging. Its own aging will presumably not only be reflected in changes of behavior but also in a changing probability of survival. It is possible that the nervous system and the immune system are the two critical limiting systems for those individuals that survive early life events and diseases. The picture being drawn here is one of an organism consisting of a complex of subsystems, each of which has a somewhat independent course over time but retains the potential for limiting the life span of the total system. What is also suggested, however, is that these subsystems are hierarchically so organized that the failure of one may have a cascading effect relative to its position in the hierarchy. In particular, it is important to note that the subsystems may not interact until certain boundary conditions are exceeded. This is sometimes referred to as the "discontinuity" hypothesis (Birren, 1959). One of the consequences of this hypothesis is that biological, psychological, and social phenomena are expected to be increasingly correlated the nearer the end of life.

Not only is biological life often limited by the functional capacity of the aging nervous system, but the quality of life is limited as well. For behavioral scientists, aging has important dual aspects in that the cellular changes of the nervous system may determine behavioral capacities at the same time that behavior patterns may influence the rate and mode of the aging of cells in the nervous system. As the prime integrating organ system of the body, the nervous system plays an even more crucial role as an initiator and disseminator of influences to other organs. In particular, the control of the endocrine system and the pituitary gland is exercised by the neural and endocrine activity of the hypothalamus. Thus the menopause may be a primary phenomenon of central nervous system regulation, with peripheral changes in the ovary being secondary or tertiary to changes in the activity of the central nervous system (Finch, 1976). If, indeed, the menopause should be looked upon less as a primary manifestation of the aging of the ovary and more as a change in the aging of the central nervous system, the question becomes one of why the nervous system loses its capability with age for timing the release of hormones. This is one example of the fact that certain biological rhythms in complex vertebrates and lower organisms require the use of time for their description.

TIME-DEPENDENT PROCESSES

The menstrual cycle illustrates a rhythm of an organism that becomes disrupted over time because of the inability of the nervous system to maintain a periodic sequential release of endocrines. In a hierarchical system, either a premature or a late release of hormones will not result in the proper expression of the primary phenomena. There are many natural rhythms of an organism such as temperature, metabolism, enzyme activity, and neural discharge. Short-term rhythms within a single day are termed *circadian rhythms* (Brown, 1972). The change in periodicity of these rhythms or spontaneous oscillations constitute part of the subject matter of aging.

According to Sampson and Jenner (1975), disorganization of the circadian rhythms can reduce mental efficiency to the extent of causing pathological states. Circadian rhythms may not only alter with age, but their function is so intimately tied with time that one may describe their outcomes as being virtually *time-dependent.*

In his review of the pineal gland, Axelrod (1974) summarized the experimental data that show that certain circadian rhythms in neurotransmitters can exercise an inhibitory effect on gonads. Especially important is the discovery that the enzyme (N-acetyltransferase) undergoes a circadian rhythm. The nucleus in the central nervous system regulating this rhythm appears to be in or near the suprachiasmatic nucleus in the hypothalamus. Such circadian rhythms are easier to observe than slower ones that occur over months or years. One of the more important biological clocks studied is one that has to do with the daily sleep–wakefulness cycle (Woodruff, this volume).

If there are subsystems of the organism that are hierarchally arranged, then perhaps we should think of an organism as consisting of a clock shop rather than as being controlled by one clock (Winfree, 1975). The study of phases in circadian and longer intervals and their experimental disruption phase appears to offer a methodological approach to experimental studies of aging.

In an earlier review of biological periodicities (Landau, 1959, p. 81), it was stated that "Time is inseparable from aging; it may be, therefore, useful in organizing our thoughts about aging to consider the role of time in some biological processes. Many processes are clocklike in their rhythmicities, while others have a characteristic duration. It may be said that most biological processes are appreciably modified by aging no matter in what sense the word is used." The hypothesis of a declining effectiveness of the aging nervous system in timing regulatory functions is an important one, although perhaps psychologists have not given it serious attention as yet because it appears to deal with the hardware of the organism to the exclusion of the software of experience and learning. It is, however, precisely because such a point of view encourages study of both the hardware and the software resulting from environmental conditions that future experiments designed to study the control by the central nervous system over bodily rhythmic activity over the life span are necessary.

AGE AS AN INDEX

Some psychologists view time as merely an index to events. It should be pointed out, however, that if this were the only status of time as a variable, it would still be an important one. Without time as an organizing concept, data become meaningless, and it is possible that there is no single variable that is more powerful as an index for organizing data than chronological age.

In examining age differences in behavior, of course, other powerful indices are also used, for example, sex, socioeconomic status, and ethnicity. As with age, in none of them is it assumed that it is the index variable in itself that causes the behavior. In the case of socioeconomic status, it is presumably not, for example, the size of the bank account of the individual that is causing the behavior. Because age is such a powerful index, it will probably always be used to classify data while we are en route to explanations using variables other than the mere ages of individuals.

Birren and Renner (1977, p. 26) have said that, "In a rigorously experimental sense, age must be approached in research as a variable that ultimately must be eliminated." This statement implies that as we approach a real understanding of why age groups differ, we will no longer use age as a variable. Presumably differences in behavior with age are associated with environmental causes, genetic causes, and individual decision-making processes.

Another source of variance is the species and unique individual genetics that influence the size, form, and function, and presumably the aging, of the organism. There are also choices in behavior that imply an interaction between environmental conditions and the genetic background resulting in the individuals changing with time. It is partly this interaction that places age in an ambiguous position as an explanatory variable.

The importance of genetics, environment, and individual decisions as variables shifts with the discipline and the kind of observations being explained. However, it must be repeated that all explanations involve time. That is to say, outcomes are consequences of antecedents, or, in functional terms, some dependent variables are a function of some independent variables. Logic itself involves time, since two concurrent processes cannot be causing one another.

Holding constant the age of animals in an experiment reduces a source of variance but must make many assumptions about the experimental effects that are obtained. In addition to the accumulation of irreversible changes that result from wear and tear, some events are determined by inherent atomic or molecular properties, such as the polymerization of protein with age. In such cases, time (and/or age) is so intimately involved that one cannot describe the system without its inclusion.

In the case of human beings, it is important to know how old an individual is and when he lived. For purposes of understanding, we want to know whether a person existed early or late historically. What gives age its importance is the fact that there are features of the organism that are not reversible. For example, time flows in one direction for the organism as well as for the universe. We can thus look for those mechanisms that act like the ratchet and cog of a watch to stop time from flowing backwards; it can only flow forwards, but there is the other question of what makes it flow forward. We can assign an age to an individual from the shifts that occur in amino composition in the bone with time.

The atomic clock is based upon the fact that known quantities of atoms disintegrate in a fixed period of time. Since the atoms that disintegrate do not reform, we are dealing with an irreversible process. In the case of the decay of radioactive atoms, the probability of any molecule disintegrating is constant, yet the proportion of molecules that have disintegrated is a function of elapsed time. Thus, probability and time are related for large numbers of atoms but not for single atoms. The portion surviving in a given population is a decreasing exponential function of age. In this sense, age does not enter the equation other than as "clock time."

Some lower animals exhibit an exponential type of survival, but in a strict sense the population doesn't show aging since the probability of survival is a constant. On the other hand, the aging of human populations does not occur in the same fashion because the probability of dying is not a constant; rather, it accelerates as a function of age, that is, the older the population, the increasingly higher the probability that individuals will not survive.

The association between atomic change and time is so close that one may alternate between using the ratio of two forms of atoms to determine the age of the sample and the use of the deterioration itself as a fundamental measure of elasped time. Landau (1959, p. 113) pointed out that there are various kinds of biological time clocks: "If a function is perturbed by experimental manipulation, its temporal behavior gives information about the underlying mechanisms. A single time constant may be adequate to describe the process if the function simply returns to normal. However, the function may not return to its original state."

In the case of complex organisms, recovery from the effects of wear and tear is presumably not complete, and there is some irreversible residue as a consequence of an event. This is not unlike the learning process, in which the age of the subjects becomes a necessary bit of information. Without such knowledge, it would be difficult to interpret not only some data about learning but about other aspects of human functioning. Another way of saying this is that there is much history involved in the age of an organism, or, in the same vein, that to understand the outcomes of an experiment one must know the organism's history.

Time then has many uses—in the measurement of elasped time as an important descriptive variable in explanation, as a dependent variable that requires explanation, or as an independent variable in the explanation of other phenomena. It is these different applications and layers of meaning in the concept of time and age that give rise to confusion in their scientific status as an area of scientific study.

In comparing the behavior of young and old individuals, many differences are immediately observable. Some of the differences may be attributed to a species pattern of biological change—that is, senescing; others to a social environmental process of change—that is, eldering; still others to a process of decision-making on the part of the individual—that is, geronting. The study of age differences is not unlike that of the differences that may be found in public-opinion surveys in which the data are divided by sex, socio-economic status, and occupation.

Birren and Renner (1977, p. 4) pointed out that age change in behavior is presumably not an exclusively biological, environmental, or social phenomenon. Their definition of aging is as follows: ". . . aging refers to the regular changes that occur in mature genetically representative organisms living under representative environmental conditions as they advance in chronological age" (ibid, p. 4).

Since studies of age differences tend to consider the individual as a passive entity, many views of age differences in behavior ascribe them to: (1) disuse, (2) wear and tear, or (3) selective reinforcement by the environment. The latter would in simple terms state that "If I act like an old person, I have been reinforced by society to act like an old person." An ontogenetic theory of aging, on the other hand, makes the individual more active as a proactive, causal agent in the changes in behavior resulting from choices and decisions. In turn, however, this probably reflects an interaction between the options provided by the environment and the values acquired in a social environment as well as the results of reasoning and choice.

The need for theory in the psychology of aging is accentuated by the increased amount of data. Salthouse (1983, p. 39) pointed out that "facts are accumulating at a rapidly accelerating pace in the field of adult cognition, and unless theoretical frameworks are available to organize these facts they may become overwhelming and consequently be ignored because they are impossible to assimilate." One of the common ways of handling theoretical issues in the psychology of aging is to use theory borrowed from another area of psychology that attempted to explain how behavior was organized in the constant aged subject, that is, the young adult. In this case, adding age as a variable results in consideration of age differences. The problem that arises, however, is that the variables considered in explaining the organization of behavior in the young adult may not be the ones involved in giving rise to differences between the young and the old organism. Salthouse pointed out that there is a difference between trying to explain age differences and age changes. Age differences can arise from many uncatalogued reasons. Age changes are the shifts in the organization of behavior that occur with age, some of them undoubtedly typical of the way the species in question ages.

THE EVOLUTION OF AGING

Various animals have characteristic lengths of life typical of their species. It is assumed that the species patterns of aging have become established in the slow time of biological evolution. The comparative approach examines the similarities of aging in mankind in comparison with other species. Basically, this approach attempts to find out what the processes of human aging have in common with the aging of other species. Presumably the pattern of aging should show a phylogenetic ordering, and the aging of mankind should be similar to that of the species closest to mankind phylogenetically. Other vertebrates, and particular primates, should show morphological, biochemical, and behavioral changes with age similar to those of human beings to the extent to which there is a common evolutionary basis for the organization of late life change.

A comparative approach to the study of

aging attempts to discover the phylogenetic similarities in the mechanisms of aging. An early symposium sponsored by the CIBA Foundation was devoted to the methodology of the study of aging (see Wolstenholme and O'Connor, 1957). In emphasizing the value of a comparative approach to aging, Muhlbock (1957, p. 115) stated, "It can be presumed that animals do not differ from man in the basic processes of aging, so that valid conclusions can be reached." In addition to the evolved common patterns of aging that adjacent species share, there are nevertheless intraspecies differences (Finch and Hayflick, 1977).

A second approach to the study of human aging is to analyze individual differences within the species. It is, in fact, more common for psychology to examine individual differences within the species than to analyze commonalities across species in a comparative approach.

Confusion can arise if investigators fail to distinguish whether their dependent variable is an intra- or inter-species characteristic of aging. Psychology tends to examine individual differences within the species, and biology tends to look at common mechanisms across species. Birren (1964) pointed out that theories of aging could be divided into three types: accident or wear-and-tear theories, genetic theories, and counterpart theories. All three possess credibility, depending upon the nature of the dependent variable being explained. An accident or wear-and-tear theory looks at differences in longevity as a function of variations in the environment. Earlier theorizing about aging seemed to regard it as implausible that there could exist an organized process of change in the old animal.

A theory of the evolution of aging must explain the selection of the characteristics a species displays long after the time of reproduction and presumably beyond the pressures of selection. Characteristics that favor survival and successful reproduction in early life presumably will be the ones that are perpetuated. Until recently it was thought that since the characteristics of late life appear so long after the age of reproduction, late life (postreproductive) characteristics of a species could not have been directly selected. However, the evidence is that species do maintain their relative order of longevity despite environmental variations. Also, individual differences within the human species are related to the longevity of previous generations, e.g., grandparents. Thus the length of life has order between species and within species, but how it arises and is organized is the scientific question. The counterpart theory suggests that regularly appearing characteristics of late life (including longevity) must be an expression of traits that were selected at the time of reproduction. "It describes a pathway through which order could have been introduced into the changes in the old, or post reproductive animal. Obviously, beyond the order implied by counterpart theory, events occur that superimpose their consequences on the organisms that in the above view have some long term programming" (Birren, 1964, p. 74).

In this view, some of the regular changes that appear in old animals are a counterpart of the early developmental characteristics that were selected. It should be pointed out that aging in this context is not simply a mirror image of early-life processes. Thus a late-life disability might be, in fact, a consequence of selection of some earlier favorable traits. Smith made this point rather well, as follows: "A high blood pressure may contribute to death from cardiac disease in old age, but cannot have consistently adverse effects on fitness, since if a high blood pressure were uniformly disadvantageous, natural selection would reduce the need level in the population. It is, therefore, probable that the deleterious effects of high blood pressure in old age are counterbalanced by advantages, perhaps earlier in life, natural selection maintaining the mean arterial pressure in the population at an optimal value" (Smith, 1957, p. 121).

Although programming of late-life characteristics on a genetic basis, including that of longevity, could emerge on the basis of counterpart selection, including behavioral selection, how much organization of late-life change is genetically programmed is open to question. It is plausible that the genetic program of aging may not be as well-organized or specific as that of development. The further that one moves from the age of reproduction, the less precise should be the genetic control over characteristics of the organism. In this sense, there is likely a *precession* of biologically favorable survival traits appearing early in life and a *recession* of unfavorable traits in later life, the latter being more difficult to remove by selective pressures. The appearance of a variety of genetic diseases of late life would fit such a view in that the longer the members of a species live, the more likely they will experience a deleterious disease difficult to eliminate by selection.

It should be pointed out that behavioral factors can be involved in the counterpart process, that is, the ordering of late-life events could arise via natural selection of long-lived and intelligent persons. Although individual differences in longevity do not appear until long after reproduction has been completed, off-spring whose parents survived a long time are themselves more favored to survive in the environment. The reasoning might be extended further to preindustrial societies in which individuals who lived a long time were more likely to accumulate wealth and provide more favorable conditions for the survival of their offspring, e.g., food and protection. In this manner, genetic selection for longevity could be accompanied by favorable late life behavioral traits. In a related manner, those individuals who show great capacity for learning, retention of information, and wisdom in late life would be more likely to provide favorable environmental circumstances for their offspring and tribe.

The probability of survival of a tribe presumably would be higher if its elders or leaders lived a long time and exercised the quality of wisdom. In contrast, the accumulation of large numbers of disabled older persons in competition for territory and food would make a tribe unfavored for survival. It would be unproductive to sketch the various circumstances that might lead to selective pressures for long-lived individuals who show behavioral characteristics favorable to the survival of their family and tribe. It is only necessary to make the point that natural selection for longevity may be coupled with favorable late-life behavioral characteristics.

The survival of complex organisms in wild or natural environments depends upon effec-

tive behavior. In this sense, behavioral selection may determine genetic characteristics. Since selection always takes place in a particular environment, the exposure of animals, including human beings, to new and unfamiliar environments may result in the appearance of characteristics never seen before. These might appear, for example, in the aging of individuals who were exposed to a new and unfamiliar environment, e.g., in the weightless conditions of space flight. Not all of the responses of organisms to a new environment are predictable, and genetic-environmental interactions can be profound. For example, Henry, Meeham, and Stevens (1967) demonstrated that inbred mice will or will not show a rise in blood pressure with age depending upon the social structure and interaction patterns in a colony. Perhaps, then, the commonly observed rise in blood pressure in late life is less an expression of a genetic characteristic than it is a manifestation of a genetic-environmental interaction, genetic factors presumably setting the range within which environmental influences can have effect. Interaction between genetic characteristics and long-term environments may lead to specialization, disuse, and loss of function. Such selective differentiation presumably led to the birds that can no longer fly, such as the kiwi or the ostrich.

Early-life behavior and experience should be expected to comprise the behavioral repertory of older adults but not in terms of a direct and literal translation. In terms of the counterpart theory, one should not expect an isomorphism between characteristics of early and late life. From the counterpart point of view, one should not expect a simple translation of early-life behavioral characteristics and experience as implied by earlier psychoanalytic points of view. In fact, what is needed is a scientific metaphor that can capture the transformation of early-life characteristics into late-life ones. Perhaps the image of a projection of early-life experience much like the projection of moving pictures onto a current scene has some promise of being extended to carry the thought that while the repertory of experience is carried forward in time, the nature of the projector and the screen onto which it is projecting shifts. This thought is expressed to guard against a too literal interpretation of late-life behavioral characteristics as being the direct expression of a presumed primacy of early-life learning. Some behaviors in late life may be phenotypically the same as those of early life but perhaps quite different in basic mechanisms.

AGING IN HUMAN SOCIETY

Previously the point was made that the way we age is a function of the way we developed, i.e., aging is a counterpart of development, although our potential for senescence is modified by the physical and social environments in which the organisms grow up and grow old. For most persons, there is a change with age in the way they dress, the way they speak, and the ways in which they relate to other persons. Since our nervous systems are in a large part programmed by our experiences in our social environments, shifts in our behavior reflect the expectations or age norms of our society. The expression "act your age" usually implies you are acting immaturely and that you should act more appropriately for someone of your age.

Culture is the organization of social status, social roles, and social rituals; it may be regarded as the "DNA" of society. Variables of culture influence the distribution of status, prestige, power, and resources. One would judge that all societies are to some extent stratified by age as well as by social class and sex. Ragan and Wales (1980, p. 386) point out that age stratification is a complex social system in which from some points of view the aged are disadvantaged, but in other ways, advantaged. The term *ageism* has been used to refer to the negative stereotypes applied to older persons. In work, old people may be disadvantaged by being pushed out of occupational roles and thereby lose income. They do, however, have a great deal more leisure time available to them. Usually in American society, older persons occupy a lower status since on average they have lower status in work and income. In addition to economic and work roles, the family, religious organizations, and other groups provide for different

forms of involvement in accordance with age, some of which are tied to the reproductive cycle of being child, parent, and grandparent. Underlying the roles assigned to people of different ages is the shifting belief structure of society that tends to change the function of older persons.

Interacting with these secular changes or drifts in customs of society related to age is the life course of the individual. Because of this interaction, the attitudes that have been early engendered may be in conflict with the changing expectations of society when one grows up. There are thus three or more "times" involved: One is the slow time of biological evolution, a second is the somewhat faster time of cultural or societal change, and the third is the still faster time of the life cycle of the individual. Clearly, one cannot only use length of life as the dependent variable in relation to the adaptations, coping, and adjustments of the individual to growing old in a particular culture.

Changes in the age of retirement and the age at which social security benefits become available are a function of the values of society and the economic resources available in periods of recession, inflation, or economic growth. Some aspects of the stratification of age and society are determined by informal norms and rules that are passed on from generation to generation and may vary between social classes.

The development of positive and negative views of old age are also influenced by the family (Bengtson and Treas, 1980). In America, young adults regard old adults as being of lower status and prestige. Having a negative image of old age, young adults therefore have a negative anticipation of growing old. Older adults in American society usually hold a more favorable view of their life circumstances than do young adults (Birren & Renner, 1980).

Studies have been made about growing up and growing old in cultures other than the United States. In comparing the U.S. with other countries, the diversity in the background of its population should be kept in mind. The U.S. is populated by many immigrant groups. Usually in other countries of the world, different racial, ethnic, and language groups tend to live in more distinctly separate regions, a fact that to some extent preserves their integrity. In a pluralistic society like ours, individual differences in aging are far more common.

Theories of aging versus psychological theories employing age differences

The psychology of aging is concerned with *differences* in behavior with age, *changes* in behavior with age, and *patterns* of behavior shown by persons of different age in different periods of time. These different points of view treat age as a variable in different manners. A study of the shift in attitudes of older persons from Victorian times to the present would conceive of historical time in a different manner than a biographer would in describing the changes in an individual life or a biologist would in examining species of animals in an attempt to identify the universal patterns of transformation with age.

It has already been pointed out that much of the contemporary psychology of aging is a collection of segments of knowledge (Birren, Cunningham, and Yamamoto, 1983). This implies that most theories in the psychology of aging are actually microtheories; they do not embrace large amounts of data from different domains of behavior. This in turn implies that different levels of explanation are used by investigators and that their explanatory positions are very close to their observed data with little reference to the kind of comprehensive concepts that would be involved in viewing man as a constantly transforming biological system moving forward in time with interactions within his own organism as well as with his social and physical environment.

Operational Issues in Studying Age

Most studies of aging utilize chronological age as a primary variable of interest in spite of considerable dissatisfaction with this practice, both conceptually and in terms of methodological implications. Clearly, the scientific study of aging requires considerably greater complexity of both concept and method than was believed necessary in the recent past. The main purpose of this section is to explore some alternatives to the employment of chronological age.

Studies of aging may be classified according to the manner in which they make use of the aging variable. There are two major approaches; from a developmental perspective, these may be characterized as "static" or "dynamic." In the "developmentally static approach," the researcher may select a particular age range or period of development to investigate and then proceed to develop theoretical statements or principles that characterize this particular age group. Here the age variable is employed primarily to identify the boundaries of the domain of study. In contrast, the "developmentally dynamic approach" seeks to develop theories or principles which characterize the process of change, that is to say, how the organism develops and what characterizes such change, how it occurs, etc. In static studies, the role of the age variable is not a difficult one, given the minor function which it plays. In contrast, the age variable is critical in studies that are developmentally dynamic.

Not only is the role of the age variable crucial in dynamic studies of development, but the manner in which age should be operationalized has been the source of considerable discussion and even heated debate. It is now generally recognized that the cross-sectional approach suffers from the possible confounding of nondevelopmental, cohort influences, which may limit the degree of certainty of an age interpretation of behavioral differences identified by this design. The longitudinal method, although conceptually sounder, suffers from a variety of limitations as well. In addition to its substantially increased costs and demands on time, selective attrition as well as time-related cultural events limit its interpretability. Finally, various sequential strategies of data structuring, which involve combinations of the simpler, basic descriptive designs, do not escape from the limitations of their constituent components and thus yield a situation that does not allow for unambiguous conclusions.

In addition to these widely discussed and debated methodological issues (Botwinick, 1978), there is also a conceptual problem. Time per se probably does not cause anything directly. What most researchers are really interested in are the changes that may occur in the nervous system or the experimental changes that are recorded there. The ultimate interest of researchers is not in the passage of time, but rather the neural and behavioral manifestations that are influenced over time and whose accumulations are crudely indexed by chronological age. Once this is recognized, there seem to be two obvious courses to follow. The first is to accept chronological age as a surrogate variable that stands for an undifferentiated conglomeration of influences and therefore recognizes chronological age as a primitive, although relatively useful, index variable that can be employed to represent the phenomena of aging. The second approach is to attempt to identify specific aspects of aging and either use these constructs to supplement chronological age, or more ambitiously, to replace chronological age.

This approach is a substantial departure from the traditional ways of studying aging and behavior, but the idea itself is hardly new. It is commonly remarked today (as it has been in the past) that a person seems old and tired for his years, or, alternatively, that it is hard to believe that a certain person is really as old as he actually is. Concretely, many people are not ready to retire from their jobs at age 65 since they are still vigorous and effective. Others may not last until age 65 and may have to retire at an earlier age.

Although chronological age is almost certainly going to remain the "meat and potatoes" variable for the bulk of aging research, attempts to augment or replace it by more specific constructs that are related to intrinsic aging processes are likely to increase in both number and sophistication in the years to come. At the very least, there is considerable potential for such research to inform and amplify results from more traditional research based on chronological age. It is not likely, and perhaps not even desirable, that such new approaches replace the traditional kind of study, but it is both desirable and likely that such new kinds of studies augment and perhaps, in some cases, enhance our theoretical understanding of the aging process.

The idea of alternative or supplementary representations of the age variable is not really a new one. Quite a few years ago, Speith (1964) considered the relationship between cognitive functioning, aging, and cardiovascular disease. His line of research has been continued by other researchers (e.g., Wilkie and Eisdorfer, 1971; Light, 1978; Elias, 1980). There are other examples as well. Recent longitudinal work (Mossey and Shapiro, 1982) has shown that subjective health indicators have significant validity for predicting mortality and supplement, in an important way, more objective indicators of health status. A number of investigators in behavioral research have provided a conceptual umbrella by introducing a conceptual distinction between *primary* (normal, disease-free) aging versus *secondary* (disease-related) aging. In biology, this distinction is commonly made and labeled as *endogenous* and *exogenous* aspects of aging. It is emphasized that the employment of chronological age implicitly involves a mixing of these influences.

Another approach to this problem is illustrated by the various studies of "functional age." Basically, such studies have usually involved the identification of variables believed to be related to age. After data have been gathered on a large sample of individuals of widely varying age, multivariate data analysis (usually multiple regression) is employed to evaluate which set of variables best predict chronological age. The primary purpose of this exercise is usually to attempt to develop a "yardstick" of functional age that will facilitate personnel decisions in industry, particularly retirement (e.g., Dirken, 1972). At an empirical level, such investigations have been very successful in that variable sets have been identified that predict a truly substantial amount of variance in chronological age—sometimes over 60 percent.

Functional age researchers have varied to the extent that they hypothesize a unitary aging process, on the one hand, or prefer to assume multiple-aging processes and various combinations of variables, each of which may be optimally employed for different situations or against different criteria.

Dirken (1972) presented the issue quite forcefully when he said that the assumption underlying this approach was either that there is a unitary force of aging or that the various forces of aging could reasonably be considered as a higher order construct. Dirken found that chronological age could very effectively be predicted from a variety of functional measures (vital capacity, grip strength, and various perceptual and cognitive abilities). His multiple correlation between chronological age and a composite functional age produced a score of 0.87. This is an impressive level of prediction.

Heron and Chown (1967) took a more cautious stance, suggesting that some veteran researchers are taken aback by the idea of a functional age and that there may be different equations for different situations or occupational categories. They explicitly disavowed the "general aging" construct approach. Nevertheless, along with Dirken, they found high correlations between a functional age composite and chronological age.

The progress of the concept of functional age has not all been clear sailing. The idea was pointedly criticized by Costa and McRae (1980). The conceptual basis for the commonest empirical approach was severely critiqued. The most common approach is to employ multiple-regression techniques to predict chronological age. If the ultimate criterion is chronological age, why not use that variable to begin with since it is easily obtained, readily verifiable, and simple to use and understand?

These authors also pointed out some unexpected outcomes of using regression procedures. Data from the Baltimore longitudinal study were presented that cast doubt on some possible implications of the functional age concept. Nevertheless, the implicit restriction in range (compared to the wider age span in both the two studies discussed here) as well as other limitations acknowledged by Costa and McRae suggest that the idea of functional age be more searchingly examined, rather than discarded. It also seems clear that greater conceptual input and construct structuring would be useful since doubts have been expressed

as to whether functional age has any real advantages, given the conceptual and empirical limitations noted above.

Interesting in this regard are the data of Heron and Chown, which have been reanalyzed (by the second author) with regard to the issue of predictability. The focus of attention here is the relative predictability of two aspects of intellectual functioning: *Figural Reasoning* (a composite of the Raven Progressive Matrices, Perceptual Mazes, and Trail Making) and *Perceptual Speed* (a variation on the Digit Symbol subtest of the WAIS). These abilities are widely believed to be relatively sensitive to the age variable. [See Heron and Chown (1967) for a more detailed description.] It was found that a functional age measure (a composite of forced expiratory volume, grip strength, and hearing loss) better predicted two intellectual abilities than did chronological age in a sample of 300 males ranging in age from 20 to 80. Although the gains in predictability were not substantial, it seems clear that a functional age construct may have empirical advantages in predictability as compared with chronological age.

Clearly, such results justify further consideration of the functional age idea. The approach of using chronological age as a criterion and employing multiple-regression procedures to develop composite weights, though undoubtedly necessary as a preliminary phase, is nevertheless overly empirical and requires further conceptual development.

There is a set of concepts about aging that is already available in the existing literature and can be brought to bear in this context. First, there is the conceptual distinction, widely accepted by behavioral gerontologists and well documented in the empirical literature, between primary aging and secondary aging, a distinction analogous to what biologists call intrinsic and extrinsic aspects of aging. This concept distinguishes between normal, disease-free aging, on the one hand, and disease-related pathological decline, on the other. Furthermore, the concept of terminal decline (Siegler, et al., 1980) has also been used to designate possible changes that may occur shortly before death to within several years of it. A number of workers in the field have suggested that these changes may be of a different magnitude, timing, and perhaps even of a different nature, than the changes related to primary and secondary aging. It is also apparent that different aspects of life style (stress, pace of life, nutrition, substance abuse, exercise, morale, socioeconomic status, and probably many others) have the potential for altering the course and perhaps the rate of secondary and primary aging. Furthermore, differing personality patterns (e.g., Type A versus Type B) may alter the course of primary aging or the expression of secondary aging.

Although the fact is often not explicitly affirmed, the concept of primary aging (versus other aspects of aging) is fundamental to current research in the psychology of aging. For example, most empirical researchers either screen their subjects for health status or report that their subjects are "healthy and community-dwelling." The assumption, often unstated, underdocumented, or inadequately operationalized, is that the area of interest is a species-specific, normative process of aging, for which disease processes are taken to be extraneous nuisance variables. This assumption cheerfully ignores the high prevalence of chronic disease even in the community-dwelling elderly. Thus, although the idea of primary aging is at the heart of most current empirical efforts in behavioral gerontology, the factor of secondary aging is of considerable potential significance. This is particularly true if generalization of these empirical findings to the elderly population is desired.

One possible approach to operationalizing a primary aging construct would be to identify variables known to be sensitive to age but not obviously dependent on a disease process. These variables would plausibly be related to the slow, gradual changes believed to reflect either a genetic aging program or a cellular, reproductive wear-and-tear program, or both. Examples of such variables from other studies might include vital capacity, grip strength, or other indicators of functional capacity.

Disease-related aging or secondary aging might involve a variety of chronic conditions influencing brain function. The commonest example in the empirical literature is cardio-

vascular disease, with indicators such as blood pressure, physician ratings, subject ratings, or health records. Naturally, other diseases (cancer, for example) are likely to be important as well. Several possible levels of explanation are possible, but it should not be overlooked that the level itself may have important implications for measurement. In positing a global health construct, for example, it would probably be necessary to rely on physical or objective global ratings. One could also opt for the measurement of the larger and critical physiological systems, for example, the cerebrovascular system, the immune system, and the hypothalamic system. Although there would be some loss in parsimony of means, there is apt to be a gain in precision of measurement. A still more analytical approach would be to attempt to evaluate specific disease/health dimensions for all of the major disease processes that might plausibly influence cognitive functioning or other behavioral variables of interest. At this level, considerable precision of measurement would be possible, and physician ratings, subjective ratings (see LaRue, et al., 1979), physiological measurements, and also laboratory tests might all be profitably deployed. It is likely that the various levels of explanation may be sufficiently interrelated to justify a hierarchical structure, from global to analytical levels, but the authors are not aware of any published study that focuses primarily on this problem.

A third major aspect of the aging process that may be abstracted from the existing literature concerns the period of approaching death, which is sometimes referred to as "negative age." One idea often discussed is terminal decline. The idea of terminal decline is that some individuals may go through a period of behavioral change that may be larger and/or qualitatively different from normal age changes in behavior. This period of time may range from months to years but is characterized by cognitive and social "slipping"—that is, a deterioration of previous levels of performance that brings about not only greater losses than expected in age-sensitive variables, but losses in variables that are usually regarded as age-insensitive. This phenomenon was first reported by Kleemeier (1962) and has been supported by various results since (see Siegler, 1975).

Another concept, which in some ways is the converse of terminal decline, is familial longevity. Clearly, some individuals have greater longevity than others. This particular factor of aging is believed to be inherited and thus widely regarded as having a genetic basis. Such biological vigor seems to manifest itself in longer stability and higher levels of performance. It is likely that a concept like *vigor* (Jalavisto, et al., 1964) would be useful as one factor of aging, though it is likely that it will be found to be strongly (if inversely) related to terminal decline.

So far, several aspects of aging have been reviewed that are not only easily conceptualized but implicitly utilized in much current research. It would appear to be an important item on the research agenda for the next decade to make their usage explicit so that they can be explicitly evaluated.

Recent conceptual and technical advances in multivariate data analysis (e.g., Joreskog and Sorbom, 1978) have provided a statistical basis for models that explicitly consider various aspects of aging. Of particular importance is the method of linear structural equation modeling. Recently published programs put this method within the grasp of nonspecialist who nevertheless have some training in multivariate statistics. They allow for the postulation and empirical testing of explicit models that incorporate different aging constructs.

An example is the Cascade Model, which posits a particular pattern of aging constructs and seeks to explain several aspects of intellectual functioning. The model is portrayed in Figure 1. On the left side of the figure are three facets of aging already discussed: primary, secondary, and tertiary aging. On the right side of the figure are three well-replicated classes of intellectual functioning, referred to as Verbal Comprehension, Reasoning, and Perceptual Speed. Verbal Comprehension involves retrieving information or knowledge that is well-known and well-practiced. Reasoning involves going beyond the information given by inference or inductive implication. These terms are used to represent theoretical distinctions made by many researchers, particularly Cattell and Horn (see Horn, 1978), and which are widely believed to be differentially related to aging. Perceptual Speed represents one class of intellectual functioning that is believed to be unusually sensitive to various aging processes and is intended to represent the speed with which information is processed in the nervous system. All classes of ability constructs in the system are "latent variables,"

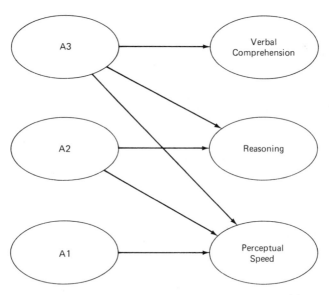

Fig. 1. The Cascade Model: *A1*—primary (normal) aging; *A2*—secondary (disease-related) aging; and *A3*—tertiary aging (terminal decline).

analogous to factors; since they are not directly observed, they are indicated by multiple variables.

Verbal Comprehension indicators would include vocabulary, comprehension, and information tests. Reasoning indicators would include inductive reasoning, abstract problem solving tasks, formal operations, etc. Perceptual Speed indicators include choice reaction time, perceptual speed tasks, and other indices of simple cognitive tasks for which speed of performance is the primary source of individual differences.

The model in Figure 1 postulates a particular pattern of causal influences. The hypothesized causal pattern is as follows. Primary aging is believed to influence Perceptual Speed but not the other aspects of intellectual functioning. Many studies in the research literature suggest that normal aging results in a slowing of the speed with which information is processed. Secondary aging is hypothesized to influence both Perceptual Speed and Reasoning. Several studies (Wilkie and Eisdorfer, 1971; Abrahams and Birren, 1973) suggest that health status, particularly cardiovascular status, may incur increased losses with age, even when chronological age is held constant. Close scrutiny of the variable curves from Schaie's (1979) Seattle project also suggests that it is in the age decade of the fifties that declines in inductive reasoning become noticeable. It is also in the age decade of the fifties that the chronic disease rate greatly increases. This population level correlation suggests the possibility of a health influence on Reasoning. The terminal decline influences of tertiary aging are viewed as being pervasive, and therefore causal links are postulated with all three aspects of intellectual functioning.

Current, but as yet unpublished, research has used archival data to evaluate this model. Although the model works well in many respects, it is apparent that a causal link from primary aging to Reasoning is needed, which violates the Cascade pattern. Moreover, the health constructs have accounted for only a disappointing amount of variance in the two classes of intellectual abilities. It may be that broader or more sophisticated indicators of health status will show a better result. It is

also possible that the indicators of primary aging may already be sensitive to the health construct and that this construct may therefore be empirically redundant. The important point, however, is that this kind of deployment of causal modeling allows for an analytical consideration of different aspects of the aging process.

Although this kind of model can be employed for a wide variety of topics in the study of human aging, it is particularly germane to research situations that are not ripe for experimental manipulation or that are intrinsically unsuited for meaningful or ethical manipulations. Although the Cascade model presented here is a decrement model, it would be possible to apply the decrement approach to other kinds of conceptualizations. For example, a decrement with compensation model could be tested if suitable constructs and related indicators were developed for factors that compensate for aging effects. Along the same lines, it would be possible to investigate cohort differences if suitable constructs and operationalizations were developed. Furthermore, various topics of adjustment and morale could be explored in the context of this type of model (e.g., Lawton, 1982). Thus, it appears that there is wide potential for the application of this approach in behavioral aging research.

Kinds of Psychological Research in Aging

Psychological research in aging can be divided into four broad categories: pre-experimental, experimental-manipulative, theoretically oriented, and intervention oriented. Although these categories are not always mutually exclusive, enough studies fall into a given category to justify this kind of a framework. Pre-experimental research is descriptive work that ideally sets the stage for the more logically incisive studies exemplified by the second and the third categories. Even in situations where a controlled experiment has already been conceptualized and meaningful manipulations already identified, it is often necessary or desirable to carry out preliminary parametric estimation studies as a prelude to further experimentation. In other situations, the nature of the phenomena being studied may limit the extent to which meaningful, ethical manipulations are possible or technically feasible. Certainly, controlled experiments are preferable. They provide a certainty of interpretation and a hardiness of inference that is rarely, if ever, possible in descriptive studies of behavior. There is little doubt that the rate of progress of various areas of study within psychology is closely related to the degree to which the experimental method is deployed. Unfortunately, not all topics within the area of behavior lend themselves readily to this approach. The third category consists of theoretically oriented research. Usually, in new areas of research, descriptive and manipulative studies lead to a crisper understanding of the phenomena of interest, which fosters the development of theories or models that attempt to explain the behavior. The fourth category concerns interventions, with the emphasis on changing behavior in a desirable way. Although such interventions are sometimes undertaken outside of the research tradition of the three other categories, it is widely believed that they are likely to be more successful when based on a firm support of the empirical results and theoretical understanding gained from previous research.

There are many examples of pre-experimental studies in aging research. In addition to an over-abundance of cross-sectional studies, an increasing number of longitudinal studies are being reported. Botwinick and Siegler (1981) recently reported descriptive results of intellectual functioning from a Duke Longitudinal Study that emphasized the role of attrition in longitudinal studies. Another example of descriptive research from the same study is that of Siegler, George, and Okum (1979) regarding personality variables. Considerable stability of personality was found with age. A project that in some ways is the most extensive yet undertaken in human development is the sequential study of Schaie (1979) and his colleagues, who followed individuals across their adult life-span for over two decades, describing age relationships for subtests of the Primary Mental Abilities Test. Schaie concluded that cohort differences played an important role in cross-sectional age differences. A number of studies of the factor structure of intellectual abilities in old age have been carried out (Cunningham and Birren, 1980; Cunningham, 1980a; 1980b; 1981). In general, it was found that ability structures were very similar in the old who were compared. However, with the young, factors tended to be more highly intercorrelated, particularly for very rapid tasks.

There are many examples of experimental manipulations. One is a study by Berg, Hertzog, and Hunt (1982) of median reaction times in several adult age groups. They varied degrees of mental rotation and practice over several days. Although practice had the effect of slowing responses in all groups, age differences were not reduced, and it was concluded that age changes in the speed of cognitive processing play an important role in responses to spatial ability tests. Kausler (1982) provides a very scholarly review of the experimental psychology of aging.

The goal of many of the studies in aging research is the achievement of theoretically oriented studies, regardless of the details of procedure. Most of the studies in the psychology of aging involve theories taken from the context of "mainline" psychology and applied to elderly individuals. In some cases, it is a matter of evaluating the extent of their generalizability. In other situations, theories developed in mainline psychology result in predictions directly applicable to older persons. One example of this is the paper by Hasher and Zacks (1979). These researchers developed a distinction between "automatic" and "effortful" processing, which involves differential attention demands in memory functioning. Implications from this conceptual distinction are drawn for various age groups, including the elderly. For example, empirical research suggests that processing frequency information is not influenced by aging or depression. Another example of theoretically oriented research concerns perception of persons and stereotypes. Brewer, Dull, and Lui (1981) investigated young people's stereotypic perception of different prototypes of elderly people in the framework of the Rosch theory of natural categories. The results suggested that stereotyping of individuals occurs in basic rather than superordinate categories.

Unfortunately, most such theoretically oriented research involves theory "borrowed" from other areas of psychology in one of the senses described above. There is a distinct shortage of efforts to establish genuine theories of behavior regarding aging in the elderly. Examples of such theories are the ideas regarding speed advanced by Birren (1965; 1974), the ideas regarding cautiousness advanced by Botwinick (1978), and the need to integrate experience in a life review proposed by Butler (1975).

An increasing number of intervention studies are oriented toward improving the behavior or circumstances of the aged. For example, Willis, Blieszer, and Baltes (1981) showed that performance of the elderly on tests of figural relations, widely believed to be age sensitive, could be improved through training procedures. Although interpretations of these findings remains in some doubt (e.g., Donaldson, 1981), the results themselves are important for a balanced understanding of the relationship between age and intellectual functioning. One of the important points is that the demonstrated improvement of an ability with practice does not contradict decrement models but does clearly show that declines are neither inevitable or immutable. The distinction between what is natural and what is inevitable is an important one for aging. Furthermore, any modifiability of behavior, even if it is subsequently found to be narrow from a transfer perspective, nonetheless serves to enrich the theoretical understanding of the phenomena of aging. Other intervention studies (e.g., Schulz and Hanusa, 1978) serve to reinforce concerns about the possible negative impact of interventions.

Theory and Selection of Experimental Variables

Psychologists use three general classes or sources of variables to explain the phenomena of aging, those arising from (1) the structure of experience, (2) individual decision and choice, and (3) biological changes in the organism. Few of the important variables can be manipulated experimentally in human beings for ethical reasons. Particularly is there reticence to alter the suspected major types of emotional experience. In a similar way, we are restricted from studying decision processes in important life circumstances—e.g., life or death choice or financial loss—and have to hope our micro experimental studies of decision processes reflect those that human beings use in complex decisions under ecologically valid circumstances. For this reason, psychologists must (1) experiment with micro learning experiments using cognitive material, hoping that it will extrapolate, (2) use natural history methods and correlational analyses, or (3) use experimental studies of other species and again hope that the results extrapolate to human aging.

If we regard the structure of experience as the result of culture, the "DNA of society," then cross-cultural studies may provide comparisons that, although not experimentally conclusive, still offer information about how behavior is organized over time. These studies do not manipulate what we suspect as being causal in aging, but we can compare them to many "natural experiments," and such comparisons can lead to inferences.

One of the models that has influenced the selection of variables in naturalistic and experimental studies is that provided by the computer. One can speak of aging as being caused by alterations in "hardware" (biology) or in "software" (experience), and perhaps to their interactions. Certainly much of the behavior shown with advancing age is the result of the programming of our software as we grow up and grow old in a particular culture. Few scientists, moreover, would contest the idea that some behavioral changes with age are hardware induced.

If we were to replace time with other putative causal variables in the software, then time would remain as a causal variable in the hardware. Ideally one would like to say that if the hardware of the organism and the decision processes were held constant, the effects of experience that have a particular effect on behavior would define aging. Logically, of course, it is impossible to hold organisms constant. Thus, the experiment can replace time with other variables only in one domain of the organism. Stated differently, time is a ubiquitous variable, and if we attempt to explain time changes as dependent on other variables, it will simultaneously appear as an independent variable for all those conditions that we cannot hold constant. Any experiment on aging involves time as a dependent and an independent variable simultaneously. The idea that experimental studies should regard time or age as a variable that should be fully eliminated, or that it is infinitely eliminable, may be an ideal principle but logically an unobtainable goal for the complex behavior of living systems (Birren, 1959).

Recent developments in neuroscience appear to offer new ways of conceiving of behavior that suggest new ways of experimenting. For example, the brain/computer model assumes point-to-point communication of information that the hardware does not modify. Contemporary neurochemistry, on the other hand, indicates that the brain has many modulator circuits in which the point-to-point communication is modified or may not be transmitted, depending upon the transient states within the modulator systems. Over 40 chemical substances that are purported to have neurotransmitter properties have been identified. Such substances modify the state of activity of cells in the brain other than the cells from which they originated. One contribution to modern neuroscience is that it describes much more of the complexity of the nervous system, a complexity we sensed must exist but for which we had no model. The importance of such findings is that they provide the means of manipulating subsystems chemically so that the behavioral effects may be observed.

For many of the neurotransmitters there are substances that will selectively enhance (agonists) or suppress (antagonists) action. For example, one of the systems that has been implicated in aging is dopamine, a neurotransmitter suspected to decline with age in the mammalian nervous system. To mimic the effects of aging experimentally or to test the hypothesis that the dopamine system declines with age, one can introduce into the organism a dopamine antagonist called haloperidol. Alternatively, if the hypothesis is that aging is the result of an increased activity of a neurotransmitter, then an agonist can be introduced into the organism to mimic these phenomena.

Not only may primary informational systems and modulators be manipulated experimentally, but a greater comparability of animal and human research may result. In addition, balances in behavior may be studied by using graded amounts of antagonists or agonists to increase the activity of one transmitter and decrease that of another. One of the characteristics of many aged persons is that they can do everything they did earlier in life but not do it so well. Thus function may be reduced with age but not categorically absent as it might be as a result of disease. Advances in neuroscience may thus lead to the design of experimental studies in which direct manipulation of neurotransmitter systems will be able to simulate the complex interactive phenomena of aging, e.g., hardware–software hypotheses.

In addition to modelling aging as a normal process of diminished or enhanced function, manipulation of the activity of selected neurotransmitters may also be used to model age-associated states such as depression or mania. As yet, we cannot reproduce Alzheimer's disease experimentally or significantly modify its course, but we can now begin to anticipate the design of such experiments. Not only is neuroscience beginning to provide a rational psychopharmacology of old age, it is also opening the door to the study of software–hardware interactions on an experimental basis. Thus, animals may learn a complex behavior and then be subjected to selective neurotransmitter modification. Conversely, the neurotransmitters may be modified in advanced of the learning. Another experimental advantage provided by current neurochemical knowledge about the brain is that it permits manipulations of different behavioral subsystems, i.e., those that are cognitive, affective, or effective, as well as those that relate to somatic regulation.

KINDS OF RESEARCH

Experimental Gerontology

Since the psychology of aging is part of the broader scientific effort of gerontology, it seems desirable to link the concerns of psychologists in explaining patterns of change with age with those of other scientists who explore the phenomena of aging from the viewpoints of physiology, biochemistry, physics, and morphology as well as the social sciences (see Verzar, 1963, pp. 4–5). This is also true of combinations of biological and neurophysiological research oriented toward behavioral issues.

Organ Systems

One of the properties of aging appears to be that the effects of experience and damage are accumulated over time. This would suggest that there are some archive-like systems of the body whose functions are more intimately related to the passage of time than are others. Special attention has been given to the immune system, the endocrine system, the nervous system, and the cardiovascular system, all of which have a high probability of limiting the longevity of the organism itself. Given the fact that experimental animals need not show cerebrovascular or cardiovascular disease with age, the frequent occurrence of diseases of the heart and brain circulation may not be intrinsically related to an evolved biological pattern of aging in human beings. In this sense, vascular disease in older adults may be a secondary phenomena of aging not reflective of a primary pacemaker of aging at the biological level. More attention has recently been given to the immune system and the nervous system in the process of aging.

RESEARCH EVALUATION

Researchers, teachers, and students are often asked to give a critique of a research report or a proposed study. Since the content of a research proposal or published article can resist dissection, it has proven useful to employ an outline that poses questions for the reader to consider in arriving at an evaluation. Advanced graduate seminars are sometimes based on the application of such an outline to various substantive areas of interest. The outline that follows has been adapted from two earlier versions (Birren, 1959a, pp. 38–40, and Birren and Renner, 1977, pp. 31–34). It covers most aspects of research from the initial question to the conclusions drawn from the empirical results.

Naturally, the evaluator must use his judgment as to which aspects of the outline are most pertinent to a given report or proposal. The components of research studies and their published reports are, characteristically, not uniformly strong in quality. It is often useful to consider each aspect separately in arriving at an evaluation of a dissertation or research proposal or in determining whether a published article represents a significant addition to knowledge. Although intuitive thinking is part of the process that accompanies the weighing of the strengths and weaknesses of a study, the following evaluation outline is presented in the hope that a more logical and analytical approach will help to guide those of us who find it necessary to make judgments about the quality and meaning of research.

(A) Problem

1. What is the purpose of the research?
2. Is the problem clearly and concisely stated so that it can be investigated or solved?
3. Does the research problem have a conceptual framework?
4. Is it clear whether this is a descriptive or normative study, a survey, a study to test a hypothesis, or some combination thereof?
5. Is the context of the problem described in such a way that it is readily apparent what is included and excluded from consideration?
6. Are the essential concepts necessary to understand the problem defined?
7. Are the terms defined clearly? Is there confusion in the definition of terms? Do they have arbitrary or multiple meanings?
8. Are assumptions stated and are they tenable in the light of existing research literature?
9. Is the literature of previous studies adequately reviewed or taken into account?
10. Is there an attempt to make a contribution to systematizing previous information?
11. Are the hypotheses and objectives stated in the context of the research problem?
12. If a hypothesis is tested, is the theory

from which it is derived sufficiently stated so that the relationship between the hypothesis and the theory can be evaluated?

13. Are the independent and dependent variables clearly identified and defined?
14. Are the consequences of possible findings pointed out?
15. Is the scope of the problem too large for the resources available and the methods which can be used? Is the proposed work only a pilot study, a kind of example of the phenomena of interest, or a small part of the whole problem? If so, is it identified as such?

(B) Experience of the Investigators

1. Are the investigators trained in the particular methods and procedures used?
2. Do the investigators have experience with the particular population studied?
3. If the study is large in scope and therefore demanding in terms of administrative responsibility, has the investigator the skills or experience to manage the project?

(C) Design

1. Was the design of the study planned and evaluated beforehand? Or does the study (as is often the case in longitudinal studies or archival expeditions) take advantage of existing data. If so, are the limitations of the available data explicitly discussed?
2. Is the design capable of providing an answer to the problem posed? Is the design applicable to, oversimplified, or unnecessarily complicated for the problem?
3. Does the design take into account all the pertinent aspects of the study: subjects and materials, environments, manipulated variables or stimuli, measurements and observations, and statistical methods?
4. Were alternative designs considered and the basis for their rejection given?
5. Are the compromises made with an ideal design described?
6. Is the design succinctly presented, as in a diagram, so that it can be readily understood?
7. Is the design an efficient one to solve the problem in terms of money, subjects, and time?
8. Are the statistical methods to be used determined before the experiment starts?
9. Was the level of significance with respect to accepting or rejecting the null hypothesis determined and discussed before the study was undertaken?

(D) Sampling of Subjects and Materials

1. Was the sample adequately described?
2. Of what population, if any, was the sample representative?
3. Was the population or subgroups of the population sampled?
4. Was the sample an appropriate one for the purposes of the study?
5. Was the sample collected for the purposes of this study or for some other purpose?
6. Was there any possibility of the introduction of a sampling bias?
7. Were the subjects selected according to the design of the study and with regard to the statistical methods to be used?
8. Was the sampling adequate to result in a standard error small enough for the purposes of the study?
9. If animals were used, have the conditions of the colony been evaluated and described?
10. Has the health of the subjects been evaluated and described?
11. Were the subjects taking medication? If so, could this have influenced the results?
12. Was there any loss of subjects or mortality in the sample, and, if so, is there a discussion of its possible effect on the results?
13. If replacement procedures for missing subjects were used, were such procedures adequate and were they sufficiently described?
14. Were the methods of sampling described as follows?
    (a) Simple random
    (b) Systematic

(c) Multistage random
(d) Stratified
   1) proportional allocation
   2) optimum allocation
   3) disproportional allocation
(e) Cluster
(f) Stratified cluster
(g) Biased
(h) Purposive
(i) Incidental
(j) Repetitive
(k) Judgment, quota.

(E) Controls

1. What controls were exercised through sampling (e.g., twins, littermates, and matching)?
2. What controls were exercised by selection of setting or natural habitat?
3. If relevant, were blind or double controls used in the gathering, evaluating, and interpretation of the data?
4. Were placebo effects controlled?
5. What controls were exercised by experimental manipulation? Were the controlled variables adequately described?
6. Were the conditions the same for all subjects or were adjustments made or a treatment given?
7. If controls were changed, were results analyzed with respect to the altered conditions?
8. Were any important controls absent that are usually found in a study of this type, and, if so, was the absence justified?

(F) Measurements and Data Collection

1. Were the techniques of measurement or observation adequately described?
2. Was a pilot study conducted, particularly if the materials were constructed for the present experiment?
3. If standardized tests were used, was there reference to normative data?
4. Were all variables of the study categorized and quantified sufficiently?
5. Were the data collected accurately and objectively? What checks were made to guard against possible error in collecting and tabulating data?
6. If several measures were taken, was a reasonable and predetermined time schedule followed?
7. Were reliability coefficients calculated between observers or examiners concerning their scoring of tests or evaluation of their subjects? Were possible examiner biases measured?
8. Were the methods and measurements suitable for testing the hypotheses and meeting the objectives of the research?
9. Were calibrations of instruments, observer differences, and other aspects of the techniques described? From the information presented could the measurements be repeated by another investigator?
10. Were the measurements or observations known to be sufficiently reliable for the study or, if new, were reliability coefficients reported?
11. Was the validity of the measurements established? Has the construct validity of the tests or measures been reported?

(G) Data Treatment

1. Were the methods of recording and the treatment of data described?
2. Were the statistical procedures clearly described?
3. Were the statistical procedures used appropriate for the research problem and the data?
4. If several different statistical analyses were made, is it clear how they are related? What contribution did each analysis make to the results?
5. Were the underlying assumptions of the statistical tests violated because of the methods, sampling, or nature of the data?
6. Were the tests of significance described and are they suitable?

(H) Results

1. Were the results or data adequately presented so that the reader can verify the author's statements about them?
2. Were the results clearly reported in tables and graphs so that others may use the data or reproduce the results? Were means and variances reported?

3. Were the essential relationships posed by the problem analyzed and tested for significance? Were trends interpreted as if they were statistically significant?
4. Were the results a logical product of the procedures and analyses, and were they relevant to the problem as originally outlined? In other words, was there a logical connection between the problem, the hypotheses, the design, the results and the conclusions?
5. Were the statistical limitations of the study appreciated and explained?
6. Were estimates of error provided and sources of error identified and qualified?
7. If several related variables were examined, were the results consistent?
8. Were the results internally consistent?
9. Were the actual results confused by unlabelled speculation or conjecture by the researcher?
10. Can the results be attributed to a treatment, spontaneous recovery, or other effects?

(I) Conclusions

1. Does the author draw conclusions about the major problem posed in the study?
2. Are the conclusions clearly supported by the data? Are there inconsistencies between the results and conclusions? Are conjectures and speculations clearly separated from the researched facts? Is there a clear, logical thread running from the problem statement through the discussion of the meaning of the findings?
3. Are the limitations of the study clearly stated?
4. Are the results generalized to the population at large? What rationale is provided, and is the generalization valid?
5. Have unexpected results been rejected merely because they do not agree with the researcher's expectations or because they appear to conflict with common sense?
6. Are statistically nonsignificant tests evaluated, or are they interpreted to be meaningless and unimportant? Are nonsignificant trends in the results section promoted to significant findings in the discussion section?
7. Are important reservations or qualifications pointed out? Are possible artifacts or spurious relations pointed out?
8. Has the author overlooked important aspects of the results?
9. Can additional questions or new hypothesis be generated from the study, and are they stated?
10. Is sufficient information presented so that the study can be replicated and cross-validated?
11. Are the results interpreted in relation to other published information, and is their significance for related fields pointed out? What are the implications of the results for knowledge in the field?
12. Are the methods used reviewed critically in the light of the obtained results?
13. Are the interpretations, implications for future research, and the development of new methods appropriate for the scope of the present study, or do they reflect an overestimation of the significance of the study?
14. What is the potential importance of the study, and what scientific or practical advances will result?
15. Are necessary modifications of theory or current interpretations of data or practice pointed out?
16. What contributions have been made to the theory of the subject?

EPILOGUE

In the previous version of this chapter (Birren and Renner, 1977), investigators were urged to undertake experimental studies on aging. It was recognized, however, that although experimental research is usually accompanied by fewer errors of interpretation, it is also difficult for psychologists to do major experimental studies of human aging for ethical reasons. Psychologists thus tend to use micro learning experiments, for example, and hope that these transfer to more complex aspects of human behavior. The other more common approach is to use description and natural history methods, correlational analyses, and occasionally "natural experiments." It is not likely that the near future will allow us to do major experimental studies of aging in which we attempt to replace the suspected independent variable involved in aging. It seems appropriate, therefore, for psychologists to continue to "encourage a descriptive and analytical psychology of aging while striving toward experimental control of the major causes of aging" (Birren, 1970, p. 135).

Aging is such a complex subject that we must approach it with many different points of view. Psychologists have been said to have four major scientific paradigms: formism, mechanism, organism, and contextualism (Pepper, 1942). Yet each of these world views seem to have some inadequacy when we contemplate what is perhaps mankind's greatest dilemma, his time-related mortality. Perhaps our bread-and-butter concepts of the organization of life are less likely to seem inadequate when dealing with issues of early-life development than when they are used to provide generalizations about aging, how the organism becomes transformed from a young to an old member of a species. One suspects that the future will bring with it new paradigms that will tell us "where" to look, how to "explain," and new ways of conducting experiments. It seems appropriate at this point to point out some trends that may prove fertile for the psychology of aging.

Molecular biology is now providing methods for identifying the actions of specific genes as well as for their localization and their transfer to new organisms. Modification of the course of life of experimental animals can soon be undertaken in efforts to understand the control that specific genes exercise on the timing of phenomena. Certainly the identification of the genes responsible for brain deterioration, as found in Alzheimer's Disease, presumably by the experimental manipulation of the expression of the genetic trait, would be a great step forward. Experimental gerontology based upon molecular biology may soon be in the repertory of laboratory methods, one from which psychologists could gain much in the understanding of aging in experimental animals.

Yet another major paradigmatic shift is underway in the neurosciences, which are providing ways of examining behavioral interactions by modifying particular neurotransmitter substances. Thus the nervous system, so important to complex behavior and the basis of *human* existence, may soon be a suitable laboratory in which to study aging. The study of the effects of behavior which may be organized on the basis of experience in relation to the effects of genetic determinants is a more perplexing prospect. Perhaps the perplexity arises because our paradigms of the nervous system do not now embrace sufficient aspects of the complexity of the organization. To this end, we introduced the thoughts of Yates since his interests lie in characterizing a science of complexity, a one-science approach than can embrace the range of phenomena from human social behavior to molecular events (Yates, 1982). Certainly psychologists are in need of new paradigms to help them ease out of the rigid molds of characterizing phenomena as either biological or social.

One example of a trend in social science research is that of Schinnar and Stewman (1978), who proposed a model of social mobility in which both age and duration in a social class were considered. In their model, "memory duration patterns" are introduced, and the authors suggest a "concept of 'social' or 'psychological' duration, called duration memory, which records duration in terms of its effect on movement, rather than by simply being a chronological 'counter' " (Schinnar and Stewman, 1978, p. 63). The model is relevant to aging since different age groups can behave differently even though they may have been in the same period of time in the same social space. Here are the beginnings of a social science modelling that embraces many of the complex features of aging and human social life that we have neglected in the past because of our limited paradigms and analytical methods.

One of the dramatic growths in social movements in recent years is the trend toward the formation of self-help groups. This has focused on groups of vulnerable individuals such as alcoholics, drug users, sex-offenders, rape victims, etc. Presumably the learning that one

maintaining an internal environment

obtains in such groups is different in some important ways from the learning individuals achieve alone, e.g., by reading. One thought is that self-help groups not only supply a large body of information in a cognitive sense but also deal with emotions and therefore provide subjective support in ways that individuals cannot secure alone. The following widely quoted comment by Mowrer is relevant: "You alone can do it, but you can't do it alone" (Mowrer, 1964). While this is not yet made explicit, self-help groups appear to assume that the human subject is interacting in a group at several levels which cannot be simply understood in either biological or social terms as we now use them. As self-help groups are developed for selected older populations or for families with older members, the new experimental opportunities presented will enable us to understand better how behavior becomes organized and the circumstances under which it become disorganized. The original chapter of this book pointed out that there is much to be optimistic about in the growth of our understanding of the processes of aging but that there is very little systematic theory to help us organize the information already existing. "Research sectarianism is another impediment to research on aging that has perhaps blocked theoretical formulations that take into account the fundamental biological as well as social nature of mankind" (Birren and Renner, 1977, p. 35).

At this point, it is perhaps appropriate to reflect upon the different obligations we have as members of a species that is hopeful of survival as well as our obligations to survive as individuals. It would seem that natural selection has favored reproduction during young adulthood when there is the least risk in terms of the possibility of defective offspring. Conceiving at an age when we are neither too young nor too old would seem to provide the circumstances under which an optimum germ cell would develop. If aging provides an advantage to the species by decreasing the probability of conception by old parents and thereby of defective offspring, it leaves to the individual an uncertain struggle for biological and psychological survival. Under optimal conditions of a changing body and changing envi-

ronment, the older person would seem to seek to maintain maximum adaptive capacity and to establish an equilibrium or homeostasis with the biological, psychological, and social forces acting upon him. This implies that the executive portion of the nervous system that is involved with voluntary activity is directing behavior toward achievement of a balance that is congruent with a lifetime of experience—a unique set of values and personality. The effort to establish a personal equilibrium among the forces that affect us results in some of us becoming wise as we grow old, more valuable to ourselves, to others, and to the broader flow of events that comprise a history of human destiny.

REFERENCES

Abrahams, J. P., and Birren, J. E. 1973. Reaction time as a function of age and behavioral predisposition to coronary heart disease. *J. of Gerontology* 28, No. 4: 471–478.

Bengtson, V., and Treas, J. 1980. The changing family content of mental health and aging. In *Handbook of Mental Health and Aging,* eds. J. E. Birren and R. B. Sloane, pp. 400–428. Englewood Cliffs, N.J.: Prentice-Hall.

Berg, D.; Hertzog, C.; and Hunt, E. 1982. Age differences in the speed of mental rotation. *Developmental Psychology* 18: 95–107.

Binstock, R., and Shanas, E. 1976. *Handbook of Aging and the Social Sciences.* New York: Van Nostrand Reinhold.

Birren, J. E. 1959a. Principles of research on aging. In *Handbook of Aging and the Individual,* ed. J. E. Birren, pp. 3–42. Chicago: University of Chicago Press.

Birren, J. E., ed. 1959b. *Handbook of Aging and the Individual.* Chicago: University of Chicago Press.

Birren, J. E. 1964. *The Psychology of Aging.* Englewood Cliffs, N.J.: Prentice-Hall.

Birren, J. E. 1965. Age changes in speed of behavior: its central nature and physiological correlates. In *Behavior, Aging, and the Nervous System,* eds. A. T. Welford and J. E. Birren, pp. 191–216. Springfield, Illinois: Charles C Thomas.

Birren, J. E. 1970. Toward an experimental psychology of aging. *American Psychologist* 25: 124–135.

Birren, J. E. 1974. Psychophysiology and speed of response. *American Psychologist* 29: 808–815.

Birren, J. E.; Cunningham, W. R.; and Yamamoto, K. 1983. Psychology of adult development and aging. *Ann. Rev. Psychology* 34: 543–575.

Birren, J. E., and Renner, V. J. 1977. In *Handbook of the Psychology of Aging,* eds. J. E. Birren and K. W. Schaie, pp. 3–38. New York: Van Nostrand Reinhold.

Birren, J. E., and Renner, V. J. 1980. Concepts of mental

health and aging. In *Handbook of Mental Health and Aging,* eds. J. E. Birren and R. B. Sloane, pp. 3–33. Englewood Cliffs, N.J.: Prentice-Hall.

Birren, J. E., and Schaie, K. W. 1977. *Handbook of the Psychology of Aging.* New York: Van Nostrand Reinhold.

Botwinick, J. *Aging and Behavior.* 1978. New York: Springer.

Botwinick, J., and Siegler, I. C. 1981. Intellectual ability among the elderly: Simultaneous cross-sectional and longitudinal comparisons. *Developmental Psychology* 41: 656–670.

Boulding, K E. 1956. *The Image: Knowledge in Life and Society.* Ann Arbor, Mich.: University of Michigan Press.

Brewer, M. B.; Dull, V.; and Lui, L. 1981. Perceptions of the elderly: Stereotypes as prototypes. *J. Pers. Soc. Psychol.* 42: 656–670.

Brown, F. A., Jr. 1972. The "clocks" timing biological rhythms. *Amer. Scient.* 60: 756–766.

Burnet, F. M., Jr. 1970a. *Immunological Surveillance,* pp. 224–257. New York: Pergamon Press.

Burnet, F. M., Jr. 1970b. An immunological approach to aging. *Lancet* 2: 358–360.

Butler, R. N. 1975. *Why Survive? Being Old in America.* New York: Harper and Row.

Comfort, A. 1956. *The Biology of Senescence.* London: Routledge and Kegan Paul.

Costa, P. T., and McCrae, R. R. 1980. Functional age: A conceptual and empirical critique. Proceedings from the second conference on the epidemiology of aging, eds. S. G. Haynes and M. Feinleib. Washington, DHHS.

Cowdry, E. V. 1952. Ageing of individual cells. In *Cowdry's Problems of Ageing,* ed. A. I. Lansing, pp. 50–88. Baltimore: Williams & Watkins.

Cowdry, E. V. 1942. *Problems in Ageing.* Baltimore: Williams & Watkins.

Cunningham, W. R. 1980a. Age comparative factor analysis of ability variables in adulthood and old age. *Intelligence* 4: 133–149.

Cunningham, W. R. 1980b. Speed, age and qualitative differences in cognitive functioning. In *Aging in the 1980's,* ed. L. W. Poon. Washington, D.C.: American Psychological Society.

Cunningham, W. R. 1981. Ability factor structure differences in adulthood and old age. *Multivariate Behavioral Research* 16: 3–22.

Cunningham, W. R., and Birren, J. E. 1980. Age changes in the factor structure of intellectual abilities in adulthood and old age. *Educational and Psychological Measurement* 40: 271–290.

Dirken, J. M. 1972. *Functional Age of Industrial Workers.* Groningen, Netherlands: Walters-Noordhoff.

Donaldson, G. 1981. Letter to the Editor. *Journal of Gerontology* 36: 634–638.

Elias, M. F. 1980. Animal models for the study of hypertension and behavior. In *Hypertension and Cognitive Processes,* eds. M. F. Elias and D. H. P. Streeten. Mt. Desert, Maine: Beech Hill.

Finch, C. E., and Hayflick, L., eds. 1977. *Handbook of the Biology of Aging.* New York: Van Nostrand Reinhold.

Fraser, J. T., ed. 1966. *The Voices of Time.* New York: George Braziller.

Gruman, G. J. 1966. *A History of Ideas about the Prolongation of Life.* Transactions of the American Philosophical Society, vol. 56. Philadelphia: The American Philosophical Society.

Hasher, L., and Zacks, R. T. 1979. Automatic and effortful processes in memory. *Journal of Experimental Psychology,* 108: 356–388.

Havighurst, R. J. 1957. The social competence of middle-aged people. *Genet. Psychol. Monograph.,* 56: 297–375.

Heron A., and Chown, S. 1967. *Age and Function.* Boston: Little Brown.

Horn, J. L. 1978. Human ability systems. In *Life-Span Development and Behavior,* ed. P. B. Baltes, vol. 1. New York: Academic Press.

Jalavisto, E.; Lindquist, C.; and Makkonene, T. 1964. Assessment of biological age, III. Mental and neural factors in longevity. *Annales Academiae Scientiarum Fennicae* 106: 3–20.

Joreskog, K. C., and Sorbom, D. 1978. Analysis of linear structural relationships by the method of maximum likelihood. Chicago: National Educational Resources.

Kausler, D. H. 1982. *Experimental Psychology of Human Aging.* New York: Wiley.

Kleemeier, R. W. 1962. Intellectual changes in the senium. Proceedings of the Social Statistics Section of the American Statistical Association.

LaRue, A.; Bank, L.; Jarvik, L.; and Hetland, M. 1979. Health in old age: How do physicians' ratings and self-ratings compare? *Journal of Gerontology* 34: 687–691.

Lawton, M. P. 1982. Kleemeier award address. Gerontological Society of America.

Light, K. C. 1978. Effects of mild cardiovascular and cerebrovascular disorders on serial reaction time performance. *Exp. Aging Res.* 4: 3–22.

Makinodan, T. 1977. Immunity and aging. In *Handbook of the Biology of Aging,* eds. C. E. Finch and L. Hayflick, pp. 379–408. New York: Van Nostrand Reinhold.

Mossey, J. M., and Shapiro, E. 1982. Self-rated health: a predictor of mortality among the elderly. *Amer. J. Pub. Health* 72: 800–808.

Mowrer, O. H. 1964. *The New Group Therapy.* New York: D. Van Nostrand.

Pepper, S. C. 1942. *World Hypotheses, a Study in Evidence.* Berkeley, Calif.: University of California Press.

Ragan, P., and Wales, J. 1980. Age stratification and the life course. In *Handbook of Mental Health and Aging,* eds. J. E. Birren and R. B. Sloane, pp. 377–399. Englewood Cliffs, N.J.: Prentice-Hall.

Reichenbach, M., and Mathers, R. A. 1959. The place of time and aging in the natural sciences and scientific philosophy. In *Handbook of Aging and the Individual,* ed. J. E. Birren, pp. 43–80. Chicago: University of Chicago Press.

Salthouse, T. A. 1983. *Adult Cognition: An Experimental Psychology of Human Aging.* New York: Springer Verlag.

Sampson, G. A., and Jenner, F. E. 1975. Circadian

rhythms and mental illness. *Psychol. Med.* 5: 4–8.

Schaie, K. W. 1979. The primary mental abilities in adulthood: An exploration in the development of psychometric intelligence. In *Life-Span Development and Behavior,* eds. P. B. Baltes and O. G. Brim. New York: Academic Press.

Schinnar, A. P., and Stewman, S. 1978. A class of Markov models of social mobility with duration memory patterns. *J. Math. Sociology* 6: 61–86.

Schroots, J. J. F. 1983. The effective consequences of technological change for older persons. (In press.)

Schroots, J. J. F., and Birren, J. E. 1980. A psychological point of view toward human aging and adaptability. In *Adaptability and Aging.* Proceedings of 9th International Conference of Social Gerontology, Quebec, Canada, pp. 43–54.

Schulz, R., and Hanusa, B. H. 1978. Long term effects of control and predictability-enhancing intervention: Findings and ethical issues. *J. Person. Soc. Psychol.* 36: 1194–1201.

Siegler, I. 1975. The terminal drop hypothesis: Fact or artifact? *Experimental Aging Research* 1: 169–185.

Siegler, I. C.: George, L. K., and Okun, M. A. 1979. Cross-sequential analysis of adult personality. *Developmental Psychology* 15: 350–351.

Siegler, I.; Nowlin, J. B.; and Blumental, J. A. 1980. Health and Behavior: Methodological considerations for adult development and aging. In *Aging in the 1980's,* ed. L. W. Poon. Washington: American Psychological Association.

Smith, J. M. 1957. Genetic variations in ageing. In *The Biology of Ageing,* eds. W. B. Yapp and G. H. Bourne, pp. 115–122. London: Institute of Biology.

Speith, W. 1964. Cardiovascular health status, age and psychological performance. *Journal of Gerontology* 19: 277–284.

Thomae, H., ed. 1976. *Patterns of Aging:* Contributions to human development, vol. 3. Basel, Switzerland: S. Karger.

Verzar, F. 1963. *Lectures in Experimental Gerontology.* Springfield, Ill.: Charles C. Thomas.

Willis, S. L.; Bleiszer, R.; Baltes, P. B. 1981. Intellectual training research in aging: Modification of performance on the fluid ability of figural relations. *Journal of Educational Psychology* 73: 41–50.

Wilkie, F., and Eisdorfer, C. 1971. Intelligence and blood pressure in the aged. *Science* 172: 959–962.

Winfree, A. T. 1975. Unclockwise behavior of biological clocks. *Nature* 253: 315–319.

Wolstenholme, G. E. W., and O'Connor, C. M., eds. 1957. *Methodology of the Study of Aging.* London: J. and A. Churchill.

Yates, F. W. 1982. Outline of a physical theory of physiological systems. *Canadian Journal of Physiology and Pharmacology* 60: 217–248.

2
EXPERIMENTAL DESIGN IN RESEARCH ON AGING

John R. Nesselroade
Pennsylvania State University

and
Erich W. Labouvie
Rutgers, The State University

INTRODUCTION: GENERAL PURPOSE OF RESEARCH DESIGN

Research designs are arranged for the purpose of gathering empirical information about variables and their interrelationships in ways that facilitate their interpretation and evaluation. As with any cumulative knowledge base, decades of practice, concern, and thought have led to a more or less formal set of principles and criteria that can be applied systematically in the pursuit of empirically based answers to research questions (Campbell and Stanley, 1963; Cattell, 1966a; Cook and Campbell, 1979; Edwards, 1950; Underwood, 1957). The formal principles, though valuable, are quite broad, and when one gets down to the level of actually integrating design concerns with substantive questions, the interdependence of the two becomes salient. In the context of research in aging, Schaie (1977) discussed the fundamental inseparability of basic assumptions about the nature of the substantive area and research design concerns. Ultimately, research designs become orchestrations of ideal arrangements, on the one hand, and constraints and limitations, on the other—some imposed by the problem and its theoretical context, some by the structural characteristics of the arrangements that provide the clearest, most unambiguous answers to questions, and some by contextual features over which the investigator has no control. The first two are the primary focus of the discussion to follow. Meshing the variety of constraints into the most efficient design possible is part of the challenge of empirical research no less in the field of aging than in any other area of empirical inquiry.

In this chapter we examine several matters that we believe need to be attended to in the design of research in aging.[1] We have built our own presentation on several extant discussions, some of which are in the initial edition of this handbook. The chapter is developed around some rather standard topical material. Some of our presentation is in the form of summary and comment, some in the form of extensions that we believe to be pertinent to the design and conduct of aging research, and some in the form of injunctions concerning the critical elements that researchers in aging cannot afford to overlook.

[1]The authors are grateful to C. K. Hertzog for his many valuable comments on an earlier version of this chapter.

35

Theoretical Context and Questions versus Principles of Design

As noted above, we will attend primarily to two general classes of conditions or limiting factors that bear on the design of empirical research. One class represents the formalized structure of general design principles that apply across disciplines and subdisciplines and are communicable essentially in the abstract. The second is the class of limitations imposed by the research question and its theoretical context. The latter includes constraints imposed both by the fundamental nature of the general phenomenon and the level of development and articulation of theory at a given time. These two classes of factors that jointly determine the optimal characteristics of a research design are not completely exclusive of one another. For instance, in some theoretical frameworks, aging involves the concept of maturational changes. In the context of experimental designs, however, maturation is often considered to be a confound to be eliminated from the effects being studied rather than a phenomenon to be examined in its own right.

The context of one's research question, broadly defined, includes metamodels, "world views," or "world hypotheses" (Overton and Reese, 1973; Reese and Overton, 1970); specific theories with conceptual definitions of constructs; measurement models with operational definitions of concepts; relevant empirical generalizations; and other products deriving from the investigation of some subset of natural events. These sources influence the design of research in a cumulative way, and their impact shows up both at a general level in the form of the questions that are asked and also at a more specific level in, for example, a particular choice of variables to be manipulated, measured, and controlled. Cattell (1966a) pointed out, for example, how Galileo *ignored* distance from the center of the earth and *controlled* pendulum mass in some early experiments whereas both decisions are now known to be fallacious in that the former greatly affects pendulum behavior and the latter does not.

Our orientation is that aging research is an aspect of developmental inquiry and, as such, should be fitted into developmental research paradigms as discussed by Baltes, Reese, and Nesselroade (1977), Wohlwill (1973), and others. These matters we will pursue more fully in subsequent sections, following an examination of general research design perspectives.

The other class of constraints that operates in effecting research designs is the formal structure of the principles that have evolved and have been articulated in discussions of design issues and procedures (e.g., Campbell and Stanley, 1963; Cook and Campbell, 1979; and Underwood, 1957). These principles, we maintain, are applicable to empirical research in general regardless of the substantive field, particular theoretical orientation, etc. Understanding such general principles well enough to know which constraints should not be abandoned (indeed, cannot be abandoned without jeopardizing the research) and which ones are "negotiable" in some sense in the design of research is critical for investigators. It is difficult, for example, to imagine in the abstract the circumstances under which controls for testing effects could be justifiably foregone in a longitudinal study. For some measurement domains, however, sound theory development may make it possible to ignore the imposition of those controls without incurring risk of interpretational ambiguity.

While arguing for a robust set of general design principles that cuts across disciplines and subdisciplines, we also acknowledge that such principles are subject to clarification, modification, reinterpretation, etc., as a normal course of knowledge generation and elaboration and as the result of refinements in the definition of fundamental concepts such as causality and its demonstration. Recall, for instance, the situation in graduate training in psychology a few years ago when the teaching of principles of research design was inextricably woven into the presentation of the analysis of variance. A course in correlational methods was nonexistent in many programs and in others it was an anomaly the content of which had little to do with the teaching of design principles. Now, Bentler (1980), for instance, has called for graduate training programs in psychology to give at least as much emphasis to teaching correlational techniques such as structural equations analysis as they give to the manipulative, experimental designs that typically culminate in some form of analysis of variance.

Exploratory Versus Hypothesis-Testing Research Purposes

Even a cursory look at discussions of empirical research impresses one with the variety of classification dimensions applied to research activities. Some prominent examples are *descriptive vs. experimental, descriptive vs. explanatory, correlational vs. experimental, differential vs. experimental,* and *exploratory vs. confirmatory.* Some of the labels reflect research purpose, and some reflect orientation and techniques of empirical research. In a general discussion of design, research purpose seems to us to be the fundamentally important classification dimension. It, in turn, is identified closely with the level of theory development in the pertinent substantive area. At some risk of oversimplification, it may be said that with respect to level of theory development, the research purpose falls between the extremes of being descriptive and exploratory or hypothesis-testing and confirmatory (Nesselroade and Baltes, 1984).

In regard to theoretical purpose, some individual research studies can be rather clearly designated exploratory or hypothesis-testing whereas others are neither solely one nor the other. Often some balance between exploration and hypothesis-testing is involved, and the two kinds of activity augment one another, if not in individual research projects, then in a series of them, as Cattell (1966b) described in discussing the inductive-hypothetico-deductive spiral of research and theory development.

The exploratory versus hypothesis-testing dimension is closely identified with strategies for proceeding from the initial description of a phenomenon to its causal-analytic explication. On the one hand, description and exploration of a domain are obviously crucial activities and must occur, to some extent, prior to serious attempts to erect a systematic theoretical framework. For developmentalists just as for any other scientists, the importance of descriptive research is critical, a fact noted emphatically in developmental methodology discussions (e.g., Baltes, Reese, and Nesselroade, 1977; Wohlwill, 1973). On the other hand, the pursuit of causal-analytic representations of phenomena is the more general and scientifically valuable goal even though the concept of causation is defined in a variety of ways and its demonstration is at best a matter of successive approximation.

There are enough general aspects of the conditions for inferring causality to permit serious discussion of research design principles in relation to it. For our purposes here, the study of causal relationships may be said to involve some four general conditions. First, *covariation* among the hypothesized cause-and-effect variables is expected to be evident. Second, there should be a *temporal sequence* to the events in question in which putative effect follows hypothesized cause in time. Third, *spurious relationships* should be ruled out. Fourth, *replication* of the relationship should be possible. As will be pointed out later, such a sequence is somewhat idealized for the developmentalist. For some questions it may be possible, for others, not. In any case, effectively combining design principles with research purposes requires not only a clear understanding of the purposes but also a clear understanding of the dimensions of research design. That is the topic to which we turn next.

DIMENSIONS OF RESEARCH DESIGN

The dichotomy presented by *descriptive versus experimental* designs is highly revered in psychology. The experimental pole has often been defined to include only manipulative research, as lamented by Cattell (1966a). Yet, students of aging and other developmental phenomena have little choice but to assault existing divisions and limits if research on aging phenomena is to proceed along a variety of potentially fruitful paths such as have been outlined by developmentalists (e.g., Baltes et al., 1977; Wohlwill, 1973). Alternative schemes are particularly helpful when they unconfound research purpose and technique. Cattell (1966a), for example, has been outspoken in arguing for the merit of examining familiar research designs in a comparative analysis and using the outcome to broaden the term *experimental* to include alternate avenues to causal explication.

Supporting the timeliness of breaking the rigid *descriptive-versus-experimental* dichotomy in characterizing research designs are several lines of development. These include the explicit identification of threats to design validity and the evaluation of a variety of quasi-experimental and experimental designs in terms of profiles of strengths and weaknesses rather than a single categorical judgment of *acceptable* or *not acceptable* (Campbell and Stanley, 1963; Cook and Campbell, 1979; Schaie, 1977) and techniques that explicitly blend together individual differences and experimental concepts in representing the relationships among psychological variables (e.g., Cattell, 1979; Tucker, 1966). Moreover, the revival and improvement of techniques for modeling hypothesized causal systems with correlational data (Bentler, 1980; Horn and McArdle, 1980; Schaie and Hertzog, Chap. 3, this volume) helps to dramatize further the erosion of the attitude that causal analysis must rest on traditional manipulative experimentation and that all one can do with so-called correlational data is descriptive work.

Cattell (1966a) has argued that research designs vary in at least six important dimensions: (1) bivariate vs. multivariate; (2) presence vs. absence of manipulation; (3) simultaneity vs. succession of observations; (4) degree of situational background control; (5) representativeness in choice of variables; and (6) representativeness in choice of experimental subjects or units. In this section we will briefly examine each of these dimensions of research design to help set the stage for a specific consideration of aging research design in subsequent sections of the chapter.

Bivariate versus Multivariate in Number of Variables

Specification of a bivariate-multivariate dichotomy is not to deny the fact that there are important situations that involve only one variable—for example, when one or more parameters of a single variable are to be estimated for a group or subpopulation of experimental units. The design of such data-gathering activities, especially the articulation of a proper sampling scheme, requires special care and effort. Our concern, however, as stated earlier, is with relationships among variables, and thus the minimum number of variables of interest is two.

The bivariate versus multivariate dimension is clearly not synonymous with experimental versus correlational design. On the one hand, designs that involve the manipulation of one or more independent variable(s) typically involve the investigation of the effects of such manipulations on one or more dependent variable(s). Moreover, available analysis techniques (e.g., multivariate analysis of variance and discriminant function analysis) permit the assessment of such effects in efficient and economical ways that take into account the structure of covariation among these dependent variables. On the other hand, research designs that involve the observation and measurement of variables with no manipulated independent variables may involve two variables or many.

The choice of a bivariate versus a multivariate design is not made in relation to one's interest in incorporating a manipulative component in the design. Instead, underlying this choice are both conceptual and methodological considerations (Cattell, 1966a). More specifically, the decision involves not only the complexity of the conceptual network (or structural model) in terms of the number of relationships one wants to investigate simultaneously, but also the complexity of one's operational definitions (or measurement model) reflected in the number of empirical indicators used to measure each concept of interest (Baltes and Nesselroade, 1973; Nesselroade, 1977).

Presence versus Absence of Manipulation

Whether or not one manipulates at least one variable in order to determine its effects on at least one other variable is, for many researchers, the central if not the only basis for discriminating among kinds of research designs (e.g., experimental versus correlational). Moreover, few would deny the importance of manipulative designs in science (astronomers, paleontologists, etc., notwithstanding). Manipulative research provides a compelling means of testing putative causal relationships for those disciplines in which it is practicable. As noted earlier, however, there are reasons for arguing that using presence or absence of manipulation as the only or even the chief among several design classification bases is no longer as viable as it once was in psychology. One reason is the "blurring" of research design categories that resulted when Campbell and Stanley (1963) systematically identified the quasi-experimental designs and evaluated them with respect to 12 classes of validity characteristics. A second reason is exemplified by the articulation and development of the variety of mathematico-statistical models for analyzing covariance structures (Bentler, 1980; Cattell, 1965; Horn and McArdle, 1980; Jöreskog, 1981; Schaie and Hertzog, Chap. 3, this volume) in relation to hypothesized structures of causal relationships among variables.

Because every relationship of interest to researchers in the field of aging does not consist of one manipulable independent variable and one observable dependent variable, other avenues to the establishment of causal relationships need to be articulated, evaluated, and assimilated into the list of acceptable research procedures. This is not to downplay the reliance that we all should freely place on relationships that are demonstrable under manipulative-experimental conditions. However, although experimental manipulation represents in many ways the most straightforward and simplest means of demonstrating causal relationships, it is often not feasible for ethical reasons or because the causal networks of interest are too complex.

Simultaneity versus Succession of Observations

The time sequence of events is one of the key components of causal explanatory analysis. Whether or not observations of different variables are made at the same time, slightly differ-

ent times, or vastly different times is also a critical feature of research design. Cattell (1966a) noted that this dimension is widely but erroneously considered to be synonymous with the manipulation dimension. Past failure to distinguish between the two dimensions is probably due to the fact that the typical experiment incorporates a temporal sequence between manipulation of the independent variable(s) and observation of the dependent one(s). In comparison, the bulk of observational studies involves the simultaneous measurement of sets of variables. However, to the extent that causes have immediate or "instantaneous" effects, experiments may require the simultaneous observation of independent and dependent variables. At the same time, observational studies need to include successive or longitudinal observations if the emphasis is, for instance, on notions of individual change.

Cattell argued that, in the search for causal relationships, it is the time sequence rather than the manipulation per se that is a *sine qua non* of causal inference. He proposed the use of the terms *prior* and *subsequent* in lieu of *causal* and *consequent* for identifying the variables in a causal relationship. We agree with this position to the extent that the temporal ordering of observations on variables helps to rule out some of the possible causal paths *a priori.* Equally or even more important from a developmental point of view (and quite apart from the issue of causal inference) is the fact that the notion of individual change necessitates the temporal sequencing of observations.

Degree of Situational Background Control

One of the most significant consequences of nature's multivariate condition is that all the pertinent variables in any given situation are not known, let alone measured. This difficulty has been one of the strongest justifications for designing research to pit one treatment condition against others (including no-treatment, placebo, etc.) and assigning experimental subjects to conditions at random with the expectation of equating unmeasured influences across treatment groups. But there are other interesting questions for which random assignment is not tactically feasible and for which a whole cluster of variables are theoretically important and ought to be investigated concomitantly.

In nature, relationships of interest are not neatly packaged in pairs of variables that are conveniently nearly independent of all other such pairs. Rather, it is more the case that relationships of particular interest are embedded in a morass or network of interrelationships. The process of designing research "pulls" some variables into the foreground for observation, possible manipulation, etc., but probably many other variables not so explicitly recognized influence those that constitute the focal point of an investigation. Are the others to be eliminated, controlled within certain limits, or left free to vary? The matter has been formally structured, for instance, by the concern of Campbell and Stanley (1963) with the *settings* dimension of the external validity of research design. For example, in investigating bivariate relationships in tightly conducted laboratory experiments, the random assignment of subjects to treatment conditions results in other variables (e.g., subject variables) being equated and still others being held constant (e.g., climatic conditions in the laboratory).

In general, the notion of situational background has been used to refer to the concurrent setting in which a particular set of manipulations or observations is embedded. From a developmental point of view, however, it can be argued that a broader concept of what constitutes relevant background needs to include the developmental history and experiences of the entities studied. Thus, when comparing different age groups in the context of age by treatment interaction designs (Baltes and Goulet, 1971), it may be possible to control (and hold constant) the concurrent setting, but it is essentially impossible to obtain age groups that are equivalent in their developmental backgrounds except for some selected aspects such as educational level. We will return to this issue when we consider the representativeness of subjects.

Representativeness of Choice of Variables

The decision to incorporate only two instead of three or more variables into the research

design (bivariate vs. multivariate dimension) and deciding exactly which variables to include are quite different matters. Electing to focus on a set of variables chosen to be representative of some domain as opposed to using particular variables because they are currently in vogue, for convenience, because of personal preference, etc., bears directly on the design of research. The matter of domain sampling or representativeness of variables (Nunnally, 1967; Campbell and Stanley, 1963; Cattell, 1952; Cronbach, Gleser, Nanda, and Rajaratnam, 1972; Humphreys, 1962) remains one of the most critical areas of design decisions because of its impact on construct validity and generalizability or external validity of relationships (Cook and Campbell, 1979). Actually, as Cattell pointed out, the design question is a more general one in that the relatives (items being related to each other) may not always be variables in the traditional sense. In some designs they may be occasions, people, etc.

Representativeness of Subjects or Experimental Units

The choice of subjects and experimental units is often thought to involve only questions of external validity or generalizability and of statistical power. As a consequence, it is usually recommended that samples be sufficiently large and representative of the population(s) studied. In our opinion, it is too often forgotten that this matter is also relevant to aspects of internal validity. One reason for this oversight may arise from the fact that the latter problem is easily taken care of in the context of experimental studies where random assignment of subjects to experimental units is not only assumed to be feasible but is also actually achieved. However, a good deal of developmental and gerontological research is more appropriately characterized as quasi-experimental in the sense that (a) it may involve comparisons of several age or cohort populations (e.g., in the context of cross-sectional designs), and (b) random assignment of subjects is often not possible. In either case, some or all of the resulting experimental units are not equivalent. As discussed for the case of cross-sectional designs (Baltes, 1968; Schaie, 1965), this nonequivalence of experimental units represents a serious threat to the internal validity of empirical comparisons and associated inferences. We will deal with this problem more explicitly in a later section.

To summarize to this point, causal-analytic work relies on the concatenation of elements of the six design dimensions identified above. The "full" treatment, for example, may involve random assignment, manipulation, etc., which act to eliminate alternative explanations of the observed effects. The concepts of internal and external validity of design (Campbell and Stanley, 1963; Cook and Campbell, 1975, 1979), although they represent a somewhat different orientation to causal-analytic research, add some valuable perspectives on these topics. We will examine these design validity topics briefly and consider some aspects of communality among the six design dimensions and the internal and external validity concepts.

INTERNAL VALIDITY OF DESIGN: ISSUES OF CONTROL

Definition of Internal Validity

Campbell and Stanley (1963) and Cook and Campbell (1975, 1979) systematized both general design forms and control issues in empirical research and provided an evaluation of the former in relation to the latter. A major focus of their discussion was how to reduce the plausibility of alternative explanations for an observed relationship among presumed antecedent and consequent variables. The more that control conditions can be instituted to reduce any ambiguity concerning the responsibility of the putative causal mechanism for the observed effect, the more internally valid the design. For Campbell and Stanley, internal validity is the *sine qua non,* without which the outcomes of research investigations are uninterpretable.

Evaluation of internal design validity centers around several conditions or situations that threaten the validity of conclusions about the interrelationships among variables (Campbell and Stanley, 1963; Cook and Campbell, 1979). Baltes, Reese, and Nesselroade (1977) and Schaie (1977) have discussed threats to internal validity with particular reference to

developmental research applications. The principal message is that the threats signify that certain fundamental matters of design need to be considered explicitly by developmentalists so that those conditions that render interpretation dubious can be subjected to some sort of control conditions (elimination by randomization; measurement of covariates and statistical adjustment, equating of effects, etc.). Thus, the introduction of internal validity into a design is a matter of careful planning involving, on the one hand, knowledge of the general principles of implementing controls and, on the other hand, capacity to make adaptations to meet the specific needs of a particular research focus. In a given situation, since it may not be possible to protect against all threats, decisions have to be made concerning those that most endanger the sought after outcomes.

Threats to Internal Validity

The influences that jeopardize the internal validity of a design were organized into eight classes by Campbell and Stanley (1963). They are effects due to: (1) history; (2) maturation; (3) testing; (4) instrumentation; (5) statistical regression; (6) selection; (7) mortality; and (8) compounds of the first seven. Cook and Campbell (1979) added (9) ambiguity about the direction of causal influence; (10) diffusion or imitation of treatments; (11) compensatory equalization of treatments; (12) compensatory rivalry by respondents receiving less desirable treatments; and (13) resentful demoralization of respondents receiving less desirable treatments. Selected sources of competing effects are examined and discussed elsewhere in summaries that emphasize their applicability to developmental research (Baltes et al., 1977; Schaie, 1977). To illustrate both the nature of such threats and the need for developmentalists to consider any special relationships they may have to their own research issues and designs, we will briefly consider here one class of such effects—those due to the phenomenon of regression toward the mean (Furby, 1973; Labouvie, 1982a; Nesselroade, Stigler, and Baltes, 1980). Effects due to selection, perhaps the most pervasive threats to the internal validity of developmental and gerontological research, will be discussed in more detail subsequently.

"Regression toward the mean" refers to the phenomenon of differential expectations of mean scores on one variable given the nature of selection on another variable. The variables involved may be different ones measured at the same or different times, or the same variable measured at different times, as in the case of change measurement. For example—in reference to Furby (1973)—Nesselroade et al. (1980, p. 264) defined regression toward the mean as follows: "For a given score on X_1 (e.g., x') the corresponding mean score on X_2 (e.g., $E(X_2|X_1 = x')$ is closer to $E(X_2)$ in standard deviation units than x' is to $E(X_1)$ in standard deviation units." In less technical terms, if one selects people for some treatment because of their extreme need (i.e., a high-scoring group), their mean score would tend to be closer to their population mean at the next time of measurement according to the regression argument. Thus, the effects of any planned treatment interpolated between two such measurements would be confounded with the expected regression effects. Accordingly, evaluation of the effectiveness of the treatment is jeopardized by the expected regression effects. Random assignment of persons to treatment groups will, on the average, control for such regression effects, but in "real life" situations random assignment is often not the optimal basis on which to allot treatments.

Nesselroade et al. (1980) studied the concept of regression toward the mean specifically from the standpoint of its impact on the measurement of developmental change. They developed expectations for later observations conditioned on initial selection values, allowing for a number of different underlying models of the score sequence (e.g., classical test theory, auto-correlation). Their conclusion was that expectations regarding regression effects varied as a function of the underlying model. Moreover, it is important to consider the effects of regression in the context of a longer sequence of observations rather than just two occasions of measurement—a point reinforced by Rogosa, Brandt, and Zimowski (1982) in discussing how to measure change. Regression is not an ubiquitous phenomenon,

as argued by Furby (1973), nor does the expectation of regression continue to hold across subsequent occasions of measurement. However, regression does occur, especially in the two occasions of measurement situation (e.g., selection and follow up), and thus it constitutes some threat to the internal validity of research designs that do not control for it. Nesselroade et al. (1980) showed that for many underlying models the effects of regression toward the mean are exhausted between the selection and first comparison occasion, a fact that suggests that the control for regression in longitudinal studies of monitoring does not change from selection on but from the first comparison measurement on. Finally, as Labouvie (1982a) pointed out, the interpretation of such effects may differ for different conceptual and operational definitions of the concept of change.

Relationships to Design Dimensions

The threats to internal validity can be grouped primarily around the following four dimensions of experimental design identified above: (1) presence versus absence of manipulation; (2) simultaneity versus succession of observations; (3) degree of situational background control, and (4) representativeness of subjects. We will consider each of these in turn, linking them to internal validity and control issues.

Presence versus absence of manipulation bears directly on the internal validity aspect in that it covers the condition of deliberate manipulation of the presumed causal variable(s) as opposed to observing a putative causal variable or variables in relation to its (their) consequences. Strictly interpreted, Campbell and Stanley (1963) limit their discussion of design validity to the case of manipulation. Obviously, absence of manipulation can apply both to cases of putative causal mechanisms that, by their nature, preclude manipulation and to cases where no discrimination among variables as to putative cause and effect is made. From the standpoint of causal analysis, presence versus absence of manipulation defines quite disparate approaches to the establishment of explanatory systems. These differences are exemplified in the so-called experimental versus differential tradition (Cronbach, 1957, 1975) and, to some extent more specifically, in the analytic traditions of analysis of variance versus path analysis and other forms of covariance structure analysis. Manipulation, especially in connection with random assignment of subjects, clearly helps to make possible the arrangement of design conditions that reduce ambiguity concerning causal relationships. But, in the absence of manipulation and/or random assignment, alternative models of causal relationships can be pitted against each other and compared for goodness of fit to one's data (Bentler, 1980). The latter may be the best that developmentalists can expect for many of their research questions.

Simultaneity versus succession of observations also bears directly on the matter of internal validity of design. To the extent that one can bring the temporal sequence aspect of the establishment of causality into play, the successive aspect of observing helps to arrange conditions for a clearer identification of the plausibility of a putative causal relationship. The use of cross-lagged panel correlation designs, for example, to study developmental phenomena (Clarke-Stewart, 1978; Rogosa, 1979) illustrates an attempt to buttress the validity of causal inference when manipulation cannot be achieved. Furthermore, as we mentioned before, the dimension of simultaneity versus succession of observation has special significance for the internal validity of developmental and gerontological research concerned with the study of individual change. Besides the fact that the notion of individual change requires a succession of observations, it is well documented that simultaneous cross-sectional observations of age differences may have little internal validity as indicators of age changes (e.g., Baltes, Reese, and Nesselroade, 1977; Wohlwill, 1973).

Degree of situational background control is a pivotal concept in that it applies to aspects of both the internal validity and, as will be noted subsequently, the external validity of designs. In relation to the internal validity of a design, situational background control involves attending to those environmental variables that may compete with "target" causal variables in the sense that their effects might plausibly include those reflected in the measurement variables to be explained. Thus, the effects of retirement from gainful employment on the sociability of older adults is confounded with such influences as age-related health status changes and increased likelihood of loss of close friends with whom one wishes to socialize.

Finally, and in a similar way, the degree of representativeness of subjects and experimental units involves not only aspects of external validity but is often critically important for the internal validity of empirical comparisons. Nonrandom assignment of subjects to experimental units (e.g., senior citizens in one retirement home are assigned to the experimental group, those in another home to the control group) and the use of convenience samples (e.g., undergraduate students in a particular college, senior citizens from a particular church group) can produce empirical evidence with little internal validity as far as causal inferences are concerned.

Control Devices

The incorporation of controls for threats to internal validity is obviously a key element in designing reliable empirical research. Ideally, corresponding strategies involve the utilization of appropriate control groups in conjunction with random assignment of subjects to the various experimental and control groups. In reality, however, this approach is often not feasible or even possible in developmental research. Thus, an alternative strategy is required. Frequently, it involves the incorporation of what might be called *a posteriori* controls. On the one hand, this approach still demands that systematic design decisions be made—in terms of targeting a selection of control variables to be measured in addition to those of primary interest—before a study is actually carried out. On the other hand, it is *a posteriori* in the sense that it takes the form of statistical corrections and estimations after the empirical evidence has been gathered. In other words, when one is studying a putative causal relationship under less than idealized control conditions, one can attempt to remove or partially remove the effects of other possible explanatory variables from the relationship of interest to determine whether or not the magnitude of the remaining relationship is consistent with a causal interpretation.

Such a posteriori control devices continue to increase in complexity and sophistication both tactically and strategically (Bentler, 1980; Games, 1979; Sörbom, 1979). For example, covariance structure analysis and causal modeling techniques offer procedures for evaluating rival explanations. This ability is the goal of all attempts to ensure internal validity, and for the developmentalist, such approaches represent the common ground between general design principles and substantive constraints discussed at the beginning of this chapter.

EXTERNAL VALIDITY OF DESIGN: ISSUES OF GENERALIZABILITY

Definition of External Validity

External validity of design, according to Campbell and Stanley (1963), refers to the degree to which relationships are generalizable to other observations. Campbell and Stanley identified four principal facets to be explicitly attended to in the matter of generalizing relationships among variables: (1) measurement variables; (2) treatment conditions; (3) settings; and (4) subgroups of individuals. Baltes, et al. (1977), added to these four a fifth—occasions of measurement—to accommodate more adequately the research foci of developmentalists. Campbell and Stanley noted that external validity is something that cannot be unequivocally determined in post hoc fashion but, rather, is insured by representative sampling of the domains of generalization. The nature of external validity is also discussed in the context of measurement generalizability (Cronbach, Gleser, Nanda, and Rajaratnam, 1972) and in the definition of covariation techniques (Cattell, 1952, 1966). Cook and Campbell's (1979) distinction between external validity and construct validity in relation to causes and effects helps to differentiate between measurement-to-construct generaliz-

ability and construct-to-construct generalizability.

Relationships that are not generalizable beyond the particular samples and situations in which they are observed cannot contribute directly to the body of scientific knowledge. At the one extreme, the straight replication of a relationship between variables is an aspect of external validity without which cumulative scientific knowledge would not be possible. At the other extreme, determining the limits of generalizability of relationships is a central aspect of theory development and testing.

Threats to External Validity

Campbell and Stanley (1963) identified four influences that jeopardize the external validity of a study: (1) reactions or interaction effects of testing or measurement and the treatment variable; (2) interaction of selection and the treatment variable; (3) reactive effects of the experimental arrangements; and (4) multiple treatment interference. For a discussion of the influence of these sources on developmental research and theorizing, the reader is referred to Baltes, et al. (1977), Hultsch and Hickey (1978), and Schaie (1977).

From our point of view, since the role of external validity in the study of aging and other developmental phenomena is a key one, direct counter-attacks on any threats to it are warranted. But in addition to the kinds of issues represented in the assertion that "What works in the lab may not work in the real world," and vice versa, there is the matter of time-boundedness of relationship as discussed by, for example, Cronbach (1975) and Gergen (1980). For instance, if there is evidence for cohort effects in developmental change functions, does that merely imply a temporal change in the quality and/or quantity of causes, or does it also suggest a temporal change and transformation in underlying processes and mechanisms?

Relationships to Design Dimensions

In relation to the six dimensions of research design identified earlier, four in particular are centrally involved in the external validity of design, as follows: (1) bivariate vs. multivariate; (2) representativeness in choice of variables; (3) representativeness in choice of experimental units; and (4) degree of situational background control.

The bivariate versus multivariate design dimension plays both a specific and a general role in relation to external validity. Specifically, it refers to the study of a relationship between only two variables or among a larger number. In the latter case, two or more variables can be selected to provide a basis for generalizing along both the treatment and measurement variables dimensions. At a more general level, the bivariate to multivariate design dimension signifies the opportunity of focusing on patterns of interrelationships of variables rather than, say, mean level as the phenomenon of interest. As such, it may delimit a configuration of treatments, a structural component of response or effect, or both.

Representativeness of choice of variables as a design dimension is closely related to aspects of external validity. To be able to state lawful relations among constructs rather than specific observables is the kind of generalization sought in theory construction. One's choice of variables, on both the treatment and the measurement variable side, can involve a narrow conception of psychological entities or a representative sampling from a universe of variables reflecting the current theoretical status of a given construct. The multivariate argument is essentially that several variables are needed to measure important constructs, and, therefore, representativeness of choice of variables depends to a large extent on construct definition. The question of how a representative sample is chosen is secondary to whether one's focus is on a domain or a particular variable or variable subset.

Representativeness in choice of experimental units and the Campbell and Stanley notion of external validity along the dimension defined by subgroups or populations to which the findings apply have much in common. Students of individual differences do not view persons as replicates of each other even though some experimental psychologists, as traditionally defined, do. Differences among people are substantial enough for the questions of representation and selection to play an important

part in most kinds of research design. Comparing extreme or contrasted groups, for example, may dramatize a particular relationship among variables, but the strength or magnitude of the association may be greatly overemphasized vis-a-vis its level in some more generally representative sample or subpopulation.

Degree of situational background control, as was noted in discussing aspects of internal validity, is a pivotal concept. From the standpoint of external validity, it is directly relatable to the Campbell and Stanley dimension of settings or background conditions. In controlling situational background variables for a cleaner investigation of the relationship among other variables, one may create a situation that severely limits generalization—a classic problem recognized in the trade-off between internal and external validity dimensions.

Incorporating a Basis for Generalization

The six dimensions of research design identified and discussed by Cattell link up with the components of internal and external validity presented by Campbell and Stanley. At the very least, these emphases serve as a grave reminder of the need to be humble about the generality of any specific observed relationship. At best, they provide a conceptual scheme within which to address questions of domain definition and sampling (Cattell, 1979; Humphreys, 1962; Nunnally, 1967) as they pertain to the study of causal explanatory systems.

Giving a study external validity is not a post hoc activity. It is, rather, a matter of designing a study which is properly representative of the dimensions along which one wishes to generalize. Typically, this will be in several directions at once.

DEVELOPMENTAL RESEARCH DESIGN

Developmental Theory and Research Objectives

After a consideration of the general design principles that apply across disciplines, it is appropriate to turn to the second class of limitations, those that arise within the theoretical context of the general phenomenon of interest. In accordance with the continuum of research purposes, these constraints deal with the question of (1) the selection and construction of raw data or empirical facts (what is to be described and explained), and (2) the conceptual interpretation of raw data (how is it to be described and explained) (see, e.g., Coombs, 1964). In our view, however, this category of limitations should not be seen as an independent set of design principles but rather as a particular clarification, elaboration, or interpretation of the more general ones.

Developmental theory and research are concerned with the study of temporal sequences and patterns of human behavior that may be constructed either as patterns of *intra*individual stability and change or as patterns of stability and change in *inter*individual differences (Labouvie, 1982b). As we will point out later, this distinction between differences in intraindividual change *versus* changes in interindividual differences has significant implications for design and data analysis. Also considered important in defining the domain of raw data is the question of "What is?" (i.e., what changes actually occur in the context of real-world conditions?) *versus* "What can be?" (i.e., what changes can occur in the context of laboratory conditions?), as discussed by McCall (1977). Although this distinction is typically made in relation to the presence or absence of experimental manipulation and considered in relation to the problem of generalizability, it can also be discussed in connection with the concept of naturalness—more specifically, the naturalness of behavior, of settings, and of treatments (Tunnell, 1977)—without the implication that greater naturalness implies greater generalizability. Finally, in response to the "what" and the "how" of explaining, developmental theories and research have often diverged by focusing either on the occurrence of a particular change ("Why, under what conditions, does this particular change occur?"), on the form of a change ("Why does the change take this particular form or pattern?"), or on both ("Why does this change occur and why does it exhibit this particular form?") (Labouvie, 1982b; Wohlwill, 1973).

Obviously, different theoretical approaches to these various issues are likely to lead to different conceptions of just which change phenomena are *truly developmental* (e.g., Baer, 1970; Baltes and Nesselroade, 1979; Baltes and Willis, 1977; Reese and Overton, 1970). For instance, *strong* conceptions of development—with their emphasis on universality, fixed sequentiality, structural transformations, and movement toward a final end state—are often more concerned with the form of change than with its occurrence. In comparison, *weak* conceptions of development tend to focus more often on the occurrence of change rather than its form and, therefore, consider almost any form of behavior as developmental.

In view of this broad range of theoretical conceptions, we believe that it is most appropriate for the purposes of this discussion to use a methodologically oriented definition of the domain of interest. Thus, following Kessen (1960) and Baltes and Nesselroade (1979), we propose that developmental/gerontological research and theory are defined[2] as the study of behaviors, B, that can be systematically linked to age, A, for some selected *age interval* $[A_m \leq A \leq A_n]$ and some selected individual or individuals, i. Descriptively, the functions $B_i(A)$ expressing such relationships represent sets that are ordered along the age dimension. Furthermore, from a formal point of view, these functions (or sets) may be defined qualitatively (e.g., an ordered sequence of states or stages) or quantitatively (e.g., ordered variations along a quantitative continuum) with the possibilities of (1) specific forms of continuity or discontinuity along the age dimension,[3] and (2) individual differences in specific characteristics.

As pointed out by Labouvie (1984), however, if the task of description is to serve its function as a necessary prerequisite for the task of explanation, more than just the empirical assessment of the $B_i(A)$ is required. De-

---

[2]From a formal mathematical point of view, this definition also includes behavior with cyclical change patterns along the age dimensions.
[3]It should be pointed out that developmentalists have been rather vague in defining their concepts of continuity/discontinuity.

scriptions become theoretically much more useful if they also include an empirical assessment of the functional relationships, $M_i(A)$, exhibited by maturational factors, M, and the environmental characteristics, $E_i(A)$, of events, E (including experimental manipulations), that are then hypothesized to relate to the $B_i(A)$. In other words, the causal analysis of age-related intraindividual change is ultimately concerned with the relationships between the $B_i(A)$, $M_i(A)$, and $E_i(A)$.

Extensions of Design Criteria

Our definition of developmental description and explanation has several implications for the design of relevant empirical research. In order to relate them more clearly to the various design principles discussed earlier, they will be considered in terms of three issues: (1) the selection of age ranges and age levels, (2) the selection of individuals, groups of individuals, and populations, and (3) the selection of variables and concepts in the three domains of behavior (B), maturational factors (M), and environmental events (E).

Selection of Age Ranges and Age Levels

In theory the paradigm stated above calls for the selection of age *intervals* with corresponding samples of age levels in order to obtain age-related functions in each of the three domains. In practice, however, actual empirical research is most often based on the selection of single age *points*. In other words, most research yields only descriptions of individual differences in behaviors, $B_i(A_m)$, in maturational factors, $M_i(A_r)$, and in environmental characteristics, $E_i(A_t)$ as they are observed at arbitrarily selected age points (A_m, A_r, and A_t). Obviously, such research circumvents the formulation of the age-functional relationships $B_i(A)$, $M_i(A)$, and $E_i(A)$ in reference to extended age intervals and yields empirical evidence that is of very limited usefulness as far as the notion of differential intraindividual change is concerned.

Regardless of the particular paradigm chosen, the selection of age levels in terms of their density and spacing along the age dimension obviously has a bearing on the internal and external validity of one's descriptions and explanations. Putting other problems aside for the moment, it would appear that a continuous recording—that is, high-density sampling of age levels requiring little interpolation—is most desirable for obtaining accurate and internally valid records of intraindividual change functions in the domains of behavior, maturation, and environment. In comparison, low-density sampling of age levels, which requires a great deal of interpolation, may lead to inaccurate and invalid representations and causal inferences. Given the fact that continuous recording of age-related functions is not practical over extended periods of time, the sampling of age levels and their spacing should be guided by hypotheses regarding the temporal location of periods of rapid versus slow change, continuity versus discontinuity, and quantitative versus qualitative changes in the three domains of interest.

Finally, the sampling of age ranges and age levels raises not only the question of valid interpolation but also that of extrapolation, that is, a problem of generalizing to age ranges not enclosed between the age levels sampled. Clearly, the willingness to make such extrapolations will depend on one's models of change and stability in the three domains of interest.

Selection of Individuals, Groups of Individuals, and Populations

According to the two paradigms identified above, the selection of individuals or groups of individuals depends, at least in part, on the selection of age levels studied. In other words, corresponding populations are defined in such a way that their members can be observed at the selected age levels. Theoretically, the larger the range of age intervals or age points of interest, the more limited the population(s) from which to select individuals. In practice, however, this constraint is often circumvented or weakened by replacing successive observations with simultaneous ones. For instance, with individuals as the unit of analysis, successive observations may be replaced by using retrospective recall to obtain observations at different age levels simultaneously.

With groups of individuals as the unit of analysis, the temporal sequentiality of observations is often short-circuited if individuals of different ages in the context of cross-sectional designs are selected and simultaneously observed. In either case, the question arises whether simultaneous observations are valid substitutes for temporally sequenced observations. Available empirical evidence on the validity of retrospective recall (e.g., Baltes and Goulet, 1971; Yarrow et al. 1970) and on the validity of cross-sectional age differences (e.g., Baltes, 1968; Schaie, 1967) suggests only a limited usefulness of such substitutes.

In considering the selection of individuals, we would like to stress again the importance of making a clear distinction between the use of individuals versus groups of individuals as the unit of analysis. First, if one is focusing on intraindividual change with the individual as the unit of analysis, it is obviously necessary to obtain successive or longitudinal observations of the same individuals at all selected age levels. In comparison, if one is interested in intra-group change, one need only observe the same type or category of individuals at the selected age levels. Such observations can be obtained by assessing independent groups sampled in the same way from the same population. For instance, such a strategy has been proposed for assessing the presence of testing effects in longitudinal, intra-group age changes (e.g., Baltes, 1968). Second, it is perhaps even more important to keep in mind that intergroup changes may have little internal and external validity as indicators of intraindividual changes, and vice versa. For instance, in the field of aging, the phenomena of terminal drop (Riegel and Riegel, 1972; Siegler, 1975) and increasing interindividual differences in behavior (Baltes et al., 1977) are just two reasons why the shapes of intraindividual and intragroup (averaged) change functions may be quite different from one another.

Finally, the selection of individuals and samples of individuals also raises the question of representativeness, with important implications for the internal and external validity of one's findings. As stated earlier, the major problem arises primarily from the use of convenience samples and a lack of randomization of subjects. It is generally recognized that the use of convenience samples is likely to impose serious limits on the generalizability of the results of both cross-sectional and longitudinal studies. Sometimes, however, it is overlooked that this practice also represents a serious threat to the internal validity of cross-sectional age comparisons, on the one hand, and of sequential cohort comparisons, on the other. For instance, when recruiting subjects over 65 from a particular church organization, subjects between 40 and 50 from a particular company, and subjects aged 20 to 25 from a particular college, one cannot be confident in the usefulness of the resulting "age" comparisons. Similarly, when recruiting subjects of different birth cohorts (e.g., an older cohort from a retirement organization, a younger cohort from a church group) through different sampling mechanisms, the resulting "cohort" comparisons become rather meaningless. Finally, the use of convenience samples in connection with a nonrandom assignment of subjects to various treatment groups/conditions in the context of an experimental study may severely limit the internal validity of the observed differences between the various control and experimental groups because of the possibility that the various groups were not equivalent before the onset of differential treatments.

In addition to both general and differential biases in age and cohort samples at the time of initial recruitment, longitudinal studies are further burdened by the possibility of subsequent changes in those biases because of selective attrition or cumulative testing effects (e.g., Baltes, 1968; Baltes, Reese, and Nesselroade, 1977; Labouvie et al., 1974; Riegel, 1968). Proposals regarding selective attrition have included assessments of its effects by comparing retestees and drop-outs retrospectively on measures obtained at the first or initial time of testing. It should be kept in mind, however, that such comparisons are of limited usefulness if individual differences at the first time of testing are relatively unrelated to differences in intraindividual changes between first and second testing. In other words, if retestees and drop-outs are found to differ on certain target characteristics at the first time of testing, it does not automatically follow that they also exhibit different change patterns over a subsequent time interval. Conversely, if the two groups are found to be similar at the first time of testing, it is still possible that their subsequent change patterns are different.

Selection of Variables and Concepts

Finally, empirical research cannot be conducted without selecting variables assumed to represent reliable and valid measures of the concepts of interest. However, although measures are primarily selected in reference to particular concepts, most developmentalists would agree that the choice of appropriate empirical indicators cannot be accomplished without also considering the range of age levels and the group(s) of individuals studied.

In general, the translation of concepts into empirical indicators, which can be cast in terms of both construct validity and the bivariate to multivariate design dimension, can be carried out in one of two ways. Following the classical bivariate research tradition, each concept is represented by a single empirical indicator or measure. In comparison, the goal of multivariate research aims at representing concepts by several empirical indicators. A major reason for using the latter approach, of course, is the belief that only part of the reliable variance of any single measure also represents valid variance, that is, variance related to the concept of interest. From the standpoint of convergent validity, the use of multiple indicators has, therefore, been proposed as a way to separate the reliable and valid variance component from the reliable but invalid variance component in each of the empirical measures. As a consequence, inferences about relationships between concepts are thought to be more generalizable and less affected by unique, though reliable, characteristics of specific empirical measures.

Besides providing a more explicit differentiation between measurement models and causal-structural models (e.g., Bentler, 1980), the multivariate representation of concepts has also led to a more detailed, empirical distinction between different types of developmental change. More specifically, changes in indicators may reflect quantitative changes in underlying concepts, changes in the relationships between indicators and concepts, or some combination of both (Baltes and Nesselroade, 1970, 1973).

Regardless of whether one chooses a univariate or multivariate representation of concepts, the selection of measures is also based on a consideration of the age ranges and groups of individuals studied. Developmentalists and gerontologists need to be aware of the fact that a given measure may have differential reliability and validity in different age groups. Thus, in order to obtain reliable and valid estimates of age-functional relationships, it is important to establish conceptual and metric equivalence of the empirical indicators across all age levels and populations studied (e.g., Labouvie, 1980). Obviously, this problem pertains not only to indicators in the domain of behaviors but also to measures of maturational factors and environmental characteristics.

Finally, the selection of variables also requires a consideration of the concept of naturalness, that is, naturalness of behaviors, naturalness of treatments, and naturalness of settings or situational backgrounds (e.g., Tunnell, 1977). There is a tendency among researchers to believe that the greater the degree of naturalness in each of the three aspects, the greater the validity and generalizability of observed relationships. However, it should be kept in mind that natural behaviors and treatments, as compared to more artificial and experimentally contrived ones, are not automatically better, that is, more reliable and valid markers of the concepts of interest. Whether or not the use of more natural behaviors, settings, and treatments yields empirical evidence that is more generalizable is itself an empirical question. However, there is agreement among gerontologists that greater naturalness may produce greater willingness among the elderly to participate in scientific studies and, therefore, less selectively in sampling and attrition.

A final aspect of variable selection to be considered here, but one that is important from a developmental point of view, concerns the choice of empirical indicators in relation to the two concepts of maturation and history. Because both concepts play such an important role in the causal analysis of developmental phenomena, it seems imperative even in studies aimed only at the description of development that measures be included that represent concepts in the domains of maturational factors and environmental/experiential history. As we will point out later, in many instances, the variables age, cohort/time of birth, and time of measurement may be very poor representatives of those two domains.

Generalizability Over Temporal Dimensions

As suggested by the two paradigms listed above, age-related intraindividual changes or individual differences—$B_i(A)$, $M_i(A)$, and $E_i(A)$—are empirically assessed for specific samples of individuals and for specific age *intervals* or age *points*. As was mentioned before, the second set of defining characteristics creates the problems of interpolation and extrapolation, that is, the question of generalizability to other age intervals and age points. In a technical sense, this problem disappears if one can achieve high-density sampling of age levels over the total human life span. In its absence, generalizations will largely depend on one's assumptions with regard to the nature of the underlying change processes, that is, assumptions concerning the constancy and stability of, as well as the regularity of change in, relevant characteristics and processes associated with the three domains of interest.

The fact that empirical evidence is gathered on specific and finite samples of individuals raises another issue of spatio-temporal generalizability. The spatial aspect of the problem refers, of course, to generalizations to some or all individuals who are contemporaries of those observed. The temporal aspect arises in connection with the notion of socio-historical change and the fact that individuals are born at, and exist during, different historical times and circumstances. As stated before, external validity may be obtained by careful enumeration and representative sampling of the domains of generalization. However, the feasibility of this definition depends on whether or not those domains can be assumed to represent fixed and invariant populations or sets of elements. Of course, one could define "all human beings" or "all elderly persons over the age of 65," including those currently living, those who lived in the past, and those yet to be born, as the domain of generalization. However, such a definition would obviously prevent a representative sampling of the domain for the simple reason that only those individuals can be sampled who are living at the time at which empirical evidence is gathered. Alternatively, if one defines the domain of generalization only as "all human beings born and / or living during a specific historical time interval," one has to introduce the concept of a constantly changing population or that of a series of potentially different populations. In either case, the issue of external validity becomes a question of replicability that needs to be assessed on an ongoing and continuous basis.

A more general implication stemming from the age interval and age point paradigms mentioned earlier is that the subscript representing individuals or groups of individuals should explicitly include an index of historical time. As pointed out by Labouvie and Nesselroade (1984) and Baltes (1968), that is most easily accomplished, at least descriptively, by categorizing individuals in terms of their time of birth, or birth cohort, T_c. In other words, the empirical data of interest are more appropriately characterized as intraindividual changes or interindividual differences $B_i(T_c,A)$, $M_i(T_c,A)$, and $E_i(T_c,A)$, with i nested within levels of T_c.

Classical Developmental Research Designs

In the past, developmental psychologists and gerontologists gathered empirical evidence for the most part by using a "simple" cross-sectional or longitudinal design. These designs are "simple" primarily in the sense that all observations are obtained either at a single time of measurement or for a single birth cohort of individuals. In other words, the resulting descriptions and associated explanations of individual development are based on an ahistorical rather than historical approach. The issues of internal and external validity associated with such an approach are significant and have been discussed quite extensively in the literature (Baltes, 1968; Baltes, Cornelius, and Nesselroade, 1978; Hultsch and Hickey, 1978; Schaie, 1965, 1977; Nesselroade and Baltes, 1974; Wohlwill, 1973). Clearly, there is no need to repeat these discussions. Suffice it to say here that cross-sectional age differences have been shown to have little internal validity as indicators of age changes and that longitudinal changes have been shown to be often rather cohort-specific.

DESCRIPTION AND EXPLANATION OF AGING AND DEVELOPMENTAL CHANGES

The General Developmental Model and Sequential Strategies

The inadequacies of simple longitudinal and cross-sectional studies, obvious for quite some time, were empirically demonstrated in the form of significant discrepancies in observed age-functional relationships (e.g., Damon, 1965; Kuhlen, 1963; Botwinick, 1977). In response to that problem and in line with Kessen's (1960) suggestion that meaningful designs for the study of developmental questions involve either the interaction of age and environmental changes or an analysis of age functions in special populations, Schaie (1965) proposed a general developmental model with three time variables: age, time of measurement, and time of birth or cohort. Kessen's (1960) proposal was reformulated by Schaie (1965), who replaced the term *special population* with *cohort* and the term *environment* with *time of measurement.* The term *cohort* refers to the total population of individuals born during the same interval of historical time. *Time of measurement* is assumed to indicate the state of the environment or its total impact at the time empirical observations are made.

Realizing the intrinsic interdependence among the three variables, that is,

Age = Time of measurement − Birth cohort

Schaie (1965) formulated three two-factorial designs for the purpose of (1) obtaining a more adequate description of behavioral change, and (2) identifying sources of those changes in relation to maturational and environmental histories. According to the *cohort-sequential method,* several cohorts are observed across the same age interval or levels, though at different times of measurement. The corresponding analytic model is based on the assumption that behavioral variation and change are related to age and cohort, but not to time of measurement. According to the *cross-sequential method,* several cohorts are assessed for the same set of times of measurement, though at different ages. The respective analytic model is based on the assumption that behavioral variation and change are related to cohort and time of measurement, but not to age. Finally, the *time-sequential method* requires the empirical observation of a given set of age levels at each of several times of measurement. The associated analytic model assumes that behavioral variation and change are related to age and time of measurement, but not to cohort. According to Schaie (1965, 1977), the systematic application of these methods together with their respective analytic models allows the identification of sources of change in behavior.

Schaie's proposal was criticized by Baltes (1968), who suggested that a classification of individuals into categories defined as intervals along one or more than one time continuum is insufficient to identify sources of behavioral change in reference to maturation, past environment, and present environment (see also Cattell, 1970). Instead, Baltes proposed that the general developmental model be used only via the cohort-sequential method for the sole purpose of obtaining a more complete *description* of behavioral changes in reference to some specific historical time period. With the Cohort X Age matrix merely serving as a guide for data collection, Baltes (1968) distinguished between longitudinal and cross-sectional *sequential strategies,* depending upon the use of repeated or independent observations along the age dimension. Schaie and Baltes (1975) subsequently tried to reconcile some of their differences. Both agreed that the description of behavioral change and development is best accomplished by using longitudinal or cross-sectional sequential strategies within a Cohort

X Age matrix. At the same time, however, they continue to disagree on the explanatory usefulness of sequential methods. In contrast to Schaie, Baltes advocates an approach that explicates the time variables more directly in terms of processes and antecedents (e.g., Baltes and Goulet, 1971; Baltes et al., 1977).

In spite of the resolution offered by Schaie and Baltes (1975), or perhaps because of it, the discussion of sequential methods and strategies is continuing (e.g., Costa and McCrae, 1982; Horn and McArdle, 1980; Labouvie and Nesselroade, 1984; Schaie and Hertzog, 1982), and its longevity suggests a need for further clarification of the underlying issues. In particular, we would like to argue that the usefulness of these methods and strategies, not in general but as they are often implemented, has been overstated with regard to both descriptive and explanatory objectives.

Although our position is similar to the one advocated by Baltes (1968), we are, nevertheless, unconvinced that the application of sequential strategies has always yielded empirical descriptions that have greater internal and external validity than those of simple designs. In fact, we think that perhaps it has not been sufficiently stressed that the implementation of these strategies requires not only a consideration of factors threatening the internal validity of age changes, but also, and perhaps more importantly, a consideration of factors that jeopardize the internal validity of observed cohort differences. In view of the notoriously poor sampling techniques and small sample sizes often employed by psychologists, internal validity is not at all routinely insured, and it is somewhat surprising that in the discussion of sequential methods and strategies most authors have been rather quiet on this topic. Without a more careful analysis of this problem and appropriate checks and controls, it is not possible to state whether, for instance, observed cohort differences reflect true differences between cohort populations, changes in sampling procedures, changes in volunteering behavior, or any combination thereof. Obviously, without a high degree of internal validity of observed cohort differences, the argument for using sequential strategies rather than simple designs becomes much less compelling.

As far as the explanatory usefulness of sequential methods is concerned, we would like to argue that it is the empirical measurement of behaviors in the absence of a parallel, though independent assessment of maturational and environmental characteristics that represents the most serious shortcoming. As stated before, in order to serve as a useful prerequisite for the task of causal analysis, the task of description requires the empirical observation of individual differences and intraindividual changes in all three domains of interest, even if one adopts a strong conception of development.

From a developmental point of view, explanatory analyses are ultimately concerned with the explication of relationships between behavior and its temporal characteristics, on the one hand, and maturational and environmental factors and their temporal characteristics, on the other. Consequently, an exclusive emphasis on the temporal characteristics of behavior can have explanatory value only if one is willing to assume complete isomorphy and synchrony between the temporal characteristics of behavior and those of maturational and environmental factors. Obviously, such an assumption is highly restrictive and of questionable validity. For instance, it is quite easy to formulate cumulative models of behavior change that do not satisfy the assumption (Labouvie, 1981).

It is also clear that the time of measurement and birth cohort variables are conceptually as vague and theoretically as empty as the age variable (Wohlwill, 1970, 1973) in spite of the high degree of precision and reliability with which they can be measured. For instance, it is questionable whether all individuals born at the same time can, in fact, be assumed to have experienced "the same environmental circumstances at the same point in their maturational sequence" (Schaie and Hertzog, 1982, p. 96) or that individuals assessed at the same time are, in fact, exposed to the same common environment. Of course, it is possible to consider alternative ways of defining both cohort and time of measurement intervals and boundaries that are conceptually more meaningful. For instance, as suggested by Rosow for the cohort variable (1978; see also Baltes, Cornelius, and Nesselroade,

1979), it may be useful to explore both variables in terms of the notion of distinctive events and associated differential effects. In our view, however, this approach seems to offer little more than the conclusion that historical events and conditions represent distal social contexts that are not likely to be experienced uniformly by different individuals.

In view of this conclusion, we agree with Baltes (1968) that a Cohort X Age matrix is sufficient to describe both *intraindividual changes*—whether in behaviors, maturational factors, or environmental factors—and *interindividual differences* in those changes, with the possibility that variance components of the latter can be expressed as social-historical shifts in population distributions irrespective of how the boundaries of cohort populations may be defined. At the same time, we also propose that Wohlwill's conclusions (1970, 1973) with regard to the role of the age variable in developmental research be extended. More specifically, we suggest that in the context of causal analyses both age and cohort be seen only as a part of all the relevant dependent and independent variables. For instance, when trying to explain individual differences in post-retirement satisfaction among several cohorts of 65–70 year olds as a function of individual differences in selected preretirement behaviors and events at earlier ages (via regression analysis or causal modeling), both age and cohort merely serve to index one's observations of the dependent and independent variables of interest and have no causal status of their own.

In summary, we believe that the increased effort and costs associated with the implementation of sequential strategies are justified and meaningful under the following conditions: (1) Sampling procedures are improved and sample sizes are made sufficiently large to provide an acceptable degree of internal validity to the description of cohort differences; and (2) the set of measured variables includes empirical indicators of maturational and environmental factors in order to make the empirical evidence amenable to more explicit forms of causal modeling. For the various reasons stated above, we do not think, for instance, that the replacement of ANOVA models with more sophisticated approaches to the model-ing of moment structures that are confined solely to the context of age, cohort, and time of measurement matrices (e.g., Horn and McArdle, 1980) represents, over the long haul, a promising approach to the explanatory analysis of intraindividual and social change. More important, however, to the extent that the practice of using convenience samples is continued, observed cohort differences as indicators of social change will have about as much accuracy and validity as cross-sectional age differences have as indicators of age changes.

Experimental Approaches

Although scientists in general view manipulative experimental investigations as the more desirable instrument for the analysis of causal relationships, some developmentalists, in particular those subscribing to a strong conception of development and aging, have questioned the usefulness of such an approach (e.g., McCall, 1977; Wohlwill, 1973). According to McCall (1977), experimental studies focus only on differences and changes that *can occur* under specific conditions in contrast to observational studies, which emphasize differences and changes as they *are occurring* under everyday life conditions. However, although this distinction between "what is" and "what can be" is a valid and useful one, it would, at least in our opinion, be misleading to suggest that the study of one or the other contributes more, let alone everything, to our understanding of human development and aging. In other words, we believe that the study of intraindividual changes that can be produced under specific, controlled conditions is as important as that of intraindividual changes that are occurring under natural conditions. In fact, it can be argued that one of the important goals of the behavioral sciences involves the formulation of social programs and policies that help to transform the "what can be" into the "what is," if that is deemed desirable.

In line with these arguments, it is helpful to view the goal of experimental approaches as a twofold one. First, the study of what changes can occur under controlled experimental conditions clearly adds to our theoretical knowledge and understanding of human organisms and their behavior. At the same time, it is of practical importance if we want to prevent, alleviate, or replace naturally occurring changes that are deemed undesirable. One of the measures used to gauge the theoretical and practical importance of such studies is, of course, the degree to which the experimentally manipulated changes can be replicated across a range of different individuals and different settings. Second, experimental investigations may directly aid our understanding of naturally occurring changes by trying to simulate the latter under experimentally controlled conditions. In this case, the focus is on the kind and degree of similarity and isomorphy between "what is" and "what can be." Before discussing developmental simulation techniques, let us first consider the range of experimental designs that may be used by developmentalists.

In order to fully utilize the insights gained in previous discussions of descriptive developmental designs, it is convenient to propose a corresponding distinction between simple and sequential experimental designs. In other words, both types of experimental designs represent straightforward extensions of the respective descriptive designs by incorporating experimental manipulations.

Simple Experimental Designs. Incorporation of experimental variables into simple cross-sectional and longitudinal designs yields what may be considered to be the most important vehicles for conducting experimental developmental research. In particular, it is the cross-sectional age X treatment interaction design that has been used most extensively to provide the bulk of empirical evidence for developmental and gerontological studies (e.g., Baltes and Goulet, 1971; Wohlwill, 1973). However, in spite of its capacity for economical and efficient implementation, it shares all the problems of descriptive cross-sectional designs. Besides the lack of any direct assessment of intraindividual change, the interpretation of observed age X treatment interactions is tentative at best. In other words, even if representative sampling and random assignment of subjects within age/cohort groups have been achieved, the causal interpretation of age/cohort differences and age/cohort X treatment interactions remains problematic because of the pre-existing nonequivalence of the various age/cohort groups with regard to a host of unknown characteristics. From a purely descriptive point of view, however, such differences and interactions may still represent internally valid indicators of corresponding population differences. Unfortunately, even that aspect of descriptive validity is often lost when, as stated earlier, the use of convenience samples introduces a multitude of unknown selection confounds (see, e.g., Krauss, 1980).

In comparison, experimental extensions of the single-cohort, longitudinal design focus directly on the manipulation of intraindividual change—in the form of differential amounts, rates, or trends over specified age intervals—thus yielding a variety of pre-test–post-test and multiple time series designs. Obviously, the internal validity of observed age X treatment interactions is threatened by factors such as (1) nonrandom assignment of subjects to treatments, (2) treatment X testing interactions, (3) treatment X attrition interactions, and (4) treatment X present environment interactions. In general, these factors are more easily controlled the shorter the age interval over which change is recorded. The longer the time intervals studied, however, the greater the possibility of "spill-over" effects—such that prolonged exposure to different treatments may motivate individuals to induce other differential changes in the environment—as well as "treatment drift"—in the sense that experimental treatments may change over time in ways other than those intended by the experimenter.

Sequential Experimental Designs. Experimental extension of sequential designs leads to strategies that involve the systematic replication of the simpler cross-sectional and longitudinal designs (Labouvie, 1980). For instance, the replication of a cross-sectional age X treatment interaction design over a series of times of measurement using independent samples represents an experimental extension of the time-sequential method. Of particular interest here, of course, is the replicability of time-specific age X treatment interactions. In comparison, the replication of an experimental longitudinal design across a series of cohorts yields an experimental extension of the cohort-sequential method. Here, the focus will be on the comparability of cohort-specific age X treatment interactions and the associated constancy or change in the differential effectiveness of different treatments across different cohorts. Finally, the repetition of a cross-sectional design over a series of times of measurement for the same samples of individuals represents an experimental extension of the cross-sequential method. In contrast to the first two methods, the latter does not represent replication in the traditional sense. Nevertheless, this design may be attractive to developmentalists because it allows the experimental study of intraindividual change in reference to a wide age span over a relatively short time period.

At a minimum, the time-sequential and cohort-sequential methods provide a series of independent replications and allow an assessment of the generality and universality of one's empirical evidence. If, however, the observed age X treatment interactions are found to vary across times of measurement or cohorts, such variations do not necessarily represent true historical changes in the relationships between target behaviors and treatment variables but could simply be the result of changes in sampling, changes in volunteering behavior, or treatment drift. Furthermore, even if these variations can be assumed to reflect true historical changes, it is still open to question whether they represent changes in treatment X maturation, or treatment X past environment, or treatment X present environment interactions. As we stated before when discussing descriptive sequential designs, solving this ambiguity requires the inclusion of empirical indicators of maturation, past environment, and present environment.

Simulation

As stated earlier, experimental studies are often used to aid our understanding of naturally occurring changes in behavior. The idea, of course, is to create experimentally controlled conditions in such a way that the resulting change patterns are similar to the naturally occurring ones, as well as to note those conditions that lead to dissimilar patterns. Furthermore, experimental simulations utilize time frames that are much shorter than those of naturally occurring changes.

Simulation studies may focus on different characteristics of change such as amount, rate, and direction. In general, it would appear that a short-term simulation of long-term changes should be primarily concerned with experimental manipulations of the rate and direction of change since it is much less likely that short-term experimental treatments can generate amounts of change that are comparable to those occurring over long time intervals. Quite apart from the question of which particular aspect of change is chosen as the target of one's simulation, there is also, of course, the problem of determining the degree to which the selected experimental treatments do, in fact, imitate or simulate naturally occurring conditions and experiences. More specifically, in view of the considerable discrepancy in time frames between a simulation study and its target, there are two particular sets of issues that become especially important to address. The two involve problems with regard to definitions of the concept of experience and also with regard to the specification of temporal characteristics of experiences in conjunction with the broader issue of the equivalence of experiences across time and age.

As Wohlwill (1973) pointed out several years ago, behavioral scientists have proposed different definitions of the concept of experience with important implications for the definition of experimental treatments and the concept of simulation. Although reminiscent of the distinction between actual environment and perceived environment, the range of definitions is broader and more general. At one extreme, experience has been defined solely in terms of the set of stimulus conditions to which an individual is, or has been, exposed. At the other extreme, experience has been viewed primarily in terms of all the behaviors that are elicited as a function of exposure to some stimulus condition. Obviously, many of the responses that are elicited are not easily observable as was, for instance, pointed out recently by Bandura (1982). From a pragmatic or practical point of view, the first approach has the advantage of generating a greater sense of control in the context of experimental simulations of intraindividual change. On the other hand, many developmentalists would probably argue that as far as long-term developmental changes are concerned, the concept of experience cannot be adequately defined and assessed solely in terms of an individual's exposure to various stimulus conditions without any regard for the great variety and amount of behaviors elicited by those conditions. For instance, according to the disuse model of aging deficits (e.g., Birren and Renner, 1977), age-related decrements in performance are not due to changes in stimulus conditions per se but rather to changes in elicited behaviors.

An important implication of the distinction between stimulus conditions and elicited behaviors is the notion that simulation may focus on both aspects to varying degrees. In general it is easier to imitate or simulate stimulus conditions than elicited behaviors, especially when longer time intervals are involved. The stimulation of elicited behaviors, however, may contribute more to our understanding of human development, especially if one adopts a strong conception of development.

From a methodological point of view, the distinction raises the specific issue of how to define the validity and equivalence of experimental treatments and simulations across time and across different age populations as well as the more general problem of how to define the temporal characteristics of experimental treatments. Again, it would appear that these problems can be more easily dealt with if experimental treatments and simulations are defined primarily in terms of stimulus conditions. However, as is well known, the repeated and/or prolonged exposure to the same stimulus conditions may produce time-related changes in elicited behaviors, changes that have been studied in the context of habituation, learning, familiarization, warm-up, and so on. In a similar sense, exposure to the same stimulus condition may elicit different sets of behaviors in individuals of different backgrounds, including individuals of different ages and cohorts. Obviously, to the extent that such changes and/or differences in elicited be-

haviors are not empirically assessed either as part of the dependent variables or as part of the independent variables, they constitute a source of invalidity or lack of equivalence of treatment variables across time and age.

From a much broader perspective, this problem raises the question whether developmental psychologists have sufficiently dealt with the issue of how to define and represent the temporal characteristics of experience, both in the case of observational and experimental studies. In general, one is reminded of classical mechanics, a field which describes and explains the spatio-temporal movement of "masspoints," that is, spatial objects without any spatial characteristics. By analogy, developmental psychology tends to describe experience in terms of "event points" that are essentially devoid of temporal characteristics (see also Campbell and Stanley, 1963 for their representation of treatments in the context of longitudinal designs). Although the strategy of referring to event points may be sufficient in the case of short-term experiments, it becomes rather questionable when longer time intervals are considered. In the latter case, the term *experience* and its associated events have been represented and empirically assessed as off-on-off sequences with a time of onset, length or duration, and a time of offset (see, e.g., Wohlwill, 1973). From a long-term developmental perspective, however, even such a representation is an extremely simplified one for two reasons. First, as is well known, human organisms can anticipate and remember events. In other words, various behaviors may be elicited prior to the onset of an event as well as after its termination. As a consequence, the representations of a given event either in terms of a set of stimulus conditions or in terms of a set of elicited behaviors may exhibit quite different temporal characteristics. Second, the representation of experience in terms of off-on-off sequences favors a focus on events that imply a sudden onset or offset of conditions rather than on events that imply more gradual changes in conditions. As exemplified by the study of stressful life events rather than stressful life conditions (see, e.g., Dohrenwend and Dohrenwend, 1974), the result may be an undue overemphasis on certain types of events and experiences as sources of intraindividual change.

Finally, it should also be pointed out that any study that is concerned with the simulation of a variety of different patterns rather than with only a single pattern of age-related intraindividual change represents at the same time a simulation of cultural change in the form of cohort-related differences in such change patterns. In other words, any set of experimental manipulations that produces differential intraindividual changes simulates potential sources and mechanisms of cultural change as long as one is willing to assume that individual differences in intraindividual changes *within* and *between* cohorts are generated by similar kinds of antecedents and mechanisms.

LINKING DESIGN TO DATA ANALYSIS

We will close this chapter with a few comments regarding selected aspects of linking together design and data analysis. Our remarks will be relatively general in light of the fact that Schaie and Hertzog (Chap. 3) discuss and illustrate the blending of data analysis and design aspects in considerable detail. In addition to some brief remarks concerning when—in the course of designing, conducting, and presenting a study—one needs to consider data analysis matters seriously, we will identify two principal aspects of the linkage between data analysis and design. In one, the role of experimental design as a mediator between theoretical purpose or questions and the analysis of data is highlighted. In the other, the choice of statistical analysis models is considered in light of the design-induced characteristics of the data to be analyzed.

If possible, data analysis considerations should be an aspect of research study planning before the data are collected. One of the frequently heard laments of statisticians, resident methodologists in psychology departments, and others to whom researchers in aging turn for data analysis advice is, "Why didn't you ask me before you gathered your data?" As two people who have occasionally been called on by students and faculty colleagues to try to work a data analysis "miracle" that will salvage a piece of empirical work, we cannot emphasize enough the desirability of some forethought about analysis in planning a study. It is not always possible, as it is in secondary data analysis, to plan for analysis before the data are collected, but such situations should be thought of as the exception, rather than the rule.

Data analysis, even in the case of secondary analysis of extant data sets, should not be thought of as an autonomous, self-contained end. Rather, it is a means to an end. There is not some ordered set of procedures that one simply applies to data, upon the completion of which one can say, "There, the data are analyzed!" Data analysis is guided by questions. Sometimes, the questions are admittedly general, such as "What are the descriptive characteristics of these data?" Other times the questions lead to precise analysis procedures such as planned comparisons or other model fitting applications. Oftentimes, the degree of specificity represented in the question falls between the two extremes just mentioned.

One's data analytic needs vary both in relation to the level of development of the theoretical framework within which research questions and issues are articulated and in relation to the experimental accessibility of the pertinent constructs. In some situations, the need is for unembellished descriptions of relationships among variables; in others, a more refined and technically precise hypothesis calls for similarly precise data analysis methods. Nesselroade and Baltes (1984) used two dichotomies, *Exploratory versus Hypothesis-Testing Theoretical Purpose* and *Explanatory versus Hypothesis-Testing Analysis Procedures,* to identify and discuss convergence and divergence between purposes and methods. One's research design can be thought of as mediating between purpose and method. Thus, by varying experimental design along the dimensions identified earlier, one can produce a wide range of data, each kind of which can be optimally exploited by a procedure or class of procedures for a particular theory-related purpose.

A second design-analysis interface of interest concerns the selection of statistical models in relation to design features that cut across the hypothesis-testing versus exploratory dichotomy. There is a host of choice points at which one can "take a wrong turn" in matching statistical models to data and, as a consequence, make inappropriate inferences about relationships among variables. Among them are application of fixed versus random effects models, use of independent observations analytic procedures on repeated measures data, performing multiple dependent significance tests without adjusting significance levels, etc.

Getting the most out of one's data clearly requires the exercise of informed judgment in selecting analysis procedures. Our argument, however, is that in the chain of events leading to the interpretation of outcomes, some very important links fall under the heading of problem identification, some under design issues, and still others under data analysis. All of them must be forged carefully and with as much concern as possible for the entire sequence to which they belong.

REFERENCES

Baer, D. M. 1970. An age-irrelevant concept of development. *Merrill-Palmer Quarterly of Behavior and Development* 16: 238–246.

Baltes, P. B. 1968. Longitudinal and cross-sectional sequences in the study of age and generation effects. *Human Development* 11: 145–171.

Baltes, P. B.; Cornelius, S. W.; and Nesselroade, J. R. 1978. Cohort effects in developmental psychology: Theoretical and methodological perspectives. In *Minnesota Symposium on Child Psychology,* ed. W. A. Collins. Vol. 2. Hillsdale, N.J.: Lawrence Erlbaum Associates.

Baltes, P. B.; Cornelius, S. W.; and Nesselroade, J. R. 1979. Cohort effects in developmental psychology. In *Longitudinal Research in the Study of Behavior and Development,* eds. J. R. Nesselroade and P. B. Baltes. New York: Academic Press.

Baltes, P. B., and Goulet, L. R. 1971. Exploration of developmental variables by simulation and manipulation of age differences in behavior. *Human Development* 14: 149–170.

Baltes, P. B., and Nesselroade, J. R. 1970. Multivariate longitudinal and cross-sectional sequences for analyzing ontogenetic and gerontological change: A methodological note. *Developmental Psychology* 2: 163–168.

Baltes, P. B., and Nesselroade, J. R. 1973. The developmental analysis of individual differences on multiple measures. In *Life-Span Developmental Psychology: Methodological issues,* eds. J. R. Nesselroade and H. W. Reese. New York: Academic Press.

Baltes, P. B., and Nesselroade, J. R. 1979. History and rationale of longitudinal research. In *Longitudinal Research in the Study of Behavior and Development,* eds. J. R. Nesselroade and P. B. Baltes. New York: Academic Press.

Baltes, P. B.; Reese, H. W.; and Nesselroade, J. R. 1977. *Life-Span Developmental Psychology: Introduction to Research Methods.* Monterey, CA: Brooks/Cole.

Baltes, P. B., and Willis, S. L. 1977. Toward psychological theories of aging and development. In *Handbook of the Psychology of Aging,* eds. J. E. Birren, and K. W. Schaie. New York: Van Nostrand Reinhold.

Bandura, A. 1982. Self-efficacy in human agency. *American Psychologist* 37: 122–147.

Bentler, P. M. 1980. Multivariate analysis with latent variables. *Annual Review of Psychology* 31: 419–456.

Birren, J. E., and Renner, V. J. 1977. Research on the psychology of aging: Principles and experimentation. In *Handbook of the Psychology of Aging,* eds. J. E. Birren and K. W. Schaie. New York: Van Nostrand Reinhold.

Botwinick, J. 1977. Intellectual abilities. In *Handbook of the psychology of aging,* eds. J. E. Birren and K. W. Schaie. New York: Van Nostrand Reinhold.

Campbell, D. T., and Stanley, J. C. 1963. Experimental and quasi-experimental designs for research in teaching. In *Handbook of Research on Teaching,* ed. N. L. Gage. Chicago: Rand McNally.

Cattell, R. B. 1952. *Factor Analysis.* New York: Harper and Row.

Cattell, R. B. 1965. Higher order factor structures and reticular-vs.-hierarchical formulae for their interpretation. In *Studies in Psychology in Honor of Sir Cyril Burt,* eds. C. Banks and P. L. Broadhurst. London: University of London Press.

Cattell, R. B. 1966a. The principles of experimental design and analysis in relation to theory building. In *Handbook of Multivariate Experimental Psychology,* ed. R. B. Cattell. Chicago: Rand McNally.

Cattell, R. B. 1966b. Psychological theory and scientific method. In *Handbook of Multivariate Experimental Psychology,* ed. R. B. Cattell. Chicago: Rand McNally.

Cattell, R. B. 1970. Separating endogenous, exogenous, ecogenic, and epogenic component curves in developmental data. *Developmental Psychology* 3: 151–162.

Cattell, R. B. 1979. *Personality and Learning Theory.* The structure of personality in its environment, vol. 1. New York: Springer Publishing Company.

Clarke-Stewart, K. A. 1978. Interactions between mothers and their young children: Characteristics and consequences. *Monographs of the Society for Research in Child Development* 38: 6–7. (Serial No. 153).

Cook. T. D., and Campbell, D. T. 1975. The design and conduct of quasi-experiments and true experiments in field settings. In *Handbook of Industrial and Organizational Research,* ed. M. D. Dunnette. Chicago: Rand McNally.

Cook, T. D., and Campbell, D. T. 1979. *Quasi-Experimentation: Design and Analysis Issues for Field Settings.* Chicago: Rand McNally.

Coombs, C. H. 1964. *A Theory of Data.* New York: Wiley.

Costa, P. T., and McCrae, R. R. 1982. An approach to

the attribution of aging, period, and cohort effects. *Psychological Bulletin* 92: 238–250.

Cronbach, L. J. 1957. The two disciplines of scientific psychology. *American Psychologist* 12: 671–684.

Cronbach, L. J. 1975. Beyond the two disciplines of scientific psychology. *American Psychologist* 30: 116–127.

Cronbach, L. J.; Gleser, G. C.; Nanda, H.; and Rajaratnam, N. 1972. *The Dependability of Behavioral Measures*. New York: Wiley.

Damon, A. 1965. Discrepancies between findings of longitudinal and cross-sectional studies in adult life: Physique and physiology. *Human Development* 8: 16–22.

Dohrenwend, B. S., and Dohrenwend, B. P. 1974. eds. *Stressful Life Events: Their Nature and Effects*. New York: Wiley.

Edwards, A. L. 1950. *Experimental Design in Psychological Research*. New York: Holt, Rinehart and Winston.

Furby, L. 1973. Interpreting regression toward the mean in developmental research. *Developmental Psychology* 8: 172–179.

Games, P. A. 1979. Assessment and statistical control of subject variables in longitudinal research. In *Longitudinal Research in the Study of Behavior and Development*, eds. J. R. Nesselroade and P. B. Baltes. New York: Academic Press

Gergen, K. J. 1980. The emerging crisis in life-span developmental theory. In *Life-Span Development and Behavior*, eds. P. B. Baltes and O. G. Brim, Jr. New York: Academic Press.

Horn, J. L., and McArdle, J. J. 1980. Perspectives on mathematical/statistical model building (MASMOB) in research on aging. In *Aging in the 1980s*, ed. L. W. Poon. Washington, D.C.: American Psychological Association.

Hultsch, D. F., and Hickey, T. 1978. External validity in the study of human development: Methodological and theoretical issues. *Human Development* 21: 76–91.

Humphreys, L. G. 1962. The organization of human abilities. *American Psychologist* 17: 475–483.

Jöreskog, K. G. 1981. Analysis of covariance structures. *Scandinavian Journal of Statistics* 8: 65–92.

Kessen, W. 1960. Research design in the study of developmental problems. In *Handbook of Research Methods in Child Development*, ed. P. H. Mussen. New York: Wiley.

Krauss, I. K. 1980. Between- and within-group comparisons in aging research. In *Aging in the 1980s: Psychological Issues*, ed. L. W. Poon. Washington, D.C.: American Psychological Association.

Kuhlen, R. G. 1963. Age and intelligence: The significance of cultural change in longitudinal vs. cross-sectional findings. *Vita Humana* 6: 113–124.

Labouvie, E. W. 1980. Identity versus equivalence of psychological measures and constructs. In *Aging in the 1980s*, ed. L. Poon. Washington, D.C.: American Psychological Association.

Labouvie, E. W. 1982a. The concept of change and regression toward the mean. *Psychological Bulletin* 92: 251–257.

Labouvie, E. W. 1982b. Issues in life-span development. In *Handbook of Developmental Psychology*, ed. B. B. Wolman. Englewood Cliffs, N.J.: Prentice-Hall.

Labouvie, E. W. 1984. Sequential strategies as quasi-experimental designs. In *Individual Development and Social Change: Explanatory Analysis*, eds. J. R. Nesselroade and A. von Eye. New York: Academic Press.

Labouvie, E. W., and Nesselroade, J. R. 1984. Age, period, and cohort analysis in developmental psychology. In *Individual Development and Social Change: Explanatory Analysis*, eds. J. R. Nesselroade and A. von Eye. New York: Academic Press.

McCall, R. B. 1977. Challenges to a science of developmental psychology. *Child Development* 48: 333–344.

Nesselroade, J. R. 1977. Issues in studying developmental change in adults from a multivariate perspective. In *Handbook of the Psychology of Aging*, eds. J. E. Birren and K. W. Schaie. New York: Van Nostrand Reinhold.

Nesselroade, J. R., and Baltes, P. B. 1984. From traditional factor analysis to structural-causal modeling in developmental research. In *Experimental Psychology in the Future*, eds. V. Sarris and A. Parducci. Hillsdale, N.J.: Erlbaum Associates.

Nesselroade, J. R.; Stigler, S. M.; and Baltes, P. B. 1980. Regression toward the mean and the study of change. *Psychological Bulletin* 88: 622–637.

Nunnally, J. C. 1967. *Psychometric Theory*. New York: McGraw-Hill.

Overton, W. F., and Reese, H. W. 1973. Models of development: Methodological implications. In *Life-Span Developmental Psychology: Methodological Issues*, eds. J. R. Nesselroade and H. W. Reese. New York: Academic Press.

Reese, H. W., and Overton, W. F. 1970. Models of development and theories of development. In *Life-Span Developmental Psychology: Research and Theory*, eds. L. R. Goulet and P. B. Baltes. New York: Academic Press.

Riegel, K. F., and Riegel, R. M. 1972. Development, drop, death. *Developmental Psychology* 6: 309–316.

Rogosa, D. 1979. Causal models in longitudinal research: Rationale, formulation, and interpretation. In *Longitudinal Research in the Study of Behavior and Development*, eds. J. R. Nesselroade and P. B. Baltes. New York: Academic Press.

Rogosa, D.; Brandt, D.; and Zimowski, M. 1982. A growth curve approach to the measurement of change. *Psychological Bulletin* 92: 726–748.

Rosow, I. 1978. What is a cohort and why? *Human Development* 21: 65–75.

Schaie, K. W. 1965. A general model for the study of developmental problems. *Psychological Bulletin* 64: 92–107.

Schaie, K. W. 1967. Age changes and age differences. *The Gerontologist* 7: 128–132.

Schaie, K. W. 1977. Quasi-experimental designs in the psychology of aging. In *Handbook of the Psychology of Aging*, eds. J. E. Birren and K. W. Schaie. New York: Van Nostrand Reinhold.

Schaie, K. W., and Baltes, P. B. 1975. On sequential strategies in developmental research and the Schaie-Baltes controversy: Description or explanation? *Human Development* 18: 384–390.

Schaie, K. W., and Hertzog, C. K. 1982. Longitudinal methods. In *Handbook of Developmental Psychology*, ed. B. B. Wolman. Englewood Cliffs, N.J.: Prentice-Hall.

Siegler, I. C. 1975. The terminal drop hypothesis: Fact or artifact? *Experimental Aging Research* 1: 169–185.

Sörbom, D. 1979. An alternative to the methodology for analysis of covariance. *Psychometrika* 43: 381–396.

Tucker, L. R. 1966. Learning theory and multivariate experiment: Illustration by determination of generalized learning curves. In *Handbook of Multivariate Experimental Psychology*, ed. R. B. Cattell. Chicago: Rand McNally.

Tunnell, G. B. 1977. Three dimensions of naturalness; an expanded definition of field research. *Psychological Bulletin* 84: 426–437.

Underwood, B. J. 1957. *Psychological Research*. New York: Appleton-Century-Crofts.

Wohlwill, J. F. 1970. The age variable in psychological research. *Psychological Review* 77: 49–64.

Wohlwill, J. F. 1973. *The Study of Behavioral Development*. New York: Academic Press.

Yarrow, M. R.; Campbell, J. D.; and Burton, R. V. 1970. Recollections of childhood: A study of the retrospective method. *Monographs of the Society for Research in Child Development* 35. (Serial No. 138).

3

MEASUREMENT IN THE PSYCHOLOGY OF ADULTHOOD AND AGING

K. Warner Schaie
and
Christopher Hertzog
Pennsylvania State University

INTRODUCTION

The purpose of this chapter is to go beyond the design recommendations made in the first edition of this Handbook (these having been brought up-to-date by Nesselroade and Labouvie in Chap. 2 of the present volume) by providing an analysis of the measurement issues in psychology that are of specific interest for researchers concerned with adult development. To do so, we shall begin with a point of view that has characterized much of our own empirical work. It is grounded in a review of many pragmatic decisions made by us and other researchers in the course of long-range studies involving the age variable in adults, but has been tempered (or constrained) by some of the dicta of classical measurement theory. The first part of this chapter will therefore be concerned with what some might term "meta-measurement problems."

After discussing issues of time and age, including directionality and reversibility, as well as the questions whether these concepts should be operationalized as dependent or independent variables and whether calendar time is their only feasible scale (cf. also Schaie, 1983a), we next turn to the characteristics of

observations, including the problem of quantifying life stages, the question of absolute magnitudes or relative position in development, whether we should be interested in estimating latent constructs or directly observable behaviors, and the role of the much maligned gain score in research on age and time.

Our next concern is with practical matters of sampling. Although psychological studies usually do not call for the rigorous construction of census-type sampling frames customary in survey research, there is still a need to consider the circumstances under which it would be preferable to utilize random samples, structured samples, or extreme groups.

The equivalence of measures across different subject groups and occasions within the same individuals is one of the central aspects of construct validity in developmentally oriented research. An analysis is provided of the implications for studies spanning several ages, cohorts, and/or time periods, including confounds presented by instrumentation, by time of measurement interactions, and by the impact of treatment effects.

The second objective of this chapter is to give the reader a guide to the quantitative assessment of developmental measures and to alternative approaches for the measurement of developmental change. Featured here are the more recent approaches to the empirical study of measurement equivalence and to methods for the estimation of reliability suitable for developmental studies. Particular attention is given to the application of covariance structure models as well as the application of restricted and unrestricted factor analysis to developmental data.

The last part of the chapter, concerned with the measurement of developmental change, first addresses the bothersome matter of distinguishing between reliability and stability in developmental data, with special attention being given to change scores. Finally, we consider structural equation models for longitudinal data (see also Schaie and Hertzog, 1982). Because of space limitations we have not covered traditional analysis of variance models. These have been given extensive previous treatment (see Schaie, 1977).

A chapter on measurement cannot be kept as nontechnical as most readers might wish without losing its usefulness. In fact, application of some of the statistical recommendations given here will require the reader to become familiar in greater depth with more technical material. Several chapters to be found in volumes edited by Nesselroade and Baltes (1979) and by Wolman (1982) are particularly useful for this purpose and will be specifically referred to as we cover the topic to which they are related.

ON THE NATURE OF TIME AND AGE

Although some would argue that preoccupations with the concepts of time and age are strictly metaphysical matters best left to philosophers (cf. Reichenbach and Mathers, 1959), they have become central to the endeavors of the developmental sciences. The distinction between time-dependent and age-related processes is not only of concern in the design of developmental studies but has implications for a number of measurement paradigms to be discussed here. In particular, for the estimation of models, causal or otherwise, it is important to understand the directionality of time-ordered observations and to ponder the question whether age or time can reasonably be treated as independent variables of central concern.

Age-Related and Time-Dependent Processes

Gerontological researchers have traditionally employed chronological or calendar age (CA) as their independent variable of primary interest. They have sometimes lost sight of the fact that although CA is a time-ordered process, there can, but need not be, a correlation with age of the time of onset or the temporal duration of a given behavior. For example, executive burnout appears to occur as a function of length of time on the job, or technological obsolescence may be related to time elapsed since initial training. Both may spuriously appear to be related to age because in a given sample there is a customary age at which one pursues initial training or becomes an executive. When the same phenomenon is observed in populations where career entry occurs over a wise age range, it becomes obvious that the phenomenon is time-dependent but not age-related.

There is every reason to believe that many developmental changes thought to be age-related, particularly those for which substantial correlations with age can only be demonstrated over limited age ranges, are more likely to be time-dependent instead. As we shall see later on, the latter are as interesting or more so than behaviors that can be characterized unambiguously as functions of age. However, it would be well for us to restrict our use of the term "age-related" to those processes that have age-specific onset, asymptote, and/or shifting points in rate of age-specific change. By contrast, we should label as time-dependent those processes that imply developmental change but exhibit wide latitude in age of onset or inflection of rate of change (see also Chap. 1, this volume).

Directionality of Time-Ordered Observations

One of the most bothersome features for measurement in the developmental sciences is the fact that data collected over time are not normally distributed but instead represent ordered sequences, albeit exhibiting a variety of forms (from the simple linear to most complex polynomial) depending upon life stage and substantive content. The most common form hypothesized in the literature to fit age-related phenomena is the well-known Gompertz curve, which assumes a steeply decelerating increment until a young adult behavioral asymptote is reached, with a slowly accelerating linear decrement thereafter. This model, which, for the study of aging, is equivalent to the irreversible decrement model (cf. Schaie, 1973a, 1977), is obviously too simplistic, if only because it does not allow for recursive phenomena, but it also does not account for the lagged phenomena so characteristic of development (see also Wohlwill, 1973, p. 273 ff.).

On the other hand, the unidirectionality of time-ordered observations presents a sound basis for causal inferences in that consequents occurring later in time ordinarily cannot be said to have "caused"' antecedent behaviors. The unidirectionality of time-ordered behaviors turns out to be a boon because it provides the major rationale for applying techniques such as cross-lagged correlation and linear structural analysis to developmental data, as well as for choosing many of the fixed parameters required in model estimation.

But the unidirectionality of time-ordered observations should not erroneously lead the investigator to assume that time-ordered changes must therefore also be unidirectional in nature. Although there are many age-related processes that are unidirectional over some portion of the life span, others are not. Indeed, it seems to be one of the characteristics of time-dependent processes that they often take a cyclical or recursive form.

Should Age Be Treated as the Independent Variable of Central Concern?

Both time and age have become recognized as having little explanatory power in themselves but rather are seen to stand as indices that represent a variety of physiological and psychological influences affecting behavioral change over time. These influences are either not yet known or cannot be measured directly, or they occur in such complex interactive patterns that they prohibit parsimonious direct measurement. A variety of alternative indices, such as mental age or functional age, have been proposed from time to time. While conceptually perhaps more satisfying, such indices have the disadvantage of ambiguous scale properties and a conceptual definition that is dependent upon arbitrary decisions by individual investigators. Calendar time has at least the advantage of being a commonly understood index and the properties of a ratio scale.

Because of the empty nature of age as an explanatory concept, Wohlwill (1973) proposed that CA should no longer be used as the developmentalist's prime independent variable, but rather that it should be made part of the dependent variable. He suggested that the use of age as a discrete independent variable in the popular ANOVA approach had come about as a function of the dominance of the cross-sectional method in developmental work. Once the fact is recognized that development is often continuous and must be measured longitudinally to understand changes within individuals, this approach becomes less attractive. As part of the dependent variable of interest, age then becomes a scaling factor that indicates the number of time units over which a developmental process has occurred and thus permits us to understand the temporal progression of developmental change.

Age (or time, for that matter) as the dependent variable may have other useful properties. For example, we could regress age upon measures of a behavior critical for survival or one having social significance to determine the chronological age at which maxima or minima are reached. Likewise, we could regress such behaviors upon time in order to determine the elapsed time from onset, when optimal maxima or intervention-demanding minima are attained.

It might then be argued that the retention of age as an independent variable is not motivated so much by its scientific status as an explanatory construct (most would agree that it has no such status) but rather for the very pragmatic reason that we live in an age-graded society. As society begins to abandon many standards based upon age, even this consideration is slowly becoming less tenable (see also Schaie, 1973b).

For those who wish to preserve the status of age as an independent variable, it becomes essential to investigate redefinitions of the construct to give it greater meaning. Despite the many theoretical and practical problems involved, it may well be timely to delve further into the complexities of what has become known as "functional age"—that is, the substitution of an age-related but substantively grounded index, which with sufficient effort might eventually attain scale properties approximating those of CA (see Heron and Chown, 1967; Nuttall, 1972; Schaie and Parr, 1981). Given an effort to understand the behavioral impact of historical events, it may also be possible to reconstruct historical time by scaling "event-time" indices that take advantage of the many environmental changes that impact upon time-dependent behaviors (see Schaie, 1983a).

CHARACTERISTICS OF OBSERVATIONS

Before we can suggest appropriate algorithms for the numerical analysis of data typically collected by psychologists studying the aging process, it is first necessary to consider the nature of the observations to be quantified. In this section, our first query addresses limitations of predictive validity resulting from the continuities and discontinuities of behavior measured over time. We next ask whether the investigator is interested in tracking directly observable behaviors or in following the course of their subjects' position on indicators of psychological constructs. After considering the scale properties of our data, we then conclude the section with a discussion of the controversy with respect to the appropriateness of using gain scores in developmental studies.

Predictive Validity

Recent discussions in the developmental literature have emphasized the fact that continui-

ties and discontinuities in the development of behavior may depend both upon a particular life stage as well as upon the substantive area involved (see Brim and Kagan, 1980). This phenomenon is most noteworthy in infancy, where many behaviors show wide ranges of individual differences and regular progressions of development that are not predictive of later behaviors (Kagan, 1980). Once certain behaviors reach an asymptote required of all surviving organisms, they cease to have predictive value because the surviving population is virtually homogeneous with respect to the predictor variable. Similarly, while there may be moderate and continuous decrement in many behaviors in old age, such behaviors may have not been predictive of later events because the magnitude of the decrement is below the threshold values that must be reached before other behavioral domains are affected.

It has already been noted that ANOVA models imply discrete levels of observation for independent variables that need not be monotonically ordered. ANOVA models would therefore be most appropriate when the investigator has theoretically defensible age boundaries, as he would in the case of stage models of aging, in the case of universal age-related phenomena, or in situations where functional age criteria are utilized. Where continuous levels of the independent variables appear more reasonable, notably in the absence of life stage assumptions, regression models would be preferred.

Latent Constructs and Observable Behaviors

With the exception of demographic and specific physiological indices, there are very few directly observable behaviors that contribute to our understanding of human behavior. In descriptive work of areas such as intellectual abilities, motivation, or personality, we are rarely interested in performance on our specific test items or measurement scales. Instead, such observations serve as indicators of the respondent's standing on some theoretically defined or empirically abstracted construct of interest. Similarly, in the clinical or psychopathology literature we are rarely interested in the occurrence of specific symptoms other than in their role as the indicators of diagnostic syndromes having broader import and future consequences. Although we measure the observable phenotype or surface trait, it is usually the unobserved genotype or source trait for which we wish to interpret developmental change. Consequently, the investigator who follows time-dependent or age-related processes will typically compare only a few independent variables that are directly observable and measure all or most dependent constructs indirectly by means of sets of observations. This is fortunate, because the equivalence of single measures for a particular construct over wide age ranges and time periods is often questionable. Fortunately, a variety of techniques are now available that permit the study of multivariate systems, including directly observable and latent constructs, some of which will be described in this chapter (see also Bentler, 1980; Jöreskog, 1979).

Scale Properties

One of the few desirable properties of chronological age as an index of development, and perhaps the only one, is that it provides an almost ideal ratio scale. That is, it has a true zero, whether defined as conception or birth, and equal scale intervals that are proportionate to one another regardless of their position on the scale. (For the classic discussion of psychophysical scales, see Stevens, 1951.) Although there are several behaviors (a notable example being reach in time) that have ratio properties, most behavior measurements do not. Nevertheless, certain methods to be found in the older, almost forgotten psychophysical literature, permit generating subjective scales that can be given a true zero point by being anchored to a physical event (Comrey, 1950). Of even greater interest for developmentalists are similarly constructable quasi-ratio scales that are anchored upon the smallest or largest discernible value of the measured behavior (Metfessel, 1947). Examples of such scales may be applied to widely varying topics ranging from the estimation of line length (Baker and Dudek, 1957) to associating colors and mood tones (Schaie, 1961a). More recent work

on multidimensional scaling approaches may be found in Shepard, Romney, and Nerlove (1972).

The investigator who does not wish to become familiar with the intricacies of psychophysical scaling, and whose work has progressed beyond mere taxonomizing, will largely deal with measures that are either ordinal or interval scales. The concern here is whether we are able to record absolute or relative measures both for the observation of behavior at one point in time and for the development of designs for the measurement of behavioral change.

Interval versus ordinal measures. Much of the work in constructing new measurement devices is concerned with the objective of creating an equal interval scale. There are both theoretical and empirical reasons why attainment of this objective may not always be realistic. For many measurement variables, even on well-constructed scales such as the Wechsler intelligence tests (Matarazzo, 1972), equal intervals may obtain over the middle range of respondents but not for the extremes. Most behaviors allow more precise judgments than the mere acknowledgement of their presence or absence, but absolute judgments of magnitude, implicit in interval scales, may be difficult to make because there is insufficient information about the quantitative characteristics of the observed behavior. Judgments of more or less or of relative position, however, can frequently be obtained even where quantification of absolute magnitude is unlikely.

In a number of instances, ordinal scales might be preferred for conceptual reasons, the most important being the study of hierarchical structures, whether within groups or individuals. In such work we are looking for ipsative measures that describe the relative position of the individual, or of a particular variate within the individual, with reference to a finite and specified set. Ipsative measures are often appropriate when we seek to create data languages or objectify judgments that are substantively subjective in nature. Such situations may range from relatively esoteric issues—such as the judgment of the relation between colors and moods (Schaie, 1961b) or the attributes of love relationships (Reedy, Birren, and Schaie, 1981)—to practical matters—such as the identification of primary patient complaints in an outpatient setting (Schaie, Chatham, and Weiss, 1961), or the perception of relative performance in competence-requiring situations (Scheidt and Schaie, 1978). Ipsative scaling usually employs the Q-technique approach introduced by Stephenson (1953).

One of the major advantages of interval scales, of course, is that they meet the basic criteria for the application of conventional parametric statistics. It should be noted, however, that parametric statistics can often be applied to ordinal data with little loss of power. Indeed, ipsative scales by their very nature meet normal distribution assumptions and control for the variability attributable to individual response styles.

Should we measure relative or absolute change? Once the scale properties of our observations have been decided, it still remains an open question whether developmental change should be treated as an absolute or relative proposition. Again, theoretical and substantive considerations must govern. Where performance criteria are at issue, we will likely be interested in changes in absolute level when making comparison between different groups or within the same individual. However, if we are concerned with individual status with respect to a constant reference group, then assessment of relative change will be more informative. Just as there are theoretical and substantive reasons to ipsatize measures within a single time frame, it may also make sense to ipsatize across occasions, that is, there may be a variety of circumstances when changes in relative position may be the crucial question of relevance. In this case, analysis of individual differences in change by means of correlational methods becomes a central focus of research, as discussed below.

SAMPLING ISSUES

It should be remembered that the sampling of populations in psychological research has a very different import than in other social sciences. There are very few studies that pre-

tend to provide national or regional population parameters for psychological variables. Indeed, it would be difficult to reach consensus whether any of our constructs have reached the status of definition that would make such an exercise profitable. Sampling from some larger universe is usually undertaken to protect the investigator from collecting data that will yield unreplicable findings because of excessive threats to the external validity of the study (Cook and Campbell, 1979). Quite often, however, psychologists' implicit rationale for a representative sample differs from that of demographers as well because its real aim is to obtain a sample that will cover the full range of occurrence of the behaviors of interest, with subjects being distributed perhaps roughly proportional to its incidence.

Within this context, there appear to be three major categories of sampling options: First, there is the random sample at the study's inception that is representative of the population to which findings are to be generalized. Second, samples are structured with respect to some desirable population attributes but with full expectation, because of nonrandom, experimental mortality, that data will be examined at the conclusion of the study only for those participants who have been examined on all test occasions. Third, a sample may be selected that is particularly appropriate to the variables or problem being studied but not necessarily representative of any identifiable population group. The latter case may arise when the researcher is interested primarily in the mechanism of a phenomenon rather than in its distribution in the population. Of course, it may also become inevitable whenever phenomena with low incidence are being studied.

Random Samples of Representative Populations

Representative populations may be obtained by census-type enumerations of all members of a population cohort for a specified age level within whatever geographical limitations are practicable for a given investigation. Such an approach is expensive and probably unnecessary for psychological investigations. Instead it may suffice to identify population frames whose demographic characteristics are known and which are broadly representative of the general population, but which are maintained over long periods of time for purposes other than a specific research project. Examples of such population frames are fraternal or religious organizations, alumni clubs, and health maintenance organizations. Random samples from the rosters of such organizations may provide as reasonable an approximation to a census type sample as may be expected for most psychological studies and may be practicable for longitudinal studies. They have the additional advantage that the selected members will be tracked by the organization from which the sample comes without expense to the research project.

No matter how representative a sample is of its parent population at the time of initial selection, it will perforce become less representative as time passes because of nonrandom sample attrition resulting from natural causes as well as from experimenter ineptitude. In fact, even if the experimenter had total control over the sample, it would most likely cease to be fully representative over time because the parent population itself may experience changes not identical to those of the sample. One of the standard features of all longitudinal studies, therefore, should be a systematic dropout analysis (e.g., Gribbin and Schaie, 1979; Schaie, Labouvie, and Barrett, 1973) to determine to what extent the residual sample differs from that originally selected.

The investigator studying population trends over time who is not particularly interested in intraindividual change can side-step the sample attrition issue by obtaining new random samples for the cohort under study at each successive measurement point. Most longitudinal studies implicitly assume a sampling-without-replacement model, that is, only members of the population frame at the study's inception are sampled at subsequent times. Because of the great mobility in today's society, this assumption may reify the problem by decreasing representativeness for the longitudinal panels previously mentioned. Consequently, it may well be that a sampling-with-replacement model that reflects the naturally occuring changes in the parent population may be more defensible, especially if generalization to the broadest possible extent is desired (cf. Gribbin, Schaie, and Stone, 1976; Schaie, 1973a, 1977).

Structured Samples

The investigator who does not have the resources for census type sampling or who cannot gain access to existing broad sampling frames is limited to samples of convenience. In this case, however, it is usually necessary to structure the sample so that it represents a sufficient range of individual differences to permit reasonable generalizability to any broader population. Whenever quota samples are structured, the matter of cell sizes is raised. Minimum sizes, of course, are strictly related to the power of the statistical test used to detect reliable nonzero effects, and standard methods for their determination are readily available (cf. Cohen, 1977). Relative cell sizes, however, are a quite different matter. Although unequal cell sizes are somewhat troublesome in certain ANOVA paradigms (cf. Cramer and Appelbaum, 1980; Schaie and Hertzog, 1982), sampling decisions must be determined conceptually rather than for analytic convenience. That is, quotas should be set so that they represent demographic incidence of the independent variable for which representation is to be obtained. The most obvious example of this principle for aging research is classification by sex: Because of differential longevity, equal sample sizes for men and women would guarantee that differential ranges of talent and other uncontrolled traits would be sampled by sex. The solution here would seem to be to fix sample sizes by sex routinely in terms of the census sex ratio for the cohort under investigation.

In selecting longitudinal panels, one is often further governed by those characteristics of potential subjects that are likely to guarantee their survival as part of the sample. Care must be taken that these characteristics are not the very ones that mediate dependent variables of interest or that reduce population variance to the point that moderate but interesting relationships cannot be explicated. Convenience samples are often obtained by offering monetary incentives for participation. Relatively little is known on how representativeness of samples is affected by such incentives. In one study, volunteer response among a stratified sample of contacts was unaffected, and performance on intellectual ability tests did not differ, but there were some minor personality differences between those who volunteered with and those who volunteered without promise of subject fees (Gribbin and Schaie, 1976).

Studying Extreme Instances

When the experimenter, is not interested in population parameters but rather wishes to study how certain behaviors express themselves at different stages of development under idealized or stress conditions, there may be good reason to argue for the selection of explicitly biased samples. For example, it may be appropriate to select two extreme samples, in one of which the behavior being studied is predicted to occur and in the other, not to occur. Or, if one wants to determine the limits of optimal functioning—as a prerequisite, say, for the development of intervention programs—it might be appropriate to select samples of the extremely well functioning.

In seeking a representative sample, we usually attempt to maximize the range of individual differences. By contrast, extreme samples should be as homogeneous as possible, and careful subject screening may be required. Where optimal performance levels are to be investigated, institutionalized populations must obviously be avoided, and routines may be needed to discourage all but the most highly motivated (for an example, see Schaie and Strother, 1968). On the other hand, if minimum levels of function compatible with survival are to be considered, then institutional populations may be highly desirable.

Generalization from extreme samples poses special hazards. When two extreme groups are to be compared (frequently those with the presence or absence of pathological symptoms), attention must be given to differential base rates. Bayesian approaches addressing this problem have been extended to longitudinal data by Geisser (1965; see also Geisser

and Kappenman, 1971). And even for extreme samples the question remains whether one should randomly sample from the available class of extreme subjects, or whether that class should be defined so narrowly that one can engage in the exhaustive study of a finite population. The former approach permits some limited generalization but also retains all the other problems of longitudinal panels. In studies of finite populations, on the other hand, measures of change are strictly relevant only to the survivors, since it would be absurd to obtain estimates for individuals who cease to be members of a finite population.

Measurement Equivalence

One of the most basic premises in science is that meaningful comparison of any two instances of a phenomenon requires use of the same measurement scale. Unfortunately for the behavioral sciences, utilization of the same questionnaire or test apparatus does not guarantee measurement equivalence. The characteristics of the individual at the time measurement occurs will determine whether or not the instrument is appropriate. In the developmental sciences we face the dilemma that no two individuals, or groups of individuals, have identical characteristics at the same point in time, nor does a given individual or group retain identical characteristics across different points in time. Measurement equivalence must therefore be demonstrated empirically, and it may be assumed that such demonstration for any directly observed behavior will indeed be difficult across groups differing in many characteristics or over significant periods of time within a single group or individual. Most approaches to the study of measurement equivalence are therefore multivariate in nature, and much of the remainder of this chapter will deal with the description of relevant methods.

The study of measurement equivalence in aging research has two fundamentally different aspects. The first is the very traditional problem, albeit with some special twists, that when a given measure is administered over several occasions, we must be concerned about the reliability of the measure. Indeed, the matter of regression to the mean (when using fallible measures) has received much attention (cf. Baltes, Nesselroade, Schaie, and Labouvie, 1972; Furby, 1973; Nesselroade, Stigler, and Baltes, 1980). The second aspect of the problem, however, is the fact that measurement equivalence would not be guaranteed, even if all the measures used were perfectly reliable, because of systematic changes in individuals that will not necessarily be uniform across *all* individuals. The issue then becomes whether an operation with adequate construct validity for a particular group of persons at one time will retain the same validity across other groups or at other times. Further problems, of course, are introduced by confounding effects that result from changes in instrumentation over time or by the differential effects of interventions occurring between measurement points.

Equivalence Across Individuals—Age and Cohort

In cross-sectional studies it is necessary to determine whether the structure of the measurement instrument is maintained across the different age groups under comparison. A task that may be a good estimate of one construct in young adulthood may measure a different construct in late life. For example, Cohen's (1957) factor analysis of the Wechsler scales showed that the digit span test shifted from being a measure of attention span to a measure of memory. Even within the same age group, one should not assume that the same measure is equally appropriate for men and women. Particularly for measures where there are life-long sex differences (e.g., spatial abilities), it is not unlikely that observable measures are differentially effective in measuring the underlying construct (cf. Cohen, Schaie, and Gribbin, 1977).

There have been some discussions of cohort-appropriate tests. In contrast to equivalence problems arising out of actual age-related changes within an individual, we are here considering attributes of the test instrument that relate to stable characteristics of the subjects. There are substantial differences in language behavior and educational exposure between successive cohorts that may readily affect test comprehension and verbal performance (cf. Gardner and Monge, 1977). Because of vast differences in life experiences between cohorts, it might be argued that older forms of some tests should be preferred in working with the cohorts upon whom those tests were constructed. Indeed, Gribbin and Schaie (1977) found that a more recent version of the PMA test had lower construct validity for older adults than did an older version of that test.

Equivalence Within Individuals Over Time—Age and Period

The equivalence problems found in the cross-sectional comparison of different age groups find a replay in the comparison of longitudinal data on the same individuals over long periods of time. Substantial questions are again raised with respect to the equivalence of the relation between observable measures and the constructs to which they refer. Although some of the evidence attests to the remarkable stability of well-measured constructs, one must expect that one of the responsibilities of investigators conducting longitudinal studies ought to be the demonstration of the measurement equivalence of their major constructs, as discussed in detail below.

Societal changes in attitudes, stereotypes, and publicly acceptable behaviors may not have much impact on ability measures, but they must certainly be expected to impact on responses to self-report inventories and other subjective sources of psychological data. Since the structural analysis of period effects can obviously be confounded by intraindividual age changes, it is best conducted on several cohorts followed over the same time period.

Confounding Effects

Measurement equivalence can also be seriously compromised by failure to control effectively for instrumentation and intervention effects. Longitudinal studies, in particular, are plagued by unavoidable shifts in project personnel, inadequate documentation leading to slight shifts in experimental protocol, as well as differential experience and motivation by project staff. In fact, we would like to suggest that the modest (and often not readily explicable) period effects found in psychological studies are likely to be due to a combination of instrumentation effects (cf. Schaie, 1983b).

There are other aspects of experimental paradigms that can and should be attended to lest their consequences serve to obscure findings of developmental change. For example, Birkhill and Schaie (1975) found that different reinforcement schedules for guessing behavior on abilities tests led to substantial differences in the performance of older persons, and Hoyer et al. (1978) showed that speed of test performance could be manipulated by rewarding subjects with trading stamps.

Covert treatment effects may also be introduced because the experimental paradigm has differential anxiety-arousing properties for persons at different levels of autonomic nervous system integration (Eisdorfer, Nowlin, and Wilkie, 1970) and for persons differing on personality traits that are related to learning parameters (Schaie and Goulet, 1977). We know as yet very little about the many behavioral "side effects" that may be attributable to experimental paradigms. Their sum total, however, cannot simply be dismissed as experimental error, particularly when many of the confounds just enumerated tend to interact systematically with many of the variables of interest in studies of human aging (see also Schaie, 1978).

QUANTITATIVE ASSESSMENT OF DEVELOPMENTAL MEASURES

In the following sections, methods are outlined more formally for assessing measurement equivalence across ages, cohorts, or specific subpopulations of interest to life-span developmental psychologists. A brief overview is provided of several different approaches to stimulating the psychometric properties of test and questionnaire items, and quantitative methods are discussed for determining measurement equivalence at different levels.

Assessing Measurement Equivalence with Covariance Structures Models

The simultaneous assessment of measurement properties in multiple groups was advanced considerably by the contributions to covariance structure analysis by K. G. Jöreskog and coworkers. Jöreskog (1970) and others (most notably, Bock and Bargmann, 1966) showed that structural models for covariance matrices can represent hypotheses about the underlying relationships among constructs that determine the empirically observed covariance structure. In these models, the covariance structure of the observed variables is determined by a linear combination of other parameters, for example, the variance components of a set of observations. Maximum likelihood methods for testing structural hypotheses about the forms of observed covariance matrices (e.g., Box, 1949) can therefore be employed to estimate the parameters of the linear model. A wide variety of useful models, including factor analysis and structural equations, can be represented and estimated using the covariance structures approach (e.g., Jöreskog, 1970, 1974).

Covariance structures models are relevant to the problem of measurement equivalence because hypotheses about the psychometric properties of empirical measures can be represented by alternative covariance structure models (Jöreskog, 1971; Rock, Werts, and Flaugher, 1978; Werts et al., 1973). The LISREL VI computer program (Jöreskog and Sörbom, 1980) represents the most recent version of the covariance structures model.[1]

In its complete form, LISREL represents a model for structural equations among unobserved variables that are determined from a set of observed variables by common factor analysis. The basis for modeling the psychometric properties of measurement instruments in LISREL is the well-known relationship of classical test theory to the parameters of a common factor analysis model (Alwin and Jackson, 1979; Jöreskog, 1971a; Lord and Novick, 1968). What is known as "the measurement model" in LISREL consists of a pair of common factor analysis models. Only one

[1]LISREL is the most widely available covariance structures model and computer program; other models are possible and arguably more advantageous in certain applications (see Horn and McArdle, 1980). We rely on LISREL because it is so widely available and because to discuss other models would introduce additional complexity to an already difficult topic.

of the measurement models is needed to assess psychometric properties. LISREL's "y-side" of the model must be used if the means of the variables are to be considered simultaneously with the covariance structure (Jöreskog and Sörbom, 1981).

The LISREL measurement model for the y-side is as follows: Assume a common factor model describing the regression of a p-order vector of observed variables upon an m-order vector of latent variables (factors), as follows:

$$y = \Lambda_y \eta + \epsilon \tag{1}$$

where y is the vector of observed variables, η the vector of latent variables, and ϵ is a vector of regression residuals. The regression coefficients, or the unstandardized factor pattern coefficients, are contained in the $p \times m$ matrix Λ_y. Equation (1) is simply a matrix representation of the usual common factor model, as follows:

$$y_1 = \lambda_{(1,1)}\eta_1 + \lambda_{(1,2)}\eta_2 + \cdots + \lambda_{(1,m)}\eta_m + \epsilon_1$$

$$y_2 = \lambda_{(2,1)}\eta_1 + \lambda_{(2,2)}\eta_2 + \cdots +$$
$$\lambda_{(2,m)}\eta_m + \epsilon_2$$

$$y_p = \lambda_{(p,1)}\eta_1 + \lambda_{(p,2)}\eta_2 + \cdots +$$
$$\lambda_{(p,m)}\eta_m + \epsilon_p \tag{2}$$

Equation (1) implies that the covariance matrix of the observed variables, defined as Σ, may be represented as

$$\Sigma = \Lambda_y \Psi \Lambda'_y + \Theta_\epsilon \tag{3}$$

where Λ_y is as before (the factor pattern matrix), Ψ is the covariance matrix of the factors in η, and Θ_ϵ is the covariance matrix of the regression residuals in Σ.

Equation (3) is a traditional factor analysis model with an infinite number of solutions. LISREL resolves the factor indeterminancy problem by *a priori* specification of a sufficient number of parameters in Λ_y, Ψ, and Θ_ϵ to identify uniquely the remaining unknown parameters (see Jöreskog, 1970). Hypotheses about the parameters are expressed by specifying them as either *fixed* or *constrained*. Fixed parameters are set equal to a specific value *a priori;* constrained parameters are not known in advance but are specified to be equal to one or more other parameters. For example, if we hypothesized that a variable was *not* de-

termined by a factor, we would fix the regression of that variable on the factor in Λ_y to zero. If we hypothesized that two factor loadings in Λ_y should be nonzero but equal to one another, we would estimate the model only under the condition that the two loadings be exactly equal.

Given a sufficient number of *a priori* restrictions, it is possible to estimate the remaining unknowns using maximum likelihood methods. Hypothesis testing is possible because LISREL models are often "overidentified," that is, they specify more restrictions than are necessary to identify the remaining unknowns. The difference between a model's estimate of Σ, or $\hat{\Sigma}$, and the sample data matrix, S, is reflected in a likelihood-ratio χ^2 test of the goodness of fit of the model to the sample data. The null hypothesis is that the sample covariance matrix was drawn from a population covariance matrix having the structure specified by the model. A significant χ^2 statistic indicates that the model does not account for the sample data. This statistic may be used for hypothesis testing by evaluating the improvement in fit, as indicated by the reduction in χ^2, between a model and an alternative model with the same basic specification but fewer restrictions. The difference in χ^2 is itself a χ^2 variable and tests the null hypothesis that the two models are drawn from the same population covariance matrix (see Jöreskog, 1971b, 1974). Less technical discussions of confirmatory factory analysis include Hertzog (1984) and Mulaik (1972).

Perhaps the most difficult aspect of LISREL for the "uninitiated" is that often one need not standardize the observed variables and analyze a correlation matrix; instead, the factor analysis is often done in the unstandardized metric of the covariance matrix. To do so, one needs to use parameter specifications to determine the metric of the factors—initially undefined in an unstandardized model—usually by fixing one factor loading to an arbitrary constant (conveniently, 1) that scales the factor variance in units of the observed variable selected (see Jöreskog, 1971b). Although unstandardized factor analysis presents unique problems in specification, interpretation analyses in covariance metric have important advantages for the analysis of psychometric properties, especially when testing the hypothesis of measurement equivalence in multiple groups (see below).

A second difficulty in employing LISREL derives from the need for an *a priori* model specification, which requires the ability to represent psychometric assumptions as covariance structure models. This difficulty is more than offset, however, by the major advantage of being able to test psychometric properties with assumptions of statistical hypothesis-testing procedures.

Treatment of Reliability Using Classical Test Theory

The LISREL approach to the problem of measurement equivalence derives from classical test theory (Cronbach, 1970; Lord and Novick, 1968). The theory conceptualizes the problem of measurement error as follows: Any empirical measure of a construct is assumed to be a function of two components: (1) a true score component, which measures the "true" status of the individual on the construct at the instant of measurement, and (2) an error component, which is a stochastic deviation from the true score caused by specific, random influences that are an unavoidable concomitant of the measurement process. Since error scores are random, the correlation of true and error components are zero, thereby implying that the variance (σ_x) of a variable, x, is

$$\sigma_x^2 = \sigma_\tau^2 + \sigma_\epsilon^2 \qquad (4)$$

which simply shows that the variance of x is the sum of two orthogonal components, the true score variance and the error variance. Equation (4) leads to a familiar set of definitions for reliability of the empirically observed variable as the ratio of true score variance to total variance, as follows:

$$\rho_{xx} = \sigma_\tau^2 / (\sigma_\tau^2 + \sigma_\epsilon^2) \qquad (5)$$

etc. (See Allen and Yen, 1979, for a useful summary of alternative formulae and their conceptual implications). Reliability in this sense is the reproducibility of the distribution of individual differences, determined by the

proportion of variance in the observed variable, which in turn is determined by individual difference in the true scores.

Classical test theory includes an important set of definitions about the levels of equivalence in psychometric properties between two or more alternative forms of the same empirical measure (Lord and Novick, 1968). According to classical test theory, alternative forms are completely interchangeable only if they are in fact "parallel" forms, that is, forms with equivalent true score and error score (and hence, observed score) variances. If the forms have equivalent true score variances but different error score variances, they are said to be "tau-equivalent." If they measure the same construct but have different true score and error score variances, they are said to be "congeneric." In general, tau-equivalent and congeneric forms are not interchangeable—that is, one would not want to assign individuals to forms randomly and then pool the individuals into a single group.

Covariance structure models for testing the psychometric properties of alternate forms make use of the fact that the definitions of parallel forms, tau-equivalent forms, etc., specify alternative levels of equivalence of true score and error score variance components between forms. Tests of equivalence of psychometric properties involve testing structured hypotheses about the equality of parameters in Λ_y, Ψ, and Θ_ϵ. Since our focus is on measurement equivalence in multiple populations or across time, we will not review the single group psychometric tests of properties in any detail (see Jöreskog, 1971a, 1974).

The covariance structures approach to measurement properties is based upon a single common factor model for alternative forms of the same measure. This single common factor model represents the hypothesis of congenerism—that is, that the tests have true scores produced by only one latent construct. A congeneric single common factor model for four alternative measures is shown in Figure 1. This hypothesis of unidimensionality is critical; if it is rejected, then the four forms are not congeneric, and reliability estimates calculated from the single factor model's parameter

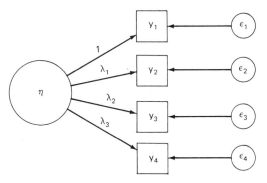

Figure 1. A single factor model for testing the psychometric properties of four alternative forms. Four observed variables (Y_1, Y_2, Y_3, Y_4) are determined by a single common factor (η_1) via the regression coefficients (λ_1, λ_2, λ_3, and λ_4). The factor (true score) variance, ψ_{11}, is shown as a self-recursive loop, as are the unique variances of the error components (ϵ_1, ϵ_2, ϵ_3, ϵ_4), θ_1, θ_2, θ_3, and θ_4. Testing the psychometric properties involves specifying different models for the λ and θ parameters (see text).

estimates will underestimate the true reliability of the forms. If the hypothesis of unidimensionality is not rejected, we cannot assume that the forms are, in fact, congeneric. There may be specific (but reliable) components in individual forms that do not covary with the components of the other forms; in this case, the reliability estimates will also be downwardly biased (Alwin and Jackson, 1979). However, the hypothesis of unidimensionality is the minimal criterion that must be achieved if parallelism is to be meaningfully tested.

The relationship of the factor analysis parameters to the true and error score components is as follows:

$$\sigma^2_{\tau_p} = \Lambda_p \psi \qquad (6)$$

$$\sigma^2_{\tilde{\epsilon}_p} = \theta_p$$

that is, the true score variance of the pth test is $\lambda_p \psi$, where ψ is the factor variance and θ_p is the error variance, assuming congenerism (see Alwin and Jackson, 1979; Jöreskog, 1971a; Werts, Linn, and Jöreskog, 1974). It is important to note that there are several ways in which the *reliabilities* of the tests might not be equal. The tests could have different observed variances and equal, or nearly equal, true score variances (as in the tau-equivalent model). On the other hand, the tests could merely be congeneric. The advantage of the covariance structures approach is that the true score and error score variance components

may be estimated under the different models. Ultimately, one can calculate an estimated reliability coefficient for the pth variable with the simple formula:

$$\rho_{pp} = \frac{\lambda_p \Psi}{\lambda_p \Psi + \Theta_p} \qquad (7)$$

This is a maximum likelihood reliability estimate based upon the factor model specified, which is, generally speaking, the best available estimator of the reliability coefficient given that the model is true (see Jöreskog, 1971a). Formulae for the reliability of a composite index also exist (see Werts et al., 1974).

Models for Measurement Equivalence in Multiple Groups

In order to examine measurement equivalence in multiple groups, we must test a series of hypotheses about the group equivalence of congeneric measures. It may be misleading merely to compare reliability coefficients from multiple groups (such as different age groups) when the groups have different true score and error score variances. The standardization implicit in the reliability coefficient may obscure important group differences in psychometric properties of the tests.

One tests the hypotheses of measurement equivalence in two or more groups by performing a series of simultaneous multiple

TABLE 1.   Test of Equality of Measurement Properties in Multiple Groups.[1]

Hypothesis	Specification	Test Statistic
1. Test of single factor model in each pop	One factor model in each group; no other constraints	Overall χ^2 (summed over groups)
2. Test of equality of scaling units	One factor model; all factor loadings in Λ_y constrained equal over groups	Difference in χ^2 between models 1 and 2
3. Test of equal true score variances	Same as 2; also, constrain ψ_{11} equal in all groups	Difference in χ^2 between models 2 and 3
4. Test of equal reliabilities	Same as 3; also, constrain all unique variances in Θ_ϵ equal over groups	Difference in χ^2 between models 3 and 4

[1] Based upon the discussion of Rock, Werts, and Flaugher, 1978.

group LISREL analyses that hypothesize varying degrees of group equivalence in Λ_y, Ψ, and Θ_ϵ parameters. Rock, Werts, and Flaugher (1978) discuss the procedure in some detail, which is summarized in Table 1.

When the primary concern is the measurement equivalence of multiple groups, the first question is whether the groups have equivalent population covariance matrices for the observed variables. Thus, a logical first step is to test the equivalence of the observed covariance matrices (Jöreskog, 1971b). If the covariance matrices differ between the groups, then additional tests are in order.

The second test of interest concerns unidimensionality—does the single factor model apply to the data from each group? If a single common factor model provides an acceptable fit to the sample data (evaluated by the χ^2 statistic), one can then test whether the factor pattern matrix, Λ_y, is invariant over the groups. This test determines whether the variables have the same scale units between groups (Rock et al., 1978). Differences in Λ_y parameters across groups would indicate an asymmetric relationship between true scores and observed scores between groups, which would be disastrous for comparisons of observed scores. After all, if a one-unit change in true scores translated into different amounts of change in observed scores for each group, how could quantitative group comparisons of ob-

served scores ever be represented as meaningful (Labouvie, 1980; Nesselroade and Baltes, 1979)? The test of the equality of Λ_y matrices over groups is therefore critical. It is obtained by calculating the improvement of fit from a single factor model in all groups, with no between-group constraints on the parameters, to a model with Λ_y constrained equally over the groups. The next two tests would involve specification of group equivalence in Ψ and Θ_ϵ parameters. The differences in χ^2 test the equality of true score variances and the equality of reliabilities, respectively.

It is important to understand the correct interpretation of the between-groups equality constraints on Λ_y, Ψ, and Θ_ϵ. When the Ψ and Θ_ϵ parameters are constrained equally across the multiple groups, parallelism among the alternative forms is *not implied*. It is not assumed that each of the observed variables has the same error variance (these are free to vary *within* groups), but it is assumed that each variable has the same error variance in all groups. Given the definitions of reliability in Eqs. (4) through (7), two groups cannot have the same reliability unless they have equal true score and error variances for a particular variable. In other words, it is possible for two groups to have equivalent true score variances but to differ in reliability, because one group has greater error variance than the other. This is the reason why simply comparing group differences in reliability coefficients is problematic. Moreover, group comparisons of the observed scores themselves would be biased in principle by group differences in reliability. On the other hand, if groups have equal scaling factors, it is possible to compare group differences on the true score means by using LISREL even though the group reliabilities differ (Rock et al., 1978).

Measuring Scale Properties with Item Factor Analysis

A common method for constructing scales of psychological constructs such as attitudes toward the elderly has been to perform exploratory factor analysis on a set of items intended to measure these constructs. Following the factor analysis, the investigator decides which items are most closely related to the factors. Factors are usually identified by a visual inspection of the magnitude of item factor loadings, and the item pool is then trimmed by deleting items with low loadings. Ultimately, scale scores are constructed by summing the item scores, usually without weighting the items as in factor score estimation procedures. Reliability estimates for the separate scales are then calculated by the internal consistency method.

Judiciously employed, such methods may be useful in defining multidimensional scales and estimating scale reliabilities, but we must emphasize several potential problems with this type of approach. First, items may factor for reasons unsuspected by the investigator—reasons that have little or nothing to do with the construct the items were designed to measure. Such components might include response bias, similarity of item formats, or social desirability of responses. There is no guarantee that factoring items will produce scales that validly measure the construct of interest. The investigator is particularly at risk when items have been constructed without prior attention to the issue of content validity and without a specific theory regarding the dimensionality of the item pool.

Second, decisions regarding the factor model (e.g., dimensions about the number of factors to extract) should not be determined arbitrarily. These issues are well covered in basic factor analysis texts (e.g., Harman, 1976; Mulaik, 1972). Here we shall consider only two illustrative points. It is well known that arbitrary decisions regarding the number of factors to be extracted can lead to badly perturbed solutions, especially when using the common default criteria in computer packages. If the number of factors is to be decided from the data, use of Cattell's scree test or related indices is preferable (Horn and Engstrom, 1979). The best procedure, however, is to design items to fit a theoretically specified multidimensional representation and then to fit the same number of factors as dimensions as the items were designed to measure.

Similar issues affect the decision regarding the selection of orthogonal versus oblique rotation. An investigator may decide that it is preferable to extract orthogonal dimensions because the resulting dependent variables will then be uncorrelated. The critical issue, however, is not whether minimally correlated scales are desirable but whether the scales are valid representations of the relationships among underlying constructs. It is of little use to construct orthogonal subscales when the multiple dimensions of interest are interrelated.

A third major problem with this approach arises at the level of scale score estimation. Although some solutions may result in simple structure—factors with a few high loadings and many near zero loadings—items will often split their loadings among two or more factors. This is especially likely when an orthogonal rotation has been forced upon dimensions that are truly oblique. Thus selection of items which are representative of a given factor may be difficult and highly arbitrary. Furthermore, simple summation of item scores by unit weighting may work against the investigator who selects a set of items based upon their high loadings and then defines a scale by summation. It is not uncommon, for example, to find that scale scores for putatively orthogonal dimensions have moderate correlations solely as an artifact of the scale definition and score estimation procedures.

Covariance Structures Approach to Item Factor Analysis

The critical feature of this approach is not the factor analysis method itself but the fact that emphasis is placed on testing hypotheses concerning the factor structure of the items. Investigators are encouraged to design items with an explicit scheme regarding the dimensionality of the construct of interest to insure that the items are constructed to represent content valid dimensions adequately and then to test empirically the conceptualization that led to the scale construction. Construct valid scales are most likely to be obtained when the item factor analysis is explicitly designed to test a hypothesis regarding the structure of the item correlations.

If the items have been selected to measure a single latent factor, the investigator will be interested in the goodness of fit test for a one factor model. The hypothesis of unidimensionality takes on special importance in item factor analysis, for it is only under the assumption of unidimensionality for the items that internal consistency estimates of reliability such as Cronbach's α may be considered valid estimates of the scale's reliability (see McDonald, 1981).

In a multidimensional solution, the investigator would be interested in testing whether or not the items relate to each other in the restricted pattern predicted by the investigator, that is, items load only on factors they were designed to measure. If this model does not fit the data, the investigator may entertain model modifications under the caveat that modifications may improve fit only by capitalizing on chance fluctuations in sample data. Whenever model modifications are anticipated, the investigator should collect a sufficiently large sample to enable split half validation procedures.

The LISREL approach is particularly well-suited to testing alternative hypotheses about intercorrelations among factors, including orthogonality (Jöreskog, 1974). When multiple, high intercorrelated factors are needed to account fully for the item covariances, the investigator may wish to determine whether a single second order factor accounts for the first order factor covariances. Liang and Bollen (1983) recently reported a reanalysis of the Philadelphia Geriatric scale suggesting that a second order factor does account for the correlations among the first order factors. Depending upon the magnitude of the second order loadings (alternatively, the magnitude of the first order factor covariances), this result can have profound implications for use of the scale as a multidimensional instrument.

The covariance structures approach is also ideally suited to performing simultaneous item factor analyses on multiple groups. If one is concerned with testing measurement equivalence of multiple item scales, the best way to do so is to perform simultaneous factor analysis in the multiple groups, determining whether there is group equivalence in the regressions of items on factors in the factor pattern matrix (e.g., Gallagher et al., 1978).

The reader should be warned, however, that there are problems associated with using LISREL for item factor analysis. The analysis of categorical (especially dichotomous) items may be highly problematic. The problem arises when the responses are not equally split between the two alternatives; in this case, there will be a tendency for the discovery of response-specific ("difficulty") factors (Ferguson, 1941). Although one can still use LISREL for the item factor analysis, no model with a reasonable number of factors will provide acceptable levels of fit to the data, as indexed by the χ^2 statistic. A theoretically better approach is to use factor analysis methods specifically designed for dichotomous variables (e.g., Muthen, 1978).

MEASUREMENT OF DEVELOPMENTAL CHANGE

Reliability versus Stability Over Time

The measurement of intraindividual change over time is a critical aspect of determining the nature and determinants of adult development. Developmental psychologists are usually interested in determining the stability of interindividual differences over time, or more precisely, in determining the consistency of interindividual differences in intraindividual change (see Baltes and Nesselroade, 1979). When we refer to the consistency of interindividual differences at the level of the construct itself, we will use the term "stability" of individual differences. Instability in individual differences will reduce the correlations of a variable (with itself) at a later longitudinal occasion. However, a test-retest correlation of an observed variable in longitudinal data will in general be less than unity for an entirely differ-ent reason—attenuation of the correlation because of the presence of measurement error. Thus, given only a low test-retest correlation for a single observed variable, it is not known whether that low correlation is a function of a high proportion of measurement error, low stability of interindividual differences over time, or both.

A general approach to the problem is to collect longitudinal data using multiple indicators that define the latent constructs of interest. The LISREL approach can then be used to estimate the disattenuated stability coefficients. When the multiple indicators are alternative forms of the same empirical measure, LISREL can be used simultaneously to estimate measurement properties and stability coefficients.

Figure 2 shows a hypothetical LISREL model for three alternate forms of the same test administered at three longitudinal occasions. The model must specify unstandardized variables since the longitudinal change in variability is an important consideration in evaluating reliability and stability over time. As discussed earlier, the reliability of the tests at each occasion may be estimated as a function of (1) the occasion-specific factor loadings of each alternative form on the latent variable, and (2) the factor variance at that occasion. The stability of interindividual differences across occasions are reflected in the factor (true score) covariances, labeled ψ_{21}, ψ_{31}, and ψ_{32}, which have been disattenuated for measurement error.

The measurement design shown in Figure 2 has some useful properties for testing hy-potheses about measurement equivalence across occasions. Assume that we have reason to believe that the measurement properties of the tests are affected by the repeated administration of the same tests to individuals in a longitudinal study. The null hypothesis of invariant true-score observed score relationships may be tested by specifying a model that constrains factor loadings to be equal across the three occasions and then testing the statistical significance of the improvement in fit obtained by relaxing this equality constraint.

An additional advantage of the LISREL model is the estimation of change in true-score variances (i.e., the factor variances in Ψ) across occasions. Stability in the magnitude of interindividual differences would be reflected in equal true-score variances across occasions. Instability in the factor variances would suggest interindividual differences in the amount of change over time.

As previously emphasized, a primary reason for using the covariance structures approach for separating reliability and stability is that the stability of interindividual differences is often underestimated when test-retest correlations are attenuated as a result of measurement error. It is also possible, however, that a lack of stability of interindividual differences might mask the high reliability of empirical measures if individual differences in the construct being measured are extremely labile. The latter pattern would occur if individual differences were situation-specific or if the attribute being measured was expected to shift in nonrandom but inconsistent ways across individuals (e.g., individual differences in emotional state). Nesselroade, Jacobs, and Pruchno (1981) used the covariance structures approach to demonstrate convincingly that low correlations on a state anxiety scale were a function of the instability of individual differences in anxiety, not a function of low reliability in the measures. Their results derived from the fact that alternative forms of state anxiety were highly correlated within occasions but virtually uncorrelated across occasions. The primary advantage of the covariance structures approach for Nesselroade et al. was that it let them show that the instability in individual differences

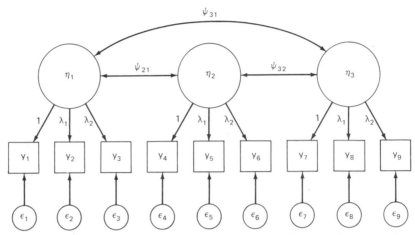

Figure 2. A model for three alternative forms administered three times to the same subjects. The reliabilities of the tests are a function of the factor loadings, factor variances, and unique variance at each occasion (see Figure 1). Tests of equality of measurement properties over occasions would involve constraining some of these elements equal over occasions. Stability of individual differences in true scores, on the other hand, are a function of the factor covariances (ψ_{21}, ψ_{31}, and ψ_{32}). Thus the principle advantage of the model is that it explicitly separates reliability of measures from stability of interindividual differences (see text).

could not be dismissed as a function of attenuation caused by measurement error in the empirical instruments.

Measurement of Developmental Change

Conceptual Issues. There is an abundant literature on the special problems associated with the statistical analysis of change over time (e.g., Bohrnstedt, 1969; Cronbach and Furby, 1970; Goldstein, 1979; Harris, 1963; Nesselroade and Baltes, 1979; Nunnally, 1978, 1982; Rogosa, Brandt, and Zimowski, 1982) and on the issues involved in appropriate selection of developmental research designs to detect such changes (e.g., Baltes, Reese, and Nesselroade, 1977; Nesselroade and Labouvie, Chap. 2, this volume; Schaie, 1977; Schaie and Hertzog, 1982). Given the contradictory positions taken in this literature, how should the developmental psychologist select an appropriate research strategy to quantify developmental change?

In discussing this problem, we shall not consider the issues involved in selecting a research design (see Nesselroade and Labouvie, this volume). Instead, we shall emphasize the importance of matching measurement techniques to conceptualizations of the nature of

the developmental phenomenon under study (and consequently, the research question being asked). Along with Baltes and Nesselroade (1970, 1973; see also Wohlwill, 1973), we would argue that the overriding issue to be addressed, conceptually and empirically, is whether (1) qualitatively different patterns of development exist in a given population of individuals, or (2) the developmental process alters the fundamental characteristics of the attributes under study. In either case, the measurement approach must attempt to specify and define the nature of such change operationally.

Along with Baltes and Nesselroade (1973), we would argue that factorial invariance across ages is a useful empirical definition of qualitative invariance constructs whenever multiple, well-defined interval or ratio scale variables are selected to measure the constructs of interest. Consequently, we will discuss methods for assessing factorial invariance in detail. Even when factorial invariance has been demonstrated, however, pooling information across subjects with different patterns of intraindividual development may have unfortunate consequences for the validity of the averaged developmental function. This is an especially important, if often ignored, issue in gerontological research since adult development is characterized by multiple patterns of development for many psychological constructs as a result of the impact of nonnormative life events, individual differences in exposure to environmental influences or physiological pathology, and other influences (see Baltes and Willis, 1977; Hultsch and Plemons, 1979; Schaie, 1983a).

If the research focus is to be placed upon developmental change *per se,* then the research design and measurement approach must be oriented toward the study of intraindividual change over time—that is, the measures must usually be made upon the same individuals in some type of longitudinal or sequential sampling design (Baltes and Nesselroade, 1979; Nesselroade and Labouvie, Chap. 2, this volume). This is especially true when explanation of individual differences in developmental change is the research goal; modelling developmental processes and their determinants requires measurement of change within individuals over time.

The sole exception to the requirement for directly measuring intraindividual change occurs whenever (1) qualitative invariance in the developmental process may be assumed (i.e., one is justified in arguing for a population or subpopulation that is homogeneous with respect to a developmental process) and (2) the research question is restricted to the description of population trends in mean or average developmental trajectories that use chronological age as the independent variable. In this case, use of cross-sectional sequences to estimate average age functions is appropriate and may even have certain advantages with respect to internal validity threats inherent in longitudinal sampling (see Schaie and Hertzog, 1982). Otherwise, the research should be oriented toward the measurement of change within individuals over time regardless of whether chronological age per se is treated as the independent variable.

Measurement of Average Developmental Functions

If average developmental functions are to be generated, the use of longitudinal sequences (Baltes, Reese, and Nesselroade, 1977) to chart the intraindividual change functions is appropriate. Hypotheses about change in levels of functioning on dependent variables may be treated in several ways. For many developmental phenomena, the descriptive utility of the orthogonal polynomial approach will suffice. A detailed discussion of the method of estimating growth curve functions using orthogonal polynomials may be found in Bock (1975, 1979; see also reviews by Guire and Kowalski, 1979; and Schaie and Hertzog, 1982). Within psychological tradition, trend analysis using least squares regression techniques has been the most common method of statistical analysis of polynomial models (or equivalently, trend analysis in repeated measures ANOVA). One of the chief advantages of the trend analysis approach is the use of hypothesis testing procedures to determine whether a lower degree polynomial may fit the data. Bock (1979) describes the polynomial approach under a set of different statistical assumptions. It is well known that, under the restrictive assumptions regarding the covariance structure of the error components, mixed model trend analysis pooling sums of squares over multiple degree of freedom subspaces provides the most powerful tests of the hypotheses of interest. However, if the mixed model assumptions are violated, multivariate profile analysis approaches to hypothesis testing should be used (Bock, 1979; Schaie and Hertzog, 1982).

A more general, but also more complex, approach that has evolved from the biometrics literature is the estimation of polynomial growth curve functions using maximum likelihood methods (Guire and Kowalski, 1979). Recently, Jöreskog (1979) described how such models may be estimated using the restricted covariance structures approach of LISREL and other programs.

Considerable complications are introduced to the estimation of developmental change functions in adult research, where one must consider the independent contributions of period effects, cohort-specific changes, and other sources of potentially confounded influences. Thus, analysis of longitudinal sequences in adult developmental studies must take into account the potential importance of effects associated with variables other than age per se (for discussion of the design issues involved, see Nesselroade and Labouvie, Chap. 2, this volume; Schaie, 1977; Schaie and Hertzog, 1982).

For purposes of description, use of the polynomial trend analysis approach on longitudinal sequences simply attempts to replicate the growth curve parameters on multiple cohort groups. This analysis represents application of trend analysis to the "cohort-sequential" design for longitudinal data (Schaie and Hertzog, 1982). We would argue along with Baltes, Cornelius, and Nesselroade (1979) that the age by cohort (cohort-sequential) matrix is the preferred arrangement of sequential data for the analysis of age effects. However, if the age-correlated effects estimated from a cohort-sequential matrix are to be treated as "pure" measures of age change, the additional assumption that period effects are absent in the cohort-sequential matrix is required. To the extent that unanalyzed period effects are present in the data, the growth curve trend coefficients will be influenced both by age and period effects (Schaie and Hertzog, 1982). For an empirical application of multivariate regression techniques for an orthogonal trend analysis of longitudinal sequences, see Schaie and Hertzog (1983).

The recent literature on analysis of sequential data matrices has included several expressions of concern that the parametric assumptions of sequential strategies may be invalid (e.g., the assumption of no period-related effects when analyzing a cohort-sequential data matrix taken from longitudinal sequences). Some of these articles have promoted the use of regression models that simultaneously estimate the effects of age, period, and cohort, under the assumption of the additivity of these effects—i.e., no interactions among these factors (George, Siegler, and Okun, 1981; Horn and McArdle, 1980). Although such approaches to the problem represent a statistical advance in modelling average developmental functions, in that they employ sophisticated applications of the general linear model, they are prone to errors of inference whenever the assumption of additivity or other parametric assumptions needed to identify the models are violated. The critical problem is that it is often not known in advance, particularly in descriptively oriented investigations, whether one form of assumptions or another is more advisable in a given application. Gerontologists interested in employing the additive effects approach should consult critical discussions of the method (e.g., Glenn, 1976, 1981) in order to understand some of its limitations before proceeding to data analysis. Glenn (1981) recently showed how the additive effects approach can lead to egregious errors when all effects from two or more of the three factors are monotonically ordered in the data under study. Certainly, there is no purely statistical solution to the problem of disentangling age, cohort, and period effects in a theory-free, descriptive manner (Hertzog and Schaie, 1982; Schaie and Hertzog, 1982).

Assessment of Individual Change: Use of Change Scores

The Role of Change Scores. The furor over the use of change scores in developmental work culminated in an influential paper by Cronbach and Furby (1970). Change scores were damned for four major reasons: (1) the variance of change scores will be greater than that found for each separate occasion; (2) the change score itself will be correlated with scores for both occasions; (3) the measurement errors from the two occasions accumulate, making change scores less reliable than the two measures from which they are derived (Nunnally, 1978); and (4) change scores may be affected by regression towards the mean occurring between the two measurement occasions.

The concerns listed above seem to have led quantitatively unsophisticated investigators virtually to abandon the use of change scores, and some journal editors have been resisting publication of change score results. Recently, however, a countermovement has appeared in the developmental literature arguing for the merits of change scores in developmental analysis (see Labouvie, 1981; Nunnally, 1982; Rogosa, Brandt, and Zimowski, 1982). The latter paper is a particularly useful review, since it provides a technically oriented counterargument to the position that the use of change scores is invalid and misleading. The issues involved in the debate are now reviewed in a more formal manner.

As indicated above, those who scorn the use of change scores suggest that these scores are unacceptably prone to the influences of measurement error. The reliability of a change score is a function of the reliability of the variable at two points in time and will be less than the reliability of the variable on either occasion—in some cases, much less. For illustrative purposes, the equation for the reliability of a change score may be simplified by assuming equal variances for the two occasions; then, following Rogosa, et al. (1982), the reliability of the change score can be expressed as:

$$\rho_{(y2-y1)} = \frac{\rho_{(y1)} + \rho_{(y2)} - 2(\rho_{y1y2})}{2(1 - \rho_{y1y2})} \quad (8)$$

where ρ_{y1} and ρ_{y2} are the reliabilities of Y_1 and Y_2 respectively and ρ_{y1y2} is the correlation between Y_1 and Y_2 (all values are assumed to be population parameters). The equation shows that the reliability of the change score is a function of (1) the reliabilities of the measure on the two occasions and (2) the correlation between the measure on the two occasions. Obviously, with low reliabilities, the reliability of the change score will also be low. Therefore, change scores should not be used with highly unreliable measures, but since highly unreliable measures should not be used *at all,* this argument cannot qualify as an admonition against the use of change scores *per se.* The more interesting case arises when the reliabilities of the measure on the two occasions are high and the correlation between them is also high. As can be seen from the equation, when ρ_{y1y2} approaches its upper limit of 1, $\rho_{(y2-y1)}$ approaches a lower limit of zero. This is one of the principle reasons why Cronbach and Furby (1970) criticized the use of simple change scores.

A recent discussion by Rogosa, et al. (1982), places this phenomenon in a rather different light. They show that the equation may be reformulated in terms of the variance of the slope of the change function from Y_1 to Y_2

(i.e., the individual differences in the amount of change from Y_1 to Y_2). If there is no variability in the amount of change, then the reliability of the change score will be zero regardless of the magnitude of measurement error or the statistical precision of the estimates. But this is entirely appropriate, for there can be no reliable rank ordering of individuals with respect to the amount of change if there are no individual differences in the amount of change!

Rogosa, et al., explicate this point by showing that stability in interindividual differences as reflected by ρ_{y1y2} is closely related to the variance of the intraindividual slope functions; the greater the stability, the lower the variance in change functions. This relationship is intuitively reasonable because perfect stability implies exact preservation of individual differences about the mean on the two occasions and equal amounts of change over time. As indicated above, however, the simple correlation ρ_{y1y2} is affected both by true stability in the underlying latent variables (i.e., $\rho_{\eta1\eta2}$) and the amount of measurement error in Y_1 and Y_2, and these two factors must be disentangled. Arguments against the use of change scores have focused on the role of measurement error and have ignored the logical implications of high stability. Given high levels of reliability on both occasions, the reliability of the change score remains high at low levels of stability.

The second issue to be considered more formally concerns the relation of initial status to amount of change. Change scores are often negatively correlated with initial status, and the argument is made that change scores should therefore be avoided because of regression toward the mean. Rogosa, et al., counter this argument with two reasons: First, when variables are standardized, as they often are, an important consequence is that the correlation between change and initial status must be less than or equal to zero. Thus, change scores should never be calculated from standard scores. Second, most of the arguments about negative correlations focus on the observed correlation of Y_1 and $Y_2 - Y_1$ and not upon the population correlation among the true score components η_1 and $\eta_2 - \eta_1$.

Rogosa, et al., show that there is a negative bias of $r_{y_1, y_2 - y_1}$ for estimating $\rho_{\eta_1, \eta_2 - \eta_1}$ and conclude that discussions regarding the negative correlation have overemphasized its importance by inadvertently focusing on observed correlations that imply values of $\rho_{\eta_1, \eta_2 - \eta_1}$ equal to or less than zero. This emphasis is unfortunate, however, because many phenomena are more likely to produce positive correlations among initial status and change at the level of the true scores—e.g., the fan spread hypothesis, which argues that gain is proportional to initial level (the rich get richer!). Inappropriate standardization and an emphasis on sample correlations between initial status and observed change have probably led to an overemphasis on the adverse impact of initial status as it relates to change.

The above argument calls into question the rationale for calculating residual change scores, in which initial level is partialed out of the change scores. One of the important advantages of the observed change score between two empirical variables is that it is an unbiased estimate of the change in the true scores across occasions. This property, and the reasons for reconsidering the logic of arguments against change scores on the basis of their correlation with initial status, led Rogosa, et al., to oppose the notion that a "fair" estimate of change requires covarying initial status with change scores. Covariance adjustments, particularly in the case of comparing change in nonequivalent groups (see below), test a different hypothesis than the analysis of simple change does. With covariance adjustment, one asks what the amount of change would have been had all individuals started at the same initial level. Leaving aside for the moment the issue of whether covariance adjustment truly provides such equating of individuals (see Reichardt, 1979), one must consider carefully whether this hypothesis of equal initial level is the one of interest before resorting to computing residualized change scores.

If we accept the proposition that assessment of individual change may justifiably be made on the basis of some form of change score, it is still necessary to decide whether the simple change score is the best indicator available for assignment into treatment groups, for post-hoc analyses of the correlates of change, or for other analyses. If simple change scores are to be used, then problems of measurement error must be addressed. Schaie (1980) has proposed use of a probable error adjustment of change scores for defining cutoffs to assign individuals to "decrement," "stability," and "increment" groups on the basis of change scores. Bayesian methods of estimating adjusted change scores, which use information about population change and variability of change, are also available (Rogosa et al., 1982; Strenio, Weisberg, and Bryk, 1983).

It should be emphasized that our relatively sympathetic view regarding use of change scores does not represent an unconditional endorsement. First, we strongly agree with those who have argued for the utility of more than two occasions of measurement in assessing change (e.g., Baltes and Nesselroade, 1979). Simple change scores are obviously relevant only for the two occasions situation; if there are more than two occasions, it may be better to estimate a growth curve and individual values for the parameters of that curve (Guire and Kowalski, 1979; Strenio et al., 1983). Second, use of the simple change score begs the issue of measurement error. A multiple indicator approach to measuring change, as in the LISREL model, is more desirable because change may be measured at the level of the latent rather than the observed variables. Under these conditions, regression to the mean caused by measurement error may be removed effectively from the analysis of the mean changes at the level of the latent variable.

Factorial Invariance and Developmental Change

In gerontological research, factor analysis of multiple indicator models is useful for determining whether the relationships between multiple indicators and factors remain invariant across multiple groups or across age levels in longitudinal data. It is only under the condition of factorial invariance that we can assume that quantitative comparisons of changes in developmental trajectories reflect changes in an isomorphic construct (Baltes and Nesselroade, 1970, 1973). There are two types of invariance to be considered: (1) invariance across multiple groups of subpopulations, and (2) invariance across occasions in the factor structure for the same individuals measured longitudinally. In each case, LISREL models may be specified that are uniquely suited to the problem of statistically testing hypotheses of factorial invariance.

Invariance in multiple groups. Assessment of factorial invariance in multiple groups would be of interest to gerontologists when either (1) cross-sectional data have been collected and the age differences in factor structure are to be investigated under the hypothesis that the group differences will reflect age changes in factor structure; (2) sequential data has been sampled and the investigator is interested in addressing the issue of factorial invariance in multiple cohort groups (Cunningham and Birren, 1980); or (3) groups are defined as being subpopulations selected from the general population on some variables of interest——e.g., comparison of depressed and mentally healthy elderly populations on measures of affect, self concept, and so on.

In spite of the conceptual problems associated with inferring developmental change in factor structure from cross-sectionally defined age groups, the first type of application has been most common in the gerontological literature. Indeed, the "dedifferentiation hypothesis," which argues for a structural reintegration of factor structure in late life development, has primarily been tested using factor analysis of multiple age/cohort groups (Cunningham, 1982; Reinert, 1970).

Many of the contradictory findings in the literature on age group differences in factor structure may be attributed to problems associated with the analysis of multiple groups using separate exploratory factor analyses of correlation matrices from each group (see Cunningham, 1978; Jöreskog, 1971b; Reinert, 1970). The principle advantages of LISREL methods for the analysis of factorial invariance in multiple groups are the use of a covariance matrix analysis and the ability to analyze simultaneously data from multiple groups while imposing between equality constraints on the factor analytic parameters (as discussed above for the analysis of measurement equivalence). These features are useful because they permit a likelihood ratio test of the hypothesis that the unstandardized regression coefficients that map variables onto factors are invariant across the multiple groups.

As shown by Meredith (1964; see also Bloxom, 1972), under the process of selection from a population into subpopulations differing in mean levels of the factors (as is the case in cross-sectionally defined groups), only the unstandardized (raw score) factor loadings may be expected to be invariant over groups. In principle, selection will produce group differences in observed variables and factors; separate standardization in each group by dividing through by the standard deviations will therefore tend to obscure factorial invariance by producing artifactual differences in standardized factor loadings (see also Cunningham, 1978; Jöreskog, 1971b). The hypothesis of factorial invariance is critically dependent upon the test of equivalence in unstandardized factor loadings across the multiple groups. Stricter forms of invariance involving group equivalence in factor covariances and unique covariance matrix may also be tested (Alwin and Jackson, 1981; Jöreskog, 1971b). Examples of applications of LISREL and related programs to simultaneous factor analysis with multiple age groups include Cunningham (1980, 1981), Hertzog and Carter (1982), and Horn and McArdle (1980).

Developmental change and longitudinal factor analysis. One of the major advantages of restricted factor analysis as represented in the LISREL model is its applicability to the unique problems of longitudinal factor analysis. When multiple indicators of a set of factors are measured at multiple longitudinal occasions, the highest values in the covariance matrix of observed variables will often be the covariances of variables with themselves on other occasions. The covariance matrix might be said to be dominated by the "test-specific" covariances. A consequence of this pattern is that traditional exploratory factor analysis of such data matrices will tend to uncover test-specific factors that collapse over the occasions of measurement. Such an analysis has interesting properties, but its parameters are not optimally suited for representing the process of change over time.

Several methodologists have developed longitudinal factor analysis models that better represent the nature of the developmental process (see Bentler, 1973; Nesselroade, 1977). Several longitudinal factor analysis models (e.g., Corballis, 1973) may be regarded as special cases of a more general LISREL model for the longitudinal factor analysis developed by Jöreskog and Sörbom (1977). Their general approach is to specify an "occasion-specific" factor model in which the factor model characterizing the structure of a single longitudinal occasion is extended or replicated to all longitudinal occasions using a covariance structure model. The Jöreskog/Sörbom model is analogous to the model for separating stability from reliability shown in Figure 2 except that the observed variables are multiple indicators of the same psychological construct rather than alternative forms of the same measure.

The Jöreskog/Sörbom model has several features of special importance for examining the consequences of interindividual differences in intraindividual change in latent variables. First, invariance of the regressions of variables on factors may be assessed by testing the hypothesis that the raw score factor pattern elements may be constrained to be equal across the different longitudinal occasions (as described for the model that examines measurement equivalence in longitudinal data). As was the case for simultaneous multiple group analysis, changes in the magnitude of individual differences over time would make it inadvisable to standardize the data prior to the analysis; under conditions of changing variance over time, only the raw score regression coefficients could be expected to be invariant over occasions.

Second, parameters of the factor covariance matrix are relevant to the hypothesis of interindividual differences in intraindividual change. Longitudinal changes in factor variances would indicate time-related changes in the magnitude of interindividual differences, which could occur only if the individuals differed in the magnitude of change over time.

The magnitude of the covariances between isomorphic factors on different occasions indicates the stability of intraindividual differences since high covariances represent little shift in interindividual differences as a function of developmental change. When rescaled to correlations, these parameter estimates should approach unity as individuals approach exact maintenance of their distribution about the factor mean over time. Conversely, low levels of covariance would indicate substantial "crossing over" of the change functions over time, which could be indicative of differential patterns of development.

The measures of individual differences discussed here are taken at the level of the latent variables or factors and not at the level of observed variables. This aspect of the model is critically important since it assures that the stability estimates as reflected in the factor covariances will be disattenuated for measurement error. Moreover, it guarantees that patterns of individual differences will be generalizable over a set of variables measuring a common construct rather than specific to an isolated empirical variable, which increases the construct validity of the observed changes.

An important additional feature of the Jöreskog/Sörbom model is that one can model covariances between residual (unique) components in Θ_ϵ. Because unique variance in factor models contains reliable specific components other than stochastic measurement error, it is usually the case that components for replicated observed variables will covary across occasions. As noted by Corballis (1973), Sörbom (1975), and others, failure to specify and estimate such "autocorrelated residuals" will perturb other parameter estimates of the model.

Jöreskog and Sörbom (1977) discuss more complex variants of the longitudinal factor model that incorporate occasion-specific and test-specific common factors. The model can easily be extended to the analysis of cohort-sequential data matrices, where multiple cohorts are measured longitudinally (Hertzog, 1984; Jöreskog and Sörbom, 1980). The model can also be expanded to include the simultaneous analysis of factor means as well as factor structure (Jöreskog and Sörbom, 1980). This feature is especially useful because the model then represents an operational method for implementing the suggestion of Baltes and Nesselroade (1973) that hypotheses about changes in developmental level and simultaneously consider the issue of qualitative invariance in the factor structure. Developmentally oriented applications of the model may be found in Olsson and Bergman (1977) and Hertzog and Schaie (1983). The latter paper also illustrates the simultaneous analysis of factor means and factor structure in sequential data.

Structural Equations Models for Longitudinal Data

If the research question focuses on explanation and prediction of interindividual differences in intraindividual change functions by antecedent and concurrent variables, then one of the better available methods for modeling change processes and their causal determinants is structural equations modeling of longitudinal data (Bentler, 1980; Jöreskog and Sörbom, 1977, 1980). Structural regression models involve the estimation of regression coefficients representing sequences of directed relationships between antecedent and consequent variables under a set of hypotheses regarding the nature of the causal relationships between constructs. The empirical measures of the constructs may be either directly observed or unobserved variables, including latent variables defined by multiple indicators. In the latter case, the structural models usually involve the use of restricted factor analysis to define the latent variables of interest. Thus the longitudinal factor analysis model just described represents a measurement model in LISREL that may define the latent variables that are to be interrelated in a structural equations model.

In the ideal case, structural regression models are intended to represent an operational representation of causal flows of influence, often involving multiple levels of causation in a single model. The critical aspect of structural modeling, then, is the representation of causal hypotheses and the testing of their consequences wherever possible by the logic of falsification (see Duncan, 1975; Heise, 1975). In structural regression, a simple zero order correlation is modeled (1) as an indication of the direct influence of one latent variable on another, (2) as an indirect influence mediated through other variables, or (3) as a causally spurious correlation.

In the longitudinal model of Jöreskog and Sörbom (1977), the endogenous latent variables are measures of constructs that have been assessed across the longitudinal occasions, whereas the exogenous latent variables are "background variables" that are pre-existing conditions at the time of the initial longitudinal sampling. The endogenous latent variables are defined as occasion-specific factors in the longitudinal factor analysis measurement model, whereas the exogenous latent variables are defined by a factor model for the background variables. For example, the longitudinal study may focus on the prediction of the mutual influence of endogenous variables measuring aspects of mental health, life satisfaction, and friendship behavior by following them over time. Exogenous variables measuring pre-existing characteristics that might influence initial status and subsequent development in the endogenous variables (e.g., parental SES, schooling, occupational area, religious background) might also be included. The critical feature of the Jöreskog/Sörbom model is that an autoregressive sequence (see also Frederiksen and Rotondo, 1979; Kenny, 1979) is modeled for the endogenous variables in such a way that each endogenous variable predicts itself at later longitudinal occasions. A first-order autoregressive sequence, which would be the most common type in psychological research, models individual differences at time $t + 1$ as a function of individual differences in the same variable at the immediately preceding longitudinal occasion t, as follows:

$$\eta_{(t+1)} = \beta_{(t+1)} \eta_{(t+1)} + \zeta_{(t+1)} \qquad (9)$$

Figure 3(a) shows a first-order autoregressive sequence for two endogenous latent variables measured at four longitudinal occasions. The autoregressive sequence is a model for the stability of interindividual differences over developmental periods; a natural consequence of the specification is that the attribute being measured will be more highly correlated at adjacent measurement occasions, with de-

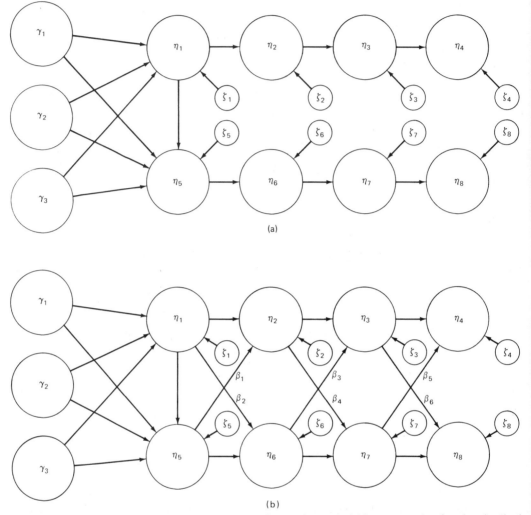

Figure 3. (a) A first-order autoregressive sequence for two latent variables measured at four longitudinal occasions. Each latent variable is predicted only by its status at the immediately preceding occasion. (b) The same sequence, but now with cross-lagged regressions, indicating reciprocal causal influences of each variable on the other (with a lag of 1). The difference between the two models is that (b) predicts that shifts in individual differences *not* accounted for by the autoregressive coefficient will covary with the individual differences in the other latent variable at the preceding occasion.

creasing correlations with increasing longitudinal separation. This pattern is a simplex for the covariance matrix of the η (see Jöreskog and Sörbom, 1977, 1979). The difference in the autoregressive model is that the simplex pattern is hypothesized to be a function of the autoregressive coefficients in β.

The utility of the autoregressive model is that it serves as the basis for examining cross-lagged influences between the endogenous variables. Figure 3(b) shows the same model with the additional specification that each endogenous variable influences the other, again with a lag of 1. This model may be viewed as a less restrictive alternative to the model of autoregression alone, since it postulates that covariances between the different η variables are determined by their direct influences upon each other and that they therefore cannot be accounted for by spurious correlations through background exogenous variables or other influences. Thus, the model of autoregression alone in Figure 3(a) is potentially falsifiable in that one may be able to show that the model with cross-lagged influences provides a more parsimonious solution and a better fit to the sample data. The importance of the cross-lagged regressions modeled in the presence of autoregressive coefficients is that they indicate shifts in interindividual differences as a function of developmental change; these shifts are systematically related to other variables—precisely the type of phenomenon of interest to developmental psychologists.

Another useful aspect of the model is that the exogenous background variables may be specified to predict only the initial status of the endogenous variables, or alternatively, to predict variance on subsequent occasions that is not predicted by the endogenous variables themselves. This alternative specification hypothesizes intraindividual change effects on interindividual differences that are systematically related to background characteristics of the individuals. For example, adjustment to retirement might be a function of pre-retirement role diversity. Again, the restrictive model, which specifies that the exogenous variables relate only to individual differences in the endogenous variables, is falsifiable from the data (see Jöreskog and Sörbom, 1977). Rogosa (1979) provides a helpful review of other aspects of cross-lagged regression models for longitudinal data.

The reader may well have noticed the similarity between the autoregressive model with cross-lagged regression and the cross-lagged correlational analysis (Kenny, 1975, 1979), which examines two observed variables at two longitudinal occasions, using the cross-lagged correlations to examine the direction of causal influence. Indeed, the cross-lagged correlation analysis is in one sense a simplified special case of the more general regression model. Rogosa (1979, 1980) has been highly critical of the cross-lagged correlation model, pointing out that the assumptions of (1) equal variances over occasions and (2) equal autocorrelations for the two variables are rarely met and that violation of these assumptions can render inferences from the cross-lagged correlation analysis completely invalid. Rogosa's critique

has stimulated a defense of the cross-lagged correlation approach by Kenny (Kenny, 1979; Kenny and Campbell, 1981).

In general, we would advocate the structural equations approach to the problem of inferring causal precedence from longitudinal data, as does Rogosa, particularly if multiple indicators are available for the constructs of interest. However, as we have indicated elsewhere (Schaie and Hertzog, 1982), cross-lagged correlation is a viable procedure when the assumptions are met (they should be tested!) and when the investigator wishes to make a provisional, exploratory examination of causal precedence before collecting more data and/or performing the more complex structural regression models. Rogosa's (1980) critique of the uncritical use of cross-lagged correlation without consideration of the viability of the enabling assumptions is well-taken; moreover, the structural equations model is the method of choice when the design includes multiple indicators, more than two longitudinal occasions, and more than two latent variables in the longitudinal sequence. Nevertheless, judicious application of cross-lagged correlation techniques is a viable approach to certain research questions (Kenny and Campbell, 1982).

Structural Equations Models for Intervention Research

One of the applications of LISREL type modeling that may well see more use in the near future involves the analysis of data from intervention research designs using comparisons of nonequivalent groups (Cook and Campbell, 1979). In many gerontological settings, it is impossible to achieve random assignment of subjects to treatment and control conditions because of ethical, logistical, or theoretical reasons. Evaluation of treatment effects must then be made on the basis of comparing treatment group change from pre-test to post-test to change in a comparison group, which in principle must be assumed to be nonequivalent. The problem then is to disentangle treatment effects from a host of rival hypotheses such as selection by maturation interactions that threaten the internal validity of the comparison.

Several statistical approaches are available for analyzing whether change in the treatment group differs from that in the comparison group, given the difficult problem that the groups will probably differ in initial pre-test performance and may differ in expected change in the absence of any intervention. Analysis of covariance is often suggested, but there are several limitations to this approach (see Cook and Campbell, 1979; Reichardt, 1979). ANCOVA assumptions are often not met, and in any case, given a fallible covariate, ANCOVA often "underadjusts" for group differences. One approach advocated by Sörbom (1978) is the use of multiple indicators for pre-test and post-test and the use of LISREL to do the ANCOVA adjustment at the level of the latent variables, testing the hypothesis that the adjusted post-test means of the latent variable differ between groups. The interested reader should also examine the alternative LISREL model for adjusted change described by Kenny and Cohen (1979).

An extension of the LISREL approach to covariance adjustment is to use predictor variables that account for the nonequivalent group differences as independent latent variables which adjust mean change or post-test differences in a post-test only design. Bentler and Woodward (1978) and Magdison and Sörbom (1980) report such analyses of the Head Start data, in which the latent variable, social class, was used to adjust post-test intellectual performance, also defined in a multiple indicator model. In principle, the method could be extended to the adjustment of growth curve models for multiple testing occasions, using group differences in variables predicting initial status to adjust group differences in change over time, where mean change is assessed at the level of the latent variables. Although these latent variable models are certainly useful in providing adjusted measures of change, they should be viewed as powerful statistical tools and not as a substitute for sound quasi-experimental designs. For example, the methods would be even more powerful if the nonequivalent group design were extended to include either (1) multiple pre-tests, so that the growth curve of the treatment group could be estimated prior to introduction of the treatment (as in interrupted time series designs) or (2) multiple treatment groups with staggered points of intervention (see Cook and Campbell, 1979, for a review of the advantages of different design characteristics).

SUMMARY

This chapter began with a nontechnical discussion of some of the major issues of concern to the gerontological researcher who is at the stage of designing measurement instruments and planning analysis schemes for complex data sets requiring comparisons across age and time. Attention was given to the nature of age and time and to the characteristics of observations. Scaling and sampling issues were briefly described. The problem of the equivalence of measures across different subject groups and occasions within individuals was identified as one of the central measurement problems in developmentally oriented research, and the role of some related confounds was analyzed.

We then grappled with the fact that there has been a revolution in multivariate methods of analysis particularly suitable for some of the central problems in gerontology. As a consequence, it was necessary to proceed with a fairly technical discussion of state-of-the-art methods for the construction of developmental measures that will deal adequately with questions of reliability and construct validity from a developmental point of view. In addition, we examined the role of structural equation models for the investigation of cross-sectional and longitudinal data sets and attempted to show why and how such models are applicable to a large number of problems investigated by gerontologists.

Some readers, no doubt, will feel that much of this chapter is too technical for their taste. We felt obliged, however, to present in some detail the consequences of the new developments in multivariate data analysis that have particular relevance for gerontological research. It is indeed fortunate for the field, albeit trying for the patience of our readers, that for perhaps the first time we now have measurement approaches that can deal adequately with many of the central issues in gerontology. We would like to end this chapter by urging every serious gerontological researcher to pay close attention to these new approaches, for they promise to bring much of the work in our discipline to a new level of sophistication and understanding.

REFERENCES

Allen, M. J., and Yen, W. M. 1979. *Introduction to Measurement Theory.* Monterey, CA: Brooks-Cole.

Alwin, D. F., and Jackson, D. J. 1979. Measurement models for response errors in surveys: Issues and applications. In *Sociological Methodology 1980,* ed. K. F. Schuessler, pp. 68–119. San Francisco: Jossey-Bass.

Alwin, D. F., and Jackson, D. J. 1981. Applications of simultaneous factor analysis to issues of factorial invariance. In *Factor Analysis and Measurement,* eds. D. J. Jackson and E. F. Borgatta, pp. 249–278. London: Sage.

Baker, K. E., and Dudek, F. J. 1957. Scaling line-lengths with a modification of the constant sum method. *American Journal of Psychology* 70: 81–86.

Baltes, P. B.; Cornelius, S.; and Nesselroade, J. R. 1979. Cohort effects in developmental psychology. In *Longitudinal Research in the Study of Behavior and Development,* eds. J. R. Nesselroade and P. B. Baltes. New York: Academic Press.

Baltes, P. B., and Nesselroade, J. R. 1970. Multivariate longitudinal and cross-sectional sequences for analyzing ontogenetic and generational change: A methodological note. *Developmental Psychology* 1: 162–168.

Baltes, P. B., and Nesselroade, J. R. 1973. The developmental analysis of individual differences on multiple measures. In *Life-Span Developmental Psychology: Methodological Issues,* eds. J. R. Nesselroade and H. W. Reese. New York: Academic Press.

Baltes, P. B., and Nesselroade, J. R. 1979. History and rationale of longitudinal research. In *Longitudinal Research in the Study of Behavior and Development,* eds. J. R. Nesselroade and P. B. Baltes. New York: Academic Press.

Baltes, P. B.; Nesselroade, J. R.; Schaie, K. W.; and Labouvie, E. W. 1972. On the dilemma of regression effects in examining ability-level-related differentials in ontogenetic patterns of intelligence. *Developmental Psychology* 6: 78–84.

Baltes, P. B.; Reese, H. W.; and Nesselroade, J. R. 1977. *Life-Span Developmental Psychology: Introduction to Research methods.* Monterey, CA: Brooks/Cole.

Baltes, P. B., and Willis, S. L. 1977. Towards psychological theories of aging and development. In *Handbook of the Psychology of Aging,* eds. J. E. Birren and K. W. Schaie. New York: Van Nostrand Reinhold.

Bentler, P. M. 1973. Assessment of developmental factor change at the individual and group level. In *Life-Span Developmental Psychology: Methodological Issues,* eds.

J. R. Nesselroade and H. W. Reese. New York: Academic Press.

Bentler, P. M. 1980. Causal modeling. *Annual Review of Psychology* 31: 332–456.

Bentler, P. M., and Woodward, J. A. 1978. A head start reevaluation: Positive effects are not yet demonstrable. *Evaluation Quarterly* 2: 493–510.

Birkhill, W. R., and Schaie, K. W. 1975. The effect of differential reinforcement of cautiousness in the intellectual performance of the elderly. *Journal of Gerontology* 30: 578–583.

Bloxom, B. 1972. Alternative approaches to factorial invariance. *Psychometrika* 37: 425–440.

Bock, R. D. 1975. *Multivariate Statistical Methods in Behavioral Research.* New York: McGraw-Hill.

Bock, R. D. 1979. Univariate and multivariate analysis of variance of time-structured data. In *Longitudinal Research in the Study of Behavior and Development,* eds. J. R. Nesselroade and P. B. Baltes. New York: Academic Press.

Bock, R. D., and Bargmann, R. E. 1966. Analyses of covariance structures. *Psychometrika* 31: 507–534.

Bohrnstedt, G. W. 1969. Observations on the measurement of change. In *Sociological Methodology: 1969,* ed. E. F. Borgatta. San Francisco: Jossey-Bass.

Box, G. E. P. 1949. A general distribution theory for a class of likelihood criteria. *Biometrika* 36: 317–346.

Brim, O. G., Jr., and Kagan, J., eds. 1980. *Constancy and Change in Human Development.* Cambridge, Mass: Harvard University Press.

Cohen, D.; Schaie, K. W.; and Gribbin, K. 1977. The organization of spatial ability in older men and women. *Journal of Gerontology* 32: 578–585.

Cohen, J. 1957. The factorial structure of the WAIS between early adulthood and old age. *Journal of Consulting Psychology* 21: 283–290.

Cohen, J. 1977. *Statistical Power Analysis for the Behavioral Sciences.* Rev. ed. New York: Academic Press.

Comrey, A. L. 1950. A proposed method for absolute ratio scaling. *Psychometrika* 15: 317–325.

Cook, T. C., and Campbell, D. T. 1979. *Quasi-experimentation: Design Analysis Issues for Field Settings.* Chicago: Rand McNally.

Corballis, M. C. 1973. A factor model for analyzing change. *British Journal of Mathematical and Statistical Psychology* 26: 90–97.

Cramer, E. M., and Appelbaum, M. I. 1980. Nonorthogonal analysis of variance—once again. *Psychological Bulletin* 87: 51–57.

Cronbach, L. J. 1970. *The Essentials of Psychological Testing.* 3rd ed. New York: Harper and Row.

Cronbach, L. J., and Furby, L. 1970. How should we measure "change"—or should we? *Psychological Bulletin* 74: 8–80.

Cunningham, W. R. 1978. Principles for identifying structural differences: Some methodological issues related to comparative factor analysis. *Journal of Gerontology* 33: 82–86.

Cunningham, W. R. 1980. Age comparative factor analysis of ability variables in adulthood and old age. *Intelligence* 4: 133–149.

Cunningham, W. R. 1981. Ability factor structure differences in adulthood and old age. *Multivariate Behavior Research* 16: 3–22.

Cunningham, W. R. 1982. Factorial invariance: A methodological issue in the study of psychological development. *Experimental Aging Research* 8: 61–66.

Cunningham, W. R., and Birren, J. E. 1980. Age changes in the factor structure of intellectual abilities in adulthood and old age. *Educational and Psychological Measurement* 40: 271–290.

Duncan, D. D. 1975. *Introduction to Structural Equation Models.* New York: Academic Press.

Eisdorfer, C.; Nowlin, J.; and Wilkie, F. 1970. Improvement of learning by modification of autonomous nervous sytem activity. *Science* 70: 1327–1328.

Ferguson, G. A. 1941. The factorial interpretation of test difficulty. *Psychometrika* 6: 323–329.

Frederiksen, C. H. and Rotondo, J. R. 1979. Time-series models and the study of longitudinal change. In *Longitudinal Research in the Study of Behavior and Development,* eds. J. R. Nesselroade and P. B. Baltes. New York: Academic Press.

Furby, L. 1973. Interpreting regression toward the mean in developmental research. *Developmental Psychology* 8: 172–179.

Gallagher, D.; McGarvey, W.; Zelinski, E. M.; and Thompson, L. W. 1978. *Age and Factor Structure of the Zung Depression Scale.* Paper presented at the 31st annual meeting of the Gerontological Society, Dallas, Texas, Nov., 1978.

Gardner, E. F., and Monge, R. H. 1977. Adult age differences in cognitive abilities and educational background. *Experimental Aging Research* 3: 337–383.

Geisser, S. A. 1965. Bayes approach for combining correlated estimates. *Journal of the American Statistical Association* 60: 601–607.

Geisser, S. A., and Kappenman, R. F. 1971. A posterior region for parallel profile differentials. *Psychometrika* 36: 71–78.

George, L. K.; Siegler, I. C.; and Okun, M. A. 1981. Separating age, cohort, and time of measurement: Analysis of variance and multiple regression. *Experimental Aging Research* 7: 297–314.

Glenn, N. D. 1976. Cohort analysts' futile quest: Statistical attempts to separate age, period and cohort effects. *American Sociological Review* 41: 900–904.

Glenn, N. D. 1981. Age, birth cohort, and drinking: An illustration of the hazards of inferring effects from cohort data. *Journal of Gerontology* 36: 362–369.

Goldstein, H. 1979. *Longitudinal Studies.* New York: Academic Press.

Gribbin, K., and Schaie, K. W. 1976. Monetary incentive, age, and cognition. *Experimental Aging Research* 2: 461–468.

Gribbin, K., and Schaie, K. W. 1977. The aging of tests: A methodological problem of longitudinal studies. Paper presented at the annual meeting of the Gerontological Society, San Francisco.

Gribbin, K., and Schaie, K. W. 1979. Selective attrition in longitudinal studies: A cohort-sequential approach. In *Recent Advances in Gerontology,* eds. H. Orino, K. Shimada, M. Iriki, and D. Maeda. Amsterdam: Excerpta Medica.

Gribbin, K.; Schaie, K. W.; and Stone, V. 1976. Ability differences between established and redefined population in sequential studies. Paper presented at the annual meeting of the American Psychological Association, Washington.

Guire, K. E., and Kowalski, C. J. 1979. Mathematical description and representation of developmental change functions on the intra- and interindividual levels. In *Longitudinal Research in the Study of Behavior and Development,* eds. J. R. Nesselroade and P. B. Baltes. New York: Academic Press.

Harman, H. H. 1976. *Modern Factor Analysis.* 3rd ed. Chicago: University of Chicago Press.

Harris, C. W., ed. 1963. *Problems in Measuring Change.* Madison: University of Wisconsin Press.

Heise, D. R. 1975. *Causal Analysis.* New York: Wiley.

Heron, A., and Chown, S. 1967. *Age and Function.* London: Churchill.

Hertzog, C. 1984. Applications of confirmatory factor analysis to the study of intelligence. In *Current Topics in Human Intelligence,* ed. D. K. Detterman. Norwood, N.J.: Ablex.

Hertzog, C., and Carter, L. 1982. Sex differences in the structure of intelligence. A confirmatory factor analysis. *Intelligence* 6: 287–303.

Hertzog, C., and Schaie, K. W. 1982. On the analysis of sequential data in life-span developmental research. Paper presented at the annual meeting of the American Psychological Association, Washington.

Hertzog, C., and Schaie, K. W. 1983. Age changes in intellectual structure: A structural equations analysis. Unpublished manuscript.

Horn, J. L., and Engstrom, R. 1979. Cattell's scree test in relation to Bartlett's chi-square test and other observations on the number of factors problem. *Multivariate Behavioral Research* 14: 283–300.

Horn, J. L., and McArdle, J. J. 1980. Perspectives on mathematical/statistical model building (MASMOB) in research on aging. In *Aging in the 1980s,* ed. L. W. Poon. Washington: American Psychological Association.

Hoyer, W. F.; Hoyer, F. J.; Treat, N. J.; and Baltes, P. B. 1978. Training response speed in young and elderly women. *International Journal of Aging and Human Development* 2.

Hultsch, D. F., and Plemons, J. K. 1979. Life events and life-span development. In *Life-Span Development and Behavior,* eds. P. B. Baltes and O. G. Brim, Jr. Vol. 2. New York: Academic Press.

Jöreskog, K. G. 1970. A general method for the analysis of covariance structures. *Biometrika* 57: 239–251.

Jöreskog, K. G. 1971a. Statistical analysis of sets of cogeneric tests. *Psychometrika* 36: 109–133.

Jöreskog, K. G. 1971b. Simultaneous factor analysis in several populations. *Psychometrika* 36: 409–426.

Jöreskog, K. G. 1974. Analyzing psychological data by structural analysis of covariance matrices. In *Contem-*

porary Developments in Mathematical Psychology, eds. D. H. Krantz, R. C. Atkinson, R. D. Luce, and P. Suppes. San Francisco: W. H. Freeman.

Jöreskog, K. G. 1979. Statistical estimation of structural models in longitudinal developmental investigations. In *Longitudinal Research in the Study of Behavior and Development,* eds. J. R. Nesselroade and P. B. Baltes. New York: Academic Press.

Jöreskog, K. G., and Sörbom, D. 1977. Statistical models and methods for analysis of longitudinal data. In *Latent Variables in Socioeconomic Models,* eds. D. J. Aigner and A. S. Goldberger. Amsterdam: North Holland Publishers.

Jöreskog, K. G., and Sörbom, D. 1979. *Advances in Factor Analysis and Structural Equations Models.* Cambridge, Mass: Abt Associates.

Jöreskog, K. G., and Sörbom, D. 1980. Simultaneous analysis of longitudinal data from several cohorts. Research Report 80–5. University Uppsala, Dept. of Statistics.

Jöreskog, K. G., and Sörbom, D. 1981. *LISREL V User's Guide.* Chicago: National Educational Resources.

Kagan, J. 1980. Perspectives on continuity. In *Constancy and Change in Human Development,* eds. O. G. Brim, Jr., and J. Kagan. Cambridge, Mass: Harvard University Press.

Kenny, D. A. 1975. Cross-lagged panel correlation: A test for superiousness. *Psychological Bulletin* 82: 887–903.

Kenny, D. A. 1979. *Correlation and Causality.* New York: Wiley.

Kenny, D. A., and Campbell, D. T. 1982. Methodological considerations in the analysis of temporal data. Unpublished manuscript.

Kenny, D. A., and Cohen, S. H. 1979. A re-examination of selection and control processes in the nonequivalent control group design. In *Sociological Methodology 1980,* ed. K. F. Schenssler. San Francisco: Jossey-Bass.

Labouvie, E. W. 1980. Measurement of individual differences in intraindividual changes. *Psychological Bulletin* 88: 54–59.

Labouvie, E. W. 1981. The study of multivariate change structures: A conceptual perspective. *Multivariate Behavior Research* 16: 23–35.

Liang, J., and Bollen, K. A. 1983. The structure of the Philadelphia Geriatric Center Morale Scale: A reinterpretation. *Journal of Gerontology,* 38: 181–189.

Lord, F. M., and Novick, M. N. 1968. *Statistical Theories of Mental Tests.* Reading, Mass: Addison-Wesley.

Magdison, J., and Sörbom, D. 1980. Adjusting for confounding factors in quasi-experiments: Another reanalysis of the Westinghouse Head Start evaluation. Paper presented at the 1980 American Statistical Association Meeting, Houston, Texas, August, 1980.

Matarazzo, J. D. 1982. *Wechsler's Measurement and Appraisal of Adult Intelligence.* 5th ed. Baltimore: Williams and Wilkins.

McDonald, R. P. 1981. The dimensionality of tests and items. *British Journal of Mathematical and Statistical Psychology* 34: 100–117.

Meredith, W. 1964. Notes on factorial invariance. *Psychometrika* 29: 177–185.

Metfessel, M. 1947. A proposal for quantitative reporting of comparative judgments. *Journal of Psychology* 24: 229–235.

Mulaik, S. A. 1972. *Foundations of Factor Analysis.* New York: McGraw-Hill.

Muthen, B. 1978. Contributions to factor analysis of dichotomous variables. *Psychometrika* 43: 551–560.

Nesselroade, J. R. 1977. Issues in studying developmental change in adults from a multivariate perspective. In *Handbook of the Psychology of Aging,* eds. J. E. Birren and K. W. Schaie. New York: Van Nostrand Reinhold.

Nesselroade, J. R., and Baltes, P. B., eds. 1979. *Longitudinal Research in the Study of Behavior and Development.* New York: Academic Press.

Nesselroade, J. R.; Jacobs, A.; and Pruchno, R. 1981. Reliability versus stability in the measurement of psychological states: An illustration with anxiety measures. Unpublished manuscript.

Nesselroade, J. R.; Stigler, S. M.; and Baltes, P. B. 1980. Regression towards the mean and the study of change. *Psychological Bulletin* 88: 622–637.

Nunnally, J. C. 1973. Research strategies and measurement methods for investigating human development. In *Life-Span Developmental Psychology: Methodological Issues,* eds. J. R. Nesselroade and H. W. Reese. New York: Academic Press.

Nunnally, J. C. 1978. *Psychometric Theory.* 2nd ed. New York: McGraw-Hill.

Nunnally, J. C. 1982. The study of human change: Measurement, research strategies, and methods of analysis. In *Handbook of Developmental Psychology,* ed. B. B. Wolman. Englewood Cliffs, N.J.: Prentice-Hall.

Nuttall, R. L. 1972. The strategy of functional age research. *Aging and Human Development* 3: 45–148.

Olsson, U., and Bergman, L. R. 1977. A longitudinal factor model for studying change in ability structure. *Multivariate Behavioral Research* 12: 221–242.

Reedy, M. N.; Birren, J. E.; and Schaie, K. W. 1981. Age and sex differences in satisfying love relationships across the adult life span. *Human Development* 24: 52–66.

Reichardt, C. S. 1979. The statistical analysis of data from nonequivalent groups designs. In *Quasi-Experimentation: Design and Analysis Issues for Field Settings,* eds. T. D. Cook and D. T. Campbell. Chicago: Rand McNally.

Reichenbach, M., and Mathers, R. M. 1959. The place of time and age in the natural sciences and scientific philosophy. In *Handbook of Aging and the Individual,* ed. J. E. Birren. Chicago: University of Chicago Press.

Reinert, G. 1970. Comparative factor analytic studies of intelligence throughout the human life-span. In *Life-Span Developmental Psychology: Research and Theory,* eds. L. R. Goulet and P. B. Baltes. New York: Academic Press.

Rock, D. A.; Werts, C. E.; and Flaugher, R. L. 1978. The use of analysis of covariance structures for comparing the psychometric properties of multiple variables across populations. *Multivariate Behavioral Research* 13: 403–418.

Rogosa, D. 1979. Causal models in longitudinal research: Rationale, formulation, and interpretation. In *Longitudinal Research in the Study of Behavior and Development,* eds. J. R. Nesselroade and P. B. Baltes. New York: Academic Press.

Rogosa, D. 1980. A critique of cross-lagged correlation. *Psychological Bulletin* 88: 245–258.

Rogosa, D.; Brandt, D.; and Zimowski, M. 1982. A growth curve approach to the measurement of change. *Psychological Bulletin* 92: 726–748.

Schaie, K. W. 1961a. A Q-sort study of color-mood association. *Journal of Projective Techniques* 25: 341–346.

Schaie, K. W. 1961b. Scaling the association between colors and mood-tones. *American Journal of Psychology* 74: 266–273.

Schaie, K. W. 1973a. Methodological problems in descriptive developmental research on adulthood and aging. In *Life-Span Developmental Psychology: Methodological Issues,* eds. J. R. Nesselroade and H. W. Reese. New York: Academic Press.

Schaie, K. W. 1973b. Reflections on papers by Looft, Peterson and Sparks: Intervention towards an ageless society? *Gerontologist* 13: 31–35.

Schaie, K. W. 1977. Quasi-experimental designs in the psychology of aging. In *Handbook of the Psychology of Aging,* eds. J. E. Birren and K. W. Schaie. New York: Van Nostrand Reinhold.

Schaie, K. W. 1978. External validity in the assessment of intellectual development in adulthood. *Journal of Gerontology* 33: 695–701.

Schaie, K. W. 1980. Intelligence and problem solving. In *Handbook of Mental Health and Aging,* eds. J. E. Birren and R. B. Sloane. Englewood Cliffs, N.J.: Prentice-Hall.

Schaie, K. W. 1983a. Historical time and cohort effects. In *Life-Span Developmental Psychology: Historical and Cohort Effects,* eds. K. A. McCloskey and H. W. Reese. New York: Academic Press.

Schaie, K. W. 1983b. The Seattle Longitudinal Study: A twenty-one year exploration of psychometric intelligence in adulthood. In *Longitudinal Studies of Adult Psychological Development,* ed. K. W. Schaie. New York: Guilford Press.

Schaie, K. W.; Chatham, L. R.; and Weiss, J. M. A. 1961. The multi-professional intake assessment of older psychiatric patients. *Journal of Psychiatric Research* 1: 92–100.

Schaie, K. W., and Goulet, L. R. 1977. Trait theory and verbal learning processes. In *Handbook of Modern Personality Theory,* eds. R. B. Goulet and R. M. Dreger. New York: Hemisphere/Halsted.

Schaie, K. W., and Hertzog, C. K. 1982. Longitudinal methods. In *Handbook of Developmental Psychology,* ed. B. B. Wolman. Englewood Cliffs, N.J.: Prentice-Hall.

Schaie, K. W., and Hertzog, C. K. 1983. Fourteen-year cohort-sequential studies of adult intellectual development. *Developmental Psychology,* 19: 531–543.

Schaie, K. W.; Labouvie, G. V.; and Barrett, T. J. 1973. Selective attrition effects in a fourteen-year study of adult intelligence. *Journal of Gerontology* 28: 328–334.

Schaie, K. W., and Parr, J. 1981. Concepts and criteria for functional age. In *Aging: A Challenge for Science and Social Policy,* ed. J. E. Birren. Vol. 3. Oxford: Oxford University Press.

Schaie, K. W., and Strother, C. R. 1968. Cognitive and personality variables in college graduates of advanced age. In *Human Behavior and Aging: Recent Advances in Research and Theory,* ed. G. A. Talland. New York: Academic Press.

Scheidt, R. J., and Schaie, K. W. 1978. Taxonomy of situations for the aged: Generating situational criteria. *Journal of Gerontology* 33: 848–857.

Shepard, R. E.; Romney, K.; and Nerlove, S. 1972. *Multidimensional Scaling-Theory and Applications in the Behavioral Sciences.* New York: Seminar Press.

Sörbom, D. 1975. Detection of correlated errors in longitudinal data. *British Journal of Mathematical and Statistical Psychology* 28: 138–151.

Sörbom, D. 1978. An alternative to the methodology for the analysis of covariance. *Psychometrika* 43: 381–396.

Stephenson, W. 1953. *The Study of Behavior: Q-Technique and Its Methodology.* Chicago: University of Chicago Press.

Stevens, S. S. 1951. Mathematics, measurement, and psychophysics. In *Handbook of Experimental Psychology,* ed. S. S. Stevens. New York: Wiley.

Strenio, J. F.; Weisberg, H. I.; and Bryk, A. S. 1983. Empirical Bayes estimation of individual growth curve parameters and their relationship to covariates. *Biometrics,* 39: 71–86.

Werts, C. E.; Linn, R. L.; and Jöreskog, K. G. 1974. Intraclass reliability estimates testing structural assumptions. *Educational and Psychological Measurement* 34: 25–35.

Wohlwill, J. F. 1973. *The Study of Behavioral Development.* New York: Academic Press.

Wolman, B. B., ed. 1982. *Handbook of Developmental Psychology.* Englewood Cliffs, N.J.: Prentice-Hall.

2 BIOLOGICAL INFLUENCES ON BEHAVIOR

4
THE NEURAL BASIS OF AGING

William Bondareff
University of Southern California

BEHAVIORAL CORRELATES OF NEURONAL AGING

The neurons and neuroglia of the brain are the focus of this review of behavioral events that characterize the process of aging. The numbers of these cells in a vertebrate brain are immense, and their interconnections, which in large part are not known, are legion. It has been estimated that the human brain after birth contains about 10^{11} neurons, each of which makes roughly 10^4 connections with other neurons (Weiss, 1973). These cells are extraordinarily active metabolically, each containing a complement of some 10^7 to 10^8 protein molecules that are renewed perhaps 10^4 times during the cell's life (Weiss, 1973). They exist in a rigidly controlled microenvironment, the properties of which they largely determine. Since the neurons synthesize and degrade large amounts of protein in a lifetime and do not reproduce themselves, there is ample opportunity for the production of abnormal protein, either by synthetic error or posttranslational modification. There are also many opportunities for neuronal metabolism to fail during a lifetime, and degenerative neuronal phenomena are common during development and aging.

Degenerative phenomena, which typically involve certain neurons at various times during the course of senescence, reflect the aging of neurons *per se*. These phenomena include: the intracytoplasmic accumulation of lipofuscin pigment; decrements in the amounts of cytoplasmic RNA and the activities of certain cytoplasmic enzymes; changes in the morphology, distribution, or reactivity of cytoplasmic organelles; and, in some cases, death and lysis of the neuron. These processes can be intrinsic to the neurons themselves or can result from extra-neuronal, age-associated changes of blood vessels, cerebrospinal fluid ventricles, intracellular channels, or neuroglia. By compromising the normal supply of ions, metabolites, and nutrients to and from neurons, such changes could well result in a neuronal pathology similar to that following a primary change in neuronal structure or chemistry. Whatever their cause, whether intra- or extraneuronal, age-related changes in neuronal metabolism affect neuronal function, and, if sufficiently extensive, they affect behavior.

It is well established that behavior changes with age—to some extent in predictable ways. Predictable changes in human behavior are not limited to the period of early development when mature structures are formed from immature ones. On the contrary, reliably defined stages are recognized during the entire life span and have been described in clinically meaningful terms (Kaplan and Sadock, 1980). These progress through a stage characterized by generative processes to a terminal integrative period. To cope successfully with each developmental stage during immature, mature, and senescent years is harmoniously to mesh an internal environment resulting from brain structure and chemistry with an external environment representing the totality of what

95

might collectively be labeled "societal living."

It would be naive to propose that human development represents a unidirectional process genetically programmed and directly reflective of age-related changes in brain structure and chemistry. Yet, when structure and chemistry are compared in young, mature, and senescent individuals, changes appear to be age-related. To some small extent, especially in rodents, these changes have been correlated with age-related changes in behavior. In human beings, the study of neuronal correlates of behavior are limited by the availability of brain specimens suitable for study; as these specimens largely come from postmortem material, their scientific suitability is usually not optimal. This review, therefore, relies heavily on data derived from the study of rodent brains, which will be correlated with age-related changes in rodent behavior and discussed as they relate to comparable changes in the human brain. Although anthropomorphic speculation is best avoided, it seems reasonable to look for relationships between age changes in animals and changes in the human condition.

EFFECTS OF AGE ON EXTRANEURONAL STRUCTURES

The various regions of the brain, although associated with highly specific functions, may have remarkably similar structures. They are, essentially, parenchymal structures derived from the primitive neurectoderm and supportive structures, which in turn derive from the mesoderm and include connective and vascular tissues. The connective tissue contributes to the meninges that provide structural support and mediate transactions between cerebrospinal fluid and brain parenchyma. Connective tissue also accompanies blood vessels into and out of the brain and mediates transactions between the brain parenchyma and the blood vessels that support its metabolism. Brain parenchyma is compartmentalized into cellular elements (neurons and neuroglia) and extracellular elements, the latter including the so-called extracellular space and the closely associated brain vasculature (see Figure 1).

Age-related changes in meninges are not well studied but appear comparable to age changes in connective tissues generally. It is believed that meninges thicken with age and that the amount of collagen increases. Brain vasculature has not been systematically studied over the life span, and as is true of meninges, it is difficult to differentiate the effects of age from those of chronic and especially subacute disease processes that accumulate with time. Fang (1976) has described a change in the tortuosity of small vessels penetrating the cerebral cortex in man, and changes in the density of capillary beds have been described both in man (Hunziker, Abdel'Al and Schulz, 1979) and rats (Burns, Kruckeberg and Gaetano, 1981; Wilkinson, Hopewell and Reinhold, 1981). Changes in regional blood flow with advanced age have been discussed (Kety, 1956; Lassen, Feinberg, and Lane, 1960; Obrist, 1979), and more recent studies demonstrating a progressive age-related fall in blood flow through gray matter are reported by Davis, et al. (1983). The effects of these changes—which may be related to age-related changes in, for example, vascular morphology or vessel diameter secondary to changing concentrations of vasoactive substances such as catecholamines—are unclear. The subject has potentially important clinical implications and has been too long neglected.

Few cells in the human body are as poorly understood as the neuroglia. They are more numerous than neurons, and at least three anatomically distinct cell types are recognized. These are the *astrocytes,* which are most numerous in gray matter; the *oligodendrocytes,* which are most numerous in white matter; and the *microcytes,* which are variously distributed in gray and white matter. The astrocytes appear to provide structural support; influence the exchange between neurons, blood, and cerebrospinal fluid; and modulate electrochemical reactions between neurons. The oligodendrocytes are known to form myelin, and the microcytes are phagocytic.

Because it is generally accepted that dead neurons are replaced in the brain by living astrocytes, it is widely held that the number of astrocytes increases with age as the number of neuronal deaths increases. Although popular, this dogma is not substantiated, and the

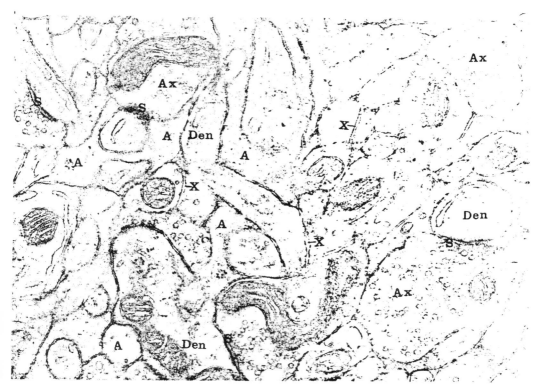

Figure 1.   Electron micrograph of molecular layer of cerebellar cortex of a 12-month-old, male Fischer-344 rat. Illustrated are representative profiles of extracellular space (X), synapses (S), dendrites (Den), axons (Ax), and astrocytes (A). Magnification: 30,000 X.

relationship between numbers of neurons and neuroglia in an aging brain remains uncertain. In one study of neuroglia in rat cerebral cortex, no age-related change in the numbers of astrocytes or oligodendrocytes was found, although there did appear to be an increase in the number of microcytes in senescence (Vaughan and Peters, 1974). In another, a light microscopic study of the rat dentate gyrus (Landfield et al. 1977), there appeared to be an age-related increase in astrocytes. In an electron microscopic analysis of the rat dentate gyrus, in which virtually all neuronal and neuroglial structures were visualized and identified in the region under study, no age-related change in the number of astrocytes was found. There was, however, a 45 percent increase in the volume fraction of astrocytic processes in senescent rats (Geinisman, Bondareff, and Dodge, 1978b), i.e., an increase in the mass of each astrocyte with no increase in the number of cells.

In the latter study, in which a minute seg-ment of rat dentate gyrus was analyzed in its entirety, there was a notable change in cellular composition but no change in overall dimensions of the brain tissue (see Table 3). There were losses of neuronal elements (dendrites and synapses), which are discussed more fully below, and a gain in astroglia (see Bondareff, 1980b). Such a gain can be reasonably presumed to result in more than mere maintenance of brain size and shape. More important, since astrocytes appear to play a major role in the regulation of the neuronal microenvironment, an increase in the astroglial volume fraction might significantly affect neuronal functioning. Astroglia have been shown to influence the spatial distribution of potassium ions in the brain (Trachtenberg and Pollen, 1970; Walz, 1982) and to respond to increased extracellular $K+$ by increasing ATPase activity (Henn, Haljamae, and Hamberger, 1972) and also by increasing intra-astrocytic Cl^- and water content (Bourke, Daze and Kimelberg, 1978; Kimelberg, Biddlecome, and Bourke, 1979). Astroglia appear to maintain the constancy of the neuronal microenvironment by controlling the composition of extracellular spaces with which neurons are in direct contact and through which neuronal exchanges with the blood and cerebrospinal fluid appear to take place. Astroglia transport electrically active amino acids, some of which (for example, GABA) appear to be important neurotransmitter substances in the mammalian brain (Henn and Hamberger, 1971). They also appear to remove other neurotransmitter substances from the extracellular space and affect the interaction between neurons and psychoactive drugs (Henn and Henn, 1980). In the rat hippocampus, astrocytic hypertrophy has been induced experimentally by the administration of corticosterone, because of which it has been suggested that changes in the astrocytic volume fraction might reflect age-related levels in circulating corticosterone (Lynch and Gerling, 1981).

In the mammalian central nervous system, the microenvironment of nerve cells is composed of extracellular channels that separate the plasma membranes of all cellular elements (cell bodies and their processes) from one another (Schmitt and Samson, 1969). These extracellular channels are of submicroscopic dimensions and can be visualized directly only with the aid of an electron microscope (see Figure 1). They appear to contain ill-defined material, believed to be acidic glycosaminoglycan or glycoprotein (see Bondareff, 1976a), and may be capable of transporting small molecules and ions by diffusion (Kuffler, Nicholls, and Orkand, 1966; Nicholls and Kuffler, 1964).

Age-related changes in the acidic glycosaminoglycan composition of the brain have been sought, and, although data are few, the relative amounts of the acidic glycosaminoglycans appear to vary with age. Since the concentration of galactosamine (presumably representing chondroitin sulfates) does not change with age, the decrease in hexosamine described in the senescent rat brain may reflect the loss of a keratan sulfate-like glycan (Vitello, et al, 1978), which might well result in decreased water-binding capacity of the proteoglycans (Bettelheim and Plessy, 1975) in aged brains. An age-related increase was

found in the sulfate/hexosamine ratio of the acidic glycosaminoglycans in the brains of old rats (Bondareff, 1976a). It is not known whether this reflects age-related changes in sulfotransferase activity or in the availability of sulfate acceptors, both of which appear to decrease with age (George, Singh, and Bachlawat, 1970; Balasubramarian and Bachlawat, 1964), or whether such changes engender age-related changes in the neuronal microenvironment.

The properties of the brain extracellular space are difficult to define, but extracellular volume, which has been estimated in rat brains at various ages, was found to diminish progressively during the first three weeks of life. After the third or fourth week, an extracellular space of about 21.7 percent was found (Bondareff and Pysh, 1968). It remained essentially unchanged until the age of 26 months (see Table 1), when the mean volume of cerebral cortex occupied by extracellular space was found to be 9.6 percent, about one-half that which is typical of young adults (Bondareff and Narotzky, 1972). These changes in the volume distribution of the extracellular compartment of the rat cerebral cortex offer a possible mechanism, with general applicability, to account for age changes in neuronal metabolism. They are, however, controversial. They support the notion (Konigsmark and Murphy, 1972) that the age-associated decrement in total brain volume is not necessarily a consequence of neuronal loss, as was once believed. They have also been corroborated by Rapo-

TABLE 1.   Changes in Volume of Brain Extracellular Space of the Rat as a Function of Age.

Age	Volume, percent*
10 days	40.5
14 days	31.8
21 days	26.3
3 mo	21.7
12 mo	20.8
26 mo	9.6

* Percent brain tissue volume estimated in electron micrographs of frozen-substituted cerebral cortex (from Bondareff and Pysh, 1968; Bondareff and Narotzky, 1972).

port, et al. (1979), who defined the extracellular compartment of brain in terms of the distribution of radioactive scrose (^{14}C sucrose) and found a 45-percent decrement in sucrose distribution space in the brains of senescent Fischer-344 rats. They are not, however, supported by the findings of Rees et al. (1982), who also used radioactive sucrose (^{3}H sucrose) to delineate the extracellular space, which was not only chemically, but also morphologically, estimated. They found an increase in extracellular space in all areas of brain with the exception of the most superficial layer of the cerebral cortex, in which the volume of extracellular space decreased in senescence.

The nature of age-related changes in the extracellular spaces of brain remains uncertain, and the role of the extracellular space in normal brain function remains largely unexplored and unknown. Bondareff and Lin-Liu (1977) have shown that ruthenium red, a charged molecule of sufficient density to be visualized in electron microcopes, penetrates less deeply into old brains than young ones. If the extracellular space of the brain contains polyanions such as glycosaminoglycans, as appears to be the case, decreased penetration of ruthenium red may indicate a greater polyanionic charge density in old than in young animals, as these polyanions are long-chain, charged molecules capable of considerable conformational change (Rees, 1972; Mathews, 1964). Relatively minor conformational changes associated with changes in charge, changes in hydration, or perhaps even changes in mechanical sieving capability would affect electro-osmotic phenomena (Ranck, 1964) and electrical conductance of perineuronal fluid (Wang et al., 1966) as well as alter the capacity of the extracellular compartment to transport metabolites and ions.

AGE CHANGES IN THE METABOLIC ACTIVITIES OF NEURONS

Whether because of age-related processes that restrict the availability of nutrients or because of changes in the intracellular membrane systems that subserve neuronal metabolism, metabolic activities appear to fail as neurons age. The failure, however, is not readily documented and still less readily related to age

changes in behavior. The accumulation of lipofuscin pigment, for example, which is often touted as a hallmark of failing neuronal metabolism (Bondareff, 1959), has never been actually proved to be deleterious. Other suggestive evidence of age-related failing neuronal metabolism includes the decline in brain concentrations of certain neurontransmitter substances that has been demonstrated in both human beings and animals. Some of these changes, which appear associated closely with age and behavior are considered below, *vis-a-vis* the neurobiological data by means of which they are most readily described.

Commonly used histological staining reactions reveal a globular or granular material in the cytoplasm of many vertebrate neurons at some stage of the life span. Depending upon the specific conditions of histological preparation, this material will appear variously colored, structured, and distributed in the neuronal cytoplasm. This cytoplasmic material, known generally as *lipofuscin* because of its lipid content and brownish coloration in unstained tissue sections, emits a characteristic yellow autofluorescence and is readily identified by fluorescence microscopy.

Neuronal lipofuscin has been the subject of numerous histochemical studies. Isolated from the human brain, it has been shown to contain a number of hydrolytic enzymes—including acid phosphatase, cathepsin, and glucosidase—and a high concentration of zinc (Siakotos and Koppang, 1973). In neurons, these hydrolytic enzymes are packaged within primary lyosomes, which are abundant in the cytoplasm of nerve cells at all ages and readily found before lipofuscin can be identified. It has been suggested that primary lysosomes are the primordia of lipofuscin (Sekhon and Maxwell, 1974), which appears to be a residuum of some sort, probably of partially destroyed cellular membrane components. It has been speculated that modification of these sequestered materials might be accomplished by peroxidation, polymerization and cross linking of lipoproteins, or by pseudoperoxidation of catechol derivatives catalyzed by metals (Barden, 1970).

Lipofuscin granules have a characteristic particulate ultrastructure (Sekhon and Maxwell, 1974) and a characteristic emission spectrum when excited with ultraviolet light (Eldred et al., 1982). Although the relationship between lysosomes and lipofuscin is well established, the involvement of the Golgi complex in the genesis of lipofuscin is still questioned. Lipofuscin and Golgi membranes are often closely associated in neurons (Bondareff, 1957), and both possess thiamine pyrophosphatase activity (Barden, 1970). In the inferior olivary nucleus of aged Rhesus monkeys, little thiamine pyrophosphatase was demonstrated, and the Golgi apparatus appeared to decrease as the amount of lipofuscin progressively increased. Golgi complex, primary lysosomes, and rough endoplasmic reticulum comprise the principle intracytoplasmic machinery by means of which neurons synthesize and degrade proteins and other membrane components. How they interact in the formation of lipofuscin has yet to be adequately elaborated.

If the accumulation of lipofuscin signals a general decline in neuronal metabolism, such a decline has not as yet been demonstrated. Lipofuscin has been considered an inert slag product of no particular importance (Bondareff, 1959). It has been noted that in the neurons of the inferior olivary nucleus, in which lipofuscin accumulates at an early age and is found in great abundance in old animals, there is no decline in the number of cells and no indication that lipofuscin accumulation is related to a loss of nerve cells (Brody, 1973). There have been few attempts to relate lipofuscin content to neuronal function; considering the attention given to the latter's dietary and pharmacological control, this lack of interest is surprising. Mann and Yates (1974) found the amount of Nissl material (rough endoplasmic reticulum) to decline as lipofuscin increased. Their study of the inferior olivary nucleus in normal and demented human beings (Mann, Yates and Stamp, 1978) suggests that the accumulation of lipofuscin impairs protein metabolism in neurons. The opposite was suggested by Davies and Fotheringham (1981), who were unable to correlate the amount of neurosecretory material with lipofuscin in neurons of supra optic nucleus in old mice. They found that the amount of lipofuscin did not affect the response of these neurons to osmotic stimuli, an observation in har-

mony with that of Rogers, Zornetzer, and Bloom (1981), who found no correlation between the amount of lipofuscin and the electrical activity of rat cerebellar Purkinje cells. Age-related impairment of Purkinje cell firing rates did not seem to correlate with the amount of lipofuscin in neurons of the inferior olivary nucleus, which are excitatory to Purkinje cells, or in the Purkinje cells themselves. Brizzee and Ordy (1979), however, were able to correlate an increase in lipofuscin in neurons of senescent rat cerebral cortex and hippocampus with an apparent loss of neurons and a reduction in short-term passive-avoidance retention. Although the accumulation of lipofuscin is probably the best known marker of neuronal aging, its effect on neuronal function is little more understood than when discussed by Murray and Stout (1947), whose early observations are still of interest. They maintained human sympathetic neurons in culture and noted that cells containing large amounts of lipofuscin-like pigment granules migrated relatively little and their nuclei stained less intensely than normal.

The accumulation of lipofuscin may relate to some functional decline, with actual cell death only occurring regionally and as a result of special circumstances, perhaps vascular. However, the accumulation of lipofuscin cannot be associated with an age-related decline in neuronal function *a priori,* and the search for other indicators of neuronal functional failure with age continues. This search has tended to focus on neuronal organelles, especially those that support intracellular transport phenomena, and on the fibrillar proteins of which they are formed. A change in these organelles, in particular neurotubules and neurofilaments, may be fundamental to neuronal functional decline in the senium.

Neurotubules, the microtubles of neurons (Wuerker and Kirkpatrick, 1972), are tubular structures about 230 nm in outside diameter; they occur singly or in groups of varying dimensions in the nerve cell body and its processes. After isolation and negative staining, they appear to be made up of 13 longitudinal protofilaments, helically arranged. When they occur in groups, they are invariably separated by a rather uniform distance, across which they are interconnected by an ill-defined dense substance. They are rich in tubulin, a dimeric protein that has been isolated and characterized (Olmsted and Borisy, 1973). Under appropriate conditions, their outside walls react with ruthenium red (Tani and Ametani, 1970), suggesting the presence of polyanionic substances presumed to be glycoproteins or glycosaminoglycans. Neurotubules, together with neurofilaments, contribute to the cytoskeleton of nerve cells. They are major determinants of neuronal shape and function in neuronal motility and intracellular transport mechanisms.

Two types of filaments are found in nerve cells (Wuerker and Kirkpatrick, 1972; Wessels, et al., 1971). Microfilaments, about 5 nm in diameter, are found immediately subjacent to the plasma membranes of many neurons and neuroglia. These appear to have contractile properties and are believed to function primarily in cellular motility (Wessels, et al., 1971). Intermediate filaments, about 10 nm in diameter, usually appear in groups arranged in parallel and seem to be involved in intracellular transport of ions and small molecules as well as having a cytoskeletal function (Reaven and Axline, 1973; Edstrom, 1974). They also seem to be biochemically different from intermediate filaments in other types of cells (Hoffman and Lasek, 1975) and from the larger 10 to 15-nm diameter filaments found in astrocytes. The latter appear to be similar to the tonofilaments found in a variety of cell types and appear to have a cytoskeletal function (Bondareff and McLone, 1973).

Although it is often assumed that neurofibrillary tangles, found commonly in a small number of neurons in the hippocampi of most normal persons more than 50 years of age (Tomlinson, 1982), develop from normal neurofibrils, with which they appear to be antigenicly similar (Gambetti, et al., 1983), fibrils in neuofibrillary tangles are structurally distinct. They are composed of paired filaments 10 to 13 nm in diameter and helically wound around each other at regular intervals of 80 nm (Iqbal, et al., 1978). These paired helical filaments, characteristic of neurofibrillary tangles, occur only in the human brain, where, depending upon their location and number, they may be associated with behavioral abnormality. They are found in large numbers in the cerebral cortex in Alzheimer disease, where they are associated with dementia (Tomlinson, 1982). They are considerably less numerous in elderly persons not afflicted by dementia.

Age-related changes in microtubules and microfilaments have been difficult to document, and sophisticated studies are few, largely because of technical limitations. Yet, age-related changes in neuronal functions, which are presumed to depend upon the integrity of microtubules and microfilaments, are regularly cited. For example, microtubules are generally thought of as major contributors to the intracellular substrate of motility. They contribute to the structure of mitotic spindles, by means of which they are involved in the movement of chromosomes, and a microtubular defect has been proposed as the cause of aneuploidy in Alzheimer disease (Heston, 1977) and perhaps (normal) old age as well (Bucton et al., 1982). The integrity of microtubules appears also to be a requirement of axoplasmic transport mechanisms in neurons (Ochs, 1972), and age-related changes in axoplasmic transport have been reported.

Transport of ^{3}H-fucose-labeled glycoprotein was shown to be materially reduced in the septo-hippocampal pathway of senescent rats (Geinisman, Bondareff, and Telser, 1977). Not only were arrival times of labeled glycoprotein in the hippocampus prolonged (suggesting a decrease in the rate of transport), but the amount of glycoprotein transported per unit time was decreased as well. Studies of axoplasmic flow in peripheral nerves, although not consistent, indicate a decrease similar to that found in the brain. Cholinesterase activity transported per time interval was decreased in a segment of sciatic nerve from senescent rats, suggesting an age-related decrement in the amount of enzyme transported (McMartin and O'Connor, 1979). The latter observation—based on the fact that accumulation of enzyme activity proximal to a ligature was less in nerves from old (as compared with young) adults—confirmed an earlier histochemical study of rat sciatic nerve reported by Gutmann and Hanzilikova (1976). Contrary results were reported by Ochs (1973), who compared the rapid axoplasmic transport of ^{3}H-leucine-labeled protein in sensory nerve fibers of old and young dogs and cats. Ochs found no significant age-related changes. In a similar study of rapid axoplasmic transport in rat sensory nerve, no consistent change was found (Stromska and Ochs, 1982).

Neurotubles, together with neurofilaments, are involved in the maintenance of cell shape, division, motility, transport, and secretion. They participate in synaptic function, and their integrity obviously affects cellular functions such as the growth of axons, the formation of new synapses, the formation and maintenance of cell membranes, the synthesis and release of neurontransmitters, and a host of other functions in such a way that a macromolecular lesion involving microtubles would (if it were age-related) have serious consequences in an aging nervous system.

Age-related differences in the distributions of neurofilaments and microtubules have been reported by Samorajski, Rolsten, and Ordy (1971), who counted them in relation to axon caliber in the pyramidal tracts of mice and found that the number of microtubules increased from the age of 8 to 26 months, whereas the number of neurofilaments decreased. The significance of these data is unclear, especially since neurofilaments and microtubles are chemically distinct, and the latter, isolated from mouse brain and analyzed on isoelectric focusing gels, have been found not to differ in mature and aged animals (von Hungon, Chin and Baxter, 1981). A reciprocal relationship between neurotubules and neurofilaments has also been claimed by Peters and Vaughn (1967), who reported the replacement of microtubules with neurofilaments in the optic nerve of old rats. However, age-related changes in microtubules *per se* remains conjectural. Neurofibrils appear to thicken with age, but their relation to the paired helical filaments of normal old age and Alzheimer disease is not known with certainty (Shelanski and Liem, 1979).

Some data support the often cited dictum that a failure of neuronal metabolism is a hallmark of old age. There may be a decrease in the number or metabolic efficiency of mito-

chrondia with age. Since it is claimed that mitochrondria isolated from the brains of old mice turn over lipids at a rate lower than that of young animals (Huemer et al., 1971; Menzies and Gold, 1972). Although little is known about the effect of advanced age or aging on the metabolic activities of neurons such as electron transport, oxidative phosphorylation, and other enzymatic reactions that depend upon the neurons' structural integrity, neuronal mitochrondria appear to remain relatively unchanged throughout life. Age-related changes in neuronal organelles that subserve protein metabolism are better documented. There is, for example, good reason to think that cytoplasmic RNA, visualized with a light microscope as stainable Nissl substance, declines in Purkinje cells of senescent mice (Andrew, 1937) and men (Ellis, 1920) and in cerebral cortical neurons of senescent rats (Kuhlenbeck, 1954) and mice (Anthony and Zerweck, 1979). The conclusion that neuronal aging is accompanied by a gradual loss of neuronal RNA is uncertain because of other reports showing no age-associated change in stainable Nissl substance (Vogt and Vogt, 1946; Wilcox, 1959; Bondareff, 1959).

Hydén (1960) approached this problem more directly. By means of microdissection, Hydén isolated neurons from the ventral horns of the spinal cord of human traffic-accident victims and found that the RNA content of these cells declines after age 60, as shown in Table 2. A decrease in RNA was also measured in pyramidal cells isolated from the CA3 zone of the hippocampus of senescent rats (Ringbörg, 1966); this decrease is also shown in Table 3. According to Hydén (1973), the age-related decline in the rate of RNA synthesis suggests that there may be fewer ribosomes available for protein synthesis in neurons of old animals. Changes in the RNA synthesized by senescent animals may be indicated by changes in the base composition of neuronal RNA as well as by data showing that the Purkinje cells and anterior horn cells of older mice incorporate less ^{3}H-Cytidine than do those of young adults (Wulff et al., 1965).

Histological studies, often difficult to quantify, suggest that metabolic impairment in DNA and protein syntheses in aged animals

TABLE 2.   Total Neuronal RNA (pg/neuron).

Human Spinal Cord (C5) Ventral Horn Cell*	Age (yrs)	Age	Rat Hippocampus Pyramidal Cell†
402 ± 28	0–20	1 day	24 ± 1
553 ± 38	21–40	6–8 wks	110 ± 10
640 ± 55	41–60	36–38 mo	53 ± 1
504 ± 31	61–80		
420 ± 3C	> 80		

* From Hyden, 1973
† From Ringborg, 1966

has functional sequelae. When, for example, the distribution and staining intensity of Nissl substance were compared in young and old rats forced to swim to exhaustion (Bondareff, 1962), it was shown that although the response to initial swimming trials was similar, there was a difference in the ability of young and old rats to recover. The Nissl pattern reverted to that characteristic of the normal, unexercised animal within 2 hours in young rats but remained "chromatolytic" in the older animals. More recently, the greater number of abnormally firing Purkinje cells in 28-month-old rats was found to correlate with an increased number of abnormally-appearing Nissl-stained Purkinje cells (Rogers et al., 1980).

ATROPHIC CHANGES IN AGING NEURONS

An age-related decline in neuronal metabolism has predictable consequences, whether the selective failure to synthesize an essential transmitter substance or a nonspecific decline in protein metabolism. Either might result in an inability to maintain the structural integrity of plasma membranes, with a consequent loss of receptor sites or synapses. Losses of axon and dendritic terminals are obvious extensions of this process, the inevitable end point of which is the loss of entire neurons. Whatever the means, the final result of each is a loss of neuronal connections, the loss of neuronal circuits, and, eventually, disruption of function. The actual loss of neurons would not appear to be an essential prerequisite of functional disruption, although it is often erroneously equated with neuronal failure in old age.

Studies of neuronal atrophy to date are too few to justify speculation about its being as reliable a benchmark of neuronal aging as the accumulation of lipofuscin. Loss of neurons, moreover, is certainly not the ubiquitous phenomenon suggested by earlier studies. Although estimates of neuronal populations in cell suspensions of whole mouse brain (Johnson and Ebner, 1971) and human visual cortex (Devaney and Johnson, 1980) showed significant losses during senescence, it is more likely that neuronal loss is a species-specific process involving only selective parts of the brain. In four parts of the human brain, a decrease in neuronal population has been reported to be greatest in the superior temporal gyrus and least in the postcentral gyrus; the neuronal loss in the precentral gyrus, area striata, and inferior temporal gyrus is intermediate (Brody, 1955). Similarly, neuronal loss in human frontal cortex has been found to be greater than that in the diencephalon, cerebellum, and brain stem (Critchley, 1942). Brody (1973), who found a progressive decline in neuronal numbers in all cortical layers after the fifth decade, reported significant neuronal loss in the superior frontal gyrus. His initial report (1955), as well as more recent studies that verify it (Anderson et al., 1983; Hendersen et al., 1980), show a loss of neurons of about 1 percent per year after age 70 in human cerebral cortex. There are, however, procedural difficulties in all these attempts to estimate total neuronal populations in cerebral cortex by morphological methods. The results of other studies that concern a variety of brain-stem nuclei—the neurons of which can be readily counted in their entirety—are seemingly antithetic, neuronal loss not having been observed. No age-related loss of neurons has been found in the motor nucleus of the facial nerve of human beings (Van Buskirk, 1945), the ventral cochelar nucleus (Konigsmark, 1969; Konigsmark and Murphy, 1972), the dentate nucleus (Höpker, 1951), or the inferior olivary nucleus (Monagle and Brody, 1974). Indeed, it seems that the nucleus locus ceruleus, in which a 48-percent loss of neurons has been shown by the ninth decade (Vijayashankar and Brody, 1979), may be a singularly involved brainstem nucleus. In the rat there appears to be no age-related loss of nucleus locus ceruleus neurons (Goldman and Coleman, 1980), and loss of cerebral cortical (Brizzee and Ordy, 1979) and hippocampal neurons (Brizzee and Ordy, 1979; Landfield et al., 1977; Bondareff and Geinisman, 1976) is uncertain.

An age-related loss of cerebellar Purkinje cells (Inukai, 1928) and frontal cerebral cortical neurons (Mufson and Stein, 1980) in the rat has been reported. Sabel and Stein (1981) found loss of neurons in the rat hypothalamus (ventromedial and lateral nuclei), septum, substantia nigra, lateral reticular formation, and amygdala. Although age-related neuronal loss is not ubiquitous in the human brain, it has been described in most of the major anatomical divisions that have evolved from developmentally early subdivisions of the neural tube. It has not been documented in the medulla but is well-known in selective regions of the cerebellar cortex and pons (nucleus locus ceruleus). In the midbrain nucleus, substantia nigra, age-related loss of dopaminergic neurons has been described (McGeer, 1978). Age changes in diencephalic derivatives are not well-studied, but there appears to be no well-documented age-related loss of neurons. Indeed, a study of the mammillary bodies found no loss of neurons (Wilkinson and Daves, 1978). Loss of neurons in cerebral cortex (discussed above) and at least one subcortical nucleus, putamen, has been reported (Bugiani et al., 1978).

If there is a general theme of age-related changes in the brain common to all vertebrates, it may include some form of neuronal atrophy. The process and its relationship to neuronal death, however, has not been adequately defined in any vertebrate, least of all human beings. Cowan (1973) has noted the remarkable constancy of neuronal populations in vertebrates, for example, in the lateral mammillary nuclei of adult cats, where the average difference in total neuronal numbers between the two hemispheres is only about 5 percent (Fry and Cowan, 1972). If cell numbers are so closely controlled in mammalian brains, a decline in the senium may be catastrophic and more reflective of serious pathology than of normal aging. But the theme of neuronal atrophy may have many variations in the aging brain depending upon differences in species, region of the brain affected, the time course of neuronal loss, and the effect of neuronal loss on behavior.

Studies of human brains indicate a gradual loss of Purkinje cells that proceeds at a very slow and gradual rate to age 60 and then begins to accelerate. The loss of neurons results in a major loss of neuronal interconnections, and it is the loss of interconnections, not that of the neurons, that is functionally important. Although the loss of neurons may proceed at different rates in various vertebrates, and may be of little significance in some, it is likely that a loss of interconnections occurs in all vertebrates. This has been variously documented in the cerebellar cortex, for example, by the loss of Purkinje cell dendritic branches and dendritic spines in aged dogs (Mervis, 1981) and by the loss of synapses in the rat (Glick and Bondareff, 1979). In both cases, there is a loss of synaptic connections between Purkinje cells and the several other neurons that synapse with them.

The time course of this loss of synaptic connections is not known, largely because electron microscopic studies in the rat have compared animals of only a few age groups and have not carefully surveyed the brain throughout the life span. The fact, however, that it is unusual to find products of neuronal degeneration in the brains of senescent animals suggests that the loss of synapses found there is the result of a prior degenerative process and that the products of degeneration have been cleared from the tissue by phagocytosis. It is unclear when synaptic loss occurs and unknown if it occurs progressively throughout adult life. If it does, the destroyed synapses must be reformed at a rate that keeps pace with destruction until late in life.

The loss of synapses in the cerebellar cortex of the senescent rat appears to be a highly selective process involving specific axodendric synapses (Glick and Bondareff, 1979). The synapses lost appeared to be between parallel-fiber axons and Purkinje-cell dendritic spines. As these synapses probably originate in large part from granule cells in the cerebellar glomeruli, it is of interest that an age-related decrease in the numerical density of glomerular synapses in the rat has been observed (Freddari and Guili, 1980). Axo-dendritic synapses between climbing-fiber axons and Purkinje-cell dendritic shafts—which probably originated largely in the inferior olivary nucleus—seemed to have been spared. The behavioral consequences of this synaptic loss are suggested by reports of age-related impairment in the electrical activity of parallel fibers, in which decrements in conduction velocity, refractory period, volley amplitude, and ability to drive Purkinje-cell unit spikes have been found (Rogers, Zornetzer, and Bloom, 1981). Unit recording from individual Purkinje cells has shown only normal, mediated-burst climbing-fiber activity in senescent rats but a significant decrease in spontaneous, simple firing rates, which largely relate to parallel-fiber activity (Rogers et al., 1980).

Even as age-related changes in the biosynthetic capabilities of neurons predict neuronal atrophy, they also predict changes in the synthesis of neurontransmitters and in the neuronal membranes with which these neurotransmitters interact at synapses. Changes reported include changes in the major systems of putative neurotransmitters; in the relative amounts of transmitter substances and their rates of turnover; in the activities of enzymes by means of which transmitter substances are synthesized; and in the neuronal processes and synapses of major chemical pathways through which these transmitters operate.

In cholinergic systems, age-associated decline is well-documented in several species, numerous parts of the brain, and in both pre- and post-synaptic elements. This decline is most adequately demonstrated by changes in

choline acetyltransferase (CAT) activity, the major enzyme of acetylocholine biosynthesis found in presynaptic terminals; most investigators report significant reductions in cerebral cortical CAT activity in elderly humans (McGeer and McGeer, 1975; Perry et al., 1977; Perry, 1980). An age-related decline in CAT activity might, therefore, be reasonably anticipated where there is a well-documented decrease in the number of excitatory synapses, such as in the rat cerebellar cortex (Glick and Bondareff, 1979), cerebral cortex (Feldman, 1976), and dentate gyrus (Bondareff and Geinisman, 1976). Surprisingly, it is unclear whether CAT activity is indeed reduced in senescent rat brain, although reduced CAT activity has been demonstrated in the cerebellum of senescent mice (Unsworth, Flemming, and Caron, 1980). Additionally, a decline in whole brain acetylcholine synthesis has been demonstrated in senescent mice and correlated with decreased ability to traverse a taught string (Gibson, Peterson, and Jenden, 1981). Cholinergic postsynaptic elements, associated with acetycholinesterase activity, seem to be more stable with advanced age (Unsworth, Fleming, and Caron, 1980; Perry, 1980), although decreases in acetylcholinesterase activity are described in mouse brains (Unsworth, Fleming, and Caron, 1980; Samorajski, Rolsten, and Ordy, 1971) and rat brains (Frolkis et al., 1973). In human beings, decreased muscarinic receptor sites in cerebral cortex, which also appear to be selectively postsynaptic, are described by some investigators (Perry, 1980; White et al., 1977) but not all of them (Davies and Verth, 1978), and an electron microscopic study of synapses in human frontal and temporal cortices, although difficult to evaluate because of sampling problems, showed no age-related difference in the number of synapses (Cragg, 1975). Nevertheless, decrements in the dendrites and dendritic spines are well-documented (see Table 3) in the cerebral cortices and hippocampi of both human beings (Scheibel et al., 1975; 1976) and rats (Feldman and Dowd, 1975; Feldman, 1976; Geinisman, Bondareff, and Dodge, 1977).

The age-related decline in noradrenergic systems is also well documented in both rodents (Samorajski, Rolsten, and Ordy, 1971;

TABLE 3.   Changes with Age in the Organization of the Rat Dentate Gyrus.

	Percent Change*
Synapses (number	
Axo-dendritic	−39.7
Axo-somatic	−14.6
Dendrites (volume)	−12.4
Astrocytes (volume)	+44.7

* Change at 28 months relative to 3-month-old young adult.

Finch, 1973; 1978) and human beings (Adolfsson et al, 1978; Carlson et al., 1980). The decline, however, appears to be highly selective in that only certain areas of the brain are involved and the involvement seems to be species specific. In senescent rats, for example, a decreased norepinephine concentration was found in one forebrain "limbic area" only (Ponzio et al., 1982), while in senescent human brains, concentrations of norepinephrine were found to be diminished in cerebral cortex and brainstem (Robinson et al., 1972). Because most, if not all, noradrenergic terminals innervating the cerebral cortex originate in the brainstem nucleus locus ceruleus, it may be significant that the number of nucleus locus ceruleus neurons declines with age in human beings (Vijayashankar and Brody, 1979), and probably in monkeys (Sladek and Sladek, 1978), but not in rats (Goldman and Coleman, 1980). A decline in cerebral cortical norepinephrine, which has been shown to be associated with impairment of memory and learning in the rat (Anlezark, Crow, and Greenway, 1973), is apparently not dependent upon a loss of neurons in the nucleus locus ceruleus. These data suggest that impaired cognition in aged human beings might be related to a decline in the amount of norepinephrine synthesized by locus ceruleus neurons, either because of damage to the neurons or to a loss in their numbers. It is tempting to consider the possibility that norepinephrine replacement therapy might be useful in the treatment of the cognitively impaired elderly, especially as the number of locus ceruleus neurons, even in the very elderly, is reduced by only 25 to 30 percent, and the loss of neurons in the cerebral cortex appears to be comparably low.

The age-related decline of dopaminergic systems seems particularly severe (Finch, 1978; Jones and Finch, 1975). The depletion of dopamine from presynaptic terminals of the corpus striatum is well-documented in old rodents (Finch, 1973) and old human beings, as is the corresponding loss of substantia nigra neurons from which these terminals originate (McGeer, 1978). A decline in dopamine concentrations appears ubiquitous and seems to involve all dopaminergie systems in the rat (Ponzio et al., 1982).

Age-related changes in serotonergic systems are not well known, although serotonin levels appear to decline in old age (Ponzio et al., 1982). GABA-ergic systems, at least in the mouse brain, are reported not to change with age (Unsworth, Fleming, and Caron, 1980). A decreased concentration of somatostatin has been found in the corpus striatum of senescent rats and human beings (Buck et al., 1981), but like GABA-ergic systems, those associated with neuropeptides have not been well studied with regard to age.

COMPENSATORY MECHANISMS IN THE AGING BRAIN

The brain of an aging individual is itself a composite of many subsystems, each having the potential to influence the whole, but at the same time having an independent time course (cf. Birren, 1959). Changes in behavior during the life of the individual are inferentially thought to reflect age-related changes in these subsystems. Their autonomy or interdependence and their relation to behavior are proper subjects for neurobiological research.

Some of these subsystems are known to deteriorate with time. The metabolic processes that decline in senescence, for example, result in degenerative changes that may progress to the loss of neurons or their processes. Other subsystems appear more "constructive," for example, the increase, with aging, in the population density of certain dendritic spines. Changes in these subsystems are usually gradual and their effects cumulative and interrelated, but they may be more autonomous and even precipitous, perhaps to the extent that the life of the individual is terminated. Although it is not known how these systems might be integrated, their integration is obviously such that aging organisms can continue to function and cope advantageously with their environment during even the terminal parts of their life span.

One, albeit speculative, way to conceptualize the integration of brain subsystems is to regard the more constructive phenomena and the more degenerative ones as being mutually compensatory. The age-related changes in the number of dendritic spines in the rat cerebral cortex, described by Connor and Diamond (1980), is an example. These investigators showed that nubbin-like spines increase with age, but that the increase is lessened by environmental enrichment. Speculating that an increase in the nubbin-like spines might make synaptic potentials more susceptible to potential changes in the dendrites, they suggested that a change in distribution of these spines could affect the integration of afferent information. A neuronal subsystem in which an increase in the relative number of dendritic spines might compensate for age-related changes in environmental interactions would help maintain the functional integrity of an individual in whose brain a gradual, age-related attenuation of dendritic spines would otherwise lead to a progressive decline in function.

It is not known to what degree dendritic spine density in the cerebral cortex is related to age or to environmental stimulation. It has been reported in a small number of cases (Buell and Coleman, 1979) that the packing density of pyramidal neuron dendrites, calculated so as to express their three-dimensional terminal (apical) distribution in the parahippocampal gyrus, is greater in brains of older persons (mean age, 79.6 years) than in younger adults (mean age, 51.2 years). Whereas these cortical neurons continue to grow with age, others degenerate and it is tempting to speculate that functional integrity, in some manner, is influenced by the integration of these two complementary processes. Were integration programmed in the genome, the decline of functional systems in senescence resulting from age-related atrophy of certain dendrites might be compensated for by age-related hypertrophy of other dendrites.

As there is evidence of compensatory processes with survival value for an aging individual involving the hypertrophy of neuronal elements, there is also evidence of similar compensatory processes involving neuroglia (see Table 3). Typically, the amount of brain tissue occupied by astrocytes increases as the neuronal mass decreases (Geinisman, Bondareff, and Dodge, 1978a), and an increase in astrocytic mass has been reported in the hippocampi of senescent rats (Geinisman, Bondareff, and Dodge, 1978b). It is, however, uncertain whether this increase results from an increase in the volume fraction occupied by astrocytic processes. The latter increase, which offers the possibility of "finer tuning" and therefore greater responsiveness to changes in the dimensions of the neuronal compartment, has been demonstrated in the rat. It remains to be demonstrated how age-related changes in the volume fraction of astrocytic cytoplasm might compensate for attrition of neuronal elements other than by filling in space; the astroglia, however, appear to modulate synaptic activity and may contribute to the general level of neuronal excitation. A superficially similar type of compensation, one that involves chemical rather that structural elements, is the age-related increase in monoamine oxidase (MAO) activity reported in human brain (Robinson, 1975). It is tempting to regard MAO activity and catecholamine concentration as a chemically integrated subsystem in which a rise in the former is coupled with an age-related decline in the latter.

In these hypothesized compensatory systems in which constructive and degenerative processes appear to be integrated, it is not now possible to predict which process leads and which follows. The actual sequence, however, may be of small consequence so long as the two processes form a mutually compensatory system. As one process would probably be as programmable in the genome as the other, survival value would depend more upon the two being mutually compensatory than upon sequence. It may also be unnecessary that a compensatory subsystem include both constructive and degradative components, since a presumably compensatory system has been described in the rat that involves the distribution of synapses on dentate gyrus granule cells in which both components are degradative (Bondareff, 1980a). Granule cells are innervated by excitatory synapses involving cholinergic axons from the septum. There is a significant loss of these axodendritic synapses, about 30 percent, in senescent rats compared with the quantity found in young adult rats. There is a simultaneous loss of inhibitory, GABA-ergic synapses on the bodies of these same neurons, and a mutually compensatory process has been proposed in which the loss of inhibitory axo-somatic synapses appears to compensate for the loss of excitatory axo-dendritic synapses in senescence. Such a system would appear overly simplistic since the inhibitory GABA-ergic interneuron appears to be innervated by noradrenergic, serotonergic, and cholinergic axons, and since the amounts of these three transmitters in the brain appear to change with age. It seems equally probable that all might be involved in a single integrated system. It is the compensatory aspect of these systems that seems to affect behavioral phenomena associated primarily with aging. The complexity may provide, secondarily, multiple mechansims for finely tuning compensatory mechanisms.

NEUROBIOLOGICAL RESEARCH IN AGING

The effects of age on human behavior are only beginning to be understood as they relate to chemical and structural changes in the brain. It is, however, becoming increasingly apparent that the brain does change with age, and that as it does, so too does its capacity to react with the ever-changing complexities of its internal and external environments. Changing states of behavior result, and some of these appear to be associated specifically with senescence.

As effects of age on the brain are reflected in behavioral changes during the course of normal adult development, they appear also to be important contributors to disease processes that affect behavior in the elderly. The clinical expression of Alzheimer's disease, for example, may be age-dependent in that there is often greater neuronal destruction and a more fulminant clinical course when the age of onset is early rather than late (Bondareff,

Mountjoy and Roth, 1982). Although histopathological findings are essentially the same in both early and late onset of Alzheimer's disease, the late onset variant appears to be more benign and its course less rampant. The life cycle of Alzheimer's disease (and other degenerative brain diseases that preferentially afflict the elderly) is actually not understood and continues to receive considerable clinical attention. The focus of biomedical scientists, however, has shifted away from the description and nosology of human behavior and its disorders that were emphasized at the turn of the present century. The turn of the next century is likely to find scientific attention focussed on the neurobiology of aging and the chemical and structural correlates of human behavior in healthy old age and in disease.

REFERENCES

Adolfsson, R.; Gottfries, C. G.; Oreland, L.; Roos, B. E.; and Winblad, B. 1978. Reduced levels of catecholamines in the brain and increased activity of monoamineoxidose inplatelets in Alzheimer's disease: Therapeutic implications. In *Aging*, eds. R. Katzman, R. D. Terry and K. L. Bick, Vol. 7, pp. 441–452. New York: Raven Press.

Anderson, J. M.; Hubbard, B. M.; Coghill, G. R.; and Slidders, W. 1983. The effect of advanced old age on the neuron content of the cerebral cortex. *Journal of the Neurological Sciences* 58: 233–244.

Andrew, W. 1937. The effects of fatigue due to muscular exercise on the Purkinje cells of the mouse, with special reference to the factor of age. *Z. Zellforsch. Mikros. Anat.* 27: 534–554.

Anlezark, G. M.; Crow, T. J.; and Greenway, A. P. 1973. Impaired learning and decreased cortical norepinephrine after belateral locus coeruleus lesions. *Science* 181: 682–684.

Anthony, A., and Zerweck, C. 1979. Scanning-integration microdesitometric analysis of age-related changes in RNA content of cerebrocortical neurons in mice subjected to auditory stimulation. *Expti. Neurol.* 65: 542–551.

Balasubramarian, A. D., and Bachhawat, B. K. 1964. Enzymatic transfer of sulfate from 3'-phosphoadenosine 5'-phosphosulphate to mucopolysaccharides in rat brain. *J. Neurochem.* 11: 887–885.

Barden, H. 1970. Relationship of Golgi thiamine phyrophosphatase and lysosomal acid phosphatase to neuromelanin and lipofuscin in cerebral neurons of the aging rhesis monkey. *J. Neuropathol. Exp. Neurol.* 29: 225–240.

Bettelheim, F. A., and Plessy, B. 1975. The hydration of proteoglycans of bovine cornea. *Biochem. Biophys. Acta.* 381: 203–214.

Birren, J. E. 1959. Principles of research on aging. In *Handbook of Aging and the Individual,* ed. J. E. Birren, pp. 3–42. Chicago: University of Chicago Press.

Bondareff, W. 1957. Genesis of intracellular pigment in the spinal ganglia of senile rats. An electron microscope study. *J. Gerontol.* 12: 364–369.

Bondareff, W. 1959. Morphology of the aging nervous system. In *Handbook of Aging and the Individual,* ed. J. Birren, pp. 136–172. Chicago: University of Chicago Press.

Bondareff, W. 1962. Distribution of Nissl substance in neurons of rat spinal ganglia as a function of age and fatigue. In *Aging Around the World,* Proceedings of the Fifth Congress of the International Association of Gerontology, ed. N. W. Shock, pp. 147–154. New York: Columbia University Press.

Bondareff, W. 1967. An intercellular substance in rat cerebral cortex: Submicroscopic distribution of ruthenium red. *Anat. Record* 157: 527–536.

Bondareff, W. 1976a. Extracellular space in the aging cerebrum. In *Neurobiology of Aging,* eds. R. D. Terry and S. Gershon, pp. 167–175. New York: Raven Press.

Bondareff, W. 1976b. The neural basis of aging. In *Handbook of the Psychology of Aging,* eds. J. E. Birren and K. W. Schaie, pp. 157–176. New York: Van Nostrand Reinhold.

Bondareff, W. 1980a. Compensatory loss of axosomatic synopsre in the dentate gyrus of the senescent rat. *Mechanisms of Aging and Development* 12: 119–221.

Bondareff, W. 1980b. Neurobiology of aging. In *Handbook of Mental Health and Aging,* eds. J. E. Birren and R. B. Sloane. New York: Van Nostrand Reinhold.

Bondareff, W., and Geinisman, Y. 1976. Loss of synapses in the dentate gyrus of the senescent rat. *Am J. Anat.* 145: 129–136.

Bondareff, W., and Lin-Liu, S. 1977. Age-related change in the neuronal microenvironment: Penetration of ruthenium red into extracellular space of brain in young adult and senescent rats. *Am. J. Anat.,* 148: 57–64.

Bondareff, W., and McLone, D. G. 1973. The external glial limiting membrane in Macaca: Ultrastructure of a laminated glioepithelium. *Am. J. Anat.* 136:277–296.

Bondareff, W., and Narotzky, R. 1972. Age changes in the neuronal microenvironment. *Science* 1976: 1135–1136.

Bondareff, W., and Pysh, J. J. 1968. Distribution of the extracellular space during postnatal maturation of rat cerebral cortex. *Anat. Record* 160: 773–780.

Bondareff, W.; Mountjoy, C. Q.; and Roth, M. 1982. Loss of neurons of origin of the adrenergic projection to cerebral cortex (nucleus locus ceruleus) in senile dementia. *Neurol.* 32: 164–168.

Bourke, R.; Daze, M.; and Kimelberg, J. 1978. Chloride transport in mamalran astroglia. In *Dynamic Properties of Glial Cells,* eds. E. Schoffeniel, G. Grank, D. Towers, and L. Hertz. Pergamon Press: New York, pp. 337–346.

Brizzee, K. R. and Ordy, J. M. 1979. Age pigments, cell loss and hippocampal function. *Mechanisms at Aging and Development* 9:143–162.

Brody, H. 1955. Organization of the cerebral cortex. III. A study of aging in the human cerebral cortex. *J. Comp. Neurol.* 102: 551–556.

Brody, H. 1973. Aging of the certebrate brain. In *Development and Aging in the Nervous System,* ed. M. Rockstein, pp. 121–134. New York: Academic Press.

Buck, S. H.; Deshmulkn, P. P.; Burks, T. F.; and Yamamura, H. I. 1981. A survey of substance P, somatostatin and neurotensin levels in aging in the rat and human central nervous system. *Neurobiology of Aging* 2: 257–264.

Buell, S. J., and Coleman, P. D. 1979. Dendritic growth in the aged human brain and failure of growth in senile dementia. *Science* 206: 854–856.

Bugiani, O.; Salvarani, S.; Perdelli, F.; Mancardi, G. L.; and Leonordi, A. 1978. Nerve cell loss with aging in the putamen. *Eur. Neurol.* 17: 286–291.

Burns, E. M.; Kruckeberg, T. W.; and Gaetano, P. K. 1981. Changes with age in cerebral capillary morphology. *Neurobiology of Aging* 2: 285–291.

Carlsson, A.; Adolfsson, R.; Aquilonius, S. M.; Gottfries, C. G.; Oreland, L.; Svennerholm, L.; and Winbland, B. 1980. Biogenic amines in human brain in normal aging, senile dementia and chronic alcoholism. In *Ergot Compounds and Brainfunction: Neuroendocrine and Neuropsychiatric Aspects,* ed. M. Goldstein. New York: Raven Press.

Connor, Jr., J. R.; Diamond, M. C.; and Johnson, R. E. 1980. Aging and environmental influences on two types of dendritic spines in the rat occipital cortex. *Exptl. Neurol.* 70: 371–379.

Cragg, B. G. 1975. The density of synapses and neurons in normal, mentally defective and aging human brains. *Brain* 98: 81–90.

Critchley, M. 1942. Ageing of the nervous system. In *Problems of Ageing,* ed. E. V. Cowdry. pp. 518–534. Baltimore: Williams & Wilkins.

Cowan, W. M. 1973. Neuronal death as a regulative mechanism in the control of cell number in the nervous system. In *Development Aging in the Nervous System.* ed. M. Rockstein, pp. 19–42. New York: Academic Press.

Davies, I., and Fotheringham, A. P. 1981. Lipofuscin—does it affect collular performance? *Exp. Gerontol.* 16: 119–125.

Davies, P., and Verth, A. H. 1978. Regional distribution of muscarnic acetylcholinc receptor in normal and Alzheimer-type dementia brains. *Brain Res.* 138:385.

Davis, S. S.; Ackerman, R. H.; Correia, J. A.; Alpert, N. M.; Chang, J.; Buonanno, F.; Kelley, R. E.; Rosner, B.; and Taveras, J. M. 1983. Cerebral blood flows and cerebrovascular CO reactivity in stroke-age normal controls. *Neurology* 33: 391–399.

Devaney, K. O., and Johnson, H. A. 1980. Neuron loss in the aging visual cortex of man. *J. Gerontol.* 35: 836–841.

Edstrom, A. 1974. Effects of Ca^{++} and MG^{++} on rapid axonal transport of proteins in vitro in frog sciatic nerves. *J. Cell Biol.* 61: 812–818.

Eldred, G. E.; Miller, G. V.; Star, W. S.; and Feeney-Burns, L. 1982. Lipofuscin: Resolutional discrepant fluorescence data. *Science* 216: 757–759.

Elkind, D. 1980. Developmental structuralism of Jean Piaget. In *Comprehensive Textbook of Psychiatry/III*, eds. H. I. Kaplan, A. M. Freedman, and B. J. Sadock, pp. 371–377. Baltimore: Williams and Wilkins.

Ellis, R. S. 1920. Norms for some structural changes in the human cerebellum from birth to old age. *J. Comp. Neurol.* 32:1–34.

Fang, H. C. H. 1976. Observations on aging characteristics of cerebral blood vessels, macroscopic and microscopic features. In *Neurobiology of Aging*, eds. R. D. Terry and S. Gershon, pp. 155–166. New York: Raven Press.

Feldman, M. L. 1976. Aging changes in morphology of cortical dendrites. In *Neurobiology of Aging*, eds. R. D. Terry and S. Gershon, pp. 211–227. New York: Raven Press.

Feldman, M. L., and Dowd, C. 1975. Loss of dendritic spines in aging cerebral cortex. *Anat. Embryol.* 148: 279–301.

Finch, C. E. 1973. Monoamine metabolism in the aging male mouse. In *Development and Aging in the Nervous System*, ed. M. Rockstein, pp. 199–218. New York: Academic Press.

Finch, C. E. 1978: Neurochemical and neruroendocrine changes during aging in rodent models. In *Alzheimer's Disease: Senile Dementia and Related Disorders*, eds. R. Katzman, R. D. Terry, and K. L. Blink, pp. 461–468. New York: Raven Press.

Frolkis, V. V.; Bezurkov, V. V.; Duplenko, Y. K.; Shchegoleva, I. V.; Shevtehuk, V. G.; and Verkhratsky, N. S. 1973. Acetylcholine metabolism and cholinergic regulation of functions of aging. *Gerontologia* 19: 45–57.

Freddari, C. B. and Giuli, C. 1980. A quantitative morphometric study of synapses of rat cerebellar glomeruli during aging. *Mechanisms of Aging and Development* 12: 127–136.

Fry, F. J., and Cowan, W. M. 1972. A study of retrograde cell degeneration in the lateral mammilary nucleus of the cat, with special reference to the role of axonal branching in the preservation of the cell. *J. Comp. Neurol.* 144: 1–24.

Gambetti, P.; Shecket, G.; Ginetti, B.; Hirano, A.; and Dahl, D. 1983. Neurofibrillary changes in human brain. *J. Neuropathol. Exp. Neurol.* 43: 69–79.

Geinisman, Y.; Bondareff, W.; and Dodge, J. T. 1977. Partial deafferentiation of neurons in the dentate gyrus of the senescent rat. *Brain Res.* 134: 541–545.

Geinisman, Y.; Bondareff, W.; and Dodge, J. T. 1978a. Dendritic atrophy in the dentate gyrus of the senescent rat. *Amer. J. Anat.* 152: 321–330.

Geinisman, Y.; Bondareff, W.; and Dodge, J. T. 1978b. Hypertrophy of astroglial processes in the denate gyrus of the senescent rat. *Am. J. Anat.* 153: 537–544.

Geinisman, Y.; Bondareff, W.; and Telser, A. 1977. Transport of (3H) fucose labeled glycoproteins in the septohippocampal pathway of young adult and senescent rats. *Brain Res.* 125: 182–186.

George, E.; Singh, M.; and Bachlawat, B. K. 1970. The nature of sulphation of uronic acid-containing glycosaminoglycans catalysed by brain sulphotransferase. *J. Neurochem.* 17: 189–200.

Gibson, G. E.; Peterson, C.; and Jenden, D. J. 1981. Brain Acetylcholine synthesis declines with senescence. *Science* 213: 674–676.

Glick, R., and Bondareff, W. 1979. Loss of synapses in the cerebellar cortex of the senescent rat. *J. Gerontol.* 34: 818–822.

Goldman, G., and Coleman, P. D. 1980. Neuron numbers in locus coeruleus do not change with age in Fisher 344 rat. *Neurobiology of Aging* 2: 33–36.

Gutman, E., and Hanzilikova, V. 1976. Fast and slow motor units in aging. *Gerontology* 22: 33–36.

Henderson, G.; Tomlinson, B. E.; and Gibson, P. H. 1980. Cell counts in human cerebral cortex in normal adults throughout life using an image analyzing computer. *J. Neurol. Sciences* 46: 113–136.

Henn, R. A., and Hamberger, A. 1971. Glial cell function: uptake of transmitter substances. *Proc. Nat. Acad. Sci., U.S.* 68: 2686–2692.

Henn, F. A., and Henn, S. W. 1980. The psychopharmacology of astroglial cells. *Progress in Neurobiology* 15: 1–17.

Henn, F. A.; Haljamae, H.; and Hamberger, A. 1972. Glial cell functions: Active control of extracellular potassium concentration. *Brain Res.* 43: 437–443.

Heston, L. L. 1977. Alzheimer's disease, trisomy 21, and myeloproliferative disorders: associations suggesting a genetic diathesis. *Science* 196: 322–323.

Hopker, W. 1951. Das Altern des Nucleus Dentatus. *Z. Alternsforsch.* 5: 256–277.

Huemer, R. P.; Bickert, C.; Lee, K. D.; and Reeves, A. E. 1971. Mitochondrial studies in senescent mice I. Turnover of brain mitochondrial lipids. *Exp. Gerontol.* 6:259–265.

Hunziker, D.; Abdel'Al, S.; and Schulz, U. 1979. The aging human cerebral cortex: A sterological characterization of changes in the capillary net. *J. Geront.* 34: 345–350.

Hyden, H. 1960. The Neuron. In *The Cell*, eds. J. Brachet and A. Mirsky. Vol. IV, p. 215. New York: Academic Press.

Hyden, H. 1973. RNA changes in brain cells during changes in behavior function. In *Macromolecules and Behavior*, eds. G. B. Ansell and P. B. Bradley, p. 62. Baltimore: University Park Press.

Iqbal, K.; Grundke-Iqbal, I.; Wisniewski, H. M.; and Terry, R. D 1978. Clinical relationship of the paired helical filaments of Alzheimer's dementia to normal human neurofilaments and neurotubles. *Brain Res.* 142: 321–322.

Inukai, T. 1928. On the loss of Purkinje cells with advancing age from the cerebellar cortex of the albino rat. *J. Comp. Neurol.* 34: 1–31.

Johnson, H. A., and Ebner, S. 1972. Neuron survival in the aging mouse. *Exp. Gerotol.* 7: 111–117.

Jones, V. J., and Finch, C. E. 1975. Senescence and dopamine uptake by subcellular fractions of the C57BL/6J male mouse brain. *Brain Res.* 91: 197–215.

Kaplan, H. I., and Sadock, B. J. 1980. *Erik Erickson.* In *Comprehensive Textbook of Psychiatry/III*, eds. H. I. Kaplan, A. M. Freedman, and B. J. Sadock, pp. 798–804. Baltimore: Williams and Wilkins.

Kety, S. S. 1956. Human cerebral blood flow and oxygen

consumption as related to aging. *Res. Publ. Assoc. Nerv. Ment. Dis.* 35: 31–45.

Kimelberg, H. K.; Biddlecome, S.; and Bourke, R. S. 1979. SITS-inhibitable Cl-transport and Na⁺-dependent H⁺ production in primary astroglial cultures. *Brain Res.* 173: 111–124.

Konigsmark, B. W. 1969. Neuronal population of the ventral cochlear nucleus in man. *Anat. Record* 163: 212–213.

Konigsmark, B. W., and Murphy, E. A. 1972. Volume of the ventral cochlear nucleus in man: Its relationship to neuronal population and age. *J. Neurophysiol., Exp. Neurol.* 31: 304–316.

Kuffler, S. W.; Nicholls, J. G.; and Orkand, R. K. 1966. Physiological properties of glial cells in the central nervous system of amphibia. *J. Neurophysiol.* 29: 768–787.

Kuhlenbeck, H. 1954. Some histologic age changes in the rat's brain and their relationship to comparable changes in the human brain. *Confinia Neurol.* 14: 329–342.

Landfield, P. W.; Rose, G.; Sandles, L.; Wohlstadter, T. C.; and Lynch, G. 1977. Patterns of astroglial hypertrophy and neuronal degeneration in the hippocampus of aged, memory-deficient rats. *J. Gerontol.* 32: 3–12.

Lassen, N. A.; Feinberg, I.; and Lane, M. H. 1960. Bilateral studies of cerebral oxygen uptake in young and aged normal subjects and in patients with organic dementia. *J. Clinical Investigation* 39: 491–500.

Litz, T. 1980. The life cycle. In *Comprehensive Textbook of Psychiatry/III*, eds. H. I. Kaplan, A. M. Freedman, and B. J. Saddocks, pp. 114–134. Baltimore: Williams and Wilkins.

Lynch, G., and Gerling, S. 1981. Aging and brain plasticity. In *Aging, Biology and Behavior*, eds. J. L. McGaugh and S. B. Kiesler, pp. 201–228. New York: Academic Press.

Mann, D. M. A., and Yates, P. O. 1974. Lipoprotein pigments—their relationship to aging in the human nervous system. I. The lipofusin content of nerve cells. 97: 481–488.

Mann, D. M.; Yates, P. O.; and Stamp, J. E. 1978. The relationship between lipofuscin pigment and ageing in the human nervous system. *J. Neurol. Sci.* 37: 83–93.

Mathews, M. B. 1964. Structural factors in cation binding to anionic polysacchardies of connective tissue. *Arch. Biochem.* 104: 394–404.

McGeer, E. G. 1978. Aging and neurotransmitter metabolism in the human brain. In *Aging*, eds. R. Katzman, R. D. Terry and K. H. Bick, vol. 7, pp. 427–440. New York: Raven Press.

McGeer, E. G., and McGeer, P. L. 1975. Age changes in the human for some enzymes associated with metabolism of catecholamines, GABA and acetylcholine. In *Neurobiology of Aging*, eds. J. M. Ordy and K. R. Brizzee, pp. 287–305. New York: Plenum Press.

McMartin, D. N., and O'Connor, Jr., J. A. 1979. Effect of age on axoplasmic transport of cholinesterase in rat sciatic nerves. *Mechanisms of Aging and Development* 10: 241–248.

Mervis, R. 1981. Cytomorphological alterations in the aging animal brain with emphasis on Golgi studies. In *Aging and Cell Structure*, ed. J. E. Johnson, vol. 1, pp. 143–186. New York: Plenum Publishing Corporation.

Menzies, R. A., and Gold, P. H. 1972. The apparent turnover of mitochondria, ribosomes and sRNA of the brain in young and aged rats. *J. Neurochem.* 19: 1671–1683.

Monagle, R. D., and Brody, H. 1974. The effects of age upon the main nucleus of the inferior olive in the human. *J. Comp. Neurol.* 155: 61–66.

Mufson, E. J., and Stein, D. G. 1980. Behavioral and morphological aspects of aging: an analyis of the rat frontal cortex. In *The Psychobiology of Aging*, ed. D. G. Stein, pp. 99–126. Amsterdam: Elsevier Scientific Publications.

Murray, M. R., and Stout, A. P. 1947. Adult human sympathetic ganglion cells cultivated in vitro. *Am. J. Anat.* 80: 225–273.

Nicholls, J. G., and Kuftler, S. W. 1964. Extracellular space as a pathway for exchange between blood and neurons in the central nervous system of the leech: Ionic composition of the glial cells and neurons. *J. Neurophysiol.* 27: 645–671.

Obrist, W. D. 1979. Cerebral circulatory changes in normal aging and dementia. In *Brain Function in Old Age*, eds. F. Hoffmeister and C. Muller, pp. 278–287. Berlin: Springer-Verlag.

Ochs, S. 1972. Fast transport of materials in mammalian nerve fibers. *Science* 176: 252–260.

Ochs, S. 1973. Effect of maturation and aging on the rate of fast axoplasmic transport in mammalian nerve. In *Neurobiological Aspects of Maturation and Aging*, ed. D. H. Ford, p. 349. Amsterdam: Elsevier Scientific Publications.

Olmsted, J. B., and Borisy, G. G. 1973. Microtubules. *Ann. Rev. Biochem.* 42: 507–540.

Perry, E. K. 1980. The cholinergic system in old age and Alzheimer's disease. *Age And Aging* 9: 1–8.

Peters, A., and Vaughn, J. E. 1967. Gierotubules and filaments in the axons and astrocytes of early postnatal rat optic nerves. *Journal of Cell Biology* 32: 113–119.

Perry, E. K.; Perry, R. H.; Gibson, P. H.; Blessed, G.; and Tomlinson, B. E. 1977. A cholinergic connection between normal aging and senile dementia in the human hippocampus. *Neurosci. Lett.* 6: 85–89.

Ponzio, F.; Calderini, G.; Lomuscio, G.; Vantini, G.; Toffano, G.; and Algeri, S. 1982. Changes in monoamines and their metabolite levels in some brain regions at aged rats. *Neurobiology of Aging* 3: 23–29.

Ranck, J. B. 1964. Synaptic "learning" due to electroosmosis: a theory. *Science* 144: 187–189.

Rapoport, S. I.; Ohno, K.; and Pettigrew, K. D. 1979. Blood-brain barrier permeability in senescent rats. *J. of Gerontol.* 34: 162–169.

Reaven, E. P., and Axline, S. G. 1973. Subplasmalemmal microfilaments and microtubules in resting and phagocytozing cultivated macrophages. *J. Cell. Biol.* 59: 12–27.

Rees, D. A. 1972. Shapely polysaccharides. *J. Biochem.* 126: 257–273.

Rees, Cragg B. G., and Everitt, A. V. 1982. Companison of extracellular space in the mature and aging rat brain using a new technique. *J. Neurol. Sci.* 53: 347–357.

Ringborg, U. 1966. Composition and content of RNA in neurons of rat hippocampus at different ages. *Brain Res.* 2: 296–298.

Robinson, D. S. 1975. Changes in monoamine oxidase and monoamines with human development and aging. *Federation Proceedings* 34: 103–107.

Robinson, A. J.; Nies, A.; Davis, J. N.; Bunney, W. E.; Davis, J. M.; Colburn, R. W.; Bourne, H. R.; Shaw, D. M.; and Coppern, A. J. 1972. Ageing, monamines, and monamine oxidase levels. *Lancet* I: 290–291.

Rogers, J.; Zornetzer, S. F.; and Bloom, R. E. 1981. Senescent pathology of cerebellum: Purkinje neurons and their parallel fiber atterents. *Neurobiology of Aging* 2: 15–25.

Rogers, J.; Silver, M. A.; Shoemaker, W. J.; and Bloom, R. E. 1980. Senescent changes in a neurobiological model system: cerebellar Purkinje cell electrophysiology and correlative anatomy. *Neurobiology of Aging* 1: 3–11.

Sabel, B. A., and Stein, D. G. 1981. Extensive loss of subcortical neurons in the aging rat brain. *Exp. Neurol.* 73: 507–516.

Samorajski, T.; Rolsten, C.; and Ordy, J. M. 1971. Changes in behavior, brain and neuroendocrine chemistry with age and stress in C57BL/10 male mice. *J. Gerontol.* 26: 168–175.

Scheibel, M. E.; Lindsay, R. D.; Tomiyasu, U.; and Scheibel, A. B. 1975. Progressive dendritic changes in aging human cortex. *Exp. Neurol.* 47: 392–403.

Scheibel, M. E.; Lindsay, R. D.; Tomiyasu, U.; and Scheibel, A. B. 1976. Progressive dendritic changes in the aging human limbic system. *Exp. Neurol.* 53: 420–430.

Schmitt, F. O.; and Samson, F. E., Jr. 1969. Brain cell microenvironment. *Neurosci. Res. Prog. Bull.* 7: 323–329.

Sekhon, S. S.; and Maxwell, D. S. 1974. Ultrastructural changes in neurons of the spinal anterior horn of aging mice with particular reference to the accumulation of lipofuscin pigment. *J. Neurocytol* 3: 59–72.

Shelanski, M. L., and Liem, R. K. 1979. Neurofilaments. *J. Neurochem.* 33: 5–13.

Siakotos, A. N.; and Koppang, N. 1973. Procedures for the isolation of lipo-pogments from brain, heart and liver, and their properties: A review. *Mech. Age Dev.* 2: 177–200.

Sladek, J. R., Jr., and Sladek, C. D. 1978. Relative quantitation of monoamine histofluorescence in young and old non-human primates. *Adv. Exp. Med. Biol.* 113: 231–239.

Stromska, D. P., and Ochs, S. 1982. Axoplasmic transport on aged rats. *Exp. Neurol.* 77: 215–224.

Tani, E., and Ametani, T. 1970. Substructure of microtubules in brain nerve cells as revealed by ruthenium red. *J. Cell Biol.* 46: 159–165.

Tomlinson, B. E. 1982. Plaques, tangles and Alzheimer's disease. *Psychological Medicine* 12: 449–459.

Trachtenberg, M. C. and Pollen, D. A. 1970. Neuroglia: Biophysical properties and physiologic function. *Science* 167: 1248–1251.

Unsworth, B. R.; Fleming, L. H.; and Caron, P. C. 1980. Neurotransmitter enzymes in telencepholom, brainstem and cerebellum during the entire lifespan of the mouse. *Mechanisms of Aging and Development* 13: 205–217.

Van Buskirk, C. 1945. The seventh nerve complex. *J. Comp. Neurol.* 82: 303–334.

Von Hungen, K.; Chin, R. C.; and Baxter, C. F. 1981. Brain tubulin microheterogeneity in the mouse during development and aging. *J. Neurochem.* 37: 511–514.

Vaughn, D. W., and Peters, A. 1974. Neuroglial cells in the cerebral cortex of rats from young adulthood to old age: An electron microscope study. *J. Neurocytol.* 3: 405–429.

Vijayashankar, N., and Brody, H. 1979. A quantitative study at the pigmented neurons in the nuclei coeruleus and sub coeruleus in man as related to aging. *J. Neuropathol. Exp. Neurol.* 38: 490–497.

Vitello, L.; Breen, M.; Weinstein, H. G.; Sittig, R. A.; and Blacik, L. J. 1978. Keratan sulfate-like glycosaminoglycan in the cerebral cortex of the brain and its variation with age. *Biochemica and Biophysica Acta* 539: 305–314.

Vogt, C., and Vogt, O. 1946. Aging of nerve cells. *Nature* 158: 304.

Walz, W. 1982. Do neuronal signals regulate potassium flow in glial cells? Evidence from an invertebrate central nervous system. *J. Neurosci. Res.* 7: 71–79.

Wang, H. H.; Tarby, T. J.; Kado, R. T.; and Adey, W. R. 1966. Periventricular cerebral impedance after intraventicular injection of calcium. *Science* 154: 1183–1184.

Weiss, P. A. 1973. *The Science of Life: The Living System—a System for Living.* Mount Kiso, New York: Futura Publishing.

Wessels, N. K.; Spooner, B. S.; Ash, J. F.; Bradley, M. O.; Luduena, M. A.; Taylor, E. L.; Wrenn, J. T.; and Yamada, K. M. 1971. Microfilaments in cellular and developmental processes. *Science* 171: 135–143.

White, P.; Hiley, C. R.; Goodhardt, M. J.; Carrasco, L. H.; Keet, J. P.; Williams, I. E. I.; and Bowen, D. M. 1977. Neocortical cholinergic neurons in elderly people. *Lancet* 1: 668–670.

Wilkinson, A., and Davies, I. 1978. The influence of age and dementia on the neurone population of the mammillary bodies. *Aging and Aging* 7: 151–159.

Wilkinson, J. H.; Hopewell, J. W.; and Reinhold, H. S. 1981. A quantitative study of age-related changes in the vascular architecture of the rat cerebral cortex. *Neuropathology and Applied Neurobiology* 7: 451–462.

Wilcox, H. H. 1959. Structural changes in the nervous system related to the process of aging. Present status of knowledge. In *The Process of Aging in the Nervous System,* eds. J. E. Birren, H. Imus, and Windle, W. F. Springfield, Illinois: Charles Thomas.

Wuerker, R. B., and Kirkpatrick, J. B. 1972. Neuronal microtubules, neurofilaments and microfilaments. In *International Review of Cytology* 33, eds. G. H. Bourne, and J. F. Danieli, pp. 45–76. New York: Academic Press.

Wulff, V. J.; Quastler, H.; Sherman, F. G.; and Samis, H. V. 1965. The effect of specific activity of H-cytidine on its incorporation into tissues of young and old mice. *J. Gerontol.* 20: 34–40.

5
BEHAVIORAL GENETICS

Gerald McClearn
and
Terryl T. Foch
The Pennsylvania State University

INTRODUCTION

This chapter is concerned with gerontological behavioral genetics—that is to say, it is concerned with the extent to which hereditary factors influence age-related changes in behavior. This three-way multidiscipline can be regarded as the intersection of the research domains of behavioral gerontology, developmental genetics, and behavioral genetics.

Considering the enormous array of theories, methods, and empirical literature of the three "basic" disciplines (if they can be so regarded) of behavioral sciences, genetics, and gerontology, the gerontological behavioral geneticist has available an exceptionally rich and varied armamentarium. Unfortunately, the work that has been built upon the sturdy foundation provided by these parental disciplines is sketchy in the extreme. In this chapter, therefore, considerable attention will be given to the foundation itself, in the expectation that from it we can infer something of the future shape of the multidisciplinary structure now abuilding.

BEHAVIORAL GERONTOLOGY

One generalization drawn from the burgeoning literature on behavioral aging is of fundamental importance to the genetic approach: Individual differences in phenomena related to aging are large and they are ubiquitous. It is important to understand that the explanatory principles of genetics are concerned with *variation* and that individual differences are the *sine qua non* for genetic research. Gerontological geneticists are concerned, for example, with explaining why some persons get Alzheimer's disease and others do not; why some retain functional competence late in a long life and others do not; why some respond adversely and some respond well to similar life events; and so on.

As will be discussed more fully later, genetic principles may also explain the *similarities* of relatives, but these similarities have meaning only in the context of the extent of *differences* among unrelated individuals. Thus, the variability that in some research areas is regarded as unwelcome noise is the very stock in trade of geneticists.

BEHAVIORAL GENETICS

The genetics of behavioral aging must be viewed against the general background of the genetics of behavior. Evidence that heredity influences behavior is about as old as the fields of psychology or sociology themselves, but the history of assimilation of the relevant data into the social and behavioral science mainstream has been a turbulent one. Without going into the record in any detail (see McClearn, 1962; Plomin, et al., 1980), it will serve here simply to note that the modern period of behavioral genetics can be dated from the decade 1951–

1960 with the publication of Hall's (1951) review chapter and the textbook of Fuller and Thompson (1960) and that the subsequent growth in number of studies, range of topics, and diversity of methods has been exponential.

A number of early studies dealt with the demonstration of classical Mendelian laws in behavioral traits. These studies provided valuable documentation of the fact that genes could indeed influence a wide variety of behavioral attributes. However, many important and interesting behavioral traits are continuously distributed and therefore not amenable to classical single-gene analyses. In order to study continuously variable traits, behavioral genetics has capitalized upon the theories and perspectives of quantitative genetics. Brief characterizations of these areas will be useful as a basis for later discussion.

Basic Concepts

Although the basic principles of heredity are elegantly simple, some of the particulars can be quite intricate. It is, for example, difficult to provide the single best definition of the *gene*. The concept of the gene has evolved to have multiple referents for different levels of analysis. For our purposes, it is most convenient to think of a gene as the functional unit that has control over the production of a specific protein. As we shall see later, genes exert their influence by directing protein synthesis. The genes are arranged linearly, like beads on a string, cn small, stringlike bodies, the *chromosomes*, which are found in the cell nucleus. The actual physical location that a particular gene occupies on a specific chromosome is that gene's *locus*, or chromosomal address. The chromosomes exist in pairs, with one member of the pair being of maternal and the other of paternal origin. The members of each pair are *homologous* to one another in the sense of having the same loci in the same order. Human beings have 23 pairs of chromosomes. Of these, the twenty-two pairs called *autosomes* are homologous as described. However, the members of the twenty-third pair, called the sex chromosomes, are of two sizes. The larger one is called the *X chromosome* and the smaller one, the *Y chromosome*. Females have paired (and homologous) X chromo-

somes, whereas males have a *heterologous* pair consisting of one X and one Y.

At some loci, the precise chemical structure of the gene may have alternate forms called *alleles*. As an example, consider the albino locus in the laboratory mouse, *Mus musculus*. There are several alleles, one symbolized by *C* and another denoted by *c*. The genotypes that are possible with these two alleles are *CC, Cc,* and *cc. CC* animals have a "full-color" phenotype. Exactly which color is fully expressed depends upon combinations of alleles at other loci. *Cc* animals are also full color; *cc* mice, on the other hand, are albino, with white coat and pink eyes. This result demonstrates the basic Mendelian phenomenon of dominance: In the case of the albino locus, one *C* allele is as effective as two, and the presence of the *c* allele in the *Cc* genotype has no apparent effect. The *C* allele is said to be dominant over the *c* allele; the latter is said to be recessive to the former. In general, dominance can be expressed as a relationship between allelic dosage and phenotypic value, as illustrated in Figure 1(A).

Dominance is not the only relationship possible between genotype and phenotype, however. In the case of some loci, when the heterozygote (with unlike alleles) gives an additive result and the phenotype is intermediate to those of the two classes of homozygote (those with like alleles), the phenotype-genotype relationship is as shown in Figure 1(B). Other intermediate relationships of partial dominance and overdominance are also possible, as displayed in Figures 1(C) and 1(D), respectively. Of the total number of genetic loci in humankind, which may number in the tens of thousands, over 300 have been identified and their location established over 23 pairs of chromosomes (Therman, 1980).

A substantial number of single loci have behavioral effects (see Fuller and Thompson, 1978; Ehrman and Parsons, 1976; Plomin, et al., 1980). A single locus, for example, accounts for red-green color blindness (with the pattern of familial distribution being complicated by the fact that the locus is on the X chromosome). In the realm of cognitive functioning, there are also examples of single-locus influence. Perhaps the best known is the condition of phenylketonuria (PKU), in which untreated individuals who are homozygous for the recessive allele at the relevant locus display severe mental retardation (if untreated). With respect to the biochemical mechanism through which these alleles exert their detrimental effect, a series of studies has shown that a defect in phenylalanine metabolism is involved. Several other single-locus conditions of mental retardation are known (e.g., Tay-Sachs, Lesch-Nyhnan, and others) in which other metabolic pathways are implicated.

In the past three decades there has been an explosion in our knowledge of genic structure and function, so that it is now possible to bridge the gap conceptually between genotype and phenotype. The hereditary material is now understood to be deoxyribonucleic acid (DNA), the structure of which is suggested in Figures 2 and 3. It is the stuff of which genes are composed. As illustrated in Figure 2, the double-stranded molecule consists of a sugar and phosphate backbone on each side, with pairs of nitrogenous bases linking the two strands. A most important characteristic of the DNA molecule is that the pairing of the bases is restricted: Adenine can bond only with thymine and guanine can bond only with cytosine (see also Figure 3). Therefore, the sequence of bases on one helix completely specifies that on the other helix. This property

permits the genetic material to replicate itself. Beginning with the single set of genetic material of the fertilized egg, many millions of copies must be made for each of the cells of the developing organism, and for the continued production of many cells even after adult body size has been attained. Very briefly, the double helix "unzips" between the bases, and, as suggested in Figure 3, each strand serves as a template to guide the synthesis of a new complementary strand. Two DNA molecules thus come to exist where there was but one previously. This copying is ordinarily accomplished with great accuracy, but on rare occasions a mistake may occur. Mechanisms exist for the repair of such mistakes, and we shall see later that these DNA repair systems may be associated with phenomena of aging.

In cellular functioning, the genetic information of the DNA is transcribed into another chemical sequence of the related substance, ribonucleic acid (RNA). The double helix of DNA separates, and one of the chains serves as a template upon which a single strand of RNA is built (see Figure 4). The base-pairing in this process is the same as for the replication of DNA except that, in RNA, uracil substitutes for thymine in pairing with adenine. The RNA strand leaves the cell nucleus and goes into the cytoplasm, where the genetic information

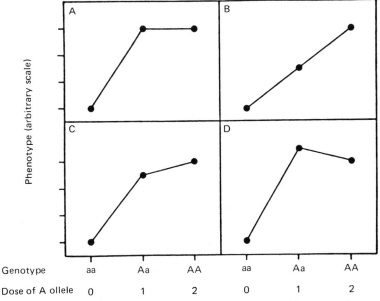

Figure 1. Diagrammatic representation of some possible relationships between phenotype and allelic dosage: (A) dominance–recessiveness; (B) additivity; (C) incomplete dominance; (D) overdominance.

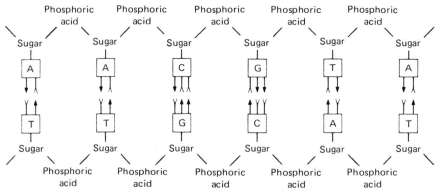

Figure 2. Flat representation of a DNA molecule. A = adenine; T = thymine; C = cytosine; G = guanine. (From *Heredity, Evolution, and Society* by I. M. Lerner. W. H. Freeman and Company. Copyright © 1968.)

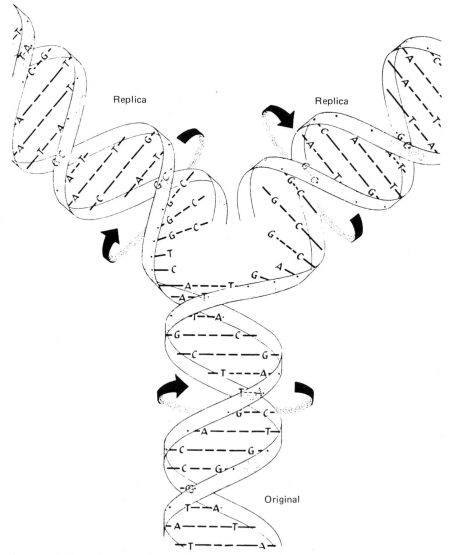

Figure 3. Replication of DNA. (After *Molecular Biology of Bacterial Viruses* by G. S. Stent. W. H. Freeman and Company. Copyright © 1963.)

is ultimately translated into a linear sequence of amino acids. The resulting chains of 100 to 500 amino acids in length form various proteins, depending on the particular sequence of amino acids. These proteins may be structural, as in the case of collagen, for example, or they may have regulatory functions or catalytic properties. The catalytic proteins—the enzymes—play a central role in all physiological functioning of the organism.

We can now amplify the meaning of some of the terms introduced earlier. A gene is a piece of DNA of several hundred or more nucleotides in length (see Harris, 1980). Each allelic form of a gene has a unique base sequence, perhaps differing from other alleles in only a single base. The polypeptides produced by different alleles usually differ in amino acid sequence. That these small differences can have large functional consequences

is well illustrated by the deadly genetic disease known as sickle-cell anemia. Intensive study of this condition has shown that the hemoglobin of sickle-cell victims is aberrant in that one of its 287 amino acids, glutamic acid, is replaced by another, valine, at one particular location. In terms of the DNA code, this implies the substitution of a single base (thymine for adenine) at a particular point in the base sequence. This difference in a single base can mean the difference between life and death.

With respect to the exemplar, phenylketonuria (PKU), some of the pathway from DNA to mental deficiency has been elucidated. The amino acid, phenylalanine, is quite widely distributed in foodstuffs. In normal persons, the ingested phenylalanine, in the presence of the enzyme phenylalanine hydroxylase, is principally metabolized to tyrosine. In those individuals who are homozygous for the recessive

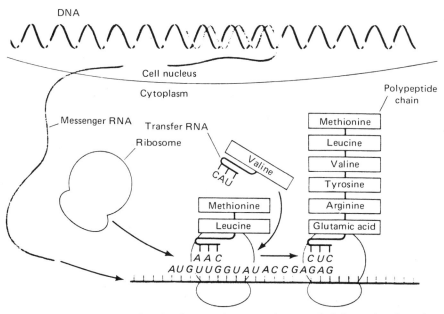

Figure 4.   The "central dogma" of molecular genetics states that genetic information flows from DNA to messenger RNA to protein. Genes are relatively short segments of the long DNA molecules in cells. The DNA molecule comprises a linear code made up of four types of nucleotide base: adenine (A), cytosine (C), guanine (G), and thymine (T). The code is expressed in two steps: first the sequence of nucleotide bases in one strand of the DNA double helix is transcribed onto a single complementary strand of messenger RNA (which has the same bases as DNA except that thymine is replaced by the closely related uracil, or U). The messenger RNA is then translated into protein by means of complementary transfer-RNA molecules, which add amino acids one by one to the growing chain as the ribosome moves along the messenger-RNA strand. Each of the 20 amino acids found in proteins is specified by a "codon" made up of three sequential RNA bases. (From "The mechanism of evolution" by F. J. Ayala. Copyright © 1978 by Scientific American, Inc. All rights reserved.)

allele, the phenylalanine hydroxylase molecule is abnormal. As a consequence, phenylalanine cannot be metabolized at a normal rate. With the resulting accumulation of large amounts of phenylalanine, other metabolic routes that normally operate at very low levels become more active (Figure 5). The accumulation of phenylalanine or of some of its metabolic products is inimical to normal development of the central nervous system.

Knowledge of this pathway has led to the ability to diagnose affected individuals early, to the development of a rational intervention (a phenylalanine-free diet), and to the capability of identifying heterozygotes who are "carriers" of the recessive allele and who might have affected offspring if mated to each other. This body of knowledge surrounding PKU serves as an exemplar of what might be hoped for when relevant single-locus conditions of aging are as thoroughly explored.

One side-effect of PKU illustrates a very important principle of gene action. Untreated homozygotes have reduced pigmentation. In addition to the mental retardation, the affected individuals are very light in complexion. Thus, the PKU locus seems to be doing more than

one thing. This phenomenon, labelled *pleiotropy,* is easily understood in terms of the branching of the metabolic pathways shown in Figure 5. Note the arrow indicating the formation of the pigment melanin. In general, though a locus may influence only one polypeptide, the effect of that polypeptide's functioning can spread out very widely downstream. The particularly well-studied pleiotropic network of the sickle-cell allele, involving a variety of organ systems as shown in Figure 6, serves as a good example.

Quantitative Inheritance

During the formation of the sex cells—ova and sperm—chromosomal replication takes place as it does in the division and proliferation of cells in somatic tissues. There is, however, one essential difference. Members of homologous chromosome pairs separate from one another during cell division so that daughter cells receive one chromosome from each pair. The result is that the genetic information is divided into exact halves. After fertilization, chromosome number is restored, and the developing zygote receives one allele at each locus from

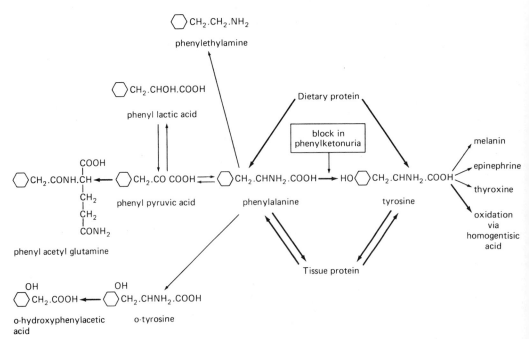

Figure 5.   Metabolic pathways involving phenylalanine, showing the site of the metabolic block in phenylketonuria.

each parent. For traits governed by single loci, this pattern of transmission makes it easy to predict the genotypes and phenotypes of offspring from particular crosses. For example, persons heterozygous for phenylketonuria will have normal phenotypes. Each heterozygous parent has a 50 percent probability of passing on a normal allele to each child and a 50 percent probability of passing on an abnormal allele. Hence, the likelihood that offspring of a union between heterozygotes will be homozygous for the recessive allele, and thus be affected, is 25 percent.

It is not particularly difficult to develop testable expectations based upon simple models of transmission that involve one or two alleles for traits whose variance falls into a few discrete classes. Many traits of interest, however, such as cognitive ability or personality, exhibit more or less continuous variation and are not susceptible to simple genetic analyses. In a classic paper, Fisher (1918) showed that a continuous distribution is exactly what would be expected if there were many loci—each acting in a Mendelian fashion and each of relatively small effect—influencing the phenotype. The elaboration and extension of this idea has led to the highly developed field of quantitative genetics (Falconer, 1981).

A general statement of the analytic model for quantitative genetics begins with the definition

$$P = G + E$$

where P is the measured trait or phenotype of an individual, G is the individual's genotypic value, and E is the contribution of environment, defined broadly to include all nongenetic effects (see Falconer, 1981).

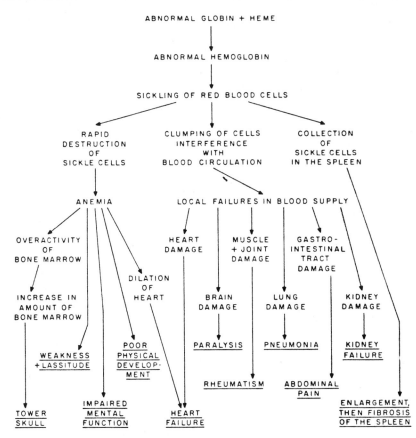

Figure 6.   A chart showing the physiological, developmental, and anatomical pathologies that follow as consequences of homozygosis for the sickling gene, a mutant gene that alters one of 287 amino acids in the hemoglobin molecule. (Reprinted by permission of the University of Chicago Press from Neel and Schull, *Human Heredity; Copyright* © 1954 University of Chicago.)

If the direction or magnitude of the effects of a particular environmental factor depends upon genotype, then the phenotype includes another factor, GXE, which is the interaction of genotype and environment. Because the genetic notion of genotype-environment interaction (GXE) is often confused with the truism that genes and environment interact during development, an example of GXE may be useful. Cortisone is a teratogenic agent that, under certain circumstances, causes the development of cleft palate in experimental animals. Fraser and coworkers (1954) explored the genetic basis of susceptibility to cortisone's effects by injecting pregnant animals from two genetically distinct strains. Cleft palate occurred in 100 percent of the offspring of one strain but in only 17 percent of the offspring of the other strain.

According to the model, phenotypic variability is thus partitionable into three components—the genotypic, environmental, and gene-environment interaction—as follows:

$$V_P = V_G + V_E + V_{GXE}$$

The ratio, V_G/V_P, or broad-sense heritability, is simply the proportion of phenotypic variance attributable to genotypic differences among individuals in the population. Of course, genetic and environmental factors participate in the development of all characteristics of an organism. Nevertheless, it is possible to ascribe proportions of the variability to particular sources. In addition to the three components already described, the covariation between genotype and environment, COV_{GE}, may be nonzero if environments favorable to a trait are occupied selectively by individuals with genotypes favorable (or unfavorable) for the trait. In some genetic designs, it is not always possible to distinguish all of these components unambiguously, and statements about the relative size of the different components must be made with the caution that interaction variance may have been "misread" as either V_G or V_E.

Some designs permit even finer resolution of particular components. For example, genetic variance can be partitioned into an additive and a nonadditive component, with the former reflecting the linear effects of "gene dosage," as illustrated in Figure 7, and the

latter attributed to dominance deviations. Similarly, environmental variance may be partitioned into pre- and post-natal components or into within-family and between-family components.

Behavioral geneticists are concerned with the operation of genotype and environment in producing a particular phenotype and with the assessment of genetic and environmental contributions to individual variation. This research requires that genotypes as well as environments be manipulated or assessed so that their individual effects might be disentangled. In animal research, the opportunity to control mating as well as to manipulate environment provides powerful research tools. Human genetic designs must rely upon the analysis of covariation among individuals who vary in the degree of shared genetic and environmental relationships. Systematic introductions to these many techniques are available (Ehrman and Parsons, 1981; Fuller and Thompson, 1978; Plomin et al., 1980); we shall describe a few that have been applied to behavioral aging.

Animal Research Techniques

The animal genetic tools of greatest relevance to the present topic are inbred strains. These strains are developed by systematic mating of

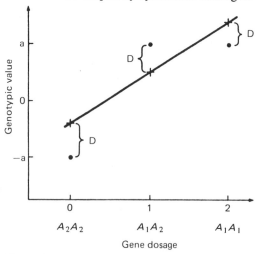

Figure 7. Genotypic values (black dots) when dominance is complete. Regression line predicts additive genetic values (crosses) based on gene dosage. Dominance deviations (D) are the difference between the additive genetic values and the actual genotypic values.

relatives, usually sibs. In simple outline, each generation of an inbred strain is the progeny of a single female and her brother. The effect of such inbreeding is to increase homozygosity, so that, after about 20 generations, all animals are homozygous in like state at about 99 percent of their loci. This condition constitutes effective genetic uniformity and offers the powerful advantage of replicate genotypes in an essentially unlimited number of different individuals. If two different inbred strains are reared and assessed in the same environmental circumstances and are found to differ in respect to some phenotype, this difference contributes *prima facie* evidence of genetic influence on the phenotype. More detailed information about the genetic system can then be derived from crosses made between the strains and from other types of matings. It is important to note that inbreeding is nondirectional. One does not inbreed *for* any phenotype. Thus, the various inbred strains that are available must be screened for the purpose of identifying those that display useful phenotypic differences for the purpose at hand.

An important limitation to the use of inbred strains emerges in multivariable research. Differences between a pair of inbred strains in two or more phenotypes do not demonstrate that those phenotypes are causally related. Because inbred strains differ at many gene loci, it is possible that strain differences in two or more phenotypes are controlled by quite separate genetic and environmental mechanisms. Putative correlations must therefore be observed in several different inbred lines or among members of a genetically heterogeneous group before the correlation can be accepted. Once the geneticist is certain that a correlation exists, multivariate genetic analyses that involve parent-offspring comparisons, for example, permit the decomposition of correlation or covariance matrices into genetic and environmental components.

Another tool available to the animal researcher is selective breeding. Not yet brought to bear fully on gerontological problems, the technique of selection has great promise for providing tailor-made research animals for the future. Beginning with a genetically heterogeneous stock, males and females with high phenotypic values are selected and are mated together. To the extent that the location of these animals in the upper part of their distributions is due to genetic factors (i.e., to the extent that the phenotype is heritable) the offspring of these matings will have a higher frequency of the "favorable" alleles than would the offspring of animals mated at random from the parental generation and should have a higher phenotypic mean than that of the population from which their parents were selected. Continued over successive generations, this procedure will yield systematically increasing means at a rate dependent upon the rigor of selection (i.e., how extreme the parents of each generation are relative to their population mean) and the heritability. Starting with the same foundation stock, selection studies typically produce two lines, one selected for high values and one selected for low values. For comparisons among lines within each generation, it is also desirable to maintain a randomly bred control line and to perform the entire study in replicate [see McClearn, et al. (1981), for a discussion of the desiderata in selection studies].

Human Research Techniques

Human research involves the assessment of familial resemblance among groups of relatives with varied genetic relationships (e.g., full sibs *versus* half sibs, adoptees *versus* biological children, and so on). In human beings, genetic resemblance is inferred from parentage: Thus, parent and offspring share one-half of their alleles; any particular pair of siblings can be more or less similar, but, on the average, they share one-half of their alleles; genetic similarity in fraternal twins (DZ or dizygotic) is the same as in siblings (but they do share more similar uterine and family environments by virtue of the shared gestation and simultaneous birth); identical (MZ or monozygotic) twins are genetically identical; adoptive parent and child are genetically unrelated; and so on.

There are many methodological problems in human research, of course. One particularly pertinent problem is that relatives who live together may be similar because of shared genes or shared environments, or both. Without other information, the simple observation of correlations between relatives is difficult to interpret.

Of the several familial methods, only the twin paradigm has been applied to normal behavioral aging. According to the simplest model, broad-sense heritability (V_G/V_P) is estimated as twice the difference between the MZ and the DZ *intra*class correlations. In addition, the relative magnitudes of the twin correlations also permit estimates of the percentage contributions to total variance by within-family and between-family environmental components (see Figure 8). This model does require the following assumptions: (1) the contribution of shared environment to the resemblances of both types of twins is equal; (2) the statistical interaction between genotypic and environmental deviations is zero; and (3) the covariation between genotypes and environments is also zero. Unfortunately, it is difficult to test the validity of these assumptions directly, but various approaches to the problem have indicated their appropriateness in the domains of cognition and personality (Jinks and Fulker, 1970; Plomin, et al., 1976; Scarr and Carter-Saltzman, 1979; Matheny, et al., 1976). These results are not directly generalizable either to different traits or to populations characterized by different subject variables. It is possible, for example, that variation in cognitive abilities among the elderly may be greatly influenced by gene-environment interaction even though that component is apparently unimportant in younger adults and children. Hence, the prudent investigator should interpret the results of classical twin analyses as an economical first step in the examination of the relative importance of genetic and environmental factors; more costly methods, such as those involving adoption, should follow.

Using these various approaches, behavioral geneticists have demonstrated a genetic influence on an enormous array of behavioral

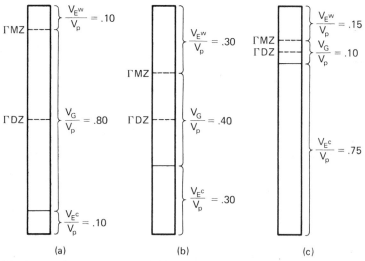

Figure 8.   Partitioning Variance with the Classical Twin Method: (a) A high MZ and a moderate DZ intraclass correlation suggest that the genetic component is the largest. Between- and within-family environments do not contribute much to individual variation. (b) Here variance is equally distributed among the between- and within-family components and the genetic component. Test unreliability is included in the V_{E^W} component. (c) When both MZ and DZ intraclass correlations are high, shared family environment is the biggest contributor to variance.

phenotypes. In addition to the numerous single-locus conditions (e.g., phenylketonuria), quantitative analyses have identified genetic components for liability to alcoholism, depressive illness, schizophrenia, time perception, cognitive factors, personality, information processing, and so on (see Plomin et al., 1980; Fuller and Thompson, 1978; Ehrman and Parsons, 1976, for reviews). It now seems reasonable to presume that genetic influence on behavior is ubiquitous.

DEVELOPMENTAL GENETICS

Gerontological genetics can be regarded as a special case of developmental genetics. A useful perspective on the genetics of aging might reasonably be expected, therefore, from a brief examination of the more intensively studied genetics of early development.

A basic principle of developmental genetics is that, even though all the genes of an individual are present from the moment of conception, they are not all effective all the time. One brief example drawn from mammalian biology will help to illustrate the point. Hemoglobin is a complex protein made of four distinct subunits or chains. In most people, six different kinds of hemoglobin chains are made throughout their development. As shown in Figure 9, an epsilon (ϵ) form predominates in early embryonic life. Between three and six weeks of gestational age, there is a brief appearance of a zeta (ζ) form. Alpha (α) and gamma (γ) chains predominate between six weeks of gestation and birth, and alpha (α) and beta (β) after birth. The temporal patterning of the relative prevalence of these different hemoglobin polypeptides is shown in Figure 9. Since different polypeptides are under the control of different loci, the picture presented is that of a continuously shifting pattern of gene activity (or at least of gene product availability).

Control of Gene Expression

The control of gene expression in eukaryotes (animals possessing cell nuclei), and particularly in multicellular eukaryotes such as ourselves, is not well understood, but some salient features are emerging from extremely active research in the area. One currently favored model is that of Britten and Davidson (1969; see also the presentation in Ham and Veomett, 1980). This model, shown in Figure 10, postulates two different types of gene: producer genes and integrator genes. The previous discussions of this chapter have concerned producer genes—producers of structural or catalytic proteins. The transcription of a producer gene is initiated at a physically adjacent receptor site when a regulatory molecule occupies the site. Regulatory molecules are produced by integrator genes and those from a single integrator gene might stimulate transcription of several producer genes. Activity of the integrator genes is stimulated when an adjacent sensor site is bound by an activator substance.

This model goes a long way toward explaining developmental phenomena of differentiation. Given any initial differences in cytoplasmic constituents of primordial cells that could provide them with different activator substances, cascading effects of subsequent metabolic processes producing ever more differentiated populations of metabolites could lead to the development of livers, brains, and all the other differentiated cells, tissues, and organs of a complex organism.

As stated so far, the Britten-Davidson model is a normative one, accounting for developmental changes that are characteristic and typical of the species (or a wider taxonomic spectrum) as a whole. In addition, the model also provides us with new ways of thinking about individual variation around this species-typical process. Not only can we think of differences in base sequences in producer genes as providing phenotypic differences, but of individuality being generated, particularly in the timing of developmental events, by similar base pair differences in receptor sites, sensor sites, and integrator genes. The Britten-Davidson model is currently under active examination and probably will be extensively revised. Nonetheless, any improved theoretical explanation of the phenomena of development will likely have many formal similarities to the present one, and we can use it as a heuristic device for approaching issues in the genetics of behavioral aging.

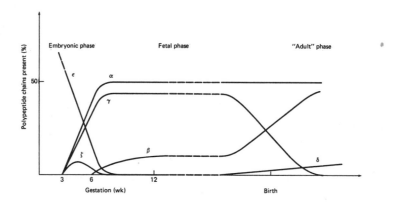

Figure 9.   Changes in the relative frequency of human hemoglobin chains during embryonic and postnatal development. The amount of each chain is shown as a percentage of total polypeptide chains present. (From Nigon, V., and Godet, J. 1976. *Int. Rev. Cytol.* 46:79.)

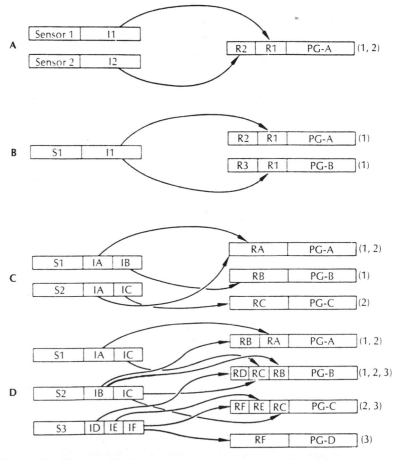

Figure 10.   Britten-Davidson model showing interactions possible with multiple receptor sites (*A* and *B*), multiple integrator genes (*C*), and multiple receptor sites plus multiple integrator genes (*D*). *S* = Sensor site; *I* = integrator gene; *R* = receptor sits; *PG* = producer gene. Numbers in parentheses to the right of each producer gene indicate which sensor sites are able to activate that producer gene. (Modified from Truman, D. E. S. 1975. *Biochemistry of Cytodifferentiation.* John Wiley & Sons, Inc., New York.)

Systems Models

In addition to the cellular and molecular approaches to the genetics of development, there have been attempts to provide conceptual bases for more molar phenomena of organ or even organism development. Particularly salient among these latter approaches has been the work of Waddington (1957). One of Waddington's valuable models is that of the epigenetic landscape, illustrated in Figure 11. In this model, the terrain is molded by the genotype. The ball represents a particular part of the egg, and its course as it rolls toward the viewer represents the developmental history of that part of the egg. Environmental forces are imagined to act laterally to displace the ball. Depending on the magnitude of the excursion and the steepness of the valley walls, the ball will return to the trajectory it was pursuing before the displacement. This process resembles homeostasis except that the tendency is to return to a trajectory rather than a set point. Waddington coined the term "homeorhesis" to describe this sort of buffering and the term "creode" to describe the trajectory that is so buffered.

Returning to the epigenetic landscape, we note that critical points exist at which an environmental nudge can cause the ball to take one path or another, and that once such a

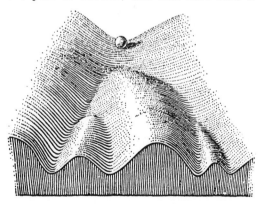

Figure 11. *Part of an Epigenetic Landscape:* The path followed by the ball, as it rolls down towards the spectator, corresponds to the developmental history of a particular part of the egg. There is first an alternative, towards the right or the left. Along the former path, a second alternative is offered; along the path to the left, the main channel continues leftwards, but there is an alternative path which, however, can only be reached over a threshold.

commitment is made, it can be difficult or impossible to undo. Note also that differences in genotype might give some individuals steeper valley walls, representing more tightly buffered developmental processes.

This model was proferred as a way of viewing histogenesis, with the troughs on the front edge representing brain, eye, liver, etc., but it can be generalized to apply to more "global" traits, such as behavioral ones, in a straightforward manner. The front edge could represent different personality traits, cognitive styles, etc. Obviously, the model is not meant to be interpreted literally but as a "rough and ready picture of the developing embryo . . . it has certain merits for those who, like myself, find it comforting to have some mental picture, however vague, for what they are trying to think about" (Waddington, 1957, p. 30).

It is significant that both genetic and environmental factors are incorporated into this model of developmental trajectories. The elegance of the quantitative treatment of genetics and environment has not as yet been fully and systematically extended to these trajectories or creodes, but certain extensions are relatively obvious. Just as the phenotypic mean can be regarded as being constituted of a genotypic value and environmental deviation, a phenotypic trajectory can be similarly regarded as a genotypic trajectory and environmental deviations from it.

Consider Figure 12(A), which shows genotypic developmental functions of a hypothetical phenotype for two individuals. The meaning of the genotypic trajectory can be most simply understood from the following: Imagine that it is possible to replicate a single genotype a very large number of times and to place some replicates in each of the environmental circumstances to which the population is exposed. The mean phenotypic trajectory of all these genetically identical individuals in diverse environments would be equal to the genotypic trajectory. Of course, each individual experiences only a single one of all possible environmental histories. The influence of this unique history can be understood to produce deviations from the individual's genotypic trajectory.

Clearly, age-related changes in a phenotype can be influenced by all sorts of environmental

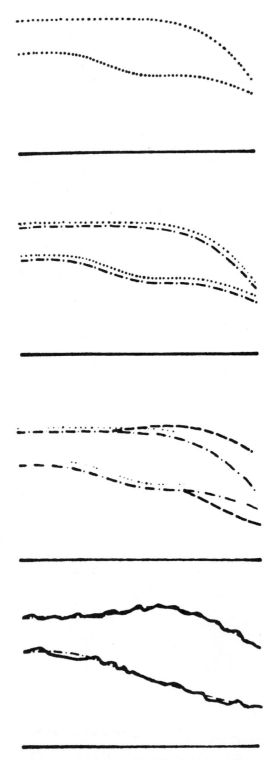

Figure 12.   A depiction of genetic developmental trajectories, with modifications caused by long-lasting, population-wide environmental (co-hort) influences; long-lasting, individual environmental effects; and short-term environmental effects. See text for explanation.

factors, some of which will have permanent and others only brief effects. In Figure 12(B), the genotypic trajectories of two of the individuals of Figure 12(A) are shown as dotted lines, with dashed-dotted lines portraying the consequences of long-lasting cohort environment effects to which both individuals were exposed. Other environmental factors may have equally persisting effects while affecting only some individuals, as shown by the dashed line in Figure 12(C). Furthermore, we must imagine the short-term environmental effects represented in Figure 12(D) as brief excursions above and below the developmental course that has been otherwise specified by the genotype and long-term environmental influences. This scheme emphasizes the desirability of examining intraindividual as well as interindividual variation in developmental research.

Considerations of developmental systems in which both genetic and environmental components may change over time imply that the heritability of traits might change during the life span. Empirical evidence is scanty on this issue, but a valuable exemplar is provided by Monteiro and Falconer (1966), who estimated variance components of body weight in mice by examining full and half siblings from birth until an age of eight weeks. As shown in Figure 13, which presents the data for males, the total phenotypic variance rises rapidly, peaks at an age of about five weeks, declines somewhat, then remains fairly level. Most of the variance is the result of between-families environmental variance, V_{Ec}, but this source peaks at four to five weeks and declines thereafter. Within-family environmental variance, V_{Ew}, rises gradually, as does additive genetic variance, V_A, so that they are of approximately equal importance at eight weeks. Heritability is estimated at 0.34 at the latter age. It is reasonable to expect that similar changes in variance components might occur in the later periods of the life span.

Developmental Behavioral Genetics

Most behavioral genetics research has dealt with phenotypes measured only at a single age. However, the work that has been concerned with age differences makes plausible the application of the general principles of developmental genetics to behavioral phenotypes. A few examples may be cited. Dixon and DeFries (1968) assessed the activity of C57BL and BALB/cJ mice at various ages, the results being shown in Figure 14. C57BL animals are more active than BALB/cJ animals at as early an age as 15 days. With increasing age, the BALB/cJ activity increases only a bit, but the C57BL activity rises substantially, so that at an age of three or four months there is a four-fold activity differential. In addition to the inbred strains, these authors tested the F_1 offspring obtained by mating animals of one strain with those of the other. Clearly, these hybrid animals resemble the C57BL parent most closely, suggesting average dominance of the relevant alleles carried by the C57BL over those of the BALB/cJ mice.

In human research, the longitudinal analyses of infant twins by Wilson and his colleagues in the Louisville twin studies have shown that MZ twins resemble one another more and more as age increases and that differential concordance for physical and behavioral traits in MZ and DZ twins is not apparent early in life (Wilson, 1978). In parent-offspring studies of intelligence, it is generally found that resemblance is low for the first several years of life but increases from the age of 6 and remains high and stable into the adult years (Honzik, 1957; Henderson, 1982).

Another type of evidence on the influence of genes on behavioral development has been provided by studies in which an environmental intervention has differential developmental consequences, depending on the genotype. For example, a relatively persistent effect of a treatment of brief duration was demonstrated by Lindzey and colleagues (1960, 1963). From the fourth through the seventh day of life, mice of four inbred strains were subjected to two minutes of intense sound. These animals were compared to untreated controls at 30 days and at 100 days of age on measures of activity and emotionality. The general outcome was that the C57BL/1 strain was more highly sensitive to this noxious infantile stimulation than were C3H, DBA/8, or JK mice.

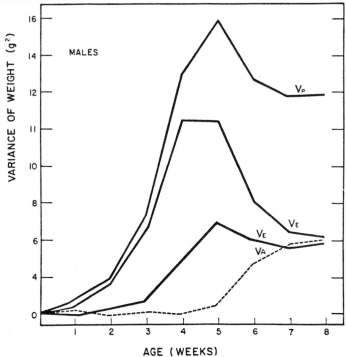

Figure 13.   Partitioning of the phenotypic variance of body weight in mice at weekly intervals from birth to eight weeks, to show changes of each component with increasing age. (*From* Monteiro and Falconer: Compensatory growth and sexual maturity in mice. *Aminal Production* 8:179–192, 1966. Copyright by Oliver and Boyd, Ltd. Reproduced with permission.)

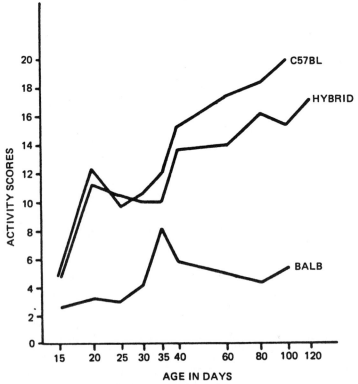

Figure 14.   Mean transformed open-field activity scores of two inbred strains of mice (BALB/cJ and C57BL/6J) and their F_1 hybrids in cross-sectional and longitudinal studies. Age is presented on a logarithmic scale.

A further example is provided by the work of Weir and DeFries (1964) and DeFries (1964), who examined the effects of stress on pregnant BALB/cJ and C57BL/6 mice on the activity of their young. Compared to offspring of untreated control mothers, the offspring of treated C57BL/6 mice had increased activity and those of treated BALB/cJ mice had reduced activity.

GENETICS OF AGING: THEORETICAL ISSUES

The foregoing review has summarized persuasive evidence that genes may influence developmental processes in general and behavioral development in particular. The focus of empirical research, however, has been aimed primarily at early parts of the life span. Nevertheless, the rich theory now growing up within the general field of developmental genetics offers several avenues to direct our thinking about gerontological phenomena. There are, in addition, some fascinating theoretical issues that are specifically pertinent to aging. (The interested reader will find the reviews in Bergsma and Harrison, 1978, and Schneider, 1978, particularly useful in providing details of these issues.)

At a systems level, a principal issue of the genetics of aging concerns whether the aging process is positively controlled by the continued unfolding of a genetic program, or whether the phenomena of aging begin to occur when the genetic program that has operated through the embryonic and fetal periods, and then through infancy, childhood, and adolescence, simply runs out. If the former, then is it the case that there are senescing genes that are turned on, or is it that antisenescing genes that have been in play throughout life are turned off?

At the level of evolutionary theory, numerous intriguing issues arise. One of the most challenging problems is to explain how natural selection could act so as to increase longevity by adding to the life span after reproductive function has ceased.

The best developed areas of inquiry into molecular genetic mechanisms and aging are normative, which is to say that they explore events and processes that are normal or typical for *all* members of the species. For example, one line of theorizing and experimentation has concerned the possibility that mutations (changes in the base sequence of a gene or aberrations of chromosome structure), which may have been induced environmentally by radiation or by certain chemicals, can accumulate with time within body cells and ultimately affect their functioning so adversely that the symptoms of aging appear.

Another related theory of aging that pertains to the basic genetic mechanism suggests that the deterioration of the mechanisms that repair damaged DNA permits the accumulation of DNA damage. In this view, although the extrinsic events are important, the key to understanding the aging process is to be found in the intrinsic DNA repair process and in whatever causes it to lose effectiveness.

Yet another theory presumes the key to be not initially in the DNA, but in the translation process. If a random error occurs in the synthesis of a protein, and if that protein happens to be one that plays a role in the protein producing machinery itself, this now-defective protein can interfere with production of many or all of the other proteins being produced within the cell. This could lead to an "error catastrophe" (Orgel, 1963) for the cell, with impairment of transcription, translation, and even of the replication of the DNA itself.

These issues are of fundamental importance to many basic biological sciences as well as to gerontology.

GENETICS OF BEHAVIORAL AGING: ANIMAL RESEARCH

Pioneering Work

Among the earliest developmental behavioral genetics studies involving mature adult animals were those of Meier (1964) and his colleague, Foshee (Meier and Foshee, 1963), who tested acquisition and reversal learning in a simple water-maze by mice of six different strains. Their cross-sectional design sampled six ages ranging from 21 to 147 days on the first day of training. Mice usually reach sexual maturity between 21 and 45 days after birth (Bronson, Dagg, and Snell, 1968), and average life-spans vary from 650 days for the relatively short-lived A/J strain to 805 days for the longer-lived C57BL/6J strain (Goodrick, 1975a). Mice in the oldest of Meier's groups were therefore mature adults but were not by any means senescent. The results demonstrated that the effects of age, sex, and strain were interdependent. Three of the strains—C57BL/6J, DBA/2 and CF/1—performed uniformly well at each age. Relative to these animals, mice from the AKR, BALB/cJ, and C3H/He strains were inferior, and for them the effects of age and sex were significant. A marked deficit was exhibited especially by BALB/cJ mice during "adolescence" and early maturity. At each age, mice within the least able strains were also more variable. Because members of an inbred strain are genetically homogeneous, the variance within any particular strain must be environmental in origin. That some of these strains were much more variable than others at specific ages suggests clearly that sensitivity to random environmental influences is modulated by genotype as well as by maturation and experience. Such interactions make it difficult to draft broad generalizations about, for example, age-related changes in learning ability.

Soon after the publication of Meier's experiments, McGaugh and Cole (1965) reported age and strain differences in the effect of distributed practice on maze learning. This research employed descendants of Tryon's selectively bred maze-bright (S_1) and maze-dull (S_3) rats. Again, the age comparison involved immature rats (29 to 33 days old) and mature rats (142 to 164 days old). Distributed practice was found to improve the performance of mature rats from both lines and of young S_1 rats. Young S_3 animals performed equally poorly in both practice conditions, but older male S_3 rats whose practice was massed performed most poorly of all. These results demonstrated that the effects of age depended upon sex and strain on the one hand and upon strain and type of practice on the other. Citing previous research that had shown very young and very old rats to be especially susceptible to convulsion-induced retrograde amnesia, McGaugh and Cole (1965) suggested that age and strain

effects might involve differential efficiency of memory.

Not until the late 1960s did researchers begin to employ animals that could be regarded as senescent in genetic designs. Since then, advances in this domain have come primarily from the efforts of three research teams headed by Elias, Goodrick, and Sprott. Elias and colleagues have looked for age-related behavioral differences in mice that had been selectively bred for extremes of blood pressure. Goodrick has chosen to compare behaviors in A/J and C57BL/6J mice, strains that differ significantly in longevity. Sprott's systematic investigations have featured avoidance learning as a paradigm in senescent DBA/2J and C57BL/6J strains, known to differ in this type of learning as juveniles and young adults. To these researchers we now turn for examples of the genetics of differential behavioral aging.

Activity and Motor Performance

In the animal literature on behavioral aging, the best substantiated observation is a marked decline in activity whether measured as distance covered in an open field (Goodrick, 1967, 1975b; Elias, Elias, and Eleftheriou, 1975; Sprott and Eleftheriou, 1974) or as revolutions in an activity wheel (Goodrick, 1974; Wax and Goodrick, 1975; Wax, 1977). In each of the studies, a cross-sectional design compared the relatively active C57BL/6J strain against either the DBA/2J or the A/J strain. In brief, older animals (in the neighborhood of 700 days old or so) are usually less active than younger animals, but the differences between old and young animals within the DBA/2J or A/J strains are not statistically significant. As compared to mice of the C57BL/6J strain, DBA/2J and A/J mice are relatively inactive throughout their lives. For the initially more active C57BL/6J strain, the senescent decline in activity is pronounced.

In a recent investigation (Wax, 1977), mice from the A/J and C57BL/6J strains were given control of ambient light, and records of revolutions in activity wheels were also kept. Mice are nocturnal creatures that are usually most active during periods of darkness. Aged mice of both strains and aged hybrid progeny chose to spend less time in darkness and were, overall, less active than younger mice. However, the senescent decline in activity of the C57BL/6J and hybrid mice was much greater than the decline of the aged A/J. This study in particular exemplifies the explanatory power of genetical designs. Young hybrid progeny were found to be even more active than young C57BL/6J mice, but there were no differences between older hybrids and older C57BL/6J mice.

When the mean of hybrid offspring deviates from the midpoint between the means of the inbred parents, the trait is said to exhibit "heterosis." For a variety of reasons, not all of which are well understood, inbreeding often diminishes the expression of traits that are closely related to biological fitness. This phenomenon of "inbreeding depression" is the reverse of the heterosis seen in hybrid progeny. Wax's data suggest that high activity levels are important for reproductive fitness in younger mice but not in older mice. Such a result demonstrates that the adaptive value of a particular trait changes during the life span and that the ecological demands upon an organism vary with age. In a less general vein, the observation of heterosis at one stage of life and not at another also leads to speculation about the genetic architecture of the trait. A geneticist would, for example, predict that there is more dominance in the direction of high activity in young mice than in old. Such predictions could be tested by examining activity in mice from the crosses of hybrids with the parental lines.

Age and strain effects in activity levels may, in part, reflect differences in neuromuscular function. Recently, Sprott (1980) found deficits in roto-rod performance as early as 18 months in C57BL/6J and DBA/2J mice. The decrement was especially pronounced for DBA/2J mice, providing another example of differential decline dependent upon genotype.

Sensory Processes

Strain differences in the magnitude and rate of decline in sensory integrity have also been discovered. Sprott (1975), for example, observed that maze learning was much more difficult for aged C57BL/6J and DBA/2J mice than for younger mice of the same strain when the solution demanded a simple black-white discrimination. There was, however, no such senescent deficit when the task required a right-left discrimination. Apparently, the ability to discriminate brightness cues is reduced in older animals of both strains, but spatial sense is spared such decrement.

Interactions between strain and age have also been observed for taste discrimination and for progressive hearing loss. Using a typical preference paradigm, Goodrick (1975b) observed that older mice were less able than younger ones to discriminate between either sucrose or quinine solutions and water. However, the magnitude of the difference between old and young groups depended upon strain. C57BL/6J mice drank more sucrose and less quinine at each age than did A/J mice, but the strain differences were greatly diminished in older groups. Strain and age differences in preferences for varying concentrations of alcohol have also been observed (Wood, 1976), and the results suggest that the ability to detect alcohol or the preference for it changes as mice mature and grow old. This work is presented in more detail in the section on alcohol preference below.

Henry (1982), in a preliminary study of progressive high-frequency hearing loss, finessed the problem of confounding motivation and other behavioral factors with sensory ability by recording the electrical discharge of the auditory nerve. Strain differences in auditory nerve response were found in both young and mature mice, and the rate and pattern of loss with respect to different frequencies varied depending upon genotype. Of special note is the fact that age-related changes as measured by auditory nerve response did not parallel changes measured by purely behavioral means (Henry and Cole, 1980).

Learning

The fact of differential decline dependent upon genotype in activity levels, sensory ability, and motor competence seems well-established. Such differences complicate the study of age-related changes in learning because apparent decline in performance might be the result of deterioration in sensory and motor skills or of differential motivation or activity. In view of these problems, Sprott and his colleagues have chosen to focus on a relatively simple paradigm, avoidance conditioning. Sprott's thorough examinations of this illusorily simple behavior have provided revealing glimpses of a complex causal nexus that includes both genetic and age-related variables. In the case of passive avoidance conditioning, for example, young C57BL/6J and mature DBA/2J mice learn passive avoidance relatively well in the presence of strong foot shock, but adult C57BL/6J mice are deficient in the presence of strong shock whereas DBA/2J mice of any age do poorly with mild shock (Sprott, 1972, 1974). During active avoidance conditioning, DBA/2J mice tend to make more escape responses than avoidance responses. In the same situation, C57BL/6J mice avoid better at all ages, but escape responses do become more frequent with advancing age (Stavnes and Sprott, 1975). Although Sprott found an age-related decrement in the passive avoidance learning of both strains, the apparent decrement in the performance of the inbreds vanished when data from older mice who died during the course of testing were eliminated (Sprott, 1978). The obvious conclusion was that the decrement in performance was simply related to failing health. However, all F_1 animals survived the testing, and the performance of the oldest groups was significantly poorer than that of younger groups. Sprott suggested that differential incage aggression was the source of the difference in mortality between hybrids and inbred mice. Inbreds engaged in more fighting than hybrids, and the fights were sometimes fatal. Sprott speculated that sickly mice may have been selectively attacked by their cage mates. Hence, inbred mice in failing health might have been eliminated as the experiment progressed. The relative tranquility of hybrid cage mates, however, permitted even sick mice to finish. If Sprott's explanation is correct, the murine senescent decline in learning may in fact be attributable to physical deterioration rather than to a specific decline in cognitive functions.

Goodrick's (1975b) battery of behavioral measures included an operant task that differentiated young and old mice in two different strains. The oldest mice had attained the ages of 50 percent mortality for their strains, 26 months in the C57BL/6J strain and 23 months in the A/J strain. These senescent mice and 5-month old mice from both strains learned a light-contingent bar-pressing task with equal facility. However, aged mice were more emotional during aquisition and more resistant to extinction. Older C57BL/6J mice, in particular, continued to respond long after reinforcement had been withheld. This strain-by-age interaction suggests that at least some of the behavioral rigidity sometimes alleged to be associated with aging is dependent upon genotype.

Alcohol Preference

Genetically mediated differences in preference for alcohol have been well established (McClearn, 1983). When offered a choice between unadulterated tap water and moderate concentrations of alcohol of 10 to 14 percent (V/V), C57BL mice consumed approximately two-thirds of their total fluid intake from the alcohol solution. In comparison, DBA/2, BALB/cJ, and A/J mice were nearly teetotalists. Wood (1976) investigated the effects of age on alcohol preference in C57BL/6J and BALB/cJ mice. When offered alcohol in concentrations varying from 4 to 18 percent (V/V), alcohol preference scores of young, mature, and old BALB/cJ mice declined sharply with increases in concentration. C57BL/6J mice consumed much more alcohol at each of the ages than did animals of other strains, but the older C57BL/6J mice drank less alcohol than did their younger strain mates. In addition, older C57BL/6J mice failed to show the marked preference for intermediate concentrations (10 to 14 percent) that was characteristic of younger mice of that strain. Similar results were reported by Goodrick (1967) who found that aged C57BL/6J mice preferred alcohol somewhat less than young C57BL/6J mice and that young and old A/J mice tended to avoid alcohol completely. More recently, Goodrick (1978) examined preference in these two strains and in their hybrid F_1 and F_2 generations. A/J mice were nonpreferrers at all ages. The preferences of the hybrid animals were intermediate, but with a mean preference value lower than mid-parent. At 14 months, hybrid preference scores dropped but recovered again at 23 months. In C57BL/6J mice, the 14-month decline was also quite dramatic, but they too drank more alcohol at later ages. The decline in preference at 14 months is a rather surprising and, as yet, unexplained phenomenon. Until the observation is replicated and related to other variables, all that can be drawn from the work is the recognition that quantitative genetic analyses of preference would yield very different conclusions about various genetic and environmental components at different ages.

Rhythmicity

Rhythmicity has also received a little attention in the context of behavioral genetics and aging. Extending their studies of genetic control in neuropsychological development, Oliverio and Malorni (1979) recorded the periodicity of wheel-running activity in 90-day-old and 24-month-old mice from the C57BL/6 and SEC/1ReJ strains. Previous research had shown that the C57BL/6 mice are the more precocial in brain and behavioral development (Oliverio, Castellano, and Puglisi-Allegra, 1975; Alleva, Castellano, and Oliverio, 1979). As adults, C57BL/6 mice maintain fairly rigid circadian rhythms even when challenged by variously shortened light–dark regimes or when subjected to constant light. The activity of SEC mice, on the other hand, was found to be synchronized by the light–dark cycles, and rhythmicity disappeared completely under constant light. At the age of 24 months, the C57BL/6 mice no longer exhibited endogenously maintained periodicity. Like SEC/ReJ mice, their activity was synchronized by light-dark schedules and was completely devoid of rhythmicity under constant light. The researchers assert that the rigid genetic mechanisms that regulate the circadian rhythm of C57BL/6 mice begin to decay in old age.

One aspect of this research that may become particularly useful in the study of aging is the use of pharmacogenetic probes to explore neurophysiological and neurochemical processes (Oliverio, Castellano, and Puglisi-Allegra, 1979; Plomin and Dietrich, 1982). The application of these techniques, for example, has revealed genetically differentiated rates of maturation in cholinergic and adrenergic neurons (Alleva, et al., 1979), but the methods have not yet been applied to the study of senescent behaviors.

Behavioral Correlates of Hypertension

With the single exception of Elias' work, selective breeding has not been applied to research on aging. Elias has studied several behaviors in old and young mice derived from Schlager's high and low blood pressure lines. Although a number of line differences and a few line-by-age interactions appeared, most were found to be independent of differences in blood pressure (Elias and Schlager, 1974; Elias, Elias, and Schlager, 1975; Elias and Pentz, 1977; Elias, 1978).

The problem in presuming causal associations among traits that differentiate "high" and "low" lines is similar to that already discussed in respect to inbred strains. In the case of inbred strain comparisons, we noted that apparently correlated differences in two or more traits do not by themselves prove that the traits are either genetically or environmentally related. Similarly, the observed differences in maze learning ability, activity, and aggressiveness between Schlager's high and low blood pressure lines cannot be attributed as causally related to the blood pressure difference. The number of breeding pairs in any one generation of selection is usually small enough to permit genes not involved with blood pressure to become fixed for different alleles in the high and low lines. It is therefore necessary to check any putative correlations between characters by examining the situation in replicate selection lines if available, or in genetically heterogeneous populations. Elias, Elias, and Schlager (1975), for example, sought behavioral correlates of blood pressure differences among the heterogeneous F_2 generation offspring of progeny derived from a cross between the high and low blood pressure lines. They confirmed only one of the correlations—that between low levels of aggression and high blood pressure—that had been suggested by line comparisons.

The central conclusion to be drawn from this review of the relevant animal research is that genotype does modulate age-related changes in behavior.

GENETICS OF BEHAVIORAL AGING: HUMAN RESEARCH

The important role of genetic factors in human aging is suggested (1) by the existence of heritable disorders with late onset or with symptoms that mimic various pathological aspects of aging; (2) by the association of chromosome loss with aging, neoplastic disease, and cognitive decline; and (3) by results of the longitudinal twin study of Kallmann, Jarvik, and their colleagues.

Presumptive Single Locus Conditions

Some apparently single-locus syndromes are curiously suggestive of accelerated aging. Among the cruelest and most bizzare of these progeroid disorders is the Hutchinson-Gilford syndrome (DeBusk, 1972; Goldstein, 1978). Progeria victims begin slowly to manifest retardation in growth at the end of their first year and seldom attain body heights of greater than 4 feet. Multiple skeletal anomalies, baldness, protuberant eyes, diminished subcutaneous fat, and disproportionately large cranial size provide the appearance of an octogenerian in miniature. Death generally occurs during the second decade of life as a result of cerebrovascular or coronary disease. The few observations of concordance in siblings and of consanguineous marriage between parents of victims are consistent with an hypothesis of transmission by an autosomal recessive gene (McKusick, 1975). However, the fact that most cases are sporadic has prompted several investigators to propose that they are the result of new mutations associated with paternal age (Jones, et al., 1975). Despite the manifold pathology of progeria, case histories describe normal intellectual and psychomotor development. The

victims of progeria seem to be children who want to do the things that other children do, but they are trapped in bodies undergoing extraordinarily rapid deterioration. If progeria does indeed represent aging in fast-forward, the conservation of psychological ability argues that decrement in mental function is not an inevitable correlate of physical senescence. Citing this compartmentalized aspect of progeria, Martin (1978) has proposed that aging occurs in a segmental fashion with the process being controlled by unique combinations of genes for each segment. Werner's disease, for example, is another progeria-type disorder that also suggests a recessive pattern of inheritance. This disease, however, involves a later onset (in the thirties or forties) of a rather different set of symptoms related to aging, including premature graying, osteoporosis, diabetes, etc. The point to be made is that no single disorder can be taken as a complete model of all normal aging processes.

Another approach to the illumination of the role of genes in aging has been to examine known single-locus conditions for any manifestations of aging phenomena. A good example provided by Martin (1978) is that of amyloidosis. Twelve genetically distinct types have been identified; nine of these are apparently dominant in inheritance pattern and three are recessive. Affected individuals show progressive cardiac failure in their forties. Upon autopsy, it is found that amyloid protein fragments have replaced many of the myocardial fibers. This phenomenon is not uncommon in normal aging, but its early onset in amyloidosis, accompanied by no other major symptoms of aging, prompts Martin to describe it as a *unimodal* progeroid condition. Elsewhere, Martin (1978) has reviewed all the known human single-locus conditions in an attempt to identify those that have some aging-like consequences. Some 690 were so identified in McKusick's (1975) catalog of human genetic conditions.

The absence of neurological dysfunction in the progerias stands in contrast to the presenile dementias of which only Huntington's disease, Alzheimer's disease, and Pick's disease will be mentioned here. In each of these progressive neurological disorders, the first morbid signs are behavioral, and these do not appear until middle age or later. Huntington's disease is a standard example of gene action late in life because its transmission as an autosomal dominant is well-documented and because the first symptoms are typically recognized in middle age (McKusick, 1975). The earliest signs of Huntington's disease may be little more than increased irritability, which later proceeds to more overt changes in personality and ends in severe dementia. If dementia precedes the appearance of choreic movement, the behavioral symptoms are easily mistaken for schizophrenia.

Although the underlying pathology of Alzheimer's and Pick's diseases are quite distinct (Corsellis, 1976), they present similar clinical pictures. Deficits in memory and judgment are the insidious prelude to progressive dementia. The greatly increased morbidity risks among relatives of Alzheimer victims have been interpreted to indicate transmission by a dominant allele (Heston and Mastri, 1977; Schenk, 1959; Sjögren, et al., 1952).

Differential Diagnosis

The presenile and senile dementias pose an engaging problem in differential diagnosis. We have already mentioned the occurrence of dementia in Huntington's, Alzheimer's, and Pick's diseases as well as in late-onset schizophrenia. In addition, dementia is not an infrequent consequence of adverse response to drugs or to nutritional insufficiency, especially among the elderly. In a recent evaluation of psychiatric diagnoses, Hoffman (1982) found the diagnosis of irreversible dementia to be inaccurate in 63 percent of the cases. Clearly the development of techniques for differential diagnosis is one of the most critical challenges to researchers in aging, and familial methods may become powerful tools in this endeavor. The recent work of Folstein and Breitner (1982) is a case in point. The Alzheimer's patients fell into two groups, based upon the presence or absence of aphasia and agraphia. The age-adjusted risk for Alzheimer's disease among the sibs and parents of patients with language dysfunction approached 50 percent, a rate consistent with autosomal dominance.

In contrast, the prevalence of dementia among relatives of nonaphasic patients was only 1 percent. It is unlikely that there are only two forms of Alzheimer's disease, one of which is familial and involves language and the other which is nonfamilial and does not, but results such as these predict that etiologically diverse dementias might be sorted out by using pedigree information along with clinical and pathological evaluations.

Chromosomal Anomalies

Various disorders of chromosome number, which are collectively referred to as *aneuploidies,* have been associated with aging (Schneider, 1978) and with malignant disease as well (Moorhead and Saksda, 1968). The most frequently occurring of the congenital aneuploidies is Down's syndrome. Most cases of the latter are believed to be the result of "nondisjunction" between the members of a particular chromosome pair during the formation of sex cells. In this commonest form of Down's syndrome, affected individuals receive the normal number of 23 chromosomes from one parent and 24 from the other. The extra chromosome induces the characteristic facial anomalies and mental retardation that are the prominent features of Down's syndrome. Victims are also stricken by premature senility, and those who live long enough develop the classical Alzheimer neuropathology (Crapper, et al., 1975). Affected persons are also particularly susceptible to malignant disease, especially leukemia (Miller, 1970). The association of Down's syndrome, hematological malignancies, and senile dementia was recently confirmed by Heston and Mastri (1977), who found heightened risks for these disorders among the relatives of Alzheimer's patients. Heston and Mastri (1977) believe that the common thread among these disorders is a genetic defect in the spatial organization of microtubules, cellular components that control the movement of chromosomes during cell divisions.

Another congenital aneuploidy that may be relevant to aging is Turner's syndrome (Turner, 1938; Engel and Forbes, 1965). Affected individuals have only 45 chromosomes—44 autosomes and a single X chromosome (Ford, et al., 1959). The typical clinical pattern of Turner's patients includes short stature, webbed neck, dysgenic ovarian tissue, and infertility. Deficiencies in spatial and mathematical abilities may also characterize this syndrome (Money, 1968, 1970, 1973). Hypertension, osteoporosis, osteoarthritis, thinning of the scalp hair, premature aging of skin, and frequent atherosclerotic and neoplastic disease suggest accelerated aging (Goldstein, 1978). How important Turner's syndrome and other congenital aneuploidies will be as models for the normal aging process remains uncertain, but they do suggest that chromosomal aberrations can accelerate the deterioration of different organ systems.

During the last 15 years, cross-sectional population studies have generally confirmed earlier observations of a correlation between age and chromosome loss (Jacobs, et al., 1966; Mattevi and Salzano, 1975; Schneider, 1978). Unfortunately, recent techniques for staining chromosomes that permit fine resolution of structural details were not available to these researchers. Thus, only gross changes in chromosomes, primarily in chromosome number, are known. Hypodiploidy (fewer chromosomes than normal), involving the X chromosome usually, is reasonably well-documented in older women. However, only one research team (Jarvik et al., 1976; Yen et al., 1976) has attempted a longitudinal assessment. The six-year followup of 11 women and 6 men (whose average age was 89.7 years at the followup) revealed significant increases in both hypodiploidy and hyperdiploidy (excess of chromosomes) in women. Among men, a tendency to lose a small chromosome, presumably the Y chromosome, was also observed but was not statistically significant. The researchers also reported slightly elevated frequencies of chromosomal aberrations among women who died during the six-year interval, but the differences between survivors and decedents in this small sample were not statistically significant.

The causes and consequences of chromosome loss are yet unclear but aneuplodies have been associated with malignant disease (Rowley, 1978; Bloom, McNeill, and Nakamura,

1974; Heston and Mastri, 1977) and with senile decline in mental function (Nielsen, et al., 1968; Nielsen, 1970; Jarvik, Altshuler, Kato, and Blumner, 1971; Bettner, Jarvik, and Blum, 1971). Nielsen et al. (1968, 1970) found that hypodiploidy was most prevalent among women diagnosed as having senile dementia. Working with a few senescent twins, the surviving participants of a twin study begun in the late 1940s, Jarvik and her colleagues observed associations between hypodiploidy and organic brain syndrome (Jarvik, et al., 1971) as well as between hypodiploidy and poor performance on the Graham-Kendall Memory for Designs Test (Jarvik and Kato, 1969) and the Stroop Color-Word Tests (Bettner, et al., 1971).

The data that suggest a correlation between cognitive ability and chromosomal loss are not yet convincing. Samples are so small that when participants are separated into groups based upon sex or type of dementia, only a few cases fall into each of the resulting categories. Furthermore, in the studies of Jarvik and her coworkers, chromosomal aberrations were related to only two of the several cognitive measures used. Finally, Jarvik and Yen (1974) failed to confirm the relation of organic brain syndrome and hypodiploidy in a sample of 78 elderly women. An important question yet to be resolved is whether the chromosomal changes observed in cultured leukocytes bear any relation to *in vivo* changes in other tissues such as, for example, the brain. In summary, an age-related increase in hypodiploidy in women is reasonably well-documented, but the correlation between behavioral change and chromosomal anomalies is still unclear.

Senescent Twins and Behavioral Aging

The longitudinal twin study of Kallmann, Jarvik, and their associates has been widely published during the last two decades. It is the sole research effort to employ a genetic design in the study of normal human behavioral aging. In 1946, Franz Kallmann and Gerhard Sander (1948, 1949) at the New York Psychiatric Institute organized a statewide survey of twins who had attained the age of 60 years. The 1603 twin index cases, members of 1019 twin pairs were followed bienially for several years to study hereditary aspects of morbidity and longevity. Intrapair differences for longevity were consistently smaller for MZ pairs than for DZ pairs (Kallmann, 1953, 1957; Falek, et al., 1960), and MZ twins were more concordant for specific diseases, including cancer (Jarvik and Falek, 1962).

From this original survey population, 75 MZ and 45 DZ same-sex pairs were selected to take part in a psychometric evaluation. The selection criteria required concordance for survival into the seventh decade, literacy, community residence, and reasonably good health. The selected twins were tested twice during the period 1947–1949, and an additional 14 pairs were added to the sample in 1949. The battery included Similarities, Digits Forward and Backward, Digit Symbol Substitution, and Block Design from the Wechsler Bellvue scale (Wechsler, 1944). A vocabulary test from the Stanford-Binet (Terman, 1916) and a Tapping test to evaluate hand-eye coordination and speed completed the battery. Although the twins were an average of 15 years older than Wechsler's oldest standardization groups, the scores of the twins at the initial sessions were similar to those of the oldest normative groups. The contribution of hereditary factors to intellectual performance was confirmed by the fact that intrapair differences were smaller in the MZ sample than in the DZ sample (Kallmann, Feingold, and Bondy, 1951).

Longitudinal assessments that involved most of the survivors occurred in 1955 (Jarvik, et al., 1957) and in 1967 (Blum, et al., 1972). In 1955, only 26 MZ pairs, 10 DZ pairs, and 7 individual twins had survived and were able or willing to complete at least a few tests in the battery. Although average performance had declined on all measures, the only statistically significant differences between the initial testing and the first 10-year follow-up involved the speeded tests, Block Design, Digit Symbol Substitution, and Tapping (Jarvik, et al., 1957). Furthermore, the surviving twins had achieved higher scores at the initial test sessions than did those who had died during the intervening years or who were otherwise unavailable for follow-up. Except for Digit Span,

the average intrapair differences remained larger for DZ twins, but, because of the diminished sample size, the differences between zygosity groups were no longer significant.

Subsequent analyses of these data and of data obtained at the third session in 1967 indicated that decline in speeded tests was a normal concomitant of aging, whereas decline in nonspeeded tasks was associated with impending mortality (Jarvik and Falek, 1963; Jarvik and Blum, 1971). In particular, an annual rate of decline of 2 percent or more on Digit Symbol Substitution, or of 10 percent or more on Similarities, or any decrement on Vocabulary comprised a quantitative definition of *critical loss* that was predictive of mortality within five years (Jarvik and Falek, 1963). Examining the scores of only intact pairs who had completed the "critical loss" tests at the first retest session, Jarvik and Blum (1971) noted that MZ pairs were more concordant (13 out of 21 pairs) for the absence of critical loss than were DZ pairs (two out of five pairs). With so few twin pairs, it is impossible to be certain that the differential concordance is a reliable finding. However, the possibility of genetic influence on the incidence of terminal drop would appear to be a gerontological genetics issue of great importance.

In 1967, the battery was appended by the addition of the Graham-Kendall Memory for Designs Test and the Stroop Color Word Test. Of the 81 surviving twins, there were only 19 intact pairs, 13 MZ and 6 DZ. Although the sample is much too small to yield reliable results, Jarvik, et al. (1972), reported that intraclass correlations for Vocabulary, Similarities, Digits Backward, and Stroop Cards 1 and 2 were statistically significant for MZ pairs only. Nevertheless, the average intrapair differences of MZ and DZ twins had converged. MZ differences had tended to increase whereas DZ differences had decreased, thus eliminating average differences between zygosity groups. The convergence of intrapair differences had also been observed for longevity data (Kallmann, 1957; Falek, et al., 1960). The gradual reduction of intrapair differences in DZ twins on cognitive measures may have been a function of their selection for concordant survival. As suggested by Bank and Jarvik (1978), survival and cognitive functioning may be related and selection for survival might constrain variation in test performance. In other words, concordance for survival may be correlated with concordance for psychological ability. Such an explanation is plausible in the light of other research that demonstrates improved longevity for the intellectually able (Baltes, Schaie, and Nardi, 1971; Jarvik, et al., 1957; Schaie, Labouvie, and Barrett, 1973). What then accounts for the increased intrapair variability of surviving MZ twins? One explanation posits that progressively less efficient regulatory mechanisms permit wider oscillations in cognitive performance. Diminished homeostatic regulation in various physiological systems has been found to accompany aging (Shock, 1977), and similar deregulation in behavioral systems could increase performance differences between members of MZ pairs. Whether such speculations may be deemed reasonable awaits the demonstration of greater intraindividual variability in elderly persons who are repeatedly observed at closely spaced test sessions.

PROSPECTS

In summary, it is probably fair to describe gerontological behavioral genetics as a sparsely populated area surrounded on all sides by vigorous disciplines and interdisciplines and with excellent prospects of maturing into a vital and exciting domain of research. To this point, the applicability of the basic principles of developmental and behavioral genetics has been amply demonstrated in the numerous examples of differential aging functions dependent upon genotype. The continued growth of this hybrid field will demand an exceptional commitment from researchers who are willing to master the methodologies of both genetics and of behavioral development.

Some brief conjectures regarding the likely course of this merger between gerontology and developmental behavioral genetics are in order. In both gerontology and behavioral genetics, cognitive functioning has been at the forefront of concern and is the subject of vigorous debate. It will, no doubt, remain a major focus, but it can be expected increasingly to share the spotlight of research interest with sensory and motor processes and with personality and emotional attributes. Sprott's (1980) critical examination of learning in aged mice serves as a fresh reminder of the distinction between performance and process. As evidence increases of differential developmental courses for different aspects of cognitive functioning as well as for the sensory and motor skills that influence its measurement, we may also expect to see the use of increasingly specific definitions of process. Certainly, for example, future genetic work on human cognitive aging will be expected to be responsive to distinctions such as that between fluid and crystallized intelligence (Horn, 1978).

That behavioral genetics will undoubtedly be characterized by a multivariate perspective is as near a certain bet as could be wished. Behavioral geneticists have not found it to be as useful or as necessary as some disciplinarians to make distinctions among biological, psychological, or social classes of variables. Such disciplinary tolerance would seem to be attuned to the growing consensus that behavioral aspects of aging cannot be fully comprehended without a matrix of information concerning biological and biomedical variables. These expected developments will open many opportunities for genetic analysis. For example, the correlations and covariances among different variables can be partitioned in a twin study in much the same way as genetic and environmental variances are estimated in the univariate case. The result will be an assessment of the underlying relations among variables. An observed correlation might be the result of common genetic influences or of common environmental factors or both. The multivariate emphasis will permit the study of genetic correlations on a grand scale, and the merger of genetic path analysis with its near relative, causal modeling, is full of promise.

In addition to the traditional areas of concern in the psychology of aging, incorporation of biological and biomedical measures will permit the student of gerontological behavioral genetics to address the vexatious problem of distinguishing "normal" aging from phenomena arising from exogenously caused diseases and also to relate to the fundamental biological theories of aging—issues of cellular clocks, of somatic or body cell mutations, of chromosomal abberations, of DNA repair mechanisms, of autoimmunity, of collagen cross-linkage, and so on. In these endeavors especially, animal models would appear to be particularly pertinent as adjuncts to human research. Inbred strains and their derived generations will, of course, remain an important tool, and it is likely that the analysis they permit will increasingly be used. As yet unused in gerontological behavioral genetics are the diallel cross and the recombinant inbred strain designs. In the diallel approach, several inbreds are intercrossed to provide all possible F_1 hybrid groups. This design permits resolution of genetic components and allows, for example, the separation of pre- and post-natal maternal effects. The recently developed methodology of recombinant inbred strains, which are derived by obtaining an F_2 between inbred strains and then creating new inbred lines starting from the F_2, offers a powerful method for searching for single-locus effects and for locating those genes, when found, on specific chromosomes. There is yet little evidence for single or major gene effects on behavioral aging in *Mus musculus,* but they have not much been sought. The recent descriptions of single loci that affect longevity as well as the possibility that progeria and other disorders of aging might be caused by single genes suggest that such a search might be worthwhile. These methods, however, rely upon the identification of differences among genetically defined groups in phenotypes of interest; to an extent, therefore, they depend upon fortuity. Selective breeding offers the researcher the enormous power of a method for building animal models to specification. Is it possible, for example, to breed selectively for animals whose fibroblast doubling number changes relatively quickly or more slowly with respect to chronological age? Will such differences be correlated with differences in longevity? In activity? In other behaviors?

There are also some truly formidable methods to be deployed in the study of heredity of human behavioral aging. The advanced methods of pedigree analysis (Cannings,

Thompson, and Skolnick, 1981; Elston, et al., 1978; Rao and Morton, 1978; Reich, Suarez, Rice, and Cloninger, 1981) employed in a multivariate framework that can illuminate issues of differential etiology might well clarify the mode of inheritance of Alzheimer's disease, of the progerias, and of other putative single gene "aging" conditions. The identification of appropriate study populations (mid-life twins and adoptees, for example) will similarly allow the utilization of the traditional analytic procedures of behavioral genetics. It is clear, however, that there are difficult problems, both theoretical and practical, to be resolved before the methods of gerontological and genetical sciences can be effectively merged. It will be, we think, well worth the trouble.

REFERENCES

Alleva, E.; Castellano, C.; and Oliverio, A. 1979. Ontogeny of behavioral development, arousal and stereotypes in two strains of mice. *Experimental Aging Research* 5: 335–350.

Baltes, P. B.; Schaie, K. W.; and Nardi, A. H. 1971. Age and experimental mortality in a seven-year longitudinal study of cognitive behavior. *Developmental Psychology* 5: 18–26

Bank, L., and Jarvik, L. F. 1978. A longitudinal study of aging human twins. In *The Genetics of Aging,* ed. E. L. Schneider, pp. 303–333. New York: Plenum Press.

Bartus, R. T.; Dean, R. L., III; Beer, B.; and Lippa, A. S. 1982. The cholinergic hypothesis of geriatric memory dysfunction. *Science* 217: 408–417.

Bergsma, D., and Harrison, D. E., eds. 1978. *Genetic Effects on Aging.* New York: Alan R. Liss.

Bettner, L. G.; Jarvik, L. F.; and Blum, J. E. 1971. Stroop color-word test, nonpsychotic organic brain syndrome and chromosome loss in aged twins. *Journal of Gerontology* 26: 458–469.

Bloom, A. D.; McNeill, J. A.; and Nakamora, F. T. 1974. Cytogenetics of lymphocyte cell lines. In *Chromosomes and Cancer,* ed. J. German, pp. 565–599. New York: John Wiley & Sons.

Blum, J. E.; Fosshage, J. L.; and Jarvik, L. F. 1972. Intellectual changes and sex differences in octogenarians: A twenty-year longitudinal study of aging. *Developmental Psychology* 7: 178–187.

Britten, R. J., and Davidson, E. H. 1969. Gene regulation for higher cells: A theory. *Science* 165: 349–357.

Bronson, F. H.; Dagg, C. P.; and Snell, G. D. 1968. Reproduction. In *Biology of the Laboratory Mouse,* ed. E. L. Green, pp. 187–204. New York: Dover Publications.

Cannings, C.; Thompson, E. A.; and Skolnick, M. 1981. Pedigree analysis of complex models. In *Theory and Methods: Current developments in anthropological ge-*

netics, eds. J. H. Mielke and M. H. Crawford, vol. 1, pp. 251–298. New York: Plenum Press.

Corsellis, J. A. N. 1976. Aging and the dementias. In *Greenfield's Neuropathology,* eds. W. Blackwood and J. A. N. Corsellis, pp. 796–848. London: Edward Arnold.

Crapper, D. R.; Dalton, A. J.; Skopitz, M.; Scott, J. W.; and Hachinski, J. C. 1975. Alzheimer degeneration in Down syndrome: Electrophysiologic alterations and histopathologic findings. *Archives Neurology* 33: 618–623.

DeBusk, F. L. 1972. The Hutchinson-Gilford progeria syndrome: Report of four cases and review of the literature. *Journal of Pediatrics* 80 (Part 2): 695–724.

DeFries, J. C. 1964. Prenatal maternal stress in mice: Differential effects on behavior. *Journal of Heredity* 55: 289–295.

Dixon, L. K., and DeFries, J. C. 1968. Development of open-field behavior in mice: Effects of age and experience. *Developmental Psychobiology* 1: 100–107.

Ehrman, L., and Parsons, P. S. 1976. *The Genetics of Behavior.* Sunderland, MA: Sinaver Associates.

Ehrman, L., and Parsons, P. A. 1981. *Behavior Genetics and Evolution.* New York: McGraw-Hill.

Elias, M. F. 1978. Some contributions of genetic selection to the study of hypertension and behavior over the life span: Methodologic considerations and useful future directions. In *Genetic Effects on Aging,* eds. D. Bergsma, D. E. Harrison, and N. W. Paul, pp. 121–156. New York: Alan R. Liss.

Elias, P. K.; Elias, M. F.; and Eleftheriou, B. E. 1975. Emotionality, exploratory behavior, and locomotion in aging inbred strains of mice. *Gerontologia,* 21: 46–55.

Elias, M. F.; Elias, J. W.; and Schlager, G. 1975. Aggressive social interaction in mice genetically selected for blood pressure extremes. *Behavioral Biology* 13: 155–166.

Elias, M. F., and Pentz, C. A., III. 1977. Blood pressure extremes and activity in aging mice. *Physiological Behavior* 19: 811–813.

Elias, M. F., and Schlager, G. 1974. Discrimination learning in mice genetically selected for high and low blood pressure. *Physiological Behavior* 13: 261–267.

Engel, E., and Forbes, A. P. 1965. Cytogenetic and clinical findings in 48 patients with congenitally defective or absent ovaries. *Medicine* 44: 135–164.

Elston, R. C.; Namboodiri, K. K.; and Kaplan, E. B. 1978. Resolution of major loci for quantitative traits. In *Genetic Epidemiology,* eds. N. E. Morton and C. S. Chung, pp. 223–253. New York: Academic Press.

Falconer, D. S. 1981. *Introduction to Quantitative Genetics.* 2nd ed. New York: Longman Inc.

Falek, A.; Kallmann, F. J.; Lorge, I.; and Jarvik, L. F. 1960. Longevity and intellectual variation in a senescent twin population. *Journal of Gerontology* 15: 305–309.

Fisher, R. A. 1918. The correlation between relatives on the supposition of Mendelian inheritance. *Transactions of the Royal Society of Edinburgh,* 52: 399–433.

Folstein, M. F., and Breitner, J. C. S. 1982. Language disorder predicts familial Alzheimer's disease. In *Alzheimer's Disease: A Report of Progress,* eds. S. Corkin,

K. L. Davis, J. H. Growden, E. Usdin, and R. J. Wurtman, vol. 19, 197–200. New York: Rowen Press.

Ford, C. E.; Kones, K. W.; Polani, P. E.; DeAlmeida, J. C.; and Briggs, J. H. 1959. A sex chromosome anomaly in a case of gonadae dysgenesis (Turner's syndrome). *Lancet* 1: 711.

Fraser, F. C.; Kalter, H.; Walker, B. E.; and Fainstat, T. D. 1954. The experimental production of cleft palate with cortisone and other hormones. *Journal of Cellular and Comparative Physiology* 43: 237–259.

Fuller, J. L., and Thompson, W. R. 1960. *Behavior Genetics.* New York: John Wiley & Sons, Inc.

Fuller, J. L., and Thompson, W. R. 1978. *Foundations of Behavior Genetics.* St. Louis: C. V. Mosby.

Goldstein, S. 1978. Human genetic disorders and premature biological aging. In *The Genetics of Aging,* ed. E. L. Schneider, pp. 171–224. New York: Plenum Press.

Goodrick, C. 1967. Behavioral characteristics of young senescent inbred female mice of the C57BL/6J strain. *Journal of Gerontology* 22: 459–464.

Goodrick, C. L. 1974. The effects of exercise on longevity and behavior of hybrid mice which differ in coat color. *Journal of Gerontology* 29: 129–133.

Goodrick, C. L. 1975a. Life span and the inheritance of longevity for inbred mice. *Journal of Gerontology* 30: 257–263.

Goodrick, C. L. 1975b. Behavioral differences in young and aged mice: Strain differences for activity measures, operant learning, sensory discrimination, and alcohol preference. *Experimental Aging Research* 1: 191–207.

Goodrick, C. 1978. Ethanol selection by inbred mice: Mode of inheritance and the effect of age on the genetic system. *Journal of Studies on Alcohol* 39: 19–38.

Hall, C. S. 1951. The genetics of behavior. In *Handbook of Experimental Psychology,* ed. S. S. Stevens, pp. 304–329. New York: John Wiley & Sons, Inc.

Ham, R. G., and Veomett, M. J. 1980. *Mechanisms of Development.* St. Louis: C. V. Mosby.

Harris, H. 1980. *The Principles of Human Biochemical Genetics.* 3rd ed. Amsterdam/New York/Oxford: Elsevier/North-Holland Biomedical Press.

Henderson, N. D. 1982. Human behavior genetics. *Annual Review of Psychology,* 33: 403–440.

Henry, K. R. 1982. Influence of genotype and age on noise-induced auditory losses. *Behavior Genetics* 12: 563–573.

Henry, K. R., and Cole, R. A. 1980. Genotypic differences in behavioral, physiological and anatomical expressions of age-related hearing loss in the laboratory mouse. *Audiology* 19: 369–383.

Heston, L. L., and Mastri, A. R. 1977. The genetics of Alzheimer's disease: Associations with hematologic malignancy and Down's syndrome. *Archives of General Psychiatry* 34: 976–981.

Hoffman, R. S. 1982. Diagnostic errors in the evaluation of behavioral disorders. *Journal of the American Medical Association* 248: 964–967.

Honzik, M. P. 1957. Developmental studies of parent-child resemblance in intelligence. *Child Development* 28: 215–228.

Horn, J. L. 1978. Human ability systems. In *Life-Span*

Development and Behavior, eds. P. B. Baltes and O. G. Brin, Jr., vol. 1, pp. 212–256. New York: Academic Press.

Jacobs, P. A., and Court Brown, W. M. 1966. Age and chromosomes. *Nature* 212: 823–824.

Jarvik, L. F.; Altshuler, K. Z.; Kato, T., and Blumner, B. 1971. Organic brain syndrome and chromosome loss in aged twins. *Diseases of the Nervous System* 32: 159–170.

Jarvik, L. F., and Blum, J. E. 1971. Cognitive decline as predictors of mortality in twin pairs: A twenty-year longitudinal study of aging. In *Prediction of Life Span,* eds. E. Palmore and F. C. Jeffers, pp. 199–211. Lexington, MA: Heath Lexington.

Jarvik, L. F.; Blum, J. E.; and Varma, A. D. 1972. Genetic components and intellectual functioning during senescence: A 20-year study of aging twins. *Behavior Genetics* 2: 159–171.

Jarvik, L. F., and Falek, A. 1962. Comparative data on cancer in aging twins. *Cancer* 15: 1009–1018.

Jarvik, L. F., and Falek, A. 1963. Intellectual stability and survival in the aged. *Journal of Gerontology* 18: 173–176.

Jarvik, L. F.; Kallmann, F. J.; Falek, A., and Klaber, M. M. 1957. Changing intellectual functions in senescent twins. *Acta Genetica et Statistica Medica* 7: 421–430.

Jarvik, L. F., and Kato, T. 1969. Chromosomes and mental changes in octogenerians: Preliminary findings. *British Journal of Psychiatry* 115: 1193–1194.

Jarvik, L. F., and Yen, F-S. 1974. Chromosomes and mental status. *Archives of General Psychiatry* 30: 186–194.

Jarvik, L. F.; Yen, F-S.; Fu, T. K.; and Matsuyama, S. S. 1976. Chromosomes in old age: A six-year longitudinal study. *Human Genetics* 33: 17–22.

Jinks, J. L., and Fulker, D. W. 1970. Comparison of the biometrical, genetical, MAVA, and classical approaches to the analysis of human behavior. *Psychological Bulletin* 73: 311–349.

Jones, K. L.; Smith, D. W.; Harvey, M. A.; Hall, B. D., and Quan, L. 1975. Older paternal age and fresh gene mutation: Data on additional disorders. *Journal of Pediatrics* 86: 84–88.

Kallmann, F. J. 1953. *Heredity in Health and Mental Disorder.* New York: W. W. Norton & Co.

Kallmann, F. J. 1957. Twin data on the genetics of aging. In *Methodology of the Study of Ageing* ("Ciba Foundation Colloquia on Ageing"), eds. G. E. Wolstenhoime and C. M. O'Connor, pp. 131–143. London: J. & A. Churchill.

Kallmann, F. J.; Feingold, L.; and Bondy, E. 1951. Comparative, adaptational, social, and psychometric data on the life histories of senescent twin pairs. *American Journal of Human Genetics* 3: 65–73.

Kallmann, F. J., and Sander, G. 1948. Twin studies on aging and longevity. *Journal of Heredity* 39: 349–357.

Kallmann, F., and Sander, G. 1949. Twin studies on senescence. *American Journal of Psychiatry* 106: 29–36.

Lindzey, G.; Lykken, D. T.; and Winston, H. D. 1960.

Infantile trauma, genetic factors, and adult temperament. *Journal of Abnormal and Social Psychology* 61: 7–14.

Lindzey, G.; Winston, H. E., and Manosevitz, M. 1963. Early experience, genotype, and temperament in *mus musculus. Journal of Comparative Physiological Psychology* 56: 622–629.

Martin, G. M. 1978. Genetic syndromes in man with potential relevance to the pathobiology of aging. In *Genetic Effects on Aging,* eds. D. Bergsma and D. E. Harrison, pp. 5–39. New York: Alan R. Liss, Inc.

Matheny, A. P.; Wilson, R. S.; and Dolan, A. B. 1976. Relations between twins similarity of appearance and behavioral similarity: Testing an assumption. *Behavior Genetics* 6: 343–352.

Mattevi, M. S., and Salzano, F. M. 1975. Senesence and human chromosome changes. *Humangenetik* 27: 1–8.

McClearn, G. E. 1962. The inheritance of behavior. In *Psychology in the Making,* ed. L. Postman, pp. 144–252. New York: Knopf.

McClearn, G. E. 1983. Genetic factors in alcohol abuse: Animal models. In *The Biology of Alcoholism,* eds. B. Kissin and H. Begleiter, vol. 6, New York: Plenum Press.

McClearn, G. E.; Deitrich, R. A.; and Erwin, V. G., eds. 1981. *Development of Animal Models as Pharmacogenetic Tools.* DHEW Publication No. (ADM) 81–1133. Washington, DC: U.S. Government Printing Office.

McGaugh, J. L., and Cole, J. M. 1965. Age and strain differences in the effect of distribution of practice on maze learning. *Psychonomic Science* 2: 253–254.

McKusick, V. A. 1975. *Mendelian Inheritance in Man—Catalogs of Autosomal Dominant, Autosomal Recessive and X-Linked Phenotypes.* Baltimore, MD: Johns Hopkins University Press.

Meier, G. W. 1964. Differences in maze performances as a function of age and strain of housemice. *Journal of Comparative and Physiological Psychology* 58: 418–422.

Meier, G. W., and Foshee, D. P. 1963. Genetics, age and the variability of learning performances. *The Journal of Genetic Psychology* 102: 267–275.

Miller, R. W. 1970. Neoplasia and Down's syndrome. *Annals of New York Academy of Science* 171: 637–644.

Money, J. 1964. Cognitive deficits in Turner's syndrome. 1968. In *Progress in Human Behavior Genetics,* ed. S. G. Vandenberg, pp. 27–30. Baltimore: Johns Hopkins University Press.

Money, J. 1970. Behavior genetics: Principles, methods and examples from XO, XXY, and XYY syndromes. *Seminars in Psychiatry* 2: 11–29.

Money, J. 1973. Turner's syndrome and parietal lobe functions. *Cortex* 9: 387–393.

Monteiro, L. S., and Falconer, D. S. 1966. Compensatory growth and sexual maturity in mice. *Animal Production* 8: 179–192.

Moorhead, P. S., and Saksda, E. 1968. Non-random chromosomal aberrations—SV40 transformed human cells. *Journal of Cellular Comparative Physiology* 62: 57–84.

Nielsen, J. 1970. Chromosomes in senile, presenile, and arteriosclerotic dementia. *Journal of Gerontology* 25: 312–315.

Nielsen, J.; Jensen, L.; Lindhardt, H.; Stottrup, L.; and Sondergaard, A. 1968. Chromosomes in senile dementia. *British Journal of Psychology* 114: 303.

Oliverio, A.; Castellano, C.; and Puglisi-Allegra, S. 1975. Effects of genetic and nutritional factors on post-natal reflex and behavioral development in the mouse. *Experimental Aging Research* 1: 41–56.

Oliverio, A.; Castellano, C.; and Puglisi-Allegra, S. 1979. A genetic approach to behavioral plasticity and rigidity. In *Theoretical Advances in Behavioral Genetics,* ed. J. R. Royce, pp. 139–165. Alphen aan den Rijn, Netherlands: Sijthoff Noordhoff International.

Oliverio, A., and Malorni, W. 1979. Wheel running and sleep in two strains of mice: Plasticity and rigidity in the expression of circadian rhythmicity. *Brain Research* 163: 121–133.

Orgel, L. E. 1963. The maintenance of the accuracy of protein synthesis and its relevance to aging. *Proceedings of the National Academy of Science* 49: 517–521.

Plomin, R.; Willerman, L.; and Loehlin, J. C. 1976. Resemblance in appearance and the equal environments assumption in twin studies of personality traits. *Behavior Genetics* 6: 43–52.

Plomin, R.; DeFries, J. C.; and McClearn, G. E. 1980. *Behavioral Genetics, A Primer.* San Francisco: Freeman.

Plomin, R., and Deitrich, R. A. 1982. Neuropharmocogenetics and behavioral genetics. *Behavior Genetics* 12: 111–121.

Rao, D. C., and Morton, N. E. 1978. IQ as a paradigm in genetic epidemiology. In *Genetic Epidemiology,* eds. N. E. Morton and C. S. Chung, pp. 145–193. New York: Academic Press.

Rao, D. C., and Morton, N. E. 1981. Path analysis of quantitative inheritance. In *Theory and Methods.* Current developments in anthropological genetics, eds. J. H. Mielke and M. H. Crawford, pp. 355–372. New York: Plenum Press.

Reich, T.; Suarez, B.; Rice, J.; and Cloninger, C. R. 1981. Current directions in genetic epidemiology. Chapter 10 in *Theory and Methods.* Current developments in anthropological genetics, eds. J. H. Mielke and M. H. Crawford, vol. I, pp. 251–298. New York: Plenum Press.

Ritter, B. 1978. Effect of chronic restraint on open field activity of aging C57BL/6N mice. *Experimental Aging Research* 4: 87–95.

Rowley, J. D. 1978. A possible role for nonrandom chromosomal changes in human hematologic malignancies. *Chromosomes Today* 6: 345–355.

Schaie, K. W.; Labouvie, G. V.; and Barrett, T. J. 1973. Selective attrition effects in a fourteen-year study of adult intelligence. *Journal of Gerontology* 25: 171–176.

Scarr, S., and Carter-Saltzman, L. 1979. Twin method: Defense of a critical assumption. *Behavior Genetics* 9: 527–542.

Schenk, V. W. D. 1959. Reexamination of a family with Pick's disease. *Annals of Human Genetics* 23: 325–333.

Schneider, E. L. 1978. Cytogenetics of aging. In *The Genetics of Aging,* ed. E. L. Schneider, pp. 27–52. New York: Plenum Press.

Shock, N. W. 1977. System integration. In *Handbook of the Biology of Aging,* eds. C. E. Finch and L. Hayflick, pp. 639–665. New York: Van Nostrand Reinhold Co.

Sjögren, T.; Sjögren, H., and Lindgren, A. G. H. 1952. Morbus Alzheimer and morbus Pick. *Acta Psychiatrica et Neurologica Scandinavica* 82(Supplement): 1–152.

Sprott, R. L. 1972. Passive-avoidance conditioning in inbred mice: Effects of shock intensity, age, and genotype. *Journal of Comparative Physiological Psychology* 80: 327–334.

Sprott, R. L. 1974. Passive-avoidance performance in mice: Evidence for single locus inheritance. *Behavioral Biology* 11: 231–237.

Sprott, R. L. 1975. Behavioral characteristics of C57BL/6J, DBA/2J, and B6D2F$_1$ mice which are potentially useful for gerontological research. *Experimental Aging Research* 1: 313–323.

Sprott, R. L. 1978. The interaction of genotype and environment in the determination of avoidance behavior of aging inbred mice. In *Genetic Effects on Aging,* eds. D. Bergsma and D. E. Harrison, pp. 109–120. New York: Alan R. Liss.

Sprott, R. L. 1980. Senescence and learning behavior in mice. In *Age, Learning Ability, and Intelligence,* ed. R. L. Sprott, pp. 26–40. New York: Van Nostrand Reinhold Co.

Sprott, R. L., and Eleftheriou, B. E. 1974. Open-field behavior in aging inbred mice. *Gerontologia* 20: 155–162.

Stavnes, K., and Sprott, R. L. 1975. Effects of age and genotype on acquisition of an active avoidance response in mice. *Developmental Psychobiology* 8: 437–445.

Stunkard, A. J., ed. 1980. *Obesity.* Philadelphia: W. B. Saunders Co.

Terman, L. M. 1916. *The Measurement of Intelligence.* Boston, MA: Houghton Mifflin.

Therman, E. 1980. *Human Chromosomes, Structure, Behavior Effects.* New York: Springer-Verlag.

Turner, H. H. 1938. A syndrome of infantilism, congenital webbed neck and cubitus valgus. *Endocrinology* 23: 566–574.

Waddington, C. H. 1957. *The Strategy of the Genes.* New York: The Macmillan Co.

Wax, T. M. 1977. Effects of age, strain and illumination intensity on activity and self-selection of light-dark schedules in mice. *Journal of Comparative Physiological Psychology* 91: 51–62.

Wax, T., and Goodrick, C. 1975. Voluntary exposure to light by young and aged albino and pigmented inbred mice as a function of light intensity. *Developmental Psychobiology* 8: 297–303.

Wechsler, D. 1944. *The Measurement of Adult Intelligence.* Baltimore, MD: Williams and Wilkins.

Weir, M. W., and DeFries, J. C. 1964. Prenatal maternal influence on behavior in mice: Evidence of a genetic basis. *Journal of Comparative Physiological Psychology* 58: 412–417.

Wilson, R. S. 1978. Synchronies in mental development: An epigenetic perspective. *Science* 202: 939–948.

Wood, W. G. 1976. Ethanol preference in C57BL/6 and BALB/c mice at three ages and eight ethanol concentrations. *Experimental Aging Research* 2:425–434.

Yen, F. S.; Matsuyama, S. S.; and Jarvik, L. F. 1976. Survival of octogenarians: Six years after initial chromosome examination. *Experimental Aging Research* 2: 17–26.

6
HEALTH BEHAVIOR RELATIONSHIPS

Ilene C. Siegler
Duke University
and
Paul T. Costa, Jr.
Laboratory of Behavioral Sciences

INTRODUCTION AND THEORETICAL ISSUES

This chapter deals with the interactions and complexities in health behavior relationships during the adult years of the life cycle. It raises two basic questions: (1) How does health affect behavior with advancing age? and (2) How does behavior affect health with advancing age? The studies reviewed in this chapter are not integrated by common theory, definitions, or methodology for the very good reason that they represent the contributions of many disciplines.

It might well be argued that health problems are so pervasive and so central to the well-being of older individuals that almost any discussion of health would be relevant to a volume on aging. However, concerns with age and behavior raise specific questions. For example, are the principles of behavioral medicine equally applicable to older individuals as well as to younger ones? Are the harmful influences of illness on social interaction amplified by the social position of many of the aged?

The division of this chapter into three parts —the effects of health on behavior, of behavior on illness, and of health-related behavior—is somewhat artificial but nevertheless represents an organizational schema related to the disciplines involved in research. Health and behavior are both broadly defined. Although health as reviewed here is primarily conceived of as physical health, the ability to distinguish physical from mental health may vary as a function of age. Physical and mental health problems may appear to be more distinct earlier in the life cycle. Moreover, disorders that present both physical and mental symptoms, as well as multiple disorders, are more likely to be seen in later life. The distinction is further blurred in the case of a disease such as dementia, where diagnosis is made purely in behavioral terms (Jarvik, 1980) or in diseases where the early symptoms are those characteristic of general poor health and declining vigor, as with many cancers (Fox, 1978).

The majority of the observations reviewed here concern data from human rather than animal studies. Behavior is considered in broad psychosocial terms to include cognitive and intellectual functioning, personality, and general coping through activities related to self-care. We are not concerned with the approximately 7 percent of the elderly whose physical limitations impose severe restrictions (Branch, 1977) but rather with the vast majority whose varying health influences their behavior in various ways, and vice versa.

Implications of Health/Behavior Relationships

Age and illness are often so intertwined that the student of behavior across the life cycle is constantly confronted with the need to distinguish them conceptually and empirically from one another. One of the ways in which individuals typically differ at different ages is in health status. Often observed differences in behavior are the result of health differences that may be correlated with, but not necessarily caused by, age differences. This fact can be documented for many different conditions (USDHEW, 1978). The economic implications of rising health care costs for older persons are well known. Subjectively, health is one of the few areas in which older Americans show lower levels of life satisfaction than the young (Campbell, Converse, and Rogers, 1976).

There are both scientific and social reasons for preferring to view aging and illness as separate entities. If we can show that age changes in a particular behavior are the result of age-related health changes, we hold out the promise of improving performance or quality of life by curing the illness—a promise that may inspire both research and increased efforts toward treatment. In addition, older persons themselves and the family members who care for them may be more inclined to seek treatment if they have reason to believe that their problem is not an inevitable consequence of the aging process (Besdine, 1981).

Busse (1969; 1978) offered one of the clearer statements of this issue by making a distinction between *primary* and *secondary* aging. Primary aging refers to the inherent, normal changes that occur with age; secondary aging, to changes that result from illnesses that accompany aging. This is a distinction that changes over time as disease processes are identified and understood. Changes once thought to be irreversible aspects of primary aging are being shifted into the category of secondary aging.

Methodological Implications

Sound empirical research in this area is beset by formidable methodological problems (Siegler, Nowlin, and Blumenthal, 1980). Methodological choices depend, in part, on perspectives that arise from decisions about the health screening of older subjects. If illness is an intrinsic part of the aging process, then data should be gathered without regard to the subjects' medical status. On the other hand, if illness is distinct from aging, subjects should be screened for certain illnesses before the effects of age are investigated. Though the latter solution is appealing, it can be carried to extremes. "Normal" aging in a group screened for all measurable diseases may produce norms characteristic of the rare biological elite only. This elite group may be of great theoretical significance but little practical importance.

Two basic research strategies are used for the resolution of these problems, and a third is to be recommended; the latter combines the two traditional approaches.

The first approach includes everyone capable of participating and makes no distinction as to health status. This method is recommended if the investigator wishes to generalize to the "complete" population within the age range of interest. It makes a powerful tool for studies in which no aging effect is hypothesized, as in studies of personality (Costa and Mc Crae, 1980a) or of crystallized intelligence (Horn, 1970). If no cross-sectional age differences are observed despite the effects of both age and whatever illness may be present, the stability of a behavior is forcefully demonstrated.

In the second approach, individuals are screened for all diseases that might be relevant. When the level of health/illness is biased toward the health side, the process can be called a "clinical clean-up." Such a clean-up is more common in multidisciplinary longitudinal studies (Shock, et al., 1984) for which detailed medical evaluations as well as behavioral data are available, and it is probably more often applied to biomedical and cognitive rather than to psychosocial data. Age differences or changes that appear despite the medical screening are thought to represent primary aging, although the failure to include the relevant medical "control" variables in the screening presents an unanswerable rival hypothesis.

The third approach combines the first two.

Most investigations of behavior and aging should take some account of health status. Researchers often use the criterion of "healthy enough to get to the laboratory." Many of those who have developed health screening questionnaires that note current diagnoses and medications fail to use this information in their analyses.

Analyses should be made of the unscreened full sample and of the screened subsample(s). Additional analyses might also distinguish between different levels of health or between different reported conditions. Following such a plan would allow the investigators to make a direct examination of the impact of health status on the behavior in question. If healthy and ill individuals of the same age perform differently, and if they are otherwise comparable, then the behavior under study may well be a function of health rather than age. Interactions in which age and health both operate to decrement performance might also be observed. In these ways, the researcher can maximize both the interpretability and generalizability of his design.

Toward the Design of Better Studies

Data collected without regard to health status often results in the absence of important data (e.g., intelligence test data from demented persons or mobility data from arthritics), data with extraordinarily high variance, or bimodality within the older group. This is particularly true of the middle and "young-old" age ranges, where variations in health are less likely to result in subjects being disqualified from a study than would be the case among the very old.

Screening individuals for health status reduces a source of between-age-group variation by making the health/illness profiles of younger and older individuals basically equivalent.

A second variant of health screening selects a younger and an older group with the same disorder and then compares them to healthy age-matched control groups. As in any cross-sectional attribution (Elias and Streeten, 1980), it is important to note that group differences may not reflect individual declines caused by the disease since these differences may have antedated the illness. It is also important that the control population be carefully drawn.

A third consideration concerns the particular disorder chosen for study. In studies that control for "health" or compare "healthy vs. ill" groups of subjects, the various diseases under study may be expected to have different behavioral consequences. For example, in their study of stress, coping, and psychological adjustment among the chronically ill, Felton and her coworkers (Felton and Revenson, 1981) chose four groups of middle-aged and older patients. Their subjects included groups with hypertension, diabetes, rheumatoid arthritis, and blood cancers in order to vary the degree of controllability and intrusiveness of the disorder and presumably the degree of stress. Groups with particular disorders may play an important role in the design of studies such as this one by Felton and her colleagues. Since particular disorders may be expected to have particular behavioral effects, populations that are likely to be subject to ill health may fail to produce consistent effects if different illnesses produce different effects. Similar considerations apply to the medications prescribed for a large collection of disorders (e.g., CNS stimulants vs. depressants).

The preferred design, which includes both healthy and carefully characterized ill subjects, can incur considerable cost, both in the gathering of the health data (for the behaviorally oriented researcher) and the behavioral data (for the medical researcher). Physician examination is always costly, but there are many cases where it may not be required. Relying on self-reports of health status (see, e.g., Hickey, 1980, Chap. 3; Siegler et al., 1980, pp. 602–605; Ware, Brook, Davies and Lohr, 1981) is a cost-effective measure that would make a useful addition to many behavioral studies. If the data thus gathered indicates the importance of health to an investigation, a later study with complete medical data may be necessary. A more troublesome problem, which arises in complex experimental designs where health parameters may interact with experimental conditions, is the need to examine additional subjects. When the cost in both time and money is proportional to the amount of information that can be reasonably gained, thought should be given to selecting extra subjects of a known health status. If simple health questionnaires are collected and analyzed routinely, this may be an efficient way of discovering when additional subjects need to be studied.

Role of Mortality Statistics in Theory Formation

A final set of theoretical concerns has to do with the role of mortality statistics in health behavior relationships. Neither survival, death, nor cause of death are random events. In general, one dies of some illness. The concept of natural death is invoked, however, whenever it appears that homeostatic mechanisms have failed to the point at which any perturbation in the system is sufficient to cause death (Fries, 1980; Fries and Crapo, 1981).

Despite the fact that cardiovascular disease is the primary cause of death in the U.S., its mortality rate has decreased by more than 30 percent in the past 30 years—with much of that gain in life expectancy occurring between 1970 and 1980 (Levy and Moskowitz, 1982). McGinnis (1982) reports that the life expectancy of a 45-year-old increased by 6.6 percent in the same decade while the life expectancy of a newborn increased by only 4 percent. Siegel (1980) reported that overall mortality during the nine-year period from 1968 to 1977 declined 18 percent for those aged 65 to 74. Additionally, if all mortality currently caused by cardiovascular disease were eliminated, the gain in life expectancy would be 12 years at birth and 11 years at age 65. If all deaths from cancer were eliminated, the corresponding figures would be 2½ and 1½ years. The changes at age 65 would be much smaller in the case of cancer because of the relatively more equal distribution of cancer across the life cycle. In the past 15 years, there has been a decline in cancer mortality in individuals under age 45 of from 20 to 43 percent, which has been countered by an increase in cancer mortality in those over 45, primarily as a result of smoking-related cancers (Frei, 1982).

These data suggest that behaviors at all stages of the life cycle, including health-related behaviors in later life, may well produce changes in life expectancy in the coming decades. Changes in mortality and patterns of mortality are important to the extent that theories of aging are designed to account for the data. When the data change, theory should also change. Mortality declined rapidly in the 1940s and early 1950s, then stabilized. In the decade 1968–1978, the mortality of the elderly declined again (Fingerhurt and Rosenberg, 1981). Recent demographic considerations suggest that the time may be at hand for revamping the assumptions that underlie current theoretical work in the biology of aging (Manton, 1982).

Geriatric Medicine

The impact of aging on health is a major concern of geriatric medicine. Various recent texts (e.g., Brocklehurst, 1978; Exton-Smith and Overstall, 1979; Friedman and Steinheber, 1976; Schrier, 1982; Steinberg, 1976) and articles in Annual Reviews (e.g., Crawford and Cohen, in press; Eisdorfer, 1980; 1981) deal with the impact of age on the body systems and on the differential presentation of symptomatology. Rarely are the potential behavioral manifestations discussed. A welcome addition is a volume dealing with the psychiatric manifestations of physical disorders (Levensen and Hall, 1981).

HEALTH AND ITS IMPACT ON BEHAVIOR

This is the traditional research area in which the topic of health/behavior relationships is raised within the psychology of aging. (See Abrahams, 1976; Eisdorfer and Wilkie, 1977; Elias, Elias, and Elias, 1977; and Siegler, 1980, for reviews.)

Ideally, this section of the chapter would be organized in the style of a matrix, with specific health conditions constituting the rows of the matrix, and various behaviors, the columns. The cells of the matrix would then report the findings of the effects (or absence of effects) of the conditions on the behaviors. However, most of the cells would be empty for lack of appropriate data. We shall therefore review the major findings to date by behavioral class.

It is clear that acute illness has profound influences on behavior. Affective responses and limitations in cognitive performance in response to illness are well known to occur across the life cycle. The effects of chronic conditions, such as heart and kidney disease, cancers, and arthritis, however, are less well understood.

Personality

Age in itself appears to have little impact on personality functioning (Neugarten, 1977). A series of longitudinal studies (Costa and Mc Crae, 1978; Leon, Gillum, Gillum, and Gooze, 1979; Mc Crae, Costa, and Arenberg, 1980; Siegler, George, and Okun, 1979) tend to find very few normative changes caused by age/cohort status. They also tend to find stability of sex differences. By and large, there is remarkable stability of individual differences, with 12-year retest coefficients rivaling the short-term retest reliability of the instruments. Since all these studies were analyzed without screening for medical/health status, it seems that neither health status nor changes in health status over the course of 8 to 12 years (for survivors) has a marked effect on personality.

The parenthetical comment, "for survivors," is important. In general, longitudinal follow-ups compare only those subjects with complete data at all measurement times of interest. Analysis of drop-outs from the Duke Second Longitudinal Study (Rusin and Siegler, 1975) indicated that those who dropped out (because of death, illness, or personal preference) were significantly more anxious or more neurotic than the long-term survivors. Similar results were reported by Costa, Mc Crae, and Arenberg (1983) for subjects in the Baltimore Longitudinal Studies of Aging (BLSA). Dementia, another cause of attrition in longitudinal studies, is known to have profound effects on personality functioning.

A detailed examination of the possible effects of hypertension on personality was undertaken in the BLSA (Costa et al., 1980). Scores on the Guilford Zimmerman Temperament Survey (GZTS) were examined in rela-

tion to measures of systolic and diastolic blood pressure taken contemporaneously over a predictive interval of from 4 to 12 years in samples of over 300 men. Initially, the sample included 796 men aged 17 to 97, with a mean age of 49.8 years. Second administration data were collected from over 500 men aged 25 to 91. When age was partialed out, blood pressure measures were essentially independent of measures of personality traits. In this study, the 101 subjects who were being medicated for hypertension were screened out. Since medication should decrease blood pressure measurements towards normal and might increase the psychological effects of knowing that one has a disease of sufficient seriousness to require medication, including such subjects might have obscured a real association between personality and hypertension. The failure to find an association even among screened subjects strengthens the conclusion that there is none.

Wood, Elias, Schultz, and Pentz (1979) examined the effects of diagnosed essential hypertension on state and trait measures of depression and anxiety. The hypertensive subjects were recruited from the hypertension examination program at Upstate Medical Center in Syracuse, New York, and were screened for hypertension-related pathologies (e.g., angina, congestive heart failure, kidney problems, CVA, MI, eyeground changes). Control subjects included screened individuals as well as community subjects. Those in the young groups ranged in age from 21 to 39; those in the older groups ranged in age from 45 to 65. Hypertensives, independent of age, were more depressed and had higher state-anxiety scores; there were no significant differences in trait anxiety. The level of these statistically significant differences was below the level of practical or clinical importance. There were significant age differences only for state anxiety (the older subjects had lower scores), and the blood pressure group-by-age interactions were not statistically significant. A closer examination of the data further suggests that the differences in depression and anxiety were primarily due to differences between young hypertensives. On the other hand, Siegler and Nowlin (1979) reported data from the Duke Second Longitudinal Study showing that middle-aged subjects who were consistently hypertensive over the course of the study (1968–1976) also had significantly higher anxiety ratings over that period. Together, these three studies suggest that an awareness of the disease or daily medication may raise state anxiety and possibly depressive effects as well, although consistent or progressive changes in trait anxiety are not exhibited.

Leon, Gillum, Gillum, and Gouze (1979) reported data on the MMPI for 71 physically healthy men tested in 1947, 1953, 1960, and 1977. They were participants in the cardiovascular disease project at the University of Minnesota and ranged in age from a mean of 49 years (range of 45 to 54) to 77 years. Starting in 1947, annual examinations were performed to evaluate the incidence of coronary heart disease in relation to physical and psychological characteristics. The original MMPI scores for subjects who developed coronary heart disease within the first 15 years were significantly higher than those of the no-illness cardiovascular control group on scale 1 (Hypochondriasis) and lower on scale 5 (Femininity), although both scores were in the normal T-score range. The authors conclude that the 30-year data indicated "remarkable stability." There were statistically significant, albeit small, changes on all of the scales, with the largest changes on scale 2 (Depression) and relatively large increases on scales 1 (Hypochondriasis) and 3 (Hysteria). These findings were seen as indicative of increases somatic concerns and preference for a more tranquil existence rather than depressive symptoms. Descriptive information on the sample indicated that 39.4 percent reported the existence of a chronic illness at the final measurement point. However, the data were not analyzed with reference to the health status of the respondents.

Coping

Felton and Revenson (1981) evaluated the influence of chronic disease on coping strategies and psychological well-being. A factor analytic procedure was used to identify six coping strategies. Both diagnosis and the illness stress scale were differentially related to coping strategies and measures of psychological well-being. For example, information seeking as a

coping strategy was related to positive affect for rheumatoid arthritic, diabetic, and hypertensive patients, but not for cancer patients. In relation to self-esteem, information seeking was beneficial in its impact only for patients with diabetes and had a mildly negative or no relationship with self-esteem for other patients. These particular associations with type of coping strategy, type of chronic disease, and measure of psychological well-being illustrate the specificity of findings that can be expected when the relevant factors are distinguished. They also illustrate the potential problem when analyses are collapsed across groups of ill subjects who have opposite responses. Whereas many studies have focused on coping with illness, Felton is one of the few to look upon coping strategies as the dependent variables.

Using a distinction proposed by Lazarus and Launier (1978), Mc Crae (1982) investigated age differences in coping response to losses, threats, and challenges in the Baltimore Longitudinal Study of Aging. Older subjects had a higher incidence of threats, most of which were illness-related. When controlled for type of stress, older subjects did not consistently differ from younger subjects in using 26 of 28 coping mechanisms, including rational action, expression of feelings, and seeking help. Middle-aged and older men and women, however, were less likely to use the immature and ineffective mechanisms of hostile reactions and escapist fantasy. Additional analyses of these data showed that threats, including health threats, elicited wishful thinking, faith, and fatalism in adults of all ages.

Intellectual Functioning

When age and health are contrasted in the same study, health rather than age appears to account for declines in intellectual functioning (Speith, 1964, 1965; Birren et al., 1963) and to reduce the increase in intelligence seen in healthy subjects when measured over a two-year period during middle age (Siegler and Nowlin, 1979).

Data from longitudinal aging studies that included health and behavioral data for adult and elderly age ranges are relatively rare.

However, data such as that from the Duke Longitudinal Studies (see Busse and Maddox, in press; Palmore, 1970, 1974; Siegler, 1983) and from the Baltimore Longitudinal Studies (see Shock et al., 1984) generally find that—as is true of the classic curves on intellectual development—longitudinal declines are generally more modest than those seen cross-sectionally.

Using subjects from the Duke First Longitudinal Study, Wilkie and Eisdorfer (1971) divided their subjects into decade-width cohorts (60–69; 70–79) and three diastolic blood pressure groups (normal, under 95 mm Hg; mild, 96 to 105 mm Hg; and high, greater than 105 mm Hg). Subjects were followed for approximately 10 years, and most of the comparisons were made between the first and the fourth visit. When a change score in WAIS was calculated, younger (60-year-old) normotensives were stable, borderline hypertensives had a significant increase in score, and hypertensives had significant declines. For the older group, none of the hypertensives survived, and both the normotensive and borderline hypertensives showed significant declines. Participation/survival status was also related to hypertensive status. Drug usage was not measured in the first longitudinal study. Thus, some of the normotensives may have been normotensive as a result of medication and have had significant underlying disease. Overall, the data indicate an interaction of measured intelligence with disease that is not actually manifest until after the end of the sixth decade.

Schultz et al. (1979) looked at WAIS performance in hypertensive vs. control subjects. The WAIS was given to the hypertensive subjects while they received a potent diuretic to lower their blood pressure. There were eight subject groups: young and old, clinic and nonclinic control groups, and young and old hypertensives who were previously medicated or nonmedicated. The young groups had mean ages in the 20s and the older groups in the 50s. Mean levels of education were between 13 and 16 years and were matched for age groups. This was a complex design that had many complex findings. Overall, hypertensives performed more poorly than normotensives, the difference being caused by differences between younger subjects only; this difference

further interacted with medication status for the younger subjects. Subjects were matched on verbal scaled score performance. An analysis of variance (ANOVA) indicated statistically significant differences for age (the younger were better) and hypertension (the normotensives were better) as well as a significant interaction, with young normotensives performing better than old normotensives, who performed better than old hypertensives, who were not different from young hypertensives. Given the relative frequency of hypertension at younger vs. older ages, these findings may also be reflective of some of the sampling problems in attempting to match on disease across broad age ranges. Schultz and Elias (1980) review their work in the context of other studies of hypertension and WAIS performance by Wilkie and coworkers. They conclude that although skill differences are observed, the absolute levels of performance shown by hypertensive subjects remains quite high. In his epilogue to the volume *Hypertension and Cognitive Processes* (1980a), Merrill Elias concludes that "it is clear that the prediction of hypertensive status from behavioral indices is poor, but it is also obvious that essential hypertensives do not perform in an inferior manner in a practically significant sense" (Elias, 1980, p. 159). In other words, cognitive dysfunction is not a characteristic of hypertensive individuals.

A longitudinal analysis by Costa and Shock (1980) evaluated the influence of hypertension on intellectual functioning as revealed by the Army Alpha test administered approximately every six years to participants of the BLSA, aged 20 to 65. Subjects were split into three age groups—20–39, 40–49, and 50–65—and three blood pressure groups—low (120/80), high (140/90), and middle (otherwise). There was no evidence of a relationship between test performance and hypertensive status. The analyses were replicated on a clinically clean sample. Those subjects on medication or with serious chronic diseases were excluded, thus reducing the number of subjects to 117, very few of them with significant hypertension (140/90). The effects were weak but suggested poorer performance for subjects with hypertension. Over the six-year interval, moreover, there was no interaction of hypertensive status and intellectual performance exhibited by those under age 65. An additional 51 subjects from the BLSA tested every year (aged 66 to 84 at the first and 74 to 93 at the sixth examination) were examined in an attempt to replicate the findings of Wilkie and Eisdorfer (1971). The hypertensives were divided into a normotensive and a borderline hypertensive group. No effect of hypertension was reported. It is important to point out that Wilkie and Eisdorfer reported that borderline hypertension was related to enhanced, rather than declining, performance, but this effect was also not observed in the Costa and Shock study.

Hertzog et al. (1978) reviewed the health records of 156 subjects who participated in Schaie's sequential studies of intellectual development and behavioral rigidity. Yearly health histories were coded using the International Classification of Disease (ICDA) codes. Problems of small N (see Siegler et al., 1980) required that a wide variety of diagnostic categories—which could be expected to have differential impact as well as different cohort groups—were added to the analysis in order to get sufficient group sizes for analysis. This made the fine-grain analysis of type of disease impossible and probably also biased against their finding anything at all. Drop-out was related to cardiovascular disease (CVD) diagnoses and maleness; hypertension, however, was not related to participation status. Three major sets of analyses of variance were performed: CVD, participation, sex, and time; CVD, cohort, sex, and time; and CVD and time. The dependent variables were always the five PMA subtests, overall indices of intellectual ability and educational aptitude, and the three factors from the test of behavioral rigidity. The results were quite detailed. In the first set of ANOVAs, CVD was related to decrements in performance on all variables except perceptual motor rigidity. Participation was related to higher performance on all dependent variables; their interaction, however, was significant for only one variable (motor cognitive rigidity). Given the relationship between participation, sex, and CVD, it is surprising that the three-way interaction was never significant and that sex by disease inter-

actions was significant only for the verbal meaning factor. Since tables of means were not presented, the direction of the interaction is unknown. In the second analysis, although cohort was always significant, the cardiovascular variables were not, and none of the cohort by disease interactions were significant. Of most interest for our purposes is the third set of analyses, in which the subjects were divided into the following groups: hypertensives, atherosclerotics, both hypertensive and atherosclerotics, cerebrovascular victims, and the undiseased. The disease groups ranged in size from 6 to 25 subjects. Due to the fact that health changes with increasing age, an individual's health status was classified according to a disease profile first in 1963 and again in 1967. Significant effects for CVD were found for none of the rigidity factors and were found only for N (number), W (word fluency), IQ, and EQ for the 1963 cutoff and only for N and IQ for the 1967 cutoff (the N for 1963 was 69; for 1967, 83). Although disease was usually related to poorer intellectual performance, this was not true of the hypertensive-only subgroup, which supports findings from the Duke studies for both middle-aged and older subjects with borderline hypertension.

Osberg, Mears, McKee, and Burnett (1982) studied kidney disease, renal failure, and dialysis patients and reported intellectual decline. Although it was clear that the majority of the patients in the studies they reviewed were adults, no mention of the age of the patients was made in their excellent and detailed tables and otherwise generally useful review of the literature.

Reaction Time

For many years, changes in reaction time have been the prototype of age-related changes (Birren, Woods, and Williams, 1980). Rabbitt (1980), however, suggests that this is true only in situations with insufficient practice. Gottsdanker (1982) reported stability in simple auditory reaction time in a cross-sectional study of men and women between 18 and 93. Among a series of conditions on a subset of subjects matched on simple RT, he showed that the traditional age differences of the magnitude of 20 percent across the life cycle were shown only under the condition where control could be exercised during a preparatory interval. Pirozzolo and Hansch (1981) studied oculomotor reaction time in two groups of older subjects (mean age in the sixties). Those with Alzheimer's disease had significantly longer RTs. Without the presence of a young control group, it is impossible to separate the impact of normal aging from any additional deficit caused by a specific disease process, but such studies can speak to the question of whether the behavior is related to health/disease status within an older population.

Wilkie and Eisdorfer (1972) investigated longitudinal change in RT as a function of hypertension. Older subjects (over 70) with hypertension (higher than 105 mm Hg) usually did not survive the 10-year period; those with borderline hypertension were found to have a slowing in RT; the normotensives exhibited no change. At initial testing, no relationship was found between blood pressure and RT, essentially the same result as was found with the same subjects on the WAIS. Light (1980) investigated RT in a group of hypertensive subjects. These subjects were the same referred to in the studies of Wood, et al., and Elias and Schultz. To assess the cause of their hypertension, they were tested under special conditions. Light (1980) reviews her own findings pertaining to RT in the context of Speith's (1965). Although hypertension in all the studies discussed was related to slower RT when compared to normotensive controls, the performance of medicated hypertensives is an issue that remains unsettled.

Learning and Memory

A set of learning and memory tasks was studied by Hulicka (1967). A group of 120 male veterans (aged 17 to 35) at a VA hospital was compared to age-matched controls. Illness severity was indexed by the number of diagnoses in the medical chart, self reports, and the number of months of hospitalization during the past five years. Within the patient group, age was related to degree of illness as follows: for age and number of diagnoses, r = .51, and for age and length of hospitalization, r = .60. A series of learning and memory tasks was

developed so that the tasks would have a high degree of face validity and be brief. The tasks included recognition of faces, memory for names and faces, logical memory, and paired associates. The results indicated that age differences favored younger patients in three of the four tasks (all except paired associates), whereas the age groups of nonpatients did not differ except on task 3 (logical memory). Comparisons within age groups suggested that patients performed more poorly than age-matched controls on all tasks. Second-order partial correlations between age and task scores with the effects of both health indices held constant indicated no patient relationship to age.

Weschler memory scale performance as a function of hypertensive status was evaluated by Wilkie, Eisdorfer, and Nowlin (1976) in the Duke Longitudinal Study over about a six-year period. There were slight declines in immediate and delayed logical memory and on paired associates, the only significant decline being in the visual reproduction task. Longitudinal change in these same subjects was evaluated by McCarty, Siegler, and Logue (1982) over intervals of 4, 10, and 20 years. As the interval increased, so did the selectivity of the subjects. Selective drop-out was also monitored. The only true longitudinal change that was unaffected by drop-out was the change in visual reproduction. These results—in conjunction with the findings of Wilkie et al.—suggest that those older hypertensives who survive to be tested repeatedly are not able to take advantage of the testings and do decline. Neuropsychological test performance on seven tests was evaluated in young and middle-aged normal and hypertensive patients by Pentz et al. (1979) and Wood and Elias (1980). As a group, hypertensives performed more poorly but were in the normal, rather than the brain-damaged, range of performance. On tests where age and hypertensive status interacted, the major differences were found between the younger hypertensives and normotensives. Since few longitudinal studies have included clinical neuropsychological tests such as the Halstead battery, we have no information about the role that hypertension may play earlier in life in the development of cognitive dysfunction later in life.

Integrated Skilled Performance

Airline pilot performance is an example of a set of skills that could be expected to be influenced by both age and health. As a case study of the interactions of health/aging/behavior issues and public policy, the question of the mandatory retirement for airline pilots at the age of 60 is quite interesting. In order to provide background information relevant to decision-making on this issue, Congress mandated NIH to review and report on the evidence regarding the validity of retiring commercial pilots at age 60. The Institute of Medicine (IoM) was commissioned to prepare a report evaluating the existing scientific evidence on this issue. Not surprisingly, the IoM (1981) report concluded that the extant data base was simply too meager to permit any firm conclusions. The report contains a list of important research questions and future directions that need to be addressed before adequate knowledge about this topic will be achieved. Incidentially, the IoM report also contains some very instructive reviews of the effects of age on various body systems.

THE EFFECTS OF BEHAVIOR ON HEALTH

Concern with the effect of behavior and behavior change on health has become a major focus of interest in the 1980s (Hamburg, 1982; Houpt et al., 1979). A 1979 report of the Surgeon General suggests that over 50 percent of all disability and disease in the U.S. is due to preventable causes under the control of individuals. For perhaps the first time in history, the proportional gain in longevity and thus health status for adults is greater than that for infants (McGinnis, 1982). Even with the mortality reductions there are still substantial differences in mortality between the sexes. Waldron (1980) reviews the major causes of mortality differentials—the mortality rate of men being at least twice that of women—and argues that behaviors related to the development of the disorders—for example, the behavioral characteristics of smoking and Type A behavior pattern that are related to heart disease—can be shown to be responsible for at least one-third of the excess mortality.

The argument is that, if behavior can be changed, so can the health status of the population. This appears to be happening in the case of smoking, diet, exercise, and other "life style" measures (see Hamburg, Elliot, and Parron, 1982). The same data and the potential for mortality reductions, moreover, have resulted in an enhanced interest in psychology (e.g., see Singer and Krantz, 1982; Stone, 1979).

The Institute of Medicine (IoM) has recently compiled a volume covering a series of conferences on health and behavior (Hamburg, Elliot, and Parron, 1982). This volume provides an excellent update on the burden that illness places on the national health and the role that behavior plays in the development of diseases. Most of the behavioral data that contribute to illness can be ascribed to "habits" such as alcohol abuse, smoking, nonadherence to proven medical regimens, and overeating to obesity. It is important, however, that data indicating behavioral predictors of health outcomes or behavioral risk factors not be overinterpreted. Until we know, for example, how personality and other behavioral factors are related to the development of cardiovascular and other diseases, we should not fall into the trap of blaming the victim (patient) for his/her disease.

Behavioral Medicine

Research in behavioral medicine (Boudewyns and Keefe, 1982; Davidson and Davidson, 1980; Pormerleau and Brady, 1979) has usually bypassed age as a factor for study. However, in clinical case reports, the age of the patient is usually reported. It is clear that most of the patients treated are adults, but few studies actually include adult age as a variable. We know from the classical and operant conditioning literature that older people, generally speaking, condition more slowly and extinguish more slowly (see Botwinick, 1979, for a review of the learning literature) and that they are amenable to various behavioral treatments for mental problems (Cautella and Mansfield, 1977; Richards and Thorpe, 1978) and physical problems (Engel, 1983). Theoretically, there is little reason to expect that different techniques will be needed. In fact, Bernard Engel (1983) in a chapter dealing with the applications of behavioral medicine to older outpatients asserts that these do not differ from those for younger patients. In his view, the only point worth noting is that certain disorders are more likely to be present in older patients. Behavioral medicine has largely proved its stripes by showing that there are useful areas of treatment for which treatments were not available before or for which present approaches are more cost effective than traditional techniques (Surwit, Williams, and Shapiro, 1982). In this regard, Engel and his colleagues have successfully developed intervention programs for treating fecal and urinary incontinence—an area where future developments can be expected to help produce an enhanced quality of life for elderly patients.

Longitudinal and prospective epidemiological studies have provided invaluable data showing that health behaviors in one phase of the life cycle are related to the development of particular disorders later on. Starfield and Pless (1980) review the major epidemiological studies of constancy and change in physical health in childhood and the predictability of adult health status. Their review suggests that it might be cost effective to consider follow-up studies of well-characterized populations seen first as children or adolescents but not seen as adults.

With data from the Grant Study at Harvard, Vaillant (1979) reported that those subjects with the best assessed mental health at the ages of 21 to 46 also had the best physical health at age 53. Multiple regression indicated that 14 percent of the variance in health deterioration was accounted for by adult adjustment when that was taken as the first variable in the equation. Obesity, alcohol use, and smoking additionally contributed less than or equal to 1 percent of the variance. When adjustment was taken as the last variable, it and alcohol abuse each accounted for 7 percent, and the other variables combined, for 4 percent.

Changes in Habits as a Function of Age

The negative impact of smoking on CHD may be reduced after age 65, as indicated by the Framingham data (Kannel and Gordon, 1980). Currently, increased cancer mortality at the older ages is primarily due to smoking-related cancers (Frei, 1982). This fact suggests that there may be a curvilinear relationship between smoking-related causes of death and the length of time of smoking, and this raises the larger question of the importance of age itself as a risk factor in the development of many disorders as well as the change in the relative importance of risk factors at various phases of the life cycle.

In a masterful review of the psychosocial influences on the health status of the elderly, Kasl and Berkman (1981) evaluate the complex and changing risk factor picture with age. Results of a study of the Pooling Project Research Group (1978) on the incidence of major coronary events in men reveals that the risk ratio goes up with age for blood pressure (and ECG abnormalities) but goes down for such risk factors as serum cholesterol, cigarette smoking, and relative weight. Andres (1980) has reached similar conclusions regarding relative weight or obesity as a mortality risk factor in most major causes of death.

Ostfeld et al. (1974), in a prospective study of stroke among those elderly free of preexisting cardiac and vascular disease, found that none of the following predicted stroke: blood pressure, ponderal index, cigarette smoking, serum cholesterol, and plasma glucose. For those with cardiac disease, only blood pressure and ponderal index were predictive of subsequent stroke.

The prevalence of alcholism may also decrease with age, as is true of substance abuse generally (Wood, 1978). How much of this is due to motivational changes, how much to an increased morbidity and mortality in the addicted population, and how much to measurement error is still unknown. Mishara and Kastenbaum (1980) provide an extensive review of the important data in the newly emerging area of aging and alcoholism. Thomas, Santora, and Shaffer (1980) considered the impact of alcohol use and smoking in a Johns Hopkins study of medical students. Their results indicate no statistically significant differences between health groups examined while they were in school or at 10- and 20-year follow-ups except for three subjects whose deaths were classified as "other"—two from cirrhosis of the liver and one who had a high blood alcohol level from an accident. Aside from these three, there was no evidence of excessive drinking. The impact of cigarette smoking on health was also assessed from a cross-sectional as well as a longitudinal analysis in 1978. Those who developed hypertension and coronary heart disease had been heavier smokers in medical school and up to age 30. These two groups had also been smokers longer.

Knowledge about the adverse impact of smoking and other bad habits may have caused many to modify their behavior without specific clinical interventions. The impact of public health measures is probably part of the reason for Schachter's (1982) finding that over the adult age range (16–79) there is a fair degree of successful self-cure for smoking and obesity.

Impact of Personality on the Development of Disease

One of the major behavioral predictors of adult disease has been the Type A behavior pattern (Jenkins, 1979). Although most of the victims of CHD are middle-aged and older, we do not know whether Type A is predictive after age 65. Haynes' data (Haynes, et al., 1978) from the Framingham Study indicated that Type A behavior pattern significantly predicts CHD among men and women 45 to 64 but not among those 65 and older (Kasl and Berkman, 1981). Also from the same Framingham Study are findings suggesting that other risk factors of coronary heart disease change their relationship in later life, with the result that hypertension increases in importance among the elderly whereas smoking and serum cholesterol appear to be less potent risk factors than during midlife (Kannel and Gordon, 1980).

Thomas and Greenstreet (1973) found the Rorschach useful in discriminating among five different disease groups in a prospective study of medical students. Specific Rorschach patterns were not identified as predictive of particular disorders except for those individuals who developed mental disorders (excluding suicides).

Studies of the usefulness of the MMPI have failed to predict morbidity or mortality from CHD (Gillum, Leon, Kamp, and Becerra-Aldama, 1980). Research on the predictability of CHD in women, reviewed by Turner (1982), however, suggested that suppressed hostility may be related to the development of CHD in clerical workers.

Disease do not, in general, have recognizable premorbid personality patterns that are predictive of them. In reviewing the evidence for psychosomatic theories of diabetes, Surwit, Scovern, and Feinglos (1982) suggest that the various approaches assuming some specific premorbid personality constellation have not been validated.

It would appear that Type A may have usefulness in the prediction of heart disease as a set of predictive behaviors rather than as a personality typology. Work by Williams et al. (1982) suggests some of the underlying physiological and neuroendocrine differences between Type A and non-Type A young men that may be related to their cardiovascular responsiveness and thus provide a potential mechanism to explain the increased incidence of heart disease in those who display Type A behavior characteristics.

Stress

Stress is sometimes seen as the major mechanism in which behavior and individual reactions can lead to health consequences. Despite this fact, the treatment of stress in most discussions of health and behavior is so general as to be theoretically useless unless the author can postulate some particular mechanism of action where stress, or a particular physiological pattern, can be shown to be reliably associated with a particular stimulus situation or behavioral manifestation.

In Eisdorfer and Wilkie (1977), the direction and organization of the current chapter were reversed in that health behavior relationships were considered as a subcategory of stress research. It should be noted that the background material in their chapter on the methodological issues in stress research as well as their models of the potential interaction of psychological stimuli as initiators of physiological stress responses is still worth reading.

A number of researchers have addressed the stress/illness link. Williams (1979) presents a model of psychological causation in which stress is taken to be the intervening variable in the development of cardiovascular disease. Rodin (1980) focuses on perceptions of control as a critical construct in understanding health/aging/stress relationships and argues that perceptions of control, which may function as a way of reducing the negative effects of stress, can also be shown to be related to reductions in psychological distress, morbidity, and mortality.

Miller (1980) presents a nice summary of current thinking that relates potential neuroendocrine/immune system approaches to potential mechanisms that give a role to behavioral interventions and can serve as an important stimulus to the design of critical experiments. Both age and health status are seen as influences not only on the events that are likely to happen but on an individual's coping ability as well. Weksler (1981) uses a more biomedical definition of stress as a construct that indicates how the homeostatic mechanisms of the CNS immune and endocrine systems operate in the regulation of healthy and nonhealthy behavior with aging. In a related fashion, Stein (1981) brings together the social stress/life events approach and the more biomedical approach of Weksler by relating his work on changes in the immune system of recent widowers and tracking the response to the "psychosocial stress" of widowerhood in a biochemical fashion. This tracking—similar to the tracking of other health and social psychological indicators—revealed that the time course of adaptation to the stressful life event was critical in observing an effect, as was shown in the Duke Longitudinal Study by Palmore et al. (1979).

The Institute of Medicine recently compiled a volume representing the findings of a blue ribbon committee's critical review of the literature on stress and health (Parron, Solomon, and Rodin, 1981). Although a number of diverse topics were examined, including stress and the environment, work and organizations, life events, and many other topics, the role of age received little attention. Of course, this lack of notice reflects its neglect in the general literature.

Perhaps the most popular operationalization of stress in the literature continues to be the stressful life events paradigm originally proposed by Holmes and Rahe (1967). Schroeder and Costa (1984) examined possible artifactual explanations of the often observed correlations between measures of live event stress and illness. They found that various kinds of measurement contamination (e.g., retrospective bias and confounds between events and physical health and neuroticism) accounted for the observed relations. If subsequent research replicates their findings, most, if not all, of the literature purportedly relating stress to illness will be called into question.

Other Predictors

Personality factors and typologies are not the only behavioral variables that have been used as predictors of disease. Thomas and her coworkers in the Precourser's Study at Johns Hopkins (Betz and Thomas, 1979; Thomas, 1976; Thomas and Greenstreet, 1973; Thomas and McCabe, 1980; Thomas, Santora, and Shaffer, 1980), began a study in 1946 of the development of five disease states (suicide, mental illness, hypertension, coronary heart disease, and tumor) in a cohort of medical students. The study was based on 1337 Johns Hopkins medical graduates in the classes of 1948 to 1964. Of these, 95.1 percent participated in the study and 88.9 percent were white males, of whom 95.2 percent graduated. At the time of the follow-up in 1971, nearly all were physicians aged between 30 and 60.

Thomas and McCabe (1980) reported data from a 1979 follow-up. Of the original 1337 students, 1046 were white men, 91 were white women, and 31 were nonwhite men and women. The disorder groups included 20 men with MIs, 53 men with essential hypertension under chemical management, 55 men with some form of cancer (of which 29 were rated as major cancers), 31 men who required hospitalization for mental illness, and 10 suicides. The healthy control group included 140 men at least 50 years old at last contact in 1978/

79. As recorded on the Habits of Nervous Tensions questionnaire that was administered approximately 30 years before the follow-up, differential responses to stress indicated significant patterns of premature death and disease for those who developed coronary occlusions, cancers, or mental illness or who committed suicide. The scale items had no relationship to the development of essential hypertension. Given the small samples, these interesting results need to be replicated by other longitudinal studies in order to be viewed as being more than suggestive.

Stress has also been shown to be an important mediator in the development of cancer (Fox, 1978; Selye, 1979; Sklar and Anisman, 1981). The experience of any illness is stress-inducing and requires coping responses. The degree to which coping with illness is a special situation that requires different mechanisms than coping with other life events is of theoretical interest. Approaches such as that presented by Cohen and Lazarus (1979) in the context of coping with illness appear to be quite promising.

Social support is often cited as the mechanism that promotes stress reduction; it functions as the inverse of social stress in many models. Schaefer, Coyne, and Lazarus (1981) investigated the health implications of social support. In an article of theoretical interest, they review not only the lack of a coherent theoretical basis for some of the work in social support but report data that fails to confirm the expected association between social support and health considerations. A similar theme has been voiced by Satariano and Syme (1981), who note that methodological problems have prevented acceptable tests of the hypothesis that a person's network of social relationships mediates the health effects of age-related life changes.

HEALTH-RELATED BEHAVIORS

As has been discussed in the previous sections, individual behavior appears to be related to the development of diseases. In this section we will be concerned with behavior that deals with illness and the health care system. It is important to understand the implications of health-related behaviors across the life cycle, particularly in later life. Older persons are major consumers of health services. Decisions made about health care may well influence the quality and length of life in old age (Fingerhurt and Rosenberg, 1981).

Models of Health Behavior

Age is only one variable among many that determines why and how people seek medical care. Among the important variables to be considered are the cohort differences and cultural background factors that influence beliefs, motives, and perceptions of self and of the elderly as a group; specific perceptions of symptoms, illnesses, and vulnerabilities; the locus of health control; the degree of faith in medical care providers; the degree of faith in the system in general; and the factors that influence access to the system.

The most formal model providing explanations of health service utilization is the health beliefs model (Rosenstock, 1966; Becker, 1974). This model employs general sociopsychological constructs such as perceptions of actions and their consequences in the prediction of health-related behaviors. Aside from some theoretical discussions such as those by Rakowski and Hickey (1980), this model has yet to be applied to data collected from older persons but should be capable of producing some useful findings if it were.

Perceptions of Health

One of the few aspects of the health beliefs model that has been applied to older persons is self-perceptions of health. Such perceptions are of central importance in understanding how health behaviors influence the attribution and appraisal of symptoms, perceived vulnerability, and decisions to seek treatment. In part, self-health perceptions parallel objective evaluations by professionals, but they are not isomorphic with health status (see Siegler et al., 1980).

Health perceptions are conditioned or influenced by a number of factors. Boyer (1980) has demonstrated that they are shaped in old age by cultural norms of activity and inactivity and, more important, by the continuation of rewarding roles and activities. In addition to objectively defined health and mobility, participation in social life and the patterns of roles and activities the elderly have available markedly influence their perceptions of health.

Health perceptions are also consistently related to levels of psychological well-being. Okun (1982) and his colleagues performed a meta analysis on 543 studies of psychological well-being that also included some measure of health status. Most of the health status measures were global self-assessments, symptom check lists, or measures of functional health. The mean correlation of psychological well-being and health status, r, equalled 0.34. When age was covaried, the resulting partial correlation of perceived health and measures of psychological well-being increased to 0.42. Thus, health is an important correlate of well-being that is independent of the age of the sample. Kaplan (1982) reported on the predictive value of self-assessments of health. His data indicated a relationship between perceived health and mortality from ischemic heart disease even when age, sex, and physical health status were held constant. Those who rated their health as poor were 2.44 times more likely to die than those who rated their health as excellent. Kaplan's data suggest that seemingly simple psychological variables may well underlie or be proxies for some important predictors of survival.

Similar findings were reported by Mossey and Shapiro (1982) using data from the Manitoba Longitudinal Study on Aging of individuals 65 and older. Increased risk as a function of poor self-rated health was shown to be true over a three-year as well as a seven-year period (2.92 and 2.77, respectively).

Symptom Self-Reports

Using data from the BLSA, Costa and Mc Crae (1980b) examined the relative influences of age and neuroticism on self-perceptions of health for several body systems and total complaints on the Cornell Medical Index (CMI). Six- and twelve-year longitudinal analyses of the 12 somatic sections of the CMI along with age and neuroticism scores from the Guilford Zimmerman Temperament Survey (GZTS) conducted on a sample of 1024 BLSA men aged 17 to 97 showed differential effects. With increasing age, modest increases (less than one-quarter item increase in six years) were observed in sensory, cardiovascular, and genito-urinary complaints. In contrast, neuroticism showed relatively more pervasive and diffuse effects. Subjects with higher neuroticism scores reported higher levels of problems or complaints on all 12 sections. Cross-sequential and time-sequential analyses (as well as supplementary long-linear analyses) of the first administration data provided firm evidence that maturational rather than generational differences or cultural change were responsible for the three observed age effects during the period of measurement. These results indicated that age, unlike neuroticism, does not produce a generalized increase in body concern or complaint; instead, specific age-related symptoms show increases (see also Costa and Mc Crae, 1982, for a further discussion of the methodological implications of these data).

Wood et al. (1978) found that hypertensive subjects report, independently of age, more symptoms (both physical and psychological) on the CMI than normotensives do and that this may reflect knowledge of the disease. Elias, Robbins, Blow, Rice, and Edgecomb (1982) considered the impact of age on symptom reporting by angina patients. Their results indicate that, even when personality characteristics such as neuroticism are taken into account, the degree of reporting tends to increase with age. Costa, Fleg, Mc Crae, and Lakatta (1982) suggest that personality characteristics, such as the stable disposition of neuroticism, may well be related to symptom reporting in later life. Thus it would appear that in populations selected for specific coronary diseases, increased symptom reporting occurs regardless of personality functioning. Nevertheless, both neuroticism and the knowledge of having a disease are more important predictors of symptom report than is age per se.

Health Concerns

Data from the adult follow-ups of the Berkeley Growth Study (BGS, birth to 36 years of age), the Oakland Growth Study (OGS, 11 to 50), and the Guidance Study (GS, birth to 42) has recently been summarized with respect to changes in health by Bayer, Whissell-Buechy, and Honzig (1981). Although the health data was not related to the wealth of behavioral data available in their data set, their study does give a picture of the health relationships observed during the first half of life and has the potential, given additional follow-ups and reanalysis of existing data, of furnishing valuable knowledge. One of their most interesting findings is the degree to which the subjects are similar to those in the National Health Survey's presentation of areas of health concerns by age. Longitudinal studies are often thought to be elite and unrepresentative of individuals in the general population, particularly in terms of psychological variables. This does not appear to be as true with respect to health variables; for example, Maddox (1962) reported a high degree of similarity with the Duke longitudinal panelists and data from the National Health Survey.

Hypochondriasis

Costa and Mc Crae's findings (1980a) contradict the prevalent notion that aging people are hypochondriacs. Although there was no evidence of a wholesale increase in somatic complaints with age, the data do not indicate that there are no elderly hypochondriacs; rather, the proportion of such people is no higher than in youth or middle age. At any age, excessive complaints are associated with neuroticism or poor psychological adjustment, factors unrelated to age.

There is some evidence to suggest that older persons are not only "remarkably low-keyed" but, in fact, often fail to report serious symptoms and illnesses. From a socio-psychological attribution perspective, Kart (1981) suggests that because age may be related to increased thresholds of pain perception and temperature sensitivity, older persons may become seriously ill before they attribute their symptoms

to illness. Gentry (1979) discussed the implications of interpretations of symptoms of coronary heart disease during the time between the onset of symptoms and the seeking of medical care. Older persons took significantly longer to seek medical help, thus decreasing the probability of their surviving a myocardial infarction. Hickey (1980) reported that older persons often experienced less pain with an MI, and thus pain perception may be a related factor.

In an excellent review of health and illness behavior in the elderly, Besdine (1980) cites data gathered by English and Scottish geriatricians that reveal disturbingly large numbers of unreported serious problems. Among the reasons given by Besdine for the tolerations of symptoms and aliments, the most common were the patient's expectations of poor health in old age, depression, cognitive impairment, fear that a serious condition would actually be found, and a fear of medical intervention and the medical care system generally.

Thus, it would appear that older persons who report the most symptoms are those whose personality traits would make such behavior predictable. To the extent that there is a problem with older persons and their self-reports of illness, it is more likely to be a problem of under- rather than of over-reporting.

Physician/Patient Relationships

Furchgott and Busemeyer (1980) investigated age preferences for professional helpers. Although older persons preferred older service providers this was not true for the choice of age of a physician. Lawton (1981) provides a useful discussion of the variables involved in the physician-older patient relationship, that should serve as a stimulus for research in this area.

Compliance

An issue related to seeking medical care is that of complying with medical regimens. Baile, Brinker, Wachspress, and Engel (1979) studied those who signed out of CCUs against medical advice. Advanced age was related to higher levels of compliance and to lower levels of signing-out against medical advice. In a very different study, one of compliance with a screening project for TB in a primarily university community, age was related to participation (Wurtle, Galanos, and Roberts, 1980).

Utilization of Health Services

Eckstein (1978) has noted that the complaints of the elderly are "remarkably low-keyed and valid," given the burden of illness and disabilities they often face. Does the absence of a general age-associated increase in physical complaints imply or translate into satisfactory or appropriate patterns of medical care utilization? Evidence bearing on this question appears to be equivocal. Haug (1980) reported the results of a health care utilization study on a national, randomly selected sample of 1509 persons aged 18 and over. Individuals 60 and older were more likely than younger individuals to visit physicians for routine checkups in the absence of symptoms and to overutilize medical care for a list of five "nonserious" complaints determined by physician judgments. There were no age differences, however, in the patterns of underutilization of care for five common symptoms judged by physicians to require medical attention.

Haug's findings illustrate some of the difficulties in determining whether the elderly overutilize health services, since older persons, primarily women, overutilize care for nonserious complaints and underutilize it for serious ones. "Misutilization" of health services by older persons may be a more accurate description.

Sex Differences

Perhaps the most frequently reported finding in health survey research is that women report symptoms of both physical and mental illness and utilize physicians and hospital services for their conditions at a higher rate than men (Nathanson, 1975). At the same time, women's life expectancy has exceeded that of men (at least since the eighteenth century) and continues to increase (Turner, 1982; Verbrugge, 1981). Reports in the literature are inconsistent about self-assessed compared to "actual"

health. Maddox and Douglass (1973) reported that women were more likely than men to report their health as worse than physician ratings would suggest. Sex differences in such "health pessimism" have not been replicated (Blazer and Houpt, 1979; La Rue et al., 1979).

Mechanic (1976) presented an illuminating discussion of the theoretical and methodological issues relevant to the question of sex differences in illness, illness behaviors, and the use of health services within the context of sex differences in response to life situations.

IMPLICATIONS FOR FURTHER RESEARCH

It is not our purpose here to recapitulate the various implications for research given throughout this chapter but rather to call attention to some general principles that relate to future research efforts.

We feel that it is important that the design of a study reflect the problem to be solved rather than the discipline of the designer. With some thought, constraints that at first glance appear to be design problems—e.g., whether to health screen subjects—can be treated as a theoretical part of the design instead.

We have provided suggestions to improve research that essentially involve (1) fuller use of the data, (2) capitalization on the characteristics of the diseases under study, and (3) attention to cost/benefit strategies in design and analysis. Although these ideas are not new with us, we hope they will act as stimuli for improved research.

The major need in this area is for more information. At our present state of knowledge, null findings and nonsignificant trends may be usefully reported. In researching the impact of behavior on health, it would be useful to report age routinely even if no age effect is observed. Although it is often appropriate not to discuss nonsignificant results, in this case it would be useful to know that age effects have been examined and found to be nonsignificant. In areas related to treatment, nonsignificant trends or clinical observations should always be reported since they often can serve as the stimuli for confirmatory research.

Data from existing longitudinal studies are

extremely valuable, but these studies are limited in various ways: sample size, geographic restrictions, or nonrepresentativeness. It is important to note where findings are consistent across a range of populations and to find ways of building linkages between the smaller, richer studies and the large, population-based epidemiological studies that have breadth but often not the depth.

In the area of health-related behaviors, we would like to encourage more psychologists to become interested in areas that have traditionally been the province of public health and medical sociology. Understanding of the behaviors (and their consequences) of middle-aged and older persons as they interact with the health care system could benefit from a psychological perspective.

A number of specific research questions have been raised in the course of this review: Do older people over- or underutilize medical resources? What are the determinants of perceptions of health and effective health behaviors? What kinds of coping strategies are most effective for reducing stress in the elderly? What are the adaptational costs and benefits of such processes as feelings of control or denial? Can longitudinal findings of stability in personality be generalized to wider groups and to individuals suffering from serious and prolonged medical conditions? Dozens of other questions worthy of immediate study might also be mentioned. Health psychology is in a period of rapid growth, as is the psychology of adult development and aging. The intersections of these two areas leave much exciting work to be done.

CONCLUDING COMMENTS

The goal of this chapter has been to review various studies that deal with health, behavior, and aging in order to improve the quality of discourse and research. To the extent that we have been successful, future aging studies will show more concern about health and illness in the design as well as the analysis phase. Similarly, research in health psychology and behavioral medicine will include age as a variable of scientific and practical interest.

The field of aging, health, and behavior is characterized more by a dawning recognition of the problem than by a comprehensive body of information. Ideally, systematic studies would be conducted among middle-aged and older persons on the effects of a range of medical conditions on all specific behaviors (e.g., mood state and memory) or on the full extent of behavioral changes that result from each specific illness (e.g., hypertension and diabetes). The identification of behavioral risk factors for various illnesses has been haphazard so far, and much more research is needed.

As a result of new research, theoretical formulations can be expected to change. The boundary between primary and secondary aging will shift as specific disease states are identified, and the concept of aging as a single process will have to be abandoned as new evidence demonstrates the multiplicity of aging processes in different individuals and systems.

Policy issues—as illustrated by the health/ aging/behavior interactions in airline pilot performance—will also prompt research. As issues of retirement policy gain increasing national attention, the measurement and interpretation of age/health/behavior interactions will require sustained attention. Thus, growth in the area of developing the knowledge base required for understanding the impact of health on behavior as a function of age will be stimulated by practical and well as scientific concerns.

When we consider the impact of behavior on health, its implications for clinical treatment and the public health are the most obvious. A full understanding of the role that age plays can be expected to help target therapeutic techniques, improve the efficacy of current treatments, and lead to the development of new treatment approaches at the individual as well as the societal level.

Acknowledgments. Dr. Siegler's effort was supported in part by NIA Grants AG00364 and AG003188 and NIMH Grant MH14660. Many colleagues were helpful in providing preprints of their work and access to their libraries. In particular, our thanks are due to Drs. H. K. H. Brodie, R. B. Williams, Jr., J. B. Nowlin, and J. A. Blumenthal at Duke University and to Drs. Robert R. Mc Crae,

Alan B. Zonderman, and Bernard T. Engel at the Gerontology Research Center, NIA.

REFERENCES

Abrahams, J. P. 1976. Psychological correlates of cardiovascular disease. In *Special Review of Experimental Aging Research,* eds. M. F. Elias, B. E. Eleftheriou, and P. K. Elias, pp. 330–349. Bar Harbor, Maine: Experimental Aging Research, Inc.

Andres, R. 1980. Influence of obesity on longevity in the aged. In *Advances in Cancer Biology Series: Aging Cancer and Cell Membranes.* New York: Stratton Intercontinental Medical Book Corporation.

Baile, W. F.; Brinker, J. A.; Wachspress, J. D.; and Engel, B. T. 1979. Signouts against medical advice from a coronary care unit. *J. Beh. Med.* 2(1): 85–92.

Bayer, L. M.; Whissell-Buechy, D.; and Honzig, M. 1981. Health in the middle years. In *Present and Past in Middle Life,* ed. D. Eichorn, pp. 55–88. New York: Academic Press.

Becker, M. H., ed. 1974. The health belief mode and personal health behavior. *Health Education Monograph* 2 (whole n. 4).

Besdine, R. W. 1980. Geriatric medicine: An overview. In *Annual Review of Gerontology and Geriatrics,* ed. C. Eisdorfer, pp. 135–153. New York: Springer.

Besdine, R. W. 1981. Health and illness behavior in the elderly. In *Health Behavior and Aging: A Research Agenda* (Interim Report No. 5), eds. D. L. Parron, F. Solomon, and J. Rodin, pp. 15–24. Washington, D.C.: Division of Mental Health and Behavioral Medicine, National Academy Press.

Betz, B. J., and Thomas, C. B. 1979. Individual temperament as a predictor of health or premature disease. *Johns Hopkins Med. J.* 144: 81–89.

Birren, J. E.; Butler, R. N.; Greenhouse, S. W.; Sokoloff, L.; and Yarrow, M. 1963. *Human Aging.* Washington, D.C.: USGPO.

Birren, J. E.; Woods, A. W.; and Williams, M. V. 1980. Behavioral slowing with age: Causes, organization and consequences. In *Aging in the 1980's: Selected Contemporary Issues,* ed. L. W. Poon, pp. 559–612. Washington, D.C.: American Psychological Association.

Blazer, D. G., and Houpt, J. L. 1979. Perception of poor health in the healthy older adult. *J. Consult. Psychol.* 27: 330–334.

Botwinick, J. 1979. *Aging and Behavior.* 2nd ed. New York: Springer.

Boudewyns, P. A., and Keefe, F. J., eds. 1982. *Behavioral Medicine in General Medical Practice.* Menlo Park: Addison-Wesley.

Boyer, E. 1980. Health perception in the elderly: Its cultural and social aspects. In *Aging in Culture and Society: Comparative Viewpoints and Strategies,* ed. C. L. Fry, pp. 198–215. New York: Praeger Press.

Branch, L. G., 1977. *Understanding the Health and Social Service Needs of the People over Age 65.* Center for Survey Research Monographs. University of Massachusetts.

Brocklehurst, J. C., ed. 1978. *Textbook of Geriatric Medicine and Gerontology.* Edinburgh: Churchill Livingstone.

Busse, E. W. 1969. Theories of aging. In *Behavior and Adaptation in Later Life,* eds. E. W. Busse and E. Pfeiffer, pp. 11–32. Boston: Little Brown.

Busse, E. W. 1978. Duke longitudinal study I: Senescence and senility. In *Alzheimer's Disease: Senile Dementia and Related Disorders,* eds. R. Katzman, R. D. Terry, and K. L. Bick, Aging, vol. 7. New York: Raven Press.

Busse, E. W., and Maddox, G. L., eds. In press. The Duke longitudinal studies of normal aging, 1955–1980: Introduction and overview of findings. New York: Springer.

Campbell, A.; Converse, P. E.; and Rogers, W. L. 1976. *The Quality of American Life: Perceptions, Evaluations and Satisfactions.* New York: Russell Sage Foundation.

Cautela, J. R., and Mansfield, L. 1977. A behavioral approach to geriatrics. *Geropsychology: A Model of Training and Clinical Service,* ed. W. D. Gentry, pp. 21–42. Cambridge: Ballinger.

Cohen, F., and Lazarus, R. S. 1979. Coping with the stresses of illness. In *Health Psychology: A Handbook,* G. C. Stone, F. Cohen, N. E. Adler, and Associates, pp. 217–254. San Francisco: Jossey-Bass.

Costa, P. T., Jr.; Fleg, J. L.; Mc Crae, R. R.; and Lakatta, E. G. 1982. Neuroticism, coronary artery disease, and chest pain complaints: Cross-sectional and longitudinal studies. *Exp. Aging Res.* 8(1): 37–44.

Costa, P. T., Jr., and Mc Crae, R. R. 1978. Objective personality assessment. In *The Clinical Psychology of Aging,* eds. M. Storandt, I. E. Siegler, and M. F. Elias. New York: Plenum Press.

Costa, P. T., Jr., and Mc Crae, R. R. 1980 (a). Still stable after all these years: Personality as a key to some issues in aging. In *Life-Span Dev. and Beh.* 3, eds. P. B. Baltes and O. G. Brim. New York: Academic Press.

Costa, P. T., Jr., and Mc Crae, R. R. 1980 (b). Somatic complaints in males a a function of age and neuroticism: A longitudinal analysis. *J. Beh. Med.* 3(3): 245–257.

Costa, P. T., Jr., and Mc Crae, R. R. 1982. An approach to the attribution of aging period and cohort effects. *Psych. Bull.* 92(1): 238–250.

Costa, P. T., Jr.; Mc Crae, R. E.; Andres, R.; and Tobin, J. D. 1980. Hypertension, somatic complaints and personality. In *Hypertension and Cognitive Processes,* eds. M. F. Elias and D. P. H. Streeten, pp. 95–110. Mt. Desert: Beech Hill Publishing Co.

Costa, P. T., Jr.; Mc Crae, R. R.; and Arenberg, D. 1983. Recent research on personality and aging. In *Longitudinal Studies of Adult Psychological Development,* ed. K. W. Schaie, pp. 222–265. New York: Guilford Press.

Costa, P. T., Jr., and Shock, N. W. 1980. New longitudinal data on the question of whether hypertension influences cognitive performance. In *Hypertension and Cognitive Processes,* eds. M. F. Elias and D. P. H. Streeten, pp. 83–93. Mt. Desert: Beech Hill Publishing Co.

Crawford, J., and Cohen, H. J. In press. Aging and neoplasia. In *Annual Review of Gerontology and Geriatrics,* ed. C. Eisdorfer. Vol. 4. New York: Springer.

Davidson, P. O., and Davidson, S. M., eds. 1980. *Behav-*

ioral Medicine: Changing Health Lifestyles. New York: Brunner/Mazel.

Eisdorfer, C., ed. 1980. *Annual Review of Gerontology and Geriatrics.* Vol. 1. New York: Springer.

Eisdorfer, C., ed. 1981. *Annual Review of Gerontology and Geriatrics.* Vol. 2. New York: Springer.

Eisdorfer, C. and Wilkie, F. 1977. Stress, disease, aging and behavior. In *Handbook of the Psychology of Aging,* eds. J. E. Birren and K.W. Schaie, pp. 251–275. New York: Van Nostrand Reinhold.

Ekstein, D. 1978. Common complaints of the elderly. In *The Geriatric Patient,* ed. W. Reichel. New York: HP Publishing.

Elias, M. F. 1980. Epilogue. In *Hypertension and Cognitive Processes,* eds. M. F. Elias and D. H. P. Streeten, pp. 159–162. Mount Desert, Maine: Beech Hill Publishing Co.

Elias, M. F.; Elias, P. K.; and Elias, J. W. 1977. *Adult Developmental Psychology.* St. Louis: C. V. Mosby.

Elias, M. F.; Robbins, M. A.; Blow, F. C.; Rice, A. P.; and Edgecomb, J. L. 1982. Symptom reporting, anxiety and depression in arteriographically classified middle-aged chest pain patients. *Exp. Aging Res.* 8(1): 45–52.

Elias, M. F., and Streeten, D. H. P., eds. 1980. *Hypertension and Cognitive Processes.* Mount Desert, Maine: Beech Hill Publishing Co.

Engel, B. T. 1983. Behavioral medicine. In *Experimental and Clinical Interventions in Aging,* eds. R. F. Walker and R. L. Cooper. New York: Marcel Dekker, Inc.

Exton-Smith, A. N., and Overstall, P. W. 1979. *Geriatric Medicine.* Baltimore: University Park Press.

Felton, B. J., and Revenson, T. A. 1981. Stress, coping and adaptability among the chronically ill. Paper presented at the American Psychological Association, Los Angeles.

Fingerhurt, L. A., and Rosenberg, H. M. 1981. Mortality among the elderly. In *Health—United States 1981.* Hyattsville, Md.: USDHSS, DSS Pub. No. (PHS) 82–1232.

Fox, B. H. 1978. Premorbid psychological factors related to cancer incidence. *J. Beh. Med.* 1(1): 45–133.

Frei, E. 1982. The national cancer chemotherapy program. *Science* 217: 600–609.

Friedman, S. A., and Steinheber, F. U. 1976. Symposium on geriatric medicine. *Med. Clin. N. Am.* 60(6), Nov. 1976.

Fries, J. 1980. Aging, natural death, and the compression of morbidity. *N. Engl. J. Med.* 303: 130–135.

Fries, J. F., and Crapo, L. M. 1981. *Vitality and Aging.* San Francisco: W. H. Freeman and Company.

Furchgott, E., and Busemeyer, J. R. 1980. Age preference for professional helpers. *J. Geront.* 36(1): 90–92.

Gentry, W. D. 1979. Preadmission behavior. In *Psychological Aspects of Myocardial Infarction and Coronary Care,* eds. W. D. Gentry and R. B. Williams, pp. 67–77. St. Louis: C. V. Mosby.

Gillum, R.; Leon, G. R.; Kamp, J.; and Becerra-Aldama, J. 1980. Prediction of cardiovascular and other disease onset and mortality from 30-year longitudinal MMPI data. *J. Consult. Clin. Psych.* 48(3): 405–406.

Gottesdanker, R. 1982. Age and simple reaction time. *J. Geront.* 37: 342–348.

Hamburg, D. A. 1982. Health and behavior. *Science* 217: 399.

Hamburg, D. A.; Elliot, G. R.; and Parron, D. L., eds. 1982. *Health and Behavior: Frontiers of Research in the Biobehavioral Sciences.* Washington, D.C.: National Academy Press.

Haug, M. R. 1980. Age and medical care utilization patterns. *J. Geront.* 36(1): 103–111.

Haynes, S. G.; Feinleib, M.; Levine, S.; Scotch, N.; and Kannel, W. B. 1978. The relationship of psychosocial factors to coronary heart disease in the Framingham study. II. Prevalence of coronary heart disease. *Am. J. Epidemiology,* 107: 384–402.

Hertzog, C.; Schaie, K. W.; and Gribbin, K. 1978. Cardiovascular diseases and changes in intellectual functioning from middle to old age. *J. Geront.* 33(6): 872–883.

Hickey, T. 1980. *Health and Aging.* Belmont, CA: Wadsworth.

Holmes, J. H., and Rahe, R. H. 1967. The social readjustment rating scale. *J. Per. Soc. Psy.* 11: 213–218.

Horn, J. L. 1970. Organization of data on life-span development of human abilities. In *Lifespan Developmental Psychology: Research and Theory,* eds. L. R. Goulet and P. B. Baltes, pp. 423–466. New York: Academic Press.

Houpt, J. L.; Orleans, C. S.; George, L. K.; and Brodie, H. K. H. 1979. *The Importance of Mental Health Services to General Health Care.* Cambridge, Massachusetts: Ballinger.

Hulicka, I. M. 1967. Short-term learning and memory efficiency as a function of age and health. *J. Am. Ger. Soc.* 15(3): 285–294.

Institute of Medicine, 1981. *Airline Pilot Age, Health and Performance: Scientific and Medical Considerations.* Washington, D.C.: National Academy of Sciences Press.

Jarvik, L. F. 1980. Diagnosis of dementia in the elderly: A 1980 perspective. In *Annual Review of Gerontology and Geriatrics,* ed. C. Eisdorfer. Vol. 1, pp. 180–203. New York: Springer.

Jenkins, C. D. 1979. The coronary prone personality. In *Preadmission Behavior,* eds. W. D. Gentry and R. B. Williams, pp. 5–30.

Kannel, W. B., and Gordon, T. 1980. Cardiovascular risk factors in the aged: The Framingham study. In *Epidemiology of Aging,* eds. S. G. Haynes and M. Feinleib, pp. 65–86. Washington, D.C.: USDHHS, PHS, NIH, NIA, NHLBI, NIH No. 80–969.

Kaplan, G. A. 1982. Psychosocial factors and ischemic heart disease mortality: A focal role for perceived health. Paper presented at the meetings of the Am. Psychol. Assn., Washington, D.C.

Kart, C. 1981. Experiencing symptoms: Attribution and misattribution of illness among the aged. In *Elderly Patients and Their Doctors,* ed. M. R. Haug, pp. 70–87. New York: Springer.

Kasl, S. V., and Berkman, L. F. 1981. Some psychosocial influences on the health status of the elderly: The perspective of social epidemiology. In *Aging: Biology and Behavior,* eds. J. L. McGaugh and S. B. Keisler, pp. 345–377. New York: Academic Press.

La Rue, A.; Bank, L.; Jarvik, L. F.; and Hetland, M. 1979. Health in old age: How do physicians' ratings and self ratings compare? *J. Geront.* 34: 687–691.

Lazarus, R. S., and Launier, R. 1978. Stress-related transactions between person and environment. In *Perspectives in Interactional Psychology,* eds. L. A. Pervin and M. Lewis. New York: Plenum Press.

Lawton, M. P. 1981. Research needs in understanding the physician-older patient relationship. In *Elderly Patients and Their Doctors,* ed. M. R. Haug, pp. 179–188. New York: Springer.

Leon, G. R.; Gillum, B.; Gillum, R.; and Gouze, M. 1979. Personality stability and change over a 30-year period–middle age to old age. *J. Consult. Clin. Psy.* 47(3): 517–524.

Levenson, A. J., and Hall, R. C. W., eds. 1981. *Neuropsychiatric Manifestations of Physical Disease in the Elderly.* Aging, vol. 14. New York: Raven Press.

Levy, R. I., and Moskowitz, J. 1982. Cardiovascular research: Decades of progress, a decade of promise. *Science* 217: 121–129.

Light, K. C. 1980. Hypertension and response slowing. In *Hypertension and Cognitive Processes,* eds. M. F. Elias and D. P. H. Streeten, pp. 17–32. Mount Desert, Maine: Beech Hill Publishing Co.

Maddox, G. L. 1962. Selected methodological issues. *Proceedings of the Social Statistics Section of the Am. Stat. Assoc.,* pp. 280–285.

Maddox, G. L., and Douglass, E. B. 1973. Self-assessments of health. *J. Heal. Soc. Beh.* 14: 87–93.

Manton, K. G. 1982. Changing concepts of morbidity and mortality in the elderly population. *Millbank Mem. Fund Q.* 60(2): 183–244.

McCarty, S. M.; Siegler; I. C.; and Logue, P. E. 1982. Cross-sectional and longitudinal patterns of three Wechsler memory scale subtests. *J. Geront.* 37(2): 169–175.

Mc Crae, R. R. 1982. Age differences in the use of coping mechanisms. *J. Geront.* 37: 454–460.

Mc Crae, R. R.; Costa, P. T. Jr.; and Arenberg, D. 1980. Constancy of adult personality structure in males: Longitudinal, cross-sectional and times-of-measurement analysis. *J. Geront.* 35(6): 877–883.

McGinnis, J. M. 1982. Recent health gains for adults. *N. Engl. J. Med.* 306(11): 671–673.

Mechanic, D. 1976. Sex, illness, illness behavior, and the use of health services. *J. Hum. Stress* 2: 29–40.

Mishara, B. L., and Kastenbaum, R. 1980. *Alcohol and Old Age.* New York: Grune and Stratton.

Miller, N. E. 1980. A perspective on the effects of stress and coping on disease and health. In *Coping and Health,* eds. S. Levine and H. Ursin, pp. 323–353. New York: Plenum Press.

Mossey, J. M., and Shapiro, E. 1982. Self-rated health: A predictor of mortality among the elderly. *Am J. Pub. Health* 72, 8: 800–808 (August).

Neugarten, B. L. 1977. Personality and Aging. In *Hand-*

book of Psychology of Aging, eds. J. E. Birren and K. W. Schaie, pp. 626–649. New York: Van Nostrand Reinhold.

Okun, M. A.; Stock, W. A.; Haring, M. J.; and Witter, R. A. Health and subjective well being: a meta-analysis. *J. of Aging and Hum. Devel.* (In press).

Osberg, J. W.; Mears, G. J.; McKee, D.; and Burnett, G. B. 1982. Intellectual functioning in renal failure and chronic dialysis. *J. Chron. Dis.* 35: 445–457.

Ostfeld, A. M.; Shekelle, R. B.; Kiawans, H.; and Tufo, H. M. 1974. Epidemiology of stroke in an elderly welfare population. *Am J. Pub. Health* 64: 450–458.

Palmore, E., ed. 1970. *Normal Aging.* Durham, North Carolina: Duke University Press.

Palmore, E., ed. 1974. *Normal Aging II.* Durham, North Carolina: Duke University Press.

Palmore, E.; Cleveland, W. P.; Nowlin, J. B.; Ramm, D.; and Siegler, I. C. 1979. Stress and adaptation in later life. *J. Geront.* 34(6): 841–851.

Parron, D. L.; Solomon, F.; and Rodin, J., eds. 1981. *Health Behavior and Aging: Research Agenda,* Interim Report No. 5. Washington, D.C.: Division of Mental Health and Behavioral Medicine, National Academy Press.

Pentz, C. A.; Elias, M. F.; Wood, W. G.; and Schultz, N. A. 1979. Relationship of age and hypertension to neurophychological test performance. *Exp. Aging Res.* 5(4): 351–372.

Pirozzolo, F. J., and Hansch, E. C. 1981. Oculomotor reaction time in dementia reflects degree of cerebral dysfunction. *Science* 214: 349–351.

Pomerleau, O. F., and Brady, J. P., eds. 1979. *Behavioral Medicine: Theory and Practice.* Baltimore: Williams and Wilkins.

Pooling Project Research Group. 1978. Relationship of blood pressure, serum cholesterol, smoking habit, relative weight, and ECG abnormalities to incidence of major coronary events: Final report of the pooling project. *J. Chron. Dis.* 31: 207–306.

Rabbitt, P. M. A. 1980. A fresh look at changes in reaction times in old age. In *The Psychobiology of Aging: Problems and Perspectives,* ed. D. G. Stein, pp. 425–442. New York: Elsevier North Holland.

Rakowski, W., and Hickey, T. 1980. Late life health behavior. *Res. on Aging* 2(3): 283–308.

Richards, W. S., and Thorpe, G. L. 1978. Behavioral approaches to the problems of later life. In *The Clinical Psychology of Aging,* eds. M. Storandt, I. C. Siegler, and M. F. Elias, pp. 253–276. New York: Plenum Press.

Rodin, J. 1980. Managing the stress of aging: The role of control and coping. In *Coping and Health,* eds. S. Levine and H. Ursin, pp. 171–202. New York: Plenum Press.

Rosenstock, I. M. 1966. Why people use health services. *Millbank Mem. Fund Q.* 44: 94–124.

Rusin, M., and Siegler, I. C. 1975. Personality differences between participants and drop-outs in a longitudinal study. Paper presented at the Gerontological Society, Louisville, KY.

Satariano, W. A., and Syme, S. L. 1981. Life changes

and disease in elderly populations. In *Aging: Biology and Behavior,* eds. J. L. Mc Gaugh and S. B. Keisler, pp. 311–327. New York: Academic Press.

Schachter, S. 1982. Recidivism and self-cure of smoking and obesity. *Am. Psychol.* 37(4): 436–444.

Schaefer, D.; Coyne, J. C.; and Lazarus, R. S. 1981. The health-related functions of social support. *J. Beh. Med.* 4(4): 381–406.

Schrier, R. W., ed. 1982. *Clinical Internal Medicine in the Aged.* Philadelphia: W. B. Saunders.

Schroeder, D. H., and Costa, P. T., Jr. 1984. The Influences of life stress on physical illness: Substantive effects of methodological flaws? *J. Pers. Soc. Psych.* 46(4):853–863.

Schultz, N. R.; Dineen, J. T.; Elias, M. F.; Pentz, C. A.; and Wood, W. G. 1979. WAIS performance for different age groups of hypertensive and control subjects during the administration of a diuretic. *J. Geront.* 34(2): 246–253.

Schultz, N. R., and Elias, M. F. 1980. The effects of hypertension on WAIS performance. In *Hypertension and Cognitive Processes,* eds. M. F. Elias and D. H. P. Streeten, pp. 33–54. Mt. Desert, Maine: Beech Hill Publishing Co.

Selye, H. 1979. Stress, cancer and the mind. In *Cancer Stress and Death,* eds. J. Tache, H. Selye, and S. B. Day, pp. 11–19. New York: Plenum.

Shock, N. W.; Grevlich, R. C.; Andres, R.; Arenberg, D.; Costa, P. T., Jr.; Lakatta, E. L.; and Tobin, J. 1984. *Normal Human Aging: The Baltimore Longitudinal Study of Aging.* U.S. Public Health Service Publication No. 84–2450. Washington, D.C.: U.S. Government Printing Office.

Siegel, J. S. 1980. Recent and prospective demographic trends for the elderly population and some implications for health care. In *Epidemiology of Aging.* eds. S. G. Haynes and M. Feinleib, pp. 289–314. Washington, D.C.: USDHHS, PHS, NIH, NIA, NHLBI, NIH No. 80–969.

Siegler, I. C. 1980. The psychology of adult development and aging. In *Handbook of Geriatric Psychiatry,* eds. E. W. Busse and D. G. Blazer, pp. 169–221. New York: Van Nostrand Reinhold.

Siegler, I. C. 1983 Psychological aspects of the Duke longitudinal studies. In *Longitudinal Studies of Adult Psychological Development,* ed. K. W. Schaie, pp. 136–190. New York: Guilford Press.

Siegler, I. C.; George, L. K.; and Okun, M. A. 1979. A cross-sequential analysis of adult personality. *Dev. Psychol.* 15(3): 350–351.

Siegler, I. C., and Nowlin, J. B. 1979. Health and behavior in the Duke longitudinal studies. Paper presented at the meetings of the Am. Psychol. Assoc. New York, September 1979.

Siegler, I. C.; Nowlin, J. B.; and Blumenthal, J. A. 1980. Health and behavior: Methodological considerations for adult development and aging. In *Aging in the 1980's: Selected Contemporary Issues,* ed. L. W. Poon, pp. 559–612. Washington, D.C.: American Psychological Association.

Singer, J. E., and Krantz, D. S. 1982. Perspectives on the interface between psychology and public health. *Am. Psychol.* 37(8): 955–960.

Sklar, L. S. and Anisman, H. 1981. Stress and cancer. *Psych. Bull.* 89(3): 369–406.

Speith, W. 1964. Cardiovascular health status, age and psychological performance. *J. Geront.* 19: 277–284.

Speith, W. 1965. Slowness of task performance and cardiovascular disease. In *Behavior, Aging and the Nervous System,* eds. A. T. Welford and J. E. Birren, pp. 366–400. Springfield, Illinois: Charles C. Thomas.

Starfield, B., and Pless, I. B. 1980. Physical health. In *Constancy and Change in Human Development,* eds. O. G. Brim and J. Kagan, pp. 272–324. Cambridge, Mass.: Harvard University Press.

Stein, M. 1981. Effects of aging on the interaction of health and behavior. In *Health Behavior and Aging: A Research Agenda,* Interim Report No. 5, eds. D. L. Parron, F. Solomon, and J. Rodin, pp. 65–73. Washington, D.C.: Division of Mental Health and Behavioral Medicine, National Academy Press.

Steinberg, F. U., ed. 1976. *Cowdry's The Care of the Geriatric Patient.* 5th ed. St. Louis: C. V. Mosby.

Stone, G. C. 1979. Psychology and the health system. In *Health Psychology: A Handbook,* eds. G. C. Stone, F. Cohen, and N. E. Adler, pp. 47–75. San Francisco: Jossey-Bass.

Surwit, R. S.; Scovern, A. W.; and Feinglos, M. N. 1982. The role of behavior in diabetes care. *Diabetes Care* 5(3): 337–342.

Surwit, R. S.; Williams, R. B.; and Shapiro, D. 1982. *Behavioral Approaches to Cardiovascular Disease.* New York: Academic Press.

Thomas, C. 1976. Precursors of premature disease and death. *Ann. Int. Med* 85: 653–658.

Thomas, C. B., and Greenstreet, R. L. 1973. Psychobiological characteristics in youth as predictors of five disease states. Suicide, mental illness, hypertension, coronary heart disease and tumor. *Johns Hopkins Med. J.* 132: 16–43.

Thomas, C. B., and McCabe, O. L. 1980. Precursors of premature disease and death: Habits of nervous tension. *Johns Hopkins Med. J.* 147: 137–145.

Thomas, C. B.; Santora, P. B.; and Shaffer, J. W. 1980. Health of physicians in midlife in relation to use of alcohol: A prospective of a cohort of former medical students. *Johns Hopkins Med. J.* 146: 1–10.

Turner, B. F. 1982. Sex-related differences in aging. In *Handbook of Developmental Psychology,* eds. B. B. Wolman and G. Stricker, pp. 912–936. New York: Prentice Hall.

U.S. Dept. Health, Education and Welfare. 1979. *Healthy people: The surgeon general's report on health promotion and disease prevention.* PHS Publication No. 79–55071. Washington, D.C.: U.S. Government Printing Office.

Vaillant, G. E. 1979. Natural history of male psychologic health: Effects of mental health on physical health. *N. Eng. J. Med.* 301(23): 1249–1254.

Verbrugge, L. M. 1981. Women and men: Mortality and health of older people. In *Leading Edges: Recent Research on Psychosocial Aging,* eds. B. B. Hess and

K. Bond, pp. 231–285. Bethesda, MD: NIH Publication 81–2390.

Waldron, I. 1980. Sex differences in longevity. In *Epidemiology of Aging*, eds. S. G. Haynes and M. Feinleib, pp. 163–82. Washington, D.C.: USDHHS, PHS, NIH, NIA, NHLBI, NIH No. 80–969.

Ware, J. E.; Brook, R. H.; Davies, A. R.; and Lohr, K. N. 1981. Choosing measures of health status for individuals in general populations. *Am. J. Pub. Health* 71 (6): 620–625.

Weksler, M. E. 1981. Three great networks: The central nervous system, endocrine system, immune system and aging. In *Health Behavior and Aging: A Research Agenda*, Interim Report No. 5, eds. D. L. Parron, F. Solomon, and J. Rodin, pp. 57–64. Washington, D.C.: Division of Mental Health and Behavioral Medicine, National Academy Press.

Wilkie, F. L., and Eisdorfer, C. 1971. Intelligence and blood pressure in the aged. *Science* 172: 959–962.

Wilkie, F., and Eisdorfer, C. 1972. Blood pressure and behavioral correlates in the aged. Paper presented at the 9th International Congress of Gerontology, Kiev, U.S.S.R.

Wilkie, F. L.; Eisdorfer, C.; and Nowlin, J. B. 1976. Memory and blood pressure in the aged. *Exp. Aging Res.* 2: 3–16.

Williams, R. B. 1979. Psychological mechanisms underlying the association between psychosocial factors and coronary disease. In *Psychosocial Aspects of Myocardial Infarction and Coronary Care*, eds. W. D. Gentry and R. B. Williams, pp. 50–64. St. Louis: C. V. Mosby.

Williams, R. B.; Lane, J. D.; Kuhn, C. M.; Melosh, W.; White, A. D.; and Schanberg, S. M. 1982. Physiological and neuroendocrine response patterns during different behavioral challenges: Differential hyperresponsivity of young type A men. *Science* 218: 483–485.

Wood, W. G. 1978. The elderly alcoholic: Some diagnostic problems and considerations. In *The Clinical Psychology of Aging*, eds. M. Storandt, I. C. Siegler, and M. F. Elias, pp. 97–116. New York: Plenum.

Wood, W. G., and Elias, M. F. 1980. Essential hypertension and neuropsychological test performance. In *Hypertension and Cognitive Processes*, eds. M. F. Elias and D. H. P. Streeten, pp. 57–80. Mt. Desert, ME: Beech Hill Publishing Co.

Wood, W. G.; Elias, M. F.; Schultz, N. R.; and Pentz, C. A. 1978. Symptoms reported on the Cornell medical index in relationship to hypertension and age. *Exp. Aging Res.* 4(5): 421–431.

Wood, W. G.; Elias, M. F.; Schultz, N. R.; and Pentz, C. A. 1979. Anxiety and depression in young and middle-aged hypertensive and normotensive subjects. *Exp. Aging Res.* 5(1): 15–30.

Wurtle, S. K.; Galanos, A. N.; and Roberts, M. C. 1980. Increasing return compliance in a tuberculosis detection drive. *J. Beh. Med.* 3(3): 311–318.

PART 3 SOCIAL INFLUENCES ON BEHAVIOR

7
THE FAMILY IN LATE LIFE: PSYCHOSOCIAL AND DEMOGRAPHIC CONSIDERATIONS

Rhonda Aizenberg
Automobile Club of Los Angeles
and
Judith Treas
University of Southern California

INTRODUCTION

The family life of the aged has been a subject of considerable debate during the past few decades. Empirical research findings on family relations in late life have conflicted with the implication of earlier sociological theory that urbanization had undermined kinship bonds in contemporary American society (Parsons, 1943; Moore, 1963; Goode, 1963). According to this perspective, the shift from the extended to the nuclear family residence and the transfer of traditional family functions to specialized institutions have attenuated family relations, leading to the social isolation of older kin members.

On the one hand, the available evidence has questioned the assumption that the emergence of the nuclear family coincided with the onset of industrialization and urbanization (Burch, 1967; Laslett and Wall, 1972; Smith, 1981). On the other hand, the work of Litwak (1960a, 1960b) and Sussman and Burchinal (1962a, 1962b) has documented the existence of a modified extended family in modern society. Subsequent studies confirm that viable relationships are typically maintained despite the residential separation of older persons and their relatives (Shanas, 1980; Lopata, 1973). Neither does it seem that older persons would prefer to coreside with kin, as research findings document a preference for intimacy at a distance among the elderly (Rosenmayr and Kockeis, 1963). Although the family's direct participation in education, recreation, economic welfare, religion, and protective activities has diminished, the importance of its affectional role has probably intensified (Cottrell, 1960). As formal bureaucracies have assumed greater responsibility for providing services to the elderly, younger kin members have become increasingly important as mediating linkages to these organizations (Kreps, 1977; Sussman, 1977; Shanas and Sussman, 1981). Rather than declining, the functions of the family with respect to the aged have been redefined in terms of a set of new tasks.

The systematic analysis of family relations in late life has been stimulated by practical concerns as well as by intellectual curiosity. As a result of broad-scale shifts in demographic processes, the profile of the American family has changed during the twentieth century. Structural and compositional differences in family memberships have been particularly noteworthy, as have alterations in the timing

169

and sequencing of the stages of the family cycle. Together these changes have had profound repercussions for the psychosocial environment and functioning of the family. They are central to understanding the climate of contemporary family life and the family transitions that older persons weather.

This chapter begins by examining macrosocietal changes in the population and proceeds to relate these changes to transformations in the structure of the family and to the timing and placement of family life stages. Consideration is then given to potential psychosocial impacts of these changes on kinship relations. The second section reviews the literature on selected dimensions of family life among the elderly, including their living arrangements and interaction patterns. In the final section, attention turns to the broader social context in which family life is embedded and synthesized. The importance of friendship is assessed, with special attention given to the issue of whether peer involvements are substitutes for, complements of, or independent from family relations. Once the research on community-based aged residents has been examined, family and friendship relations are assessed separately for their institutionalized counterparts. Finally, we conclude by suggesting possible areas for future investigation.

DEMOGRAPHIC BACKGROUND

Changes in Population Structure

Changes in family structure have closely mirrored the aggregate shifts occurring in the nation's total population. As the age distribution of the population has become more heavily weighted toward the old ages, so too has the membership profile of the family (Treas and Bengtson, 1982). While the general population grew by threefold between 1900 and 1980, the older age segment increased by over eightfold. Its proportionate share of the population climbed from 4.1 to 11.2 percent in some eighty years (Hauser, 1976; U.S. Bureau of the Census, 1981a).

Not only has the total population aged during this century, but the elderly population itself has been growing older. That is, the proportion of "old-old" persons has been on the rise. In 1900, less than 30 percent of those over 65 were at least 75 years of age and only 4 percent were 85 or over. By 1980, the comparable figures had climbed to 38 percent and 9 percent, respectively (U.S. Bureau of the Census, 1981a).

The primary factor affecting the proportionate growth of the older population has been the downward trend in fertility. Whereas women of childbearing years in 1900 had an average of 4.2 offspring, their contemporary counterparts are averaging only 1.7 (Uhlenberg, 1980; Marshall, 1981a). By reducing the relative number of younger persons in the population, this diminishment of fertility has caused the proportion of older persons to expand (Coale, 1957). Although of less significance, long-run declines in the mortality rate as well as earlier patterns of immigration have also been responsible for these trends in the "graying of America." Because of the sharp curtailment of premature deaths, old age has become "democratized" (Treas and Bengtson, 1982), allowing most individuals to survive to the later stages of life. Since they were primarily young persons who have since aged, the immigrants who entered this country prior to World War II have likewise expanded the ranks of today's elderly population.

Since death rates at the younger ages are already low, the mortality rate in the future will be largely dependent upon survivorship trends at the older ages. Some evidence shows rapid reductions in the mortality rate of elderly persons in recent years. From 1968 to 1977, death rates at ages 65 and over dropped appreciably, averaging a 1.7-percent decrement per year (Siegel, 1978), primarily as a result of declines in cardiovascular causes of death (Crimmins, 1981). Should this trend continue, life expectancy will rise considerably. Projections suggest that the expectation of life at birth in the year 2000 could range as high as 80 (Crimmins, 1981).

Since mortality declines have been far greater for females than males, newborn girls currently face an eight-year advantage in expected longevity (U.S. Public Health Service, 1981). Although males enjoy a numerical advantage at birth, the imbalance is reversed after age 25 because of the sex-selectivity in mortality. At present, there are only 68 men for every 100 women aged 65 and above and only 44 males for 100 females at the advanced old ages of 85 years and over (U.S. Bureau of the Census, 1981a). Some projections point to an even greater female excess among the aged in the future (Siegel, 1976).

Intergenerational Implications of Demographic Change

To be sure, trends in demographic processes have had significant and numerous implications for the family. Past demographic patterns have induced dramatic changes in the structural configuration of the contemporary family, and still further modifications are anticipated (Deming and Cutler, 1983; Hagestad, 1981a, 1981b; Marshall, 1981b; Siegel, 1976, 1978). One important change relates to the age composition of the family. At the same time that children have come to represent a relatively smaller component of family membership, the visibility of older members has been heightened. Consider the ratio of persons aged 65 to 84 to those 45 to 49 years of age, often cited as a measure of the dependency of aged kin to their middle-aged children. There were only 86 persons aged 65 to 84 for every 100 persons aged 45 to 49 at the beginning of the century; in recent years, there have been as many as 210 for every 100 persons (Aizenberg and Harris, 1982).

As a consequence of these broad-scale demographic trends, young people today are more likely to have older persons belonging to their kinship network than at any earlier point in history. Whereas the odds were only one-in-four that a newborn child in 1900 would have both sets of grandparents alive, this figure has since increased by more than twofold, reaching almost two-in-three by 1976 (Uhlenberg, 1980). The transition into grandparenthood having become a middle-aged experience (Troll, 1971), it is now possible for many grandchildren to reach adulthood and raise their own children during their grandparents' lifetimes. About half of all persons aged 65 years and over with surviving children belong to families spanning four generations (Shanas, 1979a).

With the average ages at marriage and childbearing declining over most of this century, the age distance between generations has fallen progressively. In the early 1900s, adjacent generations were separated by an average of 30 years; at present, the mean length of a generation is about 20 years (Troll et al., 1979). Coupled with the increase in longevity, this "generational acceleration" (Hagestad, 1981b) has made it possible for family members spanning four generations to be conceived in about the same length of time that it formerly took to form three generations (Bengtson and DeTerre, 1980).

One concomitant of the increased generational span of the family is a greater homogeneity in the ages and life stages of kin members, with families becoming more heavily weighted with individuals in the middle and later ages and stages of life. Aging families, comprised of the frail "old-old" parent and the middle-aged or "young-old" child, are becoming more frequent. In fact, Troll et al. (1979) estimate that as many as one in 10 individuals aged 65 and over has a child who also is at least 65.

Winsborough (1980, p. 75), analyzing temporal changes in survival prospects among women, concludes that the "experience for women of the death of their mother . . . is shifting from an event of the middle years to an event occurring in the immediate preretirement years. . . ." Shared lifetimes are generally longer for females than males. Mother and daughter relations are especially likely to be long-lasting. Given the sex difference in longevity, however, the chances are as high as 20 percent that a woman giving birth to a son while in her early 20s will outlive him (Metropolitan Life, 1977).

Paradoxically, the number of offspring available to the aged may have actually declined over the century as a result of reduced fertility. Although persons now approaching the threshold of old age have relatively large numbers of descendants, this situation represents what is expected to be a temporary interruption in the secular trend toward smaller families and fewer grown offspring in late life. In general, these individuals, as the parents of the baby boom, have large reservoirs of close kin on whom they can potentially depend. Their children, who presently are in the childbearing ages, are experiencing record low rates of fertility. Should their fertility levels remain unchanged, they will have relatively scarce familial resources upon which to draw in their own old age.

Marital Implications of Demographic Change

Reflecting their mortality advantage throughout the lifespan, females are more likely than males to represent the senior generation of the family lineage. Given their lower death rates and their tendency to marry men older than themselves, women experience a very high risk of outliving their husbands and being widowed in old age. Of married women aged 65 and over in 1980, only 41 percent had a living spouse and more than 50 percent were widowed. In contrast, the vast majority—80 percent—of married older men had a living spouse and only about 14 percent were widowed (U.S. Bureau of the Census, 1981b).

In addition to reflecting different mortality risks, the sex disparity in marital status can also be accounted for by the greater propensity for older men to remarry. In fact, although marriage is relatively uncommon among the elderly, men are over five times more likely to marry in old age than women. Undoubtedly, taboos concerning dating and sexual activity in late life have inhibited some elderly persons from marrying just as health, mobility, and financial limitations have constrained others (Treas and VanHilst, 1976).

That elderly males stand a greater chance of remarrying than females results from a combination of social, psychological, and demographic factors. Because of the sex disparities in death rates, there are about three times as many single women aged 65 and over as there are unmarried men in this age range (U.S. Bureau of the Census, 1981b). This numerical advantage for males is strengthened by social norms that support the marriage of men to younger women (Treas and VanHilst, 1976).

Ironically, the number of years that women can look forward to jointly surviving with their spouses has increased during the twentieth century in spite of the growing sex gap in life expectancy. Of couples currently marrying at the average age of marriage (i.e., age 22 for women and 25 for men), 64 percent can expect their marriage to last 40 years before it is disrupted by the husband's death (Uhlenberg, 1980). When the initial childless years of marriage are taken into account as well, about one-third of married life is usually spent in "the empty nest." In contrast, couples in the late 1800s could expect to live together only about 1.6 years after their last child's marriage before their own marriage was dissolved through the death of one of them, typically the husband (Glick, 1977).

Psychosocial Speculation on Family Changes

Never before have families been as heavily populated with older persons (particularly older women) as now, nor has the age distribution of elderly members been as strongly skewed towards the advanced old ages. As most elderly persons age, their kinship universe expands as more and more members and generations are added to the family lineage through marriage and childbirth. Despite this increased diversification in the kinship network, long-term declines in fertility are leading to progressive reductions in the number of immediate family members who will be available in late life.

Although familial support is not an option for familyless individuals, for those belonging to families the mere number of kin is not always a valid indicator of the behavioral and qualitative aspects of their relationships. Extensive kinship networks in the past may have facilitated the exchange of familial services and supports, but they may also have had a disruptive impact on the nature of the relationships that kin members formed with one another. Where many children are forced to compete for their parents' time and energy, parent-child relations, sibling solidarity, and marital bonds may suffer. When fertility is limited, the sum of childbearing demands is presumably reduced, and more time and effort may be expended per child. When siblings are closely spaced and born in similar stages of their parents' careers, differences arising from unequal exposure to family resources and opportunities are reduced (Hareven, 1977).

High rates of mortality probably affected

family life in the past by making people more reluctant to invest their time and effort in relationships that had a high risk of dissolving prematurely (Uhlenberg, 1980). When infant deaths were common, parents were more likely to resist becoming too emotionally involved with their children (Shorter, 1975). Today, similar concerns about the short life expectancies of their age mates may dissuade the elderly from marrying. With declines in the mortality rate, uncertainties regarding the durability of kinship ties diminish and the incentives for establishing intergenerational familial attachments increase.

Given the recent gains in longevity, relationships are longer lived than in any previous period in history (Troll et al., 1979). Although long-standing relationships may be vulnerable to stresses and conflicts resulting from maturational or developmental transformations, they are probably more highly resistant to voluntary disruptions since they involve bonds of attachment that have been forged over many decades. Involving as they do a personal investment and being based on a history of proven exchange and reciprocity, long-term relationships are likely to be strong and deeply rooted.

Changes in the age configuration of the family have probably served to reinforce intergenerational kin ties as well. Although age differences may serve to insulate the generations from competition with one another in the work force and other age-graded settings, the fact that families are assuming a more uniform age structure, with more members having made the transition into the middle or older ages, would seem to have an overall harmonious impact on intergenerational relations. When family members are of similar ages, it may be possible to attenuate resentments that ensue from age-related subordinate/superordinate relations. Intergenerational tensions arising from differences in maturational or age levels are clearly minimized. Also serving to bridge the "lineage gap" (Bengtson and Treas, 1980) is the fact that family members close in age have experienced some of the same historical events and thus may share similar social and political beliefs, values, attitudes and behaviors.

Benefits accrue to younger generations from having older relatives since the former are exposed to behavioral models of aging that provide them with anticipations of socialization in their own old age (Troll, 1977). In spite of disparities in chronological age, family members are also entering into social age peerships in ways having no historical precedent. For instance, with large numbers of older persons returning to school, parents, children, and even grandchildren may all be students at the same time. Although this example is representative of "renewal activities" initiated by the older family members, social peerships may also result from the "accelerated activities" experienced by the young ones, such as premature widowhood or early retirement (Guemple, 1969; Hagestad, 1981b). Although kin members in similar life stages may provide welcome support to one another, clear and unambiguous norms and behavioral guidelines for their relationships are lacking because of the sheer novelty of this situation, making intergenerational involvements for some kin members disorganized and anomic (Hess and Waring, 1978).

Although changes in the age distribution of family members may have led to some definite improvements in the quality of family life, they also have created the potential for intergenerational conflict and strain. With decreases in the age distance between generations and increases in life expectancy, many parents and children are finding themselves growing old together. Children typically have been the chief source of support for the aged. Particularly if they have completed launching their own children and/or are approaching retirement, adult children may feel angered when having to care for elderly kin limits their leisure activities. Kin-keeping and care-providing responsibilities become increasingly difficult to fulfill, moreover, when children are aging themselves and experiencing their own decrements in health and financial resources (Brody, 1978; Treas, 1977; Shanas, 1980).

Often filial responsibilities conflict with the other obligations that adult children face in their roles as spouse and parent. Brody (1981) has spoken of the "middle generation squeeze" to refer to the competing demands that middle-aged persons experience in attempting to balance the multiple requests and needs of aged parents and young adult children (see also Hill et al., 1970; Silverstone and Hyman, 1976; Schwartz, 1979). Although most multi-generational families today still contain only one middle generation, the number with two middle generations is growing steadily (Neugarten, 1979) as a result of the acceleration or "quickening of the family cycle" (Neugarten and Moore, 1968) as well as increased life expectancy. Although the middle-aged and "young-old" generations in some families may initially share care-providing responsibilities for the senior generation, many middle-aged kin may eventually have to cope with dependency relations involving two generations of aged parents, aging in-laws, and even aging relations from former marriages.

It is ironic as Brody (1978) has observed, that a new role of parental caretaker has emerged for individuals in the "post-parental" stage. Although the nests of these individuals have been emptied of children, they are being "refilled" both psychologically and physically with aging kin. Most of these individuals, though, will survive to experience still another family life-cycle stage. The "re-empty nest" occurs after the death of aged parents.

The capacity to fulfill filial responsibilities has been challenged in recent years by the growing tendency for middle-aged women to work for pay outside the home. Indeed, close to three in every five women aged 45 to 54, and about two in every five women aged 55 to 64 were employed in 1981 (U.S. Department of Labor, 1982). Since middle-aged women traditionally have assumed the principal responsibility for providing physical care and psychological sustenance to the elderly (Brody, 1979, 1981; Treas, 1977), their increasing participation in the labor force inevitably restricts their ability to perform care-giving functions.

KIN CONTACT AND FAMILY CONSTELLATIONS

Living Arrangements

Changes in the living arrangements of the elderly often have been taken to indicate a breakdown in contemporary patterns of inter-generational relations. During the twentieth century, living arrangements of older persons have indeed changed dramatically. Whereas over 60 percent of the population aged 65 and over were coresiding with their children in 1900, the comparable figure for recent years is below 15 percent (Smith, 1981; Shanas, 1980). Such changes have accelerated since the middle of the century. Between 1950 and 1980, the proportion of persons 65 and over who were living in nonfamilial residential arrangements rose steadily and rapidly, climbing from 21.4 percent (U.S. Bureau of the Census, 1951) to 32.2 percent (U.S. Bureau of the Census, 1981b). The overwhelming majority of these unrelated individuals (93 percent in 1980) were living alone. Partly as a result of the widening sex gap in mortality, the growth in nonfamilial living in recent decades has been particularly prominent among women.

These trends do not necessarily imply a breakdown of the family. First, even today, most older individuals continue to live in some type of family setting, either with a spouse and/or other family members, particularly grown children. In 1980, three in four males aged 65 and over were living with a spouse, as were two in five females in that age range. About 19 percent of the women and 7 percent of the men were sharing a residence with other family members (U.S. Bureau of the Census, 1981b).

Second, research studies that attempt to ascertain the household preferences of the elderly have consistently found that living with their relatives is not a desired arrangement, although they usually want to reside in the same vicinity (Shanas et al., 1968; Lopata, 1973). Older persons prefer to preserve their independence. As a consequence, the aged residing with grown offspring tend to be very old, sick, and/or poor and thus have few options.

Third, and contrary to popular belief, reconstructions of earlier household structures from censuses, parish rosters, and administrative records suggest that at no point in previous history has the extended family residence accounted for more than 10 percent of all households. Extended family households were a rarity in the past if for no other reason than the high mortality rates then existing that precluded three generations of family members from jointly surviving for any considerable length of time (Laslett and Wall, 1972).

Although temporal variations in living arrangements may reflect changes in socialization patterns and normative values that have encouraged independence and individualistic orientations (see Smith, 1981), empirical research findings highlight the role that demographic and economic changes have had in explaining these secular trends. Kobrin (1976) and Soldo (1977) both suggest that the growing trend toward nonfamilial residences, particularly solitary dwelling, has largely resulted from changes in population structure. That is, demographic shifts have led to increasing numbers of aged females and "old-old" individuals—groups especially prone to be living without kin for reasons relating to widowhood or to functional impairments warranting institutionalization. At the same time, there have been decreases in the number of middle-aged females—the most likely candidates to share households with aged relations.

Changes in the distribution of living arrangements among the elderly also have been attributed to improvements in their economic status (Pampel, 1981; Beresford and Rivlin, 1966). Particularly during the past 20 years, real income has risen significantly for the aged (Tissue and McCoy, 1981), largely as a result of rapid expansions in the Social Security system and the means-tested welfare programs for the aged. With improvements in their economic status, older persons have been afforded an unprecedented degree of flexibility in realizing their residential preferences for independent living (Michael, Fuchs, and Scott, 1981).

In recent decades, only 5 to 8 percent of American households have been composed of three generations of family members (Carter and Glick, 1976; Bane, 1976). These are probably overestimates of the "true" prevalence of multigenerational households, because studies typically fail to distinguish long-term or permanent extended-family households from those operating on a transitional, short-term basis—for example, those temporarily embracing persons who have recently experienced a personal crisis such as widowhood or divorce (see Kobrin, 1981).

Although household composition frequently is considered an important dimension of the quality of familial relations in late life, the two factors are not necessarily related in a systematic manner. Multigenerational households may facilitate day-to-day interaction and the exchange of help, but they only insure the mutual visibility of family members and do not necessarily contribute to the affective aspects of intergenerational relationships. In fact, empirical research findings reveal that older persons not living with their children are no more likely to feel neglected by them (Brown, 1970); they may even report themselves to be happier than those living with their children (Murray, 1973).

Intergenerational Contact

Despite their proclivity for living independently from their children, the majority of older Americans today reside within close geographical proximity to relatives with whom they frequently make contact. In her 1975 survey of the noninstitutionalized elderly, Shanas (1979a, 1980) found that 18 percent of respondents with surviving children coresided with one of their children and an additional 34 percent lived within 10 minutes commuting distance. Respondents who lived alone maintained the same levels of contact with offspring as respondents who resided in shared households! As many as half of the elderly with surviving children saw at least one child either the day of the interview or the previous day, and an additional 25 percent saw one of their children during the preceding week. Variations in kin contact were observed by class, sex, race, and marital status.

Although contacts with their children occur more often among older persons with working-class backgrounds than among their middle-class counterparts (Shanas et al., 1968), the reverse is true for their contacts with other relatives (Riley and Foner, 1968). This probably reflects the greater geographic dispersion and smaller size of middle-class in comparison to lower-class families (Adams, 1968; Shanas et al., 1968). The proclivity for middle-class children to live further apart from their parents is often brought about by the mobility demands of their occupation. Although great distances result in fewer visits, the contacts of middle-class families typically are of longer duration than visits among their working-class counterparts (Harris et al., 1975). Klatzky (1972) and Clark and Gordon (1979) also point to the constraining effect that distance may exert on kinship interaction. Such findings primarily relate to face-to-face contacts and not necessarily to other forms of communication such as phoning or written correspondence (Wilkening et al., 1972).

Many researchers hold that the kinship network is more integrative and important among blacks than among their white age peers. Schorr (1960) suggests that feelings of filial piety are more pervasive among black than white children, although findings reported by Seelbach and Sauer (1977) indicate that racial differences disappear when socioeconomic status is controlled. Hays and Mindel (1973) observe that interaction with extended kin and family assistance occur with greater frequency among black families than among their white counterparts. They suggest that these racial differences may be explained by different perceptions of institutional structures: Blacks are said to be more prone to view formal intervention measures as exploitative, rather than as supportive assistance. The lower socioeconomic status of blacks may encourage the exchange of aid among kin members in an attempt to ameliorate their poor economic conditions (Stack, 1974). Racial differences in family functioning may also reflect a demographic factor since blacks tend to have larger families and, thus, more extensive kin networks. Furthermore, the flow of assistance may be facilitated by their greater physical proximity, the extended or joint household being more common among blacks than among whites (Myers and Soldo, 1977). That blacks are more likely to raise and care for grandchildren may establish stronger claims on this generation for help in old age.

A gender basis for kinship interaction is seen in the more active role of females in the family network (Treas, 1977; Adams, 1970). The elderly female displays a closer relationship with her offspring, particularly with daughters, than the elderly male (Townsend, 1957; Shanas et al., 1968). Among kin visiting patterns, more frequent communication is established with maternal than with paternal relatives (Rosenberg and Anspach, 1973). This relationship persists across racial categories (Babchuk and Ballweg, 1971), age categories (Shanas et al., 1968; Rosenberg and Anspach, 1973), and social classes (Shanas et al., 1968). Females are also more likely to be dependent upon kin for material support (Rosow, 1967; Clark and Anderson, 1967). In her study of Chicago area widows, Lopata (1973) found that sons tended to be the most helpful in providing advice and managing financial affairs for their mothers, but that daughters were the primary sources of socio-emotional support and household aid. Bahr and Nye (1974) and Rosenberg and Anspach (1973) find sex-linked kinship behaviors more characteristic of the working than the middle class, however.

Never-married individuals have lower rates of kinship interaction than their married counterparts (Gibson, 1972). This probably reflects the tendency for the never-married to have a smaller pool of available kin. Townsend (1957), Berardo (1967), and Bock and Webber (1972) document the tendency for widowed individuals to be more isolated from family members than their married counterparts. Death of a spouse weakens in-law relations (Lopata, 1973) and hence reduces family interaction for the surviving member. Berardo (1967) and Adams (1968) find widowhood to have a disruptive effect on parent-child relationships as well.

Divorce, too, may disrupt kinship bonds and limit intergenerational exchange. Divorced females receive significantly less assistance from in-laws than do their currently married counterparts (Anspach, 1976), but they report receiving more assistance from members of their own families than married women (Rosenberg and Anspach, 1973). Researchers also argue that divorce typically serves to expand kinship networks since most divorced people eventually remarry (Bohannan, 1971; Sussman, 1976). Although divorce and remarriage are relatively uncommon occurrences among elderly persons, they frequently experience the impacts of these transitions indirectly through their children (Hagestad, 1981b; Furstenberg, 1981). Following a child's divorce, grandparents may become more vital to grandchildren if they fill the void left by the absent parent. Bonds with children are likewise strengthened if an aged parent provides them with needed support and assistance. Although divorced men tend to rely more heavily on parents for child care aid than divorced women, the latter frequently require financial help in addition to babysitting services.

Intergenerational Solidarity

There is little doubt that subjective social ties of a positive sort are important for the well-being of older people. Lowenthal and Haven (1968) reached this conclusion when comparing persons who had a confidant with those who did not. In a study of elderly medical patients, Snow and Crapo (1982) considered the measure of "emotional bondedness" in terms of such responses as "I can count on this person to stand by me" and "We really enjoy spending time together." Emotional bondedness was found to be an important predictor of both self-reported health and life satisfaction. In light of the fact that "objective" measures of kin contact have not revealed that interaction of itself affects morale to any great extent, studies of the subjective content of relationships become of particular interest.

Understandably, most research has tended to focus on those aspects of family life that are easiest to measure—the frequency of contact, the exchange of services, and so on. Neglected have been the qualitative aspects of family life. Bengtson, Olander, and Haddad (1976) note that "objective" *association* is only one aspect of the more general state of solidarity or cohesiveness among family members. *Consensus* in values and opinions represents a second, and a third is the "subjective" *affect,* or sentiments between relatives. No doubt, interactions are the vehicle by which consensus is forged and affect is shaped, but the qualitative nature of these encounters and exchanges (as opposed to their frequency and duration) have received scant attention.

The affective dimension of family ties has been explored in Bengtson's (1971) study of three generations within families. Respondents were queried as to the degree of trust, fairness, understanding, respect, and affection characterizing the dyadic relation. Although all three generations reported high levels of solidarity, elderly parents reported somewhat higher degrees of affective cohesion than did their middle-aged offspring. That the old perceive greater closeness between family members is attributed to differences in developmental agendas. Although the younger family members have a vested interest in establishing their independence from their parents, the old have a "developmental stake" in the continuation of their family lineage and values (Bengtson and Kuypers, 1971).

Of course, generational differences may also reflect cohort differences. The elderly may hold strong familistic values from an earlier era that lead them to attest to closer kin ties than do their descendants. Generational differences in perceptions of family solidarity may insulate the old from disappointments with their offspring, but high expectations for filial responsibility of children have been shown to lead to lower morale on the part of parents (Seelback and Sauer, 1977).

The causes and consequences of family solidarity are less well documented than its existence. Bengtson (1981) has called attention to the familial processes of aging through which perceptions are shaped and understandings are generated. This treatment points to the dynamic nature of affective family life. Four situations that serve as an impetus to family change may be identified. First, role transitions such as those brought about by retirement or widowhood may alter the expectations family members hold for one another. Second, aging may alter the balance of the autonomy and independence of family members, as epitomized in the parent-child "role reversal" that often occurs in later years. Third is the difficulty of maintaining a just and equitable balance of giving and receiving between generations when aging alters the needs and resources of each. Last are issues of the continuity of families and their traditions. Challenging continuity are geographic mobility, divorce, life style changes, and death. As Bengtson (1981) stresses, negotiation and conflict are two processes that characterize families addressing the problems of aging. Bargaining occurs continuously, with parents influencing offspring and offspring affecting parents. Conflict is an inevitable part of these continuing negotiations, but it need not be seen as a necessarily disruptive factor.

Grandchildren

In addition to the other supports they provide, children serve as mediators in the exchanges that transpire between aged parents and grandchildren (Wood and Robertson, 1978; Robertson, 1975, 1977). In fact, in their study of extended families, Hill and associates (1970, p. 62) characterize the middle generation of children as "the lineage bridge across the generations." In Robertson's (1976) study of young adults, aged 18 to 26, close to two in three grandchildren reported that their parents influenced their involvement with their grandparents. According to recent figures, as many as three in four grandparents see their grandchildren at least twice a month, and close to one in two have almost daily face-to-face contact with them (Harris, et al., 1975). Although Lopata (1973) found frequency of contact to be an important determinant of the feelings of closeness elderly widows have for their grandchildren, more recent research by Wood and Robertson (1978) fails to substantiate this relationship and suggests that such feelings prevail even when interaction with grandchildren is limited.

Despite the positive sentiments voiced, Kahana and Coe (1969) find that the grandparent role holds little significance for almost 60 percent of their sample of institutionalized respondents and over 20 percent of their community-based respondents. Among community residents, grandparenthood is viewed as providing an "anchor" or support through which they remain socially engaged. Perceiving institutionalized respondents as disengaged, the authors see them as having little need for the social roles that grandparenthood affords.

In their study of styles of grandparenting, Neugarten and Weinstein (1964) propose a five-fold classification of grandparenting types encompassing diverse responses to this familial role. "Formal," traditionally oriented grandparents have relatively rigid role expectations for themselves and their grandchildren. Interaction with grandchildren for these individuals is fairly constrained and primarily operates along authoritative lines. "Fun-seekers" enjoy engaging in playful leisure activities with grandchildren. "Surrogate parents" are noted for assuming caretaking responsibilities for their grandchildren on a regular basis. Although surrogate parenting is more typical among grandmothers, grandfathers tend to predominate among the "reservoirs of family wisdom," who provide descendants with valuable information concerning their cultural heritage and familial roots. "Distant" figures seldom interact with grandchildren except on holidays. Fun-seekers and distant figures tend to be younger grandparents; formal grandparents, to be older.

An alternative typology of grandparenting is posited by Robertson (1977) in her study of role conceptions among 125 grandmothers. Robertson distinguishes between the social dimension and the personal dimension of grandmothering. The social dimension focuses on attitudes and expectations of the grandmother role that result from macro-social influences and that emphasize societal needs. The personal dimension deals with attitudes and expectations that derive from personal factors and highlight individual needs. Based on this distinction, four types of grandmothers are categorized. At one extreme is the "apportioned" type who has high personal and social expectations and attitudes about the grandmother role. Having the greatest involvement with her grandchildren, the apportioned grandmother tends to be as concerned with indulging and enjoying them as she is with doing what is morally right for them. At the other extreme is the "remote" type of grandmother who is detached from her grandchildren, holding low social and personal expectations of the grandparent role. In between are the "symbolic" grandmothers, who emphasize the normative or moral aspects of the grandparenting role, and the "individualized" type, who emphasize the personal aspects. Robertson (1977) finds that as many as 37 percent of her respondents prefer the grandparent role to parenthood. These women perceive grandmothering to be easier, affording pleasure and gratification without requiring them to assume responsibility for the care and social life of their young kin.

Interestingly, research studies also have evaluated the meanings that grandparents have for children. Kahana and Kahana (1970a) document significant perceptual variations among children of different developmental ages. Children aged 4 to 5 prefer grandparents primarily for their indulgent characteristics whereas those aged 8 to 9 place a higher value on fun-seeking and active grandparents. Children aged 11 to 12, however, were relatively detached from their older kin. Kahana and Kahana conclude that children, as they grow older, have less preference for doting grandparents.

Robertson (1976) has also examined the perceptions that grandchildren have of grandparents. She found that the vast majority of her blue collar respondents aged 18 to 26 expressed very favorable attitudes (although such sentiments may be affected by a social desirability bias). The primary expectation that grandchildren hold for grandparents is that they provide emotional gratification in terms of nurturing behaviors. About two in three respondents think that grandchildren, once mature, have a responsibility to assist their grandparents when their help is needed and to do so without monetary reimbursement.

Intergenerational Relations of the Frail Elderly

Health status often alters the nature of contact and kinship relations. Rosencranz, Philbland, and McNevin (1968) note the tendency for *visits received by* older people from children or other relatives to be more frequent than *visits to* children by aged parents. This probably reflects the travel difficulties encountered by the elderly as a result of health impairments. Blau (1973) argues that illness eventually not only demoralizes older persons but alienates the family members who are burdened by their demands and needs.

Adult children are the major support for the sick elderly. When older people are asked who they would turn to other than a spouse in a health crisis, 90 percent designate their children, and 70 percent of the childless name another relative (Shanas, 1962). Almost 50 percent of the families examined in Litman's (1971) study, however, confide that it would be difficult to care for a sick member at home for an extended period of time; over 30 percent indicate that they would be unable to provide the needed assistance under any circumstances.

Despite the limitations of family care, only 5 percent of the older population live in institutions. As many as 10 percent are housebound or bedridden and still manage to live in the outside community. For married shut-ins, the spouse typically has the principal responsibility for meeting their needs for care, whereas children serve as the major source of care for those without a living spouse (Shanas, 1979b). Maddox and Dellinger (1978) document the high levels of involvement that kin assume in the care of the aged, noting that family members, together with friends, supply over 70 percent of the services that they receive.

To many, the dependence of older parents on their children appears to suggest a type of role-reversal; that is, the children take on the active-supportive role, assuming an increased responsibility for meeting the needs of their parents, and the parents, in turn, take on the passive-dependent role. Recognizing the long history on which parent-child relations are based and the different biological and psychological determinants of dependency in late life, Brody (1979) considers concepts such as "role reversal" and "second childhood" to be inappropriate descriptions of family dynamics among the elderly.

Similarly, Blenkner (1965) strongly contends that the role-reversal paradigm of parent-child relationships is manifested only in pathological cases and has no utility for explaining "normal" developmental changes in the relationships between parents and offspring. By the time children reach middle age, they have achieved a more "filial" role, involving both the recognition of their parents' needs and shortcomings and the assumption of responsible attitudes and behavior towards them. Filial maturity grows out of the child's emotional maturity and independence (as opposed to being based on or motivated by feelings of guilt and the desire to rectify earlier parental difficulties and conflicts). If the available resources do not completely satisfy parents' needs, filial maturity requires both parties to accept these limitations and realistically appraise the types of familial support that are possible. Resolving filial crises with parents prepares children for their own old age, according to Blenkner (1965).

SOCIAL CONTEXTS OF FAMILY RELATIONS

Friendship Relations

Although intergenerational family relations have received the most attention, friendships may also figure in important ways in the lives of older people. Research issues focus on how successfully older people make new friends and keep old ones, how meaningful such friendships are, and whether the friends are adequate substitutes for kin.

Existing studies on nonkin relations often exhibit conflicting results. Although some indicate that long-standing friendships tend to be maintained into old age, others suggest that friendships weaken (Riley and Foner, 1968). Most research points to sex differences in the development and maintenance of friendships. Studies conducted by Booth (1972), Booth and Hess (1974), and Rosow (1967) suggest that women tend to form more intimate and meaningful peer relations than men. Older males typically are more dependent upon their wives for affection and experience greater difficulties adjusting to the loss of a spouse. Women more easily rely on friends, particularly of the same sex, for intimacy when family ties have disintegrated (Blau, 1973).

Friendship patterns of married and nonmarried individuals also differ. Both Booth (1972) and Berardo (1967) report that peer relationships tend to be more extensive among married than widowed persons, in terms of both the number of friendly peers and the frequency of contacts with them. Unfortunately, the dissolution of a marriage by death or divorce often displaces individuals from the friendship networks they belonged to while married (Lopata, 1971; Hess, 1972).

Social class differences in friendship networks are amply documented. Rosow (1967) and Gubrium (1975) note the greater tendency of the middle-class elderly to retain and augment friendships than the working-class aged; the latter are more likely to develop friendships with their neighbors. Indeed, part of the reluctance of older persons to move is explained by their deeply rooted ties to their neighborhood and community and to the long-term, localized friendship bonds that they have secured (Goldscheider, 1971).

Although no conclusive evidence exists on the relationship between the morale of older people and their family involvements (Gravatt, 1953), a number of studies show that life satisfaction or happiness is positively associated with interaction with friends (Phillips, 1973; Carp, 1966; Hochschild, 1973). Lopata (1978) emphasizes the significance of peer support in facilitating widows' adjustment to the loss of their spouse. As friends most often are chosen from among people at the same stage of the life cycle and with similar characteristics, they often serve as confidants and act as important buffers against trauma in coping with the role transitions that accompany late life.

Are Friends and Family Interchangeable?

Most authors note qualitative differences between friendship and kinship associations. They argue that these differences derive from a basic difference inherent in the two relationships, namely, that family ties are foreordained whereas friendships are achieved (Adams, 1967; Bell and Boat, 1957; Blau, 1973; Babchuk, 1965).

Blau (1973) emphasizes the great importance of friendship in old age. After retirement and widowhood, new involvements need to be established with age peers who share similar needs and experiences. Because of their different life styles, the young and the old are considered to have little in common. Parent-adult child relationships are characterized by strong feelings of obligation that detract from their quality by constraining open communication and intimacy. Blau (1973, p. 67) asserts that "because friendship rests on mutual choice and mutual need and involves a voluntary exchange of sociability between equals, it sustains a person's usefulness and self-esteem more effectively than filial responsibilities." Similar conclusions are advanced by D. Adams (1971, p. 67) and by Arling (1976), who note the importance of friendship to morale of the aged.

B. Adams (1967) also recognizes the importance of friendship. Rather than suggesting its dominance over kinship, he notes the possibility for their interchangeability in the social network. Adams contrasts "positive concern" with "consensus," the latter being the sharing of values, attitudes, and interests. Although consensus is more characteristic of friendship and positive concern of kinship, both qualities are frequently found in each of these relationships. The distinctive features of kinship and friendship are likely to be blurred, and substitution of one for the other in the social network may occur.

Indeed, several studies suggest the tendency of friendship and kinship relations to overlap. In his investigation of the use of kinship terminology, Ballweg (1969) reported that about two-thirds of respondents use specific familistic expressions to refer to at least one person who is not an actual relative. Fictive kin or friends can serve as surrogate family members in modern societies. Family members, by contrast, also may be perceived as having characteristics commonly associated with friendship. In his study of informal associations among urban dwellers, Laumann (1966) observed that 15 percent of the individuals who were named as friends were, in fact, related by blood, marriage, or adoption to the respondents.

In contrast, other studies fail to substantiate the thesis of substitution in social supports and suggest a functional differentiation in support elements instead. For example, Rosow (1967) rejected the hypothesis that older persons' family and friends can serve as functional replacements for one another. Although Weiss (1969) conceded that there may be a crossover in the functions that different relationships sat-

isfy, he noted the tendency of each type of relationship to specialize and identified six alternative functions: (1) affection, (2) social integration, (3) nurturance, (4) provision or reinforcement of positive self-feelings, (5) aid, and, of less significance, (6) guidance. Both kin and nonkin resources are necessary for sustaining individual well-being because certain tasks are especially suited to and more effectively performed by one or the other.

Noting the built-in permanence of kinship, Litwak and Szeleny (1969) argued that family members are the best source for satisfying those functions that require long-term commitments (e.g., extensive custodial care). Neighbors, on the other hand, are considered the most appropriate group for socializing. Because of their proximity, they are well-suited to handling tasks that demand immediate attention, such as sudden illness and other emergencies. An intermediate role typically is filled by friends, who are portrayed as the most effective group in matters characterized by continuous change (e.g., advice on contemporary practices). Friends, neighbors, and kin alike are capable of dealing with tasks that demand only limited technical skills. For problems requiring higher levels of specialization and technical expertise, formal or bureaucratic structures prove to be the more effective agents for support (Litwak, 1968).

In contrast to the thesis of functional differentiation in social networks, Cantor (1977; 1980) developed a "hierarchical compensatory model," which posits that family members are the predominant and preferred source of social support *irrespective of the nature of the task.* When kin do not exist or are not available, the individual attempts to compensate for this absence by drawing on other support sources. Children are preferred over more distant kin, and friends and neighbors are preferred over governmental and voluntary agencies.

Although not necessarily denying the importance of friends, Hochschild (1973) finds that family and peer ties are not substitutable, family ties dominate. In fact, close kin ties were predictive of strong peer relations. When family parameters are sharply defined and rigid, the substitution of extra-familial involvements for kinship relations is unlikely.

When families are more fluid and its members more gregarious and socially oriented, high rates of familial interaction may foster high levels of nonfamilial participation.

The Institutionalized Aged

Much previous research has been primarily concerned with assessing how kin and nonkin relations operate to prevent the institutionalization of the aged. Little is known about the social relationships of older persons in institutional settings, however. The paucity of research on this subject may be attributed in large measure to the frequent, although erroneous, assumption that the institutionalized aged have been abandoned by their families and lack informal supports.

Although it is true that the older institutionalized population is disproportionately comprised of individuals who are widowed, childless, or formerly solitary dwellers (Maddox, 1975; Manard and Kart, 1976), the majority of older people with surviving kin continue to live in household settings until they reach an advanced stage of infirmity, disability, or functional limitation (Townsend, 1965; Brody, 1970; Karcher and Linden, 1974). The extent to which the family acts as a caregiving unit is dependent upon a number of factors, including the demographic structure of the family, its financial condition, the quality of the relationships among its members, and the competing demands it faces. When its resources no longer satisfy the service needs of the older individual, its effectiveness in providing care becomes increasingly questionable, and other sources of long-term care are frequently sought (Karcher and Linden, 1974; Townsend, 1965; Shanas and Maddox, 1976; Ward, 1978).

Even if the institutionalization of aged kin reduces or obviates the need to perform certain support functions (e.g., nursing care, transportation, housework), other types of assistance continue to flow between family members. For instance, kin contribute to the expenses of custodial care (Shanas and Maddox, 1976). Furthermore, emotional/affective and social supports may take on added significance after kin have been institutionalized, given that opportunities for purposeful activities, leisure roles, and the development of interpersonal associations are more limited in these settings (Hirsch, 1977; Kahana and Kahana, 1970b).

One study of the effects of institutionalization supports the idea that admission to a nursing home may foster, rather than inhibit, closer relations between elderly residents and their middle-aged offspring (Smith and Bengtson, 1979). Of families interviewed, fully 30 percent reported a renewal of parent-child closeness that had been seriously tested by the problems that led to the institutionalization. Another 15 percent reported experiencing a close parent-child relationship for the first time, and 25 percent indicated that an already close relationship was unaffected by the institutionalization. Less positive adaptations—a continuation of long-standing separateness, quantity without quality interactions, or an outright abdication of filial responsibility—were seen in only 30 percent of the cases. In sum, institutionalization served to benefit the majority of families because it alleviated the pre-admission strains arising from the needs of a sick parent, resulted in an improvement in mental or physical condition, focused kin interaction on social and emotional rather than care-taking concerns, and/or afforded the aged family member extra-familial social outlets.

Interaction among the aged, their children, and other relatives is usually not terminated once the former have been admitted to an institution. Rather, a regular pattern of visitation and/or written correspondence is taken up (Miller and Beer, 1977). If viable ties existed between the aged person and kin prior to institutionalization, these attachments persist thereafter (Sussman, 1965). Relationships also are sustained with former friends and neighbors (e.g., see Curry and Ratliff, 1973), although contacts as a rule are established less frequently with nonrelatives than with kin.

In a study of socio-familial involvements among nursing home residents (Aizenberg, 1979), face-to-face contact is found to be the most common means of communicating with both kin and non-kin who live outside the facility. Personal visits with spouse or children typically take place on a weekly basis; visits with other individuals tend to occur less frequently. Levels of contact with friends are quite high. In fact, after children, friends are the next most likely source of interaction among the nationally representative sample of residents. Although less frequent than personal visits, other means of communicating with children, siblings, and other kin are employed by a fairly large proportion of residents, telephone conversations being slightly more common than written correspondence.

Of course, there are variations in the social involvements of residents. Kosberg (1973), for example, observes that the elderly poor receive fewer visits from family and friends than their more affluent fellows. Poor residents are more likely to be welfare agency referrals and probably have little or no opportunity to choose a facility conveniently located to kin and former peers. Males are about twice as likely as females to visit outside the nursing home, probably reflecting the fact that they are more apt than women to have a surviving spouse.

Examining family-resident interaction, York and Calsyn (1977) found that its frequency is not related to the physical or mental condition of the resident. However, an inverse relationship is observed in the enjoyment families derive from visits and the amount of mental deterioration of the aged relative. Indeed, Butler (1975) acknowledges the temptation for kin to reduce the frequency of their visits over time since contact tends to enhance the awareness of the aged relative's impending death. Moreover, the administrative policies of the institution may limit contacts.

Many researchers have noted the tendency for prolonged institutionalization to be accompanied by declining involvement outside the institution (Pan, 1952). Other research findings based on a nationally representative sample of elderly nursing home residents (Aizenberg, 1979) indicate that duration of residence has no *direct* impact on the socio-familial relations of residents when other factors are controlled (e.g., characteristics of the institution and the social and economic background of the residents). Length of institutionalization affects certain types of involvement only *indirectly* by way of its relation to the resident's functional health status. It serves, on the one

hand, to reduce spousal contact but, on the other, to promote extra-familial activities.

Perceptions about the discharge prospects of the aged resident also may affect the way in which contacts are maintained with those outside the institution. When institutional residence is anticipated to be temporary or of short duration, concerted efforts may be made to remain in frequent contact. Such efforts are advantageous for both the resident and his/her significant others; they facilitate the resident's return to the community upon discharge, requiring less adaptation for all parties involved. To fill voids in other social areas, however, long-term residents may be more inclined to get involved with others in their institution.

The structural arrangements and management of the institution have serious implications for the social lives of the residents. For example, limited evidence suggests that as the size of institution increases, communication, satisfaction, and activity among residents decline (Curry and Ratliff, 1973). Curry and Ratliff (1973) note the greater tendency for friendships to develop among residents in facilities with less than 50 beds than in homes of larger size. Similarly, Handschu (1973) finds that companion relationships between nurses' aides and residents are more likely to develop in smaller (less than 100 beds) than in larger (more than 100) institutions. Presumably, smaller facilities are more prone to resemble a homelike environment and are better able to accommodate the residents' social needs (Henley and Davis, 1967).

FUTURE DIRECTIONS FOR RESEARCH ON THE FAMILY AND AGING

In this chapter we have noted that a broader social context shapes the family intimacies of later life. Demographic changes such as declining fertility, lengthening lifetimes, and widening sex gaps in mortality have created new family constellations. More than ever before, grown children have both aging parents and grandparents, generations overlap, and women become widowed. Although such changes may promote a greater emotional investment in kin and more common interests, we are woefully short of institutional solutions and behavioral guidelines for family situations that are historically unique. This fact is evidenced by the problems of middle generations caught between filial responsibilities, parental obligations, and personal aspirations.

Various social changes have altered the living arrangements of the aged—the most visible aspect of family life. The greater residential separation of the generations has not reflected a deterioration of intergenerational life, however. Numerous studies document frequent kin contact and a ready exchange of assistance and support. Within families, moreover, generations voice positive sentiments about one another. Although grandchildren and siblings may be important to older persons, the closest contacts exist between contiguous generations.

Friends also constitute a broad social network for the aged. It may well be that friends and family complement one another, serving distinctly different functions in the lives of the elderly. Alternatively, friends may substitute for a lack of family support in later life. Declines in health and functional capacity often require the involvement of professionals and specialists as well. Institutionalization, however, does not usually mean that family and friends cease to matter or that relationships are undermined.

Although much is known about the aging family, the literature is characterized by a good many discrepant findings and unanswered questions. Many of the shortcomings of these studies are attributable to theoretical and methodological problems that are endemic to research on aging. For example, the bulk of research has been based on small, local, and sometimes nonprobabilistic samples. Measurements of important concepts such as power and affect vary from study to study, with little attention paid to reliability and validity (Mangen and Peterson, 1982). Failure to employ statistical controls for confounding variables has meant that spurious relationships have sometimes gone undetected. A case in point is the disappearance of socioeconomic differentials in kin contact when residential proximity and the availability of kin are taken into account (Adams, 1968). Similarly, failure to test for nonlinearity over the life cycle may lead to incorrect inferences.

Conceptual difficulties also mar some studies. There is a common failure to distinguish age from life-cycle stage, a penchant for lumping together the vigorous young-old with the frail old-old, and a propensity to infer developmental changes in family life from cross-sectional age differences. As Hagestad (1981b) has argued, there has also been a preoccupation with modal patterns of family life to the neglect of the considerable variation in family relations. At the same time, issues of causality have been ignored in favor of correlational studies of the association between variables. This inattention to precursors and consequences in the family life of the elderly probably indicates that the theoretical underpinning of this domain of study needs to be strengthened.

It is possible to identify a number of areas in which the knowledge base is underdeveloped as well as a number of research approaches that appear to be promising. First, there is the perennial need to obtain longitudinal data on the complex dynamics of kin and nonkin relationships. For example, since the major studies of marital satisfaction in relation to aging have been based on cross-sectional, not longitudinal, study designs, the "aging" effects observed may be due to cohort differences in marital expectations, experiences, and candor. Similarly, the hypothesis of an intergenerational role reversal or ideas about the familial consequences of institutionalization can be properly assessed only if there are indicators of what family relationships were like prior to parental senescence or nursing home admission. The reversal of social roles within families needs to be investigated within a long longitudinal time frame, although a shorter before-and-after design may suffice in the case of nursing home admissions.

Second, the fact that the bulk of research on the aging family has been culturally bound has limited the generalizability of theoretical and conceptual developments. Efforts should be made to examine family relations from a cross-cultural perspective. This suggests the need not only to undertake studies of other societies but also to pursue research on minority groups within the U.S. itself. The Hispanic and Asian elderly, for example, have been largely overlooked, and recent surges of immigration make aging and family support in these communities especially timely issues.

Third, theoretical formulations involving a micro-macro synthesis are needed so that the interrelations of the family with other social institutions may be more clearly delineated. Noting that formal supports are becoming more important to the aged, Streib and Beck (1980) have observed that a fruitful area for investigation is how their informal relations, particularly those involving kin, are affected by organizational linkages and institutional transformations. Rosenfeld (1979) has considered how the growing popularity of retirement communities may affect inheritance practices, but little is known about how, say, Medicare may alter the norms for the filial behavior of grown children.

Fourth, as we have indicated, the qualitative aspects of family life have been neglected for those aspects of interaction that are more readily operationalized and quantified. There are many studies of the frequency of visits between generations but relatively little research on the extent to which the generations socialize with one another in terms of common values and traditions.

Even less is known about the affective characteristics of family relations in old age. The studies that have been undertaken have been largely descriptive. What is called for is greater knowledge of the determinants and consequences of family solidarity and further understanding of the relations between the various aspects of solidarity. For example, does intergenerational living (associational solidarity) lead to warmer sentiments between aging parents and grown children (affective solidarity)?

Fifth, investigations of family relations have typically focused on dyads such as an aging parent and a child. Families, however, are more complex networks, and important questions have gone begging because researchers have found it impractical to interview all close relatives. We do not know very much about the division of labor among siblings caring for aged parents nor about the affect of parents' aging on the relationships between brothers and sisters. Furthermore, dyadic research has more commonly dealt with parent-child dyads than with husband-wife ones. Qualita-

tive changes in marriages as a result of aging have not been adequately explored. As an example, we have little understanding of how couples cope with the differences in functional age that may emerge in later life. We do not know what life is like for the "grass widow" whose spouse has been institutionalized, nor how a marital relation is renegotiated in the face of serious impairments of one or both partners. Ironically, widowhood in old age has probably been more carefully studied than intact marriages.

In sum, research has documented that family relations are a vital aspect of life in old age. The agenda for future researchers is to extend this scholarly thrust. To do so effectively calls for recognition of the complexity of family networks, the subtle properties of kin relationships, and the developmentally and historically dynamic nature of family life in later years.

Acknowledgments: While working on research for this volume, Rhonda Aizenberg held a post-doctoral position at the Andrus Gerontology Center Research Laboratory, University of Southern California.

REFERENCES

Adams, B. 1967. Interaction theory and the social network. *Sociometry* 30: 64–78.

Adams, B. N. 1968. *Kinship in an Urban Setting.* Chicago: Markham Publishing Co.

Adams, B. N. 1970. Isolation, function, and beyond: American kinship in the 1960s. *Journal of Marriage and the Family* 32: 575–597.

Adams, D. 1971. Correlates of satisfaction among the elderly. *The Gerontologist* 11: 64–69.

Aizenberg, R. 1979. Socio-familial involvements among nursing home residents. Unpublished Ph.D. dissertation, Department of Sociology, Duke University.

Aizenberg, R., and Harris, R. 1982. Demographic changes in the family and the "middle-generation squeeze." *Generations* 7: 6–7.

Anspach, D. F. 1976. Kinship and divorce. *Journal of Marriage and the Family* 38: 323–330.

Arling, G. 1976. The elderly widow and her family, neighbors, and friends. *Journal of Marriage and the Family* 38: 757–768.

Babchuk, N. 1965. Primary friends and kin: A study of the associations of middle-class couples. *Social Forces* 43: 483–493.

Babchuk, N., and Ballweg, J. 1971. Primary and extended kin relations of Negro couples. *The Sociological Quarterly* 12: 69–77.

Bahr, H. M., and Nye, F. I. 1974. The kinship role in a contemporary community: Perceptions of obligations and sanctions. *Journal of Comparative Family Studies* 5: 17–25.

Ballweg, J. A. 1969. Extensions of meaning and use for kinship terms. *American Anthropologist* 71: 84–87.

Bane, M. J. 1976. *Here to Stay: American Families in the Twentieth Century.* New York: Basic Books, Inc.

Bank, S., and Kahn, M. D. 1975. Sisterhood-brotherhood is powerful: Sibling sub-systems and family therapy. *Family Process* 14: 311–337.

Bell, W., and Boat, H. D. 1957. Urban neighborhoods and informal social relations. *American Journal of Sociology* 62: 391–398.

Bengtson, V. L. 1971. Inter-age differences in perception and the generation gap. *The Gerontologist,* Part II: 85–90.

Bengtson, V. L. 1981. Research across the generation gap. In *Relationships: The Marriage and Family Reader,* ed. J. Rosenfeld, 2: 249–260. Glenview, IL.: Scott, Foresman.

Bengtson, V. L., and DeTerre, E. 1980. Aging and family relations. *Marriage and Family Review* 3: 51–76.

Bengtson, V. L., and Kuypers, J. A. 1971. Generational differences and the developmental stake. *Aging and Human Development* 2: 249–260.

Bengtson, V. L., and Treas, J. 1980. The changing family context of mental health and aging. In *Handbook of Mental Health and Aging,* eds. R. B. Sloane and J. E. Birren. Englewood Cliffs, N.J.: Prentice-Hall.

Bengtson, V. L.; Olander, E.; and Haddad, A. 1976. "The generation gap" and aging family members: Toward a conceptual model. In *Time, Self, and Roles in Old Age,* ed. J. F. Gubrium. New York: Behavioral Publications. Englewood Cliffs, N.J.: Prentice-Hall.

Berardo, F. M. 1967. Kinship interaction and communication among space-age migrants. *Journal of Marriage and the Family* 29: 541–554.

Beresford, J. C., and Rivlin, A. M. 1966. Privacy, poverty, and old age. *Demography* 3(1): 247–258.

Blau, Z. S. 1973. *Old Age in a Changing Society.* New York: New View Points.

Blenkner, M. 1965. Social work and family relationships in later life with some thoughts on filial maturity. In *Social Structure and the Family: Generational Relations,* eds. E. Shanas and G. Streib. Englewood Cliffs, N.J.: Prentice-Hall.

Bock, E. W., and Webber, I. L. 1972. Suicide among the elderly: Insulating widowhood and mitigating alternatives. *Journal of Marriage and the Family* 34: 24–31.

Bohannan, P., ed. 1971. *Divorce and After: An Analysis of the Emotional and Social Problems of Divorce.* New York: Anchor Books.

Booth, A. 1972. Sex and social participation. *American Sociological Review* 37: 183–192.

Booth, A., and Hess, E. 1974. Cross-sex friendship. *Journal of Marriage and the Family* 36: 38–47.

Brody, E. M. 1970. The etiquette of filial behavior. *Aging and Human Development* 1: 87–94.

Brody, E. M. 1978. The aging of the family. *The Annals of the American Academy of Political and Social Science* 438: 13–27.

Brody, E. M. 1979. Aging parents and aging children. In *Aging Parents,* ed. P. K. Ragan. Los Angeles: University of Southern California Press.

Brody, E. M. 1981. "Women in the middle" and family help to older people. *The Gerontologist* 21: 471–480.

Brown, R. G. 1970. Family structure and isolation of older persons. In *Normal Aging,* ed. E. Palmore. Vol. 1. Durham, N.C.: Duke University Press.

Burch, T. R. 1967. The size and structure of families: A comparative analysis of census data. *American Sociological Review* 32: 347–363.

Butler, R. N. 1975. Public Interest Report No. 15—Is there an ideal form of care of the old? *International Journal of Aging and Human Development* 6: 75–76.

Cantor, M. 1977. Neighbors and friends: An overlooked resource in the formal support system. Paper presented at the Annual Meetings of the Gerontological Society, San Francisco, CA.

Cantor, M. 1980. Caring for the frail elderly: Impact on family, friends and neighbors. Paper presented at the Annual Meetings of the Gerontological Society of America, San Diego, CA.

Carp, F. M. 1966. *A Future for the Aged.* Austin: University of Texas Press.

Carter, H., and Glick, P. C. 1976. *Marriage and Divorce: A Social and Economic Study.* Cambridge, MA: Harvard University Press.

Clark, M., and Anderson, B. G. 1967. *Culture and Aging.* Springfield, IL: Charles C. Thomas.

Clark, W. E., and Gordon, M. 1979. Distance, closeness, and recency of kin contact in urban Ireland. *Journal of Comparative Family Studies* 10: 217–275.

Coale, A. J. 1957. How the age distribution of a human population is determined. *Cold Spring Harbor Symposia on Quantitative Biology* 22: 83–89.

Cottrell, F. 1960. The technological and societal basis of aging. In *Handbook of Social Gerontology: Societal Aspects of Aging,* ed. C. Tibbitts. Chicago: University of Chicago Press.

Crimmins, E. 1981. The changing pattern of American mortality decline, 1940–1977, and its implications for the future. *Population and Development Review,* 7: 229–254.

Curry, T. J., and Ratliff, B. W. 1973. The effects of nursing home size on resident isolation and life satisfaction. *The Gerontologist* 13: 295–298.

Deming, M. B., and Cutler, N. E. 1983. Demography of the aged. In *Aging: Scientific Perspectives and Social Issues,* eds. D. S. Woodruff and J. E. Birren. 2nd ed. New York: Van Nostrand Reinhold.

Foner, A. 1978. Age stratification and the changing family. *American Journal of Sociology* 84: S340–S365.

Furstenberg, F. 1981. Remarriage and intergenerational relations. In *Aging: Stability and Change in the Family,* eds. R. W. Fogel, E. Hatfield, S. B. Kiesler, E. Shanas, and J. March. New York: Academic Press.

Gibson, G. 1972. Kin family network: Overheralded structure in past conceptualizations of family function. *Journal of Marriage and the Family* 34: 13–23.

Glick, P. C. 1977. Updating the life cycle of the family. *Journal of Marriage and the Family* 39: 5–14.

Goldscheider, C. 1971. *Population, Modernization, and Social Structure.* Boston, MA: Little, Brown and Company.

Goode, W. J. 1963. Industrialization and family change. In *Industrialization and Society,* eds. B. F. Hoselitz and W. E. Moore. Paris: UNESCO-Mouton.

Gravatt, A. E. 1953. Family relations in middle and old age: A review. *Journal of Gerontology* 8: 197–201.

Gubrium, J. F. 1975. Being single in old age. *Aging and Human Development* 6: 29–41.

Guemple, D. L. 1969. Human resource management: The dilemma of the aging Eskimo. *Sociological Symposium* 2: 59–74.

Hagestad, G. O. 1981a. Late twentieth century parent-child relationships. In *Human Development,* ed. T. Field. New York: John Wiley and Sons.

Hagestad, G. O. 1981b. Problems and promises in the social psychology of intergenerational relations. In *Aging: Stability and Change in the Family,* eds. R. Fogel, E. Hatfield, S. Kiesler, and J. March. New York: Academic Press.

Handschu, S. S. 1973. Profile of the nurse's aide—Expanding her role as the psycho-social companion to the nursing home resident. *The Gerontologist* 13: 315–317.

Hareven, T. K. 1977. Family time and historical time. *Daedalus* 106: 57–70.

Harris, L., and associates. 1975. *The Myth and Reality of Aging in America.* Washington, DC: The National Council on the Aging, Inc.

Hauser, P. M. 1976. Aging and world-wide population change. In *Handbook of Aging and the Social Sciences,* eds. R. H. Binstock and E. Shanas. New York: Van Nostrand Reinhold Company.

Hays, W. C., and Mindel, C. H. 1973. Extended kin relations in black and white families. *Journal of Marriage and the Family* 35: 51–57.

Henley, B., and Davis, M. S. 1967. Satisfaction and dissatisfaction: A study of the chronically-ill aged patient. *Journal of Health and Social Behavior* 8: 65–75.

Hess, B. 1972. Friendship. In *A Sociology of Age Stratification,* eds. M. W. Riley, M. Johnson, and A. Foner. Aging and Society, vol. 3: New York: Russell Sage Foundation.

Hess, B., and Waring, J. M. 1978. Parent and child in later life: Rethinking the relationship. In *Child Influences on Marital and Family Interaction.* eds. R. M. Lerner and G. B. Spanier. New York: Academic Press.

Hill, R., et al. 1970. *Family Development in Three Generations: A Longitudinal Study of Changing Family Patterns of Planning and Achievement.* Cambridge, MA: Schenkman.

Hirsch, C. S. 1977. Integrating the nursing home resident into a senior citizens center. *The Gerontologist* 17: 227–234.

Hochschild, A. R. 1973. *The Unexpected Community.* Englewood Cliffs, N.J.: Prentice-Hall, Inc.

Kahana, E., and Coe, R. M. 1969. Perceptions of grandparenthood by community and institutionalized aged. *Proceedings of the 77th Annual Convention of the American Psychological Association* 4: 735–736.

Kahana, E., and Kahana, B. 1970a. Grandparenthood from the perspective of the developing grandchild. *Developmental Psychology* 3: 98–105.

Kahana, E., and Kahana, B. 1970. The therapeutic potential of age integration. *Archives of General Psychiatry* 23: 20–29.

Karcher, C. J. and Linden, L. L. 1974. Family rejection of the aged and nursing home utilization. *International Journal of Aging and Human Development* 5: 231–244.

Klatzky, S. 1972. *Patterns of Contact with Relatives.* Washington, DC: American Sociological Association.

Kobrin, F. E. 1976. The fall of household size and the rise of the primary individual. *Demography* 13: 127–138.

Kobrin, F. E. 1981. Family extension and the elderly: Economic, demographic and family cycle factors. *Journal of Gerontology* 36: 370–377.

Kosberg, J. E. 1973. Differences in proprietary institutions caring for affluent and non-affluent elderly. *The Gerontologist* 13: 299–304.

Kreps, J. M. 1977. Intergenerational transfers and the bureaucracy. In *Family, Bureaucracy and the Elderly,* eds. E. Shanas and M. Sussman. Durham, N.C.: Duke University Press.

Laslett, P., and Wall, R. 1972. *Household and Family in Past Time.* Cambridge: Cambridge University Press.

Laumann, E. 1966. *Prestige and Association in the Urban Community.* New York: Bobbs-Merrill.

Litman, T. J. 1971. Health care and the family: A three generational analysis. *Medical Care* 9: 67–81.

Litwak, E. 1960a. Geographical mobility and extended family cohesion. *American Sociological Review* 25: 9–21.

Litwak, E. 1960b. Geographical mobility and extended family structure. *American Sociological Review* 25: 385–394.

Litwak, E. 1968. Technological innovation and theoretical functions of primary groups and bureaucratic structures. *American Journal of Sociology* 73: 468–481.

Litwak, E., and Szeleny, I. 1969. Primary group structures and their function: Kin, neighbors and friends. *American Sociological Review* 34: 465–481.

Lopata, H. Z. 1971. *Occupation: Housewife.* New York: Oxford University Press.

Lopata, H. Z. 1973. *Widowhood in an American City.* Cambridge, MA: Schenkman.

Lopata, H. Z. 1978. Contributions of extended families to the support systems of metropolitan area widows: Limitations of the modified kin network. *Journal of Marriage and the Family* 40: 355–366.

Lowenthal, M., and Haven, C. 1968. Interaction and adaptation: Intimacy as a critical variable. In *Middle Age and Aging,* ed. B. Neugarten. Chicago: University of Chicago Press.

Maddox, G. L. 1975. Families as context and resource in chronic illness. In *Long Term Care,* ed. S. Sherwood. New York: Spectrum Publishers, Inc.

Maddox, G. L., and Dellinger, D. C. 1978. Assessment of functional status in a program evaluation and resource allocation model. *Annals of the American Academy of Political and Social Science* 438: 59–70.

Manard, B. B., and Kart, C. S. 1976. Social factors and institutionalization of the elderly. In *Aging in America: Readings in Social Gerontology,* eds. C. S. Kart and B. B. Manard. New York: Alfred Publishing Company, Inc.

Mangen, D. J., and Peterson, D. A. 1982. *Research Instruments and Social Gerontology.* Vol. 2. Minneapolis: University of Minnesota Press.

Marshall, V. W. 1981a. *Social Characteristics of the Future Aged.* Quantitative Studies in Economics and Population Research Report. Hamilton, Ontario: McMaster University.

Marshall, V. W. 1981b. *The Changing Family Relationships of Older People.* Quantitative Studies in Economics and Population, Research. Hamilton, Ontario: McMaster University.

Metropolitan Life. 1977. Current patterns of dependency. *Statistical Bulletin* 58: 10–11.

Michael, R. T.; Fuchs, V.; and Scott, S. 1981. Changes in the propensity to live alone: 1950–1976. *Demography* 17: 39–59.

Miller, M. B., and Beer, S. 1977. Patterns of friendship among patients in a nursing home setting. *The Gerontologist* 17: 269–275.

Moore, W. E. 1963. *Social Change.* Englewood Cliffs, N.J.: Prentice-Hall, Inc.

Murray, J. 1973. Family structure in the preretirement years. *Social Security Bulletin* 36: 25–45.

Myers, G. C., and Soldo, B. J. 1977. Variations in living arrangements among the elderly: Identification, analyses and predictive models. Final Report. Durham, N.C.: Duke University Center for Demographic Studies.

Neugarten, B. L. 1979. The middle generations. In *Aging Parents,* ed. P. K. Ragan. Los Angeles: University of Southern California Press.

Neugarten, B. L., and Moore, J. W. 1968. The changing age status system. In *Middle Age and Aging,* ed. B. L. Neugarten. Chicago: University of Chicago Press.

Neugarten, B. L., and Weinstein, K. 1964. The changing American grandparent. *Journal of Marriage and the Family* 26: 199–204.

Pampel, F. S. 1981. *Social Change and the Aged: Recent Trends in the U.S.* Lexington, MA: Lexington Books.

Pan, J. S. 1952. Factors in the personal adjustment of old people in the Protestant church homes for the aged and old people living outside of institutions. *Journal of Social Psychology* 35: 195–203.

Parsons, T. 1943. The kinship system of the contemporary United States. *American Anthropologist* 45: 22–38.

Phillips, D. L. 1973. Social participation and happiness. In *Social Participation in Urban Society,* eds. J. N. Edwards and A. Booth. Cambridge, MA: Schenkman.

Riley, M. W., and Foner, A. 1968. *Aging and Society: An Inventory of Research Findings.* Vol. 1. New York: Russell Sage Foundation.

Riley, M. W., and Johnson, M. 1971. Age stratification of the society. Paper presented at the Annual Meetings of the American Sociological Association, Denver, CO.

Robertson, J. F. 1975. Interaction in three-generation families; parents as mediators: Toward a theoretical perspective. *International Journal of Aging and Human Development* 6: 103–110.

Robertson, J. F. 1976. Significance of grandparents: Perceptions of young adult grandchildren. *The Gerontologist* 16: 137–140.

Robertson, J. F. 1977. Grandmotherhood: A study of role conceptions. *Journal of Marriage and the Family* 39: 165–174.

Rosenberg, G. S., and Anspach, D. F. 1973. *Working Class Kinship.* Lexington, MA: D. C. Heath and Company.

Rosencranz, H. A.; Philbland, C. T.; and McNevin, T. E. 1968. Social participation of older people in the small town. Vol. 2. No. 1. Department of Sociology, University of Missouri at Columbia.

Rosenfeld, J. 1979. *The Legacy of Aging.* Norwood, N.J.: Ablex.

Rosenmayr, L., and Kockeis, E. 1963. Propositions for a sociological theory of aging and the family. *International Social Science Journal* 15: 410–426.

Rosow, I. 1967. *Social Integration of the Aged.* New York: Free Press.

Schorr, A. 1960. *Filial Responsibility in the Modern American Family.* Washington, D.C.: U.S. Government Printing Office.

Schwartz, A. N. 1979. Psychological dependency: An emphasis on the later years. In *Aging Parents,* ed. P. K. Ragan. Los Angeles: University of Southern California Press.

Seelbach, W. C., and Sauer, W. J. 1977. Filial responsibility expectations and morale among aged parents. *The Gerontologist* 17: 492–499.

Shanas, E. 1962. *The Health of Older People: A Social Survey.* Cambridge, MA: Harvard University Press.

Shanas, E. 1979a. Social myth as hypothesis: The case of the family relations of old people. *The Gerontologist* 19: 169–174.

Shanas, E. 1979b. The family as a social support system in old age. *The Gerontologist* 19: 169–174.

Shanas, E. 1980. Older people and their families: The new pioneers. *Journal of Marriage and the Family* 42: 9–18.

Shanas, E., and Maddox, G. 1976. Aging, health and organization of health resources. In *Handbook of Aging and the Social Sciences,* eds. R. H. Binstock and E. Shanas. New York: Van Nostrand Reinhold Company.

Shanas, E., and Sussman, M. B. 1981. The family in later life: Social structure and social policy. In *Aging: Stability and Change in the Family,* eds. R. W. Fogel, E. Hatfield, S. B. Kiesler, and J. March. New York: Academic Press.

Shanas, E.; Townsend, P.; Wedderburn, D.; Friis, H.; Milhöj, P.; and Stehouwer, P., eds. 1968. *Old People in Three Industrial Societies.* London: Routledge and Kegan Paul.

Shorter, E. 1975. *The Making of the Modern Family.* New York: Basic Books.

Siegel, J. S. 1976. Demographic aspects of aging and the

older population of the United States. *Current Population Reports,* Series P–23, No. 59. Washington, D.C.: Government Printing Office.

Siegel, J. S. 1978. Prospective trends in the size and structure of the elderly population, impact of mortality trends and some implications. *Current Population Reports.* Series P–23, No. 78. Washington, D.C.: Government Printing Office.

Silverstone, B., and Hyman, H. K. 1976. *You and Your Aging Parents.* New York: Pantheon Books.

Smith, D. S. 1981. Historical change in the household structure of the elderly in economically developed societies. In *Aging: Stability and Change in the Family,* eds. R. W. Fogel, E., Hatfield, S. B., Kiesler, and J. March. New York: Academic Press.

Smith, K. F., and Bengtson, V. L. 1979. Positive consequences of institutionalization: Solidarity between elderly parents and their middle-aged children. *The Gerontologist* 19: 238–447.

Snow, R., and Crapo, L. 1982. Emotional bondedness, subjective well-being, and health in elderly medical patients. *Journal of Gerontology* 37: 609–615.

Soldo, B. J. 1977. *Determinants of Temporal Variations in Living Arrangements Among the Elderly.* Unpublished Ph.D. Dissertation, Department of Sociology, Duke University.

Stack, C. B. 1974. *All Our Kin: Strategies for Survival in a Black Community.* New York: Harper & Row, Publishers.

Streib, G. F., and Beck, R. W. 1980. Older families: A decade review. *Journal of Marriage and the Family* 42: 937–958.

Sussman, M. B. 1965. Relationships of adult children with their parents in the United States. In *Social Structure and the Family: Generational Relations,* eds. E. Shanas and G. Streib. Englewood Cliffs, N.J.: Prentice-Hall.

Sussman, M. B. 1976. The family life of old people. In *Handbook of Aging and the Social Sciences,* eds. R. J. Binstock and E. Shanas. New York: Van Nostrand Reinhold Company.

Sussman, M. B. 1977. Family, bureaucracy and the elderly individual: An organizational/linkage perspective. In *Family, Bureaucracy and the Elderly,* eds. E. Shanas and M. Sussman. Durham, N.C.: Duke University Press.

Sussman, M. B., and Burchinal, L. 1962a. Parental aid to married children: Implications for family functioning. *Marriage and Family Living* 24: 320–332.

Sussman, M. B., and Burchinal, L. 1962b. Kin family network: Unheralded structure in current conceptualizations of family functioning. *Marriage and Family Living* 24: 231–240.

Tissue, T., and McCoy, J. L. 1981. Income and living arrangements among poor aged singles. *Social Security Bulletin* 44: 3–13.

Townsend, P. 1957. *The Family Life of Old People.* London: Routledge and Kegan Paul.

Townsend, P. 1965. The effects of family structure and the likelihood of admission to an institution in old age:

The application of a general theory. In *Social Structure and the Family: Generational Relations,* eds. E. Shanas and G. Streib. Englewood Cliffs, N.J.: Prentice-Hall.

Treas, J. 1977. Family support systems for the aged. Some social and demographic considerations. *The Gerontologist* 17: 486–491.

Treas, J., and Bengtson, V. L. 1982. The demography of mid and late life transitions. *The Annals of the American Academy of Political and Social Sciences* 464: 11–21.

Treas, J., and VanHilst, A. 1976. Marriage and remarriage rates among older Americans. *The Gerontologist* 16: 132–136.

Troll, L. E. 1971. The family of later-life: A decade review. *Journal of Marriage and the Family* 33: 263–290.

Troll, L. E. 1977. Society's changing age structure and the family. Presentation to the Conference on Aging in America, University of Delaware.

Troll, L. E.; Miller, S. J.; and Atchley, R. C. 1979. *Families in Later Life.* Belmont, CA: Wadsworth Publishing Co.

Uhlenberg, P. 1980. Death and the family. *Journal of Family History* 5: 313–320.

U.S. Bureau of the Census. 1951. Marital status and household characteristics: March 1950. *Current Population Reports.* Series P–20, No. 33. Washington, D.C.: Government Printing Office.

U.S. Bureau of the Census. 1981a. Age, sex, race, and Spanish origin of the population by regions, divisions, and states: 1980. *1980 Census of Population Supplementary Reports,* PC80–S1–1. Washington, D.C.: Government Printing Office.

U.S. Bureau of the Census. 1981b. Marital status and living arrangements: March 1980. *Current Population Reports,* Series P–20, No. 365. Washington, D.C.: Government Printing Office.

U.S. Department of Labor. 1982. *Employment and Earnings, January 1982.* Washington, D.C.: Government Printing Office.

U.S. Public Health Service. 1981. *Health, United States.* Washington, D.C.: Government Printing Office.

Ward, R. A. 1978. Limitations of the family as a supportive institution in the lives of the aged. *The Family Coordinator* 27: 365–373.

Weiss, R. S. 1969. The fund of sociability. *Trans-Action/Society* 6: 36–43.

Wilkening, E. A.; Guerrero, S.; and Ginsberg, S. 1972. Distance and intergenerational ties of farm families. *Sociological Quarterly* 13: 383–396.

Winsborough, H. H. 1980. A demographic approach to the life cycle. In *Life Course: Integrative Theories and Exemplary Populations,* ed. K. W. Back. Boulder, CO: Westview Press.

Wood, V., and Robertson, J. F. 1978. Friendship and kinship interaction: Differential effect on the morale of the elderly. *Journal of Marriage and the Family* 40: 367–375.

York, J. L., and Calsyn, R. J. 1977. Family involvement in nursing homes. *The Gerontologist* 17: 500–505.

8
CHANGING VALUES AND POSITIONS OF AGING IN WESTERN CULTURE

Leopold Rosenmayr
University of Vienna

CONCEPTUAL FOUNDATIONS

This chapter is an attempt to study the status of older people under different socio-structural conditions from the sociological perspective of comparative gerontology. The sometimes very careful and convincing interpretation of surveys and other sources of empirical research on the socio-structural determinants of aging and age status have rarely been able to improve the theoretical impoverishment of social gerontology. Therefore, one of the older sociological approaches of intercultural comparison has been taken here, even though it may sometimes be problematic from an epistemological and methodological point of view. As suggested by Aristotle, it would be wrong to ask for equal precision from greatly varying approaches (*Nicomachean Ethics,* 1094a 23). Research results, and middle range theories related to them, are widely used here, but they have been integrated into the more wholistic comparative perspective.

Our approach, however, is not a "culturalist" one. Culture is not being reconstructed as a unified whole that through its norms, standards, and values controls behavior directly. Instead, aging is looked at from a point of view of *culture as it is mediated through social structure.* From such a historico-cultural point of view, we focus on values and

symbols but are aware of the fact that they never act directly but are always perceived and accepted under conditions of real life forces and pressures.

This chapter does not attempt to summarize the enormous output of American social gerontology and life-course studies in their investigation of the socio-structural determinants of mid-life or later periods of the life span. An attempt is made, however, to give a little more visibility to European research, less known in the United States. Many problem areas, like the evaluation of the cohort approach or of biographical methods, are not touched upon, the author having expressed himself on some of these topics elsewhere (see Rosenmayr and Allerbeck, 1979; Rosenmayr, 1983).

Theoretical Perspectives of the Sociology of Aging (Gero-Sociology)

In studying human aging, human development, opportunities, and "paths" toward fulfillment in the second half of life, the sociologist has to unfold a complex perspective. He must ask how aging, development, and fulfilment are shaped by the changing man-environment relation, by technology and modes of production, and by models of culture, meaning, and self-interpretation. Sociologists are concerned with the impact of social structures and their power in distributing and allocating material and cultural goods and resources. Sociologists explain and interpret life history, aging, and development according to variables of social structure and cultural conditions. The longstanding relations of individuals with one another and the change in the creativity, gratification, and intensity of their being interconnected is a neglected area of research. Most data on marital relations in later life are data taken from and focused on individuals rather than on the processes of mutuality and the changes resulting therefrom.

It is only recently that elements of ideology, culture, and religion have begun to receive the attention that is due their significance for the self-interpretation of individuals as they face problems and decisions in the second half of life. This chapter is an attempt to strengthen this tendency.

Sociologists disagree on which points of view and aspects sketched here should be given preference in the study of aging. Agreement may be better on the need for a systems approach to the individual's relationship to environment, to other individuals, to social structure, and to culture if aging and development are to be properly studied. A systems approach has the advantage of allowing for the interrelation of various disciplines, and, to a certain extent, it can even link up the natural with the social sciences.

Some sociologists follow a more classical perspective and focus upon the analysis of the roles and status of the elderly (Rosow, 1976). Others have developed exchange and reciprocity concepts (Dowd, 1978; Rosenmayr, 1974a, 1978c). I propose a more risky, and to some extent less "conclusive," socio-cultural, pluridisciplinary, and interpretative approach. Interdependency, cohesion, exchange, and integration of individuals and groups of greatly different ages, especially in intergenerational relations (an important subarea of a life-course-oriented social gerontology) require the presence of a plurality of disciplines to avoid reductionism. A systems approach to human society, from our point of view, would have to relate perceptions and interpretations of reality to the position of the perceiver within the system. This is one of the reasons why history and culture (through which the human self perceives) need to be studied. Seniority, for example, coupled with age to some extent, is a status, or an element in a status system, that is viewed and defined under the impact of cultural influences and values. The gerontologist or life-course scientist needs to understand that individuals, families, groups, and institutions live and develop by interpreting their age notions and evaluations within their cultural heritage and cultural change. In this sense, the systems approach has to be supplemented by looking at individuals and groups from a historical perspective. This means that the uniqueness of their life history, cohort, or generational participation must be considered, an approach that brings biography close to literature (Rosenmayr, 1983).

In order to allow change and development, the "complex adaptive" organization of the human personality disposes of the memory that permits "the turning back of the experience of the individual upon himself" (Mead, 1934). This "reflexiveness," and thus connectedness with culture, is a special characteristic of human aging and is a necessity for human development and a prerequisite of fulfillment. Memory, in relating to one's own history, also refers to the history of the cohort and to "history at large." It seems necessary to insist on the "exploration" of these various types of events and their repercussions and effects on the individual, the sum total of which may be called experience. This, in turn, favors and increases "reflexiveness" and expands it to include more than mere cognitive elements. Experience, if it involves exposure to novel or significant events, tends to become an emotionally deep "existential reflexiveness" that is more likely to cause or facilitate human change than more cognitive speculations.

Anticipation of structured action, plus the capacity for (planned) revision, may furnish an understanding of the many conflicts and contradictions in aging and human development. Evaluation of past achievements in the light of newly visualized standards and plans for the future are the special contribution that individual consciousness may offer to homeostatic balance. Taking into account the feedback of discrepancies between past achievements and future expectations is particularly important for understanding aging and development from a sociological point of view that is based on systems theory. With this approach, *social* memory and *social* expectations may also be considered as a background of *individual* attitudes towards past and future.

The Sociocultural View of Aging as a Basis for Comparison

The key task of the sociology of aging is to relate the acting individual in its social and cultural context to the biological changes of the human organism over time. We ought to go one step further and ask that the sociologist pay special attention to profiles of aging, development, and fulfillment in terms of the socially significant factors of income, education, and occupational groups as well as ethnicity, cultural traditions, and life styles.

The sociotemporal approach (Riley and Abeles, 1982) to gerontology, however, must also include the cultural evaluation of time. To give an example, a change-oriented and innovation-based society tends to underrate continuing activities. Paradoxically, time, contemporarily, is considered extremely fugitive and overly precious, and yet the time spent on some leisure activity is valued comparatively little. Spending persistent periods of social time in certain established groups or institutions was a trait valued highly by traditional society, and the seniority principle was therefore used as a measuring stick. Modern society, with its emphasis on social mobility and learning, honors quickness and readiness for change. Post-industrial society, however, is rediscovering continuities as necessary elements for self-determined *rhythms of development* and *fulfillment.* Meditation, for example, views time in a different way. The change to post-modern values (Barnes, Kaase, et al., 1979) may emphasize the need for personal creativity to be something different from mechanical and prefabricated innovation. The capacity to wait, "to let grow," and to develop may then be valued more highly. Such a change may have positive effects on the status of older people in society.

Technological and scientific change tends to devalue the elderly. A condition for a gain in status by the aging individual would be the acceptance of a more active self-definition and creativity oriented attitude. Some evidence for a development of this sort has been described recently, it being the task of the sociologist to venture an early diagnosis of such developments in the Zeitgeist. Society, however, must be willing to accept the value of creativity if a real change in the status of older people is to occur.

The various types of aging and of the reproductive and survival systems are connected with societies and cultures in different ways. There is no single "general" path followed in the course of aging and no general model of societal and political reaction to the system of reproduction and mortality. The fertility–mortality system is both the outcome of, and an influential factor in, the development of society. An interrelation exists between the individual and "population aging," inasmuch as the proportion of older people in a society, the predominance of their needs, the resulting welfare systems, their life-styles, etc., pose additional conditions for the value climate of the society. General evaluations stemming from society's reaction to mass aging influence the self-definition of older people as well.

The cultural perspective of the society of aging can be well illustrated by studying the position of older people in preliterate societies. The study of cosmological-animistic societies reveals a close relationship between ancestor worship and great respect for older people. According to the basic tenets of animistic cosmology, the souls of ancestors act as mediators of prayers and wishes, which they accept from the living and pass on to a supreme but unknown God (Schweeger–Hefel, 1980). Cosmological-animistic belief systems vary; some make sharp distinctions between ancestors and deities; in others, there is more continuity (Rohlen, 1971). Ancestors are worshiped in particular places—sometimes in very simple, small shrines built from stones, wood, and twigs found in the vicinity—and old people play the most important roles in this veneration.

Some cosmological-animistic societies do not distinguish between (physically dead) ancestors and living elders. Differential behavior toward both ("eldership complex") is a reflection of a gerontocratic system, where juniors must honor and obey anyone senior to them (Kopytoff, 1971; Mendonsa, 1976). In return, ancestors and elders protect the younger age groups, particularly within the clan. Thus, the position of ancestors and elders not only involves privileges of respect and power but also special obligations.

The cosmological aspect is basic for non-literate cultures; it is primarily linked with a nondynamic, subsistence economy of sedentary people who have not yet developed urban centers. Magico-animistic cultures unite the visible and comprehensible with the invisible and occult, this unity being represented by a circulatory, repetitive process. Souls of deceased ancestors may return to the clan in future generations; in some cultures, they are magically identified when they return to take on life in newly born children (Rosenmayr, 1983).

If we venture a comparison between the status of the aged in societies with a cosmological-magical world-view and the status of the aged in modernized industrial cultures, we find that the old in cosmological society reinforce and intensify that world-view whereas in modernized societies they are relegated to the fringes of their culture (Eisenstadt, 1974).

INTERPLAY BETWEEN SYMBOLIC AND SOCIO-ECONOMIC FORCES AS THEY DEFINE THE AGE-STATUS

Origins of the Evaluation of Advanced Age in Western Culture

How are we to explain the dissolution of the "eldership complex" (or "ancestor syndrome") in the development of Western culture? How can we understand our outgrowing of the veneration of ancestors such as that just described? How are we to find the social and cultural motives causing the transition from the traditional dominance of the old (backed up by cosmological belief systems) to the anthropocentric development idea of modernity?

To answer these questions, one has to consider both the Judeo-Christian traditions and the basic concepts of fulfillment of Greek and Roman antiquity. According to Solon's early poetic philosophy (sixth century B.C.), Aristotle's life-stage theory, and, particularly, Cicero's dialogue "On Old Age," the individual is thought to be capable of analytical rationality and have a gift for life-long learning. To be capable of endurance and perseverance in old age, preparation for aging should include the development of life styles that combine moderation with activity. (Rosenmayr, 1978b). As we search for contemporary evaluative criteria for the status of old people in Western society, we must understand Judeo-Christian religious notions, commandments, and advice from a historico-sociological point of view. The family system became a backbone for early Judaism in its struggle to live up to its national-religious tradition in fighting against external enemies and foreign gods; it drew its strength from its traditions and kinship networks. Earlier anthropological and sociological studies claimed that status support for the elderly was linked to the *stability* of a given society (Simmons, 1970; Cowgill, 1972). To ensure an eminent status for the old, however, it would seem to suffice that a society be *integrated* internally; it need not be static and "stable," and it may exhibit dynamic characteristics such as charismatic religious movements and prophetism, and it may even be conquest-oriented toward the outside world. Religion itself may convey a message to "change the world" and still give high rank to the elderly.

An exclusive or dominating God who is demanding, who grants a covenant, and who gives powerful personal protection leaves little room for the veneration of ancestors, however. The old Babylonian, Egyptian, and Persian cultures didn't indulge in ancestor worship because special castes of priests developed. Old people, however, often accompanied religious and political leaders and heroes in their endeavors, as Jewish scripture shows (Ex. 24: 1, 9, 14; Num. 11: 24–30; I Kings 12: 6). Even in the messianic future of the "New Jerusalem," gerontocratic assistance will be necessary to the "reign of fulfillment" (Zach. 8: 4). "Grey hair is a wonderful crown" (Prov. 16: 31). The time of salvation is seen as a period in which centenarians jubilate (Jesaya 65: 20).

Longevity was important for Judaism. Many texts equate old age with religious fulfillment. The aberration of old men from the path of truth and righteousness was deplored (Dan. 13: 52), particularly if they were seduced to idolatry by foreign women (I Kings 11: 4–12). The potential for moral weakness in old age was acknowledged, and physical corruptibility and decay were feared as a source of great anxiety in late life. The time of youth should therefore be spent with care and moderation in order to prevent some of the special hardships of aging (Koh. 11: 9–12). The philosophical "preparation for aging" of the Old Testament thus comes close to thoughts later expressed by the Roman philosopher Cicero in his treatise "De senectute."

Judaism of the Second century B.C. developed an increasing sensitivity to the uniqueness and integrity of the person (Flusser, 1968) and a conviction of personal continuity and resurrection after death. The survival of the chosen people was no longer the only means for continuity. During the last two centuries B.C., trends of a general eschatological egalitarianism were spreading. A commonness of deprivation was sensed in this premessianic phase of poverty and oppression (Klausner, 1977). If the world was to be finally redeemed by a Messiah, a long life became less important and the status of the old was correspondingly diminished. More and more people came to believe that everybody, regardless of age, possessed the same rights and spiritual merits. This was the spiritual and political climate in which the "deviant" or "alternative" son, John, of the (very old) high priest Zachariah started to advocate a "democratization" of *rebirth* in a radical way. Up to then, baptism had been restricted to elite groups that performed it with ritual regularity at certain intervals. St. John's concept was that rebirth should be open at any time to all who were willing to participate in the general religio-political reform movement that he preached, regardless of age or status.

Historical Christian Ideas of Aging and the Status of Older People

The story that is the very nucleus for the Christian attitude toward the old (Jn. 3: 1–

7) must be understood in the preceding context. Secretly, by night, in order not to be discovered, the aged Pharisee (probably an educated or at least a particularly searching man) named Nicodemus approached Jesus and heard from him the famous words: "Except a man be born again, he cannot see the kingdom of God." Nicodemus replied to Jesus: "How can a man be born when he is *old?* Can he enter a second time into his mother's womb, and be born?" Jesus instructed him that rebirth means internal change and that his use of the term was in a religious and psychological sense, not in a biological one (Jn. 3: 1–7).

According to the teaching of Jesus the answer to all aspects of aging, including respect for the old, is *spiritual renewal.* Human fulfillment lies in a special form of becoming. The basic Christian message is one of hope for individual human development and a theory of fulfillment that emphasizes spiritual and psychological openness and continued reopening. The principle of "rebirth" in the Christian Gospels is grounded on a dynamic age-levelling egalitarism and therefore neglects biological age and seniority. This radicalism could not quite stand on its own. It had to be supplemented soon by the social support concepts of that early theorist of communal living, Saint Paul. The young Christian community for pastoral reasons readopted elements of the traditional Jewish "veneration" of the old. The concepts of rebirth and rejuvenation were not completely abandoned, however. The spiritual new beginning, independent of chronological age, remained an important demand. Saint Paul's letters argue that man could "put on the new nature" and even "create a new man in himself." "Rebirth" should provide the courage to assess one's psychological capacities anew continuously. The urgent appeal is that one should reorganize one's life according to new experiences and internal discoveries within a spiritual community, a network of friendships and families with strong aspects of *radical sharing.*

When the eschatological expectations of an imminent end of the world and the reappearance of Christ were not fulfilled, the Christian community had to base itself increasingly on traditional family solidarity. "Do not rebuke an older man but exhort him as you would a father; treat younger men like brothers, older women like mothers . . . (I Tim. 5: 1). This family model provided a principle of order to the community, which, in spite of its moral and spiritual radicalism that reached beyond familial interests, had to cope with problems of day-to-day living. The pastoral letters attributed to Saint Paul clearly established or reaffirmed the "filial" duty of compensation. The repayment idea of the Mosaic Law, particularly as it affected a common household, were reinstitutionalized. Paul emphasized the need for special consideration and special assistance to older members of the community (I Tim. 5: 8).

The demand for special support of the elderly is paradoxically based on both their (physical and social) *weakness* and their accumulated *strength* (life-long merits, experience, etc.). The interpretations of subsequent centuries took care of both angles, of the special *vulnerability* as well as *venerability* of persons of greater age. The weaknesses and strengths of the old were carefully juxtaposed in the abundant medieval philosophical and pastoral literature on the subject (Sprandel, 1981). Christian communities developed intensive responsibilities for the weak, the old, and the poor. If a family fails for some reason or other, the Christian community is, or ought to be, the primary agency for providing care and support for an old person in need. The pastoral letters particularly stressed this concern with regard to widows. The medieval church responded to such demands by building "hospitals" and institutions of care for the frail elderly. Those who had some financial means and could "leave" something to the church by a last will were of course in a more favored position.

The responsibilities of Christian communities were based on rather strict conditions. Older people who fulfilled certain moral standards were preferred clients. The Church could not propagandize on the basis of a completely need-oriented welfare principle. It had to show off pious and "moral" clients. Social work for the old was seen under the aspect of a personal and moral repayment that we may call "exchange." If one had behaved in a particular supportive manner towards family

and community in earlier phases of the life cycle, one's chances to be an integral part of the community in the phases of weakness and old age were much improved. The community was expected to maintain a collective consciousness with integrated moral "exchange" standards. It therefore put pressure on certain forms of human development over the life span, acting as a censor of both youthful and adult behaviors. Widows ". . . gadding about from house to house—saying what they should not" (I Tim. 5: 13–14) were unacceptable. Paul's letter to Timothy urged that the aged and widows be "honored." Honoring implied "empathic intervention" comparable to the Fourth Commandment of the decalogue. Thus, the pastoral letters explicitly reintroduced the exchange point-of-view of the Old Testament into the practice of the Christian churches.

Christian Ideas on Aging in the American Tradition

The whole span of ideas of human development and fulfillment in Western culture cannot be presented here, but such an historical attempt is increasingly viewed today as being of fundamental importance to present-day decision-making (DiFilippo, 1982). Efforts made in this direction trace, for example, the great importance of the stoic doctrine of healthy and modest living as a preparation for human dignity and philosophical (i.e., conscious and reflective) activity in the face of physical weakness. The stoic idea, most eloquently formulated by Cicero and reappearing throughout the Middle Ages in many treatises, retained its influence down to the Enlightenment and its theories of "moderate, rational, and social living" as the best preparation for an active and happy old age (Rosenmayr, 1978a).

In the United States, Christian ideas about the aged and their social position have been widely discussed in treatises reacting to the country's socio-economic and religious history since the eighteenth century (Demos, 1978). Because of the great variety and richness of its sermon literature, the Protestant tradition in America has been more readily accessible than the Catholic one. The "founding fathers" tradition has strong links with the "patriarchal piety" of the Old Testament. A brief investigation will show that certain ideas prevail for centuries but receive new meanings, and are therefore reformulated, in terms of the prevailing Zeitgeist. Concepts and notions of self-fulfillment change in keeping with changes in the general culture. The life goals of various historical periods are connected with the human development ideas of those periods and the life styles that emanate from them.

The renewed revivalist tradition in nineteenth-century American evangelical Protestantism seems to have been of great importance to the attitudes toward aging that are widely accepted today. This tradition shaped "civilized," or modern secular, morality and the moral code supporting the principles of economic expansion and the pursuit of material wealth and advancement. It aimed at some form of spiritual rebirth on the one hand, and rapid economic and ecological expansion on the other. It strove to shake off the cultural ties of parents and the past. Tradition was viewed as shackles and chains. The revivalist movements made frequent use of images adverse to a favorable picture of aging. The "old man" was constantly alluded to as a hindrance to energetic development as well as belonging to the "old" unconverted spiritual order.

Both the *real picture* of the frailty and traditionalism of the old and the *symbolic image* of spiritual stagnation were hostile to old age. In the language of the Gospels and of the Pauline letters, two sets of terms existed: *palaios* ("old") and *kainos* ("new") were used for "old" and "new" with respect to the spiritual order and *geron* and *neos* for "old" and "young" with respect to the exact chronological position in the life course. In revivalism, these two sets of terms were scrambled, not by neglect but for the ideological reasons discussed. The way of revivalist speaking about age blended both approaches, the spiritual one and the life course description. It used the picture of infirmity in old age as a warning against sins. A good old age is the fruit of a righteous life; the helpless old deservedly harvest their previous sinful life (Cole, 1980).

Revivalism in its extreme form almost never speaks of veneration for the old nor of obligations the old may still have to society. It shows no real concern for supporting or consoling the feeble. Emphasis is placed only on dying righteously. This element of Protestant Calvinist ethics was strengthened by religious revival movements that associated the values of youth with those of fast economic development. The coupling of social and economic conditions with spiritual values would seem to hold great promise for gerontology and life course science today. Such a perspective is in line with the multidisciplinary view of gerontology that is widely accepted today.

The ideas of the Enlightenment were more development-oriented than those of Calvinism and began to creep into the latter's religious traditions. In the early decades of the nineteenth century we find a growing concern for the welfare of the whole community as well as for the individual "regeneration" of man. The Rev. John Stanford in his 1829 book *Aged Christian's Adviser* (Cole, 1980) counseled his public to keep a diary in order to record the "internal warfare between the regenerated new man and the old man of the flesh." According to Cole, the highly personalized history of individual faith in the mercy of God that was documented in the diary was to be esteemed next to a man's Bible. The diary was to serve as a spiritual guide and instrument for human development. According to early Calvinist preaching, piety is the highest obligation of the old. Piety ought to serve the old for their own sanctification as well as to provide an example to younger people. Diaries, like the one of Benjamin Franklin, were written in part for the benefit of the writers' sons. Fulfillment thus takes on an intergenerational significance: The transmission of the developmental success of the father to the son becomes an important element in the fulfillment of the father's life.

There is a strong tendency to emphasize intergenerational and general societal exchange as a way of creating a righteous balance. More than 100 years ago we find sermons that read like a draft for disengagement theory: "It is an advantage to the world that men should die; that having accomplished the great purpose of life they should give place to others; and that what they have gained in any respect should go into the common stock for the good of the world at large, and for the benefit of coming generations, rather than it should be retained by themselves under the form of vast monopolies" wrote Reverend Barnes in 1868.

The Change from Devaluation of Old Age to Happy Aging—Aspects of a Joint Symbolic and Socio-Economic Interpretation

A long history of widely read advice literature for the aged has come to light through recent research. In many cases, it was written by women, from "Growing Old Gracefully" in 1832 to the medically and psychologically influenced "happiness literature" of the twentieth century. In the idea of happiness in old age, we can trace the Romantic influence of Emerson and Thoreau, which strongly differ from the revivalism and economism previously described. Development is now seen in a different way, and an emphasis on fulfillment begins to appear.

The older admonition literature had addressed itself mainly to men; the newer trend was geared to a sentimental idealization particularly open to women, children, and the aged. It laid stress on the boundaries that exist between the worldly passions that men—particularly younger and middle-aged ones— might indulge in and the Christian affections. According to this literature, such Christian affections are "naturally" available to women, children, and the aged. The world of younger men thus identified natural inhibition as a characteristic of old age. By contrast, ideas of ripening, of life-long processes of growth into a happy old age, began to appear. The special contribution of female productivity in this particular branch of advice literature was its stress upon useful activities and their continuation into old age. The early nineteenth-century female writers emphasized the need to maintain health and character as bulwarks for aging (Cole, 1980). The idealization of older (not middle-aged!) men became common as concepts of romantic fulfillment replaced the attitudes of Revivalism and the Enlightenment. Nostalgic pictures were painted of kindly, silver-haired grandfathers in rocking chairs, musing on the past before a luke-warm fire. Anne Douglas (1977) has suggested that these romanticized pictures may have masked the actual devaluation of the old that was taking place in an expanding capitalist society.

The Two-Step Formation of Social Age Categories in Industrial and Post-Modern Society

At the height of national capitalist expansion towards the end of the nineteenth century, the foundations for new social "age" categories were laid: those of the "retiree" and of the "adolescent." These categories were based upon economic necessities as well as humanitarian values; in the case of youth, they also reflected certain philosophical ideas. Under the pressure of the labor movement, various European governments introduced retirement legislation for the first time, thereby limiting the work phase of life. Slowly a new age category became accepted, that of *retirement age*. Almost at the same time, the requirements for new forms of production and of social organization were responded to by an increasingly differentiated school system. In addition to universal compulsory primary schooling, grammar schools and other forms of secondary education were established for the upper middle classes. These developments facilitated the rise of a new age category: the *adolescent*. The ambience of secondary schools for the privileged, fostered by their philosophically ambitious teachers, provided a nonfamilial environment in which adolescence took on a special ideological and, later, a social meaning. Eventually, it provided the source for a youth liberation movement. The notion of youth (as applied to adolescence) became closely associated with cultural "rebirth," however unclear the latter concept might have remained.

Adolescence, like retirement, came to be accepted as a necessary but "unproductive" life phase. Thus, two phases free of the full obligation to contribute to production were brought into being. This evolution illustrates how life stages are defined by the dynamics of production and the division of labor, although the roots of these developments in social and political movements were quite different. "Senescence" as a semantic neologism (Hall, 1922) was not hailed with anything near the attention afforded to "adolescence," which rapidly became a byword for the youth movement. The "youth" that at the turn of the century was supported to create a spiritual subculture with esthetic values became a cultural movement protesting against the middle-class world and the limitations in man's relation to nature brought about by industrialization and urbanization.

The student revolt of the nineteen-sixties created active postadolescent groups having yet another new age-status—that of "young adults"—and exhibiting a specific mentality directed toward value change. As a result, persons in midlife and the phases beyond were reminded of their own capacities for value change and for the reorganization of their lives. The classical notion of the "adult" started to loose general significance. In a sense, the genesis of the "hippie" represented the dawn for a revisionist concept of "active aging."

All these phenomena were supplemented and further advanced by the snowballing effects of cybernation (Alberoni, 1970). "Cybernetic" techniques and technologies invaded everyday life. The capabilities of the young and their eagerness for technological but also for social, cultural, and political transformation came to be seen as a new social "virtue" (Barnes, Kaase, et al., 1979). Young elites were hailed as the agents and galvanizers of technically and culturally innovative processes of change. Conversely, and unfortunately, it is these very changes that lead to premature techno-cognitive senility in midlife and beyond. What seemed to be valid bodies of knowledge yesterday are made obsolete or obsolescent by the innovations of today. The rapid succession of "generations" of various types of electronic equipment, computers in particular, exemplifies this process. On the other hand, the activism of the young stimulated and encouraged the activism of middle-aged people and the old. The recent appeals for the "activation" or "self-activation" of older people would seem to present a paradox, given the impact of the increasing socio-cultural self-definition of the young. *Such activation, in part, is a spill-over effect.*

The gradual expansion of the "alternative life styles" promoted by these newly conscious younger age groups has whetted the appetite for a new individuality and "self-realization" among middle-aged and older people. Increasingly, middle-aged and "young old" individuals become conscious of their capacities to define (or redefine) the values that are basic for the conduct of their own lives. Some of them actually do change their values and life styles. Such individuals will "age" and "develop" and define their standards of fulfillment differently from their age peers even as their concept of life changes (Luce, 1981). In one way or another, the idea of alternative life styles, however restricted in actual practice, is definitely influencing older people today (Featherstone and Kruschinski, 1981). A certain flexibility and capacity to choose is seen as a viable possibility, at least among the better educated ones. As the number of them with higher education increases and as they move into retirement age, the diversity of life style options increases. The whole profile of experienced needs, perceived biography, and search for options will undergo change in the second half of life. This is already happening wherever the impacts of education have been experienced.

The Quest for Meaning as a Social Issue in Contemporary "Mass Aging"

The developed countries in the second half of the twentieth century have arrived at a level of medical knowledge and social organization for the second half of life that provides a support and stability unprecedented in human history. To varying degrees, welfare support for meeting basic needs has become generally accepted. It is in this light that some authors increasingly regard age as "an irrelevant dimension in policy-making for old people" (Neugarten, 1982).

Longevity and the quality of life in the "later years" are important if overpublicized goals of welfare-oriented states and their bureaucracies. Nevertheless, the physical and economic deprivation of minority groups of old people still exists within welfare states (Bujard and Lange, 1978), as will be discussed later. The increase of government intervention and control over pensions and social and medical services likewise increases the power of the distributive bureaucracies, whether these are centralized or rely upon regional systems. The life course, with its various transitions and the feeling of continuity thus created takes on an unwanted air of dependency upon public means and anonymous organizations that, by their very form and structure, can rarely be influenced by personal intervention. They serve only to provide important yet stereotyped gratifications. Life opportunities are increasingly defined by public or socially organized institutional structures. Increasing longevity and the broadening scope of activities physically possible for a growing population of elderly individuals also raise the problem of which activities are to be pursued, what content of life is to be embraced, and what goals are to be looked for. Society—its churches, schools, and media—are confronted with the question of how to assist the elderly in this quest for the realization of meaning. Social institutions appear to be better equipped to respond to "aging" needs than to the satisfaction of developmental ones, not to speak of true fulfillment.

For many older people, retirement presents a new and unprepared for life situation (Rosow, 1974; Sheppard, 1976, p. 304). Ambivalence with regard to retirement (Attias-Donfut, 1978) and wide-spread hesitancy to retire (Sheppard, 1976, p. 305 ff), although often said to be motivated by economic reasons, might also be explained as the result of a fundamental lack of activities that present gratifying alternatives to work. The more or less forced withdrawal from work of those in late midlife that is currently being legislated in several European countries poses the additional problems of a search for relevance and the need for self-reinterpretation outside the existing "social models" (Gaullier, 1982, 178).

The problem of "finding a place" in postmodern society that provides status by virtue of socially esteemed activities is perhaps one of the principal issues for the contemporary sociology of aging. Diagnosis of the status issue must not be reduced to ascertaining attitudes and actions that are merely appreciative. It must include the *meaning* that aging individuals can attribute to their own activities and that their family, friends, peers, neighborhood, and the wider society can recognize. Satisfaction can result only from what is mutually deemed necessary and contributory. By "meaning" we understand cognitive content that provides emotional satisfaction and the knowledge that one's actions correspond to one's goals in a way that can be clearly formulated.

Finding coherent structures of meaningful, highly motivating goals and paths to pursue becomes difficult after midlife, particularly in the preretirement and retirement periods. The following factors may account for this difficulty:

1. The absence of "shielded areas" of moral and religious conviction and of supportive (institutionalized) environments with predictable values; the general doubt and value pluralism presented by the persuasive mass-media as new and common areas of conflict.
2. Continuous innovation in matters of fact and technology that increases the rapidity of obsolescence, which in turn encourages nonparticipation, cultural isolation, and reactions of despair in older people.
3. Innovative information and technology processes oriented not towards the needs of individuals but to standardized applications. (Activities tend to become meaningless unless they are elaborated, accepted, and applied in individualized, personal processes.)

Theories of aging will have to account for the fact that many medical and social difficulties of the elderly result from problem solutions that were repressed earlier in life. The "real" dimensions of life problems (with work, sexuality, marriage, family) that have been concealed or suppressed for a long time, are often better understood only after external factors of stress and crisis have accumulated. The need for change often becomes apparent only when the ability to change no longer exists. The decline of competence and power is suddenly realized, and the reduction of physical stamina and general health interferes with the fulfillment of personal aspirations.

GENERAL CONCEPTS OF SOCIAL GERONTOLOGY REVISITED

Position and Status: The Power of Society Versus the Subjective Resources of the Individual

The increased life expectancy of adults, the general awareness of "the adding of years to life," has created new prospects and problems. The new phase of mid-life has probably been most affected by the fact that the majority of individuals during this stage—because of the great improvements in the general health —enjoy a continued physical and psychological youthfulness. Advanced age, however, has become a mass problem. Solutions require the formulation of a social and educational policy as well as more widespread capacities for coping and self-help. As a rule, the latter cannot be planned for and transmitted by social institutions. Networks of friendship, confidence, consultation, and mutual support of a therapeutic and spiritual character, including unconventional forms of love and closeness, must be thought of as enhancing the capacities for change that are necessary for "fulfillment." Frequent, if not continuous, retraining and relearning are prerequisites for the precarious homeostasis of complex adaptive systems like human individuals and groups. Standards of vitality are being pushed far beyond those existing at the legal retirement age at the same time that economic pressures in many European countries are making early retirement mandatory. The decrease in "available work" is pushing postadolescent as well as presenescent groups into socially marginal positions. The lack of jobs has given rise to the proposition that certain phases of the life course might be designated as "vocational parking lots" —extended periods of schooling and various forms of training before joining the work force, as in the case of adolescents, or after

an early retirement. The question in many European countries is whether to lower the retirement age or tolerate higher youth unemployment rates. Both social groups tend to become restless. "Frustrated" well-educated young adults frequently deny the political legitimacy of the modern state (Habermas, 1976). Persons pushed into unprepared inactivity in late midlife feel that their lives have been deprived of meaning. Their anxiety and lack of status is shown by new French studies on the results of governmental policies increasingly favoring early retirement (Gaullier, 1982).

Society has the power to set social standards for certain age phases and to define what is "appropriate" for that stage. These standards are not based upon strict biological facts but are artificially created by society within the relatively broad limits of biological conditions. We certainly do not think only of the effects of hygiene, cosmetics, fitness-training, and geroprophylactic treatments of all kinds. A society that is conscious of human developmental necessities and the fulfillment aspirations of various age groups and that is aware of the need for an inclusive life-course policy will have to—in the words of Gaullier (1982; p. 178)—"facilitate transitions and avoid traumatic retirement, to favor individual choices, to allow the payment of a pension and the earning of a salary (forbidden to those terminated early), to be able to refer to a precise social model concerning one's category of age, etc."

Any approach to the question of the position, status, and role of the elderly will have to consider the ramifications of the basic values of the society. It will not suffice to scan merely those values that are widely held. Evaluations in detail of later life—with its perspectives on human finitude and anxieties, hopes, and escapes—necessarily lead to an examination of fundamental ideas, including religious convictions and philosophical self-interpretation. For the sociologist, the intellectual reconstruction of ultimate concerns and convictions in order to understand them is a precondition for the study of aging and the life course. In view of the religious pluralism of modern times, a more detailed "digging" into the historical past of traditions and systems of thought ought to be undertaken (Berger, 1979). We must strengthen our understanding of the connection between the ultimate concerns of individuals and groups and their life satisfaction.

Internalized psychological needs and wishes may be only casually connected with status. To attain high status in social institutions with traditionalistic criteria, important negations (such as the suppression of personal needs) and sublimations may be required. The drive to attain seniority may lead to self-destructive or self-alienating effects. Self-fulfillment (Kohut, 1977; Stein, 1979) may often be more relevant to the satisfaction and "integration" of the personality (Gould, 1978) than the pursuit of status. Fulfillment of self, however, might also mean having to sacrifice a position—a move that an aging individual worried about economic and status security might find difficult to accept.

Positions are intimately linked with the activities and behavior of individuals and can be empirically referred to from a level of concrete observation. *Status,* which is determined by converging or conflicting societal evaluations (stemming from a variety of cultural ranges) is based on changing traditions and less clearly perceived. One's status is more volatile than one's position and is subject to considerable ambivalence. What consequences for the elderly can result from this dissimilarity? The *position* of an older person in a certain occupational, political, or social network may be solidly recognized. At the same time, however, his or her *status,* because of the general societal ambivalence about aging, may be thoroughly ambiguous.

Generally speaking, the status of those of advanced age became increasingly ambiguous as a result of modernizing processes like industrialization, the mechanization of everyday life, and urbanization. Under contemporary conditions of postmodern society, a certain solidification of the status of the aged is likely to spread. The continuity, nonpragmatic knowledge, unmeasurable creativity, and nonmaterialistic values (Inglehart, 1977) that accrue from long-term life experiences are beginning to receive more favorable recognition by

society. The crises of affluent modernism, the decrease in faith in technology, and the more critical attitude toward progress and innovation are all conducive to a positive re-evaluation of advanced age.

What seems to hold true for self-realization as contrasted to status seeking may even be more true for the discordant connection between love and status. A "loving" older individual of either sex may not necessarily be granted the status that he or she deserves. Economically, socially, or politically successful old people are far more likely to be rewarded by high status. "Esteemed but not liked" was a judgment not unknown in the attitudes towards older people displayed by American "Northern Protestantism" (Demos, 1978). Many other intricacies in the conceptualization of the social status of older people become more clear when analyzed in terms of a culturally comparative sociology rather than from a functionalist point of view. Becoming a treasured partner with a "long history of shared interaction" is quite different from the kind of prestige that is determined by functionalist status definitions (Gutmann, 1977).

More theoretical and empirical work will be needed to forecast how "grey" lobbies and "grey" movements will boost the status of older people in a postaffluent society. The key issue may be whether the new cohorts of older people will be strong enough because of their dramatic gains in education to develop new models of problem-resolution for themselves. As they age, their capacity to fulfill their emotional, intellectual, and economic needs may reflect improvements as compared to earlier cohorts in the individuality of their response. Nevertheless, as the value consensus decreases even within churches and strongly ideological groups, certain weaknesses in their self-definition are bound to remain.

It is possible that the aging individual in postindustrial society will have a better chance to create a personal mixture of life-style elements. This synthesis, moreover, will increasingly be less the product of the earlier achievements of the individual or the prescriptions of society (Parsons, 1951) but of the individual's own capacity for renewed choice. In this perspective, the status of advanced age may be viewed as an "empty frame" to be filled by a "labor of consciousness" and personal experience. Position and status would thus appear modifiable by self-initiated efforts.

Age Roles Reconsidered

The sometimes used notion of social age includes definitions of the age norms operative in society. Such norms stipulate the age at which certain events, activities, or rights are "appropriate" in terms of a vaguely defined status. Empirical studies have shown that there are normative expectations of when people should marry, have children, become grandparents, and so forth (Bengtson, 1973; p. 16). Such norms often differ from legal age requirements, and different age groups may have different norms and expectations concerning the whole spectrum of the life course.

Massive demographic and sociological data on the distribution of events in the life course (such as conclusion of various types of education, onset of partnership, marriage, birth of first child, end of child-bearing phase, reentry into the job market, crucial jumps in social mobility, onset of the postparental phase, beginning of grandparenthood, death of spouse) have led sociologists to speak of *age-specific roles*. Aging is then seen as a specific form of mobility from one age category or "class" to another, with cohorts proceeding from one set of expectations to the next (Riley et al., 1972). Even those who plead for a role model theory of aging have to admit that role-notions and role-prescriptions vary substantially, depending upon any number of economic and socio-cultural variables (Tews, 1979; p. 23f.). The same roles are not valid for all social classes, ethnic groups, etc. In addition, there is no social consensus on age norms. Younger people feel much less bound to such norms than older ones, and the norms are often considered to be more appropriate for others than for oneself. The younger the individual, the greater the discrepancy between the norms they define as binding for others and those applying to themselves (Bengtson, 1975; p. 75).

The role and status of the elderly—with a very thoughtful separation of the two concepts—have been carefully considered in the context of functionalist sociology (Rosow, 1976). The description of the diminishing of roles, seen by Rosow (1976; p. 462) as "bundles of relations for which responsibilities are transferred to the person," and their subjective meanings to their actors transcend functionalism and orient our thinking towards the idea of fulfillment in aging.

Social stratification may also be defined as a system of age classes (Riley et al., 1972). Within the socio-economic system, one may rise or fall, but age classes are undirectional. Cohorts move "upwards" only; they become older. Doubts may be raised about whether role models based on age classes are fabrications independent of socio-economic structure. It is my argument that they are *products* of the internal necessities and opportunities determined or conferred by the various forces of general social structure or social change. It is questionable whether social age can be considered the result of a special role system in society (Rosenmayr, 1976a, 1978d). The *age structure* within a society and the changing and often conflicting *age norms* are derivatives that have been forged by the forces and systems of production, the educational system, and the support given to human life by forms of social care such as social security and welfare systems. Since the nineteenth century, age norms have also been the derivatives of ideologically inspired movements.

My proposed approach is based on the idea that the production system as well as the orienting and interpretative systems of a society (schools, ideologies, religious groups, and the media that diffuse values and models) "assign" different tasks to different age groups. This social division of labor shapes these groups and the individuals of which they are composed. The age structure becomes socially "utilized" and is defined by the production system and by models of interpretation of the meaning of life. The age structure results from the socio-economic processes that satisfy needs and from the models that guide social interaction (in family, work, leisure, political organization, etc.). Models of life values and spiritual and existential self-interpretation as well as the social norms represented by religion and other forces play an important role in the construction of age notions. Notions cannot become norms, however, without support from the forces of production. The age structure following such norms is thus to be considered the result of a mass of influences. The models and notions are not causally dependent on the economic structure. Interpretations of the meaning of life follow their own dynamic. Individuals let the models of meaning they have accepted govern their moral standards and some of their behaviors. Far Eastern societies (the Thai, Chinese, and Japanese, for example) found their models in ancestor worship and historical forms of "patriarchal piety." Their impact can still be seen today in face-to-face contacts in families and can in political decisions regarding services, social care, and security for the aged.

The establishment of life phases and their patterns and social interconnections are dependent upon the state of development of a society and its subunits. The social division of labor tends towards a utilization and standardization of human age that is biologically anchored, yet ontogenetically and phylogenetically modifiable. The ever-changing design of phases corresponds to historical specifications of the division of labor and ever-changing value preferences.

Historico-Sociological Dynamics Causing Socio-Economic Inequality of Older People

Having defined the general relation between social structure and the historically changing specification of life phases, we must now move to the more specific effects of socio-economic structural conditions on aging and its development and fulfillment opportunities. Extensive research on health, family relations, and the patterns of needs of older people in the United States and different European countries has led to a rejection of stereotyped approaches to aging (Shanas, 1979). Empirical research now provides a focussed and comparative understanding of social groups among the elderly (Streib, 1976). The sociological typology of aging processes is far less developed. The subsociety of the elderly was found to be more

stratified socio-economically than the younger population. We are now able to distinguish between the economic losses brought about by retirement and those that reflect special forms of deprivation. Although recent U.S. studies conclude otherwise (Neugarten, 1982), European studies indicate that the poverty of old age appears to be the hardest as well as the most difficult type to remedy (Bujard and Lange, 1978).

Historical as well as sociological evidence indicates that life expectancy differs widely in accordance with economic and social stratification (Rosenmayr, 1976a). In the past, the poorer classes did not expect to reach old age; they assumed that their life would be ended early by sickness, accident, violence, malnutrition, or lack of medical treatment, as is still the case today in many Third World countries. Those who reached old age considered it to be a hardship and were not surprised by the suffering it brought about. Rich and powerful people who gave more thought to aging were able to make good use of it or to find comfort in deploring its limitations. To the masses of the population, however, the achievement of old age came as a surprise (Stearns, 1977).

The more we approach the present, the more society began to be concerned about aging and set agencies in motion to make it more bearable. The processes of aging, however, still differ widely, individually as well as socially, and bring different hardships to people of different classes. Certain upper social groups are advantaged by advanced age. In nineteenth century France, increasing age meant a steady advancement for white collar workers—a "normal progression to higher responsibilities and higher pay" (Stearns, 1977, p. 57). These groups had definite ideas about the end of their work life, what to do and how to make a good use of their time. It is interesting to see that present patterns still largely follow this historical model (Rosenmayr, 1981). Blue collar workers, on the other hand, have historically regarded old age as the phase of exhaustion. "Repose" after a life's work was the utmost they could hope for in old age. There were pension provisions for miners and artisans as early as the middle ages. These pensions were envisaged primarily as a security for widows and children in case of accident. Pension provisions for workers were not the prime interest of labor as a social force in the nineteenth century, and this attitude remains true today. Retirement laws and public social welfare for the aged were promoted in the nineteenth century by motives of economic utility. Younger workers were expected to provide more profit than older ones. This development can be documented by substantial historical evidence; it also holds true for Germany, which established the first general retirement system in 1889.

A relatively high percentage of unskilled male laborers over 60 existed in the nineteenth century. This fact suggests that older workers had to leave their employment as skilled laborers and accept lower occupational levels in order to survive (Stearns, 1977). This pattern of having to leave one job and take on an inferior one currently continues on a large scale only in Japan (Rosenmayr, 1981). The general Western model includes wages rising over the span of employment. Retirement legislation attempts to narrow the gap between white and blue collar workers, apart from the general levelling of differences in life-styles of these groups. Differences in pensions are very great, however. The effects of multiple socio-economic stratification impinges upon retired people and aggravates the inequality of their social chances in many ways (Attias-Donfut, 1983). For most groups, retirement brings about substantial income reduction. A study of German Trade Unions reveals that the average pension of male retirees is approximately 75 percent of their final net salary; the corresponding figure for women is close to 50 percent. During the past few years, the economic gap between the working and the retired population is widening in Western Europe in spite of growing budgets for pensions, social security, medicare, etc. In spite of built-in adjustments, moreover, inflation effects are particularly hard on pensioners.

Repeated surveys since the sixties (Shanas et al., 1968; Shanas, 1971; Shanas and Sussman, 1977; Rosow, 1974; Maddox, 1976) continue to document the impact of socio-economic factors and structures on the status and life chances of older people in highly developed societies. Sociologists have been able to show that not only life expectancy, frequency or length of disease after midlife, and labor disability but also attitudes towards medical treatment and the ability to care for oneself depend heavily upon social class, education, and economic resources. The effects of these attitudes add to the limitations imposed by socio-economic conditions.

Biology, physiology, and classical medicine—the sciences prominent in early gerontology—established a general pattern of human aging. It was difficult for the newly flourishing *social* branches of gerontology to break away from this generalizing mode of thinking. Recent research permits the drafting of theories of social and cultural types of aging and life course. The sociological study of life-phases and age-groups has the task of discovering the specific social deprivations that occur in different life phases and the reasons for them. Such a developmental approach has been applied to the sociology of youth (Rosenmayr and Allerbeck, 1979) and outlined theoretically for old age (Rosenmayr and Majce, 1978), as will be demonstrated in the following section.

EFFORTS TOWARDS NEW INTERPRETATIVE AND CONCEPTUAL FOCUSING

"Cumulative Deprivation" Over the Life Course and the Genesis of a "Poverty-Personality"

The concept of "cumulative deprivation" (Rosenmayr, 1976b) demonstrates how adverse factors interact to increase deprivation. Because of the interdependency of income, education, housing, health, consumption patterns, leisure behavior, etc., lower-class elderly especially run the risk of becoming involved in a vicious circle of disadvantage. The risk becomes obvious when viewed from a life-course perspective. Poor education in youth forces individuals into jobs with low earnings and less opportunities to develop attitudes favorable to additional training and learning capacities from which they might profit in later years. Not only are their jobs less healthy compared to those of persons with higher qualifications, their health-consciousness, closely related to their health-behaviors, are also negatively influenced by their low educational level. Cumulative deprivation, therefore, is an important factor in the high proportion of healthy old people who are university graduates and the low proportion of those with only a few years of schooling.

There are far fewer opportunities for activation in the lower socio-economic classes. It is difficult to motivate deprived people to participate in the social activities offered to senior citizens. If they do participate, they usually attain only a marginal position in their group. Cumulative deprivation continues with advancing age so that there is a further deterioration of health states and a lower aptitude for activity. Lower class homes are often equipped with inadequate appliances. Deprived old persons have a special need for adequate ones, since their physical handicaps and restrictions in mobility are the more common ones.

There is a disproportionally high number of widowed women within the special subset of particularly deprived persons at or below the poverty line. Very often, they are unable to take a vacation since they are too helpless and lacking in initiative to leave their disproportionately dismal living environment. It is just where help is most needed that it is the most expensive, most time-consuming, and psychologically most difficult to offer. The greater the "neediness" in one area, the more it is accompanied by other types of deficiencies (Rosenmayr and Majce, 1978).

"Cumulative deprivation," however, ought not to be considered solely from an "objective" point of view, but also as a process of subjective internalization: The latter induces certain actions or omissions that are, to some extent, within the control of the individual. Thus, even a minimal income should permit a person to procure certain household equipment. Often there are savings that are never touched because a resigned attitude about the "short future" serves as an argument for failing to purchase the necessary goods that would enhance sanitary and functional household conditions. Bad health is often attributable to unreasonable health behavior, such as the failure to consult a physician, not following medical advice, not observing dietary restrictions properly, etc. The internalization of

deprivation is socially conditioned. Sex-specific and class-specific attitudes are generated during life-long socialization processes based on prevailing values. These values can be internalized in such a way that they become a strong impediment to rational behavior in coping with one's existence.

The educational deficiencies of deprived persons result in a lack of information, planning, self-assessment, and even a rudimentary understanding of higher order needs. Usually living in deteriorated neighborhoods with a diminished local infrastructure, they suffer from disadvantages in supply sources, often aggravated by a lack of physical mobility. Continued objective deprivation results in the development of a "poverty personality." Such a personality tends to deprive itself of remaining opportunities because of an impaired competence. It also inclines to deprive itself because of further disadvantages.

The concept of internalized cumulative deprivation is not intended to limit the well-founded recognition that poverty and social deprivation are phenomena of a *socio-structural* nature. It can be demonstrated that social deprivation relates to the structures of society and their political frame that cause or permit the unequal distribution of opportunities throughout life. Limited access to need-satisfying resources results from the structural disparities of society. The consequences of such disparity for the aged manifest themselves in a cumulative fashion as their powers of physical and economic resistance decrease and their aspirations for improvement grow weaker. In the underprivileged strata, age leads to an accelerated and extended slipping into many kinds of mutually interrelated deprivations. The same phenomenon can be studied in regard to the isolated poor old in Third World regions.

The more deprived the conditions, the fewer degrees of freedom there will be. A deprived environment with its diminished resources and opportunities allows for only a limited developmental range. Primary and secondary socialization influences dispose the deprived individual to develop an often defensive or negative self-concept. Such a self-concept leaves one powerless and at the mercy of the external forces of the neighborhood and social milieu. Internalized cumulative deprivation becomes an empirically tangible and measurable factor within general deprivation (Wieltschnig, 1981).

Although individual self-defense and motivation may become marginal, the human individual must not be regarded entirely as a "function" of social forces. It is easy to see deprived persons solely as objects of a social policy that may "grant" them higher levels of financial aid. What they need most, however, is more backing as individuals and, consequently, a transformation of aging policy to a human development policy. At the level of therapy and social work, the objective would seem to lie in encouraging various forms of self-help, improved competence, and the creation of models for development and fulfillment.

Ideological Aspects of Social Structure and Aging

Another approach to the social inequality of older people studies the political deficiencies of (and within) old populations. The direction in which social changes are sought reflects the structures of the political power system and the general economic order of the society. Thus, gerosociology is no longer isolated from an analysis of the political systems involved (Myles, 1978). Such avenues of study may significantly narrow the range of explicatory concepts to a dogmatizing few, as seen in certain adherents to the "political economy" approach, and therefore risk becoming ideological and thus reductionist.

Yet another form of analysis of social structure and aging is characterized by the criticism of ideologies developed by the state in order to "pacify," "individualize," or the like, the socio-economically marginal component of the older population. Authors writing in this vein start from the proposition that modernization policies further increase the economic gap between working and retired people (see Guillemard, 1980). Some authors make the point that scientists emphasizing opportunities for activity "play no small part in legitimizing this kind of ideology" on the part of the state (Marshall, 1981).

The destructive impacts of science and research have recently been more closely diagnosed. Lack of appropriate theory has been deplored since the late fifties. General assumptions such as those about the corrosive effects of industrialization and modernization on the status of the elderly have been criticized as leading to overexplanations and false generalizations. They may do harm not only to the analytical capacities of research but to the self-concept of older citizens. Even the uncautious interpretation of demographic data may lead to cases of overinterpretation (Comfort, 1964; Bytheway, 1981). It has been suggested that *negative portrayals* and exaggeration of problems resulting from false or misleading research generalizations may influence social attitudes towards older people and may *depress the older people themselves* (Estes, 1979). It should therefore be examined to what degree (quasi)objective survey data contain massive "orientations," particularly those that result from uncontrolled, tacit theoretical assumptions. In a media-gauged society, such results may reinforce stereotypes even when the motivation of the researcher is to assess stereotypes so that strategies may be developed to dissolve them. The relationship between social structure and aging in terms of the influences on aging processes or the status of older people in postindustrial society must be understood as being "mediated" by science. It is through the "eyes" and methods of scientists that the problems of older people become defined and recognized, and it is in this form—or in a deteriorated, oversimplified (pseudo)scientific version—that they are dealt with by decision-makers, politicians, and the public. "Reflexive modernity" (Beck, 1981) cannot remain blind towards such a scientifically produced "society" and therefore must criticize its own academic overdetermination in order to prevent an irrational public rejection of science.

The Phases of Development and Fulfillment of the Self: Old Concepts and New Transdisciplinary Interpretations

We have seen that the social study of aging and development requires some reference to a multidisciplinary theory of self-fulfilment.

It demands *complex inner revision* to arrive at a strengthening of one's self-concept (Kohut, 1979) so that new activities become feasible. Neither classical learning theories nor traditional psychoanalysis provides sufficient explanations of the kind of therapeutic help that will enable the self to turn to new assignments, new basic motivations and life processes, or a new expressiveness. The concept of self is a special, historically established "open unit" reflecting the complex adaptive system of human personality. The notion of the self relates to aspects of systems and communication theory that make it possible to conceptualize the significance of meanings—of religious, metaphysical, and ideological values —and to interpret ultimate goals for the development of consciousness and action. The notion of the self emphasizes internal flexibility (Allport, 1955) in regard to societal innovation and change. It is necessary to emphasize the connection between a *dynamic and changing culture* and the *notion of self,* since it is problematic to use the term "self" generally and uncritically (e.g., for the unity of the individual and society under conditions of a preliterate, cosmological culture). The notion of self takes on meaning only if the individual can act with at least a limited amount of socially granted freedom and a certain amount of learned and trained reflexiveness. The aged member of a clan in a society with a cosmological belief system in the strict sense does not develop self or a concept of self; as an individual, he forms a unity with his clan and society.

The typical modern notion of the self emphasizes the separation of the individual from as well as his unity with his culture and society. The self as conceived since Roman stoicism, the French moralists of the seventeenth century, and, particularly, the enlightened philosophy and religion of the eighteenth century has been accompanied by an aura of autonomy and characterized by a reflection on dialectical unity (Riegel, 1976). A revised and therefore strengthened self (which furnishes a complex set of criteria for decision-making) has the potential for making a decisively important change in its image of itself. Such a vision of a change of the self is crucial for future expectations and decisions in midlife

or in preretirement phases. Insecurity, neurotic prohibitions, compulsive constraints, and emotional fixations block the ability to change one's orientation and scope of action.

Self-image is a decisive pivotal point for the subjective regulation of one's basic orientation and becomes very important for behavior modification. Strengthening of the actual self and the resulting increased flexibility for renewal of the self-image are conditions for changing the "aspiration system" of the individual (Rosenmayr, 1974b). Changes in this system are prerequisites for a successful approach to new emotional, social, and intellectual learning fields. These fields may be of great importance in midlife or later for new sexual or erotic choices, for compensating for a loss, or for recovering after an illness. A change in one's aspiration system has important consequences both for motivating tasks and for the degree of perseverance in realizing them. Such change depends, however, on modifications in the structure of the self-image. For such modification, one needs incentives, such as strong emotional experiences. These may come from the involvement and subsequent detachment exemplified by "the separation of the lovers" (Caruso, 1968) or from a certain inner radicalness resulting from meditation or religious acts. Purposeful detachment is necessary for inner criticism and self-accepted change.

Deciding on the necessary degree and direction of changes in the self-concept during (late) middle age rests upon a paradoxical mixture of security and risk. Change may occur when both have been achieved: sufficient security to revise present evaluations and sufficient desire for and attachment to the "early dream" that is part of the ideal self. Thus, late middle age is a phase of withdrawal and must perhaps be regarded as the key phase for gerontology in its classical sense. To be able to question oneself or one's behaviorally decisive principles means being able to have better control over being defensive and regressive. The likelihood of questioning oneself is much greater in circumstances where the relationship to one's own body is not substantially threatened or made insecure, a situation that is more likely to occur at an older age. With advancing age, solutions are more likely to be sought from an already acquired psychological repertoire than by working out novel solutions (Birren, 1964). Tendencies toward stagnation and psychological redundancy that result from a lack of successful "solutions" (Watzlawick et al., 1974) may be reinforced by the expectations of others regarding one's own goals and tasks. Individuals can become trapped by such external expectations and other-directedness (Riesman et al., 1950). We have to look at learning from this point of view also.

Gerontologists were right to criticize and try to overcome the "deficit theory" that postulated a *general* decline of intelligence skills and several other accomplishments with age (Lehr, 1972). Yet, in rightly criticizing this theory, gerontology risked becoming the victim of a superficial and misleading optimism about "educability." Such optimism can be fatal for the successful education and therapy of older people both in theory and in practice and for "geronting" in general. It creates the illusion of an absolute ability to do and to learn. The illusion, which may be fortified by uncritical inferences from psychological experimentation, is that for older people to learn, they only need more time or additional encouragement. If proper results ("proper" within a certain artificial universe of experimental psychology) are misinterpreted, they can lead to overexpectations for possible change and educability in the second half of life. When the meaning of self theory is neglected, experimentally correct "findings" may lead to destructively disappointing results.

Towards a Redefinition of Solidarity in Intergenerational Relationships

In our discussion of the self, we have emphasized its integrative function. From a sociological point of view, integrative processes in the *individual* must be supported by an integrative potential in *society*, i.e., by various elements of interpersonal and group solidarity. In order to explore the importance of this notion to gerontology, we propose to study the opportunities for and obstacles to solidarity posed by intergenerational relations. Intergenerational relations of older people will be dealt with here as a "test case" for opportunities for solidarity. Many studies analyzing help patterns and similar types of intergenerational interaction have paid little attention to their *symbolic aspects*, specifically as they relate to self-definition and culturally ascribed *meanings* of the ideal as well as the actual unit of the family and its aging members. Moreover, the significance of conflict has been systematically underestimated. Findings on help patterns, however justified they may have been by some criteria, have tended to idealize the multigenerational family unit.

A contradiction is seen in the fact that many persons consider their family relations central, but proximity of living arrangements undesirable. The concept of "intimacy at a distance" had its origin in studies on the *ecological contexts* of public housing developments. We discovered that older people continue to be curious about things and that they want some participation in what is going on around them. The seemingly paradoxical inclination that couples the desire for being able to observe and be informed with the desire for staying solitary and aloof first led to the formulation of the term *"intimacy at a distance"* (Rosenmayr, 1958). Later, it was found that the same paradox holds true for *social relationships within the family*. One might expect that more positive interpersonal relationships between generations in the family would increase the desire to live in the same household. It was demonstrated, however, that this was not the case. A *separate household* located in reasonable proximity was the *favored socio-ecological basis* for intergenerational relations providing mutual sympathy and support. Since the term "intimacy at a distance" seemed appropriate, it was thus used to characterize both ecological and interpersonal, or social, relations.

I now propose that the concept of "intimacy at a distance" has explanatory value at the *socio-psychiatric* level as well. There is a reason for this theoretical assumption: reducing ambivalence without negating ties requires distance. What does ambivalence between grown-up children and their parents mean? On the one hand, children feel obligations towards parents and that they are, in some respect, "responsible" for them when they grow older. At the same time, there are unresolved problems such as the vulnerability that dates from childhood and the antagonisms and mutual disillusionment that develop in later years. Witnessing the "decline" of old parents —and their capacities to control themselves and others—may lead children to reject them. Ambivalence is the result of both these trends. The more an individual is aware of self, the more the ambivalence is discovered.

The sociologist has to learn from the psychiatrist to look at at least two contradictory aspects of a relationship: adhesion, on the one hand, and repulsion, on the other. Ambivalence seems to be the appropriate term to characterize this contradiction. Studies of various socio-ecological and socio-psychological conditions have resulted in the thesis that ecological distance (different homes, or at least different bathrooms, kitchens, etc.) and social distance (control of certain emotions, permission of secrets, acceptance of the relative autonomy of the other) help reduce ambivalence. This hypothesis also applies to life-long relationships between generations. It views individuals from a life-course perspective. Ecological arrangements, social organization, and socio-psychiatric consciousness must cohere if antagonistic (and often destructive or self-destructive) emotions and ambivalent tendencies in intergenerational relations are to be "domesticated."

For the further progress of knowledge, multidisciplinary approaches must be applied to investigating the problem of solidarity. In a system of "hierarchical dependency," strong guilt feelings accompany enforced closeness. To give an example, a seventy-five-year-old mother is housebound and needs various forms of medical care and household help. She and her gainfully employed, fifty-three-year-old spinster daughter are living together. The daughter, her only child, is not only strongly dependent upon her mother but has never lost her infantile attachment. She may have to defend herself against the guilt feelings that result from aggressive wishes to become more independent of her mother. Trying to quiet these guilt feelings, she may reject out-

side help and continue caring for her mother by herself even though she is employed and finds it difficult to combine her job with her household duties. This may lead to behavior that comes close to instrumental and psychological self-destruction. Such a battle against guilt feelings can "close up" a mother-daughter relationship to the point of making outside assistance impossible. This syndrome fits into the general type of behavior that I should like to call "hierarchical dependency."

In a family that achieves or approximates an enlightened solidarity, outside medical and social assistance can be accepted more easily. Enlightened solidarity carefully considers the individual limits under which family members can offer their help. The solidarity pattern may improve communication between the generations.

The liberation of the self and redefinition of the self-image interact in cyclical processes of enlightened solidarity. Through these processes, the linkage capacities of family members (Shanas and Sussman, 1977) might eventually bear fruit. Internal *and* external communication are furthered by an enlightened family solidarity. Empathetic and expressive behavior is more easily accepted and risks less misinterpretation. In addition, the transition from expressive to instrumental behavior, and vice versa, is facilitated. Enlightened solidarity is the product of both an attitude of "overbalancing" in exchange relations and a conscious and determined elaboration of the limits of one's self.

During the last decade, family therapy has emphasized the systemic approach. The systemic perspective views the family as a structured whole and as a changing system. It may be used to enlighten sociological research and permit a better interpretation of the linkage tasks of the family—mediating and procuring medical services, rehabilitation, and creating opportunities for life fulfillment in terms of educational and spiritual values.

Whenever a family cannot offer help or care directly, it would alleviate the task of societal care if the family would employ its strength to detect needs or find ways to implement solutions and gratifications. Normatively, the task of discovering needs should be assigned to the family. Fulfilling these needs would then be accomplished primarily by *cooperation with other institutions.* In spite of this transfer of its important functions to outside institutions, the family may continue to contribute significantly to the emotional rebalancing of its older members (Bengtson and Treas, 1980).

The number of middle-aged children who give care to one or sometimes even two older generations deserves greater scrutiny. The cliché that the middle-aged reject their dependent parents can be questioned on empirical grounds. We must rather consider the growing number of families in which two generations need assistance and efforts are being made to give it, even when these efforts may be destructive to the individuals making them.

Enlightened solidarity seems to be of great importance in understanding such family structures and may help find solutions to many problems. Women of the middle generation are especially burdened with tasks of assistance. They are charged with arduous problems concerning the young in the family, with husbands experiencing their "midlife crisis" (or other crises), with their own work, and with the difficulties of finding and defining themselves as women. On top of all these burdens, they are expected to solve the emotional and practical problems of helping their parents, parents-in-law, and sometimes their grandparents as well. Here, the establishment of some sort of limitation and hierarchy of duties can be of great socio-psychiatric avail. It is difficult for the middle-aged woman to avoid being crushed by the overload of obligations expected of her. The challenge of these obligations needs critical examination. To achieve a conscious understanding of one's dependency on aging parents that continues to exist in midlife and after requires special courage. A change is needed in the vicious circle of expectations. If members of the middle generation cannot achieve maturity vis-a-vis their own parents, it is unlikely that they will be able to offer opportunities to their children to free themselves from such over-indentification.

We are rather well informed about the amount of practical help given by family members to the old, that is, about "family pragmatism." We know far too little, however, about the quality of family relations and about what each member can offer to the fulfillment of the others in terms of revised mutual expectations. Until now, research and theory about the withdrawal from one's children in the process of generational change has received little attention. Such withdrawal, however, has central importance for the family, since its methods and processes influence the qualities of intergenerational relationships. Irrational expectations by parents with regard to their children's careers and particularly their children's partner selection or partner relationships complicate the mutual withdrawal process.

Successful withdrawal is based on "sympathetic constraint"—an important feature of enlightened solidarity. Educational programs for families assist parents in overcoming narcissistic possessiveness by fostering an attitude of "yielding" in the sense of letting go and setting free. Parent-child relations contain the seed of their own break-down if children are continually held "on a long leash" (Stierlin, 1975). Instead, parents must be capable of directing their own affairs and of developing their own capabilities for change and adaptation in later life. A central task of the adult generations in their relationships with their aging parents and grandparents is to overcome (neurotic) dependencies and replace these by "related individuation" (Stierlin, 1978). Nonnarcissistic attitudes (or revised narcissism) support enlightened solidarity. Revised narcissism does not necessarily lead to a reduction or avoidance of intergenerational relations. It may lead to a kind of relation where emotional problems (since these are bound to exist within any multigenerational interaction) can be clarified and restructured on a verbal as well as a behavioral level. Perhaps social researchers still attach too little significance to the acceptance of one's own parents as a means of liberating and renewing one's attitudes towards one's own children.

SUMMARY

It is the main purpose of this article to introduce a view of historico-comparative sociology as it applies to the social position of older people and the cultural evaluation of life phases, particularly that of old age, in Western society. The goal has been to uncover the *roots* of the status of the old in philosophical and religious systems and in the division of labor in society that defines the social value of age groups. Some sidelines explore new theoretical avenues for phenomena like the social deprivation of older people, the quest for fulfillment (by studying the notion of self), and the types of intergenerational solidarity.

This contribution to the sociology of aging (gero-sociology) is divided into four sections. First, the *nature of the approach* is explained; second, a *historico-comparative view* on aging in Western society is sketched; third, a *revision of* the usage of some *general sociological notions* for social gerontology and life course is suggested; and fourth, selected *new interpretative* and *conceptual foci* are introduced.

It is presumed that a global comparative historico-sociological understanding coupled with findings from empirical studies will have relevance to practical decision-making and policy and that it will create a conscious re-evaluation of preconceived notions, thereby permitting processes of liberation conducive to creativity both in individuals and organizations.

The sociological point of view applied here emphasizes the importance of culturally predefined meaning and orientation systems vis-à-vis decision making and priorities for action. Culture in our sense, however, is not seen as an independent entity that controls behavior directly through values and norms. Instead, aging is looked at from a point of view that sees *culture as being mediated and shaped by social structure.* Processes of the self that link the ego with culturally recognized or recommended ideals need to be studied by a systems-oriented social science of aging. Such an approach permits a better understanding of how individuals are cognitively and emotionally affected by (internalized) cultural values and norms. To give an example, seniority coupled with age is a rank-ordering status dimension heavily dependent on cultural values and one with great emotional significances for the individual.

The key question for the sociology of aging is how to relate the acting individual in its social and cultural context to the biological changes of the human organism over time.

Special attention must be paid to profiles of aging, development, and fulfillment in terms of the socially significant factors of income, education, and occupational groups, as well as ethnicity, cultural traditions, and life styles.

The various types of aging and of reproductive and survival systems are connected with societies and cultures in different ways. There is *no single "general" path of aging* and no general model of societal and political reaction to the system of reproduction and mortality. The fertility–mortality system is both the outcome of and an influential factor in the development of society. An interrelation exists between individual aging and "population aging" inasmuch as the proportion of older people in a society, the predominance of their needs, the resulting welfare systems, and their life styles are additional conditions of the general social value climate and the distribution of the resources of the society. General evaluations stemming from society's reaction to mass aging leave their mark upon the self-definition of older people. The sociological position (seen from the point of view of systems theory) does not abstract from the individual or neglect the individual, nor does it deal with social categories exclusively; rather, its concept of the individual focusses on the continued conflict and integration of the individual with and into social groups. Sociology defines systems of society and culture in order to be able to interpret the constitution, orientation, and actions of the individual.

A historically comparative sociology of aging shows that the idea of "rebirth" as a category describing and demanding spiritual and psychological renewal dates back to the messianic revivalism of Judaism and Christianity. Western philosophical and moral thought took up this idea, but here it is supplemented by a second perspective. One emphasizes the renewal of spiritual and emotional life forces (independent of biological age) by venturing to respond to developmental challenges with spiritual goals. The other emphasizes endurance. The second perspective was derived from classical Roman philosophy and redrafted by the eighteenth-century Enlightenment spirit. It defined human dignity as the fulfillment of a "properly lived" life in its late phase— properly lived because properly endured.

In our historico-comparative section, we show that it is difficult to connect the history of spiritual and moral ideas with the forms and organization of production. Although it is not possible to deduce one from the other, it is possible to give an example of mutual influence. During the rapid economic change and growth in the nineteenth century, the term "rebirth" was used in a specific economic sense. Postmodern scepticism vis-à-vis progress uses the idea of "rebirth" again, yet in quite a different sense. Present social conditions are seen as potentially favorable to a quest for "renewal" in the sense of an increase in individualization and creativity in later life.

The status of advanced age became strongly ambiguous as a result of the modernization processes of industrialization and urbanization that have been taking place since the eighteenth century. Under the conditions of contemporary postaffluent and postmodern society, there is likely to be a certain reduction of this earlier ambiguity. The advantages of continuity, nonpragmatic knowledge, unmeasurable creativity, and nonmaterialistic values that are attributable to some long-term life experiences are beginning to receive greater recognition by society.

The main theoretical perspective of this article is elaborated upon in its third section. According to this view, the *age structure* and *age norms* of a society are not separate structural properties. They are forged by the forces and systems of production, the educational system, and various forms of medical and social care, social security, and welfare systems. Age norms are *derivatives*. The production systems as well as the orientation and interpretative systems of a society (the schools, ideologies, religious groups, and media that diffuse values and models) determine the social division of labor by "assigning" different tasks to different age groups. They shape these groups and the individuals they are composed of.

The models for life values and spiritual and existential self-interpretation as well as the social norms established by religion and other forces play an important role in constructing *age notions*. The age structure is thus to be considered the result of a mass of influences.

The models mentioned are not causally dependent on the economic structure. Interpretations of the meaning of (human) life are conditioned socio-economically, however, but follow their own dynamic. Norms cannot come into being without ideological and value notions on the one hand and the socio-economic need to organize and stabilize societies and their institutions on the other. The establishment and patterns of life phases as well as their social interconnection are dependent upon the state of development of a society and its subunits. Societal organization of the division of labor tends towards a utilization and standardization of a biologically anchored, yet ontogenetically and phylogenetically modifiable, concept of human age. The ever-changing design of phases in this division of labor reflects the respective historical specifications of a society.

The division of labor in postmodern society in highly developed economic systems has created a unique situation. Because of the combination of increased life expectancy and drastic improvements in public health, leisure activities have become possible for large groups of the population over 50. In Western European countries where social policy is still following the trend of lowering the pension age, a nonemployed majority of persons over 60 has been created. Under such conditions, the problem of individual selection of *subjectively meaningful activities* takes on central significance. It coincides with the problem of "finding a place" in postmodern society. Socially acknowledged and esteemed activities may thus provide status. Diagnosis of the status issue cannot be limited to ascertaining attitudes and actions that are merely appreciative; it must take account of the *meaning* that aging individuals can attribute to their own activities and that their family, friends, peers, neighborhood, and the wider society can recognize. Satisfaction will result from what is mutually deemed necessary and contributory. By "meaning" we understand a cognitive content that provides not only emotional satisfaction but the security of knowing that one's actions correspond to one's goals in a way that can be easily grasped.

In the last section, the notion of the *cumula-*

tive deprivation of older people even under conditions of the modern welfare state is shown to remain an important topic. Limited access to need-satisfying resources is a result of the structural disparities of society. The consequences of such disparity for the aged manifest themselves in a cumulative fashion as their power of physical and economic resistance decreases and their aspirations for improvement grow weaker. Among the underprivileged strata, advancing age leads to an accelerated and extended slippage into many kinds of mutually interrelated disadvantages. The more deprived the conditions, the fewer degrees of freedom available. A deprived environment with diminished resources and opportunities allows for only a limited developmental range. Primary and secondary socialization influences dispose a deprived individual to develop an often defensive or negative self-concept. Such a self-concept can leave one powerless and at the mercy of external forces. Internalized cumulative deprivation becomes an empirically tangible and measurable factor within general deprivation.

The final subsection dealing with the notion of solidarity with special reference to kinship systems shows that solidarity under conditions of postmodern individualism requires sufficient distance between parties to accommodate efforts towards self-support as well as a readiness to permit support instead of the hierarchical dependency and clinging to one another that is typical of a closed system. Inner and outer conditions for various types of solidarity are defined. This serves to demonstrate once again the integrative aspects of systems theory, which combines the view of the individual with that of the group and thus fulfills the requirements of a sociological approach to aging.

REFERENCES

Alberoni, F. 1970. *Classe e Generazioni* (Classes and generations). Bologna: Il Mulino.

Allport, G. W. 1955. *Becoming: Basic Considerations for a Psychology of Personality.* New Haven: Yale University Press.

Attias-Donfut, C. M. 1978. Freizeit, lebenslauf und generationenbildung (Leisure, life course and the formation of generations). In *Die menschlichen Lebensalter. Kontinuität und Krisen* (Human Life Stages. Continuity and Crises), ed. L. Rosenmayr, pp. 354–375. Munich: Piper.

Attias-Donfut, C. M. 1983. La vieillesse inégale (Inegalitarian aging). *Communications* 37: 125–136.

Barnes, S. M.; Kaase, M.; et al. 1979. *Political Action. Mass Participation in Five Western Democracies.* London–Beverly Hills: Sage Publications.

Beck, U. 1981. Folgeprobleme der modernisierung und der stellung der soziologie in der praxis (Problems resulting from modernization and from the sociology-practice relation). In *Soziologie und Praxis* (Sociology and Practice), ed. U. Beck, pp. 3–23. Göttingen: Otto Schwartz & Co.

Bengtson, V. L. 1973. *The Social Psychology of Aging.* Indianapolis: Bobbs-Merrill.

Bengtson, V. L. 1975. Value socialization in three generations: cohort and lineage effects. *American Sociological Review* 33: 224–239.

Bengtson, V. L., and Treas, J. 1980. The changing family context of mental health and aging. In *Handbook of Mental Health and Aging,* eds. J. E. Birren and R. B. Sloane, pp. 400–428. N.J.: Prentice Hall.

Berger, P. L. 1979. The heretical imperative. *Contemporary Possibilities of Religious Affirmation.* New York: Anchor Press.

Birren, J. E. 1964. *The Psychology of Aging.* N.J.: Prentice Hall.

Bujard, O., and Lange, U. 1978. *Armut im Alter. Ursachen, Erscheinungsformen, politisch-administrative Reaktionen* (Poverty in old age. Causes, forms and politico-administrative responses). Weinheim–Basel: Beltz.

Bytheway, W. R. 1981. Demographic statistics and old age ideology. *Ageing and Society* 3: 347–364.

Caruso, I. 1968. *Trennung der Liebenden. Eine Phänomenologie des Todes* (Separation of the lovers. A phenomenology of death). Bern–Stuttgart: Huber.

Cole, Th. R. 1980. Past meridian: Aging and the northern middle class, 1830–1930. Unpublished doctoral dissertation. University of Rochester.

Comfort, A. 1964. *The Process of Aging.* New York: Signet Science Library.

Cowgill, D. O. 1972. The role and status of the aged in Thailand. In *Aging and Modernization,* eds. D. O. Cowgill and L. D. Holmes, pp. 91–102. New York: Appleton-Century-Crofts.

Demos, J. 1978. *A Little Commonwealth. Family Life in Plymouth Colony.* London: Oxford University Press.

DiFilippo, E. 1982. Foreword in *Aging: Spiritual Perspectives,* ed. F. V. Tiso, pp. vii–ix. Lake Worth, Florida: Sunday Publications, Inc.

Douglas, A. 1977. *The Feminization of American Culture.* New York: Alfred A. Knopf.

Dowd, J. J. 1978. Aging as exchange: a test of the distributive justice proposition. *Pacific Sociological Revue* 21: 351–375.

Eisenstadt, S. N., 1974. *Tradition, Change, and Modernity.* New York–London: John Wiley & Sons.

Estes, C. 1979. *The Aging Enterprise.* San Francisco: Jossey-Bass.

Featherstone, M., and Kruschinski, M. 1981. The older person in society. *Ageing and Society* 3: 347–364.

Flusser, D. 1968. A new sensitivity in Judaism and the Christian message. *Havard Theological Review* 61: 107–127.

Gaullier, X. 1982. *L'avenir á reculons. Chômage, retraite et temps libre* (Future backward. Leisure, withdrawal and free time). Paris: Editions Ouvrières.

Gould, P. L. 1978. *Transformations, Growth and Change in Adult Life.* New York: Simon and Schuster.

Guillemard, A. M. 1980. *La vieillesse et l'Etat* (Old age and the state). Paris: Presses Universitaires de France.

Gutmann, D. 1977. The cross-cultural perspective: Notes toward a comparative psychology of aging. In *Handbook of the Psychology of Aging,* eds. J. Birren and K. W. Schaie, pp. 302–326. New York: Van Nostrand Reinhold.

Habermas, J. 1976. *Zur Rekonstruktion des Historischen Materialismus* (On reconstruction of the historical materialism). Frankfurt: Suhrkamp.

Hall, G. S. 1922. *Senescence.* New York: Appleton–Century–Crofts.

Inglehart, R. 1977. *The Silent Revolution.* New Jersey: Princeton University Press.

Klausner, J. 1977. The rise of Christianity. In *Society and Religion in the Second Temple Period,* eds. M. Avi-Yonah and Z. Baras. Jerusalem: Massada Publishing Ltd.

Kohut, H. 1977. *Introspektion, Empathie und Psychoanalyse* (Introspection, empathy and psychoanalysis). Frankfurt: Suhrkamp.

Kohut, H. 1979. *The Restoration of the Self.* New York: International Universities Press.

Kopytoff, I. 1971. Ancestors as elders in Africa. *Africa* 2: 129–142.

Lehr, U. 1972. *Psychologie des Alterns* (Psychology of aging). Heidelberg: Quelle & Meyer.

Luce, G. G. 1981. Sage and wisdom. In *Wisdom and Age. The Adventure of Later Life,* ed. J. R. Staude, pp. 41–47. Berkeley: Ross Books.

Maddox, G. L. 1976. Scope, concepts and methods in the study of aging. In *Handbook of Aging and the Social Sciences,* eds. R. Binstock and E. Shanas, pp. 3–34. New York: Van Nostrand Reinhold.

Marshall, V. W. 1981. The changing family relationships of older people. Program for Quantitative Studies in Economics and Population, No. 5. Mc Master University of Hamilton, Ontario.

Mead, G. H. (1934) 1965. *Mind, Self and Society. From the Standpoint of a Social Behaviorist.* Chicago–London: The University of Chicago Press.

Mendonsa, E. L. 1976. Elders, office-holders and ancestors among the Sisala of northern Ghana, *Africa* 46: 57–65.

Myles, J. F. 1978. Institutionalization and sick role identification among the elderly. *American Sociological Review* 43:508–521.

Neugarten, B. 1982. New perspectives on aging and social policy. In The Leon and Josephine Winkelman Lecture, The University of Michigan, pp. 2–5.

Parsons, T. 1951. *The Social System.* Glencoe: Free Press.

Riegel, K. 1976. Toward a dialectical theory of development. *American Psychologist* 31: 689–700.

Riesman, D.; Denny, R.; and Glazer, N. 1950. *The Lonely Crowd. A Study of the Changing American Character.* New Haven: Yale University Press.

Riley, M. W.; Johnson, M.; and Foner, A. 1972. *Aging and Society: A Sociology of Age Stratification,* Vol. 3. New York: Russell Sage Foundation.

Riley, M. W., and Abeles, R., eds. 1982. *Aging from Birth to Death. Sociotemporal Perspectives,* Vol. 2. Boulder: Westview Press.

Rohlen, Th. P. 1971. Father-son dominance: Tikopia and China. In *Kinship and Culture,* ed. F. L. K. Hsu, pp. 154–173. Chicago: Aldine Publishing Company.

Rosenmayr, L. 1958. Der alte mensch in der sozialen umwelt von heute (The aged in the present social environment). *Kölner Zeitschrift für Soziologie und Sozialpsychologie* 10: 642–657.

Rosenmayr, L. 1974a. Elements of an assimilation-yield theory. Paper read at the eighth World Congress of Sociology, August 10–24, 1974. Toronto.

Rosenmayr, L. 1974b. Die revision der these vom generellen leistungsverfall im alternsprozess (Revision of the thesis of the general decline of performance related to the aging process). In *Aktivitätsprobleme des Alternden* (Activity problems of the aging), ed. K. Fellinger, pp. 101–123. Basel: Editions Roche.

Rosenmayr, L. 1976a. Schwerpunkte der soziologie des alterns (Gerosoziologie) [Main issues in the sociology of aging (Gerosociology)]. In *Familie/Alter* (Family/ old age), ed. R. König, pp. 218–406. Stuttgart: Enke.

Rosenmayr, L. 1976b. Die soziale benachteiligung alter menschen. (Social deprivation of old people). In *Scriptum Geriatricum, Vorträge des 17. Internationalen Fortbildungskurses für Geriatrie,* 1975 (Lectures at 17th international professional training in geriatrics, 1975), ed. W. Doberauer, pp. 203–219. Munich: Urban und Schwarzenberg.

Rosenmayr, L. 1978a. Die menschlichen lebensalter in deutungsversuchen der Europäischen kulturgeschichte (Human life stages as interpreted in European cultural history). In *Die menschlichen Lebensalter. Kontinuität und Krisen* (Human life stages. Continuity and crises), ed. L. Rosenmayr, pp. 23–79. Munich: Piper.

Rosenmayr, L. 1978b. Fragmente zu einer sozialwissenschaftlichen theorie der lebensalter (Fragments for a social-scientific theory of the life course). In *Die menschlichen Lebensalter . . .* (Human Life Stages . . .); op. cit., ed. L. Rosenmayr, pp. 428–457.

Rosenmayr, L. 1978c. Elemente einer allgemeinen alter(n)stheorie (Elements of a general theory of aging). In *Der alte Mensch in der Gesellschaft* (Old people in society), eds. L. and H. Rosenmayr, pp. 46–70. Reinbek/Hamburg: Rowohlt.

Rosenmayr, L. 1978d. Die soziale bewertung der alten menschen. (Social evaluation of the Old). In *Der alte Mensch . . .* (Old People in . . .); op. cit., eds. L. and H. Rosenmayr, pp. 110–132.

Rosenmayr, L. 1981. Objective and subjective perspectives of life span research. *Ageing and Society* 1: 29–49.

Rosenmayr, L. 1982. Biography and identity. In *Aging and Life Course Transitions. An Interdisciplinary Perspective,* eds. T. K. Hareven and K. J. Adams, pp. 27–54. New York: The Guilford Press.

Rosenmayr, L. 1983. *Die späte Freiheit* (Late freedom). Berlin: Severin & Siedler.

Rosenmayr, L., and Allerbeck, K. 1979. Youth and society. *Current Sociology* 2/3.

Rosenmayr, L., and Majce, G. 1978. Die soziale benachteiligung (Social deprivation). In *Der alte Mensch . . . (Old People . . .)*; op. cit., eds. L. and H. Rosenmayr, pp. 231–260.

Rosow, I. 1974. *Socialization to Old Age.* Berkeley, Calif.: University of California Press.

Rosow, I. 1976. Status and role change through the life span. In *Handbook of Aging and the Social Sciences,* eds. R. H. Binstock and E. Shanas, pp. 457–482. New York: Van Nostrand Reinhold.

Schweeger-Hefel, A. 1980. *Masken und Mythen. Sozialstrukturen der Nyonyosi und Sikonse in Obervolta* (Masks and myths. Social structures of the Nyonyosi and Sikonse in Upper Volta). Vienna: Schendl.

Shanas, E. 1971. Measuring the health needs of the aged in five countries. *Journal of Gerontology* 26: 37–40.

Shanas, E. 1979. Social myth as hypothesis: The case of the family relations of old people. *The Gerontologist* 1: 3–9.

Shanas, E., and Sussman, M. B., eds. 1977. *Family, Bureaucracy and the Elderly.* Durham: Duke University Press.

Shanas, E.; Townsend, P.; Wedderburn, D.; Friis, H.; Milhøj, P.; and Stehouwer, J. 1968. *Old People in Three Industrial Societies.* New York: Atherton Press.

Sheppard, H. L. 1976. Work and Retirement. In *Handbook of Aging and the Social Sciences,* eds. R. H. Binstock and E. Shanas, pp. 286–309. New York: Van Nostrand Reinhold.

Simmons, L. W. 1970. *The Role of the Aged in Primitive Society.* Hamden, Conn.: Archon Books.

Sprandel, R. 1981. *Altersschicksale und Altersmoral. Die Geschichte der Einstellung zum Altern nach der Pariser Bibelexegese des 12.–14. Jhds* (Fate and moral in old age. The history of attitudes towards aging according to the Paris Exegesis in the 12th to 14th Century). Stuttgart: Hiersemann.

Stearns, P. N. 1977. *Old Age in European Society.* London: Croom Helm.

Stein, H. 1979. *Psychoanalytische Selbstpsychologie und die Philosophie des Selbst* (Psychoanalytical self-psychology and the philosophy of self). Meisenheim am Glan: Anton Hain.

Stierlin, H. 1975. *Von der Psychoanalyse zur Familientherapie* (From psychoanalysis to family therapy). Stuttgart: Klett.

Stierlin, H. 1978. *Delegation und Familie* (Delegation and Family). Frankfurt: Suhrkamp.

Streib, G. F. 1976. Social stratification and aging. In *Handbook of Aging and the Social Sciences,* eds. R. H. Binstock and E. Shanas, pp. 160–188. New York: Van Nostrand Reinhold.

Tews, H. P. 1979. *Soziologie des Alterns* (Sociology of Aging). 3rd pr. Heidelberg: Quelle & Mayer.

Watzlawick, P.; Weakland, J. H.; and Fish, R. 1974. *Change. Principles of Problem Formation and Problem Resolution.* New York: W. W. Norton & Company.

Wieltschnig, E. 1981. The cumulative deprivation of retired Swiss citizens in economical difficulties. Paper presented at the XIIth International Congress of Gerontology, Hamburg, July 12–17, 1981.

9
CULTURE, BEHAVIOR, AND AGING IN THE COMPARATIVE PERSPECTIVE

Christine L. Fry, Ph.D
Loyola University of Chicago

INTRODUCTION

Wherever human beings are concerned, very few things are simple. Aging is no exception. Universally speaking, a transformation occurs between the endpoints of life—birth and death. Physiologically speaking, minds and bodies change. Socially speaking, these changes are important factors shaping behavior. Culturally speaking, the changes are interpreted and become an important part of the symbolic world by means of which people chart their lives. Culture, as a phenomenon, is often seen as made-up, artificial, and opposed to nature (Levi-Strauss, 1969). For humans, however, culture is the natural laboratory in which to study behavior and one which is diverse, indeed. Culture adds yet another dimension to our study of aging.

Precisely because culture is such an integral part of human life, it is analytically difficult to separate it from other aspects of life such as behavior or aging. Yet, culture in its diversity invites comparison to find its points of commonality. Culture, being learned, is not only highly variable but more rapidly modifiable than the biological and neurological equipment that make it possible. Each of the more than 3000 human cultures constitutes a natural experiment and a context for behavior. Although aging is experienced within these contexts, as a phenomena, it can be understood only when it is distinguished from its context. The task ahead, then, for both psychology and anthropology is to find unity in diversity.

In this review, we will examine the advances made in the comparative study of age since Simmons introduced the topic in his now classic *Role of the Aged in Primitive Society* (1945). The topics are organized under the following four general headings:

1. "Culture and Behavior: An Obvious and Not-So-Obvious Link" examines how people use culture to negotiate with others and to manage their own social identity.
2. "Age and Culture in the Comparative Perspective" examines the broad issues of longevity and culture; the cultural modeling of time and the life course; age, sex, and personality; and age and cultural values.
3. "Societies and the Experience of Aging" shifts to issues of the treatment of the aged, the consequences of change, ethnicity and aging, and age and group formation.
4. "Implications for Psychological Research on Aging" takes a look at the

strengths of comparative designs for psychological research and the subtle nature of culture, which potentially confounds the answers to our questions.

CULTURE AND BEHAVIOR: AN OBVIOUS AND NOT SO OBVIOUS LINK

In the last quarter of the twentieth century, culture is a rather obvious variable in explaining behavior. Like most concepts developed in the behavioral and social sciences, culture and its companion ethnicity have become a part of most people's vocabulary. Hence, although we are aware of it, in everyday activity it tends to be amorphous, lacking clarity until we are reminded, usually in shocking ways, of its not so obvious existence. Scientifically, we have made strides on some fronts and met with frustration on others. After its discovery during the colonial expansion of Europe, culture became superorganic (Kroeber, 1917)—a mentalistic phenomenon built upon, but transcending, the organic. In its generality, this notion served well for heuristic purposes. For analysis and interpretation, however, it has largely been abandoned for problem-specific conceptualizations (see Keesing, 1974, for a review). Recent theoretical advances have taken the direction of narrowing the concept to cover less and reveal more. A challenge remains on one front: the interface between culture and behavior and the scientific models we build to describe them.

The study of actual behavior has never been a strong point of anthropology. Anthropologists—primarily those influenced by psychology [Bateson, 1958 (original, 1936); Bateson and Mead, 1942; Arensburg, 1954, 1972]—pioneered behavioral studies cross-culturally. In spite of these efforts, the science of culture remains ideational; our models are *about* behavior, not *of* behavior. As any psychologist will tell you, behavior is highly variable and messy, especially when studied outside the controlled conditions of the laboratory. Indeed, those who have tried to find the direct effect of codes or rules upon behavior have been disappointed. Videotape recording of New York City families by Marvin Harris and his associates revealed inconsistencies with the self-reports of what had happened (De-Havernon, ND, cited in Pelto and Pelto, 1975). Similarly, analysis of Zinacantan gossip indicates that the codes are determined by contingencies (Haviland, 1978). Even rituals with explicit routines are marred by mistakes and drunken bungling (Cancian, 1965). These examples all bring home the point that behavior is shaped by a complex combination of rules and situational factors (Harris, 1964). This does not mean we should abandon the idea of the superorganic. Quite to the contrary, our theories should take culture into account in explaining how people manage the situations they get themselves into. The lesson we have learned is that the superorganic takes on a life of its own and that it alone cannot explain all behavior.

People, researchers included, reify culture. Culture is ideational, an ideal. The ideal is used to rationalize, to interpret, or even to obfuscate the real (as expressed in the folk wisdom of "Do as I say, not as I do"). Small and even flagrant discrepancies between the ideal and the actual are either minimized or overlooked unless they become the center of concern and controversy. Consequently, variability is masked. More often than not, our accounts of other people are normative and uniformist (Pelto and Pelto, 1975). We gain insights into the lives of *the* Navajo, *the* Eskimo, *the* Japanese, or *the* Tiwi, conveniently forgetting that back home there is no *the* American. Reification of concepts is a problem for all science. Because people are prone to it in their own lives, however, we are led closer to the relationship between culture, individuals, and their behavior.

Individuals are not the passive recipients of knowledge, rules and standards from enculturators who are older, bigger, stronger, or more important than they are. Knowledge, rules, and standards are not learned to be blindly followed either in motivating action or determining responses. Studies of language acquisition reveal that children actively build their ideas about language to help them generate and comprehend the speech of their community (Chomsky, 1973; McNeill, 1970). Similarly, culture is a model each individual has formed of what others know, believe, and mean. It is his or her own theory of the code being followed, of the game being played (Keesing, 1972, 1974). Linking these models with motivation and behavior has been a continuing theoretical challenge. In one study of beliefs and action in the small Maya community of Zinacantan, Francesca Cancian (1975) concluded that social identities bridge the cultural and behavioral. People use their models to generate the actions they think will lead others to validate a certain identity. People conform to rules to demonstrate to themselves and to others that they are a particular kind of person.

Culture is like a recipe we use to cook our food. We use a recipe to find instructions for what raw materials are necessary and guidelines or plans for what combinations usually work. We use culture to interpret behavior and to plot future action. Knowledge, rules, and standards are applied in formulating the strategies (Whitten and Whitten, 1972) and making the decisions (Quinn, 1975) that are needed to chart our actions. Culture attests to the superorganic, the supraindividual. It is the property of collectivities, of groups. Individuals concoct their own version of the recipe and test it by interaction, thereby affirming their own and other's identities. Social identities are complex. Since their diets of interaction vary in quality and context over time, they are not rigid; they develop and change.

For comparative purposes, anthropologists have not focused on the interior psychological experience of identity. Instead, the conventional units of analysis have been the parts or roles that people play (Linton, 1936; Goodenough, 1965). Not surprisingly, ethnologists have given the most attention to achieved roles, those that offer people more choice and options to play with. The assumption is that it is when people have alternatives that we find the greatest cultural elaboration and the greatest payoff in our search for principles and universals. Thus, in our wealth of ethnographic description and analysis, we find politics, economics, kinship, and religion well documented. Ascriptive roles, those over which we have no choice such as age and sex, have been assumed to be natural, fixed, basic, uniform, and not subject to as much cultural interpretation (LaFontaine, 1978). As we apply our ethnographic muscle to this front, we find this assumption unwarranted. Social identities and social differences are built upon combinations of ascription and achievement. Both are subject to knowledge, rules, and standards. It is now that we must turn to what we have learned about age and aging and how this knowledge is applied in building strategies and shaping identities in the comparative laboratory of anthropology.

AGE IN THE COMPARATIVE PERSPECTIVE

Comparison is the heart of our method. The comparative method, however, is neither monolithic nor singular. Instead, it is a composite of alternative research strategies for obtaining, from dissimilar societies, data that are both theoretically salient and comparable. These are discussed within two major frameworks, the holocultural and the cross-cultural.

Holocultural Considerations

Most celebrated in gerontology is Simmons' (1945, 1960) work on the aged in primitive societies. He was the first to employ the then new Human Relations Area Files (HRAF)—which had assembled and codified information on relatively complex societies ethnographers had investigated—for a study of the aged in simpler societies. As the files expanded and their usage increased, a distinctive comparative approach emerged in the seventies that was identified as "holocultural." Holocultural research involves a statistical evaluation of the relationship between two or more variables in a world sample of human societies derived from the HRAF files (Rohner, et. al., 1978; Naroll, 1970, 1976). Contemporary aging research that builds upon Simmons' pioneering efforts can be seen in the work of Maxwell and Silverman (1970) and Glascock and Feinman (1980a, 1980b, 1981).

Cross-Cultural Considerations

Cross-cultural, in contrast to holocultural, research is now reserved for multicultural studies that do not make use of the HRAF files or samples. The heterogeneity of cross-cultural research strategies should be apparent from the following examples:

1. Sending a team to investigate the same problem with the same methods in different societies—the strategy used in Myerhoff and Simic's comparative study of life histories in five cultures (1978).
2. Sending one investigator to different cultures to obtain the comparative data needed—the strategy employed by David Gutmann in his studies of personality shifts in late life (1969, 1974, 1975, 1977).
3. A re-examination of previously collected field notes by experienced researchers in a theoretically ordered selection of cultures. In their study of aging and modernization, Cowgill and Holmes (1972) invited seasoned fieldworkers to examine data they had collected for other purposes for its relevance to the problems of aging and the treatment of the aged.
4. A controlled comparison based on two or more societies similar in nearly all characteristics except one or two, the effects of the dissimilar variables being the object of investigation. Nadel's (1952) study of age grades and witchcraft in four African societies is an example.
5. An analysis of existing reports either on a regional basis or on the basis of a societal type. Press and McKool's (1972) study of the status of the aged in Meso-American peasant cultures was done on a regional basis, whereas Foner and Kertzer (1978) selected age-set societies for their study of age transitions.
6. Cross-national research is sometimes lumped with the cross-cultural but should be differentiated as yet another comparative design. Cross-national research is restricted to one societal type, the industrialized nation state, and utilizes national statistics or administers surveys to national probability samples. The study of old people in three industrial societies by Shanas, et al. (1968), and the study of retirement by Havighurst, et. al. (1969), are examples of cross-national designs.
7. A cross-ethnic design is usually used to study cultural differences within a single society that is usually either industrialized or industrializing. Bengtson's study (1979) of aging and ethnicity in three groups in Los Angeles is one example; Cool's study (1980) of the effects of ethnicity among Corsican immigrants in Paris is another.
8. By far the most utilized design is the "counter case" or "counter example," in which a familiar theory formulated in one society is evaluated in another. Often the results veto what previously was assumed to be universal (for example, Margaret Mead's famous 1928 study of adolescence in Samoa). Although this is the most familiar and most striking approach because of its emphasis on the exotic, it is also the least systematic in its methods of sampling and controlling for extraneous variables.

In the sections that follow, we will use the results obtained through these comparative methods to assess, with a world-wide perspective, what we have learned about aging.

Human Longevity in Comparative Perspective

In initially scanning the cultures of other societies, it is the exotic that catches our attention: headhunting, cannibalism, gericide. It did not take us long to discover three Shangri-las: Abkhasia in the Caucaus Mountains (USSR); Hunzakut in the Karakoram Mountains (Pakistan) and Vilcabamba in the Andes (Ecuador). Reports of numbers of people being as old as 115 or even 130 attracted physicians, gerontologists, and anthropologists to find out why (Leaf, 1973a, 1973b; Benet, 1974, 1976; Davies, 1975). No factors exclusive to these populations were found. Consequently, attention shifted to a combination of genetic and social factors (Moore, 1981). The payoff would be great, indeed. With biochemical evidence indicating a possible limit of 110 ± 10 years (Hayflick, 1965, 1977), it would be reasonable to expect extremely longevous individuals endowed with maximal inheritance for long life spans to attain super-longevity under maximal environmental conditions.

Doubts, however, have been cast upon these

Shangri-las. The anthropologists Mazess and Foreman (1979) conducted a census in Vilcabamba examining birth, marriage, and death records at three different times. They concluded that the oldest individual was 96 at death and that systematic age exaggeration begins at about the age of 70, the actual age sometimes being increased by as much as 20 to 40 years. The Abkhasian and Hunza data are now under suspicion and being subjected to greater scrutiny (Fries and Crapo, 1981). We have learned two important lessons. First, we should ask, "Under what circumstances do people distort their ages?" In Vilcabamba, age was exaggerated upward, a reversal of the "Jack Benny Complex" in the United States. Second, age may not be the ascriptive characteristic we assume it to be. Because its changes are incremental and gradual, as the Vilcabamba case indicates, age is subject to interpretation and negotiation.

In further expanding our perspective by comparing our own species with the primates, we discover the possible evolutionary significance of human longevity. Life spans are species specific. Brain size and body weight taken in conjunction are approximate predictors of maximum life potential. Human maximum life potential (MLP) is estimated to be 91 or 92 years (see Cutler, 1976, for estimates of MLP for other members of the Order Primate). On the basis of the fossil record, human MLP has remained relatively constant since the appearance of our species some 45,000 years ago. If we estimate the maximum life potential exhibited by the fossils that reveal the evolution of the hominids, we find a trend of increasing longevity (Cutler, 1975).

What selective factors have favored longer life spans? Culture itself is one of the answers. Short life spans mean shorter periods of full cultural participation, thus limiting the quantity and complexity of cultural content that can be transmitted to succeeding generations (Krantz, 1966). Increases in the complexity of culture is certainly one of the trends of the hominid revolution. Since this complexity is predicated on learning and accumulating and interpreting experience, longer life spans for some individuals would be favored. It is no accident that when anthropologists begin

a study of the culture of a preliterate people, they are usually directed to its older members. It is not because the elders have time on their hands; it is because they know more. They are the most "cultured."

Culture also shapes the way the life span is divided around the arrival of sexual maturity. Human beings go through one of the longest periods of dependency prior to sexual maturity of any animal, this being the stage during which cultural and linguistic competency is acquired. The later arrival of sexual maturity in longer life spans has concomitantly altered other life stages (Lovejoy, 1981; Washburn, 1981). A distinctively human characteristic is a long post-reproductive life. The advantages of the survival of parents until the youngest child reaches sexual maturity are obvious, but the evolutionary significance of grandparents is not so apparent. Continuity and stabilizing traditions are only part of the answer, since evolution proceeds by forces that alter the genetic composition of a population. Kin selection involving investment in existent children by post-menopausal women may not only benefit those children but increase their own genetic representation (Gaulin, 1980; Ruse, 1979; Williams, 1957).

Menopause and reduced reproductive success in advanced age is not an exclusive characteristic of human beings. Primatologists are discovering that our nearest relatives experience longer post-reproductive lives than previously suspected. A kin selection hypothesis is supported by comparative work among macaques and langurs (Hrdy, 1981). Old female macaques are nepotists to their matriline; low-ranking post-reproductive langur females are altruists and defend their "grandchildren" against younger dominant males. The intricacies of age and kin selection in the web of human kinship are only beginning to be explored (Katz, 1978).

Potential life spans and life expectancies are two different things. Age estimates of the hominid fossils indicate a low life expectancy as do those of preindustrial populations (Weiss, 1973). The most significant changes in life expectancy have occurred since industrialization, primarily as a result of reduced infant mortality. Fifty years have been added to an infant's life but only 12 years to that of a 50-year-old (Weiss, 1981). As Simmons noted in his 1960 review (p. 67), "The farther back we go into primitive and rudimentary forms of human association, the fewer old people are to be found." The available evidence, although leaving a lot to be desired, supports this conclusion. As techniques of age estimation improve and systematic census are undertaken in these societies, however, we may be in for a few surprises. For instance, we have already found a significant proportion of older adults in at least two societies that are insulated from the advantages of industry. The !Kung Bushman, a desert hunting and gathering society, had an estimated 8 percent of their population over 60 prior to 1960; during the sixties that percentage increased to 10 percent (Biesele and Howell, 1981). Among the Kirghiz, a high-altitude pastoral society in the Palmirs of Afghanistan, the percentage of those over 60 during the early seventies was 8.1. (Shahrani, 1981). Although 60 is five years short of 65, this is still not what we would expect of a nonindustrial society (Hauser, 1976), nor what we would call a young population, one with less than 4 percent over 65. Comparisons of the proportions of older adults in simpler societies are difficult since different ages (45, 50, 60) are used to define the chronological boundaries of old age. Nevertheless, estimates of 6 to 8 percent over 60 should not be viewed as overly optimistic. If anything, since most populations have experienced by now the advantages of medical care and reduced infant mortality, their age pyramids will indicate proportionately fewer older adults than they did prior to contact with Western medicine.

The length of time an organism can live and the proportion of different age groups in a society are more than simple demographic facts. Longevity and maximum life potential are indicative of the evolutionary history of a species and the interdependency between its individuals. The proportion of any age group in a society is an important variable. A cohort scarcity may make those of a particular age exotic and also a potential problem. A large cohort, on the other hand, may be able to enforce demands, and their very abundance

may become another kind of social problem (Teski, 1983). For contemporary industrialized societies, the concern about the proportion of those classed as old involves dependency ratios, economic consequences, and quality of life issues. Age differences and cohort flows affect the arena in which humans negotiate their lives. We build upon this demographic raw material in interpreting and giving meaning to lives as they unfold.

Time and Parameters of the Life Course

Time, the elusive property underlying aging, is also cultural. Like culture, it is reified and becomes implicit. Western notions of time have seldom been challenged. For research on aging, an explicit notion of time is necessary, but with few exceptions (Hendricks and Hendricks, 1976), time remains implicit and a topic of concern for philosophers, not social and behavioral scientists. Cross-culturally, we realize time is created by human beings (Durkheim, 1961; original, 1912). Oscillations in nature or human affairs combined with a sense of duration are the essentials for a notion of time (Leach, 1961b). These oscillations are the intervals between such polar opposites as night/day, winter/summer, or birth/death, which are selected to punctuate our cultural models of time. Western industrial societies are noted for the tyranny of the clock and calendar in punctuating our schedules (Woodcock, 1944). Time is a geometric metaphor of a nonrepetitive straight line, divisible into years, days, hours, minutes, stretching from past to future (Leach, 1961a). Such notions are by no means universal (Bock, 1966; Bohannan, 1953; Evans-Prichard, 1940; Maxwell, 1972; Smith, et al., 1961). The life course as an irreversible journey of personal development and aging between birth and death is reflective of this linear metaphor. Alternatively, for some societies, the image is one of a wheel or a circle through which individuals cycle from birth to death. The Hindu idea of reincarnation is one example. Another, among others, is that of the Inuit Eskimo (Guemple, 1980). Cyclical age set systems bring life full circle, with the age set of the very old soon becoming that of the new born as generations descend as a helix across time (see Baxter, 1978, p. 157, for a graphic representation of the Boran age sets) or as a circle (see Maybury-Lewis, 1974, p. 154; Maybury-Lewis, in press).

Aging involves the passage of time since it happens *through* time. Because of our linear model of time and its exactitude, to view age as chronology is a most seductive way of probing time and change. By compressing age into one dimension, we mask variability (Butler, 1968) and become caught up in time (Nydegger, 1981), confounding our variables. Developmentalists (Schaie, 1965; Baltes, 1968) have appreciated this problem in their analysis of age, cohort, and period. Researchers have been most unhappy with chronological age and in the search for more productive alternatives have differentiated between life time, historical time, and social time (Neugarten and Datan, 1973). Reckoning of age by years is alien to most nonliterate societies (the Fulani of West Africa are an exception), with age being calibrated by culturally specific social clocks. Life is punctuated by discontinuities (Benedict, 1938). Rites of passage (Van Gennep, 1960; original, 1909) transform people symbolically through a ritual death that strips them of an earlier status and temporarily places them in a marginal or liminal state so that they may ponder their predicament and be reborn into a new, but older, being. Time flows, but its stream is uneven and meanders, with its units reflecting human events, not impartial intervals of the orbit of the earth around the sun. Unevenness implies chaos, uniqueness, and almost limitless cultural elaboration. On the other hand, in spite of variability in cultural content, the human life course is conditioned by the distinctive features of *human* societies as opposed to the general features of mammalian societies.

Societies are groups of interdependent organisms sharing a habitat. People are interdependent in uniquely human ways. First, we are among the few animals who share food. Wild canids and other species regurgitate for their young, but human beings not only share with their offspring and others, they do so on a regular basis. Thus, reciprocity and the necessity to give in order to receive by creating obligations in others (Mauss, 1967; original, 1925; Malinowski, 1922; Sahlins, 1972) prods people to produce food, services, or artifacts and thus participate in sharing and exchanging. Second, human reproduction is distinctive in the length of gestation and period of dependency. In terms of the mammalian pattern, we are also unique in that estrus is suppressed. Human mating patterns instead are conditioned by cultural rules universally involving exogamy in order to avoid incest and a relatively permanent pair-bonding of partners (marriage). Consequently, parental roles are a part of adult life for both women and men. Beneath all the variance in subsistence strategies and family organization in the world's cultures, the unifying design around and through which human lives are embroidered is determined by production and reproduction.

To what extent are production and reproduction explicit or implicit components of the life course in different societies? Most ethnographies differentiate the typical life course by sex and age stage, allocating its roles by means of the etic criteria of anthropologists (i.e., those criteria based on the values of societies outside of that being studied). Predominant are economic and domestic roles followed by political and religious ones. Comparative data on the inside, or emic, view of the life course is scarce. Two studies—one of the Massai (Kirk and Burton, 1977), tribal pastoralists of East Africa, and the other of Americans in Indiana (Fry, 1980)—provide us with comparative data of this sort. Although the goals and eliciting frames of each project were different, both used informants' judgments, age as a frame of reference, and multidimensional scaling to analyze the data. The researchers independently interpreted the dimensions of the life course in these respective societies as responsibility and marriage for the Massai and responsibility-engagement and reproductive cycle for the Americans. Such convergence is exciting evidence that production and reproduction may be considered to be panhuman in any conceptualization of the life course. Before we promote them to universal status, however, we need more comparative research that will allow us to disentangle the emic from the etic and to probe beneath the status structure to the underlying cultural order.

Cultural Models of the Life Course

Culture imposes structure or embroiders upon the order in nature. Differential maturity creates age differences. Age grades or age categories merge minute differences into major ones. Life has a definite progression, the future being seen in the lives of the old and the past in those of the young. Culture codifies life into a theory of what we can expect along the way, providing guideposts to evaluate our progress. Among our discoveries in the comparative study of age is that the life course is a cultural unit (Fry and Keith, 1982). The perceptions of life course as a unit, the definitions of internal structure, the possibilities of individual differences, and the criteria and exactness with which careers are monitored vary (Keith, 1980b).

Variability in cultural conceptions of the life course is predictable, but the reasons for specific types of variation are not completely understood. Strategies for resource accumulation and opportunities for individual choice have been linked to differential factors in, and views of, the life course (LeVine, 1978a; Moore, 1973). A comparatively rare variant is that of age set societies in which the life course is explicit. Concepts of age and generation formalize cohort flow, and age strata become cognitive, socially recognized categories of people. In spite of several decades of research, we still lack a comprehensive theory of age systems (Kertzer, 1978). A number of factors including socialization (Eisenstadt, 1956) and the complementarity and opposition of different spheres of action in avoiding conflict have been suggested to account for pan-societal groups based on age. Age sets are based on the harmony and ethos of the solidarity of peers (Almagor, 1978) as opposed to the divisiveness of lineage politics and generational competition (Spencer, 1976; Maybury-Lewis, in press). Cohorts and peer bonds organize the public domain, but they never become the controllers of property nor assume the political functions of lineage and clan. Since the public domain is the male domain,

we would expect, and do indeed find, that female age sets are extremely rare and parallel male sets only slightly (Kertzer and Madison, 1981). (See Keith's forthcoming review for a discussion of the factors promoting age sets and formal groups based on age.)

What is the psychological and social import of the cultural modeling of the life course? Cultural rules define life as it should be lived. Individuals as continuous beings progressing through their life course use age-specific norms as well as long-range goals to evaluate their progress. Such guides are certainly important in maintaining a sense of self worth. Cultural rules may also facilitate the late life review, an important process in life (Butler, 1963, 1974). In parts of Africa, it is common for young adults to prepare for their own funeral. The funeral rites include an explicit accounting of the social worth of the deceased (e.g., see LeVine, 1978b, for the Fusii; Fortes, 1971, for the Tallensi; Cohen, forthcoming, for the Bura). Life reviews and continuous stocktaking are lifelong patterns established early. A tantalizing hypothesis is that whenever age categories and life trajectories are explicit, the life review is facilitated. In a controlled comparison, Nadel (1952) found that explicitness and a greater number of age categories reduces conflict. These finer distinctions more accurately match social maturity with physical ability and reduce the tensions that arise when large discrepancies occur, for example when the youngest member of the adult age category retires at age 30 because his group has moved to elderhood. Explicitness does not resolve all problems, however. Conflict over age transitions was found in all but one age set society, where, despite explicit rules, young and old negotiated and argued over their implementation (Foner and Kertzer, 1978).

Other lessons we have learned point to the salience of age criteria at different points of the life course. Among the Shavante (Maybury-Lewis, 1974), it is the younger sets that are active. By middle age, men are too involved in the politics of kinship to keep their sets active. Neugarten, Moore, and Lowie's (1965) study of age norms in Chicago has been replicated in Japan (Plath and Ikada, 1975).

In both these societies, age norms become more emotionally charged as age increases. Age as a component of a person's identity varies across the life course. As other criteria supersede age (or recede from it), age will be of lesser or greater importance (Gulliver, 1968). The studies mentioned suggest that it is during the middle period that age is of the least importance to a person's social identity and during the periods that precede and follow it that it has the greatest salience. More recent interpretations of age-set systems imply that age may be differentially expressed for the domestic and public domains. Generational age criteria may be the most salient in the domain of kinship (Kertzer, 1982), whereas chronological or explicit age criteria may be the most salient in the public domain (Keith and Kertzer, forthcoming). Cultural models are important because, like road maps, they tell us where we have been and how to get to where we are going, but more important, they tell us how we are doing.

AGE, SEX, AND PERSONALITY

Anthropology and psychology have long been allies in the study of personality. With too few exceptions, most of this effort has been concentrated on childhood and the cultural factors that shape the adult personality. The comparative study of adulthood and continued personal development has been hindered by the typical ethnographic tendency to view "the span of years between the achievement of adult status and funeral rites (as) either an ethnographic vacuum or a vast monotonous plateau of invariable behavior" (Clark, 1973, p. 86). The "new" area for studies of culture and personality, aging—outlined by Margaret Clark (1967) over a decade ago—has opened new frontiers and strengthened the alliance between the respective disciplines.

Cross-cultural psychologist David Guttman has pioneered the study of late-life personality shifts in unrelated cultures. He transferred essentially the same research design used in the analysis of TAT responses from older adults in the Kansas City study (Gutmann, 1964; Neugarten and Gutmann, 1958) to the High-

land Maya (1967), the Lowland Maya (1966), the Navajo (Goldstein and Gutmann, 1972), and the Highland Druze (1974). Among the men in each culture he found a systematic shift from "active mastery" to "passive mastery." These male personality shifts are complimented by a shift in the opposite direction for women (that is, passive to active mastery). Although personality shifts and gender differences had not previously been a focus of study, their discovery was not surprising. The ethnographic literature is full of passing observations of how postmenopausal women "become one of the boys" while their husbands become "domesticated" or turn their attentions to spiritual matters. (See Gutmann, 1977, for a review of this literature and Myerhoff, 1978b, and Myerhoff and Simic, 1978, for first-hand examples.)

Although there is little argument concerning these male/female reversals, there is little unanimity when it comes to hypotheses explaining them. Gutmann (1975) proposes a theory of gender differentiation that sees these personality reversals as being universal and linked to a panhuman pattern of parenting. The "emergency" of parenthood, of providing psychosocial and emotional security for children, results in marked gender differences. Females surrender aggressive tendencies to provide emotional support while males give up dependency needs that would interfere with physical and instrumental support. Once children assume responsibility for themselves, each gender "recaptures" the characteristics that were repressed. Other researchers emphasize relationships with adult children and shifts in core roles and power that have been developed across the life course. Older women with adult children benefit from a configuration of affect, symbolism, power over kinsmen, and freedom from earlier restrictions and find new outlets for recognition (Brown, 1982). The ethnographic literature is full of examples of senior women exerting influence on their juniors as managers of the female labor force in polygynous and extended households [e.g., among the Tiwi (Hart and Pilling, 1960) it is the old women who are the secret to the effective functioning of the collective female power in an older man's household]. In patrilineal societies, older women establish themselves in their husband's lineage (not their own) as a mother of a mature male of that lineage and supervisor of his wife (Smedly, 1974). "Bank on mother" is a strategy built upon mother/child bonds that enables Black Caribs in Belize to survive in an economy of high unemployment; mothers pool the resources of their children to redistribute in times of need (Kerns, 1980). Children are important allies, but equally important are the patterns of adult socialization and the social arenas in which influence is exerted. Male and female lives are associated with and unfold in domains with differing orientations: the domestic and the public. Child-rearing links women to the domestic while males dominate the public domain (Ortner, 1974). Each gender experiences socialization differently (Chodorow, 1974). Females endure loss (Kline, 1975) and variation in sex roles across the life span (Sinnott, 1977) and are socialized to be flexible (Cool, 1981b).

Public domains exhibit more continuity, and hence men live lives of greater consistency but less opportunity to rehearse or anticipate age-related role losses. The power of women is limited in the public domain (Sanday, 1974), with feminine influence being more informal, *de facto,* and based in the domestic sphere. Males possess the legitimate, publically acknowledged power (*de jure*), which is the kind of power ethnographers have studied and what we usually mean by power and influence. To understand the reversals in later life, an examination of both kinds of power in both the domestic and public arenas and the respective strategies each gender employs is vital. In a comparative study of societies noted for extreme gender differentiation in early life (e.g., the Corsican and Lebanese peasantry), Cool and McCabe (1983) found that women consolidated their power in later life, whereas men found their long-standing influence in the public arena diminished once they could no longer meet the physical demands of being an adult male.

Multiple hypotheses call for additional research. These hypotheses are not necessarily contradictory, but the relative effects of the complementary variables need to be determined. The question of the causes of personality shifts in later life is one which can only be resolved through comparative research. The degree of personality cross-over needs to be established on a broader sample. Two studies—one among the Mekranoti of Brazil and the other among older Irish-Americans in Chicago—indicate no cross-over occurs (Werner, 1981; Cohler and Lieberman, 1979). Both men and women display more active mastery. Societies with greater differentiation and separation between public and domestic spheres should be contrasted with those that are less differentiated. Intra-cultural as well as cross-cultural variance should be considered. Responses to psychological tests from both men and women, old and young, should be placed in their cultural contexts to determine culturally sensitive (emic) indicators of personality shifts and the effects of recent cultural changes that may differentially affect cohorts (Press, 1967). Such research will advance our knowledge on two fronts simultaneously and lead to a fuller understanding of gender differences, sexual identity, and adult personality development.

Age and Cultural Values

On a somewhat different front, Clark and Anderson discovered yet another shift. This one involved a link between values and successful aging. In their celebrated study (1967) of mentally well and mentally ill older San Franciscans, they found that those informants who continued to subscribe to prevailing American values were the ones who experienced difficulty, frustration, and hospitalization for mental problems. Informants who had successfully resolved the conflicts between their abilities and the values that define the ideal had completed one or more of five adaptive tasks for the aged. The five tasks identified by these two anthropologists are as follows:

1. Recognition of aging and definition of instrumental limitation
2. Redefinition of physical and social life space

3. Substitution of alternative sources of need-satisfaction
4. Reassessment of criteria for evaluation of the self
5. Reintegration of values and life goals.

Discontinuities involving a reordering of basic value orientations, life perspective in relation to time, and conflicts between competitiveness and cooperation and between doing and being must be resolved if adaptation is to occur in old age. Reordering of value orientations is one of the most difficult tasks to accomplish since values are rooted in sentiments and are essential to defining self-esteem. One clue as to why and how some people are able to withstand such pressures is found in their signigicant reference group. Informants who were mentally well had more social relationships and a more active social network than those with histories of hospitalization.

Dependency is a notion that triggers deeply ingrained conflicts for older Americans and older adults in other cultures. Independence/dependence are the positive/negative contrasts of the dominant value orientation prevailing in American culture (Hsu, 1961; Williams, 1970) and other Western societies. Independence is rooted in role expectations that entail reciprocity or give-and-take. As previously discussed reciprocal exchange is an essential hallmark of the human character. To be independent is to be able to "give" and maintain a balance in a relationship in which one is also "taking." Dependence, on the other hand, is nonreciprocal "taking." In her analysis of dependency, Clark (1972) points out that nonreciprocity is tolerated in certain roles with definite limitations, including illness, rites of passage, or infancy and childhood. Chronic dependence, voluntary or involuntary, borders on freeloading. In no known society do freeloaders enjoy prestige and high self-esteem.

Time and time again we learn of the importance of exchange (Dowd, 1975). The ethos of self-sufficiency masks the fact that we are all inter-dependent. Exchange between family units has been established for some time (Townsend, 1957; Sussman, 1965, 1976; Shanas, et. al., 1968). Old people in new environments have exerted their humanity by giving

and taking with peers. Men and women in public housing in Milwaukee (Jonas and Wellin, 1980; Boyer, 1980) have evolved distinct reciprocity patterns that prevent or postpone institutionalization and improve the quality of interaction with kin. Ability to exchange with staff is one critical variable discovered in a comparative study of institutional care (Kayser-Jones, 1981a, 1981b). In Scotland, patients slipped small gifts they had either made or bought to individual staff members, a recognition that fostered higher quality care for themselves and greater satisfaction to all concerned. Negative reciprocity, neglect, and even robbery were frequently reported in American institutions where patients had little opportunity to give; they could only take. The self-esteem of senior members of ethnic groups who have migrated from a common homeland is enhanced whenever they are sought out as "cultural experts" by younger members in their search for ethnic identity and roots to tell them "how it really was" (Cool, 1981a).

Dependency is not exclusively an American problem but one that is intensified by industrial organization. Families are small and residentially independent. Age norms set limits on productive activity (labor), which in turn is calculated in terms of cash (wages). Because of the cash nexus, the norms of reciprocity emphasize immediacy of return. When dependency occurs, it is apparent and painful for all. In nonindustrial societies, the household is the producing as well as the consuming unit. The onset of dependency has ramifications that are quite different (see Goody, 1976). In this case, age norms do not limit production, nor does cash define its value. Functional abilities determine the contribution of each to the household economy. Since households are often multiple-extended families that are residentially united, a dependent individual does not become the responsibility of only one or two people. Moreover, the norm of generalized reciprocity (Sahlins, 1972) does not recognize any temporal limit; reciprocity sometimes extends over an entire generation, with adult children regarding the care of their parents as reciprocity for their own nurturance in childhood. Reciprocity and maintenance of interdependence is complicated, delicate, and subtle, involving both material and nonmaterial transactions. Because of the structural differences between industrial and nonindustrial societies, an initial hypothesis was that since older people in nonindustrial societies could maintain a web of exchange and interdependence more intensively and for longer periods than those in industrialized societies, they would therefore enjoy a more elevated status and self-esteem. It is to this question that we now turn.

Societies and the Experience of Aging

With over 3,000 identifiable societies in the world, the possibility of variance would appear to be endless. In effect, it is not. There are many ways of classifying differences, depending on the problem under study. Conventionally, the principal division for aging research is made between the industrial and the nonindustrial world. Nonindustrial societies are small-scaled, low-energy societies in which family units are the primary social unit, one that is engaged in making a living through foraging, horticulture, or pastoralism and that consumes the majority of what it produces. Industrial societies are large-scaled, high-energy societies noted for a highly differentiated productive organization that is quite distinct from the state and family units. We now shift to the experience of aging and other major concerns that are found within these two societal types.

Aging in Nonindustrial Societies

Although Simmons' data (1945, 1960) indicated the presence of "thistles in paradise," the prevailing view was that older adults in nonindustrial societies were better off socially and psychologically than their counterparts in industrial societies. Nearly four decades of research (Holmes, 1976) has rectified many a misconception and dispelled many a myth both abroad and at home. Conceptual strides have been made in the disentanglement of the term "status" (to indicate prestige/esteem) from the term "role," and both from the term "old." *The* role of *the* aged is no longer thought applicable in any society. Core male

and female roles display varying degrees of continuity across the life span for the generation of esteem in old age. Defining the threshold of old age has become even more problematic in the nonindustrial world. At home, the heterogeneity of our older population has been one of the most important discoveries of gerontology. It should not surprise us, therefore, that there is no such category as *the* aged in nonindustrial societies, only older adults who have had a life time of experience to make them increasingly different. In isolating the cultural criteria that define old age, the holocultural sample of Glascock and Feinman (1980a, 1981) found that changes in social roles were the most frequently used criteria, followed by chronology (usually linked to another criterion) and changes in capabilities. In further probing the category "old," comparative researchers have discovered a distinction between different kinds of older people: the intact and the decrepit (Glascock and Feinman, 1980b, 1981; Maxwell and Silverman, 1970; Amoss and Harrell, 1981; Simmons, 1960). This finding mirrors Bernice Neugarten's contrast between the "young old" and "old old" (1974), although it doesn't constitute a direct parallel. The consequences of classification in these societies, as we shall see, are those of life or death.

The question of esteem as it relates to treatment of the aged is one frought with yet another problem—the idealization of behavior. Most people will tell an anthropologist, "Yes, we respect our elders and treat them well," and then go about their daily business. When that "business" is carefully observed or when notorious cases come to light, a considerably different picture can emerge. Even in cultures noted for holding their elders in great esteem, such as the Ibo of Nigeria (Shelton, 1965, 1972), we find cases where actual behavior deviates from the ideal (Arth, 1968, 1972). China, a nation where "old is best" and filial piety is the norm, often presents a favorable contrast to the plight of older people in Western societies. Despite this fact, research in urban Hong Kong (Ikels, 1980; Sankar, 1981) and in rural Taiwan (Harrell, 1981) casts doubt upon the extent to which the ideal is actualized except in elite culture. The norms, rules, or standards that make up the code of culture are prime candidates for reification. Ideals mask the variability that should be expected since not everyone can live up to all of the rules all of the time.

GERICIDE OR GERONTOCRACY: TREATMENT AND PRESTIGE OF OLDER ADULTS

Gericide is one of those exotic ethographic facts that fascinates investigators from industrial societies, as is evidenced by our familiarity with the shocking treatment of the old by some Eskimo groups—abandonment on ice floes. Of equal fascination are reports of gerontocracies, especially those involving polygyny. Gerontocracy and gericide are not necessarily mutually exclusive modes of treatment. In fact, most societies are Janus-faced, with both positive and negative forms of treatment, and yet are not riddled with problems of cognitive dissonance. Glascock and Feinman report (1981) that for those societies in the standard holocultural sample providing information on treatment, 84 percent displayed some kind of nonsupportive treatment. In another study (Maxwell and Maxwell, 1980), numerous cases of contempt for the elderly were discovered. What is the trigger for such attitudes and toward whom is the disdaining behavior actually directed? In all cases, death-hastening and nonsupportive treatment is directed toward the decrepit, not the intact, elderly (Glascock and Feinman, 1981, p. 27). The Maxwells' results indicate the loss of family support is the single most important trigger, followed, surprisingly, by loss of appearance and then loss of strength.

Cases of gericide among the Eskimo deserve special comment precisely because they represent an over-referenced ethnographic tidbit and because we know enough about them to dispel the myth. The Arctic is one of the harshest environments in the world, with subsistence entirely predicated on hunting and fishing. Diets are deficient in calcium (lack of vegetables), and the region is noted for fostering a variety of mental problems: Arctic hysterias and the Windigo psychosis, or fear of eating another human being (Foulks, 1972).

Prior to Westernization, Eskimo groups were noted for high rates of suicide, but reliable data accumulated over a 50-year period among the Netsklik Eskimo indicate that surprisingly few of those over 60 years old committed suicide (Balikci, 1970, p. 163). Among the St. Lawrence Eskimo we find no clearcut evidence of the aged being abandoned (Leighton and Hughes, 1955). Here, suicides occurred after persistent requests of the person wishing to die, involved groups of villagers as well as the victim, entailed ritual purification following the killing, and were motivated by illness or by a desire to save someone else from sickness or death. The internal view, or emics, of suicide and death among the Inuit Eskimo (Guemple, 1980) reveal that the victims do not "really" die. Indestructable social identities, symbolized by reactivated names, cycle endlessly as the passing generations are born and die. After a stay in the underworld, individuals are reborn to begin the cycle anew.

Killing, abandoning, and forsaking of old people are behaviors that *do* occur, but they are not the most prevalent of behaviors. The factors that are associated with them include harsh environments (tundras, deserts, savannas), subsistence based on foraging or shifting plots of cultivation, and the absence of class stratification (Glascock and Feinman, 1980b, p. 213). Esteem for elders was also found to be low in these societies. Such esteem improves in tribal and peasant societies (Sheehan, 1976) and in societies with more intensive agricultural systems (Lee and Kezis, 1981). What is it that promotes esteem for older people in these societies? Control of valued information is one determinant (Maxwell and Silverman, 1970). Social structures marked by (1) socioeconomic homogeneity, (2) role sequences that entail greater and greater responsibility, (3) continuity in role shifts, (4) resource control by older people, (5) engagement in valued activities by older adults, and (6) the dominance of extended families have been found to promote higher status and prestige (Press and McKool, 1972). Deference to older people is by no means uniform. Women receive less of it than men except in terms of service (Silverman and Maxwell, 1978), a fact that perhaps is reflective of the male and femaleness of the public and domestic domains.

Gerontocracy, rule by the old, is a world-wide phenomenon, transcending environments and societal complexity. Gerontocrats, always male, acquire their influence in myriad ways. Control of resources, offspring included, is certainly the prevalent means. In horticultural, agricultural, and pastoral societies, lineages and clans link people to scarce resources (land/cattle). Access to and eventual control of property comes through clan membership and inheritance from senior members. Elders are consequently powerful in family matters and village affairs; junior members listen, make alliances among themselves, and wait until their time has come. A dramatically opposite example is to be found among the pastoral Fulani (West Africa), where on the marriage of his youngest son, a man "gives it all away" (the remainder of his herd) to live at the periphery of his eldest son's compound, sleeping on his own grave (Stenning, 1958). Another means of exerting control is by extending social bonds through alliances with peers and affines, as we have seen among the Tiwi (Hart and Pilling, 1960) and elsewhere in Australia (Warner, 1958). Knowledge of ceremonies and other vital matters proved to be the most important road for influential Mekranoti elders in Brazil (Werner, 1981). On the other side of the world, Bakongo elders in Lower Zaire maintain their eminence by possessing technical knowledge and intervening in important life events (Missinne, 1980), as articulated in their proverb "Only the old ones can unravel the knot in a net." On the other hand, the stratification that comes with greater socioeconomic complexity obscures the gerontocratic principle since most men lack influence. The industralized United States is just as gerontocratic in many ways as many nonindustrial societies. Elite families play their strategies in a manner more similar to that of clans in tribal societies than that of their middle- or lower-class counterparts. Wealth and the decisions that concern it rest in the hands of senior family members who shape the power of the junior members and those linked to them through affinity. Even the U.S. Congress, noted for its relatively advanced age and the longevity of its members, has a seniority system that is analogous to that of the Akwi Shavante (Weatherford, 1981).

A note of caution is in order when we consider the implications of gerontocracy. The well-being of older people is not automatically promoted by it. Gerontocracy is government *by,* not *for,* the old. Other lines of allegiance take priority over age: family, class, friends, corporate interests, etc. Thus, even in Australia we find some gerontocrats and some older men who lack influence and the benefits of power. In Micronesia, four life-long strategies determine if one becomes an influential elder or just another old person: respect attained in adulthood; a desire to participate; knowledge; and control of property (Nason, 1981). In most societies, if not all, idealized, absolute success is not attainable for the majority. On the other hand, the dreaded total failure is seldom realized.

Nonindustrial societies are remnants of a world on the wane. Small-scaled egalitarian societies have become victims of progress, caught up in the riptide of opportunity and modernization. The massive changes of the past 300 years have had profound effects on the lives of all people regardless of age. Older people, however, have been viewed as being more strongly affected casualties of economic development.

Aging and Modernization

The Industrial Revolution changed social organization everywhere. Factories, firms, and corporations separated production from consumption. Nation states, bureaucracies, and social stratification expanded as population and the ability to harness and consume energy increased. Money and markets became the common denominator. Peasants flocked to the city, impelled there by its higher wages on the one hand and by the declining opportunity in the agricultural countryside on the other. Markets expanded throughout colonial empires and client states. Tribal peoples and peasants in distant parts of the world became entangled in a web of political and economic relations that eventually formed the nexus of the modern world system (Wallerstein, 1979).

What happened to older people in the process? Initially, they "disappeared" as increased fertility produced even more youthful populations (Hauser, 1976). Then, as populations aged, the old "reappeared." The developed countries were the first to experience this demographic transition, but soon the third and fourth worlds will catch up and in terms of absolute numbers of older people will surpass the developed world (Goldstein and Beall, 1982). In this changed world, how have the increased number of elders fared?

Conventional wisdom followed the "world we have lost" syndrome (Laslett, 1965). In idealized traditional societies, elders were respected; with industralization, the structural changes eroded their position. Sociologist Cowgill and anthropologist Holmes (1972) were among the first to bring qualitative, case-study evidence to this question. They assembled a team of researchers who had previously worked in societies experiencing varying degrees of modernization. They concluded that modernization brought diminished status and disadvantages to older people. A formalized model isolated economic factors, medical technology, urbanization, and education as the salient variables that interact in complicated ways to reduce the status of the aged (Cowgill, 1974, p. 141). A decade of research has sharpened our view and points toward more complex answers. Our image is no longer one of a linear decline in the status of older people with increasing modernization, but one of a cycle (Finley, 1982). The pastoral Sidamo and horticultural Ibo are the least modernized societies in the Cowgill and Holmes sample. When egalitarian foraging societies and horticultural societies in harsher environments are added to the spectrum, we find a curvilinear relation (Lee and Kezis, 1981). Initially, the status of the elderly rises to a peak with stable agricultural societies, followed by a decline with modernization. Then, in the later stages of modernization, the status of older adults again improves (Palmore and Manton, 1974), with future projections indicating a continued improvement (Palmore, 1976).

Modernization theory, in spite of its elegance in capturing the general processes that have shaped the contemporary world, when applied to aging is increasingly being met with skepticism and empirical criticism (Foner, forthcoming). Comparative attitudinal research has produced inconclusive results. An early study by Arnhoff, et. al. (1964), concluded that attitudes toward older people improved in more modernized societies, whereas a more recent study by Bengtson, et. al. (1975), demonstrated the opposite. Furthermore, Bengtson and his colleagues discovered that intracultural variance (individual modernity) was not consistent with or could not be ordered by the same principle as cross-national variance (societal modernization). Modernization has proved to be more complex than the model guiding most research on aging can handle. Alternative conceptualizations (i.e., internal colonial or world systems models) are only beginning to make their appearance (Hendricks, forthcoming; Green, 1978–79). A return to specifics is in order. The study of general processes is fascinating, since past and, hopefully, future trends can be revealed, even if these can be empirically documented only at the most superficial levels (Sahlins, 1960). The study of specific processes takes us to the heart of diverse societies and the heterogeneity of their members. The before-after of change can be empirically studied only in specific historical and cultural contexts (Laslett, 1976; Achenbaum and Sterns, 1978).

By returning to specifics, we discover that modernization is a complex of many different kinds of change. The kinds of change most detrimental to the security of older people are those that economically and demographically alter the rules and strategies they have used to build their careers. Vulnerability and dissatisfaction with their situation increases whenever change undermines their control of their resources or disrupts their strategies to accumulate wealth. In Zambia, the resettlement of the Tonga of the Gwembe district brought about by the construction of a hydroelectric dam wiped out the lineage holdings and resources of many elders during the 1950s. Many of them were not able to recoup because of the premium placed on the physical strength needed to clear new fields. It was only those who were exceptionally vigorous or able to invest in new opportunities who saw their fortunes restored (Colson and Scudder, 1981). Opportunity and wage labor are magnets that draw the young away from rural villages, leaving an older population to tend the hearth and fields. In Nepal, elderly Sherpas must face their old age alone since the emigration of the youngest sons has seriously disrupted the Sherpa family system and left otherwise active, healthy elders disappointed and dissatisfied with their lot (Goldstein and Beall, 1981). A four-fold population decline in Western Ireland has devastated the traditional gerontocracy of the Irish peasantry (Schepler-Hughs, 1983). The famous "west room" and 40-year-old "boys" reported by Arensberg in 1937 have now been replaced by high rates of schizophrenia, the collapse of community cooperation, and reduction of support by the young. An altered opportunity structure has not worked to the advantage of elderly Asmat males, former head-hunters of New Guinea. Men who aspired to be a big man or "tesmaypit" are now idle and living in a ritual void (Van Arsdale, 1981a, 1981b). Imposition of national Indonesian rule has rendered the life careers of one cohort of Asmat men meaningless. The present system of rewards favors those who speak Indonesian and can take advantage of the opportunities of the nation state—that is, the young.

Like newscasters reporting the worst, the chroniclers of change emphasize the negative. Change can and does have a positive face. Even the relocated Tonga have greater security as a result of programs that have reduced epidemics among livestock and improved public health (Colson and Scudder, 1981). In 37 years of research in the village of Tzintzuntzan, Mexico, George Foster has seen improvements in medical care, increased life expectancy, strides in educational achievement, and higher standards of living, all of which led many of his informants to conclude that "times have never been better" (Foster, 1981). Improvements in wealth, health, and functionality do not impart an ideal old age by themselves. In Tzintzuntzan, increasing age is viewed as a mix of positives and negatives and, as elsewhere, is not viewed as the best time of life (there, only childhood is thought to be worse). Change, in fact, can favor older

people only when what they have is needed by the larger society. Coast Salish elders on the Northwest coast of the United States have experienced the benefits of revivalistic change since their knowledge of the old rituals, old ways, and traditional culture is being sought out and preserved by younger tribal members in search of their roots (Amoss, 1981a, 1981b). Other native American elders are not so fortunate and experience mild anxiety when queried about old traditions that had vanished before they were born (Williams, 1980).

Not much attention is paid to continuity. The ethnographic literature is rich with examples of stable, mature economies favoring gerontocracy. Since alternative opportunities are limited, younger adults see their future in terms of their elders and wait their turn. Continuity, like change, does not produce uniformly positive or negative results. The life-term social arena described by Sally Falk Moore (1978) for Chagga (Kenya) men and women dispels notions of an idyllic old age. Instead, we see both pain and satisfaction. For these Kenyans, social isolation is a near impossibility, a situation that may be attractive from an urban perspective. Life-term arenas with a great deal of continuity, however, exact a heavy toll of another kind. One's personal history is public. It precedes one in any course of action and is interpreted and embellished in the aftermath. As disputes both large and small are settled, one's success is another's misfortune; one's loss is another's gain. The challenges of growing old and managing a career in a life-term arena are quite different from those in arenas with less continuity.

AGING IN INDUSTRIAL SOCIETIES

A comparative perspective is no stranger to industrialized societies. Such large-scaled societies, although integrated as a result of nationwide political and economic institutions, are remarkably heterogeneous (Barth, 1978). The variance seems boundless. At the most general level, populations are class-stratified and further cross-cut by ethnic differences. Negotiated solutions to problems, old and new, add to the variety of social organization on regional and local levels. From a worldwide perspective, our knowledge about aging comes mainly from populations in the industrial world. Comparative, cross-national research has dispelled many myths, most notably the supposed isolation and abandonment of the aged as families continue to shrink in size, become more geographically dispersed, and whose children experience upward mobility (Shanas, et al., 1968). As elsewhere, comparative research within industrial societies has probed the cultural and social shaping of age and behavior.

At home, cultural differences become ethnic factors, and social organization has a more fluid quality than the ethnographies we read of distant people, since we are both insiders and outsiders to our subject matter. An effective way of comprehending the organization of diversity is to view the social fabric as made up of social borders that divide the actors into "we's" and "they's" (Ross, 1975). The social world is then partitioned into "mine," "yours," "theirs," and "ours," its boundaries subject to alteration or maintenance as collectivities work for the benefit of the "we." Ethnicity is a critical factor in shaping life chances and consequently the situation of the ethnic aged. Age, in addition to grading the actors, is itself a critical factor around which borders are formed.

Ethnicity and Aging

Ethnicity is an unusual concept in that it was thrust upon the social sciences by popular culture and the ethnic revivals of the 1960s and 1970s. The melting pot became a procrustean bed in which the twin processes of acculturation and assimilation failed to make everyone fit. With the exceptions of native Americans and Wasps or Anglos, Americans became hypenated (e.g., Mexican-Americans, Afro-Americans, or Japanese-Americans). Having snuck in the back door, as it were, research on ethnic groups proceeded without conceptual definition and development (Isajiw, 1974). Ethnic categories were seen as self-perpetuating racial, cultural, linguistic, and social units that are both self-identified and recognized by others (Naroll, 1964). This definition fits most ethnographic accounts of other cultures. It fails, however, in that ethnic groups can be thought of as bounded units only *in relation to* other units. Boundaries and boundary-maintenance activities are essential to an understanding of their genesis, structure, and function by those who identify and/or are identified as ethnic (Barth, 1969). Opposition draws the boundary lines. It may take the form of political mobilization or competition for resources (Hannerz, 1974). The dialectics separating the "we's" from the "they's" are seldom singular but form a Guttman-like scale of nesting dichotomizations of inclusiveness and exclusiveness (Cohen, 1978). Since opposition and interaction give rise to ethnic borders, the saliency of ethnicity for an individual is entirely situational. It can increase or decrease during the daily round, the annual cycle, or over the life course.

Ethnicity is not a benign category. Its consequences, especially when combined with a nonwhite racial classification, are detrimental to the life chances of those on the far side of the ethnic boundary. Ethnic groups are often confused with minority groups since ethnic and racial criteria define minority status. Full economic participation and access to opportunity are limited for such groups. Discrimination assigns them the lower-paying, low-prestige jobs with no upward mobility. Impoverishment, higher rates of underemployment or unemployment, poorer health, and a life expectancy significantly less than white norms are the harvest of reduced life chances. What is the quality of life in old age for those ethnic/minority individuals who survive these perils? The coming of old age adds yet another insult to injury. Old age plus ethnic/minority status adds up to a double or even triple jeopardy (National Urban League, 1964; National Council on Aging, 1972).

Comparative data on blacks, Mexican-Americans, and whites in Los Angeles indicates a double jeopardy—both to wealth and health (Dowd and Bengtson, 1978; Bengtson, 1979). Blacks and Mexican-Americans had lower incomes and reported poorer health than whites, and both health and wealth decreased more sharply with age than among whites. A double jeopardy becomes multiple when one considers the effects of poverty on nutrition, education, and life expectancy. Other aspects of the quality of life, however, may not be jeopardized. The same study revealed inconclusive cross-ethnic/minority differences in life satisfaction and primary group interaction. Attitudes toward death improved with age regardless of ethnic/minority affiliation (Bengtson, Cuellar, and Ragan, 1977), supporting an age-as-leveler hypothesis. Data from a white, rural sample, using other techniques, indicated that sex differences are significant, older males being more anxious about death (Schulz, 1980).

Ethnicity, too, has its positive face (see Holzberg, 1982, for a review). Boundaries that exclude can also include. Those excluded from full participation in Wasp-Anglo institutions are included in a larger identity with a social organization and a web of social relations that work for its benefit. Although we should not romanticize poverty, we also should not underestimate the strengths concealed behind ethnic/minority borders. A structural intimacy in which personal rather than universal criteria are used to evaluate individual worth shields the individual from the general, abstract standards of Wasp-Anglo institutions (Kiefer, 1971). For older people, ethnicity may actually be an advantage. Older Corsican migrants in Paris who participate in Corsican associations and networks report greater satisfaction with life (Cool, 1980). Active involvement combined with knowledge of the "homeland" or the "old ways" and the interest of younger adults in this knowledge makes ethnic identity a valuable resource for exchange (Cool, 1981a). In addition to shielding them from majority attitudes, ethnicity provides the ethnic elderly with a source of esteem.

Within the past decade, research on the elderly of ethnic/minority groups has proliferated exponentially (Jackson, 1980). Demographic profiles document the extent of populations that are potentially at risk, the effects of poverty on longevity, and the racial cross-overs in later life (i.e., the greater life expectancy for minorities once a certain age is reached). From the studies of individual ethnic communities we have learned several lessons. First, once we go beyond the flat, stereotyped view that boundaries perpetuate, we discover internal differentiation, the emics of which are variable and largely situational. Second, ethnic boundaries vary in their distinctiveness (Trela and Sokolovsky, 1979). Intensity of ethnic identity, cohesiveness of community, mobilization of support, and willingness to cross ethnic boundaries to resolve problems are only a few of the issues shaped by the sharpness with which boundaries are drawn. Third, change, whether assimilative or revivalistic, continually revises border definitions. Consequently, ethnic identities show significant cohort differences (Clark, Kaufman, and Pierce, 1976). Finally, ethnicity is not a die that has been cast to force individuals to fit into an ethnic/minority mold of aging (i.e., one that generalizes *the* black, *the* Irish, *the* Italian, or *the* Korean). It is precisely because ethnicity is cultural that we find many strategies of aging reacting to and shaping the events that create individual biographies (Kiefer, 1974).

Age and Social Boundaries

Industrialization expanded the population and scale of society. It also extended the range of individual choice and the possibility of achievement, further increasing the demarcations within this complex society. What effect have these changes had on the more ubiquitous ascriptive characteristics (i.e., race, sex, kinship, age) over which humans have no choice? Have they become less salient? No, for better or worse, all are still alive and well. Age does not go away. Social age is the complex product of the interaction between choice and the range of available social options (Neugarten and Hagestad, 1976) and ambiguities plague it, but chronology leaves little room for error. Consensus on the number of adult age grades is low, and the variance in descriptive age terms is high. Adults in Indiana made age distinctions based on experience: the age heterogeneity of social networks increased the elaboration of social age categories (Fry, 1976). Age norms are often canonized into law (Cain, 1976, 1981). An age to work, an age to drink, an age to marry, an age to drive a car, an age to vote, and an age to be pensioned, all are familiar mile-posts codifying responsibility, maturity, and debility. Bureaucracies use age as a proxy, making a tradeoff between expediency and accuracy when allocating privileges and services (Neugarten, 1981). Thus age in bureaucratic societies is doubled-edged. Chronologically, it is explicit and impartial. Socially, it is functional and flexible. Whichever edge is presented, age can become the basis for a social borderline or be entangled with other borders.

"Integration not segregation!" (that is, eliminate the border) became the battle cry (Mumford, 1956) when entrepreneurs began to experiment with an alternative form of community building for the retirement market (Fry, 1977). What happened once the euphoria of newness and the advertising campaigns of the fifties wore off? A quarter of a century later the fear of geriatric ghettos now appears to have been unfounded (Perkinson, 1980). Social scientists reversed themselves, concluding that homogeneity and commonality of interest are building blocks of community life (Gans, 1972). Concentration of the elderly in apartment buildings in Cleveland increased the availability of peers. This worked to the advantage of the aged, who otherwise would outlive their peers, with profound implications for adult socialization (Rosow, 1967, 1974). Ethnographers who have probed beyond the image of "the old folks home" have found vital, dynamic communities. Age is the border; recruitment is by age-linked criteria. Appearances to the rest of the world are a major concern on the inside. Reactions from the rest of the world range from curiosity to "I wouldn't want to live with all those old people."

Keith had the rare opportunity to see a community created at Les Floralies (Keith, 1982; Ross, 1977). She traveled with informants as they moved to their new home for the first time and observed their incorporation and socialization into the evolving community (Ross, 1974a, 1974c). Social organization was a result of adapting to a new context, not a reaction to or reflection of the world outside (Ross, 1974b). Old people at Les Floralies created a community just as old people elsewhere in the United States have in retirement villages (Byrne, 1974), in high-rise apartments

(Hochchild, 1973; Jonas, 1979; Kandel and Heider, 1979; Wellin and Boyer, 1979), in homes for the aged (Hendel-Sebestyen, 1979), in senior centers (Hazan, 1980), in trailer courts (Angrosino, 1976; Deck, 1972; Fry, 1979; Johnson, 1971), and in retirement hotels (Teski, 1981). Particulars vary and local histories are idiosyncratic, but the universals are the same for age-homogenous communities as they are for utopian experiments or squatter settlements (Keith, 1980a, 1982). People bring with them qualities that serve as catalysts for community formation.

Although equality and homogeneity dominate the social fabric of such communities (Legesse, 1979), that does not mean that life there is monotonous. On the contrary, the cast of characters is differentiated into friends and factions (we/they) as visions of the future crystalize. The conflict of peers becomes especially difficult since leadership and administration are predicated on hierarchy, but such disputes indicate a committed and active involvement working toward a future.

Age-graded communities have not always been successful; many experiments have failed. Poor planning and bankruptcy have led to abandoned projects and compromised promises. Even when planning is adequate and finances secure, a viable community does not always emerge. A comparative study of elderly Eastern European Jews in age-homogenous settings in Leeds, England and Cleveland, Ohio reveals such a case (Francis, 1981). The residents of Caroll Arms in the latter city are unhappy with kin and peers. Their prior immigration experience and transiency has brought about idealized expectations for parent-child relations. An administration that undermines their involvement in community decision making and the lack of a public area for community events have left them in an atmosphere of competition and insecurity.

Age also establishes the boundaries in group formation. Age-graded clubs and voluntary associations are quite common. Age homogeneity is achieved either by formal age criteria for membership or informal recruitment by peers (Fennel, 1981). Old age is the criteria and focus for Senior Centers or Senior Citizen Clubs, although the specific age boundaries are open to interpretation. As in age-graded communities, we find people celebrating life, not sitting around waiting to die (Myerhoff, 1978a, 1978b). Through factions and friends, the future is plotted and negotiated (Cuellar, 1978). Even at the national level, age marks the boundary around which such organizations as the Grey Panthers and the AARP have crystalized.

Boundaries other than age also determine age homogeneity. Communication creates a barrier between the speaking, hearing world and the world of the deaf. For those born deaf, socialization in boarding schools for the deaf (apart from parents) promotes peer bonds and tightly knit groups. For lives built on this peer culture, growing old in silence is also growing old together (Becker, 1980). Other boundaries are designed to lead those who have been excluded to not even suspect that a boundary exists. Thus the elderly "loners" of the inner city are seen as survivors of its undesirable, deteriorating core. Even this environment that promotes so much human misery has potentials for survival (Clark, 1971). Once the border has been discovered, the otherwise unseen community emerges (Eckert, 1980). Social networks have been constructed to maintain the stance of the loner, but not his or her isolation. Social contacts are structurally dispersed, selectively intimate, and variably activated so that very few loners are devoid of social contact (Sokolovsky and Cohen, 1978, 1981; Cohen and Sokolovsky, 1980). An infrastructure of services, inexpensive hotels, and restaurants provides an adaptive niche for those who value independence and lack of intimacy (Eckert, 1979). Ethnography reveals some of the strengths of such an environment. Poor, single-room-occupancy hotel dwellers of San Diego are better fed than their middle-class counterparts (Bohannan, 1981). Ironically, however, their niche is being destroyed by the bulldozers of urban renewal whose planners see them as being underhoused, underfed, and socially isolated.

Since age itself constitutes a social boundary, a remaining question is what the future of age boundaries may be. Like everything else, boundaries are subject to change (Ross, 1975; Keith, 1981). Will age boundaries become more or less salient in postindustrial society? Our answer cannot be simple because complex industrial societies use age both chronologically and socially to demarcate borders. Use of chronological age as a proxy for other characteristics will continue since expedient bureaucracies can always be expected to categorize people and allocate their responsibilities and privileges. If mandatory retirement at the chronological threshold of 65 or 70 is eliminated, however, the age-grade of "elder," "senior citizen," or "retired" will be based on the more flexible functional criteria used by a majority of the world's cultures (Myerhoff, 1978c). Lines drawn by social age will become more acute. With the advent of larger, healthier, wealthier, and better educated cohorts of older people, organizations such as the Grey Panthers, AARP, and the National Retired Teachers Association will continue to increase in membership, and new organizations will make their appearance. In working for the benefit of their members, these organizations are erasing or modifying the stereotype that comes with the label "old." Consumer marketing is revising its age-targeted audiences. The youth culture of the 1960s has shrunk in size and economic strength. We can expect to see more ads for fade creams and "levis for men." Age conflicts will also intensify. From the comparative perspective, we know that stable, mature economies favor the middle-aged and the old, not youth. Intercohort tensions over opportunity will sharpen age boundaries. Although these are only predictions, we do know that old age is here to stay and will continue to be an important variable in behavioral research.

IMPLICATIONS FOR PSYCHOLOGICAL RESEARCH ON AGING

Culture is the target of anthropology as behavior is that of psychology. A synergistic reaction occurs when the two are combined in a comparative perspective. The study of culture and personality, once the two were linked in the 1920s, has developed into a mature area of inquiry, psychological anthropology. Comparative psychology, as Gutmann noted in his 1977 review, is only in its infancy. With new vistas to explore and basic questions to resolve, a promising future is in the offing. Since science advances on two fronts at once, the theoretical and the methodological, we will examine the implications of both these frontiers for psychological research on aging.

Theoretical Implications

If you want your pet theory vetoed, ask an anthropologist. Malinowski's work in the Trobriands (1927) resulted in a reassessment of the universality of the Oedipus Complex and Mead's study of Samoan adolescence (1928) changed our ideas about adolescent turmoil. At issue is not the cavalier destruction of theoretical icons but increasing the generalizability of our knowledge. If our endeavor is to discover what is common to all human beings as they age and to distinguish that from the population variation determined by genetics, culture, or circumstance, we must turn to the comparative laboratory. To do otherwise would be to follow the steps of the myopic experimenter, who, after construction a 4 × 3 × 2 matrix, examines only one of its cells. Although variation will be evident, we cannot know to what extent it is spurious since the factors shaping it have not been empirically studied. Thus, new ranges of variation, new combinations of variables, and new questions will be our reward when we take our old questions to this laboratory.

As Neugarten and Bengtson (1968) noted, the comparative perspective provides an opportunity to free our hypotheses from particular cultural biases. Science, being a human creation, is itself a cultural artifact, with distinctive rules, standards and concepts. Our scientific enterprise is largely a product of European and American culture, a fact that introduces unknown and extra-scientific biases. Although we have yet to examine the issue, it would be a little unsettling to discover that morale or happiness may not be a universal concern (Nydegger, 1980). The same may be said for senility or depression, two states that we consider basic psychological problems in aging. Even physicians have difficulty in certifying senility without an autopsy. Com-

paratively, we can expect the definitions, treatment, and frequency of senility to vary considerably. Depression may not even be an issue in a culture less concerned with interior psychological states than our own. Functionality, and the associated decrements that accompany increased age—the norms of which are based on predominantly U.S. male populations —may have to be reevaluated when more comparative data becomes available. Different diets, different life stresses, and different activities of daily living have rather obvious effects on individual physiology and on what is necessary to maintain one's self as an independent adult. The variety of compensation available for functional losses is also a wide-open question. To return to our myopic experimenter again, think of him as trying to improve his vision by wearing glasses—only these glasses contain a cultural prescription that eliminates all colors, leaving only black and white.

Methodological Implications

Comparability of units presents the greatest challenge for comparative researchers. Some variables are readily measured; others are not. Those which are cultural or which are culturally interpreted present the most difficulty. Difficulty does not mean impossibility. Over a century of comparative ethnographic research has also been accompanied by increasing methodological sophistication (Naroll and Cohen, 1973). We even have an entire volume devoted to cross-cultural measurement strategies for major variables in research on aging (Fry and Keith, 1980, 1982). To resolve the problem of comparability, multiple measures of the same variable increase confidence in measurement. But we must do more. From the methodological cornucopia that ethnographers have had by necessity to invent, borrow, or adapt, we learn four important lessons. First, comparative research must consider the native understanding. Second, comparative research must take into account the context in which the behavior unfolds. Third, comparative research should be long-term in an effort to overcome the normative biases inherent in short-term contact. Finally, our comparative research designs should combine qualitative and quantitative techniques in data collection and data analysis. By incorporating these lessons into our research designs, the problems of multiple realities and risks of measurement errors are minimized.

A comparative research design is an attractive one. We need more comparative research on aging and especially on the psychology of aging. Specific researchable questions, however, should be weighed with care, theoretically balancing costs against payoff. Comparative research is expensive, often involving a collaborative team effort. Team work in the four corners of the world adds social organizational issues to already complicated research problems (Finley, 1979). Nevertheless, if we are to give the full scientific treatment to what we already know about aging in one societal type, comparison is in order.

We began this chapter by looking at culture in its obvious and not so obvious aspects. In the former perspective, culture is tyrannical, the dictator of behavior. The not-so-obvious face of culture is not a totalitarian independent variable, determining and explaining all, but more an arbiter. People use culture to negotiate their daily business, their lives. Culture shapes behavior but does not determine it. Culture should therefore be added to our methodological tool kit. In fact, it is already there. We use it to communicate with our subjects and with our colleagues. Culture, however, may get in the way. It lurks in the shadows waiting to confound us, our instruments, and the relationships we are trying to discover or evaluate. For instance, the phrasing of questions may put our subjects/respondents on the defensive; inadvertently, their responses and behavior may be altered. The phrasing of questions or items can explain more of the variance than other variables, especially in areas dealing with life satisfaction or morale (Carp and Carp, 1981). An important lesson is to be learned here. Since life in the natural, human, cultural arena is a mix of positives and negatives with individuals actively negotiating them, we should employ this mix in our instruments or experiments. Instead of focusing on what is wrong with old age, we should

also ask what is good about old age. An awareness of culture, the obvious and not so obvious phenomena that make us and the people we work with human, will only work to improve our science.

Acknowledgments. The author would like to thank Loyola University of Chicago for a sabbatical leave during which this chapter was prepared and written. Especial thanks are given to Lucille McGill for her careful typing of the manuscript. Stephanie Cole deserves appreciation for her careful job of proofreading. I would also like to acknowledge the work of Margaret Perkinson for her reading of, and commentary on, the manuscript.

REFERENCES

Achenbaum, W., and Stearns, P. 1978. Essay: Old age and modernization. *Gerontologist* 18: 307–312.

Almagor, U. 1978. The ethos of equality among Dassanetch age peers. In *Age, Generation and Time*, eds. P. T. W. Baxter and U. Almagor, pp. 69–94. New York: St. Martins Press.

Amoss, P. T. 1981a. Coast Salish elders. In *Other Ways of Growing Old*, eds. P. T. Amoss and S. Harrell, pp. 227–238. Stanford: Stanford University Press.

Amoss, P. T. 1981b. Cultural centrality and prestige for the elders: The Coast Salish case. In *Dimensions: Aging Culture and Health*, ed. C. L. Fry, pp. 47–64. New York: Praeger (a J. F. Bergin Book).

Amoss, P. T., and Harrell, S. 1981. Introduction: An anthropological perspective on aging. In *Other Ways of Growing Old*, eds. P. T. Amoss and S. Harrell, pp. 1–24. Stanford: Stanford University Press.

Angrosino, M. 1976. Anthropology and the aged. *Gerontologist* 16: 174–180.

Arensberg, C. 1937. *The Irish Countrymen*. New York: Macmillan.

Arensberg, C. 1954. The community study method. *American Journal of Sociology* 60: 109–124.

Arensberg, C. 1972. Culture as behavior: Structure and emergence. *Annual Review of Anthropology* 1: 1–26.

Arnhoff, F. N.; Leon, H. V.; and Lorge, I. 1964. Cross-cultural acceptance of stereotypes toward aging. *Journal of Social Psychology* 63: 41–58.

Arth, M. 1968. Ideals and behavior, a comment on Ibo respect patterns. *Gerontologist* 8: 242–244.

Arth, M. 1972. A cross-cultural perspective. In *Research, Planning and Action for the Elderly*, eds. D. Kent, R. Kastenbaum, and S. Sherman. New York: Behavioral Publications.

Balikci, A. 1970. *The Netsilik Eskimo*. New York: Natural History Press.

Baltes, P. B. 1968. Longitudinal and cross-sectional sequences in the study of age and generation effects. *Human Development* 11: 145–171.

Barth, F. 1969. *Ethnic Groups and Boundaries: The Social Organization of Cultural Difference.* London: Allen and Unwin.

Barth, F., ed. 1978. *Scale and Social Organization.* New York: Columbia University Press.

Bateson, G. 1958 (original, 1936). *Naven.* Stanford: Stanford University Press.

Bateson, G., and Mead, M. 1942. *Balinese Character.* New York: New York Academy of Science.

Baxter, P. T. W. 1978. Boran age sets and generation sets: Gada, a puzzle or a maze? In *Age, Generation and Time,* eds. P. T. W. Baxter and U. Almagor, pp. 151–182.

Becker, G. 1980. *Growing Old in Silence.* Berkeley: University of California Press.

Benedict, R. 1938. Continuities and discontinuities in cultural conditioning. *Psychiatry* 1: 161–167.

Benet, S. 1974. *Abkhasians: The Long-Lived People of the Caucasus.* New York: Holt, Rinehart and Winston.

Benet, S. 1976. *How to Live to be 100.* New York: Dial Press.

Bengtson, V. L. 1979. Ethnicity and aging: Problems and issues in current social science inquiry. In *Ethnicity and Aging,* eds. D. E. Gelfand and A. J. Kutzik, pp. 9–31. New York: Springer Publishing Company.

Bengtson, V. L.; Cuellar, J. B.; and Ragan, P. K. 1977. Stratum contrasts and similarities in attitudes toward death. *Journal of Gerontology* 32: 76–88.

Bengtson, V. L.; Dowd, J. J.; Smith, D. H.; and Inkles, A. 1975. Modernization, modernity and perceptions of aging: A cross-cultural study. *Journal of Gerontology* 30: 688–95.

Biesele, M., and Howell, N. 1981. The old people give you life: Aging among !Kung hunter-gathers. In *Other Ways of Growing Old,* eds. P. T. Amoss and S. Harrell, pp. 77–98. Stanford: Stanford University Press.

Bock, P. K. 1966. Social time and institutional conflict. *Human Organization* 25: 96–102.

Bohannan, P. J. 1953. Concepts of time among the Tiv of Nigeria. *Southwestern Journal of Anthropology* 9: 251–262.

Bohannan, P. J. 1981. Food of old people in center city hotels. In *Dimensions: Aging, Culture and Health,* ed. C. L. Fry, pp. 185–200. New York: Praeger (a J. F. Bergin Book).

Boyer, E. 1980. Health perception in the elderly: Its cultural and social aspects. In *Aging in Culture and Society: Comparative Perspectives and Strategies,* ed. C. L. Fry, pp. 198–216. New York: Praeger (a J. F. Bergin Book).

Brown, J. K. 1982. Cross-cultural perspectives on middle-aged women. *Current Anthropology* 23: 143–156.

Butler, R. N. 1963. The life review: An interpretation of reminiscence in the aged. *Psychiatry* 26: 65–76.

Butler, R. N. 1968. The facade of chronological age. In *Middle Age and Aging,* ed. B. L. Neugarten, pp. 235–242. Chicago: University of Chicago Press.

Butler, R. N. 1974. Successful aging and the role of the life review. *Journal of the American Geriatric Society* 22: 529–535.

Byrne, S. 1974. Arden, an adult community. In *Anthropologists in Cities,* eds. G. Foster and R. Kemper, pp. 123–152. Boston: Little, Brown and Company.

Cain, L. D. 1976. Aging and the law. In *Handbook of Aging and the Social Sciences,* eds. R. H. Binstock and E. Shanas, pp. 342–368. New York: Van Nostrand Reinhold Company.

Cain, L. D. 1981. Age distinctions and their social functions: A critique of the age discrimination act of 1975. *Chicago Kent Law Review* 57: 827–832.

Cancian, Francesca. 1975. *What are Norms?: A Study of Beliefs and Actions in a Maya Community.* London: Cambridge University Press.

Cancian, Frank. 1965. *Economics and Prestige in a Maya Community.* Stanford: Stanford University Press.

Carp, F. M., and Carp, A. 1981. It may not be the answer, it may be the question. *Research on Aging* 3: 85–100.

Chodorow, N. 1974. Family structure and female personality. In *Women, Culture and Society,* eds. M. Z. Rossaldo and L. Lamphere, pp. 43–66. Stanford: Stanford University Press.

Chomsky, N. 1973. *Language and Mind,* 2nd ed. New York: Harcourt Brace Jovanovich, Inc.

Clark, M. M. 1967. The anthropology of aging: A new area for studies of culture and personality. *Gerontologist* 7: 55–65.

Clark, M. M. 1971. Patterns of aging among the elderly poor of the inner city. *Gerontologist* 11: 58–66.

Clark, M. M. 1972. Cultural values and dependency in later life. In *Aging and Modernization,* eds. D. O. Cowgill and L. D. Holmes, pp. 263–274. New York: Appleton-Century-Crofts.

Clark, M. M. 1973. Contributions of cultural anthropology to the study of the aged. In *Culture, Illness and Health: Essays on Human Adaptation,* eds. L. Nader and T. Maretzki, pp. 78–88. Washington, D.C.: American Anthropological Association.

Clark, M. M., and Anderson, B. G. 1967. *Culture and Aging: An Anthropological Study of Older Americans.* Springfield: Charles C Thomas.

Clark, M. M.; Kaufman, S.; and Pierce, R. C. 1976. Explorations of acculturation: Toward a model of ethnic identity. *Human Organization* 35: 231–238.

Cohen, C., and Sokolovsky, J. 1980. Social engagement versus isolation: The case of the aged in S.R.O. hotels. *Gerontologist* 20: 36–44.

Cohen, R. 1978. Ethnicity: Problem and focus in anthropology. In *Annual Reviews of Anthropology,* pp. 379–404. Palo Alto: Annual Reviews Inc.

Cohen, R. Age and culture as theory. Forthcoming. In *Age and Anthropological Theory,* eds. D. I. Kertzer and J. Keith. Ithaca: Cornell University Press.

Cohler, B. J., and Lieberman, M. A. 1979. Personality change across the second half of life: Findings from a study of Irish, Italian and Polish-American men and women. In *Ethnicity and Aging,* eds. D. E. Gelfand and A. J. Kutzik, pp. 227–245. New York: Springer Publishing Co.

Colson, E., and Scudder, T. 1981. Old age in Guemb District, Zambia. In *Other Ways of Growing Old,* eds. P. T. Amoss and S. Harrell, pp. 125–154. Stanford: Stanford University Press.

Cool, L. E. 1980. Ethnicity and aging: Continuity through change for elderly Corsicans. In *Aging in Culture and Society: Comparative Viewpoints and Strategies,* ed. C. L. Fry, pp. 149–169. New York: Praeger (a J. F. Bergin Book).

Cool, L. E. 1981a. Ethnic identity: A source of community esteem for the elderly. *Anthropological Quarterly* 54: 179–189.

Cool, L. E. 1981b. Role continuity or crisis in later life?: A Corsican case. *International Journal of Aging and Human Development* 13: 169–181.

Cool, L. E., and McCabe, J. 1983. The scheming hag and the dear old thing: The anthropology of aging women. In *Growing Old in Different Cultures—Cross-Cultural Perspectives,* ed. J. Sokolovsky, pp. 56–68. Belmont: Wadsworth.

Cowgill, D. O. 1974. Aging and modernization: A revision of the theory. In *Late Life: Communities and Environmental Policy,* ed. J. Gubrium, pp. 123–146. Springfield: Charles C Thomas.

Cowgill, D. O., and Holmes, L. D., eds. 1972. *Aging and Modernization.* New York: Appleton-Century-Crofts.

Cuellar, J. 1978. El senior citizens club: The older Mexican-American in the voluntary association. In *Life's Career Aging,* eds. B. G. Myerhoff and A. Simic, pp. 207–230. Beverly Hills: Sage Publications.

Cutler, R. G. 1975. Evolution of human longevity and genetic complexity governing aging rate. *Proceedings of the National Academy of Science* 72: 4664–4668.

Cutler, R. G. 1976. Evolution of longevity in primates. *Journal of Human Evolution* 5: 169–202.

Davies, D. 1975. *The Centenarians of the Andes.* London: Barne and Jenkins.

Deck, J. 1972. *Rancho Paradise: Retired Americans in a Mobile Home Park.* New York: Harcourt, Brace and Jovanovich.

Dowd, J. J. 1975. Aging as exchange: A preface to theory. *Journal of Gerontology* 30: 584–594.

Dowd, J. J. and Bengston, V. L. 1978. Aging in minority populations: An examination of the double jeopardy hypothesis. *Journal of Gerontology* 33: 427–436.

Durkheim, E. 1961 (original, 1912). *Elementary Forms of Religious Life.* Translated by J. W. Swain. New York: The Macmillan Company.

Eckert, J. K. 1979. Urban development and renewal: High risk factors for the elderly. *Gerontologist* 19: 496–502.

Eckert, J. K. 1980. *The Unseen Elderly.* San Diego: The Campanile Press.

Eisenstadt, S. N. 1956. *From generation to generation: Age groups and social structure.* New York: Free Press.

Evans-Prichard, E. E. 1940. *The Neurologist.* Oxford: Clarendon.

Fennell, V. 1981. Friendship and kindship in older women's organizations: Curlew Point, 1973. In *Dimensions: Aging, Culture and Health,* ed. C. L. Fry, pp. 131–144. New York: Praeger (a J. F. Bergin Book).

Finley, G. E. 1979. Collaborative issues in cross-national research. *International Journal of Intercultural Relations* 3: 5–13.

Finley, G. E. 1982. Modernization and aging. In *Review of Human Development,* ed. T. Field, et al. New York: Wiley-Interscience.

Foner, A. and Kertzer, D. I. 1978. Transitions over the life course: Lessons from age-set societies. *American Journal of Sociology* 83: 1081–1104.

Foner, A., and Kertzer, D. I. 1979. Intrinsic and extrinsic sources of change in life course transitions. In *Aging from Birth to Death: Interdisciplinary Perspectives,* ed. M. W. Riley, pp. 121–136. Boulder: Westview Press.

Foner, N. Forthcoming. Age and social change. In *Age and Anthropological Theory,* eds. D. Kertzer and J. Keith. Ithaca: Cornell University Press.

Fortes, M. 1971. On the concept of person among the Tallensi. In *La notion de Personne en Afrique Noire.* Colloques Internationaux du C.N.R.S.

Foster, G. M. 1981. Old age in Tzintzuntzan, Mexico. In *Aging: Biology and Behavior,* eds. J. L. McGaugh and S. B. Kiesler, pp. 115–137. New York: Academic Press.

Foulks, E. F. 1972. *The Arctic Hysterias of the North Alaskan Eskimo.* Washington, D.C.: American Anthropological Association.

Francis, D. G. 1981. Adaptive strategies of the elderly in England and Ohio. In *Dimensions: Aging, Culture and Health,* ed. C. L. Fry, pp. 85–108. New York: Praeger (a J. F. Bergin Book).

Fries, J. F., and Crapo, L. M. 1981. *Vitality and Aging.* San Francisco: W. H. Freeman and Company.

Fry, C. L. 1976. The ages of adulthood: A question of numbers. *Journal of Gerontology* 31: 170–177.

Fry, C. L. 1977. The community as a commodity: The age graded case. *Human Organization* 36: 115–123.

Fry, C. L. 1979. Structural conditions affecting community formation among the aged. In *The Ethnography of Old Age,* ed. J. Keith. Special Issue of *Anthropological Quarterly* 52: 7–18.

Fry, C. L. 1980. Cultural dimensions of age. In *Aging in Culture and Society: Comparative Perspectives and Strategies,* ed. C. L. Fry, pp. 42–64. New York: Praeger (a J. F. Bergin Book).

Fry, C. L., and Keith, J., eds. 1980. *New Methods for Old Age Research: Anthropological Alternatives.* Chicago: Center for Urban Policy, Loyola University of Chicago.

Fry, C. L., and Keith, J. 1982. The life course as a cultural unit. In *Aging from Birth to Death: Sociotemporal Perspectives,* eds. M. W. Riley, R. Abeles, and M. Teitelbaum, pp. 51–70. Boulder: Westview Press.

Fry, C. L., and Keith, J., eds. 1984. *New Methods for Old Age Research: Anthropological Alternatives.* 2nd (expanded) ed. New York: Praeger (a J. F. Bergin Book).

Gans, H. J. 1972 (original, 1967). An anatomy of suburbia. In *North American Suburbs,* ed. J. Kramer. Berkeley: Glen Dessary Press.

Gaulin, S. J. C. 1980. Sexual dimorphism in human post-reproductive lifespan: Possible causes. *Journal of Human Evolution* 9: 227–232.

Glascock, A. P., and Feinman, S. 1980a. Toward a comparative framework: Propositions concerning the treatment of the aged in non-industrial societies. In *New Methods for Old Age Research: Anthropological Alternatives,* eds. C. L. Fry and J. Keith, pp. 204–222. Chicago: Center for Urban Policy, Loyola University of Chicago.

Glascock, A. P., and Feinman, S. 1980b. A holocultural analysis of old age. *Comparative Social Research* 3: 311–332.

Glascock, A. P., and Feinman, S. 1981. Social asset or social burden: Treatment of the aged in non-industrial societies. In *Dimensions: Aging, Culture and Health,* ed. C. L. Fry, pp. 13–32. New York: Praeger (a J. F. Bergin Book).

Glascock, A. P. 1983. Death-hastening behavior: An expansion of Eastwell's thesis. *American Anthropologist* 85: 417–420.

Goldstein, M., and Beall, C. 1981. Modernization and aging in the third and fourth world: Views from the rural hinterland in Nepal. *Human Organization* 40: 48–55.

Goldstein, M., and Beall, C. 1982. Brief note on demographic aspects of aging in the less developed countries. *Association for Anthropology and Gerontology Newsletter* 3: 2.

Goldstein, T., and Gutmann, D. 1972. A TAT study of Navajo aging. *Psychiatry* 35: 373–384.

Goodenough, W. H. 1965. Rethinking 'status' and 'role': Toward a general model of the cultural organization of social relationships. In *The Relevance of Model of Social Anthropology,* ed. M. Banton, pp. 1–24. New York: Praeger.

Goody, J. 1976. Aging in non-industrial societies. In *Handbook of Aging and the Social Sciences,* eds. R. H. Binstock and E. Shanas, pp. 117–129. New York: Van Nostrand Reinhold.

Green, B. 1978–79. Internal colonialism versus the elderly: Renewal and critique for gerontological theory. *Berkeley Journal of Sociology* 23: 129–150.

Guemple, D. L. 1969. Human resource management: The dilemma of the aging Eskimo. *Sociological Symposium* 2: 59–74.

Guemple, D. L. 1980. Growing old in Inuit society. In *Aging in Canada: Social Perspectives,* ed. V. W. Marshall, pp. 95–102. Don Mills, Ontario: Fitzhenry and Witeside.

Gulliver, P. H. 1968. Age differentiation. In *International Encyclopedia of the Social Sciences,* ed. D. L. Sills. New York: McMillan and Free Press.

Gutmann, D. 1964. An exploration of ego configurations in middle and late life. In *Personality in Middle and Late Life,* ed. B. L. Neugarten. New York: Atherton Press.

Gutmann, D. 1966. Mayan aging—a comparative TAT study. *Psychiatry* 29: 246–259.

Gutmann, D. 1967. Aging among the highland Maya: A comparative study. *Journal of Personality and Social Psychology* 7.

Gutmann, D. 1969. The country of old men: Cross-cultural studies in the psychology of later life. In *Occasional Papers in Gerontology,* ed. W. Donahue. Ann Arbor: Institute of Gerontology, University of Michigan.

Gutmann, D. 1974. Alternatives to disengagement: The old men of the Highland Druze. In *Culture and Personality: Contemporary Readings,* ed. R. LeVine, pp. 232–245. Chicago: Aldine.

Gutmann, D. 1975. Parenthood: A key to the comparative study of the life cycle. In *Life-Span Developmental Psychology: Normative Life Crises,* eds. N. Datan and L. H. Ginsberg, pp. 167–184. New York: Academic Press.

Gutmann, D. 1977. The cross-cultural perspective: Notes toward a comparative psychology of aging. In *Handbook of the Psychology of Aging,* eds. J. E. Birren and K. W. Schaie, pp. 302–326. New York: Van Nostrand Reinhold.

Hannerz, U. 1974. Ethnicity and opportunity in urban America. In *Urban Ethnicity,* ed. A. Cohen. London: Tavistock.

Harrell, S. 1981. Growing old in rural Taiwan. In *Other Ways of Growing Old,* eds. P. T. Amoss and S. Harrell, pp. 193–210. Stanford: Stanford University Press.

Harris, M. 1964. *The Nature of Cultural Things.* New York: Random House.

Hart, C. W., and Pilling, A. R. 1960. *The Tiwi of Northern Australia.* New York: Holt, Reinhart and Winston.

Hauser, P. 1976. Aging and world-wide population change. In *Handbook of Aging and the Social Sciences,* eds. R. H. Binstock and E. Shanas, pp. 58–86. New York: Van Nostrand Reinhold.

Havighurst, R. J.; Munnichs; J. M. A., Neugarten, B., and Thomae, H. 1969. *Adjustment to Retirement: A Cross-National Study.* Copenhagen: Assen.

Haviland, J. B. 1978. *Gossip, Reputation and Knowledge in Zinacantan.* Chicago: University of Chicago Press.

Hayflick, L. 1965. The limited *in vitro* lifetime of human diploid cell strains. *Experimental Cell Research* 37: 614–636.

Hayflick, L. 1977. The cellular basis for biological aging. In *Handbook of the Biology of Aging,* eds. C. E. Finch and L. Hayflick. New York: Van Nostrand, Reinhold.

Hazan, H. 1980. *The Limbo People.* London: Routledge and Kegan Paul.

Hendel-Sebestyen, G. 1979. Role diversity: Toward the development of community in a total institutional setting. In *The Ethnography of Old Age,* ed. J. Keith. Special Issue of *Anthropological Quarterly,* 52, 19–28.

Hendricks, C. D., and Hendricks, J. 1976. Concepts of time and temporal construction among the aged with implications for research. In *Time, Roles and Self in Old Age,* ed. J. F. Gubrium. New York: Human Sciences Press.

Hendricks, J. Forthcoming. The elderly in society: Beyond modernization. *Social Science History.*

Hochchild, A. R. 1973. *The Unexpected Community.* Berkeley: University of California Press.

Holmes, L. D. 1976. Trends in anthropological gerontology: From Simmons to the seventies. *International Journal of Aging and Human Development* 7: 211–220.

Holzberg, C. S. 1982. Ethnicity and aging: Anthropological perspectives on more than just the minority elderly. *Gerontologist* 22: 249–256.

Hrdy, S. B. 1981. Nepotist and altruists: The behavior

of old females among macaques and langur monkeys. In *Other Ways of Growing Old,* eds. P. T. Amoss and S. Harrell, pp. 59–76. Stanford: Stanford University Press.

Hsu, F. L. K. 1961. *Psychological Anthropology: Approaches to Culture and Personality.* Homewood: Dorsey Press.

Ikels, C. 1980. The coming of age in Chinese society: Traditional patterns and contemporary Hong Kong. In *Aging in Culture and Society: Comparative Perspectives and Strategies,* ed. C. L. Fry, pp. 80–100. New York: Praeger (a J. F. Bergin Book).

Isajiw, W. W. 1974. Definitions of ethnicity. *Ethnicity* 1: 111–124.

Jackson, J. J. 1980. *Minorities and Aging.* Belmont: Wadsworth Publishing.

Johnson, S. 1971. *Idle Haven: Community Building Among the Working Class Retired.* Berkeley: University of California Press.

Jonas, K. 1979. Factors in development of community among elderly persons in age-segregated housing. In *The Ethnography of Old Age.* ed. J. Keith. Special Issue of *Anthropological Quarterly* 52: 29–38.

Jonas, K. amd Wellin, E. 1980. Dependency and reciprocity: Home health aid in an elderly population. In *Aging in Culture and Society: Comparative Perspectives and Strategies,* ed. C. L. Fry, pp. 217–238. New York: Praeger (a J. F. Bergin Book).

Kandel, R. F., and Heider, M. 1979. Friendship and factionalism in a triethnic housing complex for the elderly in north Miami. In *The Ethnography of Old Age,* ed. J. Keith. Special issue of *Anthropology Quarterly* 52: 49–60.

Katz, S. 1978. Anthropological perspectives on aging. *Annals of the American Academy of Political and Social Sciences* 438: 1–12.

Kayser-Jones, J. 1981a. *Old, Alone and Neglected.* Berkeley: University of California Press.

Kayser-Jones, J. 1981b. Quality of care for the institutionalized age: A Scottish-American comparison. In *Dimensions: Aging, Culture and Health,* ed. C. L. Fry, pp. 233–254. New York: Praeger (a J. F. Bergin Book).

Keesing, R. 1972. Paradigms lost: The new ethnography and the new linguistics. *Southwestern Journal of Anthropology* 28: 299–332.

Keesing, R. 1974. Theories of culture. *Annual Reviews of Anthropology,* pp. 73–98. Palo Alto: Annual Reviews Inc.

Keith, J. 1980a. Old age and community creation. In *Aging in Culture and Society: Comparative Perspectives and Strategies,* ed. C. L. Fry, pp. 170–197. New York: Praeger (a J. F. Bergin Book).

Keith, J. 1980b. The best is yet to be: Toward an anthropology of age. In *Annual Reviews of Anthropology,* pp. 339–364. Palo Alto: Annual Reviews Inc.

Keith, J. 1981. Old age and age differentiation: Anthropological speculations on age as a social border. In *Aging: Social Change,* eds. S. B. Kiesler, J. N. Morgan, and V. K. Oppenheimer, pp. 453–490. New York: Academic Press.

Keith, J. 1982. *Old People, New Lives: Community Cre-*

ation in a Retirement Residence. 2nd ed. Chicago: University of Chicago Press, Phoenix Books.

Keith, J. Forthcoming. Ask an anthropologist. In *Handbook of Aging and the Social Sciences,* eds. R. Binstock and E. Shanas. 2nd ed. New York: Van Nostrand Reinhold Co.

Keith, J., and Kertzer, D. I. Forthcoming. Age and anthropological theory: An introduction. In *Age and Anthropological Theory,* eds. D. I. Kertzer and J. Keith. Ithaca: Cornell University Press.

Kerns, V. 1980. Aging and mutual support relations among the Black Carib. In *Aging in Culture and Society: Comparative Perspectives and Strategies,* ed. C. L. Fry, pp. 112–125. New York: Praeger (a J. F. Bergin Book).

Kertzer, D. I. 1978. Theoretical developments in the study of age group systems. *American Ethnologist* 5: 368–374.

Kertzer, D. I. 1982. Generation and age in cross-cultural perspective. In *Aging from Birth to Death: Sociotemporal Perspectives,* eds. M. W. Riley, R. Abeles, and M. Teitelbaum, pp. 27–50. Boulder: Westview Press.

Kertzer, D. I. and Madison, O. B. B. 1981. Women's age-set systems in Africa: The Latuka of Southern Sudan. In *Dimensions: Aging, Culture and Health,* ed. C. L. Fry, pp. 109–130. New York: Praeger (a J. F. Bergin Book).

Kiefer, C. W. 1971. Notes on anthropology and the minority elderly. *Gerontologist* 11: 26–29.

Kiefer, C. W. 1974. Lessons from the Issei. In *Late Life: Communities and Environmental Policy,* ed. J. F. Gubrium, pp. 167–200. Springfield: Charles C Thomas.

Kirk, L., and Burton, M. 1977. Meaning and context: A study of contextual shifts in meaning of Maasai personality descriptions. *American Ethologist* 4: 734–761.

Kline, C. 1975. The socialization of women. *Gerontologist* 15: 485–492.

Krantz, G. S. 1966. Brain size and hunting ability in earliest man. *Current Anthropology* 9: 265.

Kroeber, A. L. 1917. The superorganic. *American Anthropologist* 19: 163–213.

LaFontaine, J. S., ed. 1978. *Sex and Age as Principles of Social Differentiation.* New York: Academic Press.

Laslett, P. 1965. *The World We Have Lost.* London: Methuen.

Laslett, P. 1976. Societal development and aging. In *Handbook of Aging and the Social Sciences,* eds. R. H. Binstock and E. Shanas, pp. 87–116. New York: Van Nostrand Reinhold.

Leach, E. R. 1961a. Chronus and chronos. In *Rethinking Anthropology,* ed. E. R. Leach. New York: Humanities Press.

Leach, E. R. 1961b. Time and false noses. In *Rethinking Anthropology,* ed. E. R. Leach. New York: Humanities Press.

Leaf, A. 1973a. Every day is a gift when you are over 100. *National Geographic* 93: 110–143.

Leaf, A. 1973b. Getting old. *Scientific American* 229: 45–52.

Lee, G. R. and Kezis, M. 1981. Societal literacy and the aged. *International Journal of Aging and Human Development* 12: 221–234.

Legesse, A. 1979. Age sets and retirement communities. In *The Ethnography of Old Age,* ed. J. Keith. Special issue of *Anthropological Quarterly,* 52: 61–69.

Leighton, A., and Hughes, C. 1955. Notes on Eskimo patterns of suicide. *Southwestern Journal of Anthropology* 3: 327–338.

Levi-Strauss, C. 1969. *The Raw and the Cooked.* New York: Harper and Row.

LeVine, R. 1978a. Adulthood and aging in cross-cultural perspective. *Items* 31/32: 1–5.

LeVine, R. 1978b. Comparative notes on the life course. In *Transitions: The Family and the Life Course in Historical Perspective,* ed. T. K. Hareven, pp. 287–297. New York: Academic Press.

Linton, R. 1936. *The Study of Man.* New York: D. Appleton Century Co.

Lovejoy, C. O. 1981. The origin of man. *Science* 211: 341–350.

McNeill, D. 1970. *The Acquisition of Language: The Study of Developmental Psycholinguistics.* New York: Harper and Row.

Malinowski, B. 1922. *Argonauts of the Western Pacific.* London: Routledge.

Malinowski, B. 1927. *Sex and Repression in Savage Societies.* London: Humanities Press.

Mauss, M. 1967 (original, 1925). *The Gift* Translated by Ian Currison. New York: W. W. Norton and Company, Inc.

Maxwell, E. K., and Maxwell, R. J. 1980. Contempt for the elderly: A cross-cultural analysis. *Current Anthropology* 21: 569–570.

Maxwell, R. J. 1972. Anthropological perspectives. In *The Future of Time,* eds. H. Yaker, et al. Garden City: Anchor Books.

Maxwell, R. J., and Silverman, P. 1970. Information and esteem. *Aging and Human Development* 1: 127–146.

Maybury-Lewis, D. 1974 (original, 1967). *Akwe-Shavante Society.* Clarendon: Oxford University Press.

Maybury-Lewis, D. Forthcoming. Age and kinship: A structural view. In *Age and Anthropological Theory,* eds. D. I. Kertzer and J. Keith. Uthaca: Cornell University Press.

Mazess, R. B., and Foreman, S. H. 1979. Longevity and age exaggeration in Vilcabamba, Ecuador. *Journal of Gerontology* 34: 94–98.

Mead, M. 1928. *Coming of age in Samoa.* New York: Morrow.

Missinne, L. E. 1980. Aging in Bakongo culture. *International Journal of Aging and Human Development* 11: 283–295.

Moore, A. 1973. *Life Cycles in Atchatlan: The Diverse Careers of Certain Guatemalans.* New York: Teachers College, Columbia University.

Moore, M. J. 1981. Physical aging: A cross-cultural perspective. In *The Dynamics of Aging,* eds. F. J. Berghorn, D. E. Schafer, et al. pp. 27–40. Boulder: Westview Press.

Moore, S. F. 1978. Old age in a life-term social arena: Some Chagga of Killimanjaro in 1974. In *Life's Career: Aging,* eds. B. G. Myerhoff and A. Simic, pp. 23–76. Beverly Hills: Sage Publications.

Mumford, L. 1956. For older people: Not segregation, but integration. *Architectural Record* 119: 191–194.

Myerhoff, B. G. 1978a. A symbol perfected in death: Continuity and ritual in the life and death of an elderly Jew. In *Life's Career: Aging,* eds. B. G. Myerhoff and A. Simic, pp. 163–206.

Myerhoff, B. G. 1978b. *Number Our Days.* New York: Dutton.

Myerhoff, B. G. 1978c. Aging and the aged in other cultures: An anthropological perspective. In *The Anthropology of Health,* ed. E. Bauwens, pp. 151–166. St. Louis: C. V. Mosby.

Myerhoff, B., and Simic, A., eds. 1978. *Life's Career: Aging: Cultural Variations in Growing Old.* Beverly Hills: Sage Publications.

Nadel, S. F. 1952. Witchcraft in four African societies. *American Anthropologist* 54: 18–29.

Naroll, R. 1964. Ethnic unit classification. *Current Anthropology* 5: 283–291.

Naroll, R. 1970. What have we learned from cross-cultural surveys? *American Anthropologist* 72: 1227–1288.

Naroll, R., et al. 1976. *World Wide Theory Testing.* New Haven: H.R.A.F. Press.

Naroll, R., and Cohen, R. 1973. *A Handbook of Method in Cultural Anthropology.* New York: Columbia University Press.

Nason, J. D. 1981. Respected elder or old person: Aging in a Micronesian community. In *Other Ways of Growing Old,* eds. P. T. Amoss and S. Harrell, pp. 155–174. Stanford: Stanford University Press.

National Council on Aging. 1972. *Triple Jeopardy: Myth or Reality.* Washington: National Council on Aging.

National Urban League. 1964. *Double Jeopardy: The Older Negro in America Today.* New York: National Urban League.

Neugarten, B. L. 1974. Age groups in American society and the rise of the young-old. *Ann. Amer. Acad.* 415: 187–198.

Neugarten, B. L. 1981. Age distinctions and their social functions. *Chicago Kent Law Review* 57: 809–826.

Neugarten, B. L., and Bengston, V. L. 1968. Cross-national studies of adulthood and aging. *Interdisciplinary Topics in Gerontology.* New York: Karger, Basel.

Neugarten, B. L., and Datan, N. 1973. Sociological perspectives on the life cycle. In *Life Span Developmental Psychology: Personality and Socialization,* eds. P. B. Baltes and K. W. Schaie, pp. 53–71. New York: Academic Press.

Neugarten, B. L., and Gutmann, D. 1958. Age and sex roles and personality in middle age: A thematic apperception study. *Psychological Monographs* 72, No. 17. Washington, D.C.: American Psychological Association.

Neugarten, B. L., and Hagestad, G. O. 1976. Age and life course. In *Handbook of Aging and the Social Sciences,* eds. R. H. Binstock and E. Shanas, pp. 35–57. New York: Van Nostrand Reinhold.

Neugarten, B. L.; Moore, J.; and Lowie, J. 1965. Age norms, age constraints and adult socialization. *American Journal of Sociology* 70: 710–717.

Nydegger, C. 1980. Measuring morale. In *New Methods*

for Old Age Research: Anthropological Alternatives, eds. C. L. Fry and J. Keith, pp. 177–195. Chicago: Center for Urban Policy, Loyola University of Chicago.

Nydegger, C. 1981. On being caught up in time. *Human Development* 24: 1–12.

Ortner, S. B. 1974. Is female to male as nature is to culture? In *Women, Culture and Society,* eds. M. Z. Rosaldo and L. Lamphere. Stanford: Stanford University Press.

Palmore, E. 1976. The future status of the aged. *Gerontologist* 16: 297–302.

Palmore, E., and Manton, K. 1974. Modernization and status of the aged. *Journal of Gerontology* 29: 205–210.

Pelto, P., and Pelto, G. 1975. Intra-cultural diversity: Some theoretical issues. *American Ethnologist* 2: 1–18.

Perkinson, M. A. 1980. Alternate roles for the elderly: An example from a Midwestern retirement community. *Human Organization* 39: 219–226.

Plath, D., and Ikada, K. 1975. After coming of age: Adult awareness of age norms. In *Socialization and Communication in Primary Groups,* ed. T. R. Williams. The Hague: Mouton.

Press, I. 1967. Maya aging: Cross-cultural projective techniques and the dilemma of interpretation. *Psychiatry* 30: 197–202.

Press, I., and McKool, M. Jr. 1972. Social structure and status of the aged: Toward some valid cross-cultural generalizations. *Aging and Human Development* 3: 297–306.

Quinn, N. 1975. Decision models of social structure. *American Ethnologist* 2: 19–45.

Rohner, R. P., et al. 1978. Guidelines of holocultural research. *Current Anthropology* 19: 128–129.

Rosow, I. 1967. *Social Integration of the Aged.* New York: Free Press.

Rosow, I. 1974. *Socialization to Old Age.* Berkeley: University of California Press.

Ross, J.-K. 1974a. Learning to be retired: Socialization into a French retirement residence. *Journal of Gerontology* 29: 211–223.

Ross, J.-K. 1974b. Life goes on: Social organization in a French retirement residence. In *Late Life: Communities and Environmental Policy,* ed. J. F. Gubrium, pp. 99–222. Springfield: Charles C Thomas.

Ross, J.-K. 1974c. Successful aging in a French retirement residence. In *Successful Aging,* ed. E. Pfeiffer. Proceedings of the Duke University Center for the Study of Gerontology. Durham: Duke University Press.

Ross, J-K. 1975. Social borders: Definitions of diversity. *Current Anthropology* 16: 53–72.

Ross, J.-K. 1977. *Old People, New Lives: Community Creation in a Retirement Residence.* Chicago: University of Chicago Press.

Ruse, Michael. 1979. *Sociobiology: Sense of Nonsense.* Boston: D. Reidel/Pallas Paperbacks.

Sahlins, M. 1960. Evolution: general and specific. In *Evolution and Culture,* eds. M. Sahlins and E. Service. Ann Arbor: University of Michigan Press.

Sahlins, M. 1972. *Stone Age Economics.* Chicago: Aldine.

Sanday, P. R. 1974. Female status in the public domain.

In *Women, Culture and Society,* eds. M. Z. Rosaldo and L. Lamphere, pp. 189–206. Stanford: Stanford University Press.

Sankar, A. 1981. The conquest of solitude: Singlehood and old age in traditional Chinese society. In *Dimensions: Aging, Culture and Health,* ed. C. L. Fry, pp. 65–84. New York: Praeger (a J. F. Bergin Book).

Schaie, K. W. 1965. A general model for the study of developmental problems. *Psychological Bulletin* 64: 92–107.

Schepler-Hughes, N. 1983. Deposed kings: The demise of the rural Irish gerontocracy. In *Growing Old in Different Cultures,* ed. J. Sokolovsky, pp. 131–146. Belmont: Wadsworth.

Schulz, C. M. 1980. Age, sex and death anxiety in a middle-class American community. In *Aging in Culture and Society: Comparative Viewpoints and Strategies,* ed. C. L. Fry, pp. 239–252. New York: Praeger (a J. F. Bergin Book).

Shahrani, M. N. 1981. Growing in respect: Aging among the Kirghiz of Afghanistan. In *Other Ways of Growing Old,* eds. P. T. Amoss and S. Harrell, pp. 175–192. Stanford: Stanford University Press.

Shanas, E., et al. 1968. *Old People in Three Industrial Societies.* New York: Atherton Press.

Sheehan, T. 1976. Senior esteem as a factor in socioeconomic complexity. *Gerontologist* 16: 433–440.

Shelton, A. 1965. Igbo aging and eldership: Notes for gerontologists and others. *Gerontologist* 5: 2–23.

Shelton, A. 1972. The aged and eldership among the Igbo. In *Aging and Modernization,* eds. D. Cowgill and L. D. Holmes, pp. 31–50. New York: Appleton-Century Crofts.

Silverman, P., and Maxwell, R. J. 1978. How do I respect thee? Let me count the ways: Deference towards elderly men and women. *Behavioral Science Research* 13: 91–108.

Simmons, L. W. 1945. *The Role of the Aged in Primitive Society.* New Haven: Yale University Press.

Simmons, L. W. 1960. Aging in preindustrial societies. In *Handbook of Social Gerontology,* ed. C. Tibbits. Chicago: University of Chicago Press.

Sinnott, J. D. 1977. Sex-role inconsistency, biology and successful aging. *Gerontologist* 17: 459–463.

Smedly, A. 1974. Women of Udu: Survival in a harsh land. In *Many Sisters: Women in Cross-Cultural Perspective,* ed. C. J. Matthhiasson, pp. 205–228. New York: Free Press.

Smith, R. J., et al. 1961. Cultural differences in the concept of time. In *Aging and Leisure,* ed. R. Kleemeier. New York: Oxford University Press.

Sokolovsky, J., and Cohen, C. 1978. The cultural meaning of personal networks for the inner city elderly. *Urban Anthropology* 7: 323–324.

Sokolovsky, J., and Cohen, C. 1981. Being old in the inner city: Support systems of the S.R.O. aged. In *Dimensions: Aging, Culture and Health,* ed. C. L. Fry, pp. 163–184. New York: Praeger (a J. F. Bergin Book).

Spencer, P. 1965. *The Samburu: A Study of Gerontocracy of a Nomadic Tribe.* Berkeley: University of California Press.

Spencer, P. 1976. Opposing streams and the gerontocratic ladder: Two models of age organization in East Africa. *Man* 11: 153–174.

Stenning, D. J. 1958. Household viability among the pastoral Fulani. In *The Developmental Cycle in Domestic Groups*, ed. A. Goody. Cambridge: Cambridge University Press.

Stewart, F. H. 1977. *Fundamentals of Age-Group Systems.* New York: Academic Press.

Sussman, M. B. 1965. Relationship of adult children with their parents. In *Social Structure and the Family*, eds. E. Shanas and G. F. Streib. Englewood Cliffs: Prentice Hall.

Sussman, M. B. 1976. The family life of old people. In *The Handbook of Aging and the Social Sciences*, eds. R. H. Binstock and E. Shanas, pp. 218–243. New York: Van Nostrand Reinhold.

Teski, M. 1981. *Living Together: An Ethnography of a Retirement Hotel.* Washington, D.C.: University Press of America.

Teski, M. 1983. The evolution of aging: Ecology and the elderly in the modern world. In *Growing Old in Different Cultures*, ed. J. Sokolovsky, pp. 14–23. Belmont: Wadsworth.

Trela, J. E., and Sokolovsky, J. H. 1979. Culture, ethnicity and policy for the aged. In *Ethnicity and Aging*, eds. D. E. Gelfand and A. J. Kutzik, pp. 117–136. New York: Springer Publishing Company.

Townsend, P. 1957. *The Family Life of Old People.* London: Routledge and Kegan Paul.

Van Arsdale, P. W. 1981a. Disintegration of the ritual support network among aged Asmat hunter-gatherers of New Guinea. In *Dimensions: Aging, Culture and Health*, ed. C. L. Fry, pp. 33–46. New York: Praeger (a J. F. Bergin Book).

Van Arsdale, P. W. 1981b. The elderly Asmat of New Guinea. In *Other Ways of Growing Old*, eds. P. T. Amoss and S. Harrell, pp. 111–124. Stanford: Stanford University Press.

Van Gennep, A. 1960 (original, 1909). *The Rites of Passage.* Chicago: University of Chicago Press.

Wallerstein, E. 1979. *The Capitalist World-Economy.* New York: Cambridge University Press.

Warner, W. L. 1958 (original, 1937). *A Black Civilization: A Study of an Australian Tribe.* New York: Harper and Row.

Washburn, S. L. 1981. Longevity in primates. In *Aging: Biology and Behavior*, eds. J. L. McGaugh and S. B. Kiesler, pp. 2–10. New York: Academic Press.

Weatherford, J. M. 1981. *Tribes on the Hill.* New York: Rawson, Wade, Inc.

Weiss, K. 1973. Model life tables for anthropological populations. *Society for American Archeology.* Memoir, No. 27.

Weiss, K. 1981. Evolutionary perspectives on human aging. In *Other Ways of Growing Old*, eds. P. T. Amoss and S. Harrell, pp. 25–58. Stanford: Stanford University Press.

Wellin, E., and Boyer, E. 1979. Adjustments of black and white elderly to the same adaptive niche. In *The Ethonography of Old Age*, ed. J. Keith. Special issue of *Anthropological Quarterly* 52: 39–48.

Werner, D. 1981. Gerontocracy among the Mekranoti of Central Brazil. *Anthropological Quarterly* 54: 15–27.

Whitten, N. E., and Whitten, D. C. 1972. Social strategies and social relationships. In *Annual Reviews in Anthropology*, pp. 247–271. Palo Alto: Annual Reviews Inc.

Williams, G. 1980. Warriors no more. In *Aging in Culture and Society: Comparative Viewpoints and Strategies*, ed. C. L. Fry, pp. 110–111. New York: Praeger (a J. F. Bergin Book).

Williams, G. C. 1957. Pleiotropy, natural selection, and the evolution of senescence. *Evolution* 2: 389–411.

Williams, R. 1970. *American Society: Sociological Interpretation.* New York: Alfred A. Knopf.

Woodcock, G. 1944. The tyranny of the clock. *Politics* 3: 265–267.

10
THE ECOLOGY OF AGING

Rick J. Scheidt
and
Paul G. Windley
Kansas State University

INTRODUCTION

Though still relatively youthful, research on the ecology of aging has proliferated at a rapid rate. There have been significant advances in the past decade in the understanding of the dynamics by which elderly individuals and processes of aging are affected by objectively and subjectively defined features of the physical and psychosocial environment. The phenomena of interest have included environmental perception and cognition, environmental preferences, community and neighborhood contexts of aging, housing for the elderly, and the adaptation of individuals to demands posed by the interaction of the environmental and intrapersonal changes that accompany aging.

The goal of this brief chapter is to offer an evaluative review of recent selective conceptual and empirical advances in the ecology of aging. It includes material published largely since the excellent, lengthier reviews of environment-aging research provided by Lawton (1977, 1980) and is intended to provide some continuity with his work. The historical perspective on the development of ecological research on aging has been provided by other sources (Lawton and Nahemow, 1973).

Specifically, the discussion is divided into three major sections. First, reflections are offered regarding the presence and influence of current theoretical perspectives that guide research in the ecology of aging. Second, exemplary profiles of innovative, on-going environmental research programs at varying levels of analysis and application are appraised. Finally, recommendations are offered that might usefully guide future research and interventive efforts on selected fronts of aging-environment relations.

Prior to discussing these issues, it would be appropriate to outline briefly the major elements of ecological aging research assumed here. The ecology of aging, like the broader field of behavioral ecology, is a general perspective on research (Willems, 1977) rather than a specific theory or method. The conceptual and procedural pluralism in this area makes it increasingly difficult and constraining to derive a single, consensually satisfying definition of its elements and dynamics. Definitions serve as useful orienting devices, however, to suggest attributes that organize the key elements and issues of the field. Lawton and Nahemow's (1973) definition is useful in this regard. These authors define the ecology of aging as "a system of continual adaptation in which both the organism and the environment change over time in a nonrandom manner" (p. 621).

First, this definition contains three "sine qua non" units of study—the organism, the environment, and, by implication, behavior

—the interactions between them. In much of the literature, these terms continue to be separated for analytical convenience, though the practice offends some theorists on epistemological grounds. There is much diversity in the specific meanings attached to these units when they are employed as first-order constructs, as will soon become apparent.

Second, the statement reflects a holistic and molar focus in that much emphasis is placed upon the "mutual and interdependent relations" between individuals, environmental contexts, and behavior (Willems, 1977). This means that individuals and environments are mutually capable of eliciting responses from one another. In a stricter sense, argument continues among competing theoretical models regarding the causal implications (e.g., reciprocal vs. unidirectional causal models) of this assumption of simultaneous influence.

Third, for most researchers, "adaptation" is the "raison d'être" for the study of the ecology of aging. Broadly, adaptation refers to the processes governing the efforts of the aging individual to respond successfully to both endogenous and exogenous changes (needs and demands) occurring over time. Thus, the study of the ecology of aging is, to a large extent, the attempt to understand the systemic orchestration of myriad personal and environmental attributes, processes, and outcomes directed toward this end.

Fourth, research in the field is largely mission-oriented; that is, the understanding gained from the study of person-environment interactions is directed toward interventive ends. For many in the field, this has meant using information gained about person-environment fit to improve the habitability of environments for older individuals (e.g., Lawton, 1980). The continuing trend, spawned by the historical emphases upon the study of natural systems, is to select everyday, real-world environments and situations for investigation (Scheidt and Schaie, 1978; Willems, 1973), which may then become targets for intervention.

Finally, research on the ecology of aging is not isolated within any single psychological subdiscipline; theoretical and empirical contributions emanate from environmental, developmental, clinical, social, and community quarters, among others. This healthy eclecticism is marked by a tendency for researchers "to borrow concepts, methods, and hypotheses freely, with little sense of preciousness about boundaries between disciplines" (Willems, 1973, p. 207).

RECENT THEORETICAL TRENDS

At the outset, it must be noted that there is very little theory-guided research in the ecology of aging. The conceptual efforts that do exist are of two types. On one front, a few prominent middle-range theories and perspectives continue to exert influence on ecological thinking, particularly in the physical environmental domain. On another front, a number of looser but rich alternative perspectives have been recently forwarded, with implications for widening the scope of aging-environment relations. A few of these contributions rely on alternative metatheoretical assumptions that should open new arenas for research.

MIDDLE RANGE THEORIES

There is a continuing need in the field for middle-range theory of effective scale—theory that is more modest and precise than grand theory, yet accommodative of broader meanings of environment, behavior, and intervention (Schooler and Rubenstein, 1980). The relative lack of such theory has been partially attributed to the youthful, evolutionary status of research on aging and to its past emphasis upon descriptive (as opposed to explanatory) documentation of age-related behavioral deficits (Lawton, 1982); it is also recognized that necessary prototheoretical work remains—e.g., the development of taxonomies for sorting out the basic units of environment and behavior (Scheidt and Schaie, 1978; Willems, 1973; Windley and Scheidt, 1980a) as well as efforts to map the broader and looser orientations that might guide future formal theory development (Rowles and Ohta, in press).

Some prominent middle-range theories do exist, however, and it is appropriate to appraise the status of three of these since the time they were last reviewed (Lawton, 1977). These are as follows: Kahana's person-environment congruence model, Lawton and Nahemow's adaptation theory, and Schooler's stress perspective (see Lawton, Windley, and Byerts, 1982, for a fuller discussion of these and other approaches).

Kahana's Congruence Model

Kahana's congruence model remains the most articulated of these three approaches. This model characterizes the optimal environment as one that offers maximum congruence between individual needs and environmental press. Incongruence between needs and press results from changes in one's life situation (e.g., movement to new housing or institutionalization) or from altered needs or capacities (Kahana, 1982). Adaptive behavior is the mechanism through which congruence is achieved or maintained, either by altering press, one's hierarchy of needs, or (for those who are able) by leaving the field. Goodness of fit is antecedent to, not synonymous with, well-being, the primary outcome variable.

Congruence is related to outcome via three distinct models. The cumulative difference model considers instances in which need-press mismatch is cumulative and continuous; the critical differences model assumes mismatch is problematic or detrimental beyond a certain critical point or range; and the optimal congruence model (after Helson's adaptation model) considers complete congruence harmful, with moderate deviations producing positive outcomes. Alternative conceptions of directionality are also posited within each model, i.e., non-, one-, and two-directional differences. The non-directional model assumes that both excessive environmental supply and demand (relative to needs) have equally deleterious effects on experienced outcome; the one-directional model assumes that only "undersupply" has negative effects; the two-directional model assumes that positive (oversupply) and negative (undersupply) have different effects, e.g., anxiety and apathy, respectively.

Using commensurate dimensions of individual preferences (P) and environmental attributes (E), Kahana, Liang, and Felton (1980) evaluated the association between the three alternative cumulative difference congruence models and morale (the outcome variable) among 124 well residents of three urban homes for the aged. A modified difference score approach was used to measure the P-E fit. Though complex, the results showed that the P-E incongruence for particular attributes explained a significant proportion of variance in morale, even with the P-E effects removed. Prediction varied by models, with incongruence in congregate living and impulse control being significant non-directional model predictors and segregate living an additional predictor in the two-directional model. Furthermore, it was found that, "depending on the dimensions involved, either an over or undersupply may have a positive effect on morale" (Kahana, Liang, and Felton, 1980, p. 594). At present, the two-directional model, by permitting the specification of different kinds of P-E fit and well-being, allows greater understanding of the ways in which fit produces positive outcome.

Eva and Boaz Kahana have recently outlined promising implications of the general congruence model for future research and intervention with more diverse older populations and environmental spheres (Kahana and Kahana, 1979; in press). Their current research extends the model to the competent or well-aged, particularly focusing upon those "adventurous aged" seeking new environmental experiences (e.g., voluntary relocation); these are persons holding a sense of optimism about personal future outcomes. A resulting typology of successful relocaters may be found in Kahana and Kahana (in press). New information from those seeking this "environmental discontinuity" should prove useful to examining the range and variety of P-E fit models (Kahana and Kahana, in press). Specific conceptual implications include (1) using the model to study prospective dynamics of P-E fit, i.e., discrepancies between anticipated outcomes vs. actual outcomes relative to increases and decreases in fit; (2) generation of different, population-appropriate dimensions of commensurate P-E congruence and outcome variables; (3) consideration of personal and environmental moderators of congruence-outcome relations; and (4) using the model as a possible index of stress resulting from lack of P-E congruence, as well as examining adaptive strategies linked to specific types and levels of incongruence. Interventive implications revolve around the provision of environmentally oriented psychotherapeutic strategies, some of which are realized in practice. The most prominent examples are the development of strategies for dealing with relocation stress (Pastalan and Bourestom, 1975) and depression resulting from P-E incongruence (Wetzel, 1978).

Although Kahana's theory has stimulated much thinking and research since its development, much work remains, e.g., testing the adequacy of alternative P-E congruence models for diverse populations. This approach holds promise as a useful heuristic device for intervention efforts (Kahana and Kahana, in press).

Other researchers also operate within a congruence perspective, though not associated with the Kahana model. Frances and Abraham Carp have conducted significant research on the Campbell, Converse, and Rogers (1976) model in an attempt to explain the greater incongruence between objective indicants of life-circumstances and self-reported domain and overall life-satisfaction for older (over 55 years) compared to younger adults. Equity (the difference between deserved and actual resources) served as a significant predictor of satisfaction at both levels for three samples of California older adults (Carp, Carp, and Millsap, in press). In related research, personal competence and situational deprivation were also found to be more significant predictors of satisfaction than was age and significantly modified the relationship between objective indices and satisfaction (Carp and Carp, 1981).

Lawton and Nahemow's Adaptation Model

Lawton and Nahemow (1973) proposed a model of adaptation and aging based upon an interactionist model of behavior [(B = (f) P, E, P × E)]. "Competence" and "environmental press" represent more limited aspects of the person and environment, respectively. Adaptive behavior is the behavioral outcome of primary interest (external criterion), though Lawton (1982) recognizes internal outcomes (morale, happiness). Competence is defined as a profile of a person's capacities, including biological health, sensation-perception, motoric behavior, and cognition. Environmental press consists of challenges or demands that activate behavior. The model assumes that individuals intrinsically strive to maintain a relatively steady state or adaptation level between external stimulation and internal sensitivity of sensory, perceptual, and cognitive states. It is also assumed that environmental stimulation slightly above or below personal adaptation level will be experienced as enjoyable, with more severe deviations experienced as deprivation or overload. The magnitude of one's adaptation level and of deviation experienced as positive affect partially vary as a positive function of personal level of competence. Broadly, the theory specifies that those who operate at higher levels of competence can adapt to a wider range of environmental press and have greater likelihood of experiencing favorable adaptive outcomes. Those of lower competence will experience a greater range of press in negative terms, exhibiting a narrower range of adaptive behavior. Adaptive behavior is judged against normative and/or teleological criteria and is mediated by both personality style and environmental cognition.

Direct work by its originators has consisted largely of theoretical elaboration of the model (Lawton, 1982; Lawton and Nahemow, 1973). Propositions derived from the model receive direct support from Lawton's own work, as well as indirectly from other gerontological research. For instance, Lawton (1982) cites numerous examples of gerontological research supporting the association of lowered competence with heightened vulnerability to environmental press (the "environmental docility" hypothesis). Despite the breadth of support for generalizations emerging from the model, little research to date has been conducted with the intent of directly testing the formal relations of the model. Greater conceptual and operational articulation of major constructs (environmental press, adaptation level, optimal range of stimulation) may facilitate such testing (Lawton, 1982). Perhaps because of this need for refinement, there has been little recent research designed to test its efficacy for diverse populations and contexts (Kiyak, 1980). This is an unfortunate research gap, considering the suggested range of personal and physical environmental qualities.

The implications of the model for intervention have not been overlooked (Lawton, 1981; Lawton and Nahemow, 1973), and this is perhaps its most important current contribution. The adaptation theory suggests alternative ways of organizing ecological interventive targeting and strategies. The most typical target is the older person who behaves maladaptively or experiences negative affect caused by decreases in overall competence or changes in the physical environment that are excessively depriving or taxing. Targeting might be directed at the individual (elevating competence) and/or the environment (reducing environmental press). Lawton (1981) has usefully elaborated the implications of the adaptation model for physical environmental design, particularly product design, that is intended to serve prosthetic, communicative, and enrichment functions for older persons.

Schooler's Stress Theoretical Perspective

Schooler's stress theoretical perspective (1978, 1980, 1982) is based upon Lazarus' cognitive theory of stress and coping (Lazarus, 1966; Lazarus, Averill, and Opton, 1974). Schooler advocates that the Lazarus model might be usefully applied to gerontological research because of the increased vulnerability of older persons to social and physical environmental hazards, as well as to provide a theory "for predicting better than we have to date the success or failure of environmental interventions" (Schooler and Rubenstein, 1980, p. 120). Lazarus' model holds that individuals engage in a persistent but fluid evaluation of "stimulus configurations" or situations to assess their potential threat value. Situations may be perceived as harmful, beneficial, or irrelevant (primary appraisal). When they are appraised as harmful or threatening, individu-

als review the range of coping alternatives that are available in their adaptive arsenals for removing the harmful stimuli (secondary appraisal). This process eventuates in some form of coping behavior (direct or intrapsychic). Both primary and secondary appraisals depend upon a variety of psychological and situational features. Responses may produce positive or negative outcomes, moderated by a variety of ecological factors (Schooler, 1978).

Schooler has applied the model, or, more accurately, terms of the model, in evaluating retest data on a sample of 521 movers and nonmovers drawn from a larger national sample of some 4,000 noninstitutionalized elderly in the U.S. (Schooler, 1975). The data were not initially collected with the intention of testing Lazarus' stress theory (Schooler, 1982). In various studies, Schooler (1978, 1982) examined the impact of three potential stressors (environmental change, residential mobility, major life events) on health and/ or morale as specific adaptive outcomes. Consistent with the theory, he also examined the degree to which both social support (club membership, confidant) and ecological factors (density of social structures) moderated the stress and health/morale relations. These data confirmed the general relations among terms in the theory (Schooler, 1982) and illustrated that the presence of social supports may affect the likelihood of situations being defined as threatening (primary appraisal) and may act as a significant coping resource (secondary appraisal).

By his own admission, Schooler's approach needs much refinement, including more attention to threat appraisal processes, to psychological (as opposed to solely social) buffers of threat, and to change over time (Schooler, 1982). It serves as a middle-range theoretical approach of potential value in framing often theory-bare evaluation research on the efficacy of environmental interventions (Schooler and Rubenstein, 1980) and illustrates the potential viability of nongerontological theory for aging-environment research. Moreover, the stress theory approach has provided a major conceptual framework for other research that assesses the relation between everyday environmental stressors and the adaptive responding of older community-based residents (Scheidt and Windley, 1981).

RECENT CONCEPTUAL CONTRIBUTIONS

Theoretical creativity in the field is at an interesting plateau, marked by increasing reflection about the appropriateness of alternative paradigms for present and future research (Howell, 1980; Howell, in press; Overton and Reese, 1977; Rowles and Ohta, in press; Windley and Scheidt, 1980a). This trend occurs for a variety of reasons, and has produced some new and promising conceptual approaches.

At the broadest conceptual level, Overton and Reese (1977) outlined three general models to guide thinking and research in man–environment relations applicable to the ecology of aging. These models emerge from alternative "paradigms" in the Kuhnian sense, i.e., from distinct metatheoretical perspectives that establish differing exclusive criteria for the form and content of formal theory, methodology, inference, and intervention. These models are as follows:

1. "Man as reducible to environment," encompassing operant and situational approaches that place greater stress upon external causality and a molecular, antecedent-consequent reductionism
2. "Environment as reducible to man," embracing psychological or phenomenal representations of the environment
3. "Man and environment as interdependent systems," entailing a holistic focus on reciprocal P-E influence, illustrated in specific theories of adaptation.

The primary contribution of the Overton and Reese (1977) treatise is to make these models explicit, with the hope of stimulating deliberate construction of alternative ecological perspectives that might compete for scientific acceptance through empirical channels. Current aging-environment theories fall largely within the third model, though much of the empirical research generated by them leans heavily upon modes of statistical inference that are more appropriately suited to the assumptions of the first model.

The most provocative alternative conceptual suggestions to date are provided by Howell (1980, in press) and Rowles (1978a, 1978b, in press). Rowles has provided a more formal model, derived from an intensive study of the "geographical experience" of a small number of older persons. For Rowles, "geographical experience" is the "totality of the individual's involvement within the spaces and places of his life" (1978a, p. xviii). This humanistic, geographical perspective is decidedly holistic, stressing modes of experience for the older individual that involve action, orientation, feeling, and fantasy. The major technique of inference is "interpersonal knowing," whereby the investigator sifts the experiences of the older individual in a kind of participant dialogue at the level of everyday events. Rowles' (1978a) formal model posits that each individual strives to maintain consistency between personal capabilities and environmental opportunities: This "adjustment results from the effort to maintain harmony or consonance between who he is as a person (identity) and the manner in which, through his geographical experience, he relates to his geographical life-space" (p. 192).

Rowles' model is clearly unique in its humanistic emphasis. It is the only formal approach to examine the possible status of environments in fantasy, including reminiscence and the projected future. This suggests new areas of research on the ecology of reminiscence and self-concept. Moreover, it has proven to be of benefit for examining long-standing gerontological issues such as attachment to place (Rowles, 1980) and the dynamics of social support (Rowles, in press).

The position of Howell (1980, in press) emerges from a similar concern with the processes by which individuals attach meaning to the (built) environment. Howell posits that a better understanding of older person-environment transactions can be gained by taking account of the influence of individual psycho-environmental histories (stored residual experiences that influence attitudes, perceptions, social interactions) and current uses of the physical environment (Howell, 1980). Moreover, she holds that stored environmental experiences may serve as salient hypothetical constructs (employed in past–present compar-isons) that moderate the content and quality of current environmental transaction and serve to test one's contextual personal identity. Adaptation may have a heavier intrapsychic component than current theories recognize, involving a continuous process of contextual and historical matching. Howell (in press) posits that (1) the meaning of place is intrinsi-cally interwoven with meanings attached to life, to self, and to specific events; (2) that place definitions may be effectively redefined when utilized over time in reminiscence, life-reviews, and problem-solving operations; (3) that place meaning may be examined through contextually specific meanings of self; (4) that environmental learning and memory, involv-ing greater emphasis on self-concept, may not be adequately described by principles that de-scribe other forms of learning and memory; and (5) that attributes of self-concept may function in parallel to attributes of place, changing over time in different ways for differ-ent populations.

Howell's perspective, like that of Rowles, is very close to Overton and Reese's (1977) second model ("environment reducible to man") and shares much in common with the dialectical environmental position (Windley and Scheidt, 1980a). The distinct paradig-matic quality of Howell's position is under-scored by the direct criticisms she has launched against the inadequacies she per-ceives in "antecedent-consequent" develop-mental models and the explanatory impotence of quantitative techniques of analysis (Howell, in press). Her position is most promising for suggesting the possible primacy of environ-mental schema in moderating or producing behavior over time. In this respect, the posi-tion is compatible with, and should draw aid from, Overton's (1976) cognitive view of envi-ronmental ontogeny, which deals with the manner in which environmental structures may be mapped into developing organismic structures. The "meaning of place," though vaguely defined, has immediate interventive implications for planners attempting to deter-mine those elements of the environment that should be retained or replaced (Howell, 1980). It also has implications, though unexamined,

for holistic clinical and counseling work with older individuals.

EMPIRICAL RESEARCH

Only systematic, illustrative, and well-estab-lished research that has been reported since the publication of the last handbook will be reviewed here. The research selected departs from traditional conceptualizations and meth-odologies and has promise for impact in areas heretofore neglected in ecology and aging re-search. It has also been our intent to focus on macroenvironmental issues as opposed to specific issues in housing or institutional facili-ties.

Social and Physical Ecology of Neighborhood: M. P. Lawton

Few have conducted research in ecology and aging as far-reaching as that of M. Powell Lawton. His studies range from design, man-agement, and policy issues in housing and in-stitutions for the elderly to assessment of city and community attributes that affect the well-being of older persons (see Lawton, 1977; Lawton and Nahemow, 1973; and Lawton, Newcomer, and Byerts, 1976). Of considerable significance is Lawton's (1980) recent compre-hensive review of research on macroenviron-mental attributes of communities and their as-sociation with social and psychological aspects of older populations. Those interested in el-derly housing issues should consult Lawton (1975) and Lawton and Hoover (1981).

Lawton, Nahemow, and Yeh (1980) found that physical attributes of neighborhoods (community size, crime risk, neighborhood ac-tivity, neighborhood resources and activity, and degree of age segregation) were signifi-cantly associated with aspects of well-being such as housing satisfaction, friendship behav-ior, activity participation, motility, morale, and contact with relatives. Generally speak-ing, quiet neighborhoods located in small and middle-sized communities with a low per-ceived risk of crime were conducive to active and satisfying lives for older people (Lawton, Nahemow, and Yeh, 1980). Specifically, cross-sectional and longitudinal findings from additional analyses regarding victimization and fear of crime indicated that the latter are central in determining psychological well-being (Lawton and Yaffe, 1980). Actual crime rate and victimization affected well-being only if perceived fear of crime intervened. Community size affected well-being only indirectly through these crime-related variables. These variables were minimally associated with the size of the social space and the activity outside the housing site (Lawton and Yaffe, 1980). It is concluded from these studies that environmentally based community interventions such as planned housing, favorable neighborhood location, and crime control can enhance well-being among the elderly.

Social area factors such as racial composition, dwelling ownership status, housing (type, quality, and value), and age composition accounted for significant degrees of variance in activity participation, housing satisfaction, friendship behavior, and motility, but not in family interaction or morale (Lawton and Nahemow, 1979). Higher neighborhood-age density was consistently associated with the well-being of housing tenants in the neighborhood, whereas neighborhood racial characteristics had minimal effects. However, a positive association existed between racial homogeniety of housing tenants and well-being (Lawton and Nahemow, 1979).

In slightly over half of these studies, the environmental features of neighborhoods and surrounding areas accounted for more variance in well-being than did the personal characteristics of older people. Although the data were correlational, it seems reasonable to hypothesize that the provision of favorable neighborhood attributes as described in these studies will lead to a higher overall well-being among older residents.

Lawton's work raises the issue of the differential impact of perceived vs. objective measurements of environmental attributes on well-being. Although Lawton (1978) has shown that perceived vs. objective environments are related statistically, it is not clear under what conditions one or the other may be the most closely associated with dimensions of well-being. Additional research questions include: Do ecological attributes at the neighborhood scale have greater impact on well-being than county

or regional factors? Does this impact vary from rural to urban settings? How do different types of housing affect older people living in differing neighborhood contexts? In a practical vein, Lawton's research cautions us against overgeneralized and mistargeted environmental intervention programs initiated by designers, planners, social agencies, and environmental managers and argues for a more discriminating definition and assessment of the ecological attributes that affect the elderly.

Ecology of Perceived Neighborhoods: V. Regnier

Complementary and countervailing relationships between the objective physical neighborhood, the perceived neighborhood, and the actual use of the neighborhood by older people have been the guiding principles in work by Regnier (1981a). Cognitive mapping is the primary method he uses to assess the perceived neighborhood. Conceptually, this technique implies that within each individual there is a neuro-psychological representation of elements of the physical environment that results from adaptive interactions with these elements (Regnier, 1981a). Successful adaptation facilitates basic orientation and navigation in time and space and fosters strong emotional ties to specific environmental settings. Cognitive representations are elicited from older individuals by asking them to sketch their urban neighborhood boundaries on blank sheets of paper and on cartographically accurate maps and to locate important neighborhood services and elements within these boundaries. These cartographic representations are later overlayed with other subjects' maps to form a consensus map for a given group of elderly individuals. Consensus maps are then compared to actual neighborhood boundaries and amenity locations (Regnier, 1981a).

Cognitive representations of neighborhoods have been found to relate to the percentage and frequency of trips taken by older residents within their neighborhood boundaries as well as to critical distances to, and utilization of, community services (Regnier, 1981a; Regnier and Rausch, 1980). Neighborhood maps also reflect perceptions of high crime areas, and, when compared to actual crime locations, show remarkable similarities (Regnier and Hamburger, 1978). The size of the perceived neighborhood maps reflects the shrinking life space of older people (Stea, 1970) that results from their reduced mobility (Regnier, 1975). The size and configuration of cognitive maps, in turn, are affected by a broad range of social and environmental delimiters and incentives. Environmental factors such as street traffic, topography, bus routes, and number of services in a neighborhood, together with such social factors as population density, crime rates, and ethnic mix, encouraged or discouraged the inclusion of certain areas within the perceived neighborhood (Regnier, 1976).

Regnier's most current studies have shown that neighborhood types, based on ethnic composition, wealth, and housing type, are now discernible in cognitive maps and contribute to further developments in policy, planning, and management of neighborhood settings (Regnier, 1981b; in press). Regnier's research demonstrates that the local neighborhood is a meaningful and definable concept both theoretically and practically for understanding the ecology of aging.

Much of the theoretical underpinnings of environmental perception and cognitive mapping research is based on the early work of Lynch (1960) and has never been developed into a fully articulated theory; however, evidence continues to show the theoretical and practical utility of this type of research. Future research efforts should be directed toward the following questions: Are the elements of neighborhood maps drawn by elderly individuals different from those of younger people? Do the elements of maps at the neighborhood scale differ from maps of cities? What is the long-term significance of cognitive mapping for coping and adaptation to environments and for general well-being among urban and nonurban elderly? Can the symbolic meaning attributed to elements in cognitive maps be identified separately from the more utilitarian or functional qualities of these same elements?

Rural and Small Town Ecology: P. Windley and R. Scheidt

Much has been learned recently about the ecology of the rural elderly through a five-year, ongoing research program investigating the mental health and well-being of older people living in small rural towns (Scheidt, 1981; Windley, 1981). This research has been investigating the effects of personal variables and perceived ecological/architectural and psychosocial attributes of 18 small towns (2,500 population or less) on a multidimensional definition of well-being among 989 older town residents. The well-being domain includes housing satisfaction, contact with friends and relatives, mobility, functional health, availability of a confidant(e), feelings of security, and activity participation. Also included are three measures of psychopathological symptomatology. Well-being is hypothesized to be indirectly affected by ecological/architectural factors, including perceived sensory stimulation and cognitive legibility of neighborhood and community, residential comfort, privacy, adaptability and control over residence, sociality of settings, community accessibility, population density, the degree of attachment to a setting, and community and residential quality or aesthetic appeal. Well-being is hypothesized to be affected directly by three psychosocial dimensions: (1) relationship, or the degree of expressed satisfaction with opportunities for social relations in the community; (2) personal development, or the degree of expressed satisfaction with community attributes that enhance personal growth and self-esteem; and (3) maintenance and change, or the rated satisfaction with community resources necessary for the survival of the town (Blake, Weigl and Perloff, 1975; Moos, 1974a).

The study utilizes a 3×3 sampling matrix composed of three degrees of county rurality (assessed by a county-based rurality index) and cross-classified with three town-size categories (populations ranging from 0 to 500, from 501 to 1500, and from 1501 to 2500). This framework permits a study of older residents in small to larger towns located in more rural to more urban counties (Scheidt and Windley, in press; Windley and Scheidt, 1980b).

Stepwise multiple-regression analyses on the factor-analyzed well-being domain against all predictor domains has shown that five factors are predicted most strongly by demographic variables, five by psychosocial variables, and seven by ecological/architectural variables. These analyses demonstrate the importance of environmental attributes, particularly ecological/architectural attributes, in the study of well-being among the rural elderly (Scheidt, 1981; Windley, 1981).

A subsequent path analysis to predict mental health for residents of all 18 communities shows that community involvement and community satisfaction have direct predictive effects, as do the age of the respondent and satisfaction with architectural features of the dwelling unit (Windley and Scheidt, 1982). The degree to which environmental barriers hinder older residents from accessing town activities and the degree to which older people feel they have high environmental jurisdiction and control at the residential level were also found to have direct effects. Indirect predictive effects were found for length of residence, years of education, and the degree to which the community is perceived as a place where people keep to themselves most of the time or where the primary emphasis is upon youth.

This path model demonstrates the advantages of a more ecological and multiple-domain (demographic, psychosocial, and ecological/architectural) approach over a single-domain approach for understanding the factors that affect the mental health of the rural elderly. Substantively, the model generally supports the position that the older people who are most involved in community affairs are psychologically happier, healthier individuals. They are also more generally satisfied with their small communities.

A short-term longitudinal study of four taxonomic groups selected from the original sample and varying in social and psychological well-being is in progress. The central thrust of this phase of the study is to investigate the coping strategies employed by these groups in dealing with perceived and actual demands of everyday behavior settings. Data gathered in this study should assist environmental designers, managers, and mental health professionals to understand better the microecology of the small community and its effect on the well-being of older residents (Scheidt and Windley, 1981).

Future research on the ecology of the rural elderly should address at least the following questions: To what extent do the effects of environmental attributes identified in small towns apply to attributes in larger metropolitan areas? What other behavioral outcomes, such as migration or patterns of institutionalization, may be affected by ecological/architectural or psychosocial town attributes? How can current population-based definitions of "rural" be augmented to include the obvious environmental and social differences of rural areas?

Ecology of Experiential Space: G. Rowles

The research of Rowles (1978a,b; 1981a) demonstrates the importance of the emerging field of humanistic geography for the study of the ecology of older people. Through "experiential field work" (a form of participant observation), small groups of older people were intensively studied over a period of two to three years to ascertain the meaning of geographical experience within the autobiographical context of their lives (Rowles, 1978a). The general hypothesis emerging from this work (Rowles, 1981a) proposes that, as a person ages, there is a gradual substitution of vicarious environmental experience (via fantasy) for physical environmental participation (action). As this substitution takes place, transitions in old people's orientation within space and in their feelings for space occur and include an intensified concern with the proximal environment (spaces close to home) and an increased emotional investment in places of significance to their life history (Rowles, 1981a). The most ecological component of this proximal environment is the residential *surveillance zone,* which includes the immediate spaces surrounding the residential unit, primarily those visible through windows from within the dwelling unit. This zone serves as a prime source of meaning, being a link between the old person within the residential unit and the world outside and providing a sense of ongoing participation in events (Rowles, 1981b). The surveillance zone has developmental significance in that the same zone during childhood is comprised of the "play area," largely defined and controlled by parents; during old age, when declining capabilities result in increasing vulnerability to environmental demands, the zone takes on a different supportive function (Rowles, 1981b).

The purpose of such life-stage research is to develop a normative developmental trajectory of environmental experience (Rowles, 1981a). For instance, Rowles (1981c) traces such a trajectory through several phases in his analysis of the relocation of Appalachian elderly that resulted in a permanent relocation: departure of children, accommodation, seasonal migration, crisis, relocation, holding on and severance, and finally gradual resolution.

Rowles' phenomenological/inductive approach has richly embellished the early work of Stea (1970), Gelwicks (1970), and Lawton and Nahemow (1973) regarding the shrinking home range of the elderly and their tendency to substitute observation for participation. His elaboration of fieldwork methodology, combined with a "small *N*" approach, provides considerable insight into the significance of older people's attachment to the geographical environment.

Future research should elaborate on the normative trajectory concept and its significance for predicting such issues as migration, life-cycle demand for housing, and historic meaning of buildings and landscapes. Further investigation should differentiate connotative from denotative meanings attributed to geographical environments. Do current substitutions of fantasy for actual environmental participation remain stable over time? How is the intensity of geographical meaning associated with such outcome variables as housing and neighborhood satisfaction, motility, activity participation, and social contact?

RECOMMENDATIONS FOR FUTURE RESEARCH

As with any emerging area of scientific study, the thinking and research on ecological aspects of aging have many significant gaps that remain to be addressed. The following suggestions pertain to those areas in most critical need of future attention:

1. There is a continuing need for articulation of middle-range theories that will guide research in this field. This applies to those theories currently in existence as well as to the development of new models. Few existing theories have stimulated much direct empirical testing. It is apparent that those theories possessing clear and detailed conceptual and operational explication continue to generate the most useful explanatory findings (Kahana, Liang, and Felton, 1980). Much of the gap between theory and empirical research appears to be due to the lack of tractable theory, not just to the descriptive and methodological preoccupations of many researchers. A significant amount of hypothesis-testing research springs from more limited context-specific models that are applicable only for particular populations of elderly individuals.

2. Recent criticism of the structural and explanatory attributes of current meta-models (paradigms) that guide research in this area, along with suggestions for alternative paradigms, serves notice that there are a variety of ways to approach aging-environment relations scientifically (Howell, 1980; in press) Windley and Scheidt 1980a) This trend should be encouraged in the future. Thus far, too few researchers have taken a "step back" from the research process to examine the trade-offs afforded by alternative perspectives on the nature and substance of ecological explanation. It is ironic, as Howell has implied, that a field concerned with the ecological context of behavior should continue to rely upon specific "antecedent-consequent" models, examining person-environment relations with statistical models that often assume unidirectional and linear causality.

3. Though much basic research is conducted within an interventive orientation, there is little evidence of the programmatic application of this research in planned interventions. Furthermore, there are few formal models to guide evaluation and program research. Though the theories reviewed here have interventive implications, none has played a prominent role in the development of evaluation models designed to

test the efficacy of intervention. Thus, it is difficult to assess the degree to which variables and mechanisms posited to produce outcomes are isomorphic and affect outcome alterations (Baltes and Willis, 1977). Basic theory development in ecological aging research might profit from information generated by theory-guided intervention research. As Baltes and Willis (1977) have noted, such a linkage might produce beneficial information about the range of aging-environment relations, as well as about the contextual validity or generalizability of basic research results. This liason between basic research and evaluation research should be developed and strengthened.

4. There is a pressing need for a taxonomy of the ecological environment—descriptive environment-behavior units that can serve as manipulatable attributes in both intervention and research. Some attempts have been made in this direction (Windley and Scheidt, 1980a; Moos, 1974b), but such taxonomies have emerged from unique theoretical perspectives and thus lack consensus, refinement, and continuity (Lawton and Nahemow, 1973).

5. Most ecological research in aging has focused on urban neighborhoods. Larger-scale area and regional ecological attributes are also likely to effect the well-being of older people, but little information of this kind is available. An exception may be the work of Windley and Scheidt (1980b), who have shown that the effects of county-level attributes accounted for differences in mental health and well-being among a sample of rural and small town older people. Researchers should not only study larger-scale environmental influences but should also direct their attention to neighborhood effects in smaller towns and rural areas.

6. The need to examine reciprocal relationships between environment and behavior, that is, those in which ecological attributes serve as both independent and dependent variables, argues for a more holistic methodology. Rowles' (1978b) field work methodology exemplifies the approach advocated by Proshansky (1976), which treats environment and behavior as a unit. Other promising methods that deal with behavior *in situ* include behavior-setting analysis, time-activity-place logs, and photography.

REFERENCES

Baltes, P. B., and Willis, S. L. 1977. Toward psychological theories of aging and development. In *Handbook of the Psychology of Aging*, eds. J. E. Birren and K. W. Schaie, pp. 128–154. New York: Van Nostrand Reinhold.

Blake, B.; Weigl, K.; and Perloff, R. 1975. Perceptions of the ideal community. *J. Appl. Psych.* 60: 612–615.

Campbell, A.; Converse, P.; and Rogers, W. 1976. *The Quality of American Life: Perceptions, Evaluations, and Satisfactions*. New York: Russell Sage.

Carp, F. M., and Carp, A. 1981. Age, deprivation, and personal competence. *Res. on Aging* 3: 279–298.

Carp, F. M.; Carp, A.; and Millsap, R. In press. Equity and satisfaction among the elderly. *Int'l J. Aging Hum. Dev.*

Gelwicks, L. 1970. Home range and use of space by an aging population. In *Spatial Behavior of Older People*, eds. L. A. Pastalan and D. H. Carson, pp. 148–161. Ann Arbor: The University of Michigan.

Howell, S. C. 1980. Environments as hypotheses in human aging research. In *Aging in the 1980's: Psychological Issues*, ed. L. Poon, pp. 424–432. Washington: American Psychological Association.

Howell, S. C. In press. The meaning of place in old age. In *Aging and Milieu: Environmental Perspectives on Growing Old*, eds. G. D. Rowles and R. J. Ohta. New York: Academic Press.

Kahana, E. 1982. A congruence model of person-environment interaction. In *Aging and the Environment: Theoretical Approaches*, eds. M. P. Lawton, P. G. Windley, and T. O. Byerts, pp. 97–121. New York: Springer Publishing Co.

Kahana, E., and Kahana, B. 1979. Person-environment fit revisited: Some new directions for gerontological research and intervention. Revised version of paper, "A congruence model of person-environment fit," presented at meeting of Gerontological Society, Washington, D.C.

Kahana, E., and Kahana, B. In press. Environmental continuity, futurity, and adaptation of the aged. In *Aging and Milieu: Environmental Perspectives on Growing Old*, eds. G. D. Rowles and R. J. Ohta. New York: Academic Press.

Kahana, E.; Liang, J.; and Felton, B. J. 1980. Alternative models of person-environment fit: Prediction of morale in three homes for the aged. *J. Geront.* 35: 584–595.

Kiyak, H. A. 1980. Environmental press and the elderly:

Impact on well-being. Paper presented at American Psychological Association meeting, Montreal, Canada.

Lawton, M. P. 1975. *Planning and Managing Housing for the Elderly.* New York: Wiley & Sons.

Lawton, M. P. 1977. The impact of the environment on aging and behavior. In *The Handbook of the Psychology of Aging,* eds. J. E. Birren and K. W. Schaie, pp. 276–301. New York: Van Nostrand Reinhold.

Lawton, M. P. 1978. The housing problems of community resident elderly. *Occasional Papers in Housing and Community Affairs,* pp. 39–74. Washington: U. S. Department of Housing and Urban Development.

Lawton, M. P. 1980. *Environment and Aging.* Monterey, CA.: Brooks/Cole Publishing Co.

Lawton, M. P. 1981. Aging in the built environment: Psychosocial Aspects. Paper presented at National Research Conference on Technology and Aging. Racine, Wisconsin.

Lawton, M. P. 1982. Competence, environmental press, and the adaptation of older people. In *Aging and Environment: Theoretical Approaches,* eds. M. P. Lawton, P. G. Windley, and T. O. Byerts, pp. 33–59. New York: Springer Publishing Co.

Lawton, M. P., and Hoover, S., eds. 1981. *Community Housing Choices for Older Americans.* New York: Springer Publishing Co.

Lawton, M. P., and Nahemow, L. 1973. Ecology and the aging process. In *The Psychology of Adult Development and Aging,* eds. C. Eisdorfer and M. P. Lawton, pp. 619–674. Washington: American Psychological Association.

Lawton, M. P., and Nahemow, L. 1979. Social areas and the well-being of tenants in housing for the elderly. *Multiv. Beh. Res.* 14: 463–484.

Lawton, M. P.; Nahemow, L.; and Yeh, T. 1980. Neighborhood environment and the well-being of older tenants in planned housing. *Int'l J. Aging Hum. Dev.* 11: 211–227.

Lawton, M. P., Newcomer, R., and Byerts, T., eds. 1976. *Community Planning for an Aging Society.* Stroudsburg: Dowden, Hutchinson and Ross.

Lawton, M. P.; Windley, P. G.; and Byerts, T. O., eds. 1982. *Aging and the Environment: Theoretical Approaches.* New York: Springer Publishing Co.

Lawton, M. P., and Yaffe, S. 1980. Victimization and fear of crime in elderly public housing tenants. *J. Geron.* 35: 768–779.

Lazarus, R. 1966. *Psychological Stress and the Coping Process.* New York: McGraw-Hill Book Co.

Lazarus, R.; Averill, J.; and Opton, E. 1974. The psychology of coping: Issues of research and assessment. In *Coping and Adaptation,* eds. G. Coelho, D. Hamburg, and J. Adams, pp. 249–315. New York: Basic Books, Inc.

Lynch, K. 1960. *Image of the City.* Cambridge: M.I.T. Press.

Moos, R. 1974a. *The Social Climate Scales: An Overview.* Palo Alto: Consulting Psychologists Press.

Moos, R. 1974b. Systems for the assessment and classification of human environments: An overview. In *Issues in Social Ecology: Human Milieus,* eds. R. H. Moos

and P. M. Insel, pp. 5–28. Palo Alto: National Press Books.

Overton, W. F. 1976. Environmental ontogeny: A cognitive view. In *The Developing Individual in a Changing World (Vol. 2): Social and Environmental Issues,* eds. K. Riegel and J. Meacham, pp. 413–420. The Hague: Mouton.

Overton, W. F., and Reese, H. W. 1977. General models for man-environment relations. In *Ecological Factors in Human Development,* ed. H. McGurk, pp. 11–20. Amsterdam: North-Holland Publishing Co.

Pastalan, L., and Bourestom, N. 1975. Forced relocation: Setting, staff, and patient effect. *Final report to the Mental Health Service Development Branch, N.I.M.H.* Ann Arbor: The University of Michigan.

Proshansky, H. M. 1976. Environmental psychology and the real world. *Am. Psychol.* 31: 303–310.

Regnier, V. 1975. Matching older person's cognition with their use of neighborhood areas. In *Man-Environment Interactions: Evaluations and Applications,* ed. D. Carson, pp. 19–40. Stroudsburg: Dowden, Hutchinson and Ross.

Regnier, V. 1976. Neighborhoods as service systems. In *Community Planning for an Aging Society,* eds. M. P. Lawton, R. Newcomer, and T. Byerts, pp. 240–257. Stroudsburg: Dowden, Hutchinson and Ross.

Regnier, V. 1981a. Neighborhood images and use: A case study. In *Community Housing Choices for Older Americans,* eds. M. P. Lawton and S. Hoover, pp. 180–197. New York: Springer Publishing Co.

Regnier, V. 1981b. *The Neighborhood Environment and Its Impact on the Older Person.* Adaptability and aging, Vol. 2. Paris: International Center for Social Gerontology.

Regnier, V. In press. Urban neighborhood cognition: Relationships between functional and symbolic resources. In *Aging and Milieu: Environmental Perspectives on Growing Old,* eds. G. Rowles and R. Ohta. New York: Academic Press.

Regnier, V., and Hamburger, J. 1978. Comparison of perceived and objective crime against the elderly. Paper presented at Annual Meeting of The Gerontological Society, Dallas, Texas.

Regnier, V., and Rausch, K. 1980. Spatial and temporal neighborhood use patterns of older low-income central city dwellers. Paper presented at Annual Conference of the Environmental Design Research Association, Charleston, South Carolina.

Rowles, G. D. 1978a. *Prisoners of Space? Exploring the Geographical Experience of Older People.* Boulder: Westview Press.

Rowles, G. D. 1978b. Reflections on experiential field work. In *Humanistic Geography: Prospects and Problems,* eds. D. Ley and M. Samuels, pp. 173–193. Chicago: Maaroufa Press, Inc.

Rowles, G. D. 1980. Toward a geography of growing old. In *The Human Experience of Space and Place,* eds. A. Buttimer and D. Seamon, pp. 55–72. London: Croom Helm Ltd.

Rowles, G. 1981a. Geographical perspectives on human development. *Hum. Dev.* 24: 67–76.

Rowles, G. D. 1981b. The surveillance zone as meaningful space for the aged. *Geront.* 3: 304–311.

Rowles, G. D. 1981c. Between worlds: A relocation dilemma for the Appalachian elderly. Paper presented at Annual Meeting of the Gerontological Society of America, Toronto, Canada.

Rowles, G. D. In press. Geographical dimensions of social support in rural Appalachia. In *Aging and Milieu: Environmental Perspectives on Growing Old*, eds. G. D. Rowles and R. J. Ohta. New York: Academic Press.

Rowles, G. D., and Ohta, R. J., eds. In press. *Aging and Milieu: Environmental Perspectives on Growing Old*, eds. G. D. Rowes and R. J. Ohta. New York: Academic Press.

Scheidt, R. J. 1981. Psychosocial environmental predictors of the mental health of the small town rural elderly. In *Toward Mental Health of the Rural Elderly*, eds. P. Kim and C. Wilson, pp. 53–80, Washington: University Press of America.

Scheidt, R. J., and Schaie, K. W. 1978. A taxonomy of situations for an older population: Generating situational criteria. *J. Geront.* 33: 848–857.

Scheidt, R. J., and Windley, P. G. 1981. A behavior setting analysis of stress and coping in older community residents: Conceptual and methodological issues. Paper presented at meeting of the Gerontological Society of America, Toronto, Canada.

Scheidt, R. J., and Windley, P. G. In press. Well-being profiles of small-town elderly in differing rural contexts. *Comm. Ment. Hlth. J.*

Schooler, K. K. 1975. A comparison of rural and non-rural elderly on selected variables. In *Rural Environments and Aging*, eds. R. C. Atchley and T. O. Byerts, pp. 27–42. Washington: Gerontological Society.

Schooler, K. K. 1978. Some effects of social environment on the relation between stress and health: Differences between urban and rural elderly. Paper presented at International Congress of Gerontology, Tokyo, Japan.

Schooler, K. K. 1982. Response of the elderly to environment: A stress-theoretical perspective. In *Aging and the Environment: Theoretical Approaches*, eds. M. P. Lawton, P. G. Windley, and T. O. Byerts, pp. 80–96. New York: Springer Publishing Co.

Schooler, K. K., and Rubenstein, D. I. 1980. The impact of the planned environment on the elderly. In *Life-span Developmental Psychology: Intervention*, eds. R. Turner and H. Reese, pp. 103–124. New York: Academic Press.

Stea, D. 1970. Home range and use of space. In *Spatial Behavior of Older People*, eds. L. A. Pastalan and D. H. Carson, pp. 138–147. Ann Arbor: University of Michigan.

Wetzel, J. W. 1978. Person-environment intervention with aging depressed women in institutions. Paper presented at meeting of the Gerontological Society, Dallas, Texas.

Willems, E. P. 1973. Behavioral ecology and experimental analysis: Courtship is not enough. In *Life-span Developmental Psychology: Methodological Issues*, eds. J. R. Nesselroade and H. W. Reese, pp. 195–217. New York: Academic Press.

Willems, E. P. 1977. Relations of models to methods in behavioral ecology. In *Ecological Factors in Human Development*, ed. H. McGurk, pp. 21–35. New York: North-Holland Publishing Co.

Windley, P. G. 1981. The effects of the ecological/architectural dimensions of small rural towns on the well-being of older people. In *Toward Mental Health of the Rural Elderly*, eds. P. Kim and C. Wilson, pp. 81–96. Washington: University Press of America.

Windley, P. G., and Scheidt, R. J. 1980a. Person-environment dialectics: Implications for competent functioning in old age. In *Aging in the 1980's: Psychological Issues*, ed. L. Poon, pp. 407–423. Washington: American Psychological Association.

Windley, P. G., and Scheidt, R. J. 1980b. The well-being of older persons in small rural towns: A town panel approach. *Educ. Geron.* 5: 355–373.

Windley, P. G., and Scheidt, R. J. 1982. An ecological model of mental health among small-town rural elderly. *J. Geront.* 37: 235–242.

4 BEHAVIORAL PROCESSES

11
AROUSAL, SLEEP, AND AGING

Diana S. Woodruff

Temple University

The purpose of this chapter is to review the recent psychophysiological literature on arousal and sleep in relation to aging, pointing out the progress that has been made in our understanding of these phenomena and assessing areas in need of further investigation.[1] In preparing this review, several issues have become clear. One is that our knowledge about sleep and aging has progressed rapidly in the last decade, with one recent review (Miles and Dement, 1980) identifying 552 articles relevant to this topic. Because this excellent and detailed review is readily available, only a brief overview of the sleep and aging literature will be included here. The other issue of note is that the topic of arousal has received relatively little attention in recent research literature. It appears that what was once a controversial area—whether overarousal or underarousal exists in the aging nervous system—is not a focus of interest to most geropsychologists today. An exhaustive computer search of the recent literature on aging in animals and humans revealed fewer than five articles published in the 1980s that specifically addressed aging and arousal. One of the major models of geropsychology is now receiving little direct research attention. Thus, a major goal of this chapter will be to point out significant unsettled issues involving aging and arousal to rekindle interest in this important area. In re-

viewing the issues of arousal here, we will concentrate on the historical importance of the model, we will update the contemporary literature, and we will consider how other issues receiving greater current research attention are related.

Although arousal and sleep represent opposite ends of the behavioral continuum, it is not unusual to discuss them together. The reason that sleep and arousal are frequently considered in conjunction is that they may be regulated by common neurophysiological and neurochemical mechanisms. Additionally, it is possible that the observed age changes in arousal in the waking state may be related to age changes in sleep patterns and/or that arousal level changes during the waking state alter requirements for sleep.

A typical measure of states of arousal and stages of sleep is electrophysiological activity, and this will be the primary measure for discussion in this chapter. The electroencephalogram (EEG) and Event Related Potentials (ERPs) have been useful in elucidating age differences in arousal and sleep in the central nervous system (CNS). Activity of the autonomic nervous system (ANS) has also received a great deal of attention, particularly in the arousal literature. No review of the literature on aging and arousal would be complete without a discussion of biochemical measures of ANS arousal (e.g., serum-free fatty acid and urinary catacholmine levels) and bioelectric

[1] The author would like to thank Dr. Donald B. Lindsley for his comments on this chapter.

measures [e.g., galvanic skin response (GSR) and heart rate].

In attempting to understand brain mechanisms in arousal, sleep, and aging, a number of related concepts and models along with empirical research, apart from psychophysiological correlates of arousal and sleep will be considered to fall within the scope of this chapter. One area of concern will be excitability and inhibition in the nervous system. The Russian physiologist Ivan Petrovich Pavlov was one of the first to point out that changes in the aging brain may involve changes in excitation and inhibition. Contemporary research supports Pavlov's assertion that inhibitory processes decline with aging. What is less clear is the relationship between decreasing inhibitory processes and arousal. It is possible that a decline in inhibition signifies more excitability and hence overarousal for the elderly. However, many possibly independent changes occur in the nervous system with age that might lead to overarousal in one system and underarousal in another. Furthermore, compensentory mechanisms occur that may result in organization at a new functioning level.

For example, Bondareff (1980) termed the loss of axosomatic synapses in the dentate gyrus of the senescent rat compensatory. He argued that the reorganization of the dentate gyrus that occurs in senescent rats includes atrophy of dendrites, hypertrophy of astrocytes, a 27-percent loss of axodendritic synapses in the molecular layer, and a coincident loss of 15 percent of the axosomatic synapses along with a 22 percent decrease in the amount of neuronal surface covered by the axosomatic synapses. Axodendritic synapses are excitatory, whereas axosomatic synapses are inhibitory. Bondareff suggested that a compensatory loss of inhibitory and excitatory synapses may result in the aging animal's ability to maintain a reasonably adaptive level of function. In spite of ongoing changes in the level of neuronal activity, functional capacity appears to be maintained, possibly as a result of the complete reorganization of the dentate gyrus in senescence.

Another related model developed from the behavioral literature on aging and perception involves stimulus persistence. This could be conceived as an excitability model that stipulates that the older nervous system responds in a prolonged fashion to stimuli. The effects of a visual or auditory stimulus persist longer in the older nervous system, implicating greater excitability and/or less inhibition. This phenomenon might be viewed as another form of overarousal, particularly if arousal is conceptualized in phasic as well as tonic terms.

The empirical literature on neuroanatomical and electrophysiological changes in the aging brain is significant for this discussion because it suggests a common origin for observed changes in arousal and sleep. A predominant and oft cited change is the loss of cortical neurons and dendritic branching in the frontal lobes (Scheibel and Scheibel, 1976) that probably underlies the observed electrophysiological changes over the frontal cortex (Michalewski, Thompson, Smith, Patterson, Bowman, Litzelman, and Brent, 1980; Pfefferbaum, Ford, Roth, Hopkins, and Kopell, 1979; Tecce, Yrchik, Meinbresse, Dessonville, and Cole, 1980). The inhibitory function of the frontal cortex on the ascending reticular arousal system (ARAS) is documented (e.g., Bronson, 1965; Campbell, Lytle, and Fibiger, 1969; Como, Joseph, Fiducia, Siegel, and Lukas, 1979; Scheibel and Scheibel, 1966; Skinner and Yingling, 1977). The frontal cortex has also been implicated in the regulation of sleep (Prinz, 1976). Thus, age changes in the frontal lobes may account in part for alterations in arousal and sleep. At the same time, other changes in the aging brain—including cell loss in various areas in addition to the anterior cortex, declines in blood flow, and alterations in neurotransmittors and synaptic mechanisms—are undoubtedly involved in age changes in sleep and arousal states. Thus, the observed age differences in sleep and arousal may involve common mechanisms, and they probably also involve independent causes.

The focus of this chapter will be on psychophysiological measures and the neurophysiological and neuroanatomical processes of aging. It should not be overlooked however, that social and behavioral phenomena are also causally involved in age differences in sleep and arousal. Retirement is a socially imposed milestone that has profound implications for sleep and wakefulness. The demands of work affect sleep patterns, energy level, attention, motivation, and arousal. The abrupt change in the work cycle caused by retirement leads to alterations in daily physical activity and altered demands for sleep, which, in turn, can affect the psychophysiological measures of these activities. A behavioral phenomenon frequently observed in aging that may profoundly affect sleep and wakefulness is depression. Social and psychological events involving loss predispose the elderly to depression, which in turn can alter sleep patterns and levels of arousal. These social and behavioral phenomena reinforce the point that most data on sleep, arousal, and aging are cross-sectional and reflect differences between groups. The age differences are not necessarily a function of ontogeny or biological aging; they may reflect different environmental demands or circumstances of the aging population.

In dealing with psychophysiological variables, it is frequently assumed that differences between young and old groups represent age changes rather than differences between cohort groups. Schaie (1965) and Baltes (1968) have pointed out that this is not a reasonable assumption. Few longitudinal studies exist in the psychophysiological literature, however. Age changes in the EEG observed in cross-sectional studies have been replicated longitudinally (e.g. Obrist, Henry, and Justiss, 1961), but ERP and sleep studies are almost exclusively cross-sectional. In this chapter, therefore, age functions will be referred to as age differences unless longitudinal data are available. It is likely that many of the cross-sectional results will be replicated in longitudinal designs because cross-sectional studies have been carried out on ERPs and on sleep among several cohorts of the aged with relatively consistent results. Nevertheless, it is important to keep in mind that the research is almost totally cross-sectional.

One goal of this chapter will be to relate age differences in sleep and arousal to changes in the brain. This goal includes the underlying assumption that there are universal biological changes in the aging brain that may lead to age changes in sleep and arousal. At the same time, it is acknowledged that most of the arousal and sleep studies are cross-sectional and reflect age differences that result, at least in part, from social and behavioral differences between young and old groups. Thus, neurophysiological changes in the brain probably cannot account for all of the age differences in sleep and arousal, and, as social and behavioral patterns of aging change, some of the arousal and sleep changes may not be replicated in future cohorts. Nevertheless, it is likely that biological aging in the brain accounts for some of the sleep and arousal differences between young and old, and it is on this aspect of aging phenomena that the chapter will focus.

SLEEP

The measure that has been used most effectively to determine the various stages of sleep is the EEG, and some of the greatest age differences in the EEG occur during sleep. The five stages of sleep in a young and old subject are depicted in Figure 1. Normal sleep can be divided into two main categories: Nonrapid eye movement (or NREM) sleep, which includes stages I through IV, and rapid eye movement (or REM) sleep. NREM sleep involves the absence of eye movements and moderately reduced muscle tonus. In stage I, the EEG pattern is of low-amplitude, irregular, rapid-frequency activity. Stage II includes synchronous waves of 12 to 16 cps (spindles) that occur against a background of low-amplitude, rapid-frequency activity. High-amplitude (75 μv, or more), slow waves (0.5 to 2.5 cps), also called *delta waves,* characterize stage III sleep and comprise 20 to 50 percent of the EEG record during this stage. When these slow waves comprise 50 percent or more of the EEG record, stage IV sleep is reached. REM sleep is characterized by low-amplitude, rapid-frequency EEG activity, similar to the EEG during wakefulness. For this reason, REM sleep is sometimes called *paradoxical sleep.* The phenomenon that gives this stage its name is the presence of bursts of rapid eye movements. Just at the onset of a REM sleep period, muscle tonus undergoes a marked decrease that is sustained throughout most of the REM period.

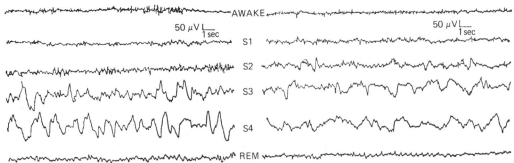

Figure 1.   The typical appearance of the EEG during waking and the stages of sleep in a young and an aged subject. Although alpha and spindle activities can be seen to be slower in the senescent EEG recordings (C4 referenced to mastoid), the most striking age difference occurs during stage III and stage IV sleep. Because of their decreased size (and apparent slowing), the delta waves in this senescent tracing do not meet conventionally defined criteria for stage IV sleep (waves of 0.5 to 3 Hz; $\geq$ 75 μv for 50 + % of the epock). (*From Prinz, 1976a.*)

According to Miles and Dement (1980, p. 198), "the most prominent EEG sign of adult aging is the steady decrease in delta wave amplitude during slow wave sleep (SWS)." The delta waves that characterize stages III and IV are greatly attenuated in amplitude. An example of this appears in the data of Prinz (1976b), who reported a study of 12 healthy subjects between the ages of 75 and 92. The subjects' EEG was recorded while they slept in their homes. The largest slow-wave amplitudes of these older subjects rarely exceeded 150 μv, whereas waves of 200 μv or greater are commonly seen in young adults. In addition to the dramatic delta-wave amplitude decrease, there is an overall decrease in the absolute amount of delta-wave activity in the all-night EEG records of old people (Feinberg, Fein, Floyd, and Aminoff, 1982). Some investigators, however, maintain that the age differences in delta-wave activity occur almost totally as a result of the decline in the amplitude of the delta waves rather than the differences in their prevalence (Webb and Dreblow, 1982).

Miles and Dement (1980) maintained that the age change in delta activity may have several causes. The enzyme monoamine oxidase increases in the brain stem with age, and such an increase could impair serotonergic functions, one of which seems to be the induction or maintenance of NREM sleep. Another possible cause of the decline in delta waves during

sleep in the aged may be the loss of the oblique-horizontal dendrite systems of layers 2, 3 and 5 pyramidal cells. The horizontal networks may facilitate cooperative or synchronous neural behavior. Feinberg (1974) proposed a model that involved brain metabolism during waking as the cause of age differences in delta waves. He hypothesized that the decrease in delta waves in the elderly was, in part, the result of reduced brain activity during waking, which would lead to a lower level of substrate for subsequent sleep.

Following the occurrence of SWS, there is typically a secretion of growth hormone that is known to promote protein synthesis and tissue repair and growth in various somatic tissues and possibly brain tissues as well (Prinz and Halter, 1980). Studies of nighttime growth-hormone release in healthy men revealed that the growth-hormone peak associated with sleep onset was significantly suppressed in men over 60 (Prinz, Blenkarn, Linnoila, and Wietzman, 1976). This age difference occurred only in growth-hormone levels secreted during the first half of the night. There were no age differences in growth-hormone secretion during the day or during the latter part of the night. At the present time, the physiological significance of the age differences in nighttime secretion of growth hormone is not apparent (Prinz and Halter, 1980).

Another age change in sleep EEG is the change in spindle activity. Senescent sleep spindles are often poorly formed and of lower amplitude, resulting in an infrequent occurrence of typical spindling activity (Feinberg, Koresko, and Heller, 1967). Spindle frequencies are often slower in older adults as well (Feinberg et al., 1967; Kales, Wilson, Kales, Jacobson, Paulson, Kollar, and Walter, 1967). Feinberg and Carlson (1968) pointed out that these changes are analogous to the changes in alpha activity, which also decrease in frequency, amplitude, and overall amount in senescence.

In addition to the altered EEG characteristics during sleep, there are also age changes in the amounts and patterning of the various sleep stages. Age changes in sleep patterns are shown in Figure 2. Most likely as a result of the reduced amplitude of sleep-related EEG slow waves that characterize stage-IV sleep, this stage is greatly reduced or absent in senescence (Feinberg et al., 1967; Foret and Webb, 1980; Kales et al., 1967; Kahn and Fisher, 1969; Prinz, 1976b). Hayashi and Endo (1982) demonstrated that this aging phenomenon occurs in Japanese elderly as well. On the basis of three consecutive nights of recording 15

healthy men and women ranging in age from 73 to 92 years, the Japanese researchers concluded, "Compared with the young adults, the aged subjects showed extraordinary reductions in stages III and IV sleep." (Hayashi and Endo, 1982, p. 277).

Although the decline in stage-IV sleep is a widely reported aging phenomenon, Webb (1982) found an increase rather than a decline in SWS in a longitudinal study of five individuals recorded initially in their early fifties and fifteen years later in their mid-sixties. Webb (1981) also reported that, after two nights of sleep deprivation, subjects in their early twenties and in their forties showed sharply reduced latencies to SWS and increased stage-IV sleep. The proportionate distribution of stage amounts and numbers was not different in the two age groups, but the younger group entered SWS more quickly. Carskadon, Harvey, and Dement (1981) reported similar results in a five-night study of sleep deprivation and recovery in adolescents. The greatest change in the sleep pattern appeared to be in stage IV, in which there was an almost 100-percent increase after one night of sleep

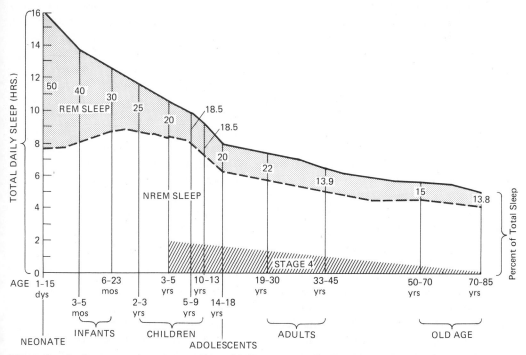

Figure 2.   A diagrammatic representation of REM and non-REM sleep (and total sleep), obtained at different ages across the life span (adapted from Roffwarg et al., 1966, with permission). Stage IV sleep values shown are based on the data of Williams et al. (1974). (*From Prinz, 1976a.*)

loss. This same five-night paradigm was used to examine sleep patterns in ten older subjects ranging in age from 61 to 77 years (Carskadon, 1982). After one night of sleep deprivation, older subjects spent significantly less time in stage I sleep and more time in stages III and IV than they had on a night preceding the sleep loss. Subjects also had fewer wakenings after sleep onset in the two nights following sleep deprivation. These results suggest that a change in sleep scheduling for the aged may be in order. Older people tend to spend more time in bed (10 to 12 hours) and more time awake in bed. Carskadon (1982) suggested that if older people would spend only six hours a night in bed, the quality of their sleep, including time spent in deep sleep, might improve. When need for sleep is increased by sleep loss, stage-IV sleep is achieved in old subjects for a time period approaching that spent by adolescents in stage IV (Carskadon, 1982).

Time spent in REM sleep also appears to diminish in studies of senescent sleep patterns (Prinz, 1976a). Intensity of the REM sleep state also appears to decline, as inferred from the diminished REM activity that normally accompanies this state. These differences in REM activity are related to mental function test scores. Among aged men selected for good health, Feinberg et al. (1967) found a correlation between time spent in REM sleep and WAIS performance and Wechsler Memory scores. These results have been replicated by Kahn and Fisher (1969) and by Prinz (1977).

An age change that receives major emphasis in the Miles and Dement (1980) review is the increased number of awakenings and time spent awake in bed among the elderly. They report an almost linear increase with age in awakenings after sleep onset, this being paralleled by a very marked increase in the occurrence of brief arousals (10 sec or less) that are not perceived or remembered and may not cause actual wakefulness. The most prominent subjective symptom in older adults is complaint of the increased number and duration of sleep disruptions. This complaint often parallels the objective finding of increased wakings after sleep onset.

One possible cause for the increase in awak-

enings per night may be related to level of arousal. A number of studies have indicated that plasma levels of norepinephrine are increased in the elderly both in the daytime and, especially, during the night (Coulombe, Dussault, and Walker, 1977; Pedersen and Christensen, 1975; Prinz and Halter, 1980; Prinz, Halter, Benedetti, and Raskind, 1979; Ziegler, Lake, and Kopin, 1976). The level of plasma norepinephrine is elevated in human beings when the sympathetic nervous system is activated. Heightened plasma norepinephrine levels may thus represent increased sympathetic activation in the aged. Such sympathetic activation has been associated with an aroused EEG pattern and behavioral alertness—two measures used in sleep research to indicate the waking state. When heightened activation resulting from increases in plasma norepinephrine occurs at night, it could interfere with sleep and promote nighttime wakefulness. Indeed, Prinz and Halter (1981) found significant correlations between sleep patterns and mean levels of plasma norepinephrine in samples of healthy men in their twenties and those over sixty. More wakefulness and less SWS and REM sleep were related to higher levels of plasma norepinephrine. Furthermore, awakenings induced by a tone stimulus approaching auditory threshold level were followed by pronounced and consistent surges in plasma norepinephrine in the old but not in the young. These observations led Prinz and Halter (1980) to conclude that either high sympathetic tonus as indexed by plasma norepinephrine levels underlies the fragmentation and deterioration of sleep in the aged or their impaired sleep results in increased sympathetic activity. They pointed out that determining the role of increased sympathetic activity in sleep abnormalities would provide an impetus for the development of new pharmacological interventions that could counteract nighttime sympathetic hyperactivity and improve the quality of sleep in the aged.

That new pharmacological interventions into the sleep of the elderly are required is becoming more apparent as more is learned about sleep and sleep dysfunction. The fastest growing body of literature on the topic of sleep and aging focuses on breathing patterns during sleep and implicates respiratory disturbances as a major cause of impaired sleep and frequent awakenings in the elderly (Ancoli-Israel, Kripke, Mason, and Messin, 1981; Bliwise, Carey, and Dement, 1983; Bliwise, Coleman, and Carey, 1982; Carskadon and Dement, 1981; Coleman, Miles, Guilleminault, Zarcone, Van Den Hoed, and Dement, 1981; Guilleminault and Dement, 1978). These respiratory disturbances are a health risk in and of themselves. More alarming, however, is the evidence that sleeping pills and alcohol increase the incidence and length of these episodes (Guilleminault, 1982).

Sleep apnea is considered to have occurred if there is a cessation of airflow for 10 seconds or longer. The occurrence of apnea or several other kinds of abnormal respiratory events at a rate of more than five per hour is considered pathological (Guilleminault and Dement, 1978). Some elderly have hundreds of these events during the night. The incidence of respiratory problems in the sleep of the elderly has been variously reported at 63 percent (Ancoli-Israel et al., 1981), 31.8 percent in women and 44.4 percent in men (Carskadon and Dement, 1981), 44 percent (Coleman et al., 1981), and 33 percent (Bliwise et al., 1983). Recent longitudinal data collected by Bliwise, Carskadone, Carey, and Dement (in Press) suggest that increases in respiratory disturbances during sleep may occur primarily during the fourth and fifth decades and remain high in subsequent years.

Coleman et al. (1981) argued that sleep apnea associated with insomnia and hypersomnia might account for the relationship between longevity and time asleep. The mortality rate for those over seventy who state that they sleep less than 4 hours or more than 10 hours per night is nearly twice the rate for those of the same age who report sleeping 7 to 8 hours. Sleep apnea is associated with life-threatening hemodynamic changes during sleep, and thus it may be directly related to longevity.

Taken as a whole, the age differences observed in sleep characteristics serve as evidence that the pattern of sleep is altered in the aged. The age differences are similar in men and women, but impairment may be greater in men (Miles and Dement, 1980). In-

creased wakefulness and decreased slow wave sleep are subjectively experienced as less-sound sleep, but it is the fragmentation of sleep most frequently caused by disturbed nighttime breathing that has been shown to be most closely related to sleepiness and reduced daytime well-being in the aged (Carskadon, Brown, and Dement, 1983). It is evident that there is a higher incidence of complaints of poor sleep and a greater usage of drugs to promote sleep among elderly individuals. It has been reported that those 60 and older in the United States consume 33 percent of all prescriptions for secobarbital and diazepam (Institute of Medicine, 1979). Advances in knowledge of respiratory disturbances associated with sleep in the aged indicate that these drugs may increase the incidence of apnea and associated cardiac arrythmia. Another behavior reported to be common among the elderly to compensate for inadequate nighttime sleep is to nap during the day. Like sleeping pills, napping may be counterindicated for the sleepless aged, and sleep deprivation studies have demonstrated that sleep loss actually improves the quality of sleep (by increasing the time spent in SWS) the next night. Thus, by avoiding sleeping pills and staying in bed at night for shorter rather than longer intervals, the aged might improve the quality of their sleep.

AROUSAL

The *Dictionary of Behavioral Science* (Wolman, 1973) defines arousal as an "increase in the complexity (amount of information, uncertainty) of neural organization manifest by desynchronization of electrical recordings made from the brain (activation)." Behavioral relationships with level of arousal had been considered in the 1920s and 1930s (Welford, 1965), but it was in the late 1940s and early 1950s that arousal theory got its major impetus with the discovery of the reticular activating system (RAS) in a series of ingenious experiments (e.g., Lindsley, Schreiner, Knowles, and Magoun, 1950; Moruzzi and Magoun, 1949). Moruzzi and Magoun observed the relationship between direct electrical stimulation from electrodes implanted in the reticular formation and behavioral arousal. This relationship is shown schematically in Figure 3, in which the electrical stimulation to the reticular formation of a cat occurs naturally from the sound of a bell input from neural collaterals from the auditory pathway. Furthermore, Lindsley et al. (1950) found that lesions to the midline reticular formation resulted in a permanent sleeping state in the animal but that the animal could be aroused by stimulation caudal to the lesion.

These discoveries led to the generation of a great body of research, and Lindsley (1952, 1960) reviewed much of this literature and organized it into a general theory of arousal. The main dependent measure in this research was the EEG, and in Lindsley's theory, various EEG-frequency bandwidths were associated with stages of arousal, ranging from deep sleep to alert problem solving. Arousal states and their EEG correlates are summarized in Table 1. In its simplest form, the theory associates very slow EEG frequencies, called *delta waves* (1 to 3 cps), with deep sleep; a band-width ranging from 4 to 7 cps, called *theta waves,* with light sleep; the transition between sleep and wakefulness, the 8- to 13-cps range called *alpha waves,* with alert wakefulness; and the faster frequencies of 14 to 30 or more cps, called *beta waves,* with thinking and problem solving.

Brain-wave frequency ranges on a continuum from 1 cps, or slower, to at least 40 cps, and a controversy has arisen as to whether it is appropriate to classify brain waves in the delta, theta, alpha, and beta bandwidths in a rigid manner and invariably to associate these bandwidths with distinct states of consciousness. For example, the states of consciousness distinctions become confusing whenever developmental and aging changes in the EEG are considered. Lindsley (1938) noted the onset of rhythmic EEG activity in occipital areas as a 3- to 4-cps rhythm that is not apparent in the record until the neonate is 3 to 4 months old. This occipital rhythm increases to 6 cps by the age of 1 year, reaches adult values by the ages of 10 to 14, and slows to 8 to 9 cps

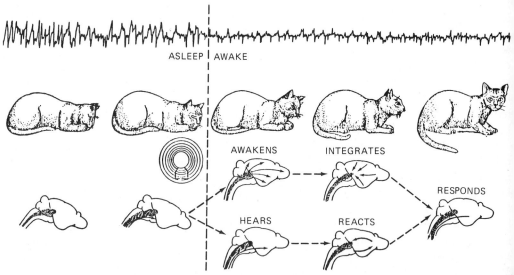

ASLEEP | AWAKE

AWAKENS INTEGRATES

RESPONDS

HEARS REACTS

Figure 3. Schematic drawing of the EEG, brain, and behavior of a cat as it passes through the arousal stages from deep sleep to waking alertness. In the first frame, the cat is in deep sleep. In the second frame, the ringing bell rouses the cat. Collaterals from the primary auditory pathway provide input to the reticular formation (shown in light grey). The cat awakens and integrates in the third and fourth frames and responds in the fifth frame. Coincidentally, in the third frame, the ARAS acts (black arrows) to awaken the cortex so that it can "hear" signals arriving in the auditory area. The EEG changes from a pattern of sleep to one of wakefulness at the end of the second frame. The ARAS then integrates brain activity so that the brain can react as a whole. The cat finally responds in the fifth frame with a motor impulse (light-grey descending arrow by reticular formation). The cat then jumps to its feet and runs away. The entire process takes place in a matter of a few seconds. (*From French, 1957.*)

TABLE 1. Psychological States and Their EEG, Conscious, and Behavioral Correlates*

Behavioral continuum	Electroencephalogram	State of awareness	Behavioral efficiency
Strong, excited emotion (fear, rage, anxiety)	Desynchronized: low to moderate amplitude; fast, mixed frequencies	Restricted awareness; divided attention; diffuse, hazy; "confusion"	Poor (lack of control, freezing-up, disorganized)
Alert attentiveness	Partially synchronized: mainly fast, low-amplitude waves	Selective attention, but may vary or shift, "concentration" anticipation, "set"	Good (efficient, selective, quick reactions); organized for serial responses
Relaxed wakefulness	Synchronized: optimal alpha rhythm	Attention wanders—not forced; favors free association	Good (routine reactions and creative thought)
Drowsiness	Reduced alpha and occasional low-amplitude, slow waves	Borderline; partial awareness; imagery and reverie; "dreamlike states"	Poor (uncoordinated, sporadic, lacking sequential timing)
Light sleep	Spindle bursts and slow waves (larger); loss of alpha	Markedly reduced consciousness (loss of consciousness); dream state	Absent
Deep sleep	Large and very slow waves (synchrony but on slow time base); random, irregular pattern	Complete loss of awareness (no memory for stimulation or for dreams)	Absent
Coma	Isoelectric to irregular, large, slow waves	Complete loss of consciousness; little or no response to stimulation; amnesia	Absent
Death	Isoelectric: gradual and permanent disappearance of all electrical activity	Complete loss of awareness as death ensues	Absent

*From Lindsley (1952).

in old age. Lindsley called this activity *alpha rhythm* when he first reported it in 1936, and he has continued to argue that because the generators for this activity are probably the same at all ages and because it is the modal rhythm at a given point in development, it should be called *alpha* regardless of frequency (Lindsley and Wicke, 1974). Obrist and Busse (1965) remarked on this issue with regard to the aged. They noted that although alpha is usually considered to indicate activity between 8 and 13 cps, because of the tendency for the rhythm to become slower in old age, investigators have often used a more liberal frequency classification, including waves of 7 cps or less. This issue is a problematical one according to Obrist and Busse, and they draw no conclusion as to whether 7-cps and slower activity

in the elderly should be classified as *slow alpha* or *theta*. Whether an elderly individual with a 7-cps modal frequency is in a quiet, alert (alpha) state or is underaroused and on the verge of sleep (theta state) is unclear.

Whether brain waves in delta, theta, alpha, and beta frequency bandwidths reflect qualitatively different states of consciousness or represent a quantitative continuum relates to the different predictions made by proponents of the arousal versus the excitability cycle hypothesis. These competing hypotheses will be described in a subsequent section of the chapter. Briefly, arousal proponents would expect to see a general relationship between brain wave frequency and performance because bandwidths of brain wave frequencies are roughly correlated with the qualitatively different states of consciousness. Within specific frequency bandwidths of theta or alpha, however, no specific one-to-one correlation between EEG frequency and reaction time is necessary to support this position. On the other hand, those who posit an excitability cycle hypothesis—either in terms of general cortical excitability or in terms of the "perceptual moment"—have to predict that EEG frequency will be correlated with performance regardless of frequency bandwidth.

Although the precise origin and mechanism for the generation of rhythmic brain activity is still unknown, it is generally agreed that the EEG generators reside in the cortex. The maintenance and regulation of all of the rhythmic activity is probably not cortical, but rather originates in subcortical pacemakers most likely located in nonspecific nuclei of the thalamus (Andersen and Andersson, 1968). The RAS synapses on the nonspecific nuclei of the thalamus. In this manner, the RAS affects the frequency of the EEG. EEG desynchronization and fast activity are related to cortical "activation," whereas slowing of the EEG frequency is an index of low arousal. The fluctuations in arousal are attributed to activity of the brain stem and thalamic reticular systems (e.g., Gastaut, 1958; Jasper, 1958), which also appear to regulate behavioral arousal and responsivity. Evidence for this relationship comes from research such as the experiments of Fuster (1957), who demonstrated that direct stimulation of the midline reticular formation of monkeys led to faster perceptual response in the visual system. More recently, Andersen and Andersson (1968) suggested that two or more rhythmic impulses from the thalamus to the cortex may be necessary to "prime" the cortex and lead to perceptual awareness. The priming time for the cortex would take longer at slower EEG frequencies.

Arousal theory received considerable attention in psychology in the 1950s, and it began to be considered in relation to aging in the late 1950s and early 1960s. It is interesting to note that in the *Handbook of Aging and the Individual* (Birren, 1959) the only brief allusion to arousal is the author's suggestion that the aged person shows a reduction in ex-

citability of the central nervous system, this being manifested in longer latencies of responses and in a relative incapacity to withhold responses. In that handbook, there is no entry for "arousal" in the index. By 1977 when the second handbook, the *Handbook of the Psychology of Aging* (Birren and Schaie, 1977), appeared, there were 38 entries under the heading of "arousal." Clearly, the 1960s and 1970s were the period when the model of aging and arousal received the most research attention.

UNDERAROUSAL

Birren (1960, pp. 326–327) first articulated the underarousal hypothesis when he stated:

> There is the possibility that the well-established psychomotor slowing of advancing age is a consequence of reduced physiological activation. This agrees with what limited literature exists on age differences in activity and drive levels. Assuming a less energized or activated organism with age, in any unit of time there will be less interaction between the individual and his environment. This reduces the opportunity for all psychological processes to take place, e.g., perception, acquisition, manipulation of symbols, and storage.

When Birren made this statement, the major evidence for the underarousal hypothesis was provided by studies of the ongoing EEG of the aged.

EEG Evidence

Investigators have reported four major changes in the brain wave activity of older adults. These include changes in the frequency and abundance of the alpha rhythm, changes in the incidence of beta activity, diffuse slowing (especially noted in institutionalized elderly), and focal slowing and abnormal activity in the temporal lobes (for reviews, see Marsh and Thompson, 1977; Obrist and Busse, 1965; and Thompson and Marsh, 1973). The most reliable age change in EEG activity is the slowing of the dominant frequency, the alpha rhythm. Since slower EEG frequencies are associated with lower states of arousal, the slowing in the aged was assumed to signify a lowered state of arousal.

As early as 1931, the scientist who discovered the human EEG, Hans Berger, noticed that patients with senile dementia had slower alpha rhythms than normal young individuals, but he assumed that the slowing was related to the patients' illness. Davies (1941) was the first to demonstrate that the alpha rhythm was slower in the aged, and her work has been upheld in subsequent research (Brazier and Finesinger, 1944; Busse and Obrist, 1963; Friedlander, 1958; Harvald, 1958; Hubbard, Sunde, and Goldensohn, 1976; Matousek, Volavka, Roubicek, and Roth, 1967; Mundy-Castle, Hurst, Beerstecher, and Prinsloo, 1954; Roubicek, 1977; Obrist, 1954, 1963; Otomo, 1966; and Silverman, Busse, and Barnes, 1955). Most of these studies have also reported a decrease in the percentage of time older subjects produce alpha rhythm, this being reported as a decrease in alpha abundance. It is in the teens and early twenties that the frequency of the alpha rhythm reaches its maximum, which is 10.0 to 10.5 cps (Brazier and Finesinger, 1944; Eeg-Olofsson, 1971). The average frequency for healthy adults in their sixties is around 9 cps, and for adults beyond 80, it is further decreased to 8 to 8.5 cps (Obrist, 1954, 1963, 1965; Obrist and Busse, 1965). In a group of ten healthy centenarians, the average alpha frequency was 8.62 cps (Hubbard et al., 1976). Alpha recordings from healthy community volunteers between the ages of 28 and 99 years showed that the alpha period (reciprocal of alpha frequency) increased at a rate of four msec per decade (Surwillo, 1963). Similar results have been reported in longitudinal studies of the EEG (Obrist, Henry, and Justiss, 1961; Wang and Busse, 1969; Wang, Obrist, and Busse, 1970).

The mechanisms underlying this change, as well as the clinical significance, remain unclear at the present time, at least in community-residing subjects. The association between measures of vascular function and EEG slowing that has been found in patient groups has raised the question of whether alpha slowing reflects changes in blood flow. Reliable relationships between slowing of alpha frequency and cognitive impairment have also been obtained in patient groups, which suggests that alpha frequency may be associated in some way with efficiency of information processing.

Attempts to find similar relationships in community-residing volunteers have been generally disappointing. Insensitivity of the behavioral and physiological measuring instruments employed in most studies may be partly responsible for the paucity of studies reporting an association between these two sets of data. For example, when Wang et al. (1970) examined the relationship between verbal and performance measures on the Wechsler Adult Intelligence Scale (WAIS) and alpha slowing, they found no relationship. When they used a more complex index of performance, verbal minus performance score, it did show a relation to alpha slowing. Since verbal scores are maintained in healthy aging individuals whereas performance measures show some decline, the difference between the two scores may more reliably mark capacity changes in the aged than performance scores alone. The careful measuring techniques of Surwillo (1961, 1963, 1964, 1968) have also yielded striking EEG and behavior relationships as a function of alpha frequency, suggesting that age changes in the EEG alpha frequency may have important behavioral consequences for the aged.

The Significance of Alpha Slowing

A domain of behavior in which alpha slowing may have significance is that related to speed and timing. Consideration of the alpha rhythm as a timing mechanism for behavior began almost with the discovery of the human EEG. In a review of the early literature, Lindsley (1952) noted that Bishop (1933) and Jasper (1936) found relationships in animals between rhythmic cortical activity and brightness enhancement. At this time, Lindsley made a distinction between alpha rhythm—the high-amplitude rhythmic activity recorded in humans from scalp electrodes and most apparent in posterior leads—and alpha activity—the periodic waxing and waning in excitability of cortical cells, which would not be recorded with scalp electrodes when large numbers of cells were not synchronized. Lindsley emphasized that alpha activity was always present in the brain even when alpha rhythm could not be recorded. He suggested that a cycle of approximately 10 cps, as reflected in the alpha rhythm, is the basic metabolic rhythm of brain cells. A large body of research literature has accumulated to support Lindsley's contention that the alpha frequency reflects a fundamental rate in the nervous system.

In a review of the literature pertaining to a periodic basis for perception and action, Sanford (1971) summarized studies demonstrating relationships between alpha rhythm and the timing of a variety of behaviors into two major categories: studies related to alpha frequency and studies related to alpha phase. Along with two major strategies for measuring alpha rhythm and behavior relationships are two general rationales or hypotheses regarding the nature of the relationship. The more general hypothesis is the previously discussed arousal hypothesis. It stipulates that brain wave frequency is associated with different states of consciousness and excitability of the cortex. Studies designed with this rationale often measure brain wave activity that is faster or slower than alpha bandwidths as well as measuring alpha. In this paradigm, slow frequencies are associated with low arousal and slow reaction time whereas faster frequencies are associated with higher arousal and faster reaction time.

The other hypothesis, the excitability cycle hypothesis, involves an attempt to relate behavioral timing to phases of the alpha wave. Sanford (1971) identified two forms of the excitability cycle hypothesis. The first suggests that the waxing and waning of excitability in the nervous system is marked by the alpha rhythm and that signals input at points in the cycle close to the point of maximal excitability will be processed and responded to more quickly than signals input at less optimal points. The other form of the hypothesis, which involves the concept of "perceptual moment," is more specific, making precise predictions about reaction time. The notion is that stimuli are sampled at discrete intervals of time. The longest reaction times will occur if a stimulus is presented when a new sample is just beginning, whereas the shortest reaction times will occur when a sample is just about to end. Since the alpha cycle (lasting 100 msec for a 10-cps alpha rhythm) is related to the points where the sample opens and closes,

there is a strong relation between the phase at which a stimulus is presented and the time it takes for the subject to recognize that it has been presented. Since the subject cannot react to the stimulus until he or she perceives it, reaction time is a function of alpha phase, and the maximum difference between reaction times obtained in this way should be equal to the duration of one "moment" or "scan" (predicted to be around 100 msec for a full alpha cycle or 50 msec if the alpha half wave represents the "scan" by Kristofferson, 1967). The arousal hypothesis and the two forms of the excitability cycle hypothesis predict that slowing of alpha frequency leads to slower perception and reaction.

Comparing the Arousal and the Excitability Cycle Hypotheses

Examinations of the excitability cycle hypothesis have involved two different approaches: (1) measuring alpha rhythm and correlating it with behavior, and (2) inputting signals on the alpha cycle and comparing behavior between points of input. Only the second approach provides direct evidence for the excitability notion, whereas the first approach can be interpreted in terms of excitability cycle or arousal.

Support for the excitability cycle hypothesis was first generated by studies demonstrating brightness enhancement in a rhythmic manner of the frequency of the alpha rhythm (Bishop, 1933; Jasper, 1936). This work was extended to the behavioral domain of movement time with correlations observed between voluntary movement and a specific phase of the alpha cycle (Bates, 1951; Kibbler, Boreham, and Richter, 1949) and writing speed and alpha frequency (Denier van der Gon and van Hinte, 1959). Using a simple tapping task, Mundy-Castle and Sugarman (1960) observed that young subjects' tapping speed was correlated with their alpha frequency, both when they tapped at normal speed and at their fastest possible rate. This result was not found in older subjects, suggesting that the central relationship between EEG and behavior could only be shown if other, more peripheral factors did not interfere (Mundy-Castle, 1962).

Direct attempts to test the notion that reaction time is faster at certain points on the alpha phase were initiated by Walsh (1952), who observed the point at which visual signals were input at various phases of alpha and found no relation between alpha phase or amplitude and reaction time. Sanford (1971) noted that this type of study is technically difficult since it assumes that alpha waves are perfectly sinusoidal. Since alpha waves are only very approximately sinusoidal, precision in determining the phase of any point on a record of alpha activity is limited. Additionally, the signal reaches the cortex slightly later and hence at a different point on the phase from the point at which it was generated. Lansing (1957) attempted to control for technique problems by dividing the alpha cycle into six time bins and inputting the visual signal into those bins. He also estimated conduction time to the cortex and corrected for that time in his calculations. With this method, Lansing did find that the fastest and slowest reaction times were obtained at input points of opposite phases of the alpha cycle, the fastest reaction times being recorded at the negative-going maxima of the alpha cycle. The perceptual moment theory—positing a serial relation between reaction time and phase, with reaction time incrementing progressively from the point of maximal excitability to the point of minimal excitability—was not supported. There was no serial ordering of reaction times between the fastest and slowest, and the difference between the two extreme reaction times was only 10 msec, a value that does not come close to approximating the 50- or 100-msec difference that would be predicted by the perceptual moment hypothesis.

Subsequent studies in the visual modality have found similar small but consistent relationships (Boswell, 1958; Callaway and Yeager, 1960). Callaway (1962) found that for a given individual there is an enduring tendency for particular phases of the alpha cycle to be associated with reaction time, but these phases were different in different individuals. The results were not replicated for auditory stimuli (Callaway, 1962; Wilkinson and Morlock, 1967). Dustman and Beck (1965) replicated Lansing's original observation of maximal excitability at the negative-going maxima

of the alpha cycle and found both reaction time and ERP amplitude to be greatest at this point. Nunn and Osselton (1974) found that masking latency was shorter when the masking stimulus was presented at certain points in the alpha cycle, and Milstein (1974) reported that alpha-blocking latency was shorter or longer as a function of the point at which the signal is input into the alpha wave.

Studies of perceptual and motor time have demonstrated relationships between alpha phase and behavior in young subjects, but an interpretation of these results is difficult. Sanford (1971) concluded that while there are relationships between alpha phase and response initiation, alpha phase and reaction time, and alpha phase and brightness, we do not understand the manner in which these relationships interact. He also concluded that while the results provide little support for the perceptual moment theory, they do not fully justify a rejection of it because of the technical difficulties involved in testing the hypothesis.

A proponent of the EEG excitability cycle hypothesis who has produced data called "startlingly convincing" (Sanford, 1971, p. 183) is Surwillo. His life-span data on EEG and behavior first led him to devise a model in which frequency of the EEG determined the timing of behavior (Surwillo, 1963, 1968). More recent data led Surwillo (1975) to revise this model into a two-factor model in which speed of information processing is governed by (1) the time characteristics of the cortical gating signal, and (2) the recovery cycle of the information-processing operations that are activated by the gating signals.

Because alpha waves seemed to be related to reaction time, and because older individuals have slower alpha waves and slower reaction time, Surwillo (1960, 1961) attempted to determine if reaction time and the duration of the alpha rhythm cycle were related. Measuring the duration of waves occurring between the onset of an auditory signal and the initiation of the subject's response, Surwillo found a statistically significant rank order correlation of 0.81 between reaction time and alpha period in a group of thirteen subjects between the ages of 18 and 72 years. On the basis of these results, Surwillo hypothesized that the period of the alpha rhythm, or some multiple of the alpha cycle, serves as the master timing mechanism in behavior.

In other investigations, Surwillo attempted to replicate his first results with a larger sample and more sophisticated reaction time tasks. Simultaneously measuring reaction time and average period of EEG between stimulus and response for 100 subjects ranging in age from 28 to 99 years, Surwillo (1963) confirmed his previous findings. In this study, a correlation of 0.72 was obtained between average reaction time and average EEG period. In another sample (Surwillo, 1964a), choice reaction time was related to alpha period with a correlation of 0.76. In both experiments, there was a low but statistically significant correlation between reaction time and age that disappeared when the brain wave period was partialled out. The presence of slow brain potentials appeared to be necessary for the occurrence of slow reaction time in old age, and this fact suggested to Surwillo that EEG frequency is the factor behind age-associated drops in the processing capacity of the brain. He further speculated that the frequency of the EEG may reflect the operation of a "biological clock" within the CNS that is a determining factor in how rapidly and effectively information can be processed (Surwillo, 1968).

Surwillo (1975) claimed that his work summarized in 1968 led to a model that could account for the prolonged reaction time in senescence. Data collected by Birren (1965), Boddy (1971), and Woodruff (1975) in attempts to replicate Surwillo's work did not provide consistent support for the model, but these failures at replication were explained in terms of technical incompatabilities between the studies. A recent attempt to carry out an exact replication of Surwillo (1963) has resulted in only a partial replication of his results (Woodruff and Baum, 1982). Between-subject correlations for alpha period and reaction time in a sample ranging in age from 20 to 75 were 0.41.

It was Surwillo's (1971) own data on children below the age of 11 that led him to modify his model from a one- to a two-factor model. Although young children's alpha rhythms as well as their reaction time are slow,

developmental changes in the EEG period could account for only a small fraction of the high correlations between age and reaction time in childhood. To explain this difficulty, Surwillo (1975) added the notion of a refractory period to his model, stipulating that gating signals could be missed if the information-processing system was still refractory when the gating signal passed. This model was supported for reaction time and EEG relationships in childhood (Surwillo and Titus, 1976), but it did not account for the reaction time data in older adults as well (Woodruff and Kramer, 1979).

A major criticism of Surwillo (1963, 1968) is that he based a model predicting causal relationships on correlational data. Aware of this problem, he stated (Surwillo, 1963, p. 113), "It is worth noting here that our hypothesis also demands that experimental alterations of brain wave frequency should be accompanied by corresponding changes in speed of response. This interesting proposition also deserves investigation." Indirect manipulation of the EEG alpha rhythm leads to changes in the timing of behavior (Creutzfelt, Arnold, Becker, Langenstein, Firsch, Wilhelm, and Wuttke, 1976; Harter, 1967; O'Hanlon, McGrath, and McCauley, 1974). However, such relationships could be mediated by metabolic factors affecting EEG and behavior independently. More direct means for affecting alpha frequency were attempted by Surwillo (1964b), who used photic driving, and by Woodruff (1975), who used biofeedback.

Surwillo (1964b) applied flickering visual stimulation at frequencies above and below the modal alpha frequency in an attempt to drive subjects' alpha at faster and slower rates. Only five of the forty subjects tested manifested adequate synchronization of alpha with flash rate, and there was some evidence of correlation between alpha period and reaction time in those subjects. These limited results did not provide conclusive support for Surwillo's model.

Using the operant conditioning technique, biofeedback, Woodruff (1975) trained ten young and ten old subjects to increase the abundance of alpha activity at modal alpha frequencies and at frequencies two cps above and two cps below the mode. Reaction time was tested when subjects reached criteria of two-thirds time in modal alpha and one-third time above baseline in the faster and slower frequencies. Comparison with control groups of young and old subjects indicated that biofeedback itself did not affect reaction time performance, and all ten of the old and seven of the ten young subjects had faster reaction times when they produced fast brain waves than when they produced slow brain waves. The reaction time differences between the fast and slow brain wave conditions were statistically significant.

In an attempt to replicate Surwillo (1963) directly, Woodruff correlated reaction time and EEG data collected in a baseline condition before biofeedback began. Although between-subject correlations were statistically significant ($r = 0.40$ and $p < .05$), they were only about half the magnitude of Surwillo's correlations. Within-subject correlations ranged from -0.31 to 0.35 and in no way approximated Surwillo's results. Woodruff used spectral analysis to assess EEG frequency. Surwillo, on the other hand, contended that spectral analysis combines amplitude and frequency information and is therefore not a "pure" frequency measure. He argued that this was the reason for Woodruff's failure to replicate. Woodruff and Baum (1982) replicated Surwillo's (1963) technique exactly by performing manual analysis of EEG alpha activity recorded during the reaction time task and again found within-subject correlations that averaged to 0. Comparison of the Surwillo (1963) and Woodruff and Baum (1982) data is presented in Figure 4.

Woodruff (1975) felt that the arousal hypothesis rather than the excitability cycle hypothesis offers the most parsimonious interpretation of the biofeedback results. Correlations between alpha period and reaction time were low between subjects and not apparent within subjects. When reaction times between biofeedback conditions were compared, however, the differences were statistically significant. This fact suggests that subjects producing fast alpha activity may have been more aroused and thus had faster reaction time. Reducing arousal level may be asso-

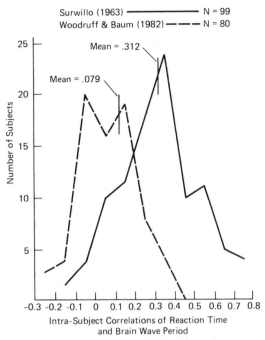

Figure 4.   Comparison of intraindividual correlations between brain wave period and reaction time for the data of Surwillo (1963) and Woodruff and Baum (1982). The latter study was not able to replicate the large number of positive correlations within individuals. (*From Woodruff and Baum, 1982.*)

ciated with production of EEG frequencies bordering on the theta range. Research indicates that reaction time and performance declines when subjects' brain waves verge into theta bandwidths (Davies and Krkovic, 1965; Groll, 1966; Kornfield, 1974; Morrell, 1966; Williams, Granda, Jones, Lubin, and Armington, 1962). Beatty, Greenberg, Deibler, and O'Hanlon (1974) used biofeedback of theta bandwidths over the right occipital hemisphere during a long radar watch and successfully achieved changes in the efficiency of detection. Operantly produced increases in theta activity decreased the efficiency of performance, whereas controlled decreases in theta activity removed the decrement.

Fast brain wave frequencies above the alpha bandwidth have not been associated with faster reaction time, but beta activity has been observed as a correlate of learning lists of nonsense syllables (Thompson and Obrist, 1964), paired associates (Freedman, Hafer, and Daniel, 1966), and backward digits (Surwillo,

1972). Thompson and Wilson (1966) also demonstrated in a group of 15 elderly subjects that "good learners" had significantly more beta activity and tended to have less slow-wave activity than "poor learners." In this study, the EEG was not measured during learning but during the course of photic stimulation, and Thompson and Wilson argued that the brain waves of poorer learners were less reactive (more sluggish alpha blocking as well as less beta activity) than the EEG of good learners.

Thompson and Wilson's poor learners were subjects over the age of 60 who had more EEG activity in the frequency range below 8 cps than subjects aged 40 or younger. Data cited previously suggest that it is when the EEG slows into the borderline theta range and below that the most consistent relationships between EEG frequency and performance are observed. With aging, the EEG slows to the borderline theta range.

At this point in time neither the excitability cycle nor the arousal hypothesis have been conclusively supported or refuted. Surwillo (1975) pointed out that, although some data in support of the EEG gating hypothesis have been reported, the presently available evidence is suggestive rather than conclusive. A number of studies interpreted in terms of the arousal model suggest a relationship between low arousal, poor performance, and EEG in the theta range, but these data do not conclusively rule out an excitability cycle interpretation. It must be noted, however, that to explain age changes in performance, the arousal concept has received far more attention and support than the excitability cycle hypothesis.

Brain wave frequency itself may not serve as a biological clock, but it may be correlated with an arousal level that does influence behavior. The fact that older individuals have slower modal brain wave frequencies and the fact that slow brain wave activity is associated with lowered states of arousal had been used as one of the rationales for suggesting that the aged are in a state of underarousal compared to young individuals (Thompson and Marsh, 1973). There have been other rationales as well.

Event Related Potentials

Electrical responses of the brain to specific stimuli are usually not apparent in recordings of ongoing EEG, but by taking a number of epochs in which the same stimulus event has occurred and summing or averaging across these epochs, the activity related to the stimulus becomes apparent. The assumption is that random activity not associated with the stimulus cancels to a flat voltage pattern, whereas activity that is time-locked to the stimulus accumulates and emerges from the random background "noise" of the ongoing EEG. This assumption has proved viable when comparisons have been made of simultaneous surface and cortical implanted-electrode recordings in animals. A number of different bioelectric signals exhibit stable temporal relationships to a definable external event, and these can be elicited in any of the sense modalities. The name for all of these signals is Event Related Potentials (ERPs).

The reviews of the ERP and aging literature that appear in Marsh and Thompson (1977) and Woodruff (1978) pertain to a number of issues that go beyond the realm of arousal theory. The subgroup of ERP studies that are most typically related to arousal are studies of sensory-evoked potentials. The sensory-evoked potential data that support the underarousal hypothesis are based upon researchers' interpretations of the significance of various evoked potential components. In sensory-evoked potential research that requires the subject to attend passively while stimuli are presented, two major types of cortically generated components have been observed and related to two different CNS systems. The primary response involving the early components is associated with the primary sensory pathways and cortical projection centers, and the secondary response is representative of more diffusely projecting pathways involving the reticular formation. More specifically, the primary response is a simple, biphasic response that usually includes a short surface-positive wave and a subsequent, slow-rising surface-negative phase. These waves occur during the first 50 to 60 mseconds of the response. (This discussion does not encompass the low-amplitude waveforms that occur in the first ten milliseconds after stimulation and that are linked to brainstem generators.) The initial surface-positive component apparently represents activation of the cortical elements (such as Golgi type II cells and pyramidal cell somata) that are found in layers IV and V of the cortex (e.g., Bishop and Clare, 1953). The origin of the subsequent surface-negative phase of the primary response has been interpreted by Bishop and Clare (1953) as antidromic conduction along the pyramidal-cell apical dendrites. Basic identifying features of the primary response include the fact that it remains unchanged under light anesthesia and, when recorded from the scalp, the primary response can be recorded only from the primary sensory area of the stimulus employed.

The post-primary response comprises any evoked activity that occurs after the primary response components and that is recorded up to 500 to 1000 msec after the stimulus. The amplitude of this activity is considerably greater than that of the primary response. Although a number of post-primary responses resemble the primary response in that they are confined principally to the primary sensory area and are not eliminated by anesthesia, the post-primary responses of relevance to arousal are the ones that are not topographically associated with the primary response and that are eliminated by either anesthesia or brain stem transection. It is widely accepted that these components are determined to a great extent by neural impulses conducted extralemniscally via the reticular formation. These post-primary responses, considered to be polysensory in nature, are seen at a latency of 100 msec or more in recordings from most association areas as well as in the long-latency portions of ERPs recorded from primary areas. Since the post-primary components are affected by conditions related to attention, consciousness, and anesthesia, it is assumed that they are related to nerve impulses conducted via the reticular formation and the unspecific midline nuclei of the thalamas.

The largest input to sensory-evoked potential data over the life span has come from the Salt Lake City laboratories of Edward Beck, Robert Dustman, and their associates (Beck and Dustman, 1975; Beck, Dustman, and Schenkenberg, 1975; Dustman and Beck, 1966, 1969; Dustman, Shearer, and Snyder, 1982; Dustman and Snyder, 1981; Dustman, Snyder, and Schlehuber, 1981; Schenkenberg, 1970; Schenkenberg, Dustman, and Beck, 1971; Snyder, Dustman, and Shearer, 1981). Since the extensive data presented by Schenkenberg (1970) are representative of the Salt Lake City laboratory, those pertain to underarousal will be discussed here.

A summary of the three patterns of age differences in ERP amplitude observed by Schenkenberg (1970) is in Figure 5. Eight age groups of human subjects, each comprised of 10 males and 10 females in the age range of 4 to 86 years, were tested on visual, auditory, and somatosensory aspects of sensory-evoked potentials. Primary components showed stability throughout childhood, adolescence, and young adulthood. Results suggested that the primary sensory systems showed two patterns of age differences. Few differences in the peak delays of auditory-evoked response (AER) or somatosensory-evoked response (SER) appeared in older subjects, but increases in the peak delay of the visual-evoked response (VER) suggested that the visual system may slow in its sensory input speed during senescence. There also appeared to be amplitude increases with old age in both VERs and AERs. Increases in amplitude and peak delay were attributed to decreased neural inhibition of primary sensory input by Straumanis, Shagass, and Schwartz (1965), who also noted increases in the amplitude and peak delay of early VER components in old age. The decline of inhibitory processes in the aging nervous system is discussed in a subsequent portion of this chapter.

Post-primary activity showed age differences at several points in the life span. Amplitude of evoked-response activity between 80 and 200 msec increased during childhood. Peak delays of the post-primary components became consistently shorter from early childhood to adolescence for all three types of evoked responses. Since myelination of non-

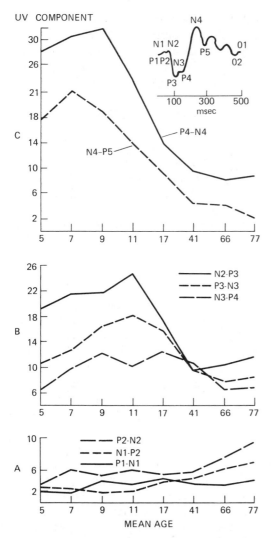

Figure 5. Component amplitudes of VERs recorded from occipital sites appeared to change with age in three basic patterns: A, B, and C. The first component, P1–N1, did not change from youth to senescence. The next two components in pattern A—N1–P2 and P2–N2—remained unchanged until early old age when abrupt increases in the amplitude of both were noted. Components in pattern B increased in amplitude steadily throughout childhood, reaching peaks in late childhood or adolescence. This rise was followed by a decline in middle age and stabilization during senescence at a level approximately equal to the level noted during childhood. The amplitude of the first component (N2–P3) in this pattern, however, decreased to a level below that noted in childhood. Pattern C components decreased dramatically in amplitude from the level reached at about age 9 to a level substantially lower during senescence. (*From Schenkenberg, 1970.*)

specific pathways and the development of collaterals to the reticular formation continued throughout childhood (Yakovlev and Lecours, 1967), the electrophysiological and neuroanatomical data were consistent. A pattern of reduced amplitude of the post-primary components was observed in the data of middle-aged and older subjects. Peak delays of VERs and SERs occurred in middle age and increased in senescence. AER peak delays did not show age differences beyond adolescence. Schenkenberg (1970) concluded that the fact that there was reduced amplitude of post-primary components in all modalities and peak delays in two of the three modalities suggested that the alerting, activating functions of the reticular system that has been implicated as the possible source of this activity becomes less effective with advancing years. This subcortical explanation is supported by the observations of Yakovlev and Lecours (1967), who noted that the reticular formations shrink and contain fewer myelinated fibers in the brains of older individuals.

The data on sensory-evoked potentials are consistent in suggesting that the old are in a state of underarousal. Nevertheless, it has been argued by Marsh and Thompson (1977) that the ERP data involving active processing of information (as opposed to the passive stimulation conditions required in sensory-evoked potential paradigms) does not consistently support the underarousal hypothesis. Smith, Thompson, and Michalewski (1980) asserted that when the elderly are stimulated passively or required to perform simple tasks, they show ERP differences consistent with reduced cortical excitability. "However, studies that have required active subject involvement and have measured the AEP (Ford, Hink, Hopkins, Roth, Pfefferbaum, and Kopell, 1979; Marsh, 1975; Smith, Tom, Brent, and Ohta, 1976) or the CNV (Harkins, Moss, Thompson, and Nowlin, 1976; Marsh and Thompson, 1973; Thompson, Marsh and Zelinski, 1981; Thompson and Nowlin, 1971) indicate that the elderly are not necessarily underaroused and can exhibit levels of cortical excitability similar to those of younger persons. (Smith et al., 1980, p. 143)."

Galvanic Skin Response and Heart Rate

The first empirical demonstration of the relationship between underarousal and aging was reported by Botwinick and Kornetsky (1959, 1960) and involved the GSR. This research initiated a series of studies carried out in a number of laboratories over the next two decades that related ANS activity to underarousal and poorer behavioral performance in the elderly. Much of this literature is excellently reviewed by Marsh and Thompson (1977). To summarize their review briefly, Botwinick and Kornetsky used a classical conditioning paradigm in which shock was the unconditioned stimulus (UCS), a tone was the conditioned stimulus (CS), and GSR was the response. The GSRs of the elderly subjects (mean age, early 70s) conditioned less readily and extinguished more quickly than the GSRs of the younger subjects, and older subjects also showed less GSR responsivity in the habituation period. The investigators concluded that autonomic reactivity was significantly decreased in the elderly. Similar results have been reported by Shmavonian and his coworkers (Shmavonian and Busse, 1963; Shmavonian, Miller, and Cohen, 1968, 1970; Shmavonian, Yarmat, and Cohen, 1965).

The underarousal hypothesis has also been supported by studies of autonomic reactivity in the aged during vigilance tasks. Surwillo (1966) reported age differences in GSR, heart rate, and skin temperature when young and old subjects monitored a Mackworth clock over an extended period. In several other studies in which young and old subjects were instructed to report the occurrence of a double advance on the ticks of a clock over a long period of time, the latency of GSR to critical stimuli was longer in the aged (Surwillo and Quilter, 1965a) and the incidence of GSR responses was less (Surwillo and Quilter, 1965b).

Heart-rate reactivity has also supported the underarousal hypothesis. Thompson and Nowlin (1973) found heart rate deceleration in a warned-reaction-time task to be much less for the old subjects than for the young. This result was also reported by Harkins, Moss, Thompson, and Nowlin (1976). Thus, taken as a whole, the bioelectric measures of ANS activity indicate the old are in a state of underarousal. Many of the studies involving bioelectric measures of ANS arousal, however, have been boring to their subjects and have involved relatively passive responses to the experimental conditions. Few of these studies supporting the underarousal hypothesis have involved active information processing on the part of the subjects. In conditions of active information processing, older and younger individuals have often been shown to be subject to equal arousal, or the old have been even more highly aroused than the young.

Overarousal

One of the first gerontologists to articulate the overarousal hypothesis was Welford (1965), who stated:

> Reduced activation would tend to lower both signal and noise, the former probably more than the latter, rendering the organism less sensitive and less responsive than it would otherwise be. At first sight the changes with age in neural structures make it seem obvious that older people would be likely to suffer from under-activation. Yet both clinical and everyday observations of middle-aged and older people often point rather to *over*-activation resulting in unduly heightened activity, tension and anxiety. (Welford, 1965, p. 14).

The most frequently used data to support the overarousal hypothesis involve the measurement of lipid mobilization, a biochemical measure related to sympathetic nervous system function. It has been demonstrated that the level of free fatty acid (FFA) in the plasma component of blood was intimately related to the level of ANS arousal (Bogdonoff, Estes, Friedberg, and Klein, 1961; Bogdonoff, Estes, Harlan, Trout, and Kirschner, 1960; Bogdonoff, Weissler, and Merritt, 1960). To obtain this measure, an indwelling needle must be placed in the subject's forearm and sequential samples of blood collected during the experimental session. Thus, regardless of the behavioral measure being assessed, a certain amount of stress is involved in this technique because of the drawing of blood.

Results of the studies using this measure

indicate that during serial learning and stressful monitoring tasks emphasizing information overload, aged subjects had initially higher FFA levels, showed increases comparable to the young while performing the tasks, and continued to show a significantly higher level for a minimum of one hour following the behavioral tests (Powell, Eisdorfer, and Bogdonoff, 1964; Troyer, Eisdorfer, Wilkie, and Bogdonoff, 1966). On the basis of these data, Eisdorfer (1968) concluded:

> It has been implicitly assumed, however, that the aged are at a resting state of low internal arousal and sustain a low drive state. Our contention is that the aged may not be at a low state of arousal. Once aroused autonomically, perhaps because of a faulty ability to suppress end organ response or because of an altered feedback system, aged Ss appear to function as if in states of high levels of heightened arousal. In any event, increasing anxiety or further exogenous stimulation has a detrimental effect on performance, as opposed to the incremental effect that we would anticipate from an organism stimulated at lower levels of arousal. It would be predicted, then, that where arousal or anxiety is diminished by experimental manipulation, older persons should improve their performance. (Eisdorfer, 1968, p. 215).

An experimental test of the overarousal hypothesis was undertaken by Eisdorfer, Nowlin, and Wilkie (1970). They administered an adrenergic blocking agent (propranolol) to one group of older subjects and a placebo to another and found fewer errors and lower FFA levels when the experimental subjects performed the serial learning task. They concluded that autonomic end organ arousal accounted for the learning deficits in the placebo-treated group and asserted that the results supported the overarousal hypothesis. Unfortunately, since a young control group was not tested, the effect of the drug on subjects who would not be expected to be "overaroused" was not assessed.

An attempt was made by Froehling (1974) to replicate these results using a within-subjects design. The results of this study did not support the hypothesis that excessive end organ activity was associated with a learning decrement in the elderly. If overarousal exists in the elderly, it may be a transitory phenomenon occurring only in the older subject's first visit to the laboratory. In a repeated measures design, the overarousal effect was not apparent.

Qualifications of the Arousal Concept

A comparison of the various studies that incorporate an arousal dimension as an explanatory construct is virtually impossible at the present time. For example, studies arguing that older people are underaroused rely heavily on traditional bioelectric measures (EEG frequency, GSR, heart rate) as indicators of physiological arousal, whereas the overarousal position stems primarily from biochemical measures related to ANS function (FFA, urinary catecholamines). Behavioral measures employed in these studies have also been decidedly different. It is obvious that greater commonality of methodology and measuring techniques is required before any resolution of the arousal, performance, and aging controversy can be realized.

A major difficulty here may rest in the limitations of traditional arousal theory as developed in the field of psychophysiology. Earlier work in this area viewed physiological indices of arousal in a unidimensional framework (i.e., the general level of arousal could be assessed at a given point in time by one of a number of physiological measures). More recent work, however, cautions against such simplistic ideas. Interrelationships among ANS measures are frequently low and make a unifying principle difficult to accept. Moreover, differential effects in the parasympathetic and sympathetic divisions of the ANS can be demonstrated, depending on the specific nature of the stressful task confronting the subject (Lacey, 1959, 1967). Lacey (1967) concluded from a series of programmatic studies over the prior decade that different forms of arousal can be separated functionally and anatomically by experimental manipulations, and furthermore, that many variables—including age—may influence the configurations of arousal responses both within and between these forms. He further affirms that the concept of arousal as a unitary phenomenon is incorrect and that electrocortical arousal, autonomic arousal, and behavioral arousal can be viewed as different forms of arousal, each of them complex in itself.

Lacey has called for experimental manipulations of arousal to clarify the nature of physiology-behavior relationships, but as of now few attempts have been made to manipulate level of arousal in the elderly to determine what effect this may have on behavioral and physiological functioning. An experiment by Eisdorfer et al. (1970) that implicated overarousal as a cause for poorer performance in the elderly and the failure of Froehling (1974) to replicate this finding have already been discussed as experimental approaches to this issue. Jeffrey (1969), in his attempt to test the hypothesis of decreased activation against the hypothesis of neural noise by having elderly subjects perform a complex reaction-time task under varying intensities of auditory white noise and increased muscular tension, found that neither hypothesis could be supported. More recently, Falk and Kline (1978) compared overarousal and underactivation hypotheses by measuring critical flicker frequency (OFF) in 16 young and 16 old subjects (8 men and 8 women in each group) under several experimental conditions. Subjects performed the task both while hearing white noise and in its absence on the one hand and both while looking through an artificial pupil and without it on the other. White noise was conceptualized as a means of increasing arousal. Increases in performance efficiency during white noise would support an underactivation hypothesis, whereas decrements in performance during white noise would implicate overarousal.

The measure of arousal was GSR. It was found that white noise impaired performance on the CFF task by old subjects, primarily older women. The authors interpreted these data to support the overarousal hypothesis, although the old men in the study did not show any GSR changes in the presence of the white noise. Woods (1980) manipulated arousal in a group of young men in their twenties and a group of older men in their sixties by testing their performance when they were in various postures. She reasoned that CNS arousal should be greatest when subjects were in the standing position and least when they were lying down. This hypothesis was supported in the old group, their reaction time being faster in the standing than in the reclining position. Body position, however, did not affect reaction time to a significant degree in the young. These data can be used to support the underarousal hypothesis since the increased CNS input resulting from standing improved performance in the old, who were presumably underaroused, but not the young, who did not suffer from underarousal. Woods also had subjects of different fitness levels in her study, and she found that old unfit subjects benefitted the most in terms of reaction time.

Although these experimental studies provide useful insights into questions of arousal level and aging, further research is clearly needed. As Lacey (1967) suggested, experimental manipulation of individual parameters of arousal in conjunction with close attention to various ANS, CNS, and behavioral measures could provide crucial data for the resolution of controversies about arousal, aging, and physiology-behavior relationships.

Lacey (1967) highlighted the importance of attending to both CNS and ANS measures of arousal in attempting to account for age-related behavioral deficits. Thompson and Marsh (1973) argued that a closer scrutiny of CNS and ANS interrelationships may be helpful in accounting for age-related changes in behavior. Support for this position can be found in the failure to obtain a significant relationship between an ANS measure (heart rate) and a CNS measure (amplitude of the CNV) in an elderly group performing a reaction time task, but a significant relationship was observed in a sample of the young (Thompson and Nowlin, 1973). Furthermore, significant correlations between speed of response and physiological measures were apparent in the young group but not in the old. A comparison of the two groups also suggested no age differences in the cortical arousal measure, but the elderly were significantly less reactive at the autonomic level. A similar finding was reported by Shmavonian et al. (1965) in a conditioning experiment that revealed greater EEG activation in old subjects than in young, but considerably less reactive autonomic measures (GSR, vasoconstriction). These discrepancies between young and old subjects in two different sets of measures employed in different experimental paradigms agree with the notion that a lack of congruence between CNS and ANS functioning may be associated with behavioral impairment in the elderly. Additional research supporting this hypothesis about the lack of congruence between the older ANS and CNA is presented in Marsh and Thompson (1977).

INHIBITION

A decrease in the inhibitory processes of the nervous system is a hypothesis that has been advanced to explain behavioral aging phenomena ever since Pavlov considered classical conditioning in aged dogs. On the basis of admittedly scanty evidence, Birren (1959b, p. 160) proposed that older persons showed a reduction in inhibitory control over behavior. The same explanation was used in studies of the classical conditioning of the eyeblink response in humans, a response that is much less efficient in old age than at younger ages (Braun and Geiselhart, 1959; Gakkel and Zinina (1953); Kimble and Pennypacker, 1963). Jerome's (1959, p. 670) description of Gakkel and Zinina's (1953) study of eyeblink conditioning and word-association was as follows: "Failure to obtain even the gross differentiation between the sounds of the buzzer and the bell was accepted as indicative of a serious impairment of the process of inhibition, and a high frequency of garrulous responses in the word-association test was regarded as supporting this conclusion."

A recent review of the evidence for the failure of inhibitory processes appears in an article on ERP research in adult aging by Smith, Thompson, and Michalewski (1980). They pointed out that the enhancement of ERP waveforms resulting from nonspecific cerebral lesions has been attributed to reduced inhibitory control of afferent stimulation. On this basis, high-amplitude ERP components observed in some neurological conditions have been interpreted as arising from deficits in central inhibition (Callner, Dustman, Madsen, Schenkenberg, and Beck, 1978; Lee and Blair, 1973). Thompson et al. (1960) also reported

on studies that indicated that one or more ERP components in the middle-latency range are significantly larger in older than in young individuals. Straumanis et al. (1965) ascribed this difference to a reduction in inhibitory activity, and subsequent research has been interpreted in the same manner (Dustman and Beck, 1969; Schenkenberg, 1970).

Recent ERP data provide even more convincing evidence for a decline in inhibitory function, at least in the visual system of the aging (Dustman and Snyder, 1981; Dustman, Snyder, and Schlehuber, 1981). In one study (Dustman and Snyder, 1981), the augmenting-reducing phenomenon was investigated in 220 male subjects aged 4 to 90. A predisposition towards augmenting or reducing is related to the level of inhibitory functioning (e.g., Buchsbaum, 1976; Knorring and Johansson, 1980; Knorring and Perris, 1981).

Subjects who reduce their ERP responses to intense stimuli have relatively strong inhibitory functions, whereas those who are augmenters are less able to dampen their responses. Furthermore, those individuals with Down's syndrome who are described as having cortical inhibitory deficits have abnormally large visual ERPs, especially in recordings from the frontal and central scalp. Their ERPs also augment substantially more in reaction to increased flash intensity than the ERPs of normal control subjects (e.g., see Galbraith, Gliddon, and Busk, 1970; Gliddon, Busk, and Galbraith, 1975). Dustman and Snyder (1981) reported that the amplitude of ERPs in reaction to flashes was greater in central scalp recording sites at waveform latencies of 90 to 110 msec, 110 to 150 msec, and 150 to 200 msec in very young (4 to 15 years) and older (50 to 90 years) individuals. These data are shown in Figure 6. Very young and old subjects were also the greater augmenters. Brighter flashes were accompanied by larger increases in ERP amplitude in these two age groups than in subjects of intermediate ages. The researchers reported that the ERPs of individuals with Down's syndrome were strikingly similar to the ERPs of the young and old subjects in their study. They pointed out that the predominant action of monoamines is thought to be inhibitory and that mono-

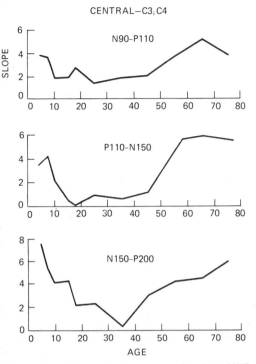

CENTRAL—C3, C4

N90-P110

P110-N150

N150-P200

AGE

Figure 6.   Amplitude slope values for three VER components from central scalp (C3 and C4 combined). Each age group included 20 male subjects. (*From Dustman and Snyder, 1981.*)

amine levels are low during childhood and old age (Beck, 1978; Kent, 1976; Nies, Robinson, Davis, and Ravaris, 1973; Robinson, Nies, Davis, Bunney, Davis, Colburn, Bourne, Shaw, and Coppen, 1972; Tryding, Tufvesson, and Nilsson, 1972). Additionally, anterior cortical areas that exert inhibitory control over the ascending reticular formation (Bronson, 1965; Campbell, Lytle, and Fibiger, 1969; Como, Joseph, Fiducia, Siegel, and Lukas, 1979; Scheibel and Scheibel, 1966; Skinner and Yingling, 1977) are immature during development and suffer cell loss in old age. This developmental course parallels the findings of Dustman and Snyder (1981), who suggested that the chemical and structural deficiencies in aging are reflected by a relative inability to suppress brain potentials elicited by repetitive and relatively meaningless stimuli. If ERP measures used by Dustman and Snyder (1981) do reflect cortical inhibitory function, loss of cortical inhibition is obvious in the recordings of individuals in the fifties and may occur a decade earlier (see Figure 6).

Dustman, Snyder, and Schlehuber (1981) examined visually evoked responses (VER's) to patterned and unpatterned flashes in the same 220 healthy males reported by Dustman and Snyder (1981). Based on the data of Harter (1971), Harter and White (1968), and Schafer and McKean (1975), Dustman et al. (1981) concluded that inhibition in the visual system is essential for the optimal detection of edges and contours. The inhibitory activity causes VERs to patterned stimuli to be more complex than those to flashes of diffuse light. Thus, reduced inhibitory function should result in less differentiated VERs to patterns. VERs to patterns and to diffuse flashes should be relatively similar in individuals having less inhibitory function, and correlations between the patterned and unpatterned conditions should be higher in those individuals. Dustman et al. (1981) found that correlations of the digital values comprising the two waveforms followed a U-shaped curve over the life span.

These interesting data are shown in Figure 7. Patterned and unpatterned flash VERs were most alike for the youngest and oldest subjects. The age effect was localized to scalp areas overlyint the visual cortex, where cortical tissue is organized to maximize the detection of lines and edges (Hubel and Wiesel, 1962, 1977.) The effects were much stronger for the earlier VER components that encompass waveforms known to be associated with checkerboard stimulation (Harter and White, 1968; Jeffrys, 1977). These results are compatible with a concept of reduced inhibitory functioning within the visual systems of the very young and the old. Dustman et al. (1981) suggested that the reduced inhibition may have been related to reduced catecholaminergic activity, although biochemical measures were not used in this study.

Another line of evidence implicating decreased inhibition in the elderly has been presented by Drechsler (1977, 1978). Studying somatosensory and visual ERPs in 65 healthy elderly subjects aged 62 to 91 and 48 normal young subjects aged 18 to 38, Drechsler (1977) reported that the amplitude of both the somatosensory and visual ERPs were significantly higher in the aged sample. The evidence

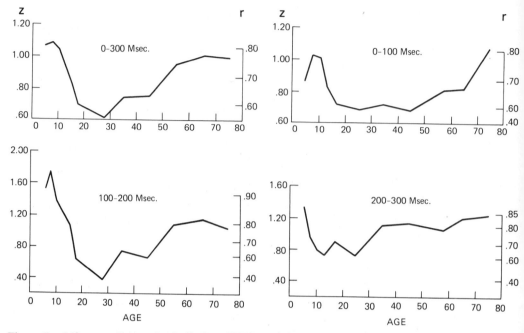

Figure 7.   Life-span changes in similarity of VER waveforms elicited by patterned and diffuse flashes for four time bands. Intensity was two logs above threshold. Each data point represents the mean correlation (r) and equivalent Fisher z-coefficient (z) obtained by correlating digital values within each time segment. Recordings were from occipital scalp. (*From Dustman, Snyder, and Schlehuber, 1981.*)

Drechsler used to suggest that inhibitory capacity was diminished in the aged was the increase in amplitude of their ERPs and the fact that the somatosensory potentials of the young were confined to the centro-parietal region but those of the aged were spread over the whole hemisphere. Drechsler (1978) attributed this phenomenon in the aged to a loss of inhibitory processes that produced a spread of cortical excitability encompassing the whole hemisphere.

It has been stated several times in this chapter that the frontal cortex is believed to exert inhibitory control over the reticular formation. Recent behavioral and electrophysiological data corroborate the neuroanatomical evidence that the frontal cortex may be an area of particular vulnerability in aging. Albert and Kaplan (1980) reviewed the neuropsychological evidence suggesting that many behavioral deficiencies apparent in the elderly resemble behavioral deficits in patients with frontal lobe lesions. Histological studies of Scheibel and Scheibel (1976) have identified losses of dendritic masses in pre-frontal and temporal areas of aging brains.

The electrophysiological measure that has implicated selective aging in anterior cortex is the Contingent Negative Variation (CNV). The term CNV denotes a class of slow-negative potential shifts that last on the order of seconds (as compared to milliseconds for most other ERPs) and that occur in conjunction with certain sensory, motor, and cognitive activities. Donchin, Ritter, and McCallum (1978) described the CNV as a cortical change that occurs when an individual's behavior is directed toward a planned action in response to a sequence of two or more events. The action referred to can be an overt motor response, the inhibition of a motor response, or a decision. The optimal situation for the production of the CNV, first demonstrated by Walter and his colleagues (1964), is a warned reaction time task in which the first stimulus (S1) serves as a ready signal for a second stimulus (S2) to which an operant motor response is made. Walter (1968) suggested that a massive depolarization of the dendrites in the frontal cortex was likely to be involved in the generation of the CNV. This waveform has been of interest to gerontologists because it has been conceived as a measure of attention and arousal (Tecce, 1972).

Initial studies yielded no age differences in CNV amplitude in scalp locations over central motor areas (Marsh and Thompson, 1973; Thompson and Nowlin, 1973). However, Loveless and Sanford (1974) found age differences in the shape of the CNV in long S1–S2 intervals, and they suggested that the aged failed to modulate arousal as efficiently as the young. Recent CNV studies involving a wider array of electrode recording sites and more complex tasks have found significant age differences. Tecce (1979) discovered what he called a "CNV rebound effect" when he added a short-term memory component to the normal CNV paradigm. As a control condition, he ran tests on subjects in the typical CNV design using the warning and imperative signals. In another condition, he added a short-term memory component to the task by presenting three letters between the S1 and S2 and requiring the subject to remember those letters. The letters were not used in all the trials, however, only in half of them. The rest of the trials were like the control condition, using a warning S1 and S2 to which the subject had to respond. A normal CNV was found in the control condition using the typical S1–S2 reaction time paradigm, but CNV amplitude was diminished when the three letters were presented between the S1 and S2. It was in that half of the trials in the short-term memory condition when the letters were not present that the CNV rebound effect occurred. CNV amplitude was greater in these trials than in the control condition or when letters were present. Reaction time to S2 was also faster when the letters were not present. Young subjects (mean age of 22 years) verbalized a strategy of recognizing that the letters would not appear after a certain time interval past S1. Then they concentrated solely on responding to S2. The supranormal increase in CNV amplitude was interpreted as reflecting a switching of attention from the divided attention set intrinsic to trials involving letters to an undivided attention set in trials without them. Tecce et al. (1980) tried this task in older subjects (mean age of 63 years) and found that the CNV rebound effect was diminished in fronto-central brain areas. None of the older subjects verbalized a strategy of realizing that no letters would be forthcoming and hence preparing only for S2, and their CNV indicated that they did not use this strategy. The older subjects also made significantly more perseverative responses than young subjects on the Wisconsin Card Sorting Test, a finding associated with frontal-lobe patients (Milner, 1963). Tecce and his colleagues concluded that the diminution of CNV rebound in the older group appeared to indicate a perseverative attention set that was significantly mediated by fronto-central brain areas and that interfered with the switching of attention. Figure 8 depicts the lower amplitude CNV found in Tecce's laboratory in the fronto-central areas of the older subjects.

Tecce, Cattanach, Yrchik, Meinbresse, and Dessonville (1982) compared the CNV rebound effect in a still older group (mean age of 75 years) to their results in subjects in their twenties and sixties. The oldest group failed to produce a reliable CNV rebound effect. The authors pointed out that in this respect the elderly group resembled Alzheimer's patients since the latter also have no CNV rebound (Tecce, Boehner, Cattanach, Branconnier, and Cole, 1981).

Using a task similar to that employed by Tecce (1979), Michalewski, Thompson, Smith, Patterson, Bowman, Litzelman, and Brent (1980) independently produced the same result. In this study, the subjects heard letters in two blocks of trials but had to remember the letters in only one of the blocks. There was also a block of trials using the classical S1–S2 CNV paradigm without letters. Frontal CNVs for the older subjects (mean age of 72 years) compared to those of the young group (mean age of 23 years) were reduced in every condition. Changes in midline activity were the same for both age groups. Although their frontal activity was diminished, subjects over the age of 70 did produce a CNV rebound effect. The discrepancy between Tecce's and Michalewski's results may reflect differences in the samples of elderly subjects. The 11 elderly subjects in the Michalewski study were alumni of the University of Southern California who were serving as

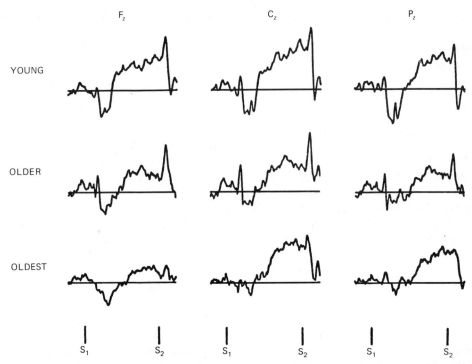

Figure 8.   Examples of CNV traces for frontal (F$_z$), central (C$_z$), and parietal (P$_z$) recording sites of one young, one older, and one oldest subject. Averaged CNVs are based on 22 trials for the young subject and 14 and 18 trials for the older and oldest subjects, respectively. Relative negatively at F$_z$, C$_z$, and P$_z$ (referenced to linked earlobes) is depicted upward. S$_1$ indicates the warning stimulus, and S$_2$ indicates the imperative stimulus to which the subject must respond. (*From Tecce, 1979.*)

volunteers at the Andrus Gerontology Center. The 23 elderly subjects in Tecce's study were selected from the general population in Boston and had an average education of 12 years.

In spite of this significant difference in their results, Michalewski et al. (1980) as well as Tecce et al. (1980) concluded that the overall reduction in frontal CNV activity in the aged suggested a process of selective aging in the frontal lobes. In another study examining ERP responses of young and old subjects to brief tones (Smith, Michalewski, Brent, and Thompson, 1980), topographical analysis of a slow potential complex consisting of components N2 and P3 and a long-latency slow wave indicated diminished frontal electrode activity in the aged. Again, the authors interpreted their results as evidence of an enhanced aging process in the frontal cortices.

A third laboratory's confirmation of diminished slow wave activity in the frontal lobes of subjects over the age of 60 was contributed by Pfefferbaum, Ford, Roth, Hopkins, and Kopell (1979). In a group of extraordinary healthy and active old women, frontal recording sites showed a marked reduction in a wave they called the late sustained potential (SP). This wave occurs as a negative wave 300 to 450 msec after a stimulus. Since the SP is maximal at frontal recording sites and is similar in form to the CNV, the brain generators of the two waveforms may be the same. Pfefferbaum et al. (1979) suggested that the diminished SP might result from a loss in dendritic mass in the frontal areas of the elderly.

Three independent laboratories have reported diminished electrophysiological activity at frontal recording sites in brains of normal subjects over the age of 60. The generators of these CNV and SP waveforms are thought to be dendritic layers in the frontal lobes. In two of the laboratories, the diminished frontal activity occurred as a correlate of diminished capacity to switch attention. These data, coupled with behavioral and histological evidence, begin to point rather compellingly to a selective aging of the frontal lobes that impairs the capacity of the elderly to modulate attention. This frontal lobe impairment might result in decreased inhibitory control of the RAS.

Smith et al. (1980) cautioned that although the evidence provided by ERP studies for a deficit in inhibition with age are provocative, they are nevertheless based on ad hoc reasoning and perhaps should not be taken seriously without more direct evidence. What is required at the present time are studies in which independent measures of inhibition are taken in the elderly along with ERP and behavioral recordings.

STIMULUS PERSISTENCE

The stimulus persistence model is essentially an overexcitability hypothesis that could be viewed in part as implying a lack of inhibitory processes. Basically, the idea is that once the aged nervous system has been stimulated, the stimulation persists longer. It reverberates within the system for a longer period of time, and the system is refractory for a longer period of time than it is in younger adults.

One of the strongest proponents of this hypothesis is Botwinick, who carefully reviewed the behavioral evidence favoring stimulus persistence in the elderly (Botwinick, 1978). Perceptual data that support this hypothesis include studies of aging and stimulus fusion, masking, after-images, and illusions.

A model of what might cause stimulus persistence at a cortical level is provided by the subcortical recordings of Landfield and Lynch (1977). These investigators recorded single-cell activity in the hippocampus of aged rats and found age-related impairment in the capacity of synapses in the rat hippocampus to respond to repetitive stimulation (Landfield and Lynch, 1977). It is possible that this refractoriness is a more general phenomenon in the aging nervous system, but as Smith et al. (1980) pointed out, there are no human ERP and aging studies of phenomena such as masking that might provide additional support for the stimulus persistence model. Landfield and Lynch's (1977) neurophysiological observation of increased nervous system refractoriness

at the unit recording level is supported by neurochemical evidence of age-related impairment of brain transmitter metabolism (Bondareff, 1977; Ordy and Kaack, 1977). Stimuli may persist longer in the aged nervous system because of the slower degradation of neurotransmitters. Neuroanatomical evidence of age-dependent degeneration of synaptic elements in cortical tissue has been provided by Geinsman, Bondareff, and Dodge (1977). The deterioration of inhibitory synapses could also be a mechanism involved in the stimulus persistence phenomenon.

Smith et al. (1980) have reviewed the ERP data relevant to the stimulus persistence hypothesis. They cite studies such as that of Celesia and Daly (1977) in which the cortical frequency of photic driving (CFPD) was examined in subjects in their early twenties and subjects over 60. CFPD is defined as the highest frequency at which a photic driving response as measured by ERPs could be obtained. In the young subjects, CFPD was 72 flashes per second; in the old subjects, 60 flashes per second. These data can be used to support the stimulus persistence hypothesis in that they can be interpreted as a demonstration that the older nervous system cannot process stimuli at as fast a rate because the stimuli persist longer. Further support for the stimulus persistence hypothesis is presented by the data of Smith et al. (1980) showing persistence of electrical positivity during the slow wave phase of the ERP response. Such positivity is usually associated with a decrease in neural reactivity, whereas slow wave negativity is thought to be associated with heightened reactivity. Thus, persistence in this case may implicate a lowered state of arousal in the elderly.

SUMMARY AND CONCLUSIONS

The greatest growth in the literature on arousal, sleep, and aging has occurred in the topic of sleep. A major impetus to research on sleep and aging is its clinical significance. Questionnaire surveys have indicated that over a third of all individuals over 60 years of age complain of problems with sleeping, and some data indicate that the quality and quantity of sleep are related to longevity. Along with the well-known earlier studies documenting the lowered incidence of high-amplitude delta-wave activity characteristic of deep sleep (stages III and IV) and the lowered incidence of REM sleep, there are some new insights about sleep in old age. Greater emphasis is now placed on the number of awakenings the elderly experience during the night and the disruptive effects of such awakenings. Not only do frequent awakenings correlate with daytime sleepiness to a greater degree than other measures of sleep, they are also related to elevated levels of norepinephrine and especially to respiratory dysfunction. An elevated incidence of sleep apnea has been documented in at least a third of the elderly population and may be exacerbated by sleeping pills. Sleep deprivation studies suggest that the elderly can achieve more SWS and fewer awakenings by missing a night of sleep and that they can improve the quality of their sleep by spending less time in bed and avoiding sleeping pills.

Taken as a whole, the evidence reviewed in this chapter on the topic of arousal indicates that the myriad changes that occur in the aging nervous system sometimes lead to contradictory predictions about behavioral outcomes. Data using measures such as the EEG, ERP, GSR, and heart rate indicate rather compellingly that the aged are in a tonic state of underarousal. Another indication of the underarousal of the elderly is the fact that their sleep is fragmented, resulting in sleepiness and a lowered state of alertness during the day. Evidence for a state of tonic underarousal in the elderly suggests a decline in the efficiency of the RAS.

The case for overarousal in the elderly has been based primarily on studies using plasma-free fatty acid levels to measure arousal level. The suggestion is that the aged may be *phasically* overaroused, especially in novel situations. Another index of ANS arousal is the norepinephrine level, which is elevated in the elderly during the day and particularly during the night. Norepinephrine studies have demonstrated that the sympathetic nervous system of aged subjects responds more to noises occurring during sleep than the sympathetic nervous system of young subjects.

A third body of evidence focusing on inhibition in the elderly nervous system has indicated that inhibitory capacity may be deficient in old age. The observed degeneration in the frontal lobes of aged subjects may be related to the decline in the inhibitory function. Less effective inhibition should result in greater excitability and a higher state of arousal. Although this may be the case in response to excitatory stimulation where brain transmitters may be degraded more slowly (resulting in stimulus persistence), it is not the case that the elderly are tonically overaroused. On the contrary, they are in a tonic state closer to the beginning stages of sleep. To explain some of these anomalies. Thompson and Marsh (1973) created the ANS-CNS desynchronization hypothesis, which stipulates that these two components of the nervous system are more poorly integrated in old age.

The model that appears most promising to the present author is the one suggested by the data of Bondareff (1980) on age changes in the dentate gyrus of the rat. He observed what he termed "compensatory" losses of excitatory and inhibitory synapses. If only one type of synapse is lost, the animal might be incapacitated, but with the loss of both types, a new balance is attained at a different level of functioning that involves fewer total synapses. If such a model were to be applied to the whole nervous system, the aging reticular formation might suffer biochemical and synaptic degradation, perhaps resulting in slower EEG frequencies, lower amplitude late ERP components, and lowered responsivity as measured by bioelectric indices of the ANS. The anterior cortex, which exerts an inhibitory influence on the reticular formation, loses cells, particularly the dendrites that provide cortico-cortico connections. Thus, integration in the frontal cortex is less efficient, and inhibitory control declines. These two age changes could result in a sort of compensation in which a new level of organization is achieved. It might be less efficient but relatively in balance as compared to that of a nervous system in which only one process partially fails. Exploration of such a model in humans, might lead us to a better understanding of how adaptation occurs in the course of aging, and it might suggest the means for maximizing compensatory mechanisms.

REFERENCES

Albert, M. S., and Kaplan, E. F. 1980. Organic implications of neuropsychological deficits in the elderly. In *New Directions in Memory and Aging: Proceedings of the George A. Talland Memorial Conference,* eds. L. W. Poon, J. Fozard, L. Cermak, D. Arenberg, and L. W. Thompson. Hillsdale, N. J.: Lawrence Erlbaum.

Ancoli-Israel, S.; Kripke, D. F.; Mason, W.; and Messin, S. 1981. Sleep apnea and nocturnal myoclonus in a senior population. *Sleep* 4: 349–358.

Andersen, P., and Andersson, A. 1968. *Physiological Basis of the Alpha Rhythm.* New York: Appleton-Century-Crofts.

Baltes, P. B. 1968. Longitudinal and cross-sectional sequences in the study of age and generation effects. *Human Development* 11: 145–171.

Bates, J. A. V. 1951. Electrical activity of the cortex accompanying movement. *Journal of Physiology* (London) 113: 240–257.

Beatty, J.; Greenberg, A.; Deibler, W.; and O'Hanlon, J. 1974. Operant control of occipital theta rhythm affects performance in a radar monitoring task. *Science* 183: 871–873.

Beck, C. H. M. 1978. Functional implications of changes in the senescent brain: A review. *Canadian Journal of Neurological Science* 5: 417–424.

Beck, E. C., and Dustman, R. E. 1975. Changes in evoked responses during maturation and aging in man and macaque. In *Behavior and Brain Electrical Activity,* eds. N. Burch and H. L. Altshuler. New York: Plenum.

Beck, E. C.; Dustman, R. E.; and Schenkenberg, T. 1975. Life span changes in the electrical activity of the human brain as reflected in the cerebral evoked response. In *Neurobiology of Aging,* eds. J. M. Ordy and K. R. Brizzee. New York: Plenum.

Birren, J. E., ed. 1959(a). *Handbook of Aging and the Individual.* Chicago: University of Chicago.

Birren, J. E. 1959(b). Psychophysiological aspects of aging. *Duke University Council on Gerontology,* pp. 157–173.

Birren, J. E. 1960. Behavioral theories of aging. In *Aging—Some Social and Biological Aspects,* ed. N. W. Shock. Washington, D.C.: American Association for the Advancement of Science.

Birren, J. E. 1965. Age changes in speed of behavior: Its central nature and physiological correlates. In *Behavior, Aging and the Nervous System,* eds. A. T. Welford and J. E. Birren. Springfield, Illinois: Charles C. Thomas.

Birren, J. E., and Schaie, K. W., eds. 1977. *Handbook of the Psychology of Aging.* New York: Van Nostrand Reinhold.

Bishop, G. H. 1933. Cyclic changes in excitability of the optic pathway of the rabbit. *American Journal of Physiology* 103: 213–224.

Bishop, G. H., and Clare, M. H. 1953. Responses of cortex to direct electrical stimuli applied at different depths. *Journal of Neurophysiology,* 16: 1–19.

Bliwise, D. L.; Carey, E.; and Dement, W. C. 1983. Nightly variation in sleep-related respiratory disturbance in older adults. *Experimental Aging Research,* 9: 77–81.

Bliwise, D. L.; Carskadone, M.; Carey, E.; and Dement, W. C. In press. Longitudinal development of sleep-related respiratory disturbance in adult humans. *Journal of Gerontology.*

Bliwise, D. L.; Coleman, R. M.; and Carey, E. 1982. Age-related prevalence and natural history of sleep apnea and nocturnal myoclonus. *Gerontologist* 22: 187.

Boddy, J. 1971. The relationship of reaction time to brain wave period: A reevaluation. *Electroencephalography and Clinical Neurophysiology* 30: 229–235.

Bogdonoff, M. D.; Estes, E. H., Jr.; Friedberg, S. J.; and Klein, R. F. 1961. Fat mobilization in man. *Annals of Internal Medicine* 55: 328–338.

Bogdonoff, M. D.; Estes, E. H., Jr.; Harlan, W. R.; Trout, D. L.; and Kirschner, N. 1960. Metabolic and cardiovascular changes during a state of acute central nervous system arousal. *Journal of Clinical Endocrine Metabolism,* 20: 1333–1340.

Bogdonoff, M. D.; Weissler, A. M.; and Merritt, F. L. 1960. Effect of autonomic ganglionic blockade upon serum-free fatty acid levels in man. *Journal of Clinical Investigation* 39: 959–965.

Bondareff, W. 1977. The neural basis of aging. In *Handbook of the Psychology of Aging,* eds. J. E. Birren and K. W. Schaie. New York: Van Nostrand Reinhold.

Bondareff, W. 1980. Compensatory loss of axosomatic synapses in the dentate gyrus of the senescent rat. *Mechanisms of Aging and Development,* 12: 221–229.

Boswell, R. S. 1958. An investigation of the phase of the alpha rhythm in relation to visual recognition. Unpublished doctoral dissertation, University of Utah.

Botwinick, J. 1978. *Aging and Behavior.* New York: Springer.

Botwinick, J., and Kornetsky, C. 1959. Age differences in the frequency of the GSR during a conditioning experiment. *Journal of Gerontology* 14: 503.

Botwinick, J., and Kornetsky, C. 1960. Age differences in the acquisition and extinction of GSR. *Journal of Gerontology* 15: 83–84.

Braun, H. W., and Geiselhart, R. 1959. Age differences in the acquisition and extinction of the conditioned eyelid response. *Journal of Experimental Psychology* 57: 386–388.

Brazier, M. A. B., and Finesinger, J. E. 1944. Characteristics of the normal electroencephalogram. I. A study of the occipital-cortical potentials in 500 normal adults. *Journal of Clinical Investigation* 23: 303–311.

Bronson, G. 1965. The hierarchical organization of the central nervous system: Implications for learning processes and critical periods in development. *Behavioral Science* 10: 7–25.

Buchsbaum, M. 1976. Self regulation of stimulus intensity: Augmenting/reducing and the average evoked response. In *Consciousness and Self-Regulation,* eds.

G. E. Schwartz and D. Shapiro. Vol. 1. New York: Plenum.

Busse, E. W., and Obrist, W. D. 1963. Significance of focal electroencephalographic changes in the elderly. *Postgraduate Medicine.* 34: 179–182.

Callaway, E. 1962. Factors influencing the relationship between alpha activity and visual reaction time. *Electroencephalography and Clinical Neurophysiology* 14: 674–682.

Callaway, E., and Yeager, C. L. 1960. Relationship between reaction time and electroencephalographic phase. *Science* 132: 1765–1766.

Callner, D. A.; Dustman, R. E.; Madsen, J. E.; Schenkenberg, T.; and Beck, E. C. 1978. Life span changes in the averaged evoked responses of Down's syndrome and nonretarded subjects. *American Journal of Mental Deficiency* 82: 398–405.

Campbell, B. A.; Lytle, L. D.; and Fibiger, G. C. 1969. Ontogeny of adrenergic arousal and cholinergic inhibitory mechanisms in the rat. *Science* 166: 635–637.

Carskadon, M. A. 1982. Sleep fragmentation, sleep loss, and sleep need in the elderly. *Gerontologist* 22: 187.

Carskadon, M. A.; Brown, E. D.; and Dement, W. C. 1983. Sleep fragmentation in the elderly: Relationship to daytime sleep tendency. *Neurobiology of Aging.*

Carskadon, M. A., and Dement, W. C. 1981. Respiration during sleep in the aged human. *Journal of Gerontology* 36: 420–423.

Carskadon, M. A.; Harvey, K.; and Dement, W. C. 1981. Sleep loss in young adolescents. *Sleep* 4: 299–312.

Celesia, G. G., and Daly, R. F. 1977. Effect of aging on visual evoked responses. *Archives of Neurology* 34: 403–407.

Coleman, R. M.; Miles, L. E., Guilleminault, C. C.; Zarcone, V. P.; Van Den Hoed, J.; and Dement, W. C. 1981. Sleep-wake disorders in the elderly: A polysomnographic analysis. *Journal of the American Geriatrics Society* 29: 289–296.

Como, P. G.; Joseph, R.; Fiducia, J. D.; Siegel, J.; and Lukas, J. 1979. Visually evoked potentials and afterdischarge as a function of arousal and frontal lesion in rats. *Society for Neuroscience Abstracts* 5: 202.

Coulombe, P. J.; Dussault, J. H.; and Walker, P. 1977. Catecholamine metabolism in thyroid disease. II. Norepinephrine secretion rate in hyperthyroidism and hypothyroidism. *Journal of Clinical Endocrinology and Metabolism* 44: 1185.

Creutzfelt, O. D.; Arnold, P. M.; Becker, D.; Langenstein, R.; Firsch, W.; Wilhelm, H.; and Wuttke, W. 1976. EEG changes during spontaneous and controlled menstrual cycles and their correlation with psychological performance. *Electroencephalography and Clinical Neurophysiology* 40: 113–131.

Davies, D. R., and Krkovic, A. 1965. Skin conductance, alpha activity and vigilance. *American Journal of Psychology* 78: 304–306.

Davies, P. A. 1941. The electroencephalogram in old age. *Diseases of the Nervous System* 2: 77.

Denier van der Gon, J. J., and van Hinte, N. 1959. The relation between the frequency of the alpha rhythm and the speed of writing. *Electroencephalography and Clinical Neurophysiology* 11: 669–674.

Donchin, E.; Ritter, W.; and McCallum, W. C. 1978. Cognitive psychophysiology: The endogenous components of the ERP. In *Event-related brain potentials in man,* eds. E. Callaway, P. Tueting, and S. Koslow. New York: Academic Press.

Drechsler, F. 1977. Determination of neurophysiological parameters of the aging CNS. I. Evoked potentials. *Aktuel-Gerontology* 7: 273–283.

Drechsler, F. 1978. Quantitative analysis of neurophysiological processes of the aging CNS. *Journal of Neurology* 218: 197–213.

Dustman, R. E., and Beck, E. C. 1965. Phase of alpha brain waves, reaction time and visually evoked potentials. *Electroencephalography and Clinical Neurophysiology* 18: 433–440.

Dustman, R. E., and Beck, E. C. 1966. Visually evoked potentials: Amplitude changes with age. *Science* 151: 1013–1015.

Dustman, R. E., and Beck, E. C. 1969. The effects of maturation and aging on the wave form of visually evoked potentials. *Electroencephalography and Clinical Neurophysiology* 26: 2–11.

Dustman, R. E., and Snyder, E. W. 1981. Life-span changes in visually evoked potentials at central scalp. *Neurobiology of Aging* 2: 303–308.

Dustman, R. E.; Shearer, D. E.; and Snyder, E. W. 1982. Age differences in augmenting/reducing of occipital visually evoked potentials. *Electroencephalography and Clinical Neurophysiology.*

Dustman, R. E.; Snyder, E. W.; and Schlehuber, C. J. 1981. Life-span alterations in visually evoked potentials and inhibitory function. *Neurobiology of Aging* 2: 187–192.

Eeg-Olofsson, O. 1971. The development of the electroencephalogram in normal children and adolescents from the age of 1 through 21 years. *Acta Paediatrics Scandinavica Supplementum* 208: 1–46.

Eisdorfer, C. 1968. Arousal and performance: Experiments in verbal learning and a tentative theory. In *Human Aging and Behavior,* ed. G. A. Talland. New York: Academic Press.

Eisdorfer, C.; Nowlin, J. B.; and Wilkie, F. 1970. Improvement of learning in the aged by modification of autonomic nervous system activity. *Science* 170: 1327–1329.

Falk, J. L., and Kline, D. W. 1978. Stimulus persistence in CFF: Overarousal or underactivation. *Experimental Aging Research* 4: 109–123.

Feinberg, I. 1974. Changes in sleep cycle patterns with age. *Journal of Psychiatric Research* 10: 283–306.

Feinberg, I., and Carlson, V. 1968. Sleep patterns as a function of normal and pathological aging in man. *Archives of General Psychiatry* 18: 239–250.

Feinberg, I.; Fein, G.; Floyd, T. C.; and Aminoff, M. J. 1983. Delta (.5–3 Hz) EEG wave forms during sleep in young and elderly normal subjects. In *Sleep Disorders: Basic and Clinical Research,* eds. M. Chase and E. D. Weitzman. New York: S. P. Medical and Scientific Books.

Feinberg, I.; Koresko, R.; and Heller, N. 1967. EEG sleep patterns as a function of normal and pathological aging in man. *Journal of Psychiatric Research* 5: 107–144.

Ford, J. M.; Hink, R. F.; Hopkins, W. F.; Roth, W. T.; Pfefferbaum, A.; and Kopell, B. S. 1979. Age effects on event-related potentials in a selective attention task. *Journal of Gerontology* 34: 388–395.

Foret, J., and Webb, W. B. 1980. Changes in temporal organization of sleep stages in man aged from 20 to 70 years. *Review of Electroencephalography and Neurophysiology Clinica* 10: 171–176.

Freedman, N. L.; Hafer, B. M.; and Daniel, R. S. 1966. EEF arousal decrement during paired associate learning. *Journal of Comparative and Physiological Psychology* 61:15–19.

Friedlander, W. J. 1958. Electroencephalographic alpha rate in adults as a function of age. *Geriatrics* 13: 29–31.

Froehling, S. 1974. Effects of propranolol on behavioral and physiological measures in elderly males. Unpublished doctoral dissertation. University of Miami (Florida).

Fuster, J. M. 1957. Tachistoscopic perception in monkeys. *Federation Proceedings* 16: 43.

Gakkel, L. B., and Zinina, N. V. 1953. Changes of higher nerve function in people over 60 years of age. *Fiziologicheskii Zhurnal SSSR im. I. M. Sechenova* 39: 533–539.

Galbraith, G. C.; Glidden, J. B.; and Busk, J. 1970. Visual evoked responses in mentally retarded and nonrelated subjects. *American Journal of Mental Deficiency* 75: 341–348.

Gastaut, H. 1958. The role of the reticular formation in establishing conditioned reactions. In *Reticular Formation of the Brain,* eds. H. H. Jasper; L. D. Proctor; R. S. Knighton; W. C. Noshay; and R. T. Costello. Boston: Little, Brown.

Geinsman, Y.; Bondareff, W.; and Dodge, J. T. 1977. Partial deafferentiation of neurons in the dentate gyrus of the senescent rat. *Brain Research* 134: 541–545.

Gliddon, J. B.; Busk, J.; and Galbraith, G. C. 1975. Visual evoked responses as a function of light intensity in Down's syndrome and nonretarded subjects. *Psychophysiology* 12: 416–422.

Groll, E. 1966. Central nervous system and peripheral activation variables during vigilance performance. *Aeitschrift Fur Experimentelle und Augewandte Psychologie* 13: 148–264.

Guilleminault, C. C. 1982. Effect of various pills on sleep and daytime alertness in the elderly. *Gerontologist* 22: 187.

Guilleminault, C. C., and Dement, W. C., eds. 1978. *Sleep apnea syndromes.* New York: Alan R. Liss.

Harkins, S. W.; Moss, S. F.; Thompson, L. W.; and Nowlin, J. B. 1976. Relationship between central and autonomic nervous system activity: Correlates of psychomotor performance in elderly men. *Experimental Aging Research* 2: 409–423.

Harter, M. R. 1967. Effects of carbon dioxide on the alpha frequency and reaction time in humans. *Electroencephalography and Clinical Neurophysiology* 23: 193–196.

Harter, M. R. 1971. Visually evoked cortical responses to the on- and off-set of patterned light in humans. *Vision Research* 11: 685–695.

Harter, M. R., and White, C. T. 1968. Effects of contour sharpness and check-size on visually evoked cortical potentials. *Vision Research* 8: 701–711.

Harter, M. R., and White, C. T. 1970. Evoked cortical responses to checkerboard patterns: Effect of check size as a function of visual acuity. *Electroencephalography and Clinical Neurophysiology* 28: 48–54.

Harvald, B. 1958. EEG in old age. *Acta Psychiatrica Scandanavice* 33: 193–196.

Hayashi, Y., and Endo, S. 1982. All-night sleep polygraphic recordings of healthy aged persons: REM and slow-wave sleep. *Sleep* 5: 277–283.

Hubbard, O.; Sunde, D.; and Goldensohn, E. S. 1976. The EEG of centenarians. *Electroencephalography and Clinical Neurophysiology* 40: 407–417.

Hubel, D. H., and Wiesel, T. N. 1962. Receptive fields, binocular interaction and functional architecture in the cat's visual cortex. *Journal of Physiology* 106: 106–154.

Hubel, D. H., and Wiesel, T. N. 1977. Functional architecture of macaque monkey visual cortex. *Proceedings of Research Society in London (Biology)* 198: 1–59.

Institute of Medicine. 1979. *Sleeping Pills, Insomnia, and Medical Practice.* Washington, D.C.: National Academy of Science.

Jasper, H. H. 1936. Cortical excitatory state and synchronism in the control of bioelectric autonomous rhythms. *Cold Spring Harbor Symposium on Quantitative Biology* 4: 320–338.

Jasper, H. H. 1958. Recent advances in our understanding of ascending activities of the reticular system. In *Reticular Formation of the Brain,* eds. H. H. Jasper, L. D. Proctor, R. S. Knighton, W. C. Noshay, and R. T. Costello. Boston: Little, Brown.

Jeffrey, D. W. 1969. Age differences in serial reaction time as a function of stimulus complexity under conditions of noise and muscular tension. Unpublished doctoral dissertation, University of Southern California.

Jeffreys, D. 1977. The physiological significance of pattern visual evoked potentials. In *Visual Evoked Potentials in Man: New Developments.* J. E. Desmedt. Oxford: Clarendon Press.

Jerome, E. A. 1959. Age and learning—experimental studies. In *Handbook of Aging and the Individual,* ed. J. E. Birren. Chicago: University of Chicago.

Kahn, E., and Fisher, C. 1969. The sleep characteristics of the normal aged male. *Journal of Nervous and Mental Disease* 148: 477–505.

Kales, A.; Wilson, T.; Kales, J.; Jacobson, A.; Paulson, M.; Kollar, E.; and Walter, R. D. 1967. Measurements of all-night sleep in normal elderly persons: Effects of aging. *Journal of the American Geriatrics Society* 15: 405–414.

Kent, S. 1976. Neurotransmitters may be a weak link in the aging brain's communication network. *Geriatrics* 31: 105–111.

Kibbler, G. O.; Boreham, J. L.; and Richter, D. 1949. Relation of the alpha rhythm of the brain to psychomotor phenomena. *Nature* (London) 164: 371.

Kimble, G. A., and Pennypacker, H. S. 1963. Eyelid conditioning in young and aged subjects. *The Journal of Genetic Psychology* 103: 283–289.

Knorring, L. von, and Johansson, F. 1980. Changes in the augmenter-reducer tendency and in pain measures as a result of treatment with a serontonin-reuptake inhibitor—Zimelidine. *Neuropsychobiology* 6: 313–318.

Knorring, L. von, and Perris, C. 1981. Biochemistry of the augmenting-reducing response in visual evoked potentials. *Neuropsychobiology* 7: 1–8.

Kornfield, C. M. 1974. EEG spectra during a prolonged compensatory tracking task. Unpublished doctoral dissertation, University of California at Los Angeles.

Kristofferson, A. B. 1967. Successiveness discrimination as a two-state, quantal process. *Science* 158: 1337–1339.

Lacey, J. I. 1959. Psychophysiological approaches to the evaluation of psychotherapeutic process and outcome. In *Research in Psychotherapy,* eds. E. A. Rubenstein and M. B. Parloff. Washington, D.C.: Psychological Association.

Lacey, J. I. 1967. Somatic response patterning and stress: Some revisions of activation theory. In *Physiological Stress: Issues in Research,* eds. M. H. Appley and R. Trumbull. New York: Appleton-Century-Crofts.

Landfield, P. W., and Lynch, G. 1977. Impaired monosynaptic potentiation in *in vitro* hippocampal slices from aged, memory-deficient rats. *Journal of Gerontology* 32: 523–533.

Lansing, R. W. 1957. Relation of brain and tremor rhythms to visual reaction time. *Electroencephalography and Clinical Neurophysiology* 9: 497–505.

Lee, R. G., and Blair, R. D. G. 1973. Evolution of EEG and visual evoked response changes in Jakob-Creutzfeldt disease. *Electroencephalography and Clinical Neurophysiology* 35: 133–142.

Lindsley, D. B. 1938. Electrical potentials of the brain in children and adults. *Journal of Genetic Psychology* 19: 285–306.

Lindsley, D. B. 1952. Physiological phenomena and the electroencephalogram. *Electroencephalography and Clinical Neurophysiology* 4: 443–456.

Lindsley, D. B. 1960. Attention, consciousness, sleep, and wakefulness. In *Handbook of Physiology,* ed. J. Field. Vol. 3, Section 1. American Physiological Society.

Lindsley, D. B.; Schreiner, L. H.; Knowles, W. B.; and Magoun, H. W. 1950. Behavioral and EEG changes following chronic brainstem lesions in the cat. *Electroencephalography and Clinical Neurophysiology* 2: 483–498.

Lindsley, D. B., and Wicke, J. D. 1974. The electroencephalogram: Autonomous electrical activity in man and animals. In *Bioelectric Recording Techniques,* eds. R. F. Thompson and M. M. Patterson. New York: Academic Press.

Loveless, N. E., and Sanford, A. J. 1974. Effects of age on the contingent negative variation and preparatory set in a reaction-time task. *Journal of Gerontology* 29: 52–63.

Marsh, G. R. 1976. Electrophysiological correlates of aging and behavior. In *Annual Review of Experimental Aging Research,* eds. B. E. Eleftheriou and M. F. Elias. Bar Harbor, Maine: Experimental Aging Research.

Marsh, G. R., and Thompson. L. W. 1973. Effects of age on the contingent negative variation in a pitch discrimination task. *Journal of Gerontology* 28: 56–62.

Marsh, G. R., and Thompson, L. W. 1977. Psychophysiology of aging. In *Handbook of the Psychology of Aging,* eds. J. E. Birren and K. W. Schaie. New York: Van Nostrand Reinhöld, 1977.

Matousek, M.; Volavka, J.; Roubicek, J.; and Roth, Z. 1967. EEG frequency analysis related to age in normal adults. *Electroencephalography and Clinical Neurophysiology* 23: 162–167.

Michalewski, H. J.; Thompson, L. W.; Smith, D. B. D.; Patterson, J. V.; Bowman, T. E.; Litzelman, D.; and Brent, G. 1980. Age differences in the contingent negative variation (CNV): Reduced frontal activity in the elderly. *Journal of Gerontology* 35: 542–549.

Miles, L. E., and Dement, W. C. 1980. Sleep and Aging. *Sleep* 3: 119–220.

Milner, B. 1963. Effects of different brain lesions on card sorting. *Archives of Neurology* 9: 90–100.

Milstein, V. 1974. Alpha wave phase and alpha attenuation. *Electroencephalography and Clinical Neurophysiology* 37: 167–172.

Morrell, L. K. 1966. EEG frequency and reaction time: A sequential analysis. *Neuropsychologica* 4: 41–48.

Moruzzi, G., and Magoun, H. W. 1949. Brain stem reticular formation and activation of the EEG. *Electroencephalography and Clinical Neurophysiology* 1: 455–473.

Mundy-Castle, A. C. 1962. Central excitability in the aged. In *Medical and Clinical Aspects of Aging,* ed. H. T. Blumenthal. New York: Columbia University.

Mundy-Castle, A. C.; Hurst, L. M.; Beerstecher, D. M.; and Prinsloo, T. 1954. The electroencephalogram in senile psychosis. *Electroencephalography and Clinical Neurophysiology* 6: 245–252.

Mundy-Castle, A. C., and Sugarman, L. 1960. Factors influencing relations between tapping speed and alpha rhythm. *Electroencephalography and Clinical Neurophysiology* 12: 895–904.

Nies, A. D.; Robinson, S.; Davis, J. M.; and Ravaris, C. L. 1973. Changes in monoamine oxidase with aging. In *Psychopharmacology and Aging,* eds. C. Eisdorfer and W. E. Fann. New York: Plenum.

Nunn, C. M. H., and Osselton, J. W. 1974. The influence of the EEG alpha rhythm on the perception of visual stimuli. *Psychophysiology* 11: 294–303.

Obrist, W. D. 1954. The electroencephalogram of normal aged adults. *Electroencephalography and Clinical Neurophysiology* 6: 235–244.

Obrist, W. D. 1963. The electroencephalogram of healthy aged males. In *Human Aging: A Biological and Behavioral Study,* eds. J. E. Birren, R. N. Butler, S. W. Greenhouse, L. Sokoloff, and M. R. Yarrow. Washington, D.C.: U.S. Government Printing Office.

Obrist, W. D. 1965. Electroencephalic approach to age changes in response speed. In *Behavior, Aging and the Nervous System,* eds. A. T. Welford and J. E. Birren. Springfield, Ill.: Charles C. Thomas.

Obrist, W. D., and Busse, E. W. 1965. The electroencephalogram in old age. In *Applications of Electroencephalography in Psychiatry,* ed. W. P. Wilson. Durham, N.C.: Duke University.

Obrist, W. D.; Henry, C. E.; and Justiss, W. A. 1961. Longitudinal study of EEG in old age. *Excerpta Medical International Congress.* Serial No. 37: 180–181.

O'Hanlon, J. F.; McGrath, J. J.; and McCauley, M. E. 1974. Body temperature and temporal acuity. *Journal of Experimental Psychology* 102: 788–794.

Ordy, J. M., and Kaack, B. 1978. Neurochemical changes in composition, metabolism and neurotransmitters in the human brain with age. In *Neurobiology of Aging,* eds. J. M. Ordy and K. R. Brizzee. New York: Plenum.

Otomo, E. 1966. Electroencephalography in old age: Dominant alpha patterns. *Electroencephalography and Clinical Neurophysiology* 21: 489–491.

Pedersen, E. B., and Christensen, N. J. 1975. Catecholamines in plasma and urine in patients with essential hypertension determined by double-isotope derivative techniques. *Acta Medica Scandinavica* 198: 373.

Pfefferbaum, A.; Ford, J. M.; Roth, W. T.; Hopkins, W. F.; and Kopell, B. S. 1979. Event-related potential changes in healthy aged females. *Electroencephalography and Clinical Neurophysiology* 46: 81–86.

Powell, A. H., Jr.; Eisdorfer, C.; and Bogdonoff, M. D. 1964. Physiologic response patterns observed in a learning task. *Archives of General Psychiatry* 10: 192–195.

Prinz, P. N. 1976(a). Sleep patterns of healthy elderly subjects: Changes in EEG slow wave activity and REM sleep. Unpublished manuscript, University of Washington.

Prinz, P. N. 1976(b). EEG during sleep and waking states. In *Annual Review of Experimental Aging Research,* eds. B. Eleftheriou and M. Elias. Bar Harbor, Maine: Experimental Aging Research.

Prinz, P. N. 1977. Sleep patterns in the healthy aged: Relationship with intellectual function. *Journal of Gerontology* 32: 179–186.

Prinz, P. N.; Blenkarn, D.; Linnoila, M.; and Wietzman, E. 1976. Growth hormone levels during sleep in elderly males. *Sleep Research* 5: 187.

Prinz, P. N., and Halter, J. B. 1980. Sleep disturbances in the aged: Some hormonal correlates and some newer therapeutic considerations. In *Psychopharmacology of Aging,* eds. C. Eisdorfer and E. Fann. New York: S. P. Medical and Scientific Books.

Prinz, P. N.; Halter, J.; Benedetti, C.; and Raskind, M. 1979. Circadian variation of plasma catecholamines in young and old men: Relation to rapid eye movement and slow wave sleep. *Journal of Clinical Endocrinology and Metabolism* 49:300–304.

Robinson, S.; Nies, A.; Davis, J. N.; Bunney, W. W.; Davis, J. M.; Colburn, R. W.; Bourne, H. P.; Shaw, D. M.; and Coppen, A. J. 1972. Aging. monoamines, and monoamine-oxidase levels. *Lancet* 1: 290–291.

Roubicek, J. 1977. The electroencephalogram in the middle-aged and the elderly. *Journal of the American Geriatrics Society* 25: 145–152.

Sanford, A. J. 1971. A periodic basis for perception and action. In *Biological Rhythms and Human Performance,* ed. W. P. Colquhoun. London: Academic Press.

Schafer, E. W. P., and McKean, C. W. 1975. Evidence that monoamines influence human evoked potentials. *Brain Research* 99: 49–58.

Schaie, K. W. 1965. A general model for the study of developmental problems. *Psychological Bulletin* 64: 92–107.

Scheibel, M. E., and Scheibel, A. B. 1966. The organization of the nucleus reticularis thalami: A Golgi study. *Brain Research* 1: 43–62.

Scheibel, M. E., and Scheibel, A. B. 1976. Structural changes in the aging brain. In *Neurobiology of Aging,* eds. R. D. Terry and S. Gerschon. New York: Raven Press.

Schenkenberg, T. 1970. Visual, auditory, and somatosensory evoked responses of normal subjects from childhood to senescence. Unpublished doctoral dissertation, University of Utah.

Schenkenberg, T.; Dustman, R. E.; and Beck, E. C. 1971. Changes in evoked responses related to age, hemisphere and sex. *Electroencephalography and Clinical Neurophysiology* 30: 163–164.

Shmavonian, B. M., and Busse, E. W. 1963. Psychophysiological techniques in the study of the aged. In *Processes of Aging,* eds. R. H. Williams, C. Tibbitts, and W. Donahue. New York: Atherton Press.

Shmavonian, B. M.; Miller, L. H.; and Cohen, S. I. 1968. Differences among age and sex groups in electro-dermal conditioning. *Psychophysiology* 5: 119–131.

Shmavonian, B. M.; Miller, L. H.; and Cohen, S. I. 1970. Differences among age and sex groups with respect to cardiovascular conditioning and reactivity. *Journal of Gerontology* 25: 87–94.

Shmavonian, B. M.; Yarmat, A. J.; and Cohen, S. I. 1965. Relationships between the ANS and CNS in age differences in behavior. In *Behavior, Aging and the Nervous System,* eds. A. T. Welford and J. E. Birren. Springfield, Ill.: Charles C. Thomas.

Silverman, A. J.; Busse, E. W.; and Barnes, R. H. 1955. Studies in the processes of aging: Electroencephalographic findings in 400 elderly subjects. *Electroencephalography and Clinical Neurophysiology* 7: 67–74.

Skinner, J. E., and Yingling, C. D. 1977. Central gating mechanisms that regulate event-related potentials and behavior. A neural model for attention. In *Progress in Clinical Neurophysiology,* ed. J. E. Desmedt. Basel: Karger.

Smith, D. B. D.; Michalewski, H. W.; Brent, G. A.; and Thompson, L. W. 1980. Auditory averaged evoked potentials and aging: Factors of stimulus, task and topography. *Biological Psychology* 11: 135–151.

Smith, D. B. D.; Thompson, L. W.; and Michalewski, H. W. 1980. Averaged evoked potential research in adult aging—Status and prospects. In *Aging in the 1980's: Psychological Issues,* ed. L. W. Poon. Washington, D. C.: American Psychological Association.

Smith, D. B. D.; Tom, C. E.; Brent, G. A.; and Ohta, R. J. 1976. Attention, evoked potentials and aging. Paper presented at the 56th Annual Meeting of the Western Psychological Association, Los Angeles, April, 1976.

Straumanis, J. J.; Shagass, C.; and Schwartz, M. 1965. Visually evoked cerebral response changes associated with chronic brain syndromes and aging. *Journal of Gerontology* 20: 498–506.

Surwillo, W. W. 1960. Central nervous system factors

in simple reaction time. *American Psychologist* 15:419.

Surwillo, W. W. 1961. Frequency of the "alpha" rhythm, reaction time and age. *Nature* 191: 823–824.

Surwillo, W. W. 1963. The relation of simple response time to brain wave frequency and the effects of age. *Electroencephalography and Clinical Neurophysiology* 15:105–114.

Surwillo, W. W. 1964(a). The relation of decision time to brain wave frequency and to age. *Electroencephalography and Clinical Neurophysiology* 16: 510–514.

Surwillo, W. W. 1964(b). Some observations on the relation of response speed to frequency of photic stimulation under conditions of EEG synchronization. *Electroencephalography and Clinical Neurophysiology* 17: 194–198.

Surwillo, W. W. 1966. On the relation of latency of alpha attenuation to alpha rhythm frequency and the influence of age. *Electroencephalography and Clinical Neurophysiology* 20: 129–132.

Surwillo, W. W. 1968. Timing of behavior in senescence and the role of the central nervous system. In *Human Aging and Behavior*, ed. G. A. Talland. New York: Academic Press.

Surwillo, W. W. 1971. Human reaction time and period of the electroencephalogram in relation to development. *Psychophysiology* 8: 468–482.

Surwillo, W. W. 1972. Latency of EEG attenuation (blocking) in relation to age and reaction time in normal children. *Developmental Psychobiology* 5: 223–230.

Surwillo, W. W. 1975. Reaction-time variability, periodicities in reaction-time distributions, and the EEG gating-signal hypothesis. *Biological Psychology* 3: 247–261.

Surwillo, W. W., and Quilter, R. E. 1965(a). The influence of age on latency time of involuntary (galvanic skin reflex) and voluntary responses. *Journal of Gerontology* 20: 173–176.

Surwillo, W. W., and Quilter, R. E. 1965(b). The relation of frequency of spontaneous skin potential responses to vigilance and to age. *Psychophysiology* 1: 272–276.

Surwillo, W. W., and Titus, T. G. 1976. Reaction time and the psychological refractory period in children and adults. *Developmental Psychobiology* 9: 517–527.

Tecce, J. J. 1972. Contingent negative variation (CNV) and psychological processes in man. *Psychological Bulletin* 77: 73–108.

Tecce, J. J. 1979. A CNV rebound effect. *Electroencephalography and Clinical Neurophysiology* 46: 546–551.

Tecce, J. J.; Boehner, M. B.; Cattanach, L.; Branconnier, R. J.; and Cole, J. O. 1981. Hydergine treatment and brain functioning (CNV rebound) in Alzheimer's patients: Preliminary findings. *Psychopharmacology Bulletin* 173: 202–206.

Tecce, J. J.; Cattanach, L.; Yrchik, D. A.; Meinbresse, D.; and Dessonville, C. L. 1982. CNV rebound and aging. *Electroencephalography and Clinical Neurophysiology* 54: 175–186.

Tecce, J. J.; Yrchik, D. A.; Meinbresse, D.; Dessonville, C. L.; and Cole, J. O. 1980. CNV rebound and aging: I. Attention functions. *Progress in Brain Research* 54: 547–551.

Thompson, L. W., and Marsh, G. R. 1973. Psychophysiological studies of aging. In *The Psychology of Adult Development and Aging*, eds. C. Eisdorder and M. P. Lawton. Washington, D.C.: American Psychological Association.

Thompson, L. W.; Marsh, G. R.; and Zelinski, L. 1981. Topographical distribution of cortical potentials as a function of verbal or spatial processing set. Unpublished manuscript, University of Southern California.

Thompson, L. W., and Nowlin, J. B. 1973. Relation of increased attention to central and autonomic nervous system states. In *Intellectual Functioning in Adults*, eds. L. F. Jarvik, C. Eisdorfer, and J. E. Blum. New York: Springer.

Thompson, L. W., and Obrist, W. D. 1964. EEG correlates of verbal learning and overlearning in the elderly. *Electroencephalography and Clinical Neurophysiology* 16: 332–342.

Thompson, L. W., and Wilson, G. 1966. Electrocortical reactivity and learning in the elderly. *Journal of Gerontology* 21: 45–51.

Troyer, W. G., Jr.; Eisdorfer, C.; Wilkie, F.; and Bogdonoff, M. D. 1966. Free fatty acid responses in the aged individual during performance of learning tasks. *Journal of Gerontology* 21: 415–419.

Tryding, N.; Tufvesson, G.; and Nilsson, S. 1972. Aging, monoamines and monoamine-oxidase levels. *Lancet* 1: 489.

Walsh, E. G. 1952. Visual reaction time and alpha rhythm, and investigation of the scanning hypothesis. *Journal of Physiology* 118:500–508.

Walter, W. G. 1968. The contingent negative variation: An electrocortical sign of sensori-motor reflex association in man. In *Progress in Brain Research*. ed. E. A. Asratyan. Vol. 22, *Brain Reflexes*. Amsterdam: Elsevier.

Walter, W. G.; Cooper, R.; Aldridge, V. J.; McCallum, W. C.; and Winter, A. L. 1964. Contingent negative variation: An electric sign of sensori-motor association and expectancy in the human brain. *Nature* (London) 203: 380–384.

Wang, H. S., and Busse, E. W. 1969. EEG of healthy old persons—A longitudinal study. I. Dominant background activity and occipital rhythm. *Journal of Gerontology* 24: 419–426.

Wang, H. S.; Obrist, W. D.; and Busse, E. W. 1970. Neurophysiological correlates of the intellectual function of elderly persons living in the community. *American Journal of Psychiatry* 126: 1205–1212.

Webb, W. B. 1981. Sleep stage responses of older and younger subjects after sleep deprivation. *Electroencephalography and Clinical Neurophysiology* 52: 368–371.

Webb, W. B. 1982. Sleep in older persons: Sleep structures of 50- to 60-year-old men and women. *Journal of Gerontology* 37: 581–586.

Webb, W. B., and Dreblow, L. M. 1982. A modified method for scoring slow wave sleep of older subjects. *Sleep* 5: 195–199.

Welford, A. T. 1965. Performance, biological mechanisms and age: a theoretical sketch. In *Behavior, Aging and the Nervous System*, eds. A. T. Welford and J. E. Birren. Springfield, Ill.: Charles C. Thomas.

Wilkinson, R. T., and Morlock, H. C., Jr. 1967. Auditory

evoked response and reaction time. *Electroencephalography and Clinical Neurophysiology* 23: 50–56.

Williams, H. L.; Granda, A. M.; Jones, R. C.; Lubin, A.; and Armington, D. C. 1962. EEG frequency and finger pulse volume as predictors of reaction time during sleep loss. *Electroencephalography and Clinical Neurophysiology* 14: 64–70.

Wolman, B. B. 1973. *Dictionary of Behavioral Science.* New York: Van Nostrand Reinhold.

Woodruff, D. S. 1975. Relationships among EEG alpha frequency, reaction time and age: A biofeedback study. *Psychophysiology* 12:673–681.

Woodruff, D. S. 1978. Brain electrical activity and behavior relationships over the life span. In *Life Span Development and Behavior,* ed. P. B. Baltes. New York: Academic Press.

Woodruff, D. S., and Baum, M. 1982. EEG and reaction time relationships in adulthood and old age. *Gerontologist* 22:151.

Woodruff, D. S., and Kramer, D. A. 1979. EEG alpha slowing, refractory period, and reaction time in aging. *Experimental Aging Research* 5:279–292.

Woods, A. M. 1980. *Age Differences in the Effect of Physical Activity and Postural Changes on Information Processing Speed.* Unpublished doctoral dissertation, University of Southern California.

Yakovlev, P. V., and Lecours, A. R. 1967. The myelogenetic cycles of regional maturation of the brain. In *Regional Development of the Brain in Early Life,* ed. A. Minkowski. Philadelphia: Davis.

Ziegler, M. G.; Lake, C. R.; and Kopin, I. J. 1976. Plasma noradrenalin increases with age. *Nature* 261:333.

12
VISION AND AGING

Donald W. Kline
University of Notre Dame
and
Frank Schieber
Soft–Chip Technology, Inc.

Our ability to cope effectively with our environment is a function of our capacity to detect, interpret, and respond appropriately to sensory information. This is particularly true of vision because the human world is in large measure a visual one. Our occupational involvements, the performance of everyday skills, and our social and psychological well-being depend upon the complex chain of visual processes that begin at the ocular media of the eye and extend all the way to high-level perceptual functions in the brain. Research findings indicate that most of the operations of this chain are altered with advancing age. Anyone who lives into old age is likely to encounter visual decline sufficient to influence daily task performance to some degree; for a significant minority, these changes are severe (Padula, 1982).

The National Center for Health Statistics estimates that of 1.4 million persons in the U.S. in 1977 suffering from severe visual impairment (inability to read newspaper print with conventional correction), 990,000 of them were over age 65 (Kirchener and Peterson, 1979). Of 550,000 persons suffering from legal blindness (20/200 or worse visual acuity and/or less than 20 degrees of visual field), almost half (230,000) were over 65. It has been projected that by the year 2000, with the increased proportion of older persons, especially in the very oldest groups, as many as 376,000

elderly persons will be legally blind and 1,760,000 will suffer from severe visual impairment (Lowman and Kirchener, 1979). Furthermore, because of a variety of methodological problems in arriving at such estimates, these prevalence figures may be overly conservative (Greenberg and Branch, 1982). In general, it appears that the incidence of visual dysfunction rises exponentially with age (see also section on Visual Pathologies). It is little wonder that at least one poll has apparently found that loss of vision is second only to cancer as a dreaded consequence of aging (cf. Cogan, 1979).

Fortunately, most older people will not experience severe visual impairment. Normally, the effects of visual aging are gradual and can be compensated for in many cases, at least to some degree. It is these more typical changes in vision that serve as the major subject matter of this chapter. We have attempted to order discussion of these changes around the natural hierarchical organization of the visual system, beginning with the effects of age on the ocular media, proceeding through the various basic visual functions and concluding with age-related differences on complex perceptual tasks. Our emphasis, where possible, is on the changes that have occurred in our understanding of visual aging since publication of the last handbook review on this topic (Fozard, Wolf, Bell, McFarland, and Podolsky, 1977). We have, in addition, attempted to refer the reader to earlier studies that either remain relevant to currently active areas of research or that continue to represent our level of understanding in areas not being actively investigated. A more extensive review of research on visual aging is available in a recently published book on the topic (cf. Sekuler, Kline, and Dismukes, 1982).

THE EYE AND THE BRAIN

On its journey to the retina, light must pass through the complex and dynamic optical apparatus that comprises part of the human eye. The structures of the eye that bend, limit, and transform light on its path toward visual effectiveness include the cornea, anterior chamber, pupil, lens, and vitreous body (see Fig. 1). All these structures change systematically with age—some greatly, others only a little.

Changes in the optic media of the eye tend to attenuate, scatter, and alter the spectral composition of the visual stimulus and are responsible for much of the reported age-related loss in visual acuity and sensitivity.

Weale (1961) has estimated that the retina of the 60-year-old receives approximately one-third the light of its 20-year-old counterpart. Visual aging, however, cannot be limited to changes in the optics of the eye. Weale (1975) has presented a careful analysis of all of the deleterious effects of senescent changes in the ocular media and has concluded that a large proportion of the exponential losses in acuity that accompany old age remains to be accounted for and must thus be due to alterations in the visual nervous system. These neural components of the visual system begin at the level of the retina, continue through the optic nerve to the lateral geniculate body, and then proceed to the visual cortex to the very highest centers of perception. There is a growing body of literature that suggests that Weale's analysis of the importance of age changes in the visual nervous system is accurate.

Cornea

The cornea is the clear, avascular anterior surface of the eyeball that provides the window

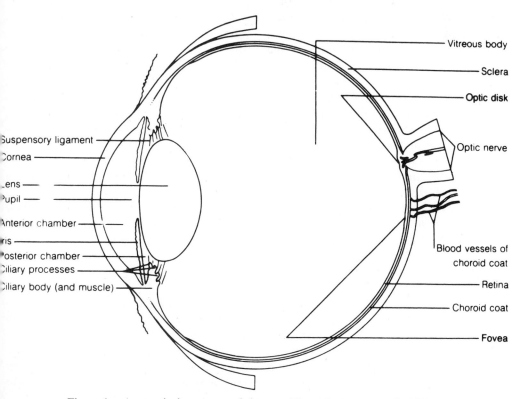

Figure 1.   Anatomical structure of the eye. (*From B. J. Anson, ed., 1966.*)

through which light enters the eye. The adjacent sclera, or white of the eye, serves as a tough, protective outer coating and ties the eye to the ocular muscles and vasculature. The principal function of the cornea is to refract, or bend, light toward a focus upon the retina. In fact, of the 65 diopters of refractive strength of the average eye (Geldard, 1972), the cornea accounts for 42 of them, or about two-thirds of this focusing power (the power of one diopter brings parallel rays of light into focus in a distance of 1 meter). Most of the remaining refractive power of the eye can be attributed to the lens.

Several age-related changes in the structural properties of the cornea appear to be of functional significance. There tends to be some flattening of the corneal surface, resulting in a slight reduction in its overall refractive power and contributing to cosmetic losses in the luster of aged eyes (Fischer, 1949; Lopping and Weale, 1965). Increased irregularity and waviness of the corneal surface structure has also been noted (Kuwabara, 1979), together with an increased incidence of corneal guttata—small deposits within the cornea that provide yet another source of optical degradation for light entering the aged eye (Anderson and Palmore, 1974). There appears to be some yellowing of the cornea in very advanced old age (Bruckner, 1959), but this yellowing may reflect increases in light scatter (chromatic abberation) rather than alterations in pigmentation (LeGrand, 1957; Fischer, 1949). Accompanying these changes is an apparent age-related increase in the incidence of corneal astigmatism. Such senescent astigmatisms tend to occur within the horizontal as opposed to the vertical axis of the eye (Leighton and Tomlinson, 1972; Marin-Amat, 1956), a tendency opposite to that observed in juvenile occurrence of astigmatism.

In addition to its refractive properties, the cornea also provides a measure of protection to the eye. In this regard, it should be noted that pressure sensitivity of the cornea decreases in advanced years—this decline being especially pronounced in the peripheral regions (Boberg-Ans, 1955). Relatedly, it has been observed that phasic lacrimal output (tearing) of the senescent eye is reduced (Henderson and Prough, 1950).

Perhaps the most commonly observed clinical manifestation of corneal aging is the gradual appearance of *arcus senilis*—a grayish-yellow ring along the border between the iris and sclera. It begins as a small arc of discoloration and gradually fuses into a complete ring with advanced age (Weale, 1963). This condition appears to result from accumulations of fatty deposits within the corneal tissue (Cogan and Kuwabara, 1959; Tschetter, 1966). Although some studies have suggested that arcus senilis occurs in up to 75 percent of elderly individuals, there is evidence that argues that it is not a universal aging phenomenon but may reflect hereditary factors instead (Burch, Murray, and Jackson, 1971; Stocker and Moore, 1975). Although advanced arcus senilis can be easily observed with the naked eye, its functional impact, if any, remains unclear.

Anterior Chamber

The anterior chamber of the eye lies between the posterior surface of the cornea and the anterior surface of the lens. It is filled with a clear fluid, the *aqueous humor,* which provides the principal means of transport for nutrients and metabolic wastes to and from the lens. The aqueous humor is a blood filtrate originating from the tissue of the ciliary body. Changes in the dynamics of aqueous production and drainage may be important factors in the genesis of glaucoma (see Visual Pathologies).

There is evidence that the depth of the anterior chamber may decline from 3.6 to 3.1 mm between the ages of 25 and 85 years (Rosengren, 1956). However, the refractive power of the structure does not appear to be altered with age (Huggert, 1948).

Iris and Pupil

The iris is a pigmented sphincter muscle parallel to the anterior surface of the lens. Through contraction and expansion, the pupillary aperture of the iris maintains maximum depth of field (focal range) under existing light conditions and also regulates the amount of light reaching the retina. Because the iris is a muscular tissue dependent upon a rich but fragile vascular supply, it is especially susceptible to systemic senile changes (Weale, 1963).

Adult aging is accompanied by a prominent reduction in pupillary diameter (e.g., Kumnick, 1956a; Weale, 1961). Known as *senile miosis,* this phenomenon results in a marked attenuation of light reaching the older retina. Birren, Casperson, and Botwinick (1950) measured pupil size in 222 subjects aged 20 to 89 years and found that pupil size inversely correlated with age under conditions of darkness (−0.70) and low-level illumination (−0.61). Weale (1963) has reported that the age difference in resting pupillary diameter appears to be most pronounced under conditions of impoverished illumination.

Researchers have offered diverse explanations to account for senile miosis. These include (1) vascular rigidity and calcification of the iris (Larsson and Osterlind, 1943; Fischer, 1949); (2) a shift with age toward autonomic parasympathetic dominance resulting in restriction of the pupil (Kumnick, 1956b); and (3) a more likely cause, atrophy of the dilator muscles of the iris (Kornzweig, 1954; Schafer and Weale, 1970; Tousimis and Fine, 1959), together with a thickening of the collagen fibers of which the iris is primarily composed (Kuwabara, 1979). One offsetting potential benefit of the reduction in pupillary diameter and the accompanying emphasis on the center of the lens is an increase in visual depth of field (e.g., Campbell, 1957). The use of small artificial pupils has been shown to increase the depth of field and sharpen figure contours in young subjects (Schurman, 1968). For these reasons, it is important that age differences in pupillary size be compensated with artificial pupils in any visual research where depth of field or retinal illuminance could be expected to play a role. This control effectively eliminates age differences resulting from senile miosis and is relatively simple to implement. Unfortunately, this problem has been too often ignored in aging research.

Aging also appears to be associated with a fading in the coloration of the iris. Pigment seems to diffuse peripherally, causing the border of the pupil to become ill-defined and probably contributing to increased scatter of the light entering the eye (Andrew, 1971).

Findings regarding age differences in the response latency of the pupil to sudden changes in illumination (i.e., the pupillary reflex) have not been completely consistent. Kumnick (1956b) measured the latency period to pupillary contraction in response to light onset and found no age differences in a group of subjects aged 7.5 to 90.8 years. Using the same group of subjects, he found a decrease with age in the velocity of constriction (Kumnick, 1956b). Other studies, however, have found an increase with age in the period between light stimulation and pupillary constriction (Peterson, 1956; Feinberg and Podolak, 1965). The difference between these studies and that of Kumnick might be attributable to methodological differences. Petersen, for example, photographed the changing pupil at a rate of 25 frames per second and may have been better able to resolve small differences in pupillary reflex than was Kumnick, who used only 10 frames per second. Feinberg and Podolak (1965) tested 86 subjects ranging in age from 14 to 67 years. With their measurement technique, the latency period was defined as the interval from the start of light stimulation to the moment when pupillary contraction velocity reached 3.5 mm/sec. Using this technique, these investigators found a significant increase with age in the mean latency period from 0.238 sec in subjects under 21 years to 0.273 sec in subjects over 50 years of age. The correlation between age and latency was 0.54. Unlike the important functional consequences of senile miosis, age changes in pupillary reflex, if any, are small and would appear to have little or no influence on visual performance.

Lens

The lens is composed of a clear, crystalline protein and provides the visual system with fine, dynamic adjustment of focus for different viewing distances. Bordered by the fluids of the anterior chamber and the vitreous body, the lens is avascular and thus completely dependent upon surrounding body fluids (primarily the aqueous humor) to maintain its metabolic and support functions. This dependency places the lens at particular risk with respect to the biological stresses that accompany the normal aging process (Spector, 1982).

The lens increases rapidly in size during early childhood and then grows at a constant linear rate across the rest of the life span (Garner and Spector, 1978). Lenticular mass doubles its neonatal value of 80 mg by puberty and grows continuously—tripling its original mass by age 70 (Salmony, cited in Weale, 1963). The growth of the lens takes place by way of a repeated differentiation of new cells in the periphery; since the lens is encapsulated in a dense membrane, no old cells are lost. In human beings, this continuous growth results in the older cells being compacted inward toward the center of the lens. This compacting of old cells along with numerous metabolic stresses (see Spector, 1982) produces several deleterious age-related changes in the functional capacity of the lens, namely: losses in transparency and optical quality, senescent lenticular "yellowing," and a marked decrease in accommodative power.

Reduced lenticular transparency can be observed in 65 percent of normal individuals between the ages of 51 and 60 and in 96 percent of those above age 60 (Alvaro, 1953). The attenuation of light that results from this opacification of the lens is not evenly distributed across the visible spectrum. Said and Weale (1959) determined age differences in the transmission of various wavelengths through the lens and found that older lens transmitted considerably less light and that the age difference was exacerbated for short wavelengths (blue and violet). Thus, the lens acts as a yellow filter to absorb complementary blue light. This yellowing appears to result from a change in pigmentation of the older cells of the lenticular nucleus as well as chromatic aberrations introduced by increased light scattering of the senescent lens (Weale, 1963).

The aging lens also appears to lose much of its malleability (Johansen, 1947), the fibers of its nucleus having a markedly increased resistance to mechanical deformation (Fisher and Pettet, 1973). This age-related change in the ability of the lens to bend is undoubtedly related to the loss of accommodative function (see also Accommodation).

Vitreous Body

The vitreous body comprises most of the volume of the eyeball and lies between the posterior surface of the lens and the retina. The vitreous, which is relatively transparent, is composed of varying proportions of gel, liquid, and well-organized microfibrils of collagen and maintains the uniform spherical shape of the eye.

Several systematic changes of the vitreous are associated with aging. There is a gradual increase from ages 40 through 80 in the proportion of the vitreous that is in the liquid state (Flood and Balazs, 1979). This changes the orientation and clustering of the collagen fibers, which, in turn, causes the vitreous to become less transparent and increases the intraocular scatter of light. Moreover, the liquefaction of the vitreous is accompanied by a shrinkage of the gel, resulting in a tendency for the vitreous body to retract anteriorly and pull itself away from the retina (Balazs and Denlinger, 1982). Eisner (1975) reported that such posterior vitreous detachment was observed in 20 percent of all clinical cases between ages 54 and 63, with an increased incidence of 49 percent in those aged 64 and above.

Posterior vitreous detachment can be accompanied by a variety of clinical manifestations, including: spontaneous occurrences of light flashes in the absence of an external stimulus (photopsia); gross distortion of the visual image; blurred vision; and most often, ephemeral, moving opacities in the vitreous that have been aptly labeled "floaters." Such detachment of the posterior vitreous can result in an excessive pull upon the retina, possibly leading to retinal detachment or hemorrhage and consequent macular edema. Since posterior vitreous detachment is usually sudden—precipitated by a jolt or other physical insult—certain classes of older workers such as truck drivers and others exposed to massive amounts of vibration may be at particularly high levels of risk (Balazs and Denlinger, 1982).

Retina

The retina is a complex photosensitive/neural network at the back of the eye that consists of several anatomically and functionally distinct layers. The activity generated by the photoreceptors—the rods and the cones—converges upon overlapping bipolar cells where information is temporally and spatially integrated within a complex, interconnected network of amacrine and horizontal cells—the structures primarily involved in the essential lateral-inhibitory processes of the retina (Ratliff, Hartline, and Miller, 1963). Sensory information is then passed on to the ganglion cells, the axons of which exit the eye to form the optic nerve. The retinal pigment epithelium (RPE) lies outside of the photoreceptors and supports the metabolic demands of the photoreceptors; it is, perhaps, the most active tissue of the human body.

Rods and cones differ in their anatomical, topographical, and functional properties. Cones mediate color perception, require high levels of luminance, and are centrally located in an area of the retina known as the *macula.* The concentration of cones in the center of the macula (the fovea) is primarily responsible for the discrimination of fine spatial detail. Rods, on the other hand, are extremely sensitive to low levels of illumination, are blind to color, and are more sparsely and peripherally distributed. The two photoreceptor types result in two functionally distinct subsystems of vision: (1) the scotopic (low illumination, peripheral vision) and (2) the photopic (high illumination, high acuity, central color vision).

Age-related changes in the retina are readily apparent upon gross examination of the fundus, or back of the eye, with an ophthalmoscope. The aged eye is characterized by more narrow and sclerotic-appearing ocular blood vessels; a progressive decrease in pigmentation of the retinal pigment epithelium, especially in the periphery, allowing the background choroidal patterns to show through; and di-

minished glistening light reflexes from the fovea and macula (Marmor, 1982). Another common age-related change is the appearance of drusen—yellow, half-moon-shaped protrusions of the choroid through the RPE—in and around the macula. The sites of such drusen are characterized by atrophic changes in overlying retinal tissue (Kuwabara, 1979). Although these changes may occur without any obvious loss of function, functional loss may also be seen in the absence of any additional ophthalmoscopic change.

Upon closer examination, the aged retina reveals more dramatic, atrophic alterations. Prominent cellular changes in the retina include the accumulation of lipofuscin (aging pigment), especially in the RPE (Kuwabara, 1979); loss of photoreceptors (Marshall, Grindle, Ansell, and Borwein, 1979); atrophy of the bipolar and ganglion cells (Kuwabara, 1979; Vrabec, 1965); and, general atrophy of the retinal capillaries (Kuwabara and Cogan, 1965). Recent data (Marshall, cited in Weale, 1978) indicates that the number of cones declines very slightly between ages 20 and 40 but then markedly decreases between ages 40 and 60. Such a loss of cones in the fovea would undoubtedly influence visual acuity and other perceptual abilities dependent upon central vision.

Aged photoreceptors are very similar in appearance to cells experimentally exposed to prolonged doses of high-intensity light. In fact, there is ample evidence suggesting that much of the photoreceptor loss accompanying old age results from the phototoxic effects of sunlight, which contains significant levels of high-energy ultraviolet radiation (Noell, Walker, Kang, and Berman, 1966; Kuwabara and Gorn, 1968; Kuwabara, 1979).

Studies of the summated electroretinogram (ERG) of the aging eye (Karpe, Rickenbach, and Thomasson, 1950; Straub and Lehnert and Wuensche, both cited in Fozard et al., 1977) indicate that the amplitude of the a-wave (largely a photopic component) declines with age, while the b-wave (more largely scotopic than photopic) undergoes an age-related increase in latency and duration as well as a decrease in amplitude. The fact that amplitude declines in the photopic component can be compensated for by increasing the level of illumination of the stimulating light suggests a lenticular attenuation factor. No such compensatory factor is apparent for the scotopic component. Although it is tempting to infer that the scotopic and photopic systems age differentially, the ERG and aging findings are difficult to interpret. For example, although it is known that the senescent lens differentially transmits light of varying wavelengths (Said and Weale, 1959) and that the ERG is extremely sensitive to color (e.g., Riggs, Johnson, and Schick, 1966), there is a paucity of data concerning age-changes in the ERG as a function of stimulus wavelength.

Visual Brain

Neurosensory codes from the retina are passed by way of the optic nerve to the lateral geniculate nucleus of the thalamus and, ultimately, to the striate cortex. Much of the topographic representation of the retina is maintained by the neural projections to the visual cortex (Geldard, 1972); however, a complex, hierarchical processing of visual information emerges at this level (e.g., Hubel and Wiesel, 1968). Psychophysical investigations indicate that a significant component of observed age differences in basic visual-perceptual processes stems from changes in these central-nervous-system structures (see Information Processing). Age-related changes in visual search (Plude and Hoyer, 1981), backward dichoptic masking (Walsh, 1976); visual perceptual latency (Kline, Schieber, Abusamra, and Coyne, 1983), and even a significant proportion of declines in visual acuity (Weale, 1975) appear to involve corresponding changes in central-nervous-system mechanisms.

In addition to inferences drawn from psychophysical investigations of visual aging, studies utilizing anatomical, biochemical, and electrophysiological procedures indicate that central-nervous-system structures and processes known to be involved in visual perception become significantly altered during normal aging. The neuronal population of the human cerebral cortex declines rapidly during old age, although some regions appear to escape this cellular loss (Brody, 1976). With respect to vision, Devaney and Johnson (1980) have reported that the number of neurons in the macular projection area of the human visual cortex falls from over 40 million per gram of tissue in the third decade to less than 30 million per gram after the sixth decade. Additional losses through age 87 were also noted by these investigators. (See Fig. 2.) In addition to the loss in sheer number of neurons, there is also evidence suggesting a qualitative change in these cells. Aged cortical neurons that do survive appear to possess decreased numbers of dendritic spines—structures essential for intercellular exchange of information (Scheibel, Lindsay, Tomiyasu, and Scheibel, 1975). Relatedly, there appears to be an age-related decline in the level of enzymes critically involved in the metabolic cycles of important neurotransmitters of the visual cortex (McGreer and McGreer, 1976).

Averaged evoked potentials, recorded from the scalp, have been used to provide gross electrophysiological indices of the location and temporal extent of sensory-perceptual processes occurring in the brain (e.g., Donchin, Ritter, and McCallum, 1978). Systematic senescent changes in the latency and amplitude of various components of this wave form have been catalogued by Beck, Dustman, and Schenkenberg (1975) and Klorman, Thompson, and Ellingston (1978). Changes in the visual evoked response that are most characteristic of advanced age include an increase in both the latency and amplitude of early, sensory components (20–100 msec) and an increase in the latency of the late components (100–300 msec), which appear to be correlated with higher-order perceptual processes such as stimulus evaluation and selective attention (Dustman and Beck, 1966; Shagass, 1972; Shaw and Cant, 1980). According to Beck, Swanson, and Dustman (1980), the latency of the P3 (late) component of the visual waveform increases by 0.8 msec per year between the ages of 28 and 63, with an acceleration of this delay to 1.6 msec per year between ages 63 and 79. Such changes probably reflect a slowing in the processing of visual perceptual information within the senescent visual system. Yet, the fact that aged individuals main-

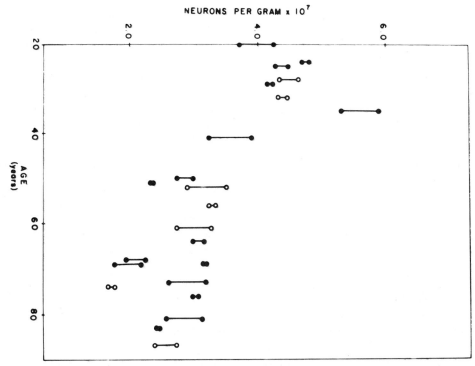

Figure 2.   Neuron population densities in the macular projection area as a function of age. Paired determinations of cell number by separate techniques are connected by vertical lines. Male subjects are indicated by closed circles; females, by open circles. (*From Devaney and Johnson, 1980.*)

tain a high degree of functional vitality in the face of such dramatic central-nervous-system losses gives evidence to the great redundancy and flexibility of the human brain. Continued research on the electrophysiological aspects of visual functioning could contribute greatly to our understanding of normal visual aging.

Visual Pathologies

Although not linked directly to the aging process, numerous pathologies of the visual system show an increased incidence among the aged population. The most common of severe age-related pathologies are cataract, glaucoma, senile macular degeneration, and diabetic retinopathy.

Greenberg and Branch (1982) have recently presented an extensive epidemiological analysis of the Westat Corporation (1976) report—a survey commissioned by the National Eye Institute. They found that three specific conditions affect a significant proportion of the older population in the United States: cataracts, glaucoma, and various retinopathies. Cata-

racts affect 5 to 7 percent, or more than one of every 20 persons over the age of 65. Glaucoma affects 3 to 5 percent, whereas retinal disorders (exclusive of diabetic retinopathy) affect 1 to 3 percent of the elderly. The incidence of cataract, glaucoma, and retinopathy was calculated to be eight, eight, and six times greater, respectively, in the aged than in the general population. In addition, diabetic retinopathy was reported to affect three to five per thousand older Americans.

Similar findings have been reported by the Duke Longitudinal Study (Anderson and Palmor, 1974) and the Framingham Study (Kahn et al., 1977) of visual impairment. Clearly, visual pathologies among the aged pose high personal, sociological, and economic costs in the United States.

Cataract. Cataract is a pathological increase in lenticular opacification that leads to markedly diminished visual acuity—often severe enough to cause blindness. Although significant yellowing and scattering of light characterizes the senescent lens, the development of cataract appears to involve numerous biochemical aspects that distinguish it from normal aging (Spector, 1982). Cataract is the leading cause of functional blindness among those over the age of 65 (Corso, 1981). Fortunately, the complete or partial blindness resulting from cataract can be surgically corrected by removal of the lens (resulting in a condition termed *aphakia*). This procedure represents the fifth most frequent major surgical operation currently performed in the U.S. (Anderson, 1971) and is reported to be successful in 95 percent of the cases (Kornzweig, 1972).

The aphakic eye requires external compensation for the refractive power lost with extraction of the lens. This is most often provided by the use of special contact lenses, which eliminate many of the deleterious visual problems associated with cataract spectacles such as ring scotoma, "jack-in-the-box" phenomenon, and severely restricted visual fields (Chylack, 1979). Studies of aphakic eyes have provided valuable information regarding the affects of lenticular aging, including its effects on color vision.

The occurrence of cataract in one eye is usually followed by its appearance in the other, although the latency varies considerably. This latency of interocular onset of cataract averages around four years for the 45-year-old and decreases by one year for each decade thereafter (Leonardi, Lumbroso, Melchionda, and Barcaroli, cited in Corso, 1981). Data from the Framingham Study (Kahn et al., 1977) suggest that cataract may be correlated with elevated blood sugar level, perhaps providing a functional link to the increased incidence of senile cataract associated with diabetes (Chylack, 1979).

There has been some speculation that life-span exposure to ultraviolet (UV) light might be a critical precursor in the genesis of cataract (e.g., Rambo and Sangol, 1960). Hallows and Moran (1981) investigated the relationship between climatic UV level and vision in 64,307 Australian aborigines and 41,254 nonaborigines. They reported a highly significant link between climatic UV light-exposure levels and prevalence of cataract for aborigines. Aborigines who lived in regions of Australia charac-

terized by higher levels of UV irradiation were more likely to acquire cataract, more likely to develop the condition earlier in life, and more likely to become visually disabled than those living in areas of low UV irradiation. Cataract among nonaborigines occurred with a prevalence rate of slightly less than two-thirds of that observed among their counterparts. Cataract among nonaborigines was not correlated with climatic UV levels. It appeared that differences in the lifestyle of nonaborigines (such as the amount of time spent indoors and the use of sunglasses) afforded significant levels of protection against the deleterious effects of environmental UV irradiation. This fact suggests that although excessive UV exposure may exacerbate the genesis of cataract, it does not appear to be a necessary precondition.

Glaucoma. Glaucoma consists of a group of disorders characterized by an increase of intraocular pressure and accompanying atrophic alteration in the optic nerve head and abnormalities of the visual fields. The elevated incidence of glaucoma found among the elderly actually represents a gradual linear increase in prevalence from age 60 through 85, as reflected in the Duke Longitudinal Study (Anderson and Palmore, 1974) and cross-sectional investigations such as the Framingham Study (Kahn et al., 1977).

An important feature of open-angle glaucoma, the most prevalent type among the elderly, is that it often remains entirely asymptomatic until the effects of irreparable damage to the retina become painfully apparent. Advanced cases reveal themselves by a characteristic cupping of the optic disk, as seen through the ophthalmoscope. However, recent advances in tonometry (estimating intraocular pressure by measuring the force needed to depress the surface of the eye) have provided a means of detecting glaucatomous increases in pressure well before significant damage can occur. Thus, regular glaucoma screening of individuals over the age of 50 would appear to be prudent.

A primary cause of glaucoma appears to be a resistance to the outflow of the aqueous humor from the anterior chamber, resulting in a gradual increase of fluid pressure within the eye and subsequent atrophic changes at the optic disk and retina. Kornzweig (1972) has speculated that age-related increases in prevalence of glaucoma might be related to normative changes in the volume of the lens and rigidity of the iris and surrounding tissue.

Intraocular pressure is correlated with systolic blood pressure. Bulpitt, Hodes, and Everitt (1975) reported that a 100-mm-Hg increase in systolic blood pressure was accompanied by a 2-mm-Hg rise in intraocular pressure. A 2-mm-Hg rise is significant, given that normal intraocular pressure ranges between 13 and 21 mm Hg (Kornzweig, 1972). Relatedly, recent studies have suggested that administration of beta adrenergic nervous-system blockers (e.g., timolol maleate) effectively controls intraocular pressure increases (Gillies and West, 1981; Strempel, 1981). This suggests that age-related increases in intraocular pressure may be also controlled by changes in nervous-system influences regulating aqueous humor dynamics.

Senile Retinopathy. Senile macular degeneration (SMD) refers to the systematic deterioration of the macula, which mediates acuity for fine detail. SMD begins with the appearance of numerous drusen throughout the macular region, followed by a progressive destruction of the surrounding neural components of the retina, pigment epithelium, and choriocapillaries. The onset of SMD is deliberate, most often bilateral, and untreatable (Lewis, 1979). It typically progresses until acuity declines to a range of 20/50 to 20/100. Reading becomes extremely difficult, but not impossible if a strong, hand-held magnifier is used. Television is reduced to a blur. Usually the damage is restricted to the macula; peripheral vision and ability to move about the local environment are maintained (Marmor, 1982).

A devastating variant of SMD is disciform macular degeneration. It is accompanied by a leakage of blood vessels which, if not halted by laser photocoagulation, will destroy the nervous tissue of the macula and central visual acuity with it. It has been estimated that 60 percent of the individuals afflicted with this pathology become legally blind within five years of the first occurrence of visual loss (Gregor, Bird, and Chisholm, 1977; Lewis, 1979).

Diabetic retinopathy also presents itself with an increased prevalence during senescence. Welch (1969) reported that diabetic retinopathy ranked only behind cataract, SMD, and glaucoma as a cause of blindness in the United States. A life course of juvenile-onset diabetes results in widespread and universal destruction of the retinal vasculature (Davis, 1971). White (1960) has estimated that over 90 percent of those having juvenile-onset diabetes for 20 years or more develop significant retinal pathology.

LIGHT SENSITIVITY AND COLOR VISION

The complementary photopic and scotopic subsystems of the human eye make it a remarkably adaptable visual instrument. Because of the ability of the subsystems to alter their responsiveness to changing illuminance, the human eye has an overall range of sensitivity of 13 log units (from about 10^{-6} to 10^7 candelas/sq m). The eye achieves this range of response through a trade-off between a relatively small range of immediate sensitivity (about 2 log units) and its potential 13-log-unit change in sensitivity over time (adaptation). It is clear that significant changes occur with age in adaptation as well as in the other operations of the photopic and scotopic subsystems.

Dark Adaptation

When confronted with a decline in illumination, the visual system increases its sensitivity in a process referred to as *dark adaptation.* This occurs first and relatively briefly (over about 8 minutes) for photopic vision; in scotopic vision, it is considerably more protracted. Dark adaptation appears to be due to both photochemical and neural processes. The photochemical processes appear to establish the ultimate sensitivity in dark adaptation; the neural processes may limit sensitivity during adaptation (Haber and Hershenson, 1980).

All studies of age and dark adaptation have found a marked elevation in the final (absolute) threshold (e.g., Birren, Bick, and Fox,

1948; Domey, McFarland, and Chadwick, 1960; Luria, 1960; McFarland, Domey, Warren, and Ward, 1960; Steven, 1946). This decline appears to be particularly marked after age 60 (see Fig. 3). A variety of factors, however, affect the eye's sensitivity to a test light after a time in the dark, including the color, size, retinal location, and duration of the test light; a variety of preadaptation parameters; and pupil size. In addition, many of these factors interact with age. Since testing conditions have varied considerably across the different aging studies, a comparison of their results is somewhat difficult. Nevertheless, a reasonable understanding of the course and cause of age differences in dark adaptation has begun to emerge.

McFarland and Fisher (1955) obtained complete dark-adaptation curves on subjects between 20 and 60 years of age. The test light was viewed through an artificial pupil to control for the age decline in pupil size. Preadaptation level and test-light duration were held constant. A correlation of 0.89 was found between age and final adaptation level; the intensity of the test light at threshold had to be approximately doubled for each 13 years of age. So strong was the relationship observed between age and final adaptation level that it could be used to predict a subject's age to

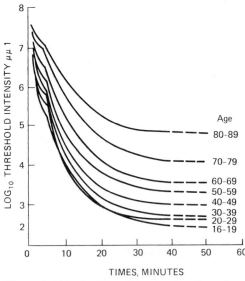

Figure 3.   Dark adaptation as a function of age. (*From McFarland, Domey, Warren and Ward, 1960.*)

within three years. McFarland, Domey, Warren, and Ward (1960) repeated this study using a more diversified group of subjects ranging in age from 16 to 89. Very high correlations were found between age and threshold throughout the adaptation period. The intercorrelations between age and threshold at different measurement intervals were so strong that Domey and McFarland (1961) were able to recommend a 13-minute adaptation procedure (3-min preexposure, 10-min adaptation) that would reliably predict ($r = 0.90$) final adaptation level. McFarland and his colleagues also concluded that rates of dark adaptation of both rods and cones as well as threshold level were inversely related to age. Noting the similarity between the effects of age on dark adaptation and those of hypoglycemia, anoxia, and vitamin A deficiency, McFarland et al. (1960) concluded that age-related decrements in retinal metabolism, rather than changes in the ocular media, were the primary cause of age-related differences in dark adaptation. There is, however, some reason to doubt both of these conclusions.

Using the data of Birren and Shock (1950), Weale (1965) has concluded that the rate of physiological dark adaptation is basically unchanged with age. He argued that the apparent reduction in rate reflects only on an age-related delay in reaching any given sensitivity level that is associated with the upward displacement of the older subjects' entire adaptation function. This delay, he concluded, results from age changes in the ocular media of the eye. There is considerable evidence consistent with this view.

Gunkel and Gouras (1963) examined the effect of test-light wavelength on age differences in dark adaptation. Their subjects, some of them with aphakic eyes, ranged in age from 16 to 86 years. At 80 years of age, a 1.0 log unit of difference was observed between the threshold of the normal and aphakic subjects. As a result, the authors concluded that changes in the transmittance of the older lens is the primary factor in the elevation of the adaptation threshold. Only a 0.3 log-unit difference was found using red light, which is passed relatively well by an older lens. Since a pupillary dilator (mydriatic) did not reduce the thresholds for older subjects, the relatively small differences at this wavelength were probably neural (Pitts, 1982).

Weale (1963) compared the absolute threshold data from five different dark-adaptation studies. Two of them controlled pupil size and used a blue target light; the other three employed a natural pupil and a white test light. For the latter studies, he also calculated the absolute visual threshold that would be expected with a pupillary correction. On the basis of this, Weale concluded that age changes in visual threshold ". . . can be accounted for largely in terms of senile miosis and alteration in the light-transmitting property of the crystalline lens" (Weale, 1963, p. 135).

Glare

Glare results when light that is excessively bright or inappropriately directed yields a reduction in visual effectiveness. Glare can be classified in a number of ways, including the one provided by Bell, Troland, and Verhoeff (cited in Carter, 1982), who divided it into veiling, dazzling, and scotomatic types. In veiling glare, stray light is distributed across a retinal image, reducing its contrast. This occurs, for example, when room lights are turned on during the projection of a slide or motion picture. Dazzling glare involves the difficulty encountered in discerning the detail in an extremely bright visual display. Scotomatic glare is the protracted reduction in sensitivity that occurs when the retina is exposed to excessive light levels, even if they are brief such as in exposure to a flash bulb. The relationship between glare and age has not been studied extensively for any glare type, particularly in the case of dazzling glare and, to a lesser degree, of scotomatic glare.

Wolf (1960) studied the effect of veiling glare on the luminance required to identify a target in 112 subjects aged 5 to 85. He observed that the illumination necessary to identify the target in the absence of glare rose significantly with age. Sensitivity to glare also increased with age, especially after age 45. Glare sensitivity, however, appears to be normal in older eyes from which the lens has been removed (Wolf, 1960), suggesting that the age-related increase in glare sensitivity is largely attributable to changes in the opacity of the lens. This conclusion is also supported by the apparent relationship between glare response and photometric measurement of the scattering of light in lens and vitreous (Wolf and Gardiner, 1965).

Other studies have also noted an increase with age in susceptibility to the effects of veiling glare (e.g., Fisher and Christie, 1965; Sturgis and Osgood, 1982). Pulling, Wolf, Sturgis, Vaillancourt, and Dolliner (1980) found a significant decline with age in headlight-glare resistance when subjects were tested in a realistic driving simulator. Sturgis and Osgood measured visual acuity and contrast sensitivity in three age groups (20 to 25, 40 to 45, and 60 to 65) over a range of background luminances and in the presence of glare. They found that the effectiveness of veiling luminance increased with age but that this did not interact with age, glare level, or background luminance. Furthermore, the age differences they noted in glare threshold were proportional to no-glare threshold differences and led them to conclude that there is not a differential glare/age effect.

Older persons also appear to show a protracted period of recovery to the effects of scotomatic glare. Burg (1967) measured form recognition ability under low illumination as well as ability to recover from glare in nearly 17,500 subjects aged 16 to 92. A progressive increase with age was found in illumination threshold for target recognition. Glare recovery time was also greater in older persons. For example, recovery times were 3.9 sec, 5.57 sec, and 6.83 sec for persons aged 20 to 24, 40 to 44 and 75 to 79 years, respectively. Age correlated with glare recovery time ($r = 0.187$) and no-glare threshold ($r = 0.249$), but the two measures were not related to one another. It should be noted that the functional significance of these data is unclear. The glare source was only 3.2 fc and was exposed for 5 seconds. Glare recovery time was timed by hand and included the latency of verbal identification of the target stimulus. Other studies, however, have also reported an increase with age in glare recovery time (Brancato, cited in Corso,

1981; Reading, 1966). Given the functional importance of recovery from glare in such tasks as night driving, there is a need for further research on this problem (Burg, 1967), including a systematic examination of age differences on the photostress test (Carter, 1982). There is evidence, at least, that those over 40 years of age take longer to recover from photostress than those under 40 (Severin, Tour, and Kershaw, 1967).

Simultaneous Brightness Contrast

McCarter and Atkeson (1977) examined the performance of young (mean age, 19.6) and old (mean age, 64.8) groups of female subjects on a simultaneous brightness-contrast comparison task. The simultaneous contrast effect refers to the situation in which differences in the illumination of the surround result in a difference of perceived brightness for two identically illuminated stimulus patches presented side by side (a gray patch of illumination is perceived as "lighter" when its surround changes from being highly illuminated to dark). This effect is presumed to be mediated by lateral-inhibitory interactions at the level of the retina (Hurvich and Jameson, 1966). The older subjects were found to exhibit larger simultaneous brightness-contrast effects than the young. This increase in the magnitude of brightness contrast in older adults was interpreted by these investigators (p. 215) as being indicative of a "degeneration of damping fibers in the visual system," that is, an age-related alteration in the neural lateral-inhibitory processes of the retina. Given the central role of lateral inhibition in the sensory coding of visual information, this possibility merits considerable additional research.

Color Vision

The degree to which aging produces an overall change in color discrimination is not clear. Neither Boice, Tinker, and Paterson (1948) nor Chapanis (1950) found a relationship between age and color vision. Dalderup and Fredericks (1969), however, observed a loss in color sensitivity that was apparent around age 70 and became more pronounced with age

thereafter. They also found considerable individual differences between the right and left eyes, suggesting different rates of color vision loss in the two eyes. Gilbert (1957) administered the Color Aptitude Test to 355 subjects ranging in age from 10 to 93 years and found that color discrimination rose until the twenties and declined steadily with advancing age. Although the discrimination of blues and greens (short wavelengths) was more difficult than of reds and yellows (long wavelengths) for all subjects, the deficiency in matching blue and green became particularly pronounced with advancing age.

The attenuation with age of light from the blue end of the spectrum (Said and Weale, 1959) shifts the appearance of white light somewhat toward yellow and results in a relative darkening of blue-colored objects and a bias of color perception toward the longer wavelengths. This shift has usually been attributed to changes in the optical media, particularly age-related yellowing of the crystalline lens. Color distortion produced by the filtering effect of the lens seems to be accentuated by senile pupillary miosis, apparently by limiting light transmission to rays passing near the center (and thickest) part of the lens (Carter, 1982). The impairment in color recognition produced by lenticular absorption, scattering, and senile miosis becomes particularly significant when ambient illumination falls to lower photopic (cone) levels. This is because both acuity and hue discrimination decline as the retina approaches the transition between cone and rod functioning (Carter, 1982).

Age differences in color discrimination may not be accounted for completely by changes in the spectral sensitivity of the lens; changes at the retina or higher levels may also be involved. That, at least, was the conclusion reached by Lakowski (1962) on the basis of color discrimination testing with young and elderly aphakic subjects. Similarly, Ferara (cited in Weiss, 1959) found that although older subjects usually required more blue light to produce the sensation of blue, among the ten aphakes in his sample, the four subjects under 55 all required less blue than the six over 55.

A relationship of possible theoretical importance has been observed between color vision and visual acuity (Chapanis, 1950; Gilbert, 1957). Kleemeier (1952) found a correlation coefficient of 0.675 between far-distance binocular acuity and color vision and suggested the importance of controlling visual acuity in studying the relationship between color vision and age.

SPATIAL RESOLUTION

Eye Movements

Oculo-motor adjustment of the eyes allows the observer to keep moving objects fixated upon the retina. Smooth-pursuit eye movements refer to voluntary, sweeping motions of the eyes used to track objects crossing the visual field. Sharpe and Sylvester (1978) have noted a distinct slowing for smooth-pursuit eye movements as well as an increased latency initiating such movements with increasing age. Young subjects could follow targets moving as fast as 30 deg/sec, whereas older ones had difficulty accurately tracking targets moving at 10 deg/sec.

Chu, Reingold, Cogan, and Williams (1979) have reported age-related changes in saccadic eye movements for a small group of elderly subjects. Maximum saccadic amplitude and peak saccadic velocity were diminished in this group. Unlike pursuit eye movements, saccades are characterized by short, rapid, ballistic movements that occur between successive fixations. Since visual processes appear to be greatly inhibited during a saccadic movement and optimized upon reaching fixation, it is possible that age-related reductions in their breadth and speed could contribute to the observed age differences in perceptual span and/or processing time.

Chamberlain (1971) has reported that old age is accompanied by a limitation in the ability to look upward, but little or no limitation in the extent of lateral or downward gaze has been reported. Age-related changes in oculo-motor abilities have generated very little interest among aging researchers up to the present. Nevertheless, the obvious importance of pursuit eye movements for dynamic visual acuity and the potential significance of saccadic eye movements for a range of perceptual processes suggest that eye movements will not remain a neglected area of visual aging research.

Field of Vision

The field of vision of an eye is the total area over which effective sight is maintained relative to a constant, straight-ahead fixation point. The extent of the visual field has consequences for everyday activity, such as driving a car, as well as being informative with respect to the detection and diagnosis of certain disease states (Pitts, 1982). Most of our knowledge concerning changes in the visual field that accompany old age comes from studies using the so-called "kinetic" method of perimetry, whereby the peripheral boundaries of threshold visual sensitivity are mapped utilizing a moving stimulus. This differs from the more rigorous "static" method of perimetry, in which changes in sensitivity across the extent of the visual field are determined. Investigations of kinetic perimetry have demonstrated that the visual field constricts with advancing age (e.g., Harrington, 1964; Wolf, 1967; Burg, 1968). An extensive examination of peripheral vision for 17,000 individuals between the ages of 16 and 92 was conducted by Burg (1968). Targets subtending 46 minutes of arc, with a luminance of 7.5 foot-candles, were presented at various positions along the horizontal meridian for both eyes, and the peripheral extent of visibility was determined for each individual. Although the extent of both temporal and nasal visual fields declined with increasing age, this effect was particularly noticeable for the temporal field. The total horizontal visual field, represented by the sum of both temporal fields, was constant up to age 35, declined slightly between ages 40 and 50, and demonstrated an accelerated loss with age thereafter.

The most typical clinical assessment of visual field utilizes the Goldmann projection perimetry technique. A spot of light of variable size and intensity is projected upon the inner surface of a wide, dimly illuminated hemispherical shell. The spot is moved from the periphery toward the central point of fixation along predetermined meridians ranging in orientation from horizontal to fully vertical. Through reckonings of maximum target eccentricity from all approach directions, the visual field of sensitivity for 360 degrees about the fixation point may be determined. This map for a stimulus of a given size is known as an *isopter* (Corso, 1981).

Wolf (1967) utilized projection perimetry to assess the full extent of the visual field for individuals ranging in age from 16 to 91 years. The isopter for a 1-sq-mm, 3.3-millilambert (mL) spot projected against a 0.02-mL background was determined for each subject. The extent of the visual field remained relatively stable through age 55, followed by a progressive shrinking of the total field through the age of 91. Total field size was particularly diminished in those over 75 years of age (see Fig. 4). Similar findings using Goldmann perimetry have been reported by Drance, Berry, and Hughes (1967), who also demonstrated a significant increase in the size of the "blindspot" with advancing age.

Wolf (1967) also found that experimentally induced hypoxia (oxygen deprivation) among young individuals resulted in a constriction of the total visual field. On the basis of this

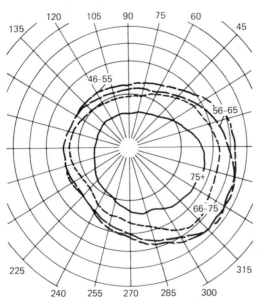

Figure 4.   Average isopters of peripheral vision for right eyes as a function of age. (*From E. Wolf, Studies on the shrinkage of visual field with age. Transportation Research Record 164, Transportation Research Board, National Academy of Sciences, 1967.*)

and related evidence, Wolf has suggested that changes in retinal metabolism may mediate age-related deficits in the fields of vision (Wolf and Nadroski, 1971).

Accommodation and Presbyopia

Accommodation refers to the ability of the eye to maintain sharply focused retinal images independent of object distance. This task is accomplished by dynamic changes in the shape of the lens as a result of forces exerted by the surrounding ciliary muscles. There is a systematic, universal loss in this accommodative ability of the lens with increasing age. Accumulated loss of accommodative reserve usually becomes noticeable during the mid-forties, resulting in a loss of near vision known as *presbyopia*.

The near point of vision—the closest distance at which a small object can be seen without blur—gradually lengthens with age. The receding near point results from a diminished ability of the senescent lens to increase its curvature and bend light to focus on the retina. The maximal refractive power of the lens, or accommodative amplitude, is represented by the dioptric equivalent of the distance between an individual's near point and the spectacle plane (14 millimeters in front of the cornea). Peak accommodative amplitude decreases gradually and linearly from childhood through age 65—with a slight acceleration in the rate of loss during the fifth decade (Bruckner, 1967). According to Weiss (1959), maximal accommodation decreases with age from about 20 diopters at age 5 until it reaches a value of 0.5 diopters at around age 60. This represents a linear loss of about 0.3 diopters of lenticular refractive power per year. Interestingly, there is some evidence that women develop presbyopia (usually defined as accommodative amplitude of less than 5.0 diopters) approximately 3 to 5 years sooner than do men (Rambo, 1953; Lebensohn, 1966).

Several theories of presbyopia have been discussed by Weale (1963); however, it is most likely that the decreased flexibility or malleability of the lens and lens capsule (Fisher, 1969; Brown, 1974) mediates senescent difficulties of accommodation. Although atrophic changes in the ciliary muscle that contracts the lens are associated with aging, Corso (1981) has discussed evidence that appears to minimize the role of ciliary-muscle changes in presbyopia. For example, electrophysiological measurements of ciliary-muscle activity during changes in monocular and binocular viewing distance (requiring an accommodative response) indicated no difference in ciliary-muscle response from age 22 through at least age 60 (Swegmark, 1969). Lenticular changes, alone, appear sufficient to account for presbyopic changes in visual function.

Static Acuity

Static visual acuity refers to the ability of the visual system to resolve fine spatial detail. Measured visual acuity is typically expressed either as the reciprocal of the threshold visual angle in minutes of arc or in the form of the Snellen fraction, which expresses the distance at which the threshold test object can be discriminated as the numerator and the distance at which the same object subtends 5 minutes of arc as the denominator (e.g., 20/20 is the so-called "normal" Snellen acuity).

Evaluated on the basis of group statistics, uncorrected visual acuity declines significantly in old age. Chapanis (1950) examined Snellen acuity of 574 persons aged 5 through 80. Acuity was reported to increase from ages 5 through 20, maintain peak levels between ages 25 to 45, and steadily decline thereafter. Pitts (1982) presented an elegant comparison of static acuity as a function of age as reported in eight major studies of visual function. On the basis of this massive condensation of data (see Figure 5), the classic pattern of age-related change in visual acuity becomes readily apparent. There is a slight increase into the second decade and then a plateau of peak acuity through the fifth decade, which is followed by a steady decline during the later years.

The Framingham study (Kahn et al., 1977) indicated that a great proportion of the acuity losses occurring during old age results from the increased prevalence of visual pathology—cataract, retinopathy, and glaucoma. These three classes of pathology, taken together, were found in 10.4, 37.1, and 88.2 percent of those with moderate to severe visual loss

in the 52 to 64-, 65 to 74-, and 75 to 85-year-old age groups, respectively. These data confirm similar findings reported by Weymouth (1960).

The vast majority of older individuals, however, do not suffer from visual pathology and maintain good to fair corrected visual acuity. Weymouth (1960) reported that many individuals maintain Snellen acuity levels of 20/20 through age 65. On the basis of a massive survey of drivers, Shinar (1977) reported that average acuity was 20/30 at age 65 and dropped significantly to 20/70 for those over age 65. Much of the slight to moderate loss in static visual acuity accompanying normal aging appears to be due to changes in the optic media of the eye. Senile miotic changes of the pupil and opacification of the lens and vitreous body tend to decrease retinal illumination and increase intraocular scatter of light markedly. These factors result in a threefold reduction in the light reaching the retina between the ages of 20 and 60 (Weale, 1961) and contribute significantly to declines in static visual acuity. The consequences of this senescent "sunglasses" effect become exacerbated under conditions of low or poor illumination. Although static acuity declines with target luminance can be observed for all age groups, the loss in visual sensitivity becomes markedly accelerated in aged individuals (e.g., Guth and McNelis, 1969; Sturgis and Osgood, 1982).

The deleterious effects of reduced retinal illumination can be compensated for by increasing the luminance and contrast of visual materials. Weston (1949) demonstrated that increases in target illumination by a factor of three produced greater improvements in acuity (Landolt rings) for older subjects than for their young counterparts. Although acuity in old subjects never reached levels achieved by the young, age-related losses in acuity were nonetheless compensated for by the simple manipulation of illumination. Similar compensation of age-related deficits in acuity through increases in target contrast have been suggested by Blackwell and Blackwell (1971). Thus, it would appear that changes in visual acuity that accompany normal adult aging are moderate and that much of the deficit that does occur may be overcome if older individu-

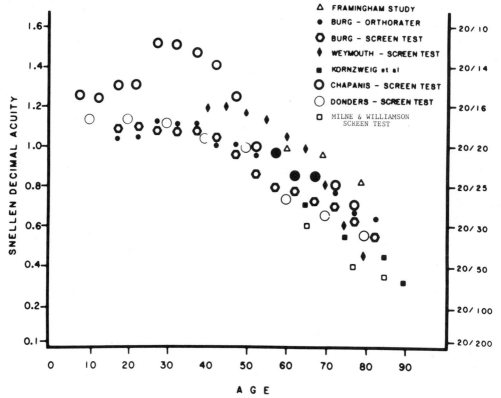

Figure 5. The composite of visual acuity as it changes with age based upon eight investigations. Acuity, here, is based on that of the best corrected eye. (*From D. G. Pitts, The effects of aging upon selected visual functions. In Aging and human visual function. New York: Alan R. Liss, 1982.*)

als are given control of environmental illumination conditions.

Dynamic Acuity

Dynamic visual acuity (DVA) refers to the ability to resolve fine spatial detail for objects in motion relative to the observer. DVA is perceptually more complex than static visual acuity processes, depending as it does upon the sharpness of the retinal image plus oculomotor coordination and higher-order visual nervous-system mechanisms (Panek, Barrett, Sterns, and Alexander, 1977). Burg (1966) examined both static and dynamic visual acuity measures obtained from a sample of more than 17,000 drivers aged 16 through 92. Acuity for moving targets was found to decline more dramatically with age than conventional measures of static acuity. Similar age-related declines in DVA have been reported by other

investigators (e.g., Farrimond, 1967; Reading, 1972).

Burg and Hulbert (1961) reported evidence indicating that an individual's ability to discriminate a moving target could not be adequately predicted on the basis of static visual acuity measures. This dissociation between static and dynamic visual acuity appears to become more pronounced in older individuals, especially as target velocity is increased (Reading, 1972). Unlike static visual acuity measures, DVA appears to have some predictive power as regards driving performance and highway safety among older, but not middle-aged, individuals (Henderson and Burg, 1974). The differential decline of DVA in older individuals, together with its predictive power for performance on complex perceptual-motor tasks such as driving, suggests that it holds the potential of providing important new information about the aging of higher-order visual functions. Additional research into age-related changes in DVA is warranted.

Contrast Sensitivity

Converging evidence from both psychophysical (e.g., Blakemore and Campbell, 1969) and electrophysiological research (e.g., Campbell and Maffei, 1970) indicates that different types of stimuli are detected by different neural channels in the visual system (cf. Levine and Shefner, 1981). Studies suggest that the human visual system contains at least two classes of channels—the "transient" and the "sustained"—which can be distinguished on their temporal response properties as well as their selectivity for targets of different size or spatial frequency. The Contrast Sensitivity Function (CSF) provides a comprehensive summary of the spatial discriminating abilities of the visual channels by relating the amount of contrast required to detect a target grating (typically sinusoidal) to the spatial frequency of the grating. *Spatial frequency* refers to the number of repetitions or cycles of the grating per degree of visual angle. A high spatial-frequency grating is a finely patterned one with a large number of cycles per degree (c/deg), and the determination of its resolution threshold is akin to a traditional visual acuity test. A low spatial-frequency grating, having relatively few c/deg, is more coarsely patterned.

The effects of aging on the CSF have only recently received serious research consideration (cf. Sekuler, 1982). Arden (1978) measured contrast sensitivity on the six plates of the Arden grating (spatial frequency of 0.2 to 6.4 c/deg) in subjects aged 11 to 70 and found no age differences. Similarly, Arden and Jacobsen (1978) observed few age differences on the Arden grating task in subjects aged 17 to 64. Skalka (1980), however, found an age decline in sensitivity across the whole range of spatial frequencies used in the Arden test. McGrath and Morrison (1980) determined CSFs for 66 subjects (aged 5 to 94) for oscilloscopically presented gratings with spatial frequency ranging from 0.33 to 40 c/deg. There was an age deficit in sensitivity for all spatial frequencies, but the point of

peak sensitivity was the same for all age groups (around 2 to 6 c/deg).

Two studies, one by Arundale (1978) and the other by Derefeldt, Lennerstrand, and Lundh (1979), revealed age deficits primarily at intermediate and high spatial frequencies (4 c/deg and higher). This outcome was just the opposite of that of Sekuler and Hutman (1980), who observed very large differences in sensitivity at the low spatial frequencies, differences that diminished as spatial frequency was increased; at the highest spatial frequency tested (16 c/deg), the sensitivity of the two groups was nearly identical.

Two recent investigations undertook to examine possible age differences with the aim of clarifying the inconsistent results of earlier investigations. Kline, Schieber, Abusamra, and Coyne (1983) used a threshold tracking method (Sekuler and Hutman, 1980) to determine CSFs for 16 young (aged 18 to 25) and 16 old (aged 55 to 70) subjects. Oscilloscopically presented sinusoidal gratings ranging in spatial frequency from 0.5 to 12 c/deg served as target stimuli. Their data were in basic agreement with those of Arundale (1978) and Derefeldt et al. (1979) in demonstrating an age-related deficit in contrast sensitivity for targets in the intermediate and high spatial-frequency range. A systematic examination of the impact of age on the CSF by Owsley, Sekuler, and Siemsen (1983) yielded similar results. Contrast sensitivity for gratings ranging in spatial frequency from 0.5 to 16 c/deg were determined for subjects from seven different age groups (age range, 19 to 87). As can be seen in Figure 6, all age groups are similar at low spatial frequencies, with a progressive age-related loss in sensitivity at the intermediate and high spatial frequencies. Sekuler and Hutman have concluded that their 1980 data are incorrect and may have resulted from a combination of factors including the small number of subjects employed as well as matching subjects for good visual acuity—i.e., high spatial-frequency sensitivity (Sekuler, personal communication, 1981). Thus, the emerging consensus appears to indicate that the major effect of aging on spatial vision is a loss in contrast sensitivity for targets whose

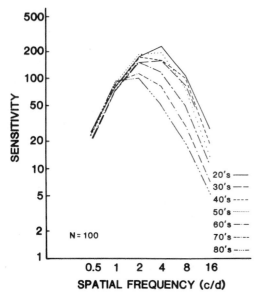

Figure 6.   Age and contrast sensitivity as a function of grating spatial frequency. (*From Owsley, Sekuler, and Siemsen, 1983.*)

Perception of Depth

The ability to localize objects in three-dimensional space despite their two-dimensional representation on the retina depends on the use of a large number of monocular and binocular depth cues. These cues vary greatly in their importance, and no one of them is absolutely essential to the perception of depth providing that others are available. These cues include texture gradient, relative height, aerial perspective, linear perspective, shading and shadow, interposition, motion parallax, accommodation, convergence, proximal brightness, and binocular disparity (stereopsis).

Depth perception and the role of these cues in mediating it has been the subject of extensive study in experimental psychology but has received only scant attention in gerontology. Furthermore, the only studies that have examined the effect of aging on depth perception have employed stereoscopic tests, although stereopsis is but one of the processes involved in depth perception (Pitts, 1982). Stereopsis is based on the integration of the disparate

images from the two eyes and may operate up to distances of 450 to 650 meters. In addition to observation distance, it is affected by several factors including luminance, lateral separation of objects, and retinal location.

Hoffman, Price, Garrett, and Rothstein (1959) compared stereopsis for young subjects with that of observers in their sixties (mean age 64) and found depth perception significantly worse in the older group. Using subjects with visual acuity of 20/40 or better in the best eye and screened for visual anomalies, Jani (1966) found little adult change in stereoacuity up to about age 45 and a steady decline thereafter. This was attributed by the author to increased image blur in the older eye.

Bell, Wolf, and Bernholz (1972) used a Verhoeff stereopter to assess age differences in stereopsis in 164 healthy veterans participating in the Normative Aging Study. The subject's task was to indicate the position (nearer or further) of one rod relative to two others as a function of viewing distance (1.0, 0.75, 0.50 and 0.25 m). They found a critical age range between 40 and 50 years at which depth perception began to deteriorate. Noting, as in Jani's study, that the decline in depth perception corresponded to the age at about which changes in accommodation, convergence, and glare sensitivity occur, the authors attributed the observed deterioration in stereopsis to changes with age in the ocular media of the eye. More generally, they suggested that early visual changes (at about 45) are associated with alterations in the anterior segments of the eye. Later changes (after 60 or so) in such functions as dark adaptation, critical flicker frequency (CFF), and visual field were ascribed to alterations in retinal function associated with metabolic change.

Corso (1981) has suggested that since no binocular interaction occurs below the level of the lateral geniculate nucleus, the stereopsic changes that have been observed actually reflect deterioration of cortical cells. Since stereopsis is dependent upon such factors as luminance and image clarity, this conclusion does not necessarily follow. Nonetheless, cells in the visual cortex do seem to respond selectively to specific degrees of retinal disparity

spatial frequency is around 2 c/deg and higher.

(Barlow, Blakemore, and Pettigrew, 1967; Hubel and Wiesel, 1970). Perhaps age-related changes in these binocular depth cells contribute to the age differences that have been observed in stereopsis.

Hofstetter and Bertsch (1976) employed the diastereo test to examine steropsis in subjects ranging in age from 8 to 46. The subjects were screened to eliminate pathologies and for monocular and binocular acuity of 20/20 or better. No age differences were observed, and it was concluded that stereopsis was unaffected by age. However, as Pitts (1982) notes, the limited age range and highly select character of the sample preclude a meaningful test of the relationship between aging and stereopsis.

Although it has not been investigated directly, it is possible that effective use of some of the cues involved in depth perception may not decline with age. Leibowitz and Judisch (1967) attempted to determine if the age decline in susceptibility to the Ponzo illusion could be accounted for by an age decline in size constancy. Seeing objects as of constant size despite their visual angle representation on the retina results from scaling image size against apparent depth. Surprisingly, in the Leibowitz and Judisch study, older adults (51 to 88) showed insignificantly better size constancy than that typically observed among college students. Minimally, these data suggest little age impairment in the use of at least one or more of the depth cues that subserve size constancy. Also, they suggest a need for systematic research on the aging of the numerous processes involved in the perception of depth.

TEMPORAL RESOLUTION

One of the most commonly observed changes with age is a decline in speed of performance. This slowing appears in both the rate at which various processes are carried out and in the latency with which they are initiated. One aspect of this change is a loss in the temporal resolving power of the visual system. Closely occurring visual events that can be readily distinguished by younger observers are often reported as fused by older ones in a wide variety of visual tasks (cf. Kline and Schieber, 1982).

Flicker Fusion

The critical flicker frequency (CFF) is the lowest frequency of a pulsating light source at which it appears to be on continuously and represents the visual system's limited ability to track rapid illumination changes. This limitation appears to be associated with the neural components in the retina; photoreceptors are capable of following flicker at rates considerably higher than the CFF. The CFF threshold is a function of a variety of factors, including retinal adaptation, target luminance, target color, target size, retinal location, and the light/dark time ratio.

Age differences in the CFF task probably represent the best documented age decline in visual temporal resolution (Brozek and Keys, 1945; Coppinger, 1955; Misiak, 1947). Wolf and Schraffa (1964) determined the CFF as a function of retinal location in 302 subjects ranging in age from 6 to 95. CFFs were obtained in the fovea and at various locations up to 60 degrees extrafoveally across the horizontal and vertical meridians. CFF thresholds were significantly lower in the older age groups, especially past 60. Although the CFF fell with increased distance from the fovea, the drop was highly similar for all age groups.

Only part of the decline in CFF appears to be associated with the reduction in retinal illuminance. McFarland, Warren, and Karis (1958) studied age differences in CFF at two illumination levels (21.9 and 0.041 fc) as a function of the relative balance of light and dark time in the flickering stimulus. The age difference was greatest when the percentage of on time of the light was low and least when the light/dark ratio was high. Age differences, however, were very similar at both illumination levels, suggesting that the age differences in CFF could not be attributed entirely to age differences in retinal luminance. Furthermore, when Weekers and Roussel (1946) compared the CFF with and without induced pupillary dilation so as to consider the effects of senile miosis, the mean difference between the young and old groups was only halved, from 8.6 to 4.4 Hz. Relatedly, Falk and Kline

(1978) found that an artificial pupil (3.5 mm) had only a negligible effect on the age difference in CFF. Semenovskaia and Verkhutina (cited in Weiss, 1959) were able to bypass entirely the effects of the optical media on the CFF by stimulating the retina directly with a pulsed, variable-rate electric current. They found that the induced phosphene critical-flicker frequency was inversely related to age and paralleled the mean values reported by Weekers and Roussel for CFF with pupils dilated.

Motion of the stimulus across the foveal area of the retina significantly elevates the CFF, presumably because of the larger number of previously unexcited, and thus nonrefractory, retinal elements stimulated in the movement condition. Simonson, Anderson, and Keiper (1967) found that increasing the rate of stimulus movement led to greater increments in CFF in young subjects than in older ones, supporting their hypothesis that a decrease in the number of excitable neural elements in the retina and visual pathways contributed to the age difference in CFF.

Stimulus Persistence

A stimulus persistence hypothesis has been offered by Axelrod (1963) and extended by Botwinick (1978) to account for age-related failures in temporal resolution. In this view, the older nervous system is slower to recover from the effects of stimulation, and, consequently, temporally contiguous stimuli are more likely to "smear" or overlap. Clearly, this hypothesis is in accord with the findings from CFF, recovery from glare, and visual masking studies. It is also generally consistent with the duration of spiral aftereffect seen in older observers (Griew, Fellows, and Howes, 1963). Relatedly, Eriksen, Hamlin and Breitmeyer (1970) used a Landolt-C detection task to determine time-intensity reciprocity in 18 subjects in three age groups: 30 to 35, 40 to 45 and 50 to 55. Their data indicated that the older subjects were able to compensate for their elevated light threshold by integrating energy over a longer interval. The authors speculated that their data might reflect an increase with age in the period of a central scanning process or psychological moment.

Data from studies specifically designed to evaluate the stimulus-persistence hypothesis have been generally, although not completely, supportive of it. Kline and Nestor (1977) measured the duration of complementary afterimages in young (mean age 18.8) and old (mean age 62.0) observers as a function of primary stimulus exposure durations of 30, 60, and 90 sec. In line with the persistence model, the old subjects showed greater afterimage persistence at all three exposure durations. Amberson, Atkeson, Pollack, and Malatesta (1979) also found support for an increase in visual persistence in a study of age differences in the dark-interval threshold. Seventy-two female subjects (12 in each of six age groups) were tested for their ability to resolve pairs of flashes. Although comparison of the age groups yielded a significant difference only between the youngest and oldest groups, dark interval threshold rose from about 65 msec (ages 20 to 29) to approximately 95 msec (ages 70 to 79). There is also evidence of an age-related increase in persistence in the mechanisms that mediate the perception of color. Kline, Ikeda, and Schieber (1982) found that older adults were significantly more likely than younger persons to fuse sequentially separated red and green flashes into an additive yellow. This effect appeared to the authors to be due more to age-related differences in neural mechanisms than to changes in the ocular media or photoreceptor activity. No support for increased persistence, however, was observed in a study of the duration of the Spiral and Waterfall aftereffects (Coyne, Eiler, Vanderplas, and Botwinick, 1979). Young (20 to 29) and old (60 to 69) subjects showed no consistent pattern of aftereffect differences across exposure durations ranging from 45 to 120 seconds.

Kline and Baffa (1976) presented young (mean, 21.3) and old (mean, 55.6) adults with word stimuli constructed of dots so that they could be presented as corresponding word halves separated by an interstimulus interval (ISI) of varied duration. They hypothesized that any increase in persistence would "bridge" the ISI and lead to superior word identification by the older subjects. Just the opposite effect was observed; the young subjects recognized more words at all levels of

ISI. The authors surmised that difficulties in perceiving the stimulus halves may have more than offset any age-related gains in performance attributable to persistence. In fact, when Kline and Orme-Rogers (1978) repeated the study, changing to a black-on-white format and eliminating the need for closure, the old subjects did identify significantly more of the words. Furthermore, in strong support of the stimulus-persistence hypothesis, the superiority of the old subjects increased as ISI was lengthened.

In a study by Walsh and Thompson (1978), a target circle was alternated cyclically with a blank ISI to determine age differences in the longest ISI at which the illusion of circle continuity could be maintained. Contrary to the persistence notion, this ISI proved to be longer for the young subjects. It has been argued (Kline and Schieber, 1980, 1982) that this outcome may have been the result of any one of several possible procedural shortcomings, including the lack of a criterion-setting practice session and the difficulty in ignoring the luminance transient that results when switching tachistoscopic fields. When Kline and Schieber (1980) repeated the Walsh and Thompson study taking these short comings into account, target persistence was in fact significantly greater among the elderly. The difference in outcome between the two studies appeared to be in the young groups; the mean persistence estimates were very similar for the old.

Although there is support for the stimulus-persistence hypothesis, its utility as a scientific heuristic is somewhat limited; it describes certain changes but it posits neither the mechanisms to explain them nor a locus for their occurrence. Clearly a model is needed that posits specific mechanisms underlying the persistence effects. Pollack (1978) has suggested a model that places the stimulus persistence mechanism in the retina. He hypothesizes that increased stimulus persistence results from age changes in the slowly decaying rod potential. No research, however, has yet directly tested this hypothesis.

Kline and Schieber (1981) have proposed a "transient/sustained shift" hypothesis of visual aging that attempts to account for a variety of age-related visual changes, including those in stimulus persistence, dynamic acuity, and integration of form in terms of the differential aging of the transient, as opposed to the sustained, channels of the visual system. The sustained channels are slow to respond when stimulated, have a relatively long integration time, and are most sensitive to high spatial-frequency targets. Transient channels respond optimally to stimulus change (flicker or motion). Accordingly, they respond quickly and briefly to low spatial-frequency targets. In addition, when activated, they appear to inhibit the persisting activity of the sustained channels (Breitmeyer and Ganz, 1976). Kline and Schieber noted that the temporal response profile of the young visual system to stimuli that evoke a "sustained type" response (e.g., high spatial frequency, long duration, and low contrast) appears to mirror the failure that occurs in temporal resolution with aging. That is, they suggest an age shift in the relationship between the transient and sustained channels, resulting in a senescent visual system that is "sustained-channel dominant" in comparison with its younger counterpart. Only a few studies are available so far to evaluate the utility of their hypothesis.

Schieber and Kline (1982) used a visual successiveness paradigm with young and old subjects and found that older subjects required significantly greater levels of stimulus offset asynchrony to discriminate offset order. Their data were interpreted as indicative of an age-related loss in the mechanisms that process visual "transients." Sturr, Kelly, Kobus, and Taub (1982) compared two young observers (mean age 27) and two older observers (mean age 45.5) on the effects of early light adaptation. They found that the older subjects manifested a longer and less vigorous recovery, a result that they viewed as consistent with the "transient/sustained shift" hypothesis.

Since the transient channels respond best to stimuli of low spatial frequency, the spatial vision losses noted earlier in the CSF are not supportive of the transient/sustained shift model. All of the studies of age and CSF used stationary stimuli, however, which optimize the likelihood of tapping the sustained channels (Harwerth and Levi, 1978) but may not expose an age difference in the transient channels. There is some evidence for this contention. Owsley, Sekuler, and Siemsen, 1983) determined the contrast threshold for a 1-c/deg grating when a transient was added (movement at 1.1 or 4.3 deg/sec). Consistent with a decline in the effectiveness of the transient channels, motion enhancement of sensitivity was very much greater for the young subjects than the old ones, particularly at the faster movement rate.

Kline, Schieber, Abusamra, and Coyne (1983) tested the transient/sustained shift hypothesis in a two-part study that examined age differences in the contrast sensitivity function and reaction time (RT) to sinusoidal gratings of varied spatial frequency (SF). As in other studies (e.g., Harwerth and Levi, 1978), they found that RT usually increased as a function of SF. This increase, like the overall relationship between RT and SF, was particularly robust among the old subjects (see Figure 7). These spatial-frequency related differences in RT could not be accounted for more than partly by age losses in contrast sensitivity. Grating visibility was most strongly correlated with RT in the young observers, particularly at the three lowest spatial frequencies where contrast sensitivity was virtually unrelated to RT in the old group. Moreover, the RT differences in the age groups did not follow the differences in contrast sensitivity. Although the age difference in sensitivity decreased from 0.5 c/deg to 2 c/deg, the RT difference increased. Also, the greatest age difference in sensitivity occurred at the intermediate spatial frequencies; the greatest RT differences were at the highest spatial frequencies. Relatedly, since contrast sensitivity at high spatial frequency corresponds to a measure of visual acuity, acuity problems do not seem to account for age differences in the RT/SF relationship. Overall, these data suggest that the age differences in RT involve age-related slowing in the visual channels at low frequencies and contrast sensitivity losses plus visual channel slowing at high spatial frequencies. An age-related shift from transient to sustained channel functioning may explain the increases in RT that cannot be attributed to losses in contrast sensitivity. These findings also question the meaning and comparability of aging studies that use response latency to figural stimuli (as opposed to a luminance transient) as a dependent variable. The spatial-frequency characteristics of the target are never specified in such studies; in this investigation, however, the age difference in response latency varied by 68 msec, or about 210 percent (from about 60 to 128 msec) as a function of SF. To evaluate this possibility adequately, however, research is needed that examines the RT/SF relationship at the higher contrast levels more likely to characterize those used in RT studies.

INFORMATION PROCESSING

The major assumption of an information-processing approach toward understanding visual function is that perception is not an immediate outcome of stimulation but the consequence of a series of neurophysiologically mediated processes that actively develop and transform systematic representations of environmental stimuli over time. Typically, the visual perceptual task is conceptualized in terms of a short-lived sensory buffer (e.g., iconic storage) whose spatial contents in ascending the visual system are selectively processed into concentrated informative codes through contour extraction and the development of organized visual "forms." At the highest levels, this visually coded form information is transformed into a meaningful semantic representation for input to more general cognitive infor-

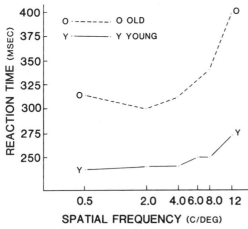

Figure 7.   The reaction time of young and old subjects as a function of the spatial frequency of the target stimulus. (*From Kline, Schieber, Abusamra, and Coyne, 1983.*)

mation processing (cf. Lindsay and Norman, 1972). Studies of masking, encoding speed, and visual search have indicated that visual perceptual processes appear to slow with increasing adult age.

Backward Masking

Backward visual masking has been the most frequently used method for investigating the time course of various phases of visual processing. In backward masking, a target stimulus (TS), which must be identified by the subject, is presented for a brief duration, followed closely by a second masking stimulus (MS) that diminishes the visual effectiveness of the TS. The interval between the onsets of the target and masking stimuli, or stimulus-onset asynchrony (SOA), during which the observer "escapes" the influence of the masking effect, can be used as an estimate of the time required for preliminary processing of the target. Through simultaneous manipulation of other stimulus variables such as stimulus energy (time × luminance intensity) and the interstimulus interval between target offset and mask onset, more complex perceptual relationships can also be examined (see Turvey, 1973).

Backward-masking studies using subjects of different ages have found that old subjects show a prolonged susceptibility to the disruptive effects of masking stimuli. Kline and Szafran (1975) examined the differences between young subjects (mean age, 23) and old ones (mean age, 66) on a backward-monoptic (both TS and MS presented to the same eye) masking task. Subjects were required to identify two-digit target stimuli of varied duration, followed by a 100-msec visual noise (randomly distributed black and white line segments) masking stimulus. As TS duration was varied from 4 to 25 msec, the interstimulus intervals (ISI) required to attain 50 percent correct TS identification were markedly greater for the old subjects. Kline and Szafran interpreted their results as indicating a significant increase in the time needed to process a single perceptual event completely.

Walsh, Till, and Williams (1978) found similar differences in a monoptic, backward-masking task when they presented young and old subjects with letter stimuli that were masked with a pattern of line segments. The old subjects processed the stimuli more slowly than the young ones at all stimulus energy levels employed. Processing time, as represented by the obtained SOA thresholds, was a power function of stimulus energy (duration × luminance) suggestive of a peripheral (at or below the primary visual cortex) masking effect as defined by Turvey (1973). An examination of identification performance as a function of energy level for nonmasked stimuli revealed little age difference, suggesting that a substantial proportion of this slowing resulted from "changes in the rate of neural net operation rather than from physical changes in the eye" (p. 242).

Kline and Birren (1975) also examined age differences in a backward-masking task where the TS and MS were dichoptically presented (to opposite eyes). It is presumed that the dichoptic procedure bypasses the possibility of a retinally mediated interaction between MS and TS in favor of a more central, postretinal locus [although this assumption has been disputed by Long (1979)]. It should be noted that these investigators used the term "central" in its more traditional, neurophysiological sense (i.e., postretinal) as opposed to Turvey's (1973) definition of the term as involving processes only above the level of the striate cortex. Single-digit target stimuli were presented to the right eye and a visual noise mask to the left. ISI thresholds for 50-percent target identification as a function of target duration were lowest for the young (mean age 23.5), intermediate for the middle-aged group (mean age 46.6) and highest for the elderly group (mean age 69.1), indicating significant perceptual slowing with age in postretinal visual processing. Kline and Birren (1975) observed no practice effects across the two sessions in which ISI masking thresholds were collected but emphasized the need for further investigation into possible age-related differences in such practice. In a subsequent study of age differences on a dichoptic masking task, Hertzog, Williams, and Walsh (1976) did demonstrate a statistically significant effect of practice for both young (mean age 18.8) and old (mean age 66.5) subjects across five successive days of performance. Since the magnitude of the practice effect was similar for both age groups, it did not lessen the observed age differences in the speed of central perceptual processing.

Walsh (1976) also studied age differences on a backward dichoptic masking task and found that older subjects (mean age 64.2) required an average ISI of 151 msec to escape the effects of a patterned line-segment mask—24 percent longer than a group of young (mean age 19.5) subjects. He concluded that there was an age-related decrease in the rate of central perceptual processes by the Turvey (1973) criteria and that, by the same token, the data of Kline and Szafran (1975) were reflective of differences in peripheral perceptual processing. Till and Franklin (1981) examined both peripheral and central masking curves for young and old subjects. They found a small but reliable age difference in peripheral masking and a marked difference between the groups on the obtained central masking curve. They concluded that age differences in central processing were larger than for peripheral processing.

Although the results of backward visual masking studies have been interpreted primarily as supporting the notion of age-related declines in the speed of the perceptual nervous system (DiLollo, Arnett, and Kruk, 1982), alternative interpretations have been presented. For example, Salthouse (1980) proposed that differences in backward masking could be understood in terms of an age-related reduction in perceptual signal-to-noise ratio rather than a decline in processing speed *per se*. He proposed that increases in temporal stimulus parameters (e.g., exposure duration and ISI) were required by older persons to escape from visual masking because of the additional processing required to extract the target signal from background perceptual noise. Salthouse conducted a masking experiment to test this hypothesis. The signal-to-noise ratio was manipulated either indirectly through variations in target stimulus-exposure duration (as is typically seen in such experiments) or directly through variations in the discriminability of the target stimulus itself. The TS consisted

of paired circles (ranging in size from 1.19 to 2.72 deg) characterized by size discrepancies of 10, 20, 30, 40, 50 or 60 minutes of arc. The subject's task was to report whether the circles were the same or different in size; the larger the discrepancy, the more discriminable were the circles. The MS consisted of two series of concentric circles ranging from 3.75 degrees to a small, solid dot. Results of the investigation were consistent with previous studies, since older subjects (mean age, 69) required greater ISIs to escape the effects of backward masking than did a younger group (mean age, 19). More interesting, however, was the finding that the same age difference observed for the ISI masking curves was demonstrated for the masking functions based upon stimulus discriminability. Salthouse interpreted this finding as indicating a "lowered signal to noise ratio" in the senescent nervous system.

Encoding Speed

Visual information focused upon the retina appears to be momentarily stored in a quickly fading sensory buffer (iconic memory). Early perceptual processes extract and encode information from this iconic "sample–and–hold" buffer and pass this structured code to primary memory where it can be processed at much higher levels (Haber and Hershenson, 1980). The basic processes of visual encoding have been extensively studied (see Coltheart, 1976). Investigations of these processes typically present strings of stimulus letters and control the time allowed to process them through the use of a backward-masking stimulus. The number of letters that are correctly identified as a function of the processing time allowed yields a characteristic, dual-process, linear recognition plot that can be used to make inferences about the qualitative and quantitative nature of the encoding processes underlying visual form perception (Sperling, 1963).

Cerella, Poon, and Fozard (1982) have examined age differences in the rate at which strings of letters are encoded for subsequent recognition and report. They used the technique of mask-induced control of the length of time that iconic memory is available for processing. Young (mean age 21) and old (mean age 64) subjects were presented with a display of seven equally spaced consonants on a CRT. The time available to encode these strings was controlled by the presentation of a patterned-noise mask at SOAs of 10 through 200 msec. For both age groups, they found that the function relating correct recognition and processing time offered a good fit to the well-demonstrated dual-process linear curve (thought to represent a cross-over from purely visual to semantic encoding). Nevertheless, there were some significant differences between the groups.

The first leg (visual encoding) of the dual-process letter-recognition function was characterized by a significant age difference in slope—representing visual encoding speeds of 27 msec/letter for the young subjects and 35 msec/letter for the old. There was also a slight difference in the slope of the second leg (semantic encoding) of the function—the processing rate estimates for the young and old groups being 142 and 153 msec/letter, respectively. The age-differential shift from the first to the second linear components of the recognition function suggested that older subjects switched from fast visual encoding to slower verbal encoding after two letters, whereas the young group switched after three letters. The investigators related these findings to previous suggestions that "perceptual span" declines with age (e.g., Schonfield and Wenger, 1975).

Visual Search

In the completion of everyday visual tasks, the individual must search for relevant information from a much wider array of stimuli. Age differences in the speed and efficiency of such visual-search behavior have been examined by several investigators. Rabbitt (1965) gave young (mean age 19) and old (mean age 63) subjects a task in which they were required to sort cards containing the letters "A" and "B" into separate piles. As the number of task-irrelevant, or distractor, letters increased, the time required to sort the cards increased more markedly for the older subjects. Rabbitt concluded that older persons were more likely to have difficulty in ignoring irrelevant or re-

dundant information and consequently were at a disadvantage in searching amongst complex patterns of stimuli. This suggestion has been challenged by Wright and Elias (1979). They have argued that, in most cases, extraneous stimuli in the visual search field are not irrelevant, insofar as they must be actively processed by the observer in order to be discriminated as target or nontarget stimuli.

An extensive examination of age differences in visual search as a function of target/display set size and practice has recently been reported by Plude and Hoyer (1981). Young (mean age 23.5) and old (mean age 74.9) subjects were required to sort cards containing one to nine letters into separate compartments based upon the occurrence of prespecified target letters. Subjects sorted 24 experimental decks of 36 cards in each of six separate sessions. Half of the participants in each age group were given the same target set for each session (consistent mapping), while the other half were given a different set of target letters for each of the sessions (varied mapping). The number of letters that could appear on a card varied from one (the target alone) to nine. Consistent with previous findings, age deficits in card-sorting speed became pronounced as display set size increased, but this effect was found only in the varied-mapping condition. In the consistent-mapping condition, where subjects got to practice with the same target letters over six sessions, little or no age differences as a function of display set size were apparent by the end of the experiment. Plude and Hoyer interpreted these findings as support for the notion that age-differences are minimal on well-practiced tasks where processing becomes "automatic" and that they are much more likely to be observed in situations requiring more active or "effortful" processing on behalf of the individual.

PERCEPTUAL ORGANIZATION AND FLEXIBILITY

Much of the early research on the effects of aging on visual perception was concerned with the global aspects of perceptual organization and flexibility. Currently these topics receive little systematic research attention. The available data do indicate that older perceivers are likely to experience greater difficulty than their younger counterparts in achieving organized perceptions from other than unambiguous, complete, clearly-structured stimuli. They also appear to be somewhat less flexible in reorganizing or reversing a perception once it has been established.

Incomplete Stimuli

Of the several studies that examine ability to identify objects from incomplete representations of them, all have found that older perceivers are inferior to at least some degree. Verville and Cameron (1946) presented young (16 to 23 years) and old (35 to 56 years) subjects with incomplete versions of common objects. The older subjects were significantly slower in achieving correct identification of the stimuli. Similarly, Comalli (1963) found that older subjects had a more difficult time than younger adults in recognizing incomplete pictures on four different perceptual closure tests. Other studies have found similar results (e.g., Basowitz and Korchin, 1957; Wallace, 1956).

Age differences in the identification of such incomplete stimuli appear to be exacerbated by less than optimal viewing conditions such as reduced inspection time (Botwinick, Brinley, and Robbin, 1958; Wallace, 1956) or small stimulus size (Thomas and Charles, 1964). With embedded figures, incomplete figures, and silhouettes of both familiar and irregular forms as their test stimuli, Crook and his co-workers (1958) varied exposure duration, luminance, contrast, and the presence or absence of a visual noise overlay. Using male subjects with normal vision, they found no effects of age under ideal viewing conditions and long exposure time. As task conditions were made more severe, however, an increasingly marked age difference was observed, although the oldest subjects were only in their late fifties.

Older perceivers appear to have particular difficulty when stimuli are irregular or unfamiliar. Kline, Culler, and Sucec (1977) presented young, middle-aged, and old subjects with a series of inconspicuous words (the let-

ters of which were formed by the unclosed space between blotches) constructed in a stylistic irregular format. Subjects were given 90 seconds to identify each word, and for young subjects the task was an extremely easy one. It was, however, a nearly impossible one for the old subjects (only three words correct out of a possible 160). Furthermore, an intervening reversible-figure training exercise had no remedial effect at all on their performance. When in a subsequent study (Kline, Hogan, and Stier, 1980) the inconspicuous words were modified slightly to conform to a traditional block-letter style, both young and old subjects performed extremely well, eliminating the age difference almost entirely.

Danziger and Salthouse (1978) investigated four possible explanations for the poorer performance of old adults on incomplete figures: (1) a higher criterion for producing a response; (2) less familiarity with the stimulus materials; (3) less adequate knowledge of the information value of particular segments of the figure, and (4) less efficient utilization of partial information. The results of their study supported the last of these possibilities.

Perceptual Flexibility

In addition to experiencing some difficulty in organizing stimuli into coherent perceptions, older persons appear less likely to modify a perception once it has been established. Korchin and Basowitz (1956) presented young (22 to 33 years) and old (65 to 85 years) adults with a picture series of 13 drawings that shifted from a cat to a dog in discrete stages. Compared to the young, the old subjects were significantly slower in making a response, reported a shift in perception at a later stage in the series, and exhibited greater vacillation in their reports subsequent to their first perceptual shift.

A similar lack of perceptual flexibility has been observed in older individuals on other tasks. Older persons report fewer oscillations on the Necker cube illusion (Heath and Orbach, 1963) and binocular rivalry task (Jalavisto, 1964), and they are less likely to report seeing the alternative stimulus in the ambiguous Boring "wife/mother-in-law" figure (Botwinick, Robbin, and Brinley, 1959). Because both young and old subjects typically reported the "wife" first, Botwinick (1962) tested the hypothesis that dominance of the figure contributed to the older persons' lower rate of perceptual modification. When he used a more balanced "husband/father-in-law" figure, old subjects were still less likely than the young to alter their initial percept. However, as the "husband" was consistently the dominant member of the pair, Botwinick (1978) has suggested that the older persons may have lacked the perceptual span to identify the alternative father-in-law figure in the first place.

Another factor that may contribute to diminished perceptual flexibility is increased cautiousness on the part of older persons. Botwinick (1962) carried out a study using the same cat/dog series employed by Korchin and Basowitz (1956), but in his study the need for perceiving a shift was indicated in advance, as were the beginning and end points of the series. Under these conditions, the shift was made earlier by the old than the young. This result suggested that given appropriate structure and direction the older person will perform with minimal difficulty on perceptual tasks such as these.

Context Effects

Several studies have shown that older observers manifest an increased sensitivity to the interfering effects of surplus or irrelevant stimuli (see also Information Processing). Age differences in the Stroop color-word task (Comalli, Wapner, and Werner, 1962), in judging verticality under conditions of body tilt (Comalli, Wapner, and Warner, 1959), and in identifying embedded figures (Eisner, 1972; Karp, 1967) are all consistent with this notion. A decline in these tasks is often interpreted as indicative of an increase with age in "field-dependence" (Eisner, 1972; Panek, 1982). In an alternative, not necessarily incompatible explanation, Layton (1975) has suggested that age differences in these and a variety of other perceptual tasks reflect an increase with age in "perceptual noise." The scientific utility of

this as well as competing hypotheses, however, remains to be determined by research.

Illusions

Age differences in the magnitude of the effect of visual illusions vary as a function of the particular illusion being examined. Both increases and decreases in susceptibility to illusions have been reported. On the basis of data from three previous studies based on the Muller-Lyer illusion, Comalli (1970) has reported that increases in adult age are accompanied by heightened magnitudes of effect. Similar findings have been reported by others (e.g., Eisner and Schaie, 1971), although Atkeson (1978) demonstrated a decrease in susceptibility to the illusion between the seventh and eighth decades of life. Another illusion that appears to increase in strength with old age is the Poggendorff illusion—the very opposite of the trend observed during early childhood development (Leibowitz and Gwozdecki, 1967).

Effects of the Titchener circles and Ponzo illusion, however, appear to decrease in magnitude with advanced age. Leibowitz and Judisch (1967) reported that susceptibility to the effects of the Ponzo illusion increased during childhood and then decreased in magnitude during late adulthood, although a subsequent study failed to demonstrate any age-related decline in the magnitude of the Ponzo illusion (Farquhar and Leibowitz, 1971). Life-span changes in the illusory strength of the Titchner circles appear to involve an increase in the magnitude of the illusion during early development and a decreased susceptibility to the effect during old age (Wapner, Werner, and Comalli, 1960).

In an attempt to make sense of these findings, Pollack and Atkeson (1978) have extended Piaget's (1969) developmental principles of perception to include senescent changes in susceptibility to visual illusions. They have proposed that differential trends in the development of sensitivity to primary (Type I) illusions such as the Muller-Lyer are mediated by age-related changes in sensory processes. Trends regarding secondary (Type II) illusions are hypothesized to result from age-related changes in higher-level perceptual processes such as spatial and temporal integration of form. The full utility of this heuristic remains to be determined by research.

CONCLUSIONS

Considering the importance of effective visual functioning for individual well-being, aging research in the visual sciences offers an important opportunity to enhance the quality of human life. The realization of this goal, however, will require significant advances in visual aging research.

Our present level of knowledge of visual aging is both very limited and uneven. Although our understanding of the extent and effect of age changes in the ocular media is relatively good, we understand very little about such important issues as changes in color vision, the extent and meaning of changes in the ERG, the possible interactive effects of age and nutrition on the visual system, or the impact of age on functions served by peripheral areas of the retina. Similarly, little progress has been made in understanding the functional significance of age changes in the speed, range, and accuracy of eye movements; dynamic visual acuity; the perception of movement; or the operations of the different visual channels. Furthermore, beyond a minimal appreciation of age differences in stereopsis, little is known about the effects of age on depth perception and the processing of the variety of cues serving it.

The present status of aging research in vision is probably a function of both the relatively small number of investigators in the field as well as limitations in the manner in which such research has been pursued. Most of the research has involved the collection of information on only a few dependent variables at any one time, an approach that frequently allows subjects to concentrate their resources on a single narrowly defined task. In some instances, especially those involving higher perceptual processes, the functional significance of this research approach is questionable. In more representative settings, the observer typically must handle a diverse and changing array of stimuli. This problem is of particular concern in studies of older persons in which irrelevant stimuli may be involved or when issues of reserve capacity and ability to shift attention continuously are likely to be of concern. In addition, such an approach is unlikely to discern important causal relationships that could have been observed if a variety of different functions were assessed in single individuals across two or more testing sessions. Furthermore, if some of this research were interdisciplinary in character, it would help to determine the important cross-variable relationships between age changes in a variety of different visual functions as well as their causal links with electrophysiological processes, prior nutritional experience, health status, and so on.

Another obstacle to progress in understanding the effects of age on vision is the lack of theory to guide research. Despite this shortcoming, visual aging currently provides a very fertile ground for theory construction and evaluation. Aging provides *in vivo* manipulations of the visual system that can be very useful in theory testing and that cannot be obtained by other means. Aging can be used to examine the utility of visual theories in another way as well. If a theory regarding any particular function is valid, it must be consistent with known age differences in that function as well with the age-directional change in the mechanisms that have been proposed to underlie it.

One approach that might foster theory development in visual aging is through research that simulates the visual effects of aging in young observers. Such research could include manipulation of ambient illumination conditions, use of artificial pupils, lens and filter-induced chromatic and refractive aberrations, state of light adaptation, and variation of stimulus size, display rate, contrast level, and retinal location. This approach could not only further our understanding of visual aging but also help to determine the human impact of various types of visual loss.

A variety of other areas of vision research also holds promise for contributing to the well-being of older persons. Currently, we are unable to specify the visual processes that are critical to the daily tasks of older persons such as walking or driving. Research is also needed to develop visual testing measures that are demonstrably valid for use with older persons; currently, most vision tests have been standardized only on younger observers. Lastly, virtually nothing is known about the way in which older individuals are able to compensate for visual decline nor the extent to which such compensations could be enhanced or their use taught to others.

Although the area of visual aging research is methodologically and technically demanding, it is an enterprise that holds great promise for advancing our understanding of the processes of vision as well as contributing significantly to the well-being of older persons. Presumably, as many of the problems of visual dysfunction become recognized by the visual sciences as aging problems, many of the limitations that have been noted in this review of the current literature will be eliminated. It is hoped that this review will serve to facilitate that process.

REFERENCES

Alvaro, M. E. 1953. Senile changes in the crystalline lens. *American Journal of Ophthalmology* 36: 1241–1244.

Amberson, J. I.; Atkeson, B. M.; Pollack, R. H.; and Malatesta, V. J. 1979. Age differences in dark interval threshold across the life-span. *Experimental Aging Research,* 5(5): 423–433.

Anderson, B. 1971. The aging eye. *Postgraduate Medicine* 50: 235–239.

Anderson, B., and Palmore, E. 1974. Longitudinal evaluation of ocular function. In *Normal Aging,* ed. E. Palmore. Durham, N. C.: Duke University Press.

Andrew, W. 1971. *The Anatomy of Aging in Man and Animals.* New York: Grune and Stratton.

Arden, G. B. 1978. The importance of measuring contrast sensitivity in cases of visual disturbance. *British Journal of Ophthalmology* 62: 198–209.

Arden, G. B., and Jacobsen, J. 1978. A simple grating test for contrast sensitivity: Preliminary results indicating value for screening in glaucoina. *Investigative Ophthalmology and Visual Sciences* 17: 23–32.

Arundale, K. 1978. An investigation into the variation of human contrast sensitivity with age and ocular pathology. *British Journal of Ophthalmology* 62: 213–315.

Atkeson, B. M. 1978. Differences in magnitude of simultaneous and successive Muller-Lyer illusions from age twenty to seventy-nine years. *Experimental Aging Research* 4: 55–66.

Axelrod, S. 1963. Cognitive tasks in several modalities. In *Processes of Aging,* vol. 1, eds. R. H. Williams, C. Tibbits, and W. Donahue. New York: Atherton Press.

Balazs, E. A., and Denlinger, J. L. 1982. Age changes in the vitreous. In *Aging and Human Visual Function,* eds. R. Sekuler, D. Kline and K. Dismukes. New York: Alan R. Liss.

Barlow, H. B.; Blakemore, C.; and Pettigrew, J. D. 1967. The neural mechanisms of binocular depth discrimination. *Journal of Physiology* 193: 327–342.

Basowitz, H., and Korchin, S. J. 1957. Age differences in the perception of closure. *Journal of Abnormal and Social Psychology* 54: 93–97.

Beck, E. C.; Dustman, R. E.; and Schenkenberg, T. 1975. Life span changes in the electrical activity of the human brain as reflected in the cerebral evoked response. In *Neurobiology of Aging,* eds. J. M. Ordy and K. R. Brizzee. New York: Plenum Press.

Beck, E. C.; Swanson, C.; and Dustman, R. E. 1980. Long latency components of the visually evoked potential in man: Effects of aging. *Experimental Aging Research* 6: 523–545.

Bell, B.; Wolf, E.; and Bernholz, C. D. 1972. Depth perception as a function of aging. *Aging and Human Development* 3: 77–81.

Birren, J. E.; Bick, M. W.; and Fox, C. 1948. Age changes in the light threshold of the dark adapted eye. *Journal of Gerontology* 3: 267–271.

Birren, J. E.; Casperson, R. C.; and Botwinick, J. 1950. Age changes in pupil size. *Journal of Gerontology* 5: 267–271.

Birren, J. E., and Shock, N. W. 1950. Age changes in rate and level of visual dark adaptation. *Journal of Applied Physiology* 2: 407–411.

Blackwell, O. M., and Blackwell, H. R. 1971. Visual performance data for 156 normal observers of various ages. *Journal of the Illuminating Engineers Society* 1: 3–13.

Blakemore, C., and Campbell, F. W. 1969. On the existence of neurones in the human visual system selectively sensitive to the orientation and size of retinal images. *Journal of Physiology* 203: 237–260.

Boberg-Ans, J. 1955. Experience in clinical examination of corneal sensitivity. *British Journal of Ophthalmology* 39: 705–726.

Boice, M. L.; Tinker, M. A.; and Paterson, D. G. 1948. Color vision and age. *American Journal of Psychology* 61: 520–526.

Botwinick, J. 1962. A research note on the problem of perceptual modification in relation to age. *Journal of Gerontology* 17: 190–192.

Botwinick, J. 1978. *Aging and Behavior.* 2nd ed. New York: Springer.

Botwinick, J.; Brinley, J. F.; and Robbin, J. S. 1958. The interaction effects of perceptual difficulty and stimulus exposure time on age differences in speed and accuracy of response. *Gerontologia* 2: 1–10.

Botwinick, J.; Robbin, J. S.; and Brinley, J. F. 1959. Reorganization of perceptions with age. *Journal of Gerontology* 14: 85–88.

Breitmeyer, B. G., and Ganz, L. 1976. Implications of sustained and transient channels for theories of visual pattern masking, saccadic suppression and information processing. *Psychological Review* 83: 1–36.

Brody, H. 1976. An examination of cerebral cortex and

brainstem aging. In *Neurobiology of Aging.* Aging, eds. R. D. Terry and S. Gerschen, vol. 3. New York: Raven.

Brown, N. 1974. The change in lens curvature with age. *Experimental Eye Research* 19: 175–183.

Brozek, J., and Keys, A. 1945. Changes in flicker-fusion frequency with age. *Journal of Consulting Psychology* 9: 87–90.

Bruckner, R. 1959. Uber Methoden longitudinaler Alternsforschung am Auge. *Ophthalmologica* 138: 59–75.

Bruckner, R. 1967. Longitudinal research in the eye. *Gerontologia Clinica* 9: 87–95.

Bulpitt, C. J.; Hodes, C.; and Everitt, M. G. 1975. Intraocular pressure and systemic pressure in the elderly. *British Journal of Ophthalmology* 59: 717–720.

Burch, P. R. J.; Murray, J. J.; and Jackson, D. 1971. The age prevalence of arcus-senilis, greying of hair, and baldness: Etiological considerations. *Journal of Gerontology* 26: 364–372.

Burg, A. 1966. Visual acuity as measured by dynamic and static tests: A comparative evaluation. *Journal of Applied Psychology* 50: 460–466.

Burg, A. 1967. Light sensitivity as related to age and sex. *Perceptual and Motor Skills* 24: 1279–1288.

Burg, A. 1968. Lateral visual field as related to age and sex. *Journal of Applied Psychology* 52: 10–15.

Burg, A., and Hulbert, S. F. 1961. Dynamic visual acuity as related to age, sex, and static acuity. *Journal of Applied Psychology* 45: 111–116.

Campbell, F. W. 1957. The depth of field of the human eye. *Optica Acta* 4: 157–164.

Campbell, F. W., and Maffei, L. 1970. Electrophysiological evidence for the existence of orientation and size detectors in the human visual system. *Journal of Physiology* 207: 635–652.

Carter, J. H. 1982. The effects of aging upon selected visual functions: Color vision, glare sensitivity, field of vision and accommodation. In *Aging and Human Visual Function,* eds. R. Sekuler, D. Kline and K. Dismukes. New York: Alan R. Liss, 1982.

Cerella, J.; Poon, L. W.; and Fozard, J. L. 1982. Age and iconic read-out. *Journal of Gerontology* 37: 197–202.

Chamberlain, W. 1971. Restriction in upward gaze with advancing age. *American Journal of Ophthalmology* 71: 241–246.

Chapanis, A. 1950. Relationships between age, visual acuity and color vision. *Human Biology* 22: 1–33.

Chu, F. C.; Reingold, D. B.; Cogan, D. G.; and Williams, A. C. 1979. The eye movement disorders of progressive supranuclear palsy. *Ophthamology* 86: 422–428.

Chylack, L. T., Jr. 1979. Aging and cataracts. In *Special Senses in Aging,* eds. S. S. Han and D. H. Coons. Ann Arbor: Institute of Gerontology, University of Michigan.

Cogan, D. G. 1979. Summary and conclusions. In *Special Senses in Aging,* eds. S. S. Han and D. H. Coons. Ann Arbor: University of Michigan.

Cogan, D. G., and Kuwabara, T. 1959. Arcus senilis. Its pathology and histochemistry. *Archives of Ophthamology* 61: 553–560.

Coltheart, M. 1976. Contemporary models of the cognitive processes. I. Iconic storage and visual masking. In *The Development of Cognitive Processes,* eds. V. Hamilton and M. Vernon. New York: Academic Press.

Comalli, P. E. 1963. Perceptual closure in middle and old age. Paper presented at Gerontological Society, Boston, MA, October, 1963.

Comalli, P. E. 1970. Life-span changes in visual perception. In *Life-Span Development Psychology: Research and Theory,* eds. L. R. Goulet and P. B. Baltes. New York: Academic Press.

Comalli, P. E., Jr.; Wapner, L; and Werner, H. 1959. Perception of verticality in middle and old age. *Journal of Psychology* 47: 259–266.

Comalli, P. E., Jr.; Wapner, S.; and Werner, H. 1962. Interference effects of Stroop color-word test in childhood, adulthood and aging. *Journal of Genetic Psychology* 100: 47–53.

Coppinger, N. W. 1955. The relationship between critical flicker frequency and chronological age for varying levels of stimulus brightness. *Journal of Gerontology* 10: 48–52.

Corso, J. F. 1981. *Aging Sensory Systems and Perception.* New York: Praeger.

Coyne, A. C.; Eiler, J. M.; Vanderplas, J.; and Botwinick, J. 1979. Stimulus persistence and age. *Experimental Aging Research* 5(3): 263–270.

Crook, M. N.; Alexander, E. A.; Anderson, E. M. S.; Coules, J.; Hanson, A.; and Jeffries, N. T. 1958. Age and form perception. USAF School of Aviation Medicine Report, No. 57–124.

Dalderup, L. M., and Fredericks, M. L. C. 1969. Colour sensitivity in old age. *Journal of the American Geriatric Society* 17: 388–390.

Danziger, W. L., and Salthouse, T. A. 1978. Age and the perception of incomplete figures. *Experimental Aging Research* 4: 67–80.

Davis, M. D. 1971. Ophthalmic problems in diabetes mellitus. In *Diabetes Mellitus: Diagnosis and Treatment,* vol. 3, eds. S. S. Fajans and K. E. Sussman. New York: American Diabetes Association.

Derefeldt, G., Lennerstrand, G., and Lundh, B. 1979. Age variations in normal human contrast sensitivity. *Acta Opthalmologia* 57: 679–689.

Devaney, K. O., and Johnson, H. A. 1980. Neuron loss in the aging visual cortex of man. *Journal of Gerontology* 35: 836–841.

DiLollo, V.; Arnett, J. L.; and Kruk, R. V. 1982. Age-related changes in rate of visual information processing. *Journal of Experimental Psychology: Human Perception and Performance* 8: 225–237.

Domey, R. G., and McFarland, R. A. 1961. Dark adaptation as a function of age: Individual prediction. *American Journal of Ophthamology* 51: 1262–1268.

Domey, R. G.; McFarland, R. A.; and Chadwick, E. 1960. Dark adaptation as a function of age and time. II. A Derivation. *Journal of Gerontology* 15: 267–279.

Donchin, E.; Ritter, W.; and McCallum, W. C. 1978. Cognitive psychophysiology: The endogenous components of the ERP. In *Event-Related Brain Potentials in Man,* eds. E. Callaway, P. Tueting, and S. H. Keslow. New York: Academic Press.

Drance, S. M.; Berry, V.; and Hughes, A. 1967. Studies of the effects of age on the central and peripheral isopters of the visual field in normal subjects. *American Journal of Ophthamology* 63: 1667–1672.

Dustman, R. E., and Beck, E. C. 1966. Visually evoked potentials: Amplitude changes with age. *Science* 151: 1013–1015.

Eisner, D. A. 1972. Developmental relationships between field independence and fixity-mobility. *Perceptual and Motor Skills* 34: 767–770.

Eisner, D. A., and Schaie, K. W. 1971. Age change in response to visual illusions from middle to old age. *Journal of Gerontology* 26: 146–150.

Eisner, G. 1975. Zur Anatomie des Glaskorpers. *Albrecht von Graefes Archiv fur Klinische und Experimentelle Ophthalmologie* 193: 33–56.

Eriksen, C. W.; Hamlin, R. M.; and Breitmeyer, B. G. 1970. Temporal factors in visual perception as related to aging. *Perception & Psychophysics* 7: 354–356.

Falk, J., and Kline, D. W. 1978. Stimulus persistence in CFF: Underactivation or overarousal? *Experimental Aging Research* 4: 109–123.

Farquhar, M., and Leibowitz, H. 1971. The magnitude of the Ponzo illusion as a function of age for large and small stimulus configurations. *Psychonomic Science* 25: 97–99.

Farrimond, T. 1967. Visual and auditory performance variations with age: Some implications. *Australian Journal of Psychology* 19: 193–201.

Feinberg, R., and Podolak, E. 1965. Latency of the pupillary reflex to light and its relationship to aging. In *Behavior, Aging and the Nervous System,* eds. A. T. Welford and J. E. Birren. Springfield, IL: Charles C Thomas.

Fischer, F. P. 1949. Growth curves and senescence of the eye. *Ophthalmologica* 117: 379–380.

Fisher, A. J., and Christie, A. W. 1965. A note on disability glare. *Vision Research:* 565–571.

Fisher, R. F. 1969. Elastic constant of the human lens capsule. *Journal of Physiology* (London) 201: 1–19.

Fisher, R. F., and Pettet, B. E. 1973. Presbyopia and the water content of the human crystalline lens. *Journal of Physiology* 234: 443–447.

Flood, M. T., and Balazs, E. A. 1979. Hyaluronic acid content in the developing and aging human liquid and gel vitreous. *Investigative Ophthalmology Supplement.* Annual Meeting of the Association for Research in Vision and Ophthalmology (ARVO).

Fozard, J. L.; Wolf, E.; Bell, B.; McFarland, R. A.; and Podolsky, S. 1977. Visual perception and communication. In *Handbook of the Psychology of Aging,* eds. J. E. Birren and K. W. Schaie. New York: Van Nostrand Reinhold.

Garner, W., and Spector, A. 1978. Racemization in human lens: Evidence of rapid insolubilization of specific polypeptides in cataract formation. *Proceedings of the National Academy of Sciences* 75: 3618–3620.

Geldard, F. A. 1972. *The Human Senses.* New York: John Wiley & Sons.

Gilbert, J. G. 1957. Age changes in color matching. *Journal of Gerontology* 12: 210–215.

Gillies, W. E., and West, R. H. 1981. Timolol maleate and intraocular pressure in low-tension glaucoma. *Transactions of the Ophthamology Society* 33: 33–35.

Greenberg, D. A., and Branch, L. G. 1982. A review of methodological issues concerning incidence and prevalence data of visual deterioration in elders. In *Aging and Human Visual Function,* eds. R. Sekuler, D. W. Kline, and K. Dismukes. New York: Alan R. Liss.

Gregor, Z.; Bird, A. C.; and Chisholm, I. H. 1977. Senile disciform macular degeneration in the second eye. *British Journal of Ophthalmology* 61: 141–147.

Griew, S.; Fellows, B. J.; and Howes, R. 1963. Duration of spiral aftereffect as a function of stimulus exposure and age. *Perceptual and Motor Skills* 17: 210.

Gunkel, R. D., and Gouras, P. 1963. Changes in scotopic visibility thresholds with age. *American Medical Association Archives of Ophthalmology* 68: 4–9.

Guth, S. K., and McNelis, J. F. 1969. Visual performance—subjective differences. *Illuminating Engineering* 64: 723–729.

Haber, R. N., and Hershenson, M. 1980. *The Psychology of Visual Perception.* New York: Holt, Rinehart and Winston.

Hallows, F., and Moran, D. 1981. Cataract—the ultraviolet risk factor. *Lancet* 8258: 1249–1253.

Harrington, D. 1964. *The Visual Field.* St. Louis: Mosby.

Harwerth, R., and Levi, D. 1978. Reaction time as a measure of suprathréshold grating detection. *Vision Research* 18: 1579–1586.

Heath, H. A., and Orbach, J. 1963. Reversibility of the necker cube: IV. Responses of elderly people. *Perceptual and Motor Skills* 17: 625–626.

Henderson, R. L., and Burg, A. 1974. *Vision and Audition in Driving.* Technical Report No. TM(L)-5297/000/00. Systems Development Corporation, Department of Transportation.

Henderson, J. W., and Prough, W. A. 1950. Influence of age and sex on flow of tears. *Archives of Ophthalmology* 43: 224–231.

Hertzog, C. K.; Williams, M. V.; and Walsh, D. A. 1976. The effect of practice on aged differences in central perceptual processing. *Journal of Gerontology* 31: 428–433.

Hoffman, C. S.; Price, A. C.; Garrett, E. S.; and Rothstein, W. 1959. Effect of age and brain damage on depth perception. *Perceptual and Motor Skills* 9: 283–286.

Hofstetter, H. W., and Bertsch, J. D. 1976. Does stereopsis change with age? *American Journal of Optometry and Physiological Optics* 53: 644–667.

Hubel, D. H., and Wiesel, T. N. 1968. Receptive fields and functional architecture of the monkey striate cortex. *Journal of Physiology* 195: 215–243.

Hubel, D. H., and Wiesel, T. N. 1970. Cells sensitive to binocular depth in area 18 of the macaque monkey cortex. *Nature* 225: 41–42.

Huggert, A. 1948. On the form of the iso-indicial surfaces of the human crystalline lens. *Acta Ophthalmologica Supplement* No. 30.

Hurvich, L. M., and Jameson, D. 1966. *The Perception*

of Brightness and Darkness. Boston: Allyn and Bacon.

Jalavisto, E. 1964. The phenomenon of retinal rivalry in the aged. *Gerontologia* 9: 1–8.

Jani, S. N. 1966. The age factor in stereopsis screening. *American Journal of Optometry and Physiological Optics* 43: 653–655.

Johansen, E. V. 1947. Undersogelse over det indbyrdes storrelesforhold mellem cornea og lens crystallina hos menneskef. *Enjar Munksgaard.*

Kahn, H. A.; Leibowitz, H. M.; Ganley, S. P.; Kini, M. M.; Colton, J.; Nickerson, R. S.; and Dawber, T. R. 1977. Framingham eye study. I. Outlines and major prevalences and findings. *American Journal of Epidemiology* 106: 17–32.

Karp, S. 1967. Field dependence and occupational activity in the aged. *Perceptual and Motor Skills* 24: 603–609.

Karpe, G.; Rickenbach, K.; and Thomasson, S. 1950. The clinical electroretinogram. I. The normal electroretinogram above fifity years of age. *Acta Ophthalmologica* 28: 301–305.

Kirchener, C., and Peterson, R. 1979. The latest data on visual disability from NCHS. *Journal of Visual Impairment and Blindness* 73(4): 151–153.

Kleemeier, R. W. 1952. The relationship between Ortho-Rater tests of acuity and color vision in a senescent group. *Journal of Applied Psychology* 36: 114–116.

Kline, D. W., and Baffa, G. 1976. Differences in the sequential integration of form as a function of age and interstimulus interval. *Experimental Aging Research* 2: 333–343.

Kline, D. W., and Birren, J. E. 1975. Age differences in backward dichoptic masking. *Experimental Aging Research* 1: 17–25.

Kline, D. W.; Culler, M. P.; and Sucec, J. 1977. Differences in inconspicuous word identification as a function of age and reversible-figure training. *Experimental Aging Research* 3: 203–213.

Kline, D. W.; Hogan, P. M.; and Stier, D. L. 1980. Age and the identification of inconspicuous words. *Experimental Aging Research* 6(2): 137–147.

Kline, D. W.; Ikeda, D.; and Schieber, F. 1982. Age and temporal resolution in color vision: When do red and green make yellow? *Journal of Gerontology* 37: 705–709.

Kline, D. W., and Nestor, S. 1977. Persistence of complementary afterimages as a function of age and stimulus duration. *Experimental Aging Research* 3: 191–201.

Kline, D. W., and Orme-Rogers, C. 1978. Examination of stimulus persistence as a basis for superior visual identification performance among older adults. *Journal of Gerontology* 33: 76–81.

Kline, D. W., and Schieber, F. 1980. What are the age differences in visual sensory memory? *Journal of Gerontology* 36: 86–89.

Kline, D. W., and Schieber, F. 1981. Visual aging: A transient/sustained shift? *Perception and Psychophysics* 29: 181–182.

Kline, D. W., and Schieber, F. J. 1982. Visual persistence and temporal resolution. In *Aging and Human Visual Function,* eds. R. Sekuler, D. W. Kline, and K. Dismukes. New York: Alan R. Liss.

Kline, D. W.; Schieber, F.; Abusamra, L. C.; and Coyne, A. C. 1983. Age and the visual channels: Contrast sensitivity and response speed. *Journal of Gerontology* 38: 211–216.

Kline, D. W., and Szafran, J. 1975. Age differences in backward monoptic visual noise masking. *Journal of Gerontology* 30: 307–311.

Klorman, R.; Thompson, L. W.; and Ellingston, R. J. 1978. Event-related potentials across the lifespan. In *Event-Related Brain Potentials in Man,* eds. E. Callaway, P. Tueting, and S. H. Koslow. New York: Academic Press.

Korchin, S. J., and Basowitz, H. 1956. The judgment of ambiguous stimuli as an index of cognitive functioning in aging. *Journal of Personality* 25: 81–95.

Kornzweig, A. L. 1954. Physiological effects of age on the visual processes. *Sight-Savers Review* 24: 130–138.

Kornzweig, A. L. 1972. The prevention of blindness in the aged. *Journal of the American Geriatrics Society* 20: 383–386.

Kumnick, L. S. 1956a. Aging and the decay of pupillary psychosensory restitution. *Journal of Gerontology* 11: 46–52.

Kumnick, L. S. 1956b. Aging and the efficiency of the pupillary mechanism. *Journal of Gerontology* 11: 160–164.

Kuwabara, T. 1979. Age-related changes of the eye. In *Special Senses in Aging,* eds. S. S. Hain and D. H. Coons. Ann Arbor: Institute of Gerontology, University of Michigan.

Kuwabara, T., and Cogan, D. G. 1965. Retinal vascular patterns. VII. A cellular change. *Investigative Ophthalmology* 4: 1049–1058.

Kuwabara, T., and Gorn, R. A. 1968. Retinal damage by visible light. An electronmicroscopic study. *Archives of Ophthalmology* 79: 69–78.

Lakowski, R. 1962. Is the deterioration of the colour discrimination with age due to lens or retinal changes? *Farbe* 11: 69–86.

Larsson, S., and Osterlind, G. 1943. Studies in the causes of senile miosis and rigidity of the pupil. *Acta Ophthalmologica* 21: 1–25.

Layton, B. 1975. Perceptual noise and aging. *Psychological Bulletin* 82: 875–883.

Lebensohn, J. E. 1966. Changes in the aging eye. *Postgraduate Medicine* 40: 746–751.

LeGrand, Y. 1957. Light, colour and vision. London: Chapman and Hall.

Leibowitz, H. W., and Gwozdecki, J. 1967. The magnitude of the Poggendorff illusion as a function of age. *Child Development* 38: 573–580.

Leibowitz, H., and Judisch, J. M. 1967. Size constancy in older persons: A function of distance. *American Journal of Psychology* 80: 294–296.

Leighton, D. A., and Tomlinson, A. 1972. Changes in axial length and other dimensions of the eyeball with increasing age. *Acta Ophthalmologica* 50: 815–825.

Levine, M. W., and Shefner, J. M. 1981. *Fundamentals of Sensation and Perception.* Menlo Park, CA: Addison-Wesley.

Lewis, R. A. 1979. Macular degeneration in the aged.

In *Special Senses in Aging,* eds. S. S. Han and D. H. Coons. Ann Arbor: Institute of Gerontology, University of Michigan.

Lindsay, P. M., and Norman, D. A. 1972. *Human Information Processing.* New York: Academic Press.

Long, G. M. 1979. The dichoptic viewing paradigm: Do the eyes have it? *Psychological Bulletin* 86: 391–403.

Lopping, B., and Weale, R. A. 1965. Changes in corneal surfaces during ocular convergence. *Vision Research* 5: 207–215.

Lowman, C., and Kirchener, C. 1979. Elderly blind and visually impaired persons: Projected numbers in the year 2000. Journal of Visual Impairment and Blindness 73(2): 73–74.

Luria, S. M. 1960. Absolute visual threshold and age. *Journal of the Optical Society of America* 50: 86–87.

Marin-Amat, M. 1956. Les variations physiologiques de la courbure de la cornee pendant la vie. Leur importance et transcendance dans la refraction oculaire. *Bulletin de le Societe belge Ophthalmologie* 113: 251–293.

Marmor, M. F. 1982. Aging and the retina. In *Aging and Human Visual Function,* eds. R. Sekuler, D. W. Kline, and K. Dismukes. New York: Alan R. Liss.

Marshall, J.; Grindle, J.; Ansell, P.; and Borwein, B. 1979. Convolution in human rods. *British Journal of Ophthalmology* 63: 181–187.

McCarter, A., and Atkeson, B. M. 1977. Simultaneous brightness contrast in young and old adults. *Experimental Aging Research* 3: 215–224.

McFarland, R. A.; Domey, R. G.; Warren, A. B.; and Ward, D. C. 1960. Dark adaptation as a function of age. I. A statistical analysis. *Journal of Gerontology* 15: 149–154.

McFarland, R. A., and Fisher, M. B. 1955. Alterations in dark adaptation as a function of age. *Journal of Geronotology* 10: 424–428.

McFarland, R. A.; Warren, B.; and Karis, C. 1958. Alterations in critical flicker frequency as a function of age and light:dark ratio. *Journal of Experimental Psychology* 56: 529–538.

McGrath, C., and Morrison, J. D. 1980. Age-related changes in spatial frequency perception. *Journal of Physiology* 310: 52.

McGreer, E., and McGreer, P. 1976. Neurotransmitter metabolism in the aging brain. In *Neurobiology of Aging.* Aging, eds. R. D. Terry and S. Gershon, vol. 3. New York: Raven.

Misiak, H. 1947. Age and sex differences in critical flicker frequency. *Journal of Experimental Psychology* 37: 318–332.

Noell, W. K.; Walker, V. S.; Kang, B. S.; and Berman, S. 1966. Retinal damage by light in rats. *Investigative Ophthalmology* 5: 45–473.

Owsley, C.; Sekuler, R.; and Siemsen, D. 1983. Contrast sensitivity throughout adulthood. *Vision Research* 23: 689–699.

Padula, W. V. 1982. Low vision related to function and service delivery in the elderly. In *Aging and Human Visual Function,* eds. R. Sekuler, D. W. Kline, and K. Dismukes. New York: Alan R. Liss.

Panek, P. E. 1982. Relationship between field-dependence/independence and personality in older adult females. *Perceptual and Motor Skills* 54: 811–814.

Panek, P. E.; Barrett, G. V.; Sterns, H. L.; and Alexander, R. A. 1977. A review of age changes in perceptual information processing ability with regard to driving. *Experimental Aging Research* 3: 387–449.

Peterson, P. 1956. Die Pupillographie und das Pupillogram. *Acta Physiological Scandinavica* 37 (Suppl. 125): 1–141.

Piaget, J. 1969. *The Mechanisms of Perception.* New York: Basic Books.

Pitts, D. G. 1982. The effects of aging on selected visual functions: Dark adaptation, visual acuity, stereopsis and brightness contrast. In *Aging and Human Visual Function,* eds. R. Sekuler, D. W. Kline, and K. Dismukes. New York: Alan R. Liss.

Plude, D. J., and Hoyer, W. J. 1981. Adult age differences in visual search as a function of stimulus mapping and processing load. *Journal of Gerontology* 36: 598–604.

Pollack, R. H. 1978. A theoretical note on the aging of the visual system. *Perception and Psychophysics* 23: 94–95.

Pollack, R. H., and Atkeson, B. M. 1978. A life-span approach to perceptual development. In *Life-Span Development and Behavior,* eds. P. B. Baltes. vol. I. New York: Academic Press.

Pulling, N. H; Wolf, E.; Sturgis, S. P.; Vaillancourt, D. R.; and Dolliner, J. J. 1980. Headlight glare resistance and driver age. *Human Factors* 22(1): 103–112.

Rabbitt, P. M. A. 1965. An age-decrement in the ability to ignore irrelevant formation. *Journal of Gerontology* 20: 233–238.

Rambo, V. C. 1953. Further notes on the varying ages at which different people develop presbyopia. *American Journal of Ophthalmology* 36: 709–710.

Rambo, V. C., and Sangal, S. P. 1960. A study of the accommodation of the people of India. *American Journal of Ophthalmology* 49: 993–1004.

Ratliff, F.; Hartline, H. K.; and Miller, W. H. 1963. Spatial and temporal aspects of retinal inhibitory interaction. *Journal of the Optical Society of America* 53: 110–120.

Reading, V. 1966. Yellow and white headlamps glare and age. *Transactions of Illuminating Engineering Society* 31: 108–121.

Reading, V. M. 1972. Visual resolution as measured by dynamic and static tests. *Pfluggers Archives* 333: 17–26.

Riggs, L. A.; Johnson, E. P.; and Schick, A. M. L. 1966. Electrical responses of the human eye to changes in wavelength of-the stimulating light. *Journal of the Optical Society of America* 56: 1621–1627.

Rosengren, B. 1956. Rise in the ocular tension produced by circumlimbal pressure on the sclera. *Transactions of the Ophthalmological Society* (U.K.) 76: 65–72.

Said, F. S., and Weale, R. A. 1959. The variation with age of the spectral transmissivity of the living human crystalline lens. *Gerontologia* 3: 213–231.

Salthouse, T. A. 1980. Age differences in visual masking: A manifestation of decline in neural signal/noise ratio? Paper presented at the thirty-third annual Scientific

Meeting of the Gerontological Society, San Diego, CA.

Schafer, W. D., and Weale, R. A. 1970. The influence of age and retinal illumination on the pupillary near reflex. *Vision Research* 10: 179–191.

Scheibel, M. E.; Lindsay, R. D.; Tomiyasu, U.; and Scheibel, A. B. 1975. Progressive dendritic changes in aging human cortex. *Experimental Neurology* 47: 392–403.

Schieber, F., and Kline, D. W. 1982. Age and the discrimination of visual successiveness. *Experimental Aging Research* 8: 159–161.

Schonfield, D., and Wenger, L. 1975. Age limitations of perceptual span. *Nature* 253: 376–377.

Schurman, D. L. 1968. Effects of an artificial pupil in visual perception. *Psychonomic Science* 2: 57.

Sekuler, R. Personal communication, November 5, 1981.

Sekuler, R. 1982. Assessing spatial vision in older humans. In *Aging and Human Visual Function*, eds. R. Sekuler, D. W. Kline, and K. Dismukes. New York: Alan R. Liss.

Sekuler, R., and Hutman, L. P. 1980. Spatial vision and aging. I. Contrast sensitivity. *Journal of Gerontology* 35: 692–699.

Sekuler, R.; Kline, D. W.; and Dismukes, K., eds. 1982. *Aging and Human Visual Function*. New York: Alan R. Liss.

Severin, S. L.; Tour, R. L.; and Kershaw, R. H. 1967. *Archives of Opthalmology* 377: 2–7.

Shagass, C. 1972. *Evoked Brain Potentials in Psychiatry*. New York: Plenum Press.

Sharpe, J. A., and Sylvester, T. O. 1978. Effects of aging on horizontal smooth pursuit. *Investigative Ophthalmology and Visual Science* 17: 465–468.

Shaw, N. A., and Cant, B. R. 1980. Age-dependent changes in the latency of the patterned visual evoked potential. *Electroencephalography and Clinical Neurophysiology* 48: 237–241.

Shinar, D. 1977. *Driver Visual Limitations: Diagnosis and Treatment*. Institute for Research in Public Safety, Department of Transportation Contract DOT-HS-5-1275, Indiana University.

Simonson, E.; Anderson, D.; and Keiper, C. 1967. Effect of stimulus movement on critical flicker fusion in young and older men. *Journal of Gerontology* 22: 353–356.

Skalka, H. W. 1980. Effect of age on Arden grating acuity. *British Journal of Opthalmology* 64: 21–23.

Spector, A. 1982. Aging of the lens and cataract formation. In *Aging and Human Visual Function*, eds. R. Sekuler, D. W. Kline, and K. Dismukes. New York: Alan R. Liss.

Sperling, G. 1963. A model for visual memory tasks. *Human Factors* 5: 19–31.

Steven, D. M. 1946. Relation between dark adaptation and age. *Nature* 157: 376–377.

Stocker, F. W., and Moore, L. W. 1975. Detecting changes in the cornea that come with age. *Geriatrics* 30: 57–69.

Strempel, E. 1981. Long-term results in the treatment of glaucoma with beta-adrenergic blocking agents. *Transactions of the Ophthalmology Society* 33: 21–23.

Sturgis, S. P., and Osgood, D. J. 1982. Effects of glare and background luminance on visual acuity and contrast sensitivity: Implications for night vision testing. *Human Factors* 24: 347–360.

Sturr, J. F.; Kelly, S.; Kobus, D. A.; and Taub, H. A. 1982. Age-dependent magnitude and time course of early light adaptation. *Perception and Psychophysics* 31(4): 402–404.

Swegmark, G. 1969. Studies with impedance cyclography on human ocular accommodation at different ages. *Acta Ophthalmologica* 47: 1186–1206.

Thomas, J. M.; and Charles, D. C. 1964. Effects of age and stimulus size on perception. *Journal of Gerontology* 19: 447–450.

Till, R. E., and Franklin, L. D. 1981. On the locus of age differences in visual information processing. *Journal of Gerontology* 36: 200–210.

Tousimis, A. J., and Fine, B. S. 1959. Ultrastructure of the iris: An electron microscopic study. *American Journal of Ophthalmology* 48: 397–417.

Tschetter, R. T. 1966. Lipid analysis of the human cornea with and without arcus senilis. *Archives of Ophthalmology* 76: 403–405.

Turvey, M. T. 1973. On periphral and central processes in vision: Inferences from an information-processing analysis of masking with patterned stimuli. *Psychological Review* 80: 1–52.

Verville, E. L., and Cameron, N. 1946. Age and sex differences in the perception of incomplete pictures by adults. *Journal of Genetic Psychology* 68: 149–157.

Vrabec, F. 1965. Senile changes in the ganglion cells of the human retina. *British Journal of Ophthalmology* 49: 561–572.

Wallace, J. G. 1956. Some studies of perception in relation to age. *British Journal of Psychology* 47: 283–297.

Walsh, D. A. 1976. Age differences in central perceptual processing: A dichoptic backward masking investigation. *Journal of Gerontology* 31: 178–185.

Walsh, D. A., and Thompson, L. W. 1978. Age differences in visual sensory memory. *Journal of Gerontology* 33: 283–297.

Walsh, D. A.; Till, R. E.; and Williams, M. V. 1978. Age differences in peripheral perceptual processing: A monoptic backward masking investigation. *Journal of Experimental Psychology: Human Perception and Performance* 4: 232–243.

Wapner, S.; Werner, H.; and Comalli, P. E. 1960. Perception of part-whole relationships in middle and old age. *Journal of Gerontology* 15: 412–415.

Weale, R. A. 1961. Retinal illumination and age. *Transactions of the Illuminating Engineering Society* 26: 95–100.

Weale, R. A. 1963. *The Aging Eye*. London: H. K. Lewis.

Weale, R. A. 1965. On the eye. In *Behavior, Aging, and the Nervous System*, eds. A. T. Welford and J. E. Birren. Springfield: Charles C Thomas.

Weale, R. A. 1975. Senile changes in visual acuity. *Transactions of the Ophthalmological Society* (U. K.) 95: 36–38.

Weale, R. A. 1978. The eye and aging. In *Interdisciplinary Topics in Gerontology*. Gerontological aspects of eye research, ed. O. Hockivin, vol. 13. New York: S. Karger.

Weekers, R., and Roussel, F. 1946. Introduction a l'étude de la fréquence de fusion en clinique. *Ophthalmologica* 112: 305–319.

Weiss, A. P. 1959. Sensory functions. In *Handbook of Aging and the Individual,* ed. J. E. Birren. Chicago: University of Chicago Press.

Welch, R. J. 1969. Causes of blindness in additions to MRA Registers for 1967. Proceedings of the 1969 Conference of Model Reporting for Blindness. Washington, D.C.: U.S. Government Printing Office.

Westat Corporation, 1976. Summary and critique of available data on the prevalence and economic and social costs of visual disorders and disabilities. National Eye Institute, Public Health Service, U.S. Department of Health, Education and Welfare.

Weston, H. C. 1949. On age and illumination in relation to visual performance. *Transactions of the Illuminating Engineering Society* (London) 14: 281–297.

Weymouth, F. W. 1960. Effect of age on visual acuity. In *Vision in the Aging Patient,* eds. M. J. Hirsch and R. E. Wick. Philadelphia: Chilton.

White, P. 1960. Childhood diabetes: Its course, and influence on the second and third generations. *Diabetes* 9: 345.

Wolf, E. 1960. Glare and age. *Archives of Ophthalmology* 60: 502–514.

Wolf, E. 1967. Studies on the shrinkage of the visual field with age. *Highway Research Record* 167: 1–7.

Wolf, E., and Gardiner, J. S. 1965. Studies on the scatter of light in the dioptric media of the eye as a basis of visual glare. *Archives of Ophthalmology* 74: 338–345.

Wolf, E., and Nadroski, A. S. 1971. Extent of the visual field changes with age and oxygen tension. *Archives of Ophthalmology* 86: 637–642.

Wolf, E., and Schraffa, A. M. 1964. Relationship between critical flicker frequency and age in flicker perimetry. *Archives of Ophthalmology* 72: 832–843.

Wright, L. L., and Elias, J. W. 1979. Age differences in the effects of perceptual noise. *Journal of Gerontology* 34: 704–708.

13
AGING AND THE AUDITORY SYSTEM

Lynne Werner Olsho, Stephen W. Harkins,
and
Martin L. Lenhardt
Virginia Commonwealth University

Auditory function appears, in many respects, to share in the basic properties of senescence. That is, age changes in hearing ability are often characterized as progressive, irreversible, and detrimental to successful adaptation in the later years of life. The purpose of this chapter is to review what is, and what is not, known concerning function-structure relationships in the aging auditory system and to highlight areas where research findings are lacking or are contradictory.

Presbycusis is the term most widely employed to refer to age-related changes in hearing ability. Hinchcliffe (1962) defined presbycusis as a syndrome that includes the following features: (1) impairment of pure-tone thresholds, particularly for high frequency tones; (2) impairment of frequency discrimination; (3) impairment of auditory temporal discrimination and sound localization ability; (4) impairment of speech discrimination ability; (5) decreased ability to understand distorted speech; and (6) decreased ability to recall long sentences. Epidemiological studies, in which presbycusis is defined in terms of pure-tone hearing loss, indicate that presbycusis is one of the, if not *the,* major sensory changes associated with aging in human beings.

Approximately 80 percent of the individuals with hearing problems are over 45 years of age and nearly 55 percent of these are 65 years or older. It has been estimated that over 20 percent of the population of the United States between the ages of 45 and 54 have some hearing loss for high frequency pure-tones. In individuals between the ages of 75 and 79 years, the frequency of hearing problems rises to about 75 percent of the population (Butler and Lewis, 1977). The impact of the elevation of pure-tone threshold on more complex auditory function, however, is poorly understood. Furthermore, the structural changes in the auditory system that are related to functional loss are poorly understood.

Early in the past decade, Riegel (1973) stressed that advances in knowledge in psychological gerontology will depend not so much on accumulation of additional data but on the success of organizing those facts already available. The present review shares this point-of-view with regard to descriptive age changes in auditory function but stresses the need for further information on the structural and physiological changes that produce the now well-documented fact of hearing loss in the later years of life.

AGE-RELATED CHANGES IN THE ANATOMY AND PHYSIOLOGY OF THE AUDITORY SYSTEM

Age-related structural changes have been reported at nearly every level of the auditory system. The intent of this section is to review the nature of these changes and to make predictions about the functional capacity of the aging auditory system. Despite the fact that we now have considerable information about the structural modifications that often accompany aging, the functional significance of these observations remains unclear. Two problems contribute to this difficulty. First is the general lack of information with regard to structure-function relationships in hearing. For example, if we find a reduction in volume of a particular nucleus in the auditory pathway, it is not known how this loss might affect hearing. Moreover, if we know that some cells in a specific nucleus are tuned to respond, say, to frequency modulated signals, whereas others respond best to interaural time differences, we have no way of knowing which of these cells are the ones that are affected by the aging process. Thus, simply knowing that structures change at a certain level is not informative as to the functional deficits, if any, that might be expected.

The second problem has to do with sampling for structural change. Generally speaking, one of two types of sampling techniques is followed in histological studies of auditory aging. In the first type, available material fitting certain age restrictions is used. From these studies, structural changes that appear to be associated with aging can be determined. Since nothing is usually known, however, about the auditory capacities of the individuals involved, it is impossible to relate structural changes to hearing ability. The second sampling technique involves histological study of individuals with known hearing impairment. This type of study usually does not include cases of mild to moderate impairment, that is, of the type typical of the aging population. Thus, although we may know that structural changes are present in the elderly deaf, it is not clear whether the same changes are present in lesser degree in cases of mild impairment. In few cases are there studies relating structural change to functional change in other than hearing *level* for pure tones. Thus, we presently do not know if certain anatomical changes in the auditory system are associated with deficits in discrimination or analytic abilities.

The research required to answer questions of structure-function relationships is difficult to carry out on humans, and animal models of the aging auditory system may come to play an increasingly important role in this context. Although some attempts have been made in this direction, the problem remains one of identifying a nonhuman species in which age-related changes in hearing are analogous to those occurring in humans (see the report of the National Research Council, 1981, for a discussion of possible candidates). Despite problems of interpretation, we are beginning to accumulate data regarding aging effects on auditory structures. In conjunction with psychoacoustic data, this information will not only allow us to predict and understand auditory function in the elderly but give us a clear picture of structure-function relationships in the normal auditory system.

Overview of the Organization of the Auditory System

Transduction of sound energy into neural impulses takes place in the ear. The human ear is typically considered to consist of three parts (Figure 1). The *outer ear* consists of the pinna and the external ear canal, structures through which sounds usually enter the ear. The *middle ear* begins at the tympanic membrane; that membrane is coupled to the ossicular chain, which serves the function of amplifying the sound and transmitting it on to the inner ear. The actual transduction process occurs in the *inner ear,* which is made up of the cochlea, the vestibule, and the semicircular canals. The auditory receptors—the hair cells—are located within the cochlea.

A schematic diagram of the auditory neural pathways is shown in Figure 2. Fibers whose cell bodies form the spiral ganglion contact the hair cells within the cochlea. The ascending fibers of these cells form the auditory nerve (eighth cranial nerve), which enters the brain at the lateral aspect of the lower pons. These first-order neurons synapse with cell bodies in the ventral and dorsal cochlear nuclei. The fibers of cells from the ventral cochlear nucleus (VCN) form the trapezoid body. Fibers of the trapezoid body synapse with the contralateral nuclei of the superior olivary complex

(SOC) or ascend via the contralateral lateral lemniscus or synapse at the ipsilateral SOC. Fibers from the dorsal cochlear nucleus (DCN) cross and ascend in the contralateral lateral lemniscus. Since the VCN gives rise to both contralateral and ipsilateral projections, the SOC receives bilateral information from the VCN.

Fibers from the trapezoid body, the SOC, and the contralateral cochlear nuclei ascend via the lateral lemniscus. The majority of these fibers synapse in the inferior colliculus (IC) at the midbrain level. Communication between the colliculi of the two sides takes place via the commissure of the inferior colliculus. Some fibers of the lateral lemniscus bypass the IC, going directly to the medial geniculate body (MGB) in the thalamus, along with fibers arising in the IC. All ascending auditory pathways synapse at the MGB.

Projections from the MGB terminate in the transverse temporal gyrus on the temporal cortex, corresponding to Brodmann's Areas 41 and 42. Area 41 is the primary auditory cortex; area 42 is the auditory association cor-

tex. These two areas communicate via short fibers. Area 42 projects to other parts of the brain as well.

The course of the efferent auditory pathways is less well established. Fibers from the olivocochlear bundle project to the hair cells. The majority of these fibers are crossed, arising in the contralateral medial superior olive, with some contributions from the trapezoid body. The uncrossed efferents arise from the lateral periolivary nucleus (Rasmussen, 1946, 1960; Luk et al., 1974). Other efferent projections have been identified from the inferior colliculus, the superior olivary complex, and the nuclei of the lateral lemniscus (Rasmussen, 1960, 1964, 1967). Fibers may also descend from the auditory cortex to the inferior colliculus and medial geniculate body.

Age-related Changes in Specific Structures

The Outer Ear
Structure and function. As stated above, the outer ear is comprised of the pinna, which

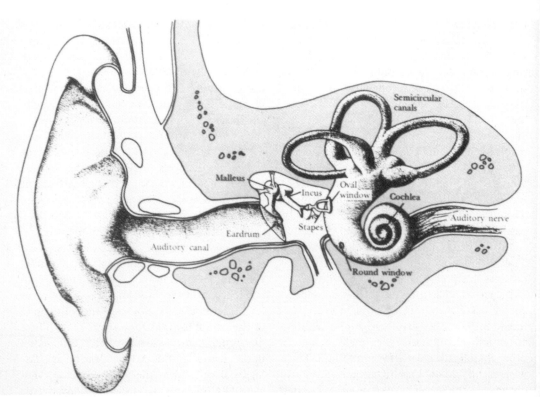

Figure 1.   The peripheral auditory system. (*From Lindsay, P. H., and Norman, D. A. 1972. Human information processing. New York: Academic Press. Reprinted by permission.*)

is the external appendage of the ear, and the auditory canal, the passage that leads to the middle ear (see Figure 1). This is the usual route by which air-conducted sound enters the auditory system. The major influence of these structures on auditory function results from their resonance characteristics: because of their size, shape, and degree of flexibility, the

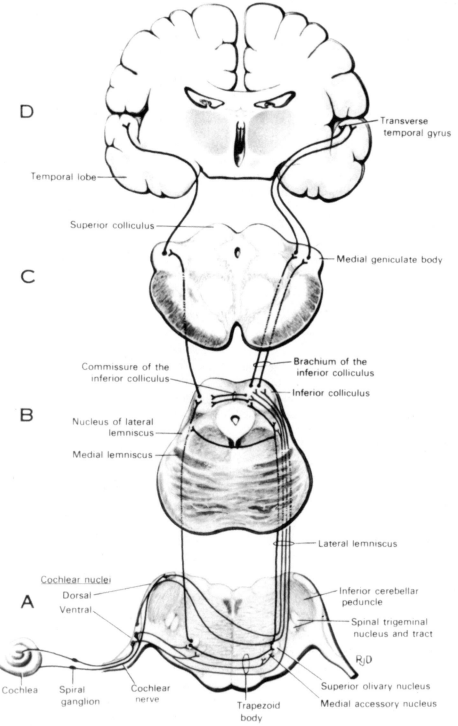

Figure 2.   The central auditory pathways. (*From Carpenter, M. B. 1978. Core text of neuroanatomy. 2nd ed. Baltimore: Williams and Wilkins. Reprinted by permission.*)

structures of the outer ear "transmit" some sound frequencies at higher amplitudes than others. Consequently, the effective sound-pressure level at the tympanic membrane will vary as a function of sound frequency.

It is commonly supposed that the *pinna* functions as a sound funnel or collector. In fact, hearing sensitivity does not appear to be affected by bypassing the pinna with tubes (Bekesy and Rosenblith, 1958). The primary function of the pinna appears to be in sound localization, particularly in monaural listening or when the sound source lies in the median plane of the head (Butler, 1975). Filling the depressions in the pinna or flattening the pinnas against the head leads to an increase in the number of errors made in a median-plane localization task (Gardner and Gardner, 1973; Roffler and Butler, 1968). Blauert (1969) suggested that such localizations could be accomplished by taking into account the degree to which the pinna acts to attenuate sounds coming from different directions. Furthermore, Batteau (1967) showed that the structures of the pinna reflect sound, so that time delays between direct and reflected sounds could be utilized in localization.

The resonance characteristics of the *auditory canal* are such that sound frequencies in the range from about 2000 to about 5000 Hz are transmitted at an amplitude as much as 15 dB higher than lower or higher frequencies. Mehrgardt and Mellert (1977) also report a relative attenuation of frequencies above 1000 Hz. Moreover, the transfer function of the auditory canal changes shape as the location of the sound source is moved from the midline toward the side (Shaw, 1974), providing the basis for spatial localization, particularly at high frequencies.

Age effects. Although age changes in the size, shape, and flexibility of the pinna have been reported (Tsai, Chou, and Cheng, 1958), it has not been determined whether these changes affect auditory localization. Magladery (1959) reported that atrophic changes in the supporting walls of the auditory canal were associated with aging. This atrophy of the ear canal may be manifested in two ways. First, because atrophy of the skin lining of the canal interferes with the expulsion of cerumen (ear wax), the elderly tend to experience

an excessive accumulation of wax, resulting in a conductive hearing loss (Corso, 1963a). Second, older individuals appear to have a higher frequency of collapsed auditory canals (Schow, Christensen, Hutchinson, and Nerbonne, 1978; Schow and Goldbaum, 1980). In a nursing home population, for example, Schow and Goldbaum (1980) found that 37 percent of residents between 65 and 79 years of age and 51 percent of those aged 80 and above showed evidence of collapse in one or both ears. Consistent with the resonant characteristics of the auditory canal, absolute thresholds were found to be affected most by the collapse at a frequency of 4000 Hz—by about 14 dB. Whether auditory canal collapse contributes significantly to hearing loss in the general elderly population has yet to be determined.

The Middle Ear

Structure and function. The middle ear is contained in the tympanic cavity, bounded laterally by the tympanic membrane (eardrum) and the promontory of the basal cochlear turn. Within this cavity is suspended the ossicular chain, which serves to transmit sound to the inner ear. In addition to its transmission function, the middle ear acts as an impedance-matching mechanism. Because air offers less opposition to the flow of sound energy than do the fluids of the inner ear (by a ratio of 4000:1), only about 0.1 percent of airborne sound energy would be transmitted to the cochlea in the absence of the middle ear. The middle ear overcomes this impedance mismatch by amplifying the level of airborne sound. Moreover, the action of this system depends on the frequency of the sound involved, the efficiency of transmission being greatest in the area of 1000 Hz and dropping off at lower and higher frequencies (Dallos, 1973). Thus, changes in middle-ear function can be expected to influence both the level and the shape of the audiogram.

The *eardrum* contributes to the transformer action of the middle ear in two ways. First, its effective area is approximately 20 times that of the oval window, where sound energy enters the cochlea. Thus the pressure applied at the oval window will be 20 times greater than that arriving at the eardrum. In addition, because the eardrum is curved, this transfer ratio is further increased (Tonndorf and Khanna, 1970). Changes in the flexibility of the membrane, then, could affect sensitivity not only by reducing the sound energy transmitted from the ear canal to the ossicular chain, but by reducing the effective area of the drum. Finally, since the displacement pattern of the eardrum is frequency-dependent, such effects may also vary as a function of sound frequency.

The *ossicular chain* also contributes to the amplification of sound energy, because the ossicles act as a lever. The lever ratio is about 1.4 for the cat, but this value is probably smaller in human beings. Deterioration of ossicular joints and other connections could be expected to reduce the lever ratio. The influence of the middle ear on auditory sensitivity is clear, at least in the cat. The total transfer ratio of the middle ear is 96.6 : 1, or 39.7 dB, a figure corresponding quite closely to the 40-dB hearing loss observed in cats following obliteration of the middle ear. Dallos (1973), moreover, showed that behavioral thresholds as a function of frequency in human beings closely resemble the middle ear transfer function.

Another factor influencing middle-ear function is the efficiency of Eustachian tube action. The *Eustachian tube* serves two purposes: (1) It acts to equalize pressure in the middle ear cavity with that in the external ear canal, and (2) it allows for drainage of fluids that would otherwise accumulate in the middle ear. Failure in either of these processes will affect hearing sensitivity by reducing the amount of energy transmitted to the cochlea.

Age effects. A variety of age-related structural changes in the middle ear have been reported, but the functional significance of these changes remains unclear. Histological observations have shown calcification of the tympanic ring (the bony annulus in which the eardrum is mounted) as well as replacement of elastic tissues in the eardrum with collagenous tissue (Belal, 1975). These impairments should result in a decline in the elasticity of the eardrum. In addition, Etholm and Belal (1974) reported that thinning and calcification of the ossicular joints becomes more common and severe with advancing age. Finally, although blockage of the Eustachian tube—resulting in fluid accumulation in the middle ear—is a common clinical finding among older individuals, this phenomenon appears to be related to the incidence of colds rather than to age (Corso, 1977). In fact, there is at least one report that Eustachian tube function actually becomes slightly more efficient with age (von Wedel and Opitz, 1978) despite histological observations of the calcification of the elastic portion of the tube (Belal, 1975).

Direct measurement of middle-ear compliance—which, in broad terms, is an index of stiffness (Dirks, 1978)—has yielded a contradictory account of the effects of the structural changes described. Studies by von Wedel and Opitz (1978) and by Nerbonne, Bliss, and Schow (1978) reported slight declines in static compliance of the middle ear with age, particularly in individuals aged 70 and older. Osterhammel and Osterhammel (1979) and Thompson, Sills, Recke, and Bui (1979), on the other hand, found no age differences in static compliance values. The source of this disparity may lie in screening procedures: Osterhammel and Osterhammel (1979) and Thompson et al. (1979) specifically excluded individuals with middle-ear disorders; the other studies did not. Although the audiograms in the studies of Osterhammel and Osterhammel and of Thompson et al. look quite similar to those published by von Wedel and Opitz and by Nerbonne et al. (and to published age-norms as well), it is possible that these latter studies included individuals with middle-ear problems. Moreover, no relationship between arthritic changes in the middle-ear joints and conductive hearing impairment has been found (Etholm and Belal, 1974). We might conclude, then, that the typical high-frequency hearing loss of presbycusis can be observed in individuals who show no sign of structural or functional middle-ear disorder. We have yet to determine, however, whether and to what extent middle-ear conductive deficits, when these exist, might contribute to age-related hearing loss.

Inner Ear

Structure and function. The transduction of sound energy to neural activity takes place within the inner ear. The inner-ear structures are found within the osseus labyrinth of the temporal bone. The *cochlea* is the most anterior portion of the inner ear. The *oval window*, the membrane-covered opening into the cochlea, is the means by which stapes footplate displacement is transmitted into the cochlea. Below the oval window is a second membranous opening known as the *round window* (see Figure 1). The *cochlear canal* is divided along its length into three sections: scala tympani, scala media, and scala vestibuli. The *scala media* is separated from the *scala vestibuli* above by Reisner's membrane and the *scala tympani* below by the basilar membrane. While the scala media is a closed duct, the scalae tympani and vestibuli are connected through an opening at the apex of the cochlea called the *helicotrema*. A schematic representation of the uncoiled cochlea is shown in Figure 3.

In cross-section (Figure 4), it can be seen that the *basilar membrane* extends from a bony ridge extending from the inner wall of the cochlea, the *spiral lamina,* to the spiral ligament along the outer wall. The basilar membrane is narrow and relatively stiff near the base of the cochlea but becomes wider and more flexible as it progresses toward the apex. *The organ of Corti,* the end organ for hearing, runs longitudinally along the basilar membrane. It contains a single row of *inner hair cells* (IHCs) and three rows of *outer hair cells* (OHCs), these being supported by various structures. The IHCs are separated from the OHCs by the tunnel of Corti, which is formed by two rows of pillar cells. There are about 50 to 70 stereocilia atop each IHC and

40 to 150 for each OHC, and these extend through the *reticular lamina* (Figure 5a). The stereocilia of the OHCs form a distinctive W-shaped pattern (Figure 5b).

The *tectorial membrane* lies over the reticular lamina (Figure 4). It is attached quite firmly on its inner edge to the *limbus* and more loosely to supporting cells lateral to the OHCs. It appears that the taller cilia of the OHCs are embedded in the tectorial membrane, whereas the cilia of the IHCs seem to be free-standing (Lim, 1973).

The transduction of mechanical to electrochemical energy in the organ of Corti is dependent upon the characteristics of the basilar membrane, the attachments of the tectorial membrane, and the manner of contact between the cilia of the hair cells and the tectorial membrane. Because of the stiffness gradient of the basilar membrane, pressure variations transmitted to the cochlear fluids by the middle ear result in a traveling wave along the basilar membrane that moves from the base (where stiffness is high) toward the apex (where stiffness is low). When a sinusoidal signal is applied to the cochlea, the envelope of the traveling wave over a complete cycle of the stimulus will have a peak amplitude of displacement at a specific point along the basilar membrane, depending upon the frequency of the signal. This peak displacement will be near the base for high frequencies, near the apex for low. The response to an impulsive stimulus, such as a click, is a traveling wave that moves from base to apex but lacks a distinct peak.

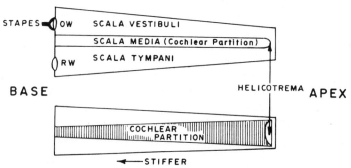

Figure 3.   Schematic representation of the uncoiled cochlea (OW—oval window). (*From Gelfand, S. A. 1981. Hearing: An introduction to psychological and physiological acoustics. New York: Dekker. Reprinted by permission.*)

The motion of the basilar membrane is translated into an electrochemical response via the shearing action of the tectorial membrane across the cilia of the OHCs. Because it is hinged, in effect, to the basilar membrane along one edge, the tectorial membrane moves relative to the basilar membrane when a traveling wave occurs. The result is a radial shearing motion across the stereocilia basal to the point of maximal displacement. This radial shear provides the excitatory stimulus for the OHCs. Since the IHCs do not make direct contact with the tectorial membrane, some other mechanism must be responsible for IHC stimulation. Dallos, Villone, Durrant, Wang, and Raynor (1972) reported that the response of the IHCs was proportional to the velocity of basilar membrane motion, whereas the OHC response depended upon the absolute displacement of the membrane. The latter investigators suggest that the IHCs are in fact stimulated by movement of the surrounding fluid relative to the basilar membrane. The extent of fluid motion would be proportional to the velocity of basilar membrane motion.

Besides differences in their effective stimuli, IHCs and OHCs also differ in innervation pattern. The dendrites of neurons whose cell bodies form the spiral ganglia enter the organ of Corti through the *habenula perforata,* openings in the osseus spiral lamina on the inner cochlear wall. Two types of fibers have been identified (Fernandez, 1951): *Radial fibers* run directly from the habenula perforata to the hair cells, whereas *longitudinal fibers* follow a course that spirals with the cochlear turns before contacting the hair cells. About 95 percent of the afferent nerve supply, mainly radial fibers, goes to the IHCs. The remaining 5 percent innervate the OHCs via the outer spiral bundle. Each of the outer spiral bundle fibers innervates about 20 OHCs. In contrast, each IHC is supplied by about 20 radial fibers. Thus, it is said that the convergent innervation pattern of the OHCs allows for summation of activity across hair cells, whereas the diver-

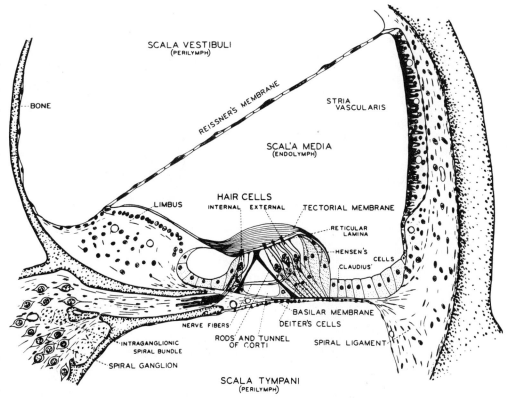

Figure 4. Cross-section of the organ of Corti. (*From Davis, H. 1961. Advances in neurophysiology and neuroanatomy of the cochlea.* J. Acoust. Soc. Am. *34: 1377–3185. Reprinted by permission.*)

gent pattern of the IHCs would not (Spoend-lin, 1975).

The differential roles of the inner and outer hair cells is still a matter of debate. Clearly one would predict, on the basis of the OHCs' connections to the tectorial membrane and their innervation pattern, that OHCs would be more sensitive to sound stimulation than would the IHCs. In fact, destruction of the OHCs produces a loss of auditory sensitivity of 30 to 40 dB (Dallos et al., 1972). It has been suggested, moreover, that OHC loss associated with certain types of hearing loss in human beings results in deficits in frequency and intensity discrimination (Jerger and Jerger, 1967). However, animal studies in which OHC destruction is produced and confirmed in the laboratory (Ryan, Dallos, and McGee, 1979; Nienhuys and Clark, 1978; Prosen, Moody, Stebbins, and Hawkins, 1981; Ryan, 1978) report no change in frequency or intensity resolution. We would expect, in fact, that

the denser innervation of the IHCs would make them better discriminators than OHCs. The implication would be that something more than OHC loss is responsible for the discrimination deficits observed in hearing-impaired human beings.

To summarize, pressure variations in the air surrounding the head are amplified and transmitted to the cochlear fluids by the middle ear. As a result, a traveling wave is set up along the basilar membrane, causing shearing motion of the tectorial membrane across the cilia of the OHCs. This shearing of the cilia results in an electrical response—the *receptor potential*—in the OHCs. Movement of the fluids surrounding the hair cells exerts drag on the cilia of the IHCs, again producing a receptor potential. This entire process is highly dependent upon the electrochemical status of the cochlear fluids. The *endolymph,* the fluid that fills the scala media, has a very high concentration of potassium and a very

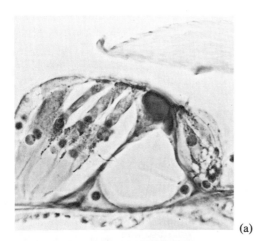

(a)

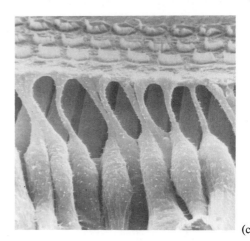

(c)

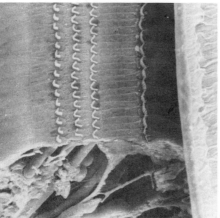

(b)

Figure 5.   (a) Light micrograph of cross section of a chinchilla organ of Corti. (b) Scanning electron micrograph of chinchilla organ of Corti. (c) Scanning electron micrograph showing supporting structure or organ of Corti at outer row of outer hair cells. (*Courtesy, Dr. Ivan Hunter-Duvar, Hospital for Sick Children, Toronto.*)

low concentration of sodium. Since the scalae tympani and vestibuli contain *perilymph,* in which the relative concentrations of potassium and sodium are reversed, the net result is a resting potential across Reissner's membrane of about +100mV. This endocochlear potential is maintained by the *stria vascularis,* a rich network of capillaries that runs along the outer wall of the scala media (Tasaki, Davis, and Eldredge, 1954; Konishi, Butler, and Fernandez, 1961; Tasaki and Spiropoulos, 1959). In addition, a negative resting potential of about −60mV has been measured within the organ of Corti (Tasaki et al., 1954). This is believed to be an intracellular potential arising from the hair cells (Dallos, 1973). The net result is a polarity difference of at least 160 mV across the reticular membrane. Since the total potential difference is far greater than what would result from the intracellular potentials of the hair cells alone, the effect is to increase the range of electrical response. Thus the integrity of this polarity difference, and, in particular, of the stria vascularis, is essential for normal auditory function.

Sound stimulation results in two types of endocochlear electrical response. The first is an ac potential, known as the *cochlear microphonic* (CM), which is a faithful reproduction of the stimulus waveform. The CM appears to be generated at the cilia-bearing ends of the hair cells (Bekesy, 1960; Tasaki et al., 1954; Konishi and Yasuna, 1963). Davis' (1965) variable-resistance model is probably the most widely accepted account of CM generation. Davis conceived of the cochlear resting potentials as biological batteries that generate a current flowing through the scala media, basilar membrane, and scala tympani. The cochlear blood supply provides a ground for the circuit. Stimulation of the hair cells would cause a change in resistance to current flow, following the stimulus waveform. The result would be an ac current that mimics the stimulus, monitored as the CM. Thus, the CM can be used as a measure of the transduction process, which depends upon the integrity of the hair cells as well as that of the stria vascularis.

The second type of electrical response to sound that is recorded in the cochlea is a dc shift known as the *summating potential* (SP).

Although the CM closely follows the envelope of the traveling wave, the SP is positive on the basal side of the displacement peak and becomes negative on the apical side (Honrubia and Ward, 1969). This suggests that the SP may serve to sharpen frequency selectivity in the cochlea by inhibiting neural excitation along the basal part of the traveling-wave envelope. Since SP polarity reverses from one side of the cilia-bearing ends of the HCs to the other (Konishi and Yasuna, 1963), the SP may be generated at the hair cell. However, there is some evidence that the average SP (measured from opposite sides of the cochlear partition) may be neural in origin (Dallos, 1971).

To this point, we have primarily considered auditory mechanisms as they influence a listener's ability to detect sound—his absolute sensitivity. Clearly, many of the structures discussed also contribute to the ability to respond differentially to sounds that vary in frequency. By the time the response to a sound reaches the auditory nerve, quite narrow "tuning" to specific frequencies has already been achieved. Kiang (1965), for example, showed that each single auditory nerve fiber responds best to a narrow range of frequencies, particularly at low intensity levels.[2] The question is, where does this sharp tuning originate? In his original observations of the basilar membrane, Bekesy (1960) pointed out that the traveling wave pattern was too wide to account for a listener's ability to distinguish pitches. Despite technical advances in the measurement of basilar membrane motion, there is surprising agreement on the degree of mechanical tuning observed. If we express degree of tuning as Q_{10}—the ratio of the center frequency to the bandwidth of the response curve 10 dB down from the peak—the basilar-membrane observations yield values ranging from about 0.5 at low frequencies to about 1.3 at high frequencies (where high values indicate better tuning). For auditory nerve fibers, on the other hand, Q_{10} values range from about 2 at low frequencies to about 9 at high frequencies. Although the shearing force exerted by the tectorial membrane is more localized than the displacement pattern of the basilar membrane

[2]Response patterns of auditory nerve fibers are discussed in detail in the next section.

(Khanna et al., 1968), it is still too broad to account for neural tuning. Moreover, Evans and Wilson (1975) found that broadening of the basilar membrane caused by perilymph drainage did not produce a corresponding loss in neural tuning when measured in the same animals. Changes in the metabolism of the cochlea, on the other hand, did reduce the sharpness of neural tuning (Evans and Wilson, 1973; Evans, 1975). Zwislocki (1974, 1975) hypothesized that the cochlear sharpening mechanism was the result of an out-of-phase relationship between IHCs and OHCs, whereas Manley (1978) and Russell and Sellick (1977) suggested that the SP mediates cochlear frequency selectivity. More recently, Khanna and Leonard (1982) report that basilar membrane tuning is, in fact, sharp enough to account for neural tuning when the trauma caused by preparation of the membrane for observation is reduced. Whatever the exact mechanism, it is clear that cochlear degeneration will not only reduce a listener's absolute sensitivity but may reduce his analytic capacity as well.

Age effects. Many investigators hold that the primary source of hearing loss in the elderly is due to loss of hair cells and/or to disturbance of inner-ear metabolism (e.g., Schuknecht, 1974; Corso, 1977, 1981). Nevertheless, mechanical changes in inner-ear structures may also influence audition in the elderly. For example, Wright and Schuknecht (1972) note pronounced acellularity in the spiral ligament, the basilar membrane's attachment to the cochlear wall, with advancing age. In addition, Hansen and Reske-Nielson (1965) observed reduced flexibility of the basilar membrane in the inner ears of older individuals. These investigators also noted an age-related thickening of the tectorial membrane and the accumulation of restrictive adhesions. When this type of degeneration becomes pronounced, the individual's audiogram apparently shows a hearing loss that gradually increases from low to high frequencies. Schuknecht et al. (1974) hold that this "inner ear conductive prebycusis" is a distinct disorder, occurring in about 23 percent of their sample of deaf elderly individuals. One is left to wonder, however, whether such mechanical deficits may also

contribute to the mild hearing loss experienced by many elderly persons. Moreover, since the mechanical portions of the inner ear provide the "first filter" in the analysis of acoustic signals, such changes may influence frequency resolution and, as a consequence, the perception of complex stimuli such as speech.

Hair-cell loss with age has been well-documented. Bredberg (1967) examined histologically the inner ears of 150 individuals ranging from 2½ months gestational age to 93 years and reported that degeneration of hair cells and supporting structures could be observed as early as the end of the second decade. This degeneration appears to increase gradually with age and is pronounced in the basal coil of the cochlea. The pattern of loss was slightly different for inner and outer hair cells. Inner hair cells tend to show only a basal degeneration, whereas outer hair-cell loss was more widespread. Outer hair-cell loss, moreover, was accentuated at the basal and apical ends of the cochlea. Johnsson and Hawkins (1972a) generally confirmed this finding. Hair-cell loss in their presbycotic material appeared to be symmetrical in the two ears and was usually confined to the lower half of the basal turn. Degeneration of the corresponding radial fibers tended to accompany hair-cell loss, but the longitudinal fibers arising in the same region did not seem to be affected. This pattern of sensory cell loss appears to be associated with an abrupt hearing loss at the higher frequencies. Schuknecht et al. (1974) termed this variety of hearing loss "sensory presbycusis" and found that approximately 12 percent of their sample of deaf individuals exhibited it. The incidence of mild loss of this type is probably higher in the general population (Keim, 1977), however, and may not become noticeable since the speech frequencies are usually not affected (Johnsson and Hawkins, 1972a).

Both Bredberg (1967) and Johnsson and Hawkins (1972a) also found a relatively severe loss of both hair cells and nerve fibers at the extreme apical end of the cochlea with advancing age. Since the extent of the degeneration is quite small, this finding may have little clinical significance. Johnsson and Hawkins suggest that this loss may result from atrophy of the stria vascularis in the apical turn.

Strial atrophy associated with aging was described by Takahashi (1971). Degeneration is indicated by an accumulation of pigment and calcium deposits, loss of cell organelles, and, in severe cases, cell and capillary loss. Takahashi distinguished between localized and diffuse types of atrophy. Since the two types were often found within the same individual, however, it seems likely that these are two stages in the degenerative process. Takahashi (1971) reported that such changes become pronounced after age 60 and that they are most often localized in the lower basal turn and most apical region of the cochlea. In contrast, Johnsson and Hawkins (1972b) found that the basal turn was less prone to atrophy than were the apical and middle turns. Gacek and Schuknecht (1969) also observed more pronounced strial atrophy in the apical and middle turns of the cochlea and found such degeneration to be associated with a flat hearing loss across frequencies. In at least one case where such loss was observed, there was little sign of either hair-cell or neural degeneration. Schuknecht and his colleagues hold that strial degeneration leads to a distinct class of age-related hearing loss—metabolic or strial presbycus—which is independent of mechanical, sensory-cell, or neural loss. Schuknecht et al. (1974) observed such strial prebycusis in about 35 percent of their sample of deaf elderly.

Since the stria vascularis functions to maintain the polarity difference between the scala media and the scalae tympani and vestibuli, atrophy of this structure should be expected to reduce the endocochlear potential. As of this writing, no study has been done to investigate this possibility. Age changes in the cochlear microphonic (CM) in rodents, however, have been observed. Pestalozza, Davis, Eldredge et al. (1957), for example, found reduced CM amplitudes in senile guinea pigs. Crowley, Swain, Schramm, and Swanson (1972) reported similar increases in CM threshold in aged rats. Moreover, in the latter study, the increased CM threshold observed in the oldest rats (24 months) appeared concurrently with a dramatic drop in outer-hair-cell count. Whether the loss of CM sensitivity was caused directly by the hair-cell loss is uncertain, because the status of the other cochlear structures was not assessed. Mikaelian (1979), in fact, found that hair-cell loss in one strain of mice was accompanied by degeneration of the strial vascularis, of the cochlear nerve supply, and of the tectorial membrane. Although caution is in order in making such cross-species comparisons, the point that atrophy of various cochlear structures may not proceed independently is worth noting. Although some investigators (e.g., Schuknecht et al., 1974) have posited distinct classes of presbycusis associated with independent degeneration of cochlear structures, there is some evidence that these deficits are rarely observed in their pure form (Johnsson and Hawkins, 1977).

To summarize, age-related anatomical changes in the mechanical structures, sensory cells, neural supply, and support structures of the inner ear are frequently observed. While degeneration of specific structures is associated with particular patterns of hearing loss, it appears that more than one type of structural change often occurs within the same individual.

The Auditory Nervous System

Writing in 1962, Hinchcliffe described presbycusis as a unitary age-related disorder that is characterized by a variety of deficits in auditory performance and concluded from his review of the then-available histological research that the anatomical locus of presbycusis lay somewhere within the brain, presumably as a result of the degeneration of second-order or higher neurons. Since that time, it has been recognized that different types of presbycusis exist, and a few studies have examined age-related structural changes in specific auditory nuclei. The general outline of the auditory pathway was described at the beginning of this section. Here we will consider the structure and functional characteristics of the major relay stations in that pathway and review what is known of the effects of aging on them.

Auditory Nerve and Spiral Ganglion

Structure and Function. The fibers of the auditory nerve, whose cell bodies are found within the spiral ganglion, leave the inner ear through the internal auditory meatus and enter the brain stem at the level of the lower pons. There are approximately 30,000 fibers in this nerve, which is tonotopically organized with low frequencies represented at the core, high frequencies in the outer layers.

The response characteristics of auditory nerve fibers have been extensively studied. Galambos and Davis (1943) first reported on the responses of individual fibers to pure tone stimulation. Fibers tend to be "tuned" to specific frequencies, showing low threshold and higher suprathreshold response rates to a relatively narrow frequency range. The curves showing threshold or response rate as a function of frequency for each unit are known as *tuning curves* (see Fig. 6). The lowest threshold or highest response rate is termed the units' characteristic frequency (CF). Tuning curves tend to rise relatively abruptly at frequencies above the CF (at the rate of 100 dB per octave or more) but more slowly at frequencies below the CF (about 25 dB per octave).

Auditory nerve fibers also show characteristic response patterns following stimulus presentation. Kiang (1965) obtained poststimulus-time (PST) histograms—the distribution of response latencies following stimulus onset—from single auditory nerve units responding to a click. He found that peaks in the distribution of responses occur at times corresponding to the period of the unit's CF. In other words, a unit whose CF was 1000 Hz, for example, would be most likely to respond at integral multiples of 1 msec following stimulus onset. In examining fibers' responses to tone bursts, Kiang showed that neural discharges tended to be phase-locked to individual cycles of the tone burst, i.e., a fiber tends to fire at a particular phase of the stimulus waveform. Sachs and Kiang (1968), furthermore, demonstrated that a unit's response to a tone at its CF can be suppressed by the concurrent presentation of a tone in adjacent frequency regions. Although this "two-tone inhibition" might be assumed to represent a neural sharpening of the tuning curves, it probably results from nonlinear cochlear processes, since it has also been demonstrated in the cochlear microphonic (Pfeiffer and Molnar, 1970; Legouix,

Remond, and Greenbaum, 1973; Dallos and Cheatham, 1974). Auditory nerve fiber responses, then, are characterized by fine tuning to specific frequencies and preserve information about the stimulus waveform.

The whole nerve action potential (AP), which represents the synchronous discharge of many auditory nerve fibers, can be measured in human beings from within the cochlea, at the round window or from the ear canal. The AP typically consists of a negative amplitude peak (N_1) at some latency following stimulus onset, followed by one or more smaller peaks (N_2, N_3, etc.). It is generally accepted that the AP response derives primarily from fibers from the basal turn of the cochlea (Tasaki, et al., 1954). Since some types of presbycusis are characterized by loss at high frequencies, we would predict age changes in the auditory nerve AP. Finally, the magnitude and latency of the AP are dependent upon stimulus intensity. The curve showing AP amplitude as a function of stimulus intensity changes slope at higher signal levels. Davis (1961) and Eggermont (1976) have suggested that the two-part curve results from the contribution of inner hair cells at higher intensities. Özdamar and Dallos (1976), however, proposed an alternate model in which the high intensity portion of the curve is held to result from an increase in the number of fibers firing at high levels. This conclusion would follow from an examination of individual tuning curves: As signal level increases, each fiber will respond to a broader frequency range.

Age effects. As mentioned in our consideration of the inner ear, loss of first-order nerve fibers, particularly of radial fibers, is often observed in the basal and apical turns of the cochlea of older people, in association with, and probably following, hair-cell loss in those regions (Bredberg, 1967, 1968; Johnsson and Hawkins, 1972b). Since lesions of the organ of Corti result in degeneration of associated nerve fibers (Powell and Cowan, 1962; Moskowitz and Liu, 1972), it may be that age-related neural loss is the result of hair-cell degeneration. However, Schuknecht et al. (1974) describe cases, comprising 31 percent of their deaf elderly sample, in which the extent of neural degeneration was far greater than would be expected from the observed receptor-cell loss. Although the loss appeared to be more severe in the basal turn, Schuknecht (1974) reported that the entire cochlea was involved to some extent. Audiological assessment of individuals with this disorder tended to show a relatively greater loss of speech discrimination than of pure tone threshold. This would imply deficits in the neural structures responsible for analysis and integration of complex stimulus waveforms, and Schuknecht (1974) suggests that degeneration at higher centers in the auditory pathway might contribute to the problem.

Johnsson and Hawkins (1972a) also observed cases in which there was severe, "patchy" degeneration of nerve fibers involving all three turns of the cochlea without correspondingly severe hair-cell loss. These investigators nevertheless point out that it was difficult to determine whether hair cells or nerve fibers had degenerated first. They suggest that what Schuknecht terms "neural" may be differentiated from sensory presbycusis by the fact that degeneration occurs in all three turns in neural presbycusis. On the other hand, Bredberg (1968) found that age-related outer-hair-cell degeneration also extended throughout the cochlea, although it was most pronounced at the basal and apical ends. Bredberg did observe one pair of cochleas exhibiting extensive patchy degeneration of the nerve throughout the cochlea with no corresponding gaps in the sensory cells.

There does not seem to be an easy answer to this chicken-and-egg question. Reports of degeneration of the internal auditory meatus (see Figure 1) with advancing age (i.e., progressive narrowing of the canal as a result of bone apposition) have been reported by Fleischer (1972) and Krmpotic-Nemanic (1972), and degeneration of arterial blood vessels has been reported by Fitsch, Doboze, and Greig (1972); either of these conditions might produce neural degeneration independent of hair-cell loss. Since the fibers carrying high-frequency information are near the outside of the nerve, they would presumably be the first to be affected. Usually, however, the pattern of spiral ganglion cell-degeneration is remarkably similar to the patterns of hair cell loss.

Fleischer (1972) studying humans and Finkiewicz (1971) studying guinea pigs both found extensive, age-related spiral-ganglion degeneration confined to the basal turn of the cochlea, that region where Bredberg (1968) reported loss of both inner and outer hair cells. Moreover, Keithley and Feldman (1979), who

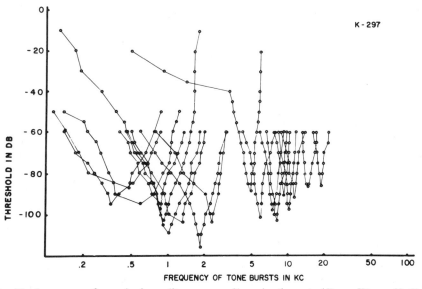

Figure 6.   Tuning curves from single auditory nerve fibers in the cat. (*From Kiang, N. Y. S. 1965. Discharge patterns of single fibers in the cat's auditory nerve. Cambridge, Mass.: MIT Press. Reprinted by permission.*)

studied rats, found distinct patterns of loss for two populations of spiral-ganglion cells. Type I cells showed degeneration earlier and were affected maximally near the base of the cochlea. Type II cells, on the other hand, were affected only in the two oldest age groups and tended to show maximal loss in the middle and apical turns, paralleling the differential loss patterns for inner and outer hair cells.

Studies of the effects of aging on the whole-nerve AP in animals do little to clarify the issue. Pestalozza et al. (1957) reported greater losses in AP amplitude than of CM amplitude in senile rats, suggesting neural damage over and above cochlear deficits. However, Crowley et al. (1972) failed to replicate this finding, and, in addition, Crowley et al. (1972) found that relatively small losses of outer hair cells correlated with reduction of the amplitude of the AP but not with change in CM voltage.

We might conclude, as did Johnsson and Hawkins (1972), that both sensory and neural degeneration are often present within the same individual, both processes resulting in the loss of first-order neurons. On the basis of the observations of Bredberg (1968) and Schuknecht et al. (1974), it appears that some cases of pure neural loss do occur, although Bredberg would probably estimate the incidence as being much lower than 31 percent of the elderly.

Finally, one study of mice (Mikaelian, 1979) examined the responses of single units in the auditory nerve of aged animals. Mikaelian found that it was difficult to find high-frequency-tuned fibers in the older mice and that the thresholds of both high and low CF fibers were elevated. In addition, the response range of single units tended to become constricted with age, and two-tone inhibition was difficult to demonstrate in the oldest animals. The latter findings must be interpreted with caution, since only moderately high levels of stimulation were used at the higher frequencies. There is the suggestion here, however, that age-related changes in frequency analysis may be found at early stages of processing.

Cochlear Nucleus

Structure and Function. The cochlear nucleus gives rise to the second-order neurons in the auditory pathway. The response characteristics of cells at this locus are more varied than those of the eighth nerve. Although the nucleus is tonotopically organized (Rose, Galambos, and Hughes, 1959; Rose, 1960), five types of discharge patterns have been identified (Kiang et al., 1965; Rose et al., 1959). Although some units respond in a manner similar to auditory nerve fibers, other units were found to produce very different PST histograms. Other investigators (Erulkar et al., 1968) have identified cochlear nucleus cells that are tuned to FM tones, an acoustic feature common to speech.

Age effects. There is some disagreement as to the effects of aging on the cochlear nucleus. Apparently only the ventral cochlear nucleus (VCN) has been examined. Kirikae and Shitara (1961) and Hansen and Reske-Nielson (1965) both reported loss of cells and other degenerative effects in the VCN. However, Konigsmark and Murphy (1970a,b) found a decrease in the volume of the VCN but no reduction in the number of cells. The latter investigators suggest that the loss of volume results from a decline in the number of myelinated axons in the nucleus, though they recognize that glial-cell or blood-vessel loss might also be contributors. Since lesions of the cochlea are known to produce degeneration of cochlear nucleus cells (e.g., Sando, 1965), what we may be seeing here are stages of degenerative process resulting from hair-cell loss. Degeneration of axon cylinders may be followed by loss of entire neurons. Note, however, that we know nothing about which types of units are being affected; various types of response patterns are found in the VCN.

Higher Level Nuclei and Auditory Cortex

Structure and Function. Examination of the other nuclei of the auditory pathways shows an even greater variety of response patterns than in the cochlear nucleus. Both narrow and broad tuning curves have been obtained from the superior olivary complex (SOC) and trapezoid body (Boudreau and Tsuchitani, 1970; Guinan, Norris, and Guinan, 1972; Katsuki, 1961; Kiang, Morest, Godfrey, Guinan, and Kane, 1973); the inferior colliculus (IC) and medial geniculate body (MGB) (Katsuki, 1961; Rose et al., 1963); and in the auditory cortex (Hind, 1960; Katsuki, Suga, and Kanno, 1962). All of these structures also exhibit tonotopic organization (Tsuchitani and Boudreau, 1966; Aitkin et al., 1970; Rose et al., 1963; Aitkin and Webster, 1971; Rose, 1949). "On" units and units responding to signal duration have been found in the IC (Rose et al., 1959); these types of units, as well as "off" cells, have been found in the MGB (Galambos, 1952; Katsuki, Watanabe, and Maruyama, 1959; Aitkin et al., 1966). The situation in the cortex is even more complex, since it has been found to contain "on" and "off" units (Hind, 1960; Katsuki et al., 1962), directionally sensitive FM units (Whitfield and Evans, 1965), and cells that respond to movement of a sound source through space (Sovijarvi and Hyvarinen, 1974).

Two types of neural coding will be discussed in some detail here. The first is binaural coding, a heavily researched topic in this context because age deficits in binaural signal processing have been demonstrated. The second is the coding of FM signals. Although this area has been less widely investigated, both physiologically and psychophysically, it is relevant to the consideration of aging since important information in speech is carried in FM signals and since, as we discuss below, the elderly often show deficits in speech discrimination over and above any loss in hearing sensitivity. Although loss of speech perception might be due to attenuation of the acoustic signal or to deficits in memory, attention, or confidence in making judgments, the degeneration of the intermediate auditory nuclei that code the acoustic features of speech sounds would also affect speech understanding.

Binaural coding in the auditory pathway is first observed at the SOC, and logically so, since this is the first site to receive input from both ears (see Fig. 3). Goldberg and Brown (1969) conducted an extensive study of binaural coding in the SOC and identified two neuron types. Excitatory-excitatory (EE) cells responded to inputs from either ear, whereas excitatory-inhibitory (EI) cells were excited by inputs from one ear and inhibited by inputs from the other. EE neurons responded on the basis of the average intensity of the two ears, but EI neurons were sensitive to interaural

intensity differences (IIDs). At low stimulus frequencies, however, a different type of response was observed. Cells tended to become phase-locked to the stimulus tone whenever there was a characteristic interaural time of arrival difference (ITD) between the ears. This finding is of interest in light of the fact that IIDs provide the best cue for high-frequency sound localization, whereas ITDs are probably used at low frequencies (Stevens and Newman, 1936).

At the IC, Rose et al. (1966) found cells that respond maximally to characteristic ITDs, regardless of signal level or frequency. Other cells were found to be tuned to specific IIDs. Benevento and Coleman (1970) identified some units that would respond to both IIDs and ITDs and others that responded to neither. Finally, some IC neurons may respond to a moving sound source (Altman, 1968).

Medial geniculate cells seem to respond in a manner similar to those of the SOC and IC. In addition, there are both short-latency (<30 msec) and long-latency (>500 msec) cells at this level (Altman, Syka, and Shmigidina, 1970). The long-latency fibers have been suggested to play a role in short-term memory for interaural differences (Gelfand, 1981).

Most cells in the auditory cortex appear to be the EI type, responding to contralateral but not to ipsilateral signals. Cells sensitive to characteristic ITDs and IIDs are found (Brugge and Merzenich, 1973; Brugge, Dubrovsky, Aitkin, and Anderson, 1969; Hall and Goldstein, 1968), as well as cells that respond to a particular direction of sound-source movement (Sovijarvi and Hyvarinen, 1974).

The situation for FM coding parallels the progressive response specificity observed by Hubel and Wiesel (1962) in the visual cortex of the cat. Erulkar et al. (1968) found units in the cochlear nucleus that responded to FM signals, but these units were not sensitive to the direction or rate of modulation and only responded to the signal if it fell within the frequency range to which the unit was tuned. Nelson et al. (1966) found the inferior colliculus to be the first site of directionally sensitive FM units. Some units were found to respond to both amplitude-modulated (AM) and FM signals. Suga (1969) reported that about 3 percent of the IC units in the bat, which uses FM signals for echolocation, were FM-specialized. At the auditory cortex, about 10 percent of the cells in the cat (Whitfield and Evans, 1965) appear to be FM-specialized. Whitfield (1969) holds that these are the first true FM-tuned cells in the pathway, since the response is dependent upon the direction, rate, and frequency range of the FM sweep.[3]

Age effects. Deficits at any of the central nuclei may play a role in observed age decrements in sound localization and speech perception. However, despite the profound implications of age-related degeneration of central auditory nerve system structures, little is known of the specific changes that occur. For example, Kirikae, Sato, and Shitara (1964) report a reduction after 68 years of age in cell size in the superior olive; irregularities in shape of cells in the inferior colliculus; and cell loss, reduction in cell size, and pigment accumulation in the medial geniculate. Hansen and Reske-Nielson (1965) also found bilateral degeneration of the inferior colliculus and a loss of cells in that nucleus. These observations, along with reported degeneration of glial cells throughout the auditory pathway (Hansen and Reske-Nielson, 1965), lead to the conclusion that information reaching the auditory cortex of older individuals will be degraded. The manner in which the input is affected and the extent of the aging effects, however, is still poorly understood.

Still less is known of age-related changes within the auditory cortex. Hansen and Reske-Nielson (1965) reported a loss of cells, accompanied by the accumulation of degenerative products, and a degeneration of myelin sheaths and axons within the temporal lobes. Furthermore, in studying rats, Vaughan and Vincent (1979) found that the cell bodies of pyramidal cells in layer II of the auditory cortex begin to shrink with advancing age and suggested that this process is related to the loss of dendrites observed by Vaughan (1977).

Vaughan and Vincent (1979) noted that age-related changes in the ultrastructure of cells in the auditory cortex proceed at different rates for cells in layers II and V. Since these two cortical layers receive different synaptic inputs, this finding may be of functional significance.

Stapedius Reflex as a Measure of Age-related Physiological Change

Characteristics of the Reflex. The middle ear contains two muscles, the tensor tympani and the stapedius. The *stapedius muscle*, innervated by the seventh cranial (facial) nerve, exits through the posterior wall of the tympanic cavity and attaches to the neck of the stapes. Contraction of the muscle pulls the stapes posteriorly. The *tensor tympani*, innervated by the fifth cranial (trigeminal) nerve, emerges from the anterior wall of the tympanic cavity and inserts at the top of the manubrium of the malleus. Contraction of the tensor tympani pulls the malleus at a right angle to its normal direction of movement.

The tensor tympani muscle contracts as part of a startle response to very intense sound (Djupesland, 1964) or to a jet of air to the eye (Klockhoff, 1961). The stapedius reflex is a bilateral contraction of the stapedius muscle elicited by intense stimulation of either ear and has been widely studied in man, particularly in audiological assessment. The function of the stapedius reflex may be to attenuate low frequencies, thus improving the signal-to-noise ratio for relevant higher-frequency environmental sounds.

In normal ears, the threshold for the stapedius reflex for pure tones ranges from about 85 to 100 dB SPL (e.g., Metz, 1952; Silman, Popelka, and Gelfand, 1978) and about 20 dB lower for wide-band noise (e.g., Silman et al., 1978). The latency to a measurable impedance change that results from the reflex is about 150 msec at 80 dB SL, decreasing to 40 msec at 100 dB SL for a 1000-Hz tone (Metz, 1951). Latencies to broad-band signals are shorter (Hung and Dallos, 1972)—on the order of 20 msec. The magnitude of the reflex grows rapidly with stimulus intensity in cases of cochlear dysfunction, where loudness re-

---

[3]Whether these responses are, in fact, *FM*-specialized has not gone unquestioned. Feth and O'Malley (1971) point out that such responses could be based on the long-term power spectrum of the signal by frequency-tuned units.

cruitment is likely to occur (Metz, 1952; Bee-dle and Harford, 1973). However, Margolis and Popelka (1975) found that the loudness levels of different signals at the reflex threshold differed by as much as 17 dB, and Block and Wightman (1977) reported that the same reflex magnitude could be elicited by signal levels as much as 10 dB apart. Thus, the relationship between the stapedius reflex and loudness is not a simple one.

Age effects. Although some controversy has been generated with regard to the effects of aging on the stapedius reflex, a few consistent findings have emerged. The threshold for elicitation of the reflex tends to decrease with age when the activating stimulus is a pure tone (Thompson, Sills, Recke, and Bui, 1980; Silman, 1979; Jerger, Hayes, Anthony, and Mauldin, 1978a; Osterhammel and Osterhammel, 1979b; Handler and Margolis, 1977; Habener and Snyder, 1974). That is to say, the minimum sensation level (level with respect to absolute threshold) required to produce the reflex is lower for older individuals, particularly after the sixth decade of life. The source of this age difference is not apparent; Jerger et al. (1978a) suggest that the reduction in reflex threshold is the result of the generation of increased cochlear distortion products, or nonlinearities, which would become pronounced at high levels but leave conventional detection thresholds unaffected. Jerger et al. point out that this would explain their findings that reflex thresholds for broad-band activating signals were not affected by age. The additional distortion products would not increase the bandwidth, and hence the loudness, of an already broad-band stimulus.

Thompson et al. (1980) also report no age difference in reflex thresholds for a filtered white noise (half-power points of 1000 Hz and 5100 Hz). Other investigators (Silman, 1979a; Handler and Margolis, 1977), however, have found an increase in the reflex threshold for broad-band signals beyond age 60. The discrepancy between Jerger et al. (1978a) and the latter studies may be due to the fact that the oldest subjects in the former study were 50 to 59 years old. Furthermore, although Thompson et al. (1980) did not find increases in reflex threshold up to age 70, the activating

stimulus in that study was actually narrower in bandwidth than that employed by Silman (1979a) or Handler and Margolis (1977).

It is possible that the observed age differences in stapedial response to tonal and broadband signals result from two different processes. Perhaps the improvement in reflex threshold for pure tones results, as Jerger et al. (1978a) suggest, from increasing distortion products, particularly if the distortion products fall within a frequency range where hearing is left relatively unimpaired. Since the amplitude of distortion products, however, does not grow as rapidly as the intensity of the stimulus (Plomp, 1965; Goldstein, 1967), it might be predicted that the amplitude and rate of growth of the reflex would be reduced in the elderly. In fact, that prediction is confirmed in three studies (Habener and Snyder, 1974; Thompson et al., 1980; and Gersdorff, 1978). In the case of a broad-band signal, the advantage conferred on the older listener by the presence of the distortion products is eliminated. However, once cochlear degeneration (as described, for example, by Bredberg, 1968) has progressed to the point where loudness summation is impaired, the differential effectiveness of the broad-band signal in eliciting the reflex is reduced. Martin (1974) and Scharf and Hellman (1966) have documented failure of loudness summation associated with cochlear disorders. Clearly, other factors, such as deterioration of the stapedial muscle or the neural elements of the reflex arc, could also contribute to age-related changes in the reflex.

AGE-RELATED CHANGES IN PERFORMANCE ON PSYCHOACOUSTIC TASKS

From our review of aging effects on the anatomy and physiology of the auditory system, we can make certain global predictions about auditory function in the elderly. First, we might expect a loss of absolute sensitivity, resulting from loss of hair cells and neural units at various loci in the pathway. Reduction in the amplitude of the evoked potential (Beagley and Sheldrake, 1978) certainly supports this prediction: Higher levels of stimulation are needed for older and younger individuals to obtain equivalent levels of neural response to younger individuals. Since hair cell loss, in particular, appears to be most pronounced in the basal cochlear turn, loss of sensitivity can be expected to be greater at high frequencies. Changes in the external and middle ears may also contribute to sensitivity loss, though perhaps not substantially.

Beyond this rather obvious prediction, it becomes more difficult to state expectations of age changes in auditory performance. If, as some believe, sharpening of the frequency-specific response is accomplished at the level of the hair cell, then the deterioration of the receptor cells and associated mechanical structures might produce deficits in the analytic capacity of the ear. Such deficits are likely to affect performance not only in discrimination tasks, but also in masking paradigms and loudness judgments (Scharf, 1970). Age changes in higher level nuclei in the auditory pathway may be reflected in binaural task performance, in ability to detect and process complex acoustic cues, such as FM glides, and in the ability to integrate information carried in different frequency-tuned channels. At this point, however, we are only making educated guesses. We are only a little closer than we were ten years ago to understanding how psychoacoustic performance is affected by specific physiological changes. Clearly there is a need for more detailed histological and physiological data, in conjunction with psychophysical work, to address structure-function relationships.

Sensitivity

Absolute Sensitivity. Probably the most well-established and widely accepted age-related change in hearing is a loss of pure-tone sensitivity. Corso (1963b) obtained audiograms from individuals aged 18 to 65 years, all of whom were subjected to otological screening and from relatively low-noise environments. Corso's audiograms for men and women are shown in Figure 7. As can be seen from the audiograms, hearing loss appears to be progressive over age—particularly for men—and is pronounced above 1000 Hz. In general, the extent of loss is greater for men

than for women. There also seems to be a sex difference in the pattern of loss over age: Hearing loss at low frequencies is barely noticeable for women prior to age 51, and the progressive age-related steepening of the high-frequency portion of the curve is more pronounced for men than women. Corso's (1963b) findings agree in most details with many other studies of auditory sensitivity (e.g., Glorig and Nixon, 1962; Hinchcliffe, 1958; Jerger, 1973; Osterhammel and Osterhammel, 1979a; Robinson and Sutton, 1979; Schaie, Baltes, and Strother, 1964). Robinson and Sutton (1979), combining data from 14 studies, generated curves showing change in hearing level between the ages of 18 and 55 as a function of frequency for different percentiles on degree of hearing loss (Figure 8). Again, note that thresholds are most affected at high frequencies and that the loss is more pronounced for males.

On the basis of these cross-sectional studies we would predict that as a person ages, hearing level will continue to deteriorate, with deterioration proceeding at a more rapid rate at the high frequencies but with a "spread" downward to the lower frequencies. However, Dayal and Nussbaum (1971) tested presbycotic individuals longitudinally for as long as 24 years and found that although hearing level deteriorated with increasing age, the shape of the individual audiograms remained stable for 72 percent of their sample. Thus progressive high-frequency loss and spread to lower frequencies may not characterize age changes within the individual. When testing large samples of even healthy, otologically screened individuals, a variety of hearing disorders may be included. If we accept Schuknecht's (1974) classification of four types of presbycusis with their associated patterns of structural and functional losses, then the standard presbycusis curves lump together sensory, neural, metabolic, and inner-ear conductive losses. Moreover, different aspects of age-related hearing loss within the same individual may stem from different physiological processes, e.g., a high-frequency loss caused by hair-cell loss and compounded by progressive strial degeneration leading to a progressive decline over the entire audiogram. Clearly, average presbycusis curves should not be taken to mean that there is a single universal pattern of hearing loss with age.

There are a number of issues to be addressed in regard to aging effects on absolute sensitivity. Perhaps one of the better researched questions is that of the etiology of presbycusis: Is the loss due to "wear and tear" on the auditory system over time or to aging effects per se? The "wear and tear" theory would predict that extent of loss would be proportional to the level of noise to which an individual has been exposed over his life span. In fact, some cross-cultural studies (e.g., Rosen et al., 1962; Rosen et al., 1964; Simonetta, 1968; Van der Sandt et al., 1969) do report less hearing loss in populations where noise levels are quite low. On the other hand, nearly all of these studies, as well as others where no cultural differences were found (Hinchcliffe, 1973; Reynaud et al., 1969), reported some elevation of threshold, particularly at high frequencies. Corso's (1963b) study of age effects on sensitivity employed subjects from relatively quiet environments who, nonetheless, displayed pronounced high-frequency loss. Thus, some type of hearing loss with age appears to occur, even where noise exposure is restricted. The extent to which factors such as disease, diet, and genetic endowment con-

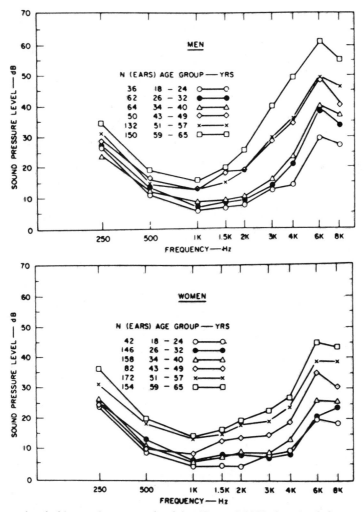

Figure 7.   Mean threshold sound pressure level in dB re: 0.0002 dyne/cm² for combined left and right ears of men and women. (*From Corso, J. F. 1963b. Aging and auditory thresholds in men and women.* Arch. Environ. Health. *6: 350–356. Reprinted by permission Heidref Publications.*)

tribute to the age effect is simply not known. However, noise exposure probably serves to accentuate age-related deficits in auditory processing (see Corso, 1981, for further discussion of this issue). It is also unclear at this point whether different types of presbycusis—e.g., Schuknecht's (1974) four categories—have different etiologies. Such issues are of considerable importance in industrial settings where decisions must be made as to the extent to which a disability such as hearing loss can be related to occupational hazards (Corso, 1980).

A related issue is the source of observed sex differences in hearing level. Corso (1963b) reported less hearing loss for women than for men, even though all of his subjects reported a negative history of noise exposure. Corso suggests that this sex difference results from "residual" differences in noise exposure between males and females. However, given sex differences in mortality rates, as well as in the incidence of other diseases (Society of Actuaries, 1979), it might also be that women are more physiologically resistant to aging influences on hearing. To date, this possibility has not been addressed.

Another question is whether published age norms for absolute sensitivity are adequate representations of the *hearing* capacity of el-

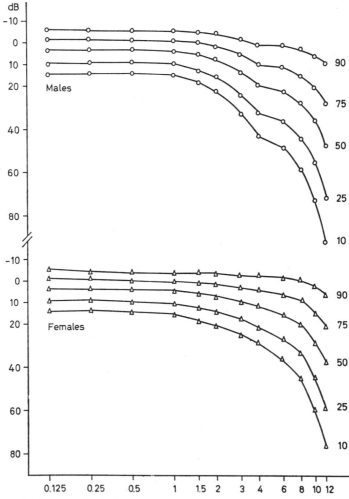

Figure 8.   Change in hearing threshold between age 18 and age 55, as a function of frequency for males and females, medians, quartiles, and deciles. (*From Robinson, D. W., and Sutton, G. J. 1979. Age effect in hearing—a comparative analysis of published threshold data. Audiology. 18: 320–334. Reprinted by permission.*)

derly individuals. As will be discussed in more detail below, it is not clear that the performance deficits of older listeners have not been exaggerated by response cautiousness (e.g., Rees and Botwinick, 1971), attentional lapses (e.g., Hoyer and Plude, 1980), and/or lack of familiarity wiht the task. These issues have not been adequately addressed by those involved in assessing age-related hearing change.

Finally, it is not known how mild to moderate presbycusis would be expected to affect an older person's daily function. Consider the case of an "average" 65-year-old male. On the basis of Corso's (1963b) data, we would predict his hearing loss to be less than 20 dB in the frequency range from 250 to 2000 Hz—a slight impairment. At 4000 Hz, the impairment might be described as moderate, on the order of 25 dB. Since most "biologically relevant" sounds, such as speech, fall in the frequency range below 4000 Hz, we probably would not expect this decline to represent a major difficulty. Moreover, studies of speech perception with young listeners indicate that normal conversation is fully intelligible even when all frequency components above 1800 Hz are filtered out (Moore, 1977). Two points are worth noting here. First, we should not expect to find serious hearing-level losses in the majority of older people. Second, given this relatively slight reduction in hearing level and the often-reported age-related difficulties in speech perception, deterioration of puretone thresholds simply does not account for many of the deficits observed in auditory processing. Efforts to document and explain age changes in absolute sensitivity have neglected other types of processing that ultimately have more serious effects on the older person's auditory function.

Differential Sensitivity. The ability to discriminate between sounds on the basis of frequency or intensity is often held to be important in the processing of complex signals such as speech (e.g., Corso, 1977; Corso, 1981; Botwinick, 1973). This belief is clearly logical since some speech sounds are distinguished by differences in frequency (e.g., vowels) or intensity (e.g., stop consonants). In fact, there is growing evidence for an association between deficits in frequency-difference thresholds and difficulty in speech discrimination among individuals suffering from sensorineural hearing loss (e.g., Drechsler and Plomp, 1980).

The data of Wier, Jesteadt, and Green (1977) provide a comprehensive account of frequency discrimination by normal young listeners. These investigators used an adaptive two-alternative, forced-choice (2AFC) psychophysical procedure to estimate difference limens (DLs) at frequencies ranging from 200 to 8000 Hz at five different sensation levels (SLs). The DLs obtained in this procedure tend to converge on the 71-percent correct point on the psychometric function. The Weber fraction, $\Delta F/F$, was a nonmomotonic function of frequency with a minimum between 1000 and 2000 Hz for all tested sensation levels. Frequency discrimination depends on both frequency and sensation level. Furthermore, the effect of increasing sensation level was found to be greater for low than for high frequencies.

For intensity discrimination, Wier, Jesteadt, and Green (1977) recently reported that when normal young listeners are asked to discriminate between tone bursts on the basis of intensity (I), the Weber fraction, $\Delta I/I$, remains constant over much of the audible range—at about 0.3, independent of signal frequency. This ratio is somewhat higher at low SLs and lower at high SLs.

Age effects. Comparison between studies of age effects in discrimination is difficult since different psychophysical procedures have been used. For example, König's (1957) study of age-related changes in frequency DL is probably the most comprehensive. His data are presented in Figure 9. All stimuli were presented at 40 dB SL. Ten individuals were tested in each decade, with approximately equal numbers of males and females. Note first that DL tends to increase with age, with greatest increases at low frequencies and somewhat greater increases at high frequencies than in the middle frequency range. It is not clear, however, that these age differences actually reflect decrements in sensory capacity. Consider first that in comparing the performance of normal young listeners in 2AFC, same-different, and yes-no tasks, Jesteadt and Sims

(1975) found that the discrepancies among procedures were greater than predicted by the TSD model of decision processes and suggested that memory factors may account for residual procedural differences. Next, consider two procedural aspects of König's study of age influences on frequency discrimination. The "AX" paradigm employed required subjects to report on each trial whether the second stimulus they heard was higher or lower in pitch than the standard stimulus, which was always presented first. Thus the subject had to remember the pitch of the standard stimulus in order to make the comparison. In addition, the subject had not only to be able to detect a difference between the standard and comparison stimuli, he had to be able to judge

the relative pitches of the two. We must consider the possibility, then, that König's data may reflect age-related changes in memory or in the ability to judge relative pitches rather than, or in addition to, decrements in the sensory capacity to detect pitch changes. Jesteadt and Sims (1975) report a doubling in their performance index from one procedure to the next. If procedural effects interact with age, then this would account for a large part of the age differences König observed. The situation is further complicated by the findings of Hallerman and Plath (1971), who reported no differences in frequency discrimination over the age range from 50 to 89 years. Listeners in the latter study, however, detected frequency modulation of a pure tone rather than

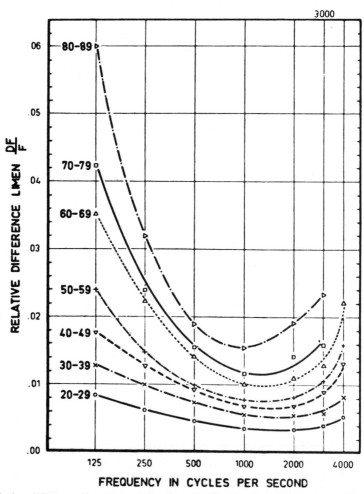

Figure 9. Relative difference limen as a function of frequency for seven age decades. (*From König, E. 1957. Pitch discrimination and age. Acta Oto-Laryngol. 48: 475–489. Reprinted by permission.*)

differences in pitch between two tones. Since the line spectra of an FM signal includes multiple components spaced at the rate of modulation (Wier et al., 1977; Kock, 1937; Stevens and Davis, 1938; Stevens 1954), it is possible that subjects used a different set of cues to perform in the FM task. Thus Hallerman and Plath's negative findings could be explained by the lack of age differences in the perception of these other spectral cues.

We must conclude, then, that age differences in the sensory capacity for frequency discrimination have not been clearly demonstrated. The situation is quite similar with respect to the issue of intensity discrimination. König (1957) reported that in a group of 15 listeners aged 60 to 89 years, intensity DLs (measured with tone bursts) were reduced when the hearing loss exceeded 30 dB. Meurmann (1953), using AM signals, failed to find any age difference in intensity DLs, but it is well-established that AM signals and tone bursts yield different results (Gelfand, 1981).

Masking and the Critical Band

We are all aware that one sound may be obscured, or made inaudible, by other sounds. This effect is known as "masking," and it is often held that elderly listeners show their greatest deficits in auditory perception under masking conditions. Besides providing a perhaps more "realistic" task (since we normally process sounds in a background of competing noise), masking paradigms "tell us a great deal about how the auditory system analyses and discriminates the various components in a mixture of sounds and the limits of this analysing faculty" (Moore, 1977, p. 90).

Hawkins and Stevens (1950) determined thresholds of young listeners for pure tones presented against a background of white noise at various spectrum levels. Basically, they found that a 10-dB increase in masker level produces a 10-dB increase in masked threshold once the masker attains an effective level. Although at low spectrum levels the noise is less effective in masking mid-frequencies, as the noise level increases, masked thresholds becomes less frequency-dependent. Over a wide range of intensities and frequencies, then,

the signal-to-noise ratio must be about 10 dB for the signal to be detected.

If we mask, say, a pure tone with a narrow band of noise (Egan and Hake, 1950), we would find that as the frequency of the tonal signal moves away from the center frequency of the masker, the signal threshold decreases. However, the relative frequencies of the signal and masker are also important. If the masker is lower in frequency than the signal, it is more effective in raising signal threshold than when the masker frequency is higher than the signal frequency. In addition, as the masker level is increased, the thresholds of higher frequency signals are affected more than those of lower frequency signals. In other words, as the overall level of sound increases, low frequencies become more and more effective in masking higher ones. This "upward spread of masking" accounts for the reduced intelligibility of speech at high levels. Despite this rule, another interesting phenomenon known as "remote masking" occurs at very intense stimulus levels. Bilger and Hirsch (1956) reported that low-frequency signals were masked by higher-frequency noise bands presented at 60 to 80 dB spectrum level. This exception to the upward spread of masking is thought to be due to cochlear distortion products generated at high intensities (Spieth, 1957; Deatherage, Davis, and Eldredge, 1957a; Deatherage, Davis, and Eldredge, 1957b) and should thus be of interest to those who suggest age-related increases in cochlear distortion products (e.g., Jerger et al., 1978b).

The results of experiments such as that performed by Egan and Hake (1950) suggests that, in white noise masking, a limited bandwidth around the tone actually contributes to masking. Fletcher (1940) introduced this concept of the "critical band" and showed that the masked threshold of a pure tone increased as the bandwidth of a masker noise—centered at the signal frequency and of constant spectrum level—was increased up to a certain bandwidth. Once that critical bandwidth was exceeded, however, further increases in masker bandwidth produced no further effect on masked threshold. The effects of critical bandwidth can be demonstrated in a variety of ways (see review by Scharf, 1970). For example, the loudness of a noise band increases with bandwidth up to the critical value; further increases produce no change in loudness judgments. Thus, the critical band is thought of as a measure of the bandwidth of an "internal filter" centered at the signal frequency and therefore reflects the frequency-resolution characteristics of the system. Critical bandwidth depends on the frequency at which it is measured, and the shape as well as the width of the filter has been investigated (e.g., Patterson, 1974).

Three additional masking paradigms are of particular interest to the study of aging. First is *psychophysical tuning curve* determination. In this task, the subject is required to detect a tonal signal in the presence of a tonal masker. The signal is typically presented at a relatively low (5 to 15 dB SL) fixed level. The level of the tonal masker that will just barely mask signals of different frequencies is determined. These curves are quite similar to the tuning curves obtained from single units in the auditory nerve since they show quite narrow tuning at the tip, steep high-frequency slopes, and shallower low-frequency "tails." The width and shape of these curves provide additional measures of frequency resolution. A related important phenomenon is *psychophysical suppression* (e.g., Houtgast, 1972), analogous to the two-tone inhibition reported in auditory nerve fibers by Sachs and Kiang (1968). In this phenomenon, adding a third tonal component just higher in frequency than the masker tone will "unmask" the signal, i.e., it will make the masker less effective. This mechanism serves to sharpen the response to the signal, and its degeneration would be expected to lead to reduced auditory selectivity. Moreover, recent findings (e.g., O'Malley and Feth, 1979) demonstrate a close relationship between tuning and two-tone suppression.

Second is *temporal masking*. Here the masker either follows (backward condition) or precedes (forward condition) the signal in time. Backward masking tends to be greater than forward masking, and little masking occurs when the interval between signal and masker is greater than about 50 msec (Elliott, 1962). Temporal masking is influenced by the relative frequencies of the signal and masker

(Elliott, 1967; Wright, 1964). Interestingly, more masking occurs when backward and forward are combined than would be predicted by adding their individual effects (Pollack, 1964; Elliott, 1969; Wilson and Carhart, 1971; Pastore, Harris, and Goldstein, 1980). The two types of masking may well result from different underlying mechanisms (Weber and Green, 1979). At least two findings lead to the inference that temporal masking involves neural, in addition to cochlear, events. First, masking is observed at signal-masker intervals longer than the time required for decay of the basilar membrane traveling wave (Elliott, 1967). Second, temporal masking occurs under dichotic (signal in one ear, masker in the other) listening conditions (Elliott, 1962). Temporal masking, therefore, not only provides information about the resolution capacity of the auditory system but a description of the time course of auditory processing as well.

Central masking is the third paradigm we will consider. As noted above, temporal masking can occur when signal and masker are presented to different ears. Central masking occurs when signal and masker are presented simultaneously to different ears and is due to an interaction of the masker and signal within the central nervous system (Zwislocki, 1972). The amount of central masking is far less than that obtained monaurally. The frequency range over which central masking occurs is limited since masker and signal must be quite close together for masking to take place. More central masking occurs at high frequencies than at low, and the amount of masking is greatest at masker onset (Zwislocki et al., 1968). Since central masking appears to be related to activity in the lower auditory pathways (Zwislocki, 1972, 1973), it provides a procedure that could be used to evaluate age effects at those levels.

Age effects. Very little work has examined the performance of older individuals under masking conditions, except when the signal to be processed has been speech. For example, Smith and Prather (1971) found that older subjects perform more poorly than young ones when asked to identify syllables against a noise background, although the size of the age effect did not increase as the noise level was raised. Green (1969) reported similar results using phonemes as signals. Consider, however, the findings of Findlay and Schuchman (1976) that subjects aged 66 to 74 actually attained somewhat higher scores than college-age listeners when required to identify monosyllables in noise. Moreover, in the studies where increases in noise level did not produce differential age-related effects, it is possible that the age effects observed stemmed from a general performance deficit rather than sensory factors.

Recently there has been an increased interest in using masking techniques to describe the analytic capacity of the aging auditory system. Bonding (1979) determined critical bandwidth by loudness summation and the degree of tuning in the psychophysical tuning curve at 1000 and 4000 Hz for a group of presbycotic listeners. Measures of critical bandwidth were not consistently larger for the presbycotic group, but tuning, as measured by the tuning curves, was found to be negatively correlated with degree of hearing loss. No presbycotic subject showed tuning within the normal range at 4000 Hz, whereas only two presbycotic subjects had normal tuning at 1000 Hz. Another interesting finding of this study was that tuning did not seem to be affected until the pure-tone hearing loss reached 30 to 40 dB. Since broadened auditory-nerve tuning curves are characteristic of cats whose outer hair cells have been destroyed (Kiang et al., 1967) but critical bandwidth is not affected by outer hair-cell loss (Nienhuys and Clark, 1979), Bonding's (1979) findings seem consistent with a model of presbycusis that posits outer hair-cell loss as a major contributing factor. Patterson and Webber (1980), however, found no age effect on auditory filter shape up to 60 years of age. Although filter width broadened for some individuals older than 60 years, for others as old as 75 years, the filter width remained quite narrow. Thus, we are warned again against treating presbycusis as a unitary or universal disorder.

Interestingly, there is one report that the elderly are less susceptible than the young to remote masking effects. Quaranta, Amoroso, and Cervella (1978) found that thresholds for tone bursts at 250, 500, and 1000 Hz were less affected by simultaneous presentation of a narrow-band masker centered at 3000 Hz at a level of 98 dB SPL for presbycotic than for normal young listeners. In fact, subjects over 70 years of age showed less masking than those between 60 to 70 years. In addition, although masking was less pronounced at 500 Hz for young listeners, the amount of masking became progressively less dependent on signal frequency with age. If, as suggested earlier, remote masking occurs as a result of cochlear nonlinearities, then these findings suggest less distortion with advancing age, at least beyond 60 years. Quaranta et al. (1978) suggest that this results from a stiffening of the cochlear partition.

At this point, then, we might conclude that some aspects of auditory analysis may deteriorate with advancing age, at least for some individuals. Although Bonding's (1979) findings are consistent with the idea that cochlear dysfunction plays a role in hearing loss with age, no data appear to be available (e.g., on central or temporal masking effects) that would allow us to assess the role of neural contributions to age-related decrements in acoustic analysis.

Binaural Hearing

Three topics are typically included under the heading of binaural hearing. The first is *sound localization,* the ability to identify the location of a sound source in space.

Lateralization, the second, on the other hand, refers to the process by which an observer will, under the appropriate conditions, perceive a binaural signal presented by means of headphones as being localized at some location within his head. The "intracranial" location of this sound image appears to move toward one ear or the other depending on the relative intensities and arrival times of the signals at the two ears. Thus, in some respects, lateralization is similar to localization occurring in the free field. Lateralization paradigms, however, offer the advantage of being able to separate interaural time from interaural intensity effects—something that can't be accomplished in the free field—and, in addition, eliminate the need to control for reflection of sound from walls and floors.

Jeffress and Taylor (1961) demonstrated that the internal sound image moves toward the ear that receives the stimulus first, or receives the more intense stimulus, just as an external image is perceived as being closer to the ear that receives the sound first. Furthermore, Yost (1974) showed that interaural time differences were effective lateralization cues only at frequencies below about 900 Hz.[4] This finding is consistent with the report of Stevens and Newman (1936) that interaural temporal difference is usable for-free field localization only at low frequencies. Yost (1974) also reported that the amount of additional interaural time difference required to discern a change in perceived internal location increases as the image is moved toward one side of the head, a finding also in agreement with free-field localization data (Mills, 1956). Finally, Mills (1960) found that the amount of interaural intensity difference required to detect a position change of an internal image at midline is independent of tone frequency. Because of the physics of sound and the size of the head, however, interaural intensity differences at low frequencies in the free field would not be large enough to be detected. Thus, in auditory localization, it appears that time differences provide the more important cue at low frequencies, whereas intensity differences become more critical at high frequencies.

The third binaural hearing issue to be considered here is *binaural masking,* or more specifically, the binaural-masking-level difference (BMLD). The phenomenon of the BMLD was first demonstrated by Licklider (1948) using speech signals and by Hirsch (1948) using pure-tone signals. To demonstrate the BMLD, a signal and masker are presented at both ears and the level of the signal adjusted until it is barely audible. If only the signal is then turned off at one ear, the signal in the other ear suddenly becomes easily audible. Thus, the threshold for the signal in the case where signal and masker occur at both ears (M_oS_o)

is higher than that where the signal occurs at one ear and the masker at both (M_oS_m). The difference between these two thresholds is about 9 dB. Subsequent work (see Green and Henning, 1969, and Green and Yost, 1975, for reviews) has led to the general conclusion that dichotic presentations yield lower thresholds than diotic presentations. For example, if the masker is presented to both ears but the signal is 180 deg out of phase at the two ears (M_oS_π), the threshold is about 15 dB lower than in the M_oS_o condition. In addition, the size of the BMLD is negatively correlated with signal frequency (Webster, 1951). Finally, conditions that produce BMLDs not only improve detection but discrimination ability as well. Gebhardt and Goldstein (1972) showed that for a given signal-to-noise ratio, antiphasic frequency DLs are substantially smaller than homophasic ones. Henning (1973), however, demonstrated that this advantage occurs only at low signal-to-noise ratios.

One might assume that the advantage conferred by dichotic masking conditions is related to spatial factors. For example, since in the M_oS_m condition the signal would be lateralized to one ear while the masker is perceived as being located at midline, it should be easier to process the signal than in the M_oS_o condition where both stimuli are perceived at the same midline position. Thus, some investigators have treated the BMLD paradigm as analogous to the "cocktail party effect," in which individuals are able to process a message coming from one speaker against a background of competing speech, presumably because the message is spatially separated from the competing sounds. Logically, then, the BMLD paradigm would provide an experimental technique for investigating the reported difficulty of the elderly in understanding speech in noisy environments (e.g., Bergman, 1971). Unfortunately, the relationship between the BMLD and perceived spatial separation is not so clear-cut. Carhart, Tillman, and Grutis (1969), for example, found the largest BMLDs under conditions where there was no clear spatial separation is not so clear-cut.

Age effects. Although there is some evi-

---

[4]Recent studies have shown, however, that high-frequency sounds can be lateralized on the basis of time cues if they are repeated or modulated at a low frequency (see Yost, 1980, for review).

dence that cochlear nerve or brain stem lesions are associated with loss of directional hearing (Tonning, 1975), it is not clear whether aging influences this capacity. Since the integrity of the external ear is essential for sound localization, changes in the characteristics of the external ear such as those described earlier might be expected to produce changes in directional hearing. To our knowledge, however, this prediction has not yet been tested.

Matzker and Springhood (1958) first reported that the minimum interaural time delay required for subjects to report a shift from the midline of the internal location of a click train increased with advancing age. Although Nordland (1964) found no effects of age on directional hearing, Herman, Warren, and Wagener (1977) also found that men 60 to 72 years old required longer time delays (ITDs) to lateralize a click. The latter investigators, however, also reported no age difference in the utilization of interaural intensity cues (IIDs). The Herman et al. (1977) study, moreover, utilized a two-alternative, forced-choice procedure that would have controlled for any age differences in response criterion. Kirikae (1969) confirmed the results of the Herman et al. study in a Japanese sample. Not only was the older age group found to require a longer time difference to discriminate a lateral shaft, but a relatively small IID was found to compensate for a large ITD. The latter finding again implies impairment in the ability to use ITD cues.

To summarize, age differences have been demonstrated in the ability to use time cues in auditory lateralization at midline, but not intensity cues. As a consequence, we would predict difficulties in the localization of low-frequency, but not high-frequency, sounds in the free field among older adults. It is not clear, however, whether these age differences are maintained, or perhaps increased, at off-midline locations. In addition, it would be interesting to test directly the frequency dependency of aging effects in both lateralization and localization.

Age differences in the BMLD for speech have been examined in several studies. Tillman, Carhart, and Nicholls (1973) determined thresholds for spondee words for men and women 18 to 27 years old, women 70 to 85 years old, and men 63 to 88 years old under 27 different binaural masking conditions. The maskers were an AM noise and two spoken sentences, all used singly and in all possible combinations. Phase differences and time delays between the two ears were also manipulated. As a group, the elderly listeners obtained smaller BMLDs than the young in all but two listening conditions, although the general pattern of BMLD change over listening conditions was similar in the two age groups. Interestingly, when the combination of masker, signal, and time delays was such that the different components were clearly lateralized at different positions (e.g., speech masker on one side, noise masker on the other side, and spondees at the midline), the age difference was particularly pronounced. Thus, the older listeners did not appear to benefit as much as young listeners from a more definite subjective separation of the stimulus components. The second study (Findlay and Schuchman, 1976) lends support to the findings of Tillman et al. (1973) by showing that the improvement in the percentage of correct identifications of monosyllables under dichotic (different messages to the two ears) relative to diotic (same messages to the two ears) listening conditions was reduced among older adults. Since Findlay and Schuchman (1976) employed different fixed signal-to-noise ratios for their young and old age groups, however, age comparisons are difficult to make.

Finally, Warren, Wagener, and Herman (1978) compared the performance of young (22 to 32 years) and old (60 to 72 years) listeners when they were required to identify monosyllables against a background of four spoken master sentences under diotic and dichotic conditions. The signal words in this study were equally distributed across five different "pitch-related phoneme categories" ranging from low (150 to 400 Hz) to high (3200 to 12000 Hz). Again, the size of BMLD was reduced in the older age group; however, no effect of pitch category on performance was observed for either age group. Given the complex nature of speech stimuli and the failure to demonstrate a pitch effect with the younger subjects, it becomes clear that some other technique must be used to assess interaction between age and frequency in BMLD. Another interesting aspect of the Warren et al. (1978) study was the failure to find any correlation between directional hearing capacity (data reported by Herman et al., 1977, for click lateralization) and the BMLD. Since the relationship between localizability and the BMLD is not as straightforward as was originally believed (e.g., Carhart et al. 1969), this finding may not be terribly surprising.

Other Issues: Loudness, Adaptation, and Pitch

Although beginnings have been made in the description, and to some extent explanation, of age-related changes in many aspects of auditory performance, there are a number of areas within audition that have been largely ignored by developmentalists. Among these neglected topics are loudness perception, pitch perception, and adaptation effects.

An examination of age differences in the perception of loudness is particularly crucial, for when we adjust the levels of stimuli to be equal in sensation level for all subjects, we make the implicit assumption that the perceived loudness of a sound grows at the same rate with increasing level for all subjects. In fact, there are a few hints already within the literature that there are age-related changes in loudness perception. For example, Corso et al. (1976) report the temporal summation is attenuated in older individuals. Inasmuch as the loudness of suprathreshold stimuli is dependent on stimulus duration (Stephens, 1974), we might expect similar age effects under suprathreshold conditions. Note also that if, in fact, critical bandwidth increases with age (e.g., Patterson and Webber, 1980), then the perceived loudness of complex sounds will also be affected. Finally, there are scattered reports (e.g., Jerger, 1973; Pestalozza and Shore, 1955) of cases of loudness recruitment in some older individuals. Since loudness recruitment is, by definition, a more rapid than normal growth in the perceived loudness of a sound, it would appear that the loudness function for at least some elderly is affected.

The most direct techniques for measuring the growth of loudness are the scaling tasks originally developed by S. S. Stevens: magnitude estimation, cross-modal matching, and magnitude production. Unfortunately, there are problems inherent in these methods that make it difficult to use them for making age comparisons. For example, if older individuals differ from young in their numbering or production behavior, this may show up as a difference in the slope of the loudness function, regardless of any difference in sensory processing. Although cross-modal matching (having the listener adjust the intensity of one stimulus, A, to match that of another, B) eliminates that problem, it is subject to regression effects, so that it is common practice to match dimension A on dimension B and dimension B on dimension A. The additional time required to run the second matching series may make this procedure unsuitable for use in elderly populations. A recently developed procedure, multimodal matching (Stevens and Marks, 1980) solves both of these problems, however, by asking subjects to rate stimuli from different modalities on the same scale in a single series. When, for example, the intensity of light that is given a certain magnitude rating is plotted against the level of sound assigned an equivalent rating, the slope of the resulting function will not be affected by differences in numbering behavior, since those effects common to numbering on the two dimensions will "cancel out." Furthermore, the need for running multiple series is eliminated. Although this method is still vulnerable to range effects —i.e., the slope of the function will be influenced by the range of stimulus intensities used —if a little care is taken, equivalent ranges for young and elderly subjects can be established. We can then hope to see this technique applied to the study of sensory aging in the near future.

In the other two neglected areas mentioned above, adaptation and pitch perception, there is little or nothing that can be said with respect to aging. One paper (Palva and Karja, 1969) has addressed the issue of age-related changes in adaptation. These investigators report no differences between young and old listeners in suprathreshold adaptation (the tendency for a continuous stimulus to be perceived as less intense over time) to 250- and 6000-Hz tones. It appears, however, that no work has been done to determine the susceptibility to, and recovery from, prolonged exposure to high levels of noise in older listeners as measured, for example, by temporary threshold shift. Such information would have practical implications for the design of environments for the elderly. Studies of pitch perception and age are totally lacking. Inasmuch as such perception is important to the processing of speech as well as to an appreciation for music, research in this area may be of practical significance as well.

In conclusion, it appears that there is much unexplored territory in the area of aging and psychoacoustics. As appropriate methodologies are developed, we can expect research in this area to lead not only to a greater understanding of the physiological and performance factors influenced by the process of aging, but to applications in audiometry, rehabilitation, and environmental design for the elderly.

Signal Detection Theory

The methodology provided by Signal Detection Theory (SDT) (Green and Swets, 1974; McNicol, 1972) allows separation of the observer's actual ability to perform an appropriate task from his willingness to respond. Since the tendency to withhold responses is thought to increase with age (Silverman, 1963), SDT provides an important methodology for the separation of an observer's actual ability from his "cautiousness" or response bias. In SDT terms, detection, discrimination or recognition ability is often termed d' and response "cautiousness" or bias denoted β. Increasing values of d' indicate better or improving performance, whereas increasing values of β indicate less willingness to hazard a response.

In audiometric evaluation of pure-tone thresholds, a tendency toward withholding a response would appear as an elevated threshold even when actual detection is not impaired. Rees and Botwinick (1971) presented results indicating that psychological factors influencing response bias may indeed artificially elevate pure-tone thresholds in the elderly. They evaluated young (18 male under-

graduate students aged 18 to 21) and elderly (15 men aged 65 to 77) for absolute threshold for a 750-Hz tone and yes-no detection performance for near-threshold 750-Hz tones. The elderly were found to have higher absolute thresholds than the young. The SDT data, however, revealed no group differences in d' but a higher β in the elderly compared to young adults. These data were interpreted to reflect an age effect on willingness to respond to near-threshold stimuli, not an actual age change in sensitivity to this low-frequency tone (Rees and Botwinick, 1971). Similar results indicating increased "caution" in elderly compared to young listeners for reporting tones in a detection paradigm have been reported (Potash and Jones, 1977). Although these results are consistent with the view of increased cautiousness in the elderly, they are characterized by several problems recently highlighted by Danziger (1980), Williams (1980), and Hertzog (1980). No systematic SDT studies of auditory detection, discrimination, or speech recognition have yet been reported in the literature.

AGE-RELATED CHANGES IN SPEECH PERCEPTION

In a recent survey of new directions in the study of aging (Poon, 1980), three trends in the area of perceptual aging emerge. First, increased effort is being directed toward the specification of the components of perceptual processing that are affected by aging (e.g., sensory coding, attention, memory). Second, cognitive influences on perceptual task performance (e.g., increased distractability) in the older adult are being explored. Third, the manner in which age-related changes in expectations, attitudes, and personal goals (top-down processes) might affect perceptual performance and the perceptual organization is arousing greater interest. Hoyer and Plude's chapter on attention and perception in Poon (1980) exemplifies these trends in the area of visual processing. In addition to such concerns, however, the area of speech perception also provides an excellent opportunity to explore the sources of perceptual difficulties in advanced age, since so much is known about the extensive interactions of sensory, perceptual, and higher-order mechanisms involved in speech processing among normal young listeners. Moreover, one explanation for the discrepancy between hearing loss and speech intelligibility among older persons could be modifications in the higher-level components of the speech-perception system.

In this section, age-related changes in psychophysical tasks involving speech stimuli will be reviewed first. A discussion of the cognitive processes that might contribute to loss of speech intelligibility will follow.

Psychoacoustics of Speech

Not surprisingly, many investigators have demonstrated impaired speech perception in hearing-impaired individuals. If the elderly are tested under ideal conditions, such as in a quiet environment with undegraded speech material, there appears to be a small but measurable deficit in speech intelligibility that is not necessarily predicted by pure-tone loss. The magnitude of this deficit when tested in ideal conditions is not well-documented but appears to be on the order of 5 to 10 dB (Punch and McConnell, 1969) relative to young listeners with similar audiograms. Speech intelligibility for the elderly listener, however, seems to be disproportionately low when the listening conditions are less than ideal.

The major problem in the interpretation of such findings rests on a lack of understanding of the site or sites responsible for the reduced intelligibility. Acoustic processing mechanisms that might account for it include attenuation of consonant sounds with high frequency loss, widening of "critical bands" (Martin, 1974)—or detuning—and loss of normal temporal integration characteristics (Corso et al. 1976). In fact, Dreschler and Plomp (1980) demonstrated a relationship between frequency resolution and SRT among hearing-impaired young listeners. Furthermore, as mentioned earlier in this chapter, there is histological evidence for age-related degeneration in brainstem nuclei and auditory cortex where acoustic speech cues such as FM signals are coded (e.g., Kirikae et al., 1964; Hansen and Reske-Nielson, 1965).

Alternatively, a cue-reduction hypothesis might include age changes in acoustic processing mechanisms but would also suggest that redundancy in speech material is lost not only because of changes in the cochlea but also of changes in central information processing. Corso (1981) has pointed out that simple peripheral-versus-central hypotheses are not likely to account for age changes in speech intelligibility. He argues instead for a "varying proportionality hypothesis." This hypothesis assumes that receptor and first-order neuron changes accrue slowly throughout life. Central degenerative changes, while slow to occur, accelerate once initiated. Thus, deficits in speech intelligibility would reflect increasing central degeneration with advancing age, this becoming most apparent under difficult listening conditions. Currently it is impossible to distinguish the relative contribution of peripheral and central factors in the elderly's hearing for speech. It is nevertheless clear that hearing for speech is at jeopardy in those over 50 years of age.

Speech intelligibility is typically assessed in terms of speech reception thresholds, speech discrimination, and speech intelligibility under difficult or stressful conditions.

Speech Reception Threshold. Speech reception thresholds (SRT) appear to decline progressively after age 50 and equally for both men and women (Plomp and Mimpen, 1979). The SRT is defined as the sound level required for some criterion performance, usually 50 percent, of correct speech identification. Punch and McConnell (1969) evaluated SRT in two groups of elderly individuals (N = 12 and mean age of 74 for both groups) that differed with respect to degree of presbycusis. The mildly impaired group had a mean pure-tone hearing loss of 13 dB between 0.5 and 2k Hz. The moderately impaired group had a mean pure-tone loss of 45 dB for the same frequency range. SRTs were approximately 14 dB and 42 dB for the minimal and moderately impaired group, respectively. The American National Standard Institute (1970) has established 19 dB SPL as normal for spondees. Although the group means for pure-tone and SRT deficit were quite similar in this study, t is often difficult to predict individual SRTs from the audiogram. Punch and McConnell 1969) did not present individual audiometric urves or individual SRTs. Jerger (1973) ound that phonetically balanced words presented near SRT (5 dB SL) resulted in dispro- ortionately poor word-identification perfor- nance in the elderly compared to a small roup of young adults with pure-tone loss sim- lar to that of the elderly group. Similar results or sentences have been reported by Plomp nd Mimpen (1979). Jerger's and, to a lesser legree, Plomp and Mimpen's data illustrate 'phonemic regression."

Gaeth (1948) defined phonemic regression s the disproportionate loss in speech intelligi- ility observed in the elderly compared to that f young individuals with comparable pure- one loss. The disproportionate loss of mean- ng for speech in the elderly indicates that uditory changes associated with aging are of different, more complex nature than those n younger people and provides circumstantial vidence for Corso's (1981) varying propor- ionality hypothesis. Elderly individuals with resbycusis do seem to utilize speech cues in he lower frequency ranges (down to 250 Hz), finding not characteristic of hearing-im- aired young listeners (Farrimond, 1961).

Although SRTs are employed extensively n clinical evaluations, there are limits to the sefulness of this test in aiding our under- tanding of age changes in speech perception. RT is usually measured under ideal condi- ions and represents a threshold measure. hese testing conditions do not parallel the onditions of everyday life. Furthermore, here appear to be no systematic longitudinal tudies of SRT nor any systematic attempt o relate SRT in the elderly to their perception f their hearing problem in the real world Noble, 1978).

Speech Discrimination. Psychoacoustic ests that more closely approximate real-world onditions include speech discrimination tests. n these tests, speech material is presented at arious intensities, and the percent of words or sentences correctly identified—or discrimi- ation score (DS)—is measured. In clinical set- ings presentation levels of 20 to 40 dB above

SRT for any given hearing-impaired individual may not mirror the degree of pure-tone loss (Jerger and Hayes, 1977; Nobel, 1978).

Word and sentence discrimination tests have appeal for the evaluation of speech intelligibility in the elderly because they involve favorable acoustical presentation but low predictability or redundancy. Thus, the DS may measure hearing ability under parallel real-word conditions such as listening to a public speaker, TV, or radio. Not surprisingly, the elderly with presbycusis appear to have an elevated threshold (approximately 5 to 10 dB) for intelligibility. That is, young listeners may perform at 30-percent intelligibility at 0 dB (re 22 dB SPL), whereas the elderly with moderate to severe high-frequency loss perform at 30-percent intelligibility at 10 dB SL (re 22 dB SPL) (Punch and McConnell, 1969). More important, the elderly show flattened intelligibility-intensity functions for phonetically balanced words presented between 0 and 40 dB SL (re 22 dB SPL) (Punch and McConnell, 1969).

Jerger and Hayes (1977) have compared performance-intensity (PI) functions for words and sentences in the same listeners. After evaluating over 3,000 patients with various types of hearing impairment, they concluded that in cochlear deficits the PI function (1) will be similar for words and sentences if the audiometric contour is relatively flat, (2) will be higher for sentences than for words if the contour slopes downward from low to high frequencies, and (3) will be higher for words than for sentences if the audiometric contour slopes upward from low to high frequencies. In the case of retrocochlear disorders, particularly those beyond the eighth nerve, the PI function for sentences will typically fall below that for words, independent of audiometric contour. In aging, the typical audiometric contour is that of a slope downward from low to high frequencies. Thus, the expected PI function for words should fall below that for sentences. Jerger and Hayes (1977), however, report that the PI function for sentences usually falls below that for words for elderly subjects. They consider this to be a special case of a central effect of speech-intelligibility scores in elderly individuals. In the elderly individual with presbycusis, Jerger and Hayes (1977) suggest that the discrepancy between the PI functions for words versus sentences yields, in combination with the audiometric contour, a rough estimate of the relative contributions of peripheral and central effects on speech intelligibility. These results are consistent with Jerger's (1973) earlier argument that, although cochlear disorders may account for the bulk of hearing loss in young adults, it is necessary to look beyond the cochlea and eighth nerve to explain speech intelligibility loss in the elderly.

Speech Intelligibility Under Adverse Listening Conditions. Although SRT and DS for speech material appears impaired in the elderly under ideal listening conditions, this effect is magnified when the speech material is degraded. In a classic study, Bergman (1971) showed that this effect begins as early as the fourth decade of life and becomes particularly apparent in the very old. Longitudinal data indicate that hearing disability for reverberated speech, speeded speech, filtered speech, and interrupted speech is also progressive (Bergman, Blumfeld, Casardo, Dask, Levitt, and Margulies, 1976). These findings are consistent with self-reports of hearing difficulty by the elderly and other cross-sectional findings of a decline in speech perception under adverse listening conditions (Jerger, 1973; Marston and Geotzinger, 1972; Plomp and Mimpen, 1979; Smith and Prather, 1971; Welsh, Luterman, and Bell, 1969).

To summarize the findings of psychoacoustic studies of speech perception, there are essentially two important phenomena to explain. First, why does the ability to identify single spoken words decline with advancing age, even when degree of hearing loss is held constant? Second, how is it that the ability to comprehend connected speech or single sentences is influenced to a greater degree by aging than is isolated word recognition, particularly under difficult conditions? One hypothesis is that in addition to a loss of hearing level, an elderly person might also experience loss of the sensory capacity to code the features of speech sounds. However, two studies of the older adult's capacity to process acoustic speech cues (Dorman and Marton, 1981; Hannley and Dobbins, 1981) found that although there were age differences in acoustic cue discrimination, these differences were not sufficient to account for the magnitude of the observed age difference in sentence identification. Thus, although degeneration of the sensory coding mechanism is probably a contributor to difficulties in speech perception, particularly the perception of isolated words, it does not appear to be severe enough to account for loss of sentence comprehension and certainly does not explain the age-related discrepancy between single-word and connected-speech performance.

More "central" mechanisms have been recognized as factors in age-related change in speech understanding for some time. Fournier (1954) and Calearo and Lazzaroni (1957) suggested that slower central neural transmission and processing time is the source of age deficits in speech intelligibility and explains why increasing the presentation rate of speech is differentially detrimental to the older listener's performance.

More recently, Corso's (1977) varying proportionality hypothesis suggests that both peripheral and central components involved in speech perception are affected by advancing age. Does this hypothesis account for the contrast between isolated word and sentence identification found in older listeners? Jerger and Hayes' (1977) observations certainly support this view: The PI functions for PB words and SSI begin to diverge only after age 55 but become increasingly divergent thereafter. The fact that no correlation between general intelligence and PB discrimination score has been found (Nash and Wepman, 1973) suggests that central factors are less involved in single-word recognition. However, is sentence identification a difficult listening task? Why should it differ from isolated-word identification? If cognitive mechanisms are involved, which specific mechanisms are they? To address these questions, we turn to a consideration of the higher-level, central processes that interact with the sensory system in the perception of fluent speech.

Cognitive Mediating Processes

From our standpoint, the most striking difference between the acoustic characteristics of a sentence and those of the isolated words of which it is composed is that much of the acoustic information available in each word is lost or modified when it is combined with others to form a sentence. Sounds are often dropped, shortened, combined, or changed in a spoken sentence (Klatt and Stevens, 1973). Moreover, the acoustic characteristics of a word in connected speech are highly variable and depend upon the speech context in which the sounds are produced (Reddy, 1976).

Not only are the characteristics of sounds within words modified, but even when a sentence is spoken at normal rates, there are often no cues within it to indicate where one word ends and the next begins. Naturally then, spoken speech is a highly ambiguous stimulus. In fact, Pollack and Pickett (1963) demonstrated that when single words were excised from recordings of conversations, only about 50 percent of them could be recognized. Thus, under many conditions, it is clear that acoustic information alone is not sufficient to identify a word.

A number of mechanisms appear to be responsible for the conversion of this ambiguous stimulus into a (usually) meaningful message. To begin with, listeners appear to take into account the fact that acoustic cues change in fluent speech contexts. Oshika, Zue, Weeks, Nue, and Aurbach (1975) found that the variations in pronunciation that occur in running speech could be described by a number of phonological rules. That listeners are aware of and use these rules in interpreting sentences is evidenced by the fact that many misperceptions of speech occur when a phonological rule is erroneously assumed to have been applied—e.g.,"inner tube" in a sentence is heard as "inter tube" (Bond and Garnes, 1980).

Besides compensating for phonological variations, listeners also appear to combine the phonological, syntactic, and semantic context with linguistic and "real world" knowledge to make judgments under conditions of reduced acoustic support. In support of this contention is Warren's (1970) demonstration of "phonemic restoration": If a phoneme in a word is replaced with a coughing sound of about the same intensity as the speech, the missing phoneme will be perceived as present. Furthermore, listeners will not be able to indi-

cate accurately where in the sentence the cough occurred. The effects of semantic and syntactic context were shown by Miller, Heise, and Lichten (1951), who found that words spoken in the presence of noise were more often identified if they occurred within a sentence than in isolation. In addition, Miller and Isard (1963) found that words-in-noise were more intelligible in syntactically and semantically normal sentences than in anomalous sentences. When the acoustic signal is ambiguous, listeners will tend to report a word rather than a nonword, even though there is acoustic support for both (Ganong, 1980), and also to report a word that is logically predictable from the sentence context (Spencer and Wollman, 1980). Finally, when a word is presented repeatedly outside of a speech context, an illusion known as the verbal transformation effect (Warren and Gregory, 1958)—in which the subject reports hearing different words on repetitions of the same acoustic stimulus—often occurs in both children and young adults.

According to one model of speech perception (Cole and Jakimik, 1980), as soon as a listener processes a speech sound, he begins to access words that would be supported by the acoustic cues. On the basis of his knowledge of phonological, syntactic, and semantic constraints, he eliminates all the "candidates" but one. When this occurs, a word is recognized, and the onset of the next word is automatically located. Some of the cognitive processes involved would be primary memory, storage and retrieval of context and knowledge from secondary memory, and use of acoustic information and knowledge to make a decision. Since primary memory, in particular, is known to be constrained by temporal factors, processing speed would also be an important variable.

There is considerable evidence that processing speed, as indexed by reaction time, does decline with age (Stern, Oster, and Newport, 1980; Birren, Woods, and Williams, 1980). Furthermore, Cerella, Poon, and Williams (1980), in a review of 18 studies of age and reaction time, concluded that age-related performance deficits become more pronounced as task complexity increases. In the context of speech perception, then, we would predict that degrading the acoustic input (which has already been degraded to some extent as a result of the degeneration of sensory coding) would result in greater age differences. Nevertheless, a direct relationship between RT and speech performance has yet to be demonstrated.

There is also evidence that aging influences primary memory processes. Although the span of primary memory seems to be little affected by age, the ability to allocate primary memory resources efficiently in complex tasks does appear to decline (Storandt, 1980; Botwinick and Storandt, 1974). In addition, there is some evidence that primary memory processes are performed more slowly by the elderly (Anders, Fozard, and Lillyquist, 1972) and that this increase in the required processing time may limit the depth of processing that the older person can achieve (Simon, 1979; Perlmutter, 1979, 1980; Smith, 1980). This might explain Petros and Chabot's (1981) finding that although young and older adults were equally able to remember the main ideas in a prose passage, older listeners remembered fewer ideas overall.

There are also indications that the elderly may have difficulty accessing lexical information from long-term memory. For example, Botwinick and Storandt (1974) found that although WAIS vocabulary scores did not decline significantly with age, older adults gave fewer of the "best" responses—i.e., the ideal synonym. Furthermore, Clark (1980) reported that normal older persons took longer to access lexical information, particularly when the words involved were low in frequency of occurrence.

Finally, we must consider the often-cited age differences in response cautiousness (e.g., Craik, 1966; Rees and Botwinick, 1971; Danziger, 1980). If an older person has experienced a progressive decline in the quality of the acoustic information available to him and finds himself making frequent misperceptions as a result, he might well be expected to require more information before making a lexical decision. In fact, such cautiousness might explain Warren and Warren's (1966) findings that the normal elderly are less susceptible to the verbal transformation effect since the older listener may not be convinced to change his response on the basis of the little acoustic support available for the illusory words.

To summarize, then, the possibility that age-related changes in the cognitive processes mediating speech perception interact with sensory change in producing difficulties in speech understanding has been established. That possibility, however, has not been directly tested. Studies relating psychoacoustic performance, speech processing, and cognitive capacities are clearly needed.

REHABILITATIVE ISSUES

Given that there is a gradual loss of speech understanding through a lifetime, how can the older person compensate for this loss? We can conceptualize the process of communication as moving through four stages, any of which can influence a listener's ability to understand a message: sender, acoustic environment, acoustic signal, and receiver. Obviously, any message begins with a sender, and perhaps as obviously, senders differ in the distinctness of their speech, the amplitude at which they speak, and the syntactic clarity and complexity of the message they produce. One way in which we might improve speech intelligibility for the elderly would be to instruct senders in appropriate speech compensations. Needless to say, it is impossible to instruct everyone with whom the elderly might interact, and there are times when compensation does not have the desired effect. Recall, for example, that speech becomes less intelligible at high levels. At the end point of the process is the receiver, whose hearing level, auditory analytic capacity, decoding skills, and cognitive abilities and strategies will all determine whether he is able to understand the spoken message. We have spent the greater part of this chapter describing these characteristics of the elderly listener, and, currently at least, the mechanical and sensorineural degeneration observed in many older persons is irreversible. Nevertheless, it is possible to modify the two middle stages of communication: The acoustic signal arriving at the receiver's ear can be modified by means of hearing aids, and the acoustic environment can be designed in such a way as to facilitate speech communication. In the remainder of this section, we will consider some of the issues to be considered when attempting such modifications.

Modifications in the Acoustic Environment

Communicative difficulties are encountered by the elderly whether they live in a private home or in an extended-care facility. Problems appear to be particularly prevalent among those who have age-related difficulties in binaural analysis, and it is this same group who could probably benefit most by modifications in the acoustic environment. However, for the most part, habilitative efforts have neglected the acoustic environment as a means to increase communication skills.

In some cases, improvements can be made at little or no cost. For example, furniture can be rearranged to provide better face-to-face contact and to remove obstructions. Noise-generating devices can be positioned so as to reduce competition with speech. Architectural factors may also prove important in influencing speech intelligibility.

Sound is absorbed in rooms by soft or rough surfaces in a frequency-dependent manner. Hard, flat surfaces tend to reflect sound, and when the sound is multiply reflected, it is said to reverberate. Reverberation time increases linearly with room volume and is inversely related to the sound absorption of the room. With the advent of digital-computer processing, it has also been found that room shape and absorber location also influence reverberation time.

Recordings made at the "ears" of an anthropometric mannequin head have been used to determine listener's preferences and speech intelligibility in rooms varying in size and shape. The results of this study (Schroeder, 1980) suggest that listeners prefer rooms with greater reverberation time (at least up to 2.2 s), narrower widths, and acoustic properties that produce greater binaural differences. Given that the elderly may suffer from degeneration of the brainstem nuclei that are responsible for binaural processing (e.g., Kirikae et al., 1964) and as a result are less sensitive to certain binaural cues (e.g., Herman et al.,

1977), rooms intended for use by older people may need to be designed to exaggerate binaural differences. Clearly, research is still necessary to determine the room characteristics most suitable for older listeners.

Modifications in the Acoustic Signal

If an elderly person complains that he cannot understand what is spoken to him, it is frequently suggested that he obtain a hearing aid. It has been estimated that about 90 percent of the people aged 60 will receive satisfaction from an aid. At age 70, 70 percent are satisfied. At age 80, less than 40 percent are satisfied (Davis and Silverman, 1970). The drop in satisfaction may result from a variety of factors, but the acoustics of the amplified sound, as they relate to changes in the auditory nervous system, will be discussed here as a major drawback.

The electric hearing aid is a separate acoustic system interposed between the acoustic environment and the receiver's auditory system. It consists of a microphone, an amplifier, and receiver, like any public address system, but is much condensed in size. Miniaturization results in limitations of its frequency response. In addition, aids typically amplify sound in the 1000- to 3000-Hz frequency range to a greater extent than other sounds; in fact, the gain is negligible at very high and very low frequencies. Moreover, because they lack perfect fidelity, distortion is often present.

Essentially, an aid increases intensity at the eardrum, but blocking the ear canal with the hearing-aid mold attenuates low frequencies. Since presbycusis also attenuates high frequencies as well, the result is a drastic reduction in the range of hearing. Since the amplification produced by two aids is never exactly equal, the IID cue is compromised. Even ITD cues are minimized because of the variability of the aid's temporal characteristics. For example, when a transient signal such as speech is fed into an aid, the output of the aid builds up gradually and does not terminate abruptly with the offset of the speech signal. If one speech signal follows a second very closely, this ringing in the aid will "smear" the temporal cues. Thus, electroacoustic hearing aids, by their very nature, cannot present signals that optimally stimulate the neural units in the brainstem that are suspected of being damaged in some presbycotics.

As mentioned earlier, noise is often disturbing to elderly individuals. Hearing aids can actually contribute to the noise level. In any given room, speech signals (and the signal-to-noise ratio for the receiver) will decay with the distance from the speaker but the ambient noise (regardless of the level) remains constant. If the receiver increases the output of the aid to compensate for the speech signal decay over distance, then the aid will not only create noise but amplify the ambient noise as well.

Finally, the acoustic characteristics of speech appear to interact with the characteristics of electroacoustic hearing aids in such a way as to make speech perception difficult. For example, since consonant identification is often dependent upon the context in which the consonant occurs, distortion produced by the hearing aid may lead to frequent misidentifications. Furthermore, since identification of a speech sound often depends on cues that occur at different times or the presence of silent intervals at certain times, poor damping by the aid can lead to temporal masking of important cues or to the elimination of silent intervals. Finally, since much of the affective information in a message is carried in the fundamental low-frequency range, the attenuation of low frequencies caused by the aid can lead to misunderstandings of intended meaning even when words are correctly identified.

There is a small but slowly growing body of literature that suggests that dichotic principals can be profitably applied to hearing-aid development. Kaplan and Pickett (1981) studied the performance of hearing-impaired elderly with mild to moderate, bilaterally symmetrical sensorineural losses on discrimination of speech mixed with noise in a variety of conditions. Regardless of whether the verbal material consisted of words or sentences, speech discrimination under dichotic conditions was statistically better than monaural listening using an earphone. These data suggest that if hearing aids incorporated dichotic principles, the speech perception of the elderly hearing-impaired listener would improve. Bin-

aural hearing aids have not been considered applicable to many elderly because of the constraints imposed by central presbycusis (e.g., Corso, 1977). Kaplan and Pickett (1981), however, found that some of the elderly with signs of central auditory-processing disorders were able to use binaural input quite well.

Although data are not presently available on elderly performance with dichotic or split-band hearing aids, there are observations on children. Franklin (1969, 1975, 1979, 1981) reported success in consonant discrimination for both normal and hearing-impaired subjects by combining a high-frequency bandpass aid in one ear with a low-frequency bandpass aid in the other (HI/LO). For subjects with profound congenital binaural sensorineural hearing loss (Franklin, 1981), there was an improvement in aided thresholds of 12 to 18 dB for the HI/LO condition compared with wide-range binaural amplification. Thus the application of dichotic (HI/LO) amplification appears to augment both threshold and discrimination of speech for some of the hearing-impaired. This type of amplification may have advantages for the elderly as well. To date, however, only a body aid is available that will produce a HI/LO fitting.

In the future, microprocessors may be installed in hearing aids to improve signal-to-noise ratios and reduce distortion. Tuning of a binaural aid may also improve synchronization and the stimulation of the superior olivary neurons that are partly responsible for speech identification. Computers may also be applied to speech (lip) reading so that video displays of articulator gestures can supplement auditory amplification. Finally, success may be realized in the use of implanted cochlear protheses, though this may be a decade away since the necessary data in auditory physiology and speech communication as well as the long term effects of electrodes in the central nervous system remain to be analyzed.

CONCLUSIONS AND IMPLICATIONS FOR FUTURE RESEARCH

To summarize, morphological and functional age-related changes in the characteristics of most auditory structures have been reported. The size, shape, and flexibility of the outer and middle ears are altered. Receptor cells and neural units within the cochlea degenerate, and mechanical and metabolic changes within the inner ear have been observed as well. The effects of aging on more central relays in the auditory pathway have not been clearly delineated, but cellular degeneration or loss is often reported.

The clearest behavioral consequence of these structural changes is a loss of absolute sensitivity. Not only is the exact cause of this loss uncertain, however, but the relationship between structural degeneration and loss of abilities other than simple detection is unknown. Although age differences have been reported in frequency resolution and binaural hearing, these are by no means well-established findings, and the abilities of the elderly in many other tasks have never been tested. In the area of speech perception, we might tentatively conclude that the major age-related decline is in the understanding of connected speech under difficult listening conditions. This loss is greater than would be predicted simply on the basis of absolute sensitivity decline and more than likely involves problems with cognitive mediating processes. Although we believe that there are many environmental and intervention modifications that could help the elderly who have pronounced loss of speech understanding, considerably more basic research will be required to identify and develop the appropriate techniques.

We have tried to highlight those areas where research is particularly needed throughout this review, but it may be fruitful to repeat them here. If we are to understand age-related structural and functional changes in the auditory system, considerable histological and physiological work will be necessary. In order for the significance of such changes to be demonstrated, however, behavioral measures correlated with structural change must be collected. Some information of this sort can be obtained through histological examination of individuals whose hearing capacity was established prior to death. A more important development in this area, though, will be identification of appropriate nonhuman animal models for the aging human auditory system. These will allow not only for correlation of structure with behavior, but for observation of physiological responses in live preparations and for the validation of hypothesized age effects by experimentally induced damage in young animals. Within the area of structure-behavior relationships, the relative contributions of peripheral and central structures to hearing loss as well as the nature of peripheral effects (mechanical, metabolic, or receptor/neural) remain unanswered questions.

Perhaps the most important issue that must be resolved before we can assess the behavioral consequences of physiological change is the separation of the sensory from the nonsensory factors that influence psychophysical performance. Although "signal-detection" type paradigms are a step in the right direction, there are a variety of variables besides response bias, such as memory and attention, that may be confounded with age. Once such variables are known and methods for their control devised, then it will be possible to assess age differences in basic acoustic processing capacity.

Realizing how little is known about the psychoacoustic performance of the elderly, there is a great temptation to try a task on young and old listeners just because it's never been tried before. We don't intend to encourage that approach. The psychoacoustical phenomena we've described here were included for one of two reasons: (1) Performance in a basic task would reasonably be expected to predict performance in a more realistic (i.e., complex or real world) task, or (2) performance differences in a task would help to explain, from a theoretical perspective, the nature of deficits in other tasks. Thus, as in any area of research and as was noted at the start, organization of the available data must precede and precipitate further data collection efforts.

Acknowledgements. We wish to thank Bruce Weber and William Yost for critical reading of earlier drafts of the manuscript and Nancy Spencer for suggestions as to the organization of the speech perception material.

REFERENCES

Aitkin, L. M.; Anderson, D. J.; and Brugge, J. F. 1970. Tonotopic organization and discharge characteristics of single neurons in nuclei of the lateral lemniscus of the cat. *J. Neurophysiol.* 33: 421–440.

Aitkin, L. M.; Dunlop, C. W.; and Webster, W. R. 1966. Click evoked response patterns in single units in the medial geniculate body of the cat. *J. Neurophysiol* 29: 109–123.

Aitkin, L. M., and Webster, W. R. 1971. Tonotopic organization in the medial geniculate body of the cat. *Brain Res.* 26: 402–405.

Altman, J. A. 1968. Are these neurons detecting direction of sound source motion? *Exp. Neurol.* 22: 13–25.

Altman, J. A.; Syka, J.; and Shmigidina, G. N. 1970. Neuronal activity in the medial geniculate body of the cat during monaural and binaural stimulation. *Exp. Brain Res.* 10: 81–93.

American National Standards Institute. 1970. *American National Standards Specifications for Audiometers (ANSI S 3.6–1069).* New York: American National Standards Institute.

Anders, T. R.; Fozard, J. L.; and Lillyquist, T. D. 1972. The effects of age upon retrieval from short-term memory. *Dev. Psychol.* 9: 214–217.

Batteau, D. W. 1967. The role of the pinna in human localization. *Proc. Roy. Soc.* (London) B168: 158–180.

Beagley, H. A., and Sheldrake, M. B. 1978. Differences in brainstem response latency with age and sex. *Br. J. Audiol.* 12: 69–77.

Beedle, R. K., and Harford, E. R. 1973. A comparison of acoustic reflex growth in normal and pathological ears. *J. Speech Hearing Res.* 16: 271–280.

Bekesy, G. 1960. *Experiments in Hearing.* New York: McGraw-Hill.

Bekesy, G., and Rosenblith, W. A. 1958. The mechanical properties of the ear. In *Handbook of Experimental Psychology,* ed. S. S. Stevens. New York: Wiley.

Belal, A. 1975. Presbycusis: physiological or pathological. *J. Laryngol.* 89: 1011–1025.

Benevento, L. A., and Coleman, P. D. 1970. Responses of single cells in cat inferior colliculus to binaural click stimuli: Combinations of intensity levels, time differences and intensity differences. *Brain Res.* 17: 387–405.

Bergman, M. 1971. Changes in hearing with age. *Gerontologist* 11(2): 148–151.

Bergman, M.; Blumenfeld, V. G.; Cascardo, D.; Dask, B.; Levitt, H.; and Margulies, M. K. 1976. Age-related decrement in hearing for speech: Sampling and longitudinal studies. *J. Gerontol.* 31: 533–538.

Bergman, M. 1971. Hearing and aging: Implications of recent research findings. *Audiology* 10: 164–171.

Bilger, R. C., and Hirsch, I. J. 1956. Masking of tones by bands of noise. *J. Acoust. Soc. Am.* 28: 623–630.

Birren, J. E.; Woods, A. M.; and Williams, M. V. 1980. Behavioral slowing with age: Causes, organization and consequences. In *Aging in the 1980's: Psychological Issues,* ed. L. W. Poon. Washington, D.C.: APA Press.

Blauert, J. 1969. Sound localization in the median plane. *Acustica* 22: 205–213.

Block, M. G., and Wightman, F. L. 1977. A statistically based measure of the acoustic reflex and its relation to stimulus loudness. *J. Acoust. Soc. Am.,* 61: 120–125.

Bond, Z. S., and Garnes, S. 1980. Misperceptions of fluent speech. In *Perception and Production of Fluent Speech,* ed. R. A. Cole. Hillsdale, N.J.: Erlbaum, pp. 115–132.

Bonding, P. 1979. Critical bandwidth in presbycusis. *Scand. Audiol.* 8: 205–225.

Botwinick, J. 1973. *Aging and Behavior.* New York: Springer.

Botwinick, J., and Storandt, M. 1974. *Memory Related Functions and Age.* Springfield, IL: Thomas.

Boudreau, J. D., and Tsuchitani, C. C. 1970. Cat superior olivary S segment cell discharge to tonal stimulation. In *Contributions to Sensory Physiology,* ed. W. D. Neff. New York: Academic Press.

Bredberg, G. 1967. The human cochlea during development and ageing. *J. Laryngol. Otol.* 81: 739–758.

Bredberg, G. 1968. Cellular pattern and nerve supply of the human organ of Corti. *Acta. Oto-laryngol.* Suppl. 236.

Brugge, J. F.; Dubrovsky, N. A.; Aitkin, L. M.; and Anderson, D. J. 1969. Sensitivity of single neurons in auditory cortex of cat to binaural tonal stimulation: Effects of varying interaural time and intensity. *J. Neurophysiol.* 32: 1005–1024.

Brugge, J. F., and Merzenich, M. M. 1973. Patterns of activity of single neurons of the auditory cortex in monkey. In *Basic Mechanisms in Hearing,* ed. A. R. Moller. New York: Academic Press.

Butler, R. A. 1975. The influence of the external and middle ear on auditory discriminations. In *Handbook of Sensory Physiology,* eds. W. D. Keidel and W. D. Neff. Vol. 5, Pt. 2, Auditory System. New York: Springer-Verlag.

Butler, R. N., and Lewis, M. 1977. *Aging and Mental Health.* St. Louis, MO: Mosby.

Calearo, C., and Lazzaroni, A., 1957. Speech intelligibility in relationship to the speed of the message. *Laryngoscope* 67: 410–419.

Campbell, F. W., and Robson, J. G. 1968. Application of Fourier analysis to the visibility of gratings. *J. Physiol.* 191: 551–566.

Carhart, R.; Tillman, T. W.; and Grutis, 1969. Release from multiple maskers: Effects of interaural time disparities. *J. Acoust. Soc. Am.* 45: 411–418.

Cerella, J.; Poon, L. W.; and Williams, D. M. 1980. Age and the complexity hypotheses. In *Aging in the 1980's: Psychological Issues,* ed. L. W. Poon. Washington, D.C.: APA Press.

Clark, E. O. 1980. Semantic and episodic memory impairment in normal and cognitively impaired elderly adults. In *Language and Communication in the Elderly,* eds. L. K. Obler and M. L. Albert. Lexington, MA: Lexington Books.

Cole, R. A., and Jakimik, J. 1980. A model of speech perception. In *Perception and Production of Fluent Speech,* ed. R. A. Cole, Hillsdale, N.J.: Erlbaum.

Corso, J. F. 1963a. Age and sex differences in pure tone thresholds. *Arch. Otolaryngol.* 77: 385–405.

Corso, J. F. 1963b. Aging and auditory thresholds in men and women. *Arch. Environ. Health* 6: 350–356.

Corso, J. F. 1977. Auditory perception and communication. In *Handbook of the Psychology of Aging,* eds.

J. E. Birren and K. W. Schaie. New York: Van Nostrand Reinhold.

Corso, J. F. 1980. Age correction factor in noise-induced hearing loss: A quantitative model. *Audiology* 19: 221–232.

Corso, J. F. 1981. *Aging Sensory Systems and Perception.* New York: Praeger Publishers.

Corso, J. F.; Wright, H. N.; and Valerio, M. 1976. Auditory temporal summation in presbycusis and noise exposure. *J. Gerontol.* 31: 58–63.

Craik, F. I. M. 1966. The effects of aging on the detection of faint auditory signals. *Proceedings of the 7th International Congress of Gerontology.* Vol. 6. Vienna.

Craik, F. I. M. 1977. Age differences in human memory. In *Handbook of the Psychology of Aging,* eds. J. E. Birren and K. W. Schaie. New York: Van Nostrand Reinhold.

Crowley, D. E.; Swain, R. E.; Schram, V. L.; and Swanson, S. N. 1972. Analysis of age-related changes in electrical responses from the inner ear of rats. *Ann. Otol. Rhinol. Laryngol.* 815: 739–746.

Dallos, P. 1971. Summating potentials of the cochlea. In *Physiology of the Auditory System,* ed. M. B. Sachs. Baltimore: National Educational Consultants.

Dallos, P. 1973. *The Auditory Periphery.* New York: Academic Press.

Dallos, P.; Villone, M. C.; Durrant, J. D.; Wang, C. Y.; and Raynor, S. 1972. Cochlear inner and outer hair cells: Functional differences. *Science* 177: 356–358.

Dallos, P., and Cheatham, M. A. 1974. Cochlear microphonic correlates of cubic difference tones. In *Facts and Models in Hearing,* eds. E. Zwicker and E. Terhardt. New York: Springer-Verlag.

Danziger, W. L. 1980. Measurement of response bias in aging research. In *Aging in the 1980's: Psychological Issues,* ed. L. W. Poon. Washington, D.C.: APA Press.

Davis, H. 1961. Peripheral coding of auditory information. In *Sensory Communication,* ed. W. A. Rosenblith. Cambridge, MA: MIT Press.

Davis, H. 1965. A model for transducer action in the cochlea. *Cold. Spr. Harbor Symp. Quant. Biol.* 30: 181–190.

Davis, H., and Silverman, S. R. 1970. *Hearing and Deafness.* 3rd ed. New York: Holt Rinehart and Winston.

Dayal, V. S., and Nussbaum, M. A. 1971. Patterns of pure tone loss in presbycusis. *Acta. Oto-laryngol.* 71: 382–384.

Deatherage, B. H.; Davis, H.; and Eldredge, D. H. 1957a. Physiological evidence for the masking of low frequencies by high. *J. Acoust. Soc. Am.* 29: 132–137.

Deatherage, B. H.; Davis, H.; and Eldridge, D. H. 1957b. Remote masking in selected frequency regions. *J. Acoust. Soc. Am.* 29: 512–514.

Dirks, D. D. 1978. Effects of hearing impairment on the auditory system. In *Handbook of Perception,* eds. E. C. Carterette and M. P. Friedman. Vol. IV, *Hearing.* New York: Academic Press.

Djupesland, G. 1964. Middle ear muscle reflexes elicited by acoustic and nonacoustic stimulation. *Acta Otol.* (Suppl.): 188.

Dorman, M. F., and Marton, K. 1981. Some preliminary observations on frequency selectivity and phonetic identification. Paper presented to the 101st meeting of the Acoustical Society of America, May, 1981. Ottawa, Ont., Canada.

Dreschler, W. A., and Plomp, R. 1980. Relation between psychophysical data and speech perception for hearing-impaired subjects. I. *J. Acoust. Soc. Am.* 68: 1608–1615.

Dutsch, L. 1972. The threshold of the stapedius reflex for pure tone and noise stimuli. *Acta Otol.* 74: 248–251.

Egan, J. P.; and Hake, H. W. 1950. On the masking pattern of a simple auditory stimulus. *J. Acoust. Soc. Am.* 22: 622–630.

Eggermont, J. J. 1976. Electrocochleography. In *Handbook of Sensory Physiology,* eds. W. D. Keidel and W. D. Neff. New York: Springer-Verlag.

Elliott, L. L. 1962. Backward and forward masking of probe tones of different frequencies. *J. Acoust. Soc. Am.* 34: 1116–1117.

Elliott, L. L. 1967. Development of auditory narrow-band frequency contours. *J. Acoust. Soc. Am.* 42: 143–153.

Elliott, L. L. 1969. Masking of tones before, during, and after brief silent periods of noise. *J. Acoust. Soc. Am.* 45: 1277–1279.

Erulkar, S. D.; Butler, R. A.; and Gerstein, G. L. 1968. Excitation and inhibition in cochlear nucleus II. Frequency modulated tones. *J. Neurophysiol.* 31: 537–548.

Etholm, B., and Belal, A., Jr. 1974. Senile changes in the middle ear joints. *Ann. Otol. Rhinol. Laryngol.* 83(1): 49–64.

Evans, E. F. 1975. The sharpening of cochlear frequency selectivity in the normal and abnormal cochlea. *Audiology* 14: 419–442.

Evans, E. F., and Wilson, J. P. 1973. Frequency selectivity of the cochlea. In *Basic Mechanisms in Hearing,* ed. A. R. Moller. New York: Academic Press.

Evans, E. F., and Wilson, J. P. 1975. Cochlear tuning properties: Concurrent basilar membrane and single nerve fiber measurements. *Science* 190: 1218–1221.

Farrimond, T. 1961. Prediction of speech hearing loss for older industrial workers. *Gerontologia* 5: 65–87.

Fernandez, C. 1951. The innervation of the cochlea (guinea pig). *Laryngoscope* 61: 1152–1172.

Feth, L. L., and O'Malley, H. 1977. Two-tone auditory spectral resolution. *J. Acoust. Soc. Am.* 62: 940–947.

Findlay, R. C., and Schuchman, G. I. 1976. Masking level difference for speech: Effects of ear dominance and age. *Audiology* 15: 232–241.

Finkiewicz, L. 1971. Micromorphology of the spiral ganglion in guinea pigs of various ages. *Folia Morphol* (Warsz) 30: 33–42.

Fitsch, V.; Dobozi, M.; and Greig, G. 1972. Degenerative changes of the arterial vessels of the internal auditory meatus during the process of aging. *Acta Oto-Laryngol.* 73: 259–266.

Fleischer, K. 1972. The aging ear: Morphological aspects. *Hals, Nase, Ohren* 20(4): 103–107.

Fletcher, H. 1940. Auditory patterns. *J. Acoust. Soc. Am.* 12: 47–65.

Fournier, J. E. L'analyse et l'identification du message

sonore. 1954. *J. Franc. Oto-Rhino-Laryngol.* 3: 257.

Franklin, B. 1969. The effect on consonant discrimination of combining a low-frequency passband in one ear and a high-frequency passband in the other ear. *J. Aud. Res.* 9: 365–379.

Franklin, B. 1975. The effect of combining low- and high-frequency passbands on consonant recognition in the hearing impaired. *J. Speech Hearing Res.* 18: 719–727.

Franklin, B. 1979. A comparison of the effect on consonant discrimination of combining low- and high-frequency passbands in normal, congenital and adventitious hearing-impaired subjects. *J. Am. Audiol. Soc.* 5: 168–176.

Franklin, B. 1981. Split-band amplification: A HI/LO hearing aid fitting. *Ear and Hearing* 2: 230–233.

Gacek, R. R., and Schuknecht, H. R. 1969. Pathology of presbycusis. *Internat. Audiol.* 8: 199–209.

Gaeth, J. H. 1948. A study of phonemic regression in relation to hearing loss. Dissertation, Northwestern University, Chicago.

Galambos, R. 1952. Microelectrode studies on medial geniculate body of cat, III. Response to pure tones. *J. Neurophysiol.* 15: 381–400.

Galambos, R., and Davis, H. 1943. The response of single auditory nerve fibers to acoustic stimulation. *J. Neurophysiol.* 6: 39–57.

Ganong, W. F. 1980. Phonetic categorization in auditory word perception. *J. Exp. Psychol.* 6: 110–125.

Gardner, M., and Gardner, R. 1973. Problem of localization in the median plane: Effect of pinnae cavity occlusion. *J. Acoust. Soc. Am.* 53: 400–408.

Gebhardt, C. J., and Goldstein, D. P. 1972. Frequency discrimination and the MLD. *J. Acoust. Soc. Am.* 51: 1228–1232.

Gelfand, S. A. 1981. *Hearing: An Introduction to Psychological and Physiological Acoustics.* New York: Dekker.

Gersdorff, M. C. H. 1978. Impedancemetric study of the variations of the auditory reflex in man as a function of age. *Audiology* 17: 260–270.

Glorig, A., and Nixon, J. 1962. Hearing loss as a function of age. *Laryngoscope* 72: 1596–1610.

Goldberg, J. M., and Brown, P. B. 1969. Response of binaural neurons of dog superior olivary complex to dichotic tonal stimuli: Some physiological mechanisms of sound localization. *J. Neurophysiol.* 32: 613–636.

Goldstein, J. L. 1967. Auditory nonlinearity. *J. Acoust. Soc. Am.* 41: 676–689.

Graham, N., and Nachmias, J. 1971. Detection of grating patterns containing two spatial frequencies: A comparison of single-channel and multiple-channel models. *Vis. Res.* 11: 251–259.

Green, D. M., and Henning, G. B. 1969. Audition. *Annual Rev. Psychol.* 20: 105–128.

Green, D. M., and Swets, J. A. 1974. *Signal Detection Theory and Psychophysics.* New York: Krieger.

Green, D. M., and Yost, W. A. 1975. Binaural analysis. In *Handbook of Sensory Physiology*, eds. W. D. Neff and W. D. Keidel. Vol. 2. New York: Springer-Verlag.

Green, J. J. 1969. Social hearing handicap: Its measurement by speech audiometry in noise. *Internat. Audiol.* 8: 182–183.

Guinan, J. J; Norris, B. E.; and Guinan, S. S. 1972. Single auditory units in the superior olivary complex II: Locations of unit categories and tonotopic organization. *Internat. J. Neurosci.* 4: 147–166.

Habener, S. A., and Snyder, J. M. 1974. Stapedius reflex amplitude and decay in normal hearing ears. *Arch. Otolaryngol.* 100: 294–297.

Hall, J. L., and Goldstein, M. H. 1968. Representation of binaural stimuli by single units in primary auditory cortex of unanesthetized cats. *J. Acoust. Soc. Am.* 43: 456–461.

Hallerman, W., and Plath, P. 1971. Effect of age on the discrimination ability of the ear. *Hals, Nase, Ohren* 19: 26–32.

Handler, S. D., and Margolis, R. H. 1977. Predicting hearing loss from stapedial reflex thresholds in patients with sensorineural impairment. *Trans. Am. Acad. Ophthalmol. Otolaryngol.* 84: 425–431.

Hannley, M., and Dobbins, E., 1981. Changes in identification of full- and partial-cue syllables in subjects with age-related hearing impairment. Paper presented to the 101st meeting of the Acoustical Society of America, May, 1981. Ottawa, Ont., Canada.

Hansen, C. C., and Reske-Nielson, E. 1965. Pathological studies in presbycusis. *Arch. Oto-Laryngol.* 82: 115–132.

Hawkins, J. E., and Stevens, S. S. 1950. The masking of pure tones and of speech by white noise. *J. Acoust. Soc. Am.* 22: 6–13.

Henning, G. B. 1973. Effect of interaural phase on frequency and amplitude discrimination. *J. Acoust. Soc. Am.* 54: 1160–1178.

Herman, G. E.; Warren, L. R.; and Wagener, J. W. 1977. Auditory lateralization: Age-differences in sensitivity to dichotic time and amplitude cues. *J. Gerontol.* 32: 187–191.

Hertzog, C. 1980. Applications of signal detection theory to the study of psychological aging: A theoretical review. In *Aging in the 1980's: Psychological Issues,* ed. L. W. Poon. Washington, D.C.: APA Press.

Hinchcliffe, R. 1958. The pattern of the threshold of perception of hearing and other special senses as a function of age. *Gerontologia* 7: 311–320.

Hinchcliffe, R. 1962. The anatomical locus of presbycusis. *J. Speech Dis.* 27: 301–310.

Hinchcliffe, R. 1973. Epidemiology of sensorineural hearing loss. *Audiology* 12: 446–452.

Hind, J. E. 1960. Unit activity in the auditory cortex. In *Neural Mechanisms of the Auditory and Vestibular Systems*, eds. G. L. Rasmussen and W. F. Windle. Springfield, IL: Thomas.

Hirsch, I. J. 1948. The influence of interaural phase on interaural summation and inhibition. *J. Acoust. Soc. Am.* 20: 536–544.

Honrubia, V., and Ward, P. H. 1969. Dependence of the cochlear microphonic and summating potential on the endocochlear potential. *J. Acoust. Soc. Am.* 46: 388–392.

Houtgast, T. 1972. Psychophysical evidence for lateral inhibition in hearing. *J. Acoust. Soc. Am.* 51: 1885–1894.

Hoyer, W. J., and Plude, D. J. 1980. Attentional and perceptual processes in the study of cognitive aging. In *Aging in the 1980's: Psychological Issues,* ed. L. W. Poon. Washington, D.C.: APA Press.

Hubel, D. H., and Wiesel, T. N. 1962. Receptive fields, binocular interaction, and functional architecture in the cat's visual cortex. *J. Physiol.* (London) 160: 106–154.

Hung, I., and Dallos, P. 1972. Study of the acoustic reflex in human beings: I. Dynamic characteristics. *J. Acoust. Soc. Am.* 52: 1168–1180.

Jeffress, L. A., and Taylor, R. W. 1961. Lateralization vs. localization. *J. Acoust. Soc. Am.* 33: 482–483.

Jepsen, O. 1963. Middle-ear muscle reflexes in man. In *Modern Developments in Audiology,* ed. J. Jerger. New York: Academic Press.

Jerger, J. 1973. Audiological findings in aging. *Advances in Otorhinolaryngol.* 20: 115–124.

Jerger, J., and Hayes, D. 1977. Diagnostic speech audiometry. *Arch Otolaryngol.* 103: 216–222.

Jerger, J., and Jerger, S. 1967. Psychoacoustic comparison of cochlear and VIIIth nerve disorders. *J. of Speech and Hearing Research* 10: 659–680.

Jerger, J.; Hayes, D.; Anthony, L.; and Mauldin, L. 1978a. Effect of age on prediction of sensorineural hearing level from the acoustic reflex. *Arch. Otolaryngol.* 104: 393–394.

Jerger, J.; Hayes, J. D.; Anthony, L.; and Mauldin, L. 1978b. Factors influencing prediction of hearing level from the acoustic reflex. *Monogr. Contemp. Audiol.* 1.

Jesteadt, W., and Sims, S. L. 1975. Decision processes in frequency discrimination. *J. Acoust. Soc. Am.* 57: 1161–1168.

Johnsson, L. G., and Hawkins, J. E., Jr. 1972a. Sensory and neural degeneration with aging, as seen in microdissections of the human inner ear. *Ann. Otol. Rhinol. Laryngol.* 81: 179–193.

Johnsson, L. G., and Hawkins, J. E., Jr. 1972b. Vascular changes in the human inner ear associated with aging. *Ann. Otol. Rhinol Laryngol.* 81: 364–376.

Johnsson, L. G., and Hawkins, J. E., Jr. 1977. Age-related degeneration of the inner ear. In *Special Senses in Aging, a Current Biological Assessment.* Proceedings of a symposium held Oct. 1977, University of Michigan. Institute of Gerontology, Ann Arbor, Michigan.

Kaplan, H., and Pickett, J. M. 1981. Effects of dichotic/diotic versus monotic presentation on speech understanding in noise in elderly hearing-impaired listeners. *Ear and Hearing* 2: 202–207.

Katsuki, Y. 1961. Neural mechanisms of auditory sensation in cats. In *Sensory communication,* ed. W. A. Rosenblith. Cambridge, MA: MIT Press.

Katsuki, Y.; Suga, N.; and Kanno, Y. 1962. Neural mechanisms of the peripheral and central auditory systems in monkeys. *J. Acoust. Soc. Am.* 32: 1396–1410.

Katsuki, Y.; Watanabe, T.; and Maruyama, N. 1959. Activity of auditory neurons in upper levels of brain of cat. *J. Neurophysiol.* 22: 343–359.

Keim, R. J. 1977. How aging affects the ear. *Geriatrics* 32: 97–99.

Keithley, E. M., and Feldman, M. L. 1979. Spiral ganglion cell counts in an age-graded series of rat cochleas. *J. Comp. Neurol.* 188: 429–442.

Khanna, S. M., and Leonard, D. G. B. 1982. Basilar membrane tuning in the cat cochlea. *Science* 215: 305–306.

Khanna, S. M.; Sears, R. E.; and Tolindorf, J. 1968. Some properties of longitudinal shear waves: A study by computer simulation. *J. Acoust. Soc. Am.* 43: 1077–1084.

Kiang, N. Y. S.; Pfeiffer, R. R.; Warr, W. B.; and Backus, A. S. 1965. Stimulus coding in the cochlear nucleus. *Ann. Otol.* 74: 463–485.

Kiang, N. Y. S. 1965. *Discharge patterns of single fibers in the cat's auditory nerve.* Cambridge, MA: MIT Press.

Kiang, N. Y. S.; Morest, D. K.; Godfrey, D. A.; Guinan, J. J.; and Kane, E. C. 1973. Stimulus coding at caudal levels of the cat's auditory nervous system: I. Response characteristics of single units. In *Basic mechanisms in hearing,* ed. A. R. Moller. New York: Academic Press.

Kiang, N. Y. S.; Sachs, N. B.; and Peake, W. T. 1967. Shapes of tuning curves for single auditory nerve fibers. *J. Acoust. Soc. Am.* 42: 1341–1342.

Kirikae, I. 1969. Auditory function in advanced age with reference to histological changes in the central auditory system. *Internat. Audiol.* 8: 221–230.

Kirikae, I., and Shitara, T. 1961. Recent advances in the study of presbycusis. *Ronenbyo* 5: 18. (Cited in Kirikae et al., 1964).

Kirikae, I.; Sato, T.; and Shitara, T. 1964. A study of hearing in advanced age. *Laryngoscope* 74: 205–220.

Klatt, D. H., and Stevens, K. N. 1973. On the automatic recognition of continuous speech: Implications of a spectrogram-reading experiment. *IEEE Transactions on Audio and Electroacoustics,* AU-21: 210–217.

Klockhoff, I. 1961. Middle-ear muscle reflexes in man. *Acta Otol.* (Suppl.): 164.

Kock, W. E. 1937. A new interpretation of the results of experiments on the differential pitch sensitivity of the ear. *J. Acoust. Soc. Am.* 9: 129–134.

Konig, E. 1957. Pitch discrimination and age. *Acta Oto-Laryngol.* 48: 475–489.

Konigsmark, B. W., and Murphy, E. A. 1970a. Neuronal populations in the human brain. *Nature* 228: 1335.

Konigsmark, B. W., and Murphy, E. A. 1970b. Volume of the ventral cochlear nucleus in man: Its relationship to neuronal population and age. *J. Neuropath. Exp. Neurol.* 31: 304–316.

Konishi, T.; Butler, R. A.; and Fernandez, C. 1961. Effect of anoxia on cochlear potentials. *J. Acoust. Soc. Am.* 33: 349–356.

Konishi, T., and Yasuna, T. 1963. Summating potential of the cochlea in the guinea pig. *J. Acoust. Soc. Am.* 35: 1448–1452.

Krmpotic-Nemanic, J. 1969. Presbycusis and retrocochlear structures. *Internat. Audiol.* 8: 210–220.

Krmpotic-Nemanic, J. 1972. Morphology of the internal auditory canal in presbycusis. *Hals, Nase, Ohren* 20: 246–249.

Labouvie-Vief, G., and Chandler, M. 1978. Idealistic vs. contextual perspectives in developmental theories. In *Life-span Development and Behavior,* ed. P. B. Baltes. Vol. 1. New York: Academic Press.

Legouix, J. P.; Remond, M. C.; and Greenbaum, H. B. 1973. Interference and two-tone inhibition. *J. Acoust. Soc. Am.* 53: 409–419.

Licklider, J. C. R. 1948. Influence of interaural phase relations upon the masking of speech by white noise. *J. Acoust. Soc. Am.* 20: 150–159.

Lim, D. J. 1973. Scanning electron microscopic morphology of the ear. In *Otolaryngology*, eds. M. M. Paparella and D. A. Shemrick. Vol. 1, *Basic Sciences and Related Disciplines*, Philadelphia: Saunders.

Luk, G. D.; Morest, N. M.; and McKenna, N. M. 1974. Origins of the crossed olivo-cochlear bundle shown by an acid phosphatase method in the cat. *Ann. Otol.* 83: 382–392.

Magladery, J. 1959. Neurophysiology of aging. In *Handbook of Aging and the Individual*, ed. J. Birren. Chicago: University of Chicago.

Manley, G. A. 1978. Cochlear frequency sharpening—A new synthesis. *Acta Otol.* 85: 167–176.

Margolis, R., and Popelka, G. 1975. Loudness and the acoustic reflex. *J. Acoust. Soc. Am.* 58: 1330–1332.

Marston, E., and Goetzinger, C. P. 1972. A comparison of sensitized words and sentences for distinguishing nonperipheral auditory changes as a function of aging. *Cortex* 8: 213–223.

Martin, M. C. 1974. Critical bands in sensorineural hearing loss. *Scand. Audiol.* 3: 133–140.

Matzker, V. J., and Springhood, E. Richtung-Shoren und Lebensalter. 1958. *Zeitschrift für Laryngologie, Rhinologie, Otologie und Ihre Grenzgebiete* 37: 739–745.

Mehrgardt, S., and Mellert, V. 1977. Transformation characteristics of the external human ear. *J. Acoust. Soc. Am.* 61: 1567–1576.

Metz, O. 1951. Studies on the contraction of the tympanic muscles as indicated by changes in impedance of the ear. *Acta Otol.* 39: 397–405.

Metz, O. 1952. Threshold of reflex contractions of muscles of the middle ear and recruitment of loudness. *Arch. Otol.* 55: 536–593.

Meurmann, O. H. 1953. Studies on the difference limen of intensity and frequency in presbycusis. *Proceedings of the First International Congress of Audiology*, Leiden 5–6 VI: 59–63.

Mikaelian, D. O. 1979. Development and degeneration of hearing in the C57/B16 mouse: Relation of electrophysiologic responses from the round window and cochlear anatomy and behavioral responses. *Laryngoscope* 89: 1–15.

Miller, G. A.; Heise, G. A.; and Lichten, H. 1951. The intelligibility of speech as a function of the context of the test materials. *J. Exp. Psychol.* 41: 329–335.

Miller, G. A., and Isard, S. 1963. Some perceptual consequences of linguistic rules. *J. Verbal Learning and Verbal Behavior* 2: 217–228.

Mills, A. H. 1956. On the minimum audible angle. *J. Acoust. Soc. Am.* 30: 237–246.

Mills, A. H. 1960. Lateralization of high-frequency tones. *J. Acoust. Soc. Am.* 32: 132–134.

Moore, B. C. J. 1977. *Introduction to the Psychology of Hearing.* London: Macmillan.

Moskowitz, N. and Liu, J. C. 1972. Central projections of the spiral ganglion of the squirrel monkey. *J. Comp. Neurol.* 144: 335–344.

Nash, M. M., and Wepman, J. M. 1973. Auditory comprehension and age. *Gerontologist* 13: 243–247.

National Research Council. 1981. *Mammalian Models for Research on Aging.* Washington, D.C.: National Academy Press.

Nelson, P. G.; Erulkar, S. D.; and Bryan, J. S. 1966. Responses of units of the inferior colliculus to time-varying acoustic stimuli. *J. Neurophysiol.* 29: 834–860.

Nerbonne, M. A.; Bliss, A. T.; and Schow, R. L. 1978. Acoustic impedance values in the elderly. *J. Am. Audiol. Soc.* 4: 57–62.

Nienhuys, T. G. W., and Clark, G. M. 1979. Critical bands following selective destruction of cochlear inner and outer hair cells. *Acta. Oto-Laryngol.* 88: 350–358.

Noble, W. G. 1978. *Assessment of Impaired Hearing: A Critique and a New Method.* New York: Academic Press.

Nordland, B. 1964. Directional audiometry. *Acta Otolaryngol.* 57: 1–18.

Obusek, C. J., and Warren, R. M. 1973. A comparison of speech perception in senile and well-preserved aged by means of the verbal transformation effect. *J. Gerontol.* 28: 184–188.

O'Malley, H., and Feth, L. L. 1979. Relationship between tuning curves and "suppression." *J. Acoust. Soc. Am.* 66: 1075–1087.

Oshika, B. T.; Zue, V. W.; Weeks, R. V.; Nue, H.; and Aurbach, I. 1975. The role of phonological rules in speech understanding research. *IEEE Transactions: Acoustics, Speech, Signal Processing* 23: 104–112.

Osterhammel, D., and Osterhammel, P. 1979a. High-frequency audiometry. Age and sex variations. *Scand. Audiol.* 8: 85–90.

Osterhammel, D., and Osterhammel, P. 1979b. Age and sex variations for the normal stapedial reflex thresholds and tympanometric compliance values. *Scand. Audiol* 8: 153–158.

Özdamar, O., and Dallos, P. 1976. Input-output function of cochlear whole-nerve action potentials: Interpretation in terms of one population of neurons. *J. Acoust. Soc. Am.* 59: 143–147.

Palva, T., and Karja, J. 1969. Suprathreshold auditory adaptation. *J. Acoust. Soc. Am.* 45: 1018–1021.

Pastore, R. E.; Harris, L. B.; and Goldstein, L. 1980. Auditory forward and backward masking interaction. *Perception & Psychophysics* 28: 547–549.

Patterson, R. D. 1974. Auditory filter shape. *J. Acoust. Soc. Am.* 55: 802–809.

Patterson, R. D.; and Webber, D. L. 1980. Auditory filter shape and age. Paper presented at the 100th Annual meeting of the Acoustical Society of America, Los Angeles, November, 17–21, 1980.

Perlmutter, M. 1979. Age differences in adults' free recall, cued recall, and recognition. *J. of Gerontol.* 34: 533–539.

Perlmutter, M. 1980. An apparent paradox about memory aging. In *New Directions in Memory and Aging: Proceedings of the George Talland Memorial Conference,* eds. L. W. Poon, J. L. Fozard, L. S. Germack, D.

Arenberg, and L. W. Thompson. Hillsdale, N.J.: Erlbaum.

Pestalozza, G.; Davis, H.; Eldredge, D. H.; et al. 1957. Decreased bioelectric potentials in the ears of senile guinea pigs. *Laryngoscope* 67: 1113–1122.

Pestalozza, G., and Shore, I. 1955. Clinical evaluation of presbycusis on the basis of different tests of auditory function. *Laryngoscope* 65: 1136–1163.

Petros, T., and Chabot, R. J. 1981. Adult age differences in sensitivity to the semantic structure of prose. In preparation.

Pfeiffer, R. R., and Molnar, C. E. 1970. Cochlear nerve fiber discharge patterns: Relationship to cochlear microphonic. *Science* 167: 1614–1616.

Plomp, R. 1965. Detectability threshold for combination tones. *J. Acoust. Soc. Am.* 37: 1116–1123.

Plomp, R., and Mimpen, A. M. 1979. Speech-reception threshold for sentences as a function of age and noise level. *J. Acoust. Soc. Am.* 66: 1333–1342.

Pollack, I. 1964. Interaction of forward and backward masking. *J. Aud. Res.* 4: 63–67.

Pollack, I., and Pickett, J. M. 1963. Intelligibility of excerpts from conversational speech. *Language and Speech* 6: 165–171.

Poon, L. W., ed. 1980. *Aging in the 1980's: Psychological Issues.* Washington, D.C.: APA Press.

Potash, M., and Jones, B. 1977. Aging and decision criteria for the detection of tones in noise. *J. Gerontol.* 32: 436–440.

Powell, T. P. S., and Cowan, W. M. 1962. An experimental study of the projection of the cochlea. *J. Anat.* 96: 269–284.

Prosen, C. A.; Moody, D. B.; Stebbins, W. C., and Hawkins, J. E. Jr. 1981. Auditory intensity discrimination after selective loss of cochlear outer hair cells. *Science* 212: 1286–1288.

Punch, J. L., and McConnell, F. 1969. The speech discrimination function of elderly adults. *J. Aud. Res.* 9: 159–166.

Quaranta, A.; Amoroso, C., and Cervella, G. 1978. Remote masking in presbycusis. *J. Aud. Res.* 18: 125–130.

Rasmussen, G. L. 1946. The olivary peduncle and other fiber projections of the superior olivary complex. *J. Comp. Neurol.* 84: 141–219.

Rasmussen, G. L. 1960. Efferent fibers of the cochlear nerve and cochlear nucleus. In *Neural Mechanisms of the Auditory and Vestibular Systems*, eds. G. L. Rasmussen and W. F. Windle. Springfield, IL: Thomas.

Rasmussen, G. L. 1964. Anatomical relationships of the ascending and descending auditory systems. In *Neurological aspects of auditory and vestibular disorders*, eds. W. S. Field and B. R. Alford. Springfield, IL: Thomas.

Rasmussen, G. L. 1967. Efferent connections of the cochlear nucleus. In *Sensorineural hearing processes and disorders*, ed. A. B. Graham. Boston: Little Brown.

Reddy, D. R. 1976. Speech recognition by machine: A review. *Proc. IEEE* 64: 501–523.

Rees, J. N., and Botwinick, J. 1971. Detection and decision of factors in auditory behavior of the elderly. *J. Gerontol.* 26: 113–136.

Reynaud, J.; Camara, M.; and Busteris, L. 1969. An investigation into presbycusis in Africans from rural and nomadic environments. *Internat. Audiol.* 8: 299–304.

Riegel, K. F. 1973. An epitaph for a paradigm: Introduction for a symposium. *Human Development* 16: 1–7.

Robinson, D. W., and Sutton, G. J. 1979. Age effect in hearing—a comparative analysis of published threshold data. *Audiology* 18: 320–334.

Roffler, S. K., and Butler, R. A. 1968. Factors that influence the localization of sound in the vertical plane. *J. Acoust. Soc. Am.* 43: 1255–1259.

Rose, J. E. 1949. The cellular structure of the auditory region of the cat. *J. Comp. Neurol.* 91: 441–466.

Rose, J. E. 1960. Organization of frequency sensitive neurons in the cochlear nuclear complex of the cat. In *Neural Mechanisms of the Auditory and Vestibular Systems*, eds. G. L. Rasmussen and W. F. Windle. Springfield, IL: Thomas.

Rose, J. E.; Galambos, R.; and Hughes, J. R. 1959. Microelectrode studies of the cochlear nuclei of the cat. *Bull. Johns Hopkins Hosp.* 104: 211–251.

Rose, J. E.; Greenwood, D. D.; Goldberg, J. M.; and Hind, J. E. 1963. Some discharge characteristics of single neurons in the inferior colliculus of the cat. I. Tonotopical organization, relation of spike-counts to tone intensity, and firing patterns of single elements. *J. Neurophysiol.* 26: 294–320.

Rose, J. E.; Gross, N. B.; Geisler, C. D.; and Hind, J. E. 1966. Some neural mechanisms in the inferior colliculus of the cat which may be relevant to localization of a sound source. *J. Neurophysiol.* 29: 288–314.

Rosen, D. E., Bergman, M.; Plester, D.; El-Mofty, A.; and Satti, M. H. 1962. Presbycusis study of a relatively noise-free population in the Sudan. *Ann. Otol. Rhinol. Laryngol.* 71: 727–743.

Rosen, S.; Plester, D.; El-Mofty A.; and Rosen, H. V. 1964. High frequency audiometry in presbycusis. *Arch. Otolaryngol.* 79: 18–32.

Russell, I. J., and Sellick, P. M. 1977. Tuning properties of cochlear hair cells. *Nature* 267: 858–860.

Ryan, A. 1978. Behavioral correlates of inner and outer hair cell damage in the chinchilla and Mongolian gerbil. Paper presented to the Association for Research in Otolaryngology, St. Petersburg, Florida.

Ryan, A.; Dallos, P.; and McGee, T. 1979. Psychophysical tuning curves and auditory thresholds after hair cell damage in the chinchilla. *J. Acoust. Soc. Am.* 66: 370–378.

Sachs, M. B., and Kiang, N. Y. S. 1968. Two-tone inhibition in auditory nerve fibers. *J. Acoust. Soc. Am.* 43: 1120–1128.

Sando, I. 1965. The anatomical interrelationships of the cochlear nerve fibers. *Acta Otol.* 59: 417–436.

Schaie, K. W.; Baltes, P.; and Strother, C. R. 1964. A study of auditory sensitivity in advanced age. *J. Gerontol.* 19: 453–457.

Scharf, B. 1970. Critical bands. In *Foundations of Modern Auditory Theory*, ed. J. V. Tobias. New York: Academic Press.

Scharf, B., and Hellman, R. P. 1966. A model of loudness

summation applied to impaired ears. *J. Acoust. Soc. Am.* 40: 71–78.

Schow, R.; Christensen, J.; Hutchinson, J.; and Nerbonne, M. 1978. *Communication Disorders of the Aged: A Guide for Health Professionals.* Baltimore: University Park Press.

Schow, R. L., and Goldbaum, D. E. 1980. Collapsed ear canals in the elderly nursing home population. *J. Speech Hearing Dis.* 45: 259–267.

Schroeder, M. R. 1980. Acoustics in human communications: Room acoustics, music, and speech. *J. Acoust. Soc. Am.* 68: 22–28.

Schuknecht, H. 1974. *Pathology of the Ear.* Cambridge, MA: Harvard University Press.

Schuknecht, H. F.; Watanuki, K.; Tukahashi, T.; Belal, A. A.; Kimura, R. S.; Jones, D. D.; and Ota, C. Y. 1974. Atrophy of the stria vascularis, a common cause for hearing loss. *Laryngoscope* 84: 1777–1821.

Shaw, E. A. G. 1974. Transformation of sound pressure level from the free field to the ear drum in the horizontal plane. *J. Acoust. Soc. Am.* 56: 1848–1861.

Silman, S. 1979a. Effects of aging on the stapedius reflex thresholds. *J. Acoust. Soc. Am.* 66: 735–738.

Silman, S. 1979b. Acoustic reflex aging and the distortion product: Reply, *J. Acoust. Soc. Am.* 66: 909–910.

Silman, S., Popelka, G., and Gelfand, S. A. 1978. Effect of sensorineural hearing loss on acoustic stapedius reflex growth functions. *J. Acoust. Soc. Am.* 64: 1406–1411.

Silverman, I. 1963. Age and the tendency to withold response. *Gerontol.* 18: 372–375.

Simmons, F. B. 1964. Perceptual theories of middle ear function. *Ann. Otol.* 73: 724–740.

Simon, E. 1979. Depth and elaboration of processing in relation to age. *J. Exp. Psychol.: Human Learn. and Mem.* 5: 115–124.

Simonetta, B. 1968. Sulla presbiacusea in tribi africane molto primitive. *Mineiva otorinolaringolocica* 18: 101–112.

Smith, A. D. 1980. Age differences in encoding, storage, and retrieval. In *New directions in memory and aging: Proceedings of the George Talland Memorial Conference,* eds. L. W. Poon, J. L. Fozard, L. S. Cermack, D. Arenberg, and L. W. Thompson. Hillsdale, N.J.: Erlbaum.

Smith, R., and Prather, W. F. 1971. Phoneme discrimination in older persons under varying signal-to-noise conditions. *J. Speech Hearing Res.* 14: 630–635.

Society of Actuaries. 1979. Report of the committee on experience under individual health insurance. *Transactions of the Society of Actuaries,* Reports Number, pp. 235–288.

Sovijarvi, A. R. A., and Hyvarinen, J. 1974. Auditory cortical neurons in the cat sensitive to the direction of sound source movement. *Brain Res.* 73: 455–471.

Spencer, N. J., and Wollman, N. 1980. Lexical access for phonetic ambiguities. *Language and Speech* 23: 171–198.

Spieth, W. 1957. Downward spread of masking. *J. Acoust. Soc. Am.* 29: 502–505.

Spoendlin, H. 1975. Neuroanatomical basis of cochlear coding mechanisms. *Audiology* 14: 383–407.

Spoendlin, H. 1979. Neural connection of the outer hair cell system. *Acta Oto-Laryngol.* 87: 381–387.

Stephens, S. D. G. 1974. Methodological factors influencing loudness of short duration tones. *J. Sound Vib.* 37: 235–246.

Stern, J. A.; Oster, P. J.; and Newport, K. 1980. Reaction time measures, hemispheric specialization and age. In *Aging in the 1980's: Psychological Issues,* ed. L. W. Poon. Washington, D.C.: APA Press.

Stevens, J. C., and Marks, L. E. 1980. Cross-modality matching functions generated by magnitude estimation. *Perception & Psychophysics* 27: 379–389.

Stevens, S. S. 1954. Pitch discrimination, Mels and Kock's contention. *J. Acoust. Soc. Am.* 26: 1075–1077.

Stevens, S. S., and Davis, H. 1938. *Hearing: Its Psychology & Physiology.* New York: Wiley.

Stevens, S. S., and Newman, E. B. 1936. The localization of actual sources of sound. *Am. J. Psychol.* 48: 297–306.

Storandt, M. 1980. Verbal memory in the elderly. In *Language and communication in the elderly,* eds. L. K. Obler and M. L. Albert. Lexington, MA: Lexington Books.

Suga, N. 1969. Classification of inferior colliculus neurons of bats in terms of responses to pure tones, FM sounds and noise bursts. *J. Physiol.* (London) 200: 555–574.

Takahashi, T. 1971. The ultrastructure of the pathologic stria vascularis and spiral prominance in man. *Ann. Otol. Rhinol. Laryngol.* 80: 721–735.

Tasaki, I.; Davis, H.; and Eldredge, D. H. 1954. Exploration of cochlear potentials in guinea pig with a microelectrode. *J. Acoust. Soc. Am.* 26: 765–773.

Tasaki, I., and Spiropoulos, C. S. 1959. Stria vascularis as a source of endocochlear potential. *J. Neurophysiol.* 22: 149–155.

Thompson, D. J.; Sills, J. A.; Recke, K. S.; and Bui, D. M. 1979. Acoustic admittance and the aging ear. *J. Speech Hearing Res.* 22: 29–36.

Thompson, D. J.; Sills, J. A.; Recke, K. S.; and Bui, D. M. 1980. Acoustic reflex growth in the aging adult. *J. Speech Hearing Res.* 23: 405–418.

Tillman, T. W.; Carhart, R.; and Nicholls, S. 1973. Release from multiple maskers in elderly persons. *J. Speech Hearing Res.* 16: 152–160.

Tonndorf, J., and Khanna, S. M. 1970. The role of tympanic membrane in middle ear transmission. *Ann. Otol.* 79: 743–753.

Tonndorf, J.; Khanna, S. M.; and Fingerhood, B. J. 1966. The input impedance of the inner ear in cats. *Ann. Otol.* 75: 752–763.

Tonning, F. M. 1975. Auditory localization and its clinical applications. *Audiology* 14: 368–380.

Tsai, H. K.; Chou, F. S.; and Cheng, T. J. 1958. On changes in ear size with age, as found among Taiwanese and Formosans of Fukienese extraction. *J. Formosan Med. Assoc.* 57: 105–111.

Tsuchitani, C., and Boudreau, J. D. 1966. Single unit analysis of cat superior olive S segment with tonal stimuli. *J. Neurophysiol.* 29: 684–697.

Van der Sandt, W.; Glorig, A.; and Dickson, R. 1969. A survey of the acuity of hearing in the Kalahari Bushman. *Internat. Audiol.* 8: 290–298.

Vaughan, D. W. 1977. Age-related deterioration of pyramidal cell basal dendrites in rat auditory cortex. *J. Comp. Neurol.* 171: 501–516.

Vaughan, P. W., and Vincent, J. M. 1979. Ultra structure of neurons in the auditory cortex of aging rats: Morphometric study. *J. Neurocytol.* 8: 215–228.

Von Wedel, H., and Opitz, H. J. 1978. The influence of aging on middle ear function. *Laryngol. Rhinol. Otol.* (Stuttg) 57: 152–158.

Warren, L. R.; Wagener, J. W.; and Herman, G. F. 1978. Binaural analysis in the aging auditory system. *J. Gerontol.* 33: 731–736.

Warren, R. M. 1970. Perceptual restoration of missing speech sounds. *Science,* 167: 393–395.

Warren, R. M., and Gregory, R. L. 1958. An auditory analogue of the visual reversible figure. *Am. J. Psychol.* 4, 71: 612–613.

Warren, R. M., and Warren, R. P. 1966. A comparison of speech perception in childhood, maturity and old age by means of the verbal tranformation effect. *J. Verbal Learning and Verbal Behavior* 5: 142–146.

Warren, R. M., and Warren, R. P. 1971. Some age differences in auditory perception. *Bull. NY. Acad. Med.* 47: 1355–1377.

Weber, D. L., and Green, D. M. 1979. Suppression effects in backward and forward masking. *J. Acoust. Soc. Am.* 65: 1258–1267.

Webster, F. A. 1951. Influence of interaural phase on masked thresholds. *J. Acoust. Soc. Am.* 23: 452–462.

Welsh, O. L.; Luterman, D. M.; and Bell, B. 1969. The effects of aging on responses to filtered speech. *J. Gerontol.* 24: 189–192.

Whitfield, I. C. 1969. Response of the auditory nervous system to simple time-dependent acoustic stimuli. *Ann. NY. Acad. Sci.* 156: 671–677.

Whitfield, I. C., and Evans, E. F. 1965. Responses of auditory cortical neurons to stimuli of changing frequency. *J. Neurophysiol.* 28: 655–672.

Wier, C. C.; Jesteadt, W.; and Green, D. M. 1977. Frequency discrimination as a function of frequency and sensation level. *J. Acoust. Soc. Am.* 61: 178–184.

Williams, M. V. 1980. Receiver operating characteristics: The effect of distribution on between-group comparisons. In *Aging in the 1980's: Psychological Issues,* ed. L. W. Poon. Washington, D.C.: APA Press.

Wilson, R. H., and Carhart, R. 1971. Forward and backward masking: Interactions and additivity. *J. Acoust. Soc. Am.* 49: 1254–1263.

Wright, H. N. 1964. Backward masking for tones in narrow-band noise. *J. Acoust. Soc. Am.* 36: 2217–2221.

Wright, J. L., and Schuknecht, H. F. 1972. Atrophy of the spiral ligament. *Arch. Oto-Laryngol.* 96: 16–21.

Yost, W. A. 1974. Discrimination of interaural phase differences. *J. Acoust. Soc. Am.* 55: 1299–1303.

Yost, W. A. 1980. Man as mammal: Psychoacoustics. In *Comparative Studies of Learning in Vertebrates,* eds. A. M. Popper and R. R. Fay. New York: Springer-Verlag.

Zwislocki, J. 1972. A theory of central masking: Its partial validation. *J. Acoust. Soc. Am.* 52: 644–659.

Zwislocki, J. 1973. In search of physiological correlates of psychoacoustic characteristics. In *Basic Mechanisms in Hearing,* ed. A. R. Moller. New York: Academic Press.

Zwislocki, J. 1974. A possible neuro-mechanical sound analysis in the cochlea. *Acustica* 31: 354–359.

Zwislocki, J. 1975. Phase opposition between inner and outer hair cells and auditory sound analysis. *Audiology* 14: 443–445.

Zwislocki, J.; Buining, E.; and Glantz, J. 1968. Frequency distribution of central masking. *J. Acoust. Soc. Am.* 43: 1267–1271.

14
NEURAL AND VESTIBULAR AGING ASSOCIATED WITH FALLS

Alfred L. Ochs
Neuro-Ophthalmology Division
Department of Neurology

Janice Newberry
Department of Physical Therapy

Martin L. Lenhardt
Department of Otolaryngology

Stephen W. Harkins
Departments of Gerontology,
Psychiatry and Psychology

Medical College of Virginia
Richmond, Virginia

This chapter reviews neurological function, balance, and falls of the elderly. Disequilibrium and falls are a major health concern in the older population, particularly in the very old. As the present chapter illustrates, little is known of central, vestibular, proprioceptive, and visual decrements in relation to the practical problems faced by elderly persons in the day-to-day negotiation of their physical environment. A better understanding awaits creative and insightful study. Ultimately, we must understand the factors predisposing one to an injurious fall and develop appropriate methods of intervention. It is unlikely that these relationships will prove to be simple.

Reaching an understanding of age changes in physiological function will take us only part of the way towards preventing falls of the elderly, for we need to know to what extent, or even if, they are themselves responsible for falls. Full understanding in this area rests on making a clear distinction between changes caused by age *per se* and those caused by disease, even though distinguishing data are not generally available at this time. As is well recognized, the interaction among health factors, behavior, and age is quite complex (Siegler, Nowlin, and Blumenthal, 1980), and it is easier to raise questions than answer them. The problem, however, is to distinguish between the healthy aged nervous system and those that are diseased and then ask how well the aged nervous system integrates degraded sensory information to control balance and react defensively to its loss.

In this review we have considered the statistical incidence of falls with age, changes in vestibular and neurological systems pertaining to equilibrium, and how the elderly perform in quantitative measures of stance and gait. We hope that this review will promote the integration of these topics, which have largely been studied separately.

FALLS AND AGING

Falls are associated with a high incidence of morbidity and mortality in the elderly population. With advancing age, falls occur with increased frequency and are life-threatening events, especially for those 75 and older. In many cases, falls and their consequences result in limited functional mobility, dependence on family members for assistance, and possible institutionalization. The impairment of postural stability further provokes fear and anxiety, resulting in self-imposed limited mobility (Bhala, O'Donnell, Thoppil, 1982).

The incidence, causes, and sequelae of falls have received increasing attention in the last 30 years. Sheldon (1948) was among the first to provide data on incidence and possible causal factors of falls in community-residing elderly. With the increase in the elderly population during the last few decades, the importance of falls has been recognized, and the interest in them has expanded. Nevertheless, even the true incidence of noninjurious falls is not accurately known. Statistics depend on recollection of the incident by persons who have fallen and by their family members or are obtained from staff reports of hospitals and long-term-care facilities. Reported are those events that the individual considers significant or that are physically or emotionally traumatic. Multiple falls are erroneously estimated when the individual forgets the exact number. To illustrate the difficulty, ask yourself: How many falls have I had in the last twelve months? Mortality is also underestimated; even though a fall preceded and contributed to an individual's death, the fall often is not listed as a cause (Waller, 1978).

As with incidence, determining the etiology of falls presents problems. It is useful to divide falls into those arising from intrinsic and extrinsic factors (Agate, 1966). Intrinsic factors are physical changes, either age or disease-related, that increase the risk of falling. Extrin-sic factors are environmental hazards such as loose rugs, slippery floors or steps, poor lighting, and uneven terrain. Within these categories, falls are further classified by descriptions of the event. Intrinsic and extrinsic factors are interrelated in that physical debility can magnify the significance of external hazards so that it is often difficult to determine which factors are implicated, and to what degree. Even though these classifications describe the types of fall and the related contributing factors, they do not suggest the underlying physiological disequilibrium that preceded the event (Isaacs, 1978).

Environmental hazards and physiological changes differ for persons living in the community, in long-term-care facilities, and in acute-care facilities. The healthy elderly, especially those residing independently, may be the ones who are the more affected by the hazards of their environment, whereas elderly in acute- and long-term-care facilities are the frail types who may be more affected by general medical debility.

Mortality From Falls

Comprehensive data on mortality from accidents is published annually by the National Safety Council in *Accident Facts.* Accidents are the fourth leading cause of death in the United States, with deaths from falls surpassed only by deaths from motor vehicle accidents. In 1980, falls accounted for 12,300 deaths, at a rate of 5.4 per 100,000. Ominously, the death rate from falls increases exponentially with advanced age (Fig. 1). Similar increases in mortality from falls are reported in the *Statistical Bulletin* (1965, 1978).

Accidents are the seventh leading cause of death in the very old, with falls even surpassing deaths from automobile accidents for persons 75 and older. Not only does the incidence of falling increase with age, but trauma from a fall threatens homeostasis, which, with age, becomes increasingly more difficult to maintain. The elderly are thus more likely to die from their injuries than are younger individuals. "Sixty-nine per cent of the deaths from falls in 1980 were of persons 65 years old or older. Of these, about three-fifths occurred in

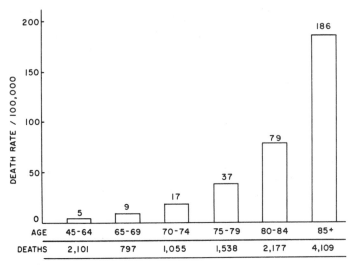

Figure 1.   Death rate from falls by age for 1978. (*From* Accident Facts (*1981*), *National Safety Council.*)

the home" (*Accident Facts,* 1981, p. 11). The higher percentage of falls in the home for this age group than for the general population surely reflects the greater amount of time spent there by elderly persons. The death rate for males is higher than for females. Table 1 shows the incidence of fatal falls in 1978 for persons 75 and older by sex.

Although mortality figures remain high, there has been a steady reduction in the rate of deaths from falls and, to a lesser extent, the death rate from all accidents. Deaths from falls declined in all age groups—from 16,926 in 1970 (8.3/100,000) to 12,300 in 1980 (5.4/ 100,000, a 35-percent drop in rate. During this 10-year period, the death rate from falls in the home declined by 31 percent, with the greatest reduction occurring in the 75+ age group. In this group, falls in and out of the home declined by 40 percent 1968 and 1978 (*Accident Facts,* 1971; 1981). Reduction in mortality from falls is helped by improved

management of medical complications, such as pneumonia and thrombophlebitis. It is also helped by an increased awareness of risk factors, leading to environmental improvement and the use of adaptive equipment, especially in age-segregated housing (Waller, 1978).

Fall of Institutionalized Elderly

Prospective studies of the elderly residing in institutional settings demonstrate a higher incidence of falls, attributable to the larger number "at risk" with predisposing medical problems. Although these individuals are within a protective environment, there is an age-related rise in the rate and severity of falls that is higher for females (718/1000) than males (551/1000). As is seen consistently throughout the literature, the rate rises with age (Gryfe, Amies, and Ashley, 1977).

Sehested and Severin-Nielsen (1977) examined falls in 511 patients in an acute-care geriatric unit over a one-year period; their mean age was 75 to 79 for males and 80 to 84 for females, and 89 percent were 65 and older. The highest fall rate was seen in the 55 to 59 age group, and this was associated with acutely ill patients who were unaccustomed to the restricted activity imposed by their disease. Acute and chronic illness itself causes instability and places an otherwise active person at a greater risk of falling. Disorientation

TABLE 1.   Death Rate by Sex for Persons 75 Years of Age and Older.
(*From* Accident Facts, *1981.*)

	DEATHS	DEATH RATE per 100,000
Males	3,020	91.7
Females	4,810	82.5
Total	7,830	85.8

on moving to a new environment is also a factor. Feist (1978) and Tinker (1979) noted a higher incidence of falling shortly after individuals are admitted to a geriatric facility.

Falls of Community-Residing Elderly

As with fatal falls, the incidence of nonfatal falls of community-residing elderly rises with successive age groups (Sheldon, 1948; Droller, 1955; Exton-Smith, 1977; Campbell, Reinken, Allen, and Martinez, 1981; Prudham and Evans, 1981). Approximately one-third of persons 65 and older have suffered one or more falls in the preceding year (Campbell, Reinken, Allen, and Martinez, 1981).

To determine the incidence and causes of falls, Droller (1955) questioned and medically examined 476 randomly chosen retired persons, of whom 35 percent had fallen. Of those aged 65, 37 percent reported falls, a figure that increased to 44.6 percent for those aged 75 and over. Unfortunately, the period during which these falls occurred is not reported. Persons who fell were described as generally "less fit," having more medical problems than those who did not report falls. Campbell, Reinken, Allen, and Martinez (1981) reported that of 553 persons aged 65 and older, 34 percent had sustained at least one fall during the previous 12-month period, and by the age 89, the incidence had increased to 45 percent. This finding is similar to that reported by Brocklehurst, Exton-Smith et al. (1978) for their non-injury control group. A slightly lower incidence has been reported by Prudham and Evans (1981). Of 2357 persons surveyed, 28 percent had fallen during the preceding year. The incidence rose steadily with age to a peak of 39.6 percent for those aged 80 to 84, after which it decreased to 35.2 percent. Of those persons who had fallen, 46.1 percent had done so on more than one occasion. The lowered incidence in this study may be partially attributed to the fitness of the subjects. Campbell et al. (1981) included some elderly from residential homes in their sample, whereas Prudham and Evans did not.

When examined by sex, females have a higher incidence of falls than males (Sheldon, 1948; Exton-Smith, 1977; Prudham and Ev-

ans, 1981). Exton-Smith reported that 30 percent of females and 13 percent of males aged 65 to 69 had fallen, figures virtually identical to the finding by Prudham and Evans of 30 percent for females and 14 percent for males. Both studies reveal an increase with age in both sexes, although differing in incidence in the older age groups. In females, the age range of most reported falls (43 to 50 percent) is 80 to 85, after which the incidence drops to 32 percent. For males, a peak of 31 percent at ages 80 to 84 was reported by Exton-Smith, with the percentage declining after age 85. Prudham and Evans, however, noted a steady rise for males, reaching as high as 41 percent for those aged 85 and older. Exton-Smith (1977, p. 47) attributed the lowered incidence of falls in the very old to "a characteristic of the biological elite whose physical fitness enables them to outlive their former contemporaries," but the decreased incidence in the oldest age groups may also be the result of a lower proportion of "at risk" elderly residing in the community, which presents the larger extrinsic risk factor.

Retrospective studies based on fallers who seek medical attention reveal an incidence of injury that ranges from 14 to 19 per 1,000 (Lucht, 1971; Waller, 1978). Waller compared 150 elderly fallers aged 60 and over to 150 matched elderly who reported no injury. Forty percent of the injured and 32 percent of the comparison sample reported at least one fall in the previous year. Brocklehurst, Exton-Smith, et al. (1978) reported an increase in prior falls, increasing with age in subjects who experienced a fracture as the result of their fall. In the 85 and over age group, 70 percent of fracture patients and 46 percent of controls reported previous falls. Waller found no increase in injury rate with age, although females who fell had a higher injury rate than males, 2.2 versus 1.4 percent.

Causes of Falls

One of the earliest studies made to determine the causes of falling was by Sheldon (1960). In this frequently cited work, 500 falls by 202 community-residing elderly were classified by the individual's description of the incident.

All subjects were at least 50, and 73 percent were 70 or over. The sample consisted of persons who reported to an emergency room (86), persons admitted to the hospital with a fracture resulting from the fall (59), persons referred by their physicians (57), and elderly persons contacted in their home (168). Although a distinction was often difficult to determine, 224 falls were attributed to environmental causes (accidents and trips) and 276 to intrinsic causes. The incidence by type per age group was not reported. Sheldon's data are summarized in Table 2.

Similar descriptive terminology has been used by other investigators (Droller, 1955; Hodkinson, 1962; Gryfe, Amies, and Ashley, 1977; Exton-Smith, 1977; Overstall, 1977; Prudham and Evans, 1981; Campbell, Reinken, Allen, and Martinez, 1981). As with incidence, the degree to which intrinsic or extrinsic factors are implicated varies with the population examined. Those residing independently in the community appear to be more susceptible to extrinsic factors. One-third to one-half of all falls are attributed to accidents or trips (Sheldon, 1960; Overstall et al., 1977; Exton-Smith, 1977). Trips occur more frequently in the younger segment of the aged population since their greater mobility exposes them to more environmental risk (Exton-

Smith, 1977; Brocklehurst, Exton-Smith, et al., 1978).

With advancing age, the importance of extrinsic factors declines, and the influence of intrinsic factors increases, seemingly as a result of both more limited mobility and increased debility. Multiple chronic medical problems are implicated as a decisive factor in the postural instability of persons in long-term-care facilities (Kalchthaler, Bascon, and Quintos, 1978) and acute-care facilities (Sehested and Severin-Nielson, 1977). The effects of medical illness and debility are also seen in community-residing elderly. Waller (1978) reported that in those elderly who had fallen repeatedly, those with medical illness outnumbered the healthy by three to one. Among the pathological mechanisms most implicated in falls are vertigo, postural hypotension, cardiac arrhythmias, vertebro-basilar insufficiency, cervical spondylolysis, and drug side effects. The significance of multiple medications and their effect on postural hypotension and falling have been demonstrated by Blumenthal and Davie (1980). Recently, previously undetected cardiac arrhythmias have been associated with a history of falling (Gordon, Huang, and Gryfe, 1982). Falls accounted for 20 percent of the total admissions to one geriatric unit during a one-year period, with cerebral ischemia the primary etiology (Naylor and Rosin, 1970). It has been speculated that changes in neuromuscular mechanisms are responsible for many of the falls categorized as accidents or trips (Droller, 1955; Sheldon, 1960; 1966; Hasselkus, 1974; Isaacs, 1978; Prudham and Evans, 1981). By comparing 47 elderly female patients 60 or over who had been hospitalized for fractured femur with a matched cohort of women hospitalized for elective orthopedic procedures, Wootton, Bryson, et al. (1982) described the typical woman who has a significantly greater risk of falling: "Her body weight is lower, probably because of loss of both fat and muscle mass; her bone density, particularly her trabecular bone density, is reduced and there is concomitant vertebral collapse. She is prone to fall, both because of poor eyesight and postural instability, and her plasma protein concentrations are lower than normal for her age. Her mental ability

TABLE 2.   Reported Causes of 500 Falls.
(*From Sheldon, 1960.*)

TYPE	INCIDENCE	PERCENTAGE
Accidental falls*	171	34.2
Drop attacks†	125	25.0
Trips	53	10.6
Vertigo	37	7.4
Recognizable CNS lesion	27	5.4
Neck hyperextension	20	4.0
Postural hypotension	18	3.6
Weakness in legs	16	3.2
Falling out of bed or chair	10	2.0
Uncertain	23	4.6
Total of all falls	500	100

*"Accidental falls" involve a loss of balance resulting from environmental hazards, excluding trips.
†"Drop attacks" are "a sudden loss of tone limited to the antigravity muscles normally concerned in the maintenance of the upright position."

appears to be significantly reduced." There have been several reports of a clustering of falls just prior to death in some older, seriously ill patients (Howell, 1971; Gryfe, Amies, and Ashley 1977). This premonitory sign of impending death is especially significant in those persons whose general weakness and disequilibrium is so severe that they are unable to rise following the fall (Wild, Nayak, and Isaacs, 1981; Murphy and Isaacs, 1982).

Summary

Little is known about the specific mechanisms that produce falls in the elderly population. What is clear is that with age there is a progressive rise in their incidence. Risk factors vary for the segment of the population examined. Younger, healthy elderly residing in the community appear to be more susceptible to accidental falls or trips produced by the hazards of the environment. Older individuals, especially those residing in long-term-care facilities or sheltered living environments, appear to be more susceptible to falls caused by intrinsic factors, either age-related or disease-produced. Females fall more often and have a higher rate of injury from their falls, but males have a higher mortality rate. The physiological reasons underlying the increasing risk are incompletely understood. Multiple risk factors in addition to age itself, such as the effects of chronic illness, general debility, cognitive deficits, and side effects of medication, have been implicated.

It is clear that many factors interact, indeed seemingly conspire, to increase dramatically the risk of falling, injury, and death in our elderly population. Intrinsic factors combine with environmental hazards in many ways, depending on health and living conditions, to increase risk and fear. In the following section we will discuss the physiological changes that form the biological substrate for this serious problem.

AGING OF THE VESTIBULAR SYSTEM

The loss of equilibrium with old age has been referred to as *presbystasis* by Krmpotic-Nemanic (1969). Although as ill-defined as pres-

bycusis in the auditory system, presbystasis is perhaps even more nebulus since sensory reception in the vestibular, visual, and proprioceptive areas are all involved, as well as many integrative functions throughout the central nervous system. The extent of presbystasis depends upon the components involved and the extent of their involvement. Certainly, aging decrement of vestibular function is a significant factor underlying the increased incidence of falls in the elderly.

Anatomy and Physiology

This section is intended to establish a background for discussing the aging of this complex system. Current research into vestibular function is active and wide-ranging. A comprehensive review of vestibular physiology and its interaction with the visual system has recently been presented and can be recommended to the specialist and nonspecialist alike (see Henn, Cohen, and Young, 1980).

One of the several end-organs concerned with equilibrium and spatial orientation is the *statokinetic labyrinth,* known commonly as the *vestibular apparatus.* Vestibular receptors are contained within the inner ear in a membranous labyrinth, consisting of a series of fluid-filled sacs fully enclosed in a bony structure. Angular acceleration of the head is detected by the semicircular canals, whereas the detection of gravity, or, more precisely, of any linear acceleration including gravity, is brought about by the *saccule* (little sack) and the *utricle* (little bottle). The saccule and utricle taken together are termed *otoliths* (or, synonomously, *statoliths*). The sensory areas of both are given the common name *macula.* Anatomically, the longitudinal axis of the utricular macula and the saccular macula are approximately perpendicular to each other. These relationships can be seen in Fig. 2. Attached to these maculae by membranous filaments are calcium-carbonate crystals, *statoconia.* Since the density of the statoconia is greater than that of the surrounding endolymphatic fluid, they move in response to both linear acceleration and the stationary acceleration of gravity. The neurosensory end-organs are *hair cells,* whose body is attached to the

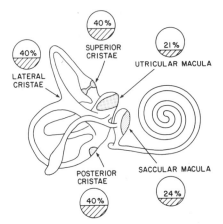

Figure 2. Anatomy of inner ear showing relationship of sensory elements. The amount of sensory element loss after age 70 is indicated in relative terms and discussed in the text. (*From Rosenhall, 1973; Engstrom, Bergstrom, and Rosenhall, 1974.*)

macula and whose hairlike appendages contact the statoconia. These hairs are bent by movement of the crystals with respect to the macula, presumably alter receptor cell membrane conductance, and so stimulate first-order vestibular neurons. The biophysics of the semicircular canals is quite similar.

The three *semicircular canals,* so named because they traverse half a circle, are planar and oriented at mutual right angles to one another. Each has a bulge at one end, an *ampulla,* which contains the sensory end-organs. The three ampullae and the opposite ends of their semicircular canals open into a common chamber—which is, in fact, the previously mentioned utrical—and are filled with *endolymph,* a free-flowing, slightly viscous fluid. The sensory end-organ, the *crista,* is homologous to the macula. Bulging into each ampulla are hairs of the sensory cells imbedded in a gelatinous membrane, which together constitute the *cupula.* Since the specific gravity of the cupula is the same as that of the endolymph, linear acceleration has no effect on it, unlike the otoliths. The structure of the sensory hair cells varies; there are two distinct types, which apparently age differently (see below). Type I cells, which are flask-shaped, are found at the summit of the cristae and in the center of the maculae. Type II cells are cylindrical and are located chiefly at the periphery of both the cristae and maculae.

When the head rotates, the endolymph (analogous to the inertial mass of the statoconia) tends to remain in place, whereas the cupula, with the hairs protruding into it, is displaced. As rotational speed becomes constant, the deviation between the endolymph and the cupula diminishes, and the cupula returns to its original position. On stopping (deceleration), the cupula is displaced in the opposite direction.

Rotation of the head in the plane of any given canal produces a counterrotation of the eyes in the plane of that canal (Ewald's First Law) and results in stronger neuronal stimulation in one direction of rotation than in the other (Ewald's Second and Third Laws, for horizontal and vertical canals, respectively) (Baloh and Honrubia, 1979). Vestibular neurons have a high resting discharge rate—e.g., 90 spikes/sec in the monkey (Goldberg and Fernandez, 1971)—and rotation of the head in the preferred direction increases neural activity sharply, whereas rotation in the opposite direction causes a mild reduction in firing. Centrally, this asymmetry is canceled by the equal but opposing asymmetry of the opposite vestibular apparatus, which is why acute unilateral vestibular loss produces profoundly debilitating vertigo. The asymmetrical discharge pattern of each canal, coupled with the normally high spontaneous discharge rate, results in a low threshold system, corresponding to a psychophysical minimum-acceleration threshold in man of approximately 0.1 deg/sec² (Clark and Stewart, 1968).

The otolith afferents have a lower resting discharge, with maximized firing depending upon head tilt—horizontal for the uticular macula and vertical for the saccular macula (Fernandez and Goldberg, 1976; Fernandez, Goldberg, and Abend, 1972; Goldberg and Fernandez, 1971). The threshold for static body tilt is 2 to 3 degrees from the vertical (McFarland, 1946, p. 361). Both otolith organs also respond to changes in linear acceleration. The vertical threshold is reported to range from 4 to 21 cm/sec² and the horizontal, from 2 to 20 cm/sec² (Armstrong, 1943). Afferent information to the brainstem is related more to head rotation than to acceleration (Fernandez and Goldberg, 1971; Melvill Jones and Milsum, 1970; Shinoda and Yoshida,

1974), and this fact may partially explain why rotary motion has such a devastating effect on some elderly patients.

Degeneration with Age

Although pathological changes with age have been extensively examined in the cochlea (Johnsson, 1974), relatively less attention has been given to documenting concomitant change in the saccule. On examining both at postmortem, one author reported no change related to age in the vestibular labyrinth (Jorgensen, 1961), whereas others noted saccular degeneration only incidentally (Schuknecht, Igarashi, and Gacek, 1965). However, Johnsson (1971) reported on 150 temporal bone dissections, wherein he observed that saccular degeneration is consistently associated with degeneration of the cochlea. Degeneration of the saccular and utricular maculae have been noted in sensory cells, neurofibers, and statoconia in older patients, as illustrated in Fig. 2.

Statoconia. Saccular degeneration, and to a lesser extent utricular degeneration, is usually accompanied by a loss of statoconia, noted in patients 60 years and older (Johnsson, 1971). This is thought to be due to mechanical wear or to defects in the normal physiological regrowth and replacement of these crystals, which occurs throughout life. The destruction of the statoconia appears to involve the dissolution of previously well-formed calcite crystals (Ross, 1977), which begins at the posterior tip and proceeds anteriorly. The surface of the statoconia first becomes pitted, followed by central dissolution, degeneration, and then usually a complete loss. The cause of statoconia loss has not yet been determined, but changes in the ionic composition of the endolymph may allow the statoconia to dissolve slowly (Ross, 1977). Further biochemical work is required to confirm this hypothesis.

Hair Cells and Nerve. Reduction of vestibular hair cells with age is graphically portrayed in Fig. 3. A 20-percent reduction in the maculae and a 40-percent reduction in the cristae for older patients (50 and over) have been found, as compared to the amounts counted

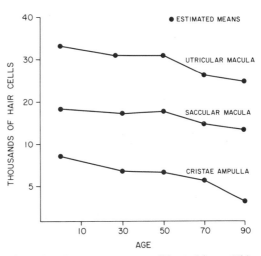

Figure 3.   Average receptor cell loss with age. This illustration ignores the considerable scatter in the original data. (*From Rosenhall, 1973.*)

in dissections from patients under 40 (Rosenhall, 1973; Engstrom, Bergstrom, and Rosenhall, 1974). Although macular degeneration is less severe in the saccule than in the utricle, pronounced utricular degeneration is confined to a small medial area; the remaining surface exhibits diffuse degeneration, as does the surface of the entire saccula (Rosenhall, 1973; Johnsson and Hawkins, 1972). The cristae show more pronounced degeneration in the summit, with less on the periphery.

Age-related degeneration results in sensory-cell loss. As a cell degenerates, it shrinks considerably, its free surface decreases, and finally it disappears. The supporting cells fill in its place, forming a scar on the reticular lamina, and the former cell is lost forever (Rosenhall and Rubin, 1975). In some older individuals, ciliary fragility may increase, and at times the cilia may clump together into a giant stalk. The latter observation might be an electron-microscopy-preparation artifact, however, and not necessarily portray the effect of natural aging accurately, even though clumping is not seen in the cila of younger individuals (Hilding and House, 1964). Metabolic disturbances prior to cell degeneration have also been found. There is usually an accumulation of lipofuscin in the sensory cells as well as in the supporting cells. Lipofuscin is also reported to accumulate more in Type I hair cells than in Type II cells (Engstrom, Ades, et al., 1977).

The normal young vestibular nerve has about 19,000 fibers, a figure that decreases by 5 percent at age 60 (Rasmussen, 1940). Krmpotic-Nemanic (1971) reported that the holes for the nerve bundles in the region of the spinal tract close and disappear. As the holes close, there is an accumulation of newly formed tissue that compresses the nerve fibers and possibly the arteries as well, an action that could contribute to the nerve fiber loss noted by Rasmussen (1940). Nerve fiber degeneration also continues into advanced age (Bredberg, 1968), not only in number but also in diameter (Bergstrom, 1973). Engstrom, Bergstrom, and Rosenhall (1974) described an approximate 40-percent reduction in saccular, utricular, and ampullar nerve fibers when comparing young against elderly groups, whereas Engstrom, Ades, et al. (1977) found degenerative changes in the synaptic membranes, suggesting an age decrement in neural transmission.

Clinical Manifestations

The loss in statoconia, hair cells, and nerve fibers observed anatomically has yet to be completely related to vestibular function in the elderly. Schukneckt (1974) drew attention to what he termed *vestibular ataxia,* which is characterized by a constant sense of disequilibrium when moving. This disorder is felt to be related to the efferent vestibular tracts, rather than to changes in the afferent pathway, and can also lead to an increased incidence of falling. Approximately 75 percent of women older than 85 reported experiencing some kind of dizziness (Steele and Crowe, 1970).

Evidence for hereditary vestibular degeneration has implications in understanding human vestibular dysfunction. Schuknecht, Igarashi, and Gacek (1965) reported hereditary cochlea-saccula degeneration in mutant strains of laboratory mammals. Although the vestibular neurons, utricle, and semicircular canals appeared grossly normal, close examination revealed collapsed saccular walls adhering to the otolithic membrane, and about half of the hair cells were missing. In human beings, a careful history may reveal the hereditary involvement of peripheral and central ves-

tibular functions. For example, some patients report that, as children, they couldn't ride in cars without becoming sick, had difficulty on swings, etc. These patients may also show much more severe vestibular effects after accidents or virus infections than expected or have vertiginous episodes when under stress (Hecker, Haug, and Herndon, 1974). Although not systematically investigated, these observations provide reason to screen subjects thoroughly, since possible genetic disposition may be misinterpreted as a severe aging effect when its clinical expression becomes manifest in later life.

Little clinical use has been made of vestibular exercises with the elderly dizzy patient, as advocated by Overstall, Hazell, and Johnson (1981). These exercises are reported to have benefited a majority of conscientious patients with movement induced vertigo (Cooksey, 1946; Hecker, Haug, and Herndon, 1974; Pfaltz, 1977; Norre and de Weerdt, 1979). Vestibular exercises could be integrated into a physical fitness program, especially in an institutional setting, and may become a viable alternative or supplement to medication in the management of vertigo.

Physiological Changes with Age

After reviewing the sensory-cell decline, particularly after age 50, it might be expected that vestibular reactivity would decrease with progressing age. The precise functional variation that correlates with anatomical change is difficult to determine, however, because of its extensive neural interconnection with other sensory-motor systems. Although it seems logical to conclude that there is less information available to the brain from aged vestibular receptors, the relationship between diminished physiological function and psychophysical limitations has been poorly explored.

Black (1977) found that energy expended in maintenance of equilibrium increases as a linear function of age from 15 years onwards. There is no evidence, however, for a corresponding loss of peripheral elements over this age span. As will be discussed in the following sections, multiple interacting factors need to be considered to determine how loss of vestibular function might impair balance and the sense of equilibrium in the elderly. Vestibular function is measured by causing endolymph to flow through at least one semicircular canal, an action that elicits a compensatory eye rotation with velocity proportional to the angular flow rate of the endolymph (Ewald's First Law; see previous discussion). Position of intended gaze is restored periodically by involuntary, rapid refixations. This "beating" of the eyes, termed *nystagmus,* is seen to have an irregular sawtooth waveshape when displayed graphically. Traditionally, nystagmus is elicited by cooling or warming an ear canal with flowing water or air, causing a continuous endolymphatic flow by thermal convection. Another method is to spin the subject and record the nystagmus caused by postrotary deceleration.

Arslan (1957) found nystagmic hypoexcitability to caloric stimulation in 30 of his 50 subjects aged 49 to 84, with 14 subjects having normal nystagmic values. Schoder (1973) described vestibular test results in subjects aged 10 to 80 and found subjects who were 60 or older had significantly stronger nystagmic reactions than middle-aged subjects. Bruner and Norris (1971) also found that intensity of the nystagmic reaction (latency, duration, slow phase velocity, amplitude, and maximum frequency) increased up to their seventh decade in dizzy patients. When healthy subjects are studied in a design with numerous age groupings, a different pattern is observed.

Mulch and Petermann (1979) studied caloric reactions in 102 healthy subjects, ranging from 11 to 70. They found that the maximum frequency and total number of nystagmus beats for the 51 to 60 age group were 40 and 57 percent greater than the corresponding values for the youngest age group, respectively. The maximum value of slow phase velocity in the 41 to 50 age group was 80 percent faster and 84 percent larger in amplitude than the corresponding values in the 21 to 30 age group. The oldest healthy subjects, aged 61 to 70, had weaker reactions on all measures. Although the conflicts of data are not completely resolved, most careful work documents a caloric hyperexcitability in mid-life (fourth and fifth decades) and a reduction in caloric

nystagmus responses in healthy elderly subjects (seventh decade) as compared with responses of healthy young subjects. The midlife increase in caloric responsivity is further supported by the work of Minnigerode, Grohmann, and Vontin (1967), who found that the maximum value for the total amplitude of postrotatory nystagmus occurred in the third decade, excluding their teenage values. Zelenka and Slanimova (1964) reported that the largest value of postrotation-induced nystagmus duration was found in the 40 to 50 age bracket.

It can thus be concluded that maximum values of typically reported nystagmus parameters are age-dependent, but not in a progressively diminishing fashion. It is in middle or late-middle age that subjects show the most intense nystagmus, but why it occurs at this time is unknown. A peak in caloric responsivity may not correlate with an increased ability to maintain equilibrium, however, nor does a mild decrease in responsivity necessarily indicate decreased vestibular function. A measurement artifact may also be involved. For example, the temperature differential across the semicircular canal is moderated by local blood flow. Age variation in vascular dilation may be partially responsible for age changes in caloric nystagmus parameters, as well as the age-related increase in their standard deviation (Bruner and Norris, 1971).

With increasing use of the servo-driven, torsion-swing chair to stimulate the vestibulo–ocular reflex directly, investigators may soon quantitate aging changes in vestibular responsivity more precisely. Preliminary evidence from a multicenter cooperative study of healthy adults conflicts with the evidence from measures of caloric and postrotary nystagmus. One group reports no change in vestibulo–ocular responsivity from ages 35 to 65, whereas another found a gradual lag in response with age only at higher sinusoidal rotation frequencies (0.08 and 0.16 Hz). In neither preliminary report is a peak manifest in late middle age at any rotational frequency (J. Parmentier, Contraves Goerz Corp., personal communication).

Both inner ears must act equally in regard to positional stimulation; otherwise, the entire reflex mechanism that regulates body position may be altered, resulting in falls or imbalance. Aging changes on each side may be qualitatively or quantitatively different, depending upon the patient's health, disease history, and possibly heredity. If the reduction in sensory-cell population after age 70, as depicted in Fig. 3, is asymmetric in the cristae or between the two ears, disequilibrium could result. Recently, there has been experimental support for the existence of functional vestibular asymmetry in the elderly. Mulch and Petermann (1979) made the interesting observation that intra-ear differences in nystagmic responsivity are age-related. Subjects in their middle years show less side-to-side difference than elderly subjects. If this observation is verified, then asymmetry in peripheral excitability, not adequately compensated for in the central vestibular pathways, may lead to disequilibrium.

CHANGES IN THE NERVOUS SYSTEM AFFECTING EQUILIBRIUM

Standing on two feet demands maintenance of static equilibrium in a narrowly stable state. A small perturbation in any horizontal direction will deflect the body's center of gravity to a point no longer directly above the feet; if this deflection is not arrested, a fall will ensue. Normal walking and running are exercises in static disequilibrium, although dynamic equilibrium is maintained by carefully timed movements of the entire body. In order to lift one foot, body weight must be transferred to the other by movement of the pelvis. Physically, the body's center of gravity is in a state of fall in the direction of intended motion (Steindler, 1955; Martin, 1967a). This narrow equilibrium is maintained by coordinated body movements under the control of a healthy nervous system. As the nervous system ages, its ability to sense and control movement is impaired.

The characteristic gait of the healthy aged has been distinguished from that of youth (Kenshalo, 1977a): "The step tends to shorten and the base tends to widen. Side-to-side sway is significantly greater in older persons than in the young (Tokumasu and Kawano, 1976). Young people tend to walk by transferring

their weight from the ball of one foot to the heel of the other. The elderly tend to shift their body weight from the ball of one foot to the ball of the other and they do not lift their feet as high as they once did. This gives their gait a shuffling appearance."

Kenshalo's description of aged gait is confirmed in virtually all respects in a detailed study of the normal walking of healthy men, to age 87, who were determined to be free of neurological disease (Murray, Kory, and Clarkson, 1969). The exception is that these healthy elderly lifted their feet higher than the younger subjects, perhaps in response to a fear of tripping. The walking patterns of older and younger healthy male subjects are illustrated in Fig. 4. Murray, Kory, and Clarkson comment that the shorter and broader

Figure 4.   "Differences in the saggital positions of the body of older (left figure) and younger (right figure) men at the instant of heel-strike. In comparison to younger men, the older men show shorter step lengths; decreased excursions of hip flexion-extension; decreased extension of the ankle and decreased elevation of the heel of the rear limbs; decreased heel-floor angle and decreased elevation of the toe of the forward limb; decreased shoulder flexion on the foreward arc of the arm swing and decreased elbow extension on the backward arc." Illustrated are walking patterns of subjects determined to be without evidence of neurological deficits except for diminished or absent vibratory sensation of the lower limbs. (*From Murray, Kory, and Clarkson, 1969. Used with permission.*)

stride apparently serves to decrease precariousness in maintaining balance. Other quantitative studies of gait with age include subjects in various states of health. Not surprisingly, aging changes in walking are magnified in the presence of disease (Finley, Cody, and Finizie, 1969; Imms and Edholm, 1981) and in those who have been hospitalized following a fall (Guimaraes and Isaacs, 1980).

"An attitude of general flexion is also one of the hallmarks of old age. Head and neck are held craned forward; there is a gentle dorsal kyphosis; upper limbs are bent at elbows and wrists; while the hips and knees are also slightly flexed . . . Thus the young actor, in assuming the role of an old man, actually adopts and unwittingly assumes many components of an extrapyramidal syndrome" (Critchley, 1956).

The Extrapyramidal Hypothesis

More than 25 years ago, the eminent neurologist MacDonald Critchley proposed on clinical grounds that the stance, gait, and attitude of the healthy aged exhibit many aspects of akinetic extrapyramidal disorder, of which Parkinson's disease is a frank pathological model (Critchley, 1956). Recent physiological, pharmacological, and biochemical evidence supports this proposal. Critchley's proposition may provide a unifying model for observing many of the subtle changes that may affect our equilibrium and agility as we age.

Barbeau (1976) inverted Critchley's argument by proposing that the basic pathogenic mechanism of Parkinson's disease is accelerated aging. He proposed that both the symptoms of Parkinson's disease and normal aging are caused by an imbalance of dopaminergic and cholinergic neurotransmitter systems within the basal ganglia, a thesis generally accepted for Parkinson's disease (Kutt and McDowell, 1979, Chap. 3). The extrapyramidal aspects of aging, arising from a decrease in dopaminergic function, were assumed to be acquired through the accumulation of random degenerative processes, accelerated by vascular, infectious, and toxic factors (Barbeau, 1976). We note that this proposed mechanism, which is a "disease model" of aging,

is not universally accepted, although it certainly holds true for many individuals.

The proposal that some deleterious changes with age are caused by extrapyramidal deterioration is supported by anatomic, physiologic, and biochemical studies in aging human beings and experimental animals. Although anatomical changes occur throughout the brain with age, this should not overshadow the finding of more specific deterioration of the basal ganglia and selective atrophy of highly pigmented neurons of the substantia nigra, which is functionally a part of the extrapyramidal system (Brizzee, Ordy, Knox, and Jirge, 1980; McGeer, McGeer, and Suzuki, 1977). Recordings of motor unit activity in healthy aged show a prolonged latency of activation of single motor units and an inability to sustain neuronal firing, as compared to young adults (Petajan and Jarcho, 1975). These defects were exaggerated in patients with Parkinson's disease and were reversible with L-dopa. Marshall and Berrios (1979) have shown that the impaired swimming posture of aged rats is improved by administering either L-dopa or the dopamine receptor stimulant, apomorphine. Beck (1978) hypothesized that dopaminergic hypofunction in the aging brain could induce the slow reflexes that are also characteristic of Parkinson's disease. Samorajski (1975), Beck (1978), and Roth (1981) have each reviewed recent biochemical literature on the dopamine system in the aging brain. Dopaminergic function is shown to be impaired both in synthesis and effect, although details vary with the type of receptor system, brain region, and the species examined. A decline in functional effectiveness of the dopamine system in aged humans has been reported in extrapyramidal nuclei (McGeer, McGeer, and Suzuki, 1977; Robinson, Sourkes, et al., 1977).

We further add a clinical description of certain elderly fitting this hypothesis. Stammering gait as described by Wright (1979) is a hesitancy or inability to initiate walking and turning seen in some elderly persons. Although an identical disorder of initiation of movement is a common feature of Parkinson's disease, the elderly with stammering gait are neurologically distinct. It is noteworthy that walking can be initiated in both by creating an obstacle over which the affected individual must first step (Wright, 1979; Martin, 1967a).

The confluence of clinical, physiological, and pharmacological reports on the similarity of normal aging with frank extrapyramidal disease forms a compelling thesis that certainly should be studied in detail. The strict association of healthy aging with mild Parkinson's disease, however, seems not to be completely correct. Aged patients with great difficulty in walking about will have no problem using their hands in playing musical instruments. Although hemiparkinsonism exists, it has not been reported to involve only the lower extremities (Sabin, 1982). Petajan and Jarcho (1975) report that their healthy aged subjects differ (see above) in that parkinsonian patients are unable to adjust the frequency of motor-unit firing whereas the healthy aged person has no difficulty in this regard. Moreover, as will be discussed below, many changes occur in the aging nervous system that also affect balance and gait but are quite unrelated to extrapyramidal function.

Reaction Time

Age-related slowing of reaction time is only peripherally related to the problem of maintaining physical equilibrium. Welford (1977), in the first volume of this Handbook, reviewed the extensive literature on this subject and discussed the physiological components of reaction time, many of which are impaired with age. Although the most important change in reactive response with age is loss of speed, the main components of this loss arise from central mechanisms. Only minor decrements in reaction time are caused by changes in sensory and motor end-organs or speed of nervous conduction (cf. Norris, Shock, and Wagman, 1953). Welford (1977) concluded his review of motor performance by noting that it is maximal movements that are most affected by age. Everyday manipulatory tasks remain relatively unaffected since they usually do not involve maximal muscle performance and can be mentally prepared for in advance, even though myographic recordings of preparatory muscle activity in the aged (60 to 90) is diminished and latency extended (Mankovsky, Mints, Lisenyuk, 1982).

Significant latency increase with age is seen when unpredictable stimuli are presented. Melvill Jones and Watt (1971a,1971b) have shown that stretch reflexes in the human gastrocnemius muscle in response to ankle jerk are too slow to contribute to the deceleration of a fall. Rather, they describe a high-order reflex, preprogrammed in the spinal cord, which is detectable myographically in normal stepping and hopping before the foot hits the ground. Spinal reflex activity alone is ineffective in preventing a fall; unless a slip can be detected centrally in time to initiate a preprogrammed neuromuscular response, a fall will occur. Accidental slips are unpredictable and no doubt contribute to falls as the aged person's reaction time lengthens. In response, it is common for an elderly person to adopt a cautious gait and so even further mimic the extrapyramidal patient.

Sensory-Motor Functions

It is reasonable to suppose that age-related changes in kinesthetic sensory receptors, afferent and efferent neurons, and skeletal muscle anatomy adversely affect equilibrium, even though these changes cause little increase in reaction time. Unfortunately, there have been very few investigations on complex movements with age. Potvine and co-workers (1980) tested 61 normal men, ranging in age from 20 to 80, with an extensive battery of quantitative neurological tests. Statistically significant age-related linear decrease in function was found in almost all measures. Complex everyday tasks showed a decline in function of 21 to 43 percent over the age span. For example, speed of handwriting and putting on a shirt declined by 30 to 40 percent, respectively. The test most sensitive to the aging process is one-legged standing with eyes closed, showing a 100-percent decline over the 20 to 80 year span (i.e., a linear regression plot of performance with age predicts the actual performance of 80-year-olds, who were all unable to perform the task). Vibration sensitivity is the next most affected measure, with the greatest decline seen in the lower extremities, a finding well documented by other workers (Rosenberg, 1958); Perret and Regli, 1970; Verrillo, 1980). Sophisticated physiological measurements, such as vestibular servo-chair testing and nerve-conduction studies, which might correlate with affected performance, were not performed. Although many physiological and anatomical changes occur in the healthy aged nervous system that are obviously involved in the maintenance of equilibrium (reviewed by Smith and Sethi, 1975; Kenshalo, 1977b; 1979), we do not know in detail how these changes degrade the sense of balance.

Vision

An important exception is our understanding of the visual system's normal "proprioceptive" role in the maintenance of equilibrium (Lee and Lishman, 1975). Closing the eyes increases body sway (Travis, 1945; Edwards, 1946), as does moving the visual environment when the eyes are open. Almost any visual perturbation will induce a compensatory body shift (Witkin and Wapner, 1950; Dichgans, Brandt, and Held, 1975; Lestienne, Soechting, and Berthoz, 1977; Bles, Kapteyn, and de Wit, 1977). For example, Lee and Lishman (1975) induced anterior-posterior sway by swinging the walls of a room past a subject standing on a stationary floor. Illusory perception of motion, *vection,* can likewise be elicited (Held, Dichgans, and Bauer, 1975; Berthoz, Pavard, and Young, 1975). A study by Brandt, Dichgans, and Koenig (1973) is especially noteworthy in its demonstration that the illusion of rotation, *circularvection,* can be induced with peripheral vision, even while appropriate but reversed optokinetic nystagmus is being elicited from the central visual field with stripes moving in the opposite direction from those of the surrounding drum. A mechanism by which vision may influence posture is suggested by microelectrode records in animal vestibular nuclei that show that visual motion modulates the vestibular neuronal firing rate (Dichgans and Brandt, 1974; Daunton and Thomson, 1979; Waespe and Henn, 1979).

Defects of vision could therefore lead to defects in posture and gait. A young individual with acquired blindness, however, can walk quite normally in a familiar environment. A visual defect will seriously manifest itself in stance and gait only when there are simultaneous defects in somatosensory and vestibular function, yet indeed this is often the condition of age. Many elderly have rather good corrected visual acuity as measured with the standard Snellen eye chart. Nevertheless, recent sophisticated tests of visual function show a decline in contrast sensitivity with age at all spatial frequencies (Skalka, 1980; Sekuler, Hutman, and Owsley, 1980; Sekuler and Hutman, 1980; Hutman and Sekuler, 1980; McGrath and Morrison, 1981; Owsley and Sekuler, 1982). The defect is independent of ocular changes associated with aging: cataract, glaucoma, and senile miosis. Rather, the change is probably neural in origin, although the exact locus (loci) and mechanism is yet to be determined. It is not unreasonable to assume that some of the decrease is related to the almost 50-percent decline in neurons in the macular projection of the human visual cortex that has been reported to occur by age 87 (Devaney and Johnson, 1980).

We speculate, as have Sekuler and co-workers (1980), that the requirement for three times as much visual contrast may well degrade the information important to visual stabilization. There are a few studies of the elderly bearing directly on this question. Tobis, Nayak and Hoehler (1981) found an age-related decrease in the accuracy of judging vertical and horizontal meridians, which was accentuated in those individuals who had suffered at least one fall in the preceding year. Brocklehurst, Robertson, and James-Groom (1982) found no statistically significant relationship between a history of falls or of body sway to defects of visual acuity as measured with a Snellen eye chart, although poor Snellen acuity is reported characteristic of elderly post-fall patients with a fractured femur (Wooton, Bryson, et al., 1982). Nevertheless, acuity determined with a Snellen eye chart is a measure of central (foveal) visual acuity, and as suggested above and demonstrated by Begbie (1967), sway is primarily stabilized with peripheral vision. We might suppose that at least some of these elderly suffered reduction in low spatial-frequency contrast sensitivity—i.e., a peripheral defect—but this variable was not examined explicitly by Brocklehurst and colleagues.

A visual object seen at a distance (e.g., at 20 m) is less effective in stabilizing body sway than a nearby visual reference (Brandt, Bles, Arnold, and Kapteyn, 1979). Furthermore, the absence of nearby visual reference induces height vertigo, that unpleasant sensation and fear of falling noted at the edge of a cliff. Should reduced contrast sensitivity correspondingly reduce visual body stabilization, the perceived result may be analogous to height vertigo, and an elderly person's fear of falling may be physiologic as well as psychologic.

BODY SWAY OF THE ELDERLY

The maintenance of postural stability and balance is dependent upon feedback mechanisms involving peripheral input from vestibular, proprioceptive, kinesthetic, and visual cues, with central integration at the brain stem, cerebellum, sensory-motor cortex, and other higher centers (Martin, 1967b; Roberts, 1978). This feedback allows for positional changes of the center of gravity without loss of equilibrium.

During quiet standing, man's center of gravity is not stationary (Hellebrand, 1938). The shifting, known as postural sway, stimulates visual, proprioceptive, and kinesthetic cues for the maintenance of stance (Hellebrand, 1938; Sheldon, 1963; Nashner, 1973; Murray, Wood, Seireg, and Sepic, 1975). Swaying movements, along with the changes in joint position, pressure distribution, and changes in muscle length and tension ". . . may provide an automatic network of feedback controls designed to equilibrate stress and maintain an upright posture" (Murray, Wood, Seireg, and Sepic, 1975, p. 154). Postural sway can thus be used as an indicator of the body's ability to balance (Hasselkus and Shambes, 1975). The amount of postural sway increases with age. Hellebrand and Braun (1939) studied the sway of 109 subjects from age 3 to 86 with kymographic recordings of a pivot platform. They found the greatest degree of sway in their youngest and oldest groups. Greatest stability, defined as least deviation of the center of gravity, was seen in subjects in their second and third decades, with a gradual deterioration occurring during the fourth decade. Sheldon (1963) utilized an apparatus

that measured sway by a framework attached to the shoulders and reported a deterioration of stability only after the sixth decade, but this was measured with less sensitive equipment.

Comparisons of the degree of postural sway in females of 20 to 30 with healthy females of 70 to 80 were reported by Hasselkus and Shambes (1975). Two positions were examined: upright stance and forward lean. In both positions, the area of sway was significantly greater in the older group, but the difference was greatest with forward lean, a more stressful position to maintain. Not only does the degree of postural sway increase with age, but the area of stability during weight-shifting activities decreases. The postural stability of three groups of males in their third, fifth, and seventh decades was compared by Murray, Wood, Seireg, and Sepic (1975). Subjects in the youngest group demonstrated the largest area over which weight could be shifted and controlled, whereas the oldest group demonstrated the least.

Sway and Falling

An increase in postural sway has been associated with a pattern of multiple falls in the elderly population. The Romberg test for posterior column disorder is a subjective clinical measure of sway when a subject stands with feet together and eyes closed. Sheldon (1960) found that one-third of his subjects who reported recent falls had moderate to severe sway in the Romberg maneuver. Overstall, Exton-Smith, Imms, and Johnson (1977) objectively measured postural sway in 306 subjects. Sway increased with age in both sexes and was greater for females in all age groups. When sway was examined in relation to fall history, it was significantly greater in those individuals who reported falls caused by a loss of balance than in those who attributed their falls to a trip. Measurements of sway were greatest in those who reported five or more falls in the previous year. Similar results were obtained by Overstall, Johnson, and Exton-Smith (1978). After examining 205 subjects with a mean age of 81.8 years in a double blind study of falls and postural sway, Fernie,

Gryfe, Holliday, and Llewellyn (1982) reported a relationship between the speed of sway and a tendency to fall. Nonfallers demonstrated a mean speed of sway which was significantly less than that of persons who experienced a fall. No sex difference was found in amplitude or velocity of sway in either of the two groups.

Brocklehurst, Robertson, and James-Groom (1982) studied the relationship of various sensory modalities to postural sway in a "frail" elderly population of ambulatory residents of a nursing home. Sway was compared with measures of visual acuity, vestibular function, proprioception, and vibration sense in three age groups: 65 to 74, 75 to 84 and 85 and over. In contrast to previously reported work, sway was not found to be significantly correlated with age. Of all the modalities tested, only vibration sense in the lower extremities was found to be correlated with increased sway, and this was only in the 75 to 84 age group. When fall history was examined, the only significant correlation with physiological performance was found in this same age group, and among these subjects, only increased sway and decreased proprioception correlated with falls in the previous year. These authors speculate that the limited relationships found may be a function of the testing done or may reflect the vulnerability of this particular group. We agree. The clinical tests employed were the relatively insensitive quantitative procedures commonly used by physicians to reveal frank disease. Quantitative laboratory measures could possibly yield different results; for all that, there is reason to suspect that the findings in this group of "frail" elderly might remain essentially the same. Brocklehurst did not mention the clinical conditions causing fraility, but we might expect a collection of diseases commonly seen in nursing homes for the elderly (Kalchthaler, Bascon, and Quintos, 1978). It appears not unreasonable to expect that a majority of the subjects were thus at risk for falls. Those who were spared may simply have been more cautious or even lucky. In this selected population, then, correlation of sway with falls or other clinical variables may be spurious a priori.

Etiology of Sway

One of the earliest contributions to our understanding of the physiology of sway, as such, is Birren's study of a young patient with bilateral vestibular loss (1945). Although this patient could not tanden walk—i.e., place each foot directly in front of the other—his body sway with eyes open or closed was within the normal range of sway recorded in unafflicted individuals. Recent, sophisticated measurements of sway in a similar patient yielded an identical result. Sway is not necessarily increased by even total loss of vestibular function (Nashner, Black, and Wall, 1982). Birren (1945) calculated angular acceleration of the vestibular canals during normal sway, showing it to be generally below the threshold of vestibular sensitivity deduced from measurements of the vestibular-ocular reflex. Nashner (1971), however, has since determined amplitude thresholds of otoliths and semicircular canals to be a complex function of angular frequency, ranging from 0.1 to 1.0 deg of sway. Apparently, the human vestibular apparatus can detect normal sway, even though loss of vestibular function does not automatically cause its increase. When ankle-joint motion and the visual surround are stabilized with a feedback mechanism such that proprioceptive and visual sense of sway is removed, loss of vestibular function is strongly manifest (Nashner, Black, and Wall, 1982). Patients with mild vestibular dysfunction sway to the limits of the experimental apparatus. It is not necessary to employ the latest in high technology, however, to make this determination clinically; one can more simply demonstrate sway by having the patient stand on foam rubber with eyes closed (Begbie, 1967; Bles, Kapteyn, and de Wit, 1977).

The role of vision in maintaining postural stability has been discussed in the preceding section. Proprioceptive sense is more difficult to manipulate and has not been well studied. Its overriding importance can be appreciated in the plight of a patient discussed by Martin (1967a). This young man received a knife wound to the cervical spinal cord, severing afferent information of body sense, while all other spinal cord functions remained unaffected. In spite of years of physical therapy, the patient could not walk in any normal fashion; rather, he staggered in a wide-based gait with arms held forward to shift his center of gravity. No mention was made of this patient's sway, except to note that he fell when he closed his eyes. Obviously neither loss of vision, vestibular sense, or both, produces this profound a disability.

Nashner, Black, and Wall have recently reported important experimental results in the feedback mechanism of sway (1982). In the anterior-posterior direction, they controlled: (1) ankle-joint motion with feedback of body sway from driving a see-saw platform, (2) visual motion sense with eye closure and with sway feedback driving the visual surround, and (3) vestibular function over a spectrum of vestibular afflictions ranging from disease in complete remission to total vestibular loss. Not all proprioceptive sense, however, could be eliminated; remaining were differential sense of weight along the feet and body sense of gravity. Removal of ankle sense alone increased sway three- to fourfold in normal subjects. With the subject's eyes shut while standing on a stationary platform, sway approximately doubled; it tripled in a stabilized visual environment, i.e., the environment swayed with the subject. Removal of ankle sense and visual cues increased sway eightfold. Under this latter condition, patients with moderate to severe vestibular dysfunction were unable to maintain balance.

We may conclude that decrement in any operative sensory modality will increase sway, with the exception of vestibular sense taken in isolation. Not surprisingly, simultaneous loss of vision and vestibular and ankle sense abolishes equilibrium. To understand the loss of equilibrium with age, however, we want to know the effect of moderate decrements in all appropriate sensory modalities applied simultaneously.

Etiology of Sway as a Function of Age

Although many have speculated on the causes of increased sway in the elderly, little hard data has been advanced. Wyke (1979) and Prudham and Evans (1981) have proposed

that proprioceptive changes may be a factor. Wyke suggests that altered proprioceptive inputs from the cervical spine contributes to abnormalities in static postural reflexes, leading to decreased control. Prudham and Evans attribute increased sway to a general proprioceptive failure. Hodkinson (1962) has suggested that the instability may be produced by a combination of the limited range of motion of lower-extremity joints and pathological motor control. Abnormal extensor plantar responses have been found without evidence of other pyramidal tract damage (Droller, 1955; Sheldon, 1960). Droller reported these responses to be four times more frequent in men who had fallen and two times more frequent in women. Sheldon attributed decreased postural control to a deficit in central processing mechanisms. He speculated that postural control is a learned response, with greatest stability attained by the mid-twenties. The deterioration of control seen in the elderly is produced by a dysfunction, primarily at the brain stem and cerebellum, that has been caused by ". . . a decrease in the number of healthy nerve cells available for the control of posture and gait" (Sheldon, 1960, p. 1698).

In a review of the literature on changes in the aging nervous system, Hasselkus (1974) suggested that decreased postural control was produced by changes in both the peripheral receptors and the central processing mechanism. Primary responsibility for the elderly's decreased ability to equilibrate postural disturbances, however, was attributed to a decrease in the ability to perceive and integrate peripheral inputs at the central level, leading to an increased reaction time. Isaacs' (1978) interpretation was similar. Murray, Wood, Seireg, and Sepic (1975) suggest that sensory inputs of the elderly may not be interpreted as accurately as they once were. A gradual decline and slowing in the ability to integrate signals from the peripheral receptors may produce the postural instability.

There is no a priori reason to suspect that any of the above suggestions do not apply to at least some of the elderly. We would criticize the suggestion that any one process is a dominant cause of sway in the aged population or even in a majority of particular aged individuals, although examples of focal defects no doubt occur. Rather, we suspect that multiple, disseminated subtle defects lead to an observable increase in sway and disequilibrium.

EPILOGUE

We have seen that degenerative changes occur with advanced age in the vestibular, visual, and proprioceptive sensory systems. Change also occurs in the central nervous system; in particular, it involves the extrapyramidal system mediating coordinated movements. Body sway increases with age, gait becomes restricted and more cautious, and the time required to react to danger increases.

The rate of falls and death from falls rises markedly by the seventh decade. It is reasonable to assume that physiological changes manifest themselves in impaired sensation and movement, which ultimately lead to a fall. Nevertheless, this is supposition, and other scenarios can be advanced in the absence of evidence. We do not know, in any detail, how physiological change manifests itself in measurable performance of a complex task. Falls occur, we suppose, while walking. Yet research on walking of the elderly is sparse, and virtually nothing has been done on the kinematics of falling. By way of exception, we note with pleasure the insightful book by Martin (1967a), *The Basal Ganglia and Posture*. We recommend this little volume to all who wish to learn the art of careful observation.

The role of disease is particularly critical. Are those who fall healthy? Statistically they are not, although better data is sorely needed. In this review, we have generally treated disease as a single entity, but clearly this is not the case. The myriad disorders commonly encountered in the elderly interact in undisclosed ways with physiological decline and place the individual at even greater risk. Along with disease, we need to consider health. Spirduso (1980) has reviewed data showing that reaction time is significantly correlated with physical fitness. Moreover, a recent report shows that speed of self-selected walking is not correlated with age *per se;* rather, it is associated with maximum aerobic uptake (cardiovascular fitness), which is independent of age (Cunningham, Rechnitzer, Pearce, and Donner, 1982).

Klaus Riegel (1973) held that advances in psychological gerontology will depend not on the further accumulation of data but on the success in organizing those data already available. We have approached the problems presented in this chapter in the spirit of Riegel's remark and perhaps have had some success in achieving his goal, for with this synthesis it is apparent that there is a need for a creative empirical study of the complex interrelationship of age and equilibrium.

REFERENCES

Accident Facts. 1981. Chicago: National Safety Council.

Accident Facts. 1971. Chicago: National Safety Council.

Agate, J. 1966. Accidents to old people in their homes. *Brit. Med J.* 2: 785–788.

Armstrong, H. G. 1943. *Principles and Practice of Aviation Medicine.* 2nd ed. Baltimore: Williams and Wilkins.

Arslan, M. 1957. The senescence of the vestibular apparatus. *Pract. Oto-Rhino-Laryngol.* 19: 475–483.

Baloh, R. W., and Honrubia, V. 1979. *Clinical Neurophysiology of the Vestibular System.* Philadelphia: F. A. Davis Co.

Barbeau, A. 1976. Parkinson's disease: Etiological considerations. In *The Basal Ganglia,* ed. M. D. Yahr, pp. 281–292. New York: Raven Press.

Beck, C. H. 1978. Functional implications of changes in the senescent brain: A review. *Canadian J. Neurol. Sci.* 5: 417–424.

Begbie, G. H. 1967. Some problems of postural sway. In *Myotatic, Kinesthetic and Vestibular Mechanisms,* eds. A. V. S. de Reuck and J. Knight, pp. 80–92. Boston: Little, Brown and Co.

Bergstrom, B. 1973. Morphology study of the vestibular nerve. III. Analysis of the calibers of the myelinated vestibular nerve fibers in man at various ages. *Acta Otolaryngol.* 76: 331–338.

Berthoz, A.; Pavard, B.; and Young, L. R. 1975. Perception of a linear horizontal self-motion induced by peripheral vision (linearvection): Basic characteristics and visual-vestibular interactions. *Exp. Brain Res.* 23: 471–489.

Bhala, R. P.; O'Donnell, J.; and Thoppil, E. 1982. Ptophobia: Phobic fear of falling and its clinical management. *Phys. Therapy* 62: 187–190.

Birren, J. E. 1945. Static equilibrium and vestibular function. *J. Exp. Psychol.* 35: 127–133.

Black, F. O. 1977. The aging vestibular system. In *Special Senses in Aging,* eds. S. S. Han and D. H. Coons, pp. 178–185. Ann Arbor: Univ. of Michigan.

Bles, W.; Kapteyn, T. S.; and de Wit, G. 1977. Effects of visual-vestibular interaction on human posture. *Adv. Oto-Rhino-Laryng.* 22: 111–118.

Blumenthal, M. D., and Davie, J. W. 1980. Dizziness

and falling in elderly psychiatric outpatients. *Amer. J. Psychiatry* 137: 203–206.

Brandt, T.; Bles, W.; Arnold, F.; and Kapteyn, T. S. 1979. Height vertigo and human posture. *Adv. Oto-Rhino-Laryng.* 25: 88–92.

Brandt, T.; Dichgans, J.; and Koenig, E. 1973. Differential effects of central versus peripheral vision on egocentric and exocentric motion perception. *Exp. Brain Res.* 16: 476–491.

Bredberg, G. 1968. Cellular pattern and nerve supply of the human organ of corti. *Acta Otolaryngol.* (Suppl. 236).

Brizzee, K. R.; Ordy, J. M.; Knox, C.; and Jirge, S. K. 1980. Morphology and aging in the brain. In *The Aging Nervous System,* eds. G. J. Maletta and F. J. Pirozzolo, pp. 10–39. New York: Praeger.

Brocklehurst, J. C.; Exton-Smith, A. N.; Lempert Barber, S. M.; Hunt, L. P.; and Palmer, M. K. 1978. Fracture of the femur in old age: A two-centre study of associated clinical factors and the cause of the fall. *Age and Ageing* 7: 7–15.

Brocklehurst, J. C.; Robertson, D.; and James-Groom, P. 1982. Clinical correlates of sway in old age—sensory modalities. *Age and Ageing* 11: 1–10.

Bruner, A., and Norris, T. W. 1971. Age related changes in caloric nystagmus. *Acta Otolaryngol.* (Suppl. 282: 1–24.)

Campbell, A. J.; Reinken, J.; Allen, B. C.; and Martinez, G. S. 1981. Falls in old age: A study of frequency and related clinical factors. *Age and Ageing* 10: 264–270.

Clark, B., and Stewart, J. 1968. Comparison of sensitivity for the perception of body rotation and the oculogyral illusion. *Percept. Psychphysiol.* 3: 253–256.

Cooksey, F. S. 1946. Rehabilitation in vestibular injuries. *Proc. Royal Soc. Med.* 39: 273–278.

Critchley, M. 1956. Neurologic changes in the aged. *J. Chronic Dis.* 3: 459–477.

Cunningham, D. A.; Rechnitzer, P. A.; Pearce, M. E.; and Donner, A. P. 1982. Determinants of self-selected walking pace across ages 19 to 66. *J. Gerontol.* 37: 560–564.

Daunton, N., and Thomsen, D. 1979. Visual modification of otolith-dependent units in cat vestibular nuclei. *Exp. Brain Res.* 37: 173–176.

Devaney, K. O., and Johnson, H. A. 1980. Neuron loss in the aging visual cortex of man. *J. Gerontol.* 35: 836–841.

Dichgans, J., and Brandt, T. 1974. The psychophysics of visually induced perception of self-motion and tilt. In *The Neurosciences: Third Study Program,* eds. F. O. Schmitt and F. G. Worden, pp. 123–129. Cambridge Mass: The MIT press.

Dichgans, J.; Brandt, T.; and Held, R. 1975. The role of vision in gravitational orientation. *Forsch. Zoologie* 23: 255–263.

Droller, H. 1955. Falls among elderly living at home. *Geriatrics* 10: 239–244.

Edwards, A. S. 1946. Body sway and vision. *J. Exp. Psychol.* 36: 526–535.

Engstrom, H.; Ades, H. W.; Engstrom, B.; Gilchrist, D.; and Bourne, G. 1977. Structural changes in the vestibular epithelia in elderly monkeys and humans. *Adv. Oto-Rhino-Laryngol.* 22: 93–110.

Engstrom, H.; Bergstrom, B.; and Rosenhall, U. 1974. Vestibular sensory epithelia. *Arch. Otolaryngol.* 100: 411–418.

Exton-Smith, A. N. 1977. Clinical manifestations. In *Care of the Elderly: Meeting the Challange of Dependency,* eds. A. N. Exton-Smith and J. G. Evans. London: Academic Press.

Feist, R. R. 1978. A survey of accidental falls in a small home for the aged. *J. Gerontol. Nursing.* 4(6): 15–17.

Fernandez, C., and Goldberg, J. M. 1976. Physiology of peripheral neurons innervating otolith organs of the squirrel monkey. I. Response to static tilts and long-duration centrifugal force. *J. Neurophysiol.* 39: 970–984.

Fernandez, C., and Goldberg, J. M. 1971. Physiology of peripheral neurons innervating semicircular canals of the squirrel monkey. II. Response to sinusoidal stimulation and dynamics of peripheral vestibular system. *J. Neurophysiol.* 34: 661–675.

Fernandez, C.; Goldberg, J. M.; and Abend, W. 1972. Response to static tilts of peripheral neurons innervating otolith organs of the squirrel monkey. *J. Neurophysiol.* 35: 978–997.

Fernie, G. R.; Gryfe, C. I.; Holliday, P. J.; and Llewellyn, A. 1982. The relationship of postural sway in standing to the incidence of falls in geriatric subjects. *Age and Ageing* 11: 11–16.

Finley, F. R.; Cody, K. A.; and Finizie, R. V. 1969. Locomotion patterns in elderly women. *Arch. Phys Med. Rehab.* 50: 140–169.

Goldberg, J. M., and Fernandez, C. 1971. Physiology of peripheral neurons innervating semicircular canals of the squirrel monkey. I. Resting discharge and response to constant angular accelerations. *J. Neurophysiol.* 34: 635–660.

Gordon, M.; Huang, M.; and Gryfe, C. I. 1982. An evaluation of falls, syncope, and dizziness by prolonged ambulatory cardiographic monitoring in a geriatric institutional setting. *J. Amer. Geriat. Soc.* 30: 6–12.

Gryfe, C. I.; Amies, A.; and Ashley, M. J. 1977. A longitudinal study of falls in an elderly population: I. Incidence and morbidity. *Age and Ageing* 6: 201–210.

Guimaraes, R. M., and Isaacs, B. 1980. Characteristics of the gait in old people who fall. *Internat. Rehab. Med.* 2: 177–180.

Hasselkus, B. R. 1974. Aging and the human nervous system. *Amer. J. Occupational Therapy* 28: 16–21.

Hasselkus, B. R., and Shambes, G. M. 1975. Aging and postural sway in women. *J. Gerontol.* 30: 661–667.

Hecker, H. C.; Haug, C. O.; and Herndon, J. W. 1974. Treatment of vertiginous patients using Cawthorne's vestibular exercises. *Laryngoscope* 84: 2065–2072.

Held, R.; Dichgans, J.; and Bauer, J. 1975. Characteristics of moving visual scenes influencing spatial orientation. *Vision Res.* 15: 357–365.

Hellebrand, F. A. 1938. Standing as a geotropic reflex. *Amer J. Physiol.* 121: 471–474.

Hellebrand, F. A., and Braun, G. L. 1939. The influence of sex and age on the postural sway of man. *Amer J. Phys. Anthropol.* 24: 347–360.

Henn, V.; Cohen, B.; and Young, L. R. 1980. Visual-vestibular interaction in motion perception and the generation of nystagmus. *Neurosci. Res. Prog. Bull.* 18: 459–651.

Hilding, D. A., and House, W. F. 1964. An evaluation of the ultrastructural findings in the utrical in Meniere's disease. *Laryngoscope* 74: 1135–1148.

Hodkinson, H. M. 1962. A study of falls and getting up from the floor in the aged. *The Practitioner* 189(8): 207–209.

Howell, T. H. 1971. Premonitory falls. *Practitioner* 206: 666–667.

Hutman, L. P., and Sekuler, R. 1980. Spatial vision and aging. I: Criterion effects. *J. Gerontol.* 35: 700–706.

Imms, F. J., and Edholm, O. G. 1981. Studies of gait and mobility in the elderly. *Age and Ageing* 10: 147–156.

Isaacs, B. 1978. Are falls a manifestation of brain failure? *Age and Ageing* 7 (Suppl.): 97–105.

Johnsson, L. G.1971. Degenerative changes and anomalies of the vestibular system in man. *Laryngoscope* 81: 1682–1694.

Johnsson, L. G. 1974. Sequence of degeneration of Corti's organ and its first-order neurons. *Ann. Otol. Rhinol. Laryngol.* 83: 294–303.

Johnsson, L. G., and Hawkins, J. E. 1972. Vascular changes in the human inner ear associated with aging. *Ann. Oto. Rhinol. Laryngol.* 81: 364–376.

Jorgensen, M. B. 1961. Changes of aging in the inner ear. *Arch. Otolaryngol.* 74: 164–170.

Kalchthaler, T.; Bascon, R. A.; and Quintos, V. 1978. Falls in the institutionalized elderly. *J. Amer Geriatrics Soc.* 26: 424–428.

Kenshalo, D. R. 1977a. Aging effects on cutaneous and kinesthetic sensibilities. In *Special Senses in Aging*, eds. S. S. Han and D. H. Coons, pp. 189–217. Ann Arbor: Univ. of Michigan.

Kenshalo, D. R. 1977b. Age changes in touch, vibration, temperature, kinesthesis and pain sensitivity. In *Handbook of the Psychology of Aging*, eds. J. E. Birren and K. W. Schaie, pp. 562–579. New York: Van Nostrand Reinhold Co.

Kenshalo, D. R. 1979. Changes in the vestibular and somesthetic systems as a function of age. In *Sensory Systems and Communication in the Elderly*, eds. J. M. Ordy and K. Brizzee, *Aging*, Vol. 10: pp. 269–282.

Krmpotic-Nemanic, J. 1969. Presbycusis, presbystasis, and presbyosmia as consequences of the analogous biological process. *Acta Otolaryngol.* 67: 217–223.

Krmpotic-Nemanic, J. 1971. A new concept of the pathogenesis of presbycusis. *Arch. Otolaryngol.* 93: 161–166.

Kutt, H., and McDowell, F. 1979. *Clinical Neuropharmacology.* New York: Churchill Livingstone.

Lee, D. N., and Lishman, J. R. 1975. Visual proprioceptive control of stance. *J. Human Movement Studies* 1: 87–95.

Lestienne, F.; Soechting, J.; and Berthoz, A. 1977. Postural readjustments induced by linear motion of visual scenes. *Exp. Brain Res.* 28: 363–384.

Lucht, U. 1971. A prospective study of accidental falls and resulting injuries in the home among elderly people. *Acta Socio-medica Scand.* 2: 105–120.

Mankovsky, N. B.; Mints, A. Y.; and Lisenyuk, V. P.

1982. Age pecularities of human motor control in aging. *Gerontology* 28: 314–322.

Marshall, J. F.; and Berrios, N. 1979. Movement disorders of aged rats: Reversal by dopamine receptor stimulation. *Science* 206: 477–479.

Martin, J. P. 1967a. *The Basal Ganglia and Posture.* Philadelphia: J. B. Lippincott.

Martin, J. P. 1967b. Role of the vestibular system in the control of posture and movement in man. In *Myotatic, Kinesthetic, and Vestibular Mechanisms*, eds. A. V. S. de Rueck and J. Knight, pp. 92–96. Boston: Little, Brown and Co.

McFarland, R. A. 1946. *Human Factors in Air Transport Design.* New York: McGraw Hill.

McGeer, P. L.; McGeer, E. G.; and Suzuki, J. S. 1977. Aging and extrapyramidal function. *Arch. Neurol.* 34: 33–35.

McGrath, C., and Morrison, J. D. 1981. The effect of age on spatial frequency perception in human subjects. *Quart. J. Exp. Physiol.* 66: 253–261.

Melvill Jones, G., and Milsum, J. H. 1970. Characteristics of neural transmission from the semicircular canals to the vestibular nuclei of cats. *J. Physiol.* (London) 209: 295–316.

Melvill Jones, G., and Watt, D. G. D. 1971a. Observations on the control of stepping and hopping movements in man. *J. Physiol.* 219: 709–727.

Melvill Jones, G., and Watt, D. G. D. 1971b. Muscular control of landing from unexpected falls in man. *J. Physiol.* 219: 729–737.

Minnigerode, B.; Grohmann, R.; and Vontin, H. 1967. Electronystagmographische Untersuchungen zum Verhalten der Labyrinthfunktion gesunder Versuchspersonen verschiedenen Lebensalters. *Pract. Otorhinolaryngol.* 29: 153–165.

Mulch, G., and Petermann, W. 1979. Influence of age on results of vestibular function tests. *Ann Otol. Rhinol. Laryngol.* 88 (Suppl. 56): 1–17.

Murphy, J., and Isaacs, B. 1982. The post-fall syndrome. *Gerontology* 28: 265–270.

Murray, M. P.; Kory, R. C.; and Clarkson, B. H. 1969. Walking patterns in healthy old men. *J. Gerontol.* 24: 169–178.

Murray, M. P.; Wood, D.; Seireg, A. A.; and Sepic, S. B. 1975. Normal postural stability and steadiness: Quantitative assessment. *J. Bone Joint Surg.* 57-A(4): 510–516.

Nashner, L. M. 1971. A model describing vestibular detection of body sway motion. *Acta Otolaryngol.* 72: 429–436.

Nashner, L. M. 1973. Vestibular and reflex control of normal standing. In *Control of Posture and Locomotion*, eds. R. B. Stein, K. G. Pearson, R. S. Smith, and J. B. Redford, pp. 291–308. New York: Plenum Press.

Nashner, L. M.; Black, F. O.; and Wall, C. 1982. Adaptation to altered support and visual conditions during stance: Patients with vestibular deficits. *J Neurosci.* 2: 536–544.

Naylor, R., and Rosin, A. J. 1970. Falling as a cause of admission to a geriatric unit. *The Practitioner* 205: 327–330.

Norre, M. E., and de Weerdt, W. 1979. II: Vestibular

habituation training. Technique and first results. *Acta Oto-Rhyno-Laryngologica.* Belgica 33: 347–364.

Norris, A. H.; Shock, N. W.; and Wagman, I. H. 1953. Age changes in the maximum conduction velocity of motor fibers of human ulnar nerves. *J. Applied Physiol.* 5: 589–593.

Overstall, P. W. 1978. Falls in the elderly—Epidemiology, aetiology, and management. In *Recent Advances in Geriatric Medicine,* ed. B. Isaacs. London: Churchill Livingstone.

Overstall, P. W.; Exton-Smith, A. N.; Imms, F. J.; and Johnson, A. L. 1977. Falls in the elderly related to postural imbalance. *Brit Med. J.* 1: 261–264.

Overstall, P. W.; Hazell, J. W. P.; and Johnson, A. L. 1981. Vertigo in the elderly. *Age and Ageing* 10: 105–109.

Overstall, P. W.; Johnson, A. L.; and Exton-Smith, A. N. 1978. Instability and falls in the elderly. *Age and Ageing* 7 (Suppl. 6): 92–96.

Owsley, C., and Sekuler, R. 1982. Spatial summation, contrast threshold, and aging. *Invest. Ophthalmol. Vis. Sci.* 22: 130–133.

Perret, E., and Regli, F. 1970. Age and the perceptual threshold for vibratory stimuli. *Europ. Neurol.* 4: 65–76.

Petajan, J. H., and Jarcho, L. W. 1975. Motor unit control in Parkinson's disease and the influence of levodopa. *Neurology* 25: 866–869.

Pfaltz, C. R. 1977. Vestibular habituation and central compensation. *Adv. Oto-Rhino-Laryng.* 22: 136–142.

Potvin, A. R.; Syndulko, K.; Tourtellotte, W. W.; Lemmon, J. A.; and Potvin, J. H. 1980. Human neurologic function and the aging process. *Amer. Geriatrics Soc.* 28: 1–9.

Prudham, D., and Evans, J. G. 1981. Factors associated with falls in the elderly. *Age and Ageing* 10: 141–146.

Rasmussen, A. T. 1940. Studies of the VIIIth cranial nerve of man. *Laryngoscope.* 50: 67–83.

Riegel, K. F. 1973. An epitaph for a paradigm: Introduction for a symposium. *Human Development* 16: 1–7.

Roberts, T. D. M. 1978. *Neurophysiology of Postural Mechanisms.* Boston: Butterworths.

Robinson, D. S.; Sourkes, T. L.; Neis, A.; Harris, L. S.; Spector, S.; Bartlett, D. L.; and Kaye, I. S. 1977. Monamine metabolism in human brain. *Arch. Gen. Psychiatry* 34: 89–92.

Rosenberg, G. 1958. Effect of age on peripheral vibratory perception. *J. Amer. Geriatric Soc.* 6: 471–481.

Rosenhall, U. 1973. Degenerative patterns in the aging human vestibular neuro-epithelia. *Acta Otolaryngol.* 76: 208–220.

Rosenhall, U., and Rubin, W. 1975. Degenerative changes in the human vestibular sensory epithelia. *Acta Otolaryngol.* 79: 67–80.

Ross, M. D. 1977. Effects of aging on the otoconia. In *Special Senses in Aging,* eds. S. S. Han and D. H. Coons, pp. 163–177. Ann Arbor: Univ. of Michigan.

Roth, G. S. 1981. Steroid and dopaminergic receptors in the aged brain. In *Aging,* Vol. 17: *Brain Neurotransmitters and Receptors in Aging and Age-Related Disorders,* eds. S. J. Enna et al., pp. 163–169. New York: Raven Press.

Sabin, T. D. 1982. Biological aspects of falls and mobility limitations in the elderly. *J Amer. Geratrics Soc.* 30: 54–58.

Samorajski, T. 1975. Age-related changes in brain biogenic amines. In *Aging,* Vol. 1: *Clinical, Morphologic, and Neurochemical Aspects in the Aging Central Nervous System,* eds. H. Brody et al., pp. 199–214. New York: Raven Press.

Schoder, H. J. 1973. Zur Reaktionweise des Vestibularsystems in Alter. *Verkehsmed Ihre Grenzgeb* 20: 180–183.

Schuknecht, H. F. 1974. *Pathology of the Ear.* Cambridge, Mass.: Harvard University Press.

Schuknecht, H. F.; Igarashi, M.; and Gacek, R. R. 1965. The pathological types of cochleo-saccular degeneration. *Acta Otolaryngol.* 59: 154–170

Sehested, P., and Severin-Nielsen, T. 1977. Falls by hospitalized elderly patients: Causes, prevention. *Geratrics* 32(4): 101–108.

Sekuler, R., and Hutman, L. P. 1980. Spatial vision and aging. I: Contrast sensitivity. *J Gerontol.* 35: 692–699.

Sekuler, R.; Hutman, L. P.; and Owsley, C. J. 1980. Human aging and spatial vision. *Science* 209: 1255–1256.

Sheldon, J. H. 1948. *The Social Medicine of Old Age.* London: Oxford Univ. Press.

Sheldon, J. H. 1960. On the natural history of falls in old age. *Brit. Med. J.* 2: 1685–1690.

Sheldon, J. H. 1963. The effect of age on the control of sway. *Gerontol. Clin.* 5: 129–138.

Sheldon, J. H. 1966. Falls in old age. In *Medicine in Old Age,* ed. J. N. Agate. Philadelphia: J. B. Lippincott Co.

Shinoda, Y., and Yoshida, K. 1974. Dynamic characteristics of responses to horizontal head acceleration in vestibuloocular pathway in the cat. *J Neurophysiol.* 37: 653–673.

Siegler, I. C.; Nowlin, J. B.; and Blumenthal, J. A. 1980. Health and behavior: Methodological considerations for adult development and aging. In *Aging in the 1980s: Psychological Issues,* ed. L. W. Poon. Washington, D.C.: American Psychological Association.

Skalka, H. W. 1980. Effect of age on Arden grating acuity. *British J. Ophthalmol.* 64: 21–23.

Smith, B. H., and Sethi, P. K. 1975. Aging and the nervous system. *Geratrics* 30(5); 109–115.

Spirduso, W. W. 1980. Physical fitness, aging, and psychomotor speed: A review. *J. Gerontol.* 35: 850–865.

Statistical Bulletin. 1965. Accidental falls: Fatal and nonfatal. Stat. Bull. of the Metropolitan Life Ins. Co. 46: 4–6.

Statistical Bulletin. 1978. Mortality from leading types of accidents. Stat. Bull. of the Metropolitan Life Ins. Co. 59(3): 10–12.

Steele, H. C., and Crowe, C. B. 1970. *How to Deal with Aging and the Elderly.* Huntsville, Ala.: Stroede Publishing Co.

Steindler, A. 1955. *Kinesiology of the Human Body.* Springfield: Charles C Thomas.

Tinker, G. M. 1979. Accidents in a geriatric department. *Age and Ageing* 8: 196–198.

Tobis, J. S.; Nayak, L. and Hoehler, F. 1981. Visual perception of verticality and horizontality among elderly fallers. *Arch. Phys. Med. Rehabil.* 62: 619–622.

Tokumasu, K., and Kawano, R. 1976. Head sway during stepping in old and young adults. *Agressologie* 17, B: 1–6.

Travis, R. C. 1945. An experimental analysis of dynamic and static equilibrium. *J. Exp. Psychol.* 35: 216–234.

Verrillo, R. T. 1980. Age related changes in the sensitivity to vibration. *J. Gerontol.* 35: 185–193.

Waespe, W., and Henn, V. 1979. Motion information in the vestibular nuclei of alert monkeys: Visual and vestibular input vs. optomotor output. *Prog. Brain Res.* 50: 683–693.

Waller, J. A. 1978. Falls among the elderly—Human and environmental factors. *Accident Evaluation Prevention* 10:21–33.

Welford, A. T. 1977. Motor Performance. In *Handbook of the Psychology of Aging,* eds. J. E. Birren and K. W. Schaie, pp. 450–496. New York: Van Nostrand Reinhold Co.

Wild, D.; Nayak, U. S. L.; and Isaacs, B. 1981. How dangerous are falls in old people at home? *Brit. Med. J.* 282: 266–268.

Witkin, H. A., and Wapner, S. 1950. Visual factors in the maintenance of upright posture. *Amer. J. Physiol.* 63: 31–50.

Wooton, R.; Bryson, E.; Ulsasser, U.; Freeman, H.; Green, J. R.; Hesp, R.; Hudson, E. A.; Klenerman, L.; Smith, T.; and Zanelli, J. 1982. Risk factors for fractured neck of femur in the elderly. *Age and Ageing* 11: 160–168.

Wright, W. B. 1979. Stammering gait. *Age and Ageing* 8: 8–12.

Wyke, B. 1979. Cervical articular contributions to posture and gait: Their relation to senile disequilibrium. *Age and Ageing* 8: 251–258.

Zelenka, J. and Slanimova, B. 1964. Changes of labyrinth function due to age. *Cesk Otolaryngol.* 13: 21–26.

15
SPEED OF BEHAVIOR AND ITS IMPLICATIONS FOR COGNITION

Timothy A. Salthouse
Department of Psychology
University of Missouri

INTRODUCTION

Seldom in psychology is a researcher at a loss for new adjectives to describe the reliability of a particular behavioral phenomenon. The phenomenon of a general slowness of behavior with increased age may be one such case, however, as the phrases already used to describe this finding include the following: "least disputed" (Surwillo, 1968, p. 2; Talland, 1965, p. 283), "most pronounced" (Tolin and Simon, 1968, p. 283), "most pervasive" (Fozard and Thomas, 1975, p. 147), "most distinctive" (Birren and Botwinick, 1955, p. 143), "most outstanding" (Bromley, 1974, p. 163), "most strongly substantiated" (Jerome, 1959, p. 661), "most characteristic" (Jarvik, 1975, p. 577; McFarland, 1968, p. 51), "least debatable" (Talland and Cairnie, 1961, p. 370), "most striking" (Loveless and Sanford, 1974, p. 52; Rabbit, 1979, p. 425; Welford, 1962, p. 335), "most clearly established" (Birren and Renner, 1977, p. 28), "most ubiquitous" (Birren, Woods, and Williams, 1979, p. 10), "most general" (Birren and Botwinick, 1955, p. 434), "most replicated" (Birren, Woods, and Williams, 1979, p. 13), "most reliable" (Birren, 1964, p. 111; Birren and Spieth, 1962, p. 390), and "most reliably documented" (Fozard and Thomas, 1975, p. 110). In fact, the slowing-with-age phenomenon is now so accepted that it sometimes appears that the only remaining quarrel concerns which phrase is "most descriptive."

The fact that there is reduced speed with increased age is not only an acknowledged laboratory result but also of considerable practical importance. For example, the increased accident rates of older adults (e.g., Barrett, Mihal, Panek, Sterns, and Alexander, 1977; Welford, 1958, pp.117–120), and the under-representation of older workers in externally paced industrial tasks (e.g., Welford, 1977, p. 487–488) have both been linked to the slowness of behavior associated with increased age. Even professional service providers appear to exhibit this trend since the time required for cavity preparation and filling among practicing dentists has been found to be longer with increased age (Klein, Dollar, and Bagdonas, 1947). It has also been reported that age-related slowness is evident in tasks of daily living such as zipping a garment, dialing a telephone, picking up coins, unwrapping a band-aid, cutting with a knife, and even putting on a shirt (e.g., Potvin, Syndulko, Tourtellotte, Lemmon, and Potvin, 1980; Potvin, Tourtellotte, Pew, Albers, Henderson, and Snyder, 1973).

Birren (e.g., 1955, 1974) has also noted that as a consequence of their slowness, older adults can be considered to be living in a functionally different environment from that of younger people. If the external environment is rapidly changing, the conditions that lead to the initiation of a particular behavior may no longer be appropriate by the time the behavior is actually executed by older adults. This could clearly lead to severe problems in operating vehicles, controlling equipment, or monitoring displays. Despite some claims to the contrary (e.g. Schaie, 1973), it appears that speed of decision and response can be quite important in our modern automated society, and, consequently, the slowness of older adults may place them at a great disadvantage relative to younger members of the population.

In introducing the chapter titled "Motor Performance" in the previous edition of this Handbook, Welford (1977) stated that two lines of research converge in the literature on motor performance and adult age. One research focus concerned questions about fundamental aging processes, whereas the other concentrated on analyses of skilled performance. Welford felt that the second area was "more coherent and systematic" than the former, and consequently he organized his review using the skilled performance perspective. In part because his survey of the literature from this perspective was so comprehensive that little more remains to be said, the current chapter will emphasize the alternative research focus mentioned by Welford, i.e., how results from motor performance studies can illuminate basic aging processes. Taking this viewpoint, therefore, the motor performance literature will be primarily considered as a means, rather than as an end, in the attempt to understand fundamental aging processes. This altered emphasis is consistent, moreover, with recent trends in contemporary cognitive psychology to use reaction time tasks in attempts to analyze cognitive processes, an approach that has met with great success.

In addition to excluding research on motor skills, the present chapter will also not discuss the growing literature on the physiological factors that contribute to the age-related slowing phenomenon. There are three reasons for the omission of this obviously important and related topic. One is simply that space limitations precluded adequate coverage of more than a few topics in a single chapter. A second

is that the biological bases for age-related slowing have recently been discussed by Birren, Woods, and Williams (1979; 1980), and this subject also received earlier comprehensive reviews by Hicks and Birren (1970) and Welford and Birren (1965). The third reason is that we wish to adopt a cognitive perspective in which the focus will be on the processing of information (software) rather than on the specific neurological substrate (hardware) of that information or its processing mechanisms. Since the literature on speed and age has not previously been considered from this perspective, the present emphasis has the potential of revealing new insights into this phenomenon.

Before examining the various hypotheses that have been proposed to account for the slowing-with-age phenomenon, it is first desirable to document its reliability and magnitude, examine apparent exceptions to it, and finally consider some of the methodological problems that have plagued the relevant research.

Reliability and Magnitude of the Slowing-with-Age Phenomenon

Figure 1 and Table 1 have been prepared to demonstrate the consistency of, and the variety of responses exhibiting, the slowing-with-age phenomenon. Figure 1 illustrates the results of two activities, finger-tapping and speeded handwriting, in adults of varying ages. (In order to minimize the influence of extraneous variation in absolute levels of performance, the ordinate in Figure 1 is expressed as a percentage of the minimum—i.e., fastest—score across all age groups.) The age difference is more dramatically apparent with the handwriting measure than with the tapping measure, but the dominant feature of the data is the longer time required with increased age both for the very simple tapping activity and for the more complicated activity of writing letters or digits.

An alternative means of expressing the association between increased age and reduced speed is by way of correlation coefficients. The importance of adult age as a factor in speed of performance can be assessed by examining the magnitude of the correlations between

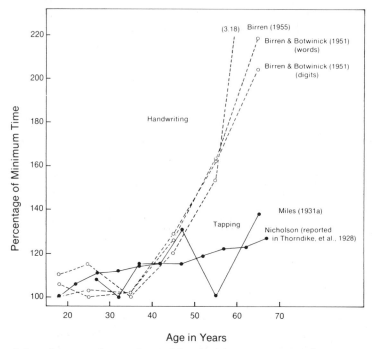

Figure 1. Speeded performance for tapping and handwriting expressed as the percentage of the mean of each age group relative to the fastest performance across all age groups.

chronological age and the time required to perform a particular activity; the larger the correlation, the greater the contribution of the age variable. This method of analysis may be somewhat misleading if there are nonlinear trends, but it does provide a rough estimate of the magnitude of the age–speed relationship. Table 1 contains over 50 such correlations across a variety of speeded activities. All correlations are positive (increased age is associated with increased time), with a median value of 0.45 and a range of 0.15 to 0.64. These results are even more impressive when it is noted that most of the speeded variables are of unknown (but certainly less than perfect) reliability, and thus the square of the correlation undoubtedly provides an underestimate of the proportion of *reliable* variance accounted for by the age variable.

Exceptions to the Slowing-with-Age Phenomenon

In light of the well-documented trend of slower behavior with increased age, apparent exceptions to this phenomenon take on special

importance. Some of the reports of no age differences in a measure of speeded performance are almost certainly due to unusual methodological characteristics or to sampling fluctuations. As an example of the latter, Welford (1958, p. 63) has noted that early investigations of simple reaction time by Miles (1931) and Galton (reported in Koga and Morant, 1923), in which the age differences were quite small, probably involved positively biased samples of older adults and therefore may have yielded unrepresentative age trends. Nevertheless, there are at least three general areas in which several studies have reported similar findings and thus warrant separate consideration.

One obvious exception to the slowing-with-age phenomenon arises when very healthy or physically fit older adults are compared with less healthy or unfit young adults. It is now clear that healthier adults (particularly with respect to cardiovascular function) have faster reaction times than less healthy adults of comparable age (e.g., Abrahams and Birren, 1973; Light, 1978; Spieth, 1964) and that older adults who regularly engage in physical exer-

TABLE 1. Age Correlations with Various Psychomotor Measures

Measure	Correlation with Age	Sample Size	Age Range	Source
Simple reaction time	0.26	316	30–69	Dirken (1972)
	0.29	687	17–102	Borkan and Norris (1980)
	0.33	460	25–57	Heikken et al. (1974)
	0.45	82	20–83	Jalavisto and Nakkonen (1963)
	0.35	130	44–93	Jalavisto et al. (1964)
	0.25	100	25–87	Miles (1931a)
	0.31	100	25–87	Miles (1931a)
	0.28	195	20–95	Miles (1931b)
	0.47	60	18–74	Potvin et al. (1973)
	0.41	96	20–80	Robertson-Tchabo and Arenberg (1976)
	0.19	100	28–99	Surwillo (1963)
Choice reaction time	0.45	70	25–64	Barrett et al. (1977)
	0.59	161	23–60	Birren and Spieth (1962)
	0.22	701	17–102	Borkan and Norris (1980)
	0.52	102	20–70	Clark (1960)
	0.29	316	30–69	Dirken (1972)
	0.37	316	30–69	Dirken (1972)
	0.49	316	30–69	Dirken (1972)
	0.42	316	30–69	Dirken (1972)
	0.41	316	30–69	Dirken (1972)
	0.46	316	30–69	Dirken (1972)
	0.42	316	30–69	Dirken (1972)
	0.42	123	25–79	Fozard et al. (1976)
	0.47	123	25–79	Fozard et al. (1976)
	0.43	50	21–69	Laufer and Schweitz (1968)
	0.54	203	18–59	Light (1976)
	0.51	96	20–80	Robertson-Tchabo and Arenberg (1976)
	0.38	65	31–75	Thomas et al. (1978)
	0.48	65	31–75	Thomas et al. (1978)
	0.64	60	25–74	Thomas et al. (1977)
Movement time	0.55	100	25–87	Miles (1931a)
	0.40	100	25–87	Miles (1931a)
	0.36	100	25–87	Miles (1931a)
	0.60	288	20–95	Miles (1931b)
	0.54	283	20–95	Miles (1931b)
	0.50	285	20–95	Miles (1931b)
Reaction plus movement time	0.33	108	18–64	Goldfarb (1941)
	0.33	108	18–64	Goldfarb (1941)
	0.36	108	18–64	Goldfarb (1941)
	0.15	60	18–54	Goldfarb (1941)
	0.24	60	18–54	Goldfarb (1941)
	0.19	60	18–54	Goldfarb (1941)
Digit-symbol substitution	0.46	933	25–64	Birren and Morrison (1961)
	0.42	161	23–60	Birren and Spieth (1962)
	0.50	108	18–64	Goldfarb (1941)
	0.48	60	18–54	Goldfarb (1941)
	0.59	460	25–57	Heikken et al. (1974)
	0.43	39	20–59	Weisenburg et al. (1936)
Trail making	0.46	120	21–80	Botwinick and Storandt (1974)
	0.52	300	20–79	Heron and Chown (1967)
	0.50	240	20–79	Heron and Chown (1967)
Digit coding	0.53	300	20–79	Heron and Chown (1967)
	0.49	240	20–79	Heron and Chown (1967)

TABLE 1   (continued)

Measure	Correlation with Age	Sample Size	Age Range	Source
Miscellaneous				
Card sorting	0.54	49	20–80	Crossman and Szafran (1956)
Clerical perceptual speed	0.41	105	20–60	Horn et al. (1981)
	0.23	147	20–60	Horn et al. (1981)
Composite speed	0.51	161	23–60	Birren and Spieth (1962)
Copying digits	0.62	120	21–80	Botwinick and Storandt (1974)
Crossing off	0.63	120	21–80	Botwinick and Storandt (1974)
Cutting with a knife	0.32	60	18–74	Potvin et al. (1973)
Dialing telephone	0.64	60	18–74	Potvin et al. (1973)
Letter comparison substitution	0.45	102	20–70	Clark (1960)
	0.54	187	20–95	Miles (1931b)
Picking up coins	0.42	60	18–74	Potvin et al. (1973)
Squeezing toothpaste	0.55	60	18–74	Potvin et al. (1973)
Transmission rate	0.26	54	34–92	Surwillo (1964a)
Unwrapping band-aid	0.48	60	18–74	Potvin et al. (1973)
Using fork	0.33	60	18–74	Potvin et al. (1973)
Zipping garment	0.64	60	18–74	Potvin et al. (1973)

cise have faster reaction times than age-matched sedentary adults (e.g., Botwinick and Thompson, 1968; Spirduso, 1975; 1980; Spirduso and Clifford, 1978). Given these trends, moreover, it is sometimes possible to obtain a sample of healthy, physically fit older adults who do not differ in speed from a sample of less healthy, physically inactive younger adults. What is not yet obvious, however, is whether "normal" age differences in behavioral speed can be accounted for by an age-related decrease in health or physical fitness. The evidence from selected populations who are all very healthy or physically fit suggests that the age differences, although possibly attenuated, are nevertheless present (e.g., Birren, Butler, Greenhouse, Sokoloff, and Yarrow, 1963; Birren and Spieth, 1962; Spirduso, 1975; Spirduso and Clifford, 1978; Szafran, 1966). It thus appears unlikely that much of the slowing phenomenon can be attributed to pathological conditions of physical health or physical fitness.

A second apparent exception to the trend of slower performance in older adults arises when vocal, rather than manual, responses are required in speeded tasks. Kaufman (1968) was apparently the first to report this phenom-

enon in the finding that age trends were more dramatic in written than in oral versions of a symbol-digit substitution task. More recently, Nebes (1978) reported that the same young and old adults exhibited a "typical" age difference with a manual response, but no age difference was apparent when a vocal response was substituted in an otherwise identical task. Salthouse and Somberg (1982a) also found that older adults were slower in manual reaction time and in various perceptual tasks, but not in vocal reaction time. The reason why vocal responses might be immune to the slowing trend is not yet known, but it should be noted that there is little consistency in the other studies employing vocal reaction time tasks. For example, various investigators have found age equivalence in at least one experimental condition with vocal reaction times (e.g., Eysenck, 1975; Howard, Lasaga, and McAndrews, 1980; Ohta, Walsh, and Krauss, 1981; Poon and Fozard, 1978; Thomas, Waugh, and Fozard, 1978; and Waugh, 1980). On the other hand, many researchers have reported that young adults were faster in vocal reaction time than older adults in one or more comparisons (e.g., Birren and Botwinick, 1955; Camp, 1981; Eriksen, Hamlin, and Daye, 1973; Howard, McAndrews, and Lasaga, 1981; Nebes, 1976; Ohta, Walsh, and Krauss, 1981; Poon and Fozard, 1978; Suci, Davidoff, and Surwillo, 1960; Thomas, Fozard, and Waugh, 1977; Thomas, Waugh, and Fozard, 1978; Waugh, 1980; and Waugh, Fozard, and Thomas, 1978). The presently available evidence is therefore not yet sufficient to determine whether vocal responses are a genuine exception to the slowing trend or simply a reflection of some unknown artifact. Nonetheless, until this situation is clarified, gerontological researchers should be cautious in their use of, and interpretation of, the results from vocal reaction time procedures.

A third possible exception to the slowing-with-age phenomenon concerns the effects of practice on age differences in speeded performance. Several years ago Murrell (1970) reported that a 57-year-old woman was able, with extensive practice, to reduce her reaction time to the level of two teen-agers. Since her initial performance was about what one would expect on the basis of previously reported age trends, this elimination of the age difference was really remarkable and would have important implications for theoretical interpretations if confirmed.

Unfortunately, later studies have not been able to replicate the major finding that age differences are completely eliminated with increased practice. Salthouse and Somberg (1982a) examined the perceptual-motor performance of eight young and eight old adults across 50 one-hour sessions and found that, although performance improved dramatically for both age groups, sizable age differences remained on nearly all dependent measures. Berg, Hertzog, and Hunt (1982); Leonard and Newman (1965); Madden and Nebes (1980); Noble, Baker, and Jones (1964); Plude and Hoyer (1981); and Rabbitt (1964) also confirmed the basic result that age differences in overall speed persist throughout at least moderate amounts of practice (4 to 50 hours). Older adults do seem to exhibit the same qualitative changes as young adults with increased experience, and therefore the quantitative relationship between the speeds of young and old adults may be altered with practice. For exam-

ple, Madden and Nebes (1980), Plude and Hoyer (1981), and Salthouse and Somberg (1982a) found that both young and old adults reduced their comparison times in memory and visual search tasks, suggesting that there is no age difference in the development of "automatic" processing. In general, however, it appears that the age difference in speed is not easily eliminated with practice, and thus the third "exception" has not yet received convincing support. This conclusion must be qualified to levels of practice that, although considered extensive from the laboratory experiment perspective, would represent a trivial period in most extralaboratory activities. For example, a skilled typist could easily execute 72,000 keystrokes per day (i.e., four hours of continuous typing at 60 words per minute and five keystrokes per word), and yet no laboratory study has even approached this number of "trials."

In summary, at least these three classes of exceptions to the slowing-with-age phenomenon have been found to be less dramatic and remarkable than sometimes claimed. It is well known that health status, amount of practice, and a number of other factors affect speed of performance, and it is now clear that age differences can be eliminated by a judicious selection of individuals in which older samples are more positively biased with respect to these variables than younger samples. Since such an outcome does not really address the issue of fundamental age differences in speed, however, these special cases are not true exceptions to the general phenomenon. The situation with respect to the differences between vocal and manual responses is not yet clear, but the available data are still too inconsistent to justify a conclusion that the type of overt response is an important determinant of the existence, or magnitude, of the slowing-with-age phenomenon.

Methodological Considerations

Although there is little doubt about the overall reliability of the finding that older adults are generally slower than young adults in most speeded activities, there is still considerable controversy as to the reasons for this age difference. One factor contributing to this situation is the existence of methodological weaknesses in many of the studies investigating age differences in speeded behavior. Indeed, Rabbitt (1980, p. 425) has suggested that it is "sad to observe that the data presently available are so inadequate that no model based upon them can be taken seriously." Although this view may be overly pessimistic, it is probably true that many of the interpretations incorporated into the psychology of aging literature have been based on results that were not appropriately analyzed, that were obtained from methodologically inadequate experiments, or that have not been confirmed in subsequent attempts at replication.

The methodological problems range from fundamental errors in experimental design and analysis to difficulties specifically associated with the use of reaction time or rate variables. Perhaps because of the important psychometric tradition in research on aging, many researchers have administered a series of different experimental conditions in the same fixed order to all individuals. Since it is possible that one age group either fatigues faster or requires more preliminary trials to reach an optimum level of performance than another age group, this confounding of condition with practice or sequence considerably weakens the value of the results of the studies that follow such a procedure.

Another serious and widespread problem is that many researchers have failed to make direct comparisons of the magnitude of age effects across experimental conditions. There are objections to the use of analysis of variance interaction tests (see below), but it is not appropriate to draw conclusions about age differences in susceptibility to condition influences by conducting separate analyses on the data from each age group. In order to make statements about age differences in the effects of some manipulation, one must directly contrast the effects in one age group with those in other age groups. Unfortunately, many of the results that form the basis of early speculations about the nature or causes of age-related slowing suffer from this defect of never having been

properly tested and are thus of limited usefulness for understanding age differences in speed.

There are also a number of less frequent, but still important, problems associated with studies investigating speed differences as a function of adult age. For example, the same individuals are sometimes used as subjects in several experiments with no concern about the restricted generality of the results because of their prior participation or about the lack of independence thereby generated across the successive statistical tests. Furthermore, because age differences are generally so pronounced, some studies rely on very small samples in each age group; such samples, although sufficient to achieve statistical significance, contribute to widely varying quantitative assessments of the magnitude of age differences under particular conditions. The latter problem is becoming more severe because of the attempts of theorists to make quantitative meta-analyses of age differences in speed (e.g., Cerella, Poon, and Williams, 1980). A relatively simple partial solution to this problem, one short of drastically increasing sample sizes, would be to administer a standardized test of speeded function as a way of assessing the representativeness of the individuals in each age group. The Digit Symbol Substitution Test from the Wechsler Adult Intelligence Scale is a reasonable candidate for such an assessment device since it is not only reliable and well-documented, but also apparently produces comparable age differences at several levels of practice (e.g., Beres and Baron, 1981; Erber, 1976; Erber, Botwinick, and Storandt, 1981; Grant, Storandt, and Botwinick, 1978; Salthouse, 1978a).

Problems arising from the use of reaction time or some other speeded measure as the dependent variable include (1) too little practice, (2) a tendency for variability to be proportional to mean time, (3) confounding of speed and accuracy, (4) extremely long task times, and (5) performing transformations without sufficient justification or awareness of the consequences. The practice problem occurs because reaction time is typically quite variable in the initial trials, particularly in complex tasks, and the measurements obtained during this unstable period provide very poor estimates of true capability. The question of how much practice is necessary before stable measurements are possible cannot be easily answered, but it seems clear that a minimum of 20 to 30 preliminary trials are desirable before attempting to measure simple tasks and proportionally more for tasks of greater complexity.

Since there are definite physiological limits on the minimum time needed to execute a response but no restrictions on the maximum time, it is likely that a shift in the mean of a distribution will often lead to a concomitant increase in the variability of the distribution. That is, as the scores move away from the measurement "floor," there is more room to exhibit variation; consequently, the variance often increases in rough proportion with the mean. This trend could be evident in the distribution of times across trials involving a single individual as well as in the distribution of mean times across individuals within an age group. In either case, the tendency for variability to be larger in the groups (or conditions) with the largest mean times can complicate the use of statistical tests that assume homogeneity of variance. It is also possible that unequal variances attributable to measurement artifacts may tempt theorists to pursue fruitless speculations based on the presumed existence of true age differences in performance variability.

The speed-accuracy confound is related to the empirical observation that speed and accuracy are often inversely related—that is, slow performance leads to high accuracy, and fast performance leads to low accuracy. Comparisons of speed with an unspecified level of accuracy may therefore be meaningless since the same speed could be produced at high accuracy in one group of individuals but only at low accuracy in another. Moreover, the possibility of this type of speed-accuracy tradeoff cannot simply be assessed by conducting separate analyses on the time and accuracy variables because nonsignificant trends in one variable could still lead to large alterations in the other variable. A more subtle and often neglected point is that speed comparisons may also be uninterpretable when accuracy is 100

percent for all groups and conditions. The difficulty here is that there is no way of determining how far one is away from the optimum speed at 100-percent accuracy (cf. Pachella, 1974; Salthouse, 1979). In one condition or one group of individuals, 100-percent accuracy might be achieved at the fastest possible speed, whereas in another condition or group, much more time than is absolutely necessary might be taken to achieve the highest accuracy. The solution to these speed-accuracy tradeoff contaminations is to make speed comparisons at a fixed, less-than-perfect level of accuracy. Since very few studies have employed such comparisons, one must be sensitive to this type of problem in drawing conclusions from most of the research on age and speed.

There are two potential difficulties when one attempts to make inferences about age differences in performance on tasks with very lengthy response times. Both problems can be illustrated by considering a card-sorting task in which the operation of interest—e.g., discrimination of the target letter—requires approximately 25 msec per card whereas all other operations consume a total of over 1000 msec. Since the operation of primary interest occupies a very small proportion of the overall task time, it is very likely that the cumulative random variability of other processes (e.g., card turning, decision, card placement) will tend to mask the small systematic effects attributable to the discrimination process. Moreover, since older adults are generally slower than young adults, the likelihood of condition effects being hidden or attenuated by the variability of other processes may be greater with increased age.

Condition effects can also be accentuated as well as attenuated in tasks producing very long response times. The effects of a manipulation may be exaggerated if the critical operation becomes so error-prone that other, more time-consuming operations, must be frequently repeated. As an example, if an error of discrimination is not discovered until the card placement is nearly completed, the incorrect response will have to be retracted and a new one substituted. Both of these actions may require considerably more time than the operation directly affected by the experimental manipulation, and thus the observed condition effect may be much greater than the added duration of the discrimination in the critical operation. It is clearly difficult to predict which of these opposing trends is operating in a given situation, but one should be sensitive to both of them whenever the condition effects of interest are small relative to the average response time of one or more age groups.

The transformation problem derives from the fact that most distributions of speeded measures are positively skewed. In order to convert these distributions to a normal approximation for purposes of statistical testing, many investigators have subjected the data to some type of mathematical transformation. There are two objections to this procedure. The first is the general argument that the statistical conclusions now pertain to the transformed data and not to the real data. In some situations, the transformation can dramatically alter the pattern of statistical effects so that one is faced with the dilemma of deciding which results to report.

A more specific objection to the use of transformations with temporal variables is that these variables are not scaled in arbitrary units as are most other dependent variables in psychology, but instead are meaningful reflections of real-time durations (cf. Pachella, 1974). In order to preserve the real-time properties of speeded variables, one should not impose transformations merely for statistical convenience. It should also be noted that the practice of employing median rather than mean measures of central tendency may be inappropriate if one wishes to use techniques such as Sternberg's (1969) additive-factors method.

These methodological problems are so pervasive that it is difficult to find many published studies that are free of all of them and still relevant to important theoretical issues. In this respect, Rabbitt's (1980) pessimism seems quite justified. Nevertheless, it is desirable to attempt to impose some organization into this literature and to identify promising theoretical approaches. We will therefore examine classes of theoretical explanation and some of the evidence relevant to each, but at all times it must be kept in mind that the data are not only sparse, but often methodologically flawed as well. Because this review is primarily concerned with theoretical issues, the coverage of material is necessarily selective. In no way should the present survey be considered an exhaustive examination of the literature in speeded behavior and aging.

CHARACTERIZING POSSIBLE CAUSES OF AGE-RELATED SLOWING

In the context of a discussion of alternative mechanisms to account for developmental differences in processing rate, Salthouse and Kail (1983) recently outlined six possible explanations to account for the time delays between input and output in two hypothetical computer systems. The six alternatives appear to encompass most of the major hypotheses that have been proposed to explain age-related slowing of behavior, and thus it is convenient to use them as a basis for organizing the present survey of theoretical interpretations in this area. Since a computer metaphor was used by Salthouse and Kail, the initial identification of possible mechanisms will be based on terminology borrowed from the field of computer science.

Input and/or Output Rate

Perhaps the simplest possibility for explaining greater delays between input and output in one computer system compared to another is a slower rate of transmitting information between the central processing unit and the peripheral input and output devices. If one system has a slower speed of peripheral communication than another, all tasks performed by that system will require more time between the initial input and final output than by an identical system performing exactly the same operations but having a faster rate of communicating with peripheral devices.

There are well-documented sensory and motor changes associated with increased age, and it is clear that the delay between input and output will be longer if environmental information takes more time to reach the brain because of such sensory or motor delays. This type of peripheral hypothesis therefore has an a priori plausibility as a potentially important factor responsible for age-related slowing. In fact, some version of this hypothesis was favored by many early investigators, and it is apparently still accepted by researchers in other areas of the psychology of aging. As an example, Burke and Light (1981) recently implied that the effects of age-related slowing in memory tasks could be controlled by manipulating the rate of stimulus presentation. Such a manipulation would successfully eliminate the slowing effects only if they were attributable simply to peripheral registration or encoding processes.

The status of this input/output class of explanation is the least ambiguous of any category of explanation to be considered here. The great majority of the evidence suggests that input and output processes can account for only a very small part of the slower behavior of older adults. One reason is that sensory and motor factors have only slight effects on speed when stimuli are as intense, or responses as simple, as those typically found in aging studies of speeded behavior. Most experimental stimuli are well above the threshold of even the most impaired older adults, and elementary key release or key press responses require minimal muscular effort or strength.

One version of the sensory-limitation hypothesis was examined 50 years ago by Koga and Morant (1923), using data originally collected by Galton. Among the measures available in the Galton battery were reaction time to a visual stimulus, reaction time to an auditory stimulus, visual acuity, and auditory sensitivity. Koga and Morant argued that if the age-related speed differences were attributable to sensory limitations one would expect the within-modality correlations (i.e., visual reaction time with visual acuity and auditory reaction time with auditory sensitivity) to be greater than the correlations between the two reaction time measures. In fact, however, the within-modality correlations were lower than the correlations between the two reaction time tasks, indicating that there was more common variance between the two speeded tasks than between a reaction time task and a measure of sensitivity in that modality. Although the measures of visual and auditory sensitivity

were rather crude and did not involve the same kind of stimuli as those used in the reaction time tests, it is interesting to note how early the peripheral hypothesis was examined and found lacking.

A straightforward prediction from an input/output rate perspective is that the time difference between young and old adults should remain constant with increases in task complexity as long as the input and output processes remain the same. That is, regardless of the number or type of processing operations, the output from one system will always be delayed a constant amount relative to the system with faster input and output processes. An early test of this expectation was conducted by Birren, Riegel, and Morrison (1962), who employed an apparatus that allowed the same stimulus and response arrangement to be used for a variety of tasks with differing translation requirements. For example, in one task the stimuli were lights appearing in a regular sequence, and the subject was instructed to press the button located below the illuminated light. In another task, the stimuli consisted of the first syllables of words, and the subject was instructed to press the buttons containing the appropriate second syllable of the word. In all tasks, the stimuli were presented in the same location and format, and the responses were always button presses.

The important result from the Birren et al. (1962) experiment was that the magnitude of the age differences was not constant across tasks but instead tended to increase with the time needed by the young adults to perform the relevant activity. As the authors stated: "In a general way the age difference in speed appears to increase as the task requires more manipulation or consideration of the stimulus before a response is given" (p. 10). A later report by Brinley (1965), in which a variety of paper-and-pencil tasks were examined in two age groups, revealed a similar pattern; age differences were not constant but instead appeared to increase with the degree of complexity of the task.

Jordan and Rabbitt (1977) have argued that the progressively greater age differences with more complex tasks is only evident at early stages of practice, but their evidence is rather equivocal. The major finding in support of their conclusion was that older adults appeared to be more affected by manipulations of task complexity in the first of four trial blocks than in later trial blocks, whereas young adults had roughly equivalent complexity effects in all trial blocks. However, several characteristics of this study lead one to question the validity of the conclusion. For example, (1) the 12 adults in each age group had previously served in two similar experiments and thus had already received some prior practice; (2) error rates were very high in the initial trials, suggesting that there was great confusion in the early phases of the experiment; (3) the complexity manipulation consisted merely of repetition or alternation of stimuli and responses and hence involved very low levels of cognitive activity; and finally, (4) although the age X complexity interaction was significant in the first trial block and not in the fourth block, there was no mention of a significant triple interaction of age/complexity/trial block as predicted by the authors' argument. For all of these reasons, the Jordan and Rabbitt result must not be considered too troublesome for the suggestion that age differences tend to increase with task complexity, although as noted earlier the specific quantitative relationship between age groups may indeed change as practice-related shifts in the mode of performance occur.

A second prediction from the class of peripheral (input/output) interpretations of the slowing phenomenon is that no age differences should be observed in the rate of internal processes when they are measured independent of the duration of input and output processes. The best known procedure for measuring such an internal process is Sternberg's (1969) memory-scanning task, in which the slope of the function relating set size to reaction time is considered an estimate of the time for mental comparison independent of the duration of all other processes. At least eight separate studies have revealed that the slope is greater with increased age (e.g., Anders and Fozard, 1973; Anders, Fozard, and Lillyquist, 1972; Eriksen, Hamlin, and Daye, 1973; Ford, Roth, Mohs, Hopkins, and Kopell, 1979; Madden, 1982;

Madden and Nebes, 1980; Salthouse and Somberg, 1982a; 1982b) although there is some evidence that the age differences in the slope parameter may be eliminated when the stimuli are so distinct, or the amount of practice so great, as to allow "automatic processing" (e.g., Madden, 1982; Plude and Hoyer, 1981; Plude, Hoyer, and Lazar, 1982; Salthouse and Somberg, 1982a).

Estimates of the rate of mental rotation derived from the procedure introduced by Shepard and his colleagues (e.g., Shepard and Metzler, 1971) are also generally consistent in indicating age differences in favor of young adults (e.g., Berg, Hertzog, and Hunt, 1982; Gaylord and Marsh, 1975; Cerella, Poon, and Fozard, 1981). An exception to this trend was reported by Jacewicz and Hartley (1979), who found no age differences in the rate of mental rotation. These investigators, however, used very few (10) adults in each age group, and in one of their two experiments they failed to find a significant main effect of age (22 vs. 56 years) on overall reaction time. It therefore seems likely that the combination of small sample sizes, restricted age range, large variability, and relatively long response times contributed to their failure to find significant age differences in duration of mental rotation.

A third prediction from the input/output rate perspective is that age differences in speed should be eliminated by bypassing either the input or the output phase of processing. For example, if the rate of executing and monitoring a response is the major factor in age-related slowing, then age differences should disappear if measurements can be obtained prior to the overt response. In fact, however, three studies (Botwinick and Thompson, 1966; Surwillo, 1968; Weiss, 1965) in which EMG recordings were used to allow measurement of pre-motor time, as well as several studies measuring the latency of evoked potential responses in the brain (see Ford and Pfefferbaum, 1980, for a review), have reported reliably faster performance in younger adults.

A large number of experiments have also demonstrated substantial age differences in the time required to achieve comparable accuracy in tachistoscopic perception when there is no time pressure concerning the occurrence of the response (see Salthouse, 1982, for a review). Fewer attempts have been made to eliminate the input stage, but the reports of sizable age differences in the rate of verbal associations when each response is triggered entirely by internal events can be interpreted as indicating age differences in speed when there is no explicit input process (e.g., Birren, Riegel, and Robbin, 1962; Riegel and Birren, 1965).

In the face of this type of evidence, it is clear that the slowing observed with increased age cannot be localized simply to either input or output processes. Peripheral factors may contribute somewhat to the slower behavior of older adults, but the bulk of the evidence suggests that such processes are not responsible for all, or even most, of the slowing-with-age phenomenon.

Software Differences

Another possibility for differences in the delay between input and output across two computer systems is the use of qualitatively different programs, or sequences of control processes, in the two systems. If one of the systems uses control processes that are less efficient in the sense of requiring more total operations than those of the other system, the former system will have a longer delay between input and output for most activities even though the two systems might be structurally identical. (Many employers of computer programmers have discovered this fact in an expensive fashion by finding that the savings of lower salaries for less experienced programmers often disappear when the cost of the additional time necessary for the computer to execute inefficient programs is taken into consideration.)

Explanations in the gerontological literature that postulate strategy differences across age groups are analogous to this type of mechanism. The strategies may be assumed to be conscious attempts at compensation for known or suspected deficits or merely unintentional and subtle shifts in the manner in which a task is approached and performed. Three specific hypotheses that have been proposed to account for findings that older adults are

slower than young adults are as follows: (1) poor preparation (e.g., Botwinick, 1965; Gottsdanker, 1980a; 1980b; Loveless and Sanford, 1974; Morris and Thompson, 1969; Thompson and Nowlin, 1973); (2) inefficient use of stimulus information (e.g., Rabbitt, 1965; 1968; Farkas and Hoyer, 1980); and (3) differential emphasis on accuracy as opposed to speed (e.g., Rabbitt, 1979; Welford, 1958).

A number of predictions can be derived from the class of theories postulating a software difference as the mechanism responsible for age-related slowing. One of these is that there should not be age differences in speed when the task is designed to minimize or eliminate variations in strategy or control processes. With respect to the accuracy-emphasis hypothesis, this prediction has not been supported, since several reports are now available that indicate that age differences in speed are still present when individuals of different ages are compared at exactly the same level of accuracy, thus eliminating any differential accuracy bias that may be present in typical reaction time tasks (Salthouse, 1979; Salthouse and Somberg, 1982c). It may well be true that older adults are often more accurate than young adults once a task has been clearly understood by both age groups (e.g., Salthouse and Somberg, 1982a), but the current evidence indicates that age differences in speed remain even when level of accuracy is equated.

The poor-preparation hypothesis exists in several different versions, but most attribute at least some of the age differences in speed to either a failure to develop optimal readiness for a specific signal or to a decreased ability to maintain a highly prepared state. One of the first manipulations employed to examine these possibilities was to vary either the duration or regularity of the preparatory interval between a warning signal and the signal indicating that a response should be made. Unfortunately, the results of these studies have been confusing since the initial reports indicated greater age differences with short preparatory intervals (e.g., Botwinick, Brinley, and Birren, 1957; Brinley and Botwinick, 1959), but later studies either failed to confirm this finding (e.g., Botwinick and Storandt, 1973; Botwinick and Thompson, 1966) or reported the opposite result, i.e., greater age differences with long preparatory intervals (e.g., Loveless and Sanford, 1974).

Several investigators have also employed psychophysiological measures of arousal or attention to investigate the differential-preparation or expectancy hypothesis, but once again the results have been inconsistent and difficult to interpret. For example, Morris and Thompson (1969) found less heart rate deceleration among older adults than young adults, and Loveless and Sanford (1974) reported different patterns of brain wave (CNV) modulation across age groups. In neither case, however, did the psychophysiological measures exhibit the same trend across conditions and foreperiods as the reaction time measure. Moreover, as Marsh and Watson (1980) point out, it is dangerous to make psychological interpretations from physiological data until one has established that the same transfer functions apply to all age groups. If the physiological process is limited by nonpsychological factors in one age group and not in another age group, then the same interpretations may not apply across age groups.

More recently, Gottsdanker (1980a) has argued that there is no age difference in the maintenance of preparation over a range of preparation intervals. His results, however, were based on adults selected to have nearly equivalent simple reaction times, and it doesn't seem reasonable to draw conclusions about the causes of performance differences when the individuals providing the data do not themselves exhibit those differences.

Taken together, it must be concluded that the data presently available provide little evidence that age differences in expectancy or preparation contribute to the slower performance of older adults in most behavioral activities. Both the theoretical interpretations and the empirical data have been confusing, inconsistent, and at least partially contradictory.

The hypothesis that older adults are slow partly because of inefficient utilization of information has not yet been supported with a finding that age differences are eliminated under conditions that maximize ease of information use. However, Rabbitt (1968) has suggested that older adults, relative to young adults, "are unable to ignore irrelevant information . . . do not ignore foresignals, which apparently never help them and often distract them . . . process information from redundant signal sources," and concluded that older adults "behave like computers that have been inefficiently programmed" (p. 88).

A second prediction from the software-differences perspective is that age differences should increase in magnitude with increases in task complexity because of the greater opportunity for the employment of differential strategies. As noted above, such a result has been observed several times in a variety of experimental tasks (e.g., Birren et al., 1962; Brinley, 1965). One might also predict from the software perspective that very simple tasks with minimal need for differential strategies would exhibit little or no age differences. This possibility has only been partially confirmed since age differences have typically been reported in simple reaction time tasks (see Table 1), although these differences are often of smaller absolute magnitude than those found with more complex tasks.

Still another prediction from the software perspective is that age differences in speed might be expected to be eliminated with prolonged practice since individuals of all ages would then be given an opportunity to acquire optimal strategies. As indicated earlier, most studies have revealed that age differences in overall speed persist through at least 50 hours of experience (e.g., Berg, Hertzog, and Hunt, 1982; Leonard and Newman, 1965; Madden and Nebes, 1980; Noble, Baker, and Jones, 1964; Plude and Hoyer, 1981; Rabbitt, 1964; and Salthouse and Somberg, 1982a).

A reasonable conclusion with respect to the possibility of strategy differences contributing to the age-related slowing is that at the present time there simply isn't much convincing evidence to support it. Age differences may exist in as yet undiscovered strategies, but those that have been examined thus far have yielded negative or inconsistent results.

Internal Representation of Control Processes

A third potential source of differences in input-output delay is the manner in which the control processes are represented in memory.

Frequently, control processes (programs) for computers are prepared in high-level languages like BASIC or FORTRAN that are easy for the programmer to produce and comprehend but are not in the optimal form for execution by a computer. In general, the speed of program execution will be faster when the control processes are represented in the form most compatible with the hardware of the particular computer (i.e., assembly or machine language).

In psychological terms, knowledge can be considered to vary in accessibility as well as presence or absence, and it is possible that many procedural operations become less available with increased age; that is, the same sequence of control processes might be employed and the physical capacity of the system may remain unchanged, but if some or all of the operations are in a low state of availability, extra time will be needed to perform many tasks.

One result that seems consistent with this type of operation-availability mechanism is the Rabbitt and Birren (1967) finding that young adults exhibited relatively more disruption than older ones whenever an unexpected signal occurred in a normally repetitive sequence of signals. It is possible that the young adults developed an efficient means of controlling their responses to regular signals that allowed them to perform better than older adults except when unexpected stimuli were presented. In the latter case, the more efficient coding appears to have actually placed them at a disadvantage since the coding had been developed for the specific situation of regular signals. The young adults were therefore operating as though they were employing a special-purpose "assembly-language" code, whereas the older adults seemed to be operating with a more general "high-level" code.

Only Rabbitt and Birren (1967), it would appear, have proposed that age differences in speed can be attributed to a possible difference in the representation of control processes. For many situations, however, the predictions would be nearly the same as those derived from the software-difference perspective. In particular, one would expect age differences in speed to be eliminated with extensive practice because recent frequency of usage should

lead to the optimum state of availability for all relevant operations. As noted above, this expectation has not been confirmed by several recent studies (e.g., Berg, Hertzog and Hunt, 1982; Leonard and Newman, 1965; Madden and Nebes, 1980; Noble, Baker, and Jones, 1964; Plude and Hoyer, 1981; Rabbitt, 1964; Salthouse and Somberg, 1982a).

Because this perspective is rather new, it is not surprising that little evidence to support the possibility of age differences in the accessibility of internal operations is currently available. The meager evidence that does exist, however, offers a mixed picture. Although the Rabbitt and Birren result can be interpreted as positive evidence, the existence of sizable differences after moderate practice must be considered negative evidence.

Capacity of Working Memory

A fourth possible source of processing delays is a smaller working memory space in one system than in another. The working memory space is used for holding all problem statements, performing computing operations, storing intermediate solutions, etc. Thus, if one system has a smaller working space than another, it will have to rely more frequently on time-consuming swapping operations to transfer information to and from the larger-capacity secondary storage system. As a consequence, many of the tasks performed by the system with the smaller working memory will require more time for completion than the same tasks performed on a system with a larger working memory.

An apparent difficulty with this class of explanation for age-related differences in speed is that some theorists have maintained that the capacity of primary or working memory is unaffected by increased age (e.g., Craik, 1977). Obviously, if the size of working memory is the same across the adult life span, one could not attempt to explain age differences in speed on the basis of nonexistent age differences in working memory. The evidence for the claim that primary memory is invariant across adulthood is still quite equivocal, however, and a recent review indicated that any conclusion would be premature on the basis of available evidence (Salthouse, 1982).

The major prediction from this capacity-of-working-memory perspective is that there should be little or no age difference for simple tasks (those that can be performed without exceeding the limits of the smaller working memory), but age differences should be pronounced and generally increasing in absolute magnitude for more complex tasks (those that require frequent exchanges of information in the system with the smaller working memory). As mentioned earlier, Birren et al. (1962) and Brinley (1965) reported increasing absolute age differences with increased complexity, but the existence of reliable age differences with simple reaction time tasks (see Table 1) is inconsistent with this hypothesis. The evidence concerning the working-memory class of explanation must therefore be considered suggestive but not yet conclusive.

Concurrent Processing Demands

A fifth basis for expecting processing delays between two computer systems is the number of jobs awaiting execution, or currently being executed, in the two systems. Consider a system with a backlog of several jobs that must be executed before the current job or a system that is performing in a time-sharing mode that allocates only a fraction of the total resources to each job (or all of the resources for only a fraction of the total time). The delay between input and output will be greater in such systems than in a system where only one task is awaiting execution and has access to all of the resources of the system. Psychological variables that might correspond to this type of situation are arousal and motivational fluctuations that lead to less than the maximum amount of resources being devoted to the experimental task.

Explanations based on the underarousal or overarousal of older adults relative to younger adults would clearly fall within this category. Unfortunately, the psychophysiological evidence is very confusing with respect to the arousal state of older adults, and recent reviews suggest that no definitive conclusion can be reached on this issue with existing evidence (e.g., Marsh and Thompson, 1977; Marsh and Watson, 1980).

One prediction from a partial-allocation-of-resources mechanism is that the age differences in speed should be eliminated if conditions are so arranged that individuals clearly benefit if they devote all of their resources to the performance of the experimental task. In reaction time studies, such conditioning has been achieved either by administering electrical shock for slow responses (Botwinick, Brinley, and Robbin, 1958; Weiss, 1965) or by providing instructional or monetary incentive for fast responses (Salthouse, 1979; Salthouse and Somberg, 1982c). Since the age difference was eliminated in neither case, it seems unlikely that a simple version of a "concurrent processing demand" interpretation will prove successful in accounting for age differences in speed of behavior. The verdict is still out with respect to more complicated versions of this hypothesis.

Hardware Differences

In view of the rapid technological advances in computers, a very likely possibility for differences in the speed of two computer systems is a hardware difference that makes the cycle time per operation faster in one system than in another. The two systems would differ in the time between input and output even if the same operations were performed in exactly the same sequence (i.e., if identical software were used) in each system. Everything done under the control of the central processing unit would simply take longer in the system with the slower cycle time. Exceptions to the slower system response would occur only when the operations are handled by an intelligent peripheral and become independent of the limitations of the central processing unit. (In psychological terms, the exceptions would occur only when the operations—by virtue of extreme practice, compatibility, or simplicity—become "automatic" and therefore exempt from processing limitations.)

A variety of hypotheses in the aging literature can be considered analogous to this hardware difference. For example, the neural-noise theory discussed by Crossman and Szafran (1957), Gregory (1957), Welford (e.g., 1958; 1959; 1965; 1977; 1981), and others is based on the assumption that neural events are slower in the older nervous system because of its need to integrate information samples for a longer time to compensate for increased levels of "neural noise." In support of this hypothesis are the reports that neural conduction time (LaFratta and Canestrari, 1966; Norris, Shock, and Wagman, 1953; Wagman and Lesse, 1952) has been found to increase slightly with advancing age. The absolute amount of increase is quite small, but when it is accumulated across a large number of neural events, the total time difference could be substantial.

For many years, Birren (e.g., 1955; 1964; 1965; 1970; 1974) has advocated the position that the time of fundamental neural events becomes slower with increasing age. He has never cited a specific physiological mechanism for this, but his (1974) analogy proposed that the older adult performs as though in a condition of electrical energy "brown out," in which the same processes are carried out as in the younger adult but at a slower rate. Birren's views have been so well articulated that the notion that increased age affects the speed of nearly all behavioral processes has come to be known as the *Birren hypothesis* (e.g., Cerella, Poon, Fozard, 1981; Jacewicz and Hartley, 1979; Salthouse, 1980).

Another hypothesis that appears formally similar to a cycle-time mechanism is the alpha-wave hypothesis of Surwillo (e.g., 1968), in which it is postulated that the alpha rhythm of the EEG serves as a central timing mechanism for most or all neural operations. If internal processing operations can be performed only at specific periods in a timing cycle and the period of the cycle is slower in one system than in another, the duration of nearly all resulting processes will be affected. Sizable correlations between age and alpha period and between alpha period and reaction time have been cited as support for this hypothesis (Surwillo, 1968), although other evidence tends to be inconsistent with this particular version of the "hardware," cycle-time mechanism. For example, Birren (1965) and Woodruff (1975) failed to find a close relationship between alpha rhythm and reaction time under slightly different conditions, and several studies (e.g.,

Arenberg, 1968; Salthouse, Wright, and Ellis, 1979; Surwillo, 1964) have reported that older adults are not poorer at time estimation as might be expected if their internal clock mechanism were operating at a slower rate than that of young adults.

One implication of the cycle-time hypothesis is that no single information processing stage should be found to be "critical," or uniquely responsible, for the age-related slowing, but instead the slowing should be generalized and evident in nearly all stages of processing. Salthouse and Somberg (1982b) used Sternberg's (1969) additive-factors method to investigate the susceptibility of encoding, comparison, and response stages to the "factor" of adult age. The major finding of this study was that increased age affected each of the three stages and that the age-related slowness could not be localized in any one of them.

A number of earlier studies in which only one processing stage was examined at a time have also supported the conclusion that age effects are evident in nearly every stage investigated. For example, the existence of interactions between age and (1) a manipulation designed to influence stimulus encoding (e.g., Simon, 1968; Simon and Pourghabagher, 1978); (2) central decision or comparison (e.g., Anders, Fozard, and Lillyquist, 1972; Anders and Fozard, 1973; Berg, Hertzog, and Hunt, 1982; Cerella, Poon, and Fozard, 1981; Eriksen, Hamlin, and Daye, 1973; Ford, Roth, Mohs, Hopkins, and Kopell, 1979; Gaylord and Marsh, 1976; Madden, 1982; Madden and Nebes, 1980); and (3) response selection or execution (e.g., Simon, 1967; 1968) have all been interpreted as signifying that the processing stage responsible for that operation was affected by increased age.

Several additional studies have reported alternative analyses in which two or more components have been identified as contributing to speeded performance. In each case, age differences have been reported in every component examined (e.g., Hines and Posner, 1976; Mortimer-Tanner and Naylor, 1973; Naylor, 1973; Poon, Fozard, Vierck, Dailey, Cerella, and Zeller, 1976; Storandt, 1976).

There are some exceptions to these findings of age differences in each information-processing stage—e.g., in response selection (Simon and Pourghabagher, 1978)—perhaps because the condition manipulations were not very effective or the statistical power was insufficient. For the most part, however, the picture presented by the information-processing analyses is reasonably consistent in indicating that age affects every processing stage.

Two attempts to employ mathematical models to isolate age differences in a particular theoretical component have led to somewhat different conclusions concerning the universality of age effects on all speeded processes. For example, Welford (e.g., 1959; 1962; 1977) has repeatedly argued that a model based on concepts from information theory is useful for distinguishing between constant (peripherally based) and proportionally increasing (centrally determined) age differences in speed. As Welford himself admits, however, the available evidence relevant to this distinction has been far from consistent. Moreover, there apparently have been very few formal statistical tests of the difference in the age trends in the two hypothetical processes, and therefore the speculations have not yet received convincing statistical support.

A similar objection can be raised against the arguments of Waugh, Fozard, Talland, and Ervin (1973) and of Fozard, Thomas, and Waugh (1976). These researchers used a model in which total reaction time was decomposed into sensory-motor and decision components and then attempted to determine which component was most affected by increased age. However, since there was no direct comparison of the magnitude of the age trends in the two components, the authors' conclusion that aging primarily affects the sensory-motor component has not yet been adequately supported. Since there was also no evidence presented concerning the validity of this technique for separating total reaction time into distinguishable components, it is questionable whether the conclusions should be accepted even if appropriate statistical tests have been conducted.

Recently, Cerella, Poon, and Fozard (1981) have distinguished between strong and weak versions of what they termed the Birren hypothesis. The weak form simply predicts that age-related slowing will be evident in all mental processes. As discussed above, this version of the hypothesis has received reasonably favorable support. The strong form of the hypothesis is that the extent of the age-related slowing should be the same in all mental processes. This is clearly a much more difficult proposition to test as it requires considerable knowledge of mental processes and much greater precision in the data than has been available. With respect to the first point, age differences might be proportional at the level of elementary operations within the nervous system, but if these operations are combined in different ways by young and old adults, it would be very difficult to predict exactly what quantitative relationship would be obtained at the grosser levels of mental process duration or overall task time.

Some of the problems with attempting to make too detailed inferences from a methodologically inadequate data base were discussed earlier. One further problem, mentioned by Salthouse and Somberg (1982b) and elaborated upon below, is that the estimate of the magnitude of the age effect in a particular processing component is heavily dependent upon the strength of the manipulation that is presumed to affect that component. As a result, quantitative comparisons of the magnitude of age effects in particular processes become difficult since it is often impossible to equate the magnitude of various manipulation effects. At the current time, therefore, it appears extremely hard to provide an adequate test of the strong version of the cycle-time hypothesis, and consequently its validity cannot yet be evaluated.

A second implication of the cycle-time perspective is that the age differences should increase in absolute magnitude as the task to be performed increases in processing complexity. The basis for this prediction is that more operations will be required with more complex tasks, and since each operation is postulated to be slower with increased age, the total time difference between young and old adults will increase directly with task complexity.

It was mentioned earlier that Birren et al (1962) and Brinley (1965) have reported results consistent with this prediction. The pro-

gressively increasing age-differences prediction can be more formally evaluated by
examining the parameters of a linear regression equation that relates the time of young
adults to the time of older adults across activities of varying complexity but comparable input and output requirements. The slope of this
equation should be greater than 1.0 to indicate
increasing absolute age differences with
greater task complexity. (Following Salthouse,
1978b, and Cerella, et al., 1980, complexity
is assumed to be proportional to the time required by the young adults to perform the
task.) The correlation coefficient should be
reasonably high to reflect a good fit of the
linear equation to the data. If all operations
are slower for older adults than for younger
ones by the same proportional amount, the
intercept should approximate zero when no
operations are performed.

These predictions were examined in several
sources of data on tasks ranging from reaction
time to paper-and-pencil tests. Salthouse and
Somberg (1982b) found that reaction time
data across eight experimental conditions fitted the equation, Old (time) = −0.31 + 2.16
Young (time), with a correlation of 0.991. An
earlier experiment by Salthouse (1978a) investigating several paper-and-pencil versions of
the Digit Symbol Substitution Test yielded
similar results, as can be seen in Figure 2.
Data were also analyzed from a number of
individual experiments with adults having
mean ages between 20 and 30 years and between 60 and 70 years, in which results from
at least ten conditions were reported. Only
studies with a relatively large number of pairs
of young-old data points were selected in order
to provide fairly definitive tests of the parameters of the regression equation. Note that the
data presented in Table 2 conform to the predictions from the cycle-time hypothesis in
each case. The slope values range between 1.58
and 2.01, the correlations are all above 0.94,
and the intercepts cluster around zero, although with more negative values than one
might expect.

Cerella, Poon, and Williams (1980) have
also analyzed the pooled data from many separate experiments and reported very similar results (i.e., high correlations, small intercepts,

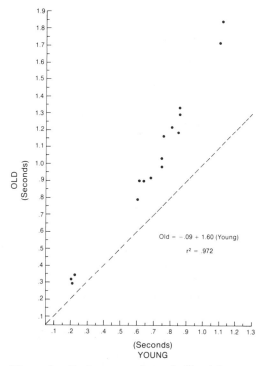

Figure 2.   Performance time of old adults as a
function of performance time of young adults
across different versions of a digit-symbol substitution task (Salthouse, 1978a). Each point represents
the time of young (abcissa) and old (ordinate)
adults in a given experimental condition.

and slopes greater than 1.0). They did suggest
that the slopes are steeper with "mental" as
opposed to "sensory/motor" tasks, but since
the mental–sensory/motor distinction was not
operationally defined, it is difficult to evaluate
this particular conclusion at the present time.
The issue of the number of parameters needed
to characterize age trends across a variety of
speeded tasks is nonetheless an important one,
and more theoretical and empirical effort in
this direction would be very desirable.

Another prediction from the cycle-time hypothesis is that the magnitude of correlations
across both speeded and unspeeded measures
should be larger with increased age. The reasoning is that both the speed and the probability of successful completion of many activities
should be affected by the general slowing (cf.,
Salthouse, 1982; Salthouse and Kail, 1983),
and thus individuals with a slow cycle time
should be slower and less accurate across a
variety of measures than individuals with a

TABLE 2   Regression Parameters of the Age-Speed Function

$$\text{Time}_{\text{Old}} = A + B\ \text{Time}_{\text{Young}}$$

Source	N(Old)	N(Young)	N(Comparisons)	Correlation	A	B
Birren and Botwinick (1955)	43	30	12	0.996	−0.309	1.87
Birren, Riegel, and Morrison (1962)[1]	23	30	22	0.961	−0.035	1.58
Botwinick, Brinley, and Robbin (1958)	34	26	12	0.975	−0.265	1.59
Brinley (1965)	51	60	21	0.986	−0.260	1.68
Cerella, Poon, and Fozard (1981)	15	14	20	0.949	−0.415	2.01

[1] The two slowest conditions in this study had extremely large variability and are omitted from the analysis to improve the fit of the regression equation to the remaining data.

fast cycle time. At present, this prediction is very gross and undoubtedly somewhat naive, as we simply don't have much knowledge about the way slower speeds of operation affect different processes. Nonetheless, there are a number of reports of higher correlations between dependent measures in older adults than in young adults (e.g., Berg, Hertzog and Hunt, 1982; Birren, 1965; Birren and Botwinick, 1955; Birren, Riegel, and Morrison, 1962; Brinley, 1965; Weber, Hochhaus, and Brown, 1981), and thus the available evidence is not inconsistent with this prediction.

Some Final Reservations

Although these six classes of alternative mechanisms encompass a large number of specific hypotheses that have or could be proposed to account for age differences in speed, the foregoing list should not be considered exhaustive, nor the alternatives mutually exclusive. With respect to the last point, it is actually very unlikely that any single mechanism would exist in isolation because a change in one aspect of the system is likely to lead to corresponding changes in other aspects. For example, a slower rate of operation (hardware difference) may cause different control processes to be employed (software difference), which may in turn lead to different degrees of operation availability (control-process-representation difference). The net result of two or more mechanisms operating simultaneously is difficult to predict, but one should not be surprised to discover a complicated pattern

of results that does not correspond exactly to any of the predictions based on a single mechanism.

It might also be expected that the particular combination of mechanisms responsible for the age difference in speed will vary across tasks. Thus, although certain fundamental mechanisms might always be operating, the demands of different tasks could lead to the employment of a variety of alternative secondary mechanisms in different situations. For example, the pattern of age differences might be altered to emphasize input and output processes by requiring fine stimulus discriminations and complicated responses (these would tend to produce a constant age difference by making peripheral factors dominant) or by keeping the stimulus and response processes simple but introducing complications in the translation processes (these should lead to a proportional age difference by stressing internal processing operations). In light of these considerations, researchers must resist the tendency to reject or accept alternatives too hastily from the results of only one or two experiments, no matter how carefully they were conducted. The quantitative age trend that one observes in a given situation is likely due to a combination of factors, and only if other tasks have a similar combination of factors would direct comparisons be meaningful.

Summary

On the basis of the evidence reviewed here, only the peripheral interpretation, which attributes age differences in speed entirely to slower sensory or motor processes, can be unequivocally rejected. The remaining classes of explanation enjoy varying degrees of support, but none has received the consistent amount of negative evidence necessary to warrant complete exclusion.

Heuristic considerations might favor the cycle-time hypothesis, since the most rapid progress in future research will probably come from attempts to investigate the class of explanation with the broadest range of application. Moreover, age differences at the cycle-time level could also be responsible for the age differences observed in other higher-order mechanisms, and there is presently at least as much empirical support for this hypothesis as for any of the remaining alternatives. It is important, however, to emphasize that this endorsement of the cycle-time interpretation is based on its potential productivity as a working hypothesis, and not because it currently has an overwhelming degree of solid support. As indicated several times already, the available data in this area are not yet adequate enough to warrant very firm conclusions about theoretical issues.

METHODOLOGICAL IMPLICATIONS

The preceding discussion of theoretical perspectives and empirical results has several implications for the design and interpretation of experiments involving age comparisons with temporal variables. Although some of these issues have not yet been satisfactorily resolved, they are sufficiently important to warrant consideration when interpretation of past research or planning of future research is undertaken.

One of the most important implications of the earlier sections concerns appropriate methods for statistical analysis. A powerful technique for attempting to identify age-specific difficulties is to examine age/treatment interactions in an analysis of variance. If older adults are found to exhibit larger treatment effects than younger adults, it is usually concluded that the treatment influences an age-sensitive mechanism. The empirical data of Table 2 and Figure 2, however, suggest that a significant interaction is likely whenever the treatment effect is large in the sample of young adults, apparently regardless of the specific manipulation (e.g., stimulus repetition or alternation, number of stimulus or response alternatives, stimulus-response compatibility, etc.).

This process-independent interaction effect can be illustrated as shown in Figure 3, where the hypothetical results in two conditions (A and B) are plotted in the form of time of older adults against time of young adults. The solid line has a slope of 1.6 to reflect the empirical findings that the slope of such a function is generally between 1.2 and 2.0. For sake of convenience, the intercept of the function is assumed to be zero. (Slight to moderate variations in these parameters would have little effect on the substance of the following argument.) Notice that the age differences are fairly small (i.e., $1.6 - 1.0 = 0.6$ units) in the "easy" condition (Condition A), but the age differences are relatively large (i.e.,

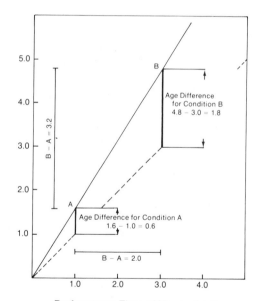

Performance Time of Young Adults

Figure 3.   Implications of the linear relationship between performance times of young and old adults. Points A and B represent the times in two experimental conditions, and the vertical lines below each point illustrate the absolute age difference in that condition. Because the slope of the solid line is greater than 1.0, the absolute magnitude of the age difference will increase directly with the performance time of young adults.

4.8 − 3.0 = 1.8 units) in the "difficult" condition (Condition B). Also observe that the difference between conditions B and A is larger among older adults than among younger adults (3.2 vs. 2.0). Since the empirical data are consistent with the trend illustrated in Figure 3, it can be seen that the absolute magnitude of the performance difference between young and old adults will tend to increase directly with the magnitude of the overall treatment effect. This trend greatly complicates the interpretation of statistical interactions because age/treatment interactions will be expected whenever treatment effects are large; consequently, the "source" of the interaction cannot be attributed simply to the effects of the treatment manipulation. In other words, the existence of age/treatment interactions may be a reflection of a general phenomenon rather than a specific deficit.

The relationship between magnitudes of treatment and age/treatment effects is a logical consequence of the fact that the slope of the function relating young to old performance is greater than 1.0, but it has also received empirical confirmation by Cerella et al. (1980) with the finding that the magnitude of the interaction effect correlated 0.89 with the magnitude of the treatment effect across 154 comparisons in 18 experimental studies. It is likely that many of the inconsistencies in the literature on age differences in speed are at least partially attributable to this type of problem. The studies with significant age interactions were probably those with the largest treatment effects, and the magnitude of the treatment effect many have been a more important determinant of the significance of the age interaction than the particular manipulation employed.

Another common practice that can be criticized on the basis of the empirical relationship observed between the processing times of young and old adults is the subtraction of the times required to perform a comparatively simple task from the times required to perform a more complex task in order to obtain "pure" measures of mental processing time. This subtraction procedure faces the same difficulty as the interaction procedure in that the magnitude of the residual time differences between age groups will vary directly with the magnitude of the difference between the experimental and control tasks in the young adults, independently of the nature of the experimental task. This is evident in Figure 3, where the B-A residual in each age group can be seen to vary with the magnitude of the B effect in the young adults.

The rationale for the subtraction procedure can also be questioned in that it assumes that the total time to perform a task can be readily partitioned into sensory/motor and mental times and that independent mechanisms are responsible for the two components. If a single general mechanism is responsible for all age-related slowing instead, then it does not make sense to attempt to attribute some of the slowness to peripheral processes and some to central processes when it all originates from the same fundamental mechanism. This, of course, is a theoretical issue, but it is important to realize that the results from any procedure are meaningful only if the theoretical assumptions underlying the procedure are valid.

Both of the problems just described relate to the suggestion of the empirical data that the temporal dimension is scaled in somewhat expanded units with increased age. Obviously, data analyses from experiments involving adults of varying ages will be greatly complicated if temporal units actually have a different meaning across age groups. One strategy that might be adopted involves imposing some type of transformation (e.g., logarithmic) on the data from one or more age groups in order to produce measurement scales with comparable intervals. This procedure should be employed with great caution, however, because using it implies the acceptance of a particular theoretical model and thus precludes proper empirical evaluation of that or other models.

An alternative empirically based strategy involves constructing a complete function such as that portrayed in Figure 2 and then examining specific conditions for data points that lie outside the predicted limits for the regression function. Only if the data point clearly deviates from the expected regression line would one be able to conclude that the age difference in that condition is attributable to factors other than those responsible for the general trend of age differences to increase in proportion to processing complexity. This would obviously require an elaborate combination of experimental conditions that would dramatically change the design of most developmental experiments involving temporal variables.

Neither of these strategies is desirable, but some such methods are apparently necessary because the empirical evidence suggests that time, when examined across the adult age span, may possess only ordinal, and not interval, measurement properties. A possible implication of the preceding arguments is that temporal variables may not be as well suited for developmental investigations of cognitive processes as for those involving more homogeneous populations.

THEORETICAL IMPLICATIONS

Although there is not yet enough evidence to distinguish confidently among most of the theoretical alternatives discussed here, it is clear that peripheral factors contribute very little to the overall slowing-with-age phenomenon. To many theorists this conclusion is discouraging because it not only implies that the central nervous system may deteriorate with age, but also seems to offer little hope for prosthetic devices or task manipulations that might remedy the problem. Nevertheless, the evidence is very convincing that central factors are involved, and neither grounds for optimism or pessimism nor ease of remediation should be used as criteria for evaluating the adequacy of a theoretical perspective.

Since central factors are implicated in the slowing phenomenon, it is reasonable to expect that other cognitive processes will share some of the causes, and perhaps be influenced by the consequences, of age-related slowing. It may be difficult to observe some of the same age trends in nontemporal dependent variables because they are typically scaled in arbitrary units that do not readily lend themselves to between-experiment comparisons. Nevertheless, it is possible that many of the same age-complexity relationships are operating in other areas of research but simply have not yet been detected.

The importance of research on speed of behavior for other cognitive processes will be particularly dramatic if the cycle-time perspective is eventually supported. This hypothesis maintains that nearly every action performed under the control of the central nervous system will be affected by the general slowing, even when the dependent variable does not appear to be obviously related to time or rate. Moreover, qualitative as well as quantitative differences can be expected, both because a slower rate of processing may lead to the adoption of different strategies of performance and because the system at any given moment will likely contain more partially processed information and thus will be more susceptible to information-overload and divided-attention effects. Only if a task can be performed without deliberate control by the central processing system—i.e., the performance is "automatic"—will a decremental effect not be expected with increased age on most activities. Response slowing, according to this perspective, is simply an overt manifestation of a mechanism affecting all processes, internal or covert as well as external or overt. The cycle-time perspective is not the only viable explanation at the current time, but all remaining alternatives that can still be considered plausible also have important implications for other cognitive processes since they too appear to involve central mechanisms.

FUTURE RESEARCH

It is always hazardous to make predictions about future trends in an active area of research, but it is particularly difficult in a field where wide-ranging implications are becoming recognized. Nevertheless, speculations can be offered as to four major directions likely to be explored in the next few years. One of these concerns the physiological basis for the slowing-with-age phenomenon. Among the important questions in this area are: Is the older nervous system slower because of focal or diffuse cell loss, because of reduced stimulation from the reticular activating system, or for still unknown reasons? Also, is the primary behavioral manifestation of this physiological change a reduced signal-to-noise ratio, a slower internal clock rate, or some other mechanism?

A related issue concerns the reasons for the apparent similarities between the slowness that is associated with increased age and the slowness that is associated with diseases such as senile dementia, Parkinson's Disease, and miscellaneous cardiovascular ailments. Similarity of effect does not necessarily imply similarity of cause, but it is nevertheless desirable to determine the extent to which aging and these various diseases share common mechanisms.

A third issue likely to receive intensive investigation in the next decade is whether the slowing is best described as specific to a limited number of processes or stages or is general across nearly all processes. It may be some time before strong versions of the Birren hypothesis (i.e., that the slowing is quantitatively equivalent in all processes) can be adequately examined, but it is certain that future researchers will actively investigate the notion that increased age leads to a slowing of all information-processing activities.

A fourth question that will undoubtedly be the subject of future research concerns the effect of speed loss on cognitive activities. Most of the theoretical hypotheses examined in the preceding sections would have consequences for a variety of cognitive processes, and it is reasonable to expect that new procedures will be developed that will allow many of the detailed predictions to be tested and evaluated.

SUMMARY

Gerontological researchers interested in speed of behavior are in the somewhat paradoxical position of working with a pervasive phenomenon about which there is considerable consensus but for which there is very little information as to its causes or consequences. In the preceding pages several theoretical approaches to this phenomenon were identified, and major methodological issues were discussed. Five classes of theoretical explanation must still be considered viable since only interpretations based exclusively on peripheral processes can be unequivocally rejected at the current time.

Methodological issues are growing in importance as the theoretical distinctions become more subtle. For example, the controversy now is not whether peripheral or central mechanisms are responsible for the slowing-with-age phenomenon but rather which particular central mechanism is the most fundamental. It is important that more theoretically motivated and methodologically sophisticated research be performed in this area because the available evidence is consistent with the hypothesis that the same mechanisms responsible for the slowing phenomenon also contribute to the other cognitive differences observed with increased age.

REFERENCES

Abrahams, J. P., and Birren, J. E. 1973. Reaction time as a function of age and behavioral predispositions to coronary heart disease. *J. Geront.* 28: 471–478.

Anders, T. R., and Fozard, J. L. 1973. Effects of age upon retrieval from primary and secondary memory. *Developmental Psychology* 9: 411–415.

Anders, T. R.; Fozard, J. L.; and Lillyquist, T. D. 1972. Effects of age upon retrieval from short-term memory. *Developmental Psychology* 6: 214–217.

Arenberg, D. 1968. Retention of time judgement in young and old adults. *J. Geront.* 23: 35–40.

Barrett, G. V.; Mihal, W. L.; Panek, P. E.; Sterns, H. L.; and Alexander, R. A. 1977. Information processing skills predictive of accident involvement for younger and older commercial drivers. *Industrial Gerontology,* 4: 173–182.

Beres, C. A., and Baron, A. 1981. Improved digit symbol substitution by older women as a result of extended practice. *J. Geront.* 36: 591–597.

Berg, C.; Hertzog, C.; and Hunt, E. 1982. Age differences in the speed of mental rotation. *Developmental Psychology* 18: 95–107.

Birren, J. E. 1955. Age changes in speed of responses and perception and their significance for complex behavior. In *Old Age in the Modern World.* London: Livingstone.

Birren, J. E. 1964. *The Psychology of Aging.* Englewood Cliffs, N.J.: Prentice-Hall.

Birren, J. E. 1965. Age changes in speed of behavior: Its central nature and physiological correlates. In *Behavior, Aging and the Nervous System,* eds. A. T. Welford and J. E. Birren. Springfield, Ill.: Charles C Thomas.

Birren, J. E. 1970. Toward an experimental psychology of aging. *American Psychologist* 25: 124–135.

Birren, J. E. 1974. Translations in gerontology—From lab to life: Psychophysiology and the speed of response. *American Psychologist* 29: 808–815.

Birren, J. E., and Botwinick, J. 1955. Speed of response

as a function of perceptual difficulty and age. *J. Geront.* 10: 433–436.

Birren, J. E.; Butler, R. N.; Greenhouse, S. W.; Sokoloff, L.; and Yarrow, M. R. 1963. *Human Aging.* Washington, D.C.: U.S. Public Health Service.

Birren, J. E., and Renner, V. J. 1977. Research on the psychology of aging: principles and experimentation. In *Handbook of the Psychology of Aging,* eds. J. E. Birren and K. W. Schaie. New York: Van Nostrand.

Birren, J. E.; Riegel, K. F.; and Morrison, D. F. 1962. Age differences in response speed as a function of controlled variations of stimulus conditions: Evidence of a general speed factor. *Gerontologia, 6,* 1–18.

Birren, J. E.; Riegel, K. F.; and Robbin, J. S. 1962. Age differences in continuous word associations measured by speech recording. *J. Geront.* 17: 95–96.

Birren, J. E., and Spieth, W. 1962. Age, response speed and cardiovascular functions. *J. Geront.,* 17: 390–391.

Birren, J. E.; Woods, A. M.; and Williams, M. V. 1979. Speed of behavior as an indicator of age changes and the integrity of the nervous system. In *Brain Function in Old Age,* eds. F. Hofmeister and C. Mueller. Berlin: Springer-Verlag.

Birren, J. E.; Woods, A. M.; and Williams, M. V. 1980. Behavioral slowing with age: Causes, organization and consequences. In *Aging in the 1980's,* ed. L. W. Poon. Washington, D.C.: American Psychological Association.

Borkan, G. A., and Norris, A. H. 1980. Assessment of biological age using a profile of physical parameters. *Journal of Gerontology* 35: 177–184.

Botwinick, J. 1965. Theories of antecedent conditions of speed of response. In *Behavior, Aging and the Nervous System,* eds. A. T. Welford and J. E. Birren. Springfield, Ill.: Charles C. Thomas.

Botwinick, J.; Brinley, J. F.; and Robbin, J. S. 1958. The effect of motivation by electric shocks on reaction in relation to age. *Amer. J. Psych.* 71: 408–411.

Botwinick, J., and Storandt, M. 1973. Age differences in reaction time as a function of experience, stimulus intensity, and preparatory interval. *J. of Genetic Psych.* 123: 209–217.

Botwinick, J., and Storandt, M. 1974. *Memory, Related Functions and Age.* Springfield, Ill.: Charles C. Thomas.

Botwinick, J., and Thompson, L. W. 1966. Components of reaction time in relation to age and sex. *J. of Genetic Psych.* 108: 175–183.

Botwinick, J., and Thompson, L. W. 1968. Age differences in reaction time: An artifact? *Gerontologist* 8: 25–28.

Brinley, J. F. 1965. Cognitive sets, speed and accuracy of performance in the elderly. In *Behavior, Aging and the Nervous System,* eds. A. T. Welford and J. E. Birren. Springfield, Ill.: Charles C. Thomas.

Brinley, J. F. and Botwinick, J. 1959. Preparation time and choice in relation to age differences in response speed. *J. Geront.* 14: 226–228.

Bromley, D. B. 1974. *The Psychology of Human Aging.* Middlesex, England: Penguin.

Burke, D. M., and Light, L. L. 1981. Memory and aging: The role of retrieval processes. *Psychological Bulletin* 90: 513–546.

Camp, C. J. 1981. The use of fact retrieval vs. inference in young and elderly adults. *J. Geront.* 36: 715–721.

Cerella, J.; Poon, L. W.; and Fozard, J. L. 1981. Mental rotation and age reconsidered. *J. Geront.* 36: 620–624.

Cerella, J.; Poon, L. W.; and Williams, D. M. 1980. Age and the complexity hypothesis. In *Aging in the 1980's,* ed. L. W. Poon. Washington, D.C.: American Psychological Association.

Clark, J. W. 1960. The aging dimension: A factorial analysis of individual differences with age on psychological and physiological measurements. *Journal of Gerontology* 15: 183–187.

Craik, F. I. M. 1977. Age differences in human memory. In *Handbook of the Psychology of Aging,* eds. J. E. Birren and K. W. Schaie. New York: Van Nostrand.

Crossman, E. R. F. W., and Szafran, J. 1957. Changes with age in the speed of information intake and discrimination. *Experientia Suppl.* 4: 128–135.

Dirken, J. M. 1972. *Functional Age of Industrial Workers.* Groningen, The Netherlands: Wolters-Noordhoff.

Erber, J. T. 1976. Age differences in learning and memory on a digit-symbol substitution task. *Exp. Aging Res.* 2: 45–53.

Erber, J. T.; Botwinick, J.; and Storandt, M. 1981. The impact of memory on age differences in digit symbol performance. *J. Geront.* 36: 586–590.

Eriksen, C. W.; Hamlin, R. M.; and Daye, C. 1973. Aging adults and rate of memory scan. *Bull. of Psychon. Soc.* 1: 259–260.

Eysenck, M. W. 1975. Retrieval from semantic memory as a function of age. *J. Geront.* 30: 174–180.

Farkas, M. S., and Hoyer, W. J. 1980. Processing consequences of perceptual grouping in selective attention. *J. Geront.* 35: 207–216.

Ford, J. M., and Pfefferbaum, A. 1980. The utility of brain potentials in determining age-related changes in central nervous system and cognitive functioning. In *Aging in the 1980's,* ed. L. W. Poon. Washington, D.C.: American Psychological Association.

Ford, J. M.; Roth, W. T.; Mohs, R. C.; Hopkins, W. F.; and Kopell, B. S. 1979. Event-related potentials recorded from young and old adults during a memory retrieval task. *Electroencep. Clin. Neurophysiol.* 47: 450–459.

Fozard, J. L., and Thomas, J. C. 1975. Psychology of aging: Basic findings and some psychiatric applications. In *Modern Perspectives in the Psychiatry of Old Age,* ed. J. G. Howells. New York: Brunner/Hassel.

Fozard, J. L.; Thomas, J. C.; and Waugh, N. C. 1976. Effects of age and frequency of stimulus repetitions on two-choice reaction time. *J. Geront.* 31: 556–563.

Gaylord, S. A., and Marsh, G. R. 1975. Age differences in the speed of a spatial cognitive process. *J. Geront.* 30: 674–678.

Goldfarb, W. 1941. *An Investigation of Reaction Time in Older Adults.* New York: Columbia Teachers College, Contributions to Education, No. 831.

Gottsdanker, R. 1980a. Aging and the maintaining of preparation. *Exp. Aging Res.* 6: 13–27.

Gottsdanker, R. 1980b. Aging and the use of advance probability information. *Journal of Motor Behavior:* 12: 133–143.

Grant, E. A.; Storandt, M.; and Botwinick, J. 1978. Incentive and practice in the psychomotor performance of the elderly. *J. Geront.* 33: 413–415.

Gregory, R. L. 1957. Increase in "neurological noise" as a factor in aging. Proceedings of the 4th Congress of the International Association of Gerontology, Merano, Italy.

Heikken, E.; Küskinen, A.; Kayhty, B.; Rimpela, M.; and Vroie, I. 1974. Assessment of biological age. *Gerontologia* 20: 33–43.

Heron, A., and Chown, S. M. 1967. *Age and Function.* London: Churchill.

Hicks, L. H., and Birren, J. E. 1970. Aging, brain damage, and psychomotor slowing. *Psych. Bull.* 74: 377–396.

Hines, T. M., and Posner, M. I. 1975. Slow but sure: A chronometric analysis of the process of aging. In *Design Conference on Decision Making and Aging,* eds. L. W. Poon and J. L. Fozard. Boston: Boston Geriatric Research Educational and Clinical Center, Technical Report 76–01.

Horn, J. L.; Donaldson, G.; and Engstrom, R. 1981. Apprehension, memory, and fluid intelligence decline in adulthood. *Research on Aging* 3: 33–84.

Howard, D. V.; Lasaga, M. I.; and McAndrews, M. P. 1980. Semantic activation during memory encoding across the adult lifespan. *J. Geront.* 35: 884–890.

Howard, D. V.; McAndrews, M. P.; and Lasaga, M. I. 1981. Semantic priming of lexical decisions in young and old adults. *J. Geront.* 36: 707–714.

Jacewicz, M. M. and Hartley, A. A. 1979. Rotation of mental images by young and old college students: The effects of familiarity. *J. Geront.* 34: 396–403.

Jalavisto, E., and Nakkonen, T. 1963. On the assessment of biological age. *Annales Academiae Scientiarum Finnicae,* Series A (V): 1–38.

Jalavisto, E.; Lindquist, C.; and Makkonen, T. 1964. Assessment of biological age III. *Annales Academiae Scientiarum Finnicae,* Series A(V): 1–20.

Jarvik, L. F. 1975. Thoughts on the psychobiology of aging. *American Psychologist* 30: 576–583.

Jerome, E. A. 1959. Age and learning: Experimental studies. In *Handbook of Aging and the Individual,* ed. J. E. Birren. Chicago: University of Chicago Press.

Jordan, T. C., and Rabbitt, P. M. A. 1977. Response times to stimuli of increasing complexity as a function of aging. *Brit. J. Psychol.* 68: 189–201.

Kaufman, A. 1968. Age and performance in oral and written versions of the substitution test. In *Psychological Functioning in the Normal Aging and Senile Aged,* eds. S. Chown and K. F. Riegel. Basel, Switzerland: S. Karger.

Klein, H.; Dollar, M. L.; and Bagdonas, J. E. 1947. Dentist time required to perform dental operations. *Journal of American Dental Association* 35: 153–160.

Koga, Y., and Morant, G. M. 1923. On the degree of association between reaction times in the case of different senses. *Biometrika* 15: 346–372.

LaFratta, C. W., and Canestrari, R. F. 1966. A comparison of sensory and motor nerve conduction velocities as related to age. *Archives of Physical Medicine and Rehabilitation* 47: 286–290.

Laufer, A. C., and Schweitz, B. 1968. Neuromuscular response tests as predictors of sensory-motor performance in aging individuals. *American Journal of Physical Medicine* 47: 250–263.

Leonard, J. A., and Newman, R. C. 1965. On the acquisition and maintenance of high speed and high accuracy in a keyboard task. *Ergonomics* 8: 281–304.

Light, K. C. 1976. Slowing of response time in young and middle-aged hypertensive patients. *Exp. Aging Res.* 1: 209–227.

Light, K. C. 1978. Effects of mild cardiovascular and cerebrovascular disorders on serial reaction time performance. *Exp. Aging Res.* 4: 3–22.

Loveless, N. E., and Sanford, A. J. 1974. Effects of age on the contingent negative variation and preparatory set in a reaction time task. *J. Geront.* 29: 52–63.

Madden, D. J. 1982. Age differences and similarities in the improvement of controlled search. *Exp. Aging Res.* 8: 91–98.

Madden, D. J., and Nebes, R. D. 1980. Aging and the development of automaticity in visual search. *Developmental Psychology* 16: 377–384.

Marsh, G. R. and Thompson, L. W. 1977. Psychophysiology of aging. In *Handbook of the Psychology of Aging,* eds. J. E. Birren and K. W. Schaie. New York: Van Nostrand.

Marsh, G. R., and Watson, W. E. 1980. Psychophysiological studies of aging effects on cognitive processes. In *Psychobiology of Aging,* ed. D. G. Stein. New York: Elsevier North Holland.

McFarland, R. A. 1968. The sensory and perceptual processes in aging. In *Theory and Methods of Research on Aging,* ed. K. W. Schaie. Morgantown, W. Va.: West Virginia University Press.

Miles, W. R. 1931a. Correlation of reaction and coordination speed with age in adults. *Am. J. Psychol.* 43: 377–391.

Miles, W. R. 1931b. Measures of certain human abilities throughout the lifespan. *Proc. Nat. Acad. Sci.* 17: 627–633.

Morris, J. D., and Thompson, L. W. 1969. Heart rate changes in a reaction time experiment with young and aged subjects. *J. Geront.* 24: 269–275.

Mortimer-Tanner, R. S. and Naylor, G. F. K. 1973. Rates of information acceptance and executive response in youthful and elderly subjects. *Austr. J. Psychol.* 25: 139–145.

Murrell, F. H. 1970. The effect of extensive practice on age differences in reaction time. *J. Geront.* 25: 268–274.

Naylor, G. F. K. 1973. The anatomy of reaction time and its relation to mental function in the elderly. *Proc. Austr. Assoc. Geront.* 2: 17–19.

Nebes, R. D. 1976. Verbal-pictorial recoding in the elderly. *J. Geront.* 31: 421–427.

Nebes, R. D. 1978. Vocal versus manual response as a determinant of age differences in simple reaction time. *J. Geront.* 33: 884–889.

Noble, C. E.; Baker, B. L.; and Jones, T. A. 1964. Age and sex parameters in psychomotor learning. *Percept. Mot. Skills* 19: 935–945.

Norris, A. H.; Shock, N. W.; and Wagman, I. H. 1953. Age changes in the maximum conduction velocity of motor fibers in human ulnar nerves. *J. Appl. Physiol.* 5: 589–593.

Ohta, R. J.; Walsh, D. A.; and Krauss, I. K. 1981. Spatial perspective-taking ability in young and elderly adults. *Exp. Aging Res.* 7: 45–63.

Pachella, R. G. 1974. The interpretation of reaction time in information-processing research. In *Tutorials in Performance and Cognition,* ed. B. Kantowitz. Hillsdale, N.J.: Lawrence Erlbaum Associates.

Plude, D. J., and Hoyer, W. J. 1981. Adult age differences in visual search as a function of stimulus mapping and processing level. *J. Geront.* 36: 598–604.

Plude, D. J.; Hoyer, W. J.; and Lazar, J. 1982. Age, response complexity and target consistency in visual search. *Exp. Aging Res.* 8: 99–102.

Poon, L. W., and Fozard, J. L. 1978. Speed of retrieval from long-term memory in relation to age, familiarity, and datedness of information. *J. Geront.* 33: 711–717.

Poon, L. W.; Fozard, J. L.; Vierck, B., Dailey, B. F.; Cerella, J. and Zeller, P. 1976. The effects of practice and information feedback on age-related differences in performance speed, variability and error rates in a two-choice decision task. In *Design Conference on Decision Making and Aging,* eds. L. W. Poon and J. L. Fozard. Boston: Boston Geriatric Research Educational and Clinical Center, Technical Report 76–01.

Potvin, A. R.; Syndulko, K.; Tourtellotte, W. W.; Lemmon, J. A.; and Potvin, J. H. 1980. Human neurologic function and the aging process. *J. Amer. Ger. Soc.* 28: 1–9.

Potvin, A. R.; Tourtellotte, W. W.; Pew, R. W.; Albers, J. W.; Henderson, W. G.; and Snyder, D. N. 1973. The importance of age effects on performance in the assessment of clinical trials. *J. Chron. Dis.* 26: 699–717.

Rabbitt, P. M. A. 1964. Set and age in a choice response task. *J. Geront.* 19: 301–306.

Rabbitt, P. M. A. 1965. Age and discrimination between complex stimuli. In *Behavior, Aging and the Nervous System,* eds. A. T. Welford and J. E. Birren. Springfield, Ill.: Charles C. Thomas.

Rabbitt, P. M. A. 1968. Age and the use of structure in transmitted information. In *Human Aging and Behavior,* ed. G. A. Talland. New York: Academic Press.

Rabbitt, P. M. A. 1979. How old and young subjects monitor and control responses for accuracy and speed. *Brit. J. Psychol.* 70: 305–311.

Rabbitt, P. M. A., and Birren, J. E. 1967. Age and responses to sequences of repetitive and interruptive signals. *J. Geront.* 22: 143–150.

Riegel, K. F., and Birren, J. E. 1965. Age differences in associative behavior. *J. Geront.* 20: 125–130.

Robertson-Tchabo, E. A., and Arenberg, D. 1976. Age differences in cognition in healthy educated men: A factor analysis of experimental measures. *Exp. Aging Res.* 2: 75–89.

Salthouse, T. A. 1978a. The role of memory in the age decline in digit-symbol substitution performance. *J. Geront.* 33: 232–238.

Salthouse, T. A. 1978b. Age and speed: The nature of the relationship. Unpublished manuscript.

Salthouse, T. A. 1979. Adult age and the speed-accuracy tradeoff. *Ergonomics* 22: 811–821.

Salthouse, T. A. 1980. Age and memory: Strategies for localizing the loss. In *New Directions in Memory and Aging,* eds. L. W. Poon, J. L. Fozard, L. Cernak, D. Arenberg and L. W. Thompson. Hillsdale, N.J.: Lawrence Erlbaum Associates.

Salthouse, T. A. 1982. *Adult Cognition: An Experimental Psychology of Human Aging.* New York: Springer-Verlag.

Salthouse, T. A., and Kail, R. (1983). Memory development throughout the lifespan: The role of processing rate. In *Life Span Development and Behavior,* eds. P. B. Baltes and O. G. Brim, Vol. 5. New York: Academic Press.

Salthouse, T. A., and Somberg, B. L. 1982a. Skilled performance: The effects of adult age and experience on elementary processes. *J. Exp. Psychol. Gen.* 111: 176–207.

Salthouse, T. A. and Somberg, B. L. 1982b. Isolating the age deficit in speeded performance. *J. Geront.* 37: 59–63.

Salthouse, T. A., and Somberg, B. L. 1982c. Time-accuracy relationships in young and old adults. *J. Geront.* 37: 349–353.

Salthouse, T. A.; Wright, R.; and Ellis, C. L. 1979. Adult age and the rate of an internal clock. *J. Geront.* 34: 53–57.

Schaie, K. W. 1973. Reflections on papers by Looft, Paterson, and Sparks: Interventions towards an ageless society. *Gerontologist* 13: 31–35.

Shepard, T. N., and Metzler, J. 1971. Mental rotation of three-dimensional objects, *Science* 171: 701–703.

Simon, J. R. 1967. Choice reaction time as a function of auditory S-R correspondence, age and sex. *Ergonomics* 10: 659–664.

Simon, J. R. 1968. Signal processing time as a function of aging. *J. Exp. Psychol.* 78: 76–80.

Simon, J. R., and Pouraghabagher, A. R. 1978. The effect of aging on the stages of processing in a choice reaction time task. *J. Geront.* 33: 553–561.

Spieth, W. 1964. Cardiovascular health status, age, and psychological performance. *J. Geront.* 19: 277–284.

Spirduso, W. W. 1975. Reaction and movement time as a function of age and physical activity level. *J. Geront.* 30: 435–440.

Spirduso, W. W. 1980. Physical fitness, aging and psychomotor speed: A review. *J. Geront.* 35: 850–865.

Spirduso, W. W., and Clifford, P. 1978. Neuromuscular speed and consistency of performance as a function of age, physical activity level and type of physical activity. *J. Geront.* 33: 26–30.

Sternberg, S. 1969a. The discovery of processing stages: Extensions of Donders' method. In *Attention and performance II,* ed. W. G. Koster. Amsterdam: North Holland.

Sternberg, S. 1969b. Memory scanning: Mental processes revealed by reaction time experiments. *Am. Scientist* 57: 421–457.

Storandt, M. 1976. Speed and coding effects in relation to age and ability level. *Developmental Psychology,* 12: 177–178.

Suci, G. J.; Davidoff, M. D.; and Surwillo, W. W. 1960. Reaction time as a function of stimulus information and age. *J. Exp. Psychol.* 60: 242–244.

Surwillo, W. W. 1963. The relation of simple response time to brain-wave frequency and the effects of age. *Electroenceph. Clin. Neurophysiol.* 15: 105–114.

Surwillo, W. W. 1964a. The relation of decision time to brain wave frequency and to age. *Electroenceph. Clin. Neurophysiol.* 16: 510–514.

Surwillo, W. W. 1968. Timing of behavior in senescence and the role of the central nervous system. In *Human Aging and Behavior,* ed. G. A. Talland. New York: Academic Press.

Szafran, J. 1966. Age differences in the rate of gain of information, signal detection strategy and cardiovascular status among pilots. *Gerontologia* 12: 6–17.

Talland, G. A. 1965. Initiation of response, and reaction time in aging, and with brain damage. In *Behavior, Aging and the Nervous System,* eds. A. T. Welford and J. E. Birren. Springfield, Ill.: Charles C. Thomas.

Talland, G. A., and Cairnie, J. 1961. Aging effects of simple, disjunctive and alerted finger reaction time. *J. Geront.* 16: 370–374.

Thomas, J. C.; Fozard, J. L., and Waugh, N. C. 1977. Age related differences in naming latency. *Am. J. Psychol.* 90: 499–509.

Thomas, J. C.; Waugh, N. C.; and Fozard, J. L. 1978. Age and familiarity in memory scanning. *J. Geront.* 33: 528–533.

Thompson, L. W., and Nowlin, J. B. 1973. Relation of increased attention to central and autonomic nervous system states. In *Intellectual Functioning in Adults: Psychological and Biological Factors,* eds. J. Jarvik, C. Eisdorfer, and J. Blum. New York: Springer.

Thorndike, E. L.; Bregman, E. O.; Tilton, J. W.; and E. Woodyard. 1928. *Adult Learning.* New York: Macmillan.

Tolin, P., and Simon, J. R. 1968. Effect of task complexity and stimulus duration on perceptual-motor performance of two disparate age groups. *Ergonomics* 11: 283–290.

Wagman, I. H., and Lesse, H. 1952. Maximum conduction velocities of motor fibers of ulnar nerves in human subjects of various ages and sizes. *J. Neurophysiol.* 15: 235–244.

Waugh, N. C. 1980. Age-related differences in the acquisition of a verbal habit. *Perceptual and Motor Skills,* 50: 435–438.

Waugh, N. C.; Fozard, J. L.; Talland, G. A.; and Erwin, D. E. 1973. Effects of age and stimulus repetition on two-choice reaction time. *J. Geront.* 28: 466–470.

Waugh, N. C., Fozard, J. L. and Thomas, J. C. 1978. Age-related differences in serial binary classification. *Exp. Aging Res.* 4: 433–441.

Weber, R. J.; Hochhaus, L.; and Brown, W. D. 1981. Equivalence of perceptual and imaginal representation: Developmental changes. In *Attention and Performance,* eds. J. Long and A. Baddeley, IX. Hillsdale, N.J.: Lawrence Erlbaum Associates.

Weisenburg, T.; Roe, A.; and McBride, K. E. 1936. *Adult Intelligence.* New York: The Commonwealth Fund.

Weiss, A. D. 1965. The locus of reaction time change with set, motivation and age. *J. Geront.* 20: 60–64.

Welford, A. T. 1958. *Aging and Human Skill.* London: Oxford University Press.

Welford, A. T. 1959. Psychomotor Performance. In *Handbook of Aging and the Individual,* ed. J. E. Birren. Chicago: University of Chicago Press.

Welford, A. T. 1962. Changes in the speed of performance with age and their industrial significance. *Ergonomics* 5: 139–145.

Welford, A. T. 1965. Performance, biological mechanisms and age: A theoretical sketch. In *Behavior, Aging, and the Nervous System,* eds. A. T. Welford and J. E. Birren. Springfield, Ill.: Charles C. Thomas.

Welford, A. T. 1977. Motor performance. In *Handbook of the Psychology of Aging,* eds. J. E. Birren and K. W. Schiae. New York: Van Nostrand.

Welford, A. T. 1981. Signal, noise, performance, and age. *Human Factors* 23: 97–109.

Welford, A. T., and Birren, J. E. 1965. *Behavior, Aging and the Nervous System.* Springfield, Ill.: Charles C. Thomas.

Woodruff, D. S. 1975. Relationships among EEG, alpha frequency, reaction time and age: A biofeedback study. *Psychophysiology* 12: 673–681.

16
DIFFERENCES IN HUMAN MEMORY WITH AGING: NATURE, CAUSES, AND CLINICAL IMPLICATIONS

Leonard W. Poon

Veterans Administration Outpatient Clinic, Boston
Harvard Medical School

The feeling that one's ability to remember and to retrieve information is not as good as it used to be is a universal complaint among middle-aged and elderly persons. The effort to substantiate these complaints and to clarify issues surrounding age-related differences in memory abilities has become the single most concentrated activity in psychological aging research. A survey of the content areas in the psychological sections of gerontological journals shows that 68 percent of the papers in the period 1963–1968 were in this area, as were 72 percent in 1964–1974, and 58 percent in 1979–1980 (Abrahams, Hoyer, Elias, and Bradigan, 1975; Poon, Krauss, and Bowles, 1981).

Literature reviews on memory and aging from the 1950s to 1980s reflect the *Zeitgeist* of memory research. The first reviews by Kay (1959) and Jerome (1959) demonstrated the interest in learning and acquisition processes that prevailed in the 1950s. Major reviews in the 1970s by Botwinick (1973), Craik (1977), and Kausler (1970) emphasized the information-processing approach and the search for age differences in specific stages of information flow. Proceedings of a conference on memory and aging (Poon, Fozard, Cermak, Arenberg, and Thompson, 1980) and at least 17

general and specific reviews published in the early 1980s (see Table 1) explored a widening concern for issues regarding individual differences, clinical memory diagnosis and remediation, and neuropsychological and psychopharmacological models.

Investigators in recent reviews are becoming more cognizant of the multivariate nature of memory and are beginning to subscribe to the notion that no one hypothesis can adequately account for all the observed age differences in performance. This chapter intends to highlight and support the current trend of research toward the study of interactional effects among individuals the environment and the task demands on the memory performance of young and elderly adults. The chapter is divided into four parts. The first part provides a selected review of prominent findings on the nature of age differences. The second part explores the adequacy of several biological, processing, and contextual hypotheses in accounting for the variability of age differences in memory. The third part discusses the dilemma of the clinician who needs to make clinical diagnoses and recommend remedial strategies while faced with incomplete information about the relative influences of biological, environmental, and processing factors on the

TABLE 1. RECENT REVIEWS OF MEMORY AND AGING

Authors	Sensory memory	Primary memory	Secondary memory	Encoding	Storage	Retrieval	Remote memory	Speed	Contextual semantic processing	Spatial	Mnemonic organization	Metamemory	Noncognitive factors	Attentional resources	Diagnostic battery	Intervention	Neuro-psychological correlates	Episodic/ Semantic
Albert and Kaplan, 1980														●	●		●	
Burke and Light, 1981				●		●			●									
Cavanaugh and Perlmuter, 1982												●						
Craik, 1977	●	●	●	●	●	●								●				
Craik and Simon, 1980				●		●								●				
Erber, 1981						●												
Erber, 1982	●	●	●	●	●	●	●					●	●					
Erickson, Poon, and Walsh-Sweeney, 1980															●			
Fozard, 1980	●	●	●	●				●								●		
Hartley, Harker, and Walsh, 1980		●	●	●				●										
Hines and Fozard, 1980		●	●	●					●	●	●							
Kausler, 1982	●	●	●	●	●	●	●		●	●	●	●	●	●		●	●	●
Labouvie-Vief and Schell, 1982	●	●	●	●	●	●	●		●		●		●					
Poon, Walsh-Sweeney, and Fozard, 1980			●	●							●					●		
Salthouse, 1982	●				●	●	●	●	●	●		●	●	●				
Schonfield and Stone, 1979		●					●		●									
Smith, 1980				●	●	●					●							
Smith and Fullerton, 1981	●	●	●	●	●	●	●				●							
Walsh and Prasse, 1980	●								●		●			●				

presenting memory complaints and performance. Finally, the fourth part provides several examples of current research that attempt to examine the interactive impact of individual differences and environmental influences on the cognitive performance of young and elderly adults.

NATURE OF AGE DIFFERENCES

Laboratory studies in the last two decades of age-related differences in memory processes have been dominated by an information-processing model (e.g., Murdock, 1967) that is based on three major assumptions. The model assumes that an individual is an active participant in the learning and retrieval processes, that both qualitative and quantitative patterns of responses can be analyzed, and that information flow can be traced through several hypothetical stages or memory stores. The stores are a modality-specific sensory memory, a short-term primary memory, and a long-term secondary memory that is a repository of newly learned information. Permanent or remote information is stored in a tertiary memory.

Sensory Memory

At the very early stage of information flow is sensory memory, in which new information is initially registered. This brief storage of peripheral information is referred to as *iconic memory* in the visual system and as *echoic memory* in the auditory system. Although practically no information on echoic memory and aging is available, Crowder (1980) has provided a review of the theoretical framework developed with young adults, together with suggested directions for aging research. Information on sensory memory and age is derived primarily from limited work on iconic memory.

Decline in the visual system of older adults includes changes in the accommodative power, refractive index, and yellowing of the lens, shrinkage of the retina and visual fields and decreased sensitivity to low levels of illumination (see Fozard, Wolf, Bell, McFarland, and Podolsky, 1977, for a detailed review).

Given these changes, it is surprising to find only small age differences in the capacity of young and elderly adults to identify briefly presented stimuli.

In a series of studies using the backward masking technique, Walsh and his colleagues showed that the time necessary for identifying a single letter does not change, or changes only a small amount, with age. In this procedure, a target stimulus is presented, followed by an interfering (masking) stimulus that effectively terminates the display. No age difference was found in exposure thresholds when unmasked letters were employed (Walsh, Till, and Williams, 1978). A slight slowing with age (by a factor of 1.4) was obtained in the time necessary to establish a legible icon when a diffused mask was employed (Walsh et al, 1978). Finally, a similarly small age decline was found when a patterned mask was employed (Walsh, 1976).

Cerella, Poon, and Fozard (1982) extended Walsh's investigation from the detection of a single element to the detection of multiple-element displays. Seven-letter strings were presented followed by a mask. Figure 1 shows the number of letters correctly identified by young and elderly adults for display durations of 10 to 200 msec. Younger adults were able to identify three letters at a rate of 27 msec per letter, a value similar to those reported by Coltheart (1972) and Sperling (1963). Any additional letters were identified at a slower rate. In contrast, older individuals were able to identify two letters at a rate of 35 msec per letter. The age decline in the rate of letter

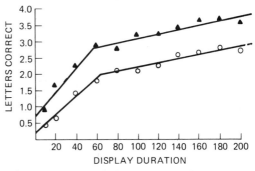

Fig. 1.   Number of letters reported from a seven-letter string as a function of string duration (msec). Triangles = young adults; circles = old adults. (*From Cerella, Poon, and Fozard, 1982.*)

identification is by a factor of 1.3, similar to that found by Walsh.

Walsh and Thompson (reported in Walsh and Prasse, 1980) found an age difference in iconic memory in a study employing the partial report paradigm (Averbach and Corriell, 1961). One should exercise caution in drawing conclusions about the age effect from this paradigm, which employs the tachistoscopic display of a matrix of stimuli (e.g., a 3 × 3 array) the same with stimulus size for young and elderly subjects. Two methodological problems may confound the results. First, if the parafoveal discriminability is not equated for the young and elderly subjects, differences in iconic readout can be caused by differences in parafoveal discrimination. In two experiments, Cerella and Poon (1981) demonstrated a significant reduction in the parafoveal field of the elderly: their identification latencies increased more rapidly as a function of retinal locus. Age differences became minimal after the sizes of parafoveal targets were adjusted to compensate for the loss in discrimination.

A related problem, elaborated by Grossberg (1980) and Walsh and Prasse (1980), is that the partial report task may not be appropriate for aging research because elderly people find it difficult to complete. In this task, other cognitive processes, such as selective attention, pattern recognition, and component integration, may confound and contribute to the poorer iconic memory performance of the elderly.

Finally, there is the question of whether the persistance or duration of the iconic image is longer or shorter for older adults. Contrasting conclusions were drawn from data obtained from two different paradigms. Kline and Orme-Rogers (1978) employed a word identification technique in which a select portion of the dot matrix of a word was presented for a brief duration, followed by a varying interval, after which the remaining portion of the matrix was presented. The subject's task was to identify the complete word. The data showed that no age difference was found at the short interval but that older persons could identify more words at longer intervals, suggesting a longer persistence.

Walsh and Thompson (1978), on the other hand, employed a procedure, reported by Haber and Standing (1969), in which repetitive flashes of a circle were separated by dark intervals of varying length. The subject's task was to report whether the stimulus was continuous or flashing, and the dependent variable was the longest interval at which the subject saw the circle as continuous. The data showed that the older subjects had a shorter stimulus persistance interval (O = 252 msec; Y = 306 msec).

In a recent study, Kline and Schieber (1981) pointed out one possible methodological problem in the Walsh and Thompson experiment (1978). There seemed to be high intraindividual variability in the reported stimulus continuity data, which could have resulted from the inevitable luminance transcience produced by switching tachistoscopic fields, i.e., a flicker in the stimulus that appears to contradict its continuity. Kline and Schieber (1981) hypothesized that if older subjects are not able to ignore the flicker, the estimates might reflect this inability. In their study, Kline and Schieber (1981) obtained persistence measures free of luminance summation effects by presenting the target stimuli in white-on-black as well as black-on-white formats. They found reduced intraindividual variability for the older subjects in their data in comparison to that of Walsh and Thompson's, as well as longer stimulus persistance (O = 262 msec; Y = 183 msec).

The limited data on iconic memory present an optimistic picture of the magnitude of age differences in this sensory store. A practical question is whether a modest loss in sensory memory contributes significantly to the learning and retrieval difficulties experienced by the elderly. Craik (1977), Walsh and Thompson (1978), and Smith and Fullerton (1981) believe that differences in sensory memory may underlie the shorter perceptual span of the elderly. It is unlikely, however, that a modest sensory memory loss would significantly contribute to the observed deficits in secondary memory since primary memory, the next stage of the information processing system, is also relatively unaffected by age.

Primary Memory

A theoretical division into primary and secondary memory (e.g., Waugh and Norman, 1965) is usually employed to describe the acquisition and retention of new information. Primary memory is conceptualized as an ephemeral, limited-capacity store in which information is still "in mind," as it is being used. If the information is stored, it enters secondary memory, which is conceptualized as an unlimited, permanent store of newly acquired information. Although primary memory represents a temporary repository with a small capacity, it plays an important role in the control and assimilation of information and is thus an important process to study in cognitive aging research (Craik, 1977).

A comprehensive review of primary memory and aging has been presented by Craik (1977). Fozard (1980) provided an update by adding examples of studies on primary memory that clarified the relationship between primary and secondary memory. The findings of all primary memory paradigms seem clear: except for differences in response time, primary memory is relatively unaffected by age.

Since primary memory is conceptualized as a temporary, limited-capacity memory store, research emphasis has been placed on whether the capacity and the retention rate changes with age. In terms of primary memory capacity, most studies found no significant age difference in digit span (e.g., Bromley, 1958; Craik, 1968; Drachman and Leavitt, 1972), whereas some studies reported a slight age decrement (e.g., Botwinick and Storandt, 1974). Botwinick and Storandt (1974) reported that the memory span for letters presented auditorially was about six to seven letters for individuals in their 20s and about five and a half letters for those in their 70s. In terms of retrieval efficiency, there was no age difference in the retrieval of the last few items presented in a list for free recall (Craik, 1968; Smith, 1975) or for the most recently presented items in a continuous recognition task (Poon and Fozard, 1980). The speed of recall of the most recently presented items, however, was found to be slightly slower for elderly subjects (e.g., Waugh, Thomas, and Fozard, 1978).

Secondary Memory

In contrast to the finding of minimal age differences in iconic and primary memory, comparatively larger age differences are evident whenever the material to be remembered exceeds the span of primary memory. Consequently, the mechanisms of secondary memory have been the most studied in the literature and have aroused the most speculation.

Figure 2 presents patterns of age differences in six subtests of the Guild Memory Test reported by Gilbert and Levee (1971). The figure shows a slight age difference in digit span and a substantial age difference in typical tests of secondary memory, e.g., immediate and delayed tests of memory for paired-associates, designs, and paragraphs.

An important question in assessing age differences in secondary memory retrieval is whether an obtained difference is due to a deficit in learning new information (i.e., the information is not successfully committed to secondary memory) or difficulty in retrieving the learned information (Kausler, 1970). It has

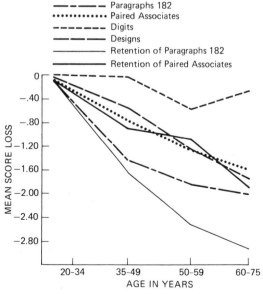

Fig. 2. Differential decline on memory tests throughout maturity (*Gilbert and Levee, 1971.*)

been well documented that older adults exhibit slower acquisition rates in paired associate learning (see Jerome, 1959; Winn, Elias, and Marshall, 1976). Figure 3 presents functions for the retrieval of 12 paired-associates by young, middle-aged, and elderly adults at one hour and at four, eight, twelve, and sixteen months after asymptotic learning was demon-

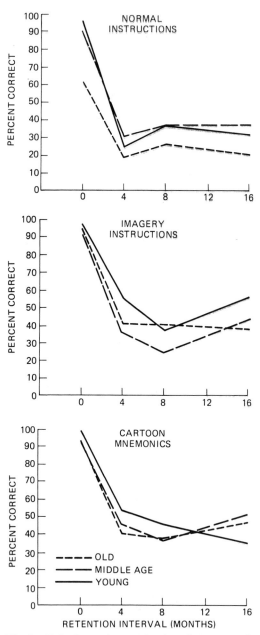

Fig. 3. Paired-associate retrieval performances of young, middle-aged and elderly subjects over a 16-month span. (*From Thomas and Ruben, 1973.*)

strated (Thomas and Ruben, 1973). The paired-associates were learned under one of three conditions: (1) standard no-instruction condition, (2) interacting imagery condition, or (3) cartoon mnemonics condition, in which bizarre interactions relating the stimulus and response items were depicted. This study is particularly noteworthy because it contained testing intervals much longer than those employed by most paired-associate learning studies. As expected, a substantial decline in retrieval performance was found for all groups over the retention periods. Subjects in the imagery instruction and cartoon mnemonics groups performed very similarly, however, at the four-, eight-, and sixteen-month retention intervals. The elderly performed at a lower level at all testing intervals under standard instructions, but no age difference was found between the imagery instructions and cartoon mnemonics at any test interval. It was noted that there was a marked age difference at the one-hour retrieval interval in the control condition, whereas no such difference was evident in the experimental conditions.

The data in the Thomas and Ruben study demonstrated several robust results: (1) Older subjects perform at a lower level in a standard no instruction condition; (2) organizational techniques tend to elevate performance; and (3) older persons in most studies tend to benefit more from organizational techniques, with the result that the observed age difference under the standard condition is minimized (Poon, Walsh-Sweeney, and Fozard, 1980). The results suggest that older people tend to be inefficient spontaneous organizers. When efficient strategies such as appropriate elaborative or orienting instructions are provided, however, older subjects are able to utilize them and to improve their memory performance (see Smith, 1980, for a detailed review).

Although significant age differences are found in free recall, smaller or no age differences are found in recognition or cued recall (e.g., Schonfield and Robertson, 1966; Hultsch, 1975). When the target items are presented in the context of a recognition test, retrieval is assumed to be an easier task. Smith (1977) examined the effects of semantic (category labels) and structural (initial letters) cues

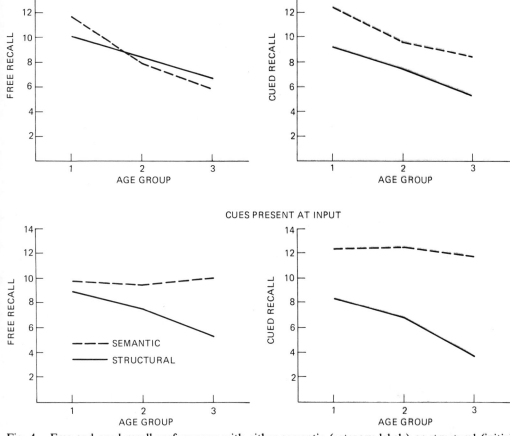

Fig. 4.   Free and cued recall performance with either semantic (category labels) or structural (initial letters) cues for three age groups: Group 1, aged 20–39; Group 2, 40–59; Group 3, 60–80. (*From Smith, 1977.*)

during presentation and recall. Figure 4 shows that minimal age differences were found when semantic cues were provided at input, suggesting that poor retrieval performance could be a by-product of faulty processing during acquisition.

Smaller age differences were reported when (1) the pacing of the experiment was modified to a pace more suitable to the subject, (2) sufficient practice was given, and (3) the stimulus material was familiar to the subject. Figure 5 presents the results of a paired-associate learning study (Canestrari, 1963) that showed significantly greater improvement in the performance of the older subjects under a self-paced versus an experimenter-paced condition. A similar finding of improved pair-as-

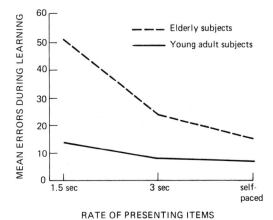

Fig. 5.   Age differences in paired-associate learning proficiency as affected by rate of presenting items. (*Adapted from Canestrari, 1963, and Kausler, 1982.*)

sociate performance was also reported when subjects used self-provided versus experimenter-provided imageries (Treat and Reese, 1976). The data suggest that the old subject who is give enough time or a mode of learning that is most suitable to his or her style can perform at a higher level, thus minimizing the age difference.

Figure 6 shows the effect of practice on paired-associate learning with young and old adults (Treat, Poon, and Fozard, 1981). Subjects were divided into mnemonic or control groups, and they learned two different lists per session in each of three sessions separated by a two-week period. The data showed (1) significant age and mnemonic effects, (2) near-asymptotic performance for the young subjects throughout the study, (3) significant transfer of learning from the first to the second list in each session for the old subjects, (4) a "relearning" effect evident at the beginning of each session for the old but not for the young subjects, and (5) a significantly smaller age effect in the third session. The mechanisms involved in this improved performance of the elderly have not been clearly identified. However, practice is indeed a powerful variable in improving the performance of older adults (see also Murrell, 1970).

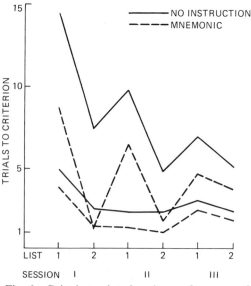

Fig. 6. Paired-associate learning performance of young (Y) and old (O) subjects in mnemonic and no-instruction conditions. (*From Treat, Poon, and Fozard, 1981.*)

Item familiarity is another factor that has been demonstrated to reduce age differences in retrieval from secondary memory. Barrett and Wright (1981) tested for the effects of both differential word familiarity and number of semantic tasks on recall in young and older adults following semantic processing. They found that both variables had a strong effect on recall. Young and old adults benefited equally from additional semantic processing. Furthermore, older subjects outperformed the young on recall of words more familiar to them. Similar patterns of age by familiarity interaction were reported by Poon and Fozard (1978) in a naming latency task and by Hultsch and Dixon (1983) in a text recall task. Although the finding of better recall for more familiar stimuli should not be a surprising one, it serves to highlight the flexibility of the secondary memory performance of older adults.

With regard to individual ability variables, research thus far suggests that vocabulary level might influence the magnitude of age differences in secondary memory retrieval of verbal material. In a study of recognition memory for words, Bowles and Poon (1982) found no age difference between young and old samples with a high vocabulary level, but a significant age difference was obtained between those samples with a low vocabulary level. A retrospective analysis was conducted in the literature to examine the available information on the vocabulary levels of the subject samples in word-recognition memory studies. The analysis suggested that the vocabulary level of subjects might be one factor that could account for the report of significant age effects in some studies (e.g., Rankin and Kausler, 1979; Harkins, Chapman, and Eisdorfer, 1979; and Erber, 1974) and the lack of age effects in others (e.g., Schonfield and Robertson, 1966; Gordon and Clark, 1974).

The concomitant effect of vocabulary level on recall was corroborated in a study of adult's retention of TV programs. Cavanaugh (1983) discovered that older low-verbal adults were consistently poorer than their younger counterparts in free recall, probed recall, and recognition of the program contents. On the other hand, no significant age difference was found in any of the dependent measures for high-verbal adults. A similar age by vocabulary interaction was found for the retention of prose material by Taub (1979).

Although the bulk of research on age differences in secondary memory has examined memory for discrete words or pairs, findings from a limited amount of work on memory of discourse allow some comparison and generalization of findings to memory of the more contextual information found in everyday activities. Some parallels can be drawn between findings using different types of materials. First, significant age differences are observed when rote recall or recall of verbatim surface information is required (Gilbert and Levee, 1971; Craik and Masani, 1967). Second, when elaboration is required in the processing of text to draw meaning, gist, or implication, young and old adults are usually observed to perform at equivalent levels in prose recall.

Meyer, Rice, Knight, and Jensen (1979a) presented short (about 200 words) passages to young, middle-aged, and elderly adults to read for later recall. No age difference was found in subjects' performance on free recall, one-sentence summary, or outline listing of main ideas. In a second study (Meyer et al., 1979b), the finding of no age difference in prose recall was replicated with a longer passage (about 600 words). In a metamemory study in which prose recall was administered as one of the memory tests, Zelinski, Gilewski, and Thompson (1980) also reported no age difference in the recall of propositions at the superordinate level. The results of the Zelinski study differed, however, from the Meyer studies as to which age group was superior in the recall of propositions at the subordinate levels. Till and Walsh (1980), using sentence recall task, found that the activity of drawing implications from sentences was a major contributing factor in obtaining equivalent recall performance from young and elderly subjects. In another study of prose learning comparing the young and elderly, Labouvie-Vief, Campbell, Weaver, and Tannenhaus (1979) found elderly subjects to be more efficient on memory for gist but younger subjects more efficient on memory for verbatim surface information.

Third, practice, verbal ability, and content familiarity variables that tend to interact with age in word memory studies may exert some of the same influences in discourse memory. Taub and Kline (1978) found an initial age difference in prose recall, but the difference disappeared in subsequent trials. As mentioned earlier, Taub (1979) found an age difference in prose recall for those adults with "average verbal" vocabulary scores but not for adults with "bright average" scores. Hultsch and Dixon (1983) found that the presence or absence of an age difference can be dependent on the familiarity of the contents of the prose. In studies where age decrements in prose recall were reported (e.g., Gordon and Clark, 1974; Cohen, 1979), it is difficult to ascertain how practice, prose content, and subject selection variables influenced the results, or how different scoring systems of discourse passages affected the outcome (Hartley, Harker, and Walsh, 1980).

In general, evidence to date shows minimal age differences in memory for familiar discourse materials that may be found in the everyday environment. Studies of age differences in memory for discourse, as well as studies of face recognition and face-name retention (e.g., Smith and Winograd, 1978; Ferris, Crook, Clark, McCarthy, and Rae, 1980) are examples of some first attempts by researchers to examine secondary memory processes in everyday activities (c.f. Gruneberg, Morris, and Sykes, 1978; Neiser, 1978). In addition, recent studies have provided some preliminary information on how older adults feel about their memory failures, use of memory aids, and methods of remembering everyday information (e.g., appointments).

Cavanaugh, Grady, and Perlmutter (1983) asked young and elderly adults to keep diaries of their experiences of memory failures and use of memory aids. They found that older adults reported more memory failures, corroborating results from questionnaires and interview studies (e.g., Lowenthal, Berkman, Beuhler, et al., 1967) as well as laboratory results that indicated problems in secondary memory. Memory failures included forgetting names, faces, objects, appointments, locations, routines, addresses, and phone numbers. Older adults reported more incidences of forgetting names, routines, and objects than young adults. Memory failures seemed to occur more frequently when the older adults were out of their normal routines or when they were required to remember information not used recently, whereas younger adults reported that most problems occurred when they were under "stress."

The data showed that older adults were the more likely to be upset when they experienced a memory failure. This finding corroborates the point made by Zarit, Cole, and Guider (1981) that older adults are more sensitive about their memory failures, which could be one factor influencing their self-assessment of memory function.

Younger and older adults were similar in the types of information for which they used memory aids and in the types of memory aids used. Older adults reported a higher frequency of employing aids, but the proportion of external aids (e.g., notes and lists) to internal aids (e.g., imagery and association) was about the same (about 7:3) for young and old adults

The use of a high proportion of external aids in remembering information by both young and old adults was reported in a study of remembering appointments (Poon and Schaffer, 1981). Subjects were asked to call a designated telephone number at specific times over a three-week period (analogous to a situation of reminding a sick aunt to take her medication). Half of the scheduled calls were determined by the subject and half by the experimenter (within the constraints of the subject's activities). One third of the subjects were given a flat fee ($10) to participate in the study; another third's fee was contingent on performance; the remaining third was asked to volunteer for the experiment. The data showed that the elderly remembered more calls, called closer to the target time, were more consistent over the three-week period, and were more cognizant of the incentive contingency than the young. A question of interest is why the younger adults performed relatively poorly. Did they fail to remember the calls, or were they less motivated to do well because they had more things to occupy their time?

An examination of the interview data obtained after the study seems to eliminate memory as a contributing factor. All subjects were asked about their awareness of missed calls, and they were asked to give an account of both those calls missed and those made. An examination of the obtained patterns showed that although the young adults missed more calls, they were able to account for both missed and completed calls. The overall level of recall was similar for both young and elderly adults. Because the elderly were significantly more influenced by the incentive manipulation, their higher level of motivation may have contributed to their better performance.

Finally, the subjects were asked what methods they used to remember calls. About 80 percent of both young and old subjects reported that they depended on external aids to remind them of their daily calls.

Tertiary (Remote) Memory

A common question about memory asked by elderly adults is why they experience difficulty in recalling recent events, whereas events that happened years ago can often be recalled with great accuracy. Perhaps this type of ancedotal evidence contributed to the formulation of Ribot's Law (1982), which states that information is forgotten in the reverse order from which it was acquired. A review of data on remote memory suggests that age differences are minimal, and although remote memory stays fairly intact with older adults, it is not superior to the recall of recent events (Erber, 1981).

Questionnaire testing for the recognition and/or recall of public events is a common means of evaluating remote memory (e.g., Botwinick and Storandt, 1974; Perlmutter, Metzger, Miller, and Nezworski, 1980; Poon, Fozard, Paulshock, and Thomas, 1979; Warrington and Sanders, 1971). The questionnaire method takes advantage of public knowledge that is assumed to be available to all subjects. Figure 7 shows data from a questionnaire study in which public events from each decade from the 1920s to the 1970s were presented to subjects aged 20 to 80 (Poon, Fozard, Paulshock, and Thomas, 1979). The data show

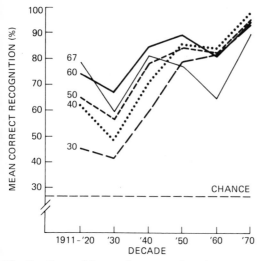

Fig. 7. Recognition performance of public events from 1910 to 1970 among five age groups. (*From Poon, Fozard, Paulshock, and Thomas, 1979.*)

that (1) there was no age difference in the recall of events from the 1970s; (2) the remote memory of the older groups was maintained at a fairly high level over the 50-year span of history; and (3) older subjects performed better than the younger subjects. The age comparison, however, is inappropriate since the older subjects might have acquired the information through personal experience whereas the younger subjects might have had to depend on secondary sources.

The finding of minimal forgetting of remote events for older adults is consistent across questionnaire studies. For recent events, however, Botwinick and Storandt (1974) found a slight but significant superiority for young adults, whereas Perlmutter et al. (1980) and Poon et al. (1979) found a similar but statistically insignificant trend. Differences in the results across studies could be due to differences in the selection of questionnaire items, which might be familiar to some subjects and not to others. One method of compensating for differential familiarity is to examine personal events of equal salience to all subjects. One such study was conducted by Bahrick, Bahrick, and Wittlinger (1975), who tested high school graduates aged 17 to 74 for recognition of their classmates' faces (in yearbook pictures) and the matching of faces and names.

Recognition of classmates' faces was consistently high (at 90 percent) up to 15 years after graduation, and free recall of names as long as 48 years after graduation for the older group declined only to 60 percent. Another study reporting good remote memory performance by the aged was conducted by Bahrick (1979), using recall of geographic knowledge of one's college town. Although item familiarity can be partially controlled by the examination of personal events, the method is not practical for general assessment of remote memory because of the difficulty in verification of responses. Little evidence for Ribot's law has been found, however, that is independent of the method used for assessment.

Summary

The literature is fairly consistent in describing the nature of memory differences between young and elderly subjects. There are minimal age differences in iconic, primary, and tertiary memory, but a significant decline with age in the acquisition and retrieval of new information from secondary memory.

A considerable amount of variability in age differences is found in secondary memory. Age decrements are found when the memory task requires spontaneous organizational and elaborative processes (e.g., paired-associate learning, list learning, and orienting tasks). The initial magnitude of age differences can be reduced, however, through the use of organization and elaboration techniques, more familiar stimuli, more practice, and self-regulation of pace and methods of learning. In some verbal memory tasks, minimal age differences were found in adults with high-verbal abilities. Furthermore, elderly adults sometimes performed better than young adults, especially in certain familiar, ecologically based tasks.

CAUSES OF AGE DIFFERENCES

As early as 1928, Thorndike (Thorndike et al., 1928) hypothesized that the learning problems of older people were associated with their susceptibility to negative transfer. In 1934, Ruch considered the possibility that learning problems in adults were related to their difficulties in reorganizing habits. The causes of age-related differences and the interpretation of data supporting specific models of memory and aging are controversial at present. Some of the interpretation problems are due in part to our limited knowledge of the influence of the biological systems on memory functioning, as well as the influence of the lawful interaction between the individual, the environment, and the task demands on the observed performance.

Selected examples of three types of memory and aging models are discussed in this section. First, biological hypotheses attempt to define age-related differences in memory capacities in terms of biological differences (Albert and Kaplan, 1980; Kinsbourne, 1980), including differences in the central nervous system (Birren, Woods, and Williams, 1980; Salthouse, 1980). These hypotheses set limits on the cognitive processes. Second, processing explanations have come to constitute the majority of hypotheses since the information processing tradition has come to dominate memory and aging research. Some hypotheses attempt to isolate the deficit in a discrete stage of memory processing, such as encoding or retrieval. Other hypotheses address the failure or inability of the elderly to use optimal processing strategies (Kausler, 1970; Eysenck, 1974, 1977). Finally, contextual hypotheses (Hultsch and Pentz, 1980; Labouvie-Vief and Schnell, 1982) adapt the model of memory proposed by Bartlett (1932), which viewed learning and memory within the context of an interaction between the individual and an event. This perspective emphasizes the differences attributable to experiences and motivation, as well as to perceptual, linguistic, personality, and cultural factors in understanding the observed performance of young and elderly adults.

Biological Hypotheses

Neuropsychological Bases of Attention and Age. Several well-documented neurological, physiological, and biological changes are known to occur with normal aging. Examples include an increase in senile plaques and neurofibrillary tangles, changes in neuronal metabolism, and neuronal depletion. How do these changes affect the behavior of the aged in general, and what are their relations to memory function in particular?

Preliminary neurochemical and pharmacological work on peptide and cholinergic drugs with both animal and human subjects showed that changes in neurotransmitter and neuroendocrine functions in the later years of healthy individuals could be responsible for some of the decline observed in cognitive functions (see Marsh, 1980; Hines and Fozard, 1980, for reviews). For example, Deutsch (1971, 1973) reported that it is the cholinergic neuronal system that is involved in memory function and that performance is sensitive to the levels of neurotransmitter at the postsynaptic receptor sites. Drachman (1976, 1977; Drachman and Leavitt, 1972) showed that administration of an acetylcholine (ACh) antagonist—a receptor blocker—resulted in memory performances by young adults similar to those observed in the elderly. This condition can be reversed with the administration of an ACh agonist.

Two recent neuropsychological hypotheses have linked age-related changes in memory to neurological factors that have been shown to compromise an individual's ability to attend. Since attention is needed for encoding and retrieval, attentional deficits would be linked with memory deficits (Craik and Simon, 1980). Kinsbourne (1980) described a general model of how attention might be affected, given diffused or localized brain dysfunction in the elderly. Albert and Kaplan (1980) further proposed that selective-attention deficits in the age could be isolated as deficits in the frontal system of the elderly brain. Although both hypotheses are based on preliminary findings and need further development and verification, they could provide a possible biological basis for the attentional deficits observed in elderly subjects.

Kinsbourne's Model. Kinsbourne (1980) hypothesized that brain integrity and behavior in older individuals may be compromised in three general ways: (1) by diffuse neuronal depletion, which may affect the various cerebral "processors"; (2) by topographically skewed neuronal depletion, which may interfere with the proper balance and flexibility of opponent systems; and (3) by intense focal damage, which may generate specific neuro-psychological symptoms.

Intense focal damage that generates specific behavioral symptoms (including memory dys-function) is far from unique to the elderly pop-ulation and is a concern of clinical neuropsy-chology. Diffuse and topographically skewed neuronal depletion may also be found in pre-senile dementia of the middle-aged and in Down's syndrome during late adolescence. These problems are, however, disproportion-ately prevalent in older adults.

Kinsbourne (1980) employed two principle sources to argue that diffuse or uneven neu-ronal depletion may have some impact on se-lective attention. He cited the hypothesis of Lashley (1942) and his associates that certain intellectual abilities are tied not to specific loci but to the integrity of wide cerebral areas. Diffuse impairment might leave specific func-tions intact and yet render its victim slow in response, lacking in vigilance, and resistant to changes in mental set. A second part of Kinsbourne's postulation was based on the no-tion that much of the central nervous system is controlled by opponent processes (e.g., Sher-rington, 1906) and that mutually inhibitory interaction over a range of settings is needed for adaptive behavior. If neuronal depletion is more pronounced at one site than another, however, the opposite balance is upset, leading to quantitative excess in some behavior and the absence of some other behavior. It is postu-lated that a lack of opponent control would result in dysfunctions associated with lateral-ity of attention, focus of attention, and dura-tion of attention.

How can remembering become more diffi-cult with diffuse or focal damage to the brain? Kinsbourne suggested that focal lesions might limit the range and transform the nature of a particular experience. Furthermore, he ar-gued that older persons with selective atten-tional dysfunction resulting from diffuse dam-age may have their experience determined more by details, even irrelevant ones, than by generalities. As a consequence, the usual cuing for remembering may not work, and more spe-cific and concrete cuing may be necessary.

Kinsbourne's preliminary postulation is tantalizing particularly because little is known about the relationship between neuronal de-pletion in old age and memory behaviors. To make this speculation into a working model for both neuropsychologists and cognitive psy-chologists, a detailed accounting is needed to provide explicit, testable hypotheses about specific behaviors and the range of circum-stances under which those behaviors would be compromised.

Albert and Kaplan's Model. Albert and Ka-plan (1980) postulated a neuropsychological model of aging based on the comparison of cognitive patterns of normal elderly and brain-damaged patients. They suggested that two areas of performance dysfunction in older adults—changes in arousal/attention and vis-uospatial performance—may signal focal neu-ropathological change in the frontal system (Nauta, 1971).

Evidence from electrophysiological mea-surements of the autonomic nervous system that are correlated with arousal and attention provides some support for the hypothesis that the elderly are underaroused and have a selec-tive attention deficit. Measurement of the gal-vanic skin response showed reduced respon-sivity in older subjects in a classical conditioning paradigm (Botwinick and Kor-netsky, 1960) and a vigilance task (Surwillo, 1966). Underarousal of the aged was proposed as one possible mechanism for the lower level of performance in these studies. Another elec-trophysiological measure that has been useful as a measure of central nervous system activity and that is also correlated with changes in attention and/or activation (Karlin, 1970) is the late component (P3) of the Average Evoked Potential (AEP). The magnitude of P3 has been shown to decrease with age (Dust-man and Beck, 1969; Marsh and Thompson, 1977) and is correlated with decline in cogni-tive performance. Furthermore, Schenkenberg (1970) suggested that decrease in P3 could be due to a diminished effectiveness of the reticular activating system.

Another component of the AEP, the Con-tingent Negative Variation (CNV)—which is correlated with the preparatory set of the subject—was reduced in elderly subjects in a simple reaction time task with random interstimulus intervals. Loveless and Sanford (1974) argued that reduced CNV was a reflection of the elderly's difficulty in initiating a preparatory set at an appropriate time. Tecce (1978) also measured the magnitude of the CNV and found it to be significantly smaller in the frontal area for the elderly in comparison to young controls, but not in the parietal area.

In addition to their review of the electrophysiological literature, Albert and Kaplan also found evidence in the cognitive literature (Craik, 1977; Hoyer and Plude, 1980) suggesting that there is a change in arousal and attention in the cognitive performance of the elderly. Given that an intact frontal system is needed for selective attention and set, the lower level of arousal and attention of the elderly seems to suggest an inadequacy in the frontal system.

A second source of evidence to support the frontal-system deficit hypothesis came from qualitative analysis of the elderly's perfor-

mance in a set of visuospatial tasks. Albert and Kaplan analyzed the steps taken by the elderly toward the solutions of several neuropsychological tasks and concluded that the processes the elderly employed were similar to those of patients with frontal impairment. The elderly subjects in this study were also participants in the Framingham Heart Study, for whom detailed health information was available. Trained observers recorded the order or sequence of steps taken to complete a set of visuospatial tasks (i.e., the flag figure on the visual reproduction subtest of the Wechsler Memory Scale, the Draw a Clock test, the Hooper Visual Organization Test, and a task to test motor agraphia). In performing these visuospatial tasks, patients with frontal system damage tended to perceive the units of a drawing accurately but to reproduce them in distorted ways. Examples of the results of the Draw a Clock test are presented in Figure 8. Subjects were instructed: "Draw a clock. Set the hands at 10 after 11." Figure 8A shows the drawings of the high-scoring subjects. Sev-

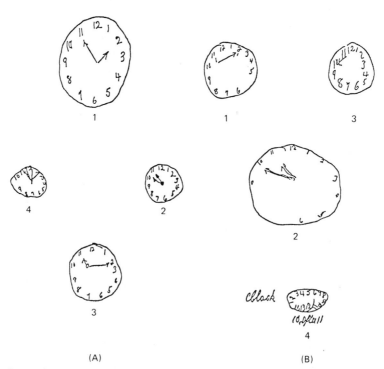

(A)   (B)

Fig. 8. Clock drawings by elderly subjects with high (A) and low (B) scores on a neuropsychological screening battery. (*From Albert and Kaplan, 1980.*)

eral abnormalities are observed: the length of the hands is inappropriately drawn (Nos. 1 through 4); the center is pulled over toward the 11 (No. 3); and one hand is set on the 10 and the other on the 11 (No. 2). The drawings of the low-scorers were more severely defective (Figure 8B), but the patterns were similar.

Albert and Kaplan found similar patterns of performance in the other visuospatial tasks. Subjects tended to segment stimulus information, and their errors seemed to be the result of a pull to the most prominent feature, with a lack of appreciation of the relationships between the parts and of the parts to the whole. The similarity of the overall patterns of behavior between healthy older volunteers in the Framingham Heart study and patients with frontal area dysfunction led Albert and Kaplan to postulate that processes controlled by the frontal area may be impaired in the older adults.

Models of Behavioral Slowing and Age. For 25 years, Birren has maintained that the most pervasive age-related change is the slowing of behavior (see Birren et al., 1980, for a review). He has systematically examined the causes, organization, and consequences of behavioral slowing with age and reported that a wide range of functions (e.g., intelligence, peripheral and central processing, health status, brain damage, depression, physical fitness) are related to the slowing. Although no one specific biological component was implicated, according to Birren, the most parsimonious explanation of the slowing phenomenon involves a general mediating mechanism within the central nervous system that influences cortical, cerebellar, and brainstem functions simultaneously. Slowing, in his view, underlies many of the cognitive difficulties manifested by older people.

Salthouse (1980) has elaborated Birren's general behavioral hypothesis that general speed loss is an explanatory factor for cognitive loss. Salthouse holds that all memory mechanisms that are sensitive to temporal parameters lead to poorer performance in the elderly. Postulating that the memory process

most likely to be slowed with age is rehearsal, he has proposed a model of how differences in the speed of rehearsal between young adults and the elderly could influence their memory performance.

Salthouse measured the rehearsal speed of young and old subjects for one- and three-syllable words as well as the percentage of correct recall of the words following rehearsal. He noted that both increased age and an increased number of syllables affected rehearsal speed and recall and suggested that the reason older people have poor recall is that they perform slowly. According to Salthouse, the memory processes of the elderly are similar to those of younger adults but function at a slower rate.

In summary, the general implication of biological hypotheses is that the degree of impairment in memory functions corresponds to the integrity of the biological system of the older adult. This line of research defining the brain-behavior relationship needs to be further developed to answer the following two questions: Under what conditions are the observed memory deficits of older adults the result of biological deterioration and under what conditions are they caused by processing changes? And under what conditions are these deficits reversible? Questions of functional reversibility are of central importance to biological and behavioral sciences as well as to clinicians concerned with memory diagnosis and remediation issues.

It is hoped that answers to the above questions will be forthcoming in the future. At present, the relationship between specific biological deterioration and memory functions is more evident in subjects with advanced pathological dysfunctions. The usefulness of generalized neuronal depletion or generalized slowing models would depend on the specificity of these models in predicting the critical threshold of deficit that begins to compromise behavior. Generalized biological deficit models provide little explanatory power with regard to performance in the large proportion of healthy, community-dwelling older adults. Furthermore, these hypotheses by themselves cannot account for equivalent performance by old and young in some situations or superior performance by older adults in others.

Processing Hypotheses

Because memory processing is thought to involve encoding, storage, and retrieval of information, some cognitive researchers have attempted to isolate the locus of age-related deficits to one or a combination of these stages. This section examines briefly the available hypotheses on memory processing in the sequence of their development (see also reviews by Smith, 1980; Smith and Fullerton, 1981; Hartley, Harker, and Walsh, 1980; and Burke and Light, 1981).

Storage-Deficit Hypothesis. Because early research on memory concentrated on learning and acquisition, it is reasonable to find that one of the first hypotheses on memory and aging held that poorer performance by the elderly was due to greater susceptibility to interference with the stored information (Kay, 1959; Welford, 1958). The underlying premise of the storage-deficit hypothesis is that prior (proactive interference) or subsequent (retroactive interference) learning interferes with the strength of the memory traces and that this interference is more prominent for the older adult during the retrieval period. Data in the literature, however, failed to support this view (Craik, 1977): Older persons were not more vulnerable to proactive (Craik, 1968; Fozard, and Waugh, 1969) or retroactive (e.g., Smith, 1974; 1975) interference. Kausler (1970) cautioned that, since levels of acquisition were not equated in many early studies, differences in forgetting could be due to differences in the original level of learning. Indeed, in studies in which original learning levels have been equated, no age differences in forgetting rates have been found (e.g., Poon and Fozard, 1980; Fozard, Waugh, and Thomas, 1975).

Retrieval-Deficit Hypothesis. Instead of attributing age differences to interference with the memory trace, the retrieval hypothesis attributes memory difficulties to a failure to access the stored information during retrieval.

The evidence most often cited in support of a retrieval deficit is the comparison of recall and recognition performances of young and elderly adults (Schonfield, 1965; Schonfield and Robertson, 1966; Erber, 1974). The well-replicated finding of small age deficits for recognition, compared to the large deficits found for recall, suggests that information was in the memory store and that retrieval rather than storage is thus the locus of the age deficit.

Additional data in support of the retrieval hypothesis come from the comparison of age differences in cued and free recall. If age effects are due to retrieval differences, then retrieval cues should minimize the age effect. The fact that age effects were greatly reduced when category cues were provided (Hultsch, 1975; Laurence, 1967) suggests that the recall deficit is associated with retrieval.

A major problem of the retrieval explanation is that retrieval efficiency is dependent on encoding; it is difficult, if not impossible, to untangle the two stages (Smith, 1980). Alternatively, encoding explanations could account for some of the data cited as support for the retrieval hypothesis. Several investigators (e.g., Griffith, 1975; Winograd and Smith, 1978) have showed that recall and recognition are differentially affected by different encoding strategies. For example, organization of the input stimuli was of benefit on a recall test, but not on a recognition test. When the recognition test provided the possible alternatives during retrieval, encoding strategies may not have been as critical. It is possible, therefore, that the large age differences observed in free recall, but not in recognition, are due to inefficient encoding strategies used by older adults.

An encoding explanation for the smaller age difference in cued recall was suggested by Smith (1977; see Figure 4). Smith showed that in order for the category cues to be effective the stimuli had to be organized during acquisition. Category cues provided at acquisition were sufficient to minimize age differences, whereas cues at retrieval alone did not improve performance. There is a high likelihood that there is a retrieval deficit in older adults (see also Burke and Light, 1981); retrieval alone, however, cannot account for all the processing deficits observed in the data.

Encoding-Deficit Hypothesis. The data from secondary memory studies reviewed earlier suggest that older adults are deficient in encoding. In the study by Thomas and Ruben (1973) described earlier (Figure 3), for example, older subjects performed at a lower level than young subjects in the standard no-instruction condition. When organizational aids such as visual imagery instructions or cartoon mnemonics were provided at acquisition, no age difference in retrieval was observed for up to 16 months. These results are typical of studies examining the encoding-deficit hypothesis. Smith (1980) and Smith and Fullerton (1981) differentiated three types of encoding deficits: (1) verbal elaboration—the degree to which each item is distinctly encoded; (2) visual elaboration—the use of imagery as a type of encoding; and (3) organization—the degree to which the items are related to each other during acquisition. Data are available to support all three types of encoding deficits in memory performances of older adults.

To investigate the possibility of a verbal elaboration deficit in older adults, Eysenck (1974) employed an incidental orienting task in which varying levels of elaboration of words were required. Subjects were required either to count letters of words, to generate rhymes, or to generate appropriate adjectives. A control group received no elaboration instructions. In a later free recall test, older subjects showed increasing decrements from letters to rhymes to adjectives, with the largest decrement in the no-elaboration control task. The results suggested that the more elaborative the processing required by a task, the larger the age difference will be in later recall performance.

Data supporting an age deficit in visual elaboration can be found in studies of imagery mnemonics and recall performance (Poon, Walsh-Sweeney, and Fozard, 1980). Imagery mnemonics have been found to facilitate the recall performance of older adults and reduce the magnitude of age differences. Smith and Fullerton (1981), however, cautioned that imagery mnemonics could increase organization of the items as well as visual elaboration, and the literature is not clear whether one or both processes are involved in imagery mnemonics.

Finally, organizational deficits, in terms of grouping items at acquisition, were demonstrated for older adults in experiments in which different types of organization instructions were manipulated. For example, Hultsch (1969) provided subjects with either general or specific instructions to organize a list of words, while a control group received no instructions. The results showed that the age decrement found in the no-instruction condition was reduced in the general-instruction condition; the decrement was further reduced in the specific-instruction condition.

In summary, although it is difficult to disentangle the different stages of memory empirically, the available data suggest that both encoding and retrieval deficits are implicated in the lower level of performance of older adults. Some investigators have argued that it is not likely that cognitive deficits can be isolated to one stage or component but rather that deficits are widespread in the entire cognitive system (e.g., Craik and Lockhart, 1972; Norman, 1968). Since it has been suggested that fundamental processes in encoding and retrieval are very similar, a dysfunction in encoding would also be found in retrieval. Decreased efficiency in verbal elaboration, visual imagery, organization, and failure to spontaneously process "deeply" (Craik and Simon, 1980) are some of the causes found to contribute to the elderly's deficit.

Contextural Perspectives

As information on the memory of elderly adults accumulates, a question inevitably arises regarding how changes in learning milieu affect memory processes. How do changes in learning habits and motivation, increased knowledge base, and cumulative experience influence the memory processes and strategies of the older adult? Essentially, these are the same type of questions posed by Bartlett (1932) in his study of prose retention some 50 years ago. Not only did he find that subjects' recall contained a high proportion of inaccuracies but that the contents of the recall protocols were transformed and modified according to the subjects' social and environmental conditions. Bartlett postulated that memory is a reconstructive and elaborative process involving the application and integration of an individual's existing schemata and prior experience. Thus, individual differences in motivation, abilities, and personality, as well as in social and cultural background, all interact with the stimulus event. These interactions could contribute in significant ways to the study of differences in memory performance between young and old adults.

Bartlett's (1932) contextual approach lay dormant for many years until recent investigators began to incorporate his ideas into their concepts of learning and memory (e.g., Flavell, 1981; Hultsch and Pentz, 1980; Jenkins, 1979; and Meacham, 1977). Hultsch and Pentz (1980) have emphasized that there is no one contextual model of learning and memory. It can be said that there are no models at all but, rather, frameworks describing the interactive nature of the various individual, environmental, and task variables that contribute to the understanding of an event. For example, emphasis may be placed on the stimulus material (e.g., Craik and Lockhart, 1972; Jenkins, 1974; Kintsch, 1974), the individual's pre-experimental knowledge (e.g., Brockway, Chmielewski, and Cofer, 1974), the individual's expectations and goals (e.g., Cofer, 1977; Kintsch, 1978), or the sociocultural context (e.g., Kvale, 1977). From the contextualist view, there is no complete definition of context, and the usefulness of any one analysis is dependent on the questions asked.

Labouvie-Vief and Schell (1982) proposed that the contextual approach can be viewed as a generalization of the current information-processing approach, and that both approaches can complement one another in furthering the understanding of the learning and memory processes of the older adult. The available literature has already demonstrated the usefulness of this interactive approach. For example, age has been found to interact with verbal abilities (Bowles and Poon, 1982; Cavanaugh, (1983); Taub, 1979), motivation and motivation-related variables (Kahn and Miller, 1978; Miller, 1975; Weckowicz, Nutter, Cruise, and Yonge, 1972; Poon and Fozard, 1978; Welford, 1980), monetary incentives (Leech and Witte, 1971; Erber, Feely,

and Botwinick, 1980), and item familarity (Barrett and Wright, 1981; Poon and Fozard, 1978; Hultsch and Dixon, in press). These studies help to estimate the relative contribution of chronological age as well as the contributions of ability, motivation, task demands, and other contextual variables on the observed performances.

Labouvie-Vief and Schell (1982) further proposed that qualitative processing styles employed by young and elderly adults should be carefully examined. Some observed inefficient processing behaviors may actually reflect adaptive changes for older adults. It is possible that new modes of processing are employed to replace old modes as the latter lose efficiency. An example of adaptive modes of processing can be found in the prose memory literature. Although age decrement is observed in the retention of subordinate prose structure, no age decrement is found in the retention of superordinate ideas (Meyer et al., 1979a,b). It has been suggested that, with aging, there is an adaptive trade-off of low-structured detail for higher-ordered units of meaning (Labouvie-Vief and Schell, 1982). Qualitative age differences found in styles of processing—such as in categorization (Kogan, 1974; Sabatini and Labouvie-Vief, 1979), word association (Perlmutter, 1978; Reigel, 1968), and sorting-and-recall (Hultsch, 1971) tasks—may very well reflect cohort differences in experience and not necessarily a deficit in the processing system of the older adult.

In summary, the incorporation of contextual perspectives into the information-processing framework could provide at least two innovative ways of viewing memory differences between young and old adults. One, it may not be useful to label all performance differences between older community-dwelling volunteers and younger college students as "deficits," since there are dramatic individual and environmental differences between these populations. Although the interaction on memory of these concomitant variables with age is not clearly understood, the evidence suggests that it could alter the magnitude and direction of age differences. Two, there are patterns of information processing that may be adaptive for different stages of development. It would be useful to identify both adaptive and maladaptive processes with the older adults.

Summary

Proponents of the biological, processing, and contextual hypotheses have, by and large, pursued the understanding of memory processes of older adults from their separate perspectives. Although biological and environmental influences are not well understood, it is argued that they have to be integrated in the understanding of memory processes.

The bulk of memory and aging studies have attempted to locate age differences in encoding, storage, and/or retrieval mechanisms. Other models postulated the nature of these deficits in terms of whether older adults suffer from an inability to process in a particular way or simply from a disuse of efficient strategies (see Reese, 1976; Eysenck, 1974). Most of the work attempts to account for the deficits in secondary memory of older adults. The available hypotheses have yet to explain (1) the apparently good performance of older adults in iconic memory even though some peripheral decline is detected; (2) the processes involved in the transition between primary memory, where minimal age difference is found, and secondary memory, where a substantial age difference is evident; (3) the differences in the retrieval processes from secondary memory and tertiary memory, where a large age difference is detected in secondary memory but a minimal difference is found in tertiary memory; and (4) the mechanisms involved in situations where age differences are attenuated, eliminated, or reversed (e.g., practice and superordinate level retention in prose recall).

The next section describes the dilemma faced by clinicians who need to make diagnoses and to recommend remediation strategies for older adults in the face of incomplete knowledge about biological, processing, and contextual influences on memory performance.

MEMORY TESTING AND INTERVENTION

Researchers agree on the importance of the progression "from lab to life" (Birren, 1974; Schaie, 1974; Schonfield, 1974; Poon, Fozard, and Treat, 1978), but few steps actually have been taken to translate information obtained in the laboratory to the clinical setting.

In their review of clinical assessment and aging, Schaie and Schaie (1977) summarized the state of the art in clinical testing. They wrote: "Although for the first few decades in the history of clinical psychology, psychometrics and psychological assessment ruled supreme, in the fifties, disenchantment set in. As in the fairy tale we suddenly discovered the emperor had no clothes; we found our elaborate techniques lacked validity or were simply irrelevant to the kind of questions mental health professionals wanted answers for. In retrospect, it seems today that the techniques may have been sounder than we suspected, but that our error was to put the cart before the horse. That is, we developed elegant techniques before we knew what should be asked" (p. 692).

Practical problems in clinical assessment and remediation encountered by clinicians can be linked directly to the state of current theoretical knowledge: (1) The current research has not yet identified all the major factors involved in memory performance of the aged, and, more important, the interactions among the factors that could alter the patterns of observed performance are not well defined. (2) The assumptions, paradigms, and results derived in the laboratory rarely translate directly into clinical applications (Thompson, 1980). Clinicians cannot assume that cognitive processes inferred from laboratory studies can be equated with those long-term changes in cognitive processes in a remedial program. In addition, clinicians cannot be sure that the strategies employed in memory tasks are similar for both laboratory volunteers and patients in a clinical setting. Even with incomplete knowledge, clinicians need to provide useful diagnosis and effective remediation. From the perspective of the practicing clinician, experimental psychological methods give minimal attention to the needs and constraints of the clinical setting, while theoretical memory models are too esoteric to address the many memory complaints of the client (Erickson, Poon, and Walsh-Sweeney, 1980). As a consequence, most memory assessment batteries still depend chiefly on the time-worn Wechsler Memory Scale, subtests of the Wechsler Adult Intelligence Scale, or the Primary Mental Ability Tests. As for memory training techniques, there has been little progress since ancient times (e.g., the method of loci).

Memory complaints flow from many of the elderly people living in the community. Although the primary goal of memory diagnosis is to differentiate cases of "benign senescent forgetfulness" from cases of pathology or "malignant memory loss" (Kral, 1962), the diagnostic instrument can also be used to monitor functional changes if memory problems are detected and to provide a strategy for remediation. Erickson, Poon, and Walsh-Sweeney (1980) have defined a series of questions that address the immediate concerns of the client, the family, and the treatment personnel in a clinical setting. Elderly people who perceive some memory loss want to know, in layman's language, what has gone wrong with their ability to attend, learn, and remember. Is the loss normal with aging, or does it signal some abnormal change? What can be done about it; what is the prognosis?

The treatment personnel also have questions about etiology and prognosis: What are the motivational, environmental, and health influences on the status of the patient? How, when, and with what tools do the diagnosis and remediation proceed? These questions are pragmatic and specific and reflect the need for clear answers to pressing problems.

Clinical Memory Tests

Unfortunately, there are no agreed upon criteria for memory tests used for diagnostic purposes (see Butters, 1980; Gallagher, Thompson, and Levy, 1980; Raskin and Jarvik, 1979; and Schaie and Schaie, 1977). Until criteria are established and tests developed, clinicians have two alternatives—to pick their tests from among the available memory paradigms or to try their hand at developing tests to fit the memory problems of their patient populations. Conflicting needs complicate the administration of clinical memory tests. On the one hand, there is usually little time available for the testing, and, on the other, not only the different types of memory but other concomitant factors that influence memory in the aged need to be evaluated. The selection of a battery or a testing strategy to satisfy both these needs presents a challenge for the future.

Table 2 illustrates the dilemma of subtest selection in nine memory batteries. The batteries were evaluated for the presence or absence of 18 memory-assessment features compiled by Erickson, Poon, and Walsh-Sweeney (1980). The table shows that different combinations of memory components are deemed important in different batteries. In general, the batteries attempt to sample short- and long-term retention of verbal and spatial materials. Some batteries assess auditory memory, and all stress brevity and convenience, but orientation, remote memory, motor skill learning, and acquisition and retrieval of the kind of information subjects use everyday (e.g., telephone numbers, name/face) are typically not assessed. Furthermore, few instruments provide alternative forms, standardization, validation of tests with regard to everyday behavior, or norms for elderly persons.

Theoretical orientations have sometimes guided the design of subtests. For example, the Wechsler Memory Scale (WMS) was originally designed to isolate organic problems associated with memory disorders. It has been shown, however, that the test does not differentiate between psychotic, neurotic, and organic problems once the age and IQ of patients are controlled (Cohen, 1950). Factor analysis of the WMS (Kear-Colwell, 1973) revealed that only demented patients exhibited overall memory dysfunction and that some subjects with confirmed lesions produced no measurable memory deficits whatsoever.

Neuropsychological and general memory models have provided some guidance in subtest selection. The examination of verbal, spatial, and motor reaction time, as well as of integration and learning skills in different sensory modalities, provides neuropsychological information on the integrity of different parts of the cortex associated with memory functions (e.g., Barbizet, 1970; Luria, 1973; Talland, 1965; Milner, 1970; Butters and Cermak, 1975). Information-processing models also

TABLE 2. INVENTORY OF SELECTED FEATURES OF EIGHT MEMORY BATTERIES. (From Erickson, Poon, and Walsh-Sweeney, 1980.)

	Wechsler Memory Scale	Inglis	Cronholm	Meyer and Falconer	Williams	Barbizet and Cany	Patten	Pershad	Number of tests reflecting each criterion
Orientation	?*	No	No	No	No	No	?*	?*	0+
Remote memory	?	No	No	No	?	?	?	Yes	1+
Short-term auditory memory	Yes	Yes	No	No	Yes	Yes	Yes	Yes	6
Short-term visual memory	No	Yes	No	No	No	Yes	No	No	2
Learning-to-criterion (Verbal stimuli)	No	Yes	No	Yes	No	No	?	No	2+
Learning-to-criterion (Visual stimuli)	No	Yes	No	Yes	No	Yes	?	No	3+
Delayed retention (Verbal stimuli)	No	No	Yes	No	Yes	Yes	Yes	Yes	4
Delayed retention (Visual stimuli)	No	No	Yes	No	Yes	Yes	Yes	Yes	5
Motor skills learning	No	No	No	No	No	No	No	No	0
Alternate procedure for verbal response	No	Yes	No	Yes	Yes	No	No	No	2
Alternate procedure for motor response	No	Yes	Yes	Yes	Yes	Yes	Yes	Yes	7
Common verbal stimuli	Yes	Yes	Yes	Yes	Yes	Yes	Yes	Yes	8
Common visual stimuli	No	Yes	Yes	Yes	Yes	Yes	Yes	Yes	7
Brevity and convenience	Yes	Yes	Yes	Yes	Yes	Yes	Yes	Yes	8
Alternate forms	Yes	No	Yes	Yes	Yes	No	No	No	4
Standardized	Yes	No	?	No	Yes	No	No	Yes	3+
Validated on everyday behaviors	No	?	No	No	No	No	No	No	0+
Elderly norms available	Yes	Yes	No	No	Yes	Yes	No	No	4
Number of criteria met on each test	6+	10+	7+	8	9+	10+	7+	9+	

* ? = minimal or inadequate.

suggest that the processing capacity and efficiency of the different memory stores should be assessed.

The disarray found in clinical memory testing reflects the lack of confidence by clinicians in the ability of available instruments to evaluate the presenting symptoms accurately and to identify underlying causes of organic, processing, and/or environmental factors. Clinicians have realized that memory may be affected by different factors, and current thinking about necessary aspects of the diagnostic battery includes: (1) the evaluation of the self-perception of memory function; (2) measures of the concomitant factors of environment, personality, affective states, health, neurological status, etc. that may influence changes in memory functions; and (3) a clinical examination of memory behavior employing either psychometric or information-processing designs (Gallagher et al., 1980; Erickson et al., 1980).

Thompson (1980) has provided one possible diagnostic sequence. If a person who complains often of memory problems is shown to have normal memory performance but an elevated level of depression, the depression may be contributing to the self-perceived memory problems. If memory complaints are many when memory performance is normal and there are no signs of depression, then some stress or anxiety may be underlying the complaints. If memory performance and memory complaints are both low in the absence of depression, then some neurological or physiological dysfunction is indicated, and neurological and health examinations could verify the initial diagnosis. Next, if complaints are high and performance is low in the presence of depression, then diagnosis is more difficult. If treatment for depression does not improve the memory performance, brain damage may be indicated. Qualitative performance differences observed between individuals with known neurological deficits and community-dwelling adults with memory problems might provide cues to other contributing factors.

Pharmacological Intervention

The influences of processing and biological hypotheses are most evident in the types of pharmacological treatment used for cognitive problems associated with aging (see also Reisberg, Ferris, and Gershon, 1981, for a review). When learning and memory problems of older adults were thought to be influenced by arteriosclerotic vascular changes and cerebral blood flow deficiencies, treatment involving cerebral vasodialators (e.g., Bazo, 1973) hyperbaric oxygenation (e.g., Jacobs, Winter, Alvis, et al., 1969) and anticoagulants (Walsh, Walsh, and Maloney, 1978) was recommended. When depression was found to influence memory, a wide variety of psychostimulants were prescribed (e.g., Darvill, 1954; Prien, 1973), including a broad category of "rejuventor" (Gerovital H3) and "mood elevators" and "attention enhancers" (e.g., methylphenidate and pentylenetetrazol). Other drugs thought to enhance learning—e.g., mootropics, neuropeptides, and neurotransmitters—are being tested, but only equivocal results have been obtained so far.

Since changes in neurotransmitter and neuroendocrine functions with advancing age could set limits on the function of the cognitive system, would the administration of pharmacological agents improve these functions? Current research with aged animals suggests some positive trends. For example, Cooper, McNamara, Thompson, and Marsh (1980) reported that systematic treatment with lysine vasopressin improved the retention performance and slowed the rate of extinction in old rats. Bartus (1980) tested young and aged monkeys for the effects of physostigmine on a delayed recall task. Performance in the aged monkeys improved somewhat with the drug, though the improvement varied with dose levels. Jenson, Messing, Martinez, Vasquez, and McGaugh (1980), however, reported that although naloxone improved the retention performances of young rats in inhibitory-avoidance and swim-escape tasks, it impaired the performances of old rats.

Pharmacological intervention with older adults has had some disappointing results so far (for reviews, see Hines and Fozard, 1980; Marsh, 1980). Ferris, Reisberg, and Gershon (1980) found predominantly negative results in their review of representative studies of neuropeptides (ACTH4–10 and ACTH4–9) in normal and cognitively impaired subjects.

Some positive results have been reported in clinical studies with small samples in which the effects of vasopressin on cognitive functions were observed (see Ferris et al., 1980). Legros, Gilot, Seron, Claessena, Adam, Moeglen, Audibert, and Berchier (1978) reported significant improvements in tests of memory and attention when vasopressin was administered to elderly inpatients, but their results may have been contaminated by practice effects (Poon, 1978). Mohs, Davis, and Darley (1980) reported no substantial effect of choline chloride in a series of four memory studies with young and elderly adults.

Two primary methodological problem areas need to be addressed in the study of pharmacological intervention with elderly subjects: (1) Variability is large in the pretreatment cognitive abilities of the elderly and between cognitive impaired and normal elderly controls. Cognitive tests employed to evaluate the efficacy of the drug treatment must be sensitive to possible floor and ceiling performance effects as well as to the specific cognitive process that the drug is purported to influence. A report of no improvement may be due to the ineffectiveness of the drug for a specific cognitive process or to the insensitivity of the measuring instrument. (2) Variability is large in the sensitivity of subjects to some drugs, e.g., physostigmine. Underdosage produces no facilitation, and overdosage can produce poor performance. Only a narrow range of dose levels may facilitate the performance of a particular subject. A pilot study reported by Mohs et al. (1980), in which dosages were designed for each individual, showed some promising facilitation effects.

Memory Retraining

Minimal attention has been paid to memory retraining for either young or elderly adults (Neiser, 1978). Nevertheless, some studies have found that neurologically compromised adults can learn mnemonics (memory aids) and can improve their memory functions (e.g., Pattern, 1972; Jones, 1974; Baddeley and Warrington, 1973; Lewinsohn, Danaher, and Kikel, 1977). Data from studies on age differences in elaboration, organization, and visual mnemonics show fairly conclusively that older adults can learn to improve their memory as well as younger ones. In a review of visual mnemonics, Poon, Walsh-Sweeney, and Fozard (1980) found that 14 of 17 studies reported that the use of a mnemonic immediately improved the paired-associate and list-learning performances of the elderly. The results also showed the importance of pacing, self-provided imagery, and practice in assisting older learners to improve their performance. Recent studies of mnemonics and aging have further examined the appropriateness of bizarre imagery for older adults and found that elderly subjects tended not to want to use them; natural, interacting imagery worked just as well (Poon and Walsh-Sweeney, 1981). This finding corroborated the results reported by Morris (1978), who found that bizarre imagery tends not to be useful in ordinary or natural situations.

Several experiments have shown that the results obtained in mnemonic training with paired-associate learning can be replicated in name/face learning. Visual mnemonics can improve name/face performance for older adults. This improvement is further enhanced when the elderly subject is provided with an elaboration technique, i.e., judgment of pleasantness of the image (e.g., Yesavage, Rose, and Bower, 1983). The mnemonics-plus-elaboration technique seemed to work in a similar manner for the method of loci (Yesavage and Rose, 1982). Furthermore, practice was shown to be an important factor in improving name/face recall (Yesavage and Rose, 1982).

Although elderly subjects as a group have usually improved their performance when provided with a mnemonic, the data reported in the mnemonic literature and in clinical experience associated with memory training programs varies considerably (see Schaffer and Poon, 1982). Two important points emerge: (1) Not everyone can benefit from mnemonic training, and no single method is viable for every individual or all situations. (2) Maintenance of learned techniques over time has not been demonstrated. A limited number of studies examining the extended use of mnemonics showed that older adults do not use the learned techniques unless they are reminded to do so (e.g., Robertson-Tchabo, Hausman, and Arenberg, 1976; Schaffer and Poon, 1982). This finding brings into question the usefulness of current techniques if the learner tends not to use them over time. Some researchers have argued that the available techniques are sound but that not enough attention is paid to motivating subjects to use them consistently. Others have argued that techniques should be made compatible with the environment of the subjects (Glasgow and Rosen, 1978).

It is noted that "internal" memory aids, such as elaboration, organization, and visual imageries, are seldom used by either young or elderly adults in everyday situations (Cavanaugh et al., (1983); Poon and Schaffer, 1982; Harris, 1978). Instead, external memory aids (e.g., note, diary, string tied on the finger, etc.) are employed most of the time. It would be useful for future research on memory improvement to examine the uses and criterion of uses of both internal and external aids, and also their success rates.

Summary

It should not be surprising that the development of useful clinical assessment and intervention techniques depends on the comprehensiveness of available theories of memory and aging. Until theories can account for a reasonable amount of performance variability based on biological, processing, and contextual factors, clinical diagnoses and remediation strategies will continue the present trend toward "shot gun" approaches. Some investigators argue that our knowledge of age differences in memory would accrue more rapidly in the context of an active intervention program (Fozard, 1980). Intervention or research programs that attempt to examine the impact of individual differences, environment, and task demands would be immensely helpful to clinicians who need to separate out the impacts of environmental influences, organicity, processing capacity, and ability on perceived and observed performance. Furthermore, it would be helpful to clinicians to ascertain which psychometric or information-processing tests are sensitive to changes in the different factors associated with memory dysfunc-

tion. What degree of specificity is needed in making a diagnosis and how much is enough? Finally, the question of the "ecological validity" of psychometric and information-processing tests needs to be settled by both clinicians and researchers (Neiser, 1978). What do these tests measure with respect to real life situations? And how much confidence can one place in the obtained measures in predicting "similar" types of behavior in everyday situations? Salthouse (1982; p. 204) stated:

Cognitive psychologists have made reasonable progress in identifying a limited number of basic processes or operations thought to be responsible for the performance of different laboratory tasks, although there is admittedly little evidence documenting that the same processes are involved in what appear to be related tasks. What is markedly deficient, however, is adequate knowledge about the specific processes involved in various real-world activities. Until detailed job analyses are conducted, one must be content to rely on speculation and intuition in attempting to relate laboratory findings to extralaboratory situations.

INTERACTIVE VIEWS OF MEMORY AND AGING

Perlmutter (1980; p. 352) made the observation:

Most researchers have been confident in anecdotal reports of age-related decline in memory, and have been busy carrying out experiments designed to illuminate the mechanisms underlying this deterioration. The results of these experiments have led us to a point of almost complete confidence in the assumption that memory deteriorates with age.

Among the available deficit hypotheses, biological hypotheses are of limited use at this state of their development for the description of memory functions for a large proportion of the active, independent, and fairly healthy community-dwelling older population. Their usefulness would significantly increase if the relationship between biological and performance variables was made more precise. On the other hand, clinical experience teaches us that processing hypotheses alone cannot adequately account for the variability in observed memory performance. The search for explanations for the variability in memory performance observed in recent years has brought researchers to examine models of memory involving interactions among the task, the individual, and the environment (e.g., Jenkins, 1979; Flavell and Wellman, 1977; Labouvie-Vief and Schell, 1982). Three preliminary research efforts are highlighted in this remaining section to illustrate some current attempts at investigating individual differences and the interactive effects of the individual, the task, and the environment on memory and cognitive performance in older adults.

Post Hoc Analyses of Concomitant Effects

A common concern of cognitive-aging investigators involves the selection of subjects in cross-sectional studies. Since young controls are typically college students, whereas older adults are selected from community volunteers, the concern of researchers centers on whether differences in health, ability, education, or gender distributions among the samples could confound the obtained age effects (Browning and Spilich, 1981; Poon, Krauss, and Bowles, 1981). In response to this concern, Krauss, Poon, Gilewski, and Schaie (1982) reported on the preliminary results of an ongoing study that performed a series of post hoc, Monte Carlo-type analyses to evaluate possible confounding in a large pool of existing data. The data are from a longitudinal study (Schaie, 1979) carried out in Seattle over a period of 21 years. The total number of available subjects was 2,814. Demographic information as well as several subtests of the Primary Mental Abilities test (Thurstone and Thurstone, 1949) were available, the latter examining verbal meaning, spatial rotation, reasoning, number, and word fluency.

Two types of preliminary post hoc analyses were conducted. The first examined the replicability of the age effect across the different PMA subtests, given different sampling procedures (with and without replacement), sample sizes (N = 16 or 20), and different numbers of cohort groups in the comparison (20s vs. 70s or 20s vs. 30s vs. 40s vs. 50s vs. 60s vs. 70s). These different sampling procedures were thought to reflect practices current in the literature. The second type of analyses purposely biased the subject characteristics of the samples. First, age effects were examined across samples of healthy, well-educated, and high-ability subjects only; other analyses involved samples with only one gender, contrasting samples of high and low health, education, and abilities for the different age groups, as well as samples drawn in a random fashion. Care was exercised to select an equal number of subjects across each age range. Furthermore, the age ranges were intentionally biased so that a small age range was obtained for the young subjects (21 to 33 years) and a large age range was used for the older subjects (60 to 80 years). This is also a common procedure found in the literature.

Preliminary results of the replication analyses (Schaie, 1979) showed that the age effects obtained from the small samples were not as strong as those reported for the whole population—a reflection of sample size. Although robust age effects were obtained for verbal meaning, space, and reasoning, age differences were not present for the number subtest in those analyses comparing a small age range of young subjects with a large age range of older subjects. Age differences in the number subtest were only significant in the analysis that compared the performances of the six cohort groups. Aside from the increased statistical power, inspection of group means showed that the addition of the middle-aged cohorts contributed significantly to the obtained age effect. The sampling method, with as well as without replacement, also seemed to have an impact on the consistency of the replications. Three of the five samples obtained with replacement showed significant age differences on the number subtest, whereas only marginally significant age effects were obtained when the samples were obtained without replacement.

In the biased samples, gender effects were found for number and word fluency in large but not small samples. For the six ability subtests, the age effects obtained were similar for samples reflecting the gender distributions across the six cohorts and samples with an equal number of males and females. Education appeared to have a significant effect on verbal meaning, reasoning, and word fluency. Age effects were significantly reduced when education of the samples was statistically controlled.

Although the results reported by Krauss et al. (1982) were preliminary and are at present incomplete, these post hoc analyses represent one systematic method of exploring the effects of individual differences and sampling procedures on aging studies. Similar studies can be conducted on other large data bases to evaluate the consistency of results and conclusions. These studies could parametrically confirm or reject some researchers' intuitively derived concerns about possible confounding effects of certain concomitant variables on chronological age and the cognitive measure under investigation.

Causal Modeling

Another method proposed to examine main and interactional effects in memory and aging was recommended by Cavanaugh (1982). He noted that memory is multidimensional and that the study of memory requires a multivariate method. He proposed the use of causal modeling based on linear structural equations (Bentler, 1980; Bentler and Weeks, 1980) to explore the relations among relevant variables in memory and aging. In this technique, one employs theoretical constructs in order to evaluate plausible directional relations between the constructs. More important, the relations must be explicit, measurable, and testable. Causal modeling could overcome four shortcomings of previous work in adult memory development because: (1) it allows examination of a complex system of variables; (2) it allows consideration of hypothetical constructs that may be impossible to measure directly or with one single index; (3) it provides a way to examine previously ignored factors, and (4) it represents a way to test and modify hypotheses about memory.

Cavanaugh (1982) further provided an example of a causal model to account for the use of memory strategies. Constructs were selected on several levels, and interrelationships were predicated on available hypotheses. The first level of constructs in Cavanaugh's model included age, task, and social context; the second, knowledge and personality; the third, belief, followed by motivation, strategy selection, and response production. Each construct had an operational definition with hypothesized directional relationships. Although no data are available at present to demonstrate the viability of the model, Cavanaugh's causal modeling does illustrate the importance of interactive effects on the output response; it also provides a means to explain contradictory results when only simple variables are manipulated. Perhaps complex issues do indeed necessitate a complex model.

Knowledge Actualization

Lachman and Lachman (1980) introduced the notion "actualization of world knowledge," which describes the accumulation, access, and use of knowledge and information in the natural environment. Several pertinent questions are involved: What knowledge do people acquire in the course of everyday living? How is the knowledge acquired? How is the process represented in the memory system? How do people access the knowledge and use it? Do older adults use their knowledge as efficiently as young adults? At present there are few answers to these questions, and the methodolgies needed for answering them are either in the experimental stages or not yet created.

How do people actualize knowledge? The Lachmans conceptualized three basic processes: (1) retrieval, the process of locating specific information for some purpose; (2) inference, the constructive process used when retrieval of explicit information is not possible; and (3) the metamemory process, or knowledge about the functioning of the memory system.

Retrieval of available, familiar knowledge may be automatic, unconscious, and strategy free, but some of it may be intentional and effortful, particularly if the information cannot be located at the first try. The Lachmans proposed a resolution of the apparent paradox that a significant age decrement is observed in some studies but none at all in others. They suggested that attention should be paid to the efficiency as well as quantity of the retrieval (e.g., number of errors). Efficiency may be calculated as the ratio of the number of correctly retrieved items to the size of the knowledge base. Comparisons of age groups should thus consider the size of the knowledge base, which is thought to increase in a person's lifetime.

An experiment was designed to examine differences between young, middle-aged, and elderly samples in estimated total knowledge and retrieval efficiency. A set of 190 questions on a variety of topics was constructed (i.e., current events, movies, sports, history, the Bible, and geography), and the subjects were tested on recall. The incorrectly recalled items were tested again in a multichoice recognition format. The estimated total knowledge was calculated as the sum of the correctly recalled and recognized items, correcting for the false positives. The efficiency index was calculated by dividing the recall score by the estimated total knowledge. The results showed that estimated knowledge increased from young to middle-age, whereas no difference was found between middle-aged and older adults. The efficiency coefficient, however, was similar across all three age groups.

Examination of retrieval efficiency in terms of an estimated knowledge base is a potentially fruitful research method for comparing the retrieval of young and old adults. This method adjusts for the type of information as well as the knowledge base of that information so that subjects are not penalized if questions are asked outside their field of expertise or if they have a small information base. It must be noted, however, that the size of the knowledge base is difficult to estimate (Perlmutter, 1980; Nickerson, 1980). Inaccurate estimates would provide different pictures of retrieval efficiency.

Perlmutter (1980) suggested that although older adults probably have less efficient memory mechanisms, their rich experience possibly allows them to perform some taks at the same or higher level than younger adults. The questions of how knowledge is accumulated and how experience can be used to compensate for failing memory are therefore two revealing areas for the study of memory in everyday life. For example, consider the retrieval of facts by young and old engineers. If the knowledge base could be accurately estimated, would retrieval efficiency for different engineering information be qualitatively similar or different for young and older, more experi-

enced engineers? How does experience help or hinder the older engineers? How does the retrieval of known facts relate to the inferential and metamemory processes? How does the size of the knowledge base relate to the retrieval of well learned compared to recently learned information?

Another fruitful area of research would be to evaluate whether a salience parameter would improve the retrieval efficiency equation. Perhaps salience could be weighed 0 to 1.0 so that the relative importance to the individual regarding an item to be retrieved could be accounted for. Salience, as it is related to motivation and attitude, has been suggested as an important factor in memory performance. How does salience affect retrieval in relation to the size of the available data base?

The distinction between retrieval of explicit facts and inferentially derived knowledge, in the Lachman's conception of real world information retrieval, reminds us that most of what we know is not learned explicitly (Nickerson, 1977). The possible difficulty of distinguishing explicit and implicit information stored in memory was pointed out by Bartlett (1932), who demonstrated that much of remembered information is transformed according to one's social and environmental context. Studies in prose recall reviewed earlier showed that older adults tend not to perform as well as young adults in the recall of verbatim surface structures but as well or better when the recall of gist or superordinate structures is required. The findings suggest that the constructive and inferential processes stay fairly intact with aging and are important processes for study by memory and aging investigators. Unfortunately, little is known about inferential skills across adulthood.

Several questions may guide research on age differences in inferential abilities and memory performance. As in the investigation of explicit fact retrieval, the quantitative and qualitative aspects of the knowledge base may have some effect on the inferential process. Under what circumstances could prior experiences help or hinder the inferential processes? Do the types of inferences or the process change as a result of the accumulation of experience? Finally, the retrieval and inferential processes involved in knowledge actualization are guided by metamemory, the knowledge of the functioning of the memory system. Metamemory has been long regarded as an important factor in furthering the understanding of memory. Memory theorists, especially those proponents of the contextual and constructionist viewpoints (e.g., Jenkins, 1979; Flavell and Wellman, 1977), believe that memory knowledge can guide a person toward a selection of executive strategies that will have a significant impact on output behavior. A frequently cited example is the development of an expert chess player, in which performance is dependent on the utilization of past experiences (Chase and Simons, 1973; Charness, 1981). In a critical review of the current status of metamemory research, Cavanaugh and Perlmutter (1982) concluded that much needs to be done to clarify operational definitions of the metamemory concept, assessment methods, and most of all the relations between metamemory and memory.

In research on older adults, the relationship between self-assessment of memory and memory performance is not clear. In studies attempting to appraise metamemory simply by asking subjects to assess their general memory functions or by administering a memory questionnaire (e.g., Herman and Neiser, 1978), no correlation was found between general memory assessment and memory performance on paired-associate, list, or prose memory (e.g., Kahn, Zarit, Hilbert, and Neiderehe, 1975; Zarit, Cole, and Guider, 1981; Poon and Schaffer, 1982). When older subjects were asked to predict their actual performance, however, or when a questionnaire was employed including ratings of memory functions in specific memory activities, a significant correlation between prediction and performance was found (Poon and Schaffer, 1982; Zelinski et al., 1980). The inconsistency of the obtained correlations may be due to the impreciseness of the prediction or the memory assessment instrument. Cavanaugh and Perlmutter (1982) reported similar inconsistent correlations for young adults and suggested that the correlational method is weak in assessing the relationship between metamemory and memory for several reasons: (1) The reasons for the selection of questionnaire items are often obscure;

(2) frequently, only one index of assessing metamemory (e.g., verbal report) is used; (3) the selection of appropriate tasks to assess memory functions is problematic; and (4) there are no strong theoretical grounds on which to predict when either a strong or a weak relationship will be found.

Is there an age difference in the subjective feeling-of-knowing between young and old adults? Preliminary results seem to show a consistent trend. Lachman and Lachman (1980) measured the decision latencies and confidence ratings of young and old subjects in their subjective feeling-of-knowing, as well as their performances on a set of general knowledge questions. The Lachmans found no age difference in the accuracy of predicting whether the questions can be answered, nor in the response times, nor the after-the-fact confidence ratings on choices in a multiple choice test. Similarly, Perlmutter (1978) found no age differences in subjects' accuracy in predicting recall or recognition performances, in feeling-of-knowing judgments, or in confidence ratings.

If these preliminary findings of no age difference in the feeling-of-knowing hold true, then can older adults use their knowledge about memory functions and about memory strategy as effectively as younger adults? Data from mnemonic studies reviewed earlier show some inconsistencies in the use of memory strategies by older adults, suggesting that they may not utilize their memory knowledge as effectively: (1) They tend not to use effective organizational strategies when they first encounter a laboratory learning task; (2) when a mnemonic is provided, they can utilize it to improve performance; and (3) when they are not reminded to use it, they tend not to, and their performance declines. As a group, older adults may be deficient in using memory strategies to guide their actions towards a specific goal. It would be fruitful to examine metamemory processes in young and old adults in relation to a model proposed by Flavell (1981), in which performance is based on the interaction between stored information, metamemory knowledge, cognitive goals, and cognitive actions.

In summary, post hoc analysis of available data bases, causal modeling, and the study of knowledge actualization are examples of three immensely creative areas for the study of differences in memory behavior between young and old adults. The following points may be made: (1) These research areas emphasize the effects of individual differences in accumulated knowledge and problem-solving styles as well as task demands on observed performance. The examination of interactions among these variables should help to clarify our current understanding of memory and aging. (2) New ideas in methodologies and concepts are shown to be needed. (3) Questions posed in knowledge actualization can be used to guide the description or catalogue of memory usage in the everyday environment. (4) Interactive models of memory (e.g., Lachman and Lachman, 1980; Jenkins, 1979; Flavell, 1981) can serve to describe and evaluate successful as well as inefficient usage of memory in young and old adults.

SUMMARY

In comparing memory performances of community-dwelling young and elderly adults, minimal age differences are found in iconic, primary, and tertiary memory, whereas substantial differences are found in the acquisition and retrieval of new information from secondary memory. Since there is a well-documented biological decline with advancing age, and learning habits and experiences are different between young and elderly adults, how much of the observed age differences in performance are due to the respective biological, processing, and contextual factors? And how do changes in one factor influence the other factors in the observed performance?

At present, deficit hypotheses alone cannot adequately account for the variability in the observed performances of older adults. Generalized biological deficit hypotheses provide little explanatory power for secondary memory problems of the majority of healthy, independent, and community-dwelling elderly adults. The usefulness of biological models will increase in proportion to their increased specificity in describing the interaction between biological decline and cognitive performance.

Concurrently, memory and aging researchers are exploring the effects of interaction between the individual, the environment, and the task demands on the processing abilities of older adults. In the last decade, research associated with the processing hypothesis has identified difficulties in the encoding and retrieval processes of older adults and suggested that difficulties in verbal elaboration, visual elaboration, and organization are some of the causes of the observed difficulties. Research in the 1980s has begun to further the examination of how these processes interact with environmental, motivational, and other individual difference variables. Some investigators have highlighted the milieu of older adults and suggested that some age differences in performance are normal and adaptive in nature. Others have pointed out the differences in the knowledge base of young and elderly adults and suggested that retrieval efficiency may interact with the knowledge base. Systematic post hoc analyses are being carried out to determine how some individual difference variables may affect cognitive performance. Multivariate methods are proposed to describe how different variables interact to influence output performance. Not only could this type of interactional research help to advance the description of memory performance throughout the life span, it would significantly benefit clinicians who need to evaluate the impact of environmental influences, organicity, and processing abilities on memory complaints and performance.

It has been said that the understanding of memory has evolved slowly; in fact, that it has not adequately advanced beyond the work of Ebbinghaus over 100 years ago (Neisser, 1978; Tulving and Madigan, 1970). At no previous time has there been such a proliferation of reviews on memory and aging within a two-year span as at present. Although quantity per se does not guarantee substantive advance, the raising of the combined consciousness of researchers and clinicians on theoretical and practical issues provides an exciting prospect for research in this decade.

Acknowledgment. Preparation of this chapter was supported by the VA Medical Research Service. The author is grateful to Drs. N. Bowles, F. I. M. Craik, C. Feier, J. Fozard, M. Hakami, D. Plude, and A. Smith for their critical comments on earlier drafts, and to D. Lowe, P. Tun, and D. Williams for their assistance in manuscript preparation.

REFERENCES

Abrahams, J. P.; Hoyer, W. J.; Elias, M. F.; and Bradigan, B. 1975. Gerontological research in psychology published in the Journal of Gerontology 1963–74: Perspectives and progress. *Journal of Gerontology* 30: 668–673.

Albert, M. S., and Kaplan, E. 1980. Organic implications of neuropsychological deficits in the elderly. In *New Directions in Memory and Aging: Proceedings of the George A. Talland Memorial Conference,* eds. L. W. Poon, J. L. Fozard, L. S. Cermak, D. Arenberg, and L. W. Thompson. Hillsdale, N.J.: Lawrence Erlbaum Assoc.

Averbach, E., and Corriell, H. S. 1961. Short-term memory in vision. *Bell System Technical Journal* 40: 309–328.

Baddeley, A. D., and Warrington, E. K. 1973. Memory coding and amnesia. *Neuropsychologia* 11: 159–165.

Bahrick, H. P. 1979. Maintenance of knowledge: Questions about memory we forgot to ask. *Journal of Experimental Psychology: General* 108: 296–308.

Bahrick, H. P.; Bahrick, P. P.; and Wittlinger, R. P. 1975. Fifty years of memory for names and faces: A cross-sectional approach. *Journal of Experimental Psychology* 104: 54–75.

Barbizet, J. 1970. *Human Memory and Its Pathology.* San Francisco: W. H. Freeman.

Barrett, T. R., and Wright, M. 1981. Age-related facilitation in recall following semantic processing. *Journal of Gerontology* 36: 194–199.

Bartlett, F. C. 1932. *Remembering: A Study in Experimental and Social Psychology.* Cambridge: At the University Press.

Bartus, R. T. 1980. Cholinergic drug effects on memory and cognition in animals. In *Aging in the 1980s: Psychological Issues,* ed. L. W. Poon. Washington, D.C.: American Psychological Association.

Bazo, A. J. 1973. An ergot alkaloid preparation (hydergine) versus papaverine in treating common complaints of the aged: Double-blind study. *Journal of the American Geriatric Society* 21: 63–71.

Bentler, P. M. 1980. Multivariate analysis with latent variables: Causal modeling. *Annual Review of Psychology* 31: 419–456.

Bentler, P. M., and Weeks, D. G. 1980. Linear structural equations with latent variables. *Psychometrika* 45: 289–308.

Birren, J. E. 1974. Translations in gerontology—from lab to life: Psychophysiology and speed of response. *American Psychologist* 29: 808–815.

Birren, J. E.; Woods, A. M.; and Williams, M. V. 1980. Behavioral slowing with age: Causes, organization, and consequences. In *Aging in the 1980s: Psychological Issues,* ed. L. W. Poon. Washington, D.C.: American Psychological Association.

Botwinick, J. 1973. *Aging and Behavior.* New York: Springer.

Botwinick, J., and Kornetsky, C. 1960. Age differences in the acquisition and extinction of GSR. *Journal of Gerontology* 15: 83–84.

Botwinick, J., and Storandt, M. 1974. *Memory, Related Functions and Age.* Springfield, Ill.: Charles C Thomas.

Bowles, N. L., and Poon, L. W. 1982. An analysis of the effect of aging on memory. *Journal of Gerontology* 37: 212–219.

Brockway, J. P.; Chmielewski, D.; and Cofer, C. N. 1974. Remembering prose: Productivity and accuracy constraints in recognition memory. *Journal of Verbal Learning and Verbal Behavior* 13: 184–208.

Bromley, D. B. 1958. Some effects of age on short term learning and remembering. *Journal of Gerontology* 13: 398–406.

Browning, G. B., and Spilich, G. J. 1981. Some important methodological issues in the study of aging and cognition. *Experimental Aging Research* 7: 175–188.

Burke, D. M., and Light, L. L. 1981. Memory and aging: The role of retrieval processes. *Psychological Bulletin* 90: 513–546.

Butters, N. 1980. Potential contributions of neuropsychology to our understanding of the memory capacities of the elderly. In *New Directions in Aging in Memory and Aging: Proceedings of the George A. Talland Memorial Conference,* eds. L. W. Poon, J. L. Fozard, L. S. Cermak, D. Arenberg, and L. W. Thompson. Hillsdale, N.J.: Lawrence Erlbaum Assoc.

Butters, N., and Cermak, L. S. 1975. Some analyses of amnesic syndromes in brain damaged patients. In *The Hippocampus,* eds. R. L. Isaacson and K. H. Pribram. Vol. 2. New York: Plenum.

Canestrari, R. E., Jr. 1963. Paced and self-paced learning in young and elderly adults. *Journal of Gerontology* 18: 165–168.

Cavanaugh, J. C. 1982. Memory in everyday life: Theoretical and empirical needs. *The Gerontologist* 22: 104. (Abstract.)

Cavanaugh, J. C. 1983. Comprehension and retention of television programs by 20- and 60-year olds. *Journal of Gerontology* 38: 190–196.

Cavanaugh, J. C.; Grady, J. G.; and Perlmutter, M. P. 1983. Forgetting and use of memory aids in 20- and 70-year olds' everyday life. *International Journal of Aging and Human Development.*

Cavanaugh, J. C., and Perlmutter, M. 1982. Metamemory: A critical examination. *Child Development* 53: 11–28 17:113–122.

Cerella, J., and Poon, L. W. 1981. Age and parafoveal sensitivity. *The Gerontologist* 76. (Abstract.)

Cerella, J.; Poon, L. W.; and Fozard, J. L. 1982. Age and iconic read-out. *Journal of Gerontology* 37: 197–202.

Charness, N. 1981. Aging and skilled problem solving. *Journal of Experimental Psychology: General* 110: 21–38.

Chase, W. G., and Simons, H. A. 1973. The mind's eye in chess. In *Visual Information Processing,* ed. W. G. Chase. New York: Academic Press.

Cofer, C. N. 1977. On the constructive theory of memory. In *The Structuring of Experience,* eds. F. Weizman and I. C. Uzgiris. New York: Plenum.

Cohen, G. 1979. Language comprehension in old age. *Cognitive Psychology* 11: 412–429.

Cohen, J. 1950. Wechsler Memory Scale performance of psychoneurotic, organic, and schizophrenic groups. *Journal of Consulting Psychology* 14: 371–375.

Coltheart, M. 1972. Visual information processing. In *New Horizons in Psychology,* ed. P. C. Dodwell. Harmondsworth: Penguin.

Cooper, R. L., McNamara, M. C.; Thompson, W. G.; and Marsh, G. R. 1980. Vasopressin modulation of learning and memory in the rat. In *Aging in the 1980s: Psychological Issues,* ed. L. W. Poon. Washington, D.C.: American Psychological Association.

Craik, F. I. M. 1968. Two components in free recall. *Journal of Verbal Learning and Verbal Behavior* 7: 996–1004.

Craik, F. I. M. 1977. Age differences in human memory. In *Handbook of the Psychology of Aging,* eds. J. E. Birren and K. W. Schaie. New York: Van Nostrand Reinhold.

Craik, F. I. M., and Lockhart, R. S. 1972. Levels of processing: A framework for memory research. *Journal of Verbal Learning and Verbal Behavior* 11: 671–684.

Craik, F. I. M., and Masani, P. A. 1967. Age differences in the temporal integration of language. *British Journal of Psychology* 58: 291–299.

Craik, F. I. M., and Simon, E. 1980. Age differences in memory: The roles of attention and depth of processing. In *New Directions in Memory and Aging: Proceedings of the George A. Talland Memorial Conference,* eds. L. W. Poon, J. L. Fozard, L. S. Cermak, D. Arenberg, and L. W. Thompson. Hillsdale, N.J.: Lawrence Erlbaum Assoc.

Crowder, R. G. 1980. Echoic memory and the study of aging memory systems. In *New Directions in Memory and Aging: Proceedings of the George A. Talland Memorial Conference,* eds. L. W. Poon, J. L. Fozard, L. S. Cermak, D. Arenberg, and L. W. Thompson. Hillsdale, N.J.: Lawrence Erlbaum Assoc.

Darvill, F. T., Jr. 1954. Double-blind evaluation of methylphenidate (Ritalin) hydrochloride. *Journal of the American Medical Association* 169: 1739–1741.

Deutsch, J. A. 1971. The cholinergic synapse and the site of memory. *Science* 174: 788–794.

Deutsch, J. A., ed. 1973. *The Physiological Basis of Memory.* New York: Academic Press.

Drachman, D. A. 1976. Memory and cholinergic function. In *Neurotransmitter Function,* ed. W. S. Fields. New York: Statton International Medical Book.

Drachman, D. A. 1977. Memory and cognitive function in man: Does the cholinergic system have a specific code? *Neurology* 27: 783–790.

Drachman, D. A., and Leavitt, J. 1972. Memory impairment in the aged: Storage versus retrieval deficit. *Journal of Experimental Psychology* 93: 302–308.

Dustman, R. E., and Beck, E. C. 1969. The effects of maturation and aging on the wave form of visually evoked potentials. *Electroencephalography and Clinical Neurophysiology* 26: 2–11.

Erber, J. T. 1974. Age differences in recognition memory. *Journal of Gerontology* 29: 177–181.

Erber, J. T. 1981. Remote memory and age: A review. *Experimental Aging Research* 1: 189–199.

Erber, J. T. 1982. Memory and age. In *Review of Human Development,* eds. T. Field, W. Overton, H. Quay, L. Troll, and G. Finley. New York: Wiley-Interscience.

Erber, J.; Feely, C.; and Botwinick, J. 1980. Reward conditions and socioeconomic status in the learning of older adults. *Journal of Gerontology* 35: 565–570.

Erickson, R. C.; Poon, L. W.; and Walsh-Sweeney, L. 1980. Clinical memory testing of the elderly. In *New Directions in Memory and Aging: Proceedings of the George A. Talland Memorial Conference,* eds. L. W. Poon, J. L. Fozard, L. S. Cermak, D. Arenberg, and L. W. Thompson. Hillsdale, N.J.: Lawrence Erlbaum Assoc.

Eysenck, M. W. 1974. Age differences in incidental learning. *Developmental Psychology* 10: 936–941.

Eysenck, M. W. 1977. *Human Memory: Theory Research and Individual Differences.* Oxford: Pergamon Press Ltd.

Ferris, S. H.; Crook, T.; Clark, E.; McCarthy, M.; and Rae, D. 1980. Facial recognition memory deficits in normal and senile dementia. *Journal of Gerontology* 35: 707–714.

Ferris, S. H.; Reisberg, B.; and Gershon, S. 1980. Neuropeptide modulation of cognition and memory in humans. In *Aging in the 1980s: Psychological Issues,* ed. L. W. Poon. Washington, D.C.: American Psychological Association.

Flavell, J. H. 1981. Cognitive monitoring. In *Children's Oral Communication Skills,* ed. P. Dickson. New York: Academic Press.

Flavell, J. H., and Wellman, H. W. 1977. Metamemory. In *Perspectives on the Development of Memory and Cognition,* eds. R. V. Kail and J. W. Hagen. Hillsdale, N.J.: Lawrence Erlbaum Assoc.

Fozard, J. L. 1980. The time for remembering. In *New Directions in Memory and Aging: Proceedings of the George A. Talland Memorial Conference,* eds. L. W. Poon, J. L. Fozard, L. S. Cermak, D. Arenberg, and L. W. Thompson. Hillsdale, N.J.: Lawrence Erlbaum Assoc.

Fozard, J. L., and Waugh, N. C. 1969. Proactive inhibition of prompted items. *Psychonomic Science* 17: 67–68.

Fozard, J. L.; Waugh, N. C.; and Thomas, J. C. 1975. Effects of age on long-term retention of pictures. *Proceedings of the Tenth International Congress of Gerontology* (Jerusalem) 2: 137. (Abstract.)

Fozard, J. L.; Wolf, E.; Bell, B.; McFarland, R. A.; and Podolsky, S. 1977. Visual perception and communication. In *Handbook of the Psychology of Aging,* eds. J. E. Birren and K. W. Schaie. New York: Van Nostrand Reinhold.

Gallagher, D.; Thompson, L. W.; and Levy, S. M. 1980. Clinical psychological assessment of older adults. In *Aging in the 1980s: Psychological Issues,* ed. L. W.

Poon. Washington, D.C.: American Psychological Association.

Gilbert, J. G., and Levee, R. F. 1971. Patterns of declining memory. *Journal of Gerontology* 26: 70–75.

Glasgow, R. E., and Rosen, G. M. 1978. Behavioral bibliotherapy: A review of self-help behavior manuals. *Psychological Bulletin* 85: 1–23.

Gordon, S. K., and Clark, W. C. 1974. Application of signal detection theory to prose recall and recognition in elderly and young adults. *Journal of Gerontology* 29: 64–72.

Griffith, D. 1975. Comparison of control processes for recognition and recall. *Journal of Experimental Psychology: Human Learning and Memory* 1: 223–228.

Grossberg, M. 1980. Individual age-related differences in sensory memory. In *New Directions in Memory and Aging: Proceedings of the George A. Talland Memorial Conference,* eds. L. W. Poon, J. L. Fozard, L. S. Cermak, D. Arenberg, and L. W. Thompson. Hillsdale, N.J.: Lawrence Erlbaum Assoc.

Gruneberg, M. M., Morris, P. E., and Sykes, R. N. 1978. *Practical Aspects of Memory.* London: Academic Press.

Haber, R. N., and Standing, L. G. 1969. Direct measures of short-term visual storage. *Quarterly Journal of Experimental Psychology* 21: 43–54.

Harkins, S. W.; Chapman, C. R., and Eisdorfer, C. 1979. Memory loss and response bias in senescence. *Journal of Gerontology* 34: 66–72.

Harris, C. S. 1978. *Fact Book on Aging: A Profile of America's Older Population.* Washington, D.C.: National Council on the Aging.

Hartley, J. T.; Harker, J. O.; and Walsh, D. A. 1980. Contemporary issues and new directions in adult development of learning and memory. In *Aging in the 1980s: Psychological Issues,* ed. L. W. Poon. Washington, D.C.: American Psychological Association.

Hermann, D. J., and Neisser, U. 1978. An inventory of everyday memory experiences. In *Practical Aspects of Memory,* eds. M. M. Gruneberg, P. E. Morris, and R. N. Sykes. London: Academic Press.

Hines, T., and Fozard, J. L. 1980. Memory and aging: Relevance of recent developments for research and application. In *Annual Review of Gerontology & Geriatrics,* Vol. 1. New York: Springer.

Hoyer, W. J., and Plude, D. J. 1980. Attentional and perceptual processes in the study of cognitive aging. In *New Directions in Memory and Aging: Proceedings of the George A. Talland Memorial Conference,* eds. L. W. Poon, J. L. Fozard, L. S. Cermak, D. Arenberg, and L. W. Thompson. Hillsdale, N.J.: Lawrence Erlbaum Assoc.

Hultsch, D. 1969. Adult age differences in the organization of free recall. *Developmental Psychology* 1: 673–678.

Hultsch, D. 1971. Adult age differences in free classification and free recall. *Developmental Psychology* 4: 338–342.

Hultsch, D. 1975. Adult age differences in retrieval: Trace-dependent and cue-dependent forgetting. *Developmental Psychology* 11: 197–201.

Hultsch, D. F., and Dixon, R. A. 1983. The role of pre-experimental knowledge in text processing in adulthood. *Experimental Aging Research* 9: 17–22.

Hultsch, D. F., and Pentz, C. A. 1980. Encoding, storage and retrieval in adult memory: The role of model assumptions. In *New Directions in Memory and Aging: Proceedings of the George A. Talland Memorial Conference,* eds. L. W. Poon, J. L. Fozard, L. S. Cermak, D. Arenberg, and L. W. Thompson. Hillsdale, N.J.: Lawrence Erlbaum Assoc.

Jacobs, E. A., Winter, P. M., Alvis, H. J., et al. 1969. Hyperoxygenation effects on cognitive functioning in the aged. *New England Journal of Medicine* 281: 753–757.

Jenkins, J. J. 1974. Remember that old theory of memory? Well forget it. *American Psychologist* 29: 785–795.

Jenkins, J. J. 1979. Four points to remember: A tetrahedral model of memory experiments. In *Levels of Processing in Human Memory,* eds. L. S. Cermak and F. I. M. Craik. Hillsdale, N.J.: Lawrence Erlbaum Assoc.

Jenson, R. A., Messing, R. B., Martinez, J. L., Vasquez, B. J., and McGaugh, J. L. 1980. Opiate modulation of learning and memory in the rat. In *Aging in the 1980s: Psychological Issues,* ed. L. W. Poon. Washington, D.C.: American Psychological Association.

Jerome, E. A. 1959. Age and learning—experimental studies. In *Handbook of Aging and the Individual: Psychological and Biological Aspects,* ed. J. E. Birren. Chicago: University of Chicago Press.

Jones, M. K. 1974. Imagery as a mnemonic aid after left temproal lobectomy: Contrast between material-specific and generalized memory disorders. *Neuropsychologia* 12: 21–30.

Kahn, R., and Miller, N. 1978. Adaptational factors in memory impairment in the aged. *Experimental Aging Research* 4: 273–290.

Kahn, R. L.; Zarit, S. H.; Hilbert, N. M.; and Niederehe, M. A. 1975. Memory complaint and impairment in the aged: The effect of depression and altered brain function. *Archive of General Psychiatry* 32: 1569–1573.

Karlin, L. 1970. Cognition, preparation, and sensory-evoked potentials. *Psychological Bulletin* 73: 122–136.

Kausler, D. H. 1970. Retention-forgetting as a nomological network for developmental research. In *Life-Span Developmental Psychology,* eds. L. R. Goulet & P. B. Baltes. New York: Academic Press.

Kausler, D. H. 1982. *Experimental Psychology and Human Aging.* New York: John Wiley & Sons.

Kay, H. 1959. Theories of learning and aging. In *Handbook of Aging and the Individual,* ed. J. E. Birren. Chicago: University of Chicago Press.

Kear-Colwell, J. J. 1973. The structure of the Wechsler Memory Scale and its relationship to "brain damage." *British Journal of Social and Clinical Psychology* 12: 384–392.

Kinsbourne, M. 1980. Attentional dysfunctions in the elderly: Theoretical models and research perspectives. In *New Directions in Memory and Aging: Proceedings of the George A. Talland Memorial Conference,* eds.

L. W. Poon, J. L. Fozard, L. S. Cermak, D. Arenberg, and L. W. Thompson. Hillsdale, N.J.: Lawrence Erlbaum Assoc.

Kintsch, W. 1974. *The Representation of Meaning in Memory.* Hillsdale, N.J.: Lawrence Erlbaum Assoc.

Kintsch, W. 1978. On comprehending stories. In *Cognitive Processes in Comprehension,* eds. M. A. Just and P. A. Carpenter. Hillsdale, N.J.: Lawrence Erlbaum Assoc.

Kline, D. W., and Orme-Rogers, C. 1978. Examination of stimulus persistences as the basis for superior visual identification performance among older adults. *Journal of Gerontology* 33: 76–81.

Kline, D. W., and Schieber, F. 1981. What are the age differences in visual sensory memory? *Journal of Gerontology* 36: 86–89.

Kogan, N. 1974. Categorizing and conceptualizing styles in younger and older adults. *Human Development* 17: 218–230.

Kral, V. A. 1962. Senescent forgetfulness: Benign and malignant. *Canadian Medical Association Journal* 86: 257–260.

Krauss, I.; Poon, L. W.; Gilewski, M.; and Schaie, K. W. 1982. Effects of biased sampling on cognitive performances. *The Gerontologist* 22: 104. (Abstract.)

Kvale, S. 1977. Dialectics and research on remembering. In *Life-Span Developmental Psychology: Dialectical Perspectives on Experimental Research,* eds. N. Datan and H. W. Reese. New York: Academic Press.

Labouvie-Vief, G.; Campbell, S.; Weaver, S.; and Tannenhaus, M. 1979. *Metaphoric Processing in Young and Old Adults.* Paper presented at the annual meeting of the Gerontological Society, Washington, D.C., Nov. 1979.

Labouvie-Vief, G., and Schell, D. A. 1982. Learning and memory in later life. In *Handbook of Developmental Psychology,* ed. B. B. Welman. Englewood Cliffs, N.J.: Prentice-Hall.

Lachman, J. L., and Lachman, R. 1980. Age and the actualization of world knowledge. In *New Directions in Memory and Aging: Proceedings of the George A. Talland Memorial Conference,* eds. L. W. Poon, J. L. Fozard, L. S. Cermak, D. Arenberg, and L. W. Thompson. Hillsdale, N.J.: Lawrence Erlbaum Assoc.

Lashley, K. S. 1942. The problem of cerebral organization in vision. In *Visual Mechanisms.* Biological Symposia, vol. 7. Lancaster, Pa: Jacques Cattel Press.

Laurence, M. W. 1967. Memory loss with age: A test of two strategies for its retardation. *Psychonomic Science* 9: 209–210.

Leech, S., and Witte, K. L. 1971. Paired-associate learning in elderly adults as related to pacing and incentive conditions. *Developmental Psychology* 5: 180.

Legros, J. J.; Gilot, P.; Seron, X.; Claessena, J.; Adam, A.; Moeglen, J. M.; Audibert, A.; and Berchier, P. 1978. Influence of vasopressin on learning and memory. *Lancet* 1: 41–42.

Lewinsohn, P. M.; Danaher, B. G.; and Kikel, S. 1977. Visual imagery as a mnemonic aid for brain-injured

persons. *Journal of Consulting and Clinical Psychology* 45: 717–723.

Loveless, N. E., and Sanford, A. J. 1974. Effects of age on the contingent negative variation and preparatory set in a reaction-time task. *Journal of Gerontology* 29: 52–63.

Lowenthal, M. F.; Berkman, P. L.; Beuhler, J. A.; Pierce, R. C.; Robinson, B. C.; and Trier, M. L. 1967. *Aging and Mental Disorder in San Francisco.* San Francisco: Jossey-Bass.

Luria, A. R. 1973. *The Working Brain.* New York: Basic Books.

Marsh, G. R. 1980. Psychopharmacological issues. In *Aging in the 1980s: Psychological Issues,* ed. L. W. Poon. Washington, D.C.: American Psychological Association.

Marsh, G. R., and Thompson, L. W. 1977. Psychophysiology of aging. In *Handbook of the Psychology of Aging,* eds. J. E. Birren and K. W. Schaie. New York: Van Nostrand Reinhold.

Meyer, B. J. F.; Rice, G. E.; Knight, C. C.; and Jensen, J. L. 1979a. *Differences in the Type of Information Remembered from Prose by Young, Middle, and Old Adults.* Research Report No. 5, Prose Learning Series. Tempe: Arizona State University, Department of Educational Psychology, College of Education, Summer 1979.

Meyer, B. J. F.; Rice, G. E.; Knight, C. C.; and Jensen, J. L. 1979b. *Effects of Comparative and Descriptive Discourse Types on the Reading Performance of Young, Middle, and Old Adults.* Research Report No. 7, Prose Learning Series. Tempe: Arizona State University, Department of Educational Psychology, College of Education, Summer 1979.

Miller, W. 1975. Psychological deficit in depression. *Psychological Bulletin* 82: 238–260.

Milner, B. 1970. Memory and the medial temporal region of the brain. In *Biology of Memory,* eds. K. Pribram and D. E. Broadbent. New York: Academic Press.

Mohs, R. C., Davis, K. L., and Darley, C. 1980. Cholinergic drug effects on memory and cognition in humans. In *Aging in the 1980s: Psychological Issues,* ed. L. W. Poon. Washington, D.C.: American Psychological Association.

Morris, P. E. 1978. Sense and nonsense in traditional mnemonics. In *Practical Aspects of Memory,* eds. M. M. Gruenberg, P. E. Morris, and R. N. Sykes. London: Academic Press.

Murdock, B. B. 1967. Recent developments in short-term memory. *British Journal of Psychology* 58: 421–433.

Murrell, F. H. 1970. The effect of extensive practice on age differences in reaction time. *Journal of Gerontology* 25: 268–274.

Nauta, W. J. H. 1971. The problem of the frontal lobe: A reinterpretation. *Journal of Psychiatric Research* 8: 167–187.

Neiser, U. 1978. Memory: What are the important questions? In *Practical Aspects of Memory,* eds. M. M. Gruenberg, P. E. Morris, and R. N. Sykes. New York: Academic Press.

Nickerson, R. S. 1980. Retrieval efficiency, knowledge assessment and age: Comments on some welcome findings. In *New Directions in Memory and Aging: Proceedings of the George A. Talland Memorial Conference,* eds. L. W. Poon, J. L. Fozard, L. S. Cermak, D. Arenberg, and L. W. Thompson. Hillsdale, N.J.: Lawrence Erlbaum Assoc.

Nickerson, R. S. 1977. Some comments on human archival memory as a very large data base. *Proceedings on Very Large Data Bases.* Third International Conference on Very Large Data Bases, Tokyo, Japan, Oct., 1977, pp. 159–168.

Norman, D. A. 1968. Toward a theory of memory and attention. *Psychological Review* 75: 522–536.

Pattern, B. M. 1972. The ancient art of memory—usefulness in treatment. *Archives of Neurology* 26: 25–31.

Perlmutter, M. 1978. What is memory aging the aging of? *Developmental Psychology* 14: 330–345.

Perlmutter, M. 1980. An apparent paradox about memory aging. In *New Directions in Memory and Aging: Proceedings of the George A. Talland Memorial Conference,* eds. L. W. Poon, J. L. Fozard, L. S. Cermak, D. Arenberg, and L. W. Thompson. Hillsdale, N.J.: Lawrence Erlbaum Assoc.

Perlmutter, M.; Metzger, R.; Miller, K.; and Nezworski, T. 1980. Memory of historical events. *Experimental Aging Research* 6: 47–60.

Poon, L. W. 1978. Vasopressin and memory. *Lancet* 1: 557.

Poon, L. W. 1981a. Ecological validity and aging research. Paper presented in the symposium, "Spatial cognition in older adults: from lab to life." Biennial meeting of the Society for Research in Child Development, Boston, Mass., April, 1981.

Poon, L. W. 1981b. New directions in memory and aging research. *12th International Congress of Gerontology Abstract* 1: 156.

Poon, L. W., and Fozard, J. L. 1978. Speed of retrieval from long-term memory in relation to age, familiarity and datedness of information. *Journal of Gerontology* 5: 711–717.

Poon, L. W., and Fozard, J. L. 1980. Age and word frequency effects in continuous recognition memory. *Journal of Gerontology,* 35: 77–86.

Poon, L. W.; Fozard, J. L.; Cermak, L. S.; Arenberg, D.; and Thompson, L. W., eds. 1980. *New Directions in Memory and Aging: Proceedings of the George A. Talland Memorial Conference.* Hillsdale, N.J.: Lawrence Erlbaum Assoc.

Poon, L. W., Fozard, J. L., Paulshock, D. R., and Thomas, J. C. 1979. A questionnaire assessment of age differences in retention of recent and remote events. *Experimental Aging Research,* 5: 401–411.

Poon, L. W.; Fozard, J. L.; and Treat, N. J. 1978. From clinical and research findings to intervention programs. *Experimental Aging Research* 4: 235–254.

Poon, L. W.; Krauss, I. K.; and Bowles, N. L. 1981. Subject selection issues in cognitive aging research. *The Gerontologist* 21: 104. (Abstract.)

Poon, L. W., and Schaffer, G. 1982. Prospective memory in young and elderly adults. Presented at the American Psychologist Association, Washington, D.C.

Poon, L. W., and Walsh-Sweeney, L. 1981. Effects of bizzare and interacting imagery on learning and retrieval of the aged. *Experimental Aging Research* 7: 65–70.

Poon, L. W.; Walsh-Sweeney, L.; and Fozard, J. L. 1980. Memory skill training for the elderly: Salient issues on the use of imagery mnemonics. In *New Directions in Memory and Aging: Proceedings of the George A. Talland Memorial Conference,* eds. L. W. Poon, J. L. Fozard, L. S. Cermak, D. Arenberg, and L. W. Thompson. Hillsdale, N.J.: Lawrence Erlbaum Assoc.

Prien, R. F. 1973. Chemotherapy in chronic organic brain syndrome—a review of the literature. *Psychopharmacology Bulletin* 9: 5–20.

Rankin, J. L., and Kausler, D. H. 1979. Adult age differences in false recognitions. *Journal of Gerontology* 34: 58–65.

Raskin, A., and Jarvik, L. F., eds. 1979. *Psychiatric Symptoms and Cognitive Loss in the Elderly.* Washington, D.C.: Hemisphere Publishing Co.

Reese, H. W. 1976. The development of memory: Lifespan perspectives. In *Advances in Child Development and Behavior,* ed. H. W. Reese. Vol. 11. New York: Academic Press.

Reigel, K. F. 1968. Changes in psycholinguistic performance with age. In *Human Aging and Behavior,* ed. G. A. Talland. New York: Academic Press.

Reisberg, B.; Ferris, S. H.; and Gershon, S. 1981. An overview of pharmacologic treatment of cognitive decline in the aged. *American Journal of Psychiatry* 138: 593–600.

Ribot, T. 1982. *Diseases of Memory.* New York: Appleton.

Robertson-Tchabo, E. A.; Hausman, C. P.; and Arenberg, D. 1976. A classical mnemonic for older learners: A trip that works. *Educational Gerontology* 1: 215–226.

Ruch, F. L. 1934. The differentiative effects of age upon human learning. *Journal of General Psychology* 11: 261–268.

Sabatini, P., and Labouvie-Vief, G. 1979. *Age and Professional Specialization in Formal Reasoning.* Paper presented at the 1979 annual meeting of the American Gerontological Society, Washington, D.C., Nov. 1979.

Salthouse, T. A. 1980. Age and memory: Strategies for localizing the loss. In *New Directions in Memory and Aging: Proceedings of the George A. Talland Memorial Conference,* eds. L. W. Poon, J. L. Fozard, L. S. Cermak, D. Arenberg, and L. W. Thompson. Hillsdale, N.J.: Lawrence Erlbaum Assoc.

Salthouse, T. A. 1982. *Adult Cognition: An Experimental Psychology of Human Aging.* New York: Springer-Verlag.

Schaffer, G., and Poon, L. W. 1982. Individual variability in memory training with the elderly. *Educational Gerontology* 8: 217–229.

Schaie, K. W. 1974. Translation in gerontology—from lab to life: Intellectual functioning. *American Psychologist* 29: 802–807.

Schaie, K. W. 1979. The primary mental abilities in adulthood: An exploration in the development of psychometric intelligence. In *Lifespan Development and Behavior*, eds. P. B. Baltes and O. G. Brim. Vol. 2. New York: Academic Press.

Schaie, K. W., and Schaie, T. P. 1977. Clinical assessment and aging. In *Handbook of the Psychology of Aging*, eds. J. E. Birren and K. W. Schaie. New York: Van Nostrand Reinhold.

Schenkenberg, T. 1970. *Visual, Auditory, and Somatosensory, Evoked Responses of Normal Subjects from Childhood to Senescence.* Unpublished doctoral dissertation, University of Utah.

Schonfield, D. 1965. Memory changes with age. *Nature* 208: 918.

Schonfield, D. 1974. Translation in gerontology—from lab to life: utilizating information. *American Psychologist* 29: 796–801.

Schonfield, D., and Robertson, B. A. 1966. Memory storage and aging. *Canadian Journal of Psychology*, 20: 228–236.

Schonfield, D., and Stone, M. J. 1979. Remembering and aging. In *Functional Disorders of Memory*, eds. J. F. Kihlstrom and F. J. Evans. Hillsdale, N.J.: Lawrence Erlbaum Assoc.

Sherrington, C. S. 1906. *The Integrative Action of the Nervous System.* New Haven: Yale University Press.

Smith, A. D. 1974. Response interference with organized recall in the aged. *Developmental Psychology* 10: 867–870.

Smith, A. D. 1975. Aging and interference with memory. *Journal of Gerontology* 30: 319–325.

Smith, A. D. 1977. Adult age differences in cued recall. *Developmental Psychology* 13: 326–331.

Smith, A. D. 1980. Age differences in encoding, storage, and retrieval. In *New Directions in Memory and Aging: Proceedings of the George A. Talland Memorial Conference*, eds. L. W. Poon, J. L. Fozard, L. S. Cermak, D. Arenberg, and L. W. Thompson. Hillsdale, N.J.: Lawrence Erlbaum Assoc.

Smith, A. D., and Fullerton, A. M. 1981. Age differences in episodic and semantic memory: implications for language and cognition. In *Communication Processes and Disorders*, eds. S. Beasley and L. Davis. New York: Grune & Stratton.

Smith, A. D., and Winograd, E. 1978. Adult age differences in remembering faces. *Developmental Psychology* 14: 443–444.

Sperling, G. 1963. A model for visual memory tasks. *Human Factors* 5: 19–31.

Surwillo, W. W. 1966. The relation of autonomic activity to age differences in vigilance. *Journal of Gerontology* 21: 257–260.

Talland, G. A. 1965. *Deranged Memory.* New York: Academic Press.

Taub, H. A. 1979. Comprehension and memory of prose materials by young and old adults. *Experimental Aging Research* 5: 3–13.

Tecce, J. J. 1978. Contingent negative variation and attention functions in the aged. In *Event-related Brain Potentials in Man*, eds. E. Callaway, P. Tueting, and S. H. Koslow. New York: Academic Press.

Thomas, J. C., and Ruben, H. 1973. *Age and Mnemonic Techniques in Paired Associate Learning.* Presented at the Gerontological Society meeting, Miami, Florida.

Thompson, L. W. 1980. Testing and mnemonic strategies. In *New Directions in Memory and Aging: Proceedings of the George A. Talland Memorial Conference*, eds. L. W. Poon, J. L. Fozard, L. S. Cermak, D. Arenberg, and L. W. Thompson. Hillsdale, N.J.: Lawrence Erlbaum Assoc.

Thorndike, E. L.; Bregman, E. O.; Tilton, J. W.; and Woodward, E. 1928. *Adult Learning.* New York: Macmillan.

Thurstone, L. L., and Thurstone, T. G. 1949. *SRA Primary Mental Abilities.* Chicago: Science Research Assoc.

Till, R. E., and Walsh, D. A. 1980. Encoding and retrieval factors in adult memory for implicational sentences. *Journal of Verbal Learning and Verbal Behavior* 19: 1–16.

Treat, N. J.; Poon, L. W.; and Fozard, J. L. 1981. Age, imagery and practice in paired associate learning. *Experimental Aging Research* 7: 337–342.

Treat, N. J., and Reese, H. W. 1976. Age, imagery, and pacing in paired-associate learning. *Developmental Psychology* 12: 119–124.

Tulving, E., and Madigan, S. A. 1970. Memory and verbal learning. *Annual Review of Psychology* 21: 437–484.

Walsh, A. C.; Walsh, B. H.; Maloney, C. 1978. Senile-presenile dementia: follow-up data on an effective psychotherapy-anticoagulant regimen. *Journal of the American Geriatric Society* 26:467–470.

Walsh, D. A. 1976. Age differences in central perceptual processing: A dichoptic backward masking investigation. *Journal of Gerontology* 31: 178–185.

Walsh, D. A., and Prasse, M. J. 1980. Iconic memory and attentional processes in aged. In *New Directions in Memory and Aging: Proceedings of the George A. Talland Memorial Conference*, eds. L. W. Poon, J. L. Fozard, L. S. Cermak, D. Arenberg, and L. W. Thompson. Hillsdale, N.J.: Lawrence Erlbaum Assoc.

Walsh, D. A., and Thompson, L. W. 1978. Age differences in visual sensory memory. *Journal of Gerontology* 33: 383–387.

Walsh, D. A.; Till, R. E.; and Williams, M. V. 1978. Age differences in peripheral perceptual processing: A monoptic backward masking investigation. *Journal of Experimental Psychology: Human Perception and Performance* 4: 232–243.

Warrington, E. K., and Sanders, H. I. 1971. The fate of old memories. *Quarterly Journal of Experimental Psychology* 23: 432–442.

Waugh, N. C., and Norman, D. A. 1965. Primary memory. *Psychological Review* 72: 89–104.

Waugh, N. C.; Thomas, J. C.; and Fozard, J. L. 1978. Retrieval time from different memory stores. *Journal of Gerontology* 33: 718–724.

Weckowicz, T. E.; Nutter, R. W.; Cruise, D. G.; and Yonge, K. A. 1972. Speed in test performance in relation to depressive illness and age. *Journal of the Canadian Psychiatric Association* 17: 241–250.

Welford, A. T. 1958. *Aging and Human Skill.* London: Oxford University Press.

Welford, A. T. 1980. Memory and age: A prespective view. In *New Directions in Memory and Aging: Proceedings of the George A. Talland Memorial Conference,* eds. L. W. Poon, J. L. Fozard, L. S. Cermak, D. Arenberg, and L. W. Thompson. Hillsdale, N.J.: Lawrence Erlbaum Assoc.

Winn, F. J., Jr., Elias, J. W., and Marshall, P. H. 1976. Meaningfulness and interference as factors in paired-associate learning. *Educational Gerontology* 1:297–306.

Winograd, E., and Smith, A. D. 1978. When do semantic orienting tasks hinder recall? *Bulletin of the Psychonomic Society* 11: 165–167.

Yesavage, J. A. and Rose, T. 1982. Assessment and treatment of affective and cognitive disorders in the elderly. *GRECC Technical Report* Palo Alto: Veterans Administration Medical Center Publications.

Yesavage, J. A.; Rose, T. L.; and Bower, G. H. 1983. Interactive imagery and affective judgments improve face-name learning in the elderly. *Journal of Gerontology* 38: 197–203.

Zarit, S. H.; Cole, K. D.; and Guider, R. L. 1981. Memory training strategies and subjective complaints of memory in the aged. *The Gerontologist* 21: 158–164.

Zelinski, E. M.; Gilewski, M. J., and Thompson, L. W. 1980. Do laboratory memory tests relate to everyday remembering and forgetting? In *New Directions in Memory and Aging: Proceedings of the George A. Talland Memorial Conference,* eds. L. W. Poon, J. L. Fozard, L. S. Cermak, D. Arenberg, and L. W. Thompson. Hillsdale, N.J.: Lawrence Erlbaum Assoc.

17
Language Skills Across Adulthood

Loraine K. Obler
and
Martin L. Albert
Boston University School of Medicine

In the common parlance, we tend to think of language as a unitary phenomenon acquired *in toto* sometime during childhood. "She knows French and Japanese" we may say, or "Einstein acquired language at age 3." In fact, however, it is more appropriate to speak of (relatively) discrete *language skills* that may be differentially acquired or exploited or lost across the life span. Thus we say, "She reads French like a native but speaks with an accent," or "Einstein began speaking only at age 3 but appeared to understand everything that was said to him long before."

In the tradition of thinking of language as unitary, we usually assume that people have learned their native language by adolescence and may need only to have certain skills refined, such as writing, or that they may choose to develop skills, such as new and speedier reading styles. In the same vein, neuropsychologists will assert that some quantum *language* is spared with aging relative to *performance* abilities. In fact, one ought to consider the diverse language skills separately, because it is becoming clear that different skills have different life spans of their own; they may develop, mature, and evolve in different ways at different ages.

LATERALIZATION FOR LANGUAGE

We often tend to think of language use as "correct" or "incorrect" when in fact what is considered correct changes over time and what was once labelled correct becomes archaic. In order to distance ourselves from such value judgments on how language is used, it would be worthwhile to consider first what neuropsychology knows about the significance of brain lateralization for language across adulthood. In the child, the cerebral hemispheres appear to have a certain plasticity that permits the right hemisphere to take over language skills in the event the left hemisphere becomes damaged (Dennis and Kohn, 1975; Dennis and Whitaker, 1976; Rasmussen and Milner, 1977). Although there is some debate as to when this plasticity is lost, puberty has been the latest age suggested (Lenneberg, 1967; see Krashen 1973 for an earlier boundary). Implicit in neuropsychological theories until 1975 was the belief that brain organization for language remained stable after puberty unless brain damage interfered. In 1975, Brown and Jaffee noted that the type of aphasia—language disturbance caused by brain damage—resulting from a given lesion differed across the life span. They therefore suggested that either (1) language organization within the left hemisphere changes across the life span, or (2) the relative degree of left-hemisphere responsibility for language increases across the life span. (Note that these possibilities are not mutually exclusive; both may be true, as Brown and Jaffee (1975) and Brown (1978) indicated.) More recent work has confirmed that aphasia type correlates with age (e.g. Obler, 1978; Miceli et al., 1981), that is to say, fluent aphasias of the Wernicke type are predominantly seen in older adulthood (60s and 70s), whereas nonfluent aphasia of the Broca type predominates in the 50s. Obler (1978) speculated that this age by aphasia-type correlation might relate to changes in brain organization for language across adulthood. These findings might also be accounted for, however, by patients' being prone to strokes in different locations at different ages (Obler et al., 1980).

One indication linking different organization for language within the left hemisphere with increased age comes from Harry Whitaker (1980), who has proposed that language becomes more automatized with increased use. Indeed in our own work, using a task of reciting automatic sequences (reciting numbers from 1 through 21) in which subjects were not instructed to speak at any particular rate, we noted that there was no change in the time needed to perform the task across the age groups 30, 50, 60, and 70. This finding is particularly striking in the context of generalized slowing with advanced age. Such language behaviors must be linked to brain function, of course, but the current methods we have for observing the left hemisphere—such as computerized axial tomography, evoked potential, or blood flow studies—are either too gross to provide the information we need or too limited in application.

In research employing cortical stimulation, for example, only naming skills can be easily tested. New technologies currently being developed, such as the positron emission scan (PET scan), may provide us the means for a more sophisticated study of brain organization for the dynamics of language processing within the next decade. Thus the hypotheses of Jaffee and Brown about increasing specialization within the left hemisphere and of Harry Whitaker regarding increasing automatization with age cannot be rigorously examined as yet.

As to the second component of the Brown-Jaffee hypothesis, studies conducted to explore lateralization in healthy individuals across adulthood have yielded conflicting results. Some researchers (e.g., Clark and Knowles, 1973; Johnson et al., 1979) have demonstrated increased left lateralization with age, whereas others (Borod and Goodglass 1980; Nebes, Madden, and Berg, 1980) have demonstrated no changes with aging. In this regard, it is important to consider methodological artifacts that may be obtained when one studies lateralization in a population varying in age. For lateralization of auditory language, one uses a dichotic listening technique. In this procedure, different stimuli are presented to each of the subject's ears. Subjects are required to report what they have heard, and laterality scores are calculated by comparing the number of words reported from the right ear with the number of words reported from the left ear. Clearly, differential hearing loss would bias the results. Since the standard application of this methodology involves children or young adults who are unlikely to show hearing loss, however, audiometric screening is rarely done. With respect to older adults, systematic biases in hearing have been reported (e.g., Kannan and Lipscomb, 1974; Schaie, Baltes, and Strother, 1964); sex differences have also been reported (Tait, 1877). Borod, Obler, and Albert (1981) have recently reported an increase in right-ear superiority for pure-tone audition across adulthood for their 181 male subjects, although not for their 79 female subjects. This discrepancy in pure-tone hearing may well be interacting in the studies of lateralization across adult aging, since the two studies that did not screen subjects for pure-tone hearing were the two that found increased right-ear (allegedly left-hemisphere) effects with aging, whereas the two studies that did perform auditory screening and ruled out subjects with marked ear differences for pure-tone hearing —and were therefore, we maintain, more accurate—found no change in lateralization for language with age.

Degree of lateralization, we tentatively conclude, does not change with age, but it remains possible that organization for language within the left hemisphere does change. Let us turn then to those language performance aspects that we can record and analyze. From observing patterns of their change with aging and their breakdown with dementia, we can start to infer more general patterns of age-related change in brain-language systems.

LEXICON

Among linguistic skills, lexical skills are the ones most studied by psychologists, probably because lexical items are both meaningful and discrete. In particular, naming skills and defining abilities have been charted through late adulthood, as have the abilities to learn lists of lexical items. As verbal learning will be treated elsewhere in this volume (see Arenberg's chapter), we will focus on naming and its complement, definition.

It is taken for granted that as people get older they tend to forget the names for things. Researchers have confirmed this finding. Kaplan, Goodglass, and Weintraub (1976), for example, constructed the *Boston Naming Test,* an 85-item, object-naming task to elicit lexical items varying in frequency from *tree, pencil,* and *bed* to *spiral, yoke,* and *trellis.* Borod, Goodglass, and Kaplan (1980) and Goodglass (1980) report that correctness scores on this test increase between ages 30 and 50, hold steady among 60-year-olds, and then decrease among 70-year-olds, largely because of very poor performance on the part of some 70-year-olds (that is to say, the standard deviation of performance increases from the 60-year-olds to the 70-year-olds). When Goodglass divided his elderly population for statistical purposes into the institutionalized and the noninstitutionalized, he found that the institutionalized elderly performed worse. (Among the large population of institutionalized elderly, only the cognitively sound were tested.) Error analysis indicated that the institutionalized make a large number of misperception errors and circumlocutory responses, whereas the noninstitutionalized make relatively more semantic association errors and self corrections.

The present authors conducted a naming study using the Boston Naming Test with 160 noninstitutionalized elderly subjects (Obler, Albert, and Goodglass, 1981). Our qualitative analysis of responses on this task showed that the percentage of semantic substitutions did not change systematically with age. The proportion of phonologically similar words decreased from 8.4 percent for the 30-year-olds to 2.6 percent for the 70-year-olds. Two sorts of errors increased with age: comments on the task or item and circumlocutions that described the item but did not name it. Related to this finding was the analysis of strategies used in order to arrive at *correct* responses. Again, the number of comments and circumlocutions increased linearly with age, as did the number of augmented responses and self-corrected namings of semantically related words. For a number of items on this test, moreover, the object to be named is drawn with a heavy line, whereas its context is dotted (e.g., the *paddle* to be named is sketched in heavy lines next to a dotted *canoe.*) The mean number of times a subject mentioned the denoted context of the item rather than the specific item increased with age. Such findings are similar to the increased elaborateness of speech style with advancing age that we shall describe in the section on discourse. On other measures, it should be noted, there were no age-related changes. For example, when subjects could not name an item, they were given first semantic and then phonetic cues. No pattern of response was discernible across age for these cues, but the phonological cues were more helpful than the semantic in every instance.

Lest it be thought that the recall of nouns is impaired whereas that of other lexical classes is not, we tested both proper nouns—names of famous people—and verbs. We developed the Action Naming Test (Obler and Albert, 1979) to access verbs of frequency varying from that of *to eat* and *to sleep* to that of *to juggle* and *to knight.* For both verbs and proper nouns, the pattern of results was similar to those for the common nouns of the Boston Naming Test. Subjects showed little change up to age 70 and then showed diminished correctness and increased time to complete the test. Indeed, the correlations between the two tests for both correctness and time to respond are significant at the 0.001 level. For correctness, the correlation is 0.671; for time, it is 0.775 (Obler, Albert, Goodglass, 1981).

One difference between the Borod and

Goodglass report of norms on the Boston Naming Test and that of Obler et al. (1981) lay in the results from the scores of the younger subjects. Borod and Goodglass report that males under 40 performed worse than the 50-year-olds, giving a U-curve over adulthood. Obler et al. report a similar pattern for 30-year-old males but not for 30-year old females. As a result, for the population as a whole tested in the latter study, there was no change in performance between age 30 and age 60. This significant gender difference for that population might be linked to the slightly higher education levels of the 30-year-old females ($\bar{x}$ = 15.7 years) as compared to those of the males ($\bar{x}$ = 14.9 years).

We must conclude, then, that naming scores for verbs as well as nouns decrease with age for 70-year-olds as a group. Whether they increase between 30 and 50 or 60, or simply hold stable, would seem to depend on the subject population studied. Even among 70-year-olds, different mean scores will be obtained, depending on the relative health of the subject population.

Definition skills present a somewhat different picture. The definition task most commonly discussed is the vocabulary-subtest of the Wechsler Adult Intelligence Scale, WAIS (Wechsler, 1958). Subjects are instructed, "I want you to tell me the meanings of some words. Let's start with _____ ; what does _____ mean?" Since the entire WAIS is scaled for age, it is of note that a score of 43 for a 70-year-old is equivalent to a score of 50 in a 30-year-old. This suggests minimal (as compared to those of other WAIS subtests) but reliable "deficits" in an older adult population. Botwinick and Storandt (1974) have cogently demonstrated that these putative deficits result from the scoring procedure. If one gives full credit to good definitions that consist of more than one word—"good explanations" in the terms of Botwinick and Storandt (1974)—the score differences between young (age $\bar{x}$ = 18.4) and old (age $\bar{x}$ = 70.6) subjects is not significant (young $\bar{x}$ = 17.1; old $\bar{x}$ = 16). If one judges single-word synonyms as the best response, however, young adults perform significantly better than old ones. What Botwinick, West, and Storandt

(1975) do not mention (but their data indicate) is that the tendency toward multi-word responses commences between the 30- and 40-year-old groups and then ceases to increase further until the 70-year-old group. This tendency towards elaborate speech may also be seen in discourse.

DISCOURSE

Asked to tell a story or write a description of a picture, adults of various ages will perform differently along an elaborateness/brevity dimension. Cross-sectional data from a population of 30- to 80-year-olds suggest a U-curve, with more elaborate speech at the two ends of the scale, and briefest speech among the 50-year-olds. In the writing modality, the abbreviated style of the 50-year-olds often renders sentences incomplete—e.g., "woman washing dishes." The more elaborate speech of the 30-year-olds and the 70- and 80-year-olds includes complex, embedded sentences and much modification of nouns and verbs. In oral speech, elaboration additionally includes metalinguistic comments, personalization, repetition of items, and redundancy (Obler, 1980). Repetition and redundancy, it should be noted, may be considered poor form in high-school composition class, but in oral language they perform important rhythmic and structuring functions.[1]

Factors other than age should be eliminated, of course, before we can conclusively maintain that discourse becomes more elaborate with age. Henry James' writing style became more "convoluted"—i.e., elaborate—with advancing age according to his biographer Leon Edel (1953). It should be noted, however, that the typewriter came into common use in James' lifetime and that around age

---

[1] The structural importance of repetition and redundancy, and elaborate speech style in general, is particularly relevant in cultures where tale-telling is a prominent activity. We have found that the renowned tale-tellers in a Palestinian village were the three oldest subjects interviewed, all in their 60s or above. A fourth person, age 78, was identified to us as a well-known tale-teller. In retrospect, we realize that our great difficulty in interpreting the stories that we recorded from him was the result of his dementia; the elaborate tale structures remained, but the coherence was lost.

fifty he stopped writing his materials in long-hand and began dictating them. Until systematic longitudinal studies are evaluated, we cannot be sure if it is not cohort rather than age effects that are producing the increasingly elaborate discourse style of later adulthood. The parallels across cultures, however, convince us that age-related factors may well be responsible for the more elaborate discourse.

COMPREHENSION OF SPOKEN LANGUAGE

Ideally, we would study comprehension in aging in its pure form—i.e., without the intervening variable of decreased hearing abilities—but this is not possible in Western society, where both pure-tone and speech discrimination scores decrease consistently after age 30 in the great majority of the population (e.g., Corso 1977). Whatever life-span changes in comprehension we document must be considered in light of the question: Are we documenting changes in comprehension *per se* or rather strategies of dealing with impaired hearing that subjects of any age with equal hearing loss would display? Stevenson (1975), for example, determined that the types of phonological errors in perception made by presbycusic subjects on a speech perception task are the same *types* of errors that poor-hearing younger subjects make.

One way to circumvent differences in absolute abilities on comprehension strategies across aging is to administer tests under two conditions to all subjects and then compare the relative performance on the two tasks. Thus Nickerson, Green, Stevens, and Kalikow (1975) employed a group of 19 young (aged 15 to 21) and 22 old (aged 60 to 87) good-hearing (better than 20-dB) subjects in their speech-perception-in-noise task.

Subjects had to write down the last word of each sentence they heard. Half of the sentences had last words that were highly predictable for the context (e.g., a rose bush has prickly *thorns*), and half had last words that were hard to predict (e.g., the boy can't talk about the *thorns*). Contrary to the researchers' expectations, old and young subjects relied equally successfully on context. We confirmed

their findings using the same materials with subjects aged 30 to 79 divided into four age groups. We found lower absolute scores for the elderly for both low-probability and high-probability sentences, but an equal decrement (11 points) for all four age groups. Although one might argue that the percent of decrease was greater for the older than the younger group, this is not a zero-based scale, and the probability is low that all four groups should be impaired to the same degree.

Bergman (1980, pp. 113–118), it should be noted, reported a contradictory finding in a study in which he appears to have asked subjects to repeat individual words. Twenty subjects in their 20s benefitted relatively more than twenty 60-year-olds from the experimental limitation of the set of words that might be heard. That is, all subjects performed better when the set of possible target words was shown them, as compared to when the targets were the open set of all the words in the language. The younger adults, however, performed relatively better than the older adults in the closed-set condition. Bergman (1980) also reported an age-related decline in performance for various forms of distorted speech (masked, interrupted, speeded, compressed, and expanded) and for more complex, centrally embedded sentence structures as compared to simple, right-branching structures. Bergman emphasized percentage differences rather than absolute differences on this task of speech perception in noise. This is a good example of how choices made in the type of analysis to be used influence one's findings. The present authors chose to look at the *absolute decrement* between high- and low-probability items and as a result reported no age differences; Bergman chose to look at the *percentage of decrement* and as a result reported age differences. Currently then, the question of how context interacts with comprehension in aging remains unresolved.

In an analogous study, we tested 90 healthy men aged 28 to 78 on a comprehension battery presented to each subject under two conditions: with a video picture and without. The items and ordering of the condition were counterbalanced across subjects within each age group. Although absolute scores were lower for our oldest group (who had a mean hearing threshold of better than 35 dB), the absolute difference between the with-video and without-video conditions was the same for the three groups. We concluded, then, that younger subjects do not rely any less than older subjects on visual/face-reading clues in comprehension of oral speech.

One series of studies suggests qualitatively different comprehension on the part of older subjects. (Warren, 1961; Warren and Warren, 1966; and Obusek and Warren, 1973). They report that a verbal-transformation effect occurs when subjects hear a brief tape loop played over and over repeating a syllable like *tress.* The illusion is that one hears different sound sequences from time to time. Obusek and Warren report age-related changes in both the frequency and quality of the transformations reported. The oldest adult subjects report the fewest transformations, and quite appropriately, as indeed there are none. Furthermore, older adults report only real words (e.g., *stress*) whereas younger adults also report nonwords that conform to English word-formation constraints (e.g., *estre*). Children also report nonwords that could not exist in English (e.g., *sress*). This finding nicely illustrates the various ways we may label the performance of the elderly (or indeed of any group). Are we to call the elderly rigid or realistic? Working from common sense or working with limited imagination or creativity? Better not to choose such value-laden terms, we conclude, and let the description suffice.

METALINGUISTIC SKILLS

Irigaray (1973) has reported that dementing patients show diminished abilities on various metalinguistic tasks—for example, list generation, morphological antonyms (e.g., the opposite of *visible* is *invisible*), and naming the months of the year backwards. Since there are no age norms for such tests, we carried out a similar series of tests on a healthy aging population.

List generation is measured by counting the number of correct items given (without repetition) in a given period of time, usually 60

seconds. Two forms of this task are widely used, one asking subjects to list within a broad semantic field (e.g., animals) and the second to list by phonological/orthographic properties (e.g., all words beginning with the letter F). Slight but consistent decrements with age have been reported on this task (Lezak, 1976). We hypothesized that older subjects might be able to generate lists that would be equal to those of younger subjects if longer intervals were given. Accordingly, we measured the number of words generated over periods of 60 and 90 seconds. In the task of listing by initial letter, we did not find age-related decrements for either period. On the animal listing task, by contrast, there was a significant decrement with age for both periods. Older subjects continued listing after 60 seconds, but they did not catch up to the younger subjects. Nevertheless, the 70-year-olds produced more items in 90 seconds than the younger group had produced in 60.

We also observed age decline on a second metalinguistic task—the Stroop task. In this task (Stroop, 1935), subjects are first asked to label the ink-colors of 100 designs and then to label the ink-colors of 100 words. The words are *blue, black, red, green,* and *brown,* and the ink colors are not the same as the color described by the word. Speaking the written word rather than the label of the ink color is likely because of the interference; it results in both increased time to respond and in errors. Note in Table 1 that both time and errors increased with age:

TABLE 1.   Time and Error Scores on the Stroop Test

Age	x̄ time in seconds	SD	x̄ errors	SD
30	99	20	2.0	2.0
50	115	15	2.7	2.4
60	130	32	4.1	5.9
70	145	31	4.6	3.6

Performance on this metalinguistic task, it would appear, is sensitive to interference effects as well as generally increased response time latencies with age.

On the test of morphological antonyms, we

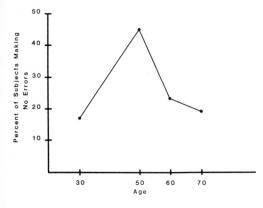

Fig. 1. Metalinguistic performance on Morphological Antonyms Test.

LANGUAGE IN THE APHASIAS AND DEMENTIAS

Because aphasias and dementias are medical phenomena that predominantly affect older adults in our society (Albert, 1980, 1981), we must consider what the language changes brought about by these conditions indicate about language skills in aging.

The type of aphasia resulting from a lesion of the posterior language area of the left hemisphere changes over the life span. In the child, a period of muteness with or without impaired comprehension is followed by a slow return of speech; in the 60-year-old adult with a stroke in this area, poor comprehension is accompanied by a fluent, empty speech, such as is rarely if ever heard in the child. Younger adults respond to stroke with less fluent types of aphasias, although this may also relate to the fact that they are more prone to strokes in the anterior cortical regions traditionally associated with nonfluent aphasias (Obler et al., 1980).

found an inverted U-curve for the males (see Figure 1). Scores were highest among the 50-year-olds (45 percent made no errors) and lowest among the 30- and 70-year-olds (17 and 19 percent, respectively, made no errors). Among the 60-year-olds, 23 percent made no errors. For reciting months of the year backwards, a U-curve was also obtained (see Figure 2). The 30- and 70-year-old males took the longest to respond ($\bar{x} = 15.0$ sec each). On this task, it was the 60-year-olds who performed best ($\bar{x} = 11.6$ sec) and the 50-year-olds who performed medially ($\bar{x} = 13.0$ sec). We confess that these U-curves, like the curve found for elaborate speech, are difficult to explain at this point. Although we suspect that the 30-year-olds and the 70-year-olds perform similarly but for different reasons, we simply cannot say with authority what these reasons would be.

The quality of discourse in the most fluent aphasic differs from the elaborate speech style of the elderly in that it includes few substantives, or modifiers, or logical conjunctions other than *ands* and a few *ors* or *buts* (Gleason et al., 1980). It is of interest to note that the logical conjunctions such as *so, because,* and *although* are preserved in the dementias, although the logic underlying them may be violated in the discourse.

The quality of naming response differs among aphasic groups. For aphasics as a group, lexical substitutions are more likely to bear phonetic relation to the target item, whereas for the normal elderly, semantic similarities influence substitutions (Goodglass, 1980). For older, fluent aphasics—those with posterior lesions—comprehension disturbance is, by definition, severe. There has been little study to date, however, that distinguishes their comprehension deficits from those of hard-of-hearing but otherwise healthy elderly.

Among the dementias, both cortical and subcortical types must be compared with healthy aging (Albert, 1978). Subcortical dementias such as might occur in Parkinson's disease and Progressive Supranuclear Palsy

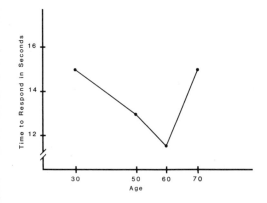

Fig. 2. Metalinguistic performance on Months Backwards Test.

manifest more speech disorder than language disorder. What language disorder can be observed occurs at the two levels of morphological and lexical selection. Thus, patients will produce gramatically incorrect sentences (paragrammatisms) as a result of one or both of these deficits. A sentence such as "The children comes around" reflects the addition of morphological inflection on two items rather than one, a curious error of commission seen in patients with subcortical dementing diseases more frequently than errors of omission. A sentence such as "The wolf took a liking to Little Red Riding Hood's basket" reflects an error in idiom selection, resulting in the humorous collocation of *take a liking to* and the inanimate *basket* (Obler, 1983).

In the predominantly cortical aphasias, such as Alzheimer's Dementia and Pick's Disease, discourse includes many neologisms (that is, jargon or nonsense words that nevertheless conform to English morphophonological constraints). Words that resemble other words phonologically rather than semantically may be substituted in conversation (e.g., *jogging* for *juggling*), and semantic boundaries break down systematically (Schwartz, Marin, and Saffran, 1979; Bayles, Tomoeda, and Boone, 1983). Comprehension is impaired, at least in part as a result of attentional disturbances (Obler, 1983; Curtiss, Kempler, and La Rue, 1982); thus, one sees patients respond to a single word in a question by giving an answer they guess may have been asked about it or providing a free association suggested by it. Discourse pragmatics—the overall structure of a discourse—breaks down, an example being violations of conversational continuity (Hutchinson and Jensen, 1980; Bayles, 1981; Whitaker, 1976).

Recently, several authors have observed the deterioration of language skills over the course of a dementing disease and divided the progressive decline of language skills into three periods: early, mid, and late (Obler and Albert, 1981; Bayles, 1982; Horner and Heyman, 1982). In the early stage, syntax, phonology, and interactional pragmatics are preserved. The patient experiences only mild difficulties in word finding and comprehension. In the realm of discourse, the patient may diverge

from a story but will frequently be able to return to it. Bayles observes increased reliance on stereotypic conversation and cliches; Horner and Heyman note brief pauses that interrupt the flow of speech, probably because of word-finding difficulties.

By the middle stage, the patient is making some uncorrected naming errors from semantic fields related to the target. Comprehension is impaired. In discourse, patients will make fragmented false starts and will repeat themselves at the sentence and story level. Some patients will use predominantly noncomplex syntactic constructions and become less talkative (Bayles, 1982), whereas others are given to uninterruptible press-of-speech and continue to use complex logical conjunctions (Obler and Albert, 1981). Tangential and self-referential comments will also be observed (Horner and Heyman, 1982). In writing, morphological errors occur, as well as spelling errors.

In the later, florid stage of the disease, neologistic nonsense terms enter speech, and real word names become semantically distant from the target. Conversation is empty of content; discourse is disorganized and stereotypic; syntactic errors occur (paragrammatisms). Bayles notes that pragmatic skills are lost at this point. Patients are unable to appreciate humor or sarcasm and do not interpret speech in terms of its context.

In sum, naming is impaired in the early stages of dementia, comprehension and discourse start to evidence substantial deficits in the middle stage, and pragmatic skills become severely damaged at a late stage.

CONCLUSION

Across the life span, we find styles of language use highly variable. On the numerous language tasks we have discussed, researchers have found standard deviations to increase among older adults, indicating relatively greater diversity of language behavior with age both across groups and within individuals. It must be stressed, then, particularly with regard to studies of language behavior across the life span, that results depend not only on what one tests and how one tests it (as mentioned in the introduction) but also on whom one selects to test (Poon, Krauss, and Bowles, 1981). We thus may see differences in the language behavior of institutionalized and non-institutionalized elderly (Goodglass, 1980; Hutchinson and Jensen, 1980), between women and men (Obler, 1980), between native and nonnative speakers of a language (Bergman, 1980), and between individuals with high and low levels of education on certain language tasks such as object or action naming (Obler, Albert, and Goodglass, 1981). Certainly, differences will be found if we choose exclusively healthy elderly subjects or if we choose a random sample of elderly that includes aphasic and demented patients. Procedures of subject selection always have great influence on the direction of our findings.

Cohort effects may be expected to be similarly influential on tests of language skills in realms beyond test-taking style. Story-telling, composition, and conversation conventions are facets of language that may be expected to change relatively quickly over time. As Broyard (1982) mentions in his article *The Talking Age,* "Though to be a good talker today is often regarded as a bore, to be one [in his youth] was our ambition." Changes we see in comparisons of young and old adults may reflect the historical change of a language rather than age-related changes in language use. Studying several age groups cross-sectionally may permit us to disconfirm hypotheses about linear historical (or age-related) change, whereas longitudinal studies are more likely to distill such changes. In any event, we must expect that age-related factors will interact with cohort effects on language-usage patterns. If we consider only one young and one old group in order to discover the truth about aging, however, we eliminate any possibility of determining progressive changes in language-use styles over time.

We should not be surprised to find a plethora of patterns when we study different language skills: linear patterns of increase or decrease for tasks such as recitation or paragraph-recall, respectively; U-curves for such functions as elaborateness of speech; and horizontal lack of change for such skills as appreciation for face reading in comprehension. To the extent that language is a window on the mind, we may expect that future work on linguistic abilities across the life span will document interactions between pure language abilities and lifespan developments in cognition, memory, attention, pacing, and emotion.

Acknowledgment: This project was funded in part by grants from the Veterans Administration and NIH grant R23AG01243 and NIH grant PHS 2PO INS 06209–16.

REFERENCES

Albert, M. L. Subcortical Dementia. 1978. In *Alzheimer's Disease, Senile Dementia, and Related Disorders,* eds. R. Katzman, R. Terry, and K. Bick. New York: Raven Press.

Albert, M. L. 1980. Language in normal and dementing elderly. In *Language and Communication in the Elderly: Clinical, Therapeutic, and Experimental Issues,* eds. L. Obler and M. Albert. Lexington, MA: D. C. Heath and Company.

Albert, M. L. 1981. Changes in language with aging. *Seminars in Neurology* 1: 43–46

Albert, M. S. 1979. *Famous Faces Test,* Experimental Edition.

Bayles, K. 1981. Comprehension deficits in several dementing diseases. Paper presented at Linguistic Society of America Meeting, New York City, Dec. 1981.

Bayles, K., and Tomoeda, C. 1983. Naming impairment in dementia. *Brain and Language* 19: 98–114.

Bayles, K. 1982. The use of language tasks in identifying etiologically different dementias. Paper presented at International Neuropsychological Society Meeting, Pittsburgh.

Bergman, M. 1980. *Aging and the Perception of Speech.* Baltimore: University Park Press.

Borod, J., and Goodglass, H. 1980. Lateralization of linguistic and melodic processing with age. *Neuropsychologia* 18: 79–83.

Borod, J.; Goodglass, H.; and Kaplan, E. 1980. Normative data on the Boston diagnostic aphasia examination, parietal lobe battery, and the Boston Naming Test. *Journal of Clinical Neuropsychology* 2: 209–215.

Botwinick, J., and Storandt, M. 1974. Vocabulary ability in later life. *The Journal of Genetic Psychology* 125: 303–308.

Botwinick, J.; West, R.; and Storandt, M. 1975. Qualitative vocabulary responses and age. *Journal of Gerontology* 30: 574–577.

Brown, J. 1978. Lateralization: A brain model. *Brain and Language* 5: 258–261.

Brown, J., and Jaffe, J. 1975. Hypothesis on cerebral dominance. *Neuropsychologia* 13: 107–110.

Broyard, A. Jan. 24, 1982. The talking age. *New York Times Book Review Section,* p. 35.

Clark, L., and Knowles, J. B. 1973. Age differences in

dichotic listening performance. *Journal of Gerontology* 28: 173–178.

Curtiss, S.; Kempler, D.; and La Rue, L. 1982. Language and cognition in dementia: A case study. UCLA Working Papers in Cognitive Linguistics.

Corso, J. 1977. Auditory perception and communication. In *The Psychology of Aging,* eds. J. Birren and K. W. Schaie, pp. 535–553. New York: Van Nostrand Reinhold Company.

Dennis, M., and Kohn, B. 1975. Comprehension of syntax in infantile hemiplegics after cerebral hemidecortication: Left hemisphere superiority. *Brain and Language* 2: 472–482.

Dennis, M., and Whitaker, H. 1976. Language acquisition following hemidecortication: Linguistic superiority of the left over the right hemisphere. *Brain and Language* 3: 404–433.

Edel, L. 1953. *Henry James.* Philadelphia: J. P. Lippincott.

Gleason, J.; Goodglass, H.; Green, E.; Obler, L.; Hyde, M.; and Weintraub, S. 1980. Narrative strategies in aphasic and normal subjects. *Journal of Speech and Hearing Disorders,* 23: 370–382.

Goodglass, H. 1980. Naming disorders in aphasia and aging. In *Language and Communication in the Elderly,* eds. L. Obler and M. Albert. Lexington, MA: D. C. Heath.

Horner, J., and Heyman, A. 1982. Characteristics of spoken language in Alzheimer's Dementia. Paper presented at International Neuropsychological Society, Pittsburgh, 1982.

Hutchinson, J., and Jensen, M. 1980. A Pragmatic Evaluation of Discourse Communication in Normal and Senile Elderly in a Nursing Home. In *Language and Communication in the Elderly,* eds. L. Obler and M. Albert. Lexington, MA: D.C. Heath Co.

Irigaray, L. 1973. *Le langage des dements.* The Hague: Mouton.

Johnson, R. C.; Cole, R. E.; Bowers, J. K.; Foiles, S. V.; Nikaido, A. M.; Patrick, J. W.; and Woliver, R. E. 1979. Hemispheric efficiency in middle and later adulthood. *Cortex* 15: 109–119.

Kannan, T. M., and Lipscomb, D. M. 1974. Bilateral hearing asymmetry in a large population. *J. Acoust. Soc. Am.* 55: 1092–1094.

Kaplan, E.; Goodglass, H.; and Weintraub, S. 1976. *Boston Naming Test,* Experimental Edition.

Krashen, S. 1973. Lateralization, language learning and the critical period: Some new evidence. *Language Learning* 23: 63–74.

Lenneberg, E. 1967. *Biological Foundations of Language.* New York: Wiley Press.

Lezak, M. 1976. *Neuropsychological Assessment.* New York: Oxford University Press.

Miceli, G.; Caltagirone, C.; Gainotti, G.; Masullo, C.; Silveri, M.; and Villa, G. 1981. Influence of age, sex, literacy, and pathologic lesion on incidence, severity, and type of aphasia. *Acta Neurologica Scandinavica* 64: 370–382.

Nebes, R. D.; Madden, D. J.; and Berg, W. D. 1980.

The effects of age on hemispheric asymmetry in visual and auditory identification. Paper presented at the Gerontological Society Meeting, San Diego.

Nickerson, R.; Green, D.; Stevens, K.; and Kalikow, D. 1975. Some experimental tasks for the study of effects of aging on cognitive performance. In *Design Conference on Decision Making and Aging,* eds. L. Poon and J. Fozard. Technical Report 76–01 of the Normative Aging Study: 136–175.

Obler, L. 1978. Tale-telling Conventions in Three Elderly Palestinians. Paper presented at MESA meeting, Ann Arbor, MI.

Obler, L. 1980. Narrative discourse style in the elderly. In *Language and Communication in the Elderly,* eds. L. Obler and M. Albert. Lexington, MA: D. C. Heath Co.

Obler, L. 1981. Review of Le Langage Des Dements. *Brain and Language* 12: 375–386.

Obler, L. 1983. Language dysfunction and brain organization in dementia. In *Language Functions and Brain Organization,* ed. S. Segalowitz. New York: Academic Press.

Obler, L., and Albert, M. 1979. *Action Naming Test,* Experimental Edition.

Obler, L., and Albert, M. 1981. Language in the senile patient and the elderly aphasic patient. In *Acquired Aphasia,* ed. M. Sarno, pp. 385–398. New York: Academic Press.

Obler, L.; Albert, M. L.; Caplan, L.; Mohr, P. T.; and Geer, D. 1980. Stroke type, aphasia type, sex differences and aging. Academy of Aphasia, Bass River, MA.

Obler, L.; Albert, M. L.; and Goodglass, H. 1981. The word finding difficulties of aging and dementia. Annual Meeting of Gerontological Society of America, Toronto, Nov. 1981.

Obler, L.; Albert, M.; Goodglass, H.; and Benson, D. F. 1978. Aging and aphasia type. *Brain and Language,* 6: 318–322.

Obler, L.; Borod, J.; and Albert, M. L. 1981. Perception of pure tones: Ear asymmetries. Annual Meeting of Gerontological Society of America, Toronto, Nov. 1981.

Obusek, C.; and Warren, R. 1973. A comparison of speech perception in senile and well-preserved aged by means of the verbal transformation effect. *Journal of Gerontology* 28: 184–188.

Poon, L.; Krauss, I.; and Bowles, N. 1981. Subject selection in cognitive aging research. Paper presented at Gerontological Society of America Annual Meeting, Toronto, Nov. 1981.

Rasmussen, T., and Milner, B. 1977. The role of early left-brain injury in determining lateralization of cerebral speech functions. In *Evolution and Lateralization of the Brain,* eds. S. Dimond and D. Blizard. Annals of the New York Academy of Sciences. New York: Academic Press.

Schaie, K. W.; Baltes, P.; and Strother, C. 1964. A study of auditory sensitivity in advanced age. *Journal of Gerontology* 19: 453–547.

Schwartz, M.; Marin, O.; and Saffran, E. 1979. Dissociations of language functions in dementia: A case study. *Brain and Language* 7: 277–306.

Stevenson, P. 1975. Responses to speech audiometry and phonemic discrimination patterns in the elderly. *Audiology* 14: 183–231.

Stroop, J. 1935. Studies of interference in serial verbal reactions. *Journal of Experimental Psychology* 18: 643–662.

Tait, L. 1877. Galton's whistles. *Nature* 15: 294.

Warren, R. M. 1961. Illusory changes in repeated words: Differences between young adults and the aged. *American Journal of Psychology* 74: 506–516.

Warren, R. M. and R. P. Warren, 1966. A Comparison of Speech Perception in Childhood, Maturity, and Old Age by Means of the Verbal Transformation Effect, *Journal of Verbal Learning and Verbal Behavior,* 5, 142–146.

Wechsler, D. 1958. *The Measurement and Appraisal of Adult Intelligence.* Baltimore: Williams and Wilkins.

Whitaker, H. 1976. A case of the isolation of the language function. In *Studies in Neurolinguistics,* eds. H. and H. Whitaker, vol. 2, pp. 1–58. New York: Academic Press.

Whitaker, H. 1980. Neurofunctional approach to second language acquisition. Paper presented at Neurolinguistics of Second Language Learning Symposium, Rio de Janeiro.

18
PROBLEM SOLVING AND COMPLEX DECISION MAKING

Hayne W. Reese
West Virginia University
and
Dean Rodeheaver
University of Wisconsin, Green Bay

INTRODUCTION

This chapter deals with problem solving and decision making in the period from young adulthood through old age. We begin with definitions of problem solving and decision making, then describe conceptual issues in research on aging and problem solving/decision making, and finally review the relevant research, organizing the studies by type of task.[1]

Definitions

All problems can be defined as referring to the transformation of a situation from some initial state to some other state (Reitman, 1964). Problem solving, then, involves assessing the present state, defining the desired state,

and finding ways to transform the former to the latter. Decision making refers to the evaluation of these possible solutions and selection of one for implementation. Deliberately choosing not to solve the problem—by withdrawing from the situation or withholding a response, for example—implies that this was one of the possible solutions that had been evaluated.

Conceptual Issues

Theories of problem solving are available in every major approach to psychology, including empirical behaviorism (e.g., Parsons, 1976; Skinner, 1969), theoretical behaviorism (e.g., Gholson and Beilin, 1979; Kendler, 1979), cognitive psychology (e.g., Klahr and Siegler, 1978), dialectical materialism (e.g., Luria, 1976; Vygotsky, 1978), Gestalt psychology (e.g., Mayer, 1977, Chap. 3), organismic psychology (see references in the section on Piagetian tasks), and other approaches. None of these theories, however, has been used systematically in research on problem solving among the aged. Consequently, a major obstacle to interpreting and integrating research in this area is the absence of any theory on which interpretation and integration can be based.

---

[1]Because of space limitations we have deleted a section on creativity and a section on theories of problem solving. For a review of the literature on real-life creative production and aging, see Botwinick (1967, pp. 176–182); for psychometric research, see Alpaugh and Birren (1975, 1977), Jaquish and Ripple (1981), and Romaniuk and Romaniuk (1981); and for training research, see Engelman (1978) and Romaniuk (1978). We regret having had to delete the section on theories of problem solving because, as noted in our introductory section, research on problem solving and aging has lacked a systematic theoretical stance. Copies of this section are available from the authors.

The Piagetian perspective might be a candidate for such a theory in that it has been used frequently in the relevant research, were it not for the fact that the procedures and the criteria for inferring competence from performance have often been inconsistent with the orthodox Piagetian perspective, thus making its usefulness more limited than it might appear at first.

Because of the lack of an integrative theoretical framework, we have organized our review of the research around a set of conceptual issues about cognitive aging in general. These issues are discussed in the next subsection.

The Competence-Performance Distinction

Role of extraneous variables.   Competence refers to what persons can do under ideal conditions; performance, to what persons do under actual conditions. The difference is attributable to the effects of variables that are extraneous to competence but nevertheless influence performance: memory, attention, motivation, and task familiarity.

An example is a study of Cohen and Square (1980), in which subjects were given practice on reading 50 word-triads backward on each of three consecutive days and then again on a fourth day about 13 weeks later. The subjects were apparently middle-aged adults (the mean ages reported were in middle age) and included amnesic patients and normal control subjects. Reading speed improved with practice in all subjects, and the performance level reached was maintained over the 13-week interval. All subjects also exhibited faster reading speed when triads were repeated than with new triads, but the amnesic patients much less so than the normal subjects, indicating that they had acquired the skill of backward reading like the normal subjects but had poor memory for the words actually read. In other words, backward-reading *performance* is influenced not only by backward-reading *competence* but also by memory.

Memory often influences performance in situations intended to assess competence in other domains, such as problem solving (Brinley, Jovick, and McLaughlin, 1974; Rabbitt, 1977; Welford, 1958, pp. 220–223). Problem-solving tasks usually require subjects to re-

member a variety of stimulus features and possible solutions that have already been tried and rejected. Consequently, although memory is not in itself a problem-solving ability, it can be an aid to problem solving—and, indeed, often a necessary one. Therefore, any variables that interfere with memory will usually interfere with problem solving. For example, as early as 1831, Upham speculated that the elderly have trouble remembering recent events because of a decline in sensory abilities and in attention. He suggested that the decline in attention reflects a decline in interest (pp. 472–475)—a suggestion that implies multiple causes of decline in problem-solving performance. Decline in sensory abilities represents neurological decay, and decline in interest represents changes in nonintellective factors.

Other variables that are extraneous to problem-solving competence per se and that have been implicated in performance differences include attention, motivation, and task familiarity. Hoyer, Rebok, and Sved (1979) found that increasing the number of irrelevant stimuli in a selective-attention problem-solving task reduced performance speed and increased errors and that the effect was stronger in elderly adults than in young adults. Hoyer et al. interpreted these results as indicating an age effect on the ability to attend selectively to relevant information and to ignore irrelevant information. An age difference in selective attention could also account for a finding by Rabbitt (1965) that irrelevant information slowed solution times to a greater extent in elderly adults than in young adults (but had no differential effect on the number of errors). Selective attention is not a problem-solving ability in itself, but as these studies indicate, it can be an aid to problem solving.

Neimark and Stead (1981) concluded from a study of diary entries by college students—keeping the diaries was a course requirement—that "the average individual is too lazy, unmotivated, or otherwise disinclined, for a variety of reasons, to indulge in high level cerebration when not compelled to do so" (p. 483). Labouvie-Vief (1977) suggested that similar nonintellective factors influence the performance of children and elderly subjects—factors "such as, in particular, test-taking attitudes, high levels of anxiety and apprehensiveness, low self-esteem, cautiousness" (p. 254; see also Baltes and Labouvie, 1973). Fatigue and contextual variables also influence performance (Furry and Baltes, 1973).

Sanders, Sanders, Mayes, and Sielski (1976) discussed another performance-related factor—familiarization with the task—and noted that its effects can be distinguished from competence effects by the inclusion of a control condition such as the one they and Sanders, Sterns, Smith, and Sanders (1975) used: practice on the task with feedback as to the correctness of responses but without specific strategy training. (In both studies, this control condition yielded significantly less improvement from pretest to posttest than strategy training.)

Production deficiency. As shown above, competence is not reflected fully by performance when the support system is deficient or inappropriate. Neither will competence be reflected fully when a *production deficiency* occurs. Production deficiency means that although a particular cognitive strategy may be in a person's repertoire, it is not used spontaneously but is used if prompted.

Young adults tend to use kinds of cognitive strategies that are more effective for problem solving than the kinds elderly adults and young children tend to use. However, the latter age groups can sometimes be induced to use the more effective kinds of strategies by prompting. One method of prompting, found to be effective for both elderly adults and young children, is modeling and/or explaining a particular strategy.

Strategy modeling improves performance in concept identification tasks (e.g., see review by Denney, 1979). Moreover, Denney, Jones, and Krigel (1979) noted that modeling a strategy for this kind of task provides information about (1) how to classify stimuli, (2) how to ask constraint-seeking questions, and (3) how to use the information gained from the answers to such questions. Denney et al. separated these components into different treatment conditions administered to young children (6 years old) and elderly adults (60 to 90 years old) and found that performance was significantly facilitated only by training

the subjects in how to ask constraint-seeking questions. In a follow-up experiment, again with young children (4 to 6 years old) and elderly adults (64 to 85 years old), Denney et al. examined two components of this training—giving examples of constraint-seeking questions and giving the rule for generating such questions—and found that these components were about equally effective in prompting use of the constraint-seeking strategy. Evidently, then, the failure of both age groups to use this strategy spontaneously is a production deficiency.

A production deficiency may occur when a strategy is effortful and the subject is unwilling or unable to expend the required effort. Alternatively, it may occur when the subprocesses involved in use of a strategy are effortful and the strategy can be performed efficiently only if the subprocesses are automatic. In either case, subjects would presumably avoid using the strategy, either because its cost in cognitive effort is excessive or because its benefit is minimal. The alternative is the usual explanation of production deficiency in early childhood, when the child has not yet practiced the subprocesses sufficiently to make them automatic. The usual explanation of production deficiency in old age is similar, except that automaticity is assumed to have been lost (or reduced) because of disuse.

Sanders et al. (1975) argued against the disuse hypothesis on the ground that practice on their cognitive task facilitated the concept-attainment performance of elderly subjects little if at all. Under the disuse hypothesis, however, practice on a cognitive task is not what is expected to be facilitative, but rather practice of a specific cognitive skill that is relevant and effective. On the positive side, they demonstrated that a programmed training procedure, analogous to operant shaping, was effective in inducing efficient concept-attainment performance. Sanders et al. (1976) found that this kind of training was also successful in prompting use of an effective strategy in a more complex concept-attainment task (requiring identification of a bidimensional conjunctive concept).

Modeling, instruction, feedback, and practice techniques have yielded improved performance in figural relations, concept attainment, 20 questions, and conservation tasks (Baltes and Baltes, 1982; Denney, 1979; Perlmutter and List, 1982; Plemons, Willis, and Baltes, 1978; Schultz and Hoyer, 1976). Intervention strategies are more effective when they are direct than when they are more indirect—that is, when they are aimed at motivation, confidence, practice, and increased time to plan strategies (Denney, 1980a). Although this finding suggests that the aged are learning new skills through intervention, the rapidity with which the training effect occurs suggests otherwise.

Modeling and training effects are obtained very rapidly in older subjects. For example, the training in the studies by Sanders et al. (1975, 1976) was given in three 30-minute sessions. Even more rapid effects have been obtained in other situations. For example, in a study of paired-associates learning, Treat and Reese (1976) found that merely instructing elderly subjects to use an elaboration strategy was effective and under the most favorable conditions yielded performance as good as that of young adults. The rapidity of these training effects can be taken as evidence against the disuse hypothesis. More extensive retraining would be required to weaken the presumed tendency to use ineffective strategies and to re-educate the subjects on how to use the forgotten effective strategy. Denney (1979) has interpreted such a readiness to learn to mean that the aged are competent to use other strategies but that they either prefer their natural strategies or find them better adapted to their needs.

An alternative to the disuse hypothesis has been suggested by Goulet (1973). He concluded from a review of research that "there is not one whit of evidence to suggest that the decline in learning efficiency after middle adulthood is attributable to the 'forgetting' of enactive skills" (pp. 294–295). He argued that "the decline in learning efficiency in the aged, and indeed, more rapid forgetting, is attributable to the inhibition of enactive (e.g., mediational) skills and habits rather than the inability of aged subjects to use such skills in learning and memory" (p. 295).

Problem-solving training research in general, therefore, supports the distinction between competence and performance. The distinction is obvious, once noted, and would be uninteresting were it not so often ignored by researchers. All too often, researchers dismiss the possibility of threats to the internal validity of the inference that poor performance reflects deficient ability (competence). So many variables other than ability influence performance that this inference requires explicit justification.

Deficit Vs Difference

The realization that a group can be *different* without being *deficient* or *inferior* seems to have appeared earlier in anthropology than in psychology; for example, it was promoted as early as 1911 by Franz Boas (Klineberg, 1980), but it is still relatively rare among developmental psychologists.

Labouvie-Vief has stressed that much of what is usually characterized as cognitive *deficit* in late adulthood and old age is better characterized as cognitive *difference,* reflecting not loss of desirable abilities but gain of other, more desirable abilities (e.g., Labouvie-Vief, 1977, 1981, 1982a, 1982b; Labouvie-Vief and Blanchard-Fields, 1982).

Cautiousness

Evidence for increased cautiousness. Okun (1976) noted that a presumed increase in cautiousness in old age has been "invoked as a *post hoc* explanation for observed differences in performance between younger and older subjects on a wide range of tasks including perceptual tasks . . . , verbal tasks . . . , and memory tasks. . . ." (p. 220; references deleted). Cautiousness in this sense is inferred primarily on the basis of (1) the occurrence of errors of omission, and (2) slow reaction times, as follows:

1. In verbal learning tasks, young adults tend to make more errors of commission and old adults tend to make more errors of omission (e.g., Botwinick, 1967, p. 61; Eisdorfer, 1965, 1968; Korchin and Basowitz, 1957; Okun, Siegler, and George, 1978). Leech and Witte (1971) found that reinforcing commission errors did

not affect the rate at which they were committed but significantly reduced the rate of omission errors and trials to attain the learning criterion. Evidently, then, omission errors do not relect incomplete learning of associations or lack of competence; presumably, they reflect cautiousness.

2. One of the best established findings in gerontological research is the slowing in the speed of responding and cognitive processing that occurs with aging. The slowed speed of performance is sometimes accompanied by increased accuracy, although sometimes accuracy as well as speed declines (Botwinick, 1967, p. 172). Botwinick hypothesized that either (1) the slowing is a primary effect of aging, is beyond the control of the person, and may produce accuracy as a by-product; or (2) the slowing is deliberate—a "purposeful slow down with age in order to obtain accuracy either because of an increased value on carefulness or because of increased tendencies to make errors" (Botwinick, 1959, p. 763). After more than two decades of further research, both hypotheses are still tenable, but both are also controversial (Salthouse and Somberg, 1982).

Causes of increased cautiousness.   Okun (1976) reviewed the literature on cautiousness, and suggested that adulthood age differences in cautiousness could reflect the effects of five kinds of variables: physiological, rational, cultural, motivational, and generational. For example:

1. The *physiological* aging of the nervous system is associated with slow response time, leading to cautiousness in situations in which fast responses are required.

2. Cautiousness is *rational* when it reflects a realization that performing well will be difficult because the required abilities have declined. (This and the former possibility are essentially the same as those suggested by Botwinick, 1967, as is mentioned above.)

3. The *cultural* variables that lead to disen-

gagement result in lower self-esteem. "As a consequence of lowered self-esteem, the aged view themselves as less competent and, in turn, exhibit greater cautiousness as a means of keeping their egos intact" (Okun, 1976, p. 221).

4. Increased cautiousness in old age could reflect *motivational* changes, such as an increase in fear of failure and consequent decrease in achievement motivation.

5. Differences in cautiousness during adulthood may reflect *generational* or cohort differences rather than, or in addition to, age differences.

An alternative interpretation.   An alternative interpretation of the adulthood age differences in cautiousness is that they do not reflect an increase in cautiousness with increasing age but rather reflect a decrease in risk-taking. If this alternative interpretation is correct, then the theoretical problem is to explain why young adults take risks rather than why old adults are cautious. For example, older adults seem to avoid taking risks altogether if they can; if they cannot, they tend to avoid taking risks on tasks of intermediate difficulty. Failure on difficult tasks can be attributed to the tasks themselves; failure on easier tasks is less easily attributable to task difficulty and therefore requires some evaluation of one's own abilities.

Thus, compared with young adults, older adults are not as eager to have their abilities evaluated; "older adults attempt to protect themselves from engaging in self-evaluation" (Okun, 1976, p. 231). By contrast, the risk-taking of young adults suggests that they pursue evaluations of their abilities.

The unwillingness of older adults to take risks can be modified by increasing the direct payoff of risk-taking (Okun and Elias, 1977) and by differential reinforcement of omissions and risk-taking (Birkhill and Schaie, 1975). That is, old adults are more willing to take risks when evaluations are more likely to be positive.

Effects of Sex, Education, and Intelligence

The effects of subjects' sex, education, and intelligence have been widely studied in psychology as a whole but not widely studied in research on problem solving and aging. The available evidence is reviewed in the present chapter, even though preliminary considerations cast some doubt on their importance.

Kesler, Denney, and Whitely (1976) reviewed 13 studies of problem solving of various kinds in middle-aged and elderly subjects and found no sex differences in problem-solving performance. This conclusion is surprising in light of other literature on sex differences—for example, that of psychometric research where findings show differences in declines in psychometric intelligence (e.g., Blum, Fossage, and Jarvik, 1972). One criticism is that the problem-solving and decision-making tasks used in research often include only male central characters and problem issues. However, Heyn, Barry, and Pollack (1978) varied the sex role of central characters in one problem-solving task and still found no sex differences in performance.

Performance on cognitive tasks is often correlated more highly with education than with age (e.g., Sharp, Cole, and Lave, 1979). The issue of education is critical in assessing adult age differences in problem solving because older adults may have had different amounts and kinds of educational experiences from those of younger adults (Baltes and Schaie, 1974). Therefore, any differences observed in problem-solving performance between elderly and young adults might reflect to a large extent cohort differences in education and not only age differences.

Finally, several authors (e.g., Hooper, Fitzgerald, and Papalia, 1971) have noted a similarity in the developmental patterns of fluid intelligence (e.g., Horn and Cattell, 1966) and problem solving—negatively accelerated growth in childhood and positively accelerated decline in adulthood—and have suggested that the decline in adulthood results at least in part from the decline in fluid intelligence (cf. Siegler, 1980). The decline in fluid intelligence has been attributed to neurological decline (Horn and Cattell, 1966) and to nonintellective variables—attention and practice, for example (e.g. Kamin, 1957; Willis, Cornelius, Blow, and Baltes, in press). However, results of a study by Hayslip and Sterns (1979) questioned the validity of predictions of problem-solving performance based on Horn and Cattell's theory of intelligence. They found only slight differences in the correlations of fluid and crystallized intelligence to problem solving.

TYPES OF RESEARCH TASKS

The tasks used in problem-solving/decision-making research can be divided into three major categories: real-life tasks, laboratory simulations of real-life tasks, and artificial tasks. We have used these categories to organize our review of the relevant aging research, treating each of them in a separate section.

REAL-LIFE TASKS

In general, real-life tasks view the aging individual in an environmental context that is dealt with through a variety of cognitive strategies; that is, problem solving and decision making are the cognitive links between the individual and the environment. This view implies that the aged (or any) individual may use a number of problem-solving strategies to meet environmental demands—reacting to demands by using or adjusting one's strategies, ignoring demands, or manipulating the environment to change its demands (Collins, 1975). Given this perspective, we would suggest that the actual problem-solving research on this subject, which deals most typically with the first strategy alone—i.e., reacting to environmental (experimental) demands—has seriously underrepresented the construct of problem solving.

Naturalistic studies, which utilize tasks that older adults face in their own lives, should, ideally, be sensitive to the entire range of problem-solving strategies. This ideal has not been attained, however. Capon and Kuhn (1979), for example, used an ecologically valid task— grocery shopping—to assess a formal operation (i.e., use of a proportional reasoning strategy). Shoppers in a supermarket were asked to determine which of two sizes was the better buy for two products. Although the task was a real-life one, Capon and Kuhn's evaluation was not sensitive to all problem-solving strategies. They considered the best response to be estimating or calculating price differences and buying the size with the lower price per ounce. An alternative strategy would be to ignore the price aspect of the experimenters' question and to reply, "Who cares? I always buy my favorite brand because it works best," or "I always buy the largest because I can only get to the store every two weeks." In short, using criteria for evaluating performance on a laboratory task, such as reaction to an experimenter's demands, in a natural setting undermines the ecological validity of the task.

Demming and Pressey (1957) were also concerned with ecological validity in their study of problem solving. They developed a questionnaire dealing with tasks such as use of the yellow pages in the telephone directory, knowledge of common legal terms, and identification of occupations providing necessary services. These items did not deal with problem solving per se, but rather with the knowledge required to begin to solve a problem. This limitation is perhaps a product of the method inasmuch as questionnaires are more effective for assessment of knowledge useful in solving problems than for assessment of actual problem solving.

Although we lack the space to deal with issues of life events, coping, and adaptation, we would suggest that they are important examples of real-life problem-solving situations. To the extent that responses to life events include reacting to demands, ignoring demands (disengagement), or manipulating demands, these responses also reflect problem-solving strategies.

The problems in real-life tasks revolve around the question, "Mastery for what purposes?" No single criterion situation, such as academic performance for the young, exists for the problems of everyday living faced by older adults (Schaie, 1978). Scheidt and Schaie (1978) attempted to develop a taxonomy of specific real-life situations to address this problem. The concrete situations they identified (e.g., weekly shopping or completing tax returns) are characterized by varying behavioral requirements, situational constraints, and potentials for response. Underlying competencies may then be abstracted from adaptive performance across a variety of situations commonly faced by the aged. Research is needed to determine how useful this taxonomy will be.

LABORATORY SIMULATIONS

Results of both problem-solving and memory research conducted by Denney and Palmer (1981) indicate that making tasks meaningful does not equalize the performance of young and elderly subjects. The actual meaningfulness of most of their tasks, however, remains questionable.

Denney and Palmer gave their subjects nine situations designed to simulate real-life problems, such as (1) dealing with a refrigerator that is warm inside, (2) dealing with a flooded basement, (3) being stranded on a highway in a blizzard, (4) witnessing a mugging, and (5) receiving a threatening telephone call. Responses to each problem were scored separately, the scores being based on the nature of the problem and the possible responses. For example, a warm refrigerator might elicit no response at all (1 point), a solution involving total reliance on another person (2 points), some self-action but only one solution (3 points), or self-action and more than one solution (4 points). Denney and Palmer found that middle-aged (40–59) subjects performed better on these problems than younger and older subjects. The total number of questions asked increased with age, and the number of constraint-seeking questions asked decreased.

The Denney and Palmer study demonstrates that laboratory simulations of real-life tasks are subject to the same validity problems that real-life tasks themselves are. Denney and Palmer suggested that more intensive research is needed to determine whether the differences they obtained reflected a developmental function or the frequency with which their subjects encountered the problems included in the study. An additional problem centers around their scoring method—as with real-life tasks, this method of evaluation does not represent all the possible solutions. Someone who has a great deal of experience with appliances, for example, would not be expected to respond in the same way to a broken refrigerator as someone who has been shocked by electrical appliances in the past. For each individual, the best response to the problem is unique.

Charness (1981a, 1981b) studied solutions of chess problems by tournament chess players ranging in age from 16 to 64 years. They had current, official ratings of skill covering a wide range; the lowest and highest skill ratings differed by 3.9 standard deviations. He found that the quality of solutions varied significantly with skill but not with age, implying that the older players either were not deficient in chess skills or had developed competencies that compensated for deficiencies. Charness noted that the older players exhibited memory deficits characteristic of aging and that they apparently took short cuts on some of the steps in solving the problems; this finding led him to support the *deficit-with-compensation* explanation.

Charness's study illustrates a problem that is the converse of the problem in the Denney and Palmer (1981) study. If individual differences in experiences and abilities must be assessed in order to establish ecological validity, the generalizability of the results is undermined. Thus, Charness (1981a, 1981b) has considered the individual skill level of tournament chess players, but the generalizability of his results to other groups of elderly must be seriously questioned.

ARTIFICIAL TASKS

Most of the research on problem solving in adulthood and old age (not to mention childhood) has involved artificial laboratory tasks. The advantage of using such tasks is that they permit control of independent and contextual variables and delimitation of dependent variables (response possibilities). The disadvantage is that they may lack ecological validity, as noted in the section on real-life situations.

Various procedures have been used to study subjects' problem-solving strategies. Often, however, no attempt is made to determine what strategies were used, the intent being to identify age differences or the lack of them.

Concept Attainment

A decline in speed of concept attainment has been amply demonstrated across adult age groups (e.g., Hayslip and Sterns, 1979; Hoyer et al., 1979; Offenbach, 1974; Wiersma and Klausmeier, 1965). Here we will emphasize the studies that were aimed at identification of age differences in the strategies used.

In concept attainment tasks, a set of items is divided into subsets in accordance with some predetermined rule (Giambra and Arenberg, 1980). In the simplest case, the set consists of two items that differ in a single dimension, and the subsets are defined by the difference in this dimension, one subset usually being identified as positive and the other negative—that is, the choice of one item is correct and the choice of the other incorrect. For example, if the items differ only in color—red or green—the red one might be correct (the *positive instance*) and the green one incorrect (the *negative instance*). The relevant rule here might be "Choose the red one," "Avoid the green one," or "Choose the red one and avoid the green one."

In more complicated cases, the items are multidimensional, and the task may be to identify the positive instances or to sort the items on the basis of some rule. In either case, the relevant rule may refer to one dimension or to a combination of dimensions. If the task is to identify positive instances, it is called *discrimination learning,* as is the simplest case just described. If the task is to sort the items, the task is called *classification* or *sorting.* In both cases, the stimuli can be presented either one at a time or in arrays (e.g., pairs of stimuli), and the subject must identify the subset to which each stimulus belongs. In discrimination learning tasks, the appropriate subsets are always determined by the experimenter. In sorting tasks, the subsets are also determined by the experimenter unless the task involves free classification, in which case they are determined by the subject. The distinction between discrimination learning and sorting becomes clear-cut only when the latter involves free classification.

A study by Crovitz (1966) illustrates the

fuzzy distinction between discrimination learning and sorting. The subjects were community-dwelling males averaging about 72 years of age. A control group was given a standard discrimination learning task, and an experimental group was given a modified sorting task in which the experimenter did the sorting and then asked the subjects what the basis for sorting was. The control subjects required considerably more trials to reach criterion (mean 53.0) than did the experimental subjects (6.5) and were considerably more variable (standard deviation, 43.6) than the latter (S.D. 12.4). Rapid learning was associated with appropriate verbalization of the relevant stimulus dimensions in both conditions.

Discrimination Learning

Hypothesis testing. Offenbach (1974) developed a method for determining the sequence of *hypotheses* that subjects test in solving the multidimensional, two-choice discrimination learning task. Following each choice, subjects must indicate the stimulus attribute on which they based it. They are then told whether their choice was correct, but not whether it was based on the correct attribute. For example, if the attributes are "large" and "small," "red" and "blue," "circle" and "square," and "left position" and "right position," and "red" is the correct attribute, choice of the large red circle on the left would be correct even if the subject had based the choice on the attribute "large." A possible problem with this method is that it requires subjects to designate a single attribute as the basis for any one choice and can therefore yield misleading data if subjects actually base their choices on compounds of attributes, such as "red circle."

In comparing children, college sophomores, and elderly adults from a senior center, Offenbach found that the probability of repeating a hypothesis following a correct response increased during childhood ($p = 0.69$ at age 7) and peaked in young adulthood ($p = 0.88$) whereas the probability of repeating an hypothesis following an incorrect response decreased during childhood ($p = 0.125$ at age 7) and reached a minimum in young adult-

hood ($p = 0.094$). These results are consistent with previous findings based on the use of "blank-trial probes" (for definition, see Offenbach). Offenbach also found that following a correct response the elderly subjects were as likely to change their hypothesis as to repeat it ($p = 0.50$) and that following an incorrect response they repeated their hypothesis 20 percent of the time even though they had been informed that their response was incorrect and should have clearly realized that their hypothesis was also incorrect. The random changing and repeating of hypotheses following a correct response would be consistent with an assumption of no memory retention from trial to trial, but the nonrandom behavior following an incorrect response—changing hypotheses 80 percent of the time—would indicate trial-to-trial retention. Perhaps the elderly subjects were responding to compounds of attributes, thus making the technique yield a false analysis of their hypothesis-testing behavior.

Meaningfulness of stimuli. The stimuli used in most concept-attainment studies are relatively meaningless in the sense that the dimensions and dimensional values used are arbitrarily selected and combined, as in the example described earlier. However, Arenberg (1968) used highly meaningful stimuli in a discrimination learning task in which the subjects were presented with descriptions of meals, each consisting of three foods, and were told whether the diner would live or die as a result of eating them. The subject's task was to identify which one of nine foods was poisoned. Although the use of meaningless, unfamiliar stimuli was not always found to disrupt the performance of old subjects more than that of younger ones in earlier studies, Arenberg found that younger subjects (aged 17 to 22) were superior in performance to older subjects (aged 60 to 77) despite the vital meaningfulness of his task. Older subjects seemed to be particularly misled when the poisoned food did not change from one meal to the next.

Hayslip and Sterns (1979) used the same poisoned foods task and found that young and old adults differed from one another but not from middle-aged adults. Older adults required the most trials to criterion and also committed the most errors.

Hartley (1981) used a somewhat different poisoned-foods task. Each meal consisted of three courses with four alternative foods, and the subject's task was to determine which two courses had been tampered with. The solution required use of an inclusive disjunction rule; for example, illness resulted if the meal had *"either oysters or pie or both"* (p. 701). Two groups of old subjects (mean ages, 65.4 and 71.5) were found to be significantly less likely to solve the problem than two younger groups (mean ages, 20.0 and 41.4). The major problems were failure to realize that uncertain information does not establish the irrelevance of a dimension, failure to ignore irrelevant information, and fixation on hunches. Despite the use of a meaningful task, then, the elderly exhibit the same kinds of inefficiencies in problem solving as observed in studies with relatively meaningless stimuli.

Sex differences. Offenbach (1974) obtained no significant sex differences in a discrimination learning study, testing groups with mean ages of 7.1, 9.0, 11.2, 19.3, and 74.7 years. Sanders et al. (1975, 1976) obtained no significant sex differences in the effects of training on concept attainment in subjects with a mean age of 71 years.

Education and intelligence. The effects of education on discrimination learning in old age have not been studied. In the one study we found on the effects of intelligence, Wetherick (1966, Exp. 2) found that performance was positively correlated with fluid intelligence (Raven's matrices).

Effects of training. Sanders et al. (1975, 1976) showed that training involving successive approximation (operant shaping) of skills is effective. In both studies, training was given in only three half-hour sessions. The rapidity of the training effect can be interpreted to mean that training affected performance rather than competence, as argued above in the section on the competence-performance distinction.

Twenty Questions

The task. The 20 questions task is a concept identification task in which the positive subset contains a single item, that is, the task is to identify the one item in an array that is "correct." Subjects are allowed to ask any questions that can be answered "yes" or "no." The questions are analyzed to determine what questioning strategies the subjects use spontaneously.

In the 20 questions task, and concept attainment tasks in general, the most efficient strategy is to ask a series of constraint-seeking questions, each eliminating a set of possible answers. Asking "hypothesis-scanning" questions—each referring to a single possible answer—is an inefficient strategy. Another kind of question, "pseudo-constraint-seeking," has the form of a constraint-seeking question but the implicit content of a hypothesis-scanning question (Mosher and Hornsby, 1966). For example, if the items are a cat, a cow, and a pig, drawn the same size but varying in color (e.g., black, brown, and white) and posture (e.g., lying, sitting, and standing), to ask the question "Is it a color?" is constraint-seeking, to ask "Is it the standing white cat?" is hypothesis-scanning, and to ask "Does it moo?" is pseudo-constraint-seeking.

Age differences. Kesler, Denney, and Whitely (1976) gave middled-aged and elderly subjects three types of problem-solving tasks—a 20 questions task, a motoric analogue of the 20 questions task, and seven insight type problems. Factor analysis of the scores revealed only one factor, and percentage of constraint-seeking questions in the 20 questions task had the highest factor loading, followed by number of questions in this task; the elderly subjects were worse than the middle-aged subjects on all scores, but the age differences were statistically significant only on these two scores, perhaps because the sample sizes were small (15 men and 15 women per age level) and the power of the tests was therefore low. Sex of subjects had no significant effects.

The age difference in strategies used was supported by Denney and Denney (1973), who found that elderly subjects asked more hypothesis-scanning questions, asked more questions overall, and asked more redundant questions than younger subjects. The constraint-seeking questions they did ask were often based on perceptual attributes ("Does it have wings?").

Sex differences. As mentioned above, Kesler et al. (1976) found no significant sex differences in middle and old age. Sex differences were not examined in the other studies cited, but Denney et al. (1979) found no significant sex difference in the effects of training questioning skills in two experiments.

Education and intelligence. Kesler et al. (1976) found that performance was positively related to education and nonverbal (fluid) intelligence. The latter was the better predictor of performance.

Effects of training. Denney and Denney (1974) and Denney et al. (1979) demonstrated that training facilitates the performance of elderly subjects on the 20 questions task. Evidently, training most effects how constraint-seeking questions are asked (Denney et al., 1979). However, Denney (1980b) demonstrated that elderly subjects can be induced to use constraint-seeking questions without direct training, by manipulation of task characteristics (eliminating the visual display; using playing cards instead of the usual type of array). Thus, the difference between elderly and middle-aged adults in reference to the type of question asked is evidently not a difference in competence (a difference in the strategies available in their repertoires) but rather is a difference in the use of these strategies.

Other Concept Attainment Tasks

Age differences. Sanford (1973) compared young (mean age, 20.3) and old (mean age, 74.6) adults on a search task in which an object was hidden in one of 20 holes covered with identical lids. The problem was to find the object in as few moves as possible, replacing each lid after looking in the hole. The young and old subjects were found to use the same strategies on the first two trials, but on the next three, the old subjects were more likely to use a random search strategy and the young subjects a systematic, stepwise search strategy. The correct locations were not the same from trial to trial, and the old subjects had apparently either failed to discover that fact or failed to act on the discovery. In spite of the apparent randomness of their search strategy, the old subjects were not ignoring previous trials but rather were carrying over hunches from trial to trial. This interpretation, which is Sanford's, agrees with our interpretation of the results of Offenbach (1974), to wit, that his old subjects were exhibiting an inefficient strategy from trial to trial rather than zero memory. The results of the other concept attainment studies reviewed herein are also consistent with this interpretation.

Wetherick (1964) used a kind of task that could be considered a motoric analogue of the 20 questions task. The experimental apparatus contained four switches, each with three possible positions, and a target light. The subject's task was to determine which position each switch must have in order to light the target light. Wetherick tested three groups of men (mean ages, 26.2, 44.7, and 67.1). They were matched on Raven Progressive Matrices scores, which reflect fluid intelligence, and were given three increasingly difficult problems. The old group performed more poorly than the younger groups on the second problem but improved on the third, whereas the performance of the younger groups declined. The age groups did not differ in overall performance nor in the amount of redundant information their problem-solving strategies yielded. The author concluded that old adults can "learn from experience" and "compete with younger subjects who are equal or even superior to them in non-verbal intelligence" (p. 177). Although the "or even superior" seems not to accord with the reported matching, the results suggest—if indeed the age groups were matched on fluid intelligence—that problem solving of the type assessed is related to fluid intelligence.

Young (1966, 1971) has also used motoric problem-solving tasks. In one (the Logical Analysis Device), the experimental apparatus contains a circular array of nine lights with pushbuttons, a center (goal) light, and a time light that is on for 3 sec and off for 3 sec (Young, 1966). The lights in the circular array can be *effectors, combinors,* or *preventors* of the onset of the center light. Two age groups were tested (age ranges, 29 to 45, 54 to 76) after having been given training designed to impose order in the search for information and to decrease the demands on short-term memory. In spite of the training, fewer old than young subjects solved problems on all forms of the task and at every level of difficulty. The old subjects could not maintain strategies in the face of irrelevant information and did not use effective solution strategies even after they were repeatedly demonstrated. Although these results are consistent with the results of other concept attainment studies, they were unexpected because the age groups did not differ in fluid intelligence as assessed by the Raven Progressive Matrices. Evidently, more than fluid intelligence is involved in solving problems of this type, but what that "more" might be is not revealed by this study.

Arenberg (1974) used this same task in a cohort-sequential study and found that in cross-sectional comparisons, using subjects from age 40 to over age 70, the number of problems solved decreased with increasing age. However, in longitudinal comparisons over a seven-year span, performance improved in all cohorts except those originally over 70.

Young (1971) used a simpler lights-and-switches task (the Heuristic Evaluation Problem Programmer) and obtained significant age effects for men but not for women, as described below.

Effects of sex, education, and intelligence. Young (1971) found that the means and ranges of women's scores on the Heuristic Evaluation Problem Programmer varied little with age, even though the older women had less education than the younger. The extremes of the range of possible scores were not approached closely enough to suggest floor or ceiling effects. For the men, in contrast, the 50s were a transitional period—performance of those in their 50s equalled that of those in their 40s on simple tasks but resembled that of those in their 60s and 70s on more difficult tasks. Men in their 40s—and, on simple tasks, in their 50s as well—were more efficient than women the same age, but in the 50s on difficult tasks and in the 60s and 70s on all tasks, the sex differences faded.

As noted above, the results of the studies of Wetherick (1964) and Young (1966) imply that motoric problem solving is positively related to fluid intelligence. Young (1971) obtained results that do not contradict this implication, although they do not directly confirm

it because she used a measure of omnibus intelligence (i.e., with no differentiation between fluid and crystallized intelligence) and she obtained a sex difference. Omnibus intelligence was positively correlated with performance on all problems for the men but on only one problem for the women. Amount of education was positively correlated with performance on two of three problems for the men but was not correlated with performance for the women.

CLASSIFICATION

The Task
In free classification tasks—also called categorization and sorting tasks—subjects are instructed to classify, categorize, or sort stimuli that may be unidimensional or multidimensional, meaningful or meaningless, and presented one at a time or simultaneously. For example, Kogan (1974) used ink-drawings of common objects in one stimulus set and photographs of human faces in another, each set in a separate deck that was handed to the subject. Denney and Lennon (1972) used cardboard figures that varied in color, shape, and size and were randomly spread on a table prior to testing. The groupings that the subjects form are then analyzed to determine the criteria used to classify the stimuli.

Types of Classification Criteria
Classification is said to be based on *complementary* criteria if the items "share some interrelationship either in the subject's past experience or in the experimental situation" (Denney, 1974b, p. 41), and to be based on *similarity* criteria if the items are similar perceptually or functionally. An example of the use of complementarity is grouping items on the basis of functional or graphic relations. On this basis, a triangle and a square might be grouped together because they form a house. An example of the use of similarity is grouping on the basis of superordinate categories.

The same criteria are reflected in word association tasks, in which use of complementary criteria yields "syntagmatic" associations and use of similarity criteria yields "paradigmatic" associations. An association is *syntagmatic* if the response word is a different part of speech, or form-class, from the stimulus word and could fit into a sentence with the stimulus word (e.g., deep—hole). An association is *paradigmatic* if the response word "is the same part of speech as the stimulus word and could take its place in a sentence (e.g., deep—shallow)" (Denney, 1974b, p. 43). Word associations in the elderly are more likely to be syntagmatic; in the young adult, paradigmatic (Riegel, 1968).

Age Differences
Evidence reviewed by Denney (1974b) indicates that young children use complementary criteria and older children and young adults use similarity criteria, with a transition occurring between 6 and 9 years of age. In old age, the use of complementary criteria increases again (Annett, 1959; Cicirelli, 1976; Denney, 1974a; Denney and Lennon, 1972; Kogan, 1974; Papalia and Bielby, 1974; Riegel, 1970). Denney (1974b) suggested that the reversal to complementarity in old age is attributable to environmental factors rather than competence. Young children and the elderly are subjected to no educational or occupational "pressure for categorizing in any particular way; under such circumstances, complementary categorization would seem to be the most natural. After all, complementary items are grouped naturally in time and space" (p. 48). That is, the age trend occurs because the demand for classification based on similarity is associated with formal schooling and occupation, and the more "natural" use of complementarity appears before formal schooling and after retirement. In support, Denney (1974a, Exp. 2) found that complementarity was used more by nonprofessional than by professional men and women (aged 25 to 69). Sex and age differences were nonsignificant.

In support of the naturalness of complementarity, Denney (1974b) cited research by Cole et al. on unschooled African children and adults, whose classifications were based on what they called *functional entailment.* Functional entailment means that the objects are paired such that "the first went with, or operated on, the second" (Cole, Gay, Glick, and

Sharp, 1971, p. 79). Functional entailment is the same as complementarity.

Essentially the same phenomenon was observed by Luria (1976). He found that traditional, uneducated peasants in Uzbekistan and Kirghizia evidenced *situational* (concrete) thinking, and collective farm members, who had some education, evidenced *abstract* thinking. Situational thinking is the same as the use of complementarity (syntagmatic association, functional entailment), and abstract thinking is the same as the use of similarity (paradigmatic association).

Deficit Vs Difference
The evidence just reviewed implies that abstract thinking is required in formal schooling and some occupations but does not reflect the more natural or preferred mode of situational or concrete thinking. As shown by the studies cited, concrete thinking is found more than abstract thinking in young children, uneducated people (including uneducated adults), and old people. It is also found more in individuals who are brain-injured (Sigel, 1964) or psychotic (Cameron and Magaret, 1951, pp. 511–515). It is therefore characterizable as a *primitive* form of thought, especially because of the tendency of many psychologists to use the performance of young adults—actually, college students—as the pinnacle of mature intelligence and therefore to interpret *different* performance as *deficient* (Labouvie-Vief, 1980). However, as Kogan (1974, p. 228) noted, in discussing the results of his own classification study, the shift from similarity to complementary criteria between young and old adulthood reflects the use of criteria that are adaptive for the respective age groups. College students favor criteria adaptive for high-level abstract functioning. Older adults have not lost the ability to use those criteria, but they are "more willing to indulge an alternative mode when the circumstances permit it." The alternative mode, based on complementarity, offers greater imaginative scope, as Kogan noted.

Evidence that the elderly have not lost the capacity or competence to use similarity criteria is conclusive. For example, Kogan (1974)

found that old adults used complementarity (functional relationships) more often than young adults and used similarity (taxonomic categories) less often, but both age groups used similarity the most often (taxonomic categories: 80 to 81 percent for young adults, 71 to 74 percent for old adults), and even the young adults sometimes used complementarity (functional relationships: 13 percent for young adults, 24 to 25 percent for old adults). Both age groups seldom used another similarity basis—physical attributes (5 to 6 percent for young adults, 1 to 4 percent for old adults). Contradictory results were obtained by Denney and Lennon (1972), who found that old adults used complementarity and young adults similarity. However, the old adults (mean age, 80) were nursing home residents, and Kogan's old adults (mean age, 71) were members of an incorporated "nonprofit gerontological research and service organization" (Kogan, 1974, p. 221). Furthermore, Denney and Lennon used meaningless items and Kogan used meaningful ones. Finally, Denney (1974a) failed to replicate the Denney and Lennon finding and, in fact, obtained even more frequent use of similarity by the elderly than did Kogan (89 vs 71 to 74 percent). Denney suggested that the difference in findings resulted from a difference in instructions. Denney and Lennon instructed subjects to "put together what goes together"; Denney instructed subjects to "put together what is alike or the same." (Kogan instructed his subjects to group the objects into "the most comfortable number of categories.")

Further evidence relevant to the question of the competence of old adults to use similarity was obtained by Denney (1974a). Elderly subjects who did not initially use similarity were given training in its use. The trained subjects used similarity after the training, and although they did not generalize its use to unfamiliar stimuli, the effectiveness of the training indicates that the failure to use it does not have a neurological basis.

Effects of Sex and Intelligence

Kogan (1974) found that in classification tasks with meaningful items and also with photographs of faces, young and old females created more categories than young and old males (the difference was significant for classifying male and female faces but not for classifying meaningful items.) The females left significantly fewer meaningful items unclassified than the males, but nonsignificantly more faces. The implications of this pattern of results are unclear (for discussion, see Kogan, 1974). Although Denney (1974a, Exp. 2) found no significant sex difference in classification, she obtained a significant age-by-sex interaction in a variation of the task (Exp. 1). The frequency of complementary classifications was high in elderly men and both middle-aged and elderly women but lower in middle-aged men.

The effects of intelligence were not assessed in these studies, but Annett (1959) reported a positive correlation between vocabulary and complexity of the explanations adults (aged 18 to 73) gave for their classifications.

Effects of Training

Modeling has been found to be effective for training elderly subjects to classify according to similarity, but the training effects have not been found to generalize to the classifying of kinds of stimuli other than those used in training (Denney, 1974a; Denney and Lennon, 1972).

PIAGETIAN TASKS

Studies of aging and performance on Piagetian tasks are reviewed in the present section. We do not describe the tasks herein, because most of them are complex and our page allotment is limited. Readers who are interested in the tasks but are unfamiliar with them can find descriptions in Sigel and Hooper (1968) and in many of the references cited in this chapter.

The review is not limited to those studies in which orthodox Piagetian procedures were used. In fact, as will be shown, important deviations from these procedures have been fairly common in this research.

General Issues

Interpretation of findings.   In the preceding edition of this *Handbook,* Rabbitt (1977,

p. 607) said of the research on aging and performance on Piagetian tasks:

> The evidence so far available does not encourage me beyond the simplistic view that Piagetian tasks offer a series of problems of graded difficulty, and that it is not surprising that old people should find the harder problems intractable and the easier soluble. I do not feel that our understanding as to what makes a hard problem difficult and a simple problem easy, either for adults or old people, has been as yet much advanced by this work.

We consider this statement to be still valid. The fact that different studies have often yielded different results leads to this conclusion. Even more important, many of the studies have involved deviations from the standard procedures for administering and interpreting Piagetian tasks, and therefore their results are ambiguous with respect to Piagetian theory.

Interpretation is always theory-based, and Piaget's theory deals with cognitive development in childhood, ending at the stage of formal operations—the mature stage—in early adolescence (for overviews of the theory, see Piaget, 1970, 1972). The applicability of the theory to changes in adulthood and old age is, therefore, highly questionable. Several studies of performance by adults on Piagetian tasks have been interpreted to show that older adults perform at a more primitive level than younger adults, but the data show only that they perform at a *different* level. This level is phenotypically like that of children in some ways, but since the possibility that it is genotypically different cannot be ruled out, the inference that the performance reflects a primitive level of competence is unwarranted.

Familiarity of materials. Data reported by Sinnott (1975) suggest that the use of familiar materials in Piagetian tasks instead of the usual formal materials may improve performance, especially in older subjects and especially when the use of formal materials makes the task either very simple and perhaps unmotivating or very difficult and perhaps confusing. These suggestions are tentative, however, because they are based on quantitative scoring of performance.

Quantitative scoring. The orthodox way to use Piagetian tasks is as a basis for categorizing subjects—for example, as *nonconserving, transitional,* or *conserving.* Since a person cannot be an 80-percent conserver, for example, only the qualitative treatment of performance is meaningful from the viewpoint of Piagetian theory. Nevertheless, many researchers treat Piagetian tasks as psychometric tests yielding *scores* that are interpreted to assess cognition as a quantitative variable (e.g., Gallagher and Reid, 1978; Rubin, 1973; Rubin, Attewell, Tierney, and Tumolo, 1973; Sinnott, 1975; Sinnott and Guttmann, 1978).

For example, Rubin (1973) and Rubin et al. (1973) assessed conservation on five tasks —two-dimensional space, number, substance (mass), weight, and continuous quantity— awarded one point per correct judgment and one point per correct explanation on each problem, and then summed the points to obtain a composite conservation score. The quantitative approach seems especially inappropriate in these studies because the tasks used vary in difficulty in childhood (that is, they exhibit horizontal décalage) and might therefore be expected to vary in difficulty in adulthood and old age.

Judgments and explanations. In the standard procedure for Piagetian tasks, a situation is presented, the subject is asked to make a judgment about it, and then the subject is asked to justify or explain the judgment. Many researchers ask only for judgments, but Reese and Schack (1974) argued that explanations as well as judgments should be used in order to reduce the possibility of false positives (correct judgments generated from false premises). The evidence relevant to this argument is ambiguous.

Papalia, Kennedy, and Sheehan (1973) categorized elderly subjects (age range, 63 to 92) as *conservers* and *nonconservers* (surface area) and found that judgments plus explanations yielded the same classifications as judgments alone. In a more extensive study, with subjects ranging from 6 to over 65 years of age and with four conservation tests (number, substance, weight, volume), Papalia (1972) found that in 384 assessments (96 subjects, each given four tests), the classification changed from *conserver* to *nonconserver* only 13 times (3.4 percent) when explanations were added to judgments. Insofar as the *conserver* criterion based on judgments was not overly strict, these two studies provide strong evidence contradicting Reese and Schack's argument.

The issue is not settled, however, because Rubin (1976) reported evidence supporting Reese and Schack's argument. The subjects ranged from Grade 2 (mean age, 7) to community-dwelling elderly (mean age, 74) and institutionalized elderly (mean age, 82). They were given tests of continuous and discontinuous quantity conservation. Those who exhibited conservation were given extinction trials in which a glass with a false bottom was used to give the appearance of nonconservation. Rubin reported that 12.15 percent of the correct resistance-to-extinction explanations followed incorrect judgments. Thus, if only judgments had been used, conservation (resistance to extinction) would have been underestimated by about one-eighth.

Overview of Findings

Papalia and Bielby (1974) reviewed studies of performance on Piagetian tasks in adulthood and old age and came to three general conclusions:

1. Many adults do not attain the highest level of cognitive functioning—formal operations.
2. Cognitive operations decline in the reverse order of their acquisition (which is also the reverse order of their complexity).
3. The apparent cognitive regression in old age may be an artifact of the exclusive use of cross-sectional methods in the relevant studies. Alternatively, if the regression is real, the cause may be (a) neurological decrement, (b) isolation from occupational, educational, and social experiences, (c) *terminal drop,* which begins a few years before death from natural causes, or (d) any combination of these. Hooper, Fitzgerald, and Papalia (1971) suggested another possibility—a decline in *fluid intelligence* (Horn and Cattell, 1966). Papalia and Bielby also noted a need for tasks that "validly measure the same cognitive ability at all

stages of the life span" (p. 439), implying that the apparent regression might reflect changes in the validity of the tasks used. All too often, researchers have interpreted performance differences as differences in ability, capacity, or competence without attempting to rule out differences in the motivational, contextual, and other systems that affect performance but are unrelated to competence.

Class Inclusion and Multiple Classification
Age differences. Denney and Cornelius (1975) studied class inclusion and multiple classification in middle-aged and elderly adults and found that the former outperformed the latter on both tasks. (Denney and Cornelius also assessed the effects of sex, institutionalization, and education, as will be discussed subsequently.) The data are hard to interpret because the researchers assessed performance quantitatively and apparently asked only for judgments. Also, as in other cross-sectional studies of performance by adults on Piagetian tasks, the elderly were assumed to have attained the stage of concrete operational thought at some time in their lives, and therefore their performing more poorly than younger adults was interpreted as reflecting cognitive disorganization or deterioration. However, the investigators presented no evidence that really supports the assumption of disorganization or deterioration.

Sheehan and Papalia (1974) assessed class inclusion in subjects ranging in age from 6 to over 65 years. They found that it increased during childhood, as expected from other research and from Piagetian theory. They also found, however, that it peaked in adulthood, a result contrary to the theory because class inclusion should reflect concrete operational thought and therefore should reach its peak in childhood rather than adulthood. Sheehan and Papalia failed to confirm the decline in class inclusion found by Denney and Cornelius in old age. The reason for the discrepancy is not apparent.

Storck, Looft, and Hooper (1972) found that multiple seriation was easier than multiple classification in adults aged 55 to 79, as it is in childhood. This finding supports Papalia and Bielby's (1974) second conclusion (with the usual caveats about inferring age change from cross-sectional data), in that both should have been attained by the end of childhood and therefore the performance difference implies that multiple classification competence had declined (with the usual caveats about inferring competence from performance).

Effects of sex, institutionalization, and education.   Denney and Cornelius (1975) gave class inclusion and multiple classification tasks to middle-aged and elderly subjects, the latter divided into community-dwelling and institutionalized, and all subgroups divided into low and high education subgroups. The age difference was discussed above. Among the elderly, the community-dwelling outperformed the institutionalized on both tasks. Sex and education had no significant effects on class inclusion; on multiple classification, however, high education facilitated the performance of men but had no effect on the performance of women.

Effects of intelligence.   Storck et al. found that performance on multiple seriation and multiple classification tasks was significantly correlated with fluid intelligence in later adulthood (age 55 to 79), as Hooper et al. (1971) had predicted it would be.

Conservation

Age differences.   As mentioned above, Rubin et al. (1973) assessed performance on five conservation tasks—two-dimensional space, number, substance, weight, and continuous quantity—and combined the tasks to obtain a composite quantitative score. They administered the tasks to five age groups, with mean ages of 7.6, 11.6, 21.1, 44.1, and 76.3 years.

The oldest group had a significantly lower composite score than the other two adult groups, but no other age differences were reliable.

Using qualitative scoring, Papalia (1972) assessed four kinds of conservation in subjects ranging from 6 to over 65 years of age. She found that conservation of number was invariant after early childhood, but that conservation of substance, weight, and volume increased throughout childhood and declined in old age (with the usual caveats about inferring age changes from cross-sectional data). As shown in Table 1, the order in which the various kinds of conservation declined in old age was the reverse of the order in which they increased in childhood. This finding confirms research in the European literature, according to Papalia (for the relevant references, see Papalia, 1972).

The ordering of the tasks in old age has been confirmed for substance, weight, and volume conservation (Papalia, Salverson, and True, 1973) and for weight and volume conservation (Storck et al., 1972), as shown in Table 2. However, as shown in Table 3, Chance, Overcast, and Dollinger (1978) obtained inconsistent results in that they found no evidence of regression in conservation of substance, surface area, or weight, or of interior, occupied, or displaced volume.

The conservation of volume may reflect formal operations (Phillips, 1975, pp. 100, 128–129), and therefore the high percentages of conservers imply that the subjects tested by Chance et al. were a select group. As a matter of fact, they were deliberately a select group and furthermore were tested only on the second or third visit to their homes. Papalia-Fin-

TABLE 1.   PERCENTAGES OF CONSERVERS IN THE PAPALIA STUDY*

Years	Mean Age	Number	Substance	Weight	Volume
6–7	6.7	75	56	38	6
11–13	11.8	100	69	50	12
18–19	18.5	100	100	100	50
30–54	43.6	100	88	82	38
55–64	60.0	100	100	94	75
over 65	74.8	100	62	50	6

*From Table 1, Papalia, 1972, p. 235. Used by permission.

TABLE 2.   PERCENTAGES OF ELDERLY CONSERVERS

Note: The studies are by Hornblum and Overton (1976); Hughston and Protinsky (1978); Protinsky and Hughston (1978); Papalia, Salverson, and True (1973); Papalia-Finlay, Blackburn, Davis, Dellmann, and Roberts (1980); and Storck, Looft, and Hooper (1972). The Eisner (1973) study is not included because only a secondary source was available. For description of substance problem, see Protinsky and Hughston (1978); for description of other problems, see Hornblum and Overton (1976).

Study	Sex	Age range	Sub-stance	Area[a]	Area[b]	Surface area	Weight	Interior volume	Occupied volume	Displaced volume
Hornblum and Overton	F	65–76		70 (72)[d]	62 (63)[d]	43 (48)[d]		75 (77)[d]	63 (73)[d]	57 (77)[d]
Hughston and Protinsky	M FL[c]	65–92	100			96		92		
	M CN[c]	65–86	100			76		94		
	F FL[c]	65–87	58			62		85		
	F CN[c]	63–80	100			82		96		
Papalia et al.	M F	64–85	67				44		21	
Papalia-Finlay et al.	F	65–87		100[e]	100[e]	100[e]		100[e]	100[e]	100[e]
Storck et al.	M F	55–79					100	f	f	f

[a]"Method One" (Hornblum and Overton, 1976).
[b]"Method Two" (Hornblum and Overton, 1976).
[c]FL: Tampa, Florida; CN: New Haven, Connecticut.
[d]Percentages in parenthesis include subjects classified as partial conservers.
[e]Percentages are conservers plus two partial conservers.
[f]Percentages not reported for individual tasks; 54 percent met the conservation criterion for the combined tasks.

lay, Blackburn, Davis, Dellmann, and Roberts (1980) also tested a select sample—described as being elite educationally, economically, and socially—and obtained at least partial conservation in all subjects, as shown in Table 2. Eisner (1973) obtained virtually perfect conservation in a group that may have been less elite than those tested by Chance et al. and Papalia-Finlay et al.

Inconsistent results of another kind have

TABLE 3.   CONSERVATION IN THE CHANCE, OVERCAST, AND DOLLINGER STUDY

Conservation task	Age group	
	18–20	65–94
Substance	100	100
Surface area	94	88
Weight	100	100
Interior volume	100	100
Occupied volume[a]	50	88
Occupied volume[b]	100	94
Displaced volume	77	76

[a]Task same as that used by Papalia, Salverson, and True (1973): Do plasticine balls take up the same space?
[b]Task same as that used by Lovell and Ogilvie (1961): Does submerging a pile of plastic cubes in a gallon pitcher mean that the pitcher will hold less water?

also been obtained. As shown in Table 2, the ordering of the conservations obtained in some studies has been erratic, relative to the ordering in childhood (Hornblum and Overton, 1976; Hughston and Protinsky, 1978; Protinsky and Hughston, 1978). Also, marked variations in the percentages of conservers are evident in cross-study comparisons (see Table 2). Two studies of conservation of surface area yielded percentages close to one another, but considerably lower than those in Table 2. Sanders, Laurendeau, and Bergeron (1966) found 84 percent conservation at 20 to 39 years of age, 72 percent at 40 to 59, and 23 percent at 60 and older. Papalia, Kennedy, and Sheehan (1973) tested only elderly subjects, 63 to 92 years old, and found 27 percent conservation, confirming the Sanders et al. percentage for the elderly.

A final complication is that these percentages may not reflect true conservation. Rubin (1976) has argued that a resistance-to-extinction test is needed to assess true conservation. In a cross-sectional life-span study, Rubin studied resistance to extinction in the conservation of continuous and discontinuous quantity. He used only judgments to categorize subjects (he also obtained explanations but treated them as quantitative scores in a separate analysis). His classification criteria, however, were strict: Only subjects with 12 correct judgments on 12 conservation trials were classified as conservers, and only those with no correct judgments on 12 resistance-to-extinction trials were classified as exhibiting extinction of conservation. (Rubin reported that the elderly subjects who did not meet the conservation criterion gave correct judgments on from 8 to 11 of the 12 conservation trials.) The results are shown in Table 4. Percentages of conservers did not vary with age, but resistance to extinction increased during childhood, peaked in young adulthood, and declined after young adulthood. The relevant point here is that many apparent conservers in middle and old age fail to resist extinction and therefore apparently fail to grasp the logical necessity of conservation. For Piaget, logical necessity is an essential feature of true conservation.

Sex differences. The evidence on sex differences in conservation is clear-cut. Gallagher and Reid (1978), Rubin et al. (1973), and Rubin (1973) obtained no significant sex differences in, respectively, childhood (kindergarten, first and second grades), childhood through old age (mean ages, 7.6 to 76.3), and old age (age range, 70 to 85). Quantitative conservation scores were used in these studies

and in the last two reflected performance on five tests of conservation. As noted earlier, the use of quantitative scores makes interpretation uncertain. Other studies, however, have also revealed no significant sex differences for number [Papalia (1972), age range, 6 to 65 and over], surface area [Papalia, Kennedy, and Sheehan (1973), 63 to 92; Sanders et al. (1966), 20 to 60 and over], substance [Papalia (1972), 6 to 65 and over; Papalia, Salverson, and True (1973), 64 to 85; Selzer and Denney (1980), 30 to 93], and volume [Papalia (1972), 6 to 65 and over; Papalia, Salverson, and True (1973), 64 to 85; Selzer and Denney (1980), 30 to 93; Storck et al. (1972), 55 to 79]. For weight, the sex difference was nonsignificant in two studies [Papalia (1972), 6 to 65 and over; Selzer and Denney (1980), 30 to 93] and significant in one, favoring males [Papalia, Salverson, and True (1973), 64 to 85]. Evidently, then, sex differences in conservation are generally negligible.

Effects of education. The results of the Chance et al. and Papalia-Finlay et al. studies, in comparison with the results of other studies in Table 2, imply that education and perhaps intelligence have an important influence on performance in conservation tasks. Hornblum and Overton did not report the relation of education and intelligence to conservation. However, they reported that 8 nonconservers and 14 partial conservers—selected for partici-

TABLE 4. PERCENTAGES OF CONSERVERS AND EXTINGUISHERS IN THE RUBIN STUDY

Note: After Rubin, 1976, p. 53 and Table 1, p. 54.

Group	Mean age	Percentage of group who conserved[a]	Percentage of conservers who extinguished[b]
Grade 2			
trained	7.0	60[c]	75
untrained	7.0	100	70
Grade 5	10.4	100	60
Grade 7	12.6	100	35
Young adult	22.2	100	5
Middle-aged adult	47.3	95	10.5
Old adult			
noninstitution	73.6	92	20.8
institution	81.8	95	42.1

[a]Criterion for conservation: 12 correct judgments on 12 trials.
[b]Criterion for extinction: no correct judgments on 12 trials.
[c]On posttest following training.

pation in a further study—were significantly below the full sample of 60 subjects in mean educational level. The full sample included conservers as well as these 22 subjects.

Papalia, Kennedy, and Sheehan (1973) studied the effects of education on conservation of surface area in men and women ranging in age from 63 to 92 years and in education from 5 to 19 years. The correlation between education and performance was 0.74; with age partialled out, 0.98. (The correlation between age and performance, with education partialled out, was nonsignificant.) The relation is evidently complicated, however, because Sanders et al. (1966) and Storck et al. (1972) found no significant correlation between education and conservation of surface area in elderly men and women. [Sanders et al. also found no significant correlation in middle-aged men and women (40 to 59) but found a significant correlation in young men and women (20 to 39).] Papalia (1972) found no significant correlation between education and conservation of number, substance, weight, and volume in subjects ranging from 30 to over 65; Rubin (1976) obtained no significant correlation for conservation of continuous and discontinuous quantity in a similar age range; and Rubin et al. (1973) obtained no significant correlation for a composite score reflecting conservation of two-dimensional space, number, substance, weight, and continuous quantity in groups with mean ages of 44.1 and 76.3 years.

A further complication is that, although other researchers have obtained significant correlations between education and conservation in the elderly, the correlations have been much lower than the 0.74 obtained by Papalia, Kennedy, and Sheehan. Selzer and Denney (1980) obtained a correlation of 0.33 between education and a composite score reflecting substance, weight, and volume conservation in men and women in the age range, 30 to 93; and Papalia, Salverson, and True (1973) obtained correlations of 0.32 and 0.40 for substance conservation, 0.15 and 0.21 for weight conservation, and 0.59 and 0.37 for volume conservation in men and women, respectively, in the age range, 64 to 85. The correlations for weight conservation were nonsignificant.

Effects of intelligence. The effects of intelligence are unclear. As noted previously (in the subsection on class inclusion and multiple classification), Storck et al. (1972) confirmed the Hooper et al. (1971) prediction of a relation between fluid intelligence and concrete operational thought, as reflected by multiple seriation and multiple classification; as will be noted in the subsection on formal operations, however, Clayton and Overton (1973) obtained only partial confirmation. Hornblum and Overton (1976) found that the 22 previously mentioned subjects who were nonconservers or partial conservers had a lower mean intelligence than the full sample (110.5 and 117.3, respectively), but the difference did not attain an acceptable level of statistical significance. We found no other relevant evidence in the literature on aging and conservation, except that Eisner (1973) reported that elderly men with moderate to severe brain damage did less well than normal elderly men on conservation of space, number, substance, continuous and discontinuous quantity, weight, and volume.

Effects of institutionalization. Effects of institutionalization have also been studied, but without conclusive results. The study by Clayton and Overton (1973), tangential here because it involved Piagetian tasks other than conservation, revealed no significant effect of institutionalization in elderly women (aged 70 to 79). More directly relevant here, Selzer and Denney (1980) found no significant effect of institutionalization on conservation of substance, weight, and volume by elderly subjects (aged 70 to 93). Rubin (1973) obtained a significant effect of institutionalization in elderly subjects (aged 70 to 85), favoring the noninstitutionalized. As mentioned above, however, Rubin (1973) used a composite score reflecting performance on five conservation tasks, and the meaning of his finding is therefore unclear, though suggestive. Rubin also obtained suggestive evidence in another study (1976): Noninstitutionalized elderly subjects were about twice as likely as institutionalized elderly subjects to resist extinction of conservation of continuous and discontinuous quantity (Table 3), but the difference was statistically nonsignificant. Further suggestive evidence was reported by Kominsky and Coppinger (1968) in a study of conservation of surface area in institutionalized male veterans. Three age groups were tested (50 to 59, 60 to 69, and 70 and beyond), and all three were reported to perform at low levels of conservation ability. Relatively high levels of conservation of surface area have been found in elderly non-institutionalized subjects in some studies (Chance et al., 1978; Hughston and Protinsky, 1978; Papalia-Finlay et al., 1980; Protinsky and Hughston, 1978), but low levels have been obtained in other studies (Papalia, Kennedy, and Sheehan, 1973; Sanders et al., 1966).

Effects of training. Hornblum and Overton (1976) studied the effects of training on conservation in elderly subjects who had been nonconservers of surface area and partial conservers of pattern area and of volume. The training consisted of unguided practice on a surface-area task with feedback as to the correctness of responses. Control subjects were given the same unguided practice but without feedback. An immediate posttest consisted of conservation of surface area—to assess the direct effect of training; two other tests of area conservation—to assess near transfer; and three tests of volume conservation—to assess far transfer. Although Hornblum and Overton asked for explanations as well as judgments on these tests, they treated the data as quantitative scores for the primary analyses. The training group was found to be significantly superior to the control group on these scores for all but one test. The exception was conservation of displaced volume, which might be a formal operational task and therefore irrelevant here, in that the training task (and the other tasks) involved concrete operations. Thus, the training led to both near and far transfer, as assessed by conservation scores, a result arguing for a generalized rather than a specific effect on performance.

Hornblum and Overton argued that the training affected performance and not competence. Rubin (1976) criticized these investigators for (1) assuming that the nonconserving elderly subjects had at some earlier age attained the ability to solve conservation problems, and (2) failing to include resistance-to-extinction or delayed posttests to provide an adequate test of competence following training. Rubin, however, failed to take adequate note that the training used by Hornblum and Overton involved only unguided practice with feedback as to correctness of responding, that the effect of training occurred very rapidly, that the training produced far as well as near transfer, and that the training effects persisted in a delayed (six-week) posttest given to a small subsample of the subjects.

Formal Operations

Clayton and Overton (1973) obtained evidence in line with Papalia and Bielby's second conclusion (operations decline in reverse order of their acquisition), in that performance on two formal operations tasks (the pendulum problem and a card-sorting task) declined significantly in old age whereas performance on a concrete operations task (transitive inference) did not. They also found that performance on the formal operations tasks was significantly correlated with a measure of fluid intelligence, confirming the prediction of Hooper et al. (1971). On the other hand, they found that performance on the concrete operations task was not significantly correlated with fluid intelligence but was significantly *negatively* correlated with crystallized intelligence. This negative correlation may reflect sampling error; it makes no sense theoretically.

Serious theoretical and empirical doubts have been raised about the universality of formal operations. For example, Kuhn, Langer, Kohlberg, and Haan (1977) assessed formal operational thought in four groups, with age ranges of 10 to 15, 16 to 20, 21 to 30, and 45 to 50 years. Only about 30 percent of the adults were found to have completed the transition to consolidated formal operations—the highest level of thinking—and 11 percent evidenced no formal operational thought at all. Tomlinson-Keasey (1972) obtained even lower percentages in three groups of females with mean ages of 11.9, 19.7, and 54.0. The percentages who had entered the stage of formal operations were, respectively, 32, 67, and 54 percent, and the percentages who were at the highest level of formal operations were 4, 23, and 17 percent. A brief period of training increased the percentages, and the effect persisted across a one-week delay; the effect did not transfer from the tasks used in training to other tests of formal operations, however, indicating that the training influenced performance rather than competence.

Tomlinson-Keasey commented that "attainment of the highest stage of formal operations was rare and seemed to be dependent on available structures, experiences, use, and *possibly even preference*" (p. 364, emphasis added). Chandler (1980, p. 82) noted that the elderly "generally dislike bookish, abstract, or childish tasks of low meaningfulness. . . . [Investigators who use such tasks] set out to determine what the elderly *can* and *cannot* do, only to learn what they were and were not willing to *try*. In other words, research instruments intended to capture differences in competence often succeeded only in snaring more trivial differences in performance." The triviality of most of the differences is shown by the ease with which prompting and brief training can eliminate them.

Piaget (1972, p. 10) suggested that the failure of many adults to reach the stage of formal operations may be more apparent than real: "However, they reach this stage in different areas according to their aptitudes and their professional specializations (advanced studies or different types of apprenticeship for the various trades); the way in which these formal structures are used, however, is not necessarily the same in all cases." In effect, Piaget was suggesting that no one test of formal operational thought is universally valid.

SUMMARY

In general, old and young adults perform differently on problem-solving tasks. On concept identification tasks, the elderly use less efficient strategies, are less successful at attaining solutions, commit more errors, and are less likely to change strategies when their responses are incorrect. On classification and categorization tasks, old adults use more "primitive" strategies. Finally, on Piagetian tasks, the performance of old adults tends to be poorer than the performance of young adults on the more difficult tasks (and in some groups on the easier tasks as well). With re-

spect to problem solving, this review leads to the same conclusions as previous reviews (e.g., Arenberg, 1973; Hooper and Sheehan, 1977; Papalia and Bielby, 1974). Despite the addition of several years' research since those reviews, however, we are not much closer to understanding the causes of the age differences in problem-solving performance.

The overriding problem in the research is the absence of a consistent theory of adult age changes in problem solving. As a consequence, several free-standing conceptual issues undermine the results of research. Differences in performance cannot be definitively interpreted as deficits in competence. The rapidity of training effects, the influence of memory and selective attention, the positive correlation between performance and fluid intelligence, and the persistent use by old adults of hunches and ineffective strategies in the face of corrective feedback all strongly suggest that the elderly possess the competence to solve experimental problems more efficiently but often do not utilize this competence. The reasons for this are not entirely clear. Research suggests that the strategies old adults actually use may be more closely attuned to their needs than the strategies researchers would like to elicit—for example, a similarity criterion for classification is not necessarily useful to all old adults. Furthermore, the unwillingness of the elderly to risk having their performance evaluated (cautiousness) suggests a substantial difference in the way old and young subjects approach problem-solving situations. In other words, problem-solving situations may have different meanings or validities for different age groups.

Finally, we have suggested that the variety of problem-solving responses that the elderly might actually resort to has been seriously underestimated in the problem-solving research. They may, for example, choose to ignore a problem or to change its conditions as a way of dealing with it. Such seemingly natural responses have been ignored in the problem-solving research. The preponderant use of experimental problems may yield a very distorted view of aging and problem solving.

In sum, we must agree with Seltzer's (1975) assessment that "the quality of research is strained." It is strained because, although older adults have been shown to respond differently from young adults in many problem situations, few significant steps have been taken toward understanding the nature of the differences.

REFERENCES

Alpaugh, P. K., and Birren, J. E. 1975. Are there sex differences in creativity across the adult life span? *Hum. Dev.* 18: 461–465.

Alpaugh, P. K., and Birren, J. E. 1977. Variables affecting creative contributions across the adult life span. *Hum. Dev.* 20: 240–248.

Annett, M. 1959. The classification of instances of four common class concepts by children and adults. *Br. J. Educ. Psychol.* 29: 223–236.

Arenberg, D. 1968. Concept problem solving in young and old adults. *J. Geront.* 23: 279–282.

Arenberg, D. 1973. Cognition and aging: Verbal learning, memory, and problem solving. In *The Psychology of Adult Development and Aging*, eds. C. Eisdorfer and M. P. Lawton. Washington, D.C.: American Psychological Association.

Arenberg, D. 1974. A longitudinal study of problem solving in adults. *J. Geront.* 29: 650–658.

Baltes, M. M., and Baltes, P. B. 1982. Microanalytic research on environmental factors and plasticity in psychological aging. In *Review of Human Development*, eds. T. M. Field, A. Huston, H. C. Quay, L. E. Troll, and G. E. Finley. New York: John Wiley & Sons.

Baltes, P. B., and Labouvie, G. V. 1973. Adult development of intellectual performance: Description, explanation, and modification. In *The Psychology of Adult Development and Aging*, eds. C. Eisdorfer and M. P. Lawton. Washington, D.C.: American Psychological Association.

Baltes, P. B., and Schaie, K. W. 1974. Aging and IQ: The myth of the twilight years. *Psychology Today* 40: 35–38.

Birkhill, W. R., and Schaie, K. W. 1975. The effect of differential reinforcement of cautiousness in intellectual performance among the elderly. *J. Geront.* 30: 578–583.

Blum, J. E.; Fosshage, J. L.; and Jarvik, L. F. 1972. Intellectual changes and sex differences in octogenarians: A twenty-year longitudinal study of aging. *Devl. Psychol.* 7: 178–187.

Botwinick, J. 1959. Drives, expectations, and emotions. In *Handbook of Aging and the Individual*, ed. J. E. Birren. Chicago: University of Chicago Press.

Botwinick, J. 1967. *Cognitive Processes in Maturity and Old Age.* New York: Springer.

Brinley, J. F.; Jovick, T. J.; and McLaughlin, L. M. 1974. Age, reasoning, and memory in adults. *J. Geront.* 29: 182–189.

Cameron, N., and Magaret, A. 1951. *Behavior Pathology.* Boston: Houghton Mifflin.

Capon, N., and Kuhn, D. 1979. Logical reasoning in the supermarket: Adult females' use of a proportional

reasoning strategy in an everyday context. *Devl. Psychol.* 15: 450–452.

Chance, J.; Overcast, T.; and Dollinger, S. J. 1978. Aging and cognitive regression: Contrary findings. *J. Psychol.* 98: 177–183.

Chandler, M. J. 1980. Life-span intervention as a symptom of conversion hysteria. In *Life-Span Developmental Psychology: Intervention*, eds. R. R. Turner and H. W. Reese. New York: Academic Press.

Charness, N. 1981a. Aging and skilled problem solving. *J. Exp. Psychol.: Gen.* 110: 21–38.

Charness, N. 1981b. Search in chess: Age and skill differences. *J. Exp. Psychol.: Hum. Percep. Perf.* 7: 467–476.

Cicirelli, V. G. 1976. Categorization behavior in aging subjects. *J. Geront.* 31: 676–680.

Clayton, V., and Overton, W. F. 1973. The role of formal operational thought in the aging process. Paper presented at the meeting of the Gerontological Society, Miami, Fla. (Cited in Papalia and Bielby, 1974, and Hooper and Sheehan, 1977, as Overton and Clayton, unpublished manuscript, 1972.)

Cohen, N. J., and Square, L. R. 1980. Preserved learning and retention of pattern-analyzing skill in amnesia: Dissociation of knowing how and knowing that. *Science* 210: 207–210.

Cole, M.; Gay, J.; Glick, J. A.; and Sharp, D. W. 1971. *The Cultural Context of Learning and Thinking.* New York: Basic Books.

Collins, R. 1957. *Conflict Sociology: Toward an Explanatory Science.* New York: Academic Press.

Crovitz, E. 1966. Reversing a learning deficit in the aged. *J. Geront.* 21: 236–238.

Demming, J. A., and Pressey, S. L. 1957. Tests "indigenous" to the adult and older years. *J. Couns. Psychol.* 4: 144–148.

Denney, D. R., and Denney, N. W. 1973. The use of classification for problem solving: A comparison of middle and old age. *Devl. Psychol.* 9: 275–278.

Denney, N. W. 1974a. Classification abilities in the elderly. *J. Geront.* 29: 309–314.

Denney, N. W. 1974b. Evidence for developmental changes in categorization criteria for children and adults. *Hum. Dev.* 17: 41–53.

Denney, N. W. 1979. Problem solving in later adulthood: Intervention research. In *Life-Span Development and Behavior*, eds. P. B. Baltes and O. G. Brim, Jr., vol. 2. New York: Academic Press.

Denney, N. W. 1980a. The effect of manipulation of peripheral, noncognitive variables on problem-solving performance of the elderly. *Hum. Dev.* 23: 268–277.

Denney, N. W. 1980b. Task demands and problem-solving strategies in middle-aged and older adults. *J. Geront.* 35: 559–564.

Denney, N. W., and Cornelius, S. W. 1975. Class inclusion and multiple classification in middle and old age. *Devl. Psychol.* 11: 521–522.

Denney, N. W., and Denney, D. R. 1974. Modeling effects on the questioning strategies of the elderly. *Devl. Psychol.* 10: 458.

Denney, N. W.; Jones, F. W.; and Krigel, S. H. 1979.

Modifying the questioning strategies of young children and elderly adults with strategy-modeling techniques. *Hum. Dev.* 22: 23–36.

Denney, N. W., and Lennon, M. L. 1972. Classification: A comparison of middle and old age. *Devl. Psychol.* 7: 210–213.

Denney, N. W., and Palmer, A. M. 1981. Adult age differences on traditional and practical problem-solving measures. *J. Geront.* 36: 323–328.

Eisdorfer, C. 1965. Verbal learning and response time in the aged. *J. Genet. Psychol.* 107: 15–22.

Eisdorfer, C. 1968. Arousal and performance: Experiments in verbal learning and a tentative theory. In *Human Aging and Behavior: Recent Advances in Research and Theory,* ed. G. A. Talland. New York: Academic Press.

Eisner, D. 1973. The effect of chronic brain syndrome upon concrete and formal operations in elderly men. Unpublished manuscript. (Cited in Papalia and Bielby, 1974.)

Engelman, M. A. 1978. The response of older women to a creative problem-solving program. Abstracted in *J. Creat. Behav.* 12: 278.

Furry, C. A., and Baltes, P. B. 1973. The effect of age differences in ability-extraneous performance variables on the assessment of intelligence in children, adults, and the elderly. *J. Geront.* 28: 73–80.

Gallagher, J. McC., and Reid, D. K. 1978. An empirical test of judgments and explanations in Piagetian-type problems of conservation of continuous quantity. *Percept. Mot. Skills* 46: 363–368.

Gholson, B., and Beilin, H. 1979. A developmental model of human learning. In *Advances in Child Development and Behavior,* ed. H. W. Reese, Vol. 13. New York: Academic Press.

Giambra, L. M., and Arenberg, D. 1980. Problem solving, concept learning, and aging. In *Aging in the 1980s,* ed. L. Poon. Washington, D.C.: Gerontological Society.

Goulet, L. R. 1973. The interfaces of acquisition: Models and methods for studying the active, developing organism. In *Life-Span Developmental Psychology: Methodological Issues,* eds. J. R. Nesselroade and H. W. Reese. New York: Academic Press.

Hartley, A. A. 1981. Adult age differences in deductive reasoning processes. *J. Geront.* 36: 700–706.

Hayslip, B., and Sterns, H. L. 1979. Age differences in relationships between crystallized and fluid intelligences and problem solving. *J. Geront.* 34: 404–414.

Heyn, J. F.; Barry, J. R.; and Pollack, R. H. 1978. Problem solving as a function of age, sex, and the role appropriateness of the problem content. *Expl. Aging Res.* 4: 505–519.

Hooper, F. H.; Fitzgerald, J.; and Papalia, D. 1971. Piagetian theory and the aging process: Extensions and speculations. *Aging Hum. Dev.* 2: 3–20.

Hooper, F. H., and Sheehan, N. W. 1977. Logical concept attainment during the aging years: Issues in the neo-Piagetian research literature. In *Knowledge and Development.* Vol. 1: *Advances in Research and Theory,* eds. W. F. Overton and J. McC. Gallagher. New York: Plenum.

Horn, J. L., and Cattell, R. B. 1966. Refinement and test of the theory of fluid and crystallized general intelligences. *J. Educ. Psychol.* 57: 253–270.

Hornblum, J. N., and Overton, W. F. 1976. Area and volume conservation among the elderly: Assessment and training. *Devl. Psychol.* 12: 68–74.

Hoyer, W. J.; Rebok, G. W.; and Sved, S. M. 1979. Effects of varying irrelevant information in adult age differences in problem solving. *J. Geront.* 34: 553–560.

Hughston, G. A., and Protinsky, H. W. 1978. Conservation abilities of elderly men and women: A comparative investigation. *J. Psychol.* 98: 23–26.

Jaquish, G. A., and Ripple, R. E. 1981. Cognitive creative abilities and self-esteem across the adult life-span. *Hum. Dev.* 24: 110–119.

Kamin, L. J. 1957. Differential changes in mental abilities in old age. *J. Geront.* 12: 66–70.

Kendler, T. S. 1979. The development of discrimination learning: A levels-of-functioning explanation. In *Advances in Child Development and Behavior,* eds. H. W. Reese and L. P. Lipsitt, vol. 13. New York: Academic Press.

Kesler, M. S.; Denney, N. W.; and Whitely, S. E. 1976. Factors influencing problem-solving in middle-aged and elderly adults. *Hum. Dev.* 19: 310–320.

Klahr, D., and Siegler, R. S. 1978. The representation of children's knowledge. In *Advances in Child Development and Behavior,* eds. H. W. Reese and L. P. Lipsitt, vol. 12. New York: Academic Press.

Klineberg, O. 1980. Historical perspectives: Cross-cultural psychology before 1960. In *Handbook of Cross-Cultural Psychology.* Vol. 1: *Perspectives,* eds. H. C. Triandis and W. W. Lambert. Boston: Allyn & Bacon.

Kogan, N. 1974. Categorizing and conceptualizing styles in younger and older adults. *Hum. Dev.* 17: 218–230.

Kominsky, C., and Coppinger, N. 1968. The Muller-Lyer illusion and Piaget's test for the conservation of space in a group of older institutionalized veterans. Unpublished manuscript. (Cited in Papalia and Bielby, 1974.)

Korchin, S. J., and Basowitz, H. 1957. Age differences in verbal learning. *J. Abnorm. Soc., Psychol.* 54: 64–69.

Kuhn, D.; Langer, J.; Kohlberg, L.; and Haan, N. S. 1977. The development of formal operations in logical and moral judgment. *Genet. Psychol. Monogr.* 95: 97–188.

Labouvie-Vief, G. 1977. Adult cognitive development: In search of alternative interpretations. *Merrill-Palmer Q. Behavl. Dev.* 23: 227–263.

Labouvie-Vief, G. 1980. Beyond formal operations: Uses and limits of pure logic in life-span development. *Hum. Dev.* 23: 141–161.

Labouvie-Vief, G. 1981. Proactive and reactive aspects of constructivism: Growth and aging in life-span perspective. In *Individuals as Producers of Their Development,* eds. R. M. Lerner and N. A. Busch-Rossnagel. New York: Academic Press.

Labouvie-Vief, G. 1982a. Dynamic development and mature autonomy: A theoretical prologue. *Hum. Dev.* 25: 161–191.

Labouvie-Vief, G. 1982b. Growth and aging in life-span perspective. *Hum. Dev.* 25: 65–79.

Labouvie-Vief, G., and Blanchard-Fields, F. 1982. Cognitive ageing and psychological growth. *Ageing and Society* 2 (Pt. 2): 183–209.

Leech, S., and Witte, K. L. 1971. Paired-associate learning in elderly adults as related to pacing and incentive conditions. *Devl. Psychol.* 5: 180.

Lovell, K., and Ogilvie, E. 1961. The growth of the concept of volume in junior school children. *J. Child Psychol. Psychiat.* 2: 118–126.

Luria, A. R. 1976. *Cognitive Development: Its Cultural and Social Foundations,* ed. M. Cole. Translated by M. Lopez-Morillas and L. Solataroff. Cambridge, Mass.: Harvard University Press.

Mayer, R. E. 1977. *Thinking and Problem Solving: An Introduction to Human Cognition and Learning.* Glenview, Ill.: Scott, Foresman.

Mosher, F. A., and Hornsby, J. R. 1966. On asking questions. In *Studies in Cognitive Growth,* eds. J. S. Bruner, R. R. Olver, P. M. Greenfield, et al. New York: John Wiley & Sons.

Neimark, E. D., and Stead, C. 1981. Everyday thinking by college women: Analysis of journal entries. *Merrill-Palmer Q. Behavl. Dev.* 27: 471–488.

Offenbach, S. I. 1974. A developmental study of hypothesis testing and cue selection strategies. *Devl. Psychol.* 10: 484–490.

Okun, M. A. 1976. Adult age and cautiousness in decision: A review of the literature. *Hum. Dev.* 19: 220–233.

Okun, M. A., and Elias, C. S. 1977. Cautiousness in adulthood as a function of age and payoff structure. *J. Geront.* 32: 451–455.

Okun, M. A.; Siegler, I. C.; and George, L. K. 1978. Cautiousness and verbal learning in adulthood. *J. Geront.* 33: 94–97.

Papalia, D. E. 1972. The status of several conservation abilities across the life-span. *Hum. Dev.* 15: 229–243.

Papalia, D. E., and Bielby, D. D. V. 1974. Cognitive functioning in middle and old age adults: A review of research based on Piaget's theory. *Hum. Dev.* 17: 424–443.

Papalia, D. E.; Kennedy, E.; and Sheehan, N. 1973. Conservation of space in noninstitutionalized old people. *J. psychol.* 84: 75–79.

Papalia, D. E.; Salverson, S. M.; and True, M. 1973. An evaluation of quantity conservation performance during old age. *Int. J. Aging Hum. Dev.* 4: 103–109.

Papalia-Finlay, D.; Blackburn, J.; Davis, E.; Dellmann, M.; and Roberts, P. 1980. Training cognitive functioning in the elderly—inability to replicate previous findings. *Int. J. Aging Hum. Dev.* 12: 111–117.

Parsons, J. A. 1976. Conditioning precurrent (problem solving) behavior of children. *R. Mexic. Anál. Conduct.* 2: 190–206.

Perlmutter, M., and List, J. A. 1982. Learning in later adulthood. In *Review of Human Development,* eds. T. M. Field, A. Huston, H. C. Quay, L. E. Troll, and G. E. Finley. New York: John Wiley & Sons.

Phillips, J. L., Jr. 1975. *The Origins of Intellect: Piaget's Theory.* 2nd ed. San Francisco: Freeman.

Piaget, J. 1970. Piaget's theory. In *Carmichael's Manual of Child Psychology,* ed. P. H. Mussen, vol. 1. 3rd ed. New York: Wiley.

Piaget, J. 1972. Intellectual evolution from adolescence to adulthood. *Hum. Dev.* 15: 1–12.

Plemons, J. K.; Willis, S. L.; and Baltes, P. B. 1978. Modifiability of fluid intelligence in aging: A short-term longitudinal training approach. *J. Geront.* 33: 224–231.

Protinsky, H., and Hughston, G. 1978. Conservation in elderly males: An empirical investigation. *Devl. Psychol.* 14: 114.

Rabbitt, P. 1965. An age-decrement in the ability to ignore irrelevant information. *J. Geront.* 20: 233–238.

Rabbitt, P. 1977. Changes in problem solving ability in old age. In *Handbook of the Psychology of Aging,* eds. J. E. Birren and K. W. Schaie. New York: Van Nostrand Reinhold.

Reese, H. W., and Schack, M. L. 1974. Comment on Brainerd's criteria for cognitive structures. *Psychol. Bull.* 81: 67–69.

Reitman, W. R. 1964. Heuristic decision procedures, open constraints, and the structure of ill-defined problems. In *Human Judgments and Optimality,* eds. M. W. Shelly, II, and G. L. Bryan. New York: John Wiley & Sons.

Riegel, K. F. 1968. Changes in psycholinguistic performances with age. In *Human Aging and Behavior: Recent Advances in Research and Theory,* ed. G. A. Talland. New York: Academic Press.

Riegel, K. F. 1970. The language acquisition process: A reinterpretation of selected research findings. In *Life-Span Developmental Psychology: Research and Theory,* eds. L. R. Goulet and P. B. Baltes. New York: Academic Press.

Romaniuk, J. G. 1978. Creative thinking in action: Reactions to a workshop designed for older adults. *J. Creat. Behav.* 12: 274–276.

Romaniuk, J. G., and Romaniuk, M. 1981. Creativity across the life span: A measurement perspective. *Hum. Dev.* 24: 366–381.

Rubin, K. H. 1973. Decentration skills in institutionalized and noninstitutionalized elderly. *Proc. 81st Annu. Conv. APA* 8 (Pt. 2): 759–760.

Rubin, K. H. 1976. Extinction of conservation: A life-span investigation. *Devl. Psychol.* 12: 51–56.

Rubin, K. H.; Attewell, P. W.; Tierney, M. C.; and Tumolo, P. 1973. Development of spatial egocentrism and conservation across the life span. *Devl. Psychol.* 9: 432.

Salthouse, T. A., and Somberg, B. L. 1982. Time-accuracy relationships in young and old adults. *J. Geront.* 37: 349–353.

Sanders, J. A. C.; Sterns, H. L.; Smith, M.; and Sanders, R. E. 1975. Modification of concept identification performance in older adults. *Devl. Psychol.* 11: 824–829.

Sanders, R. E.; Sanders, J. A. C.; Mayes, G. J.; and Sielski, K. A. 1976. Enhancement of conjunctive concept attainment in older adults. *Devl. Psychol.* 12: 485–486.

Sanders, S.; Laurendeau, M.; and Bergeron, J. 1966. Aging and the concept of space: The conservation of surfaces. *J. Geront.* 21: 281–286.

Sanford, A. J. 1973. Age-related differences in strategies for locating hidden targets. *Gerontologia* 19: 16–21.

Schaie, K. W. 1978. External validity in the assessment of intellectual development in adulthood. *J. Geront.* 33: 695–701.

Scheidt, R. J., and Schaie, K. W. 1978. A taxonomy of situations for an elderly population: Generating situational criteria. *J. Geront.* 33: 848–857.

Schultz, N. R., and Hoyer, W. J. 1976. Feedback effects on spatial egocentrism in old age. *J. Geront.* 31: 72–75.

Seltzer, M. M. 1975. The quality of research is strained. *Gerontologist* 15: 503–507.

Selzer, S. C., and Denney, N. W. 1980. Conservation abilities in middle-aged and elderly adults. *Int. J. Aging Hum. Dev.* 11: 135–146.

Sharp, D.; Cole, M.; and Lave, C. 1979. Education and cognitive development: The evidence from experimental research. *Monogr. Soc. Res. Child Dev.* 44 (1–2, Serial No. 178).

Sheehan, N., and Papalia, D. 1974. The nature of the life concept across the life-span. Paper presented at the meeting of the Gerontological Society, Portland, Oregon. (Cited in Hooper and Sheehan, 1977.)

Siegler, I. C. 1980. The psychology of adult development and aging. In *Handbook of Geriatric Psychiatry,* eds. E. W. Busse and D. G. Blazer. New York: Van Nostrand Reinhold.

Sigel, I. E. 1964. The attainment of concepts. In *Review of Child Development Research,* eds. M. L. Hoffman and L. W. Hoffman, vol. 1. New York: Russell Sage Foundation.

Sigel, I. E., and Hooper, F. H., eds. 1968. *Logical Thinking in Children: Research Based on Piaget's Theory.* New York: Holt, Rinehart & Winston.

Sinnott, J. D. 1975. Everyday thinking and Piagetian operativity in adults. *Hum. Dev.* 18: 430–443.

Sinnott, J., and Guttmann, D. 1978. Dialectics of decision making in older adults. *Hum. Dev.* 21: 190–200.

Skinner, B. F. 1969. *Contingencies of Reinforcement: A Theoretical Analysis.* Englewood Cliffs, N.J.: Prentice-Hall.

Storck, P. A.; Looft, W. R.; and Hooper, F. H. 1972. Interrelationships among Piagetian tasks and traditional measures of cognitive abilities in mature and aged adults. *J. Geront.* 27: 461–465.

Tomlinson-Keasey, C. 1972. Formal operations in females from eleven to fifty-four years of age. *Devl. Psychol.* 6: 364.

Treat, N. J., and Reese, H. W. 1976. Age, pacing, and imagery in paired-associate learning. *Devl. Psychol.* 12: 119–124.

Upham, T. C. 1831. *Elements of Mental Philosophy.* Vol. 1. Boston: Hilliard, Gray & Co., and Wells & Lilly.

Vygotsky, L. S. 1978. *Mind in Society: The Development of Higher Psychological Processes,* eds. M. Cole, V. John-Steiner, S. Scribner, and E. Souberman. Cambridge, Mass.: Harvard University Press.

Welford, A. T. 1958. *Ageing and Human Skill.* London: Oxford University Press.

Wetherick, N. E. 1964. A comparison of the problem-solving ability of young, middle-aged and old subjects. *Gerontologia* 9: 164–178.

Wetherick, N. E. 1966. The inferential basis of concept attainment. *Br. J. Psychol.* 57: 61–69.

Wiersma, W., and Klausmeier, H. J. 1965. The effect of age upon speed of concept attainment. *J. Geront.* 20: 398–400.

Willis, S. L.; Cornelius, S. W.; Blow, F. C.; and Baltes, P. B. In press. Training research in aging: Attentional processes. *J. Educ. Psychol.*

Young, M. L. 1966. Problem solving performance in two age groups. *J. Geront.* 21: 505–509.

Young, M. L. 1971. Age and sex differences in problem solving. *J. Geront.* 26: 330–336.

19
INTELLIGENCE AND COGNITION

Gisela Labouvie-Vief
Wayne State University

The different images of aging evoked in different social, cultural, and historical contexts partially formulate questions and anticipate answers for both laymen and scientists who are concerned with the study of aging. Writing nearly a quarter century ago on intellectual functions in the precursor to this volume,[1] Jones (1959, p. 700) summarized the evidence thus:

> In the first two decades the effects are chiefly positive and are defined in terms of growth or maturation. In later maturity negative changes are apparent, with progressive age reductions in functional efficiency.

Nearly 20 years later, Botwinick (1977, p. 580) concluded in the first edition of this volume:

> . . . after reviewing the available literature, both recent and old, the conclusion here is that decline in intellectual ability is clearly part of the aging picture. The more recent literature, however, is bringing attention to what has been underemphasized in the older literature, via., these declines may start later in life than heretofore thought and they may be smaller in magnitude; they may also include fewer functions.

As Botwinick notes, the question of whether intellectual functions decline in aging is no longer rhetorical but rather has become the subject of some controversy. The dispute surrounding the issue is not so much a matter

of a lack of consistent data but rather has its basis in a deeper theoretical disagreement. Indeed, the body of evidence itself has remained amazingly stable. Despite this fact, there has been a proliferation of opinions concerning what to make of it. Are we to adhere, for example, to the notion that such deficits are normative and universal, or are we to explain them by variations in the contexts in which individuals age? Are we to concentrate our efforts on more refined descriptions of this pattern of intellectual decline, or are we to aim at altering its very course? These questions, we shall argue, are new and interesting ones that may well reflect an emerging paradigm shift in our conceptualizations of aging, and—since the concept of aging inevitably presumes a concept of that from which aging represents a deviation (i.e., a concept of progressive growth and adaptive maturity)—of psychological growth as well. Thus Jones' equation of intellectual growth with the first two decades of life is highly consistent with models of development (such as those of Piaget and Freud) that have defined psychological growth as nearly coterminous with physical maturity and that have, in essence, visualized its completion in late adolescence.

As the age structure of our society is shifting upward, however, and as expectations have been raised not only for a longer, but also for a more healthful life span, attempts to show that adulthood should be viewed not merely

---

[1]*Handbook of Aging and the Individual* (Birren, 1959).

in terms of decline and loss of youthful vigor, but also in terms of potential gains and growth, are proliferating. These efforts are exemplified in a flurry of recent writings that address adult developmental changes in cognitive and intellectual functions (e.g., Labouvie-Vief, 1980, 1982; Pascual-Leone, in press; Riegel, 1973; Schaie, 1977/78) as well as more general questions about the stages of adult adaptation (e.g., Cytrynbaum et al., 1980; Levinson et al., 1977; Vaillant, 1977). Notably, too, such efforts are joined by a parallel concern of child developmentalists who are also currently viewing age-span-specific concepts of growth, stability, and regression as quite limited (Gilligan and Murphy, 1979; Kegan, 1982; Labouvie-Vief, 1982; Perry, 1968). Thus to think of "maturity" as a characteristic of youth is being revealed as a foreclosed concept, and notions of maturity now delay its attainment until later in adulthood. In the same vein, the concept of aging as usually understood is displaced and compressed beyond this hypothetical apogee. The view here, then, is that the very concept of aging, including the aging of intellectual functions, is undergoing a shift in theoretical emphasis. The question "Is there decline in aging per se?" may be no longer the most useful one to pose, since the answer will be influenced by varying theoretical conceptions of the process of life-course development. Indeed, the somewhat controversial nature of the question can be seen to derive from this very pluralism of ideas. To some readers, no doubt, such pluralism may represent a regrettable state of confusion. Still, we may point to the fact that the coexistence of a variety of competing interpretations is usually the concomitant of paradigmatic transitions (Kuhn, 1970), and that, as such, it can also be seen as a sign of the vigor a field needs to reorganize itself and define, in preliminary fashion, the shape of novel issues.

The primary objective of the present chapter, therefore, is not to provide an exhaustive summary of recent literature on adult cognition. Many excellent summaries (e.g., Baltes and Labouvie, 1973; Botwinick, 1977; Denney, 1981; Horn, 1970, 1976; Labouvie-Vief, 1977; Schaie, 1980) have been provided, and

the interested reader may wish to consult these. We are hoping, instead, that this chapter may serve as an opportunity for theoretical self-reflection and for pondering on the trajectories that research in later life cognition took during its formative years prior to Jones' writing, on the turning points it now appears to be negotiating, and on the possible directions it may assume in the future.

In this discussion, we intend to synopsize a number of areas that are seemingly diverse and only tangentially related to the topic of aging and intelligence per se. To provide the reader with a sense of continuity and direction across this superficially discursive presentation, it will be helpful to discuss its organization at the outset.

This chapter consists of five main sections. The first of these provides a brief review of the area of intellectual aging and demonstrates that the issues of variability that have arisen can no longer be accounted for by traditional models of aging and intelligence. In the second section, we argue that these issues call for a re-examination of the concept of intelligence as an adaptive capacity. In particular, new models are needed in which notions of *cultural* evolution supersede past notions of biological evolution as primary explanatory concepts in the aging field. Thus, adulthood is no longer to be seen as the cessation of growth and development (and, consequently, as the beginning of aging) but as a life stage programmed for plasticity and further growth.

This primarily theoretical notion is further explicated in the remaining three sections. The third section reviews a series of studies that suggest that biological growth processes continue into adulthood, given proper conditions of stimulation. The fourth section reviews research from a more behavioral perspective and argues that behavioral growth may similarly continue into late life, given proper ecological supports. These "supports" may be both external (e.g., training) and internal (e.g., internalized notions of competence—incompetence). The fifth and final section discusses the implications of recent models of adult intelligence that stress the possibility of continued structural growth and adaptive reorganization in adulthood.

EXPLANANDA: PATTERNS OF COGNITIVE AGING

Let us begin by briefly summarizing the body of evidence we are to discuss. Precursors to studies of intellectual functions over the adult life span established a pattern of pronounced decrements in these functions beginning in the early twenties and suggested a unitary and regressive course for them thereafter. A famous example is Galton's large-scale anthropometric assessment of over 9,000 visitors at the 1884 International Health Exhibition in London. This assessment was based on such measures as sensory acuity, reaction times, and so forth (Ruger and Stoessiger, 1927). Such measures are no longer thought to be signs of intelligence per se, although they may impact on declines in intellectual functioning.

The view that intelligence displays a unitary pattern and expresses a unitary capacity, however, continued to exert an influence once intelligence tests proper were established in this century. This assumption found expression both in factor analytic views of intelligence as being globally or unidimensionally structured and in the finding that global measures of intelligence showed a steady decrement from young adulthood onward. It soon became apparent, however, that neither the structure of intelligence nor life-course pattern could adequately be described within a unifactorial conception (see Baltes and Nesselroade, 1973). Intelligence came to be better conceived as a collection of somewhat independent factors, and if age performance functions were examined in this light, it became apparent that both decrement and stability—or even growth—over the adulthood period were the rule.

Differential Pattern

Perhaps the most comprehensive integration of this evidence so far was offered in the theory of fluid and crystallized intelligence proposed by Cattell (1963) and extended by Horn (Horn, 1970; Horn and Donaldson, 1980). According to this two-factor model, crystallized intelligence refers to those cognitive processes and primary abilities that are imbedded in a context of cultural meaning and that are relatively "age-insensitive" (Botwinick, 1978). Fluid intelligence, by contrast, typically concerns the processing of information in a context of low meaningfulness and exhibits profound age differences between younger and older adults. The prediction of differential decline rates in crystallized and fluid intelligence subsumes an enormous body of empirical evidence (for summaries, see Baltes and Labouvie, 1973; Botwinick, 1978; Horn, 1970) and offers one explanation for the frequent demonstration that the elderly typically perform well on tests of stored information while evidencing apparent deficits on tests of immediate memory, spatial relations, and abstract reasoning. Both these differences in performance, as well as the changes in structural organization on which they are thought to rest, are said to reflect the dual interplay between life-long cumulative learning on the one hand and "normal" maturational aging on the other. Thus Horn (1970, p. 466) proposes:

> At first [fluid intelligence] and [crystallized intelligence] are indistinguishable. . . . The accumulation of CNS injuries is masked by rapid [neurological] development in childhood, but in adulthood the effects become more obvious. Fluid intelligence, based upon this, thus shows a decline as soon as the development of CNS structures is exceeded by the rate of CNS breakdown. Experience and learning accumulate throughout development: The influence of these is felt in the development of crystallized intelligence which increases through adulthood. It, too, will decline after the rate of loss of structure supporting intelligence behavior exceeds the rate of acquisition of new aids to compensate for limited anlage functions.

Horn's hypothesized interplay over adulthood between these sources of variation is schematically represented in Figure 1. Here we must note that this hypothesis captures, in effect, a widely accepted notion about the relationship between biological decrements and their effects on intellectual functioning. This is the hypothesis that performance decrements in cognitive tasks primarily reflect the aging of those brain centers responsible for either the most complex or the most hierarchically superior mental operations. Hence, aging is seen as a regressive process that pro-

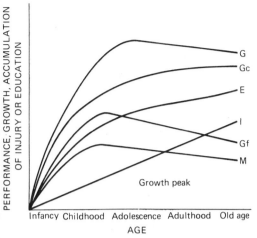

Figure 1. Hypothetical relationship of the development of fluid intelligence (Gf) and crystallized intelligence (Gc) and their correlation with maturational growth and decline of neural structures (M), accumulation of injury to neural structures (I), accumulation of educational exposures (E), and overall ability (G). (*From J. L. Horn, 1970. Copyright 1970 by Academic Press. Reprinted by permission.*)

ceeds from "higher" to "lower" levels of functioning and that involves the loss of the hierarchic integration of functions. The aging individual, therefore, functions at a more concrete, lower level of organization. Rubinstein (1968, p. 409) has expressed this "law of the regression of intellectual functioning in pathology and aging" as follows:

> Regression first affects more complex organizations. In mnemonic organization the 'new' dies prior to the old, the complex before the simple. Thus in old age one will often remember events long past while forgetting recent ones. . . . Volitional control is lost first, the control of automatic action later. In this way cognitive disorganization follows the reverse order of its development through sequential stages [author's translation].

Indeed, this hypothesis appears to account for the wide range of claims that the primary deficits brought about by aging lie in the abstraction and integration of novel information. Thus, aging of the memory system has been said to be due to a failure to utilize more abstract codes and a return to more shallow, inefficient processing modes (Craik, 1977); deficits in language processing have been attributed to a failure of inferential organization of information (Cohen, 1979); and above all,

adulthood has been claimed to bring about a disintegration of formal-logical thought (Denney, 1981; Hooper, Fitzgerald and Papalia, 1971). At the most general level, therefore, cognitive aging is attributed to a disintegration of the kinds of higher-order executive and control operations that permit powerful integration and transfer of information (Craik, 1977; Pascual-Leone, in press; Hebb, 1978; Horn and Donaldson, 1980; see also Poon, this volume).

Aging and Variability

If Horn's model remained the broadest and most integrative one until about a decade ago, the interval since has witnessed a proliferation of data that are not always readily compatible with it or that present rather serious conceptual challenges, depending upon one's theoretical emphasis. Horn's and related models suggest that cognitive aging results, in part, from biological (presumably, largely genetic) limitations on an organism's fluidity or its capacity for plasticity. The assumption of such limitations may be based on an artifact, however, as research has often failed to account for the multitude of ways in which individual development is influenced by socio-cultural factors.

This interpenetration *between* individual (ontogenetic) development and socio-historical context remained a rather neglected topic until the early 60s. To be sure, research reports demonstrating a strong correlation between variables of intellectual competence and those of experiential backgrounds had been available before. For example, Foster and Taylor had already offered a detailed analysis of these issues in 1920. Somewhat later, Tuddenham (1948) reported that the median intelligence test score of World War II recruits corresponded to the eighty-fourth percentile of the troops in World War I. Such contributions remained, however, somewhat sporadic and minor in impact until Schaie and his collaborators (1974) put forward the notion that much of what would appear age-related variance can, in fact, be traced to socio-historical change.

Schaie's starting point was the observation that, ever since the first life-span studies on intellectual development, researchers had reported striking discrepancies between cross-sectional and longitudinal studies (e.g., Bayley, 1970; Bailey and Oden, 1955; Schaie, 1965). The cross-sectional studies reported earlier and more dramatic losses than the longitudinal ones. Although such discrepancies were usually attributed to such methodological factors as the greater heterogeneity of

cross-sectional samples and the higher selectiveness of longitudinal ones, Schaie argued that more systematic factors were at work—in particular, the changing cultural backgrounds of the age-cohort samples involved in the cross-sectional research. To support this argument, Schaie performed follow-up studies on different age-cohort groups, permitting a plotting of cross-sectional and longitudinal data

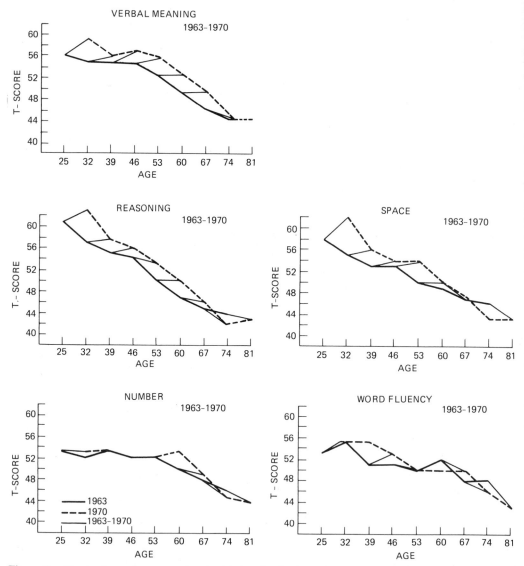

Figure 2.   Comparison of cross-sectional with longitudinal gradients (dotted lines) in Schaie's cohort-sequential research on adult intelligence. (*From "Generational versus ontogenetic components of change in adult cognitive behavior: A fourteen-year cross-sequential study" by K. W. Schaie and G. Labouvie-Vief. Developmental Psychology, 1974, 10: 305–320. Copyright 1974 by the American Psychological Association. Reprinted by permission.*)

in a single grid (see Figure 2). This method yielded a latticelike picture in which, on many of the subtests, each cohort occupied a rather stable trajectory for as long as 14 years, with the younger cohorts tending to show systematically higher positions than older ones (e.g., Nesselroade, Schaie, and Baltes, 1972; Schaie and Labouvie-Vief, 1974; Schaie and Strother, 1968). Thus it appeared that "most of the adult life span is characterized by an absence of decisive intellectual decrements. In times of rapid cultural and technological change it is primarily in relation to younger populations that the aged can be described as deficient, and it is erroneous to interpret such cross-sectional age differences as indicating ontogenic change patterns" (Schaie and Labouvie-Vief, 1974, p. 15).

This conclusion seems not unreasonable since the cohort differences reported by Schaie and collaborators show close parallels with changes that have occurred during this century both in the quality and quantity of education. It is important that these changes may not impact only on such "crystallized" functions as information-related tests (Verbal Meaning and Number in Figure 2), but also on ones much closer to fluid functions (Reasoning and, to a less extent, Space).

Still, not all of the age-group variance in aging may be accounted for by such cohort differences, and this issue has been the focus of a rather animated debate (e.g., Baltes and Schaie, 1976; Botwinick, 1977; Horn and Donaldson, 1976). Botwinick (1977), for example, has argued that the increasing selectivity of Schaie's longitudinal sample may have served to underestimate declines that are both earlier and steeper in more representative samples. It must be noted, however, that cohort variance in Schaie's data (see Schaie and Labouvie-Vief, 1974) was primarily predominant in the period up to the 60s or early 70s. Age-related variance, and indeed nearly linear declines, appear to be much more predominant thereafter (Schaie and Parham, 1977). Part of the disagreement may therefore arise from the fact that researchers have focused their conclusions on disparate age spans. For example, Botwinick and Siegler (1980) failed to sub-

stantiate Schaie and Labouvie-Vief's (1974) claim. Since their samples consisted of adults older than 60, however, their data are not in actual disagreement with the cohort argument.

At the very least, then, the argument for differentiating age and cohort variance has called attention to the fact that significant decrements are considerably delayed into the far end of the 60- to 70-year-old spectrum. In addition, however, it has also highlighted the need for systematic attention to sources of variability that are separate from those of aging per se (Baltes and Willis, 1981). This attention has attracted interest away from research whose aim is primarily descriptive towards an explanatory analysis of sources of variability (both inter- and intra-individual) that are statistically correlated with, but conceptually separate from, involutional change.

One issue, for example, has been the notion that traditional age-performance functions primarily address such life-history variables as education, professional training, and similar cultural changes related to the educational system. A second issue builds upon this one and suggests that if age-related "deficits" largely reflect a variance accidentally related with age, these deficits may be reduced in turn by treatments oriented at eliminating such variance. Such an orientation, then, rejects the notion of a lack of plasticity in the aging organism and sets out not merely to describe age-related functional decline in cognition and intelligence, but to alter its very course. Research adopting this approach is substantial at the present time; the reader is referred to Baltes and Baltes (1980), Labouvie-Vief (1977), and Denney (1981).

A third issue addresses the very conceptualization of "intelligence" and cognitive competence that has underlain investigations heretofore. Its claim is that many so-called deficits are strictly relative to the youth-centered standards adopted by researchers. The issue, then, is the validity of the assessment instruments from which these deficits are inferred. Thus, it is claimed that the seeming appearance of maladaptation in later life may actually reflect the anomalous situation that virtually all developmental models have addressed themselves to the problems of youth rather than those of adulthood proper. This notion has been expressed particularly well by Demming and Pressey (1957, p. 147):

> Most investigations of adult traits appear to involve this problem. For instance, the July 1956 issue of the *Journal of Gerontology* contains two excellent reports indicating decrease in problem solving in older years, as shown by an alphabet maze and puzzle board. But should not problems and matter usual in adult life, rather than in childhood and school, be employed in such investigations? Might some of these adults have then been found decidedly competent in dealing with problems in their world and of concern to them? Wechsler seems to have gone even further when he urged the probability that not only human abilities change with age, but that the significance of the abilities themselves are altered at different ages . . . and with different levels of functions at the same level. . . . It would seem that we ought to have special tests of intelligence for older individuals just as we now have them for young children.

Such issues, then, have greatly heightened researchers' methodological awareness, as reflected in the proliferation of writings on the subject (see Baltes and Labouvie, 1973, Baltes and Willis, 1980).

It should be noted that these issues are not "merely" methodological; they reflect a shift in emphasis in theorizing about aging as well. Specifically, they suggest a move away from a concept of aging that is primarily understood as "normative," chronologically defined, and transcendent of sociocultural processes to one that looks at aging processes inherently from a *differential* perspective (Baltes, 1982; Baltes and Baltes, 1980; Baltes and Willis, 1980). This altered theoretical perspective deserves more extensive examination.

AGING, ADAPTATION, AND INTELLIGENCE

Of the plethora of theoretically oriented definitions of aging, a common nucleus is constituted by the view of aging as a normative adaptational failure that eventually results in organismic breakdown. From this common core, a number of threads diverge. Issues such

as the universal or differential nature of this process and its intrinsic or extrinsic control, onset, and age-functional course are far from agreed upon. Nevertheless, all these various issues take their departure from a shared concept, even though it is often implicit, of what constitutes mature adult adaptation. Indeed, by defining aging as a deviation from this hypothetical optimum, the concepts of aging and of mature adaptation come to be logical and methodological correlates.

Models of intelligence and general notions of biological and evolutionary adaptation tend to be closely associated since intelligence, in the view of many writers, is intricately related to the ability to negotiate environmental demands successfully. This rather ambitious general definition, however, has proven rather more fluid than was healthful for the vigorous development of a measurement methodology, and many researchers in the field eventually appear to have concurred with Boring's (1950) advice to lay to rest such lofty theoretical claims in favor of concrete and reliable assessment methods. The concept of intelligence thus yielded to the pressures of operationism and took on the more pragmatic meaning of "that which intelligence tests measure."

Still, a number of authors have questioned whether such theoretical neutralism is indeed possible and pointed out that in the attempt to steer away from theoretical controversy, the concept of intelligence has taken on rather specialized meanings whose controversial nature was to become apparent only in the aftermath (e.g., Gould, 1981; Kamin, 1974; McClelland, 1973). Often, as biologist Gould (1981, p. 324) noted when writing about concepts of intelligence and their presumed biological underpinnings, "previous claims for a direct biological mapping of human affairs have recorded cultural prejudice and not nature. . . ." Riegel (1977, p. 7) similarly commented on the way in which notions of "maturity" become infused with time and culture-specific models of social structure and economic realities:

> The main criterion for intellectual and personal excellence was the amount of information accumulated, just as the criterion for social respect-

ability was the amount of wealth and property acquired . . . It is not surprising . . . (therefore) . . . that the adult white male engaged in manufacturing or trade appeared as the most successful competitor and became the standard for comparisons. None of the other individuals—the young and the old, the delinquent and the deprived, the female and the colonial subject—were evaluated on their own terms but rather compared against this single yardstick. They were described in negative terms only, as deficient, deteriorated, retarded, or simply deviant.

It is important, therefore, to return to the question of adaptation tabled by Boring. Indeed, to do so will highlight not only the claim that concepts of adaptation profoundly bear on theories of intellectual aging, but will also help to clarify associated methodological questions of how to study them.

Aging and the "Compression" of Senescence: An Example

Since our concepts of intellectual and biological adaptation are so very closely associated, it will be useful to consider a parallel from the biology of aging. Age-related changes in the probability of survival typically yield exponentially accelerated declines after the age of 30 (see Fries, 1980). Joined by data indicating that the functional capacity of various organs declines linearly from early adulthood (e.g., Shock, 1977), such data impress on us the view that most of adulthood consists of a long period of gradually worsening debility and that aging in essence is a counterpart of physical maturation: If maturation is aimed at growth and perfection, aging is aimed in the opposite direction. This view of adulthood was, in fact, anticipated by G. Stanley Hall when he entitled his treatise on aging *Senescence: The Second Half of Life* (Hall, 1922).

As is well known, however, the average life span has increased by some 26 years during this century. Such data, as Fries (1980) notes, might lead to the ominous prediction of "an ever older, ever more feeble, and ever more expensive-to-care for populace" (p. 130). This view is not borne out by the data, however, since it assumes that age-related mortality rates have merely been stretched over a longer

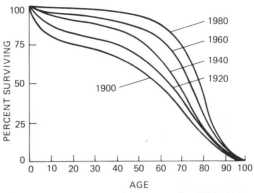

Figure 3.   Human survival curves for 1900, 1920, 1940, 1960, and 1980, showing an increase of life expectancy as a result of increase in median age at death with fixed maximum age of survival.

time interval while otherwise preserving the shape of the time-survival relationship. Instead, the prolongation of the life span has been achieved by a gradual rectangularization of mortality curves such that accelerated decline sets in at a later age (see Figure 3). Thus, although the mean age at death has risen, the maximum life span has most likely remained fixed at an estimated 85 years. Such a picture, then, suggests that the view of *gradual aging* must be displaced by the ideal of a vigorous adult life span followed by a brief and *precipitous senescence*.

The view of gradual aging implies that aging is an *intrinsic* process, i.e., one that is not primarily influenced by cultural exigencies but rather by biologically determined decreases in plasticity, the eventual outcome of which is death. The fact that the actual (i.e., overt) cause of death is usually due to some form of illness or pathology can then be viewed as a direct consequence of the biological decrease in self-regulating capacity. Indeed, pathology and aging come to be so inextricably linked at a conceptual and methodological level that one might be tempted to say, with little danger of exaggerating, that pathology becomes the idealized model case for the study of aging.

In actuality, however, the cultural changes in mortality rates have been paralleled by profound changes in the very causes of aging as well (see Fries, 1980; Fries and Crapo, 1981).

Specifically, acute disease has been virtually eliminated and come to be replaced by chronic disease as a major cause of nonaccidental death. Since chronic disease is strongly associated with life-style variables such as diet, physical health habits, and psychological coping mechanisms, illness has therefore acquired the status of a *secondary* causal variable. That is, although aging in general results from homeostatic failures and reduced capacity for self-repair (see also Sacher, 1978), in specific it is a highly variable and idiosyncratic process whose rate and specific course are under the control of nonbiological factors. Hence, the primary causes of aging and the control of its rate are shifting to variables previously termed *extrinsic;* the mechanisms of aging are shifting from biology alone to culture and individual psychology in interaction with biology. Fries (1980, p. 133) comments on this conceptual shift:

> The complex nature of the major diseases calls attention to multifactorial influences on outcome, in particular social and psychological factors. Outcome is related to choice; assumption of personal responsibility, education for making decisions about personal health, and ability to encourage self-care are clearly essential to changing health behaviors.

This change in emphasis, in turn, has wide-ranging implications for the causal analysis of aging processes. If emphasis was formerly put upon the measurement of statistical trends that confound aging and pathology, it becomes imperative to unconfound these processes by the comparison of criterion samples and the systematic exploration of sources of variability that are now conceived as influencing rates of aging. In this attempt—based as it is on a concept of "ideal aging"—interest shifts away from a primarily descriptive goal to one that is aimed at explanation and an exploration of those processes that may alter aging rates. The very concept of biological causation thus shifts from one that is deterministic to one that is interactive: The individual not only passively submits to a predetermined aging program, but also—within limits—actively participates in this course, affecting it through his or her own behavior and decision making.

Aging and Universal Competencies

If an increased attention to sources of individual variability, then, characterizes a theoretical shift in the health field, a similar theoretical trend is observable in thinking about intelligence as well. The intellectual climate in which research into intellectual aging first began has been variously characterized as positivism, operationism, or logical empiricism, and from this general orientation, the definitions of intelligence and cognition derived both their content and interpretive framework. Ebbinghaus' approach (1885/1913) to the study of memory offers a telling example. Quite conscious of the complexities introduced by the historicity of subjects' memories, Ebbinghaus resolved to table the problem until learning and retention of "very simple" material (i.e., nonsense syllables) in rigidly controlled and laboratory settings were better understood. This, he believed, "offered a possibility of indirectly approaching the problem . . . in a small and definitely limited sphere and, by means of keeping aloof for a while from any theory, perhaps of constructing one" (p. 65).

The hope, then, was to construct a theory upon the initial study of pure processes that might eventually be assimilated with the contexts of individual activities and meanings that characterize "everyday" cognition. In so doing, however, the concept of intelligence becomes removed from those parameters by means of which individuals express "intelligent" behaviors in ecological contexts (e.g., Neisser, 1976). For example, the Ebbinghaus approach is in striking contrast to that of Bartlett (1932), whose view has only recently gained prominence in the study of cognitive processes. It was Bartlett's view (see also Neisser, 1976) that memory and cognition in principle are personalized processes that arise from the schematizing and generalizing activities individuals apply to their personal (and, to that extent, concrete) experience. Thus, individually imparted meaning becomes *intrinsic* to the definition of cognition, *not derived* from it.

The study of aging and development in abstraction from such personalized meaning-giving activity was greatly influenced by the ascendancy of Darwinian thought (see also Riegel, 1977). Primary interest lay in those universal components of growth and decline that reflected a species-specific pattern, presumably selected through Darwinian processes linked to sexual reproduction (see Gould, 1981). This model, then, favors the view that development is primarily age-correlated and essentially (though not perfectly) independent of environmental regulation.

Note, now, however, that by primarily examining those functions that are very robust across different cultures and their subcultural strata, we are likely to come across a set of physical growth processes, or psychological growth processes that are correlated with them. We can then assume with reasonable confidence that such growth processes are regulated by Darwinian genetic processes, or processes that are quite species specific and buffered against environmental influences. Baltes (e.g., Baltes and Willis, 1981) has proposed that such processes be called "normative," thereby reinforcing the assumption that (as is true of Darwinian processes in general) they highly constrain any further adult aging and/or development.

There is some evidence, indeed, that part of cognitive growth may be regulated in such a Darwinian fashion. For example, the brain undergoes regular growth spurts during development that may be correlated with general improvements in the capacities for attending, schematizing, and memorizing (Kagan, 1981). Similarly, some organic processes—such as the already mentioned linear decline in homeostatic organ capacity—may be strongly constrained in this way, even though experiential variance may be considerable.

In general, this viewpoint not only lends strong credence to notions of development that are highly conditioned by physical maturation, but also asserts that psychological aging must be highly correlated with the cessation of reproductive capacity since Darwinian selection no longer operates in the postreproductive period. Any further growth processes are thus precluded, even though rates of aging may be indirectly affected through selection of growth processes (Birren and Renner, 1977).

It is often impossible, however, to extend processes related to sexual maturation to the understanding of individual differences in adulthood, especially if one considers intellectual functions. Jerison (1973), for example, has forcefully argued that many of the parameters related to the maturational growth of the brain (size, volume, etc.) may not be adduced as explanatory variables for variations in adult intelligence. Gould (1981), moreover, has shown that early research aimed at correlating certain brain size parameters with variations in adult intelligence were conceptually, methodologically, and even ethically flawed. Thus he discusses the systematic efforts to eliminate variables such as sex, education, ethnic background, and literacy that characterized early stages of the development of intellectual assessment methodology. Riegel (1977) has also commented on the fact that such data, in the Zeitgeist of logical empiricism, failed to make a critical impress and were attributed to error rather than systematic variance. More specifically, Baltes and Labouvie (1973) have extensively discussed the way in which presumably universal age-performance functions of intelligence are usually a confound between aging processes proper and such secondary variables as pathology, educational and cohort differences, and other life history variables.

To some theoreticians dealing with the process of development and aging such arguments represent no more than a confusion between universals and particulars. It must be emphasized here, however, that this re-emergence of "the particular case" by no means represents mere confusion but rather mirrors the changes of conceptualization that have occurred in many spheres touching upon discussions of intelligence. In this general view, development (as usually defined, i.e., correlated with physical growth) may well be highly constrained by Darwinian processes. It is, however, geared at openness, inherently equipping the mature organism with the capacity to be influenced by its environment on levels that are *both* psychological and biological.

Maturity and Variability

Gould (1977) provided an extensive discussion of this issue in his book *Ontogeny and Phylogeny*. Noting that earlier theoreticians have tended to characterize the relationship between evolutionary change and individual development as one of *recapitualation,* he rejects this view as conflicting with much of the evidence. Gould proposes that recapitulation is merely one possible case in a range of phenomena in which changes in developmental timing produce parallels between the stages of ontogeny and phylogeny. Such changes in timing, in general, are referred to as *heterochrony.* Recapitulation theory, for example, holds that such timing has worked to push ancestral forms into the juvenile stages of descendants, and hence the notion that the childlike, "primitive," and aged occupy similar levels of development.

The most important form of heterochrony in human evolution, however, is that of *neoteny.* Unlike recapitulation, it is a developmental *retardation* rather than acceleration. At the human level, it is shown in a high degree of nervous system immaturity and plasticity altogether unlike the finished form of ancestral adults. According to Gould, this key feature of *paedomorphosis* (the retention of youthful traits in adult forms) characterizes all of human development and gives increased importance to the higher cortical functions, prolonging their growth until quite late in human life—indeed, into adulthood.

Gould argues that such paedomorphosis of the brain and the cognitive functions the brain subserves is an important factor in human evolution, which relies on techniques of socialization and information transmission. Thus,

> Human evolution has emphasized one feature of . . . common primate heritage—delayed development, particularly as expressed in late instruction and extended childhood. This retardation has reacted synergistically with other hallmarks of hominization—with intelligence (by enlarging the brain through prolongation of fetal growth tendencies and by providing a longer period of childhood learning) and with socialization (by cementing family units through increased parental care of slowly developing off-spring). It is hard to imagine how the distinctive suite of human characters could have emerged outside the context of delayed development (p. 400).

Several implications of Gould's statements are of prime importance in this context. First, is the significant implication that brain growth processes must be conceived of as partially independent from physical maturation processes. Thus the earlier contention that intellectual growth and aging operate, in part, independently from physical growth and that aging can be seen to have strong theoretical underpinnings. The latter processes are, indeed, strongly controlled by Darwinian sexual maturation, but the former, in contrast, are highly plastic. In a succeeding volume, *The Mismeasure of Man,* Gould (1981) observes

> Cultural evolution can proceed so quickly because it operates, as biological evolution does not, in the "Lamarckian" mode—by the inheritance of acquired characters. Whatever one generation learns, it can pass to the next by writing, instruction, inculcation, ritual, tradition, and a host of methods that humans have developed to assure continuity in culture. Darwinian evolution, on the other hand, is an indirect process: genetic variation must first be available to construct an advantageous feature, and natural selection must then preserve it. Since genetic variation arises at random, not preferentially directed toward advantageous features, the Darwinian process works slowly. Cultural evolution is not only rapid; it is also readily reversible because its products are not coded in our genes (p. 325).

The second implication, therefore, is that much of the variability of adult behavior is better accounted for by a model of cultural evolution than by one of biological evolution alone. The argument for cultural evolution does not reject the biological nature of intelligence, however, but rather points out that intelligence and its biological roots participate in a bidirectional causal bond:

> The classical arguments of biological determinism fail because the features they invoke to make distinctions among groups are usually the products of cultural evolution . . . We now believe that different attitudes and styles of thought among human groups are usually the nongenetic products of cultural evolution. In short, the biological basis of human uniqueness leads us to reject biological determinism. Our large brain is the biological foundation of intelligence; intelligence is the ground of culture; and cultural transmission builds a new mode of evolution more

effective than Darwinian processes in its limited realm—the "inheritance" and modification of learned behavior. As philosopher Stephen Toulmin stated . . . : "Culture has the power to impose itself on nature from within." (Gould, 1981, p. 325)

The final and perhaps major, implication of Gould's views is that a useful model of adaptive adult intelligence *demands* a model of cultural evolution. The instructional techniques, symbolic products, and behavioral adaptations that shape the intellectual capacities of the young and that form, in effect, the selective context of their adaptation, are, after all, creations of the adults of a culture. This generative role of the adult may be only very loosely related to the growth and decline of those biological parameters that are already subject to Darwinian selection since many of the generative adaptive capacities simply lie outside of those models of aging that are primarily tied to the decline of reproductive capacity, biological vigor, and health parameters.

In advancing this view, we are not proposing that we deny the reality of aging through the invocation of irresponsible idealism (see Horn and Donaldson, 1976) but, suggesting that "reality" be re-defined as a mere subset of possible outcomes. To that extent, the "idealism" we advocate merely reflects the "idealism" native to all scientific progress that is aimed not just at recording, but at transforming, actualities (e.g., Inhelder and Piaget, 1958). Of course, such a transformation involves the submission of all its efforts to systematic empirical analysis. These issues, then, and their implications for an altered view of the process of cognitive aging, will be considered in the remainder of this chapter.

BIOLOGICAL MECHANISMS

A decrease in intellectual adaptability with advancing age has been suggested by an enormous body of data indicating that adulthood—at a biological-organismic level—is characterized both by a plethora of pathological changes related to intellectual functioning and by more normative changes that may reduce the biological self-regulating capacities of the individual. As to the first, pathologies of the cardiovascular system may reduce oxygenation of the brain, result in strokes, and in general affect the efficiency of the cerebrovascular system (Jarvik and Cohen, 1973; Obrist et al., 1962; Wang, 1973). Apart from such gross pathology, however, the aging brain appears to be characterized by more normative changes that are thought to be involutional. For example, cross-sectional evidence suggests that the brain over the adult life span may experience a degree of atrophy, with an 11-percent reduction of brain weight from young adulthood to the mid 80s (Dekaban and Sadowsky, 1978), a loss of neurons (Brody, 1955, 1978), a variety of intra-cellular abnormalities (Wisniewski and Terry, 1973), and changes in neurotransmitter activity (Valenstein, 1981).

All such changes, since they are essentially irreversible, would seem to lend overwhelming support to the view that intellectual adaptability and plasticity are inherently restricted. Nevertheless, a variety of arguments have been advanced over the past decade or so which may render this conclusion overly restrictive, and possibly in need of correction.

Normal and Pathological Changes

Changes Secondary to Pathology. A first argument draws attention to the fact that neither decline in intelligence nor the biological alterations on which they are based are normally distributed in adulthood, but rather are characteristic of subpopulations characterized by pathology, poor health, and/or nearness to death (Birren, 1970).

Earlier research, for instance, seemed to indicate a correlation of indices reflecting brain alterations (e.g., cerebral blood flow, EEG) on the one hand, and intellectual malfunctioning on the other (Jarvik and Cohen, 1973; Obrist, Busse, Eisdorfer, and Kleemeier, 1962; Wang, Obrist, and Busse, 1970). More recent data, however, suggest that such relationships may not hold as systematically for the elderly who are in reasonable health. There is a strong indication in the literature (Obrist, 1978; Wang and Busse, 1975) of a positive correlation between the degree of brain impairment (as revealed by histopathological, pneumoencephalographic, electroencephalographic, or cerebral blood flow study) and intellectual malfunctioning in institutionalized patients who have various neuropsychiatric or brain disorders. Such a relationship is exceptional, on the other hand, in elderly persons who live in the community in relatively good health. When care is taken to exclude patients with even minimal dementia or systemic disease, cerebral oxygen consumption may not differ between young and old adults.

In a similar vein, data reported by Eisdorfer and Wilkie (1973) indicates that the relationship between intellectual decline and elevated blood pressure may be secondary to pathologic processes and not merely an index of "normal" age-related deterioration. Only in those subjects with blood pressure *elevated above a critical level* were there consistent blood pressure–intelligence relationships.

Finally, this argument is also supported by a set of findings that have emerged from various major longitudinal projects (Eisdorfer and Wilkie, 1973; Riegel and Riegel, 1972) in which it was possible to examine retrospectively the performance changes associated with death. This research on dying subjects convincingly showed that decrement related to chronological age is an artifactual result, since performance changes were revealed to be a function of distance from death rather than from birth. Throughout most of their adult life span, individual subjects maintained a more or less stable level, the dramatic changes occurring primarily in the (approximately five) years immediately preceding death. Hence, the continuous rate of decrement suggested by group-average data simply arises out of the correlations of age and mortality with the age-related increase in the incidence of pathological alterations associated with, and that eventually lead to, natural death (Baltes and Labouvie, 1973; Riegel and Riegel, 1972). In the absence of such a statistical artifact, in turn, these data may well support Fries' claim (Fries and Crapo, 1981) of a brief and precipitous period of death-related decline.

More generally, many of the parameters relating to brain morphology and physiology currently being counted among normal age-related changes may well result from the inclusion of subjects who are demented or otherwise suffer from systemic disease. Tomlinson, Blessed, and Roth (1968), for example, reported only a slight reduction of brain weight in adults over 62 compared to those under 50. This reduction, moreover, was significant in the male subsample only. Furthermore, within the group aged 62 to 95, brain weight and age were not correlated.

Similarly, although some authors (e.g., Terry, 1978) have felt that diseases such as senile dementia (e.g., Alzheimer's disease) are merely the extreme of a spectrum of *normal* aging changes, others have argued that they are changes of different qualitative order. For example, recent neurochemical analyses of healthy and demented aging brains (see Valenstein, 1981) reveal dramatic qualitative differences (see also below). The implications of such findings are summarized by Valenstein (1981, p. 96): "It is certainly of pragmatic value to consider Alzheimer's dementia a disease, rather than an inevitable accompaniment of aging, since investigation and treatment are better served by this approach."

Age vs. Intelligence. A second argument points out that even though some brain changes may indeed be normative with advancing age, their bearing on intellectual deficits is not by any means clear. It may be tempting, for example, to speculate that slight degrees of cortical atrophy play a profound role in intellectual deficits. However, it appears that moderate atrophy may be compatible with normal intellectual functioning and in fact may be more closely associated with age than with intelligence (Roberts and Caird, 1976).

Price et al. (1980) have recently pointed out that we rarely know the significance of hypothesized or observed alterations of the brain for adaptive or maladaptive outcomes in later adulthood. Data, therefore, is often based on mere comparisons between young and old adults, and interpretations may be advanced from patterns known to be maladaptive for young adults. For example, although patterns of intellectual performance in the elderly may parallel those of young adults with various degrees of brain damage, they often occur in elderly subjects *with no demonstrable deficit,* and, indeed, with apparently excellent health and social adaption, and may thus arise from sources that are qualitatively different. As Price et al. (1980, p. 84) point out:

> The lack of valid norms for neuropsychological tests is apparent and emphasizes the need for caution by clinicians in interpreting neuropsychological test scores of the elderly. Many other researchers have made similar points in the past, but the continued inadequacy of norms remains a problem, as is clearly demonstrated by the performance of the CRTA subjects. They are especially well-functioning, active, and involved elderly citizens who show little, if any, clinical evidence of neuropathology. Yet their performance on the WAIS and the Halstead-Reitan Neuropsychological Battery may be conventionally interpreted as indicating brain damage. While most normal elderly may in fact have significant brain impairment compared with young adults, the behavioral manifestations of such impairment are not usually clinically meaningful in terms of the decisions that neuropsychologists have to make about elderly individuals.

In sum, there are strong suggestions that the status of apparent normal deficits in aging is not clear by any means. Although a variety of cognitive impairments do characterize the process of aging, in a statistically normative sense, these impairments may be secondary to pathology rather than typical of aging per se.

Plasticity and the Adult Brain

The reader may object, of course, that the arguments thus far advanced are far too idealistic, since in much descriptive research we are interested in statistical expectations for a population. Nevertheless, we must point out that such statistical trends will merely tell us about aging trends that occur under given conditions—e.g., in an environment characterized by certain patterns of disease. Such "normative" patterns may indeed have an overwhelming extrinsic component.

In the past, therefore, we may have taken recourse to biological data and arguments in order to rule out environmental effects. This strategy assumes that causative influences between biology and behavior are strictly unidirectional. Such an assumption is severely limiting, however, since, as Walsh (1981, p. 15) notes, in the study of "environmental effects on brain and behavior it is probably dangerous to assume that any stimulus is incapable of causing detectable effects."

Environment and Brain Structure in Mammals. Arguments about the brain's lack of environmentally supported plasticity sometimes point out that, unlike muscle tissue, the brain is supplied with a fixed number of neurons and is thus unlikely to respond to "exercise" with growth. Nevertheless, as Cajal (cited in Walsh, 1981, p. 33) conjectured nearly a century ago:

> One might suppose that cerebral exercise, since it cannot produce new cells, carries further than usual, protoplasmic expansion and neural collaterals, forcing the establishment of new and more extended intercortical connections.

Evidence of such plasticity has been forthcoming from studies examing the effects of differential rearing conditions on brain morphology and physiology in rats (Rosenzweig and Bennett, 1978; Bennett, Diamond, Krech, and Rosenzweig, 1964; see Walsh, 1981, for review). Such research has demonstrated that young animals reared in complex environments differ significantly from those reared in impoverished ones on a number of parameters. Specifically, they are found to have higher cortical weight, depth, and width, more extensive dendritic arborization and numbers of spines, an increase of about 25 percent in synapses, as well as significantly altered neurochemical activity. The temporal course of these changes is not, however, insignificant, as these complexity-isolation differences tend to diminish after 30 days and are only very slightly in evidence by 160 days (see Walsh, 1981, p. 57).

Whereas most of these studies were originally performed by placing animals in different environments from weaning, subsequent research has shown similar effects with 105-day-old animals that were sexually mature and had achieved almost full adult brain weight. Thus Bennett et al. (1964, p. 616) state: "We conclude that the adult brain shows increases in cortical weight and total acetylcholesterase activity as readily as the young brain."

Although similar research has forced a slow retreat from the assumption of brain immutability, it is still widely assumed that environment-induced growth changes may not be maintained as animals age, nor occur *de novo* in the geriatric brain. A study by Cummins, Walsh, Budtz-Olsen, Konstantinas, and Horsfall (1973), in contrast, found evidence challenging both of these views. Rats reared in differential complexity environments from weaning to 509 days were subsequently removed from these respective environments and underwent daily maze testing for 21 days. Not only were the usual differences between isolation and enrichment found, but for the isolates, subsequent testing also appeared to have stimulated brain growth.

In a second study, Walsh and Cummins (1977) reared rats from weaning in differential environments for 900 days. By this time, 50 percent of the animals had died, and the remainder appeared "truly geriatric." One-third of the survivors were then sacrificed, and the rest placed in enriched environments. Again, the effect of rearing was similar to that found in young animals. Furthermore, the effect of placing isolates into enriched conditions was such that by the end of 36 days the effects of the prior 900 days had been largely overcome.

In a somewhat similar study, Warren, Zerweck, and Anthony (1981) placed mice in enriched environments from 600 to 750 days. Results showed enriched mice to be superior to control mice on several behavioral tests and to have more cortical cells with high RNA levels. This was true despite the fact that the control animals, unlike in the studies cited previously, had been reared in social groups (as opposed to isolation) to day 600, after which they were placed in individual cages. Thus, these results possibly suggest that negative changes in environmental complexity at a very old age have a debilitating effect.

In sum, then, it appears that plasticity is by no means a characteristic of the maturing brain only; growth processes may continue significantly even in adults and aged organisms, if at a less gross level than during maturation. As Walsh (1981, p. 58) states:

It is obvious that, contrary to previous thinking, the mammalian brain may not only maintain structural and behavioral changes originally elicited in youth, but may also retain a considerable degree of cerebral plasticity in extreme old age, and the effects of previous experiential deprivation may be largely reversible. Such findings would seem to hold widespread theoretical and practical implications and to suggest that the adaptive potential of the geriatric brain may have been considerably underestimated.

Environment and Brain Structure in Humans.

We cannot yet be perfectly certain that the mammalian data just discussed fully apply to humans as well. For example, compared to rearing in wild, unrestricted environments, most of the experimental environments used are rather impoverished, and one might thus be assessing degrees of deviation from some normal baseline. Despite these cautions, however, there are strong reasons why the argument may hold at the human level and may indeed do so in a more powerful sense. Lerner (1981) has recently provided an excellent summary of the rapidly expanding literature on this subject, and here we shall merely reiterate a few of the points he develops.

First, although many writers on aging have tended to point to the deleterious effects of changes in brain mass over the adult life span, it is no longer at all certain that this factor necessarily bears on intellectual functioning to any significant extent. As we ascend the evolutionary scale, the significant factor is the relative amount of association of cortex to sensory cortex, and since this ratio is highest in humans, the structural basis for plasticity is very considerable because the specific interconnections between neurons are highly variable and virtually unlimited (Thompson, 1981).

Second, this plasticity derives from the fact that specific modes of function and realized circuitry are highly influenced by experience. As Cowan (1979, p. 129) notes,

. . . one of the most striking features of the development of neurons is . . . their adaption of a particular mode of transmission (either action potentials or decremental transmission) and the selection of one of two modes of interaction with other cells—either by the formation of convention synapses, providing for the release of chemical transmitters, or by the formation of gap junctions, providing for electrical interaction among cells.

We have already summarized the evidence for such environment-induced changes in mammals. Here, it remains to be added that the morphology of the human brain as well does not merely follow a genetic "hard-wiring" but is highly influenced by specific experience (Lynch and Gall, 1979).

A specific example of such plasticity at the human level, and at an advanced age, has been pointed out in a study by Buell and Coleman (1979). In a sample of normal old adults (79.6 years), these researchers found dendritic arborization more extensive than that in middle-aged subjects (51.2 years). This extensive branching was in marked contrast to a group of the aged (76.0 years) with senile dementia, who displayed less extensive dendritic trees. Buell and Coleman argue from this evidence that there is evidence for considerable plasticity in the mature and old human brain. Proposing that the aged brain might consist of two populations of neurons—one dying and with shrinking dendritic trees, one surviving and with expanding trees—they note that, in normal aging, the healthy population appears to predominate.

As Lerner (1981) notes, such lines of evidence have indeed remarkable implications for reconceptualizations of brain–cognition relationships in adulthood and aging. There is already considerable evidence to suggest that neurochemical changes can be produced by environmental manipulations as well as micromorphological changes. Moreover, the fact that such manipulations may be indirect and brought about by behavior and cognitive-behavior therapeutic techniques lends considerable support to Fries' (1980) notion that aging research will give considerable attention in the future to those intellective factors aimed at the prevention and retardation of cognitive deficits heretofore thought "normal."

THE ECOLOGY OF INTELLECTUAL AGING

The close interdependence of biological and environmental change serves to remind geropsychologists once again that our analyses of aging and cognitive functioning must be closely allied with more ethnographic approaches in which the adaptive demands and opportunities and the resulting intellectual repertoires of the individual are reintegrated. Let us survey, therefore, several of the ways in which this interaction between the individual and his/her cultural setting may impact on the process of cognitive aging and its analysis.

Education

Education and Age. We have already reviewed data that relates patterns of aging to cohort differences. It is not certain, of course, exactly what mediates such cohort differences, but a prime candidate is certainly the fact that, currently, cohorts of varying age levels differ dramatically in their educational backgrounds. To what extent may such differences impact on descriptive aging patterns?

The most careful study thus far of education-related effects on patterns of intellectual aging is that by Green (1969), which was based upon the Spanish standardization of the WAIS. Green compared age trends of stratified random samples with others that were obtained after this sample had been educationally balanced through randomly selecting and deselecting subjects so as to equalize educational level across age groups. When the former procedure was undertaken, the typical age-related declines in full and performance scale scores were found, although these declines showed a striking parallel to a declining gradient of educational level (see Figure 4a). In contrast, the education-balanced groups showed an essential elimination of these declines (Figure 4b). Green concluded, therefore, that it "is surprising that . . . (similar evidence) . . . has not eroded belief in the decline hypothesis" (p. 618) and asserted that "intelligence as measured by the WAIS does not decline . . . before age 65" (p. 626).

Cultural Change.   Green's (1969) analysis also receives support from research that has specifically examined the impact of educational changes in a variety of cultures. Such comparisons are especially significant since the elderly in our culture sometimes give re-

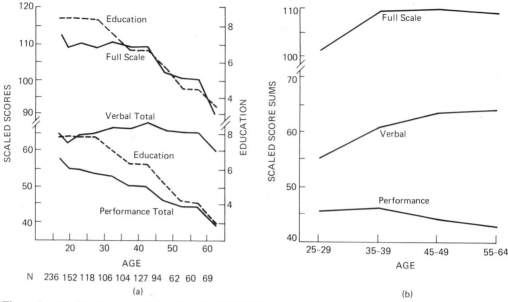

Figure 4.   Age intelligence relationships for WAIS Verbal, Performance, and Full Scale Scores in Standardization Sample (Figure 4a) as compared to education-balanced groups (Figure 4b). (*From "Age-intelligence relationships between ages sixteen and sixty-four: A Rising trend" by R. F. Green.* Developmental Psychology, *1969, 1: 618–627. Copyright 1969 by the American Psychological Association. Reprinted by permission.*)

sponses quite like those of unschooled people in other cultures.

As an example, take such relatively well-researched tasks as the classification of objects or the solution of formal syllogisms of the type used in Luria's (1976) study of schooled and unschooled people in Central Asia:

> In the far north all bears are white. Novaya Zemlya is in the far north. What colors are the bears there?

As is true of older populations in Western cultures (see Botwinick, 1978; Denney, 1974, for review), uneducated people produce high error rates on such tasks. Such errors have suggested a deficit in the integration and retention of logical relationships.

Upon closer examination, one usually encounters a number of rather consistent sources of such error. As reported by Luria (1976) and elaborated by Scribner (1979), for example, uneducated people will often simply resist a solution to the task. They may assert, for example, that it is unanswerable in principle, as when replying, "You should ask the people who have been there and seen them," or "We always speak of only what we see; we don't

talk about what we haven't seen." Scribner (1979) refers to this stylistic tendency as a concrete bias and shows (as does Luria) that it is profoundly affected by formal education (see also Scribner and Cole, 1981).

Thus, Green's conclusions are substantiated by cross-cultural research. In addition, however, he also demonstrates that such thought patterns can be modified. This is true even if culture-related changes in formal education are initiated relatively late in ontogeny. One of Luria's (1976) subsamples, for instance, shifted to a theoretical approach after only a few weeks of exposure to formal education.

Even if adults, not formally trained, are not familiar with the theoretical approach, however, it is doubtful that their thinking can be captured at all by a deficit model. According to such deficit interpretations, one might argue, of course, that the concrete bias of the uneducated and/or the old reflects an inherent restriction on abstract thinking. Yet Scribner (1979) rejects such a notion. First, many subjects will occasionally adopt a primarily formal or "theoretical" approach to the problem, and if they do, they *always* produce correct answers. Second, subjects often assimilate the information presented in the problem to their own ways of conceptualizing reality; they construct new premises and correctly operate upon those. The following excerpt from Luria's study will serve as a good example. Three subjects were first shown a picture of a saw, an ax, and a hammer and then asked if a "log" belonged to the same category (i.e., tools).

Experimenter (E): Would you say these things are tools? All three subjects (S-1, S-2, S-3): Yes
E: What about a log?
S-1: It also belongs with these. We make all sort of things out of logs—handles, doors, and the handles of tools.
S-2: We say a log is a tool because it works with tools to make things.
E: But one man said a log isn't a tool since it can't saw or chop.
S-3: Yes you can—you can make handles out of it! . . .
E: Name all the tools used to produce things . . .
S-1: We have a saying: take a look in the fields and you'll see tools. (Luria, 1976, pp. 94–95.)

If presented with the same task, city-educated subjects will almost inevitably exclude "log" from the category of tools, and from this fact Luria argues that the uneducated display a deficit in classificatory behavior. Yet one also senses here a different dimension; these Uzbekistan peasants appear engaged in a bantering argument about the proper definition of "tool," rejecting any one concrete definition and arguing for a more flexible and perhaps even creative stance. And indeed, although the experimenter attempts to guide the subjects towards a "correct" definition of tools, one is hard put to judge who is more "rigid" or "concrete"—the subjects or the experimenter!

Bloom (1981) has similarly argued that cultural differences may reflect a different mode of thinking about problems, and one which cannot readily be interpreted as a deficit. In a related vein, the author (Labouvie-Vief, 1980) has reported that many older adults may also fail to see any point in adopting the experimenter's view of a cognitive problem. Indeed, although young Western adults often show a certain submissive compliance that refuses to question the validity of such tasks, older and more mature adults will often express a vigorous interest in such issues.

When evaluating notions of cognitive decrement, therefore, one must calibrate one's standard to the modes—often linguistic—that a culture, subculture, or even individual has developed in order to deal with, and to encode, complex information. Hymes (1974) has referred to such modes as *genres;* Bartlett (1932), as *schemata.* The Soviet psychologist Leontiev (1977) has gone even further by suggesting that such schemata create specific brain-based "functional organs" that serve to assimilate knowledge into pre-existing modes of organization. In any case, the end result of such concepts is a somewhat altered view of development, one in which the individual becomes socialized and specialized to deal with such genres. Conversely, a failure to comprehend or integrate information may not in any way reflect a generalized decrement, but rather the individual's lack of familiarity with the genre used by the experimenter.

Environmental Complexity. It is true, nevertheless, that a considerable proportion of elderly individuals do experience deficits that may not be so easily explained by stylistic differences. As already mentioned, the cohort-based argument, even in Schaie's research, seemed to hold more strongly for the young to middle-aged than for old adults. Thus, some authors (e.g., Botwinick, 1978; Horn and Donaldson, 1976) have concluded that arguments of the type presented here may well displace the peak of intellectual performance into later adulthood; even if they do, however, they may not qualitatively alter the view of age-related intellectual deterioration.

Nevertheless, this conclusion may present an overly conservative view, and it definitely contrasts with a series of models that have more specifically addressed the issue of age-related *decline* (e.g., Baltes and Schaie, 1976; Rosenmayr and Rosenmayr, 1978; Labouvie-Vief, 1977). The best known prototype of such models is perhaps Bengtson and Kuyper's "social breakdown model" (c.f. Bengtson, 1973). In this conceptualization, the relationship between aging and intellectual functioning is to be viewed as a feedback loop that actively induces social groups in marginal positions into a role of social and intellectual incompetence. Once begun, this loop initiates a cycle of self-fulfilling prophecies that is buttressed by mythologies and sterotypes surrounding socially held views of "normal" aging. As a result, a two-fold socialization process is reinforced. First, many social institutions actively discourage competent behaviors. Second, the target individuals themselves are subjected to a life-long socialization process that leads them to internalize negative expectations. Rosenmayr has coined the poignant phrase, a "societally induced individual responsibility," to capture the idea that many elderly surrender to negative social sterotypes and thereby contribute towards their own decline (c.f. Rosenmayr and Rosenmayr, 1978).

Demonstrations of such a self-fulfilling cycle are to be found particularly in marginal groups of the elderly, such as those who are institutionalized. Often, the social expectation in such groups is one of irreversible decrement and one in which interactions with patients becomes actively translated into a discouragement of competence-related behaviors by the caretakers and staff of institutions (Baltes and Baltes, 1977; Macdonald and Butler, 1974). Yet relatively minor interventions into this breakdown cycle have often resulted in dramatic effects. Schultz (1976) and Langer and Rodin (1979), for example, have shown that patients' subjective control of events affect their cognitive, emotional, and even physical well-being. Such control may be heightened simply by involving patients in decisions about everyday happenings such as taking care of plants or being aware of visitation schedules. In the same vein, Langer (e.g., Langer et al., 1979) has argued that memory deficits may result from institutional failures to make events memorable. Even more dramatically, the increased mortality following institutional relocation that is often reported has been significantly alleviated when administrators implemented programs to familiarize and involve patients with the events and circumstances of the move (Schultz and Brenner, 1977).

In this context, it is significant to note that similar effects might well explain part of the apparently more normative declines in cognitive functioning in the late 60s to early 70s. This age period is typically marked by retirement. It is one of dramatic constriction in economic and cultural participation and as such may often remove a viable supportive context (Baltes and Baltes, 1977; Labouvie-Vief et al., 1974). With the exception of Schaie's (Gribbin, Schaie, and Parham, 1980), we still don't know of any large-scale research addressing this important issue.

Training Research.   Although little is known as yet about the relationship of intellectual change in later life to changes in ecological settings, the last decade or two have witnessed a vigorous effort to establish such environment-based mechanisms in experimental settings. The rationale of such research is that, if deficits are indeed induced by variables related to a general restriction of environmental complexity, the resulting deficits are not necessarily irreversible and can possibly be reversed (Labouvie-Vief et al., 1974).

The evidence relating to training efforts has been reviewed by Labouvie-Vief (1977), Baltes and Willis (1981), and Denney (1981). In general, it shows rather overwhelmingly that significant performance gains can be affected, often with very minor interventions. Specific treatments have covered a great diversity of approaches, ranging from physical exercise and its hypothesized mediating effect on intellectual functioning (e.g., Barry et al., 1966; Powell, 1974) to performance factors that may be relatively extraneous yet related to cognitive performance (such as the older person's reluctance to guess, Birkhill and Schaie, 1975) or to others that are specifically aimed at highlighting task dimensions (e.g., Denney, 1974; Hornblum and Overton, 1976; Sanders et al., 1975) or that provide training in component strategies (e.g., Labouvie-Vief and Gonda, 1976; Baltes and Willis, 1981; Schultz and Hoyer, 1976; Zaks and Labouvie-Vief, 1980).

One objection often raised against such research (e.g., Donaldson, 1981; Horn and Donaldson, 1976) is that training in actuality may not modify intellectual functions per se but rather provide more extraneous assistance through motivational, social, and other supports. This differentiation between ability-specific and ability-extraneous training effects has been addressed most specifically in Baltes' and Willis' (e.g., Baltes and Willis, 1981) large-scale training project. An original study (Plemons et al., 1978) using eight training sessions and two delayed posttests after 25 days and 23 weeks demonstrated a hierarchical transfer pattern in which training effects arranged themselves in descending order of magnitude from those directly related to the training task (a sign of fluid intelligence) to ones less related. Similar effects have since been established in further studies using different target abilities (e.g., Baltes and Willis, 1981; Blieszner et al., 1981) and support the conclusion that specific cognitive plasticity does indeed seem to be apparent in later life.

A second question has been raised regarding the failure to use young control groups in this research; the argument here is that if the environmental hypothesis were true, one should not find similarly large training effects in "nondeprived" younger controls (e.g., Botwinick, 1978; Donaldson, 1981). The failure to use young controls does not, however, invalidate the plasticity hypothesis. As Baltes and Willis (1981, p. 638) point out:

> The key question in the use of younger controls in aging research is to examine what such groups can assess or control for . . . Use of younger controls can be seriously misleading in studying the range of modifiability of behavior in current older cohorts. Age differences based on cross-sectional data are indicative of a large class of life history differences, not only ability differences. Further, it is unclear whether current elderly cohorts . . . performed at comparable levels with today's youth when at a younger age . . . Assuming . . . that a younger control group would provide information about "true" age changes in ability is naive and reflects misunderstanding of the complexities involved in developmental research.

STRUCTURAL ASPECTS OF ADULT COGNITION

Much of the research and arguments so far surveyed has made it clear that descriptive aging patterns are profoundly determined by the contexts in which individuals age. We still do not know whether quantitative differences between the young and old will disappear if such differences are eliminated. Even if they do not, however, it is still not certain that some differences in the cognitive behavior of young and old are primarily a matter of deficit, since it is possible that adulthood and aging bring qualitative changes that may mimic decrements but in fact signal adaptive reorganizations.

This issue is not a novel one (see, e.g., Baltes, 1982, for a review of historical precursors). It has gained increasing importance, however, with the realization of the considerable contextual plasticity and multidirectionality of gerontological cognition. If, for example, training programs are effective, which ones ought we select? What target adaptive behaviors are we to focus on? Here, the fact that most gerontological research in cognition and intelligence is still validated by youth-oriented criteria may become extremely limiting and ethically problematic.

Thus, the issue of potential qualitative reorganizations has experienced a flurry of investigation since the first edition of this handbook. Many of these studies do raise rather cogent arguments for the continuance of structural change after youth, thereby suggesting that the processes that are primarily implicated in the acquisition of cognitive structures and functions during childhood and the early adult phase may not be the same as those involved in the maintenance and reorganization required of these structures and functions to meet the demands of later life (Flavell, 1970).

Validity Issues

The resulting issues of research validity were foreshadowed by Lorge (1936), who had already shown in the 1930s that age-comparisons between young and old adults can be manipulated to suggest increments or decrements depending upon the specific words used. Some 20 years later, Demming and Pressey (1954) demonstrated that if tests are constructed so as to tap the knowledge base relevant to mid- and later life (e.g., use of the yellow pages of a telephone directory, common legal terms, and knowledge of occupations), the usual decrements found with increasing age were reversed. More recently, Gardner and Monge (1977) have demonstrated similar, systematic age/cohort differences in familarity with specific vocabularies. Young adults, for example, were found to have more expertise in vocabularies dealing with the usual school-based forms of information. Older adults, conversely, excelled at information relating to modes of transportation, knowledge of finance management, categories of disease, etc.

Such research, however, though suggestive, is not conclusive, being based primarily on specific items of information rather than the mode by which they are organized and interrelated. A study by Kogan (1974), in turn, provides more specific evidence for structural changes. Building on previous findings (e.g., Denney, 1974; Papalia and Del Vento Bielby, 1974) that have interpreted adult age differences in classificatory behavior as indicating formal regression—the young tend to use similarity criteria based on lexical categories, whereas the old tend to use functional criteria much like those of Luria's subjects (see p. 228)—Kogan (1974) argued that a stylistic analysis of the older adults' responses failed to show any evidence of regression. In fact, he suggested that older subjects' preference for thematic groupings offered a greater imaginative scope. Hence, it is possible

> that judicious selection of tasks can yield stylistic differences between age groups that are equally adaptive for both. It is no surprise that college students should strongly favor the superordinate inferential groupings typical of high-level abstract functioning. It is doubtful, however, whether educated healthy older adults have lost the capacity for such groupings. Rather, they appear more willing to indulge an alternative mode when circumstances permit (p. 228).

In the domain of psychometric intelligence, this possibility of structural change is also suggested by findings reporting age-related changes in the number and composition of intelligence factors (e.g., Baltes et al. 1980; Reinert, 1970). Baltes et al. (1980) for example, suggest from such evidence that later life witnesses a "neointegration" of "dedifferentiation" of abilities.

Theoretical Issues

The question of whether or not adult intelligence experiences a reorganization is not solely a matter of methodology but touches on some deeper theoretical issues as well. For example, mature cognitive adaptability as exemplified in the fluid-crystallized model has often been gauged by models of inference borrowed from logical theory. Theories of formal logic, however, leave open the important issue of the relationship of such formal models to the concrete demands of adult adaptation. Thus, although the picture of intellectual maturity derived from such tests may be particularly germane in youth or in educational settings, it may lack validity when applied to more mature adults and to new, nonacademic situations.

What is this youthful image of cognitive maturity? Adolescence, according to Piaget (1972), brings about a movement from the concrete to the hypothetical, permitting young people to operate in a world of possibility rather than just presently perceived reality. The result is a high degree of flexibility. Rather than being fixed in a concrete viewpoint, youth are able to approach any subject matter from multiple perspectives. New possibilities and viewpoints alien to youth's background cannot only be comprehended, but also generated by permutation. Problems can be examined for their logical cohesiveness in a purely abstract, formal way, and personal likes and dislikes, and even pragmatic utility, can be excluded from judgment.

It is possible, however, that the ability to engage in abstraction *outside of* the context of pragmatic considerations is particularly adaptive as a trait of youth who are involved in exercising newly acquired skills. As Schaie (1977, 1978) put it, this is an acquisitive phase, a phase of taking in, a time of perfecting one's skills while reserving judgment as to their concrete value or utility, a period in which foreclosure must be avoided in order to permit the development of mature commitments.

Much as the theme of youth is flexibility, however, that of adulthood is commitment. Careers must be started, intimacy bonds formed, children raised. Here, amidst a world of a multitude of possible alternatives, there is a need to adopt *one* course of action. This conscious commitment to one pathway and the concomitant disregard of others may indeed mark the onset of adult cognitive maturity.

It is possible to suggest, therefore, that the "pure" logic of the adolescent or youth that has served as the measurement standard of all adults is based on a merely budding, but not yet mature, mode of thinking. Indeed, this is just what Piaget (1967) suggests:

> With the advent of formal intelligence, thinking takes wings and it is not surprising that at first this unexpected power is both used and abused . . . each new mental ability starts off by incorporating the world in a process of egocentric assimilation. Adolescent egocentricity is manifested by a belief in the ominpotence of reflection, as though the world should submit itself to idealistic schemes rather than to systems of reality (pp. 63–64).

and

> True adaptation to society comes automatically when the adolescent reformer attempts to put his ideas to work. Just as experience reconciles formal thought with the reality of things, so does effective and enduring work, undertaking in concrete and well-defined situations, cure dreams (pp. 68–69).

Schaie (1977, 1978) has similarly argued that the skills construed to indicate adaptive maturity may be primarily significant for childhood and youth, the tasks of which are acquisitive—i.e., aimed at an initial mastery of cultural knowledge systems. Middle and later adulthood, in turn, bring concerns that can no longer be gauged by these tasks. They are focused, instead, on issues of responsibility and stability.

Traditional concerns with responsibility and stability have often been said to be earmarks of "conservatism" and/or "rigidity" in later adulthood. Such qualities, however, may be of supreme adaptive importance. Ethologists, for example, have long pointed out that, in any species that relies on the passing of information from generation to generation, the older organism brings adaptive assets. Sometimes the exploratory behavior of the young may serve to introduce innovative technology.

Kawai's (1965) description of the acquisition by Japanese macaques of a potato washing technique is a particularly striking example. Although most of these monkeys clumsily attempted to clean sweet potatoes by wiping off the sand, a young monkey named Imo was first observed in 1953 to rinse potatoes in water. This efficient technique was quickly adopted by other monkeys. Significantly, however, it propagated along generational lines, being first picked up by age peers and then spreading more slowly to the older cohorts. In fact, only two of the eleven older monkeys had adopted it eleven years later! Similar generational propagation has also been reported by Hinde (1974) and Jolly (1972).

The adaptive significance of differential attraction to innovation is often attributed to the fact that the exploratory curiosity of the young can be detrimental to the troop since it may embrace adaptive and maladaptive techniques with undifferentiated, naive enthusiasm; the more "rigid" behavior of the older animals thus serves to select those innovations that are more likely to be adaptive. "Rigidity" may be too derogatory a term here, however; in actuality, it may reflect a degree of accumulated wisdom that increases adaptive advantages for the troop. For example, older members of a troop are often seen to serve as leaders by exerting control over exploratory behavior (Hinde, 1974; Rowell, 1966) even though they may no longer be the strongest physically. As Kummer (1971, p. 129) suggests:

> . . . there is little doubt that conservatism, too, is adaptive. The inflexible adults of the Koshima troop form a safety reservoir of the previous behavioral variant, which will survive the intervention for at least ten years. If the new behavior should turn out to be harmful, say because of parasitic infection, they would survive. In spreading new behaviors, adult rigidity has the same function as low mutation rates in evolution.

Theoretical Models

How, then, do such adaptive potentials change after youth? Perry (1968) addressed this issue in his study of college students and their encounter with (and eventual resolution of) the multiple concerns of university life. Such youth are usually searching for a single perspective on truth and are profoundly confused and troubled by the fact that no *one* correct view is apparent, whether in academic matters or in personal decisions. The role of authority, in their mind, is to offer "correct" interpretations; as a result, they often display a high dependence on authority, the role of which they view as one that will remove ambiguity. Their failure to realize that everyone ultimately must accept responsibility for his or her own thought—with no guarantees of certainty—can create a kind of obsession with finding safe techniques to secure truth.

Labouvie-Vief (1982) argues that this *intrasystemic* logical mode is but a precursor to mature cognition. In its assumption of universal truth criteria, it is a mode that displays both a profound dependence on those who define truth and a failure to differentiate between one's self and one's own thought and others and their thoughts.

This mode, in turn, gives way to a stage of *intersystemic* thought, in which the individual learns to order true and false assumptions from the perspective of multiple systems. This allowance for uncertainty, in turn, initiates a further step in which truth criteria are redefined by the individual's ability to establish new commitments out of this confrontation with multiplicity. This autonomous mode, Labouvie-Vief (1982) argues, permits, in turn, a responsible commitment to the generative tasks of participating in the construction of new systems of knowledge and to a concern with efforts that are directed at maintaining the stability of the social system. In the same vein, Gilligan (1982), Kegan (1982), Loevinger (1976), and Pascual-Leone (in press) point out that the autonomy that arises from an awareness of the genuine complexity of the social system represents a new qualitative step. However, like Labouvie-Vief (1982), all of these authors believe that the attainment of this plateau is a somewhat idealized step that may not be reached by all adults.

Empirical Research

As Schaie (1977, 1978) notes, theoretical adult stage models will demand an altogether new approach to the study of adult cognition and intelligence. If mature thinkers, as argued by Labouvie-Vief and Blanchard-Fields (1982), are apt to redefine the "space" of problems, then tasks must be designed that can assess the nature of the qualitative reorganization involved. Youth, for example, will tend to "stick with the facts" and look for "correct" solutions. For more mature adults, however, the task is inherently open-ended and ambiguous, and their approach to problems is one of isolating those dimensions that may decrease the ambiguity. The ease of working with ambiguity creatively has been noted by a number of authors as a hallmark of mature thinking (e.g., Arlin, 1983; Basseches, 1980; Labouvie-Vief and Blanchard-Fields, 1982).

As an example, consider the study by Allen (c.f. Welford, 1958) in which young and older adults were presented with logically inconsistent statements. Although the younger subjects took the information presented as given and concentrated on the analysis needed to reach conclusions, the older adults were found to focus on an analysis of the premises. They would comment on them, question them, and/or introduce supplementary premises that might resolve the logical inconsistencies. They went, then, beyond the information given and expanded upon it on the basis of their own personal experience and knowledge.

Welford concluded that this approach demonstrated a failure to comprehend material and to organize it logically, as well as a tendency to allow "interference" from one's real-world knowledge. Yet our earlier analysis would also permit another interpretation. Noting logical inconsistencies, these older adults realize that they are inconsistent only in the context of the information given and proceed to rely on the kind of information that might resolve them, thereby displaying the knowledge that logical truth cannot be ultimately separated from the truth of the premises on which it rests.

Allen's study was not directly designed to test a progressive interpretation. Somewhat more direct evidence comes, however, from a study by Sabatini and Labouvie-Vief (1979) in which elderly subjects cogently argued that they found a formal approach to problem solution unsatisfactory and oversimplified. When pressed to proceed with a formal approach nevertheless, one elderly subject commented, "I know what you want me to do, but it just isn't true," revealing his consternation at being asked to simplify what he knew to be more complex.

A similar phenomenon was reported in a study by Newman-Hornblum, Attig, and Kramer (1980) in which older adults responded to a Piagetian surface conversation task. This task presented its subjects with a green surface (a "meadow") on which miniature houses could be arranged in different ways and then asked whether the spatial arrangement of the houses would affect the amount of grass left to mow—thus, presumably, the total open surface. The older subjects did not give the "correct" solution, in terms of which the spatial arrangement of houses is not significant. Instead, they noted that mowing would be harder and take more time if the arrangement was such as to leave many small spaces between the individual houses rather than one large open space. Time, energy, and the spatial differentiation of the surface were thus seen to be critical variables, and these "practical" concerns were related to task solution. Obviously, within these pragmatic parameters the older subjects' thinking was perfectly coherent, rational, and indeed logical.

In problems designed specifically for children or adolescents, such a pragmatic mode of thinking may not, of course, strike us as particularly adaptive. In problems for others, however, an awareness of the complex embedding of logical operations in a social matrix may permit an altogether more powerful approach. This is particularly well demonstrated in Birren's (1969) analysis of the decision-making of successful career men and women in two different age groups. First, problems were defined differently by the two groups. The younger ones tended to define them from the narrow, individualistic (but, of course, stage-appropriate) perspective of their own career advancement, seizing upon an opportunity to demonstrate their competence to do a job single-handedly, even if at the cost of intellectual and work overload (and, no doubt,

occasional blunders). Two older adults, in contrast, defined the problems as one of maximizing benefits and minimizing risks for the system within which they operated. They had come to realize and admit individual restrictions in such an endeavour and relied instead on the intercoordination of experts and advisors whose pooled resources might guarantee a more stable payoff.

This more socially centered reasoning allows older adults to make use of the complex social matrix to optimize their decisions. A study by Fengler (1976) illustrates the payoffs on such an approach. In his study of 150 members of the 1973–74 Vermont legislature, he found that younger legislators produced twice as many bills as older ones, yet the likelihood of an older legislator's bill being passed was twice that of a younger legislator's bill. Thus, productivity defined by sheer quantity favored the younger legislators, whereas productivity defined by effective outcome favored the older ones. The former tended to work on a trial-and-error basis with much more risk taking, whereas the older legislators' style reflected greater caution and deliberation.

As argued by Labouvie-Vief and Blanchard-Fields (1982), modes of thinking that integrate social dimensions indeed represent a higher degree of complexity, involving as they do a knowledge of self and others as well as of the specific dimensions of a given task and requiring as they do an integration of these differing perspectives. In support of this contention, they cite several studies that demonstrate that middle-aged adults are better interpreters of conflicting information—for example, the tensions or incongruities between verbal statements and seemingly contradictory facial or gestural expressions. Shantz (1983), in turn, points out that youthful adults in such ambiguous tasks tend to rely on the linguistic information and disregard the other evidence.

Kuhn, Pennington, and Leadbeater (1983) also observed that the ability to integrate information from ambiguous and conflicting sources may increase throughout adulthood. These authors examined reasoning strategies of jurors (aged 21 to 73) on jury duty. Here, reasoning was represented by the ability to take into account all possible versions of the crime under review. Wide individual differences were observed in the ability of jurors to base their inferences on more comprehensive data, in coordinating information, and in avoiding basing their conclusions on isolated issues. This study did not make any correlations with age. Lougee and Packard (1981), however, asserted that the older adult is commonly judged to be a more competent evaluator of such social information.

Elsewhere (Labouvie-Vief, 1982), we have argued that this social integration of thinking can be viewed as a direct extension of Piaget's model of the preadolescent development of cognitive structures. The model we have proposed is akin to Piaget's model of egocentrism in spatial relations and moral behavior, in which object-derived abstract relationships must be relativized according to varying interindividual perspectives. Similarly, it is claimed that formal operations must be relativized in a parallel fashion, though at a level of higher abstraction. Thus, cognitive maturity is defined as a further structural extension in which the individual differentiates the logical algorithms first acquired relatively automatically and in restricted contexts and, by decoupling ("dissociating") them from the contexts, becomes aware of the self as an interpreter occupying but one perspective in an interpersonal space. This process of continuing differentiation, then, permits a further transcendence of egocentricity and a progressive regard for "the self" in relation to "the other."

This gradual process of differentiation was observed in a study (Labouvie-Vief, Adams, Hakim-Larson, and Hayden, 1983) involving preadolescents (age 9–10), adolescents (14–15), young adults (20–25), and mature adults (30 and over). Interpretations of ten syllogisms embedded in brief frame stories were solicited. One of the stories told of a woman who threatened to leave her drunkard husband if he came home drunk one more time. The subjects were asked what the woman would do if he then came home drunk anyway. Their answers were scored according to a five-level scheme indicating a progression from "automatic" logical responses with no awareness of other interpretations of the problem, through acknowledgements of interpretive ambiguity, to

an integration of the "logical" and contextual possibilities. The results revealed a systematic progression through these five levels with advancing age, the correlation between age and level being 0.75.

Blanchard-Fields (1983) has applied a similar scoring scheme to adolescents' and adults' integration of information from conflicting sources and reports evidence highly congruent with the preceding. Thus, the adolescents' failure to differentiate between an account and its interpretation is seen to be related to an egocentric and distorting tendency to side with just one of a variety of possible interpretations. Mature adults, in turn, clearly differentiate between an account and its interpretation and in so doing demonstrate a less egocentric and more integrated approach to information processing.

Implications

What are the implications of such reassessments for the study of intellectual processes in later life? Consider, for example, the study by Cohen (1979) in which college students and older adults were tested on the inferences to be derived from information of the sort contained in the following passage:

> Downstairs, there are three rooms: the kitchen, the dining-room, and the sitting-room. The sitting-room is in the front of the house, and the kitchen and dining-room face onto the vegetable garden at the back of the house. The noise of the traffic is very disturbing in the front rooms. Mother is in the kitchen cooking and Grandfather is reading the paper in the sitting-room. The children are at school and won't be home til tea-time.

When asked who is being disturbed by the traffic noise, college students almost invariably answer "the grandfather," thus giving evidence of having processed the logical relationships embedded in the test: that it is about midafternoon and the traffic thus likely to be noisy, especially in the front rooms, and so forth. Older adults, on the other hand, do not appear to engage in this mode of analysis and thus fail to infer that it is only the grandfather who might be disturbed.

On this basis, Cohen proposes that failures

of processing information are due to a decline in the ability to interrelate information logically, thus adhering to a major theoretical tradition according to which adulthood intellectual decline is marked by a breakdown of logical reasoning.

Is it not possible, however, that the adults in this study perceived *different* logical relationships from the ones of interest to the experimenter rather than none at all? In the study previously cited (Labouvie-Vief et al., 1983), such a hypothesis of qualitative differences in modes of logical analysis was addressed, and evidence found that it may be the case. For example, many adults might point out that the grandfather may have been deaf or that the noise may not have been disturbing at the moment in question. Indeed, some might invert the causal direction readily adopted by Cohen's college students by arguing that the grandfather could not possibly have been disturbed since, had that been the case, he would not have chosen to read in the sitting room or would have chosen to leave it.

One senses, then, a kind of psychological causality that differs from the purely formal, syllogistic causality adopted by Cohen's college students and that is not necessarily regressive. It is a causality in which the grandfather's behavior can be seen as motivated, free, and responsible, and in light of this *causality of choice,* a reason is postulated, given that he made no attempt to leave, why he should tolerate the noise if it were unbearable. From this perspective, the college students' behavior appears to reflect a degree of naively literal interpretation. Thus Labouvie-Vief and Blanchard-Fields (1982, p. 203) propose that

. . . such data reflect profoundly different interpretations of the experimental setting by the young and mature adult. College students, for example, in information processing tasks focus on an analysis of logical and semantic surface relationships of propositions explicitly contained in text. They isolate units of information *as if* they referred to abstract entities, but do not integrate them with the psychologically complex transformations they permit. Task structures are accepted at face value, performance is motivated out of compliance with authority, the search is for 'correct' solutions.

The findings and considerations outlined above, therefore, are of great significance in the context of discussions about intellectual aging. They demonstrate that what in one context appears as a high level of flexibility, in another can be characterized as maladaptive and rigid behavior. Even though stage-appropriate for the youthful adult, this behavior may in the mature and aging adult be indicative of a problematic adaptation. Thus Labouvie-Vief (in press) has summarized the data that indicates that the interpersonal egocentrism and denial of affective parameters related to the youthful mode may, if not transformed by the passage of time, lead to profoundly maladaptive outcomes. Such outcomes may maintain cognitive and adaptive rigidity, but they may also have harmful consequences on interpersonal adaptation and health. Hence, failures to transcend youthful egocentricity and proceed to a level of cognitive autonomy may, as argued by Fries (1980), come to constitute the primary variable that prevents individuals from influencing their own aging rates.

SUMMARY AND CONCLUSIONS

In sum, we have proposed in this chapter that research on aging and cognition be reinterpreted within a theoretical framework appropriate for adult adaptation. Most research on the cognitive capacities of mature and aging adults is still performed using models that address themselves to youth rather than adulthood. Thus the cognitive abilities of adults are inevitably interpreted with a regression-oriented bias.

The predominance of regression-oriented views, and, indeed, their strong logical appeal, may have resulted from a view of psychological development that largely equates maturational growth with psychological adaptation. It is no mere coincidence that most major theories of psychological development still (if only implicitly) propose a temporal parallelism between biological maturation and the emergence of psychological maturity. Yet such a "zoological" model is becoming increasingly inadequate as the partial independence of biological and cultural evolution has become increasingly stressed by biologists and social scientists alike.

In a model that stresses the importance of cultural evolution, then, adult cognitive development is seen to possess two important features. First, it profoundly mirrors aspects of the social structure and the distribution of resources and opportunities within that structure. Second, it also displays the attempts of mature adults to differentiate themselves from that structure and to define their adaptive role within it.

As a result of these further attempts at differentiation, the baseline, as it were, of adult intellectual competence will need to be redefined within criteria of successful cultural adaptation: those of responsibility and generativity. In this view, we suggest, traditional criteria of intellectual and cognitive competence may be severely restrictive and misplaced, confusing, as they do, sheer egocentric exercise of logical prowess with its measured exercise in the context of the adaptive constraints that arise out of the role of adults as the planners and caretakers of the social system.

Acknowledgement: Preparation of this chapter was supported by Research Career Development Award NIA 5K04 AG00018 to the author.

REFERENCES

Arlin, P. K. 1983. Adolescent and adult thought: A structural interpretation. In *Post-Formal Operations*, eds. N. Commons and S. Benack. New York: Praeger.

Bailey, N., and Oden, M. H. 1955. The maintenance of intellectual ability in gifted adults. *J. Gerontol.* 10: 91–107.

Bailey, N. 1970. Development of mental abilities. In *Carmichael's Manual of Child Psychology*, ed. P. H. Mussen, pp. 1163–1209. New York: Wiley.

Baltes, P. B. 1982. Developmental psychology: Observations on history and theory revisited. In *Developmental Psychology: Historical and Philosophical Perspectives*, ed. R. M. Lerner. Hillsdale, N.J.: Lawrence Erlbaum.

Baltes, M. M., and Baltes, P. B. 1977. The ecopsychological relativity and plasticity of psychological aging: Convergent perspectives of cohort effects and operant psychology. *Zeitschrift fur Experimentelle and Angewandte Psychologie* 24: 179–197.

Baltes, P. B., and Baltes, M. M. 1980. Plasticity and variability in psychological aging: Methodological and theoretical issues. In *Determining the Effects of Aging on the Nervous System*, ed. G. Gorsk. Berlin: Schering.

Baltes, P. B.; Cornelius, S. W.; Spiro, A.; Nesselroade, J. R.; and Willis, S. L. 1980. Integration versus differentiation of fluid-crystallized intelligence in old age. *Developmental Psychology* 16: 625–635.

Baltes, P. B., and Labouvie, G. V. 1973. Adult development of intellectual performance: Description, explanation, and modification. In *The Psychology of Adult Development and Aging*, eds. C. Eisdorfer and M. P. Lawton, pp. 157–219. Washington, D.C.: American Psychological Association.

Baltes, P. B., and Nesselroade, J. R. 1973. The developmental analysis of individual differences on multiple measures. In *Life-Span Developmental Psychology: Methodological Issues*, eds. J. R. Nesselroade and H. W. Reese, pp. 219–251. New York: Academic Press.

Baltes, P. B., and Schaie, K. W. 1976. On the plasticity of adult and gerontological intelligence: Where Horn and Donaldson fail. *American Psychologist* 31: 720–725.

Baltes, P. B., and Willis, S. L. 1981. Enhancement (plasticity) of intellectual functioning: Penn State's Adult Development and Enrichment Project (ADEPT). In *Aging and Cognitive Processes*, eds. F. I. M. Craik and S. E. Trehub. New York: Plenum Press.

Barry, A. J.; Steinmetz, J. R.; Page, H. F.; and Rodahl, K. 1966. The effects of physical conditioning on older individuals. II. Motor performance and cognitive function. *J. Gerontol.* 21: 182–191.

Bartlett, F. C. 1932. *Remembering.* Cambridge, England: University Press.

Basseches, M. 1980. Dialectical schemata: A framework for the empirical study of the development of dialectical thinking. *Hum. Develop.* 23: 400–421.

Bengtson, V. L. 1973. *The Social Psychology of Aging.* New York: Bobbs-Merrill.

Bennett, E. L.; Diamond, M. C.; Krech, D.; and Rosenzweig, M. R. 1964. Chemical and anatomical plasticity of brain. *Science* 146: 610–619.

Birkhill, W. R., and Schaie, K. W. 1975. The effect of differential reinforcement of cautiousness in intellectual performance among the elderly. *J. Gerontol.* 30: 578–583.

Birren, J. E., ed. 1959. *Handbook of Aging and the Individual.* Chicago: University of Chicago Press.

Birren, J. E. 1969. Age and decision strategies. *Interdisciplinary Topics in Gerontology.* Basel: Karger.

Birren, J. E. 1970. Toward an experimental psychology of aging. *American Psychologist* 25: 124–135.

Birren, J. E., and Renner, V. J. 1977. Research on the psychology of aging: Principles and experimentation. In *Handbook of the Psychology of Aging*, eds. J. E. Birren and K. W. Schaie, pp. 3–38. New York: Van Nostrand Reinhold.

Blanchard-Fields, F. 1983. The social integration of logic from adolescence to mature adulthood. Unpublished dissertation, Wayne State University.

Blieszner, R.; Willis, S.; and Baltes, P. 1981. Training research in aging on the fluid ability of inductive reasoning. *J. Appl. Develop. Psych.* In press.

Bloom, A. H. 1981. *Linguistic Shaping of Thought: Study in the Impact of Languages on Thinking in China and the West.* Hillsdale, N.J.: Lawrence Erlbaum Associates.

Boring, E. G. 1950. *A History of Experimental Psychology.* 2nd ed. New York: Appleton Century Crofts.

Botwinick, J. 1977. Intellectual Abilities. In *Handbook of the Psychology of Aging,* eds. J. E. Birren and K. W. Schaie, pp. 580–605. New York: Van Nostrand Reinhold.

Botwinick, J. 1977. *Aging and Behavior.* 2nd ed. New York: Springer.

Botwinick, J., and Siegler, I. C. 1980. Intellectual ability among the elderly: Simultaneous cross-sectional and longitudinal comparisons. *Developmental Psychology* 16: 49–53.

Braitenberg, V. 1977. *On the Texture of Brains.* New York: Springer.

Bransford, J. D., and Franks, J. J. 1971. The abstraction of linguistic ideas. *Cog. Psychol.* 2: 331–350.

Brody, H. 1955. Organization of the cerebral cortex. III. A study of aging in the human cerebral cortex. *J. Comp. Neurol.* 102: 511–556.

Brody, H. 1978. Cell counts in cerebral cortex and brainstem in Alzheimer's disease: Senile dementia and related disorders. In *Alzheimer's Disease: Senile Dementia and Related Disorders,* eds. R. Katzman, R. D. Terry, and K. L. Bick, pp. 345–351. New York: Raven Press.

Buell, S. J., and Coleman, P. D. 1979. Dendritic growth in the aged human brain and failure of growth in senile dementia. *Science* 206: 854–856.

Cattell, R. B. 1963. Theory of fluid and crystallized intelligence: A critical experiment. *J. Educ. Psychol.* 54: 1–22.

Cohen, G. 1979. Language and comprehension in old age. *Cog. Psychol.* 11: 412–429.

Cowan, W. M. 1979. The development of the brain. *Scient. Am.* 241: 113–133.

Craik, F. I. M. 1977. Age differences in human memory. In *Handbook of the Psychology of Aging,* eds. J. E. Birren and K. W. Schaie, pp. 384–420. New York: Van Nostrand Reinhold.

Cummins, R. A.; Walsh, R. N.; Budtz-Olsen, O. E.; Konstantinas, T.; and Horsfall, C. R. 1973. Environmentally induced brain changes in elderly rats. *Nature* 243: 516–518.

Cytrynbaum, S.; Blum, L.; Patrick, R.; Stein, J.; Wadner, D.; and Wilk, C. 1980. Midlife development: Personality and social systems perspective. In *Aging in the 1980s,* ed. L. Poon, pp. 463–474. Washington, D.C.: American Psychological Association.

Dekaban, A. S., and Sadowsky, D. 1978. Changes in brain weights during the span of human life: Relation of brain weights to body heights and body weights. *Ann. Neurol.* 4: 345–356.

Demming, J. A., and Pressey, S. L. 1957. Tests "indigenous" to the adult and older years. *J. Counsel. Psychol.* 4: 144–148.

Denney, N. 1974. Classification abilities in the elderly. *J. Gerontol.* 29: 309–314.

Denney, N. W. 1981. Adult cognitive development. In *Aging: Communications Processes and Disorders,* eds. D. S. Beasley and G. A. Davis, pp. 123–137. New York: Grune & Stratton.

Donaldson, G. 1981. Letter to the editor. *J. Gerontol.* 36: 634–636.

Ebbinghaus, H. 1913. *Memory.* New York: Teachers College Press. (Originally published, 1885).

Eisdorfer, C., and Wilkie, F. 1973. Intellectual changes with advancing age. In *Intellectual Functioning in Adults,* eds. L. F. Jarvik, C. Eisdorfer, and J. C. Blum, pp. 21–29. New York: Springer.

Fengler, A. P. 1976. Productivity and representation: The elderly legislator in state politics. Paper presented at the meeting of the Gerontological Society, New York.

Flavell, J. 1970. Cognitive changes in adulthood. In *Life-Span Developmental Psychology.* ed. P. B. Baltes & L. R. Goulet. New York: Academic Press.

Foster, J. C., and Taylor, G. A. 1920. The application of mental tests to persons over 50. *J. Appl. Psychol.* 4: 29–58.

Fries, J. F. 1980. Aging, natural death, and the compression of morbidity. *New Engl. J. Med.* 303: 130–135.

Fries, J. F., and Crapo, L. M. 1981. *Vitality and Aging.* San Francisco: Freeman.

Gardner, E. F., and Monge, R. H. 1977. Adult age differences in cognitive abilities and educational background. *Experimental Aging Research* 3: 337–383.

Gilligan, C. 1982. *In a Different Voice.* Cambridge, MA: Harvard University Press.

Gilligan, C., and Murphy, J. M. 1979. Development from adolescence to adulthood: The philosopher and the dilemma of the fact. In *Intellectual Development Beyond Childhood,* ed. D. Kuhn, pp. 85–99. New York: Jossey-Bass.

Gould, S. J. 1977. *Ontogeny and Phylogeny.* Cambridge, MA: Harvard University Press.

Gould, S. J. 1981. *The Mismeasure of Man.* New York: W. W. Norton.

Green, R. F. 1969. Age-intelligence relationships between ages sixteen and sixty-four: A rising trend. *Developmental Psychology* 1: 618–627.

Gribbon, K.; Schaie, K. W.; and Parham, I. A. 1980. Complexity of life style and maintenance of intellectual abilities. *Journal of Social Issues* 36: 47–61.

Hall, S. G. 1922. *Senescence: The Last Half of Life.* New York: D. Appleton & Co.

Hebb, D. 1978. On watching myself grow old. *Psychology Today* 12: 15–34.

Hinde, R. A. 1974. *Biological Bases of Human Social Behavior.* New York: McGraw-Hill.

Hooper, F.; Fitzgerald, J.; and Papalia, D. 1971. Piagetian theory and the aging process: Extensions and speculations. *Aging and Human Development,* 2: 3–20.

Hooper, F., and Sheehan, N. 1977. Logical concept attainment during the aging years: Issues in the neo-Piagetian research literature. In *Yearbook of Developmental Epistemology* I, eds. W. Overton and Gallagher, pp. 205–253. New York: Plenum Press.

Horn, J. L. 1970. Organization of data on life-span development of human abilities. In *Life-Span Developmental Psychology: Research and Theory,* eds. L. R. Goulet and P. B. Baltes, pp. 424–466. New York: Academic Press.

Horn, J. L. 1976. Human abilities: A review of research and theory in the early 1970's. *Annual Review of Psychology* 27: 437–485.

Horn, J. L., and Donaldson, G. 1976. On the myth of intellectual decline in adulthood. *American Psychologist* 31: 701–709.

Horn, J. L., and Donaldson, G. 1980. Cognitive development in adulthood. In *Constancy and Change in Human Development,* eds. O. G. Brim and J. Kagan, pp. 445–529. Cambridge, MA: Harvard University Press.

Hornblum, J. N., and Overton, W. F. 1976. Area and volume conservation among the elderly: Assessment and training. *Developmental Psychologist* 12: 68–74.

Hymes, D. 1974. Ways of speaking. In *Exploration in the Ethnography of Speaking,* eds. R. Bauman and J. Scherzer, pp. 433–451. London: Cambridge University Press.

Inhelder, B., and Piaget, J. 1958. *The Growth of Logical Thinking From Childhood to Adolescence.* New York: Basic Books.

Jarvik, L. F., and Cohen, A. 1973. A biobehavioral approach to intellectual changes with aging. In *The Psychology of Adult Development and Aging,* eds. C. Eisdorfer and M. P. Lawton, pp. 220–280. Washington, D.C.: American Psychological Association.

Jerison, H. J. 1973. *Evolution of the Brain and Intelligence.* New York: Academic Press.

Jolly, A. 1972. *The Evolution of Primate Behavior.* New York: Macmillan.

Jones, H. E. 1959. Intelligence and problem solving. In *Handbook of Aging and the Individual,* ed. J. E. Birren, pp. 700–738. Chicago: University of Chicago Press.

Kagan, J. 1981. *The Second Year: The Emergence of Self-Awareness.* Cambridge, MA: Harvard University Press.

Kamin, L. J. 1974. *The Science and Politics of IQ.* Hillsdale, NJ: Lawrence Erlbaum.

Kaszniak, A. W.; Garron, D. C.; Fox, J. H.; Bergen, D.; and Huckman, M. 1979. Cerebral atrophy, EEG slowing, age, education, and cognitive functioning in suspected dementia. *Neurology* 29: 1273–1279.

Kawai, M. 1965. Newly acquired precultural behavior of the natural troop of Japanese monkeys on Koshima Island. *Primates* 6: 1–30.

Kegan, R. 1982. *The Evolving Self.* Cambridge, MA: Harvard University Press.

Kogan, N. 1974. Categorizing and conceptualizing styles in younger and older adults. *Hum. Develop.* 17: 218–230.

Kuhn, D.; Pennington, N.; and Leadbeater, B. 1983. Adult thinking in developmental perspective. In *Life-Span Development and Behavior,* eds. P. B. Baltes and O. G. Brim, Jr. New York: Academic Press.

Kuhn, T. S. 1970. *The Structure of Scientific Revolutions.* 2nd ed. Chicago: University of Chicago Press.

Kummer, H. 1976. *Primate Societies: Group Techniques of Ecological Adaptation.* Chicago: Aldine Publishing Co.

Labouvie-Vief, G. 1977. Adult cognitive development: In search of alternative interpretations. *Merrill-Palmer Quarterly* 23: 227–263.

Labouvie-Vief, G. 1980. Beyond formal operations: Uses and limits of pure logic in life-span development. *Hum. Develop.* 23: 141–161.

Labouvie-Vief, G. 1982. Dynamic development and mature autonomy: A theoretical prologue. *Hum. Develop.* 25: 161–191.

Labouvie-Vief, G.; Adams, C.; Hakim-Larson, J.; and Hayden, M. 1983. Contexts of logic: The growth of interpretation from pre-adolescence to mature adulthood. Paper presented at the meeting of the Society for Research in Child Development, Detroit.

Labouvie-Vief, G., and Blanchard-Fields, F. 1982. Cognitive aging and psychological growth. *Ageing and Society* 2: 183–209.

Labouvie-Vief, G., and Chandler, M. J. 1978. Cognitive development and life-span developmental theory. Idealistic versus contextual perspectives. In *Life-Span Development and Behavior,* ed. P. B. Baltes, pp. 181–210. New York: Academic Press.

Labouvie-Vief, G., and Gonda, J. N. 1976. Cognitive strategy training and intellectual performance in the elderly. *J. Gerontol.* 31: 327–332.

Labouvie-Vief, G.; Hoyer, W. J.; Baltes, M. M.; and Baltes, J. B. 1974. Operant analysis of intellectual behavior in old age. *Hum. Develop.* 17: 259–272.

Langer, E., and Rodin, J. 1979. The effects of choice and enhanced personal responsibility: A field experiment in an institutional setting. *J. Pers. Soc. Psychol.* 34: 191–198.

Langer, E.; Rodin, J.; Beck, P.; Weinman, C.; and Spitzer, L. 1979. Environmental determinants of memory improvement in late adulthood. *Soc. Psychol.* 37: 2003–2013.

Leontiev, A. N. 1977. Probleme der Entwicklung des Psychischen. 2nd ed. West Germany: Fischer.

Lerner, R. M. 1981. On the nature and limits of human plasticity: Implications for intervention with children and adolescents. Paper presented at the 2nd Planning Conference on "Child Development in Life-Span Perspective," Max Planck Institute for Development and Education, Berlin.

Levinson, D. J.; Darrow, C. N.; Klein, E. B.; Levinson, M. H.; and McKee, B. 1977. *The Seasons of a Man's Life.* New York: Ballantine.

Lockett, D. W. 1980. The relationship between levels of cognitive development and ego development in adult women. Paper presented at the Sixth Biennial Southeastern Conference on Human Development, Alexandria, Va.

Loevinger, J. 1976. *Ego Development.* San Francisco: Jossey Bass.

Lorge, I. 1936. The influence of the test upon the nature of mental decline as a function of age. *J. Educ. Psychol.* 27: 100–110.

Lougee, M., and Packard, G. 1981. Conformity and perceived competence in adulthood. Paper presented at the bi-annual meeting of the Society for Research in Child Development, Boston, MA.

Luria, A. R. 1976. *Cognitive Development: Its Cultural and Social Foundations.* Cambridge, MA: Harvard University Press.

Lynch, G., and Gall, G. 1979. Organization and re-organization in the central nervous system: Evolving of brain plasticity. In *Human Growth, Vol. 3. Neurobiology and Nutrition,* eds. F. T. Falkner and J. M. Tanner. New York: Plenum Press.

MacDonald, M. L., and Butler, A. K. 1974. Reversal of helplessness: Producing walking behavior in wheel chair residents using behavior modification procedures. *J. Gerontol.* 29: 97–101.

McClelland, D. C. 1973. Testing for competence rather than for "intelligence." *American Psychologist* 28: 1–14.

Neisser, V. 1976. *Cognition and Reality.* San Francisco: W. A. Freeman.

Nesselroade, J. R.; Schaie, K. W.; and Baltes, P. B. 1972. Ontogenetic and generational components of structural and quantitative change in adult cognitive behavior. *J. Gerontol* 27: 222–228.

Newman-Hornblum, J.; Attig, M.; and Kramer, D. A. 1980. The use of sex-relevant Piagetian tasks in assessing cognitive competence among the elderly. Paper presented at the Conference of the American Psychological Association, Toronto.

Norris, J. E. 1979. Social cognition in adulthood: Perceiving the complexity of others. Paper presented at the Meeting of the Gerontological Society, Washington, D.C.

Obrist, W. D. 1978. Noninvasive studies of cerebral blood flow in aging and dementia. In *Alzheimer's Disease: Senile Dementia and Related Disorders,* eds. R. Katzman, R. D. Terry, and K. L. Bick, pp. 213–217 (Aging, vol. 7). New York: Raven Press.

Obrist, W. D.; Busse, E. W.; Eisdorfer, C.; and Kleemeier, R. W. 1962. Relation of the electroencephalogram to intellectual function in senescence. *J. Gerontol.* 17: 197–206.

Owens, W. A., Jr. 1962. Age and mental abilities: A second adult follow-up. *J. Educ. Psychol.* 51: 311–325.

Papalia, D. E., and Del Vento Bielby, D. 1974. Cognitive functioning in middle and old adults: A review of research based on Piaget's theory. *Hum. Develop.* 17: 424–443.

Pascual-Leone, J. In press. Growing to human maturity: Towards a meta-subjective theory of adulthood stages. In *Life-Span Development and Behavior,* eds. P. B. Baltes and O. G. Brim, Jr. New York: Academic Press.

Perry, W. I. 1968. *Forms of Intellectual and Ethical Development in the College Years.* New York: Holt, Rinehart, & Winston.

Piaget, J. 1967. *Six Psychological Studies.* New York: Random House.

Piaget, J. 1972. Intellectual evolution from adolescence to adulthood. *Hum. Develop.* 15: 1–12.

Plemons, J. K., Willis, S. L., and Baltes, P. B. 1978. Modifiability of fluid intelligence in aging: A short-term longitudinal training approach. *J. Gerontol.* 33: 224–231.

Powell, P. M. 1980. Advanced social role-taking and cognitive development in gifted adults. *International Journal of Aging and Human Development,* 11: 117–192.

Powell, R. R. 1974. Psychological effects of exercise therapy upon institutionalized geriatric mental patients. *J. Gerontol.* 29: 157–161.

Price, L. J.; Fein, G.; and Feinberg, I. 1980. Neuropsychological assessement of cognitive function in the elderly. In *Aging in the 1980s,* ed. L. W. Poon, pp. 78–85. Washington, D.C.: American Psychological Association.

Reinert, G. 1970. Comparative factor analytic studies of intelligence throughout the human life-span. In *Life-Span Developmental Psychology,* eds. L. R. Goulet and P. B. Baltes, pp. 467–484. New York: Academic Press.

Riegel, K. F. 1973. Dialetic operations: The final period of cognitive development. *Hum. Develop.* 16: 346–370.

Riegel, K. F. 1977. History of psychological gerontology. In *Handbook of Psychology of Aging,* eds. J. E. Birren and K. W. Schaie, pp. 70–102. New York: Van Nostrand Reinhold.

Riegel, K. F., and Riegel, R. M. 1972. Development, drop, and death. *Developmental Psychology* 6: 306–319.

Roberts, M. A., and Caird, F. L. 1976. Computerized tomography and intellectual impairment in the elderly. *J. Neurol., Neurosurg., Psychiat.* 39: 986–989.

Rosenmayr, L., and Rosenmayr, H., eds. 1978. *Der alte Mensch in der Gesellschaft.* Reinbek, West Germany: Rowohlt.

Rowell, T. 1966. Forest living baboons in Uganda. *J. Zool.* 147: 344–364.

Rosenzweig, M. R., and Bennett, E. L. 1978. Experiential influences on brain anatomy and chemistry in rodents. In *Studies on the Development of Behavior and the Nervous System,* ed. G. Gottlieb, vol. 4. New York: Academic Press.

Rubinstein, S. L. 1968. *Grundlagen der allgemeinen Psychologie.* Berlin: Volkseigener Verlag.

Ruger, H. A., and Stoessinger, B. 1927. On the growth of curves of certain characteristics in man (males). *Ann. Eugen.* 2: 76–111.

Sabatini, P., and Labouvie-Vief, G. 1979. Age and professional specialization in formal reasoning. Paper presented at the 1979 Annual Meeting of the American Gerontological Society, Washington, D.C.

Sacher, G. A. 1978. Longevity, aging, and death: An evolutionary perspective. *Gerontologist* 18: 112–120.

Sanders, J. C.; Sterns, H. L., Smith, M., and Sanders, J. E. 1975. Modification of concept identification performance in older adults. *Developmental Psychology* 11: 824–830.

Schaie, K. W. 1965. A general model for the study of developmental problems. *Psychol. Bull.* 64: 92–107.

Schaie, K. W. 1977/78. Towards a stage theory of adult development. *International Journal of Aging and Human Development* 8: 129–138.

Schaie, K. W., 1980. Intelligence and problem solving. In *Handbook of Mental Health and Aging,* eds. J. E. Birren and R. B. Sloane, pp. 262–284. Englewood Cliffs, NJ: Prentice-Hall, Inc.

Schaie, K. W., and Labouvie-Vief, G. 1974. Generational versus ontogenetic components of change in adult cognitive behavior: A fourteen-year cross sequential study. *Developmental Psychology* 10: 305–320.

Schaie, K. W., and Parham, I. A. 1977. Cohort-sequential analysis of adult intellectual development. *Developmental Psychology* 13: 649–653.

Schaie, K. W., and Strother, C. R. 1968. A cross-sectional

study of age changes in cognitive behavior. *Psychol. Bull.* 70: 671–680.

Schultz, R. 1976. Aging and control. In *Cognition and Social Behavior,* eds. J. S. Carroll and J. W. Payne. New York: John Wiley.

Schultz, R., and Brenner, G. 1977. Relocation of the aged: A review and theoretical analysis. *J. Gerontol.* 32: 323–333.

Schultz, N. R., and Hoyer, W. J. 1976. Feedback effects on spatial egocentrism in old age. *J. Gerontol.* 31: 72–75.

Scribner, S. 1979. Modes of thinking and ways of speaking: Culture and logic reconsidered. In *New Directions in Discourse Processing,* ed. R. O. Freedle, vol. 2. Norwood, NJ: Ablex.

Scribner, S., and Cole, M. 1981. *The Psychology of Literacy.* Cambridge, MA: Harvard University Press.

Shock, N. W. 1977. Biological theories of aging. In *Handbook of the Psychology of Aging,* eds. J. E. Birren and K. W. Schaie, pp. 103–115. New York: Van Nostrand Reinhold.

Selye, H. 1970. Stress and aging. *J. Am. Geriat. Soc.* 18: 660–681.

Shantz, C. U. 1983. Social cognition. In *Cognitive Development,* eds. J. H. Flavell and E. Markman. Vol. 3, *Handbook of Child Psychology,* ed. P. Mussen. 4th ed. New York: Wiley.

Terry, R. D. 1978. Aging, senile dementia, and Alzheimer's disease. In *Alzheimer's Disease: Senile Dementia and Related Disorders,* eds. R. Katzman, R. D. Terry, and K. L. Bick, pp. 11–14. New York: Raven Press.

Thompson, R. F. 1981. *The Brain.* Unpublished manuscript, Stanford University.

Tomlinson, B. E., Blessed, G., and Roth, M. 1968. Observations on the brains of nondemented old people. *J. Neurol. Sci.* 331–356.

Tomlinson-Keasey, C. 1972. Formal operations in females from eleven to fifty-four years of age. *Developmental Psychology* 6: 364.

Tuddenham, R. D. 1948. Soldier intelligence in World Wars I and II. *American Psychologist* 3: 149–159.

Vaillant, G. E. 1977. *Adaptation to Life.* Boston, MA: Little Brown.

Valenstein, E. 1981. Age-related changes in the human central nervous system. In *Aging: Communication Processes and Disorders,* eds. D. S. Beasley, and G. A. Davis, pp. 87–106. New York: Grune & Stratton.

Walsh, R. N. 1981. *Towards an Ecology of Brain.* New York: SP Medical & Scientific Books.

Walsh, R. N., and Cummins, R. A. 1977. Old brains can. Paper presented at the 6th World Congress of Psychiatry, Honolulu.

Wang, H. S. 1973. Cerebral correlates of intellectual functioning in senescence. In *Intellectual Functioning in Adults,* eds. L. F. Jarvik, C. Eisdorfer, and J. E. Blum, pp. 95–106. New York: Springer.

Wang, H. S., and Busse, E. W. 1975. Correlates of regional cerebral blood flow in elderly community residents. In *Blood Flow and Metabolism in the Brain,* eds. A. M. Harper, W. B. Jennett, J. D. Miller, and J. O. Rowan. London: Churchill Livingstone.

Wang, H. S., Obrist, W. D., and Busse, E. W. 1970. Neurophysiological correlates of the intellectual function of elderly persons living in the community. *Am. J. Psychiat.* 126: 1205–1212.

Warren, J. M.; Zerweck, C.; and Anthony, A. 1982. Effects of environmental enrichment on old mice. *Developmental Psychobiology* 15: 13–18.

Welford, A. T. 1958. *Aging and Human Skill.* London: Oxford University Press.

Wisniewski, H. M., and Terry, R. D. 1973. Morphology of the aging brain, human and animal. In *Neurobiological Aspects of Maturation and Aging,* ed. D. H. Ford. Amsterdam: Elsevier Scientific Publishing Co.

Zaks, P. M., and Labouvie-Vief, G. 1980. Spatial perspective taking and referential communication skills in the elderly: A training study. *Journal of Gerontology* 35: 217–224.

20
EMOTION AND AFFECT

Richard Schulz, Ph.D.
Department of Psychiatry
University of Pittsburgh

There is a virtually universal consensus that emotion and affect exist in human beings, that they are ubiquitous and important, and that specific emotions and affective states are easily and similarly defined by members of a culture sharing a common language. Common usage suggests that terms such as "affect" and "emotion" are used to denote personal, subjective feelings. These feelings may vary in intensity, may induce bodily state and behavior, and are thought to occur in particular situations.

When we use these terms in our daily affairs, any or all of these meanings may be implied even if not specifically stated. This lack of precision is found in more formal definitions as well, emotions sometimes being defined as a state of the organism that affects behavior or simply as a response. Thus, as a state, emotions are sometimes defined as mentalistic and other times as physiological events. Similarly, as a response, emotions are sometimes seen as physiological and other times as behavioral events (Strongman, 1978).

Although there are hundreds of studies carried out and reported each year in which emotions are either manipulated and/or measured, the subject itself is rarely addressed from an adult developmental perspective. Major textbooks on adult development and aging devote little space to it; moreover, major theories regarding the determinants of human emotions and affect (Arnold, 1970; Bindra, 1969; Cannon, 1927; Duffy, 1962; Izard, 1972; James, 1890; Lazarus, 1968; Leventhal, 1974; Lindsley, 1970; Mandler, 1976; Plutchick, 1970; Pribram, 1970; Schachter, 1972; Tomkins, 1963; Young, 1961) have little to say about emotionality through middle and old age. It is unclear whether this neglect is due to oversight, to the unavailability of the necessary data, or to the assumption that age, beyond early adulthood, is an irrelevant dimension for the understanding of emotionality. The aim of this chapter, therefore, is to focus on and synthesize the literature on emotionality and adult development.

Terms such as "mood," "emotion," and "affect" are used interchangeably by both professionals and lay persons. The first part of this chapter will concentrate on some of the semantic issues concerning their use. The second part will identify not only the major theories of emotionality but the major constructs derived from them. None of the existing theories specifically address the issue of intraindividual developmental change in emotionality. It may be possible, however, to lay the ground for predictions regarding such change by examining the social-psychological and biological changes associated with growing old in the context of these same theories. This will be a principal aim of parts three and four. The available relevant data on emotionality and aging will be examined in the fifth part, including data on both the episodic and long-term emotional responses of older persons,

531

with special emphasis being placed on the situational factors that elicit such responses as well as on the experimental attempts that have been aimed at manipulating their emotional status. An integrative summary completes this discussion.

DEFINING EMOTIONS

There are literally hundreds of descriptive terms regularly used to discuss moods and emotions, as well as dozens of instruments designed to measure a wide variety of affective states ranging from any one extreme (e.g., elation) to another (e.g., depression). From a Whorfian perspective, this richness in our language reflects the strong interest in—and importance of—this domain to our culture. From a researcher's perspective, such a large lexicon of emotion-related terms can be either an asset or a liability. On the one hand, it presents opportunities for precision and nuance; on the other, it invites confusion and obfuscation.

Since the terms "emotion," "mood," and "affect" are frequently used interchangeably, the first question to ask is whether one can distinguish between them. According to one researcher (Buss, 1973), the states signified by these terms can be differentiated on the basis of the level of arousal underlying each of them. Thus, emotions such as rage and fear occupy the extreme end of the arousal continuum, whereas states such as grief, disgust, love, and shame are characterized by more moderate degrees of arousal and should properly be called "moods" or "affective states." One critical distinguishing factor between emotions and moods, then, is level of arousal. In particular, arousal well beyond the range of normal wakefulness is believed to be crucial for the generation of emotions.

A second useful distinction between emotions and moods can be made on the basis of the localizability of their principal effects or consequences. Strong emotions result in behaviors directed at the external environment; weaker emotions or moods are more commonly "localizable within the reacting organism rather than the exteroceptive environment" (Brady, 1970, p. 70). Implicit in Brady's and Buss's discussions is the idea that emotions are relatively rare and short-lived, whereas moods and affective states are more common and longer in duration. By adding this third dimension—duration—we can differentiate not only emotions and moods but also several personality types.

The preceding analysis is illustrated in Table 1. Strong emotions are defined as involving extreme levels of arousal, they are likely to alter the organism's relationship to the environment, and they are brief in duration. Moods or affective states are characterized by moderate levels of arousal, their effects are localizable primarily within the individual, and they are of moderate time duration. Finally, certain affective disorders (e.g., dysthymic disorder or depressive neurosis) have all the characteristics of affective states except that they are longer lasting. Thus, when we talk about an individual being in a bad mood, it is with the expectation that the mood will

TABLE 1. Dimensions Used To Differentiate Emotions, Moods, And Personality Types

	Dimensions		
Affective Category	Intensity of Arousal	Primary Locus of Effects	Duration
Strong emotions	High	Emotions	Short (e.g., minutes)
Moderate emotions, moods	Moderate	Individual	Moderate (e.g., hours, days)
Affective disorders	Moderate	Individual	Long (e.g., years)

change at some time; when we say that an individual is a depressive type, we are suggesting that change is unlikely.

Thus far we have tried to draw some theoretical distinctions between several emotion-related terms without attempting to isolate and define the many specific, qualitatively different types of emotions commonly experienced. Two approaches have been taken to the latter task. One claims the existence of six to twelve independent monopolar factors, such as sadness, anxiety, anger, elation, and so forth. Tomkins (Tomkins and McCarter, 1964) is representative of this approach, claiming the existence of eight primary "affects": interest, enjoyment, surprise, distress, fear, shame, contempt, and rage.

A second perspective is provided by those (e.g., Frijda, 1969; Schlosberg, 1952) who claim that emotions do not exist as discrete entities but are instead related to each other in a highly systematic fashion. A current advocate of this view is Russell (1980), who asserts that emotions are organized in accordance with two dimensions, pleasure–displeasure and degree of arousal. His circumplex model (see Fig. 1) provides a structure of affective expression as assessed through self-report and as a representation of the cognitive structure that lay persons use to conceptualize emotions.

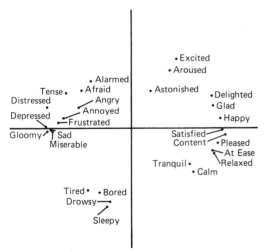

Figure 1.   Two principal components of twenty-eight assent words based on self-report data. (*From Russell, 1980.*)

The "lay person" in Russell's research, as in most studies on emotions, is the ubiquitous college student. Whether older adults would yield factor structures similar to those reported by Russell is an empirical question in need of further study. Indeed, this represents only one of several important questions one might ask concerning emotions and affect when viewed from an adult developmental perspective. A more complete list of questions might be posed as follows:

1. *Intensity.* Is the intensity of emotional experiences stronger or weaker among the aged than it is among the young? One of the popular stereotypes of the aged suggests that, while they experience emotions, the intensity of their feelings is subdued relative to that of younger cohorts. For example, the aged are often thought of as being happy but rarely as elated.

2. *Duration.* Once an emotional experience is instigated, do older persons experience a longer or shorter duration of that emotion? Is it more difficult for an aged individual to return to a neutral baseline?

3. *Variability.* Do the aged show less day-to-day or same-day variability in emotional states? Implicit in the popular view of the aged as more rigid than the young is the idea that they have reduced lability, that they are more set in their ways, and that they are therefore less likely to experience mood swings.

4. *Frequency.* Are particular types of emotional experiences more or less frequent among the aged? Another stereotype of the aged suggests that negative affective states are more common among the aged than the young. Are there data to support this belief?

5. *Quality.* Are there qualitative differences in the experience of specific emotional states among the aged? For example, is an emotion such as love a qualitatively different experience for the aged than for the young?

6. *Elicitors, instigators.* Do the types of events that elicit emotional experiences

change with age? What are the attributes of the instigators of emotional experiences for the aged?

Information concerning each of these questions will be presented here. A prerequisite to any attempt at answering them, however, is an understanding of (1) the biological and social-psychological changes that occur with age and their likely impact on the organism's ability to experience affect, and (2) the theories regarding the determinants of emotions. If we believe, for example, that emotions are largely physiologically determined, and we know that there are relevant physical changes associated with age, then age differences in the intensity of emotions may be largely attributable to biological aging. In contrast, we might find that the aged are exposed to particular environmental events that precipitate a characteristic set of emotional or affective reactions that differentiate them from younger people.

THEORIES OF EMOTION

The goal of a theory of emotion is to integrate three of its identifiable components. One component concerns the motor behavior associated with emotions (What is expressed?), the second concerns the experiential aspect (What is felt?), and the third concerns the underlying central and peripheral physiological mechanisms (What happens inside the body?). Each of these components receives some attention in all existing theories, although the emphasis varies.

Many theories have been advanced. If we restrict our attention to formal theories proposed in the last 100 years, we can identify at least four general perspectives and as many as thirty individual theories. The early period begins with the James/Lange theory (James, 1884; Lange, 1885) and includes several alternative theories later proposed by Cannon (1927), McDougall (1923), Watson (1929), and Papez (1937). From an historical point of view, these five theorists represent the classic tradition in theory development. A second group of theories represented by the work of Duffy (1962), Lindsley (1970), Young (1964), and Bindra (1969) is strongly focused on moti-

vation and arousal as explanatory mechanisms for the emotions. This group also distinguishes itself from others in that it favors the use, whether explicit or implicit, of concepts—such as arousal, etc.—thought to be scientifically less vague and hence more useful than that of emotion.

Behavioral theories of emotion have their origin in the work of Watson (1929) and are represented by advocates such as Harlow and Stagner (1933), Millenson (1967), and Gray (1971). The psychoanalytic and phenomenological tradition is represented by the work of Rapaport (1950), Hillman (1960), and Sartre (1948). Theories emphasizing cognitive approaches to emotion have been proposed by Bull (1951), Siminov (1970), Leventhal (1974), Schachter (1972), Arnold (1970), and Lazarus (1968). A sociological perspective can also be discerned. The emphasis here is on the cultural conditions that affect both the experience and expression of emotions (e.g., Kemper, 1978; Shott, 1979).

Finally, there is the "grand approach" (Strongman, 1971) to the study of emotion, exemplified by a small group of individuals who have attempted to develop comprehensive, all-embracing theories. Included among this group are individuals such as Leeper (1948), Pribram (1970), Plutchick (1970), Tomkins (1962, 1963), Mandler (1976), and Izard (1972). It would obviously require far too much space to discuss in detail the many theories of emotionality currently available (see Strongman, 1978, for a detailed discussion of each of these theories). Instead, summaries are presented here of those theoretical constructs likely to be important from an adult developmental perspective.

Physiology

All theories of emotionality include the idea that the activation of physiological systems is correlated with emotional experiences. There is general consensus that both parasympathetic and sympathetic systems are involved, that the limbic system and reticular formation play an important role, and that to the extent that cognitive processes are thought to mediate emotional experiences, those structures of the brain that serve processing, learning, and memory functions must also be included. In short, there is little of the central nervous system that does not play a part. From the perspective of an aging organism, the important question to be answered, therefore, is whether there are structural and functional age changes in the central nervous system that might systematically affect the individual's experience of emotions.

Adaptation

A second common characteristic of all theories of emotion is the concept of an adaptation level or some relatively neutral background against which deviations manifest themselves. Adaptation can be specified as a physiological and/or cognitive state, with the emphasis on one or the other varying, depending on the particular theorist. Because the adaptation level of an organism is largely a function of prior input and because the aged have by definition a longer history of prior experiences, this factor is likely to play an important part in our efforts to understand emotionality in the aged.

Instigators

How is an emotional experience instigated, and how does it come to be defined as a particular emotional state? The answer to these questions constitutes the heart of most theories of emotionality. In many cases, the instigating event is also the defining event. For example, Kemper (1978) suggests that a socially related event such as loss of power not only instigates an emotional experience, but also defines the particular emotion (e.g., fear) elicited. For other theorists (Schachter and Singer, 1962), a two-stage process is suggested that begins with the perception of sympathetic arousal and is then followed by a search for an appropriate explanation in the physical and social environment.

Instigating events can also be described in varying degrees of abstractness. At one extreme, we have concrete interpersonal events that can perturb the system (e.g., Kemper), whereas at the other, the density of neural firing elicited by external events is identified as the instigator of particular emotional experiences (e.g., Tomkins). Somewhere in between lie the appraisal mechanisms identified by Pribram and Melges (1967); these activate processes that either bring the system back to baseline (preparatory processes) or that accommodate the system to the perturbing input (participatory processes). Perhaps these different perspectives could be integrated if we took the point of view that different theorists are focusing on different facets of the input continuum.

Emotion and Motivation

This topic is discussed in detail by several theorists (e.g., Solomon and Corbit, 1974; Pribram and Melges, 1967; Tomkins, 1970). For the purposes of this discussion, it should suffice to point out that in none of the theories of emotionality are human organisms viewed as passive receptacles of emotional experiences. Emotional experiences are actively constructed via interpretive and appraisal processes, and certain emotional experiences are actively sought out whereas others are avoided (Lazarus, 1975). It is perhaps a truism, but most persons prefer to feel good and avoid feeling bad, and much of human behavior can be explained as serving those ends.

Emotion and Control

A persistent theme in several of the theories discussed is the idea that control plays an important part in determining emotional experiences (Pribram and Melges, 1967; Tomkins, 1967; Tomkins, 1970; Kemper, 1978). If we accept the basic premise that most persons desire to maximize positive feelings and minimize negative feelings, then each of these theories suggests means for achieving this goal. In each case, it is achieved by exercising control, whether over social interactions or the rate of stimulation. It follows, therefore, that the degree to which individuals feel capable of controlling the density of stimulation (Tomkins, 1970), assimilability of stimulus input (Pribram and Melges, 1967), and/or the outcomes of social interactions (Kemper, 1978), the more likely they are to experience positive as opposed to negative emotions.

EMOTION AND BIOLOGICAL AGING

No one would deny the fact that important, clearly perceivable physical changes occur as humans age and, moreover, that there are profound although less detectable changes that occur beneath the skin, particularly in the central nervous system. The observable structural and metabolic functional changes within the central nervous system are described in detail by Brody and Vijayashankar (1977), Bondareff (1980), and Adams (1980). Some of the more significant changes include the loss of neurons and synapses, atrophy of dendrites, accumulation of lipofuscin in the cytoplasm of neurons, and the appearance of neurofibrillary tangles and senile plaques. The production of neurotransmitters also seems to be affected. Research carried out with animals indicates that the quantity of catecholamine, indoleamine, as well as norepinephrine, dopamine, and serotonin are decreased in the senescent brain (Bondareff, 1980).

For the purposes of this discussion, the important question is whether there are functional or behavioral consequences of these age-related changes. Many changes in the structure and composition of the brain do not have clearly identifiable behavioral correlates; however, it is generally believed that certain neuronal changes are correlated with the appearance of specific behavioral symptomatology (such as those associated with dementia). Moreover, the high rates of depression observed in the aged may be attributable to reduced levels of noradrenaline and/or serotonin. McGeer and McGeer (1980, p. 26), for example, "speculate that the imbalance in neurotransmitter systems may not only account for the shuffling gait, tardy movement initiation, and rapid fatiguing seen in the elderly but possibly also for changes in sexual function, sleep disturbances, and the increasing frequency of depressive illness."

Another functional consequence of aging is the reduction in the regulatory effectiveness of the central nervous system. The heart of this system, the hypothalamus, is more sensitive in older than younger organisms to direct injections of certain substances such as catecholamines but less sensitive to endogenous peripheral hormonal substances (Renner and Birren, 1980). This susceptibility may contribute to the slower responding of the organism to external stressors as well as to the reduced reliability of the homeostatic mechanisms in general (Wigdor, 1980). In particular, it appears that once an aged system is activated, it is more prone to overactivity (Welford, 1980) and exhibits a decreased ability to return to baseline. According to Kaack, Ordy, and Trapp (1975), decreasing homeostatic adaptation to environmental challenges is one of the most fundamental manifestations of aging.

In sum, current data on age-related biological changes suggest that the aged, when compared to the young, reach higher levels of arousal when confronted with novel stress-inducing situations and may require more time to return to baseline once aroused. Applied to emotionality, the latter two points suggest that the intensity and duration of certain emotional experiences may increase with age.

COGNITIVE CHANGES

One universal characteristic of aging is the accumulation of a large number of experiences, many of which are stored in long-term memory. Since emotional experiences are frequently some of the most salient of these, it is likely that they also become some of the most memorable (Schonfield, 1980). They very likely provide the context against which any new emotion-related events are evaluated.

The accumulated store of emotion-related experiences may affect future emotional experiences in two ways. First, other things remaining constant, the greater the number and variety of stored emotional experiences, the higher the adaptation level for similar emotion-arousing events (Tomkins, 1962). This reasoning would suggest, for example, that the threshold for falling in love the second time is a little higher than it is the first time.

A second and related consequence is that emotions become first more differentiated and then more mixed with age. From a developmental perspective, it is probably true that a few general affective states become differentiated into several specific identifiable emotions. For example, research carried out by Bridges (1932) suggests that infants evolve from a state of being able to experience unpleasant and pleasant states to one where, later in childhood and early adulthood, they are able to differentiate approximately nine different emotional experiences. In addition, there is a growing body of recent research indicating that emotions are rarely experienced as discrete, pure states by adults (Polivy, 1981). Any given experience is likely to elicit not just a single emotional response but several related emotions as well. For example, laboratory inductions aimed at making an individual feel depressed also frequently elicit high levels of anxiety and hostility (Polivy, 1981). The negative emotions of hostility, depression, and anxiety especially appear to co-vary. They may be triggered sequentially or simultaneously.

These cognitive changes have particular relevance for the aged. First, if the types of experiences encountered during old age are essentially similar to those stored in long-term memory, their impact is likely to be relatively low because of changing adaptation levels. Second, it is likely that events that elicited predominantly positive emotions in the past acquire negative loadings over time and events that elicited predominantly negative emotions in the past acquire positive loadings over time. This idea is reflected in the popular notion that, with increasing age, persons increasingly see the bad side of good things and the good side of bad things. In sum, this reasoning suggests that there may be a decrease in the frequency of emotional experiences associated with age but that the proportion of positive and negative feelings remain roughly the same over time.

Alternatively, it can be argued that the aged are exposed to a class of new emotion-arousing events that can be broadly identified as losses (e.g., a loss of spouse, a health crisis, a decrease in physical mobility). Such events, in part because of their novelty, are likely to elicit immediate, intense, and long-lasting emotional responses that are generally negative in character. Given this greater predominance of objectively negative events experienced by older persons, one would expect a higher incidence of negative affective states among the old than the young. Put another way, as one grows older, the number of new positive events decreases while the number of new negative events either stays the same or increases. Moreover, since the adaptation level for familiar positive events is likely to be higher than that for unfamiliar negative events, the net impact of positive and negative events for the aged is likely to be weighted on the negative side.

Another line of reasoning, based on theories of emotionality, leads to a similar conclusion. It was pointed out earlier that the degree to which individuals feel capable of controlling the density and/or the assimilability of stimulus input, and/or the outcomes of social interactions, they are more likely to experience positive as opposed to negative emotions. However, the ability of older persons to control these factors is reduced for a variety of reasons, including decreased physical and cognitive capacity as well as the dimunition of available resources. This impairment again suggests an increase in negative emotional experiences with age.

These converging lines of thought might lead one to the conclusion that human aging should be associated with a steady increase in negative affect. Some support for this notion is found in the relatively high rates of depression among the aged. Nevertheless, the majority of the data indicate that most old persons are not particularly depressed, angry, or afraid most of the time. In fact, it would be difficult to argue that the aged as a group evidence any more negative affect than do younger persons (Cameron, 1975).

A partial solution to this puzzle can perhaps be found if we ask the question, How do persons determine how they feel? What is the process individuals go through to arrive at either a negative, positive, or neutral affective state? We have already rejected the idea that emotions are determined exclusively by internal physiological responses and have stressed the importance of context—viewed as both an immediate situation and an individual's cognitions about that situation—as a vital contributor to that individual's affective state. An elaboration and some slight alteration of these ideas may provide an answer to the puzzle.

With the possible exception of extreme cases, how we respond to a wide array of stimuli, particularly social stimuli, is not a function of absolute levels of input but rather a function of the discrepancy between expected and actual levels of input (Thomae, 1980). Expectations may be based on a composite or average of similar past encounters, as adaptation level theory would suggest, or on standards currently existing within a society or a subgroup of society.

Put another way, individuals can make *historical* or *temporal* comparisons based on similar events in their past and/or *contemporary* comparisons by noting how relevant others react to similar situations. Regardless of the source of these expectations or standards, any time the outcomes fall short of what is expected, negative affective experiences should result, whereas outcomes that exceed expectations should result in positive affect.

The important question with respect to the aged, then, is the types of comparisons (temporal or contemporary) they make when evaluating their outcomes. Or, put another way, what is the source of their expectations? The answer to this question, as we shall see, has important implications for their general emotional status.

Given the many real declines associated with the onset of old age (e.g., declines in physical and cognitive ability or economic resources), comparisons based on the past are likely to yield negative discrepancies and hence negative affective states. Thus, individuals who compare present events and circumstances with past abilities, accomplishments, and outcomes are likely to encounter many negative discrepancies. On the other hand, those who use a contemporary context to evaluate their outcomes are less likely to encounter such discrepancies and hence negative affective states.

As an example, consider institutionalized older persons and the types of events they are likely to encounter. Clearly, if they compare past housing conditions, leisure activities, physical mobility, and daily events in general with present conditions, they are likely to experience negative affect. However, if they base their comparison on the outcomes of similar individuals in their immediate environment (other institutionalized old persons), there will be less likelihood of experiencing negative discrepancies.

In sum, two sets of opposing mechanisms can be identified as important determinants of the emotional status of the aged. Absolute changes in the adaptation level for positive events, the increased probability of novel negative events, and the decreased ability to control external events should all contribute to an increased incidence of negative affect. Counteracting these mechanisms are changes in the individual's reference groups and expectation levels. Although there are few data that bear on this analysis, it is anticipated that the two mechanisms in conjunction tend to promote stability over time in the emotional status of aging individuals.

THE DATA: EVIDENCE ON AFFECT AND EMOTION IN THE AGED

Much of the discussion thus far has focused on theories of emotion and speculation about their relevance to the aged, thereby providing a point of departure for the final portion of this chapter, which will concentrate on the available data regarding mood, emotionality, and aging.

Four types of data will be discussed: (1) data on personality changes characteristically associated with growing old; (2) evidence on common emotional problems of the aged; (3) determinants of mood and emotion in the aged primarily in terms of their contextual correlates; and (4) data from several field experiments in which mood states of the aged were altered as byproducts of interventions aimed at increasing their level of competence and their ability to control and predict their environment.

Personality Changes and Aging

Are there characteristic personality changes associated with growing old? This question can be answered at several levels. From the theoretical perspective of psychoanalysis or ego psychologists (e.g., Buhler, 1959; Erikson,

1959; Jung, 1933), the answer is a decided yes. There is some agreement among most of these theorists that introversion increases in middle and later life. A contrasting view is presented by a variety of social psychologists, symbolic interactionists, and role theorists, who emphasize the situational or environmental determinants of dispositional characteristics and play down the internal or intrapersonal changes associated with aging. Even representatives of the latter group would agree, however, that there are important changes correlated with age. Their argument is over the ultimate cause of those changes rather than their presence or absence.

Many cross-sectional and several longitudinal studies could be cited (see Neugarten, 1977, and Thomae, 1980, for reviews) in support of or against the notion that personalities undergo changes with age. The findings from these studies are largely inconclusive, primarily because of the many different measurement instruments used and the large variety of populations sampled. One generalization can be made from this work, however, namely that persons exhibit relative stability over time in major personality traits such as anxiety, openness, and extraversion (Costa and McCrae, 1980). Data have been reported for other traits, but they are at best suggestive; older individuals, for example, may be higher in rigidity and control and lower in impulsivity, activity, heterosexuality, and need for achievement (Fozard and Thomas, 1975).

Long-Term Emotional Problems of the Aged

The most common affective disturbance of late life is depression. Although the reported incidence and prevalence rates vary widely, depending on the criteria used, it is estimated that between 21 and 54 percent of all geriatric admissions to hospitals are diagnosed as depressed. Among nonpatient populations, it is estimated that between 2 and 10 percent of the elderly warrant a clinical diagnosis of depression (Zarit, 1980). Indeed, some researchers have noted the many behavioral similarities between the depressed and the elderly in general (e.g., Lewinsohn, 1974). On the posi-

tive side, the elderly depressed patient does appear to have a relatively good prognosis.

A second common response among the aged to traumatic events, such as the loss of a loved one, is frequently referred to as adjustment reaction of late life. It is characterized by a variety of emotional and physical disturbances, the most prominent of which is anxiety. "Fear sometimes to the point of panic, perplexity, emotional lability, tearfulness, and feelings of helplessness dominate the psychological symptomology" (Pfeiffer, 1977, p. 658).

Affect and Mood in the Aged

Data bearing on affect and mood are less available than data on extreme emotional states, although items that reflect mood are frequently found in life satisfaction and morale scales. Of those studies assessing mood directly (Bradburn and Caplowitz, 1965; Gurin et al., 1968), Cameron's (1975) is probably the most extensive and carefully executed. Mood states of 6,452 persons aged 4 to 99 were assessed in four different situations: leisure, home, school, and work. Social class, sex, and situational differences in mood were found but no significant age differences were discovered. The frequency of happy, sad, and neutral moods were identical among the young and old.

The second major source of mood data consists of the numerous studies assessing life satisfaction, morale, and happiness. Life satisfaction is typically viewed as an assessment of "life in general" or "life as a whole," always using a long-term referent. The meaning of morale is more ambiguous. As George (1981) points out, some conceptualize morale in terms of affect; others, as a cognitive assessment of life quality. Cross-cutting this distinction is another based on the time referent. Sometimes morale is viewed as a stable personal attribute; other times, as a transitory mood state. The conceptualization of happiness is simple by comparison. It is viewed as an affective assessment of subjective life quality and usually has a short-term time referent (George, 1981).

The centrality of emotions or affect to subjective well-being is further substantiated by a factor analysis of well-being scales. Such an analysis repeatedly yields three factors: cognitive evaluation, positive affect, and negative affect (George, 1981).

Are there age-related differences in well-being? Larson (1978) found that subjective well-being was most strongly related to health, followed by socio-economic status, degree of social interaction, marital status, housing, and availability of transportation. No differences in subjective well-being were found as a function of age. George (1981) in her review of this literature is more tentative: "Currently we do not know whether life satisfaction, happiness, morale, and psychological distress exhibit consistent, identifiable age changes over the life course" (p. 377). This picture is further complicated by the findings of Campbell, Converse, and Rodgers (1976) who report that older people are less likely than younger people to describe themselves as "very happy" but are more likely to report a higher level of overall life satisfaction.

Experimental Data

Experimental research has long been a tradition in adult development and aging, although its main focus has been on biological processes and sensory and cognitive abilities. Experimental research on social-psychological aspects of aging is still relatively rare, and studies of affect and emotions are almost nonexistent. Nevertheless, some data on the affective consequences of a variety of experimental interventions are now available. In particular, a growing body of research demonstrating the impact of social-psychological variables on the health and psychological status of the aged has coincidentally yielded some important findings regarding affect and emotions.

The underlying premise for much of the existing research (Schulz and Hanusa, 1980) is that aging is characterized by many losses, the combined impact of which is to induce feelings of lack of control and helplessness. Several studies have been aimed at showing that giving aged individuals increased control over, and responsibility for, important out-

comes has positive effects on their well-being (see Schulz and Hanusa, 1980, for a review). In these studies, affective states were also altered by these interventions. Schulz (1976), for example, found that levels of happiness, hope, and "zest for life" were significantly higher and depression lower among individuals who were given control over an important event.

These data might lead one to the conclusion that affective states are directly related to absolute levels of control and hence to the argument that the aged, since they experience absolute declines in their ability to control important outcomes, should exhibit more negative affect than younger cohorts. This may be true for individuals occupying the extreme ends of the control continuum, but for those individuals occupying the middle range of this continuum, affective responses should be the result of relative changes occurring over a short period of time rather than of absolute levels of control. Put another way, what we are suggesting is that individuals have expectations for controlling outcomes largely determined by their own reference group. It is likely that, just as absolute levels of control decline with age, so do the expectations for control, and it is only when the level of available control diverges from expected levels that positive or negative affect result.

CONCLUSION

Our discussion began with a list of questions concerning aging and emotionality. Our attempt to find answers has led us through a diverse literature spanning numerous disciplines including psychology, sociology, biology, and neurophysiology. It is appropriate now to return to those questions to summarize what we know and still need to know.

1. *Is the intensity of emotional experiences stronger or weaker among the aged when compared to that of the young?* The physiological data indicating a tendency toward over-activity of the central nervous system as well as higher levels of arousal would suggest that the aged experience emotions at least as intense as

those of younger cohorts. The reduced coping capacity attributed to the aged also suggests that intensity, at least with respect to negative emotions, does not decrease with age.

2. *Does the duration of emotional experiences vary with age?* Here again, age-related physiological changes in the central nervous system suggest that once a strong emotion is instigated, it may take longer for an older person to return to baseline. This view is supported by the fact that the aged exhibit decreased homeostatic adaptation capacities.

3. *Do the aged show less variability in emotional states?* The decrease in homeostatic adaptation capacities in the aged also suggests that variability in emotional states, at least in the short run (e.g., same-day), is reduced. Little is known about the day-to-day variability of these states among different age groups.

4. *Are particular types of emotional experiences more or less frequent among the aged?* Given the increased number of novel and negative events (e.g., loss of spouse, health crisis, loss of mobility) that are associated with increased age and the higher adaptation level for positive events, one would expect a higher incidence of negative emotional states and a lower incidence of positive ones among the aged. It has also been pointed out that the aged have decreased instrumental control over their environment. Together, these processes suggest that human aging may be associated with increased negative affect. Counteracting these mechanisms, however, are changes in individual expectations of probable negative events and of the ability to control environmental events. The net impact of these opposing forces may be to promote stability over time in the emotional status of the aging individual. Some existing data, however, suggest that the frequency with which older persons are happy is reduced.

5. *Are there qualitative differences in the experience of specific emotional states among the aged?* It is likely that emotional responses become less unidimensional with age. Events that elicited predominantly positive emotions in the past acquire negative associations over time, and vice versa. Emotions such as those aroused by love, for example, may be less euphoric and become a little more bittersweet the second, third or fourth time around.

6. *Do the types of events that elicit emotional experiences change with age?* The answer to this question is affirmative. We have already indicated that identical events may elicit different emotions over time. In addition, changes in adaptation levels as well as in expectancies suggest that types of eliciting events change with age. In general, to the extent that aging is correlated with changes in social context, the types of eliciting events are likely to change as well.

This chapter represents only the tip of the iceberg in terms of what might be examined in a discussion of emotionality and aging. We have identified many questions and have provided a few speculative answers. Since issues of emotionality and affect are central to the study of aging, they deserve a direct assault by researchers and theoreticians in addition to the incidental consideration they already receive in the context of research on stress and well-being.

Unfortunately, certain inherent methodological difficulties arise in attempting to answer even the most basic questions concerning emotionality and aging. For example, although it is possible to describe age differences in, say, the intensity of emotional responses, it is much more difficult to identify the underlying cause of these differences. As in other domains of adult development, the demonstration of age changes in emotionality requires the ability to untangle cohort and time-of-measurement effects from ontogenetic change. This problem is further compounded by the fact that each of these potential contributors to observed differences may exert their influence at any one of several stages in the process that culminates in an emotional experience. They may affect the way a stimulus is perceived and processed; they may affect the way it is experienced; and finally, they may determine whether an emotion is expressed or not, and how.

These problems present formidable but not impossible challenges. We have available to us ever more powerful research methodologies (e.g., Nesselroade and Baltes, 1979) and analytical talents that will allow us to break down this topic into manageable units. The reward for our efforts will be a very fundamental understanding of human development.

REFERENCES

Adams, L. 1969. Analysis of life satisfaction index. *Journal of Gerontology.* 24: 470–474.

Adams, R. D. 1980. The morphological aspects of aging in the human nervous system. In *Handbook of mental health and aging,* eds. J. E. Birren and R. B. Sloane. Englewood Cliffs, N.J.: Prentice-Hall.

Arnold, M. B. 1970. *Feelings and emotions: The Loyola Symposium.* New York: Academic Press.

Bindra, D. 1969. A unified interpretation of emotion and motivation. *Ann. New York. Acad. Sci.* 159: 1071–1083.

Birren, J. E., and Schaie, K. W., eds. 1977. *Handbook of the psychology of aging.* New York: Van Nostrand Reinhold.

Bondareff, W. 1980. Neurobiology of aging. In *Handbook of mental health and aging,* eds. J. E. Birren and R. B. Sloane. Englewood Cliffs, N.J.: Prentice-Hall.

Bradburn, N., and Caplowitz,D. 1965. *Report on happiness.* Aldine, Chicago.

Brady, J. V. 1970. Emotion: Some conceptual problems and psychological experiments. In *Feelings and emotions,* ed. M. B. Arnold. New York: Academic Press.

Bridges, K. M. B. 1932. Emotional development in early infancy. *Child Development* 3: 324–341.

Brody, H., and Vijayashankar, N. 1977. Anatomical changes in the nervous system. In *Handbook of the biology of aging,* eds. C. E. Finch and L. Hayflick. New York: Van Nostrand Reinhold.

Buhler, C. 1959. *Der Menschliche Lebenslauf als Psychologisches Problem.* 2nd ed. Gottingen, West Germany: Hogrefe.

Bull, N. 1951. The attitude theory of emotion. *Nerv. Ment. Dis. Monogr.* No. 81.

Buss, A. 1973. *Psychology: Man in perspective.* New York: John Wiley & Sons.

Cameron, P. 1975. Mood as an indicant of happiness: Age, sex, social class and situational differences. *Journal of Gerontology* 30: 216–224.

Campbell, W.; Converse, P. E.; and Rodgers, W. L. 1976. *The quality of American life.* New York: Russell Sage Foundation.

Cannon, W. B. 1927. The James-Lange theory of emotions: A critical examination and an alternative theory. *American Journal of Psychology* 39: 106–124.

Costa, P. T. Jr., and McCrae, R. R. 1980. Still stable after all these years: Personality as a key to some issues in adulthood and old age. In *Life span development and behavior,* vol. 3, eds. P. B. Baltes and O. G. Brim, Jr. New York: Academic Press.

Duffy, E. 1962. *Activities and behaviour.* New York: Wiley.

Erikson, E. R. 1959. *Identity and life cycle. Psychological issues I.* New York: International Universities Press.

Fozard, J. L., and Thomas, J. C. 1975. Psychology of aging. In *Modern perspectives in the psychiatry of old age,* ed. J. G. Howell. New York: Bruner/Mazel.

Frijda, N. H. 1969. Recognition of emotion. In *Advances in Experimental Social Psychology,* vol. 4, ed. L. Berkowitz pp. 167–223.

George, L. K. 1981. Subjective well-being: Conceptual and methodological issues. In *Annual review of gerontology and geriatrics,* vol. 2, ed. C. Eisdorfer. New York: Springer.

Gray, J. A. 1971. *The psychology of fear and stress.* London: Weidenfeld and Nicolson.

Gurin, G.; Veroff, J.; and Feld, S. 1968. *Americans view their mental health.* New York: Basic Books.

Harlow, H. F., and Stagner, R. 1933. Psychology of feelings and emotions. II. Theory of emotions. *Psychological Review,* 40: 184–194.

Hillman, J. 1968. *Emotion.* London: Routledge and Kegan Paul.

Izard, C. E. 1972. *The face of emotion.* New York: Appleton-Century-Crofts.

James, W. 1884. What is an emotion? *Mind* 9: 188–205.

James, W. 1890. *The principles of psychology.* New York: Henry Holt.

Jung, C. C. 1933. *Modern man in search of a soul.* New York: Harcourt, Brace, and World.

Kaack, B.; Ordy, J.; and Trapp, B. 1975. Changes in limbic, neuropendocrine and autonomic systems, adaptation, homeostasis during aging. In *Neurobiology of aging,* eds. J. Ordy and K. Brizzee. New York: Plenum Press.

Kemper, T. D. 1978. *A social interactional theory of emotions.* New York: John Wiley and Sons.

Lange, C. G. 1885. *The emotions.* Baltimore: Williams and Wilkins.

Larson, R. 1978. Thirty years of research on the subjective well-being of older Americans. *Journal of Gerontology* 33: 109–125.

Lawton, M. P. 1972. The dimensions of morale. In *Research, planning and action for the elderly,* eds. D. Kent, R. Kastenbaum, and S. Sherwood. New York: Behavioral Publ.

Lazarus, R. S. 1968. Emotions and adaptation: Conceptual and empirical relations. In *Nebraska symposium on motivation,* ed. W. J. Arnold. Lincoln, Nebraska: University of Nebraska Press.

Lazarus, R. S. 1975. The self-regulation of emotion. In *Emotions: Their parameters and measurement,* ed. L. Levi. New York: Raven.

Leeper, R. W. 1948. A motivational theory of emotion to replace "emotion as disorganized response." *Psychological Review*, 55: 5–21.

Leventhal, H. 1974. Emotions: A basic problem for social psychology. In *Social psychology: Classic and contemporary integrations*, ed. C. Nemeth. Chicago: Rand-McNally.

Lewinsohn, P. M. 1974. A behavioral approach to depression. In *The psychology of depression: Contemporary theory and research*. eds. R. J. Friedman and M. M. Katz. Washington, D.C.: Winston and Sons.

Lindsley, D. G. 1970. The role of nonspecific reticulothalamocortical systems in emotion. In *Physiological Correlates of Emotion*, ed. P. Black. New York: Academic Press.

Mandler, G. 1976. *Mind and emotion*. New York: Wiley.

McGeer, P. L., and McGeer, E. G. 1980. Chemistry of mood and emotions. In *Annual review of psychology*, vol. 31, eds. M. R. Rosenzweig and L. W. Porter. Palo Alto, CA: Annual Reviews Inc.

McDougall, W. 1923. *Outline of psychology*. New York: C. Scribner's.

Millenson, J. R. 1967. *Principles of behavioral analysis*. New York: Macmillan.

Nesselroade, J. R., and Baltes, P. B. 1979. *Longitudinal research in the behavior and development*. New York: Academic Press.

Neugarten, B. L. 1977. Personality and aging. In *Handbook of the psychology of aging*, eds. J. E. Birren and K. W. Schaie. Van Nostrand Reinhold.

Papez, J. W. 1937. A proposed mechanism of emotion. *Archives of neurological psychiatry* 38: 725–743.

Pfeiffer, E. 1977. Psychopathology and social pathology. In *Handbook of the psychology of aging*, eds. E. Birren and K. W. Schaie. New York: Van Nostrand Reinhold.

Plutchick, R. 1970. Emotions, evolution and adaptive processes. In *Feelings and emotions: The Loyola Symposium*, ed. M. B. Arnold. New York: Academic Press.

Polivy, J. 1981. On the induction of emotion in the laboratory: Discrete moods or multiple affect states? *Journal of Personality and Social Psychology* 41: 803–817.

Pribram, K. H. 1970. Feelings as monitors. In *Feelings and emotions: The Loyola Symposium*, ed. M. B. Arnold. New York: Academic Press.

Pribram, K. H., and Melges, F. T. 1967. Psychophysiological basis of emotion. In *Neurophysiology and emotion*, ed. D. C. Glass. New York: Rockefeller University Press.

Rapaport, D. 1950. *Emotions and memory*. New York: International Universities Press.

Renner, V. J., and Birren, J. E. 1980. Stress: Physiological and psychological mechanisms. In *Handbook of mental health and aging*, eds. J. E. Birren and R. B. Sloane. Englewood Cliffs, N.J.: Prentice Hall.

Russell, J. A. 1980. A circumplex model of emotion. *Journal of Personality and Social Psychology* 39: 1161–1178.

Sartre, J. P. 1948. *The emotions*. New York: Philosophical Library.

Schachter, S. 1972. *Emotion, obesity and crime*. New York: Academic Press.

Schachter, S., and Singer, J. E. 1962. Cognitive, social and physiological determinants of emotional state. *Psychological Review* 69: 379–397.

Schlosberg, H. 1954. Three dimensions of emotion. *Psychological Review* 61: 81–88.

Schonfield, A. E. D. 1980. Learning, memory and aging. In *Handbook of mental health and aging*, eds. J. E. Birren and R. B. Sloane. Englewood Cliffs, N.J.: Prentice Hall.

Schulz, R. 1982. Emotionality and aging: A theoretical and empirical analysis. *Journal of Gerontology* 37: 42–52.

Schulz, R. 1976. The effects of control and predictability on the psychological and physical well-being of the institutionalized aged. *Journal of Personality and Social Psychology* 33: 563–573.

Schulz, R., and Hanusa, B. H. 1980. Experimental social gerontology. *Journal of Social Issues* 36: 30–46.

Shott, S. 1979. Emotion and social life: A symbolic interactionist analysis. *American Journal of Sociology* 85: 1317–1334.

Siminov, P. V. 1970. The information theory of emotion. In *Feelings and emotions: The Loyola Symposium*, ed. M. B. Arnold. New York: Academic Press.

Solomon, R. L., and Corbit, J. D. 1974. An opponent-process theory of motivation: I. Temporal dynamic of affect. *Psychological Review* 81: 119–145.

Strongman, K. T. 1978. *The psychology of emotion*. 2nd ed. New York: John Wiley and Sons.

Thomae, H. 1980. Personality and adjustment in aging. In *Handbook of mental health and aging*, eds. J. E. Birren and R. B. Sloane. Englewood Cliffs, N.J.: Prentice Hall.

Tomkins, S. S., and McCarter, R. 1964. What and where are the primary affects? Some evidence for a theory. *Perceptual and Motor Skills* 18: 119–158.

Tomkins, S. S. 1962. *Affect, imagery and consciousness: Vol. I, The positive affects*. New York: Springer.

Tomkins, S. S. 1963. *Affect, imagery and consciousness: Vol. II, The Negative Affects*. New York: Springer.

Tomkins, S. S. 1970. Affect as the primary motivational system. In *Feelings and emotions*, ed. M. B. Arnold. New York: Academic Press.

Watson, J. B. 1929. *Psychology. From the standpoint of a behavorist*. 3d rev. ed. Philadelphia: J. B. Lippincott.

Welford, A. 1980. Sensory, perceptual and motor processes in older adults. In *Handbook of mental health and aging*, eds. J. E. Birren and R. B. Sloane. Englewood Cliffs, N.J.: Prentice Hall.

Wigdor, B. T. 1980. Drives and motivation with aging. In *Handbook of mental health and aging*, eds. J. E. Birren and R. B. Sloane. Englewood Cliffs, N.J.: Prentice Hall.

Young, P. T. 1961. *Motivation and emotion*. New York: Wiley.

Zarit, S. H. 1980. *Aging and mental disorders*. New York: Free Press.

21
AGING AND SELF-CONCEPTIONS: PERSONALITY PROCESSES AND SOCIAL CONTEXTS

Vern L. Bengtson
University of Southern California
Margaret N. Reedy
Pacific Coast Psychological Center, Long Beach
and
Chad Gordon
Rice University

INTRODUCTION: THE "LITTER-ATURE" ON PERSONALITY AND AGING

Does personality change with aging? To what extent is selfhood "fixed" by the time individuals reach adulthood? Does negative self-evaluation increase with old age?

Whether there are characteristic changes in personality over the life course remains one of the most enduring puzzles in the social psychology of aging. For much of the twentieth century, researchers and theoreticians seemed to be in agreement with William James, who wrote almost 100 years ago, "For most of us, by the age of 30, the character has set like plaster, and will never soften again" (1892, p. 124). However, the premise of unswerving personality constancy was challenged by the growth of "life-span" developmental research in the 1970s, which documented age differences in personality indicators across stages of adulthood (reviewed in Schaie and Parham, 1976; Baltes, 1979; Baltes, Reese, and Lipsitt, 1980).

Within the past decade, there has been a resurgence in the stability *versus* change debate among those interested in life-span personality. The claim for distinct changes was exemplified in popular literature by Gail Sheehy's (1976) phenomenally successful portraiture of distinct "passages" in adult personality. It was continued in the more conventionally documented analyses of Levinson (1978), Gould (1978), and Vaillant (1977). In the past five years there has been a counterattack by scholars (e.g., Brim and Kagan, 1980; Costa and McCrae, 1980b), whose evidence emphasizes stability in personality dispositions throughout the adult lifespan.

What is one to make of these conflicting claims? What meaningful conclusions can be drawn from what has been derisively labeled the "litter-ature" on personality and adulthood (Block, 1977)? In the first edition of this handbook, Bernice Neugarten's (1977) review provided a broad conceptual and empirical context. She summarized the developmental perspective necessary to examine adult personality, the major theories of adult change, the best-documented empirical assessments of age-related change in personality, and recent theoretical formulations. Her conclusion was cautious, however, and, according to some observers (e.g., Costa and McCrae, 1980b), overly pessimistic. Neugarten wondered, as did Schaie and Marquette (1971) and Rubin (1981), whether there were any propositional statements that could be asserted with confidence concerning personality and aging, given the methodological and conceptual problems that have characterized research.

An implication of previous reviews of personality and aging is that investigators have been casting their nets too broadly. Perhaps a more limited, and certainly a more well-defined, conceptual focus is required in order to escape the dual problems that appear to characterize the field: Although broad concepts (often clinically inspired) may be unoperationalizable, narrow concepts (experimentally tested and validated) may be trivial.

We view the current controversy in the field of aging and personality as intellectually constructive, since it poses challenges for researchers to reconceptualize their approaches and refine their constructs. In particular, it suggests the need to focus on more limited aspects of personality dispositions throughout the life course.

One approach that appears to us particularly useful is to focus on the "self" and its empirical manifestations: *self-conceptions.* We suggest that a review of research on self-conceptions offers an instructive contribution to the debate over stability versus change in thoughts, feelings, and behavioral orientations that may accompany aging. This perspective is congruent with a long tradition, rooted in the beginnings of social psychology but addressed most frequently in recent years by sociologists. Furthermore, we suggest that it would be useful to approach self-conceptions as complex systems of *attitudes,* enabling the investigator to draw upon the long conceptual and empirical tradition of attitude study in social psychology (see McGuire, 1969).

A second approach to the study of self-perceptions used by personality psychologists is to focus on a contemporary version of person-

ality traits, since these evidence stability or change over the life course (Costa and McCrae, 1980b). Traits are defined as generalized tendencies toward thoughts, feelings, and behaviors that can be reliably measured in large, age-heterogeneous populations or in longitudinal designs. The investigator infers the respondent's position on the abstractly conceived trait from a mathematical combination of the respondent's self-ratings on a number of specific scale items, each reflecting constructs termed "traits." Examples are ego-strength, sex-role rigidity, optimism, and androgyny. Current formulations of trait theory and measurement seek to avoid many of the conceptual and methodological problems of earlier trait formulations.

The purpose of this chapter is to review theory and research concerning patterns of stability or change in self-conceptions. We will first discuss conceptual issues: what most researchers mean by self-conceptions, and what dimensions or modes constitute their varied manifestations throughout life. In the second section, we will consider the methodological problems involved in researching self-conceptions and the life course. In the following three sections, we will review the existing empirical evidence for stability and change in self-conceptions throughout adulthood, focusing in turn on their cognitive, affective, and conative aspects. There has been an astonishing growth in recent years in the number of studies of continuity or discontinuity in both self-conceptions and personality traits reflecting the self, and our concluding section will present a number of propositions that can be asserted (with some confidence borne of replicated findings) concerning stability or change throughout the adult years.

This chapter attempts to integrate research on self-conceptions (typically conducted by sociologists) with research on personality traits (typically conducted by psychologists). These two domains have often been seen as separate; in truth, they are somewhat different conceptually, since self-conception refers to inferences made directly by the subject, whereas personality traits refer most commonly to inferences made by a trained observer. Operationally, however, both are grounded in one or another form of self-report, and thus the two are inextricably intertwined. We propose that self-conceptions and measures of personality traits may be meaningfully integrated within the framework of cognition, evaluation, and conation that is suggested by attitude theory and research. This orientation can provide a fresh perspective on the issues of stability and change throughout adulthood.

CONCEPTUAL ISSUES: SELF-CONCEPTION STRUCTURES AND PROCESSES

What is "the self" in empirical terms? What are its component elements, "self-conceptions," and how can they best be measured, especially over time? How do self-conceptions develop and change over the life course, and how do they resist change in content and structural interrelationships? What processes may allow the self to maintain a sense of continuity in the face of onslaughts from the social environment and to defend against internal intrusions of unwelcome conceptions? How do changes in self-conception shape changes in subsequent behavior? Important theoretical questions such as these cannot be posed properly without delineation of the conceptual dimensions of self-conception.

Perspectives on Self and Systems of Self-Conceptions

The terms "self" and "self-concept" invoke some of the oldest, most enduring, and yet most perplexing themes in social psychology; these themes originated in philosophy—especially phenomenology. Their nature, their social and intrapsychic determinants, and their development over time have been the source of continuing debate for almost a century.

The "I" and the "Me". In 1892, James framed the special nature of reflexive thought, feeling, and motivation to self-oriented actions by his differentiation between the self as subject (the "I") and the self as object (the "Me"), as follows:

> Whatever I may be thinking of, I am always at the same time more or less aware of *myself,*

of my *personal existence.* At the same time it is *I* who am aware; so that the total self of me, being as it were duplex, partly known and partly knower, partly object and partly subject, must have two aspects discriminated in it, of which for shortness we may call one the *Me* and the other the *I* (p. 176).

But James went further and proposed a conceptual distinction we have found useful in organizing our review of contemporary empirical literature:

> Understanding the Me in this widest sense, we may begin by dividing the history of it into three parts, relating respectively to (a) Its constituents; (b) The feeling and emotions they arouse—*self-appreciation;* (c) the acts to which they prompt—*self-seeking* and *self-preservation* (pp. 176–177; emphases in original).

The same tripartite division has been suggested in other contexts by Hilgard (1980) and Allport (1954). The phenomenology of the self is a complex topic (c.f. Gordon and Gergen, Part III, 1968; Rosenberg, 1979; Gecas, 1982). There has been little resolution of some classic ambiguities despite the appearance of nearly 2,000 studies relating to self variables published before 1971 (Gergen, 1971). Indeed, in response to the many definitions and approaches that had been devised in grappling with "self" as a construct, Allport (1955) suggested that the term itself be discarded, using instead the Latin word *proprium.* That suggestion did not deter subsequent writers, however, and we shall follow the more recent usage and attempt to clarify the relevance for self for gerontology, as well as for social and developmental psychology.

Conceptual models of the "self" and theory about self-conceptions have undergone substantial development over the last twenty years. Wylie's (1961) original comprehensive review of major reflexive concepts and their typical measurement strategies has been revised and expanded to two large volumes (Wylie, 1974, 1978), and the collection of classic and contemporary self theory and research edited by Gordon and Gergen (1968) has been updated and expanded to cover the work of the 1970s (Rosenberg and Kaplan, 1982). Major new domains of dependent variables have been linked to various aspects of self in an effort to explain subsequent behavior more fully. For example, Gordon (1972) developed implications of self theory for educational and occupational achievement orientations. Schwartz and Stryker (1971) and Kaplan (1975, 1976) examined self-concept correlates of deviant behavior. Webster and Sobieszek (1974) dealt with laboratory group interaction and self-conceptions. Gergen (1971) synthesized much of the psychological and social-psychological literature on the implications of self-conceptions, whreas McCall and Simmons (1966) made self-conceived role identities the heart of their theory of social interaction. At the macro-social level, Zurcher (1977) related mutability of self-conceptions to rapidly changing institutional structures, and Rosenberg (1981) has most recently codified some of the ways in which the self can be a social force as well as a social product. Finally, there have been significant developments in research methodologies designed to tap either the broad range of self-conception dimensions (cf. Gordon, 1969; Mortimer, Finch, and Kumka, 1982) or the specifically evaluative dimensions (Wylie, 1974, 1978; Wells and Marwell, 1976).

Two very recent integrative efforts can be drawn upon to establish a single coherent framework with which to guide the next round of self theory and research. These two reviews (Rosenberg, 1979; Gecas, 1982) attempt to integrate self theory and research. We have drawn extensively on these reviews for many of the components of the model to be presented below.

This chapter focuses on the self as object, not as subject; thus, our focus is on the *self-concept*, not the *phenomenological self*. Our definition of the self-concept follows Rosenberg's (1979, p. 9): "The totality of the individual's thoughts and feelings that have reference to himself as an object." Note that these orientations are multiple; as will be discussed later, they vary by context and referent. Thus, we think it necessary to speak of "self-conceptions" (plural) not "the self-concept" (singular).

Attitudes Toward the Self. Self-conceptions are most usefully considered as *attitudes;* as such, they are amenable to analysis and interpretation in much the same way as other attitudes. In his monumental review of the history of attitude research, McGuire (1969, p. 155) notes that:

> Philosophers at diverse times and places have arrived at the same conclusion, that there are basically three existential stances that man can take with respect to the human condition: knowing, feeling, and acting. Throughout the classical tradition, from Plato and Aristotle on, theorists repeatedly proposed the same three components of attitude under their Latinized names of cognitive, affective and conative.

We find it useful to follow this division, originally noted by James (1892) and recently described by Hilgard (1980) as the trilogy of mind: cognition, affection, and conation. We will look at self-conceptions that reflect three major components of attitudes toward the self.

The *cognitive* component of attitude refers to how the attitude object is perceived, its conceptual connotation, informational value, or "stereotype." In terms of self-conceptions, this component involves the content of the self as perceived by the individual—the factual attributes, usually stated in nouns and adjectives, that the person believes describes him or her. It also can be said to constitute the social meanings that reflect "identity" (Gordon, 1968a; Breytspraak and George, 1979, 1982; Gecas, 1982).

The *affective* component (also called the feeling, emotional, or evaluative aspect of attitude) deals with the person's liking or disliking for the object. In this evaluative dimension, the emphasis is with the valence (positive or negative) of evaluations that the individual feels with respect to given self-cognitions and the resultant feelings of pride, shame, or guilt generated by the evaluations. Within the sociological tradition, Cooley (1902) wrote of these affective aspects under the heading "Varieties of Self-Feeling."

The *conative* (action, volition, striving, behavior-oriented) component refers to the person's orientations to action insofar as these orientations reflect the self. The issue here is how the individual acts on the basis of motivation deriving from particular self-conceptions. Especially relevant are those attempts to change the self that are based on discrepancies between what the individual would like to be and what he feels he currently is. The conative dimension, though infrequently researched, is particularly important in analyzing change or stability of the self through time.

Pursuing this three-part division of self-concept as attitude, we feel, can impose structure and clarify ambiguity when we examine change and continuity in personality dispositions over time. In the following section, we present a more general model for the structure of self-conceptions, elaborating a view of them as being divisible into cognitive, affective, and behavioral components.

The Structure of Self-Conceptions

We propose a general typology for the structure of self-conceptions in aging that reflects six frequently employed constructs in the theoretical literature. These constructs can be categorized as modes of self-conception structures.

The term "self-conception" does *not* refer to the "I" that does the perceiving, interpreting, or evaluating, but rather to the *aspects* of the "me" that are perceived, interpreted, and evaluated. This distinction was amply developed by James (1892, pp. 176–216) and Mead (1934). It is the key feature of Gordon's (1968a) distinction between "active reflexive consciousness" and "the resultant accruing *structure of self-conceptions* (the special system of self-referential meanings available to this active consciousness)" (Gordon, 1968a, p. 116; emphasis in original). The six modes described below represent different planes of self-conception (Rosenberg and Kaplan, 1982, p. 7–9), each with a structure of its own but interpenetrating with the other self-conception modes. Specification of these analytic dimensions can be used to summarize much of the major theoretical work on self over the past two decades. Such specification also reveals the benefits of treating each self-structure in terms of general attitude theory, the stance taken in this chapter (see also Rosenberg, 1965). We will indicate where each fits within the cognitive, affective, and conative dimensions that we are employing to review age

changes and age differences in aspects of self-conceptions throughout the life course.

The Current Self-Conceptions Structure (Cognitive Dimensions). By far the greatest amount of theory and research on self-conceptions has been devoted to what James (1892, p. 191) called the "empirical self" and the "immediate and actual" as contrasted with the "remote and potential." Turner (1968, p. 94) describes self-conceptions as "the picture that carries with it the sense of "the real me—I myself as I really am . . . felt as inescapable fact by the individual." Rosenberg (1979, p. 38) calls this the *extant* self-concept: "what the individual sees and feels when he reflects upon himself at a given point in time."

This structure of current self-conceptions is primarily cognitive in character, indexed by the nouns of personal identity and the adjectives of personal characteristics. However, any of these may take on affective tone, since they are interpreted by the individual to be congruent or incongruent with the relevant contents of the second and third modes discussed below. All these meanings and their interrelations are addressed by the person-conceptions system for computer analyzed content analysis (Gordon, 1967), as will be discussed in the second section.

The Idealized Self-Conceptions Structure (Affective). Many self-conceptions refer to "what I should be, could be, must be, want to be, am trying to be, plan to be," and other forms of idealized identities and attributes. These affective images (of especially desirable roles, moral stances, and optimal characteristics) serve as evaluative standards against which relevant roles, stances, and characteristics within the structure of current self-conceptions can be judged. In terms of moral standards, the evaluation may be very difficult, if not impossible, to live up to; in terms of "realistic" goals, it is derived from the same or somewhat different values. Idealized self-conceptions vary considerably. On the one hand, there are the cruelly demanding images of total perfection and success that Horney (1945) placed at the center of her theory of neurosis; on the other hand, there are the rather ordinary "good husband" or "good lawyer" images that shape our judgments about how well we are actually playing out such roles.

Although idealized self-conceptions obviously have an evaluative character, they are also cognitive. Moreover, they often form the informational bases for the conative dimension and thus for self change since the perceived differences between *current* self-conceptions and relevant *idealized* conceptions provide much of the conative motivation for change.

Changes or stability across the life course can be readily researched by examining idealized self-conceptions. One hypothesis (untested to date) can be stated as follows. In young adulthood, a wide range of valued adult roles are contained within the structure of idealized self-conceptions, since these roles are considered both good and not yet attained (e.g., good parent, famous novelist, and cherished grandparent), but with increasing age, role-acquisition, and experience with the concrete ways in which roles are actually constructed and played (by oneself and by others), the idealized conceptions may be adjusted downward in the interest of avoiding the continuing pain of perceived imperfection and failure.

The Disvalued Self-Conceptions Structure (Affective). A third component, also affective, consists of negative identities and attributes. These attributes motivate much of our conduct and cause us much pain throughout the life course. Many disvalued and rejected conceptions may be only the echoes of names we may have been called in childhood (e.g., "fatso," "skinny," "foureyes"), whereas others are the result of inferences from previous interaction sequences that did not go well (e.g., "loser" at sports, "second-best" at poker, "reject" from unsuccessful job interviews). No one is as creative, intelligent, wealthy, or skillful as he or she would like to be, and the person's past experiences with any of the risky elements of social life may also have implanted a negative image of being—at least potentially—a thief, a drunk, an addict, a degener-

ate, a sinner, or some other negative role identity.

Negative role images and disvalued self-conceptions may exist only as *potential* self-conception elements, never actually being framed within a current self-conceptions structure. They may function only as cautionary warnings against imprudent actions, as was suggested by Klapp in his *Heroes, Villains and Fools* (1962). In other cases, however, disvalued self-conceptions derived from past behavior patterns or suggestions by significant others may exist as defensively repressed and ordinarily unconscious mental images. These disvalued conceptions may appear only as consciously perceived potentials, or they may be *actual* elements of current self-conception under conditions of fatigue, depression, projective testing, dreams, hypnosis, drug ingestion, or extreme embarrassment. For some individuals, the negative images may become firmly and unshakeably incorporated into the structure of current self-conception, as in the case of an anorexic girl believing she is still too fat.

Disvalued self-conceptions, especially the differences between them and their relevant current self-conceptions, provide major avoidance motivations as additional components of conative strivings. Since much in American culture stereotypes older persons in quite negative terms (e.g., sick, weak, blind, deaf, senile, sexless, poor, rigid, narrow, out-of-date, dependent, near-dead), increasing age and specific life events impacting on relevant current self-conceptions may increase their identification with disvalued conceptions, thus producing much negative self-valuation.

The Presented Self-Conceptions Structure (Conative). The presented self includes the identities and characteristics we present to others in situations. Some of this presentation is consciously manipulated; some, beyond conscious control. In either case, this fourth mode clearly reflects the "conative" aspects of attitudes. The arts of impression management, as Goffman has analyzed them in his many writings (especially 1955, 1959, 1963), are designed to optimize the degree to which an individual's claimed current self-conceptions and interactive "line" accomplish the following: (1) *match* relevant idealized self-conceptions; (2) *avoid* resemblance to disvalued conceptions; and yet (3) *fit* meaningfully under the frame of the social demands of the particular interactive situation. This is an incredibly complex juggling act, requiring the individual to represent his identities, skills, moral character, background, and intentions as at least acceptable—if not altogether desirable—to the significant others in the situation and also as at least acceptable to himself. In short, the presented self is structured largely around conative striving, in attempts to confirm, protect, and possibly enhance one's cognitive current self-conceptions in light of affective judgments concerning valued and disvalued images.

Five considerations add to the complexity. First, each of the various persons in any given situation has a distinct set of values and expectations regarding this particular type of situation and the apparent type of presenter addressing it. Thus, the individual will be at least minimally aware that the claims and stylistics that may favorably impress one significant other might well fail totally with another in the same setting.

Second, each situation or occasion has its own set of social demands; thus, the same presenter will present very differently conceived arrays of appropriate identities and attributes at different times. It is therefore meaningful to raise the theoretical and pragmatic issue of just what sense it makes to call our individual "the same" presenter, as has been pointed out by Gergen (1968, 1982).

Third, persons have a very special motive for self-perceived consistency in interaction that operates to maintain identity coherence over time and avoid negative self-conceptions, such as phony, hypocrite, liar, or crazy.

Fourth, social situations and the significant others in them do not vary at random or even over a tremendous range; we move through more or less familiar types of situations and deal mostly with familiar types of other persons.

Finally, the other people with whom we interact have a strong vested interest in perceiving us as the same person they dealt with yesterday, as having at least roughly similar capacities, identities, and characteristics. These others will tend to reward at least similar presentations (perhaps edited only to indicate improvement along desirable dimensions) and will apply unpleasant sanctions against any presenter who is so changeable as to precipitate any negative self-conceptions that the presenter already holds.

Conceptions of Significant Others' Responses (Cognitive). This structure contains an individual's fragmentary impressions of other persons' reactions and perceptions of him or her. Each person in the given situation who notices an individual at all will have a unique set of perceptions, interpretations, appraisals, and emotional reactions, depending on his or her own values, previous experiences, and expectations for that type of individual in that type of situation.

To the degree that the various persons share some major values, experiences, or expectations with one another, they may show some consistency in their interpretations of the individual's presentations, but the individual will never know precisely what any or all of these others make of him. Their interpretations will be too individualistic, too well masked by tact and social convention, and too fleeting to be grasped with accuracy.

Conceptions of Inferred Self-Images (Conative). The individual will attempt to interpret the appraisals of the significant others in the situation and to integrate them with a composite situational self-image (Turner, 1968, p. 102). This integration occurs through a combination of (1) selective attention to cues concerning others' responses; (2) granting centrality to only a few dimensions from among the entire range; (3) attributing generally positive portrayals to oneself; and (4) selecting only those referents of social comparison that render one's own reflected performances most creditable (Rosenberg, 1979, pp. 62–77 and 260–278).

These momentary situational self-images, these inferences regarding the way the significant others are apparently appraising the presenter, must then be integrated and generalized across different types of signficant others, across different replays of similar situations in a short period of time, and over more situations and more significant others. Interactions, especially those that Turner (1968) calls "task-directed interaction," may produce relatively little information that might disconfirm the presenter's line of identity and attribute claims. In these cases, the motivations of the presenter toward self-confidence and security are supported, and self-consciousness may be minimal. On the other hand, when the interaction introduces conflicting claims or accusations of incompetency, immorality, mental aberration, or other forms of social risk, self-consciousness will rise greatly—often to extremely painful levels—and communication will tend to become, in Turner's terms, identity-directed or even explicitly diagnostic so that the presenter is inescapably faced with information that may reflect in severely negative terms on the claims for identities and attributes being presented.

The six modes of self-conceptions outlined above can be viewed as self-attitudes conforming to the three dimensions suggested by traditional research, as follows:

Cognition is involved in almost every mode, especially regarding the specific contents, the generalized inferences, the formal or structural attributes of the self-cognitions, and the selective/deceptive process by which the cognitions are formed to be maximally pleasurable to the individual.

Evaluation of the various contents is dealt with explicitly in modes 2 and 3 and in a more abstract inferential manner in the other modes. Self-consciousness deals for the most part with negative evaluations, although evaluations of self can bring about positive changes. Obviously, the whole point of self-striving efforts is to produce evaluative tones that are maximally satisfying to the self. It should be explicitly noted that the maximally satisfying evaluative tone for a particular individual need *not* be positive. Those who conceive of themselves as sinners, losers, wimps, unattractive, unlovable, or some other negative image may actually derive satisfaction

when the situational feedback (their conceptions of the inferred self-images) confirms their current negative self-conceptions.

Finally, *conation* involves striving to make presented self-images approximate desired self-conceptions and trying to obtain interactive support for these approximations, in turn, in ways that will eventually allow current self-conceptions to approximate the desired conceptions. These maneuvers are particularly apparent in modes 4 and 6.

With this typology of the modes of self-conception as background, we can turn to issues of operationalization and measurement in recent empirical work on self-conceptions and aging and then map out the substantive findings that indicate stability or change across the adult life course.

METHODOLOGICAL ISSUES: EXPLORING SELF-CONCEPTIONS AND AGING

Four major methodological issues confront those engaged in researching self-conceptions across the adult life span. These issues are related to (1) definition and measurement of self-attitudes, (2) research design, (3) statistical analysis and data interpretation, and (4) population sampling. As will be clear from the literature reviewed in this chapter, any attempt to sort out, integrate, or develop propositions about change or stability in self-attitudes in adulthood eventually depends upon these methodological challenges. Generally speaking, we suggest that the explicit categorization of methodological problems is one key to resolving the current controversy over stability versus change in more general explorations of personality and aging.

Definition and Measurement of Self-Attitudes

Problems in the definition and measurement of self-conception constructs include: (1) lack of agreement on definitions of primary constructs (e.g., self-concept, self-esteem, self-regard, self-image); (2) ambiguity about how these constructs are related to one another; (3) insufficient attention to developing measures that adequately represent concepts; and

(4) inadequate technology for coding qualitative data.

There has been a proliferation of instruments for measuring self-conceptions over the past 20 years (Wylie, 1974; Gordon, 1969; Gecas, 1982; Wells and Marwell, 1976; Block, 1977; Breytspraak and George, 1979, 1982). Nevertheless, inadequate attention has been devoted to issues of reliability and validity. In their review of the measurement of self-concept and self-esteem in gerontological literature, Breytspraak and George (1982) note that the majority of instruments they examined did not report internal consistency or split-half or test-retest reliablities. Instruments initially developed on young subjects and later used with older age groups have rarely reported reliability data for the older sample, although reliability estimates should be reported for all age groups under study. Block (1977) notes that when measurement reliabilities are unknown or not taken into account, it is unclear whether low intercorrelations are actually low or merely the result of defective measures. Validity data on self-conceptions and self-esteem are also inadequate as a rule, and face validity is the most commonly cited form of validation. There has usually been a failure to replicate studies, or even to repeat the use of the same measuring instrument. Frequently, moreover, there is a failure to clarify the relevance of instrument content to the self-attitude construct dimensions being studied. Few self-conception studies have employed multitrait–multimethod approaches to assess validity (Wylie, 1974, pp. 107–123).

Breytspraak and George (1982) note the need for studies on self-concept and aging that (1) clearly specify the construct of interest, (2) assess the construct validity and factorial invariance of the measure across age groups, and (3) assess the appropriateness of the measure with regard to the characteristics of the population studied (e.g., community residing versus nursing home; poorly versus highly educated) as well as potential difficulties in administering the instrument to an older population (e.g., greater fatigue in responding to questionnaires).

As Moss and Susman (1980) point out, different methods of measuring self-conceptions are likely to result in different information about stability and change in self-attitudes during adulthood. Investigators using self-report measuring instruments to assess self-conceptions are implicitly operating under two basic assumptions: that self-attitudes are consciously available to the individual and that self-attitudes can be adequately measured by self-report methods (Breytspraak and George, 1982). Both assumptions reflect the notion that individuals can and will accurately report their self-conceptions. There is not consensus on this issue; some researchers have argued that some self-conceptions are not conscious phenomena or that self-reporting measures simply assess what an individual would like the investigator to think his personality is like. The question of distortion (unconscious or deliberate) has rarely been considered in the literature on adult development and self-attitudes. Certainly this issue merits additional empirical investigation.

Coding is an additional problem, especially in self-report measures of self-conceptions. Although may coding schemes have been developed to capture some of the modes indicated in the previous section (cf. Kuhn and McPartland, 1954; Wylie, 1961, 1974, 1978; Gordon, 1969), coding categories have been problematic. Perhaps the most promising innovation to date is the Person-Conceptions (PC) System of computer-assisted content analysis (Gordon, 1967, 1976). The computer dictionary includes a wide range of meanings in a single comprehensive approach to analyzing the data of unstructured self-descriptions such as the "Who am I?" (Twenty Statements Test) or other open-ended instruments. Subjects' responses to the "Who am I?" instrument are first entered verbatim into a computer file. Then the computer dictionary analyzes the response in terms of 243 possible codes, reflecting the Persons Conceptions categories. The PC System assumes that there is a continuum of increasing abstraction within any of the six structures or modes of self-conceptions reviewed earlier (Gordon, 1967, pp. 9–15).

Issues of Research Design

Cross-sectional studies not only far outnumber longitudinal studies of self-conceptions and aging, they also yield different results. As will be demonstrated later, cross-sectional studies usually show large age differences in self-attitudes; however, because of the confounding of age and cohort variables, these contrasts may be more indicative of cohort differences in self-conceptions than of age changes. Longitudinal studies of single cohorts ordinarily point to considerable stability in self-conceptions. However, as Schaie (1965) and Baltes and Nesselroade (1970) have argued, longitudinal studies of self-attitudes confound age changes with the effects of time of measurement. The additional confounding variables of the unique historical experience of the birth cohort under study, as well as repeated testing and selective attrition, make the interpretation of longitudinal changes ambiguous.

To overcome the limitations of both longitudinal and cross-sectional research designs, Schaie and Parham (1976) have argued for the utility of a time-sequential design in personality research. In sequential design, several birth cohorts are followed longitudinally in order to get a more accurate assessment of the impact of aging, cohort membership, and social/cultural events on self-conceptions. In fact, as Costa and McCrae point out (1982), no design can provide unambiguous interpretations, since aging, time of measurement, and birth cohort are inevitably confounded. Although few studies of self-conceptions using sequential strategies exist, these usually show few age-related changes in self-conceptions and instead point to significant differences between generations in self-conceptions, as well as to social and cultural influences on changes in self-attitudes (Schaie and Parham, 1976; Douglas and Arenberg, 1978).

Additional problems in cross-sectional and longitudinal studies include the age range of individuals studied and the length of time the study is pursued. Moss and Sussman (1980) propose that the wider the age range and the longer the time frame of study, the more likely that change rather than stability will be observed. This generalization seems to hold true from infancy into adulthood, but after that, the pattern is much less clear. The data of McCrae, Costa, and Arenberg (1980) suggest that older men are no more stable than younger men in some of the traits that reflect conceptions of self.

Issues in Statistical Analysis

In the research to date, four major approaches have been used to assess stability or change in self-attitudes: structural invariance, correlational stability, level stability, and ipsative stability (Mortimer, Finch, and Kumka, 1982). The first type, *structural invariance*, refers to the examination of stability in the structure, organization, or dimensionality of self-conceptions, typically assessed through factor or cluster analysis techniques. Structural invariance is said to exist when a self-attitude construct maintains the same dimensions and relationships among component attributes over time. The issue of structural invariance in comparing age-group contrasts has been widely discussed (Baltes and Nesselroade, 1970; Nesselroade, Schaie, and Baltes, 1972; Bengtson, 1975; Moss and Sussman, 1980), with some developmentalists (e.g., Nesselroade, 1977) arguing that a demonstration of structural invariance of a construct or self-concept dimension must precede an examination of other kinds of stability.

Correlational stability, or "rank-order stability" (Mortimer, Finch, and Kumka, 1982), focuses on assessing stability or change in an individual's self-conception position relative to others over time. The most frequently used approach for investigating developmental constancy or change, correlational stability is typically measured by examining Pearsonian, Spearman, or Kendall correlation coefficients between measures of self-concept attributes or personality traits across time in a group of individuals. Such an approach allows the investigator to determine the extent to which individuals maintain their relative standing in relation to other members of the group between Time 1 and Time 2 of measurement.

In the investigation of *level stability*, the focus is on constancy or change in the measured value of an attribute over time. Stability or change in an individual's scores at different ages for an attribute or at a group level is analyzed by noting increases or decreases in group mean scores over time. Also different age groups can be contrasted by comparing group means on self-conception measures. An important issue related to the assessment of level stability is the extent to which group variances on measured attributes remain stable over time. Increases in variance between particular times or age periods would be indicative of increased individual differences in a trait, even though mean scores might be stable.

The fourth type, *ipsative stability,* is the least frequently investigated. It involves examination of intraindividual consistency in self-attributes, that is, of the stability or change in the relative ordering of attributes within a given person over time, as assessed by profile analysis.

Obviously, the method used to assess stability affects the type of information obtained. Although correlational stability measurement provides information about the consistency of the scores of individuals across time, this approach provides no information about the relative strength or importance of the attributes of a single individual or about the extent to which an attribute shifts in absolute levels across time. Although mean-level analyses give quantitative information about age differences or changes for a group, significant individual change may be obscured in grouped data. The application of different methods of analysis to the same data results in different conclusions about developmental consistency or change in self-attitudes (Mussen et al, 1980; Block, 1971). For example, Mortimer, Finch, and Kumka (1982) examined structural, rank order, mean-level, and ipsative stability of self-image using panel data collected from male students over a 14-year period. Their results revealed a four-dimensional self-concept that showed stability over three periods of measurement in three of the four types of assessments: structural, rank-order, and ipsative. In their analysis of mean-level stability, however, they found significant changes in level, with some decrease in self-evaluation during college years and improvement over the next 10 years. Thus, the finding of stability using one method of analysis does not necessarily imply other types of stability; moreover, change in mean-level can occur along with rank-order stability.

A fifth problem related to method of analysis concerns the size of the coefficients necessary to establish consistency or change. Although there is an increasing body of literature that points to considerable consistency in self-conceptions (as will be demonstrated subsequently), there is no agreed-upon standard for defining the level of correlation that constitutes stability. This lack of a standard gives rise to different interpretations of the same correlation coefficients (Mortimer et al., 1982; Chiriboga, 1982; also see Schaie and Hertzog in Chap. 3 of this handbook).

With some exceptions involving well-developed inventories (Costa and McCrae, 1977–78), correlation coefficients in longitudinal personality studies are usually modest and rarely more than 0.50. A correlation of 0.50 leaves 75 percent of the variance unaccounted for. Some recent discussions (Nesselroade, Seigler, and Baltes, 1981) suggest that measurement-error unreliability is a major factor that limits these correlations. Instrument unreliability places a limit on the stability that can be observed, and researchers like Block (1971) recommend correction for unreliability. When corrected for unreliability, some personality trait studies find stability accounting for 80 to 100 percent of the reliable variance (McCrae, Costa, and Arenberg, 1980). A number of investigators (Moss and Sussman, 1980; Mortimer et al., 1982) argue that relatively high unexplained variance points to the potential for plasticity and change in self-attitudes.

As with correlational data, the interpretation of significant shifts in mean-level score is also problematic. Correlations are easily interpreted in terms of the proportion of variance accounted for, but changes in mean-levels are usually reported only in terms of statistical significance. A more accurate perception of the degree of change would be afforded by a measure of effect size. Since publications such as the *Journal of Gerontology* have only recently begun to require reports of effect size, it is not yet possible to review studies systematically in this light.

A few publications do provide the necessary data concerning effect size, and the results can be quite revealing. For example, Chiriboga (1982) analyzed the effects of stress and aging on measures of well-being and psychological symptoms. He reported that significant stress effects accounted for 2.6 to 9.0 percent of the variance, and aging/time accounted for 0.9 to 6.0 percent. Retest correlations showed that baseline data on well-being and symptoms accounted for from 0.4 to 23.0 percent of the variance in these variables five years later. These figures suggest that stability accounted for about three times as much variance as did assessments of change. Although measures of well-being and symptoms are designed to be sensitive to change, measures of personality traits are designed to be more stable and may be expected to show a much larger proportion of stable-to-changing variance. In evaluating the literature examining mean-level stability of self-attitudes reviewed in this chapter, the reader should be aware that assessments of effect size are not generally reported; thus, effects that are statistically significant may account for only a very small percentage of variance (Bengtson, 1975).

Issues of Population Sampling

A fourth source of conflicting findings in the research literature on self-conceptions in adulthood involves contrast among populations and sampling procedures. Respondents vary widely across studies on such factors as sex, marital situation, health, socio-economic status, ethnic background, and birth-cohort membership. These factors are rarely examined for their impact on developmental change or stability in self-conceptions (for an exception, see Rosenberg, 1979). As in most of the developmental literature, studies on self-attitudes cover wide variations in age ranges of subjects. Some studies compare young persons with middle-aged persons, others middle-aged with the elderly, and still others the "young old" and the "old old." Apparent inconsistencies and substantive contradictions in the vast literature on self-concept may relate to these differences. For example, if self-esteem over the life course follows a curvilinear trend, increasing from adolescence to middle age and then decreasing from middle to old age, such a pattern would not be evident when the focus is continually on comparing "younger" and "older" groups.

It has been generally argued that age is a variable having major and direct impact on self-attitudes. There is no theoretical reason, however, for asserting that age has a direct impact on self-conceptions (Bengtson, 1973; George, 1980). Instead, researchers are beginning to maintain that life-stage, or life-events that may or may not be correlated with age, are more significant markers of the life course than age (Gordon, 1971, 1976; Lowenthal, Thurnher, and Chiriboga, 1975; Chiriboga, 1982; Breytspraak and George, 1982; Feldman, Biringen, and Nash, 1981). Rather than reporting chronological age contrasts, it may be more useful and illuminating to organize groups by life-stage or by major developmental events presumed to have an impact on attitudes toward the self.

Given these four major types of methodological problems in studying self-attitudes and aging, it is not surprising, as Neugarten (1977) noted, that the empirical literature is replete with inconsistent and contradictory findings. In the following three sections, we review the empirical evidence concerning self-attitudes in terms of the three distinctive components of attitude: the cognitive, the evaluative, and the conative.

COGNITIVE COMPONENTS: CONTENTS OF SELF-CONCEPTIONS

Do self-cognitions (the current self-conceptions structure) change or remain stable across the adult life span? Are some dimensions of current self-conceptions more stable than others over time? What factors other than age (e.g., cohort membership, gender, physical health, finances, life events) influence stability or change in the content of self-conceptions during aging?

Self-cognitions are the ideas or thoughts that an individual has about himself or herself. They include such dimensions as social self-identities, body image, ideas about what one's personality is like. Existing empirical studies can be categorized as two kinds: The first focuses on constructs specifically identified by the researcher as reflecting the construct of self-concept, and the second on trait-type personality studies involving self-report data, which may be interpreted as reflecting self-conceptions. When a self-report personality inventory (such as the Minnesota Multiphase

Personality Inventory, Guilford-Zimmerman Temperament Survey, or the Cattell 16 Personality Factors Inventory) is administered, it is usually interpreted by researchers to reflect dimensions of personality. The same items could be understood equally, however, as indicators of self-conceptions (McCrae, 1982; McCrae and Costa, 1982). The assumption here is that an individual's response to each item on a personality inventory tells us what that individual thinks some aspect of himself or herself is like.

In this section, a total of 38 studies are reviewed, with 21 of them reflecting a focus on traditional measures of self-conceptions (primarily cognitive) and 17 specifically reflecting assessments of personality traits or dimensions and aging. The criteria for including a study in our review were that: (1) it examined age differences or age changes explicitly; (2) it was published, or, if not published, enough of its details were available in a review article; and (3) it was judged to be representative or has been cited in the literature on self-conceptions and aging. As will be evident, the studies cited are not consistently adequate in terms of methodology; in general, however, they are typical of what is available in the literature.

Studies Using Self-Conception Scales

Table 1 lists the 21 self-conception studies that have investigated age differences or changes and describes the sample, design, variables assessed, measures used, and results. Fifteen studies reviewed were cross-sectional; six were longitudinal. No studies employing sequential data-collection strategies (Schaie, 1965) were found in the literature. In the majority of studies (17), the issue of stability or change in self-conception during aging was assessed from the perspective of mean-level analyses. Five studies included correlational analyses of stability, and two involved percentage analyses of age differences. Five examined stability of self-conception and aging, using more than one type of stability measurement approach. Sixteen different self-conception scales were used in the 21 studies, only four of them being used more than once.

To summarize what will be evident in the following paragraphs, there is little agreement among the studies on whether there is change or stability of self-conception with aging. This lack of consistency may be attributed to a variety of sources, including differences in (1) design methodology (longitudinal versus cross-sectional); (2) type of stability investigated (structural, correlational, mean-level, ipsative); (3) age range studied (young/middle-age; young/old; middle-age/old; young/old-old); (4) populations sampled (healthy versus institutionalized; SES, education); and (5) contrasting measures used to assess the same self-conception dimensions.

Structures of Self-Conceptions. Three studies offer evidence for substantial stability in both the nature and the interrelationships of self-concept dimensions with aging. Nevertheless, each of these studies also indicates, to a lesser degree, some changes or shifts with age.

Pierce and Chiriboga (1979) investigated the structural stability of self-conceptions as part of a longitudinal investigation of several hundred individuals (begun in 1969–1970). At the time of the first assessment, the subjects chosen were shortly to undergo one of four major adult transitions: high school seniors leaving home, birth of first child of newlyweds, departure of youngest child from home of middle-aged parents, and retirement for older workers (see Lowenthal et al., 1975, for a detailed description of the sample). Pierce and Chiriboga found stability in the structure and interrelationships of self-conception dimensions over a five-year period among individuals in the four life-stage groups. Their cluster analysis yielded six dimensions of the self at the first time of measurement and seven dimensions at the second. Personal security, amiability, and assertion were stable self-conception dimensions, but changes were noted in other dimensions: social poise, self-control, and hostility. At least some dimensions of self-conceptions were significantly influenced by culture and history, as well as by maturation.

Similar results were reported in an analysis of the structural invariance of self-conceptions over a 14-year period in subjects who were initially tested as college freshmen and thereafter periodically tested until 10 years after graduation. Mortimer, Finch, and Kumka (1982) used confirmatory factor analysis techniques to identify four self-concept dimensions (well-being, sociability, competence, and unconventionality). Each of the four dimensions showed substantial structural stability over the 14 years of early adulthood.

In a third study, comprised of individuals aged 9 to 89, Monge (1975) identified four self-conception dimensions: achievement–leadership, congeniality–sociability, masculinity–femininity, and adjustment. Monge found no significant age differences in factor structure in this large cross-sectional sample.

The results of these studies tentatively suggest structural stability of self-conception dimensions that are either personality- or temperament-related. In particular, the three studies suggest that three self-conception dimensions (personal well-being–security–adjustment; sociability–amiability; and competence–assertion–achievement) appear to be structurally stable across cohorts and during aging.

Mean Levels of Self-Conceptions. A different approach to assessing change or stability in self-conceptions with aging is found in those studies using mean-level analyses. Since the majority of these studies are cross-sectional, they may reflect cohort differences instead of maturational changes. Findings of studies investigating mean-level change or stability in self-conceptions are markedly inconsistent (see Table 1). Some studies show age differences; some show no age differences; and some show age differences or changes for some but not all variables under consideration. A part of the confusion and apparent contradictions in the self-concept and aging literature disappears, however, if we move away from the too general and simplistic question of whether or not "*the* self-concept" changes with aging. Instead, it is more meaningful and relevant to ask: (1) What are the most salient dimensions or categories of self-conceptions?, and (2) Which of these show change and which show stability with aging? As was discussed in the first section of this chapter, self-concep-

tions include a number of distinguishable categories, such as abilities and temperamental traits, role indentifications (family, occupational, sex role identities), and body image.

Body Image. A general expectation is that aging brings about significant shifts in body image, but the empirical literature on age and body image is extremely sparse, and the studies reviewed here are cross-sectional. The available research suggests that age does not necessarily have a negative impact on body image. Thompson's (1972) review of studies using the Physical Self Subscale of the Tennessee Self-Concept Scale suggests that older people usually have less positive views of their physical selves, but other studies of body image and physical attractiveness (Plutchik, Weiner, and Conte, 1971; Plutchik, Conte, and Weiner, 1973; Berscheid, Walster, and Bohrnstedt, 1973) suggest that middle-aged and older individuals may be just as satisfied with their bodies and body image as younger individuals. Thus, the limited literature does not support the public view that old people consider themselves to be unattractive. More systematic research would be useful to examine the extent to which body image may be stable across time, what factors may contribute to positive body image despite aging and negative social views of the elderly as unattractive, and relationships between body image and other domains of self-conceptions (e.g., self-esteem and public behaviors such as assertiveness and sociability).

Gender Contrasts and Sex-Role Identity. Self-conception dimensions of sex role identity are usually summarized in two dimensions that have been drawn from recent Western culture. The male or masculine dimension is often described as instrumental-competence and includes descriptions of the self as ambitious, achievement-oriented, dominant, assertive, and independent. The female or feminine dimension is called warmth-expressiveness and includes such self-concept descriptions as nurturing, tender, sensitive, sociable, and submissive/dependent. There is substantial evidence that self-conceptions of younger adult men are characterized more by instrumental-

TABLE 1 Summary of Research on Age Changes or Age Differences in Cognitive Components of Self-Concept: Studies Using Self-Conception Scales.

Authors	Sample	Method	Variables	Measures	Results
Back (1971)	502 F,M Age, 45–70	X-sectional Mean scores	Personal background Personal characteristics Personal values	Kuhn and McPartland 20 Statements Test	Age × sex differences in mean level for all three variables
Berschied, Walster, and Bohrnstedt (1973)	2,000 M,F Adol. to 45+	X-sectional Mean scores	Body image	Rated satisfaction with 24 body parts	No age differences in stated satisfaction with body parts Trend toward increased body satisfaction with age
Feldman, Biringen, and Nash (1981)	804 F,M Eight family-stage groupings: Adolescent–grandparents	X-sectional Mean scores	Instrumental variables: (Leadership, Autonomy, Acquiescence, Non-assertiveness, Self-ascribed masculinity) Expressive variables: (Compassion, Tenderness, Social inhibition) Mixed variables: (Immaturity, Athletic)	Bem Sex-Role Inventory	Stage × sex differences in mean level for most instrumental and expressive variables Majority of effects related to stage of life, not age
Fitzgerald (1978)	180 M,F Mean age, 18 60 M,F Mean age, 68	X-sectional Mean scores	Managing Narcissistic Aggressive Distrustful Passive-submissive Docile-dependent Cooperative-overconventional Overly generous	Leary Interpersonal Checklist	Age × sex differences in mean level on six of eight variables

Study	Sample	Design	Variables	Instrument	Findings
Foley and Murphy (1977)	65 F, 37 M Age, 65–85; 53 Ss College age (Elman, 1970)	X-sectional Mean scores	Male-valued competence Female-valued warmth-expressiveness	Revised Broverman Sex-Role Measure	Age × sex differences in mean level on both variables
George (1975)	380 M,F Age, 55–78	Longitudinal × 6 years Correlation	Self concept Ideal self Social self	Duke Semantic-Differential Scale	Correlational stability for all three variables
Hyde and Phillis (1979)	289 M,F Age, 13–85	X-sectional Regression and categorical scoring using percentages	Masculinity Femininity Androgeny	ModifiedBem Sex-Role Inventory	Regression analysis showed no age differences Categorical analysis showed age × sex differences in percent androgynous
Kahana and Coe (1969)	36 Ss Age, 50–92 Institutionalized	X-sectional Percentages	Role membership Affective responses Personality characteristics Interpersonal characteristics Physical/health characteristics Global	Kuhn and McPartland 20 Statements Test	No age differences in percentage of responses falling into these six categories
Lachman (1984)	1212 M,F Age, 36–63 Studied from 1968 to 1972; divided into seven age cohort groups	Longitudinal × 4 years Mean Scores	Personal efficacy	Three-Item Efficacy Scale	Mean level and correlational stability within cohorts No significant cohort differences in personal efficacy; trend for middle aged to be lower
Lowenthal, Thurnher, and Chiriboga (1975)	216 M,F High school Newlyweds Middle-aged Pre-retirement	X-sectional Mean scores	Ego diffusion Feminine self-concept Masculine self-concept Negative self-concept Positive self-concept Self-criticism	70 item ACL derived from Block Q-set	Stage, sex, and stage × sex differences for self-concept variables

TABLE 1 (*Continued*)

Authors	Sample	Method	Variables	Measures	Results
Monge (1975)	2741 F, 1799 M, Age, 9–89	X-sectional, Factor analysis, Mean scores	Achievement-leadership, Congeniality-sociability, Adjustment, Masculinity-femininity	Monge Semantic-Differential Scale	No age differences in factor structure; Age × sex differences in mean level for all 4 variables
Mortimer, Finch, and Kumka (1982)	368 M, College freshman, 1962–63, Seniors, 1966–67, 10 years later, 1976	Longitudinal × 14 years, Factor analysis, Mean scores, Correlation, Ipsative	Well-being, Sociability, Competence, Unconventionality	"Myself as a Person" Sematic-Differential Scale	Stability of factor structure; normative and ipsative stability; Mean level decreases in self-image in college years; increases in self-image (well-being and competence) after college; decreases in unconventionality after college; decreases in sociability over 14-year period
Mortimer and Lorence (1979)	435 M, 1966–1967 college grads studied in college and follow-up 10 years later	Longitudinal × 10 years, Correlation, Mean scores	Self-competence	Four-Item Scale derived from "Myself as a Person" Semantic-Differential Scale	Correlational stability (0.78); Increases in mean level over 10-year period
Nehrke, Hulicka, and Morganti (1980)	99 M, Age, 50–70+	X-sectional, Mean scores	Locus of Control	Rotter I-E Scale	No age differences in internal-external control
Pierce and Chiriboga (1979)	216 M,F in 1970, 189 M,F in 1975 (4 age/stage groups)	Longitudinal × 5 years, Cluster analysis	Personal security, Amiability, Assertion, Social poise, Self control	70-item ACL from Block Q-set	Structural stability for personal security, amiability, and assertion; Structural shifts in self-control, hostility, and social

Study	Sample	Design/Analysis	Variables	Measures	Findings
Plutchik, Weiner, and Conte (1971)	99 M,F Age 70+; mostly institutionalized; varying in physical and mental health / 35 M,F Mental patients / 36 M,F College students	X-sectional Mean scores	Body worries Body discomfort	Body worries Body discomfort Form	No significant difference between groups on either variable / Elderly with mental illness or in less supportive environment tended to score higher on worries and discomforts
Plutchik, Conte, and Weiner (1973)	94 M,F Age 70+; mostly institutionalized; varying in physical and mental health / 35 M,F Mental patients / 74 M,F College students	X-sectional Mean scores	Body image	Accidents Questionnaire	Value of body parts invariant across age groups / Advanced age less important than psychiatric status in impaired body image
Ryckman and Malikiosi (1975)	100 F,M College age / 383 F,M Age, 21–79	X-sectional Mean scores	Personal control Powerful others Chance	Levinson's I-E Scale	Age differences in personal control, perceived control by powerful others, and chance
Smith (1966)	140 Ss Age, 65+	X-sectional Mean scores	Number of details reported Reference on self vs. others	Kuhn and McPartland 20 Statements Test	No age differences in number of responses or reference to self vs. others
Thompson (1972)	626 M,F Age, 12–68 (Fitts, 1965) / 60 M Age 60 to 80+ (Postema, 1970)	X-sectional Mean scores	Physical self Moral-ethical self Social self	Tennessee Self-Concept Scale	Age differences in mean level for physical, moral-ethical, and social self

TABLE 1 *(Concluded)*

Authors	Sample	Method	Variables	Measures	Results
Thurnher (1981)	180 M,F Four age/sex groups of young M,F and old M,F (Transition Study)	Longitudinal × 8 years Mean scores	"Subjective" variables: Self Interpersonal relations Activities Affect "Objective" variables: Amiability Insecurity Assertion Self control Hostility Dysphoria	Open-ended self-descriptions 70-Item ACL from Block Q-set	"Subjective" self showed more change over time than "objective" self Age difference in perceived change in "subjective self" over time Age change in only one of "objective" self measures (assertion)

competence than those of younger women, whereas younger women see themselves as being relatively more warm-expressive than younger men (see the review of this topic in Tavris and Offir, 1977).

Cross-sectional studies focusing on sex-role-related attributes typically find that older individuals are more likely to incorporate opposite-sex characteristics (traditionally defined) into the self (Neugarten, 1977). This finding suggests that sex-role self-conceptions probably change with life circumstances and as a function of family or occupational life stage.

For example, Monge (1975) has reported that age and sex interact significantly on the dimensions of achievement, masculinity, congeniality/sociability, and adjustment. The greatest sex difference in achievement was evident in middle-age, with men scoring higher than women. For the overall summary dimension of masculinity, men scored higher than women, but this sex difference was less evident with increasing age. Females scored higher on congeniality/sociability, and males scored higher on adjustment, except in the 65–89 age group, where no sex differences along these dimensions were observed. Foley and Murphy (1977) present similar findings, suggesting that sex-role-related self-conception differences may be less evident in older men and women than younger men and women.

Hyde and Phyllis (1979) and Ryff and Baltes (1976) also suggest that traditional sex differences in self-conceptions are less evident in older men and women compared with younger ones. Fitzgerald (1978) investigated sex-role related self-conceptions using the Leary Interpersonal Checklist, a measure designed to assess eight interpersonal dimensions of the self that reflect variations of two major orthogonal dimensions: nurturance and dominance. By this instrument, college males described themselves as more aggressive than older males did, whereas older males scored higher on cooperation and nurturance. Although younger women scored higher than men on docile/dependence and cooperative/unconventional dimensions, older men scored only slightly higher on dominance than older women.

Stage of life, rather than age *per se*, may have a significant impact on self-conceptions (Bengtson, 1973). For example, in a cross-sectional study of the relationship between life-stage, sex, and self-conceptions, Feldman, Biringen, and Nash (1981) used the Bem Sex-Role Inventory to assess male-instrumental and female-expressive self-conceptions in a sample of over 800 men and women divided into eight family life-cycle-stage groups, from the adolescent through the grandparent stages. Their analyses demonstrated that the majority of effects on self-conception variables were related to stage of life, not age. Sex differences waxed and waned as a function of the respondents' stage in the family life cycle. The largest sex differences in traditional male-instrumental versus female-expressive scores occured during the parenting stages. By contrast, postparental males and females were more likely to identify cross-sex traits in their self-conceptions (expressiveness for men, autonomy for women).

In their review of age changes in sex roles, Troll and Perron (1981) concluded that although each sex maintains its own sex-role self-conceptions as a dominant mode, men in later life come to integrate a greater sense of nurturance, tenderness, or dependency in their self-views. Older women often come to see themselves as relatively more autonomous, assertive, or dominant. Gutmann (1975) has suggested that this shift in sex roles and tendency toward a "normal unisex of later life" may result from the increased freedom and decreased need for traditional sex roles in the post-parental years.

Locus of Control. There is little empirical research examining the developmental course of self-perceived locus of control in adulthood. The few cross-sectional studies using mean-level analyses suggest that age differences in locus of control may be only minor until late in life. Ryckman and Malikiosi (1975) investigated the variable of perceived personal control cross-sectionally in 100 college-aged students and nearly 400 men and women aged 21 to 79. Using Rotter's internal-external control scale, they found some age differences in personal control, with a higher mean for each age group until the seventh decade. Lachman

(1984) investigated personal efficacy in 1,212 men and women aged 36 to 63. She found no evidence for significant cohort differences in personal efficacy, although there was a trend for middle-aged individuals to score *lower* than their younger or older counterparts. Nehrke, Hulicka, and Morganti (1980) examined locus of control using Rotter's Internal-External Control Scale in 99 men aged 50 to 70 and found no age differences in this middle-aged and older group. Research on change or stability of attributional style in adulthood would appear to be a particularly important area for future research. A growing body of literature suggests that an internal, global, and stable attributional style in relation to uncontrollable or nonnormative events may predispose individuals to depression and life-threatening illnesses, such as cancer, in later life (Seligman, unpublished manuscript).

Temperament Variables. The few longitudinal studies of mean-level changes in self-conception dimensions suggest that temperamental variables (such as activity level, sociability/extroversion, anxiety, unconventionality, well-being, or competence) show significant change over time, at least during the period from late adolescence into young adulthood. Mortimer, Finch, and Kumka (1982) found that the dimensions of well-being and competence declined during the college years but increased after that. Unconventionality showed a nonsignificant positive increase from the freshman to senior years, then a significant decline in the 10 years following graduation. Sociability decreased over the entire 14-year period. Mean level scores for competence items also increased from senior year of college until 10 years after graduation (Mortimer and Lorence, 1979).

After examining these mean temperament scores, Mortimer et al. considered the standard deviations of the individuals' factor scores at each of the three time periods. Results suggested increasing stability with age. Three constructs (well-being, competence, and unconventionality) showed declining interindividual variability; however, sociability showed a divergent trend with interindividual variability increasing over the 14-year period.

Thompson (1972) also reports that older adults showed more variability than did younger persons on measures of physical, social, and moral self-conception.

Checklist Versus Open-Ended Assessment. It should be noted that the method of measurement (adjective checklist versus open-ended) in assessing temperament variables affects results. Thurnher (1981) analyzed variables similar to those studied by Mortimer et al. (1982) over a greater range of the adult life span. For purposes of analysis, Thurnher divided her Transitions Study sample into four age–sex groups (young men, older men, young women, and older women). She studied both subjective (open-ended) and objective (adjective checklist) self-descriptions. Objective self-concept was assessed using a 70-item adjective checklist derived from the Block Q-Sort; the data were analyzed in terms of the six stable factors identified by Pierce and Chiriboga (1979): amiability, insecurity, assertion, self-control, hostility, and dysphoria. Thurnher found that subjective self-conceptions showed more change over the eight-year period than did the objective self-ratings. Age differences were evident in perceptions of subjective change in the self, with more younger (70 percent) than older (29 percent) subjects reporting subjective changes. Mean-level analyses of the adjective checklist data showed stability for all six objective dimensions of self-conceptions over the eight-year period.

In contrast to the findings of Mortimer et al. (1982) of shifts in mean-level for temperamental variables over a 14-year period from late adolescence to young adulthood, Thurnher's findings suggest relatively more stability. Additionally, Thurnher's data suggest that subjective, open-ended assessments of the self show more change over time than do scores derived from an objective self-rating scale. They also suggest that older individuals show somewhat less subjective change than do their younger counterparts.

Studies using open-ended measures to examine self-conceptions are relatively rare in the adult life-span literature. Two out of three cross-sectional studies reviewed that use the

Kuhn and McPartland Twenty Statements Test in samples of middle-aged and elderly individuals did show age differences in self-conceptions. Back (1971) coded the responses of his middle-aged and older respondents in terms of their use of three domains of the self: personal background, personal characteristics, and personal values. Back found that older women perceived themselves more in terms of personal characteristics and values and less in terms of personal background factors than did middle-aged women. Smith (1966) used the Twenty Statements Test to investigate self-conceptions among individuals aged 65 and over who were ill and impaired in their functioning. Compared to a younger reference sample, the impaired and ill elderly reported significantly fewer details about themselves and were significantly more introspective. In the physically ill and impaired old person, self-conceptions may be less differentiated and there may be a greater tendency toward interiority (see also Kahana and Coe, 1969).

In short, when self-conceptions are measured using open-ended procedures, age differences or age change in self-conceptions are frequently found. These studies suggest that plasticity or alteration of self-conceptions occurs even into advanced age, perhaps largely as a result of health changes, changing social circumstances, or institutionalization.

Correlational and Ipsative Stability. Correlational studies usually show significant stability over the period of study. For example, in addition to mean-level analyses, Mortimer and associates (1979, 1982) examined correlational stability of self-conception variables across 4-, 10-, and 14-year intervals. They found that individual scores were fairly consistent over time. Correlations across the four-year college period ranged from 0.63 for well-being to 0.68 for competence; for the senior year to 10-year follow-up, correlations ranged from 0.51 for well-being to 0.63 for unconventionality. They also reported considerable ipsative stability for the self-conception variables measured, with an average rho of 0.59 over the college period and 0.57 over the following decade, indicating stability of hierarchial ordering of self-concept

dimensions within individuals over time. Stability correlations for competence for the senior year until the 10-year follow-up were 0.79.

It appears, therefore, that the relative ordering of individual self-concept scores is usually preserved over time, despite the many role changes and shifts in life experience that are likely to occur during the young adult years.

This conclusion is supported by another study. George (1975) used the Duke Sematic Differential Scale on subjects in the Duke Longitudinal Study to assess self-concept, ideal self, and social self over a six-year period. Cross-wave correlations between the self-ratings on individual scale items ranged from 0.67 to 0.93, again suggesting substantial stability in self-conceptions over time.

Studies Using Personality Scales

Seventeen studies using responses to personality inventories and scales were reviewed to investigate age-related stability or change in self-conceptions. As noted previously, personality inventories and scales can be taken as measures of self-conceptions (McCrae and Costa, 1982; McCrae, 1982), because they assess how an individual rates himself or herself on aspects of personality provided by the investigator.

Table 2 summarizes these 17 studies. Four are cross-sectional in design, three are longitudinal, five involve the analysis of both cross-sectional and longitudinal data, and five are cross-sequential.

The majority of studies (13) examined the issue of stability or change by using mean-level analyses. Four studies made correlational analyses of stability; three investigated structural invariance. Only three studies used more than one type of stability measurement approach. A variety of different inventories were used to examine personality change during aging. In fact, twelve different instruments were used in the 17 studies reviewed here, only three of which—Cattell's 16 Personality Factors (16PF) Inventory, the Guilford-Zimmerman Temperament Survey, and the Edwards Personal Preference Schedule (EPSS)—were used more than once.

TABLE 2 Summary of Studies Using Personality Scales: Age Changes or Age Differences in the Cognitive Components of Self-Concept

Authors	Sample	Method	Variables	Measures	Results
Ahammer and Baltes (1972)	120 F,M Age, 15–74	X-sectional Mean scores	Affiliation Achievement Autonomy Nurturance	Derived from Jackson Personality Inventory	Age differences on affiliation and achievement
Bray and Howard (1983)	422 M Age in 20s, 1956–1960 266 M 20 year follow-up 204 M,F Age in 20s, 1977 (AT&T Longitudinal Studies of Managers)	Longitudinal × 20 years X-sectional Mean level	15 personality needs	Edwards Personal Preference Schedule	Age change on eight needs; need autonomy increased the most No cohort differences in need autonomy; cohort differences in need dominance
Costa and McCrae (1976)	140 M Age, 25–34 711 M Age, 35–54 118 M Age, 55–82 (Normative Aging Study)	X-sectional Cluster analysis	Anxiety/neuroticism Extraversion Openness to experience	16 PF	Structural stability for anxiety and extroversion
Costa and McCrae (1977–78)	104 M Age, 25–35 711 M Age, 35–54 118 M Age, 55–82 (Normative Aging Study)	Longitudinal × 10 years X-sectional Correlation	Anxiety/neuroticism Extraversion Openness to experience	16 PF	Correlational stability across age groups and over time for all three dimensions (r = 0.58 to 0.84 over 10 years)

Study	Sample	Variables	Instrument	Design/Analysis	Results
McCrae, Costa, and Arenberg (1980)	114 M Age, 17–85; three age groups; three measurement points	10 personality variables	Guilford-Zimmerman Temperament Survey	X-Sequential × 12 years Correlation	Correlational stability across age groups and over time ($r = 0.59$ to 0.87 over 12 years)
Costa and McCrae (1978)	206 M Age, 36–51 132 M Age, 52–57 197 M Age, 58–85 140 M Age, 25–82; retested at 10 years	Neuroticism Extraversion Openness to experience	16 PF	X-sectional Longitudinal × 10 years Mean level Factor Analysis	Structural stability of three personality dimensions across age groups Stability of means over 10 years
Douglas and Arenberg (1978)	915 M Age, 17–98; tested 1958–74 336 M Retested seven years later (Baltimore Longitudinal Study)	10 personality variables	Guilford-Zimmerman Temperament Survey	X-Sequential × seven years Mean scores	Mean level stability with aging for emotional health and sociability Maturational decline in general activity and masculine interests Later born cohorts lower on restraint; higher on ascendance Period declines for thoughtfulness, personal relations, friendliness Significant attrition effects
Kelly (1955)	227 couples Age, 25 and 45	Many personality variables	Bernreuter Personality Inventory 36-Trait Personality Rating Scale	Longitudinal × 20 years Mean scores Correlation	Mean level stability for most personality variables; decrease in energy Correlational stability for personality variables
Leon, Gillum, Gillum, and Gouze (1979)	71 M Age, 49–77; four measurement points	MMPI Validity and Clinical Scales	MMPI	Longitudinal × 30 years Mean scores Correlation	Mean level increases in depression, hypochondriasis, hysteria, and introversion Correlational stability, with extroversion most stable

TABLE 2 *(Continued)*

Authors	Sample	Method	Variables	Measures	Results
McCrae, Costa, and Arenberg (1980)	769 M Age, 17–97 346 M Age, 25–91 171 M Age, 33–86 (Baltimore Longitudinal Study)	X-sequential × nine years; three measurement periods Factor analysis	Emotional health Extraversion Thinking introversion	Guilford-Zimmerman Temperament Survey	Structural stability of three factors in three age groups and across time
Reedy (1982)	204 M,F Age, 23–84; three age groups	X-sectional Mean scores	15 personal needs	EPPS	Age × sex effect, with no sex differences in young adults, but traditional sex differences in middle-aged group and older group for autonomy, affiliation, dominance, abasement, and nurturance
Schaie and Parham (1974)	2151 M,F Age, 21–84; independent X-sectional and repeated meas. data, tested in 1956, 1963, 1970	X-sequential Mean scores	Social responsibility	Social Responsibility Scale	Social responsibility showed a differential course over time as a function of cohort and sex
Schaie and Parham (1976)	2500+ F,M Age, 21–84; tested in 1963, 1970	X-sequential × seven years Mean scores	13 personality variables 6 attitudinal variables	75-Item Questionnaire	Maturation effects on two of 19 variables Cohort effects on 10 out of 19 variables Period effects on seven out of 19 variables

Study	Sample	Design	Variables	Instrument	Findings
Siegler, George, and Okun (1979)	331 M,F Age, 45–70	Longitudinal × two years Mean scores	16 personality variables	16 PF	Stability over time for variables reflecting neuroticism and extroversion Traditional sex differences across cohorts Sex × time effect for self-confidence
Spence and Helmreich (1979)	1170 H.S. students 612 College students 602 parents 1572 college-age parents	X-sectional Mean scores	Expressive Instrumental	Derived from Personal Attributes Questionnaire	Age × sex effect, with no sex differences in younger group but traditional sex differences in college-age parent group
Whitbourne and Waterman (1979)	76 M, 71 F College age in 1966; Age 30 in 1976 224 F,M College age in 1976	Longitudinal × 10 years X-sectional Mean scores	Overall: Trust-mistrust Autonomy-shame Initiative-guilt Industry-inferiority Identity-diffusion Intimacy-isolation	Inventory of Psychosocial Development	Found maturational trend toward increased psychosocial development Period effects found to have differential impact on male-female development
Woodruff and Birren (1972)	54 M,F Age, 20 and 45; tested in 1944 and 1969 34 M,F Age, 19 43 M,F Age, 16; tested in 1969	Longitudinal × 25 years X-sectional Mean scores	Personal adjustment	California Test of Personality	No age-change in personal adjustment Cohort differences Subjective perception of positive change in the self

Structural Invariance. Designs examining structural invariance ordinarily indicate stability in personality-related self-conceptions between cohorts and across time. Costa and McCrae have been the most prominent researchers addressing the issue of structural invariance in adulthood. They have published cluster- and factor-analytic studies of data (Costa and McCrae, 1976, 1978, 1980b; McCrae, Costa, and Arenberg, 1980) from the Baltimore Longitudinal Study (12 years) and the Normative Aging Study (seven years) of hundreds of men across the adult life span. These studies used Cattell's 16PF Inventory and the Guilford-Zimmerman Temperament Survey.

Costa and his colleagues report substantial factor invariance across time for three dimensions of personality structure: neuroticism, extroversion, and openness to experience. This finding has led Costa and McCrae (1980b) to propose a formal trait model—the NEO model—that integrates the three major personality dimensions (neuroticism, extroversion, and openness) which show structural invariance during adult development.

Mean-Level Stability. Empirical evidence regarding mean-level change across age groups is markedly inconsistent. Cross-sectional studies of personality self-conceptions usually show age differences, but these may be due mainly to cohort differences.

In their study of adolescent, middle-aged, and older adults, Ahammer and Baltes (1972) found cross-sectional age differences for two personality dimensions. Specifically, adolescents and older subjects described themselves as more affiliative, compared with the middle-aged group; adolescents were significantly lower on achievement when compared with the two older groups.

In contrast to studies using direct self-conception measures, studies using investigator-inferred personality measures often find more sex differentiation among the elderly than among the young. A cross-sectional study by Reedy (1977; summarized in Reedy, 1982) suggests that traditional sex differences in personality are less likely to characterize young adult men and women than they do middle-aged and older individuals. In analyzing the personality needs of 102 married couples aged 20 to 80, she found that young adult men and women showed no significant difference for five personality needs: autonomy, affiliation, dominance, abasement, and nurturance. However, significant sex differences along traditional lines were evident for the middle-aged and older men and women.

Spence and Helmreich's (1979) study of nearly 4,000 individuals ranging in age from high school students to parents of college-age children yielded findings similar to those of Reedy. Older groups (both male and female) were usually more traditional in their sex-role personality attributes than were younger subjects. The results of these studies could be interpreted as reflecting cohort differences in generational values, with the younger respondents embracing more androgynous views of themselves. Alternatively, these results might reflect differences in role expectations and demands characteristic of different life stages, with traditional sex-role demands, and hence self-descriptions, characterizing the parents more than the students.

Longitudinal and cross-sequential studies usually show mean-level stability in personality self-descriptions for some, but not for all, variables. Scores for personality variables reflecting the domain of neuroticism and anxiety appear to be the most stable. Also stable, but less so, are the scores for extroversion. Self-confidence, autonomy, and energy level more frequently show some mean-level shifts with age. For example, in a longitudinal study of 331 men and women over age 45, Siegler, George and Okun (1979) found no main effects for time or cohort on scales reflecting neuroticism or extroversion. However, their data did reveal traditional sex differences in personality across all cohorts, with women more submissive, tender-minded, naive, and tense than men. Additionally, a sex-by-time interaction effect was significant, revealing *increasing* self-confidence for men but *decreasing* self-confidence for women over the two-year period studied. Similarly, in a 10-year longitudinal follow-up of 140 men aged 25 to 82, Costa and McCrae (1978) found mean-level stability for 16PF scales reflecting neuroticism (suspicious, guilt-prone, over-controlled, tense) and extroversion (outgoing, assertive, happy-go-lucky, adventurous).

In a cross-sequential analysis of 915 participants in the Baltimore Longitudinal Study, Douglas and Arenberg (1978) demonstrated no changes attributable to aging on the Guilford-Zimmerman Temperament Survey factor of emotional health. Although they found an increase in stability with aging for the extroversion scale of sociability, two dimensions of the self were interpreted as showing maturational effects. Beginning at age 50, general activity decreased and masculine interests declined steadily with age. Two scales showed cohort effects, with cohorts born later scoring lower on restraint and higher on ascendance. Period declines were found for thoughtfulness, personal relations, and friendliness. Douglas and Arenberg also examined personality differences between drop-outs and repeaters of the study. Much as in other investigations of subject mortality in studies of mental abilities (Baltes, Schaie, and Nardi, 1971; Schaie, Labouvie-Vief, and Barrett, 1973), they found that individuals who drop out of longitudinal studies tend to be less advantaged, emotionally and psychologically, than those who remain as participants and continue to furnish data.

In his now classic 20-year longitudinal study of 227 couples at ages 25 and 45, Kelly (1955) reported stability in mean-level for most personality and interest variables he examined. However, Kelly noted decreases in energy, personal appearance, and breadth of interests in both men and women, although women showed an increase in self-confidence from young adulthood into middle-age. More recently, Whitborne and Waterman (1979) reported their longitudinal research on 147 men and women studied in college and 10 years later, at age 30. Their findings show mean-level increases in overall psychosocial development, especially for the dimensions of industry, identity, and intimacy. These findings are similar to those of Mortimer et al. (1982) reported earlier.

Increased male self-confidence and autonomy with age is reported by Bray and Howard (in press) in their recent report of 20-year data from the American Telephone and Telegraph

Company longitudinal study of managers. At the 20-year follow-up, middle-aged Bell System managers had shown this increase most significantly in the Edwards Personal Preference Survey (EPPS) variables of need for achievement and need for autonomy, with these changes characterizing both college-educated and noncollege-educated managers. There were also shifts in mean-level for other test scores, including a decline in motivation to make and enjoy friends, to understand others' motives or feelings, and to conform to authority and regulations. These were interpreted by the investigators as suggesting increased self-competence, autonomy, and independence, decreased sociability, and increased "toughness" from young adulthood into middle-age. Comparing 1956 and 1977 cohorts of young managers on EPPS scores, cohort differences were evident for dominance but not for autonomy, providing evidence that the increase in need for autonomy over the 20-year period is an aging-related change. Taken together, these studies suggest an increase in well-being, competence, self-confidence, and autonomy from late adolescence into the middle years. A limitation of these studies is that their respondents were relatively advantaged and educated; mean-level shifts in personality in less educated individuals may not follow the same course.

Most of the studies finding mean-level shifts in personality variables have focused on the period from young adulthood to middle-age. Leon, Gillum, Gillum, and Gouze (1979) found an increase from middle to old age in mean scores on MMPI scales for depression, hypochondriasis, hysteria, and social introversion (n = 71; 30 years). Although it must be noted that these age differences are relatively small (Costa and McCrae, 1980b), they do stand in contrast to other findings (Costa and McCrae, 1978; Douglas and Arenberg, 1978). If generalizable, these findings suggest that later life may lead to some mild increase in neuroticism and introversion.

Studies with cross-sectional and longitudinal data suggest that cohort and period effects are at least as important as maturational effects, if not more so, in affecting personality-related self-conceptions. Using the California

Test of Personality, for example, Woodruff and Birren (1972) found no measured age changes in personal adjustment but found large cohort differences: The younger cohorts had lower adjustment scores. In contrast to the objectively measured findings of no change, Woodruff and Birren found that middle-aged individuals subjectively perceived themselves as having changed significantly over the time period studied. This is similar to the findings of Thurnher (1981) described earlier.

The personal adjustment measure Woodruff and Birren used may be construed as a measure of social conformity. A cross-sequential study with independent samples by Schaie and Parham (1974) suggests similar cohort differences for a similar self-conception variable, social responsibility. Controlling for the effects of attrition and testing, Schaie and Parham found that the life course of social responsibility was affected most strongly by period effects, differentially affecting men and women of different generations. Specifically, the study showed a temporal drop in social responsibility, with younger men increasing and older men decreasing their self-conceptions of being socially responsible.

In another study by Schaie and Parham (1976), 13 personality and six attitudinal variables were assessed over a seven-year period in a sample of over 2,500 men and women aged 21 to 84. Maturational effects were evident for only two variables, excitability and humanitarian concern, each of which showed increases with age. Cohort effects, however, were demonstrated for 10 variables. Older cohorts described themselves as less morally constrained and more candid; middle cohorts, aged 43 to 56, rated higher in self-conceptions reflecting dominance, assertiveness, vulnerability, and sensitivity to criticism; and younger cohorts, aged 22 to 42, rated higher on self-conceptions reflecting flexibility, restraint, and concern with honesty and morality. Period effects were found for seven of the 19 variables, with trends across all cohorts toward the following: increased conservatism, group dependency, and practicality along with decreased trust, excitability, concern about universal political issues, and interest in the financial support of society.

In sum, studies of mean-level change or stability in personality-related self-conceptions give evidence of stability in variables reflecting neuroticism and extroversion (but with small increases in neuroticism and decreases in extroversion at advanced ages); of increases in autonomy, self-competence, and self-confidence from young adulthood into at least middle age; of decreases in energy perhaps as early as the 40s; and of increased differentiation of traditional sex differences in personality with increasing age.

Correlational Studies. Correlational studies of personality in adulthood point to significant continuity in self-conceptions for a variety of different personality measures. Siegler, George, and Okun (1979) demonstrated correlational stability with their sample of 331 men and women aged 45 to 70 over a two-year period on the scales of the 16PF, with an average correlation of 0.50. Similarly, Kelly (1955) reported stability coefficients to average 0.5 for the personality variables he examined in his sample of 224 married couples over a 20-year period. Leon, Gillum, Gillum, and Gouze (1979) reported significant rank-order stability over a 30-year period, using the MMPI in their sample of 71 healthy men with an average age of 77 at retest. The median retest correlation was 0.39, with personality variables reflecting somatic concerns and schizoid tendencies being relatively unstable ($r = 0.28$), whereas social introversion-extroversion showed the greatest stability ($r = 0.74$). Costa and his colleagues (Costa and McCrae, 1977–1978, 1980b; Costa, McCrae, and Arenberg, 1980) have consistently observed that there is correlational stability for extroversion and neuroticism, as well as openness to experience. In a 10-year study using the 16PF, they report correlations from 0.58 for young (aged 25 to 34) subjects on the dimension of anxiety to 0.84 for extroversion in the old group (aged 55 to 82) (Costa and McCrae, 1977–1978). In another study, correlational stability over a 12-year period on the 10 scales of the Guilford-Zimmerman Temperament Survey ranged from 0.59 to 0.87 (Costa, McCrae, and Arenberg, 1980). As noted previously, whereas Costa and McCrae (1980b) conclude that there is correlational stability with r's of

0.58 or higher, Moss and Susman (1980) argue from the same data that there is evidence for change and plasticity in self-conceptions.

Conclusions

Within the past decade, a number of well-designed studies have been assessing self-cognitions using personality-trait assessments. These studies suggest the following conclusions:

1. Correlational studies indicate considerable (but not uniform) *stability* across age ranges in adulthood. Dimensions such as introversion-extroversion and neuroticism, in particular, appear quite stable over most of the adult life-span.
2. Mean-level studies have demonstrated inconsistent results. For example, studies using explicit self-conception measures lead to the conclusion that individuals incorporate opposite sex characteristics into the self as they age, whereas studies using personality-trait measures often find more sex differentiation among the elderly than the young.
3. Subjective perceptions of the self (as measured in open-ended questions) show more change with age than do objective assessments. Individuals subjectively perceive more change in themselves than is evident from more objective indicators.
4. Cohort membership, gender, social/cultural trends, and life-stage experiences have more significant impact on self-conceptions than maturation does. Since many of the studies examined here are cross-sectional in design, age contrasts may in fact reflect cohort differences rather than maturational changes or stability.

AFFECTIVE COMPONENTS: EVALUATIONS OF SELF-CONCEPTIONS

To what extent do self-evaluations—the affective component of self-conceptions—change or remain stable throughout the course of adulthood? How much do idealized self-conceptions change after adolescence? Do disvalued self-conceptions change as much? What factors other than age (such as sex, physical health, finances, life events) appear to vary with stability or change in self-evaluations?

Self-esteem refers to the evaluative and affective aspects of self-attitudes. Two dimensions of this evaluation have been noted in several analyses: (1) self-esteem based on a sense of personal competence, power, or efficacy, and (2) self-esteem based on a sense of personal virtue or moral worth (Gordon, 1968a, 1968b). Most of the gerontological literature on self-esteem does not reflect this potentially important and useful distinction but rather attempts to assess the individual's overall positive self-evaluation as a single variable.

Our review includes 17 studies that have examined age differences in self-esteem (see Table 3). Since all 17 studies are cross-sectional in design, age change is potentially confounded in each with cohort or generational differences. A total of 10 different instruments was used in these studies to assess self-esteem, reflecting their lack of consistent intrumentation (Breytspraak and George, 1982; Gecas, 1982). Findings are likely to be confounded, therefore, not only by the uniform use of cross-sectional methodology, but also by the variability of the measuring instruments. The most frequently employed scale was the Total Positive Scale from the Tennessee Self-Concept Scale (used in five studies). The Rosenberg Self-Esteem Scale and the Monge Semantic Differential Scale were also used more than twice.

In relation to stability change or differences in self-esteem during aging, eight studies showed a positive relationship between age and self-esteem, and seven showed no age differences in self-esteem. A finding that surprised us is that only one study found older cohorts to be lower in self-esteem than younger cohorts. One study found a curvilinear relationship between age and self-esteem, the latter reaching its peak in the fourth decade.

Higher Self-Esteem Among Older Age Groups

Eight studies showed a significant positive relationship between self-esteem and age. In a survey of over 3,000 men and women, Atchley

TABLE 3 Summary of Research on Self-Esteem: Age Changes and Age Differences

Authors	Sample	Method	Variables	Measures	Results
Atchley (1969, 1976)	1385 M, 2167 F Age, –79 5024 M,F High-school age (Rosenberg, 1970)	X-sectional Mean scores	Self-esteem	Rosenberg Self-Esteem Scale	Higher self-esteem for older subjects
Bloom (1961)	83 M Age, 20–69	X-Sectional Mean scores	Self-acceptance	Bloom Adjective Checklist	Curvilinear relationship between age and self-acceptance; peak at 40-49
Clark and Anderson (1967)	206 M, 229 F Age, 62–94	X-Sectional Mean scores	Self-evaluation	Clark and Anderson Self-Evaluation Scale	No age differences
Erdwins, Mellinger, and Tyer (1981)	120 F Age, 18–75; four age groups	X-Sectional Mean scores	Self-esteem	Total Positive TSCS	No age differences
Erdwins, Tyer, and Mellinger (1980)	80 M Age, 29–45; two age groups	X-Sectional Mean scores	Self-esteem	Total Positive TSCS	No age differences
Gaitz and Scott (1972)	1441 M,F Age, 20–79	X-Sectional Mean scores Percentages	Self-satisfaction	Global Question (Satisfaction as a person)	Slight age differences; old higher
Grant (1967)	500 M,F Age, 20–60	X-Sectional Mean scores	Self-esteem	Total positive TSCS	Age differences; old higher
Hess and Bradshaw (1970)	177 F,M Age, high school to 65	X-Sectional Mean scores	Congruity of self and ideal-self	Gough and Heilbrun Adjective Checklist	Increases in self/ideal-self congruency with age No age difference in self/ideal-self congruency
Kahana and Coe (1969)	36 F,M Age, 50–92	X-Sectional Percentages	Self-evaluation	Kuhn and McPartland 20 Statements Test	No age differences

Study	Sample	Design	Variable	Scale	Results
Kaplan and Po-korny (1969)	Age, 30–60+	X-Sectional Correlation	Self-esteem	Scale	Self-esteem signifcantly related to life events, finances
Kitching (1972)	200 F Age, 25–55	X-Sectional Correlation	Self-acceptance Positive self-concept	Index of Adjustment and Values	Positive self-concept positively correlated with age
Mason (1954a, 1954b)	30 F,M Age, 34 90 M,F Age, 73	X-Sectional Correlation	Positive self-judgment	Self-Concept Question-naire	Positive correlation with age
Nehrke (1974)	75 F Age, 19–74	X-Sectional Mean scores	Positive self-concept	Monge Smantic-Differ-ential Scale	No age differences
Nehrke, Hulicka, and Morganti (1980)	99 M Age, 50–70+	X-Sectional Mean scores	Positive self-concept	Monge Semantic-Dif-ferential Scale	Age differences; old higher
Thompson (1972)	626 M,F Age, 12–68 (Fitts, 1965) 60 M Age, 60–80+ (Postema, 1970)	X-Sectional Mean scores	Self-esteem	Total Positive TSCS	Higher self-esteem for elderly sample
Trimakas and Ni-colay (1974)	162 F Age, 66–88	X-Sectional Mean scores	Self-esteem	Total Positive TSCS	Higher self-esteem for old compared to nor-mative sample on which TSCS was de-veloped Trend for increased self-esteem with age for older respondents
Ward (1977)	323 F,M Age, 60–92	X-Sectional Correlation	Self-esteem	Rosenberg Self-Esteem Scale	Negative correlation of age with self-esteem Positive correlation of health with self-es-teem

(1976) used the Rosenberg Scale and found higher self-esteem for older cohorts than for younger cohorts. Mason (1954a, 1954b) used his own self-concept questionnaire to assess positive self-judgment in a cross-sectional study of 30 men and women with an average age of 34 and 90 men and women with an average age of 73. Findings showed a small but significant positive correlation between positive self-judgment and age. Grant (1967) investigated self-esteem using the Total Positive Scale from the Tennessee Self-Concept Scale (TSCS) in a sample of 500 men and women aged 20 to 60. He found significant age differences, the old being higher in self-esteem. Using the same positive scale, Thompson (1972) reviewed the findings from Fitts' (1965) sample of 626 males and females aged 12 to 68 and Postema's (1970) sample of 60 men aged 60 to 80 and found that the older groups had higher self-esteem. Kitching (1972) conducted a study of 200 females aged 25 to 55. Using the Index of Adjustment and Values to assess self-acceptance and positive self-concept, he found that positive self-concept showed a significant positive correlation with age. Nehrke, Hulicka, and Morganti (1980) used the Monge Semantic Differential Scale to measure positive self-evaluation in 99 males aged 50 to 70 and over. Age differences were found in positive self-evaluations, with the older group scoring higher than the middle-aged subjects.

Trimikas and Nicholay (1974) studied 162 females aged 66 to 68 from low-income senior housing. Using the TSCS Total Positive Scale to assess self-esteem, they found that their older sample's self-esteem level was higher than that of the younger normative group on which the scale was standardized (Fitts, 1965). Within their sample of young-old and old-old women, however, Trimikas and Nicholay found no significant relationship between self-esteem and age. However, they found self-esteem to be correlated significantly and positively with a measure of defensiveness and adjustment. They also assessed one potential correlate of self-esteem—altruism. Subjects were given an opportunity to contribute some money to the entertainment fund of the building in which they were living. The investiga-

tors found that individuals who were high in self-esteem were more altruistic than those who were low. They concluded that higher self-esteem in the elderly may be a positive force contributing to group cohesiveness and reduced social isolation.

Self-esteem appears to be correlated with other age-related variables. Data from the Houston study of leisure and mental health (Gaitz and Scott, 1972) were used to examine relationships between age and mental health. Their sample consisted of 1,441 community-dwelling respondents aged 20 to 94 from three major ethnic groups in the Houston area: Anglos, Blacks, and Mexican-Americans. Gaitz and Scott concluded that older people appear to be more relaxed and at ease with themselves but more concerned about poorer health status and increased memory problems. Data from the Bradburn Affect Balance Scale suggested that the older age groups reported both less positive affect and less negative affect. Finally, the older the respondent, the higher the self-satisfaction (as expressed by a single global question), especially among women.

Specific self-evaluations were also analyzed (Gordon, Gaitz, and Scott, 1975) in an effort to discover the relation of age/stage to three other variables: self-rated intelligence, self-rated work skills competence, and a 17-item leisure skills index. This differentiation into specific self-evaluations was based on Gordon's approach (1968a, 1968b) to what he calls "systemic senses of self" (competence, self-determination, unity, and moral worth). He argues that these systemic senses are the person's reflexive interpretations of how he or she is doing with regard to the four major problems that must be dealt with, according to Parsonian action theory, by any continuing system. The validity and usefulness of going beyond a single global self-esteem dimension has been demonstrated in research on a successful Career Options Program for a group of women aged 18 to 55 who were planning to enter the job market (Gordon and Gordon, 1982). This research revealed that measures of these "systemic senses" changed in different ways over the course of the program.

In the Houston sample, self-rated intelligence was essentially equal in all five age groups, but self-ratings of work skills were significantly lower in the older age groups (particularly after ages 45 to 64). The leisure competence index also revealed a pattern of lower mean scores in each older age group, especially after ages 30 to 44. The fact that these three patterns are distinctly different from that observed with the self-satisfaction ratings (which were found to be higher in the older age groups) again demonstrates the value of theorizing, measuring, and analyzing self-evaluations as differentiated concepts, rather than in global terms.

No Age Differences

Although the eight cross-sectional studies just discussed suggest that older cohorts consistently show higher self-esteem than younger cohorts, seven other studies reviewed showed no age differences in self-evaluation. Clark and Anderson (1967) studied 206 men and 229 women aged 62 to 94. Using their own Self Evaluation Scale to assess self-esteem, they found no age differences. Kaplan and Pokorny (1969) investigated self-esteem using Rosenberg's Self-Esteem Scale with 500 men and women aged 30 to 60. Although they found no age differences in self-esteem, they did find that self-esteem was related to recent life events, congruence between current and desired standard of living, fear of being left alone in childhood, and present household composition. Kahana and Coe (1969) used the Twenty Statements Test to assess self-evaluation in 36 institutionalized subjects aged 50 to 92 and also found no significant age differences.

Hess and Bradshaw (1970) studied 55 high school students, 63 college students, 39 subjects aged 35 to 50, and 20 subjects aged 55 to 65, the older respondents being healthy, community-residing individuals of higher socio-economic status. They used the Gough and Heilbrun Adjective Checklist to assess the degree of match between current and ideal self-preferences, interpreting this match as a measure of self-acceptance. Both current-self and ideal-self scores proved to be more favorable for older cohorts than for younger cohorts, a result the investigators suggested might be due to the higher socio-economic status of the older subjects. Since there were no clear age trends for the current-self/ideal-self congruency measure, no age difference in self-acceptance could be discerned.

Nehrke (1974) used Monge's Semantic Differential Scale to measure positive self-concept in 75 women aged 19 to 74; there were no age differences in positive self-concept. Erdwins, Tyer, and Mellinger (1980), using the Total Positive Scale of the Tennessee Self Concept Scale, found no significant age differences in self-esteem in women aged 29 to 39 and 40 to 45. In another study, Erdwins, Mellinger, and Tyer (1981) studied self-esteem in 120 women divided into four age groups: 18 to 22, 29 to 39, 40 to 55, and 60 to 75. Using the Total Positive Score from the TSCS, they found no age differences in self-esteem in this wider age range of women.

Most of the studies reviewed, for all of their different measurement instruments, suggest that the self-esteem of middle-aged or older individuals equals or surpasses that of younger subjects. One possible explanation is that of cohort differences, the older respondents simply having had higher levels of self-esteem throughout their lives than younger cohorts do now. A maturational explanation is also plausible: that the results reflect ontogenetic change and that individuals are able to maintain or even increase their level of self-esteem with aging despite the losses and assaults that often accompany it. A third possible explanation involves survivorship: People with higher self-esteem have greater longevity. Although there are no longitudinal studies that examine the relationship between subject attrition and level of self-esteem, Antonovsky (1981) presents evidence that self-esteem is a protective factor, increasing an individual's resistance to stress and thereby contributing to physical health.

An important but neglected research issue is how the four processes of self-esteem formation (reflected appraisals, social comparison, self-attribution, and psychological centrality) proposed by Rosenberg (1979) might contribute to cohort differences in self-esteem. Especially relevant is how these processes relate to the observed maintenance or enhancement of self-esteem with aging.

Age Contrasts in Determinants of Self-Esteem

From another perspective, it may be the case that the bases or determinants of self-esteem are different in old age than at previous life-cycle stages (Ward, 1977). Self-esteem in the elderly may be related to general attitudes toward old people, as well as to self-age identification and age-related deprivation changes. Ward examined relations among these variables in a survey of 323 noninstitutionalized volunteers aged 60 to 92. Respondents were asked to select their age identification category, the two most frequently selected being elderly (55 percent) and middle-aged (45 percent). Attitudes towards old people were then assessed using 19 statements about old people in general. Self-esteem was assessed using the Rosenberg Self-Esteem Scale. An age-related deprivation scale was designed to assess eight possible life changes since age 55, including retirement, widowhood, decreased finances, decreased health, decreased ability to do household chores, decreased socializing, decreased ability to do favorite activities, and residential relocation. Activity level was assessed on the basis of respondents' reported participation in twelve activities.

The results indicated that only the scale of attitudes toward older people was reliably predictive of higher or lower self-esteem. Shifts in age-identity were related to several factors, ordered as follows: age-related deprivation, chronological age, health, activity, employment status, and gender (women usually making a younger age-identification). Age-identity made no significant contribution to self-esteem. Attitudes toward old people, however, were related to level of self-esteem regardless of age-identification. Those with negative attitudes toward old people also displayed lower levels of self-esteem, even when personal change and current situation variables were controlled.

Sex differences were also noted. Education and income were found to be more important to male self-esteem, suggesting that men are more affected by SES. Age-related deprivation and current activity were more important to female self-esteem, suggesting that women are more affected by their current situation and loss experiences.

Ward concluded that the acceptance of the age-identity "old" was not related to attitudes toward old people in general but rather to change in continuity of life or the self as a result of retirement, health problems, and other external factors. Ward hypothesized that the basis of consistency of self-identity in old age lies in both continuity of personal relationships and the lack of age-related deprivations. Transformation in self-image occurs in response to personal changes in roles, SES, current situations, and loss experiences, rather than being intrinsically related to chronological aging.

Conclusions

Despite the importance of the topic of self-esteem and aging and the recent resurgence of interest in self-phenomena in psychology and sociology, there are relatively few recent studies of self-esteem and aging. From those reviewed here, several conclusions emerge:

1. The majority of studies showed either no age differences in self-esteem or higher self-esteem in older cohorts. This fact suggests either that today's older cohorts started out with a more favorable self-evaluation than did younger generations, or, more possibly, that self-esteem typically is maintained or increased as individuals age.

2. All of the studies are cross-sectional, so that cohort differences and maturational change are confounded in the results. There is clearly a need to introduce cross-sequential strategies to this research area.

3. The limited available research investigating factors other than age that contribute to self-esteem suggests that social, situational, and personal life changes, along with attitudes toward old people, are at least as important as age itself.

4. The determinants of age-identification and self-esteem may be different in old age than at other stages in the life course. This possibility remains a hypothesis for

further cross-age-group investigations. Another hypothesis is that there are sex differences in sources of self-esteem in old age.

5. Unfortunately, no research has investigated the process by which self-esteem is enhanced or maintained during aging in terms of Rosenberg's (1979) four proposed determinants of self-esteem (reflected appraisals, social comparison, self-attribution, psychological centrality). Also unresearched is how age-identification is related to self-esteem during adulthood. All these topics reflect important research areas for the future.

CONATIVE COMPONENTS: BEHAVIORS REFLECTING SELF-STRIVING

To what extent are striving and behavioral orientations toward self-enhancement or self-maintenance stable across the adult life span? If there is change, what dimensions or behavioral orientations reflecting the self show this change? What factors other than age contribute to behavior that reflects maintenance of self-conceptions through adulthood?

This section focuses on the limited empirical literature on aging, self-striving, and behaviors reflecting the self. We found seven studies that reflect the striving or action component of self-conceptions. All involve clinical ratings—that is, evaluations of such variables as aggressiveness, self-confidence, and expressiveness—made by clinically trained examiners working from a wide range of observational or interview protocols. With one exception, all are longitudinal studies that were conducted at the University of California at Berkeley beginning in 1930. A description of the studies covered by this review may be found in Table 4.

Evidence from Clinical Ratings

The seven studies display inconsistent findings concerning stability or change in self-attitudes as observed in behaviors reflecting the self. Two of them examine stability of self from childhood or adolescence into young adulthood. The first, by Tuddinham (1959), pre-

sented an analysis of one of the earlier developmental studies of behaviors from late adolescence into adulthood. Its data, based on the longitudinal Oakland Growth Study, involved 72 individuals who were evaluated as adolescents and again in their mid-30s. Many self-related variables were inferred from observational and interview data. The average correlation from adolescence to the mid-30s (across all variables) was 0.27 for men and 0.24 for women. Aggression was found to be the most stable dimension for men (r = 0.68), along with self-assertiveness. Social prestige was found to be the most stable dimension for women (r = 0.67). Expressiveness was stable for both men and women, but there was a lack of stability for attractiveness, self-confidence, and achievement. In general, the Tuddinham study suggests a significant stability of behavior-related self-attitudes from late adolescence into adulthood, but with different patterns for men and women.

Using data from the parallel longitudinal Berkeley Guidance Study, Bronson (1966) studied data from 85 children aged 5 to 16, who were re-evaluated at age 30. The interviews were quantified using the 100-item California Q-Sort. For both males and females, stability was found for expressiveness/withdrawal and placidity/reactivity.

Four of the studies reviewed examine the relationship between personality type and age. In their now classic investigation of adjustment to retirement, Reichard, Livson, and Peterson (1962) studied 87 men aged 55–84, half of whom were retired and half of whom were facing retirement. Based on personality ratings derived from interviews with the men, the investigators identified five personality types. Three of the personality types were seen as adapting well to aging and retirement: the "mature," the "rocking-chair," and the "armored" categories. Two personality types, the "angry" and the "self-haters," were seen as adapting poorly. The investigators found no relationship between age and personality type.

In another classic study of personality and aging, Neugarten, Crotty, and Tobin (1964) studied 88 men and women aged 56 to 90 from the Kansas City Study of Adult Life to examine the relationships between personal-

TABLE 4 Summary of Studies Reflecting the Conative Component of Self-Conceptions: Behavior-Observer Rating Studies

Authors	Sample	Method	Variables	Measures	Results
Block (1971)	170 F,M Age, adol. to mid-30s (Oakland Guidance and Berkeley Growth Studies)	Longitudinal × 25 years Correlation Mean scores Factor analysis	100	Naturalistic plus interview data quantified on California Q-sort	S/B Correlational stability over time for many variables; sex differences Mean level change over time, with sex differences evident Ipsative analyses revealed interindividual differences in extent of personal consistency over time
Bronson (1966)	85 M,F Age, 5–16 and 30 (Berkeley Guidance Study)	Longitudinal × 25 years Correlation	100	Interviews quantified on 100-item California Q-sort	No age differences on variables of expressiveness—withdrawal, placidity, reactivity
Maas and Kuypers (1974)	95 F, 47 M Age, 20–82	Longitudinal × 60 years Factor analysis	100	Clinical ratings on Q-sort and ego-defense scales based on interview data	Stability over time varied by personality type
Mussen, Eichorn, Honzik, Bieber, and Meredith (1980)	53 F Age, 30 and 70 (mothers from Child Guidance Study)	Longitudinal × 40 years Correlation Mean scores Factor analysis	16 personality-social variables 5 cognitive variables	Clinical ratings	All five cognitive variables plus 10 out of 16 personality variables showed significant (>0.05) interage correlation Six out of 10 personality variables showed trend toward change in mean level over 40-year period

580

Study	Sample	Design	Variables	Data	Results
Neugarten, Crotty, and Tobin (1964)	45 F, 43 M Age, 56–90	X-Sectional Mean scores Factor analysis	45 personality variables	Clinical ratings on five-point scale based on clinically structured and open-ended projective data.	Three factors common to age 30 and 70: (1) cognitive style (2) adjustment/anxiety (3) energy/outgoingness
Reichard, Livson, and Peterson (1962)	87 M Age, 55–84	Longitudinal	Five personality types	Personality ratings derived from interviews	No age changes
Tuddenham (1959)	72 M,F Age, adol. to mid-30s	Longitudinal × 20 years Correlation	Many	Ratings based on observation and interview data	Variables showed different patterns of stability for men and women

ity type, sex, age, and adjustment. Forty-five personality variables were assessed using clinical ratings based on clinical, structured and open-ended interviews. The investigators identified six personality types: integrated, passive-dependent, defended-constricted, self-doubting, competitive and unintegrated. No relationship was found between chronological age and an individual's personality type. The investigators concluded that there appeared to be consistency over time in these personality classifications, each of which reflect observed behavioral consistency in the presented self over time.

Two studies have examined the relationship between age, personality type, and consistency or change in self-perceptions. Block (1971) examined the relationship between age, personality type (based on clinical ratings of interview data), and consistency of personality attributes over a period of two decades. Using data from both the Oakland Growth and the Berkeley Guidance studies, Block analyzed data from 170 males and females from adolescence into their mid-30s. He used naturalistic and interview data to assess many self-variables that were then quantified on the California Q-Sort through judges' ratings. When Block examined stability of the personality variables over the period of study, he observed that 60 percent of the personality variables were correlated significantly across time beyond the 0.05 level. In particular, he found stability for behaviors reflecting dependability and impulsivity in young men and stability for behaviors reflecting passive-conforming versus expressive-aggressive autonomy in women. In contrast to the generalized finding of stability of behaviors from the correlational analysis, Block's mean-level analysis of age-related change in personality variables gave evidence for more change than stability. In particular, men showed an increase in self-control, self-confidence, and seriousness and a decrease in the need for reassurance and favorable social comparison. The females showed an increase in conventional femininity, social ease, psychological mindedness, and dependability and a decrease in the importance they placed on sexuality.

In an additional analysis of the data, Block computed "personal consistency correlations" to assess ipsative stability over the period of study. Correlations on variables for individuals ranged from -0.02 to 1.00 for subjects from junior to senior high school, and from -0.49 to 0.99 for subjects from senior high school into the mid-30s. Block concluded that mean correlations for a group are uninformative about any particular individual, with some subjects remaining stable over the time period of study and others exhibiting considerable changes in behaviors reflecting the self. Block then grouped subjects into two categories— "changers" and "non-changers"—and found that changers were systematically different in their personality makeup than non-changers. In contrast to non-changers, changers were insecure, defensive, and having problems in interpersonal relations.

Maas and Kuypers (1974) followed up on the 142 parents from the Berkeley Guidance Sample (see the previous discussion of Bronson's study). Those parents were initially interviewed in their 20s and 30s and again in their 70s. Many dimensions of personality were assessed, including energy output, freshness, restlessness, talkativeness, excitability, self-assurance, criticalness, open-mindedness, and frankness. Ratings were made by the California Q-Sort scale, as well as by ego-defense scales employing all available interview data. Using a factor analysis of the personality ratings, Maas and Kuypers identified four consistent female personality types and three male types from the data gathered on their by now elderly (aged 60 to 82) subjects. The female types included person-oriented mothers, fearful-ordering mothers, autonomous mothers, and anxious-asserting mothers. The male personality types were identified as person-oriented fathers, active-competent fathers, and conservative-ordering fathers.

Maas and Kuypers report differential stability across the 40-year period of study by personality type. The greatest stability for older subjects was found among those high in anxiety and ego-disorganization, e.g., the fearful-ordering and anxious-asserting mothers. Their results imply that individuals with less functional personality characteristics may exhibit less change over time in behaviors reflecting the self. Another important suggestion of the study is that evidence of change in personality may be lost whenever researchers average the scores on personality scales of individuals who are of different personality types.

It should be noted that Block's (1971) findings on "changers" and "non-changers" are not consistent with those of Maas and Kuypers (1974) in their older sample of grandparents. One possible explanation is that younger individuals who are less functional in their personality organization tend to change *more,* whereas similar older individuals with dysfunctional personality characteristics tend to change less.

Mussen, Eichorn, Honzik, Bieber, and Meredith (1980) report the most recent analyses of the Berkeley data: an assessment of the 40-year longitudinal study of 53 mothers of children from the Child Guidance Study. These investigators examined clinical ratings for the 53 mothers at ages 30 and 70 for five cognitive variables and 16 personality/social variables. Just as the findings from Block's (1971) study did, correlational analysis and mean-score analysis yielded different results. As with Block's findings, the correlational analysis suggested more stability; the mean-score analysis, more change in behaviors reflecting the self. Mussen et al. report that, based on their interage correlational analysis, all five cognitive variables and 10 out of the 16 personality social variables showed statistically significant interage correlations. The correlations ranged from −0.01 for the tendency to criticize children to 0.52 for talkativeness. By contrast, six out of 16 personality-social variables showed a trend toward change in mean-level over the 40-year period of study; specifically, the trend was for freshness, self-assurance, tendency to criticize, and personal appearance to decline over the period of study, and for open-mindedness and frankness to increase.

Mussen et al. (1980) used a new factor analytic method to extract three factors common to both age groups, two factors specific to respondents at age 30, and three specific to those at age 70. Although these unique factors were difficult for the investigators to interpret, the three common factors were (1) cognitive style (accuracy in thinking, good use of language, open-mindedness); (2) adjustment (lack of worrisomeness, self-assurance, satisfaction with life); and (3) energy/outgoingness (excit-ability, energy level, talkativeness, restlessness). Overall, correlations of scores for the three factors across all individuals from age 30 to 70 were 0.28, 0.34 and 0.24, respectively. These coefficients suggested that energy/outgoingness, cognitive style, and adjustment appear to be relatively more stable than other types of self-attitude traits. Since these correlations, while signficant, are not large, the investigators concluded that there is some, but not great, continuity over the 40-year period. These findings are remarkably consistent with those from the Baltimore Longitudinal Studies reported by McCrae and his colleagues using personality inventories to assess stability and change in self. The study of Mussen et al. further suggests that interests, attitudes, self-assurance, and life satisfaction are less stable and that, over all, correlations over time on behaviors reflecting the self are quite modest.

Conclusions

Five general findings emerge from these studies of behaviors reflecting the self, based on clinical ratings:

1. The degree of stability over time in self-attitudes varies in accordance with the particular dimension under study, with gender, and with personality type. Correlational analyses show somewhat greater stability than do mean-level analyses.

2. As revealed by correlational analyses, some self-attitude variables that reflect action or striving seem to be more stable than others; specifically, personality dimensions that reflect cognitive style, adjustment-anxiety, and energy-outgoingness are relatively more stable than other behavioral dimensions reflecting the self. This finding is consistent with child-developmental literature. It leads to the hypothesis that "process-oriented" dimensions of the self (i.e., dimensions reflecting temperamental or constitutional differences, influence of heredity or genes, or early learning experiences) are more stable. "Content-oriented" dimensions of the self (such as interests, role-related behaviors, and attitudes) are less

stable because they are more affected by impact of life events, history, culture, and individual specific experiences (Mussen et al., 1980). Stability for the behavioral variables reflecting adjustment-anxiety and energy-outgoingness coincides with stability found for the variables for anxiety-neuroticism and extroversion when using personality inventories.

3. Both correlational and mean-level analyses suggest that behaviors reflecting the self differ for men and women and exhibit different patterns of stability and change over the adult life course. No consistent age patterns of change for men and women are evident so far from the available data.

4. Although correlations across time for behaviors reflecting the self may be significant, mean correlations for a group of individuals are uninformative and may mask change and stability for any individual subject. Ipsative analyses suggest that younger individuals with less functional self-characteristics may be more likely to change over time, whereas older individuals with less functional self-characteristics may show more stability over time.

5. Correlations for behaviors reflecting the self over time are not large, suggesting that personal consistency or stability is far from complete. Notably, correlational analyses of behavioral data points to less stability over time than do studies using personal inventories. The greater impact of situational factors, lower reliability of clinical ratings, and/or lower validity of behavior ratings in assessing the construct of interest may contribute to the lower correlational stability found in clinical-behavioral studies.

SELF-ATTITUDE STABILITY AND LIFE EVENTS

The studies reviewed in previous sections suggest tendencies toward considerable stability for many self-attitude variables and for many individuals. Life-span developmental theorists

and researchers are increasingly turning their attention to understanding and explaining those findings.

A most promising approach focuses on possible impacts of changing life circumstances and changes in self-conceptions (Moss and Susman, 1980; McCrae and Costa, 1982; Mortimer, Finch, and Kumka, 1982; Gecas, 1982; Seligman, 1975; Schmitz-Scherzer and Thomae, 1983). Self-attitude stability or change is not necessarily the result of some intrapsychic dynamic or of remote forces (such as early childhood experiences) but may be the result of stabilities or discontinuities in current life circumstances and social roles. In this view, self-attitudes are influenced by environmental conditions. Glenn (1980), for example, maintains that as the social environment becomes more stable during adulthood, some attitudes and values become more stable. Age-graded, normative events and less predictable nonnormative events may be sources of self-concept stability or redirection (Baltes et al., 1980). Gordon (1971, 1976) has proposed a "stage-developmental" model to explore changes in self-attitudes over the life span.

Individuals are not simply passive respondents to life stresses and circumstances. Self-attitudes may be highly influential as individuals create, maintain, or change their life situations (Rosenberg, 1979; Neugarten, 1977; Cottrell, 1969).

There is a growing body of literature suggesting that distant as well as current life experiences are significant forces influencing self-concept stability and change during the late-adolescent through early-adult years (Rosenberg, 1979; Simmons et al., 1979; Brooks and Elliott, 1971). For example, Mortimer et al. (1982) and Mortimer and Lorence (1979) demonstrated that life experiences during the decade following college have significant effects (independent of prior self-conceptions) on self-competence at a 10-year follow up. Employment insecurity had a negative impact on self-competence, whereas income, work autonomy, and close relations with father had positive effects.

Other studies suggest that self-conceptions shape and influence the kinds of life stresses and lifestyles that individuals experience. A preliminary report by Seligman (unpublished manuscript) of additional analyses of data taken from the longitudinal Grant Study (Vaillant, 1977) suggests that the attributional style of college men in 1946 is a significant predictor (r = 0.396) of health status 40 years later. Similarly, Seligman's preliminary re-analyses of data from the Berkeley-Oakland Growth Study reveals the attributional style for fathers in 1943 to be significantly related to perceived self-defeat (r = 0.71), personal meaning (r = 0.61), and economic strain (r = 0.59) 27 years later.

Costa and his colleagues (Costa and McCrae, 1980a; McCrae and Costa, 1982; Costa, McCrae, and Norris, 1980) report data suggesting that individuals higher on self-atti-tude dimensions reflecting neuroticism tend to be more crisis-prone. These self-conceptions are also predictive of job dissatisfaction, mari-tal troubles, concerns over failing health, and low subjective well-being. Similarly, in an older sample, George (1978) found that per-sonality variables from the 16PF—those de-scribed as including conscientious, tender-minded, practical, group-dependent, relaxed, and aroused—were better predictors of well-being than social-status variables. Thurnher's (1981) analysis of an eight-year longitudinal study of developmental turning points and self-conceptions suggests that respondents' scores on objective self-conception measures at the outset of the study were significantly related to their later perceptions of the impact of turning points. Individuals judged high in self-control were more likely to perceive turn-ing points positively. By contrast, individuals high in dysphoria perceived later developmen-tal events negatively. Also, individuals high in insecurity and in hostility tended to see developmental milestones in a negative light. Schmitz-Scherzer and Thomae (1983) and Bray and Howard (1983) suggest that individ-uals may be differentiated into two groups, reflecting the way they age: (1) those with increasingly positive self-image attributes who also receive positive reinforcement from their social environment, and (2) those with de-creasing self-images who also perceive more negative environmental stress.

Taken together, this pattern of findings sug-gests the following conclusions: (1) individuals with more "adjusted" self-conceptions may achieve objectively and subjectively better life situations, which in turn enhance self-concep-tions; (2) certain personality self-conceptions are predisposed to well-being, independent of life events. In sum, the life-span developmen-tal course of self-attitudes and the reciprocal relationships between life events and self-con-ceptions has gained the attention of a diverse set of investigators. Research to date suggests that earlier self-conceptions significantly im-pact on later objective and subjective events and that these events then contribute to fur-ther stability or shifts in self-conceptions.

SUMMARY AND CONCLUSIONS: FUTURE DIRECTIONS FOR RESEARCH AND THEORY ON THE SELF AND AGING

Does aging affect personality? And does per-sonality affect aging? We began this review by noting that existing answers to these sim-plistic questions are complex and that the con-temporary "litter-ature" of personality and aging has produced some healthy controver-sies that may lead to a much needed reconcep-tualization and narrowing of focus. Our con-cern in this chapter has been to unravel some of the current confusion surrounding stability versus change in personality dispositions dur-ing aging by trying to delimit and conceptually integrate the field.

The first section presented our basic argu-ment: A focus on "self-conceptions" as atti-tude structures (in contrast to the more ab-stract and global notions of "personality") may be the most fruitful approach for develop-ing an empirically valid theory concerning sta-bility or change over the life course. We pro-posed the orientation of *attitudes toward the self,* thus drawing on a long empirical and theoretical tradition in the social psychology and sociology of attitude formation and change.

In this section, we also presented our con-ceptual and theoretical bases for an examina-tion of self-conceptions as they undergo expe-riences of stability or change during the life course. We argued that a coherent examination of self-conceptions in terms of aging (based on the reflexive "me" of oneself as object in contrast to the "I" of actual action—following the distinction of George Herbert Mead) involved consideration of the three traditionally defined components of attitude: cognition (the "content" of the self), evaluation (the "feeling" toward the self), and conation (the "striving" toward confirmation, protection, enhancement, and fulfillment of the self). We presented a conceptual typology of self-conception that suggested six distinct modalities that are amenable to empirical investigation and can be related explicitly in theory. The six modes are: (1) current self-conceptions structure; (2) idealized self-conceptions; (3) negative or disvalued self-conceptions; (4) presented self-conceptions; (5) conceptions of responses by significant others; and (6) conceptions of inferred self-images. We discussed major analytic dimensions pertaining to the measurement possibilities and conceptual properties of each of the six modes, with the suggestion that this typology be employed in future research on aging and self-conceptions.

In the second section, we discussed the major methodological issues that have created difficulty for those attempting to examine age changes or similarity in self-conceptions across time. We suggested that outlining these problems makes an important contribution in itself to understanding the "disarray" of personality and aging literature currently evident. The four major issues can be examined as follows: (1) problems in definition and measurement of self-attitudes; (2) issues in statistical analyses; (3) difficulties in population and sampling; and (4) issues related to interpretation of findings.

In sections three, four, and five, we reviewed the existing literature on self-conceptions and aging, focusing on the empirical evidence of change versus stability in the three components of attitudes toward the self. A total of 62 empirical analyses were examined. Our review pointed to the difficulty of making generalizations concerning age-related stability or change because of the methodological difficulties highlighted in the second section. In particular, we found that a majority of the research is cross-sectional and that the age differences observed cannot therefore be attributed conclusively to either ontogenetic (maturational) or cohort (historical) effects.

Our review does suggest, however, some generalizations that have sufficient support in existing studies—whatever their methodological limitations—that they can be stated in the form of tentative propositions. These propositions are, more correctly, hypotheses that can be used to guide future research and theory building concerning the interrelations of self-conceptions and aging.

In terms of the *content* of self-conceptions (cognitions about the self), the following hypotheses may be advanced:

Proposition 1: There is substantial *structural stability* of those self-conception dimensions that are most closely related to temperament (especially personal well-being, security/adjustment, sociability/amiability, and competence/assertion/achievement).

Proposition 2: Mean levels of "objectively" measured self-conception variables (from use of adjective checklists or semantic differential self-ratings) show substantial stability in longitudinal research (especially such self-attitude dimensions as amiability, insecurity, assertion, self-control, hostility, dysphoria, adjustment/anxiety, extroversion/introversion, openness to experience, and neuroticism).

Proposition 3: Mean-level change in longitudinal research has been found in many variables: autonomy, self-competence, self-confidence, excitability, and humanitarian concern, all of which tend to increase from young adulthood at least into middle age; energy, which can decrease as early as the 40s; and social responsibility, which in older men's self-conceptions tends to decrease.

Proposition 4: "Subjective" self-conceptions (revealed by using open-ended procedures that measure the percentage utilization of particular noun-like categories or adjectival attributes) show greater change than "objective" self-ratings.

Proposition 5: Correlational studies indicate considerable (but not uniform) *stability* across age ranges in adulthood (especially in introversion/extroversion and neuroticism).

Proposition 6: There is an increased tendency with age to incorporate traditionally defined opposite-sex characteristics into self-conceptions (especially warmth/expressiveness in aging men and instrumentality/autonomy in aging women).

Proposition 7: Cohort membership, sex, sociocultural trends, and life stage experiences have more significant impact on self-conceptions than does maturation; since many of the studies examined in this review are cross-sectional in design, even those *age differences* that would seem to indicate *age changes* may in fact reflect cohort differences rather than maturation.

In terms of *self-evaluations* (the affective components of self-conception), the following propositions emerge from our review of the literature and call for confirmation in future empirical research:

Proposition 8: Since all of the studies reviewed are cross-sectional, cohort differences and maturational changes are confounded in the results; there is a clear need for the introduction of cross-sequential strategies to future research on self-esteem and aging.

Proposition 9: The majority of studies reviewed showed either no age differences in self-esteem or higher self-esteem in older cohorts, suggesting either that recent older cohorts started out with more favorable self-evaluation than did younger cohorts and/or that self-esteem is typically maintained or increased as individuals age.

Proposition 10: Although global self-esteem may be as high or higher among older persons, the specific dimensions related to competence may decline with age.

Proposition 11: The limited research investigating the contributions to self-esteem other than age suggests that social, situational, and personal life changes, along with attitudes toward older people, are at least as important as chronological age itself.

Proposition 12: The determinants of age-identification and self-esteem may be different in old age; moreover, there are sex differences in sources of self-esteem in old age.

In assessing the issue of *behavioral orientations* reflecting the self (the conative aspects of self-conception that suggest striving or motivation toward self-enhancement, protection, confirmation, etc.), the following tentative propositions are suggested but await empirical validation in future studies:

Proposition 13: Individuals of different personality types (as determined from clinical ratings) tend to adapt differently to age-related life-cycle events (such as retirement or widowhood) and also show different patterns of stability and change in self-related variables.

Proposition 14: Based on clinical ratings, expressiveness seems to be quite stable for both men and women between adolescence and their mid-30s; in addition, aggression, self-assertiveness, impulsivity, and dependability seem to be stable for men and social prestige and passive-conformity for women. For both sexes, substantial change seems more characteristic of the dimensions of attractiveness, self-confidence, and achievement.

Proposition 15: Older individuals possessing relatively "dysfunctional" personality types may exhibit *less* change in behaviors reflecting the self over time (especially those who are high in anxiety and ego-disorganization), whereas younger adults possessing dysfunctional personalities may experience *more* change.

These fifteen propositions suggest a rich research agenda for future investigators who wish to clarify the question of stability versus change in self-conceptions and personality characteristics throughout later life.

Acknowledgments: We are grateful to a number of colleagues for helpful reviews of an earlier draft of this paper: Robert Atchley, Paul Baltes, Paul Costa, David Chiriboga, Viktor Gecas, Dale Lund, Jeylene Mortimer, and Robert Trevethian. We also want to acknowledge our debt to Mike Lucero, Sheila Miyazaki, and Citas Vanderpool for extraordinary assistance in word processing and literature review, and to Miriam Kmet for editing.

REFERENCES

Ahammer, J. M., and Baltes, P. B. 1972. Objective versus perceived age differences in personality: How do adolescents, adults, and older people view themselves and others? *Journal of Gerontology* 27: 46–51.

Allport, G. W. 1954. The historical background of modern social psychology. In *Handbook of Social Psychology,* ed. G. Lindzey, Reading, MA: Addison-Wesley.

Allport, G. 1955. *Becoming.* New Haven, CT: Yale University Press.

Andrews, G.; Tennant, C.; Hewson, D. M.; and Vaillant, G. E. 1978. Life event stress, social support, coping style, and risk of psychological impairment. *Journal of Nervous and Mental Disease* 166: 307–320.

Antonovsky, I. 1981. *Health, Stress and Coping.* San Francisco: Jossey-Bass.

Antonucci, T.; Gillett, N.; and Hoyer, F. W. 1979. Values and self-esteem in three generations of men and women. *Journal of Gerontology* 34: 5–422.

Atchley, R. 1969. Respondents vs. refusers in an interview study of retired women. *Journal of Gerontology* 24: 42–47.

Atchley, R. C. 1976. Selected social and psychological differences between men and women in later life. *Journal of Gerontology* 31: 204–211.

Atchley, R. C. 1982. The Aging Self. *Psychotherapy: Theory, Research and Practice* 19(4): 338–396.

Back, K. W. 1971. Transition to aging and the self-image. *Aging and Human Development* 2: 296–304.

Baltes, Paul B. 1979. "Life-span developmental psychology: Some converging observations on history and theory. In *Life-Span Development and Behavior,* eds. Paul B. Baltes and Orville G. Brim, Jr., pp. 256–274. New York: Academic Press.

Baltes, P. B., and Nesselroade, J. R. 1970. Longitudinal and cross-sectional sequences for analyzing ontogenetic and generational change: A methodological note. *Developmental Psychology* 2: 163–168.

Baltes, P. B.; Schaie, K. W.; and Nardi, J. 1971. Age and experimentality in a seven-year longitudinal study of cognitive behavior. *Developmental Psychology* 5: 18–26.

Baltes, P. B.; Reese, H. W.; and Lipsitt, C. P. 1980. Lifespan developmental psychology. *Annual Review of Psychology* 31: 65–110.

Barrett, C. J. 1978. Effectiveness of widows' groups in facilitating change. *Journal of Consulting and Clinical Psychology* 46: 20–31.

Bellucci, G., and Hoyer, W. J. 1975. Feedback effects on the performance and self-reinforcing behavior of elderly and young adult women. *Journal of Gerontology* 30: 456–460.

Bengtson, V. L. 1973. *The Social Psychology of Aging.* Chicago: Bobbs-Merrill.

Bengtson, V. L. 1975. Generation and family effects in value socialization. *American Sociological Review* 40(3): 358–371.

Bengtson, V. L.; Kasschau, P. L.; and Ragan, P. K. 1977. The impact of social structure on aging individuals. In *Handbook of the Psychology of Aging,* eds. J. E. Birren and K. W. Schaie. New York: Van Nostrand Reinhold.

Berscheid, E.; Walster, E.; and Bohrnstedt, G. 1973. The happy American body: A survey report. *Psychology Today,* Nov. 1973: 119ff.

Block, J. 1971. *Lives through Time.* Berkeley, CA: Bancroft Books.

Block, J. 1977. Advancing the psychology of personality: Paradigmatic shift or improving the quality of research. In *Personality at the Crossroads: Current Issues in Interactional Psychology,* eds. D. Magnussen and N. S. Endler, pp. 37–63. Hillsdale, N.J.: Erlbaum.

Bloom, K. L. 1961. Age and the self-concept. *American Journal of Psychiatry* 118: 534–538.

Bourne, E. 1977. Can we describe an individual's personality? Agreement on stereotype versus individual attributes. *Journal of Personality and Social Psychology* 35: 863–872.

Bray, D. W., and Howard, A. 1983. The AT&T longitudinal studies of managers. In *Longitudinal Studies of Adult Psychological Development,* ed. K. W. Schaie. New York: The Guilford Press.

Breytspraak, L. M. 1974. Achievement and the self-concept in middle age. In *Normal Aging II: Reports from the Duke Longitudinal Studies, 1970–73,* ed. E. Palmore. Durham, NC: Duke University Press.

Breytspraak, L. M. 1975. Self-concept in adulthood: Emergent issues and the response to the symbolic interactionist perspective. Paper presented at annual meetings of the Gerontological Society, Louisville, KY.

Breytspraak, L. M., and George, L. K. 1977. Measurement of self-concept and self-esteem in older people: State of the art. Paper presented at the annual meetings of the Gerontological Society, San Francisco, CA.

Breytspraak, L. M., and George, L. K. 1979. Measurement of self-concept and self-esteem in older people: State of the art. *Experimental Aging Research* 5: 137–148.

Breytspraak, L. M., and George, L. K. 1982. Self-concept and self-esteem. In *Clinical and Social Psychology,* eds. D. J. Mangen and W. A. Peterson. *Research Instruments in Social Gerontology,* vol. 1, pp. 241–302. Minneapolis: University of Minnesota Press.

Brim, O. G., Jr. 1966. Socialization through the life cycle. In *Socialization after Childhood: Two Essays,* eds. P. Baltes and O. G. Brim. New York: John Wiley and Sons.

Brim, O. G., Jr. 1974. The sense of personal control over one's life. Presentation at the annual meetings of the American Psychological Association, New Orleans, LA.

Brim, O. G., Jr. 1975. Life span development of the theory of oneself. Presented at 4th Biennial Conference, International Society for the Study of Behavioural Development, Guildford, Surrey, England.

Brim, O. G., and Kagan, J. 1980. Constancy and change:

A view of the issues. In *Constancy and Change in Human Development,* eds. O. G. Brim and J. Kagan. Cambridge, MA: Harvard University Press.

Brim, O. G., Jr., and Ryff, C. D. 1980. On the properties of life events. In *Life-Span Development and Behavior,* eds. P. B. Baltes and O. G. Brim, vol. 3, pp. 367–388. New York: Academic Press.

Britton, J. H., and Britton, J. O. 1972. *Personality Changes in Aging: A Longitudinal Study of Community Residents.* New York: Springer.

Brooks, J. B., and Elliott, D. M. 1971. Prediction of psychological adjustment at age thirty from leisure time activities and satisfactions in childhood. *Human Development* 14: 51–61.

Brubaker, T. H., and Powers, E. A. 1976. The stereotype of "old:" A review and alternative approach. *Journal of Gerontology* 31: 441–447.

Burke, P. J. 1980. The self: Measurement requirements from an interactionist perspective. *Social Psychology Quarterly* 43: 18–29.

Burke, P. J., and Weir, T. 1976. Some personality differences between members of one-career and two-career families. *Journal of Marriage and the Family* 38: 453–459.

Burne, P. J., and Reitzes, D. C. 1981. The link between identity and role performance. *Social Psychology Quarterly* 44: 83–92.

Cattell, R. B. 1957. *Personality and Maturation Structure.* New York: World.

Chiriboga, D. A. 1973. The adult self-concept: A longitudinal analysis. Paper presented at Western Psychological Association meetings, Anaheim, CA.

Chiriboga, D. A. 1982. An examination of life events as possible antecedents to change. *Journal of Gerontology* 37: 597–601.

Cicirelli, V. G. 1977. Relationship of siblings to the elderly person's feelings and concerns. *Journal of Gerontology* 32: 317–322.

Clark, M., and Anderson, B. 1967. *Culture and Aging: An Anthropological Study of Older Americans.* Springfield, IL: Charles C Thomas.

Cohn, R. M. 1978. The effect of employment status change on self-attitudes. *Social Psychology Quarterly* 41: 81–93.

Cooley, C. H. 1902. *Human Nature and the Social Order.* New York: Charles Scribner's.

Costa, P. T., Jr., and McCrae, R. R. 1976. Age differences in personality structure: A cluster analytic approach. *Journal of Gerontology* 31: 564–570.

Costa, P. T., Jr., and McCrae, R. R. 1977–78. Age differences in personality structure revisited: Studies in validity, stability and change. *International Journal of Aging and Human Development* 8: 261–275.

Costa, P. T., and McCrae, R. R. 1978. Objective personality assessment. In *The Clinical Psychology of Aging,* eds. M. Storandt, I. C. Siegler, M. F. Elias. New York: Plenum.

Costa, P. T., Jr., and McCrae, R. R. 1980a. Influence of extroversion and neuroticism on subjective well-being: Happy and unhappy people. *Journal of Personality and Social Psychology* 38: 668–678.

Costa, P. T., Jr., and McCrae, R. R. 1980b. Still stable after all these years: Personality as a key to some issues in adulthood and old age. In *Life Span Development and Behavior,* eds. P. Baltes and O. Brim, vol. 3, pp. 65–102. New York: Academic Press.

Costa, P. T., Jr., and McCrae, R. R. 1982. An approach to the attribution of aging, period, and cohort effects. *Psychological Bulletin* 92(1): 238–250.

Costa, P. T., Jr.; McCrae, R. R.; and Arenberg, D. 1980. Enduring dispositions in adult males. *Journal of Personality and Social Psychology* 38: 793–800.

Costa, P. T., Jr.; McCrae, R. R.; and Norris, A. H. 1980. Personal adjustment to aging: Longitudinal prediction from neuroticism and extroversion. *Journal of Gerontology* 36: 78–85.

Cottrell, L. S. 1969. Interpersonal interaction and the development of the self. In *Handbook of Socialization Theory and Research,* ed. D. A. Goslin. Chicago: Rand McNally.

Coyne, A. C.; Whitbourne, S. K.; and Glenwick, D. S. 1978. Adult age differences in reflection-impulsivity. *Journal of Gerontology* 33: 402–407.

Cutler, N. E. 1979. Age variations in the dimensionality of life satisfaction. *Journal of Gerontology* 34: 573–578.

Douglas, K., and Arenberg, D. 1978. Age changes, cohort differences, and cultural change on the Guilford-Zimmerman Temperament Survey. *Journal of Gerontology* 33: 737–747.

Edwards, J. N., and Klemmack, D. L. 1973. Correlates of life satisfaction: A reexamination. *Journal of Gerontology* 28: 497–502.

Erdwins, C. J.; Mellinger, J. C.; and Tyer, Z. E. 1981. A comparison of different aspects of self-concept for young, middle-aged and older women. *Journal of Clinical Psychology* 37: 484–490.

Erdwins, C. J.; Tyer, Z. E.; and Mellinger, J. C. 1980. Personality traits of mature women in student versus homemaker roles. *The Journal of Psychology* 105: 189–195.

Fazio, R. H.; Effrein, E. A.; and Falender, V. J. 1981. Self-perceptions following social interaction. *Journal of Personality and Social Psychology* 41: 232–242.

Feldman, S. S.; Biringen, Z. C.; and Nash, S. C. 1981. Fluctuations of sex-related self-attributions as a function of stage of family life cycle. *Developmental Psychology* 17: 24–35.

Filsinger, E., and Sauer, W. J. 1978. An empirical typology of adjustment to aging. *Journal of Gerontology* 33: 437–445.

Fitts, W. H. 1965. *Manual: Tennessee Self-Concept Scale.* Nashville, TN: Counselor Recordings and Tests.

Fitzgerald, J. M. 1978. Actual and perceived sex and generational differences in interpersonal style: Structural and quantitative issues. *Journal of Gerontology* 33: 394–401.

Foley, J. M., and Murphy, D. M. 1977. Sex role identity in the aged. Paper presented at the annual meetings of the Gerontological Society, San Francisco, CA.

Gaitz, C. M., and Scott, J. 1972. Age and the measurement of mental health. *Journal of Health and Social Behavior* 13: 55–67.

Gecas, V. 1982. The self-concept. In *Annual Review of Sociology,* eds. R. Turner and I. Short, vol. 8, pp. 1–34. Palo Alto, CA: Annual Reviews, Inc.

George, L. K. 1975. Subjective awareness of self and age in middle age and later life. Ph.d. Dissertation, Duke University.

George, L. K. 1978. The impact of personality and social status factors upon levels of activity and psychological well-being. *Journal of Gerontology* 33: 840–847.

George, L. K. 1980. *The Role Transitions of Later Life.* Monterey, CA: Brooks/Cole.

George, L. K., and Maddox, G. L. 1977. Subjective adaptation to loss of the workrole: A longitudinal study. *Journal of Gerontology* 32: 456–462.

Gergen, K. J. 1968. Personal consistency and the presentations of self. In *The Self in Social Interaction: Classic and Contemporary Perspectives,* eds. C. Gordon and K. J. Gergen. New York: Wiley.

Gergen, K. J. 1971. *The Concept of Self.* New York: Holt, Rinehart and Winston.

Gergen, K. J. 1982. *Toward Transformation in Social Knowledge.* New York: Springer-Verlag.

Gergen, K. J., and Back, K. W. 1966. Communication in the interview and the disengaged respondent. *Public Opinion Quarterly* 30: 385–398.

Gillum, R.; Leon, G. R.; Kamp, J.; and Becerra-Aldama, J. 1980. Prediction of cradiovascular and other disease onset and mortality from 30-year longitudinal MMPI data. *Journal of Consulting and Clinical Psychology* 48: 405–406.

Glenn, N. D. 1980. *Values, Attitudes, and Beliefs.* Beverly Hills, CA: Sage.

Goffman, E. 1955. On facework: An analysis of ritual elements in social interaction. *Psychiatry* 18: 213–231.

Goffman, E. 1959. *Presentation of Self in Every Day Life.* Garden City, NY: Doubleday Anchor.

Goffman, E. 1963. *Behavior in Public Places.* Gencoe, IL: Free Press.

Gordon, C. 1967. A person-conceptions analytic system for the general inquirer. Mimeograph, Social Relations Department, Sociology Department, Rice University (Rev., 1974).

Gordon, C. 1968a. Self-conceptions: Configurations of content. In *The Self in Social Interaction: Classic and Contemporary Perspectives,* eds. C. Gordon and K. J. Gergen. New York: Wiley.

Gordon, C. 1968b. Systemic senses of self. *Sociological Inquiry* 38: 161–178.

Gordon, C. 1969. Self-conceptions methodologies. *Journal of Nervous and Mental Disease* 148: 328–364.

Gordon, C. 1971. Role and value development across the life cycle. In *Sociological Studies IV. Role,* ed. John Jackson, pp. 65–105. London, Eng.: Cambridge University Press.

Gordon, C. 1972. Looking Ahead: Self-conceptions, race and family as determinants of adolescent orientations to achievement. Washington, D.C.: American Sociological Association's Rose Monograph Series.

Gordon, C. 1976. Development of evaluated role identities. In *Annual Review of Sociology* 2, ed. A. Inkeles, pp. 405–433. Palo Alto, CA: Annual Reviews, Inc.

Gordon, C.; Gaitz, C. M.; and Scott, J. 1975. Self-evaluation of competence and worth in adulthood. In. *American Handbook of Psychiatry,* ed. S. Arieti. 2nd ed. New York: Basic Books.

Gordon, C., and Gergen, K. J., eds. 1968. *The Self in Social Interaction: Classic and Contemporary Perspectives.* New York: Wiley.

Gordon, C., and Gordon, P. 1982. Changing roles, goals and self-conceptions process and results in a program for women's employment. In *Personality, Roles, and Social Behavior,* eds. W. Ickes and E. S. Knowles. New York: Springer-Verlag.

Gould, R. 1978. *Transformations.* New York: Simon and Schuster.

Grant, C. R. H. 1967. Age differences in self-concept from early adulthood through old age. Ph.D. dissertation, University of Nebraska.

Gutmann, D. L. 1975. Parenthood: Key to comparative study of the life cycle. In *Life-Span Developmental Psychology: Normative Life Crises,* eds. N. Datan and L. Ginsberg. New York: Academic Press.

Herzog, A. R., and Rodgers, W. L. 1981. The structure of subjective well-being in different age groups. *Journal of Gerontology* 36: 472–479.

Hess, A. L., and Bradshaw, H. L. 1970. Positiveness of self-concept and ideal-self as a function of age. *Journal of Genetic Psychology* 177: 57–67.

Hilgard, E. R. 1980. The trilogy of mind; cognition, affection, and conation. *Journal of the History of the Behavioral Sciences* 16: 107–117.

Horney, K. 1945. *Our Neurotic Conflicts.* New York: Norton.

Hyde, J. S., and Phillis, D. E. 1979. Androgyny across the life span. *Developmental Psychology* 15: 334–336.

James, W. 1892. *Psychology.* New York: Henry Holt. (Adapted in Gordon and Gergen, 1968, Ch. 3.)

Jellison, J. M., and Green, J. 1981. A self-presentation approach to the fundamental attribution error: The norm of internality. *Journal of Personality and Social Psychology* 40: 643–649.

Johnson, E. S. and Bursk, B. J. 1981. Relations between the elderly and their adult children. *The Gerontologist* 21(1): 91–102.

Jung, C. G. 1933. The stages of life. In *Modern Man in Search of a Soul,* pp. 95–114. Translated by W. S. Dell and C. F. Baynes. New York: Harcourt, Brace.

Kagan, J. 1976. Emergent themes in human development. *American Scientist* 64: 186–196.

Kahana, E., and Coe, R. M. 1969. Self and staff conceptions of institutionalized aged. *The Gerontologist* 9: 264–267.

Kahle, L. R.; Kulka, R. A.; and Klingel, D. M. 1980. Low adolescent self-esteem leads to multiple interpersonal problems: A test of social-adaptation theory. *Journal of Personality and Social Psychology* 39: 496–502.

Kaplan, H. B. 1975. *Self-Attitudes and Deviant Behavior.* Pacific Palisades, CA: Goodyear.

Kaplan, H. B. 1976. The self-attitude and deviant response. *Social Forces* 54: 788–801.

Kaplan, H. B., and Pokorny, A. D. 1969. Self-derogation

and psychosocial adjustment. *Journal of Nervous and Mental Diseases* 149: 421–434.

Kelly, E. L. 1955. Consistency of the adult personality. *American Psychologist* 10: 659–681.

Kivett, V. R.; Watson, J. A.; and Busch, J. C. 1977. The relative importance of physical, psychological, and social variables to locus of control orientation in middle age. *Journal of Gerontology* 32: 203–210.

Klapp, O. 1962. *Heroes, Villains and Fools.* Englewood Cliffs, NJ: Prentice-Hall.

Kline, R. 1972. Age, sex, and task difficulty as predictors of social conformity. *Journal of Gerontology* 27: 229–235.

Kuhn, M. H., and McPartland, T. S. 1954. An empirical investigation of self-attitudes. *American Sociological Review* 19: 68–76.

Kuypers, J. A. 1972. Internal-external locus of control, ego functioning, and personality characteristics in old age. *The Gerontologist* 12: 168–173.

Kuypers, J. A. 1974. Ego functioning in old age: Early adult life antecedents. *International Journal of Aging and Human Development* 5: 157–178.

Lachman, M. E. 1984. Personality efficacy in middle and old age: Differential and normative patterns of change. In *Life Course Dynamics: 1968 to the 1980's,* ed. G. H. Elder, Jr. New York: Academic Press.

Larson, R. 1978. Thirty years of research on the subjective well-being of older Americans. *Journal of Gerontology* 33: 109–125.

Lehr, U. 1978. Changes in family occupational roles of women. Symposium on "Continuities in the Development of Women," presented at the 5th Biennial Conference of the International Society for the Study of Behavioral Development: Continuity and Discontinuity in Behavioral Development, Lund, Sweden.

Lehr, U. 1980a. Altersstereotypien und altersnormen—Das bild des alten menschen in unserer gesellschaft. In *Fortschritte der Markpsychologie, Rand 2, Grundlagen—Methoden—Anwendungen,* eds. K. D. Harmann and K. F. Koppler, pp. 327–338. Frankfurt: Factbuchhandlund f. Psychologie GmbH.

Lehr, U. 1980b. Alterszustand und alternsprozesse—Biographische determinanten. *Gerontologia* 13: 442–457.

Lehr, U. 1980c. Personality development in older age: Differential aspects. Paper presented at the 22nd International Congress of Psychology, Liepzig, Germany.

Leon, G. R.; Butcher, J. N.; Kleinman, H.; Goldberg, A.; and Alonagor, M. 1981. Survivors of the holocaust and their children: Current status and adjustment. *Journal of Consulting and Clinical Psychology* 47: 517–524.

Leon, G. R.; Gillum, B.; Gillum, R.; and Gouze, M. 1979. Personality stability and change over a 30-year period—middle age to old age. *Journal of Consulting and Clinical Psychology* 47: 517–524.

Leon, G. R.; Kamp, J.; Gillum, R.; and Gillum, B. 1981. Life stress and dimensions of functioning in old age. *Journal of Gerontology* 36(1): 66–69.

Levinson, D. J. 1978. *The Seasons of a Man's Life.* New York: Knopf.

Levinson, D. J.; Darrow, C. N.; Klein, E. G.; Levinson, M. H.; and McKee, B. 1974. The psychosocial development of men in early adulthood and the midlife transition. In *Life History Research in Psychopathology* 3, eds. D. F. Ricks, A. Thomas, and M. Roff. Minneapolis: University of Minnesota Press.

Lewis, C. N. 1971. Reminiscing and self-concept in old age. *Journal of Gerontology* 26: 240–243.

Liang, J.; Dvorkin, L.; Kahana, E.; and Mazian, F. 1980. Social integration and morale: A re-examination. *Journal of Gerontology* 35: 746–757.

Longino, C. F.; McClelland, K. A.; and Peterson, W. A. 1980. The aged subculture hypothesis: Social integration, gerontophilia and self-conception. *Journal of Gerontology* 35: 758–767.

Lowenthal, M. F.; Thurnher, M.; and Chiriboga, D. 1975. *Four Stages of Life.* San Francisco: Jossey-Bass.

Lundgren, D. C. 1978. Public esteem, self-esteem, and interpersonal stress. *Social Psychology Quarterly* 41: 68–73.

Lutsky, N. S. 1980. Attitudes toward old age and elderly persons. *Annual Review of Gerontology and Geriatrics* 1: 287–311.

Lutsky, N. S. 1981. Trends in research on attitudes toward elderly persons. Paper presented at the XII International Congress of Gerontology, Hamburg, Germany.

Maas, H. S., and Kuypers, J. A. 1974. *From Thirty to Seventy.* San Francisco: Jossey-Bass.

Markides, K. S., and Martin, H. W. A causal model of life satisfaction among the elderly. *Journal of Gerontology* 14: 81–93.

Mason, E. P. 1954a. Some correlates of self-judgements of the aged. *Journal of Gerontology* 9: 324–337.

Mason, E. P. 1954b. Some factors in self-judgements. *Journal of Clinical Psychology* 10: 336–340.

McCall, G. J., and Simmons, J. L. 1966. *Identities and Interactions.* Rev. ed. 1978. New York: Free Press.

McCrae, R. R. 1982. Consensual validation of personality traits: Evidence from self-reports and ratings. *Journal of Personality and Social Psychology* 43: 293–303.

McCrae, R. R.; Costa, P. T., Jr.; and Arenberg, D. 1980. Constancy of adult personality structure in males: Longitudinal, cross-sectional and times-of-measurement analysis. *Journal of Gerontology* 35: 877–883.

McCrae, R. R., and Costa, P. T., Jr. 1982. Self-concept and the stability of personality: Cross-sectional comparisons of self-reports and ratings. *Journal of Personality and Social Psychology* 43: 1282–1292.

McGuire, W. J. 1969. The nature of attitudes and attitude change. In *The Handbook of Social Psychology,* eds. G. Lindzey and E. Aronson. 2nd ed. Reading, MA: Addison-Wesley.

Mead, G. H. 1934. *Mind, Self, and Society,* ed. (posthumous) C. W. Morris. Chicago: University of Chicago Press.

Monge, R. H. 1975. Structure of the self-concept from adolescence through old age. *Experimental Aging Research* 1: 281–291.

Morgan, L. A. 1982. Social roles in later life: Some recent research trends. In *Annual Review of Gerontology and Geriatrics,* ed. C. Eisdorfer, vol. 3. New York: Springer.

Mortimer, J. T.; Finch, M. D.; and Kumka, D. 1982. Persistence and change in development: The multidimensional self-concept. In *Life Span Development and Behavior,* vol. 4, pp. 263–313. New York: Academic Press.

Mortimer, J. T., and Lorence, J. 1979. Occupational experience and the self-concept—A longitudinal study. *Social Psychology Quarterly* 42: 307–323.

Moss, H. A., and Susman, E. J. 1980. Longitudinal study of personality development. In *Constancy and Change in Human Development,* eds. O. G. Brim, Jr., and J. Kagan. Cambridge, MA: Harvard University Press.

Mussen, P.; Eichorn, D. H.; Honzik, M. P.; Bieber, S. L.; and Meredith, W. M. 1980. Continuity and change in women's characteristics over four decades. *International Journal of Behavioral Development* 3: 333–334.

Nehrke, M. F. 1974. Actual and perceived attitudes toward death and self-concept in three generational families. Paper presented at the annual meeting of the Gerontological Society, Portland, OR.

Nehrke, M. F.; Hulicka, I. M.; and Morganti, J. B. 1980. Age differences in life satisfaction, locus of control, and self-concept. *International Journal of Aging and Human Development* 11: 25–33.

Nesselroade, J. R. 1977. Issues in studying developmental change in adults from a multivariate perspective. In *Handbook of the Psychology of Aging,* eds. J. E. Birren and K. W. Schaie, pp. 59–69. New York, Van Nostrand.

Nesselroade, J. R., and Baltes, P. 1974. Adolescent personality development and historical change: 1970–1972. *Monographs of the Society for Research in Child Development* 39: (1, Whole No. 154).

Nesselroade, J. R.; Schaie, K. W.; and Baltes, P. G. 1972. Ontogenetic and generational components of structural and qualitative change in adult behavior. *Journal of Gerontology* 27: 222–228.

Neugarten, B. L. 1977. Personality and aging. In *Handbook of the Psychology of Aging,* eds. J. E. Birren and K. W. Schaie, pp. 626–649. New York: Van Nostrand Reinhold.

Neugarten, B. L., and associates. 1964. *Personality in Middle and Later Life.* New York: Atherton.

Neugarten, B. L.; Crotty, W. J.; and Tobin, S. S. 1964. Personality types in an aged population. In *Personality in Middle and Later Life,* ed. B. L. Neugarten and associates. New York: Atherton Press.

Neugarten, B. L., and Gutmann, D. L. 1968. Age-sex roles and personality in middle age: A thematic apperception study. In *Middle Age and Aging,* ed. B. L. Neugarten, pp. 58–71. Chicago: Chicago University Press.

Neugarten, B.; Havighurst, R.; and Tobin, S. 1968. Personality and patterns of aging. In *Middle Age and Aging,* ed. B. Neugarten, pp. 173–177. Chicago: University of Chicago Press.

Okun, M. A., and Elias, C. S. 1977. Cautiousness in adulthood as a function of age and payoff structure. *Journal of Gerontology* 32: 451–455.

Palmore, E.; Cleveland, W. P.; Nowlin, J. B.; Ramm, D.; and Siegler, H. C. 1979. Stress and adaptation in later life. *Journal of Gerontology* 34: 841–851.

Palmore, E., and Kivett, V. 1977. Change in life satisfaction: A longitudinal study of persons aged 46–70. *Journal of Gerontology* 32: 311–316.

Pierce, R. C., and Chiriboga, D. A. 1979. Dimensions of adult self-concept. *Journal of Gerontology* 34: 83–85.

Plutchik, R.; Weiner, M. B.; and Conte, H. 1971. Studies of body image I: Body worries and body discomforts. *Journal of Gerontology* 26(3): 344–350.

Plutchik, R.; Conte, H.; and Weiner, M. B. 1973. Studies of body image II: Dollar values of body parts. *Journal of Gerontology* 28(1): 89–91.

Postema, L. J. 1970. *Reminiscing, Time Orientation and Self-Concept in Aged Men.* Ph.D. dissertation, Michigan State University.

Reedy, M. N. 1982. Personality and aging. In *Aging: Scientific Perspective and Social Issues,* eds. D. S. Woodruff and J. E. Birren, pp. 112–136. Monterey, Ca.: Brooks/Cole.

Reichard, S.; Livson, F.; and Peterson, P. G. 1962. *Aging and Personality.* New York: John Wiley and Sons.

Rosenberg, M. 1965. *Society and the Adolescent Self-Images.* New York: Basic Books.

Rosenberg, M. 1979. *Conceiving the Self.* New York: Basic Books.

Rosenberg, M. 1981. The sociology of the self-concept. In *Social Psychology: Sociological Perspectives,* eds. M. Rosenberg and R. H. Turner. New York: Basic Books.

Rosenberg, M., and Kaplan, H. B. 1982. *Social Psychology of the Self-Concept.* Arlington Heights, IL: Harlan Davidson.

Rosenberg, M., and Pearlin, L. I. 1978. Social class and self-esteem among children and adults. *American Journal of Sociology* 84: 53–77.

Rubin, Z. 1981. Does personality really change after 20? *Psychology Today,* May: 18–27.

Ryckman, R. M., and Malikiosi, M. X. 1975. Relationship between locus of control and chronological age. *Psychological Reports* 36: 655–658.

Ryff, C., and Baltes, P. B. 1976. Value transition and adult development in women. The instrumentality-terminality hypothesis. *Developmental Psychology* 12: 567–568.

Schaie, K. W. 1965. A general model for the study of developmental problems. *Psychological Bulletin* 64: 92–107.

Schaie, K. W.; Labouvie-Vief, G. V.; and Barrett, T. J. 1973. Selective attrition effects in a fourteen year study of intelligence. *Journal of Gerontology* 28: 328–334.

Schaie, K. W., and Labouvie-Vief, G. V. 1974. Generational versus ontogenetic components of change in adult cognitive behavior: A fourteen-year cross-sectional sequence. *Developmental Psychology* 10: 305–320.

Schaie, K. W., and Marquette, B. W. 1971. Personality and maturity in old age. In *Multivariate Personality Research: Contributions to the Understanding of Personality,* ed. R. M. Dreger, pp. 612–632. Baton Rouge, LA: Claitor's Publishing Division.

Schaie, K. W., and Parham, I. A. 1974. Social responsibility in adulthood: Ontogenetic and sociocultural change. *Journal of Personality and Social Psychology* 30: 483–492.

Schaie, K. W., and Parham, I. A. 1976. Stability of adult personality traits: Fact or fable? *Journal of Personality and Social Psychology* 34: 146–158.

Schlenker, B. R.; Forsyth, D. R.; Leary, M. R.; and Miller, R. S. 1980. Self-presentational analysis of the effects of incentives on attitude change following counterattitudinal behavior. *Journal of Personality and Social Psychology* 39: 553–557.

Schmitz-Scherzer, R., and Thomae, H. 1983. Constancy and change of behavior in old age: Findings from the Bonn longitudinal study on aging. In *Longitudinal Studies of Adult Psychological Development,* ed. K. W. Schaie. New York: The Guilford Press.

Schwartz, M., and Stryker, S. 1971. *Deviance, Selves and Others.* Washington, D.C.: American Sociological Association, Rose Monograph Series.

Secord, P., and Backman, C. 1976. *Understanding Social Life.* New York: McGraw Hill.

Seligman, M. E. P. 1975. *Helplessness: On Depression, Development, and Death.* San Francisco: Freeman.

Sheehy, G. 1976. *Passages: The Predictable Crisis of Adult Life.* New York: E. P. Dutton.

Siegler, H. C.; George, L. K.; and Okun, M. A. 1979. Cross-sequential analysis of adult personality. *Journal of Personality and Social Psychology* 15: 350–354.

Simmons, R. G.; Blyth, D. A.; VanCleave, E. F.; and Bush, D. M. 1979. Entry into early adolescence: The impact of school structure, puberty and early dating on self-esteem. *American Sociological Review* 44: 948–967.

Smith, J. 1966. Narrowing social world of the aged. In *Social Aspects of Aging,* ed. I. H. Simpson and J. C. McKinney, pp. 226–242. Durham, NC: Duke University Press.

Snyder, M., and Cantor, N. 1980. Thinking about ourselves and others: Self-monitoring and social knowledge. *Journal of Personality and Social Psychology* 39: 222–234.

Spence, J. T., and Helmreich, R. L. 1979. Comparison of masculine and feminine personality attributes and sex-role attitudes across age groups. *Developmental Psychology* 15: 583–584.

Steitz, M. 1977. Value change: A life course perspective. Paper presented at the annual meetings of the Gerontological Society, San Francisco, CA.

Tavris, C., and Offir, C. 1977. *The Longest War: Sex Differences in Perspective.* New York: Harcourt Brace Jovanovich, Inc.

Tesser, A., and Campbell, J. 1980. Self-definition: The impact of the relative performance and similarity of others. *Social Psychology Quarterly* 43: 341–347.

Thomae, H. 1970. Theory of aging and cognitive theory of personality. *Human Development* 13: 1–16.

Thomae, H. 1980. Personality and adjustment to aging. In *Handbook of Mental Health and Aging,* eds. J. E.

Birren and R. B. Sloane, pp. 285–309. Englewood Cliffs, NJ: Prentice-Hall.

Thompson, W. 1972. *Correlates of the Self-Concept.* Monograph No. 6. Nashville, TN: Counselor Recordings and Tests.

Thurnher, M. 1977. Value change: A life course perspective. Paper presented at the annual meetings of the Gerontological Society, San Francisco, CA.

Thurnher, M. 1981. Turning points and developmental change: Subjective and "objective" assessments. *American Journal of Orthopsychiatry* 37(1): 349–361.

Trimikas, K., and Nicholay, R. C. 1974. Self-concept and altruism in old age. *Journal of Gerontology* 29: 434–439.

Troll, L. E., and Perron, E. M. 1981. Age changes in sex roles amid changing sex roles: The double shift. In *Annual Review of Gerontology and Geriatrics,* ed. C. Eisdorfer, vol. 2, pp. 118–143. New York: Springer Publishing Co.

Tuddenham, R. D. 1959. Constancy of personality ratings over two decades. *Genetic Psychology Monograph* 60: 3–29.

Turner, R. H. 1968. The self-conception in social interaction. In *The Self in Social Interaction: Classic and Contemporary Perspectives,* eds. C. Gordon and K. G. Gergen, pp. 93–106. New York: Wiley.

Urberg, K. A., and Labouvie-Vief, G. 1976. Conceptualization of sex roles: A life-span developmental study. *Developmental Psychology* 12: 15–23.

Vaillant, G. E. 1977. *Adaption to Life.* Boston: Little, Brown.

Wallach, M. A., and Kogan, N. 1961. Aspects of judgement and decision-making: Inter-relationships and changes with age. *Behavioral Sciences* 6: 23–36.

Ward, R. A. 1977. The impact of subjective age and stigma on older persons. *Journal of Gerontology* 32: 227–232.

Webster, M. A., and Sobieszek, B. I. 1974. *Sources of Self-Evaluation: A Formal Theory of Significant Others and Social Influence.* New York: Wiley.

Wells, L. E., and Marwell, G. 1976. *Self-Esteem: Its Conceptualization and Measurement.* Beverly Hills, CA: Sage.

Whitbourne, S. K., and Waterman, A. S. 1979. Psychosocial development during the adult years: Age and cohort comparisons. *Developmental Psychology* 15(4): 373–378.

Woodruff, D. E., and Birren, J. E. 1972. Age changes and cohort differences in personality. *Development Psychology* 6: 252–259.

Wylie, R. C. 1961. *The Self-Concept.* Lincoln, NB: University of Nebraska Press.

Wylie, R. C. 1974. *The Self-Concept.* Rev. ed., vol. I. Lincoln, NB: University of Nebraska Press.

Wylie, R. C. 1978. *The Self-Concept.* Rev. ed., vol. II. Lincoln, NB: University of Nebraska Press.

Zurcher, L. A. 1977. *The Mutable Self: A Self-Concept for Social Change.* Beverly Hills, CA: Sage.

22
THE PSYCHOLOGICAL CONSTRUCTION OF THE LIFE SPAN

Susan Krauss Whitbourne

University of Rochester

COPING AND ADAPTATION IN THE CONTEXT OF A LIFE COURSE PERSPECTIVE

Coping and adaptation processes have been the perennial concern of researchers and practitioners in the field of mental health who are interested in how people manage not only the stresses of major life events but the everyday concerns of living. Models of coping and adaptation have emerged from this work that have considerable relevance for understanding how such processes develop over the accumulated life experiences of the individual. Unfortunately, this relevance has not been exploited. Workers in the coping and adaptation fields have usually not paid attention to the ages of the people in their samples or else have based their conclusions on data collected from young adults in stress-simulation laboratory experiments. Gerontological research, theory, and practice, on the contrary, have all been directed at understanding how coping is accomplished in a specific time frame—the latter years of adulthood—and how these adults adapt to changes in physical, psychological, and social functioning. In focusing on the qualities of later life that are specific to loss, gerontological research on adaptation has tended to diverge from the work on coping and adaptation being conducted in the mental health field.

It is the purpose of the present chapter to bridge the gap between coping and adaptation research, on the one hand, and the tradition within gerontological research and theory that focuses on adaptation as a developmental process, on the other. Three models of adaptation are to be analyzed in terms of a developmental perspective: the "life events" model, the "cognitive appraisal" model, and the "subjective well-being" model. All three of these are based on research on adults of varying ages but are not specifically targeted at adaptation in adulthood as a developmental process. As a result, they do not make specific references to adaptation to situations and events in relation to their sequential occurrence over the individual's lifetime.

The position to be taken here is that it is the individual's own construction of the life course that is central to adaptation in adulthood. This approach combines elements within gerontological research and theory that focus on the ways in which conceptions of the life course influence adaptation. Thus, within the life-span psychoanalytic framework of Erikson (1963), there is concern with how individuals confronted with impending death arrive at an integrated sense of the life they have lived. The related concepts of age-grading, age-related normative expectations, and the "timing" of events in the life course have been the focus of social gerontologists (Clausen, 1972; Elder, 1975; Neugarten and Hagestad, 1976; Riley, 1971). In this sense, conceptions of the life course are seen as providing a set of normative criteria (Atchley, 1981). Age norms are seen as serving to orient members of society to the tasks they are expected to accomplish, or at least to be attempting to accomplish, at various points in the life course. The individual's failure to meet the requirements of these age-linked expectations is assumed to result in negative self-evaluations. Sociologists of different schools of thought give varying accounts for the process through which age norms serve to influence people's self-concepts (Gubrium and Buckholdt, 1977). These approaches concur that age norms influence the individual's behavior, albeit through different mechanisms. None of them, however, takes into account the role that social expectations play in the cognitive and affective structuring by the individual of his or her life. Age expectations are seen as being "out there" rather than within the psychological realm of the individual's stance toward his or her own life as organized around age-related expectations. As a result, there is no way that they can directly influence personal adaptation. It is being assumed here that it is only when age norms are given a personal "stamp" by the individual that age norms can stimulate the process of adaptation.

THE LIFE-SPAN CONSTRUCT: A PRELIMINARY FORMULATION

The term "life-span construct" will be used here to contrast the individual's unique conception of his or her own life course from the age norms and expectations that exist within society at large. The life-span construct is viewed as a unified sense of past, present, and future events linked by their common occurrence to the individual. It is cognitive in the sense of being an organizer of experience —a prototype (Cantor and Mischel, 1977) against which all events are measured. It is affective in the sense that the individual's evaluation of events in terms of it lead to positive or negative feeling-states. The life-span construct possessed by the individual is shaped by identity in that self-attributions of physical,

psychological, and social qualities serve to determine its content. The individual's values further contribute to this content, whether it is organized around family, work, self-development, or involvement in the social welfare of the community. The life-span construct develops transactionally with identity, changing identity as it itself is changed. Social context also influences the life-span construct through the mechanisms that influence identity—for example, those described by George (1980).

Two manifestations of the life-span construct serve as its basic structural components. The first of these is what I call the "scenario"; it consists of expectations about the future. With the initial emergence of identity in adolescence (Erikson, 1963), individuals begin to gain a sense of what they will do with their lives and to project a future place for themselves in life (Kastenbaum, 1966). The scenario is the translation of the life-span construct into such plans for the future in the area or areas that have been defined by identity as important. The use of the term "scenario" is derived from its hypothetical nature as an organized sequence of scripts (Schanck and Abelson, 1977) that extend far into the future and have a beginning, a peak, an anticlimax, and a resolution. The scenario is strongly influenced by age norms that define the transition points and associated "acceptable" ages for making these transitions. Individuals will vary, however, in the extent to which these ages conform to the standard social sequence according to their evaluation of their specific backgrounds, their perceptions of their abilities to meet the implicit demands, and their susceptibility to being molded by outside forces—all of which are features of identity (Whitbourne and Weinstock, 1979).

As the individual begins to advance into the positions defined by the scenario, it will inevitably be revised. These revisions may be purposeful, taking place as the result of planned change, or inadvertent, as the outcome of unexpected intrusions from the outside world. At the same time, the individual begins to build the "life story" (Lieberman and Falk, 1965), which is the second manifestation of the life-span construct. The life story incorporates past events into an organized sequence, giving them a personal meaning and a sense of continuity. It is called a "story" to convey that its retelling by the individual to self and others causes it to take on a rehearsed quality that eventually becomes stylized and stereotyped.

Some of the alterations of the life story brought about by its retelling are a function of cognitive processes, as in the simplification process noted by Bartlett (1932). Changes may also occur as a result of the highlighting of nuclear scenes (Carlson, 1981), that is, the amplification and intensification of past events of broad emotional significance (Tomkins, 1979). Other transformations of events from the initial perception of them to some altered form in the life story occur as the result of motivational biases such as egocentrism, beneficence, and cognitive conservatism (Greenwald, 1980). These biases may be seen as various forms of psychological selectivity designed to maintain and preserve the individual's identity (Rosenberg, 1968) by facilitating assessments of experiences that are compatible with that identity (Sampson, 1978). As a function of the life-span construct, these distortions will occur in a way that allows the individual to feel "on time" rather than "off-time" by maximizing the congruence between the belief in "acceptable" age-linked guideposts and the actual sequence and timing of events that have caused the alteration (Neugarten, Moore, and Lowe, 1965). Particular aspects of events may also influence how the events are interpreted and the eventual shape they will take within the life story. These include various informational biases such as salience (Pryor and Kriss, 1977), representativeness (Kahneman and Tversky, 1973), and correspondence between actions and settings (Jones and Davis, 1965). Since the life-span construct may itself be altered as a function of interchanges between the individual and the environment, however, the life story may also undergo transformations that make it more congruent with the objective aspects of past events.

The life-span construct as a psychological entity has been alluded to in the writings of several researchers and theorists (Bortner and Hultsch, 1974; Bourque and Back, 1977; Gubrium and Buckholdt, 1977; Hughes, 1957;

Raynor and Entin, 1982), but its fundamental characteristics as the organizer of the self's experiences through time unique to the individual have not been explicitly postulated. From another perspective, Markus (1977) has hypothesized the existence of "self-schemata," psychological constructs of the self, but her definition of self-schemata does not impart that unity over time to them that is implied by the life-span construct. The life-span construct may be seen as an entity distinct from other types of information about the self, since it is specific to the sense of time over the life span that is continuously experienced by the individual. Taken together, the observations of most writers converge on the idea that the individual possesses a unique sense of the life-span as a totality that serves as an organizer principle of all life experiences. Before elaborating upon the ways in which the life-span construct facilitates adaptation to life events, mediates the cognitive appraisal of stress and copes with it, and determines subjective well-being, I shall review the models of adaptation that deal with each of these three processes.

MODELS OF ADAPTATION IN ADULTHOOD

Attempts to define the terms "stress," "coping," and "adaptation" have been a recurrent theme in research on the response of individuals to situations involving the direct possibility of physical harm (Selye, 1956) or indirect effects on health status (Dohrenwend and Dohrenwend, 1969). As a result, there is much confusion in the literature over the proper usage of these terms (cf. Levine and Scotch, 1970; Appley and Trumbull, 1967). Rather then add to the array of definitions, those meanings that seem to have the greatest potential for operationalization will be restated here and used in all subsequent references.

Following Lazarus (1981, p. 193), "stress" will be regarded as "demands . . . from within or without . . . that tax or exceed available resources of the individual, social system, or tissue system." The definition of "coping" will be adopted from Pearlin and Schooler (1978, p. 3) as "any response to external life strains that serves to prevent, avoid, or control emotional distress." The term "adaptation" is more nebulous than stress or coping, and it is usually not explicitly defined. Often, it is used interchangeably with coping (e.g., Moos, 1976). White (1974) has made the most direct attempt to grapple with defining adaptation in the context of this literature. Although he did not offer a single, concise definition of adaptation, what emerges from his description of adaptive strategies is the use of the term to refer to the range of behaviors needed to meet adequately the demands of almost any situation, from mechanical, smoothly running habits, to small problems and frustrations, through complex defenses against anxiety—in short (p. 52), "a part of the whole tapestry of living . . . a striving toward acceptable compromise" with the environment.

The outcome of the adaptation process is usually considered to be the preservation of the physical health and psychological well-being of the individual. This result is also posited to be the motivating force behind processes that facilitate adaptation. Although the particular models to be examined differ in the specific feature of the adaptation process they emphasize, each appears to be in agreement on this fundamental point.

The Life Events Model of Adaptation

The Impact of Life Events. The part of the adaptation process highlighted in the life events model is the origin of the process in experiences with the potential of harming the individual by creating a disruption of the normal everyday routine of living. It is assumed that the normal state of the individual is one of homeostasis and that life events that require change are crises to the extent that they require time and energy to return to a steady state of functioning. Stress is assumed to be a mediator between an event and adaptation to the event, causing damage to physical and psychological systems the longer and more intense the disruption of the individual's usual life patterns (Holmes and Masuda, 1974).

The basic research tool used to measure stress within the context of the life events model is a checklist of the number of events that have occurred to the individual over a specified interval of time prior to the administration of the questionnaire. The original instrument of this kind found a clustering of events at or shortly before the time of disease onset in a large number of individuals (Rahe, Meyer, Smith, Kjaer, and Holmes, 1964). This instrument, the Schedule of Recent Events (SRE), was based on the assumption that it was the sheer number of events, not their desirability, psychological meaning, duration, or emotional impact, that determined the degree of stress placed on the individual. It was subsequently modified (Holmes and Rahe, 1967) to form the Social Readjustment Rating Scale (SRRS). As its name implies, the SRRS took into account, as an additional factor, the degree of readjustment required by an event. Readjustment was based on the judgments made by a sample of almost 400 adults, who were asked to rate the 43 life events on the SRE with respect to their intensity and the length of time needed to accommodate to them but not to their desirability or their particular meaning to the individual.

Tests of the life events model have involved attempts to determine whether life events questionnaires are predictive of illness. As a rule, the correspondence between life event scores and subsequent emotional or physical disturbances has proven to be low to moderate (Rabkin and Streuning, 1976). Critics have argued that this failure to demonstrate the effects of stressful events on health is due to a faulty conceptualization about the nature of life events. In the first place, the basic assumption of the model that any type of change brought about by a life event has a negative impact on a person's life, ignores the possibility that it may have a positive impact. Even the type of change that may be considered negative by the person experiencing it may have a growth-stimulating outcome (Eisdorfer and Wilkie, 1977). Related to this consideration is the importance of taking into account the individual's stance with respect to the timing of the event, since an initially negative event may turn out well at a later point (Levine and Scotch, 1970). These criticisms are based on the assumption that an event has a meaning that can be palpably positive or negative. Others have questioned the underlying assumption of the life events model that any type of change creates stress and is thus negative in its effects and have emphasized the need to take into account the individual's definition of the event as positive or negative (Chiriboga and Cutler, 1980). The "crisis" approach represented by the life events research in which a causal role is attributed to life events because of their vividness, recency, and apparent magnitude to the observer fails to take into account the cumulative impact of smaller, less obvious changes in the circumstances of daily living (Brim and Ryff, 1980). In addition to including events that have actually occurred, it has also been suggested that "nonevents" may be stressful if the events that did not occur were desired or anticipated (Gersten, Langner, Eisenberg, and Orzek, 1974). The low reliability of life events measures is cited as another reason for the lack of a strong relationship between life events and illness measures. This is in part due to the failure to make correction for errors of omission or commission (Rabkin and Streuning, 1976).

It has also been noted that the relationship between life events and subsequent illness has been inflated by the inclusion in the life events measure of changes that themselves may be symptoms of physical or psychological disturbance (Rabkin and Streuning, 1976). In addition, the severity of the illnesses that follow life changes has often not been considered. If a respiratory infection and a myocardial infarction are both counted as illness outcomes of a life change, it is likely that the reported magnitude of the relationship between life changes and illness would be overestimated (Dohrenwend and Dohrenwend, 1974). There may also be a spurious relationship between life changes and reported illness to the extent that individuals adopt the role of an invalid as a result of discontent with their activities (Mechanic, 1974a).

In response to such challenges of the basic assumptions of the measures developed within the life events model, alternative instruments have been developed that take into account the individual's personal interpretation of a life event (Lowenthal, Thurnher, and Chiriboga, 1975; Sarason, Johnson, and Siegel,

1978). Other modifications have categorized life events according to content rather than summing them into a total score (Chiriboga and Dean, 1978; Redfield and Stone, 1979).

The need to consider those features of life events that might bring on a stress reaction has led to the development of categorization schemes based on underlying dimensions of life changes. Using a stress scale specific to parenting, Weinberg and Richardson (1981) found stressful responses to vary along several dimensions, a result suggesting that even one life event may have multiple meanings. Hultsch and Plemons (1979) classified events along individual-cultural and concurrent-distal dimensions. Attributes of events were further categorized according to the degree of control held by the individual over their occurrence, whether the change involved gain or loss, and whether the change was required in the proximal interpersonal context. Criteria of an epidemiological nature were suggested by Brim and Ryff (1980), who used three frequency properties of life events: the correlation of the event with age, the probability of the event's occurrence, and the number of people who experience the event. Along these lines, Pearlin (1980) has distinguished between scheduled and nonscheduled events.

Life events were categorized by Myers et al. (1972) according to a different underlying set of characteristics in a longitudinal study investigating the effect of change in the number of events over a two-year period on psychiatric symptoms in a community sample of adults. The three dimensions of life events were area of social activity, entrance- versus exit-related events, and desirable versus undesirable events. Exit-related events were found to have the most negative impact on mental health.

The differing significance of life events according to the individual's movement through adulthood (Bengston, Kasschau, and Ragan, 1977) has been used in analyzing the reactions of older persons to major life changes in old age. This line of research has contributed data to the question of whether fewer life events are experienced by older adults (Masuda and Holmes, 1978). It has been argued that most events in the lives of older people have a negative impact because they involve role loss and also represent a rejection by society (Butler, 1975). This position has recently come under criticism as representing an overdramatization of the plight of old people and a distortion of the available data on their adaptation to major transitions (Atchley, 1981; Blank, 1982; Eisdorfer and Wilkie, 1977; George, 1980). Variations in the impact of several life events typically experienced by older adults—such as retirement, the moving out of children from the nuclear family, death of significant others, and illness—have been compared by using the life events rating scales. The effects of these events have been found to vary according to the individual's age and sex (Bourque and Back, 1977; Chiriboga and Dean, 1978; Pearlin, 1980). Across age groups of adults, it has also been suggested that socioeconomic status has a mediating role in the relationship between life changes and illness outcomes (Mechanic, 1974a; Rabkin and Streuning, 1976). Consideration of the effects of social status begins to add another level of complexity to the basic life events/illness model heretofore discussed, this being the conditioning effect of both personal and social resources on the outcome of a major life change.

Resources. The individual's response to a life change is increasingly being understood as a function of personal resources at the time the event occurs. Age, sex, and socioeconomic status are only very crude indicators, at best, of what the individual brings to bear on a change in life situation. A match between the individual's situation and personal and social characteristics was suggested as a necessary condition for adaptation in a study of a large sample of telephone workers by Hinkle (1974). He found considerable overlap between healthy and frequently ill workers in the possession of these resources, suggesting that those who were capable of sustaining personal deprivation without becoming ill were those who were "insulated" from social demands and difficulties.

Such results are suggestive of a general observation, which has taken hold in the life events literature, that both personal disposition and social status are contributory factors

to the ability to withstand stress. Included in the personal domain are physical status, cognitive abilities, personality traits, morale, psychological defenses, past experience, a sense of mastery over one's fate, knowledge of available means for dealing with stress, anticipatory socialization, time-perspective, self-concept, and cognitive style. Social resources are represented by age, education, occupation, and income (Hultsch and Plemons, 1979; Rabkin and Streuning, 1976).

A more elaborate system of classifying resources was proposed by George (1980) in the context of a general model of social adjustment in later life. Personal resources were defined as "the broad range of reserves and aids individuals can draw on in times of need" (p. 25), including the following four types: finances, social support, health, and education of the sort that fosters problem-solving strategies. These were distinguished from personality traits and coping skills that facilitate prevention, alleviation, or response to stressful situations. Social resources were further subdivided into the two broad categories of social status and socialization experiences. Social status includes occupation, gender, marital status, and ethnic group membership. Socialization experiences are those that prepare individuals for life events by providing for the learning of necessary skills. All four types of resources were regarded as conditioning variables that mediate between life events and adaptation in situations of retirement, the exiting of children from the nuclear family, widowhood, remarriage, relocation, and institutionalization. The model based on the effects of these resources brought together in a useful way a considerable amount of previous research on life events in later life.

Research on the Duke longitudinal sample of older adults by Palmore, Cleveland, Nowlin, Ramm, and Siegler (1979) demonstrated that the effect of resources—classified in their system as health, psychological, and social resources—varied according to the number of events experienced by the individual and the specific adaptational outcome. Adaptation was subdivided into physical, social-psychological (satisfaction), self-esteem, and activity dimensions. The simultaneous occurrence of several events tended to have long-term effects on those individuals lacking one or more of the ascribed resources. The possibility that the effects of resources may also vary according to sex was suggested in a study of a national sample of adults over 50. Elwell and Maltbie-Crannell (1981) found that financial security was a more important resource for men, whereas social participation was more critical for women as a mediator of life events.

It appears necessary, then, to include the individual's resources—or even more important, the balance of the individual's resources as measured against deficits (Lowenthal et al., 1975)—as moderators of reactions to life events in adulthood. These seem to have their primary effect on adaptation by fostering the process of coping.

Coping. Within the life events model, coping involves the individual's attempts to restore order into his or her life following a stressful event, that is, to re-establish the status quo that existed prior to the disruptive event. Coping involves securing information about the adaptation requirements posed by the stressful event (Hamburg and Adams, 1967; Sarason, 1980; Tyler, 1978), appraising the range of alternative actions, reaching a tentative behavioral plan, acting on this plan, and then adhering to it (Janis, 1974). Coping may also involve taking actions to prevent the stressful event, to prepare for it through anticipating its impact before it happens, to rehearse ways of dealing with it if it does happen, or to minimize its importance as a threat (McGrath, 1970). The stress created by a life event may also be coped with by endurance (Pearlin and Schooler, 1978). Avoidance is another way of reducing the stress created by a life event that has a negative impact on adaptation (Mechanic, 1974b). Some writers, however, have considered behaviors that do not involve a full appreciation of the magnitude of a situation to be a defensive rather than a coping mechanism (e.g. Haan, 1977). A pragmatic solution to this question is to consider as defensive any avoidance attempts that are not well-suited to the type of event at hand (Pearlin, 1980) and are therefore not capable of facilitating adaptation (White, 1974).

Summary. In its most highly articulated version, the life events model takes into account resources and coping strategies as mediators of the effect of stress-provoking life events on adaptation. This version of the life events model is schematically represented in Figure 1. The life event is one that precipitates stress because it involves a change in the individual's characteristic everyday routine or in some way drains his or her physical and psychological reserves. Stress is regarded as the degree of readjustment necessitated by the event. It may be created by the actual occurrence of the event or the anticipation of its inevitability. Coping strategies are a function of the abilities, attitudes, and knowledge that the individual brings to bear on the situation and promote adaptation by reducing the event-produced stress. The outcome of this process is either physical or mental illness if the coping strategy has been unsuccessful in reducing stress, or restoration of equilibrium if the stress has been alleviated. Although some variations of the life-events model include more complex, interactive processes (e.g., George, 1980), the basic premise remains that it is a single event, a series of events, or day-to-day disruptions that initiates the actions resulting in adaptation. In research designed to test the basic life-events/adaptation sequence, the life event is considered to be the independent variable and either illness, or lack of adverse symptoms, the dependent variable. The emphasis in this research is on specifying those life events that result in physical or psychological disturbances rather than determining how life events produce their effects.

Evaluation. The major contribution of the life events model of adaptation is that it dimensionalizes the qualities of events that create stress and the characteristics of the individuals that mediate its impact. Its limitation,

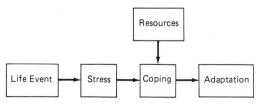

Figure 1.   The life events model of adaptation.

however, is that the investigator must make judgments about the effect of life events and about the strengths and weaknesses of individuals in their adaptation to them (Dohrenwend and Dohrenwend, 1974). By focusing on the observable components of the adaptation process, the personal meaning the individual attributes to the event and its effect are lost (Schlossberg, 1981). Moreover, the underlying assumption that stress is the result of disruption of homeostatis fails to account for human behavior that seeks disequilibrium and change for the sake of mastering them (Mechanic, 1974b). Thus, the lack of regard for subjective meanings of life events and the negative connotations attached to change are two inherent weaknesses of models that try to explain adaptation in terms of adjustment to changes in life patterns as measured through universal life-event classification systems. It is probably for these reasons that empirical tests of the life events model have resulted in only weak support for its major premises.

The Cognitive Appraisal Model

The role played by subjectivity in the process of adaptation has been given its most comprehensive treatment in the cognitive appraisal model formulated by Lazarus (1966). This model has received only limited attention in the life-span development literature (e.g., Chiriboga and Cutler, 1980; Eisdorfer and Wilkie, 1977; Schooler, 1975), although its underlying premises are entirely consistent with dialectical (e.g., Riegel, 1976) and transactional (e.g., Glenwick and Whitbourne, 1977) models applied to development in adulthood and old age.[1] Stress is not regarded simply as a mediator between the event and the reaction to that event as it is in the life events model; it is also regarded as the outcome of the event, the stimulator of subsequent reactions, and the result of these reactions. It is subjective in the sense of being the result of attempts by the individual to interpret situations and then to deal with the requirements generated

by the interpretation, this leading, in turn, to reinterpretations of the significance of the event. This emphasis on transactional processes in adaptation to events as subjective phenomena with an impact on the individual's psychological well-being is crucial to the elaboration of the life-span construct as a model of adaptation in adulthood.

Cognitive Appraisal. Lazarus describes his approach to understanding adaptation as "cognitive-phenomenological," by which he means that the way in which the individual appraises his or her relationship with the environment determines the emotional reaction to the environment. An appraisal is a judgment of the significance of the event to well-being. The appraisal process is seen as a function of motivational constructs such as beliefs, goals, and values; such constructs, along with learning, memory, and perception, are labeled "cognitive" (Lazarus, 1966; Lazarus, Kanner, and Folkman, 1980). The role of appraisal was first inferred from a series of experimental studies on college students in which physiological and psychological stressful reactions were monitored under conditions involving the manipulation of preparatory information about gory films (e.g., portrayal of tribal circumcision rites, serious accidents).

Cognitive appraisal is applied to situations with a potential impact on well-being because they allow for or thwart important motives. Appraisals, once made, represent an inseparable fusion of the person and the environment since it is not possible to define the "environment" independently of the individual's assessment of it (Lazarus, 1966), and each is changed as the result of this transaction (Lazarus, 1981).

Primary Appraisal. Evaluation of the significance of an event for its impact or possible impact on well-being constitutes the process of primary appraisal. Primary appraisal results in an evaluation of the situation as either irrelevant, benign or positive, or stressful. If appraised as stressful, the reason may be that it has already caused harm or loss, that it indicates the possibility of future injury and therefore constitutes a threat, or that it signi-

---

[1] In an article that appeared after this chapter was written, Lazarus and DeLongis (1983) addressed some of the developmental issues raised here.

fies challenge by presenting the opportunity for growth, mastery, or gain (Lazarus, 1981; Lazarus et al., 1974; Lazarus et al., 1980). The primary appraisal of a situation determines the emotional response to the transaction. If benign or positive, the appraisal is accompanied by joy, contentment, relief, or exhilaration; if harmful or threatening, it is accompanied by anxiety, fear, anger, guilt, envy, or depression. Challenge promotes excitement, hope, eagerness, and joy (Lazarus et al., 1980). Each emotion is predicted to have its own appraisal pattern (Lazarus, 1981).

As is implied by the transactional nature of the appraisal process in general, primary appraisal involves the mutually influencing effects of individual and situational factors. This transaction can be illustrated in several ways. The involvement of strong motives increases the degree of threat or challenge. Imminence of harm tends to increase the perception of threat, but appraisal of a situation as threatening has the result of altering the perception of its imminence, making the dreaded event appear to arrive sooner than it does in actuality (Lazarus, 1966), thereby slowing down the internal clock. The appraisal of a situation as threatening or challenging is also a function of the individual's perception of his or her own capabilities for meeting its demands. This evaluation constitutes the basis for the secondary appraisal process.

Secondary Appraisal. Secondary appraisal involves evaluating what personal and social resources are available, how well a particular mode of coping will meet the situational demands, and the "costs" of that coping, that is, whether new problems will result from the actions taken to reduce the threat or meet the challenge. Secondary appraisal is influenced by personal motivations and skills and the situational indicators of harm or gain that are mediated by the primary appraisal.

Reappraisal. When changes in the encounter between the individual and the environment occur as the result of the person's actions on the environment and the counteractions of the environment, both the situation and the person's coping capacities must be reassessed. This comprises reappraisal, and it can apply to any appraisal reached through either or both of the primary and secondary processes. Reappraisal may take the form of a change in the judged significance of an encounter to well-being as the result of information absorbed during the encounter. This form of the reappraisal process is dependent upon situational cues actually present during the encounter. In the second form of reappraisal, the change in the judged significance is due to an alteration of the individual's thoughts about the situation and his or her capacity to handle it in a way that will reduce the stressful emotions rather than change the actual nature of the relationship with the environment. Both forms of reappraisal are necessary to establish the transactional nature of the cognitive appraisal processes over time. The principle of reappraisal also serves as an important link between efforts by the individual to interpret the situation and the activities involved in responding to that interpretation.

Coping. Coping refers to the strategy employed by individuals to reduce a stressful reaction or act upon a challenging opportunity. Coping modes can serve two functions, an instrumental and a palliative one, towards the general end of either reducing stress or fulfilling a challenge (Lazarus and Launier, 1978). The instrumental function changes the nature of the person-environment relationship, whereas the palliative function is served when the nature of the person's emotional reaction to the situation is improved. Coping modes differ according to the relative degree to which they meet one or the other of these functions (Lazarus, 1981).

The direct-action coping mode is basically instrumental in its function. Intrapsychic coping modes are purely alterations of cognitions, mainly as a result of reappraisal, and thus serve the palliative function. Sometimes intrapsychic coping serves an instrumental function indirectly, if by reducing the reactions that are part of the emotional experience of stress it allows the individual to solve problems in a more clear-headed fashion or approach situations with less trepidation. Information-seeking is a mode of coping that can serve either an instrumental or a palliative function. The former is achieved by scanning those features of a situation that might reduce stress or turn a challenging appraisal into action. Information-seeking is palliative whenever actions taken in the past are rationalized or reappraisal alters the perception of threat without actually changing the situation.

Finally, inhibition of action is itself an instrumental coping mode, in that the individual, by not taking action, avoids creating a situation where coping activity would lead to further danger. This coping mode follows directly from the secondary appraisal that the "cost" of coping would exceed the gain (Lazarus, 1966). Direct-action, intrapsychic, and information-seeking coping modes may be directed at the self or the environment. Coping efforts may also be directed at situations that have already taken place, are occurring at present, or are anticipated in the future (Lazarus, 1981).

The relationship between the particular coping strategy employed by the individual and the appraisal of the situation involved was investigated by Folkman and Lazarus (1980). Stressful episodes in daily experiences over a 12-month period were evaluated by 100 adults, aged 45 to 64, using the "Ways of Coping" questionnaire. It was found that coping strategies serving palliative functions were used when situations were appraised as not offering the opportunity for action. In contrast, in situations that respondents viewed as amenable to problem-solving, more frequent use of coping directed at instrumental functions was reported.

Positive Emotions. The role of positive emotions aroused by challenging or even stressful appraisals of situations has been receiving increasing attention throughout the development of the cognitive appraisal model. Lazarus et al. (1980) dealt with this issue in some detail, relating different functions of positive emotions according to their point of origin in the coping process. Lazarus calls a break from an ongoing stressful encounter a "breather." Positive emotions can also serve as "sustainers" of coping during an episode

in which coping proves to be successful or by maintaining hope when coping does not appear to be having its intended effects. If the final results of coping are not successful, positive emotions that he calls "restorers" operate to facilitate recovery by augmenting the individual's psychological resources.

Hassles and Uplifts. Another recent development in the cognitive appraisal model has been its translation from extreme-danger situations to the everyday-life situations that can also generate appraisals, emotions, and coping (Kanner, Coyne, Schaefer, and Lazarus, 1981). These situations, categorized into "hassles" and "uplifts," were proposed to be stronger predictors of well-being than the number of major life events. The study designed to test this expectation was based on the sample used by Folkman and Lazarus (1980), who completed a questionnaire rating of the frequency of hassles and uplifts, a psychological symptoms checklist, and a measure of affect balance over the course of a 10-month period. Hassles proved to be the most closely related to well-being, whereas the number of major life events had little effect apart from its relationship to hassles. Thus, this study signified the relative importance to adaptation of daily events as compared to life crises. It should be noted, however, that hassles and uplifts were not assigned the role of mediators of stress; in keeping with the cognitive appraisal model, they were intended to reflect the evaluation of an everyday situation as favorable or unfavorable.

Summary. The cognitive appraisal model describes a complex and multifaceted process of adaptation to events that have significance for the individual's well-being. The types of events that present a potential for harm or benefit range from everyday annoyances and accomplishments to dangers that test the individual's resources for survival. Although diagramming such an intricate model carries the risk of oversimplification, a schematic representation of its essential characteristics to illustrate its transactional properties is given in Figure 2.

Although adaptation is not shown in this

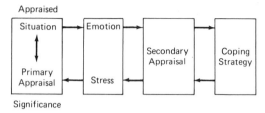

Figure 2.   Transactional processes in the cognitive appraisal model.

figure as a separate step within the process, it may be considered to occur whenever a stressful reaction is reduced or a positive emotion experienced. The process of reappraisal is indicated by the arrows moving from right to left, through which a situation's originally appraised signficance is altered. This process may continue through more cycles than are shown in Figure 2, depending on the length of the individual's involvement in the situation.

Evaluation. A tendency toward tautological explanations has plagued the stress research field since the first attempts were made to systematize the study of stress and coping. For instance, labeling of a situation as stressful because it leads to a stressful reaction does not allow for independent evaluations of situations and responses to those situations, nor does it allow for causal analyses. The cognitive appraisal model partially overcomes these shortcomings by allowing for numerous predictions about specific variables within the individual and the situation that might influence the appraisal and coping processes. Each statement of the model, as it has become more fully elaborated, has been based on experimental manipulations of stress-induced reactions, clinical observation, and naturalistic reports of reactions both to disasters and to daily events.

One particular area in which causal analyses become strained, however, is in the presumed dependence of coping strategies on secondary appraisal, that is, that the strategy chosen is based on the greater potential it offers for resolving the dilemma. It is not clear, however, to what extent the decision made in the secondary appraisal process is informed by pro-

jection into the future of whatever particular path is followed. Does the individual choose a palliative strategy, for instance, because he or she knows that it will reduce the stress-related emotion? Or does the reappraisal of a threatening situation as benign follow from some other combination of factors so that the outcome (stress reduction) is only an incidental result of the coping strategy? This issue was not addressed in the Folkman and Lazarus (1980) study of coping strategies, since all data were retrospective.

Other points will almost certainly receive clarification as the role of positive emotions becomes more fully incorporated in the cognitive appraisal model. In this regard, it would also be desirable to specify how coping mechanisms involved in positive emotional experiences differ, if at all, from those stimulated by negative emotions. Also, it would be of value to extend to negative emotions the analysis of the functions served by positive emotions at different points in the coping process.

A related issue that has not received much attention is whether the model proposed by Lazarus is based on the same assumption as the life events model—that is, that events that cause stress do so because of their disruptive effects on the otherwise homeostatic relationship between the individual and the environment. If positive emotions and the positive effects of stressful interactions with the environment were given greater emphasis as contributing factors to a favorable, growth-enhancing state of disequilibrium, the model might more closely approximate the dialectical approaches that Lazarus favorably compares to his own (Lazarus, 1981).

A final concern about the underlying logic of the cognitive appraisal model pertains to its coping classification scheme. This aspect of the model has been subject to the most modification over the course of Lazarus' writings and still seems to present a nagging problem. If the model is to have continued useful empirical applications, such overlaps as those that exist between information-seeking and intrapsychic coping and between both of these processes and the reappraisal mechanism will have to be reduced or eliminated. The "Ways of Coping" questionnaire is a step toward the clarification of coping strategies, but the distinction between the instrumental and palliative functions implicit in it does not serve to separate the coping modes.

Paradoxically, it is exactly this sort of definitional problem that can be interpreted as a result of the major contribution of the cognitive appraisal model: treating coping as dependent on the individual's perception of the situation. Two features that detract from the life events model as a basis for understanding the coping process are its failure to take into account the individual's interpretation of an event and its lack of regard for the appropriateness of the coping strategy in terms of that interpretation. The cognitive appraisal model incorporates both these factors as well as the way they change over the course of a stressful encounter and thus provides for a more refined specification of adaptation as a process.

Given this set of complications and the problem of obtaining valid self-report data on coping (Lazarus, 1981), it is probable that a taxonomy that completely distinguishes among coping strategies will never be formulated nor would it be useful in and of itself. More important for the purpose of integrating the model developed by Lazarus into a life-span developmental framework is the concept of appraisal and the way in which it affects, and is affected by, the individual's changing view of self and the environment throughout adulthood. Further insight into this process can be gained from the research on subjective well-being in adulthood that addresses variables having a direct bearing on cognitive appraisal as reflected in the outcome, satisfaction.

The Subjective Well-Being Model

In contrast to the cognitive appraisal model, which focuses on processes of adaptation through coping, the subjective well-being model has developed from attempts to understand the result of these processes. It is assumed that adaptation is reflected in satisfaction, which in turn evolves from the individual's appraisal of personal and social resources. Variations within this model exist according to the degree to which subjective

evaluations of self and environment include affective as well as cognitive components (Campbell, 1980). The general approach, however, is characterized by an overall concern for the perceived quality of life of the individual. Adaptation is viewed as the result of a continuous evaluation of life experiences rather than as reactions to discrete, stress-provoking crises as it is in the life events model. The subjective well-being model is also focused predominantly on "positive" features of adaptation rather than reactions against stress. As in the cognitive appraisal model, subjective evaluation forms the basis for the individual's reaction to experiences, and coping follows from this reaction. The subjective well-being model also provides for mechanisms that modify the appraisal of the environment as a result of coping. The two models arrived at their similarity in describing adaptation methods through entirely different routes, however. The survey method on which the subjective well-being model is based allows for generalization to adults of varying ages, ethnicity, and social status groups. The cognitive appraisal model was developed with more limited samples that were studied more intensively and therefore provides a more complete description of the processes of adaptation within these samples. The fact that the two models converge on the importance of perception as a determinant of adaptation despite their radically different approaches provides a source of convergent validity for this basic principle. In addition, research on the subjective well-being model permits further insight into the specific appraisal process through which the life-span construct influences adaptation.

Background. There have been two traditions of research on well-being as an index of adaptation in adults. The first has been mainly the concern of gerontologists: the prediction of well-being from the independent variables of social status, income, and activity levels (reviewed in Larson, 1978), personality (George, 1978), and the mediating effects of personality (Neugarten, 1977), social status (Markides and Martin, 1979), and availability of transportation (Cutler, 1972) on the relationship between activity and well-being. Perceived health has also been examined in relation to well-being in old age, and its effects have been found to be significant (Edwards and Klemmack, 1973). Much of this research was stimulated by the controversy over activity versus disengagement theory as a means of accounting for the relationship between social participation and morale in old age. This debate has been supplanted by the interest in predicting well-being through causal modeling in order to avoid the circularity implicit in simple correlational analyses.

The individual's perception of his or her life situation as a determinant of well-being has usually not been examined within the gerontological research tradition. In contrast, in the second research approach represented most recently by the work of Andrews and Withey (1976) and Campbell, Converse, and Rodgers (1976), subjectivity has assumed prime importance as a predictor of well-being, operationalized as satisfaction with life's quality. Because of its broader sampling base across the entire age range of adulthood, research based on this measure provides a more general model of subjective well-being than that derived from research based only on older adult samples. The principle of adaptation that has emerged from the global well-being research is one that applies throughout the adult years, even though some of the specific factors that contribute to overall satisfaction may differ somewhat for older adult groups (Herzog and Rodgers, 1981).

Measurement. In a study of Campbell et al. (1976), respondents were asked to reply to the question "How satisfied are you with your life as a whole these days?" by choosing a number from 1 (completely satisfied) to 7 (completely dissatisfied). Andrews and Withey (1976) requested their respondents to reply to the question "How do you feel about your life as a whole?" on a scale ranging from 1 (terrible) to 7 (delighted), the points between these extremes indicating the degree of satisfaction. The single-item indicator was combined with semantic differential ratings of global features of life by Campbell et al. (1976). It was made more stable by Andrews

and Withey (1976), who averaged two global satisfaction ratings taken over the course of their interview. Although the global satisfaction rating is not as elaborate as other well-being measures that cover a wider range of evaluations, George (1981) concluded that the single-item-based rating scales compare favorably on various psychometric criteria with the more complex measures of well-being.

Mechanisms of Adaptation. Aspiration level is the major factor that has emerged from research on subjective well-being as the determinant of whether an aspect of life will be perceived positively or negatively. In their survey of over 2100 adults, Campbell et al. (1976) noted instances of the apparent effects of aspiration level in producing discrepancies between global subjective assessments and "objective" qualities, particularly in the areas of housing and education, where objective indices were most readily available. The role of aspiration level in promoting adaptation was inferred from observing discrepanices between measures of happiness and satisfaction in old and young adults. Although older adults reported lower levels of happiness, they were also the more satisfied. The opposite attitude was observed among young adults. The latter finding was replicated in the surveys of over 5000 adults by Andrews and Withey (1976), who noted, moreover, that young adults believed that their well-being had improved more in the past five years and would improve still more in the next five years than did older people.

The analyses by Campbell et al. (1976) of discrepancies between objectively assessed and subjectively perceived conditions and of age differences in happiness and satisfaction, in addition to their data on life changes, led to the development of a model whose major features are displayed in Figure 3. This model represents a feedback process in which the dependent variable, satisfaction, is the outcome of the comparison between expectations set by the aspiration level and the reality of the current situation. Adaptation is fostered when the aspiration level rises or falls in accordance with the individual's meeting or failing to meet important life goals.

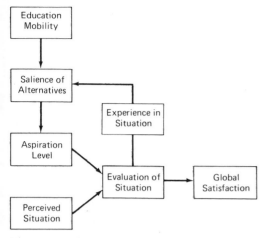

Figure 3.   The subjective well-being model of adaptation.

The Effects of Experience. In the subjective well-being model, mobility and education are considered to exert an influence on satisfaction in that increasing diversity of experience either directly (through mobility) or indirectly (through learning about other places or cultures) produces a cognitive state in which alternatives to one's situation are made more salient. Awareness of alternatives, in turn, are seen as heightening aspiration level so that past accomplishments or decisions may be devalued. For example, college dropouts have been found to depart from the curve showing greater satisfaction with higher levels of education across many domains. This was not because their objective circumstances were particularly unhappy, but because their level of aspiration had been raised while they were in college, and their self-evaluations had fallen short when they compared themselves to their peers who had managed to complete their college education.

Coping. Modification of aspiration level either upwards or downwards leads to a revised evaluation of the situation, and this, in turn, leads to alterations in satisfaction. Generally speaking, aspirations are lowered when the salience of alternatives diminishes, and the individual recognizes that alternatives have become inaccessible. This type of feedback process would account for the relatively high satisfaction of poorly educated older adults who, Campbell et al. (1976) assumed, had progressively lowered their expectations as the result of a lifetime's accumulation of experiences signifying that these expectations would not be met. A variant of this process can be seen in the adaptation to a fixed situation over a long term period that is made possible by forgetting about the existence of alternatives. Another accommodation process occurs as a resolution of feelings about commitments not easily changed, such as choice of a marriage partner or a place to live. Following an initial period of pleasure with the choice, flaws may be discerned and satisfaction reduced to a commensurate degree. If the individual maintains the commitment despite this dissatisfaction, evaluation of the situation will gradually become more favorable through an accommodation process that reduces the salience of deficiences. A situation that involves a major, unexpected, and negatively evaluated change in life circumstances results in a more accentuated accommodation process than the more gradual mechanisms described thus far. In such a situation, accommodation occurs through a drifting downward of aspiration level in response to circumstances that seem unlikely to change.

All of these accommodation routes may be considered intrapsychic forms of coping—in terms of the cognitive appraisal model. This is because they involve reappraisal and other cognitive manipulations of the individual's evaluation of the environment rather than actual changes in the characteristics of the individual or the environment.

Motivation. The need to preserve feelings of positive self-esteem is the stimulus for the feedback mechanism through which the salience of alternatives is reduced or the aspiration level lowered. A related tendency is to discount the importance of an area in which dissatisfaction is expressed. Andrews and Withey (1976) observed that the average respondent's self-rating of satisfaction was higher than the rating assigned to the "typical" American and also higher than the rating of the nearest neighbor of the same sex. This positive bias was more obvious in areas with central relationships to global well-being. Andrews and Withey (1976, p. 333) concluded that the tendency to view oneself favorably was a factor critical to adjustment: "Optimism is another apparent phenomenon that keeps people from assimilating some of the sting of current conditions . . . the hope of better things is undoubtedly a help in one's acceptance of present circumstance."

Evaluation. The cognitive appraisal and subjective well-being models present radically different views on the adaptive value of purely intrapsychic modes of coping. The point of departure may be posed in terms of Hamlet's question to himself (*Hamlet*, III, i) "Whether 'tis nobler in the mind to suffer/the slings and arrows of outrageous fortune/Or to take arms against a sea of troubles/And by opposing end them?" Clearly, the subjective well-being model advocates the "suffer" approach; all coping strategies described within it are intrapsychic. By contrast, the cognitive appraisal model of direct action involves coping modes that are aimed at changing the environment to produce satisfaction or reduce unhappiness. This model has therefore avoided the trap into which the subjective well-being model falls of treating the individual as passively avoiding unpleasantness in life rather than as actively taking control over situations, including situations that provoke discontent as well as those that are potentially rewarding.

Indeed, the very concept of satisfaction conveys a passive sense of resignation, particularly as operationalized by Campbell et al. (1976). Andrews and Withey (1976), who included affective states and end-points in their satisfaction rating scale ("Delighted" and "Terrible"), made more of an attempt to distinguish between satisfaction as passive acceptance and satisfaction as active joy or exhilaration. In both cases, however, satisfaction is regarded as the result of changes in the individual's perception of the state of his or her life conditions or expectations, not changes in the external circumstances that may be causing unhappiness.

This emphasis on passivity in the subjective well-being model makes it difficult to understand the basis for the assertion by Campbell (1980) that a sense of control over one's life is an essential factor in promoting well-being. The only possible resolution of this problem appears to be that the control that people high in well-being possess is actually an illusion. It is only the individual's ability to control a situation by distorting the perception of it that contributes to well-being; the circumstances themselves are not subject to control.

It should also be noted that the conclusion that coping occurs as a result of internal processes alone may have been a function of the kinds of questions people were asked in the surveys on subjective well-being. Adaptation models were imposed on the questionnaire data in a post-hoc fashion, and only the responses concerning the end-product of adaptation, well-being, were available for analysis. Inferences concerning adjustment of aspiration level were made by comparing responses of specific demographically defined subgroups, and ratings were based on how satisfied these groups "should" have been with their externally rated resources. No direct attempt was made to ask people how they coped with feelings of unhappiness or how they tried to change unsatisfactory circumstances.

If it is assumed that the adjustment of aspiration level is just another form of coping, rather than the *only* mode of adaptation, then the research conducted within the subjective well-being model can provide useful principles for expanding upon the life-span construct as a model of adaptation. Unlike the life events model, it has identified coping mechanisms that operate continuously, not just as a result of life crises, and it focuses on psychological health rather than physical illness as manifestation of the adaptation process. The concept of aspiration level, although not new to this model, forms a link between appraisals and identity in the adaptation process. The finding that individuals distort their recall of past experiences and alter their projections of the future in ways that are intended to facilitate self-esteem complements the theory of the psychological career proposed by Raynor and Entin (1982) and supports that portion of the life-span construct model that deals with changes in the interpretation of life experiences to make them consistent with the life-span construct. To the extent that the life-span construct involves motivated distortions of life experiences, the subjective well-being research provides evidence across large samples of adults that subjectivity is indeed an important feature of adaptation.

THE LIFE-SPAN CONSTRUCT AS A MODEL OF ADAPTATION

With the specification of the traditional approaches to adaptation represented by the life events, cognitive appraisal, and subjective well-being models, it is now possible to expand upon the processes described at the outset of the chapter as functions of the life-span construct. This restatement will involve a re-evaluation of the strengths and weaknesses of the three traditional models, focusing on the subjective meaning of events, the interaction between subjective perceptions and coping, distinctions among types of coping strategies, and the outcome of adaptation. This re-evaluation will then form the basis for a model of adaptation based on the life-span construct.

Life Events

From the research conducted in the context of the life events model, it has become clear that a distinction must be made between events on the basis of their positive or negative impact on the individual if adaptation to these events is to be understood. The lack of coherence among the schemes for cataloging all possible types of events, major and minor, that can be experienced by adults further suggests that events should not be prespecified in terms of either content or evaluative quality in any attempt to determine how or whether an individual will change. Life events models that specify coping strategies as attempts to reduce stress have illustrated the difficulties inherent in describing such strategies from a point of reference external to the individual. It is particularly difficult in this regard to distinguish between coping and defense mechanisms. The outcome of the coping strategy as positive adaptation, on the one hand, or illness, on the other, is seen to reflect the success or failure of the coping strategy, but in this case as well, using criteria external to the individual in distinguishing illness from health is fraught with difficulties. Finally, the assumption that homeostasis is the basic form of being creates problems for a developmental model of adaptation.

Cognitive Appraisal

The cognitive appraisal model helps to overcome some of the above difficulties with the life events model. In the first place, the entire process is viewed as transactional, so that coping is treated as a function of the perception of stress, which in turn is influenced by the success of the coping strategy. Events are not predefined in terms of whether their effects will be positive or negative; the individual's appraisal is the determinant of how they will be evaluated. Both major disruptive events and ordinary events of everyday life are seen as having the potential to stimulate the appraisal process and, hence, coping. Although the classification of coping strategies offered by this model requires refinement, the concept of defining coping in terms of the appraisal of the event helps to avert the problems of classifying coping strategies according to the tenuous distinction of whether or not they distort reality. Adaptation is not singled out as a separate step in the coping process; it may be assumed that reduction of stress or meeting a challenge represents positive adaptation and that the continued experiencing of a stressful reaction is maladaptive.

Subjective Well-Being

Finally, the subjective well-being model reinforces the premise of the cognitive appraisal model that the evaluation of a situation is a judgmental process, and that it is this evaluation, not the "objective" features of the person or the situation, that determines whether the situation will be adapted to favorably or unfavorably. As in the cognitive appraisal model, it is assumed that individuals are evaluating a range of events in terms of well-being. A deliberate attempt is made to avoid regarding external evaluative criteria as being synonymous with the individual's interpretation of an event as positive or negative. Research based on the subjective well-being model in which large samples of adults were given survey-type interviews has substantiated the presence of the feedback mechanism postulated by the cognitive appraisal model—from evaluation of the situation, to coping, to re-evaluation in light of the altered appraisal. The major deficiency of the subjective well-being model is its failure to consider strategies that change the nature of the environment as forms of coping. Instead, the model describes only passive forms of accommodation (through changes in aspiration levels) as ways of dealing with situations that fall short of expectations.

The Role of Motivational Biases

The latter point is particularly important for the further elaboration of the life-span construct model. In the initial description of the life-span construct, support for the principle that the life story involves distortion was drawn from research demonstrating the role played by motivational biases in serving the goal of identity preservation and maintenance of self-esteem. Indeed, Greenwald's (1980) description of motivational biases that serve the "totalitarian ego" and Raynor and Entin's (1982) extension of similar processes as part of the way in which self-esteem is maintained over a lifetime suggest that individuals seldom interpret events outside the framework of their own motive to see themselves in a favorable light. According to this view, changes in self-perception or actions taken to alter the environment or one's perception of the environment occur rarely, if ever. As a result, the individual is portrayed as static, self-serving, and unrealistic—in short, as maintaining a defensive posture against the environment. When dissatisfaction arouses a perceived need for change, it is accomplished by altering one's view of what is considered desirable so as not to threaten self-esteem or "make waves" in the environment.

To avoid this antidevelopmental portrayal of adaptation, it is necessary to build mechanisms into the adaptation model that will promote changes in the life-span construct as the result of experiences that are incongruent with it. In addition, ways of changing the environ-

ment, not just one's perceptions of it, must be recognized as coping strategies.

Restatement of the Life-Span Construct

Identity is considered to be the primary source of the life-span construct and determines its content, being that area around which the individual's sense of self is defined and towards which the greatest commitment of identity is made. The content of the life-span construct also determines the content, level, and timing of the individual's aspirations. It is these aspirations that form the basis for appraising the significance of events. Coping may result in an altered life story so that the meaning of events is distorted according to one's biases toward the maintenance of self-esteem. Coping may also result in altered aspiration levels through any revision of the life-span construct involving a changed scenario. Rather than viewing this process as a passive form of adaptation emerging from a need to reconcile an unhappy situation with the desire to maintain a positive outlook on life, it is regarded as an active process and involves restructuring identity in response to a real need to make changes in one's estimation of one's capacities toward greater congruence with one's actual competencies. The motivation for identity restructuring is not simply self-esteem maintenance; It is the desire to solve the problems of everyday living more effectively and to experience a sense of accomplishment from tasks successfully completed over the course of a lifetime. Coping strategies that alter the life story in such a way as to portray the individual as the hero may temporarily serve the same purpose, but eventually they must break down because not all events can be transformed through intrapsychic processes alone (Lazarus, 1981). Finally, coping may also take the form of changing the environment when it is apparent that failure to achieve one's aspirations does not stem from self-limitations alone. Attempts to change the environment may be premature and unsuccessful if the individual has not adequately confronted the possibility that this failure may be internally induced. Thus, actions directed toward the environment may not have their intended effects, but it is critical that the possibility of such actions be recognized as a coping mechanism.

Adaptation Processes

The general processes implied in the life span construct model of adaptation are shown in Figure 4. The adaptational outcomes of this process consist of both the affective state associated with the event and the further growth of identity. Whether these two outcomes operate in complementary or opposing ways, they are distinct features of adaptation that must be regarded as independent.

The adaptation process takes on different configurations depending on whether the event is consistent or inconsistent with the individual scenario. An event consistent with the scenario is evaluated favorably and is integrated into the individual's life story virtually as it happened. Furthermore, because it has fitted in with desired goals and expectations in line with motives derived from identity, it is incorporated into identity in a confirmatory fashion. Interpretation of the event in a favorable manner does not imply that it is necessarily positive in its impact on the individual's life, however. On the contrary, it may be an experience that creates discomfort, loss, or unhappiness. Nevertheless, the fact that it is consistent with the scenario allows it to be adapted to with greater ease than if it had been unexpected. In effect, the scenario provides a framework for anticipatory coping.

Confronting an event that does not conform to the scenario is far more complex and may have alternative outcomes. The first possibility is for the event to be incorporated in the life

story in fairly accurate form; that is, the individual, when reconstructing the event, describes it in a way that closely resembles the details of its antecedents and outcome. It is not transformed so as to make it congruent with the individual's identity; no motivational biases are applied to its recall. As a result of the experience, the individual alters his or her identity, which in turn modifies the life-span construct and results in a revised scenario that takes into account the fact that the original goal could not be achieved according to the original scenario. New events are then interpreted in light of their fit with the altered scenario. This process is comparable to the form of reappraisal described by Lazarus (1981), in which the individual uses information from the initial transaction with the environment to evaluate more realistically the altered person-environment relationship. As a coping strategy, this reappraisal becomes an information-seeking mode directed toward the environment.

The second possible route following an event that is not consistent with the scenario involves distortion of the causes and/or nature of the event in order to make it more consistent with identity. In applying motivational biases to the retelling of the event, its features, or the circumstances surrounding it, are transformed so that the original details are no longer available to memory. The individual actually believes that the event occurred in the way it is reconstructed. Once the modified event has been incorporated in the life story, the scenario for future events will be revised, perhaps by extending or foreshortening its time lines to account for the delay or earlier arrival of an event than expected. Each new event will then be reappraised in light of the revised scenario, but not with any new insights about the individual's identity or a commensurate change in the life-span construct. This reaction is similar to the intrapsychic form of reappraisal described by Lazarus (1981), in which the subjective but not the objective features of the situation are changed. The coping mode to which it corresponds is information-seeking directed toward the self, in which information of a negative nature is ignored or distorted.

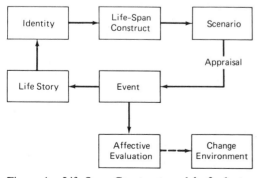

Figure 4.   Life-Span Construct model of adaptation.

The third possible result of the individual's encounter with an unanticipated event or one that conflicts with the scenario is a change in the person-environment relationship. This reaction, which corresponds to the coping strategy of direct action against the environment, is depicted as a broken line in Figure 4. The individual may abandon the environment if it is totally antagonistic toward the achievement of the goals defined within the scenario. Environmental modifications might not be undertaken until previous attempts at achievement were found to be impossible within the context of that environment. Attempts to change the existing environment may occur if it is not overly constraining. The scenario may be revised to take into account those changes necessitated by the new environmental inputs, but there would be no alteration of the individual's identity.

The Role of Events. It should be pointed out that the events that create congruence or dissonance with the scenario need not be restricted to those requiring major life changes. In keeping with the concept of "strains" (Pearlin, 1980) and "hassles" (Lazarus et al., 1980), the possibility that relatively minor events can trigger the processes described, whether in an isolated or cumulative fashion, must be built into the life-span construct model of adaptation. Indeed, the definition of an event in terms of magnitude will depend on its significance to the individual's scenario.

It is not necessarily the case that an event is "known" by the individual as one that has significance for the life-span construct before it is experienced. Significance is determined as the result of the appraisal process that may not take place until well after the event has occurred or before its ramifications have been considered. As previously implied, the individual may be unprepared for an event that had been planned for in the scenario but had occurred before anticipatory coping had taken place. If the event was not only unprepared for but not even a part of the original scenario, the individual will be forced to incorporate it in the scenario as well as make it a part of the life story. This double strain would account for the fact that unanticipated events

require greater adaptational efforts on the part of the individual than events that occur before their time but were expected to happen eventually. Of course, pleasant unexpected "surprises" may be experienced positively if they are congruent with the goals defined by the original scenario, even though they may require its readjustment.

Relationship to Traditional Models

The assumption that an event is not definable apart from the interpretation the individual places upon it forms the outstanding link of convergence between the life-span construct model and those traditional models that take into account subjective perceptions of experiences as critical to adaptation. The individual's perception of an event is a function of the structure imposed on it from identity through the life-span construct and cannot be predicted from a categorization system based on external criteria defined by an observer. The transactional nature of the life-span construct model of adaptation is also exemplified by the fact that past, present, and future become linked in a continuous interchange of appraisals and reappraisals, a process emphasized in the cognitive appraisal model and to a lesser extent in the subjective well-being model. The interpretation of future experiences depends on the way in which past events were perceived. The latter are continuously reinterpreted in light of present and anticipated experiences. This continuous interchange between the individual and the environment in the process of encountering events over time places the life-span construct model well within the conceptualization of development as a dialectical process.

In keeping with the assumptions of both dialectical and transactional models of development, the individual is portrayed as having an active role in structuring development. Although the life-span construct model of adaptation does carry with it the undesirable potential of regarding changes in the individual as reactions to environmental disruptions, it must be emphasized that it is only within the individual that the potential for developmental change can be activated. It is through the scenario that the individual sets the goals against which events will be evaluated and their role in stimulating change promoted. The scenario, in turn, is a function of the life-span construct, which is heavily influenced by identity. Moreover, homeostasis is not necessarily the only state in which positive affect is experienced by the individual as it is assumed to be in reactive models of adaptation. As in the cognitive appraisal model, challenge is considered to be a state in which the individual's sense of well-being is heightened, even though this state may involve discontinuity between goals and experiences. A search for change may also be built into the scenario, so that periods of placidity and equilibrium are not seen as end-states of being. To be sure, the motivation for revising events so that they are compatible with the life story may be seen as serving the goal of conserving one's self-image. This tendency, however, is not seen as a stable one in face of the continued input of conflicting evidence that is bound to occur when distortion of events become the predominant mode of coping with life events that are considered discrepant with the scenario.

As a transactional model of adaptation, the life-span construct model adds a dimension to the traditional adaptation models by incorporating into the subjective appraisal process the individual's view of how his or her life has been and will be shaped. At the same time, it integrates the individual's cognitive and emotional frames of reference into the life-course perspective, a connection heretofore not explicitly made.

Applications of the Life-Span Construct Model

Measurement. Current life-event rating scales are not suitable for the purpose of testing the life-span construct model since they are based on normative principles of the nature of life events and do not provide a sense of how past events have been either perceived or timed over the individual's life. They also give no measures of future expectations. Although modifications of standard life-event instruments take into account individual variations in perceptions of life events by means of impact rating scales (Lowenthal et al., 1975; Sarason et al., 1978), these still carry the assumption of universality across individuals in the occurrence of particular events and the nonoccurrence of others. Others measure both past and future life-course interpretations. The life graph (Back and Bourque, 1970) is a tool that roughly approximates an ideographic measure of perceptions of the life span but is nevertheless practical for large-sample studies. The Life Evaluation Chart developed by Lowenthal et al. (1975) is a variation on this measure, one with a more extensive specification of the evaluative criteria to be applied to life events. Both these measures, however, contain an undesirable restriction in that the vertical dimension is predefined as satisfaction, prohibiting respondents from including events not relevant to this dimension. In addition, since the horizontal axis is divided into equal time intervals, the respondents are not given the opportunity to apply differential weighting to events and periods in their lives according to perceived importance. For these reasons, the life graph and its variant are more properly regarded as expanded satisfaction-rating scales than as indicators of how people impose organization on their lives as was originally intended by investigators interested in perceptions of the life course.

A measure called the "life drawing" was designed by Whitbourne and Dannefer (in press) to yield scores indicative of the individual's unique perception of the life span without placing undue constraints on respondents to indicate particular events, years, or evaluations. A similar method was described by Sanguiliano (1980) for clinical purposes. The procedure for administering the life drawing involves presenting the respondent with a horizontally oriented sheet of paper with a line near the bottom. This line forms the horizontal axis and is labeled "age and/or year" to provide a basis for scaling according to a personal or social time dimension. The respondent is asked to "draw your life" in whatever way he or she wishes, the only instruction being that eras or marker points, if they are shown, be labeled so that their content can be understood. Thus, the respondent can construct whatever basis for evaluation of events he or she believes to be relevant. From this relatively open-ended technique, several variables can be derived that relate to the individual's sense of the life span as a psychological entity.

The instrument was administered to a sample of 94 adults (47 men and 47 women) ranging in age from 24 to 60 years (mean = 40.64 years) and randomly selected from residents of Rochester, New York, and its immediate suburbs. They completed the life drawing as part of a three-hour interview on identity and life history. A group of 55 respondents (22 men and 33 women) responded to a mailed retest of the life drawing one year later, and of these, 40 provided usable life drawings. From the retest data, evidence for the reliability and validity (sensitivity to life changes) of the instrument was obtained. At retest, the respondents were asked to list significant life changes on a separate open-ended questionnaire. Among the 20 who indicated no significant changes, the time perspective of the most significant period in terms of past versus present timing (the portion of the drawing with greatest relative space devoted to it) was stable in 75 percent of the cases. Among those who stated that significant life changes had occurred, the test-retest agreement was significantly lower (45 percent). A change from past to present orientation was noted in 83 percent of these 20 cases. Thus, the life drawing measure proved to be sensitive to life events, a change in life circumstances being reflected in increased preoccupation with the present. Extension of the life drawing into the future also showed test-retest stability in 75 percent of the cases, but agreement between testings did not show sensitivity to life-event changes.

Reference to specific age markers in the life drawing showed low consistency between testings; in the original sample, regular age or year intervals comparable to "stages" in adulthood were not observed with any regularity. Results of research on samples more representative than the ones used by advocates of age-stage analyses of adult transitions (e.g., Gould, 1978; Levinson, Darrow, Klein, Levinson, and McKee, 1978) support the observations derived from the life drawing, suggesting that most adults do not perceive their lives as having been characterized by major, age-related shifts (Campbell, 1980). It is possible that when stages are found it is only because they are expected by the investigator [see Gubrium and Buckholdt's (1977) critique of Kimmel's (1974) case histories]. Even if the Levinson-type age stages are apparent in a particular individual's drawing, however, the technique by itself cannot verify whether they actually occurred or if their presence signifies a representation of the expected life course portrayed in a stereotypic fashion. Verification through external sources, if possible, and interviewing would help to resolve this question.

Test of the Model. In the research conducted to date on the life drawing, past orientation may be seen as reflecting an imposition of the life story on the interpretation of the present, whereas future extension can be taken as representative of the scenario. Changes or life events appear to bring the present more sharply into focus, making the life story less predominant, perhaps, as the event's implications are integrated into identity. Nevertheless, the life drawing measure has not yet been fully exploited as an instrument for tapping the life story and scenario. In future research, it could be considered as a rough diagram of the individual's life-span construct. As such, it could be used as the starting point for interviewing adults about why they chose to represent their lives as they did and hence for developing a more complete picture of the two components of the life-span construct that it indexes. Correlations linking the effect of life events on the individual's scenario and life story with the openness-to-experience inventory (Costa and McCrae, 1978) would provide further empirical verification. Thus, it could be predicted that individuals who are more open to experience would be more likely to integrate events into their life stories without distortion and to revise their scenarios more in keeping with the events that have occurred rather than in terms of expectations derived from identity through the life-span construct. [See Coan (1974) for a fuller treatment of this issue.]

Practice. The life drawing used in the context of the life-span-construct model of adaptation can also be used in applied settings as a way for individuals to clarify their perceptions about their expectations for the future and their recollections of the past. The life-drawing technique can be modified so that the individual is asked to project plans for the future. Once the scenario has been made explicit on paper, it can be determined whether the goals set for the future can reasonably be met or if they, or coping strategies for achieving them, would profit by some adjustment. If individuals are incapable of producing a future time line, this incapacity in itself would be significant, and facilitating the preparation of one could help them see their present life in the perspective of the future. Retaining life drawings obtained at periodic intervals would constitute a "future diary" that would permit them to compare projected with actualized goals.

The life drawing can also be used to help the individual incorporate events from the past in the life story and thus serve to promote adjustment through the life review process (Butler, 1963). Walaskay, Whitbourne, and Nehrke (1983–1984) found that some aged individuals were able to avert this process and still negotiate successfully the psychosocial crisis of ego integrity versus despair described by Erikson (1963). Among a healthy-community sample of 40 adults ranging in age from 65 to 90 years, 10 of the 20 adults who had achieved favorable resolution of the integrity crisis (defined in terms of positive affect balance, low death anxiety, appropriate death preparation, and questionnaire and intensive interview responses signifying ego integrity) showed no evidence of their having significantly engaged in reminiscing. This finding would suggest that the life story of an aged person who does not achieve ego integrity by means of the life review may be one in which identity-preserving qualities facilitate adaptation rather than richness of detail regarding past experiences. Intervention may be deemed desirable if the life story begins to disintegrate when unresolved events enter awareness. In this case, the life drawing can be of value in helping the individual reconcile these events into a revised life story.

SUMMARY

As a means of bringing together theories of coping and adaptation with gerontological research, theory, and practice, three traditional models of adaptation in adulthood have been considered: life-events, cognitive appraisal, and subjective well-being. Each model has its own particular strengths, but each was also found to have limitations as far as providing a developmental basis for an adaptation model focused around the life-span construct is concerned. A new model was proposed that builds upon features of all three, and an experimental approach designed to explore its validity was described. The life-span construct and the life-drawing technique aimed at measuring it are based on the underlying premise that it is the individual's cognitive and emotional construction of the life span that will ultimately determine how that individual will develop through the experiences of a lifetime. It is hoped that the model based on this construct will contribute to a conceptually integrated approach to understanding adaptation over the life course.

Acknowledgment: This paper was prepared while the author was at the University of Rochester. Support for some of the research on which it was based was provided by a University of Rochester BRSG-SUB grant and funding from the Spencer Foundation, W. Dale Dannefer, Co-Principal Investigator.

REFERENCES

Andrews, F. M., and Withey, S. B. 1976. *Social Indicators of Well-Being: Americans' Perceptions of Life Quality.* New York: Plenum.

Atchley, R. C. 1981. *The Social Forces in Later Life.* 3rd ed. Belmont, CA: Wadsworth.

Atkinson, J. W., and Feather, N. T., eds. 1966. *A Theory of Achievement Motivation.* New York: Wiley.

Appley, M. H., and Trumbull, R., eds. 1967. *Psychological Stress.* New York: Appleton-Century-Croft.

Back, K. W., and Bourque, L. 1970. Life graphs: Aging and cohort effect. *Journal of Gerontology* 25: 249–255.

Bartlett, F. C. 1932. *Remembering.* Cambridge: Cambridge University Press.

Bengston, V. L.; Kasschau, P. L.; and Ragan, P. K. 1977. The impact of social structure on aging individuals. In *Handbook of the Psychology of Aging,* eds. J. E. Birren and K. W. Schaie. New York: Van Nostrand Rheinhold. .

Blank, T. O. *A Social Psychology of Developing Adults.* 1982. New York: Wiley.

Bortner, R. W., and Hultsch, D. F. 1974. Patterns of subjective deprivation in adulthood. *Developmental Psychology* 10: 534–545.

Bourque, L. B., and Back, K. W. 1977. Life graphs and life events. *Journal of Gerontology* 32: 669–674.

Brim, O. J., and Ryff, C. D. 1980. On the properties of life events. *Life-Span Development and Behavior,* vol. 3. New York: Academic Press.

Butler, R. N. 1963. The life review: An interpretation of reminiscing in the aged. *Psychiatry* 26: 65–76.

Butler, R. N. 1975. *Why Survive? Being Old in America.* New York: Harper and Row.

Campbell, A. *The Sense of Well-Being in America.* 1980. New York: McGraw-Hill.

Campbell, A.; Converse, P. E.; and Rodgers, W. L. 1976. *The Quality of American Life.* New York: Russell Sage Foundation.

Cantor, N., and Mischel, W. 1977. Traits as prototypes: Effects on recognition memory. *Journal of Personality and Social Psychology* 35: 38–48.

Carlson, R. 1981. Studies in script theory: I. Adult analogs of a childhood nuclear scene. *Journal of Personality and Social Psychology* 40: 501–510.

Chiriboga, D. A., and Cutler, L. 1980. Stress and adaptation: Life span perspectives. In *Aging in the 80's,* ed. L. Poon. Washington, D.C.: American Psychological Association.

Chiriboga, D. A., and Dean, H. 1978. Dimensions of stress: Perspectives from a longitudinal study. *Journal of Psychosomatic Research* 22: 47–55.

Clausen, J. 1972. The life course of individuals. In *Aging and Society,* eds. M. W. Riley, M. Johnson, and A. Toner, vol. II. New York: Russell Sage.

Coan, R. W. 1974. *The Optimal Personality.* New York: Columbia University Press.

Costa, P. T., Jr., and McCrae, R. R. 1978. Objective personality assessment. In *The Clinical Psychology of Aging,* eds. M. Storandt, I. C. Siegler, and M. F. Elias. New York: Plenum Press.

Cutler, S. J. 1972. The availability of personal transportation, residential location and life satisfaction among the aged. *Journal of Gerontology* 27: 383–389.

Dohrenwend, B. P., and Dohrenwend, B. S., 1969. *Social Status and Psychological Disorder.* New York: Wiley.

Dohrenwend, B. S., and Dohrenwend, B. P. 1974. Overview and prospects for research on stressful life events. In *Stressful Life Events,* eds. B. S. Dohrenwend and B. P. Dohrenwend. New York: Wiley.

Edwards, J. N., and Klemmack, D. L. 1973. Correlates of life satisfaction: A re-examination. *Journal of Gerontology* 28: 497–502.

Eisdorfer, D., and Wilkie, F. 1977. Stress, disease, aging and behavior. In *Handbook of the Psychology of Aging,*

eds. J. E. Birren and K. W. Schaie. New York: Van Nostrand Rheinhold.

Elder, G. 1975. Age differentiation and the life course. *Annual Review of Sociology* 1: 165–190.

Elwell, F., and Maltbie-Crannell, A. D. 1981. The impact of role loss upon coping resources and life satisfaction of the elderly. *Journal of Gerontology* 36: 223–232.

Erikson, E. H. 1963. *Childhood and Society.* 2nd ed. New York: Norton.

Folkman, S., and Lazarus, R. S. 1980. An analysis of coping in a middle-aged community sample. *Journal of Health and Social Behavior* 21: 219–239.

George, L. K. 1978. The impact of personality and social status factors upon levels of activity and psychological well-being. *Journal of Gerontology* 33: 840–847.

George, L. K. 1980. *Role Transitions in Later Life.* Belmont, CA.: Wadsworth.

George, L. K. 1981. Subjective well-being: Conceptual and methodological issues. In *Annual Review of Gerontology and Geriatrics,* ed. C. Eisdorfer, vol. 2. New York: Springer.

Gersten, J. C., Langner, T. S., Eisenberg, J. G., and Orzek, L. 1974. Child behavior and life events: Undesirable change or change per se? In *Stressful Life Events,* eds. B. S. Dohrenwend and B. P. Dohrenwend. New York: Wiley.

Glenwick, D. S., and Whitbourne, S. K. 1977–78. Beyond despair and disengagement: A transactional model of personality development in later life. *International Journal of Aging and Human Development* 8: 261–267.

Gould, R. L. 1978. *Transformations: Growth and Change in Adult Life.* New York: Simon and Schuster.

Greenwald, A. G. 1980. The totalitarian ego: Fabrication and revision of personal history. *American Psychologist* 35: 603–618.

Gubrium, J. F. and Buckholdt, D. R. 1977. *Toward Maturity.* San Francisco: Jossey-Bass.

Haan, N. 1977. *Coping and Defending.* New York: Academic Press.

Hamburg, D. A., and Adams, J. E. 1967. A perspective on coping behavior: Seeking and utilizing information in major transitions. *Archives of General Psychiatry* 17: 277–284.

Herzog, A. R., and Rodgers, W. L. 1981. The structure of subjective well-being in different age groups. *Journal of Gerontology* 36: 472–479.

Hinkle, L. E. Jr. 1974. The effect of exposure to culture change, social change, and changes in interpersonal relationships on health. In *Stressful Life Events,* eds. B. S. Dohrenwend and B. P. Dohrenwend. New York: Wiley.

Holmes, T. H., and Masuda, M. 1974. Life change and illness susceptibility. In *Stressful Life Events,* eds. B. S. Dohrenwend and B. P. Dohrenwend. New York: Wiley.

Holmes, T. H., and Rahe, R. H. 1967. The Social Readjustment Rating Scale. *Journal of Psychosomatic Research* 11: 213–218.

Hughes, E. C. 1957. Institutional office and the person. *American Journal of Sociology* 43: 404–413.

Hultsch, D. F., and Plemons, J. K. 1979. Life events and life-span development. In *Life-Span Development and Behavior,* eds. P. B. Baltes and O. G. Brim, vol. 2. New York: Academic Press.

Janis, I. L. 1974. Vigilance and decision-making in personal crises. In *Coping and Adaptation,* eds. G. V. Coelho, D. Hamburg, and J. Adams. New York: Basic Books, 1965.

Jones, E. E., and Davis, K. E. 1965. From acts to dispositions. In *Advances in Experimental Social Psychology,* ed. L. Berkowitz. New York: Academic Press.

Kahneman, D., and Tversky, A. 1973. On the psychology of prediction. *Psychological Review* 80: 237–51.

Kanner, A. D.; Coyne, J. C.; Schaefer, C.; and Lazarus, R. S. 1981. Comparison of two modes of stress measurement: Daily hassles and uplifts versus major life events. *Journal of Behavioral Medicine* 4: 1–39.

Kastenbaum, R. 1966. On the meaning of time in later life. *Journal of Genetic Psychology* 109: 2–25.

Kimmel, D. 1974. *Adulthood and Aging.* New York: Wiley.

Larson, R. 1978. Thirty years of research on the subjective well-being of older Americans. *Journal of Geronotology* 33: 109–125.

Lazarus, R. S. 1966. *Psychological Stress and the Coping Process.* New York: McGraw Hill.

Lazarus, R. S. 1981. The stress and coping paradigm. In *Theoretical Bases in Psychopathology,* eds. C. Eisdorfer, D. Cohen, A. Kleinman, and P. Maxim. New York: Spectrum.

Lazarus, R. S.; Averill, J.; and Opton, E. M. 1974. The psychology of coping: Issues of research and assessment. In *Coping and Adaptation,* eds. G. V. Coelho, D. Hamburg, and J. Adams. New York: Basic Books.

Lazarus, R. S., and DeLongis, A. 1983. Psychological stress and coping in aging. *American Psychologist* 38: 245–254.

Lazarus, R. S.; Kanner, A.; and Folkman, S. 1980. Emotions: A cognitive-phenomenological analysis. In *Theories of Emotion,* eds. R. Plutchik and H. Kellerman. New York: Academic Press.

Lazarus, R. S., and Launier, R. 1978. Stress-related transactions between person and environment. In *Perspectives in Interactional Psychology,* eds. L. Pervin and M. Lewis. New York: Plenum.

Levine, S., and Scotch, N. A., eds. 1970. *Social Stress.* Chicago: Aldine Press.

Levinson, D. J.; Darrow, C. N.; Klein, E. B.; Levinson, M. H.; and McKee, B. 1978. *The Seasons of a Man's Life.* New York: Alfred A. Knopf.

Lieberman, M. A. and Falk, J. M. 1965. The remembered past as a source of data for research on the life cycle. *Human Development* 14: 132–141.

Lowenthal, M. F.; Thurnher, M.; and Chiriboga, D. 1975. *Four Stages of Life.* San Francisco: Jossey-Bass.

McGrath, J. E., ed. 1970. *Social and Psychological Factors in Stress.* New York: Holt, Rinehart, and Winston.

Markides, K. S., and Martin, H. M. 1979. A causal model of life satisfaction among the elderly. *Journal of Gerontology* 34: 86–93.

Markus, H. 1977. Self-schemata and processing information about the self. *Journal of Personality and Social Psychology* 35: 63–78.

Masuda, M., and Holmes, T. H. 1978. Life events: Perceptions and frequencies. *Psychosomatic Medicine* 40: 236–261.

Myers, J. K.; Lindenthal, J. J.; Pepper, M. P.; and Ostrander, D. R. 1972. Life events and mental status: A longitudinal study. *Journal of Health and Social Behavior* 13: 398–406.

Mechanic, D. 1974a. Discussion of research programs on relations between stressful life events and episodes of physical illness. In *Stressful Life Events,* eds. B. S. Dohrenwend, and B. P. Dohrenwend. New York: Wiley.

Mechanic, D. 1974b. Social structure and personal adaptation: Some neglected dimensions. In *Coping and Adaptation,* eds. G. V. Coelho, D. Hamburg, and J. Adams. New York: Basic Books.

Moos, R. H., ed. 1976. *Human Adaptation: Coping with Life Crises.* Lexington, MA.: D. C. Heath and Co.

Neugarten, B. 1977. Personality and aging. In *Handbook of the Psychology of Aging,* eds. J. E. Birren and K. W. Schaie. New York: Van Nostrand Rheinhold.

Neugarten, B. L., and Hagestad, G. O. 1976. Age and the life course. In *Handbook of Aging and the Social Sciences,* eds. R. H. Binstock and E. Shanas. New York: Van Nostrand Rheinhold.

Neugarten, B. L.; Moore, J. W.; and Lowe, J. C. 1965. Age norms, age constraints, and adult socialization. *American Journal of Sociology* 70: 710–717.

Palmore, E.; Cleveland, W. P.; Nowlin, J. B.; Ramm, D.; and Siegler, I. 1979. Stress and adaptation in later life. *Journal of Gerontology* 34: 841–851.

Pearlin, L. I. 1980. Life strains and psychological distress among adults. In *Themes of Work and Love in Adulthood,* eds. N. J. Smelser, and E. H. Erikson. Cambridge, MA: Harvard University Press.

Pearlin, L. I., and Schooler, C. 1978. The structure of coping. *Journal of Health and Social Behavior* 19: 2–21.

Pryor, J. B., and Kriss, M. 1977. The cognitive dynamics of salience in the attribution process. *Journal of Personality and Social Psychology* 35: 49–55.

Rabkin, J., and Streuning, E. 1976. Life events, stress, and illness. *Science* 174: 1013–1020.

Rahe, R. H. 1974. The pathway between subjects' recent life changes and their near-future illness reports: Representative results and methodological issues. In *Stressful Life Events,* eds. B. S. Dohrenwend and B. P. Dohrenwend. New York: Wiley.

Rahe, R. H.; Meyer, M.; Smith, M.; Kjaer, G.; and Holmes, T. H. 1964. Social stress and illness onset. *Journal of Psychosomatic Research* 15: 19–24.

Raynor, J. O., and Entin, E. E., eds. 1982. *Motivation, Career Striving, and Aging.* Washington: Hemisphere.

Redfield, J., and Stone, A. 1979. Individual viewpoints of stressful life events. *Journal of Consulting and Clinical Psychology* 47: 147–154.

Riegel, K. F. 1976. The dialectics of human development.

American Psychologist 31: 689–700.

Riley, M. W. 1971. Social gerontology and the age stratification of society. *The Gerontologist* 11 (No. 1, Part I): 79–87.

Rosenberg, M. 1968. Psychological selectivity in self-esteem formation. In *The Self in Social Interaction,* eds. C. Gordon and K. J. Gergen. New York: Wiley.

Sampson, E. E. 1978. Personality and the location of identity. *Journal of Personality* 46: 552–568.

Sanguiliano, I. 1980. *In Her Time.* New York: Morrow Quill Paperbacks.

Sarason, I. G. 1980. Life stress, self-preoccupation, and social supports. In *Stress and Anxiety,* eds. I. G. Sarason and C. D. Spielberger, vol. 7. Washington, D.C.: Hemisphere.

Sarason, I. G.; Johnson, J. H.; and Siegel, J. M. 1978. Assessing the impact of life changes: Development of the life experiences survey. *Journal of Consulting and Clinical Psychology* 46: 932–946.

Schanck, R., and Abelson, R. 1977. *Scripts, plans, goals, and understanding.* Hillsdale, NJ: Erlbaum.

Schlossberg, N. K. 1981. A model for analyzing human adaptation to transition. *The Counseling Psychologist* 9: 2–18.

Schooler, K. K. 1975. Response of the elderly to environment: A stress-theorectic perspective. In *Theory Development in Environment and Aging,* eds. P. G. Windley and G. Ernst. Washington, D.C.: Gerontological Society.

Selye, H. 1956. *The Stress of Life.* New York: McGraw-Hill.

Stebbins, R. A. 1970. Career: The subjective approach. *The Sociology Quarterly* 11: 32–49.

Tomkins, S. S. 1979. Script theory: Differential magnification of affects. In *Nebraska Symposium on Motivation,* eds. H. E. Howe, Jr., and R. A. Dienstbier, vol. 26. Lincoln: University of Nebraska Press.

Tyler, F. B. 1978. Individual psychosocial competence: A personality configuration. *Educational and Psychological Measurement* 38: 309–323.

Walaskay, M.; Whitbourne, S. K.; and Nehrke, M. F. 1983–1984. Construction and validation of an ego status integrity interview. *International Journal of Aging and Human Development* 18: 61–72.

Weinberg, S. L., and Richardson, M. S. 1981. Dimensions of stress in early parenting. *Journal of Consulting and Clinical Psychology* 49: 686–693.

Whitbourne, S. K., and Dannefer, W. D. In Press. The life drawing as a measure of time perspective in adulthood. *International Journal of Aging and Human Development.*

Whitbourne, S. K., and Weinstock, C. S. 1979. *Adult Development: The Differentiation of Experience.* New York: Holt, Rinehart, and Winston.

White, R. W. 1974. Strategies of adaptation: An attempt at systematic description. In *Coping and Adaptation,* eds. G. V. Coelho, D. Hamburg, and J. Adams. New York: Basic Books.

23
DYING AND DEATH:
A LIFE-SPAN APPROACH

Robert Kastenbaum
Arizona State University

INTRODUCTION

No journey is more familiar to humankind than the procession from cradle to grave. It is only in recent years, however, that psychologists and their colleagues in related fields have started to explore the full sweep of human life from infancy through old age, including the central fact of mortality. The independent histories of life-span developmental psychology (e.g., Charles, 1970; Havighurst, 1973) and studies of dying and death (e.g., Kastenbaum, 1981) have been told elsewhere. Here we shall examine selected aspects of the interface. The aim is not to catalog and critique every study but to suggest connections between what is being learned about life-span development and the field that some call *thanatology*. Basic reviews of research on death-related topics are already available (e.g., Kalish, 1983; Kastenbaum, 1978; Kastenbaum and Costa, 1977; Marshall, 1980; Meyers, 1978; Rowland, 1977). These leave us free to formulate and pursue a set of guiding hypotheses.

The approach taken here, then, cannot follow the usual contours of the gerontologist's landscape. Instead, we must find a new path among concepts, studies, and clinical observations that are not usually considered within the same framework.

The first section offers two views of the social context of aging and death. We begin by considering normative expectations for earlier and later portions of the total life span. Doing so provides a framework for understanding both the phenomena and the meanings associated with dying, death, and bereavement in old age. Particular attention is given to the increasing discrepancy between social expectation and immediate reality as the individual ages. Next, it is proposed that our attitudes toward the elderly may imply a principle of compensation, this being, perhaps, a special case of equity theory (Adams, 1965). The motives and consequences associated with compensatory benefits for the elderly and the life-threatened are examined.

The second section is devoted to death orientations throughout the life span. It attempts to track the continuities as well as the discontinuities in our relationship to mortality over time.

In the third section, we treat specific problems associated with dying and terminal care in later life. Recent developments in the hospice movement are given particular attention. A brief final section suggests a research and social action agenda.

EXPECTATIONS OF GROWTH AND DECLINE

A developmental curve of functional growth and decline is evident in many tabulations of

619

data from mouse through man. Standards exist against which the career of the individual can be plotted. The fetal mouse knows less about the eventual length of his/her own tail than does the ardent comparative developmentalist. Well before this pre-mouse reaches seniority, probable senile changes in the tendons of the tail-to-be can be cleverly guessed by the gerorodontologist. Patterns of growth and decline for large populations are also familiar to the life sciences, being expressed, for example, in mortality rates. Whether focus is on the individual or a population, there are data-based expectations for life-span development within a particular species. At this point in our knowledge, expectations for growth are more precise and abundant than those for decline. A child who has not learned to walk or speak "on schedule," for example, is more likely to be noticed than an adult whose fluid intelligence has started to dry up. Specific developmental schedules for the early years of life have not yet been supplemented by equally detailed and verified schedules for midlife and older adults.

The species that describes itself as sapient, however, has two additional frameworks for expectation and takes into consideration other dimensions than the barebones, functional ones. We each apply a personal frame of reference as individuals, and, collectively, we participate in the social or interpersonal expectation set. In other words, we compare our personal growth and decline against our own expectations and at the same time judge the developmental status of other people (who judge us right back). Furthermore, our expectations of self and others include dimensions of value and utility. These dimensions have a complex relationship to functional status. The infant, for example, may be highly valued by its family even though it does not earn wages or mow the lawn. Adults unable to obtain employment may judge themselves as useless in terms of their own private standards even though they have many of the abilities and skills expected of them by society. The perceived worth of a person is not independent of functional and status variables. Nevertheless, value or utility cannot properly be reduced to measures of objective performance or rank in society.

Shifting Patterns of Expectation Across the Life Span

These intersecting frames of expectation—the scientific, the personal, and the interpersonal—all bear upon our relationship to death and loss throughout the life span. Here are some of the specific assumptions and background facts:

1. Expectations for continued growth are high and consistent for the early years of life. The developmentalist, the parent, and the child all anticipate the pattern of change known as growth or maturation.

2. Expectations for decline, loss, and death are low and consistent for the early years of life. This situation has not always existed, being the result, in part, of the significant reduction in infant and childhood mortality during the twentieth century (Kent, 1980).

3. Expectations for growth, decline, loss, and death are mixed and inconsistent for the later years of life (Gruman, 1978). This breakdown in consensus is a phenomenon that must be taken into account before the particulars are addressed. Both social policy and the attitudes and psychodynamics of individuals are influenced by such variables as the clarity, specificity, and consistency of expectation (e.g., Shaver, 1977).

4. Expectations for growth, decline, loss, and death are influenced by the individual's developmental level of cognition, whether the focus is on one's own status or the status of another. Selman (1980), for example, has formulated data-based phases of interpersonal understanding in childhood. The meaning of growth and decline is best considered within the context of the individual's general frame of reference; this, in turn, is closely related to developmental level.

Death as the Proper Concern of the Old

With these general points in mind, we can now proceed to more substantive problems. A major implication of what has already been suggested is that we are highly socialized for expectations of growth in early life. Actual instances of decline, loss, or death run counter to our expectations. Even in our "enlightened" era of death awareness, it is still common practice for schools to evade social recognition of a child's death, and, predictably, the media apply the adjective "untimely" to the deaths of the young and only the young. One might hold that the anguish occasioned by the death of a child has its source in the high value we place on the young rather than in its discrepancy with our expectations. Certainly, we do place high value on our children, and certainly this evaluation does contribute to the depth of our grief. Nevertheless, there is a relationship between childhood mortality and the value placed on the young. Stannard (1975), for example, notes that Puritan parents were urged not to become too fond or too familiar with their children because so many would perish. Before taking their nuptial vows, Swedish couples in past generations would walk together to the local graveyard and there select the burial sites for some of the children they would bring into the world (Inge, 1982). History is abundant with examples of how the perceived value of a child depends to some extent on expectations for its survival.

The effects of discrepancy with congruent and strongly socialized expectations should not be underestimated. Our overall pattern of life, both as individuals and as a society, draws much of its stability from shared expectations. Losses are less disruptive when they are "scheduled," or when we persuade ourselves that they *can* be scheduled (Glaser and Strauss, 1966; 1967). The persuasion process can be seen in the explanations of death often given by parents to their children, e.g., "Grandmother was old." Advanced age and death are linked in attitudes and explanations. This association has the effect of liberating the earlier years of life from anxieties associated with decline, loss, and death. The elderly become our specialists in vulnerability and mortality.

This exaggerated expectation is supported in part by the desire to keep death and other forms of loss at a distance. Feifel and his colleagues, for example, have studied orientations toward death at the level of direct self-report

but also by techniques intended to elicit responses below the level of self-awareness (e.g., Feifel and Branscomb, 1973; Feifel, 1974). Summarizing his findings, Feifel concludes that "The governing conscious response to fear of death is one of limited fear; on the fantasy level, one of ambivalence; and on the nonconscious level, one of outright aversion. This patterning appears to serve adaptational requirements, allowing us to maintain communal associations and yet organize our resources to contend with oncoming death" (Feifel, 1977, p. 10). Strong expectations that death is a prime concern of the elderly but not of the young comprise one of society's ways of maintaining communal associations and organizing our resources.

This is not the only source, however, of such bifurcated expectations. The lack of clear, positive expectations for development during the adult years also contributes to the attribution of normative loss. Scientific, personal, and interpersonal expectations for growth start to diminish with the middle adult years and continue to fade with advancing age, making it easier to project an eventual "specialization in loss." Expectations for death-by-sequence break to the surface when a person dies out of sequence. The old person tends to be seen as the most suitable selection in the pecking order of death (Kastenbaum, 1975). Sorrow may follow the death of the person whose name appears atop the list, but the very fact that one's expectations have been confirmed provides a measure of psychological security. Death is "playing the game" according to the rules that we would like to believe have been established.

Ambivalence Toward the Old and "Regressive Intervention"

There are at least two further contributing sources for such expectations, or, perhaps, one fundamental source with two channels of flow. The historical perspective suggests that society's attitudes toward its elderly have always been tinged with ambivalence. Affectional ties, respect, and practical utility are countered by the desire to shake free of gerontocratic control and allocate scarce resources to the young (e.g., Haraven, 1979; Kastenbaum and Ross, 1975). By viewing the older person as one who is meant to suffer, lose, or disengage, we remove a competitor. Notice that those theories of psychosocial development that have found any "task" at all for the elderly person tend to emphasize life review and preparing one's self for death. Whatever else might be true of such theories, they have the effect of strengthening the bifurcated expectation that active life is for the young and death is the proper concern of the old. This attitude finds more specific expression in the systematic allocation of social and economic resources. Cost-containment exercises typically involve limitation of health and other services to the elderly. Disability and death are seen as more appropriate to the elderly than to the young, and fiscal decisions predictably follow this attitudinal orientation.

Watson and Maxwell (1977) have expressed what both they and many other observers have witnessed in their concept of "regressive intervention." This is defined as "the process of reducing the frequency of social commingling and gradually withdrawing the allocation of highly trained professionals and other resources from the organization of care for a person whose physical and/or mental processes are severely and irreversibly impaired" (Watson and Maxwell, p. 125). This process begins after it is decided that a person's illness cannot be reversed. The person in question need not be at death's door, however. "Old" may be treated as a status equivalent to "chronically ill," and "chronically ill" as equivalent to "severely impaired." Within the medical and institutional context, advanced age makes one a better candidate for regressive intervention, although a parallel process operates within the community as well. Keeping our focus on the health system, however, we can see, along with Watson and Maxwell, that the elderly patient's "impairment and probable increasing disability become socially sanctioned, albeit by default. An inadvertent consequence of segregation through regressive intervention can be the acceleration of dying. Studies of sudden and unexplained deaths are suggestive of this conclusion" (Watson and Maxwell, p. 126).

Self-Perceived Continuity and Discontinuity

The mental segregation of decline, loss, and death to the later years of the life span does have its pragmatic consequences, then. These consequences also include a contamination of terms such as "old," "elderly," and "aged" with the kiss of death. It is hardly surprising that many people of advanced years reject such descriptors, laden as they are with the projected fears of a society that prefers to keep disability and death as far as possible from its dominant self-image.

A sense of the life span as a whole is difficult to achieve when growth is so firmly attributed to the early years, while the later years are associated primarily with decline, loss, and death. Continuity can be discerned within an objective or scientific framework. A sampling of behavioral and cognitive variables, for example, will tend to provide a picture of continuity rather than abrupt breaks or shifts in function. This is true, for example, of the diverse phenomena that indicate a behavioral slowing with age (Birren, Woods, and Williams, 1980). One can select from a variety of graphs that display age-associated changes, their specific shapes depending on research strategy, data-analysis procedures, and study populations. All will suggest continuity more than radical break, especially until the old-old echelon is reached, at which point conclusions may be premature. Yet these objective charts tell us nothing directly about *perceived* continuity, whether of self or others. The drastic shift in emotional/attitudinal valences makes it difficult for the individual to move psychologically along the time gradient.

We know little about the conditions under which a person reclassifies himself as old (and, therefore, properly subject to decline, loss, and death). Up to, let us say, age 50, a particular individual may have viewed old age from the interpersonal framework. This individual participated in the expectational set of society at large, applying the classification of "old" to others. The force of habit may now be reinforced by an unfavorable balance of incentive and threat. Normatively, little in the way of favorable gains is to be expected by classifying one's self as old, whereas there is almost everything to lose. This does not mean that elderly people necessarily have either reduced life satisfaction or competence. Indeed, there are data to suggest otherwise (e.g., Giesen and Datan, 1979). At issue here, however, is the individual's state of mind whenever circumstances suggest that one might now reclassify one's self as old.

Somewhere along the line we run into our own expectancies. Adolescents and young adults, for example, tend to project dysphoric events to their remote futures (Kastenbaum, 1959), and the "novice" phase of adulthood may be characterized by a life perspective that does not prepare one well for the challenges of middle and later life (Levinson, 1978). Individuals cope with this challenge in a variety of ways (including, for some, the rejection of their previous, less reflective ideas about what it means to be old). The most relevant aspect for us here is that the aging person must find some solution to the decline/loss/death barrier. If the individual cannot find a way to cross this psychological barrier, then it will be very difficult to develop a sense of selfhood over the entire life span. Crossing over to the identity of old-vulnerable-and-mortal may also be accomplished at the sacrifice of perceived continuity. The force of circumstance (e.g., retirement, illness, death of loved ones) may lead the individual to cross over without having built a psychological bridge between then and now. It is not enough, then, simply to establish that a person has or has not accepted the self-as-old frame of reference. We must also learn whether a sense of continuity has been preserved. One of the more interesting research challenges is to discover how some people do manage to spin out a continuing sense of identity across the life span despite the social stereotypes that preserve the illusive expectation of growth and invulnerability in youth at the cost of burdening age with a heavy expectation of disability and loss.

A PRINCIPLE OF COMPENSATION?

There may be an underlying principle that makes it easier for society to add grim expectations to the serious enough realities of later life. All that can be done here is to sketch this possibility briefly, with the suggestion that those with the opportunity to make additional observations keep this one in mind.

The *principle of compensation* holds that there is a need for perceived equity in what befalls a person (Berkowitz and Walster). Perhaps this need derives from what some believe to be a stage of moral development at which a strong sense of fairness dominates (e.g., Kohlberg and Turiel, 1974). As adults, we may know better. The deserving may be ruined and the rascals enriched. Nevertheless, it may be comforting to act upon the assumption of equity, if only to salve our conscience or as grounds for rationalizations. The assumptions of compensation requires a supportive set of assumptions about the universe, even if these assumptions are not made explicit. All that needs to be mentioned here is the central assumption that human intentions and actions are linked to the cosmos. What we think and feel and do somehow matters to the universe.

How might the principle of compensation apply in the context of aging and death? The general rule must be that the old or dying or old-*and*-dying person receives something of equal value for losses suffered. There are precedents earlier in the life span, e.g., the shiny penny (or nickel, dime, quarter, depending on age echelon) left under childhood's pillow by a solicitous tooth fairy. This was a direct cash payment, or bribery, to compensate for a small and normative loss to the integrity of the body. What payment for loss of heath, agility, and life itself?

One mode of compensation takes the form of replacement and displacement. The individual's loss of additional time on this earth is compensated by life everlasting. Structurally, this compensatory exchange has much to recommend itself. The quality of remaining time-on-earth has been compromised. One will have a higher quality of existence in the life to come. Furthermore, there is a quantitative advantage as well. Although eternity and time are not thoroughly compatible concepts, most of us do replace "endless" or "unlimited" time with the even more abstract idea of "the eternal." Actual and prospective loss, then, are not only well compensated by life everlasting but, in a sense, even help to pay for this transformation. In the ideal situation, both the terminally ill person and the others regard present limitations and suffering as an expected (and therefore acceptable) prelude to the compensatory state. There is no reason for the dying person to cling to what remains of this flawed and temporary life when eternity waits in the wings. This reasoning also removes any pressure that care-givers might have felt to take measures that might extend life.

Eternity as compensation has other adaptive functions as well:

1. It enables the dying person and the survivors to share a frame of reference.
2. It relieves the rehearsal anxiety of the others, i.e., helps them to draw reassuring implications from their participation in somebody else's death.
3. It supports the others' hoped-for conclusion that they have done right by the deceased.
4. It provides a socio-theological reinforcement for the practice of regressive intervention (e.g., "There is nothing more that could have or should have been done.").
5. It minimizes the social disruption of dying and death (e.g., "We do not have to take time out to mourn. She is so much happier now!").

This mode of compensation helps to support the status quo, both in terms of individual psychodynamics and the interpersonal network. It is not difficult to collect illustrations of the kinds of attitudes and behaviors described here. Unfortunately, perhaps, the future of this compensatory mode is in doubt. The first wave of data from the National Hospice Study indicates, among other things, that few elderly people facing death draw strength from the prospect of an afterlife (Kastenbaum, Kastenbaum, and Morris, in prep.). A national sample of 390 terminally ill adults (201 women, 189 men) was asked to describe their greatest sources of strength in adversity as part of a larger and continuing study. In this sample of predominantly older people (85.3 per-

cent over the age of 60), only 3.2 percent mentioned the compensatory benefit of surviving into an afterlife. Nearly half the respondents described themselves as holding strong religious values, but the afterlife as a source of strength or comfort was mentioned by few —only three women and ten men. Another possible source of compensation for impending loss of life might have been the comfort in knowing that descendants would survive and carry forward the dying person's name and tradition. This also proved of little consolation (cited by only 2.3 percent). Perceived compensation for death, then, was seldom paramount in the minds of older people who were just a few weeks from the end of their lives. The most common source of strength cited was support from family and friends (56.9 percent). [Additional information on the National Hospice Study can be obtained from Mor (1982), Morris (1982), or the author.]

The general trend toward reduced salience of the afterlife belief will gradually encompass an increasingly higher proportion of the elderly and the terminally ill, barring new developments from some unexpected quarter. The limited research available indicates that passing the torch holds little compensatory value for people of our time (Kastenbaum, 1974a), as we have seen further expressed in data from the National Hospice Study. Nevertheless, the dynamics of compensation through the gift of eternity will remian instructive for those interested in understanding individual and social response to the situation of the aged and the terminally ill.

More evident today are compensatory techniques that attribute certain psychological or spiritual qualities to the aged and the dying. These are at times completely distinct populations, of course, but the principle of compensation operates whether the individual is aged, dying, or both (in the latter case, perhaps most vigorously). Examples are abundant, but seldom if ever recognized as serving the purpose of compensation for loss. To older people, social scientists have attributed internal states such as heightened interiority (e.g., Henry, 1965) and life review (e.g., Butler, 1963). Inspirational literature is replete with references to the wisdom and spirituality of the old. Seen as less active, less needed, and less legitimate a claimant on social resources, the older person may be transformed into a sage or saint. What has been lost and what will still be lost (including life itself) is counterbalanced by the attribution of "heightened" or "deepened" (contrary but interchangeable terms) spiritual wisdom. Such a person is obviously too pure for this imperfect life on earth and must put on the robes of eternity to find suitable companionship.

One does not have to reach quite so extreme a point to find utility in the principle of compensation by attributed wisdom and spirituality. Elevation to this status is preceded or accompanied by the removal of almost all practical decision-making power on the part of the old person. Moral radiance is acceptable because there is little danger of interference with the bread-and-butter issues of concern to others. The new spiritual plane of existence attained by (or, rather, attributed to) old people places them beyond the trivialities and frustrations of everyday life. This distancing makes it possible, of course, to limit their options and withdraw services. Additionally, one can hold on a little longer to the troubled assumption that "fair is fair," that a deserving person somehow gets back something valuable for what is lost.

We have here, then, the other side of the coin from the kind of attitudes that demean and reject people on the basis of age. The assumption that "old means incompetent" is replaced by "old means wise." Both assumptions have in common a control technique that serves the interests of their advocates as well as the knack of ignoring individual reality in favor of generalized expectancies. This compensatory mode can be based on varying shades of objective fact. Some aged people and some dying people whatever their age do seem to discover a more universal, transcendent, or spiritual view of life. In such instances, family and care-givers have only to recognize the transformation and perhaps marvel. In other situations, however, the needs of the other people involved contribute mightily to such attributions of spiritual exaltation.

For various reasons—including the maintenance of faith in a universe that somehow computes and cares—we want to see the aged and the dying compensated for what they are losing.

Observations made for either clinical or research purposes must take into account both types of bias toward the aged and the dying: the perhaps more familiar attitude that people in this condition have already lost much of their value, and the opposite orientation that attributes new and singular value to those who are approaching the ends of their lives. Although opposite in their direction, both sets of attitudes (1) assume that a crucial change in human value has taken place with age and illness, (2) seldom fully test this assumption against reality, and (3) have implications for what is actually done to, for, and with the affected individual. It is our challenge to find a way to see the old, the dying, or the old-and-dying person in their distinctive individuality without invoking either demeaning stereotypes or uncontrolled fantasies of compensatory miracles.

DEATH ORIENTATIONS THROUGHOUT THE LIFE SPAN

Everyone lives in relationship to death at every point in the life span. This perspective can enrich our understanding of orientations toward death in old age. We will draw here not only from research specific to death attitudes, but also on studies of cognition, time perspective, and interpersonal relationships, although this approach must be selective and illustrative rather than comprehensive. General cognitive level and style are relevant because death-related thoughts are formulated within the context of the individual's overall ability to interpret self and world. Time perspective is relevant because personal death is always a future prospect at the same time that past bereavements, separations, and other encounters with loss and threat help to form the subjects of retrospection. The roots of death orientation can be found in early interpersonal experiences, and since relationships with others continue to be influential throughout life, they are therefore relevant here.

Infancy and Early Childhood

A superficial view of cognitive development might rule out in advance the possibility that infants and young children could have any knowledge of death. Piaget's influential work includes the concept of *formal operations*. It is only toward adolescence that most people develop the ability to "think about thought," to engage in flexible and abstract intellectual operations (e.g., Piaget, 1954). Even the preliminary stage of *concrete operations* does not usually appear until well into the latency period. It would seem, then, that the very young are incapable of forming concepts of any kind and can therefore grasp nothing of that highly abstract concept, death. Such a conclusion would accord with the beliefs of many parents and teachers who have long assumed that children do not, cannot, and should not understand death.

Nevertheless, the very young *do* show awareness of death-related matters (Bluebond-Langner, 1977; Kastenbaum, 1974b; Rosemeir and Minsel, 1982), and this demonstrated fact turns out to be consistent with cognitive-developmental theory when one examines it with more care. Central to Piaget is the view that intelligence is a biological adaptational function. This function does not suddenly snap into place in adolescence or with the activation of conceptual thought. The infant and young child display intelligent activity right from the start, although this takes forms far removed from adult cognitions. Acting intelligently in the world can be distinguished from the possession of highly developed cognitive structures. Furthermore, the extreme vulnerability of the very young person would seem to require the ability to sense danger and seek assistance. Loss of the protective adult is a kind of death threat. The infant does not require formal intellectual operations in order to scan its environment anxiously when its well-being is jeopardized. No human being is ever too young to be subject to the threat of separation or abandonment. We will sample some empirical observations shortly. The point here is simply that preconceptual modes of intelligent activity exist very early in life and have, as one of their most critical objects, the preservation of life itself.

A further look at Piagetian theory is useful because of its emphasis upon the development of *object permanence* and *conservation*. Theory and research within the Piagetian approach suggest that the related concepts of permanence and conservation start to develop gradually during the first two years of life and then develop specifically through a process of continuous interaction with the environment. People and other objects change their position in space with relationship to the child. To track successfully all the transformations that occur within its perceptual field, the child must develop the awareness of *invariance* through change. Mother is still Mother whether she is a relatively small object on the other side of the room or looming large right over baby's face; the cat that has just come in the door is the same cat that went out the door just a moment ago, and so on. This emphasis on the development of object permanence and conservation has an important role in the overall theory that attempts to explain how the growing individual gradually constructs reality.

Unfortunately, a bias has crept in. Fascination with constancy, permanence, and conservation has relegated *transience* to second-class treatment. The world that each developing individual is attempting to construct includes unique, periodic, and evanescent events as well as invariants. Without the ability to recognize and track object permanence, the child might be subject to a fragmented or chaotic, certainly an undependable, view of reality. On the other hand, without the ability to recognize transience and loss, the child would also be captive to a severely limited vision of reality. In fact, "constancy of the object itself has little or no meaning if the child has not already come to appreciate the phenomena of change, destruction, and disappearance. The basic notion of constancy implies the possibility of nonconstancy" (Kastenbaum and Aisenberg, 1976, p. 29).

Note that mental activity early in life is less differentiated (or more global) than it will eventually become (e.g., Werner, 1957). At age 2, for example, abstract concepts such as time, permanence, and death are a long way off. Nevertheless, the child is already processing experiences that are shaping such concepts but without drawing fine distinctions. "Gone," "gone for a long time," and "gone forever" (or "dead") have not yet been distinguished, and therefore any disappearance, transformation, separation, or loss has the potential to be coded (preconceptually) in the category from which concepts of "death" and "dead" will eventually emerge. What might be called "the death of the object" (Kastenbaum and Aisenberg, 1976), then, could be one of the earliest and most important protoconcepts in the child's long progression toward mature cognitive functioning. It will require further experience and cognitive maturation before a reliable differentiation can be made between "death of the object" and "death of the self," since the infant and young child are still highly embedded in the proximal environment. Construction of a predictable and stable world through mental operations requires the ability to recognize and differentiate that which is unpredictable, unstable, and "all gone." What is being proposed here is not inimical to Piagetian theory when the bias toward exploiting constancy is corrected; it is, in fact, indispensable to any theory that attempts to explain the life-span development of cognitive structures.

There is a rich and varied array of observations on death-related orientations among the very young, but we cannot expect the same type of methodology here that we do in studies of older children and adults. Naturalistic observation, including of the play situation, is a particularly useful approach when supplemented by miniature experiments. Therapeutic interventions also provide opportunity for intensive observation. Nonverbal responses should also be given close attention. Differences in methodology are among the factors that recommend caution when one compares death-related orientations of the very young with those of their seniors, but the descriptions themselves have much to offer.

Bowlby (1980) has given careful consideration to the psychosocial consequences of loss in early childhood. Observations of children as young as 12 months of age reveal determined efforts to recover the lost mother when placed with strangers. There is first "protest" and "urgent effort" at recovery. For days the child will cry loudly, throw himself about, and search eagerly, as though hopefully, toward "any sight or sound which might prove to be his missing mother" (Bowlby, 1980, p. 9). Alternations between urgent distress and hopeful scanning often continue for a week or so. "Sooner or later, however, despair sets in. The longing for mother's return does not diminish, but the hope of it being realized fades. Ultimately . . . the demands cease; he becomes apathetic and withdrawn, a despair broken only perhaps by an intermittent and monotonous wail. He is in a state of unutterable misery" (Bowlby, 1980).

This pattern of response can also be observed in people who clearly do know that they have suffered bereavement or some other catastrophic loss. Indeed, it is all too familiar a sight among institutionalized geriatric patients. The behavioral response, then, is one that can readily be associated with perception of critical loss. The yearling does not have to form the verbal concept that "Mother is gone"; this concept is embodied in all his actions. The fact that an underlying pattern familiar in adult response to grief has been repeatedly observed among infants suggests that some perception of loss, equivalent or consonant with death, can occur. Other studies reviewed by Bowlby demonstrate that the grief response in childhood can be of long duration. When stricken by loss of the mother-figure, a young child shows remarkable persistence of action and affect despite all assumptions about memory limitations. Observers perceptive enough to notice apparently incidental nonverbal behaviors often find additional evidence for persistence of grief in very young children. Furman (1974) has given poignant examples of toddlers leading their surviving parent on rounds they had previously enjoyed with their now deceased mother or father and insisting on repeating every little action and step of the journey, this seeming to be both an acknowledgement of the loss and an attempt at reconstitution.

Therapists have made detailed observations of young children's death-related play. Such observations are particularly valuable because the child's actions can be placed in their naturalistic context. That a two-year old knows something about death can hardly be doubted from careful case reports. Lopez and Kliman (1979), for example, show that "Diane's" self-injurious experiments with falling and her entire altered pattern of behavior were clearly in response to her mother's death (suicide, by leaping off a cliff). Clinical approaches at times do more than verify the death/separation awareness of young children and provide therapeutic intervention; they also demonstrate some of the ways in which death-related experiences interact with the child's developmental level to create themes and concerns that can dominate the individual throughout the life span. Kliman (1976), Mahler (1961), and Nagera (1970) are among others who have examined the dynamics of death awareness and mourning in young children.

Reports are not limited to very young children whose problems have lead to clinical intervention. Maurer (1966, p. 36) offers a provocative analysis of games often played by the very young. "Peek-a-boo," which enters the infant's repertoire at about three months of age, "replays in safe circumstances the alternate terror and delight, confirming his sense of self by risking and regaining complete consciousness. A light cloth spread over his face and body will elicit a forceful and immediate reaction. Short, sharp intakes of breath, vigorous thrashing of arms and legs removes the erstwhile shroud to reveal widely staring eyes that scan the scene with frantic alertness until they lock glances with the smiling mother, whereupon he will wriggle and laugh with joy . . . it is obvious that he enjoyed the temporary dimming of the light, the blotting out of the reassuring face and the suggestion of a lack of air which his own efforts enabled him to restore, his aliveness additionally confirmed by the glad greeting implicit in the eye-to-eye oneness with another human." Maurer also sees a burgeoning sense of death-awareness in the young child's fascination with games of hidings and disappearances, including the pleasures of flushing objects and making them "all gone." Naturalistic observations of this kind are not to be mistaken for definitive studies, of course, but do provide guiding hypotheses and call our attention to common behaviors that we might not understand as well as we think.

Opportunistic observations of very young children have added many accounts suggestive of death awareness (e.g., Brent, 1977; Kastenbaum, 1973; 1974b). Because the situational context is known and follow-up observations possible, a response that might be dismissed at first as too mature for a two or three year-old sometimes is seen to be part of a consistent and determined pattern. Retrospective reports also suggest that specific death experiences make an impression on the very young. In his pioneering book on *Senescence,* G. Stanley Hall (1922) included data on the childhood memories of older adults. He found many vivid reports of early experiences with death, so vivid, in fact, that Hall suggested that percepts had been forced to carry the load of emotion through the years because the child did not have verbal concepts available at the time of the experience. Contemporary studies in which adults are asked to retrieve and share their earliest memory also include many examples of death and other loss experiences (e.g., Tobin, 1972). Should one consult the extensive and scattered literature on effects of early bereavement on later personality, again much circumstantial evidence arises to testify to the impact of death-related experiences, although there are no easy generalizations (e.g., Bendiksen and Fulton, 1975). Immediate observation of children's behavior and retrospective reports both converge, then, to suggest that the very young can at times register death-relevant experiences, and, moreover, that these experiences can become part of the individual's orientation to life over an extended period of time.

Later Childhood Through Adolescence

Children of all ages have death-related thoughts (e.g., Anthony, 1972; Bluebond-Langner, 1976) whether they themselves are healthy or faced with life-threatening illness, and whether they are experiencing psychological difficulties or are as normal as apple pie without polysyllabic additives. Much remains to be learned, however, about the place of death-related thoughts in the general pattern of cognitive, affective, and interpersonal development. Results of an influential early study (Nagy, 1948, reprinted in Feifel, 1959) suggested that concepts of death pass through two preliminary stages before reaching the adult level. During the preschool years, children seem to view death as a temporary state that involves a diminution rather than complete cessation of life (e.g., "dead people don't get hungry—well, maybe just a *little!*"). An intermediate stage follows in which the child realizes that death is final but does not consider it inevitable and universal. While they were in this stage, Anthony's respondents aged 5 through 9 often personified death (represented it as a person). Around age 10, the child understands that death is not only final but will be the fate of every living creature, including one's self. Follow-up studies have tended to support the existence of a stage-like pattern but rarely find personification responses at any age (e.g., Childers and Wimmer, 1971; Kane, 1979; Koocher, 1973; Safier, 1964). The level of death conceptualization has been shown to be more closely related to general level of cognitive maturation rather than to age per se (Koocher, 1973).

Increased attention to children who have been stricken with terminal illness suggests that life experiences may count for as much or more than age or developmental level. Bluebond-Langner (1977) has described systematic growth in the understanding of death on the part of terminally ill children. The finality, inevitability, and completeness of death are grasped even by the ones who should be too young to understand, if general research on cognitive development or on death concepts in particular were to be taken as guidelines. These children learn from changes in their own condition but also from the responses (and nonresponses) of parents, doctors and nurses. Mostly, however, they seem to learn from the experiences of other terminally ill children whose plight they have observed over time. "To these children (regardless of age), death and dying are mutilating experiences,

bringing in their wake separation and loss of identity. Death is part of the disease cycle, and the life cycle as it has become for these children" (Bluebond-Langner, 1977, p. 60).

The time perspective of terminally ill children clearly represents their knowledge of impending death. As the disease progresses, "conversations about the future declined noticeably. The future was limited to the next holiday or occasion. At the same time, the child also tried to rush these holidays and occasions, to bring them closer to the present" (Bluebond-Langner, 1977, p. 58). Former long-range goals and plans are never mentioned, e.g., what the child expects to be when grown up. Adults often have great difficulty with this realistic shift in time perspective. Bluebond-Langner reports a physician trying to get a child's cooperation with a procedure by saying, "I thought you would understand, Sandy. You told me once you wanted to be a doctor." The boy replied by screaming, "I'm not going to be anything!" and hurled an empty syringe at the physician. A nurse standing nearby asked, "What are you going to be?" "A ghost," said Sandy, and turned away from them. It is also striking that references to living with God in Heaven are seldom heard. The afterlife as a form of futurity is conspicuously absent from the conversation of terminally ill children. The principle of compensation applied to the aged and the terminally ill did not show itself in Bluebond-Langner's careful work with children; they acted as though any comforts or satisfactions had to come quickly if they were to come at all.

The perceived relationship between the prospect of death and one's view of the future in general has most often been discussed with respect to the aged or, at least, those old enough to review many years of life and come to terms with their mortality. What is known about time perspective across the life span, however, suggests that concepts of futurity and death are mutually influential from at least middle childhood onward (Kastenbaum, 1983). Each individual has a personal history of working with the related concepts of futurity and death well before either advanced age or the close prospect of death are encountered.

Bluebond-Langner's continuing studies focus on children facing the extreme circumstances of pain, disability, and impending death. Nevertheless, her findings are applicable to children in more ordinary situations as well. It is obvious that children form their ideas and feelings about death in part through their interpersonal relationships, including with one another. Recent studies (reviewed by Masters, 1981) strengthen the view that cognitions develop within a social as well as personal-maturational context. Our general knowledge of cognitive and social development will be incomplete until the role of death-related thoughts has been fully considered; likewise, our knowledge of the life-span development of death cognitions will be incomplete until placed firmly within the larger context of psychosocial maturation. Comprehension of death cognitions in adulthood and old age could also be enriched by attending to the individual's interpersonal context, e.g., who is available to share death-related experiences and how is one affected by the way others respond or fail to respond? The interpersonal context of thought does not vanish after childhood, although one might be excused for thinking so because of the relative neglect of this topic by theoreticians and researchers.

Although the cognitive possibilities of childhood remain open to question, adolescence has been singled out for special recognition in this field from G. S. Hall (1904) to Piaget (1967) and beyond (Elkind, 1974). Hall's controversial theory of human development called for society to cultivate a cadre of elite adolescents in every generation in order to improve our species. He argued that it is in adolescence that we find a unique mixture of intellectual capacity and flexibility or openness to experience. The so-called idealism of youth should be harnessed for the good of society. Piaget's very different approach has sketched a series of developmental steps leading up to the attainment of formal intellectual operations in adolescence. That intellectual development might actually continue beyond adolescence to even higher levels of functioning has been proposed by Riegel (1973) but tends to be shrugged off by mainstream researchers (e.g.,

Niemark, 1982). Although Hall's grand plans for the adolescent are not conspicuous on the current scene, experts in cognitive development continue to laud the awakening of intellectual energies at this time in life. More than ever before, the adolescent "attempts to make sense of all aspects of experience . . . a general broadening of horizons on all dimensions. Issues that have never or rarely been considered by the adolescent will take on enlarged significance and meaning. Topics of identity, society, existence, religion, justice, morality, friendship, and so on, are examined in detail with high emotion as well as increased cognitive capacity. The spark for such consideration is not purely cognitive, of course; there are many lines of development converging with special significance for the adolescent. But at least some of the motivation for this stretching and breaking of old limits is probably cognitive in the purest sense: 'Cogito ergo sum' " (Keating, 1980, p. 214). This fresh and probing examination of life is "all the more exciting and attractive" because the adolescent now has more sophisticated cognitive tools with which to work.

From this characterization we might well expect the adolescent to think long, hard, and perhaps brilliantly about "final things." Able to transcend the present situation with new powers of abstract thought, the adolescent might soar with wings of imagination through a variety of possible futures, a mental journey even more exhilarating because more than fifty years of continued life can be expected at this point. At no other point in the life span will there be such a combination of high intellectual potential and extensive probable life expectancy.

The actual findings, however, do not provide clear support for this view. To begin with, the adolescence research establishment has for the most part ignored either the meaning of death or the actual prospect of death at this time of life. The otherwise authoritative *Handbook of Adolescent Psychology* (Adelson, 1980) and the widely used *Adolescence in the Life Cycle* (Dragastin and Elder, 1975) devote no attention to this topic in their combined 948 pages. "Death," "dying," and "mortality" are not even indexed. Furthermore, the index to a 960-page tome, *Handbook of Developmental Psychology* (Wolman, 1982) likewise does not find space to cover death-related cognitions, affects, or behaviors in adolescence. It is possible somehow to discuss topics such as social development without considering the effects of bereavement, moral development without considering the possibility of existential orientations toward death, and personality and development without considering how adolescents come to terms with concepts of limits and endings. There is neither empirical nor theoretical justification for this neglect, especially since so much emphasis is otherwise given to the adolescent's enlarged capacity and interest in examining *all* facets of reality. We are left to wonder about the influence of general stereotypes on the scientific enterprise: Death remains the specialty of the elderly and can therefore be ignored in mainstream research on adolescence.

Working from the adolescent literature toward death orientations is not very productive, but if one begins with studies of thanatology instead, there is appreciably more information available. Lanetto takes us up to the brink of adolescence, concluding that although older children do have "an emerging belief in the mortality of the self," nevertheless, for them, "death is far in the future and remains in the domain of the aged" (Lanetto, 1980, p. 157). In company with a number of other observers, Lanetto adds that most people reach adolescence in our society with little help from that society in conceptualizing and coping with death. With the advent of "death education" in high schools and colleges across the nation, there has been more opportunity for adolescents to explore death-related topics. Instructors have quickly discovered that many students had been keeping emotion-laden death concerns to themselves for lack of opportunity to discuss them (e.g., McLendon, 1979). These concerns often focus on specific people and events in their lives, as distinguished from abstractions and ideas. The experience of death educators suggests, in fact, that the freedom to deal with mortality on a conceptual level is often hindered by unresolved problems of

a close and personal nature. There is some evidence that the supportive classroom environment as well as the specific material presented does help the adolescent student to develop more flexible and comfortable orientations toward death (e.g., Wittmaier, 1979; McDonald, 1981).

Although it has been speculated that death anxiety may be at its peak during adolescence, the available data do not coalesce into a clear pattern, some studies indicating more fears among the young (e.g., Cautela, Wincze, and Kastenbaum, 1972) and others (e.g., Templer, Ruff, and Franks, 1971) finding no age-related differences. It is probable that death-related fears are mediated by a variety of variables, including past experience, current social support, and cognitive maturation. Enough is known, however, to indicate that affective as well as cognitive factors must be taken into account in attempting to understand the adolescent's orientation toward death.

Actual death—as distinguished sharply from thoughts and feelings—is more salient in adolescence than might be supposed. The death rate for all causes is continuing to rise for adolescents and young adults in the United States. Suicide and indirect forms of self-destruction are a particular concern (Farberow, 1980). In the course of his extensive review and analysis of suicide across the life span, Maris (1981) suggests that people are especially vulnerable at transition points, including the adolescent's move from one major role and status to another. Acknowledging that an adequate data base is not yet available to test broad hypotheses such as this, Maris nevertheless draws interesting parallels between the suicide potential of the adolescent on the brink of adulthood, and the adult on the brink of old age, both of whom are faced with discontinuity and transition. This offers a useful alternative to a linear model of suicide across the life span and is worth further investigation.

A word must be added about individual differences in adolescence. There are marked differences in the inclination to scan the distant future among adolescents (e.g., Kastenbaum, 1959; 1961), with corresponding differences in the conceptualization of death. Those individual differences that gerontology has learned to recognize among older adults have their start many years before, and the adolescent period of life may hold some of the answers to questions that surface in old age.

Adulthood Through Old Age

Problems in Following the Developmental Thread. The thread of "pure" development becomes ever more difficult to follow as we move through the adult years. It is obvious enough that the conditions of life change. Apart from each individual's particular circumstances, there is the universal (statistical) expectation of increased mortality, both for one's self and for one's elders and peers. Regardless of the individual's own cognitions and attitudes, then, death becomes an ever more conspicuous shadow along life's journey.

From a theoretical standpoint, one might look for the degree of concordance between objective and personal orientations toward death. Do adults reshape their thinking to take death increasingly into account? If so, does this accommodation occur gradually or by sudden bumps and leaps (e.g., in response to specific life experiences?). In other words, is a crisis model more appropriate, or should we look instead for a continuous, underlying process of transformation yet to be identified? (Kastenbaum, 1975). Both disengagement (Cumming and Henry, 1961) and life review theory (Butler, 1963) imply that the individual normatively initiates a new process of self-reflection that results in an altered relationship with mortality. Although these influential theories performed the service of calling attention both to the inner life of older adults and to the confrontation with death, neither can be said to have been established by empirical fact. Time perspective does not necessarily contract as the individual ages or even as death comes into close prospect (e.g., Chappell, 1975). The older adult's sense of futurity may depend more on perceived control over the environment than empty variables such as chronological age or probable distance from death (Schulz and Hanusa, 1977; Chang, 1979).

Furthermore, individual differences are slighted. Some people review (or are even obsessed by) issues of life and death from early on, whereas others, of a less reflective disposition, move into advanced old age true to their habitual one-day-at-a-time approach. The variance of interpersonal and cognitive-level influences on orientations toward death have not been thoroughly examined. Another factor almost entirely ignored in this realm is the possible effect of social desirability and expectation variables. Many older adults know they are expected to say wise and gracious things about life and death, and some may well succumb to these expectations. It is true enough that some people do review their relationship to death and develop a revised, even a transformed, set of beliefs and attitudes. Much remains to be learned, however, about the personality and situational conditions that favor such a development. Disengagement and life review theories give us some possibilities to explore but have not demonstrated a normative, universal developmental process that eventuates in an altered psychological relationship to death.

Potentially useful clues to death orientation in the adult years may come from study of practical decisions as well as verbal formulations. Has this person made a will or revised it to keep up with changed circumstances? Has that person changed exercise, dietary, and drinking habits out of concern for longevity? How about those who continue to smoke heavily despite the presence of warning symptoms? Are seriously ill friends and relations visited or avoided? Does one turn to the obituary page or determinedly skip over it? And what steps (in her mind or in reality) has the potential widow taken to adjust to the probable death of her husband? Questions of this kind, centered on specific decisions and actions, could well be pursued from a theoretical standpoint (although they have not been completely neglected in research with limited and applied aims).

Cognitive dissonance theory may also have its relevance here. The more the aging adult takes death-related factors into account, the more consonance is achieved between reality and cognitive representation. However, death-tinged thoughts may themselves create cognitive dissonance, conflicting with well-entrenched attitudes. Should we remain young and immortal in our secret hearts, thereby drifting away from the press of reality, or should we allow death a greater share of our thoughts, thereby stirring up a sort of cognitive indigestion? There are both gains and losses in revising one's mental life to acknowledge death, and the strategies we use must to some extent be influenced by everything that influences us at every age: level of cognitive maturation, interpersonal support and stress, health, and so on. Life-span and gerontological investigators have yet to achieve theoretical integrations of strategic and developmental processes in this realm.

What has been learned so far about death attitudes through adulthood emphasizes the same diversity already noted in adolescence (e.g., Munnichs, 1966). Predicting orientation toward death from chronological age alone has not proven especially productive. There have been mixed results in trying to relate death concerns to other variables as well. A random sample representative of elderly people in the United States was drawn by Oleshansky, Gamsky, and Ramsmeyer (in press). Death anxiety could not be predicted from knowledge of the participants' activity level, purpose in life, or tendency toward repression. As the authors noted, the limitations of all of the procedures employed (which are among the more popular techniques in this field) must be taken into account. There is justifiable controversy about precisely what is assessed by measures intended to reveal death anxiety or concern. Bell and Batterson (1979) formulated three causal models that might have been expected to predict the death attitudes of older adults; they didn't! "Confusing and contradictory" was the term applied by Bell and Batterson as they attempted to make sense both of their own findings and other data in the literature. The most promising lead emerging from their investigation has to do with the relatively greater strength of past or historical forces as compared with current variables in shaping death attitudes. They conclude with the thought that *"How, when,* and *under what circumstances* death attitudes are formed should become the primary focus of empirical investigation"* (Bell and Batterson, 1979, p.

72). This is one more call, then, for intensifying our efforts in the life-span approach.

Correlates of Death Concern. Theories attempting to explain and predict death attitudes in adulthood have, in general, not fared well when put to empirical test. There are so many methodological problems involved that one cannot firmly attribute the failure to either the conceptualization or the operationalization. Although academic-type studies of death concern continue to have their difficulties, we continue to learn from clinical and other applied investigations. McCrae, Bartone, and Costa (1976) studied nearly a thousand men ranging in age from 25 to 90 years and found that some of them had high, moderate, or low levels of expressed anxiety at every age level. The young and middle-aged men with high anxiety reported more illnesses than their physicians could diagnose. Highly anxious old men, however, underreported their ailments. Who reported his health concerns accurately, then? The "well-adjusted" (not highly anxious) old man was the most likely to do so. It was as though the anxious old man felt he must protect himself from recognition of an actual threat to life, whereas the anxious young man could afford to focus on symptoms because he did not truly believe his life to be in danger. The practical implications here are obvious; for example, the patient's level of anxiety (and mode of coping with it) should be partialled into clinical assessments, and reports of health concerns by the elderly should be taken quite seriously.

Promising research has been done on time perspective and sense of purpose in life as related to death concern in later adulthood. Bascue (1973) found that elderly women with higher self-report death-anxiety scores also displayed a sense of possessiveness toward time and uneasiness about its rapid passage. Durlak (1972) reported a similar finding, again with an all-female sample. Quinn and Reznikoff (in press) studied another sample of healthy older women, employing a battery of six well-established measures. One of the more methodologically sophisticated studies in this area, the Quinn and Reznikoff investigation partialled out the contribution of general state and trait anxiety and social desirability. This approach increases the likelihood that the obtained correlations do represent death anxiety rather than contaminating variables. A significant negative correlation was found between death anxiety as indexed by the Templer Scale (Templer, 1970) and having a sense of meaning in life as indexed by the Crumbaugh and Maholic (1964) Purpose-in-Life Test. Furthermore, women with high self-report death anxiety were more sensitive to the rapid passage of time, as assessed by the Time Metaphors Test (Knapp and Garbutt, 1958) and the Temporal Experience Questionnaire (Wessman, 1973). This finding is consistent with Bascue's and suggests that death concern in adulthood might be inferred from the individual's pattern of relating to the everyday passage of time. All three studies drew samples of elderly women in good health. It would be useful to repeat these procedures with men as well as women and encompass a broader spectrum of health conditions, as well as to take ethnic diversities into account.

Perhaps studies that rely exclusively on verbal responses should be given less emphasis, and more attention paid to thoughts and actions within carefully observed naturalistic situations. This approach will create problems for theorists who have linked their concepts almost exclusively to clean and shiny variables amenable to easy data collection and traditional multivariate analysis. The future of life-span psychology may depend to some extent on how well this challenge is met.

Suicide and Self-Destructive Behavior. If adult orientations toward death cannot be understood fully through verbal responses, then perhaps that most extreme of nonverbal behaviors—suicide—can prove instructive.

Choosing death over life is a phenomenon that occurs at all age levels from childhood through old age, for both sexes, for all rungs of the socio-economic ladder, and in all ethnic groups. The frequency, modality, and context of suicide differ appreciably, however, across these categories. Here we will focus on some aspects of suicide among middle-aged and older adults with just enough background to provide perspective. There are clear gender differences in frequency and mode of suicide. The male suicide rate in the United States is almost three times as high as that for females, and this discrepancy has been marked ever since statistics have been collected (Frederick, 1978; Diggory, 1976). Males tend to employ more violent and active modalities, e.g., shooting, cutting, and leaping, whereas females more typically use drugs. Native Americans have a suicide rate appreciably higher than either whites or blacks (Frederick, 1978).

Suicide rates for both sexes increase with chronological age from childhood until young adulthood (specifically, the age 20 to 24 category). The female suicide rate continues to increase until the mid-forties and then declines through the mid-eighties (the last age category encompassed by national statistics). The male suicide rate rises and dips slightly between the ages of 25 and 40 (remaining at all times well above the female rate in relative frequency). Instead of levelling off in mid-life and then declining, however, male suicides become increasingly frequent with age until the eighth decade. Taking gender differences into account is essential in trying to understand age-related patterns in suicide. In the 75 to 79 age range, for example, there are 42.5 male suicides per 100,000 as compared with 7.5 for females—a discrepancy that makes the overall suicide rate of 21.2 for that age level a rather misleading statistic.

Attention must also be given to time trends in suicide. The overall suicide rate in America has generally shown an increase throughout the twentieth century, although with occasional peaks and dips. Most of this increase is age-specific: from ages 10 through 24 (there are not adequate data available on suicides for children younger than 10). Over a recent 20-year span, there has been an increase of 223 percent for male and 161 percent for female suicide in the 20 to 24 age range, where the largest number of completed suicides are concentrated. More than three thousand 20- to 24-year-olds kill themselves annually in the United States, as compared with approximately nine hundred people in the 75 to 79 age range. Old white males continue to have the highest suicide rates within the general population (but matched by Native American youths). Two sets of facts must be kept in mind, then: Older white Americans remain those most at risk from suicide, but time-trends show a slight but steady decline in suicide among the elderly, accompanied by a marked increase in youth suicide.

Why? Seiden (in press) suggests that the white/nonwhite suicide differential in middle and old age can be attributed to six factors: (1) differential life expectancy; (2) deviant burnout; (3) screening out of the violence-prone; (4) role and status of the elderly; (5) traditional values; and (6) age-specific motives. His review of the ethnic literature indicates that all the above factors operate in the direction of holding down the suicide rates of elderly nonwhites. Loss of status with age is seen as less traumatic to nonwhites, who often enough have been for all their lives "shut out of most positions of occupational power and authority; consequently retirement and diminished income do not lead to the same loss of status as for many whites. If you have been used to little you are not quite as disappointed as when you have great expectations which are unfulfilled. Perhaps, then, one lesson we can learn is to be more realistic about adjusting our aspirations" (Seiden, p. 20). He adds two other lessons from the review of nonwhite support systems, that there is greater respect for the older person and greater self-acceptance of aging and that there is much less sense of interpersonal relations and uselessness. The nonwhite community, according to Seiden, "by necessity as much as design, provides a role and status for elderly persons" and thereby makes suicide a much less attractive alternative.

Further clues emerge from a study that tested ten hypotheses regarding the high rate of suicide in older white men. Robins, West, and Murphy (1977) drew a sample of men between the ages of 45 and 65 (specifically to avoid the complications of retirement status), with both whites and blacks represented among the subgroups of psychiatric patient, medical patient, and healthy adult. Suicidal ideation for both blacks and whites was clearly associated with being unmarried, seeing few friends, lack of belief in an afterlife, and a state of clinical depression. Among blacks, sui-

cidal thoughts were also associated with loss of contact with a child and fearing that relatives would treat one badly when old, as well as with a family history of depression and multiple previous episodes of depression. Knowing somebody who had committed suicide was the only variable present among whites with self-destructive thoughts that was not also present among blacks. Men who had dysphoric views about growing older and anticipated few and unsatisfactory roles tended to be more suicidal regardless of their race. The investigators concluded that "there is reason to believe that the mechanism for unleashing suicidal thoughts are no different in blacks and whites. When these characteristics occur in blacks, they can be expected to be associated with an increase in the risk of suicide" (Robbins, West, and Murphy, p. 14). In company with many other recent investigators, Robbins et al. found a multifactorial view of suicide more appropriate and useful than any existing unified theory.

Boldt (1982) has contributed to our understanding of time trends by finding generational differences in the acceptance of suicide as a solution to one's problems. Respondents in this Canadian study were drawn from two generations within the same families. The younger generation held more accepting attitudes toward suicide than did their elders. Interestingly, the younger generation also reported a more accepting attitude toward death in general. As Boldt notes, "Perception of death as punitive or pleasant may be suicide inhibiting or suicide promoting" (Boldt, p. 153). It would be unwarranted to assume a causal relationship between the more accepting attitudes toward suicide and death among the young and their increasing suicide rate, but Boldt's findings do emphasize the possible importance of cohort influences. Furthermore, even the older generation reported itself more accepting of suicide and death than during its younger days. The parental generation, according to Boldt, has shown a life-long openness to change, moving some distance from its early socialization that instilled punitive and shunning attitudes toward suicide.

Still other studies have found a relationship between environmental constraint and self-injurious behavior among elderly residents of nursing homes and mental hospitals (Kastenbaum and Mishara, 1971; Mishara and Kastenbaum, 1973; Nelson and Farberow, 1977). Although such studies have focused on behaviors that seldom lead to a direct lethal outcome, there is often a mental accompaniment of suicidal ideation and the potential for premature death by one route or another. These studies suggest that many institutionalized elders have frequent and serious inclinations to bring their lives to a rapid end. The *fatalistic* type of suicide discussed by Durkheim (1897) comes to mind here. Durkheim pointed out that suicide can emerge from a context of relentless social oppression; he then promptly dismissed this type of suicide as having much interest for our civilized times in which liberty and opportunity were at hand for all. Visiting a geriatric facility today (or some of our reservations for Native Americans), Durkheim might take his own concept more seriously.

Completed suicides are relatively infrequent, even in the highest risk age/sex/race categories. Orientations toward self-destruction are much more common, however. These manifest as suicide ideation, suicide attempts, and a variety of behaviors that substantially increase the risk to one's life (Farberow, 1980). To understand possible changes in death orientation with advancing age, then, we must also be alert to the ever-present option of suicide. Greater awareness of suicidal thinking and self-injurious behaviors in later life can help us become more adept both as care-givers and researchers. Concern about the increased dependency as well as the possible pain of terminal illness is one source of heightened consideration of suicide in middle and old age. Progress in terminal care might therefore have a subtle additional benefit in its reduction of suicidal ideation and attempts.

Dying and Terminal Care

How the older person faces death and what type of care is most useful are topics that have been long obscured by assumption and bias. The concept of regressive intervention has already been mentioned. Sudnow (1967) was among the first to describe a systematic organization of events through which institutions attempt to conceal the near dead and the dead. Watson (1976) subsequently showed that being old and sick (or sick*er* than other age peers) tends to stimulate the same process. Decisions to discontinue active treatment occur more frequently in the case of patients who are seen as either very sick or dying. The distinction between "very sick" and "dying" is often blurred in the case of the aged. Furthermore, along with discontinuation of active treatment, there may also be a sharp reduction in the amount and quality of interpersonal contact. If, in some instances, this leads to the premature withdrawal of active treatment for old people who are sick but not necessarily dying, in other instances, the terminally ill have been classified as psychiatric patients and placed in dismal custodial settings (Markson and Hand, 1970). Case examples make it clear that some sick-and-old people written off as "terminal" do, in fact, retain viability when given sensitive and attentive care (e.g., Miller, 1976). The danger of a self-fulfilling prophecy must always be addressed, then, for socio-emotional as well as technical abandonment of the patient can lead to death where recovery might have been possible.

Another obscuring factor has been the uncritical acceptance of the so-called "stages of dying" (Kubler-Ross, 1969). Empirically, this theory has not been confirmed (e.g., Hinton, 1975; Schulz and Aderman, 1974; Metzger, 1979), and many of its conceptual and methodological deficiencies have been pointed out (e.g., Kastenbaum and Costa, 1977; Kastenbaum, 1981; Shneidman, 1980). Of most relevance here has been the tendency to limit attention to the hypothetical states. This offers the illusion of control through naming and predicting phases of response. Fortunately, the abuse of stage theory as an anxiety-reducing formula by some health personnel seems now to be waning. And, fortunately, theory and research into the dying process also appears to be liberating itself from the stimulating but inadequate stage theory.

The growth of hospice services is producing a larger cadre of skillful and compassionate care-givers and, more slowly, a new wave of research that is directed primarily to applied problems. From St. Christopher's Hospice alone, for example, have come useful studies of pain relief (Twycross, 1974) and family dimensions of care (Parkes, 1975), with further studies continuously in progress. The hospice approach emphasizes the individuality of each patient and the needs and rights of families and care-givers as well. Experience with hospice care usually includes significant work with the elderly. The opportunity to receive care at home when this is preferred to hospitalization has been made available to elderly as well as younger patients (Lack, 1978) and seems to be working (e.g., Buckingham and Foley, 1978). Within the hospice movement, if not yet within the total health care system, supportive care for the older terminally ill patient is becoming well established. Caughill (1976), for example, has introduced a life-span approach to terminal care that firmly includes the older person. She particularly emphasizes the anxiety felt by many people who, old and sick, must also contend with major environmental changes. Caughill notes that admission to a nursing home sometimes results in heightened death anxiety even when there is no immediate or obvious life jeopardy involved. The hospice approach, dedicated to helping the individual remain in a familiar and comforting environment, may be of even more value to the aged than to other populations. The entrenched pattern of less-than-first-rate care for the aged does not apply, in general, to hospice services (Hamilton and Reid, 1980). Furthermore, elderly people have proven themselves valuable providers as well as recipients of hospice care. The maturity and coping skills of many older people have made them welcome as hospice volunteers.

The hospice influence is reaching also into more conventional medical practice and perhaps will result in improved care for the terminally ill aged in all settings. Attention has already been given to certain problems occurring with greater frequency among the elderly. Howell (1980), for example, reports that sudden falls often signal the onset of terminal deterioration and should therefore be taken very seriously. Unlike the better recognized pattern of gradual decline, there is another pathway to death that is less expected

and more discontinuous. The frail but apparently not terminally ill old person may show signs of rapid recovery from a fall, only to suffer a relapse and die. Care-providers must learn, then, to recognize alternative patterns of terminal decline among the elderly and to offer more appropriate services.

We can expect further knowledge to be gained concerning terminal care of the older person as, for example, through the ongoing National Hospice Study (Mor, 1982; Morris, 1982). Theoretical issues, however, are seldom addressed in these studies, which typically are intended to evaluate the effectiveness of care. Two questions of theoretical as well as applied interest are worth brief attention here, although the available data are meager: (1) Is dying an extension of the aging process?, and (2) Does the death of an old person have a profound psychological effect on the survivors?

There is a tradition of casual proclamations about the relationships among development, aging, and dying. "We start aging/dying from the moment of conception" is the way this view is sometimes expressed. Is there really a continuity here, an underlying process that at one point in time is recognized as "development" but later earns the terms "aging" and "dying"? Or is this all just loose talk?

The biological work of Hayflick (1977) and others has raised the possibility of a built-in program that encompasses development, aging, and death. After approximately 50 doublings, human fibroblasts lose their ability for continued proliferation and survival. Known as the *Phase III phenomenon,* this is an intrinsic process to be regarded "as a manifestation of senescence at the cellular level" (Hayflick, 1977, p. 161). Terminal decline is prefigured, then, in the earliest phases of development that are inevitably transformed into senile changes. Virtually all research on this topic has been on the cellular and tissue levels. Nevertheless, there are substantial implications for psychology. A few of these will be touched on very briefly.

First, Metchnikoff (1908), and then Freud (1920), formulated the concept of a *death instinct.* Despite the eminence of both writers, this concept has been almost completely neglected on all sides—by gerontology, thanatology, and the hospice movement (although still the subject of occasional philosophical papers in psychoanalytic journals). Was the concept of a death instinct simply too much ahead of its time? Have we been too quick to set it aside as a hopelessly vague philosophical notion? One must certainly be aware of the problems inherent in this concept and of the temptation to use it carelessly. Nevertheless, the concept retains interest on formal grounds (e.g., as an attempted integration of phenomena on multiple levels) and may yet have something to offer as new empirical data continue to emerge. We do not have so many major concepts available in the intersecting areas of gerontology that we can afford to dismiss the death instinct without a fresh look. The less than nourishing results gleaned from superficial "death anxiety" scales certainly recommends an alternative approach, as do the interesting but fragmented findings yielded by naturalistic studies.

Within mainstream gerontology, there is at least one research topic that bears on the question of dying as a direct outcome of the aging process. The phenomenon known as *terminal drop* is taken into account by most experienced researchers who are attempting to interpret longitudinal data. Perhaps a less clumsy phrase such as *differential survival* would be preferable. In any event, the literature includes some important demonstrations that cognitive decline can predict (or postdict) mortality (e.g., Lieberman, 1965; Granick and Patterson, 1971; Riegel, 1971; Palmore and Cleveland, 1980). Beyond the methodological implications, however, are questions bearing on terminal decline itself. Do the affected individuals have premonitions of impending death that the people around them fail to identify (Weisman and Kastenbaum, 1968)? Are there some meanings and resonations to the pattern of terminal decline that gerontology has failed to identify (because we have limited ourselves to behavioristic approaches)? Is the pattern of cognitive decline that eventuates in death the same as patterns that can be reversed? These are a few of the many questions that cannot be firmly answered at this time.

Our understanding of the relationships among development, aging, and dying will depend not only upon more research, but also upon more careful conceptualization. It is at the least premature to hold that there is an inevitable link between aging and dying, for example, in the face of data displaying the diversity of cognition, affect, and behavior during the terminal phase.

That not all deaths have the same meaning or result in the same level of social disruption is familiar in anthropology and sociology. Glaser (1966) was perhaps the first to introduce into gerontology the contention that the death of aged people has relatively little impact on society. More recently, Owen, Fulton, and Markusen (1983) compared grief responses among adults who had lost either a spouse, a parent, or a child. It was found that "the death of elderly parents is less disruptive, less emotionally debilitating and generally less significant for surviving adult children in terms of the continuity and stability of established behavioral patterns than for the other two groups." The survivors of parental death were less likely to utilize traditional funerary rituals and less likely to become ill in subsequent months. Owen et al. suggest that much of the potential emotional response to the death of an elderly parent has been attenuated by its predictability, as well as by geographic and other factors that have diminished the power of the nuclear family. Sanders (1979) has also found relatively less grief response to the death of an elderly parent than to the death of spouse or child.

Moss and Moss (1980) suggest the existence of a phenomenon that has not yet been studied directly. Although the adult child may apparently show relatively less disturbance over the death of a parent, there may be an important adaptive function taking place. "The adult child recurrently considers and rehearses the potential death of a parent. There is certainly less taboo in anticipating one's parent's death than the death of a spouse or a child. The cognitive and affective process of anticipatory orphanhood may occur over decades, thus preparing the adult child for the fact of parental death" (Moss and Moss, pp. 8–9). Possibly, this process also includes subtle preparations for one's own death. This is one more instance in which the life-span approach provides a useful perspective; the adult child's response to the death of a parent may begin long before the fact, and continue long afterward.

Again, it would be premature to draw firm conclusions on this topic, but a disturbing question has been raised. Do we, in fact, care less about the deaths of our elders? If so, is this a transposition of attitudes once held toward the expected death of young children? How is this attitude linked with other attitudes—and behaviors—directed toward older people while they are still with us? And what happens when, as discussed earlier, the individual is faced with pressures to move from self-definitions of "young" to "old"? Is there perhaps a process of silent grief involved? ("I am to become one of those who will not be missed . . . so perhaps I should become accustomed to not missing myself")? To the usual call for more research, might also be added here, "more understanding."

TOWARD AN AGENDA FOR THEORY, RESEARCH, AND APPLICATION

Developmental psychology has been inching its way along the time continuum toward a life-span approach. Useful as many child-oriented theories have been, it has proven necessary to work toward concepts and methods that do more justice to the total arc of life. Similarly, gerontology has been increasing its familiarity with dying, death, and bereavement. The range of convenience for existing psychological and gerontological theory, however, also appears to fall short of comprehending death-related phenomena on their own terms. We run the risk of bending or reducing the problem of mortality to conform with the theories and methods that happen to be on the surface of psychogerontology today. Those who have resisted thinking of the old person as a variant of the child have now the further challenge of distinguishing our relationship to death from the more standard topics that keep our data mills grinding. There is already a tendency in our society for the existential

problem of death to be transformed and manipulated by bureaucracies until it becomes a bland impersonation of the real thing (Kastenbaum, 1982). Perhaps we should not become too comfortable with this topic too soon. Perhaps there is more to the human encounter with death than self-report questionnaires can measure and routine theories explain. Despite the assortment of data and theories presented in this chapter, death-related phenomena in adulthood and old age—indeed, throughout the entire lifespan—have yet to be adequately addressed.

External incentive for responding to this challenge is becoming more evident all the time. Fries (1980), for example, has offered a new model for national health in the influential pages of *The New England Journal of Medicine*. Reviewing data from several fields, including gerontological psychology, Fries predicts a "continued decline in premature death and emergence of a pattern of natural death at the end of a natural life span" (Fries, pp. 134–135). In other words, if living out our full life expectancies becoming normative, so will the fact of dying old. Criticizing current social policies, Fries argues that "The older person requires opportunity for expression and experience and autonomy and accomplishment, not support and care and feeding and sympathy. High-level medical technology applied at the end of a natural life span epitomizes the absurd. The hospice becomes more attractive than the hospital. Human interaction, rather than respirators and dialysis and other mechanical support for failing organs, is indicated at the time of the 'terminal drop' " (Fries, p. 135).

This model appears to be still another formulation of the activity theory of aging, emphasizing as it does constant diligence and vigilance on the part of every individual to "maintain organ capacity." There is much that is appealing here. Fries is proposing a broad social and individual commitment to "postpone chronic illness, to maintain vigor, and to slow social and psychologic involution." The data cited are new, but the spirit is old-fashioned American activism and optimism. Notice that this proposed integration of scientific knowledge and social policy barely pauses to consider our psychological relationship to death. Both morbidity and mortality are to be increasingly compressed into a compact little end-piece of time after many years of healthy life. Death, then, is really not so much of a problem after all! Such an approach, although sophisticated in some of its detail, at center is hollow and naive. It repeats in modern language and cadence a theme often voiced in the history of alchemy and science: We do not really have to face death at all, so long as we dissolve that pearl in wine, eat that yogurt, or jog that track.

The caution expressed here does not pertain to specific recommendations for maintaining health and vigor, or for more enlightened social policy. My concern is that the combined power of science and social policy has issued a fresh if implicit invitation to trivialize and compartmentalize death. Any of us might choose to select this option as individuals. Continued postponement and evasion of our intimate reckonings with death, however, could prove hazardous to the "completion of being" (Van Tassel, 1979). The precept that dying and becoming are intimately related has a tradition of its own, recently expressed again by Erikson (1979). The "potential for what adulthood may become" (Erikson, p. 57) has been viewed by some as a deeper, more demanding, and less comfortable matter than enacting new legislation and keeping our bodies tuned. Is it possible for life-span developmental psychology to plumb other levels of experience, innovate other methods of study, and discover other principles of functioning? Or have we already fashioned a discipline that must cling to the coast line and forego ventures into the unknown? Just as the future of development psychology has required its extension into later adulthood, so the new life-span psychology perhaps requires the willingness to revise and expand our conceptual horizons by considering the human relationship to death on its own terms rather than through the limitations of current theory and method. Specific research topics and gaps are of less importance than the willingness to go beyond the methods and concepts that have brought us this far. Erikson reminds us "how uncon-

vincing a sense of integrity can be if it does not remain answerable to some existential despair" (Erikson, p. 59). There is an implicit research agenda in these words. Are we ready to seek it?

REFERENCES

Adams, J. S. 1965. Inequity in social exchange. *Adv. Exp. Soc. Psychol.* 2: 267–300.

Adelson, J., ed. 1980. *Handbook of Adolescent Psychology.* New York: Wiley Interscience.

Anthony, S. 1972. *The Discovery of Death in Childhood and After.* New York: Basic Books, Inc.

Bascue, L. 1973. *A Study of the Relationship of Time Orientation and Time Attitudes to Death Anxiety in Elderly People.* Doctoral dissertation, University of Maryland, Ann Arbor, Michigan. University Microfilms, No. 7318234.

Bell, B. D., and Batterson, C. T. 1979. The death attitudes of older adults: A path-analytic exploration. *Omega* 10: 59–76.

Bendiksen, R., and Fulton, R. 1975. Death and the child: An anterospective test of the childhood bereavement and later behavior disorder hypothesis. *Omega* 6: 45–60.

Berkowitz, L., and Walster, E., eds. 1976. *Advances in Experimental Social Psychology.* Vol. 9. *Equity Theory: Toward a General Theory of Social Interaction.* New York: Academic Press.

Birren, J. E.; Woods, A. M.; and Williams, M. V. 1980. Behavioral slowing with age: Causes, organization, and consequences. In *Aging in the 1980s: Psychological Issues,* ed. L. W. Poon, pp. 293–308. Washington, D.C.: American Psychological Assoc.

Bluebond-Langner, M. 1976. Field research on children's and adults' views of death. Unpublished fieldnotes.

Bluebond-Langner, M. 1977. Meanings of death to children. In *New Meanings of Death,* ed. H. Feifel, pp. 47–66. New York: McGraw-Hill.

Boldt, M. 1982. Normative evaluation of suicide and death: A cross-generational study. *Omega* 10: 145–158.

Bowlby, J. 1980. *Loss.* New York: Basic Books.

Brent, S. B. 1977. Puns, metaphors, and misunderstandings in a two-year old's conception of death. *Omega* 8: 285–294.

Buckingham, R. W., and Foley, S. H. 1978. A guide to evaluation research in terminal care programs. *Death Education* 2: 127–144.

Butler, R. N. 1963. The life review: An interpretation of reminescence in the aged. *Psychiatry* 26: 65–76.

Caughill, R. E. 1976. Supportive care and age of the dying patient. In *The Dying Patient,* ed. R. E. Caughill, pp. 191–224. Boston: Little, Brown.

Cautela, J. R.; Wincze, J. P.; and Kastenbaum, R. 1972. The use of the Fear Survey Schedule and the Reinforcement Survey Schedule to survey possible reinforcing and aversive stimuli among juvenile offenders. *J. Genetic Psychol.* 121: 255–261.

Chang, B. L. 1977. The relationship of generalized expectancies and situational control of daily activities to morale of the institutionalized aged. Gerontological Society, San Francisco.

Chappell, N. L. 1975. Awareness of death in the disengagement theory: A conceptualization and an empirical investigation. *Omega* 6: 325–344.

Charles, C. C. 1970. Historical antecedents of life-span developmental psychology. In *Life-span Developmental Psychology*, eds. L. R. Goulet and P. B. Baltes, pp. 24–53. New York: Academic Press.

Childers, P., and Wimmer, M. 1971. The concept of death in early childhood. *Child Development* 42: 705–715.

Crumbaugh, J., and Maholic, L. 1964. An experimental study in existentialism: The psychometric approach to Frankl's concept of noogenic neurosis. *J. Clin. Psychol.* 20: 200–207.

Cumming, E. M., and Henry, W. E. 1961. *Growing Old.* New York: Basic Books.

Diggory, J. C. 1976. United States suicide rates, 1933–1968: An analysis of some trends. In *Suicidology: Contemporary Developments*, ed. E. S. Shneidman. New York: Grune & Stratton, Inc.

Dragastin, S. E., and Elder, G. H., Jr., eds. 1975. *Adolescence in the Life Cycle.* Washington, D.C.: Hemisphere/Halstead Press.

Durkheim, E. *Le Suicide.* 1951. Translated by J. A. Spaulding and G. Simpson. New York: The Free Press. (Originally published, 1897.)

Durlak, J. 1972. Relationship between attitudes toward life and death among elderly women. *Develop. Psychol.* 8: 146.

Elkind, D. 1974. *Children and Adolescents: Interpretive Essays on Jean Piaget.* 2nd ed. New York: Oxford University Press.

Erikson, E. H. 1979. Reflections on Dr. Borg's life cycle. In *Aging, Death, and the Completion of Being*, ed. D. D. Van Tassel, pp. 29–68. University of Pennsylvania Press.

Farberow, N. L., ed. 1980. *The Many Faces of Suicide.* New York: McGraw-Hill.

Feifel, H., ed. 1959. *The Meaning of Death.* New York: McGraw-Hill.

Feifel, H. 1974. Religious conviction and fear of death among the healthy and terminally ill. *J. Sci. Study Relig.* 13: 353–360.

Feifel, H. 1977. Death in contemporary America. In *New Meanings of Death*, ed. H. Feifel, pp. 4–11. New York: McGraw-Hill.

Feifel, H., and Branscomb, A. B. 1973. Who's afraid of death? *J. Abn. Psychol.* 81: 282–288.

Frederick, C. J. 1978. Current trends in suicidal behavior in the United States. *Am. J. Psychother.* 32: 172–200.

Freud, S. 1920. Beyond the pleasure principle. In *Standard Edition of the Complete Psychological Works*, vol. 18, pp. 3–64. London: The Hogarth Press, 1953–1965.

Fries, J. F. 1980. Aging, natural death, and the compression of morbidity. *New England J. Med.*, July 17, 1980: 130–135.

Furman, E. *A Child's Parent Dies.* 1974. New Haven: Yale University Press.

Giesen, C. B., and Datan, N. 1979. The competent older woman. In *Transitions of Aging*, eds. N. Datan and N. Lohmann, pp. 57–74. New York: Academic Press.

Glaser, B. G., and Strauss, A. L. 1966. *Awareness of Dying.* Chicago: Aldine Publishing Co.

Glaser, B. G., and Strauss, A. L. 1967. *Time for Dying.* Chicago: Aldine Publishing Co.

Granick, S., and Patterson, R. D., eds. 1971. *Human Aging II: An Eleven-year Followup Biomedical and Behavioral Study.* Washington, D.C.: U.S. Government Printing Office.

Gruman, G. J. 1978. Cultural origins of present-day "ageism": The modernization of the life cycle. In *Aging and the Elderly: Humanistic Perspectives in Gerontology*, eds. S. F. Spicker, K. M. Woodward, and D. D. Van Tassel. Atlantic Highlands, N.J.: Humanities Press, Inc.

Hall, G. S. 1904. *Adolescence: Its Psychology and Its Relations to Physiology, Anthropology, Sociology, Sex, Crime, Religion and Education.* Englewood Cliffs, N.J.: Prentice-Hall.

Hall, G. S. 1922. *Senescence.* New York: Appleton.

Hamilton, M., and Reid, H., eds. 1980. *A Hospice Handbook.* Grand Rapids: Eerdmans.

Haraven, T. K. 1979. The last stage: Historical adulthood and old age. In *Aging, Death, and the Completion of Being*, ed. D. D. Van Tassel, pp. 165–192. Philadelphia: University of Pennsylvania Press.

Havighurst, R. J. 1973. History of developmental psychology: socialization and personality development through the life span. In *Life-span Developmental Psychology: Personality and Socialization*, eds. P. B. Baltes and K. W. Schaie, pp. 4–25. New York: Academic Press.

Hayflick, L. 1977. The cellular basis for biological aging. In *Handbook of the Biology of Aging*, eds. C. E. Finch and L. Hayflick, pp. 159–188. New York: Van Nostrand Reinhold.

Henry, W. E. 1965. Engagement and disengagement: Toward a theory of human development. In *Contributions to the Psychobiology of Aging*, ed. R. Kastenbaum, pp. 19–36. New York: Springer Publishing Co., Inc.

Hinton, J. 1975. The influence of previous personality on reactions to having terminal cancer. *Omega* 6: 95–112.

Howell, T. W. 1980. Some terminal aspects of disease in old age: A clinical study of 300 patients. In *Thanatological Aspects of Aging*, eds. M. Tallmer, D. J. Cherico, A. H. Kutscher, and D. E. Sanders, pp. 147–152. New York: Highly Specialized Promotions.

Inge, G. 1982. Life and death in Swedish folk customs. Presented at International Work Group on Death and Dying, Rosenheim, Sweden.

Kalish, R. A. 1983. Death and dying in a social context. In *Handbook of Aging and the Social Sciences.* 3rd ed. New York: Van Nostrand.

Kane, B. 1979. Children's concept of death. *J. Genet. Psychol.* 134: 141–153.

Kastenbaum, R. 1959. Time and death in adolescence. In *The Meaning of Death*, ed. H. Feifel, pp. 99–113. New York: McGraw-Hill.

Kastenbaum, R. 1961. The dimensions of future time

perspective, an experimental analysis. *J. Genet. Psychol.* 65: 203–218.

Kastenbaum, R. 1973. The kingdom where nobody dies. *Saturday Review/Science,* January: 33–38.

Kastenbaum, R. 1974a. Fertility and the fear of death. *J. Social Issues* 30: 63–78.

Kastenbaum, R. 1974b. Childhood: The kingdom where creatures die. *J. Clin. Child Psychol.* 3: 11–13.

Kastenbaum, R. 1975. Is death a life crisis? On the confrontation with death in theory and practice. In *Life-span Developmental Psychology: Normative Life Crisis,* eds. N. Datan and L. Ginsberg, pp. 19–50. New York: Academic Press.

Kastenbaum, R. 1978. Death, dying, and bereavement in old age: New developments and their possible implications for psychosocial care. *Aged Care and Services Review* 1: 1–10.

Kastenbaum, R. 1981. *Death, Society and Human Experience.* 2nd ed. St. Louis: C. V. Mosby Co.

Kastenbaum, R. 1982. New fantasies in the American death system. *Death Education* 6: 155–166.

Kastenbaum, R. 1983. Time course and time perspective in later life. In *Annual Review of Gerontology and Geriatrics,* ed. C. Eisdorfer. New York: Springer Publishing Co.

Kastenbaum, R., and Aisenberg, R. B. 1976. *The Psychology of Death.* Rev. ed. New York: Springer Publishing Co.

Kastenbaum, R., and Costa, P. T., Jr. 1977. Psychological perspectives on death. In *Annual Review of Psychology,* eds. M. R. Rosenzweig and L. W. Porters, vol. 28, pp. 225–250. Palo Alto, CA: Stanford University Press.

Kastenbaum, R.; Kastenbaum, B. K.; and Morris, J. Strengths and preferences of the terminally ill: Data from the National Hospice Demonstration Study. In preparation.

Kastenbaum, R., and Mishara, B. L. 1970. Premature death and self-injurious behavior in old age. *Geriatrics* 26: 71–81.

Kastenbaum, R., and Ross, B. 1975. Historical perspectives on the care of the elderly. In *Modern Perspectives in the Psychiatry of Old Age,* ed. J. G. Howells, pp. 421–449. New York: Brunner/Maazel.

Keating, D. P. 1980. Thinking processes in adolescence. In *Handbook of Adolescent Psychology,* ed. J. Adelson, pp. 211–246. New York: Wiley Interscience.

Kent, S. 1980. The evolution of longevity. *Geriatrics* 35:98–104.

Kliman, G. W. 1976. Analyst in the nursery. In *The Psychoanalytic Study of the Child,* eds. A. J. Solnit, R. S. Eissler, A. Freud, M. Kris, and P. B. Neubauer, vol. 30, pp. 477–510. New Haven: Yale University Press.

Knapp, R., and Garbutt, J. 1958. Time imagery and the achievement motive. *J. Pers.* 26: 426–434.

Kohlberg, L., and Turiel, E. 1974. Overview—Cultural universals in morality. In *Recent Research in Moral Development,* eds. L. Kohlberg and E. Turiel. New York: Holt, Rinehart & Winston.

Koocher, G. 1973. Childhood, death, and cognitive development. *Develop. Psychol.* 9: 369–375.

Kubler-Ross, E. 1969. *On Death and Dying.* New York: Macmillan.

Lack, S. A. 1978. Characteristics of a hospice program of care. *Death Education* 2: 41–52.

Lanetto, R. 1980. *Children's Conceptions of Death.* New York: Springer Publishing Co.

Levinson, D. J. 1978. *The Seasons of a Man's Life.* New York: Alfred A. Knopf.

Lieberman, M. A. 1965. Psychological correlates of impending death. *J. Geront.* 20: 181–190.

Lieberman, M. A., and Falk, J. M. 1971. The remembered past as a source of data for research on the lifecycle. *Human Develop.* 14: 132–141.

Lopez, T., and Kliman, G. W. 1979. Memory, reconstruction, and mourning in the analysis of a 4-year-old child: Maternal bereavement in the second year of life. In *The Psychoanalytic Study of the Child,* eds. A. J. Solnit, R. S. Eissler, A. Freud, M. Kris, and P. B. Neubauer, vol. 34, pp. 235–272. New Haven: Yale University Press.

Mahler, M. S. 1961. On sadness and grief in infancy and childhood. In *The Psychoanalytic Study of the Child,* eds. A. J. Solnit, R. S. Eissler, A. Freud, M. Kris, and P. B. Neubauer, vol. 16, pp. 332–351. New Haven: Yale University Press.

Maris, R. W. 1981. *Pathways to Suicide.* Baltimore: Johns Hopkins Press.

Markson, E. W., and Hand, J. 1970. Referral for death: Low status of the aged and referral for psychiatric hospitalization. *Int. J. Aging and Human Develop.* 1: 261–272.

Marshall, W. 1980. *Last Chapters: A Sociology of Aging and Dying.* California: Brooks/Cole.

Masters, J. C. 1981. Developmental psychology. In *Annual Review of Psychology,* eds. M. R. Rosenzweig and L. W. Porter, vol. 32, pp. 117–152. Palo Alto, CA: Annual Reviews, Inc.

Maurer, A. 1966. Maturation of concepts of death. *Brit. J. Medicine & Psychol.* 39: 35–41.

McLendon, G. H. 1979. One teacher's experience with death education for adults. *Death Education* 3: 57–66.

McDonald, R. T. 1981. The effect of death education on specific attitudes toward death in college students. *Death Education* 5: 59–66.

McCrae, R. R.; Bartone, P. T.; and Costa, P. T., Jr. 1976. Age, personality, and self-reported health. *Int. J. Aging & Human Develop.* 6: 49–58.

Metchnikoff, E. 1908. *The Prolongation of Life.* New York: Putnam.

Metzger, A. M. 1979. A Q-methodological study of the Kubler-Ross stage theory. *Omega* 10: 291–302.

Meyers, G. C. 1978. *Cross-national Trends in Mortality Rates among the Elderly.* Unpublished manuscript, Duke University Center for Demographic Studies, March, 1978.

Miller, M. B. 1976. *The Interdisciplinary Role of the Nursing Home Medical Director.* Wakefield, MA: Contemporary Publishing.

Mishara, B. L., and Kastenbaum, R. 1973. Self-injurious behavior and environmental changes in the institutionalized elderly. *Int. J. Aging & Hum. Develop.* 4: 133–145.

Mor, V. 1982 (and continuing). The National Hospice Study: Progress reports. School of Medicine, Brown University, Providence, R.I.

Morris, J. 1982 (and continuing). Technical reports, National Hospice Study. Hebrew Home for Rehabilitation of the Aged: Social Gerontology Research Unit, Boston, Mass.

Moss, M. S., and Moss, S. Z. 1980. The impact of parental death on middle-aged children. Presented at 38th Annual Meeting of American Association of Marriage and Family Therapy, Toronto, Nov. 8, 1980.

Munnichs, J. M. A. 1966. *Old Age and Finitude.* Basel: S. Karger.

Nagera, H. 1970. Children's reaction to the death of important objects. In *The Psychoanalytic Study of the Child,* eds. A. J. Solnit, R. S. Eissler, A. Freud, M. Kris, and P. B. Neubauer, vol. 25, pp. 360–400. New Haven: Yale University Press.

Nagy, M. H. 1948. The child's theories concerning death. *J. Genet. Psychol.* 73: 3–27.

Nelson, F. L., and Farberow, N. L. 1977. Indirect suicide in the elderly chronically ill patient. In *Suicide Research,* eds. K. A. Achte and J. Lonnqvist. Helsinki: Psychiatria Fennica.

Niemark, E. D. 1982. Adolescent thought: Transition to formal operations. In *Handbook of Developmental Psychology,* ed. B. B. Wolman, pp. 486–502. Englewood Cliffs, N.J.: Prentice-Hall.

Oleshansky, M. E.; Gamsky, N. R.; and Ramseyer, G. C. Activity level, purpose in life and repression as predictions of death anxiety in the aged. *Omega.* In press.

Owen, G.; Fulton, R.; and Markusen, E. 1983. Death at a distance: A study of family survivors. *Omega* 13: 191–226.

Palmore, E., and Cleveland, W. 1980. Aging, terminal decline, and terminal drop. In *Thanatological Aspects of Aging,* eds. M. Tallmer, D. J. Cherico, A. H. Kutscher, and D. E. Sanders, pp. 1–6. New York: Highly Specialized Promotions.

Parkes, C. M. P. 1975. Evaluation of family care in terminal illness. Alexander Ming Fisher Lecture, Columbia University.

Piaget, J. 1954. *The Construction of Reality in the Child.* New York: Basic Books.

Piaget, J. 1967. *Six Psychological Studies.* New York: Random House.

Quinn, P. K., and Reznikoff, M. In press. The relationship between death anxiety and the subjective experience of time in the elderly. *Omega.*

Riegel, K. 1971. The prediction of death and longevity in longitudinal research. In *Prediction of Lifespan,* eds. E. Palmore and F. Jeffers. Lexington: D. C. Heath.

Riegel, K. F. 1973. Dialectic operations: The final period of cognitive development. *Research Bulletin RB-73-3.* Princeton: Educational Testing Service.

Robins, L. N., West, P. A., and Murphy, G. E. 1977. The high rate of suicide in older white men: A study testing ten hypotheses. *Soc. Psychiat.* 12: 1–20.

Rosemeier, H. P., and Minsel, W. R. 1982. Das kranke Kind und der Tod. Presented at Thanato-Psychologie Symposien, Vechta, West Germany, Nov. 5, 1982.

Rowland, K. F. 1977. Environmental events predicting death for the elderly. *Psychol. Bull.* 84: 349–372.

Safier, G. 1964. A study in relationships between the life and death concepts in children. *J. Genet. Psychol.* 105: 283–294.

Sanders, C. M. 1979. A comparison of adult bereavement in the death of a spouse, child and parent. *Omega* 10: 303–322.

Schulz, R., and Aderman, D. 1974. Clinical research and the stages of dying. *Omega* 5: 137–144.

Schulz, R., and Hanusa, B. H. 1977. Long term effects of control and predictability enhancing interventions: Findings and ethical issues. Gerontological Society, San Francisco.

Seiden, R. H. In press. Mellowing with age: Factors influencing the nonwhite suicide rate. *Omega.*

Selman, R. L. 1980. *The Growth of Interpersonal Understanding: Developmental and Clinical Analyses.* New York: Academic Press.

Shaver, K. G. 1977. *Principles of Social Psychology.* Cambridge, MA: Winthrop.

Shneidman, E. S. 1980. *Voices of Death.* New York: Harper & Row, Publishers.

Stannard, D. E. 1975. Death and the Puritan child. In *Death in America,* ed. D. E. Stannard, pp. 9–29. Philadelphia: Univ. of Pennsylvania Press.

Sudnow, D. 1967. *Passing On.* Englewood Cliffs, N.J.: Prentice-Hall.

Templer, D. 1970. The construction and validation of a death anxiety scale. *J. General Psychol.* 82: 165–177.

Templer, D.; Ruff, C.; and Franks, C. 1971. Death anxiety: Age, sex and parental resemblance in diverse populations. *Develop. Psychol.* 4: 108–114.

Tobin, S. 1972. The earliest memory as data for research in aging. In *Research, Planning, and Action for the Elderly,* eds. D. P. Kent, R. Kastenbaum, and S. Sherwood. New York: Behavioral Publications, Inc.

Twycross, R. G. 1974. Clinical experience with diamorphine in advanced malignant disease. *Int. J. Clinic. Pharm., Therapy & Toxic.* 9: 184–198.

Van Tassel, D. D., ed. 1979. *Aging, Death, and the Completion of Being.* Philadelphia: Univ. of Pennsylvania Press.

Watson, W. H. 1976. The aging sick and the near dead: A study of some distinguishing characteristics and social effects. *Omega* 7: 115–124.

Watson, W. H., and Maxwell, R. J. 1977. *Human Aging and Dying.* New York: St. Martin's Press.

Weisman, A. D., and Kastenbaum, R. 1968. *The Psychological Autopsy: A Study of the Terminal Phase of Life.* New York: Behavioral Publications, Inc.

Werner, H. 1957. *Comparative Psychology of Mental Development.* New York: McGraw-Hill.

Wessman, A. 1973. Personality and the subjective experience of time. *J. Pers. Assmnt.* 37: 103–114.

Wittmaier, B. C. 1979. Some unexpected attitudinal consequences of a short course on death. *Omega* 10: 271–275.

Wolman, B. B., ed. 1982. *Handbook of Developmental Psychology.* Englewood Cliffs, N.J.: Prentice-Hall.

PART 5 PSYCHOLOGICAL APPLICATIONS TO THE INDIVIDUAL

24
REHABILITATION AND THE OLDER ADULT

Bryan Kemp
Rancho Los Amigos Hospital
Downey, CA

ORIENTATION TO DISABILITY AND REHABILITATION

The disabled elderly have truly become the most forgotten and neglected segment of our society. Despite the high incidence of disability among the aged, they have received only minimal attention in all areas of health care, including rehabilitation services. This neglect contributes to the high percentage of isolated, chronically impaired, and dependent elderly in our society. This chapter is about some of the special considerations that must be addressed in order to bring about their rehabilitation. The purposes of this chapter are to define the field; to illustrate the need for rehabilitation services that will help alleviate the chronic health problems of the elderly; to examine the principles, especially psychological ones, that can improve the functioning of the elderly; and to discuss implications of these findings for rehabilitation programs.

Rehabilitation means literally to *re*-habilitate—or make capable of living again. Rehabilitation services seek to maximize the use of the disabled person's remaining abilities by procedures, therapy, and education and to minimize the consequences of the impairments suffered in order to facilitate the disabled person's participation in all aspects of life.

Rehabilitation is required whenever a disability causes a permanent, widespread disruption of the normal equilibrium between a person and the environment. Disabilities can be the result of physical illness (such as diabetes or cardiovascular disease), an injury (such as spinal cord trauma), or a "mental" illness (such as schizophrenia or Alzheimer disease). Impairments of any nature can be defined as disabilities if the consequences of them are widespread and more or less permanent so that they interfere with the everyday functioning of an individual (Kaarlela, 1973). An impairment does not necessarily produce a disability since some of them are temporary, curable, or self-limiting. According to Hunt (1980), a disability is a decrement in any one of, or a combination of, a person's capacities for mobility, communication, social interaction, activities of daily living, or thinking.

In order to define a disorder as a disability, therefore, it must meet the following criteria:

1. It must be caused by a physical injury or physical or mental illness.
2. It must produce relatively permanent impairments in daily functioning.
3. It must cause a disruption in the way a person normally relates to the physical and/or social environment.

Demographics of Disability and Old Age

Disabilities do not occur randomly across the life span. Most of the major activity-limiting disabilities occur far more frequently in older age, with a steady increase in incidence across the life span. Overall estimates of the percentage of disabled persons over age 65 range from 15 percent (Shanas, 1962) to 32 percent (Henriksen, 1978).

The National Center for Health Statistics (1976) has reported on the kinds of conditions causing limitations of activity. Although these data may be somewhat limited since they were based on household interviews and do not reflect physician assessments, they can still provide some useful comparisons, among them the following.

The percentage of persons with arthritis increased from 1 percent for the less-than-17-years-old group to about 25 percent for the over-65 group. Heart conditions increased from 2.4 percent for the less-than-17 group to 23.4 percent for the over-65 group. Strokes, degenerative neurological disorders, pulmonary disorders, metabolic disorders, and most orthopedic disabilities increase with age on a similar scale. Visual and hearing disorders increase as well. Significant eye abnormalities increase from 12 percent at age 17 to 89 percent for the 65-to-74 age group. The prevalence of mental disorders increases with age as well. The percentage of persons with a major depression is about 11 percent among community-dwelling elderly. The percentage of elderly with some degree of dementia is about 11 percent (Butler and Lewis, 1978).

When older persons become disabled, they are limited to a greater extent than younger persons because they often suffer from multiple chronic conditions and more frequently develop acute illnesses as well. Older persons spend three times as long in bed as the result of a disability than do younger persons.

Minority elderly and the old-old (over 75) have even higher percentages of disabilities that cause limitations in daily functioning. Among those over 74, approximately 50 percent have at least one major disability (Kane, Solomon, Beck, Keeler, and Kane, 1980). Blacks not only have a shorter life span than whites but more disabilities. Elderly Hispanics have a higher percentage of physical impairments as well as major depressions (Lopez-Aqueres, Kemp, Plopper, and Staples, 1982).

The elderly American Indian has a higher percentage of impairments as well.

Another way to view the situation is to note that there are approximately 22 million disabled persons in the United States. Of these, about 40 percent, or nine million, are elderly (Henriksen, 1978). With an increase in the percentage of people living to age 75, this number will grow even more in the years ahead. A great many of these disabled persons live in institutions. More than 85 percent of the population of nursing homes is elderly. Although only 5 percent of the elderly are in these institutions at any one time, nearly all of them are disabled. Furthermore, about 20 percent of the elderly population, most of them disabled, will spend some part of their life in an institution (Pegels, 1980).

The disabled elderly are vastly underrepresented in rehabilitation programs. Although they represent 40 percent of the disabled population, they receive less than 10 percent of the services rendered by state departments of rehabilitation. Ten to 20 percent of services to the blind are for the elderly, although they constitute about 50 percent of the blind population (Kaarlela, 1973). Very few programs address the special needs of the disabled older person. There are no good data on this question, but it can be conservatively estimated that only about 30 percent of the disabled elderly who could profit from rehabilitation services actually receive them.

How did this situation come to be? What can be done about it? It came about through three principal causes. First, no one has adequately protested about the situation. It has been easier to ignore the elderly or build nursing homes than to attempt to provide for their rehabilitation. Second, a general attitude has prevailed that expects the elderly to be disabled and ill, that considers such debilities a part of normal aging. Few people have taken the time to find out what might be done to rehabilitate this group of persons. Third, professionals have not been attracted to the problem. For example, of the 49,000 medical school faculty in the United States in 1978, only 20 indicated that geriatrics was an area of personal interest (Pegels, 1980; Kane et al., 1980). It is only within the last few years that health professionals have begun to take the health needs of the elderly population seriously.

It is the contention of this chapter that the practice of rehabilitation has much to offer the aging population, that it can assist disabled elderly persons to live more normal and useful lives. We live in an era when chronic illnesses are commonplace (c.f. Fordyce, 1981) and even more common among the elderly. We do not need to invent new systems of care for the elderly as much as we need to use the systems we already have.

GENERAL PRINCIPLES OF REHABILITATION

Rehabilitation as a discipline has specific philosophical, technical, and operational characteristics that distinguish it from acute medical practice. The focus of acute medicine is on the diagnosis and correction of *disease processes*. The training of most physicians is organ-system-oriented. By contrast, the key word in rehabilitation is not *disease* but *function*. Knowledge of a person's diagnosis does not translate adequately into knowledge about what that person can *do*. A diagnosis of rheumatoid arthritis by itself does not allow one to know whether the person afflicted with it is capable of working, cooking, walking, or most other functional activities. One of the underlying assumptions of acute medicine is that if an individual's underlying disease is corrected, that individual will return to his or her pre-illness state more or less automatically. Such is not the case with a chronic disability. By its very nature, a chronic disability leaves permanent impairment. Moreover, it always affects many different functions. Arthritis, for example, affects mobility, work performance, social participation, and the ability to perform home chores. Any disability affects people psychologically in a substantial way as well. Most important of these psychological injuries is the disruption of a person's self-concept, or view of self in relation to the former, pre-disability self. This, in turn, can affect overall emotional, cognitive, and interpersonal functioning. The main technological approach of rehabilitation is to assess and treat the disabled person's functional deficits and to improve functional abilities.

Society's view of people with disabilities is also important. Unfortunately, negative reactions to disabled people tend to be more common than positive ones. Vash (1981) succinctly summarizes the reactions of society in one word: *devaluation.* Society's view of disabled persons is not only that they are different (as red hair is different from blond) but that they are less important, inferior to, less valuable, and more trouble than nondisabled persons. This devaluation has led to segregated care, education, and social participation at all ages. Rehabilitation efforts have to deal not only with the physical recovery of individuals but with society's acceptance of them. Older disabled persons have another strike against them—their age as well as their disability. Brody (1973) has called this "double jeopardy."

The philosophical foundation of rehabilitation stresses that disabled persons deserve, as much as anyone else, the opportunity to participate in all aspects of life. The focus in rehabilitation is to maximize individual functioning, thereby promoting personal independence. Most rehabilitation efforts are thus also directed toward helping the disabled person return to participation in society. Full integration is the objective. Separate education, work, legal rights, and social participation are not acceptable.

Although rehabilitation is concerned with the disabled person's functional participation in society, there are limits to how much the disabled individual can adapt or adjust to what some (c.f. Vash, 1981) call a "handicapping world." Examples of the handicapping world abound: architectural barriers, discriminating laws, adverse social attitudes, job discrimination, and prejudicial personal relations. For this reason, rehabilitation also distinguishes itself by placing strong emphasis on the influence of environmental factors in attaining independence. This attitude is manifested in several ways. First is the recognition that optimum improvement does not occur in hospitals. Most people do not live in hospitals; they live in homes within communities. A rehabilitation program, therefore, only *starts* in a hospital; it is continued at home. For this reason, rehabilitation programs must always assess the patient's home environment and make contact with the other people who are a part of that environment. (The home environment is also considered to include the work environment and school environment, if appropriate.) It will sometimes be necessary to modify the home environment to make it more convenient for the disabled person, for example, building ramps to make entering the home easier, providing devices that will improve reaching from a wheelchair, or installing hand controls on a car. The ability of applied technology to improve the functioning of disabled persons can be seen in such programs as the Rehabilitation Engineering Centers sponsored by the National Institute of Handicapped Research and by Project Threshold at Rancho Los Amigos Hospital in Downey, California. The rehabilitation movement also influences the "dehandicapping of society" by encouraging corrective legislation, promoting positive role models in the media, and conducting research on related topics.

The general principles of physical/medical management of the rehabilitation patient have been summarized by several authors including Hunt (1977). These are (1) control of the underlying disease, (2) prevention of secondary disabilities (e.g., pressure sores, contractures), (3) restoration of functional abilities, and (4) adaptation of the patient and patient education. To this should be added (5) modification and preparation of the environment.

The elderly are different from the young in many ways that affect rehabilitation. Physically, the elderly are more likely to have multiple chronic illnesses rather than just one. The presentation of many clinical illnesses is also different in the elderly. A myocardial infarct may present as confusion instead of pain. The elderly are also more prone to developing secondary disabilities, among them pressure sores, dehydration, bladder infections, deconditioning, and pain (c.f., Hunt, 1976). The older person is more apt to have cognitive impairment as well as a medical condition. The elderly also metabolize medicines differently than the young do, making dosage and proper drug selection important. The elderly

are particularly susceptible to the ill effects of immobility. With elderly patients, as little as three days confinement in bed can have very deleterious results (c.f., Hunt, 1976).

The elderly, particularly the disabled elderly, suffer from the highest incidence of psychiatric disorders. Chief among these is depression, which has been reported to be present in as many as 40 percent of the disabled elderly (Blazer, 1982). Deliriums are also relatively common among ill, hospitalized older patients. Paranoid symptomatology may also arise in hospitalized patients, particularly among those with sensory impairments. Unless properly managed, psychiatric disorders can undermine the benefits of rehabilitation.

Attitudes toward the elderly are negative among 40 to 50 percent of health professionals (Kosberg and Harris, 1978). These attitudes can degrade the quality of care for older people in rehabilitation. The elderly themselves may consider disability a normal accompaniment of advanced age and not insist on receiving the rehabilitation services they need (Tayback et al., 1977).

The goals of rehabilitation are frequently different for older patients. Historically, rehabilitation efforts have stressed a return to family life and to work as indicators of success. Most elderly persons are past the age of employment, however, and many lack families to return to, particularly older women. The prospects of returning home and getting back to work frequently motivate younger people to improve their abilities. Such motivational sources are all too often lacking among the elderly. The goal of rehabilitation with them should stress return to independent living and previous life styles as much as possible (Hunt, 1976; Sherman and Gingras, 1965). The absence of significant others among the older population may lead to lower levels of support when they return home (Hirschberg, Lewis, and Vaughn, 1976). Levels of interpersonal support have been shown to be related to the improvement of younger people after discharge (Kemp and Vash, 1971). The reinforcement needed to maintain the behavior of many people is peer approval and peer support. Lacking this, the older person discharged to the community may show more rapid declines in functioning than a person with more peer support.

Older people are also more frequently near or below the poverty line (Brody, 1973). This means that they will have a more difficult time securing private medical care in the community, proper nutrition, adequate transportation, and home assistance.

Owing to these multiple differences, older people unquestionably progress more slowly in rehabilitation than younger ones (Rusk and Lee, 1971; Hunt, 1977; Hunt, 1980). Nevertheless, the evidence (to be discussed) also indicates that older people do profit from rehabilitation and can be expected to return to independent living.

Interdisciplinary Team Approach

As the previous discussion has indicated, rehabilitation focuses on assessing and treating the functional deficits of the elderly in order to promote greater independence. Functional areas of concern include communication, mobility, hand dexterity, sensory abilities, emotional stability, activities of daily living, cognition, and health maintenance. These areas are not the usual domain of traditional medical and nursing practice. The allied health professions have developed in part to meet just such needs. Medical and allied health personnel are sometimes organized into an interdisciplinary rehabilitation team. Interdisciplinary team treatment is the key to rehabilitation success. Since the elderly, as noted, are more likely to have *multiple* chronic conditions, periodic acute medical problems, psychiatric complications, less family support, and less visibility in society, they are especially in need of this approach.

An interdisciplinary team can be composed in a variety of ways, depending upon the needs of the individual patient. For the older person with chronic impairments, the following team members are considered essential. First is the *physician,* who can be a psychiatrist or other specialist such as an internist or family doctor. The physician acts as leader of the interdisciplinary team. The most important characteristics for a physician in geriatrics are a strong commitment to the field (including teaching

and research interests as well as service), a realistically optimistic attitude about the older person's potentials, and an ability to communicate effectively with other team members, patients, and their families.

Because of the higher than average frequency of mental and emotional disorders among the elderly, a *psychiatrist* with a special interest in the problems of geriatric patients is also essential. The older patient in rehabilitation is highly susceptible to many factors that can bring about an acute psychiatric disturbance. These include underlying medical conditions, medicines, relocation trauma, sensory restriction, social isolation, and interpersonal problems. Careful assessment and treatment of these problems will not only assist the overall rehabilitation program but prevent the inappropriate placement of many older persons. In addition, one of the primary diagnoses for many older persons in rehabilitation will be a psychiatric one, such as dementia or a major depression.

The *adult nurse practitioner* is a highly valuable member of the geriatric rehabilitation team. The nurse practitioner is responsible for much of the physical care of the older person and often for coordination of services. Nurse practitioners may conduct physical examinations, take histories, perform certain physical procedures, administer medicines, and assess health maintenance. They also counsel patients and families about their health care and refer patients for additional health services. The nurse practitioner will see patients in a variety of settings, including the patient's home and a hospital or clinic.

Other nursing personnel, including registered nurses and vocational nurses, are essential to patient care. The *physical therapist* assesses and treats problems of muscle strength, range of motion, mobility, and overall endurance. He or she also assesses the need for assistive devices in the home (such as a ramp) and more personal aids such as braces, altered shoes, wheelchairs, or canes. Older patients have an inordinately high number of problems requiring a physical therapist. Approximately 50 percent of those who are disabled have some kind of mobility problem that limits their ability to get around at home or in the community. Many of them suffer from extreme decon-ditioning and low physical endurance caused by a lack of exercise or excessive bed rest.

The *occupational therapist* evaluates and treats problems concerning activities of daily living such as dressing, cooking, grooming, eating and toileting. The orientation and train-ing of occupational therapists also prepare them to help patients to adjust to family, work, leisure, and community roles by teach-ing adaptive techniques that can overcome limitations. Occupational therapists, like physical therapists, may work with either indi-vidual patients or groups of patients. For many older people, the ability to perform their own household activities is the factor that most highly correlates with self-satisfaction and that most reassures their family that they are able to stay in the community.

The *clinical psychologist* evaluates and treats the patient's emotional and mental func-tioning, family status and dynamics, and any psychological factors that impinge on rehabili-tation success. Unlike the psychiatrist, the psychologist does not medically treat patients. Both, however, may provide individual and group psychotherapy to patients and family members. An important function of the geria-tric psychologist is to perform neuropsycho-logical testing on patients suspected or known to have cognitive impairments. This assess-ment may help to establish treatment goals as well as provide a baseline level on patient's abilities for future comparison.

The *social worker* assesses family patterns of functioning, provides family counseling or therapy, arranges for community services for the patient, takes care of discharge planning from the hospital, conducts group treatment programs, provides individual psychotherapy, and helps secure financial benefits. The social worker frequently gets in touch with commu-nity agencies to identify persons in need of services and facilitate their entry into rehabili-tation programs.

The *nutritionist* evaluates and prescribes diets in accord with the patient's medical con-dition, customs, and energy demands. The *pharmacist* secures a drug history on each pa-tient and counsels patients on drug usage, safety, interactions, and economy. The *audiol-*

ogist conducts an evaluation of the older per-son's hearing, diagnoses hearing impairments, and recommends corrective measures. The *speech therapist* diagnoses communication problems and treats them through retraining or possibly artificial speech devices.

The geriatric rehabilitation team must also have access to other disciplines, including other medical specialists, dentists, orthodon-tists, recreation therapists, and respiratory therapists.

The interdisciplinary team approach to care is different from merely making a variety of health disciplines available. A variety of health professionals could operate independently of one another, each of them doing his or her own part, and still not be interdisciplinary. Interdisciplinary team care differs in that the desired outcome can be achieved only by the *interactive* process of the entire team (For-dyce, 1981).

The principles of interdisciplinary team care include the following:

1. Each person has a role as both a health specialist and a team member. As a spe-cialist, he or she has the responsibility of assessing and treating problems in his or her unique area of expertise. As a team member, each has the responsibility of informing the others of the implications of his or her findings and for coordinat-ing care of the patient in the manner that the team, with the physician as leader, prescribes.

2. Each member of the team understands the function of every other team member and how best to utilize it for the patient's needs.

3. The team shares decision making and responsibility for the patient. Each pro-fessional contributes to the overall evalu-ation, plan, and treatment of the patient in a team setting. At any given time, the most important treatment for a par-ticular patient may be the province of any of the disciplines. At times, physi-cian care may not be the most vital part of the patient's program.

4. The team provides support for the efforts of all its members. One of the conse-

quences of working with chronically impaired older persons is that it can place a heavy work burden on staff members. Team functioning provides support and morale for alleviating this burden.

5. Team members may cross traditional professional lines or roles at times to help the patient. For example, a physical therapist may be the person the patient is most comfortable with discussing sexual function, although this is not frequently a role that physical therapists perform.

6. Coordination of patient care is accomplished through team review of patients as well as by specific assignment.

7. The patient and his or her family are part of the team. Family conferences are conducted by members of the team to provide continuity of care, answer questions about the patient, and provide support for family members.

The effectiveness of the team approach in geriatric rehabilitation appears to be good, although there have been no properly controlled experimental studies to compare different approaches. The evidence concerning geriatric rehabilitation comes from a variety of sources. Several studies show a reasonably high degree of success with this approach (Kaplan and Ford, 1975; King, Vaughn, and Clausen, 1978; Leeming and Luke, 1977). Kaplan and Ford found a 61 percent rate of return to independent living after an interdisciplinary approach. Strax and Ledebur (1979) found an 82 percent return.

Williams, Hill, Fairbank, and Knox (1973) reported on a sample of 332 older persons (80 percent over age 70) who were seen in an evaluation clinic. After a review and screening, 112 of them were referred for rehabilitation services. Of these, 75 percent, or 85, were then able to live either independently or with a lower level of care. These patients had a variety of disabilities, and most had more than one major disability.

Few studies have measured specific increases in abilities after rehabilitation efforts with older persons. However, Feigenson, McDowell, Meese, McCarthy, and Greenberg (1977) and Feigenson, McCarthy, Greenberg, and Feigenson (1977) reported on two different samples of elderly patients with cerebral vascular accidents. After rehabilitation, 51 percent proved to be independent in the activities of daily living, and 79 percent returned home. There were no significant relationships between age and the measured outcomes in the age range of 40 to 80.

What is presently needed in the field are some well controlled studies with appropriate measures and adequate long term follow up. The results of several outcome studies are summarized in Table 1.

TABLE 1. Summary of Major Studies of Elderly Persons in Rehabilitation.

Authors	Sample Size	Age	Disabilities Included	Improvement In Function, Percent	Discharged to Independent Living, Percent	Nature of Program
Williams et al., 1973	112	70 (82%)	Various	Unspecified	75	Evaluation with referral
Kaplan and Ford, 1975	1135	62–99	Various	Unspecified	61	Interdisciplinary
Reyes et al., 1977	105	M = 64	Lower extremity amputation	92	97	Interdisciplinary
Reed and Gessner, 1979	401	7 > 70	Various	Unspecified	20	Very ill patients already in extended care facilities
Feigenson et al., 1977	248	17–98	CVA	52	80	Interdisciplinary
Feigenson et al., 1977	318	17–98	CVA	51	78	Interdisciplinary
Henriksen, 1978	75	M = 65	Various	67	53	Interdisciplinary

PSYCHOSOCIAL ASPECTS OF GERIATRIC REHABILITATION

The Effects of Disability Across the Life Span

The impact a disability has on an individual's life is a function of the nature of the disability, the stage of life at which it occurs, the number of alterations in life style it produces, the way in which it is perceived by the individual, and how it is responded to by that individual and others.

Some disabilities do not occur as frequently as others across the life span; certain kinds are more prevalent at certain ages. The age at which a disability occurs is very important in determining how it will influence a person's life. Developmental disabilities, such as mental retardation and cerebral palsy, occur in the beginnings of life. Such disabilities are caused by perinatal and even postnatal factors. Other disabilities, such as leukemia, multiple fractures of the extremities, brain injury, and some spinal cord injuries frequently have their onsets prior to adulthood. Disabilities of this kind are typically the result of accidents or viruses. Diseases with a typical mid-life onset often reflect life-style stressors, environmental pollutants, and genetic predisposition, including rheumatoid arthritis, multiple sclerosis, diabetes, heart disease, and various cancers. Disabilities with an onset in late life are more likely to include cerebral vascular accidents, Parkinson's disease, osteoarthritis, and Alzheimer disease. These disabilities seem to reflect the slow accumulation of multiple degenerative, viral, and/or autoimmune processes.

The impact these disabilities have on psychological processes and functioning in educational, vocational, social, familial, sexual, leisure, and economic spheres is more than can be explained by the medical condition alone. One must look to the interaction of the medical condition, the stage of the life style, the person's own attributes, and general social attitudes for a fuller explanation of the how people respond to a disability.

Disabilities with an onset at birth or in early childhood have a particularly devastating ef-
fect on the family as well as the individual. At the beginning, the family may feel guilty, angry, resentful, and anxious about having a disabled child. They must then learn how to steel themselves to the difficulties of providing constant care and the emotional conflict that goes with their love of the child and their feelings of burden. The child soon learns the meaning of "environmental barrier," "handicapped," and "different." To realize that you will never grow up like other children is one of the most horrendous experiences a child can have. Every developmental phase and every daily task is different for the disabled child. In Erikson's (1959) terms, the critical ego development issues of trust, autonomy, initiative, and industry that normal children go through, as well as all future stages of development, are vastly different for the disabled child. Development of the senses of trust and autonomy requires a consistent environment and equal opportunity for play, schooling, and interaction. Basic attachments, control over self and things, decision making, exploration, creativity, and a sense of competence begin at this stage. These experiences may be missing or radically altered for the disabled child. Making friends, going to school, and learning role identification are all altered. The disabled child growing into a disabled adult will experience work, career, romance, family, and parenthood in a very irregular way. The experience of the self will also be quite different (c.f. Vash, 1981). For many psychologists involved with disability, self-image, self-concept, and self-esteem are the most important theoretical concepts. These attributes are learned early in life and are not easily modified thereafter; the child who acquires a negative self-image maintains it. Aging among people with a childhood disability may even occur faster than normal as a result of the strain on their biological systems (Hunt, 1980).

Disabilities with an onset in late adolesence or early adulthood carry yet another set of consequences. Although some of the early phases and tasks of psychosocial development have been negotiated, the crises of sexual identity and intimacy and the demands of work, education, marriage, and family remain. In addition, if the young adult acquires a catastrophic disability (e.g., spinal cord injury) even the fruit of early stages of development (trust, autonomy, initiative, and industry) may be affected. The person may feel, and often is, less autonomous. Adolescent disabilities occur just when the person is beginning to establish himself or herself as an individual, to be like his or her friends and yet different. Sexual interest and identity are at critical heights. The individual may have just reached a physical peak, and concern over appearance and bodily beauty are all important. As a result of the disability, relationships end or change, popularity is affected, career goals have to be reassessed, and most of all, the person's self concept is altered.

Disabilities that occur in middle age, after the "settling down" stage, present still different complications. The family has reached its maximum size and the children are more or less grown. The person has nearly reached his or her maximum earning power. The woman has passed some of the more difficult child-rearing stages. A disability at this time either brings the family to the support of its disabled member or, in troubled marriages, adds to the difficulty of keeping it together. Family support is a critical factor in adjustment to disability at this age (c.f. Kemp and Vash, 1971). The disability can plunge a person's now soundly developed identity into crisis and pathos, although the crisis is usually only temporary. The effect of a disability on work is problematic since between 60 and 70 percent of previously employed persons return to work. Like a disabled young adult, the middle-aged person may have to relearn or adjust to certain early psychodynamic stages, particularly the crises of intimacy, identity, and generativity. Sexual adjustment after a heretofore established pattern is difficult for many couples. Presence of a disability is also one of the major risk factors in late life suicide (Blazer, 1982). The unexpectedness of the disability exacerbates concerns about death for many and leads to a re-examination of personal values. Starting over in so many areas is more than a struggle, it is a searing family and personal crisis.

Disabilities that occur in late life have a unique character. There is frequently an absence of a spouse (especially among women), the children are usually gone, the man is retired, and the individual lives on a fixed income. A disability frequently marks *the* major loss in the older person's life, excluding the loss of a spouse. Depression is the most likely psychological result of disability. Among disabled older people, the rate of major depressions approaches 40 percent (compared to about 25 percent for younger disabled persons). For many of them, the onset of the disability marks the line between not being old and being old. It becomes the "sign of aging." When the elderly woman cannot bounce back from the broken hip as quickly as she might have before, she feels immeasurably older. When the older man is retired because of a disability, he attributes it to his age. The self-concept and self-esteem of the older person, so dependent upon being optimally functional, is at least temporarily crushed by a disability. The previous roles of worker or parent to fall back upon for hope or regaining purpose in life are usually not at hand. Discouragement if rehabilitation does not occur early foretells of further illnesses and decreasing independence. In Erickson's terms, the older person is also thrust back to earlier crises that must be resolved all over again, particularly the struggle of integrity against despair. The older person frequently feels a great lessening of control, of self-direction, and of purpose, the very attributes most directly related to survival and adaptation in late life (Butler, 1967). The family, when there is one, all too often infantilizes the older disabled person with undue protection. It is unfortunately true that many older persons "give up" and succumb to their disability. For many of these, proper timing of rehabilitative intervention can prevent further decline. The person who has limited abilities to perform personal and home tasks is at high risk of institutionalization after a disability. The combination of limited mobility, incontinence, and poor family support dramatically increases the risks of institutionalization. This is not true of the younger person with the same disability—a fact all too often overlooked in health care. Unfortunately, a disability in old age frequently turns out to be the difference between spending one's remaining years with integrity or in despair.

Adjustment to Crisis

A disability presents a crisis in a person's life, a crisis that is relatively long lasting and encompasses many aspects of existence that are not resolved by the stabilization of the underlying physical causes. Several writers (Steger, 1976; Athelstan, 1981) have reviewed crisis-oriented models of adjustment to disability. A certain regularity or pattern becomes apparent in people's attempts to adjust.

The first phase has been labeled *shock,* during which the person must make vigorous attempts to maintain an internal equilibrium both physically and psychologically. Individuals in this state may not even be aware of what has happened because their powers of perception, reasoning, and responding are malfunctioning. During this phase, others may need to take a greater role in caring for such individuals since they may be unable to care for themselves.

The next phase of adjustment, called *defensive retreat,* occurs when the person finally realizes what has happened, is terrified by it, and begins trying to cope with it. During this phase, defense mechanisms are put into play, often to extremes, in order to ward off the anxiety, depression, and panic that would otherwise accompany the realization of the full extent of the blow. Denial of the extent, permanence, or severity of the disability frequently occurs. Anything opposed to this denial is so painful that it will be avoided, even friends, family, and staff. Such denial is common, but any form of defense mechanism or behavior may take a similar extreme form. Even schizophrenic-like episodes to avoid the reality of the event are not uncommon. Motivation for rehabilitation is less than optimal at such a time because the disability is not perceived to be real or permanent. There are no time limits on this phase of adjustment; it may last in some form from weeks to years. It may also be all-encompassing or limited

to a few areas of life. This is not a time for fruitful psychological intervention because defensiveness is at such a high level. Nevertheless, if this phase interferes with rehabilitation efforts, it must be confronted by the appropriate staff.

When the disability does not change dramatically and denial processes do not succeed in eliminating all its sources of stress, the person is finally forced to recognize its existence. This frequently leads to a phase called *acknowledgment.* During this phase of adjustment, there is usually a great deal of anxiety, worry, depression, and grief. There may also be feelings of hopelessness, lost opportunities, uselessness, and alienation from others. This is the time when staff intervention can be most helpful. Appropriate psychological intervention can help the person to begin to integrate the disability, both emotionally and pragmatically, into an acceptable life style.

The final phase of adjustment is called *adaptation.* This phase is life-long, for the disabled person continues to encounter new challenges and new barriers as long as life remains.

Although there are no vigorous studies of the subject, clinical evidence suggests that the elderly do not necessarily show the same reaction pattern to a disability as younger persons. Typically, the loss produced by their disability is another addition to a myriad of other losses —of spouse, job, children, important roles, and so forth. The older person's very self-esteem is at stake, and at a time when there are fewer resources and supports to fall back upon. Grief and depression are more frequent and long-lasting among the elderly. This grief is more typical than clinical depression and should be accepted and treated as such. It is the reaction to tangible loss—in this case, the loss of one's sense of self, of health, and of life as it has formerly been enjoyed. The elderly also have a different set of comparisons on which to base their worth and functioning. Whereas younger persons are likely to compare themselves to others, older persons compare themselves to how they were before their disability. The young can find other disabled persons to serve as role models for work, play, and marriage. The older person has fewer chances to do so. As a result, outside factors play a larger role in the older person's depression and grief as opposed to the internalized guilt and anger found in the younger disabled. The elderly disabled person is also at a disadvantage because the people around him often *expect* him to have a disability in late life and to accept it as an inevitable by-product of aging. As Wright (1956) points out, society as a whole may need older people to give up some of the normal functions of life and to suffer from their loss in order to prove that they were important in the first place. Having had to deal already with fewer resources and the decrease in status, roles, and authority that aging brings, the elderly who have the added affliction of a disability need timely and effective psychosocial intervention to regain their maximum independence.

Motivation

Motivation for rehabilitation is generally agreed to be one of the more important factors for its success. Despite its importance, motivation is one of the least understood concepts in psychology. In attempts to explain why people choose one way of behaving instead of another and how much effort they are willing to put forth, we frequently invoke motivation as the cause.

Two models of motivation appear to be especially helpful in rehabilitation. Abraham Maslow's theory of need satisfaction is one well suited for practice. In this theory, needs are arranged in a hierarchy from physiological concerns to safety to love and from belonging to esteem to self-actualization. Human development progresses up the hierarchy, the more basic needs requiring satisfaction before the higher ones can be met. People choose a variety of ways of satisfying these needs and in the process develop learning styles and personality characteristics that set them apart from others. A disability disrupts normal need satisfaction and the ways people have learned to satisfy their needs. It therefore follows that much of the behavior observed in rehabilitation efforts is directed toward satisfying needs the patient feels are important to him or her at that time and in those circumstances.

When important needs are not met over an extended period of time, frustration, stress and serious psychopathology can result. When the older person's need for security, for example, cannot be met because of an ever-changing hospital or home environment that is beyond understanding, serious maladjustment can set in. Older people are more likely than the young to experience deprivation of respect, approval, and admiration. They are far more likely to have little or no family. If there is no one to give approval for effort or no one to care, why should they exert themselves? Nevertheless, the older person has a strong need to maintain a sense of worth in the face of a disability, and much of the depression of old age is a result of this need's not being met. Development of a "sick role" by some older patients can be viewed as a way of attempting to maintain some degree of need satisfaction (perhaps for interpersonal contact or control) in the absence of any perceived alternatives.

An additional model of motivation is one based upon the works of Atkinson, Bastian, Earl, and Litwin (1960) and McDaniel (1969). It is expressed by the equation

$$M = \frac{P(Os) \times V}{C}$$

In this model, which has excellent value in applied settings, motivation (M) is seen as a complex set of factors. Behavior is seldom the result of a single factor. In this case, motivation (choice of behavior and effort) is a function of the subjective probability of a successful outcome, $P(Os)$—given that the choice is made or effort put forth—the utility or value (V) of the outcome if it is achieved, and the cost of that outcome (C). The cost can be in terms of money, energy, self-concept, interpersonal relations, emotions, or even in terms of giving up other rewarding experiences.

If an older person does not believe a particular task can be accomplished, this model would predict, all other things being equal, that little effort will be made. If seeing himself in long-leg braces "costs" him too much in self-concept terms, an elderly man will probably not use them. If the therapist's goals (values) are not the patient's goals, the patient won't "cooperate" fully. In fact, one of the bigger problems in geriatric rehabilitation is the absence of many of the customary goals that help motivate the young, such as return to work, rejoining family members, and raising children.

In general, maximizing the numerator and minimizing the denominator of this model of motivation will enhance performance. Disabled people often find themselves in a conflict about a particular activity. For example, an older woman may resist following diet instructions even though she knows they will help her diabetes and hence her eyesight. Exploration of both aspects of the conflict (the numerator and denominator of the model) will usually reveal the true nature of the difficulty.

Staff motivation to work with the elderly is similarly determined. If professional staff see little hope of being able to help an older person [$P(Os)$], or see no value in it because the older person will not return to a job (V), or feel that it will cost them too much in time expended or in what others may think of them (C), then they will not be motivated to give the elderly as much assistance as they need. Unfortunately, this situation appears to be the case, being reflected in the low percentage of older persons who are able to participate in a variety of health systems.

The documented age differences in motivation that should be taken into account in rehabilitation include the following:

1. Today's older individuals grew up with a different set of values, experiences, and customs. These value differences must be considered in attempting to assist them. When it comes to such things as refinancing the family home in order to live better, accepting outside assistance, or discussing feelings about sexual relations, these value differences become apparent.
2. Older adults are more cautious and less risk-taking (Botwinick, 1978). They are less likely to want to take chances or make significant changes in the way they have always done things. Whereas a younger person's behavior can often be described as stemming from a "hope of

success," an older person is more likely to be motivated by a "fear of failure."
3. It is well documented that older persons are more anxious in social situations and at learning tasks (e.g., Eisdorfer, 1981). Since rehabilitation consists in large part of the relearning of many tasks, efforts should be made to reduce this anxiety as much as possible.
4. The elderly person, already suffering from many losses, is often fearful of "looking bad" or "losing face" in new situations. Such "costs" can be reduced by focusing on the positive aspects of behavior and sufficiently simplifying tasks so as to build in positive reinforcement.

Improving Motivation

One of the psychologist's key roles in rehabilitation is that of analyzing and helping to improve motivation toward rehabilitation by reducing the barriers to participation or enhancing its benefits. Using the motivation model presented earlier, the psychologist can begin to examine the costs and benefits to the patient of a particular behavior. Specific examination of the patient's *perception* of a situation is required since these are often based upon erroneous assumptions or information. Barriers to motivation in the elderly are frequently founded in mistaken beliefs that life is over, that improvement will be of no avail, that too much physical effort will be required, that too much is to be overcome, or that a more dependent and safer, albeit less functional, existence will have to be given up. The majority of motivational problems can be pinpointed and mitigated by following this model.

One of the main points to consider is that virtually no patient, whether young or old, is unmotivated. He or she may be motivated to do something different than the staff would like, but even that behavior is motivated. Specific steps for improving motivation in elderly patients include the following:

1. Verbally exploring with the patient his or her outlook in terms of feelings of achieving success, goals, values, and

costs. Listening for and observing less-than-conscious conflicts, such as whether an improvement might reduce another family member's attention. Counseling will usually help to overcome mistaken beliefs and resolve conflicts.

2. Giving credence to the patient's goals and needs and prioritizing services that will benefit the older person even if it means postponing staff goals.

3. Simplifying the steps needed to achieve a rehabilitation objective in order to improve the opportunities for its success and lessen fears of failure (which are already all too prevalent among the elderly). If resocialization with the public is the objective, "safer" outings should be favored to begin with, such as trips with staff or passive involvement in patient meetings.

4. Encouraging and supporting involvement in peer group activities, such as a resocialization group, "rap" group, or exercise group. The group process will help reinforce further efforts.

5. Applauding efforts made by the patient and either ignoring or minimizing the impact of perceived failure.

6. *Never* engaging the older person in activities that might result in diminished self-esteem or loss of face. All efforts must reflect positively on the older person.

PSYCHOLOGICAL INTERVENTION IN GERIATRIC REHABILITATION

This section will focus on psychological techniques to improve the functioning of disabled older persons. The objectives of psychological intervention are as follows:

1. To conduct assessments of patients—including their cognitive, affective, and functional status—in order to contribute to a team treatment plan.

2. To help resolve the crises of disability, grieving, and depression.

3. To help patients meet their own needs and maintain independence.

4. To identify suspected organic ailments that may impair optimal functioning

(e.g., disorientation, drug interactions, acute psychotic episodes).

5. To promote self-esteem.

6. To help improve family relations.

Several methods are available to the psychologist to help achieve these objectives, but there must first be a thorough evaluation.

Assessment

A psychological assessment of the older person for rehabilitation purposes should include at least the following:

1. A mental status examination to assess major cognitive and emotional difficulties and help define the proper psychological treatment, based upon standard methods and procedures (e.g., Birren and Sloane, 1981).

2. A social and vocational history focusing on previous roles, marriages, and sexual history, sources of life satisfaction, achievements, and values.

3. A personality assessment focused on the individual's self-perception, character, method of dealing with crises in the past, interpersonal relations, responses to stress, and nature of previous losses. In a study of younger persons, Kemp and Vash (1971) found that patients' responses to their biggest loss—that is, to their disability—was one of the more important predictors of their adjustment to it.

4. The person's own perception of the rehabilitation process and motivation for improvement.

5. Current family situation, including relations with family members, sources of support, quality of housing, and the presence of other sick or disabled persons.

6. An assessment of the home environment through a visit to determine architectural barriers, nature of neighborhood, how the person functions at home (as opposed to functioning in a hospital), and community resources.

7. Interview of patient's family (if agreeable with the patient) to determine their view of the patient, concerns, and resources.

Psychotherapy

Individual psychotherapy with elderly patients is an effective way of promoting improved functioning and mental health (Butler and Lewis, 1978). Psychotherapy within the context of rehabilitation is not totally different than it is in other situations. Some differences will be noted later. What is most important is that elderly persons have the opportunity to receive it. Psychotherapy for the older rehabilitation patient is more similar to psychotherapy for the younger patient than it is dissimilar, but certain characteristics are worth noting.

Therapy must be considered within the context of the aged person's development and personality as well as the context of the rehabilitation effort (Steger, 1976). The older patient has multiple, interrelated problems that affect his recovery, including biological, psychological, functional, and social ones. The older person has characteristically suffered a large number of losses. Aging has already stripped him or her of income, family, vigor, and prestige. As a result, older people frequently have feelings of impaired self-confidence, helplessness, and lack of purpose. They are frequently less competitive, less achievement-oriented, and less motivated by promises of future rewards. In the face of these multiple losses, they need to maintain adequate defensiveness in order to function. The goal of therapy is not to reduce this defensiveness but to replace it with better alternatives. The older disabled person under stress, such as that which rehabilitation participation creates, may express their emotional turmoil in bodily symptoms (e.g., appetite disturbance, constipation) or in exacerbation of pain. Careful assessment of biological versus emotional causes must be undertaken to produce the proper improvement.

Techniques of psychotherapy must therefore take these contextual and substantive differences into account. Nevertheless, the essence of psychotherapy with older disabled persons is exactly the same as it is for younger and nondisabled persons, namely, the creation of an interpersonal environment comfortable enough and supportive enough to allow patients to experience "how they are" (i.e., their feelings, attitudes, intentions, behavior, etc.) in relation to anything germane to their life and to find the most personally satisfying way of living it. Timing of psychological intervention is critical, especially during the early phases of adjustment (Athelstan, 1981). If the clinician attempts to intervene while the patient is still in the denial phase of adjustment, he may arouse pain and anxiety and destroy a potentially beneficial relationship. Defensiveness is appropriate and necessary to carry the patient through certain phases of adjustment. Encouraging the use of defenses at such times should therefore not be considered negative.

Once patients begin to cope adequately, insight-oriented therapy can become effective. Therapy that allows them to acknowledge the totality of their experience—including their feelings, attitude, goals, and behavior—can help move them from a more or less helpless state to a functioning state. The skilled clinician should not be afraid to bring up topics the older person may not spontaneously discuss, such as death, suicide and sexual needs, if the timing is right. Patients will usually be relieved that it's all right to discuss them and be comforted that someone understands and considers natural their own feelings and concerns.

The topic of death is common among disabled elderly persons. Many of them desire an opportunity to put their life in perspective, to review it, and to reconcile themselves to its course. This train of thought can often be initiated in therapy by asking about early life experiences, people who influenced the patient, or childhood interests. Since older persons are always attempting to adjust to their many losses, the clinician should try to find substitutes for these losses whenever possible, either symbolically or factually. These might include making a firm commitment for patient care, scheduling specific and consistent appointments, taking a personal interest in the patient's life, doing the patient extra favors, and suggesting substitutes for lost relationships (e.g., a pet).

Since the promise of rewards in the future can be of less importance, it is important to do something concrete and utilitarian for older patients by reducing their functional deficits as well as conveying a commitment of concern. Clinicians should not feel it is out of their professional role to help correct an erroneous utility bill or arrange for an appointment for a needed professional service such as social work, physical therapy, or audiology. By taking some kind of action, like starting an exercise regimen or correcting a nutritional deficiency, the older patient's psychological state will often improve as well.

Many authors stress the importance of increased socialization as an important objective for the elderly disabled person (e.g., Steger, 1976; MacBride, Rogers, Whylie, and Freeman, 1980; Wallach, Kelley, and Abrahams, 1979; Woods and Britton, 1977). The reasons for this are two-fold. First, increased socialization is important in its own right because of the social needs it satisfies. Second, socialization provides a reason and incentive for looking and doing one's best. Regardless of age or disability, all people maintain a need for the approval of others. Peer and intergenerational socialization of the elderly substitutes for the work, play, and parental roles of an earlier age. All geriatric rehabilitation programs should therefore include an appropriate group program.

No mode of individual psychotherapy should be overlooked for the elderly. Dream analysis has been found by the author to be equally helpful for young and old alike. (One patient, striving to accept the recent death of her husband and reestablish her life, dreamed of other persons in her past, including a dream of her mother closing a door on her.) Gestalt techniques of integrating bodily symptoms and psychological states have also proven useful both in providing self-insight and alleviating biological distress. Older subjects are also candidates for hypnosis. Many of them make significant gains after a brief period of hypnotic treatment. Biofeedback methods can also benefit the elderly, both in learning how to combat stress and for muscle retraining.

In no other part of psychological practice is it more important for the psychologist to have access to a psychiatrist than in geriatrics. The psychologist cannot and should not substitute for the latter. Problems of organicity, biologically determined mood states, psychosis, drug interactions, and medical-psychiatric interrelations require the services of a *psychiatrist interested in geriatrics*. The intricate interrelationships between biological and psychological factors in the aged are so common that a large part of the disabled elderly population requires such psychiatric evaluation and treatment.

Group Psychotherapy

Group therapeutic approaches are highly desirable for the elderly because they are highly effective (Butler and Lewis, 1978). Group therapy is able to provide several benefits that may not be as readily available in individual therapy. Peer support from those in similar circumstances is valuable for bolstering morale and an understanding of others. Socialization, as already mentioned, helps to maintain healthy functioning. The universality of experiences that people discover in a group helps them realize that others are facing the same kind of problems. Groups also provide a way of imparting information, whether it be about available resources, new services for disabled persons, or psychological insights. Clinical experience indicates that disabled persons of all ages can be successfully gathered together in therapeutic groups. However, grouping disabled and nondisabled persons, as useful as it might appear, is difficult because of the different issues that confront each.

Family Involvement

An important aspect of geriatric rehabilitation is the need to involve the family. Rehabilitation does not take place in the hospital alone but in the home environment as well. It is as much a learning process as a medical process, and the family plays an important role in how well that learning is acquired. Even severely demented older persons can remain in the community as long as they have family support. In working with families, Blazer (1978) recommends that seven important factors be considered:

1. Evaluation of the family for their perceptions of the patient, internal conflicts, resources, and models of communication.
2. Identification of desired and undesired target behaviors for the patient and discovery of any maladaptive behavior.
3. Information for the family about community resources.
4. Explanation of the patient's capabilities and limitations.
5. Specific training on transfers, incontinence, medications, etc.
6. Encouragement of occasional respite care to help give the family relief.
7. Exploration of feelings, conflicts, and ideas that might be helpful in the care of the elderly person.

Johnson and Bursk (1977) found that health status and attitudes toward the older person were the two most crucial factors for a positive relationship between young and old family members. The importance of family assistance in maintaining the health gains of the elderly and keeping them at home rather than in an institution can scarcely be overemphasized.

REFERENCES

Abrahams, J. P.; Wallach, H. F.; and Divens, S. 1979. Behavioral improvement in L.T. geriatric patients during an age-integrated psychosocial rehabilitation program. *J. Am. Geriatrics Soc.* 27: 218–21.

Athelstan, Gary T. 1981. Psychosocial adjustment to chronic disease and disability. In *Handbook of Severe Disabilities*, eds. Walter C. Stolov and Michael R. Clowers. U.S. Dept. of Education, Washington, D.C.

Atkinson, J. W.; Bastian, J. R.; Earl, R. W.; and Litwin, G. H. 1960. The achievement motive, goal setting, and probability preference. *J. Abnormal Soc. Psychol.* 60: 27–36.

Barry, J. R., and Bozarth, J. 1980. Rehabilitation of the aging. *J. Rehab.* 46: 50–51.

Birren, J. E., and Sloane, B. R. 1981. *Handbook of Aging and Mental Health.* Philadelphia: Lippincott.

Blazer, D. 1978. Working with the elderly patient's family. *Geriatrics* 33: 117–23.

Blazer, D. 1982. *Depression in Late Life.* St. Louis, MO: Mosby.

Botwinick, J. 1978. *Aging and Behavior.* New York: Springer.

Brody, S. 1973. Comprehensive health care for the elderly: An analysis. *Gerontologist* 13: 412–18.

Buch, J.; Basavarajv, N.; Charatan, F.; and Kamen, S. 1976. Preventive medicine in a long-term care institution. *Geriatrics* 31: 99–105.

Butler, R. 1967. Aspects of survival and adaptation in human aging. *American J. Psych.* 123: 1233–1243.

Butler, R., and Lewis, M. I. 1978. *Aging and Mental Health.* 2nd ed. St. Louis: C. V. Mosby.

Dzav, R. E., and Boehme, A. R. 1978. Stroke rehabilitation: A family team education program. *Arch. Phys. Med. and Rehab.* 59: 236–239.

Eisdorfer, C. 1981. Care of the aged: The barriers of traditions. *Annals Int. Med.* 94: 256–260.

Erikson, E. H. 1959. Identity and the life cycle. *Psychological Issues* 1: Monograph No. 1.

Feigenson, J. S.; McDowell, F. H.; Meese, P.; McCarthy, M. L.; and Greenberg, S. D. 1977. Factors influencing outcome and length of stay in a stroke rehabilitation unit. Part 1. *Stroke* 8: 651–656.

Feigenson, J. S.; McCarthy, M. L.; Greenberg, S. D.; Feigenson, W. D. 1977. Factors influencing outcome and length of stay in a stroke rehabilitation unit. Part 2. *Stroke* 8: 657–662.

Fordyce, W. 1981. On interdisciplinary peers. *Arch. Phy. Med. and Rehab.* 62: 51–53.

Henriksen, J. D. 1978. Problems in rehabilitation after age sixty-five. *J. American Geriatrics Soc.* 26: 510–512.

Hirschberg, G. G.; Lewis, L.; and Vaughn, P. 1976. *Rehabilitation: A Manual for the Care of the Disabled and Elderly.* Philadelphia: J. B. Lippincott.

Hunt, T. E. 1976. Management of chronic non-rheumatic pain in the elderly. *J. Amer. Geriatrics Soc.* 24: 402–406.

Hunt, T. E. 1977. Rehabilitation of the elderly. *Hospice Practice* 16: 89–97.

Hunt, T. E. 1980. Practical considerations in the rehabilitation of the aged. *J. Amer. Geriatrics Soc.* 28: 59–64.

Johnson, E., and Bursk, B. 1977. Relationships between the elderly and their adult children. *Gerontologist* 17: 70–81.

Kaarlela, R. 1973. Problems of disability for the older American. In *The Neglected Older American,* eds. Cull, J. D. and Hardy, R. E. Springfield, IL: Charles C. Thomas.

Kane, R. L.; Solomon, D. H.; Beck, J. C.; Keeler, E.; and Kane, R. A. 1980. *Geriatrics in the United States: Manpower Projections and Training Considerations.* Santa Monica, CA: Rand Corp.

Kaplan, J., and Ford, C. S. 1975. Rehabilitation for the elderly: An eleven year assessment. *Gerontologist* 15: 393–397.

Kavanagh, T. 1971. Home and outpatient rehabilitation. A two year comparative study. *Canadian Medical Association Journal* 105: 65–69.

Kemp, B. J., and Vash, C. L. 1971. Productivity after injury in a sample of spinal cord injured persons. *J. Chron. Dis.* 27: 337–343.

Kern, Richard A. 1971. Emotional problems in relation to aging and old age. *Geriatrics* 26: 82–93.

King, G.; Vaughn, I. and Clausen, K. 1978. Challenges of geriatric care—new ways to cope. *RN* 41: 47–53.

Kinsey, L. R.; Roberts, J. L.; and Logan, D. L. 1972. Death, dying, and denial in the aged. *Am. J. Psychiatry* 129: 75–80.

Kosberg, J., and Harris, A. 1978. Attitudes toward elderly clients. *Health and Soc. Work* 3: 66–90.

Leeming, J. T., and Luke, A. 1977. Multidisciplinary meetings with relatives of elderly hospital patients in continuing care wards. *Age and Aging* 6: 1–5.

Lipner, J., and Sherman, E. 1975. Hip fractures in the elderly; a psychodynamic approach. *Social Casework* 56: 97–103.

Lopez-Aqueres, W.; Kemp, B.; Plopper, M.; and Staples, F. 1982. Rehabilitation needs, physical health and mental health needs of older Hispanics in Los Angeles County. Unpublished manuscript.

MacBride, A.; Rogers, J.; Whylie, B.; and Freeman, S. 1980. Psychosocial factors in the rehabilitation of elderly amputees. *Psychosomatics* 21: 258–265.

McDaniel, J. 1969. *Physical Disability and Human Behavior.* Elmsford, NY: Pergament Press.

Moore, J. T. 1973. Functional disability of geriatric patients in a family medicine program: Implications for patient care, education, and research. *J. Family Practice* 7: 1159–1166.

National Center for Health Statistics. 1976. Vital Statistics of the United States, vol. II, Part A. Washington, D.C.: U.S. Government Printing Office.

Pegels, Carl C. 1980. *Health Care and the Elderly.* Rockville, MD: Aspen.

Policoff, L. D. 1973. The rehabilitation of the aged disabled. *J. Med. Soc. N.J.* 70: 586–588.

Reed, J. W., and Gessner, J. E. 1979. Rehabilitation in the extended care facility. *J. Amer. Geriatrics Soc.* 27: 325–329.

Reyes, R. L.; Leaher, E. B.; and Leaher, E. B., Jr. 1977. Elderly patients with lower extremity amputations: Three-year study in a rehabilitation setting. *Arch. Phys. Med. Rehabil.* 58: 116–123.

Rusk, H. A. 1973. Dynamic rehabilitation in geriatrics. *Bull. N.Y. Acad. Med.* 49: 1137–1142.

Rusk, H. A., and Lee, M. H. 1971. Rehabilitation of the aging. *Bull. N.Y. Acad. Med.* 47: 1383–1388.

Shanas, E. 1962. The health of older people: A social survey. Cambridge, MA: Harvard University Press.

Sherman, E. D., and Gingras, G. 1965. Rehabilitation of the aged. *Canad. MAJ* 93: 799.

Steger, H. G. 1976. Understanding the psychologic factors in rehabilitation. *Geriatrics* 31: 68–73.

Strax, T., and Ledebur, J. 1979. Rehabilitating the geriatric patient: Potential and limitations. *Geriatrics* 65: 99–101.

Tayback, M.; Krompholz, B.; and Folkemer, D. 1977. Community care of the disabled aged. *Clinical Medicine* 84: 18–24.

Vash, C. 1981. *The Psychology of Disability.* New York: Springer.

Wallach, H. C.; Kelley, F.; and Abrahams, J. 1979. Psychosocial rehabilitation for chronic geriatric patients. An intergenerational approach. *Gerontologist* 19: 464–470.

Wilcock, G. K. 1981. A comparison of total hip replacement in patients aged 69 years or less and 70 years or over. *Gerontology* 27: 85–88.

Williams, T. F.; Hill, J. G.; Fairbank, M. A.; and Knox, K. G. 1973. Appropriate placement of the chronically ill and aged. *J. AMA* 226: 1332–1335.

Woods, R. T., and Britton, P. G. 1977. Psychological approaches to the treatment of the elderly. *Age and Aging* 6: 104–112.

Wright, B. 1956. *The Psychology of Disability.* New York: Wiley.

25
AGING AND MENTAL DISORDERS

Asenath La Rue,* Ph.D.

Connie Dessonville, Ph.D.

Lissy F. Jarvik,* M.D., Ph.D.

Department of Psychiatry and Biobehavioral Sciences, UCLA
* Also, West Los Angeles VA Medical Center, Brentwood Div.

INTRODUCTION

Older people with mental disorders constitute a small but significant subgroup of the aged population. At least 10 percent of them over the age of 65 have emotional or cognitive problems severe enough to warrant professional attention (Birren and Sloane, 1977; U.S. DHEW, 1979), but, for a variety of reasons, a much smaller percentage are actually receiving mental health services (Birren and Sloane, 1977; Gurland and Cross, 1982; Lowenthal, Berkman, and associates, 1967; NIMH, 1978; Redick, Kramer, and Taube, 1973). Traditionally, it has been neither fashionable nor lucrative to work with psychiatrically ill old people, and theory and data to guide such work have been few and far between (cf. Gatz, Smyer, and Lawton, 1980; Guttmann, 1981; Kastenbaum, 1978; Stenmark and Dunn, 1982; Storandt, 1977).

Publication on the topic of aging and mental disorders has expanded significantly since the first edition of this handbook was prepared, and there are several recent texts and edited volumes that review the relevant literature in detail (e.g., Birren and Sloane, 1980; Jarvik and Small, 1982; Zarit, 1980). It is our impression, however, that secondary sources on aging and mental disorders have expanded more

rapidly than basic and clinical research in this area, and we concur with the observation of Stenmark and Dunn (1982, p. 87) that "the simple fact remains that comprehensive and systematic research focusing on the prevalence of psychiatric symptomatology in the latter half of the life span has yet to be done." The same can be said for the assessment and treatment of late-life psychopathology. In addition, exchange of ideas between students of normal and pathological aging has been limited, and even the more recent investigations of the relationships of aging and mental disorders usually fail to incorporate the methodological or theoretical developments that one finds in studies of normal aging.

This chapter presents a selective review of the field, examining evidence for and against an age-stratified conceptualization of mental disorders. It is restricted to studies of prevalence, diagnosis, and hypothesized etiologic factors. As a backdrop, it is important to note that in the classification scheme of DSM-III (Diagnostic and Statistical Manual of the American Psychiatric Association, 1982), a clear distinction is made between disorders arising in infancy, childhood, or adolescence and those that normally begin in adulthood. By contrast, there is little reference to aging or the aged except for separate classification codes for "dementias arising in the senium." In this and most other diagnostic systems, it appears that continuity is assumed between adulthood and old age in the nature and manifestation of mental disorders. We are a long way from refuting that assumption, although some intriguing age differences have been reported.

Most of what we know about aging and mental disorders comes from one of two sources: (1) investigations in which the sample is limited to old people, but findings are interpreted with reference to previous studies of younger adults; and (2) cross-sectional studies comparing two or more age groups—e.g., young vs. old or "young-old" vs. "old-old." There have been very few longitudinal studies of the development of psychiatric conditions through the latter half of the life span, and no cohort- or cross-sequential investigations. By and large, then, the data pertain to age differences, rather than age changes, and it is impossible at present to disentangle "true" age effects from cohort and time-of-measurement influences.

On the level of age differences, however, three general but important observations have been made. The first concerns the distribution of different types of mental disorder at different points in adult life. There are some conditions (e.g., Alzheimer type dementia, and possibly, the late-onset paranoid disorder termed *paraphrenia* by British geriatricians) that occur almost exclusively in old age. By contrast, schizophrenia and mania rarely begin late in life (cf. Post, 1976). Figure 1 summarizes data on first admissions to state and county mental hospitals in the United States for various psychiatric disorders as a function of age. Although alcoholism and schizophrenia are the mental disorders with the highest incidence among young and middle-aged adults—accounting for roughly 40 to 50 percent of all mental illness between age 25 and 45 compared to less than 4 percent for "brain syndromes"—they become so infrequent by age 75 that, together with all mental disorders other than brain syndromes, they are reported to account for only 15 percent of first admissions of older adults. Figure 1 also illustrates that the rates of brain syndromes double for

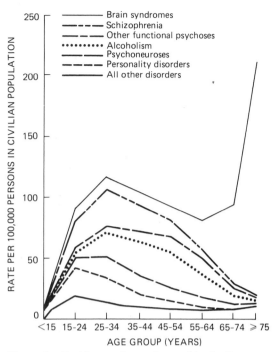

Figure 1.   Incidence of organic psychiatric disorders as determined by first-admission rates (From Kramer, M. 1969. *Application of mental health statistics.* Geneva: WHO.

the last decade, from 100 per 100,000 at age 65 to over 200 at age 75 and above. Caution is advised in interpreting these data, as differences in diagnostic styles may be as important as differences in true incidence in creating age associated discrepancies. Nonetheless, there is little doubt that certain types of organic mental disorder occur with disproportionate frequency in old age. The striking difference in the distributions for young adult and aged groups certainly has practical implications in terms of the facilities and programs required for different age groups. The disparity in distributions also bears on the theoretical issue of qualitative change in the organization of behavior with advancing age (cf. Baltes and Willis, 1977; Overton and Reese, 1973). It may be appropriate, for example, to conceptualize new "aging syndromes" (e.g., depressive pseudodementia), even if they are poorly defined and researched at the present time.

A second, and related, observation is that older people perform differently than young or middle-aged adults do on virtually all psychodiagnostic instruments; this is true of personality and mood scales as well as tests of cognitive function (see Chap. 27 in this volume by Zarit, Eiler, and Hassinger; see also Albert, 1981; Kramer and Jarvik, 1979; Lawton, Whelihan, and Belsky, 1980; Miller, 1980; Schaie and Schaie, 1977; Storandt, Siegler, and Elias, 1978). This observation raises the question as to whether specific disorders may be over- or underdiagnosed in the aged relative to the young and has led to a wave of studies attempting to "recalibrate" existing assessment instruments for use with older people. The lack of appropriate age norms for psychodiagnostic instruments creates a "catch 22" vis-a-vis estimates of the prevalence of mental disorders; that is, if we are not sure how to diagnose a particular disorder in older people, how can we estimate its frequency? The issue of age norms is probably most significant for diagnosing disorders of mild severity and may account, at least in part, for the fact that we are unable to distinguish between early forms of dementia and the mental changes normally expected in old age which Kral (1978) has termed benign senescent forgetfulness. Clearly, assessment problems contribute to current confusion about the presence or absence of age differences in mental disorders.

A third general observation concerns age differences in risk factors associated with mental illness. Sensory deficits, physical illness, poverty, bereavement, and social or geographic isolation are all more common among the old than the young. High rates of physical or psychosocial disability may inflate the prevalence of certain conditions—e.g., adjustment disorders or mild depression—in aged samples. It is not clear how these risk factors contribute to other, more serious, disorders—e.g., major depression or various forms of dementia. There may well be explanatory discontinuity (cf. Baltes and Willis, 1977) in the manner in which antecedent conditions combine to produce mental disorders at different points in the life span. For example, Post (1976), Jarvik and Perl (1981), Verwoerdt (1981), and others maintain that there is a particularly close association between physical and psychiatric disorders in the aged; however, the nature of this interaction, and how it differs from that observed in younger age groups, has not

been adequately researched. At this point we assume that base rates of risk factors differ as a function of age, but we know neither how the risk factors affect development of mental disorders in older people, nor whether they have a differential effect upon the old as compared to younger adults.

Each of these observations—possible age-related discontinuity in distributions of mental disorder, lack of appropriately normed assessment techniques, and age differences in potential risk factors—will be re-examined below when specific disorders are discussed. Taking the overview, however, a peculiarly developmental dilemma becomes apparent throughout this literature. A portion of the research can be construed as attempting to demonstrate qualitative age differences. Definition and documentation of syndromes unique to the elderly fall in this category, as do discussions of special, age-linked expressions of common disorders such as depression. The remainder of the research seems to proceed from the assumption that the behavior of older adults is quantitatively different, but qualitatively similar, to that of younger people, and that similar disorders are likely to be observed throughout adulthood, provided only that we apply the proper, age-normed, assessment techniques. As indicated subsequently, evidence for uniqueness of mental disorders in the aged varies for different conditions.

SPECIFIC MENTAL DISORDERS IN THE AGED

Depression

Depression is one of the most common, and most treatable, of the psychiatric disorders affecting the elderly. Estimates of its prevalence vary widely (cf. Blazer and Williams, 1980; Gerner, 1979; Gurland and Cross, 1982), reflecting differences in sample characteristics (varying age cohorts and nationalities, community vs. patient samples), methods of assessment (self-report, observer ratings, or clinical evaluation), and most important, criteria for case identification (see Gurland, 1976, for a discussion). Some community surveys have reported depressive symptoms in as many as

TABLE 1 Diagnostic Criteria for Major Depressive Episodes

(From *Diagnostic and Statistical Manual of Mental Disorders.* 1980. Edition 3, pp. 213–214. Washington, D.C.: American Psychiatric Association. With permission.)

A. Dysphoric mood or loss of interest or pleasure in all or almost all usual activities and pastimes. The dysphoric mood is characterized by symptoms such as described by the adjectives "depressed," "sad," "blue," "hopeless," "low," "down in the dumps." "irritable." The mood disturbance must be prominent and relatively persistent, if not necessarily the most dominant symptom, and does not include momentary shifts from one dysphoric mood to another dysphoric mood—e.g., anxiety to depression to anger—such as are seen in states of acute psychotic turmoil. (For children under six, a dysphoric mood may have to be inferred from a persistently sad facial expression.)

B. At least four of the following symptoms have each been present nearly every day for a period of at least two weeks (in children under six, at least three of the first four):
   (1) Poor appetite or significant weight loss (when not dieting) or increased appetite or significant weight gain; in children under six, consider failure to make expected weight gains
   (2) Insomnia or hypersomnia
   (3) Psychomotor agitation or retardation (but not merely subjective feelings of restlessness or being slowed down); in children under six, hypoactivity
   (4) Loss of interest or pleasure in usual activities or decrease in sexual drive not limited to a period when delusional or hallucinating; in children under six; signs of apathy
   (5) Loss of energy; fatigue
   (6) Feelings of worthlessness, self-reproach, or excessive or inappropriate guilt (either may be delusional)
   (7) Complaints or evidence of diminished ability to think or concentrate, such as slowed thinking, or indecisiveness not associated with marked loosening of associations or incoherence
   (8) Recurrent thoughts of death, suicidal ideation, wishes to be dead, or suicide attempt

C. Neither of the following dominates the clinical picture when an affective syndrome is absent (i.e., symptoms in criteria A and B above):
   (1) Preoccupation with a mood-incongruent delusion or hallucination
   (2) bizarre behavior

D. Not superimposed on either schizophrenia, schizophreniform disorder, or a paranoid disorder

E. Not due to any organic mental disorder or uncomplicated bereavement

30 to 65 percent of persons over 60 (Dovenmuehle, Recklass, and Newman, 1970; Pfeiffer and Busse, 1973; Raymond, Michals and Steer, 1980; Zung, 1967). By contrast, the full sympton complex of major depression, as defined by DSM-III (see Table 1), may be present in only 2 to 6 percent (Blazer and Williams, 1980; Gurland and Cross, 1982; Weissman and Myers, 1978). Depressions severe enough to warrant intervention are generally estimated to affect 10 to 15 percent of the geriatric population (Gurland and Cross, 1982; Post, 1976). Frequencies of both mild and severe depressions are generally reported to be higher for women than men (e.g., Weissman and Klerman, 1977), although this trend may be reversed in persons over the age of 80 (Gurland, Dean, Cross, and Golden, 1980).

Affective disorders are estimated to account for nearly half of the admissions of older adults to acute-care psychiatric hospitals in the U.S. (Gurland and Cross, 1982; Myers, Sheldon, and Robinson, 1963; Redick and Taube, 1980). A significant proportion of these cases—perhaps as high as 50 percent, judging from earlier British studies (e.g., Roth and Kay, 1956)—are first admissions. Unipolar depressions are much more common than bipolar illness among elderly patients (Post, 1978). In fact, the onset of manic-depressive illness after the age of 65 is rare (Jamison, 1979), although some cases of late-onset mania have been reported (Shulman and Post, 1980).

Depressive illness appears to affect older individuals in much the same way as younger ones, and although the same range of treatments (e.g. psychotherapy, drugs, ECT) is appropriate regardless of age, we are just beginning to learn about age-associated differences in response. Aging has also been hypothesized to affect both the pattern of depressive symptoms and the elderly individual's susceptibility to depression.

Symptoms of Depression in the Aged

Major depressive episodes are defined in DSM-III by the presence of persistent dysphoric mood or loss of interest in almost all usual activities, and at least four of the following associated symptoms: appetite or weight loss; sleep disturbance; psychomotor retardation or agitation; loss of interest or pleasure in activities; feelings of worthlessness, guilt, or self-reproach; cognitive complaints; suicidal ideation or behavior (see Table 1). If the symptoms are severe and disabling, a diagnosis of *Major Depression* (296.xx) is made; a less pronounced but relatively chronic pattern of depressive symptoms is denoted as *Dysthymic Disorder* (300.40). *Bipolar Disorder* (296.xx) is diagnosed when there is evidence in the individual's history of both clear-cut manic and depressive episodes, whereas the category of *Cyclothymic Disorder* (301.13) applies when the mood swings and concomitant symptoms appear to have been less severe. The categories of *Atypical Bipolar Disorder* (296.70) and *Atypical Depression* (296.82) are reserved for cases of suspected affective disorder that fail, at a given point in time, to meet the full set of criteria for the more clearly delineated disorders previously denoted. Other diagnoses in which depressive symptoms are prominent include *Adjustment Disorder with Depressed Mood* (309.00), *Uncomplicated Bereavement* (v62.82), and *Dementia with Depression* (290.21).

One of the "aging issues" vis-a-vis diagnosis of depression centers on the concern that older persons without mental disorder may exhibit symptoms of depression—particularly, somatic or cognitive complaints—because of physical illness or normal aging changes (Gaitz, 1977; Raskin, 1979). Attention to these symptoms could sometimes lead to overdiagnosis of depression and unnecessary or inappropriate treatment. Alternatively, cases of "true" depression could go unnoticed because clinicians may assume that fatigue, sleep problems, or memory complaints are a natural consequence of aging.

Several studies have indicated that the normal vs. depressed distinction may indeed be more difficult to draw in elderly populations than in younger ones, particularly if self-report measures are used. Zung (1967) found that 40 percent of the community-resident elderly studied by him scored in the depressed range on his Self-Rating Depression Scale relative to the range cut-offs established for this instrument with younger adults. Gaitz and Scott (1972), and Schwab, Holzer, and Warheit (1973) also reported higher frequencies of depressive symptoms (particularly somatic ones) among elderly than younger normals.

Nonetheless, marked differences between clinically depressed samples and normal elderly groups are clearly demonstrable by comparing scores on depression rating scales. Dessonville, Gallagher, Thompson, Finnell, and Lewinsohn (1982) compared elderly (aged 55 to 91 years) normals and outpatients with major depressive disorder on five summary scales of the Schedule for Affective Disorders and Schizophrenia (or SADS; see Endicott and Spitzer, 1978). Highly significant differences were observed on each scale (Depressive Mood and Ideation, Endogenous Features, Depressive Associated Features, Suicidal Ideation and Behavior, and Anxiety). Moreover, even for the normal elderly subgroup most likely to be mislabeled as depressed—i.e., "old-old," unhealthy individuals—mean scores on each scale differed by at least one standard deviation from those obtained for younger, physically healthy, depressed individuals. In a five-institution collaborative study, Raskin and Rae (1981) also found clear differences between elderly normals and elderly depressed patients in terms of observer ratings, relatives' ratings, and self-reports of psychiatric symptomatology. In a separate analysis, Raskin and Rae (1981) reported that cognitive complaints were markedly higher among the elderly depressed patients relative to the elderly normals (52 percent of the depressed sample and 13 percent of the normal group reported at least occasional problems with memory).

There is substantial circularity in contrasting depressed patient samples with presumably normal controls using scores on symptom rating scales as a basis, since the symptoms that constitute such scales are essentially the same ones used in making the clinical diagnosis. Results of such studies do indicate however, that older adults who seek treatment for depression and are diagnosed clinically as major depressives differ substantially in affective, cognitive, and somatic symptomatology from older adults not in treatment. Conversely, the risk of older persons being diagnosed as clinically depressed merely because of their advanced age or physical health problems is quite low.

The opposite concern, that depression may actually be "underdiagnosed" in the elderly, has also been expressed in the literature. Reference has repeatedly been made to the possibility that "masked depressions," where dysphoric affect is minimal and somatic complaints predominant, may be more common among the aged than in other populations (e.g., Gerner, 1979; Lehmann, 1982; Goldfarb, 1975; Epstein, 1976; Lesse, 1974; Pichot and Hassan, 1974). Theoretically, there is a good possibility that "masked depression" is more common among the aged since there is an increase in the occurrence of physical illness with increasing age. All can recall clinical examples of patients' denying any dysphoric affect, complaining of somatic symptoms only. Nevertheless, there is little systematic information about the prevalence of these conditions or their response to treatment, and the conceptual and empirical status of "masked depressions" remains unclear.

Differential diagnosis of depression and dementia is another topic that has received a great deal of attention in the geropsychiatry literature. Although it has long been observed that cognitive impairment may occur in conjunction with a variety of "functional" disorders (e.g., hysterical neurosis, schizophrenia) in patients of all ages, the syndrome of "depressive pseudodementia" first described two decades ago (Kiloh, 1961) has gained increasing attention (cf. DSM-III, pp. 111 and 212).

There have been a sufficient number of case examples (cf. Kiloh, 1961; Post, 1975; Folstein and McHugh, 1978; and more recently, McAllister and Price, 1982) to substantiate that elderly individuals may present major cognitive deficits that later remit spontaneously or im-

prove with treatment for depression. Follow-up studies that indicate that 30 percent or more of "dementia" cases may be misdiagnosed (Ron, Toone, Garralda, and Lishman, 1979; Marsden and Harrison, 1972; Nott and Fleminger, 1975) also underscore the need to consider depressive pseudodementia (and other potentially treatable conditions; c.f. Task Force Report, 1980) as a cause of cognitive impairment.

However, pseudodementia, like masked depression, is so poorly defined and unsystematically studied that its prevalence, etiology, pathogenesis, and prognosis remain largely unknown. In practice, all definitive cases of pseudodementia are identified retrospectively; i.e., if an individual's cognitive deficits improve with antidepressant medication, ECT, psychotherapy, or the passage of time, then it is inferred that the initial symptoms represented a pseudodementia rather than a true dementia. The number of individuals with similar symptoms that worsen or fail to respond to treatment is typically not specified. The clinical recommendation in suspected cases of depressive pseudodementia is usually "When in doubt, treat," a recommendation intended to counteract the therapeutic passivity that has characterized work with the aged but one that could possibly engender further, iatrogenic disability (e.g., drug-related falls and fractures).

Of the various attempts to delineate the clinical features of pseudodementia (Kiloh, 1961; Post, 1975; Wells, 1979), the list proposed by Wells, summarized in Table 2, is representative. Clinicians familiar with elderly patients will recognize that none of the distinguishing features listed in this table is invariant; indeed, some have been contradicted in print (e.g., Whitehead, 1973, reported equally common rates of "don't know" answers on memory tests for both demented and depressed subjects). Moreover, the number and pattern of features necessary for diagnostic distinction remains unspecified. Thus, although these clinical criteria are undoubtedly capable of distinguishing groups of depressed from groups of demented patients, their validity in individual cases needs to be established.

There have been other attempts to differen-

TABLE 2   Clinical Features of Pseudodementia and True Dementia

(Adapted from Wells, C. E. 1980. The differential diagnosis of psychiatric disorders in the elderly. In *Psychopathology in the Aged,* eds. J. O. Cole and J. E. Barrett. New York: Raven Press.)

	Pseudodementia	Dementia
Duration of symptoms before physician consulted	Short	Long
Onset can be dated with some precision	Usual	Unusual
Family aware of dysfunction and severity	Usual	Variable* (rare in early stages; usual in late stages)
Rapid progression of symptoms	Usual	Unusual
History of prior psychopathology	Usual	Unusual
Patient's complaints of cognitive loss	Emphasized	Variable* (minimized in later stages)
Patient's description of cognitive loss	Detailed	Vague
Patient's disability	Emphasized	Variable* (concealed in later stages)
Patient's valuation of accomplishments	Minimized	Variable*
Patient's efforts in attempting to perform tasks	Small	Great
Patient's efforts to cope with dysfunction	Minimal	Maximal
Patient's emotional reaction	Great distress	Variable (unconcerned in later stages)
Patient's affect	Depressed	Labile, blunted, or depressed
Loss of social skills	Early	Late
Behavior congruent with severity of cognitive loss	Unusual	Usual
Attention and concentration	Often good	Often poor
"Don't know" answers	Usual	Unusual
"Near miss" answers	Unusual	Variable† (usual in later stages)
Memory loss for recent versus remote events	About equal	Greater
Specific memory gaps ("patchy memory loss")	Usual	Unusual
Performance on tasks of similar difficulty	Variable	Consistent

*Wells lists the characteristics of the later states. In our clinical experience, these manifestations are variable early in the course of dementia and are helpful in the differential diagnosis only if they are in the direction seen in later stages of dementia.

tiate depression-related cognitive deficits from those caused by dementia on the basis of mental status questionnaires and psychological testing. As would be expected, elderly patients diagnosed as demented usually score much lower than those diagnosed as depressed on most commonly used psychometric and neuropsychological tests (e.g., Bolton, Savage, and Roth, 1967; Hilbert, Niederehe, and Kahn, 1976; Inglis, 1959; Irving, Robinson, and McAdam, 1970; Kahn, Zarit, Hilbert, and Niederehe, 1975; Kendrick and Post, 1967; Kendrick, Parboosingh, and Post, 1965; Miller and Lewis, 1977; Roth and Hopkins, 1953, Whitehead, 1973). For all that, the depressed patients may actually complain more of cognitive losses than patients with dementia, a distinction that may in itself be clinically useful (Kahn et al., 1975; Raskin and Rae, 1981), Nevertheless, distributions of psychological test scores for depressed and demented samples certainly show overlap, and classifications based on quantitative cutting scores will invariably misidentify some depressed patients as demented.

An alternative but complementary use of psychological test data involves the examination of qualitative features of performance, such as the nature and distribution of errors or sensitivity to various forms of cueing. The recent work of Weingartner and his associates (see Weingartner and Silberman, 1982, for a review) exemplifies this approach. Analyzing data from a number of learning and memory tasks, these investigators suggest that the cognitive failures in depression are qualitatively different from those associated with progressive dementia. In particular, they postulate that depressed patients retain the ability to use organizational or semantic properties of events as a basis for encoding and retrieving information, whereas demented patients do not. As a result, although both depressed and demented patients might have problems learning a list of random words, their performance could be expected to diverge on the learning of categorized lists (depressed patients improving; demented patients staying the same). Other distinctive features noted in the literature on depression include conservative or cautious response criteria by depressed patients (Miller and Lewis, 1977), a relatively high rate of omission orrors with a low rate of random or confabulatory errors (Whitehead, 1973), underestimation of ability, and preoccupation with negative feedback (Miller, 1975; Weingartner and Silberman, 1982).

None of these observations has been validated by means of prospective studies, and pseudodementia is likely to remain a diagnostic gray area until such validation occurs. As a scientific construct, pseudodementia may well prove useless since it is possible that when the cognitive concomitants of depression are more widely recognized and better understood, it may no longer be necessary to posit a specific "depressive pseudodementia" syndrome. Alternatively, elderly people whose depression manifests itself primarily as a cognitive disturbance could prove to have a different illness than those for whom dysphoria or somatic complaints are the most prominent symptoms. At present, the main value of the construct of pseudodementia is its role in consciousness-raising, encouraging practitioners to look before they leap in making the diagnosis of dementia (cf. Small and Jarvik, 1982).

The frustration engendered by ambiguous, behavioral diagnostic criteria has led to attempts to identify biological markers of different psychiatric disorders, including depression. Carroll and his associates (Carroll, Feinberg, Greden, Tarika, Albala, Haskett, James, Kronfal, Lohr, Steiner, de Vigne, and Young, 1981) have promoted the use of the dexamethasone suppression test (DST) as a means of identifying a subgroup of "endogenous" depressives particularly responsive to somatic therapies (Brown, Johnston, and Mayfield, 1979; Brown and Shuey, 1980). This test is performed by administering 1 milligram of dexamethasone orally at 11:30 P.M. and measuring serum cortisol at 4 P.M. and 11

P.M. the next day. In normals, dexamethasone suppresses plasma cortisol levels for over 24 hours; "endogenous" depressives, however, exhibit an early escape from suppression and produce greater plasma cortisol levels approximately 24 hours following ingestion of the dexamethasone than do normal individuals. Accordingly, a cortisol level of 0.5 mg/ml is considered diagnostic of depression, if confounding medical and drug factors are avoided. [For example, major medical illnesses, such as uncontrolled diabetes, and certain drugs, such as barbiturates, can produce abnormal DST responses (Carroll et al., 1981).] The diagnostic utility of the DST with elderly patients is an open question. According to one study, young and elderly men exhibit similar plasma cortisol responses to dexamethasone (Tourigny-Rivard, Raskind, and Rivard, 1981). Other preliminary findings however, suggest that as many as 50 percent of dementia patients without any symptoms of depression may also have a positive DST (Spar and Gerner, 1982; Raskind, Peskind, Rivard, Veith, and Barnes, 1982). Moreover, elderly nonsuppressors may actually be less responsive to somatic therapy than elderly suppressors (Spar and La Rue, 1983), a finding that differs from the greater response rates expected in younger nonsuppressors as opposed to younger suppressors.

Nonetheless, it would be difficult at present to justify a change in diagnostic criteria for depression specifically geared for the aged. Normal older persons do have unusually high rates of some depressive symptoms (e.g., sleep disturbance), but the likelihood that major depression is currently being overdiagnosed does not appear great. Although the risk of underdiagnosis may be more significant, this remains unknown in the absence of data on the incidence and prevalence of "masked depression" and "pseudodementia," the two forms of atypical depression cited most frequently in the clinical research literature.

Correlates of Depression in the Aged

Central Nervous System Function. Several theories of depression have been proposed that attribute the occurrence of depressive symptoms to inadequate availability of specific neurotransmitter substances (e.g., catecholamines and indoleamines) or more generalized neurotransmitters imbalance (e.g., Akiskal and McKinney, 1973; Maas, 1978; Schildkraut and Kety, 1967). Since age differences have been observed in a number of neurotransmitter systems (cf. McGeer and McGeer, 1976; Lipton and Nemeroff, 1978), there has been considerable speculation about the etiologic connection between biogenic amines and depression in the aged. It is clear that depressive symptoms in the elderly are often drug responsive (cf. Gerner, 1979; Gerner and Jarvik, in press; Jarvik, Mintz, Steuer, and Gerner, 1982; Gerner, Estabrook, Steuer, Waltuch, Kakkar, and Jarvik, 1980) but there are too few controlled investigations as yet to link individual differences in responsiveness to neurotransmitter function.

Neurobehavioral models of depression have also been proposed, most of them emphasizing the role of the nondominant hemisphere (see Weingartner and Silberman, 1982, for a review). Impairments of right-hemisphere functions have been observed in neuropsychological tests of depressives (Flor-Henry, 1979; Goldstein, Filskow, Weaver, and Ives, 1977), as have lateralized EEG abnormalities (Davidson, Schwartz, Saron, Bennett, and Goleman, 1979). The number of studies reporting such findings is still small, and age differences have not been investigated. Pronounced age-related differences on visuoperceptual and visuospatial tasks have been described, however, leading to the suggestion of a parallel between aging and nondominant hemisphere disease (e.g., Klisz, 1978). The combined effects of depression and aging on dominant vs. nondominant hemisphere function may be a worthwhile area of study.

Physical Health. There appears to be a strong correlation between physical illness and depression in the aged (Jarvik and Perl, 1981). Evidence for this relationship comes from community surveys as well as from studies of hospitalized patients. In their recent survey of over 900 people aged 65 and above from the OARS-Durham sample, Blazer and Williams (1980) found that 44 percent of the respondents with depressive symptoms (DSM-III criteria) were medically ill. Studies of morale or life satisfaction also emphasize the importance of health status as a correlate of a sense of well-being (Lowenthal and Haven, 1968; Morgan, 1976).

In an early study of hospitalized patients, Roth and Kay (1956) examined rates and types of illness in 231 men and women over the age of 60 who had been admitted to an inpatient psychiatric service as a result of "a manic or depressive symptom complex." Slightly more than half ($n = 120$) had been previously hospitalized for similar conditions (early-onset cases), but for the remainder, this was the first psychiatric admission (late-onset cases). Illness was prevalent throughout the sample, but more so among men than women, and among late-onset as opposed to early-onset cases. Fifty percent of the men with recurrent affective disorder had significant medical conditions, compared to 71 percent with late-onset depression or mania; among women, the corresponding rates of medical illness were 42 and 65 percent for early- and late-onset cases, respectively. Men who become severely depressed for the first time after age 60 were particularly likely to have undergone operations shortly before their psychiatric admission, had unusually high rates of chronic illness (especially cardiovascular and urogenital conditions), and were more likely than the other patients to suffer from multiple medical conditions.

In discussing their findings, Roth and Kay (1956) noted that illness could not be considered the sole etiologic factor in late-onset affective disorder, since in a fair proportion of the cases (29 percent of the men and 35 percent of the women), there was no evidence of medical illness or sensory impairment and since the psychiatric and medical symptoms often failed to follow a parallel course. Nonetheless, physical or sensory disability was judged to be an important contributing factor, particularly in men who had avoided affective disorder until old age.

There are several reasons why physical illness and depression might occur together (see Jarvik, in press; Jarvik and Perl, 1981; Ouslander, 1982; Verwoerdt, 1976). Feelings of sadness, anxiety, or fatigue are to be expected in response to awareness of illness or in reaction to pain or disability; in some cases, these reactions become protracted or severe enough to constitute a depression. Symptoms of depression may also be a direct consequence of illness (see Table 3) or a side effect of medications (see Table 4). Finally, longitudinal and retrospective studies (Vaillant, 1979; Wigdor and Morris, 1977) have pointed out that individuals who are depressed may be predisposed to develop physical illness, so that often a cycle of physical and emotional illness becomes established.

Given the current state of knowledge in this area, disentangling cause and effect is difficult whenever psychiatric and physical illness coexist. Future research that incorporates detailed time series analyses of the affective and somatic symptoms of individual hospitalized patients would help to address this issue. In addition, the application of statistical techniques, such as path analysis to data from larger samples of medically ill elderly patients, would be elucidating.

Bereavement.   Like physical illness, bereavement is a disproportionately common occurrence among the elderly; 51.0 percent of women, and 13.6 percent of men over the age of 65 have been widowed at least once (U.S. Bureau of the Census, 1981). Several studies have documented increased morbidity and mortality among widows and widowers (see reviews by Jacobs and Ostfeld, 1977; Clayton, 1973), and bereavement has been reported to be a common precipitating factor among elderly patients hospitalized for depression (Turner and Sternberg, 1978). However, longitudinal investigations of widows and widowers (Clayton, Halikas, and Maurice, 1972; Bornstein, Clayton, Halikas, Maurice, and Robins, 1973) have reported relatively low overall rates of clinical depression (33 percent at one month following spousal death and 13 percent at one year). The same investigations indicate that symptoms of depression in bereaved individuals are usually fewer and less severe than those in persons hospitalized for depression. Similarly, in a recent study comparing elderly widows, depressed outpatients, and normal

TABLE 3   Disorders that Cause Depression

(From Lehmann, H. E. 1982. Affective disorders in the aged. *Psychiatric Clinics of North America* 5:33.)

Disorder	Examples
Neoplasm	Carcinomatosis, cancer of the pancreas, primary cerebral tumor, cerebral metastasis
Infection	Tuberculosis, subacute bacterial endocarditis, neurosyphilis, hepatitis, encephalitis, post-encephalitic states
Cardiovascular disease	Post-myocardial infarction, congestive heart failure
Metabolic disorders	Hyperthyroidism, hypothyroidism, hyperparathyroidism, Cushing's disease, Addison's disease, hyponatremia, hypokalemia, pernicious anemia, severe anemia (any cause), protein deficiency, avitaminosis (especially vitamin B deficiencies), diabetes, uremia, hepatic disease, Wilson's disease
Degenerative disease	Parkinson's disease, Huntington's disease, primary degenerative dementia
Miscellaneous conditions	Pancreatitis, collagen vascular disorders, chronic subdural hematoma
Drug effects	Neuroleptics, barbiturates, meprobamate, benzodiazepines, alcohol, steroids, L-dopa, digitalis, methyldopa, reserpine, propranolol, hydralazine, guanethidine, clonidine

TABLE 4 Psychiatric Symptoms Caused by Drugs Used to Treat Medical Conditions

(From Ouslander, J. G. 1982. Illness and psychopathology in the elderly. *Psychiatric Clinics of North America* 5:155.)

Drug	Symptom
Antihypertensives Reserpine Methyldopa Propranolol Clonidine Hydralazine Guanethidine Diuretics	Sedation, fatigue, depression, constipation, weakness, confusion
Analgesics	

Narcotic
  Morphine
  Codeine
  Meperidine
  Pentazocine
  Propoxyphene
	Sedation, constipation, confusion, hallucinations, withdrawal

Non-narcotic Indomethacia	Headache, dizziness, confusion, depression
Antiparkinsonian L-dopa Carbidopa Bromocriptine Trihexyphenidyl	Confusion, hallucinations, depression
Antihistamines Dipheniramine Hydroxyzine	Sedation, anxiety, confusion, delirium
Antimicrobials Gentamicin Isoniazid	Psychosis, depression, agitation, hallucinations, memory disturbance
Cardiovascular Digitalis* Lidocaine* Atropine	Fatigue, psychosis, irritability, confusion
Hypoglycemics† Insulin Sulfonylureas (Tolinase, Diabinese)	Anxiety, irritability, confusion, lethargy
Steroids Glucocorticoids Estrogen	Lability, euphoria, mania, depression, psychosis
Others Cimetidine	Confusion
Cancer chemotherapeutic agents	Somnolence, apathy, lethargy
Laxatives	Habituation, withdrawal, irritability, insomnia, confusion

*Symptoms are noted with toxic levels of this drug.
†The use of hypoglycemics may result in psychiatric symptoms by causing hypoglycemia.

controls on the Beck Depression Inventory, bereaved individuals had significantly lower total scores than depressed patients and were less likely to endorse self-deprecatory items (Gallagher, Breckenridge, Thompson, Dessonville, and Amaral, 1982).

Based on this limited set of investigations, it appears that bereavement reactions in the aged can often be differentiated from major depression, provided that careful attention is paid to the severity and pattern of depressive symptoms. Relatively few older people appear to develop protracted and disabling depressive illness following age-appropriate loss of loved ones.

Isolation.   Depressed people often complain of loneliness and social or emotional isolation. Social support may act as a buffer against depressive reactions in response to loss (Warheit, 1979). Nonetheless, isolation is not strongly associated with an increased frequency of severe depression in the elderly (Bennett and Cook, 1980; de Alarcon, 1971). With milder depressions, it may be a stronger contributing factor since correlations between frequency of social interactions and measures of morale or life satisfaction have been noted in a number of studies (Lowenthal and Haven, 1968; Lemon, Bengtson, and Peterson, 1972). In most cases, the important variable appears to be the availability of close personal relationships, especially of confidants, rather than social contact per se. The direction of cause and effect is unclear in most of these studies, and low morale cannot be equated with depression, although research suggests that they are significantly related (Morris, 1975; Gilleard, Willmott, and Vaddadi, 1981). At present, it seems reasonable to assume that involuntary separations from significant others may be contributory to the high rates of mild depression observed among older people.

Retirement and Relocation.   Although it has commonly been assumed that retirement is associated with adverse outcomes for the retiree, research in the area of retirement usually does not support this assumption. Atchley (1980) notes that men of retirement age do not exhibit increased rates of depression and suicide, and most retirees adjust to retirement with little trauma (George, 1980). Nonetheless, several studies (Palmore, Cleveland, Nowlin, Ramm, and Siegler, 1979; Thompson, 1973; Streib, 1956) found that retirement is related to decreased life satisfaction and lower morale. These negative outcomes may be explained in part, however, by factors other than retirement, such as the retiree's health status and income.

Relocation to a different residential setting has also often been thought to contribute to depression in the elderly. Several studies of involuntary relocation (Kasteler, Gray, and Carruth, 1968; Brand and Smith, 1974; Kasl, Ostfeld, Brody, Snell, and Price, 1980) have found lower life satisfaction following forced relocation. However, the relationship between residential change and adjustment is a complex one, being influenced by many variables such as the desirability of the move, the nature and quality of the residential setting, the degree of disruption of the individual's social network, and other factors, such as declining physical health, that may have precipitated the individual's need to relocate in the first place (Kasl and Rosenfield, 1980).

Summary

In the absence of adequate data, the idea that depression may develop in the elderly in reaction to age-related stresses and losses is generally given considerable support by researchers and reviewers. According to Blazer and Williams (1980, p. 442), for example, "Much of what is called 'depression' in the elderly may actually represent decreased life satisfaction and periodic episodes of grief secondary to the physical, social, and economic difficulties encountered by aging individuals. . . ." Lehmann (1982, p. 29) makes the same observation in more dramatic terms: "Aging may be regarded as an ongoing process of increasing entropy or a continuous chain of losses. Since depression is the normal reaction to any significant loss, the aging individual seems to be prone, in a tragic existential scenario, to become easy prey to depression." As previously indicated, however, only a small minority of older people are clinically depressed, and adaptation, rather than decompensation, appears to be the modal reaction to any single loss such as bereavement or retirement.

It would be helpful if future investigations would make clear the distinctions between clinical depression (DSM-III diagnoses) and existential sadness, between mild and severe depressions, and between recurrent and late-onset depressions. It is not clear whether mild and severe depressive states represent variants of the same illness; each may have a different set of causes and may respond to different treatments. Similarly, individuals who become depressed for the first time in old age may differ in important ways from those who have recurrent depressive illness. British geriatricians have searched for differences along these lines more carefully than American investigators (e.g., Roth and Kay, 1956; Post, 1972), and it is fair to say that the findings have been equivocal to date. These questions are crucial ones for a life-span model of depression, however, and more extensive study is warranted.

Dementia

The prevalence of organic mental disorders in the aged has been estimated at approximately 5 percent if moderate to severe conditions are taken into account and at 15 percent if mild disorders are included (Gurland and Cross, 1982; Katzman, 1976; Terry and Davies, 1980). Prevalence and incidence are age-related, with only a minute percentage of persons under 60 being affected, compared with 20 percent or more of those over 80 (Bergman, Kay, Foster, McKechnie, and Roth, 1971; Gianturco and Busse, 1978; Kay, Bergmann, Foster, McKechnie, and Roth, 1970; Jarvik, Ruth, and Matsuyama, 1980).

Of the total group of older people with organic mental disorders, an estimated 10 to 20 percent have remediable, or partially remediable, afflictions (Fox, Topel, and Huckman, 1975; Marsden and Harrison, 1972; Smith and Kiloh, 1981; Wells, 1978). These include patients with space-occupying lesions and focal neurological damage, as well as those with cognitive disturbance caused by alcohol, medications, malnutrition, infection, metabolic dis-

orders, and depression (see discussions by Small, Liston, and Jarvik, 1981; Spar, 1982; Task Force Report, 1980; and Wells, 1977). The remaining 80 percent of cases are believed to result from primary degenerative dementia (Alzheimer type), multi-infarct dementia, or a mixture of both (Freeman, 1965; Katzman, 1978; Marsden and Harrison, 1972; Tomlinson, Blessed, and Roth, 1970). Dementia of the Alzheimer type (DAT) is thought to be most common, accounting singly or in combination for at least 60 percent of the cases, compared to 15 to 25 percent attributable to multi-infarct disease (MID), with the rest probably being mixed DAT/MID (Freeman, 1965; Marsden and Harrison, 1972; see also Wells, 1978). Pick disease, Creutzfeld-Jakob, and other degenerative brain diseases are so rare as not to affect data on incidence or prevalence.

There is general agreement that primary degenerative and multi-infarct dementia are disorders that predominantly affect the aged. As discussed subsequently, however, there is substantial concern about the accuracy of current diagnostic procedures and a great deal of uncertainty about the role of both biological and nonbiological etiologic factors.

Symptoms of Dementia in the Elderly

DSM-III criteria for diagnosis of dementia consist of (1) loss of intellectual ability severe enough to interfere with social or occupational functioning; (2) memory impairment; (3) impairment in abstract thinking, judgment, higher cortical functions, or personality change; (4) clear state of consciousness; and (5) documented or presumed evidence of an organic cause (see Table 5).

When the behavioral syndrome of dementia is presumed due to a known cause (e.g., Huntington disease, subdural hematoma, or vitamin B-12 deficiency), the appropriate Axis I DSM-III code is 294.10, and the disease producing the dementia is specified on Axis III. A diagnosis of multi-infarct dementia (290.4x) is made when there is a "patchy" distribution of cognitive deficits and a stepwise deteriorating course, combined with evidence of significant cerebrovascular disease and focal neurological signs and symptoms. Primary

TABLE 5   Diagnostic Criteria for Dementia

(*From American Psychiatric Association: Diagnostic and Statistical Manual of Mental Disorders. Edition 3. Washington, D.C., American Psychiatric Association, 1980, pp. 111–112, with permission.)

A.   A loss of intellectual abilities of sufficient severity to interfere with social or occupational functioning

B.   Memory impairment

C.   At least one of the following:
    (1)   Impairment of abstract thinking as manifested by concrete interpretation of proverbs, inability to find similarities and differences between related words, difficulty in defining words and concepts, and other similar tasks
    (2)   Impaired judgment
    (3)   Other disturbances of higher cortical function, such as aphasia (disorder of language due to brain dysfunction), apraxia (inability to carry out motor activities despite intact comprehension and motor function), agnosia (failure to recognize or identify objects despite intact sensory function, "constructional difficulty" (e.g., inability to copy three-dimensional figures, assemble blocks, or arrange sticks in specific designs)
    (4)   Personality change, i.e., alteration or accentuation of premorbid traits

D.   State of consciousness not clouded (i.e., does not meet the criteria for delirium or intoxication, although these may be superimposed)

E.   Either (1) or (2):
    (1)   Evidence from the history, physical examination, or laboratory tests of a specific organic factor that is judged to be etiologically related to the disturbance
    (2)   In the absence of such evidence, an organic factor necessary for the development of the syndrome can be presumed if conditions other than organic mental disorders have been reasonably excluded and if the behavioral change represents cognitive impairment in a variety of areas

degenerative dementia (290.xx) is diagnosed when the history suggests a uniformly progressive course of cognitive decline and when all specific causes of such decline have been ruled out.

There are a variety of laboratory and neurodiagnostic tests that can be used to identify specific causes of dementia (see Table 6). Usually, however, all of these show normal results, and the diagnostic choice is limited to either MID or PDD, the PDD label being used to include Pick disease, subcortical dementias, and Creutzfeld-Jakob disease, as well as dementia of the Alzheimer type (DAT).

For multi-infarct dementia, CT scan evidence of small areas of hemorrhage or infarction, or focal EEG abnormalities, may help to confirm a diagnostic impression, but the absence of such findings cannot be used to rule out the diagnosis because the lesions have to be at least 1 millimeter in size in order to be visible on the CT scan. From the behavioral standpoint, it may be hard to operationalize criteria such as "patchy deficits" or "stepwise deterioration." Quantitative rating scales such as the Hachinski Ischemic Index (Hachinski,

Itiff, Zilhka, DuBoulay, McAllister, Marshall, Russell, and Symon, 1975; see also revision by Rosen, Terry, Fuld, Katzman, and Peck, 1980) do not resolve the diagnostic problem, since they contain the same ambiguous items as the DSM-III criteria themselves. Psychological testing has also not been very helpful in confirming multi-infarct dementia, since post-mortem diagnostic confirmation is usually lacking. Perez and colleagues (Perez, Gay, and Taylor, 1975; Perez, Gay, Taylor, and Rivera, 1975; Perez, Rivera, Meyer, Gay, Taylor, and Matthew, 1975) reported that the effects of imipramine on WAIS and Wechsler Memory Scale subtests was less uniform and less severe in a sample of suspected multi-infarct than in DAT patients, but there is no way of determining whether or not the two samples were equivalent with regard to duration or overall severity of illness. In our analysis of a small sample of patients, there was a wider range of WAIS subtest scores among MID than DAT patients diagnosed clinically and matched for age, sex, and duration of illness, but, in accordance with previous observation (Clark, 1982), there was no particular

TABLE 6   Screening Tests for Evaluating Dementia*

(From Small, G. W., Liston, E. H., and Jarvik, L. F. 1981. Diagnosis and treatment of dementia in the aged. *The Western Journal of Medicine* 135:477.)

1. Complete blood count with sedimentation rate
2. Analysis of urine
3. Stool examination for occult blood
4. Serum urea nitrogen and glucose; serum electrolytes (sodium, potassium, carbon dioxide content, chloride, calcium, phosphorus); bilirubin; serum vitamin B_{12}, folic acid
5. Tests for thyroid function
6. Serological test for syphilis
7. Roentgenogram of the chest
8. Electrocardiogram
9. Computerized tomography (CT scan) of the brain

*Recommended by the Task Force sponsored by the National Institute on Aging.

pattern of preservation and impairment that characterized the patients with MID. Albert (1978) and Benson (1982) classify multi-infarct disease as a subcortical dementia, with behavioral deficits presumably limited to psychomotor slowing, memory impairment, and "dilapidation" of reasoning and abstraction, but the distinction between cortical and subcortical dementias needs to be verified by further behavioral and autopsy studies.

There are no neurodiagnostic procedures that unequivocally confirm the presence of primary degenerative dementia. Cortical atrophy as measured by CT scans is correlated to some extent with degree of behavioral impairment in patients with the clinical diagnosis of PDD (e.g., de Leon, Ferris, George, Reisberg, Kricheff, and Gerson, 1980; Fox, Topel, and Huckman, 1975; Huckman, Fox, and Topel, 1975; Kazniak, Garron, Fox, Huckman, and Ramsey; 1975; Roberts, Caird, Grossart, and Stevens, 1976), but atrophy is also age-related (Earnest, Heston, Wilkinson, and Manke, 1979; Fox, Kazniak, and Huckman, 1979; Hughes and Gado, 1981), and measures of sulci and ventricle enlargement are usually considered insufficient to rule in a diagnosis of DAT (cf. Wells and Buchanan, 1977; Task Force Report, 1980). Whether analyses based on CT number (e.g., Bondareff, Mountjoy,

and Roth, 1981; Naeser, Gebhardt, and Levine, 1980) will prove to be diagnostically useful remains to be established; moreover, quantitative CT data are often not available in clinical settings.

Current electrophysiological measures are not diagnostically specific either. In general, EEG slowing is correlated with degree of functional impairment (Barnes, Busse, and Friedman, 1956; Busse, 1978; Obrist, Busse, Eisdorfer, and Kleemeier, 1962; Wang, 1973; Wilson, Musella, and Short, 1977), but normal EEGs may be obtained, particularly in early stages of dementia (Nott and Fleminger, 1975; Liston, 1979; Loeb, 1980). Increased latency of the P300 component of event-related potentials has been reported to differentiate between patients with the clinical diagnosis of DAT and normal elderly controls (Goodin, Squires, and Starr, 1978; Squires, Chippendale, Wrege, Goodin, and Starr, 1980; Syndulko, Hansch, Cohen, Pearce, Goldbert, Monton, Tourtellotte, and Potvin, in press), but exceptions to this finding have also been observed (Brown, Marsh, and La Rue, 1982).

Because of the limitations of current neuroradiologic and electrophysiologic techniques, the diagnosis of dementia is made on clinical grounds, and once specific etiologies have been ruled out, a premium is placed on accurate description of the extent and pattern of behavioral impairment.

Several quantitative mental status questionnaires have been developed to assist in screening for the behavioral impairments characteristic of dementia. In their autopsy study of 60 elderly patients, Blessed, Tomlinson, and Roth (1968) correlated senile plaque counts with scores prior to death. Questions tapped orientation to person, place, and time, remote memory and delayed recall, and attention/ concentration (such as counting backwards). The test scores of patients diagnosed as having senile dementia were markedly lower than those of other diagnostic groups, with mean corrected scores of 10.5, 20.8, 28.6, and 31.8 observed for patients with dementia, delirium, depression, and physical illness, respectively. A significant negative correlation ($r = -0.59$) was obtained between test scores and senile plaque counts, suggesting that this brief mental status instrument was sensitive to varying degrees of neurodegenerative change. There were notable exceptions, however, with good mental status performance shown by some patients with extensive brain damage and poor performance by some with minimal brain changes.

The mental status questionnaire most widely used in the United States (Kahn, Goldfarb, Pollock, and Peck, 1960) consists of 10 items that assess orientation and recent and remote recall. Three or more errors on this scale (MSQ) are usually considered sufficient to raise the possibility of dementia, provided that the patient does not suffer from an acute confusional state (delirium). The MSQ was originally validated against clinical ratings of organic impairment and has been examined more recently in relation to performance on formal memory tests (Zarit, Miller, and Kahn, 1978). Subjects in the latter study included 153 patients, and in some cases their spouses, evaluated at an outpatient gerontology clinic; mean age for the sample was 65 years. Psychometric tests included story recall, learning and recall of pairs of words, and repeating strings of digits forward and backward. Increasing numbers of errors on the MSQ were associated with progressively poorer scores on each of the tests of memory, with the exception of digit span repeated forward. An unexpected finding was that one or two incorrect answers on the MSQ, usually considered to be of little clinical significance, correlated positively and significantly with poor memory test performance.

Folstein, Folstein, and McHugh (1975) developed a mental status instrument, the "mini-mental state" examination (MMS), which taps a broader range of functions than the Kahn-Goldfarb MSQ. The MSS includes items measuring attention/concentration, immediate and delayed recall, language, visuographic ability, and orientation. Scores on the MMS were found to differentiate 63 normal elderly controls from 206 psychiatric inpatients with varying diagnoses. Mean scores (out of a possible 30) were as follows: 27.6 for normal individuals, 25.1 for depressed patients without cognitive deficits, 19.0 for depressed patients with cognitive deficits, and 9.6 for patients

with dementia. When patients were retested following appropriate treatment, the scores of the patients with dementia remained stable over time, but there were small gains for depressed patients without significant cognitive symptoms, and noticeable gains for patients with "pseudodementia" (that is, depressed patients who initially showed signs of cognitive impairment). In a five-institution collaborative study of 384 elderly subjects (Raskin and Rae, 1980), the mean MMS scores for normal individuals, depressed patients, and demented patients with and without depression were 26.4, 25.5, 19.1, and 20.3, respectively. Patients with dementia scored worse than normal elderly persons on all items, whereas depressed patients differed from normal individuals primarily in their lower scores on delayed three-item recall.

Use of screening instruments such as the MSQ, MMS, or other mental status measures (Jacobs, Bernhard, and Delgado, 1977; Pfeiffer, 1975) can presumably reduce certain types of diagnostic error (especially misclassification of normal older people as demented), but it is important to note that these brief questionnaires are not intended to aid in distinguishing among different subtypes or causes of cognitive impairment. Although most patients with PDD will obtain scores in the abnormal range, a high MSQ score is obviously not pathognomic of this condition. Also, none except the Blessed scale has been validated against postmortem findings.

Numerous studies have attempted to document and quantify changes on psychological tests attributable to organic mental disorders in elderly patients and to differentiate such changes from those associated with normal aging or with affective disorders (see Crook, 1979; Eisdorfer and Cohen, 1978; Kramer and Jarvik, 1979; La Rue, 1982; Miller, 1980; Savage, 1973; Schaie and Schaie, 1977; Wells and Buchanan, 1977, for reviews). In a majority of these studies, however, samples are either poorly described or based on populations with a mixture of disorders so that the performance of clinically diagnosed patients with DAT is averaged with that of other organically impaired subgroups (e.g., Bolton, Savage, and Roth, 1967; Botwinick and Birren, 1951;

Crook, Ferris, McCarthy, and Rae, 1980; Crookes, 1974; Crookes and McDonald, 1972; Ferris, Crook, Clark, McCarthy, and Rae, 1980; Gilleard, 1980; Hall, Savage, Bolton, Pidwell, and Blessed, 1972; Hilbert et al., 1976; Inglis, 1957, 1959; Irving et al., 1970; Kahn et al., 1975; Kendrick and Post, 1967; Kendrick et al., 1965; McCarthy, Ferris, Clark, and Crook, 1981; Overall and Gorham, 1972; Savage, 1973). Moreover, persons considered as part of normal aging groups are usually not described in terms of physical health status. It is not surprising, then, that there is little consistency from study to study in the tests or factors observed to be most "organicity-sensitive" and that this literature does not delineate the cognitive deficits characteristic of a particular disease, such as DAT.

Table 7 summarizes procedures and results of a few studies in which the patient samples were restricted to persons suspected of having Alzheimer-type dementia. Even in these studies, however, specific diagnostic procedures are only vaguely described, although they make explicit reference to the exclusion of suspected multi-infarct and treatable dementia cases. Roth and Hopkins report distinct differences in distributions of scores between demented and affectively impaired groups on all of the measures they studied, as did Bigler et al. (1981). Both samples probably contained only relatively severely impaired individuals. Miller and Lewis concentrated on presenile patients whom he described as "early cases" (1977, p. 50) and documented deficits in both short-term and long-term memory; he interpreted his findings from both cognitive-psychological and neuropsychological perspectives, and suggested that the pattern of memory loss seen in primary degenerative dementia may be distinct from that observed in some other amnestic syndromes (e.g., bilateral mesial temporal lesions). Weingartner, Kaye, Smallberg, Ebert, Gillin, and Sitaram (1981) described their patients as being in "the earliest stages" of a progressive dementia (p. 188); their results demonstrated some preservation of verbal intelligence among the dementia patients, while simultaneously showing marked differences between patients and normals on tests of learning and memory. The

difficulties encountered by patients with dementia were attributed to an inability to access semantic memory structures, which, in turn, made it difficult to encode new information.

Even within these few studies, some clinically significant contradictions and limitations are apparent. For example, from the results reported by Bigler et al. (1981), one would surmise that PDD patients are likely to perform in the impaired range on all types of psychological tests. Actually, Weingartner's patients maintained verbal intelligence, and some types of memory tasks were reported to be more severely disrupted than others. As suggested above, the discrepancies are presumed due to the fact that the patients studied by Bigler and colleagues were, in all likelihood, in later stages of the dementing process than Weingartner's patients. Lack of control (or even description) of the stage or severity of illness is the norm rather than the exception in studies of dementia, and one is left with the impression that a given test may or may not be effective in identifying dementia, depending on sample variations. Besides, none of these studies described their findings in terms of cutting scores that might be used in assigning clinical judgments on the presence or absence of dementia. This omission is understandable in view of the small samples and unstandardized procedures, but it does little to resolve the current diagnostic quandary. Finally, in the absence of longitudinal follow-ups or autopsy verification, it is important to underscore the *presumptive* nature of diagnostic categories in the preceding studies.

Although the prospects of quick resolution of diagnostic ambiguity via psychological testing are dim, there is evidence that poor performance on cognitive tests is correlated with positive findings on neuroradiologic and electrophysiologic measures and that it is also linked to survival duration. Kaszniak et al. (1979) found that scores on memory and language tests could be used to predict survival within a sample of 47 senile and presenile dementia patients (diagnoses based on clinical evaluation and an extensive neurodiagnostic screening battery, including CT scans and EEGs). Discriminant function analyses of the psychological test scores predicted one-year

TABLE 7   Studies Contrasting Clinically Diagnosed Alzheimer Patients with Depressives or Normal Controls on Measures of Cognitive Functioning

Study	Samples	Measures	Results
Roth and Hopkins (1953)	Affective disorders group (n = 46); "consisted mainly of patients with the depressive-symptom complex"; median age = 67 years Senile psychotics (n = 20); clinical diagnosis excluding specific causes; did not include arteriosclerotic dementia cases; median age = 78 years All were recent hospital admissions	Wechsler-Bellevue Vocabulary Wechsler-Bellevue Digit Span Progressive Matrices Information test (analogous to MSQ)	Scores of senile psychotics lower on all measures, most strikingly so on Matrices and Information tests
Miller (1975)	*Experiment I:* Presenile dementia patients (n = 14); clinical diagnosis and air encephalogram; mean age = 60.5 years Normal controls (n = 14); mean age = 60.0 years	Free recall of 20 lists of common words	Dementia patients < controls on mean number of words recalled; differences in both recency (STM) and primacy (LTM) components of the serial position curve
	Experiment II: Presenile dementia patients (n = 12); mean age = 58.7 years Normal controls (n = 12); mean age = 57.5 years	Same as in Experiment I, with presentation rate varied	Same as above; dementia patients' performance not improved by slower presentation rate
Miller (1975)	Alzheimer dementia patients (n = 15); clinical diagnosis and air encephalogram; mean age = 58.2 years Hospitalized controls (n = 15); neurological patients with extracranial lesions or patients recovering from pulmonary tuberculosis; mean age = 58.6 years	Word span established; subject then required to learn tests of length span +1, span +2, span +3	Alzheimer patients < controls on word span (STM) and supraspan learning (LTM)
Miller and Lewis (1977)	Depressed inpatients (n = 20); no subtype control Demented inpatients (n = 20); "brain atrophy" diagnosis Normals (n = 20); community residents All subjects over 65 years of age (M = 77.5 years); three groups matched for age and sex; diagnostic procedures unspecified	Picture recognition task using geometric designs; continuous recognition procedure; hit rates and false positives used to calculate d' and B as specified by signal detection model	d': Normals = depressives > dements B: Normals = dements > depressives Hit rates = 86%, 69%, and 50% for normals, depressives, and dements, respectively False positives = 15%, 9%, and 28% for normals, depressives, and dements, respectively
Bigler, Steinman, and Newton (1981)	Degenerative disease patients (n = 19); most were "probable Alzheimer cases" but two "probable Pick's" included; clinical diagnosis and CT scans; excluded patients with cerebrovascular disease or specific causes of dementia	WAIS WMS Halstead-Reitan tests (Category, Trail Making, Aphasia Screen, Sensory Exam, Motor Exam)	Dementia patients < controls on all subtests and summary scores, with the exception of errors on Trails A and the Motor Exam

TABLE 7 (Continued)

Study	Samples	Measures	Results
Weingartner et al. (1981)	Primary ideopathic dementia cases (n = 14); clinical diagnoses based on "several detailed neurological examinations" and psychiatric exam; none being treated for medical disorders Normal controls (n = 14), matched with patients for age, education, and SES	WAIS WMS Free recall of related and unrelated words Serial learning of unrelated words Free recall with selective reminding Continuous association tasks with letters or words as stimuli	Dementia patients < controls on Performance IQ, WMS scores, and all laboratory tests of learning and memory; unlike controls, patients' recall was equally poor for categorized and uncategorized lists; patients much less fluent in naming of associations

survival with 97 percent accuracy, compared with the 77 percent accuracy achieved by EEG findings and nonsignificant prediction based on CT measurements of ventricle and sulci width. In light of our discussion in the preceding pages, it is not surprising that the routine CT measures correlate only marginally with survival, but it remains to be explained why results of psychological tests do appear to be relatively reliable predictors, not only among inpatients with dementia (cf. also Naguib and Levy, 1982) but in community resident normal elderly as well (e.g., Jarvik and Blum, 1971; Kleemeier, 1962; Riegel, Riegel, and Meyer, 1967; Siegler, 1975). Kaszniak and colleagues (1979) have also reported on interrelationships between psychological test data and either CT or EEG findings. In a study of 78 well-screened patients with PDD (mean age, 68 years), cerebral atrophy was reported to affect memory performance independently of age. Presence vs. absence of atrophy (based on sulci and ventricle measurements) influenced performance on several memory or attention tasks (Digits Forward, Digits Backward, and Mental Control, from the WMS) that were not affected by age. On other measures of memory (associate learning, paragraph recall, and visual reproduction), there were both age and atrophy effects, but no interaction. In a second study (Kaszniak et al., 1979), additional evidence for the independence of age and atrophy effects was obtained, and a strong pattern of intercorrelations was noted between EEG slowing and cognitive impairment. Such results suggest that combinations of positive findings (e.g., EEG slowing, atrophy on CT,

and impaired psychological test performance) may be useful for distinguishing pathological impairments from normal aging changes.

One direction for future studies would be to follow some questionable cases (e.g., mildly forgetful people or individuals who are both depressed and forgetful) to get a better picture of how often improvement, stability, or decline is likely to emerge (cf. Jarvik, Ruth, and Matsuyama, 1980). A number of longitudinal studies in progress (cf. Hughes and Gado, 1981; Jarvik et al., 1982; Reisberg and Ferris, 1982) are attempting to clarify the natural history of dementing illness, and more are in the planning phase. There is also a need to examine subgroups within the population of clinically diagnosed DAT patients, distinguished on the basis of either behavioral or biological measures. What is now called DAT may well represent several diseases with distinct etiologies and patterns of progression.

Correlates of Dementia

Biological Correlates. The characteristic neuropathology of DAT, first described by Alzheimer, has been known since the turn of the century. Cortical atrophy and dilatation of cerebral ventricles are typically evident on gross examination, although the degree of atrophy sometimes does not exceed that seen in normal individuals of advanced age. The microscopic findings include senile plaques, neurofibrillary tangles, granulovacuolar degeneration of the neurons, and congophilic angiopathy. Senile plaques are composites of dead cell fragments with an amyloid core that are found in spaces between cells. Neurofibril-

neurons in which the cytoplasm has been replaced by densely packed, twisted protein microfibrils. Granulovacuolar degeneration refers to clumps of granular material within the cytoplasm of neurons, most often observed in the hippocampal pyramidal cells. Congophilic angiopathy denotes amyloid deposits within cerebral blood vessels. Pathological examination is ordinarily considered necessary to verify a diagnosis of DAT, but it is important to note that since each of the characteristic changes can be observed to some extent in brains of nondemented individuals, confirmation must be based on quantitative criteria that may vary among laboratories.

It is only in recent years that other biological correlates of DAT have begun to be extensively investigated. Several studies have shown that neurotransmitter systems are disrupted in DAT. The most consistent finding (cf. review by Bartus, Dean, Beer, and Lippa, 1982) has been reduced choline acetyltransferase (CAT) in the hippocampus and some parts of the frontal cortex, including the nucleus basalis (Whitehouse, Price, Clark, Coyle, and DeLong, 1981). CAT is essential for the synthesis of the neurotransmitter acetylcholine that is believed to be involved in processes of learning and memory (e.g., Davis, Mohs, Tinklenberg, Hollister, Pfefferbaum, and Kopell, 1978; Drachman and Leavitt, 1974; Sitaram, Weingartner, and Gillin, 1978). Decreased levels of noradrenaline (Adolfsson, Gottfries, Oreland, Roos, and Winblad, 1978; Bondareff, Mountjoy, and Roth, 1981), dopamine (Adolfsson et al., 1978; Carlsson, 1981), and somatostatin (Davies, Katzman, and Terry, 1980) have also been reported in the brains of DAT patients. Other lines of investigation suggest increased accumulations of aluminum in neurons, especially those with neurofibrillary temples (Crapper-McLachlan, Krishnan, and Dalton, 1973; Perl and Brody, 1980), decreased concentrations of circulating immunoglobulins (Eisdorfer, Cohen, and Buckley, 1978), and reduced philothermal response in peripheral leukocytes (Matsuyama, Jarvik, Kessler, Fu, Tsai, and Clark, 1981) among individuals with DAT relative to age-matched controls. Pedigree, twin, and family studies (cf. review by Matsuyama and Jarvik, 1980) suggest that genetic factors may play

a role in the development of DAT, although no single genetic model has been offered to date that adequately accounts for all of the findings in this area. Chromosomal abnormalities have been implicated by studies showing high rates of chromosome loss among individuals diagnosed clinically as having DAT (Jarvik, Altshuler, Kato, and Blummer, 1971; Nielsen, 1968; Ward, Cook, Robinson, and Austin, 1979) and by Heston's (1976) observation of increased frequencies of Down syndrome and myeloproliferative diseases within families of patients with early-onset DAT.

As evidence of biological correlates of DAT accumulates, hopes for understanding the pathogenesis of this disorder and for developing effective treatments also increase. At present, however, the etiologic role of the various biological correlates remains unknown, and no clinically significant somatic treatment has been identified. Pharmacologic interventions have been disappointing (cf. Crook and Gerson, 1981). The most promising treatment strategy in recent years has involved the use of cholinomimetic agents, either alone or in combination with other drugs. There is evidence that drugs such as physostigmine or arecholine can produce mild improvements in learning and memory performance for short periods of time, particularly in normal and mildly impaired individuals, but longer-term treatments based on the acetylcholine precursors choline and lecithin have usually failed to yield positive outcomes (Barbeau, Growdon, and Wurtman, 1979; Bartus et al., 1982). There is even less support available for the efficacy of other experimental treatments such as aluminum chelation, vitamin supplementation, or intravenous injections of opiate blockers (i.e., Naloxone).

Although the prospects for discovering the causes of DAT in the near future appear dim, one or more *in vivo* biological markers may soon be identified; these would reduce diagnostic ambiguity and facilitate sample selection for future research.

Psychosocial Influences.   The case for psychosocial influences in the development of dementia is largely circumstantial. Verwoerdt (1976, p. 35) described the complicating role of nonbiological causative factors as follows:

Although brain impairment is usually accompanied by deficits of those cognitive functions which depend on the intactness of the tissue involved, the pathogenic role of organic factors should not be overemphasized. Usually, multiple factors are operating, either simultaneously or as successive links in a cause-and-effect chain. These factors may be physical, psychological, or social and environmental, and may have various effects on each other. The outcome of such interactions is the formation of one or more vicious cycles: one pathogenic process exerting a positive feedback effect on another. Hence, it is useful to consider organic brain syndrome as being sociopsychosomatic in origin and nature.

Similar points have been made by other authors experienced in the evaluation and treatment of dementia (Gianotti, 1975; Kahn, 1977; Amster and Kraus, 1974; Gurland, 1981). A check of references cited in support of these statements is usually disappointing, however, there appear to be few, if any, investigations documenting an increased incidence of dementia as a function of such factors as bereavement, isolation, relocation, or accumulated stress and life-style changes.

Gurland (1981) provides a detailed discussion of relationships between levels of education and diagnoses of dementia. A number of studies are cited that show that older people with minimal education are more often diagnosed as demented than their better-educated peers, particularly if the diagnosis is based on mental status questionnaires rather than clinical assessment. This finding would usually be interpreted as indicating that the diagnostic error rate may be greater for less educated people, but Gurland discusses the alternative possibility, i.e., that more poorly educated individuals may actually be at greater risk for developing dementia. Exposure to neurotoxic substances, malnutrition, etc., may vary systematically with education and other indices of socioeconomic status, and these may affect susceptibility to degenerative brain diseases in old age. Such hypotheses are plausible, but there are few data available as yet to support the etiologic interpretation.

In conjunction with a long-term follow-up of a sample of aging twins, La Rue and Jarvik (1980) reported that the likelihood of developing dementia may vary with premorbid intellectual levels. The subjects were 65 survivors of an original sample of 268 who had entered the New York State Psychiatric Institute Study of Aging Twins between 1947 and 1949. All were over the age of 60 at the time of initial assessment (mean age, 70 years; range, 60 to 89). The assessment consisted of personal and family history interviews and psychological testing (Similarities, Digit Span, Digit Symbol Substitution, and Block Design Subtests from the Wechsler-Bellevue; Vocabulary from the Stanford-Binet; and a tapping test of psychomotor speed). Between 1966 and 1968, medical and psychiatric evaluations were conducted on most of the surviving participants. The survivors then ranged in age between 78 and 94 years, with a mean age of approximately 85 years. Of the 65 seen for medical and psychiatric evaluation, 36 had no signs of cognitive impairment, but 29 were diagnosed clinically as having dementia. The severity of dementia was rated as mild, moderate, or severe based on Goldfarb's (1964) criteria. Analyses of covariance indicated that participants diagnosed as demented in the 1966–68 evaluation had scored significantly lower than those who did not develop dementia on a subset of psychological tests (Vocabulary, Similarities, Digit Symbol) administered some 20 years earlier (during the 1946–49 assessment). As was the case with the findings cited by Gurland (1981), our results might be interpreted as indicating only that the probability of clinical diagnostic error increases for less intelligent individuals. The individuals who eventually were diagnosed as having developed dementia, however, not only obtained lower test scores initially, but also declined more rapidly during the succeeding two decades than did those diagnosed as without dementia. The two groups were statistically comparable in terms of other potentially confounding factors such as education, activities, and physical health (Jarvik and La Rue, 1979). Instead of representing increased diagnostic errors, the higher rates of dementia in the initially lower scoring group may indicate that early changes in mental performance preceded the diagnosis of dementia by as much as 20 years. Lengthy and gradual decline may well reflect underlying organic changes.

At the moment, there is no way of identifying individuals at risk for developing dementia of the Alzheimer type (other than strong family history), and the role of psychological, social, and environmental characteristics as predisposing factors remains unclear. There is less controversy, however, about the phenomenon of "excess disabilities," i.e., the exhibition of cognitive or functional deficits more severe than those warranted by dementing illness alone (e.g., Kleban, Lawton, Brody, and Moss, 1975; Loew and Silverstone, 1971). Perhaps because dementia reduces basic capacities to cope and compensate, individuals with DAT or other neurodegenerative conditions often appear to suffer disproportionately when adequate stimulation, diet, and medical care are lacking. In this regard, then, environmental and psychosocial variables appear to have a definite impact on the severity and progression of dementia symptoms.

Summary

The dementias of old age represent a heterogeneous group of disorders, each of which eventually produces a diffuse pattern of impairments in judgment, orientation, personality, and higher order cognitive functions. Dementia of the Alzheimer type may itself consist of several different diseases that are indistinguishable by means of current diagnostic techniques.

Dementias are among the most difficult of mental disorders that confront both professionals and family members, in part because a diagnosis is hard to establish antemortem, and also, because so little can be done to ameliorate the impairments. Faced with the prospect of caring for someone with dementia, family members often ask for concrete information about the nature of the disease and about what lies ahead in terms of further deterioration and disability. It is clear from the preceding review that little can be said about the reasons why dementias occur, and even less can be predicted about their future course, since the longitudinal studies need to answer that question have not been conducted.

Current research on dementia consists primarily of cataloging and contrasting, i.e., of describing in detail the behavioral and biological characteristics of individuals clinically diagnosed as demented and comparing the resultant biobehavioral profiles with those observed in normal aging and other neurologic and psychiatric disorders. Although such descriptive research has been in progress for several decades, at least with regard to behavioral characteristics, results of some of the older studies are difficult to interpret because samples were either sketchily described or lumped individuals with many different types of disorders into a single "organic" category. Sample characteristics have also been poorly defined in many of the biological investigations; for example, participants are frequently described only as having been "carefully selected" to represent cases of DAT (or MID, Parkinson disease, etc.), without the severity or type of behavioral dysfunctions observed being specified. Future research may produce more interpretable results if (1) participants are evaluated longitudinally rather than at a single point in time, (2) pathological verification of diagnosis is obtained via autopsy, and (3) multidisciplinary evaluations are performed, so that both behavioral and biological characteristics are adequately documented.

Other Conditions

Although depression and dementia are by no means the only psychiatric disorders observed in old age, they are the most prevalent, and certainly the most thoroughly researched, of all of the late-life mental disorders. A wide range of other disorders occurs among older adults, but unfortunately, even less is known about their diagnosis and etiology than that of dementia or depression. Several of the more intriguing and problematic of these conditions are briefly discussed in this section.

Schizophrenic and Paranoid Disorders

Unlike depression or dementia, schizophrenia is a relatively rare condition in the general geriatric population (cf. Gurland and Cross, 1982). Population studies and larger-scale community surveys estimate prevalence of schizophrenic disorder in persons over the age of 60 at 1 percent (Bollerup, 1975; Kay, Beamish and Roth, 1964; Nielson, 1962). About

90 percent of elderly patients with schizophrenia acquired the disorder before the age of 40 (Kay, 1972) and continue to exhibit symptoms or consequences as they age. Among late-onset cases, paranoid symptoms are almost always present (Roth, 1955; Fish, 1960).

Long-term follow-up studies of patients diagnosed as schizophrenic (see Post, 1980, for a review) indicate that mortality is higher in this group than in the age-matched general population, in part because of its higher rates of suicide and traumatic death. Among schizophrenics who survive to old age, differences in symptomatology (e.g., catatonic vs. hebephrenic subtypes) tend to disappear (Ciompi and Müller, 1976), and there is said to be an overall decrease in its severity of symptoms (Bleuler, 1972; Lawton, 1972; Müller, 1959; Ruemke, 1963; Wenger, 1958). Some 20 percent of patients diagnosed as schizophrenic appear to make lasting recoveries following their initial psychotic episode (Bleuler, 1972), 10 percent (Bleuler, 1974) to 23 percent (Ciompi and Müller, 1976) have been more or less permanently institutionalized, and the remainder have had histories characterized by episodic attacks alternating with periods of adequate function. In terms of psychosocial function, however, schizophrenic individuals who survive to old age outside of institutions often continue to have isolated or marginally integrated social lifestyles (Ciompi and Müller, 1976). Since the management and treatment of schizophrenia has changed dramatically in the past few decades, it has not been possible for follow-up studies to discern a clear picture of the natural course of this disease unconfounded by effects of institutionalization and varying treatment regimens.

Classification of late-onset paranoid disorders has been a confusing and controversial topic for many years (see discussions by Bridge and Wyatt, 1980a,b). In the British literature, the term *paraphrenia* is often used to denote the paranoid conditions that affect older people. Roth (1955) used this term to refer to a paranoid, schizophrenic-like disorder distinguishable from schizophrenia *per se* primarily on the basis of its later onset. Diagnostic criteria are onset of paranoid ideation and hallucinations beginning after age 60 in

an individual with well-preserved personality without dementia and without primary affective disorder. Roth reported that about 10 percent of psychiatric first-admissions in elderly patients were due to paraphrenia and that the condition was most common among women thought to have a paranoid or schizoid premorbid personality.

Other European researchers have stressed the existence of different subtypes of paraphrenia (e.g., Post, 1966), although the etiologic or predictive usefulness of subtyping has not been clearly established. Retterstöl (1966, 1968), while not specifically concerned with the elderly, characterized paranoid patients as a heterogeneous group, with affective symptoms clearly present in some and schizophrenic symptoms in others. Unlike Roth, Retterstöl and other Scandinavian researchers have emphasized the reactive nature of paranoid states.

In the United States, the term *paranoia* and *paraphrenia* have been loosely and inconsistently used (Varner and Gaitz, 1982), and there has been very little research on such conditions in the aged (Berger and Zarit, 1978; Bridge and Wyatt, 1980a,b). In DSM-III, paranoid disorders are considered as a distinct diagnostic category (see criteria summarized in Table 8), to be differentiated from schizo-

TABLE 8   Diagnostic Criteria for Paranoid Disorder

(From Diagnostic and Statistical Manual of Mental Disorders. Edition 3. Washington, D.C., American Psychiatric Association, 1980, p. 196. With permission.)

A. Persistent persecutory delusions or delusional jealousy

B. Emotion and behavior appropriate to the content of the delusional system

C. Duration of illness of at least one week

D. None of the symptoms of criterion of schizophrenia such as bizarre delusions, incoherence, or marked loosening of association

E. No prominent hallucinations

F. The full depressive or manic syndrome is either not present, developed after any psychotic symptoms, or was brief in duration relative to the duration of the psychotic symptoms

G. Not due to an organic mental disorder

phrenia, affective illness, and organic mental conditions. Applying these diagnostic criteria to more than 800 geropsychiatric patients (aged 65 and over) seen at Texas Research Institute of Mental Sciences between 1973 and 1978, Varner and Gaitz (1982) reported an incidence of 2 percent for paranoid conditions among outpatients and 4.6 percent among inpatients. There appears to be a much larger percentage of geriatric inpatients who meet some, but not all, of the DSM-III criteria for paranoid states (cf. Whanger, 1973).

Descriptive studies by Kay and Cooper found that patients with paraphrenia as defined by Roth were more likely than affectively ill patients to have never married, to have few or no surviving children, to have been living alone before admission, to have hearing losses affecting their ability to process conversations, and to have a family history of schizophrenia (Cooper, Garside, and Kay, 1976; Cooper and Porter, 1976; Kay, Cooper, Garside, and Roth, 1976). In contrast to the high rates of physical illness observed among aged depressed individuals, physical health problems are not particularly common among patients with paranoid conditions (Post, 1966; Kay, 1959, 1963). It is worth emphasizing, however, that these generalizations are based on only a small number of studies, and conclusions about the significance of possible etiologic factors are difficult to draw because of inconsistencies in diagnostic criteria from study to study. In many older people with prominent paranoid symptoms, cognition and overall functional ability are well preserved. Why disabling paranoid disorders develop in such people, after many years of relatively effective adjustment and coping, is an intriguing and unanswered question.

Studies of therapy outcome suggest that elderly paraphrenics can usually be treated successfully with major tranquilizers. In a three-year follow-up study (Post, 1966) of 65 patients who initially responded favorably to phenothiazines, 34 percent remained free of symptoms throughout the follow-up period, 38 percent exhibited a fluctuating course, and 28 percent continued to experience consistent paranoid delusions. The patients with most favorable long-term outcomes were those who had responded to initial treatment with complete remission of delusions and who continued compliance with drug treatment over the three-year interval. As Post (1980) points out, the greatest obstacle to intervention with late-onset paranoid disorders is that patients with these problems seldom seek treatment and are usually suspicious of medications or any other form of therapy that identifies them as being ill. Post recommends that internists or general practitioners should be trained to recognize and treat paraphrenic illness, since such patients may be more comfortable seeking and accepting help for a somatic condition than a psychiatric one. Post and others point out that attempts to reason individuals with persistent paranoid delusions out of their delusional beliefs are typically counterproductive, and that a sympathetic recognition of the distress engendered by the paranoia is more likely to promote a therapeutic relationship with the patient. Given a degree of acceptance and support by professionals and family members, many elderly persons with paranoid symptoms can establish reasonably effective and comfortable everyday lives in spite of recurrent fears.

Somatoform Disorders

There are several DSM-III diagnoses in which the principal features consist of somatic complaints or loss of or alteration in physical functioning. These include the following:

1. Somatization Disorder (300.81), in which there are multiple somatic symptoms of several years' duration
2. Conversion Disorder (300.11), in which there is a disturbance of physical functioning that cannot be explained by a known physical disorder
3. Psychogenic Pain Disorder (307.80), with severe and prolonged pain in the absence of known organic pathology
4. Hypochondriasis (300.70), characterized by body preoccupation and unrealistic fear or belief of having a serious disease
5. Atypical Somatoform Disorder (300.70). The incidence of most subtypes of somatoform disorder in the aged is not known, but hypochondriasis is believed to be common in older age groups.

Busse and Blazer (1980) estimate the incidence of hypochondriasis in community resident elderly as between 10 and 20 percent. Maddox (1964) classified 31 percent of aged subjects participating in a longitudinal study as "health pessimists," because their self-perceptions of health were negative even though their medical examinations failed to reveal any significant medical findings. Also, as noted earlier in the chapter, hypochondriachal behaviors often accompany depression in the elderly. In one study (de Alarcon, 1964) 64 percent of aged hospitalized depressives had physically unjustified somatic complaints. In nearly half of these cases, the illness started with the appearance of hypochondriacal symptoms, other depressive symptoms emerging later. Complaints about constipation and other digestive system problems were most common, followed by headaches, burning sensations, and tightness and pressure in the head. According to reports of relatives and friends, some of these patients had shown a lifelong preoccupation with health, but in 80 percent of them, the somatic complaints were seen as a new or unusual problem. The most striking finding reported by de Alarcon was that suicide attempts were noted for 25 percent of the patients with hypochondriacal complaints compared to only 7 percent of the other depressed individuals.

Busse (1976) states that new cases of hypochondriasis peak between the ages of 60 and 65 and that a greater portion of women are affected than men. Busse conceptualizes this disorder as a response to accumulated stress that is particularly likely to occur in social situations in which the individual suffers prolonged criticism, when there is isolation induced by economic restrictions, or when there is a decline in marital satisfaction because of a spouse's disability. The hypochondriacal behaviors are seen as indicative of (1) a withdrawal of psychic interest from other people and objects with a centering of interest on the self, (2) a shift of anxiety from psychic topics to less threatening concerns about physical disease, and (3) the use of physical symptoms as a means of self-punishment for unacceptable hostile feelings toward significant others. Verwoerdt (1981) also emphasizes

disengagement and self-absorption as characteristic of hypochondriasis and notes that among chronic complainers, there may be a secondary narcissistic pleasure derived from the physical complaints and concern. Goldstein and Birnbom (1976) emphasize the social system aspects of hypochondriasis, the central feature being an inability to convey feelings directly and honestly to significant others.

The prognosis associated with hypochondriasis is uncertain. Busse (1976) maintains that hypochondriacal reactions in the elderly are often transient and self-remitting, but provides no supporting data. Verwoerdt's (1981) recommendations, which are also provided without substantiating evidence, include (1) an acceptance of the need for the hypochondriacal defense, (2) provision of symptomatic treatment, and (3) continued availability of the physician-therapist for follow-up appointments. Goldstein and Birnbom (1976) reported improvement in hypochondriacal symptoms in eight elderly depressed patients for whom the primary treatment was family therapy; in eight additional cases, all considered treatment failures at a 6-month follow-up, family therapy either proved to be impractical or was refused. Specific therapeutic techniques were not described, nor were any alternative treatments discussed or evaluated.

In an initial contact with an older person with multiple somatic complaints, it is difficult to determine whether these complaints represent prodromal symptoms of depressive illness, a somatoform disorder independent of depression, or a direct response to physical illness that may or may not have been diagnosed. Referral to a physician with the skill and patience to pursue the complaints is appropriate; if the evaluation proves negative, treatment for depression should be considered. Further studies are needed, however, to determine the treatments that are most likely to be effective in alleviating hypochondriacal symptoms, whether or not these are accompanied by features of depression.

Alcohol and Drug Abuse

Studies to date suggest that the use of illegal drugs is infrequent among the aged compared to younger adults. According to DuPont (1976), 2 percent of the population over 50 in the United States report having tried marijuana at least once in contrast to 56 percent of individuals aged 18 to 21. Similarly, Ball and Chambers (1970) found that less than 4 percent of total hospital admissions for opiate addiction in two metropolitan areas involved individuals over the age of 60. The apparent low prevalence of heroin addiction in the aged has been attributed in part to attrition and also to a hypothesized "maturing out process" (Winick, 1962), in which addiction is believed to remit spontaneously as a result of life cycle changes in stresses and patterns of coping. However, many aging addicts do not seem to follow this trend (e.g., Capel, Goldsmith, Waddell, and Stewart, 1972), and some researchers have predicted that there will be a marked increase in the addicted older population in future decades (cf. Capel and Stewart, 1971; Pascarelli and Fischer, 1974).

Alcohol abuse and dependence (DSM-III 305.0x and 305.9x) are also usually reported to be less prevalent among the aged than the younger adult groups (Simon, 1980; U.S. Department of Health, Education, and Welfare, 1974). According to a national survey conducted in the 1960s (Cahalan, Cisin, and Crossley, 1969), the proportion of heavy drinkers is lower for both sexes past the age of 49 than it is for younger age groups; for men, an additional decrement in heavy drinking occurs after the age of 65. Approximately 5 percent of men and 1 percent of women 66 years and older were judged to be heavy drinkers, compared to 35 to 40 percent of men and 60 percent of women who abstained from all alcohol consumption. Some of these age differences may have resulted from sampling bias, since problem drinkers are less likely to survive to old age. However, Calahan and associates found that half of the elderly abstainers described themselves as former drinkers, and men and women who continued to drink in old age reported that the amount they consumed was considerably reduced compared to former years. Concern has been expressed (Glantz, 1981) that the apparent age decline in alcoholism may actually reflect generational differences; young and middle-aged adults are currently less likely to have grown up in environments that emphasize temperance, and as these individuals reach old age, high rates for late-life alcoholism may become the rule.

Within the subgroup of elderly people who do have drinking problems, two-thirds or more have had the problem for many years (Rosin and Glatt, 1971). The remainder appear to have intensified earlier moderate drinking patterns in response to age-related events, such as retirement and bereavement (Rosin and Glatt, 1971; Zimberg, 1974). Elderly alcoholics have been reported to consume less alcohol per drinking occasion than younger alcoholics (Harford, 1977; Schuckit and Pastor, 1978; Zimberg, 1978), but they appear to be more likely to drink on a daily basis. There is some evidence to suggest that many late-onset problem drinkers may be women, in contrast to the predominance of male alcoholics noted at earlier ages (cf. U.S. Department of Health, Education, and Welfare, 1974). Twenty percent or more of elderly patients hospitalized for psychiatric conditions may be diagnosed as alcoholic (Simon, Epstein, and Reynolds, 1968; Whittier and Korenyi, 1961).

A number of neuropsychological investigations indicate that cognitive deficits associated with alcohol abuse are likely to be more pronounced in elderly alcoholics than in younger people with comparable drinking histories (Brandt, Butters, Ryan, and Bayog, 1983; Ryan and Butters, 1980; Parson and Leber, 1981). For example, Ryan and Butters (1980) observed main effects of both age and alcohol abuse on a battery of learning and memory tasks; the 34- to 49-year-old alcoholics were similar to the 60- to 65-year-old controls. Findings were interpreted as supporting a "premature aging" hypothesis, in which alcoholism is seen as accelerating normal decremental aging changes in central nervous system function. It also appears that former alcoholics may have an increased risk of developing cognitive problems as they age. Studies indicate that there is some recovery of cognitive function with increased duration of abstinence (see Parson and Leber, 1981, for a review), but that long-term alcohol abusers months or years after detoxification still perform more poorly than age-matched controls on tests of perceptual-motor speed, tactual-motor ability, and abstraction (Parson and Leber, 1981), as well as on tests of learning and recall of new information (Brandt et al., 1983).

The neuropsychological studies indicate clearly that excessive alcohol consumption can markedly impair an older person's functioning and that a history of such consumption may leave negative residual effects. The pros and cons of moderate social drinking are open to debate. Older people who drink occasionally or in moderation tend to be more active and sociable and perceive themselves as being in better health than elderly alcohol abstainers (U.S. Department of Health, Education, and Welfare, 1974); beneficial effects on mood and social interaction have also been reported to result from introduction of opportunities for limited social drinking in nursing homes (Chien, 1971; Chien, Stotsky, and Cole, 1973). By contrast, Parker and Noble (1977) observed mild, but statistically significant, deficits in cognitive performance in social drinkers compared to abstainers. Programs incorporating "medicinal" use of alcohol are not universally viewed as positive; on the contrary, they have been interpreted by some as a further sign of excessive reliance on pharmacologic approaches to managing problems of the aged (Glantz, 1981).

For most old people, iatrogenic, medication-related illness is a much greater problem than alcoholism. Community surveys of legal drug use in different age groups (see Petersen, Whittington, and Beer, 1979, for a review) indicate that the elderly have a higher overall rate of drug intake than any other age group (Warheit, Arey, and Swanson, 1976), as well as higher usage rates for several specific types of prescription medications, including psychoactive drugs such as tranquilizers, sedatives, and hypnotics (Chambers, 1971; Parry, Balter, Mellinger, Cisin, and Manheimer, 1973; Mellinger, Balter, Parry, Manheimer, and Cisin, 1974; Warheit et al., 1976). According to one survey of community residents over the age of 60 living in the Capital District of New York State (Chien, Townsend, and Townsend, 1978), 66.6 percent reported that

they had taken analgesics, 33.5 percent were using cardiovascular drugs, 30.6 percent laxatives, 29.3 percent vitamins, 26.4 percent antacids, 22.3 percent antianxiety agents, and 16.5 percent diuretics. In addition, 33.1 percent reported taking medications that they could not specifically identify. The mean number of drugs per respondent was 3.8; 83 percent were taking two or more medications; and only 8 percent stated that they were taking no drugs. Guttman (1978) also reported high rates of drug intake within a stratified random sample of more than 5,000 persons over the age of 60 living in the Washington, D.C., area. Sixty-two percent of the participants in this survey reported that they were taking prescription drugs, with the most commonly cited types being cardiovascular medications (39.3 percent), sedatives/tranquilizers (13.6 percent), and antiarthritic drugs (9.4 percent). Sixty-nine percent of the respondents also reported use of over-the-counter medications, most commonly analgesics. In institutional settings, rates of psychotropic medication use alone range as high as 92 percent (Salzman, in press), and polypharmacy—i.e., the prescription of multiple medications—is common in both residential-care and hospital settings (see Table 9).

A strongly held belief among health care professionals is that the risk of drug misuse increases proportionally with the frequency and quantity of drug intake. There are few adequate investigations of the extent of drug misuse among older adults, but some interesting preliminary statistics are available. Studies indicate that elderly individuals comprise only a small percentage (2 to 6 percent) of patients seen in acute-care medical settings for drug-related emergencies (Heller and Wynne, 1975; Petersen and Thomas, 1975). Most overdose reactions in the aged involve misuse of a psychotropic drug (mainly Valium, Tuinal, Luminal, and Darvon), in contrast to the pattern seen among younger patients for whom illicit drugs (especially heroin and cocaine) figure prominently in drug-related emergencies (Inciardi, McBride, Busse, and Wells, 1978; Petersen and Thomas, 1975). Other data suggest that emergency-room statistics severely under-

TABLE 9   Clinical Examples of Polypharmacy in a General Hospital Elderly Population

(From Salzman, C. 1982. Key concepts in geriatric psychopharmacology. *Psychiatric Clinics of North America* 5:186.)

Desired Effect	Clinical Indication	Psychotropic Drug	Drug Combination
Sleep	Insomnia likely in elderly; worse in unfamiliar surroundings or when anxious, as in a hospital	Flurazepam	Often used with other central nervous system sedatives, analgesics, and sedating psychotropic drugs
Daytime sedation	Agitation, postsurgical confusion, precarious medical condition	Diazepam Chlorpromazine Thioridazine Amitriptyline	Often combined with narcotic analgesics and nighttime sedatives
Anti-anxiety	Anxiety common in elderly with declining health and support systems, as well as those with medical disease	Diazepam almost routinely prescribed in hospital survey; other benzodiazepines have limited use	Often combined with analgesics
Anti-agitation	Toxic confusion, organic brain syndrome, intensive care unit disorientation	Haloperidol Thioridazine Chlorpromazine	Often combined with other central nervous system sedatives and analgesics

estimate the extent of total drug misuse among the elderly. A number of studies have shown the elderly to be more likely than other age groups to fail to comply with doctors' instructions in taking medications (Brand, Smith, and Brand, 1977; Neely and Patrick, 1968; Schwartz, Wang, Zeitz, and Goss, 1962). Persons in their seventies have been reported to fail to follow physicians' medication instructions more than twice as often as those in their forties (Brand et al., 1977); the same study reported a high noncompliance rate (62 percent) among patients over 80. Schwartz et al. (1962) found omissions of medication to be the major form of noncompliance in the aged, accounting for 47 percent of medication mistakes, followed by inaccurate information (20 percent), self-medication (17 percent), incorrect dosage (10 percent), and incorrect sequence or timing of dose (4 percent). Factors contributing to these mistakes appeared to include incomplete communication between physician and patient, decreased mental competence of the patient, and inadequate supervision of drug regimen by either professionals or family members. In the Brand et al. study, the most frequently cited reason for noncompliance was economic; more than one-third of the older patients in this study reported that they couldn't afford to take their medications in the manner prescribed.

Since misuse of medications in the aged usually occurs in the context of medical treatment, the physical or psychological impairments that result cannot be classified as substance-abuse disorders by DSM-III criteria. Dependence can develop, however, particularly in anxious, depressed, or hypochondriacal older adults. In addition, symptoms such as lethargy, confusion, fatigue, depression, and anxiety are commonly observed side effects of many of the medications taken by the elderly (see Table 4). Medications remain the treatment of choice for many of the illnesses that affect older people, and the global recommendation that aged people should take fewer drugs appears to be an over-simplified answer to a difficult problem (cf. Lamy, 1980). Guidelines for management of medications in the aged are gradually becoming available (e.g., Levenson, 1979), and these may help to reduce the risk of medication-related incidents.

Personality Disorders

Community and population surveys conducted in the 1950s and 1960s place the prevalence of personality disorders in older adults at 2.8 to 11 percent (Bollerup, 1975; Bremer, 1951; Essen-Moller, 1956; Kay, Beamish, and Roth, 1964; Nielson, 1962). Older people with personality disorders, however, are seldom seen in either community mental health centers or psychiatric hospitals (Redick et al., 1973). Incidence of personality disorders has been reported to decrease in old age (Vaillant and Perry, 1980; see also Figure 1), but this impression may be due in part to patterns of service utilization rather than rates of disorder per se.

According to Straker (1982), schizoid, histrionic, antisocial, or borderline disorders are not commonly found among elderly patients, whereas paranoid, compulsive, narcissistic, or dependent personalities may be more adversely affected by the changes that accompany aging and may therefore come to a psychologist's or psychiatrist's attention. Dependency is particularly painful for many older people. On the one hand, becoming dependent appears to be a prominent fear in old age; on the other, learning to do without the help to which one has become accustomed can also present problems. Goldfarb (1975) recommends that dependency needs be viewed in a somewhat different light for old as opposed to young adults and suggests that it may be therapeutically beneficial to accept the development of positive transference on the part of some dependent, elderly patients.

The prevalence and incidence of personality disorders as defined by DSM-III have not been investigated in aged samples. This is going to be a particularly difficult area to study because of the absence of clear reference points for normal aging changes in personality, and

caution is warranted in diagnosing personality disorders at the present time.

CONCLUSIONS AND IMPLICATIONS

Having reviewed current data on several of the mental disorders observed in old age, it is our impression that the hypothesis of age differences in the nature and expression of psychopathology during adulthood is reasonably well supported. This impression is based in part on the shifting prominence (in terms of incidence, prevalence, and severity of symptoms) of illnesses such as dementia, paraphrenia, hypochondriasis, schizophrenia, and alcoholism. Age changes in the distribution of specific illnesses appear to result from several factors. Since there is increased mortality associated with disorders such as schizophrenia and alcoholism, many individuals acquiring them in early life do not survive to older ages. In addition, the biological and social changes that currently accompany aging seem to predispose those who do survive to clinically significant expressions of dementia, paranoic symptoms, hypochondriasis, and iatrogenic, drug-related problems. That there may also be considerable artifice in current opinions about age changes in the prevalence of psychopathologies is an undeniable possibility. Since scientific and clinical interest is itself unevenly distributed, the conditions about which we have learned the most in a given age group are the ones that we come to see as most common and significant.

A second recurrent theme throughout this review pertains to age difference in the context (biological, psychological, and socioenvironmental) of mental disorders. For mental health professionals who primarily serve young or middle-aged adults, it is rare to encounter individuals with emotional or cognitive problems who are also affected by multiple chronic physical illnesses, taking several types of medications, and adjusting to a series of potentially traumatic life changes such as bereavement, retirement, or hospitalization. Yet, such combinations of complicating circumstances are commonplace in the caseload of geriatric practice. If true mental disorder is viewed as "signal" and the context of extenuating factors as "noise," then surely the signal-to-noise ratio is lower for elderly patients, and the diagnosis and treatment of these disorders in old people is necessarily a chancier enterprise.

A number of problems observed among the elderly do not seem to fit well into any of the diagnostic categories of DMS-III. A good proportion of the diagnostically ambiguous cases are ones in which symptoms of several different disorders are present in varying degrees. Pseudodementia is one example; certain somatoform disorders and paraphrenia also fall into this category. The diagnostic quandary in these instances is not solely due to a lack of appropriate assessment instruments; rather, the difficulty appears to be on a more basic conceptual level, since too little effort has been devoted to date to the definition and theoretical specification of these atypical or mixed conditions.

On an empirical level, the greatest challenge for specialists in aging is to arrive at a clearer understanding of the causes and cures of dementing illnesses. Dementia of the Alzheimer type, currently believed to be the most common neurodegenerative condition, has been described by Lewis Thomas (1981) as the disease of the century. The appellation does justice to the sheer enormity of the disability the disease engenders and the costs associated with the care of the many who are, or will be, affected. Although research on dementia is rapidly expanding, data are still disquietingly descriptive, and in Lewis' opinion, a very long period of focused investigation may be needed to produce advances.

Given our state of knowledge, working clinically with old people who suffer from mental disorders is challenging, to say the least. A tolerance for ambiguity is necessary, and since many of the professionals in the field are young, considerable humility about one's inexperience with being old is also in order. There is a feeling among many who work with the aged that, because combinations of problems are the rule rather than the exception, one must be prepared to extend professional roles beyond the specific skills or approaches typically taught in graduate or medical school. How best to incorporate this generalist emphasis within curricula increasingly devoted to specialization may be the Rhubik's cube in clinical geriatrics for many years to come.

REFERENCES

Adolfsson, R.; Gottfries, C. G.; Oreland, L.; Roos, B. E.; and Winblad, B. 1978. Reduced level of catecholamines in the brain and increased activity of monoamine oxidase in platelets in Alzheimer's disease: Therapeutic implications. In *Alzheimer's Disease: Senile Dementia and Related Disorders,* eds. R. Katzman, R. D. Terry, and K. L. Bick. *Aging,* vol. 7, pp. 441–451. New York: Raven Press.

Akiskal, H. S., and McKinney, W. T. Jr. 1973. Depressive disorders: Toward a unified hypothesis. *Science* 182: 20–29.

Albert, M. L. 1978. Subcortical dementia. In *Alzheimer's Disease: Senile Dementia and Related Disorders,* eds. R. Katzman, R. D. Terry, and K. L. Bick. *Aging,* vol. 7, pp. 173–180. New York: Raven Press.

Albert, M. S. 1981. Geriatric neuropsychology. *Journal of Consulting and Clinical Psychology* 49: 835–850.

Amster, L. E., and Kraus, H. H. 1974. The relationship between life crises and mental deterioration in old age. *Int. J. Aging Hum. Dev.* 5(1): 51–55.

Atchley, R. 1980. Aging and suicide: Reflection of the quality of life. In *Proceedings of the Second Conference on the Epidemiology of Aging,* eds. S. Haynes and M. Feinleib. National Institute of Health. Washington, D.C.: U.S. Government Printing Office.

Ball, J. C., and Chambers, C. D. eds. 1970. *The Epidemiology of Opiate Addiction in the United States.* Springfield, IL: C. C. Thomas Publisher.

Baltes, P. B., and Willis, S. I. 1977. Toward psychological theories of aging and development. In *Handbook of the Psychology of Aging,* eds. J. E. Birren and K. W. Schaie, pp. 128–154. New York: Van Nostrand Reinhold.

Barbeau, A.; Growdon, J. H.; and Wurtman, R. J. 1979. Nutrition and the brain. In *Choline and Lecithin in Brain Disorders,* eds. A. Barbeau, J. H. Gordon, and R. J. Wurtman, vol. 5. New York: Raven Press.

Barnes, R. H.; Busse, E. W.; and Friedman, E. L. 1956. The psychological function of aged individuals with normal and abnormal electroencephalograms. II. A study of hospitalized individuals. *J. Nerv. Ment. Dis.* 124: 585–593.

Bartus, R. T.; Dean, R. L. III; Beer, B.; and Lippa, A. S. 1982. The cholinergic hypothesis of geriatric memory dysfunction. *Science* 217: 408–417.

Bennett, R., and Cook, D. 1980. *Isolation of the Aged in New York City in Planning for the Elderly in New York City.* New York: Community Council of Greater New York.

Benson, D. F. 1982. The use of positron emission scanning techniques in the diagnosis of Alzheimer's disease. In

Alzheimer Disease: A Report of Progress in Research, eds. S. Corkin, K. L. Davis, J. H. Growdon, E. Usdin, and R. J. Wurtman, pp. 79–82. New York: Raven Press.

Berger, K. S., and Zarit, S. H. 1978. Late-life paranoid states: Assessment and treatment. *Am. J. Orthopsychiatry* 48: 528–538.

Bergmann, K.; Kay, D. W. K.; Foster, E. M.; McKechnie, A. A.; and Roth, M. 1971. A follow-up study of randomly selected community residents to assess the effects of chronic brain syndrome and cerebrovascular disease. *Psychiatry,* Part II, pp. 856–865. *Proceedings of the V World Congress of Psychiatry,* Mexico.

Bigler, E. D., Steinman, D. R., and Newton, J. S. 1981. Clinical assessment of cognitive deficit in neurologic disorder. 1: Effects of age and degenerative disease. *Clinical Neuropsychology* 3: 5–12.

Birren, J. E., and Sloane, R. B. 1980. *Handbook of Mental Health and Aging.* Englewood Cliffs, NJ: Prentice-Hall.

Birren, J. E., and Sloane, R. B. 1977. Manpower and training needs in mental health and illness of the aging. Los Angeles: Ethel Percy Andrus Gerontology Center, University of Southern California.

Blazer, D., and Williams, C. D. 1980. Epidemiology of dysphoria and depression in the elderly population. *Am. J. Psychiatry* 137(4): 439–444.

Blessed, G.; Tomlinson, B. E.; and Roth, M. 1968. The association between quantitative measures of dementia and of senile change in the cerebral grey matter of elderly subjects. *Br. J. Psychiatry* 114: 797–811.

Bleuler, M. 1972. *Die Schizophreneu Geistesstorungen.* Stuttgart: Thiene.

Bleuler, M. 1974. The long-term course of the schizophrenic psychoses. *Psychol. Med.* 4: 244–254.

Bollerup, T. 1975. Prevalence of mental illness among 70-year-olds domiciled in nine Copenhagen suburbs. *Acta Psychiatr. Scand.* 51: 327–339.

Bolton, N.; Savage, R. D.; and Roth, M. 1967. The modified word learning test and the aged psychiatric patient. *Am. J. Psychiatry,* 113: 1139–1140.

Bondareff, W.; Mountjoy, C. G.; and Roth, M. 1981. Loss of neurones of origin of the adrenergic projection to cerebral cortex (nucleus locus coeruleus) in senile dementia. *Lancet* 1: 782–783.

Bornstein, P. E.; Clayton, P. J.; Halikas, J. A.; Maurice, W. L.; and Robins, E. 1973. The depression of widowhood after thirteen months. *Br. J. Psychiatry* 122: 561–566.

Botwinick, J., and Birren, J. E. 1951. Differential decline in the Wechsler-Bellevue subtests in the senile psychoses. *J. Gerontol.* 6: 365–368.

Brand, F. N., and Smith, R. T. 1974. Life adjustment and relocation of the elderly. *J. Gerontol.* 29: 336–340.

Brand, F. N., Smith, R. T., and Brand, P. A. 1977. Effect of economic barriers to medical care on patients noncompliance. *Public Health Reports* 92: 72–78.

Brandt, J.; Butters, N.; Ryan, C.; and Bayog, R. 1983. Cognitive loss and recovery in chronic alcohol abusers. *Arch. Gen. Psychiatry* 40: 435–442.

Bremer, J. 1951. A social psychiatric investigation of a small community in northern Norway. *Acta Psychiatr. Neurol. Scand.* 62 (Suppl.)

Bridge, T. B., and Wyatt, R. J. 1980a. Paraphrenia: Paranoid states of late life. I. European research. *J. Am. Geriatr. Soc.* 28: 193–200.

Bridge, T. B., and Wyatt, R. J. 1980b. Paraphrenia: Paranoid states of late life. II. American research. *J. Am. Geriatr. Soc.* 28: 210–205.

Brown, W. A.; Johnston, R.; and Mayfield, D. 1979. The 24-hour dexamethasone suppression test in a clinical setting: Relationship to diagnosis symptoms and response to treatment. *Am. J. Psychiatry* 136: 543–547.

Brown, W. S.; Marsh, J. T.; and La Rue, A. 1982. Event-related potentials in psychiatry: Differentiating depression and dementia in the elderly. *Bulletin of the Los Angeles Neurological Societies* 47: 91–107.

Brown, W. A., and Shuey, I. 1980. Response to dexamethasone and subtype of depression. *Arch. Gen. Psychiatry* 37: 747–751.

Busse, E. W. 1978. The Duke longitudinal study I: Senescence and senility. In *Alzheimer's Disease: Senile Dementia and Related Disorders,* eds. R. Katzman, R. D. Terry, and K. L. Bick, pp. 59–68. New York: Raven Press.

Busse, E. W. 1976. Hypochondriasis in the elderly: A reaction to social stress. *J. Am. Geriatr. Soc.* 24: 145–149.

Busse, E. W., and Blazer, D. 1980. Disorders related to biological functioning. In *Handbook of Geriatric Psychiatry,* eds. E. W. Busse and D. Blazer, pp. 390–414. New York: Van Nostrand Reinhold.

Cahalan, D.; Cisin, I. H.; and Crossley, H. M. 1969. American drinking practices: A national survey of drinking behavior and attitudes. Monogram No. 6. New Brunswick, N.J.: Rutgers Center of Alcohol Studies.

Capel, W. C.; Goldsmith, B. M.; Waddell, K. J.; and Stewart, G. T. 1972. The aging narcotic addict—An increasing problem for the next decade. *J. Gerontol.* 27: 102–106.

Capel, W. C., and Stewart, G. T. 1971. The management of drug abuse in aging populations: New Orleans findings. *Journal of Drug Issues* 1: 114–121.

Carlsson, A. 1981. Aging and brain neurotransmitters. In *Strategies for the Development of an Effective Treatment for Senile Dementia,* eds. T. Crook and S. Gerson, pp. 93–104. New Canaan, CT: Mark Pawley Association.

Carroll, B. J.; Feinberg, M.; Greden, J. F.; Tarika, J.; Albala, A. A., Haskett, R. F., James, N. M.; Kronfal, Z.; Lohr, N.; Steiner, M.; de Vigne, J. P.; and Young, E. 1981. A specific laboratory test for the diagnosis of melancholia. *Arch. Gen Psychiatry* 38: 15–22.

Chambers, C. D. 1971. An assessment of drug use in the general population. New York: New York State Narcotic Addiction Control Commission.

Chien, C. P. 1971. Psychiatric treatment for geriatric patients; "Pub" or drug? *Am. J. Psychiatry* 127: 1070–1075.

Chien, C. P.; Stotsky, B. A.; and Cole, J. O. 1973. Psychiatric treatment for nursing home patients: Drug, alcohol and milieu. *Am. J. Psychiatry* 130: 543–548.

Chien, C. P.; Townsend, E. J.; and Townsend, A. R. 1978. Substance use and abuse among the community elderly: The medical aspect. *Addictive Diseases: An International Journal* 3(3): 357–372.

Ciompi, L., and Müller, C. 1976. *Lebensweg und Alter der Schizophreneu.* Berlin: Springer Verlag.

Clark, E. 1982. Test profiles in Alzheimer and multi-infarct dementia. Paper presented at a meeting of the American Psychological Association, Washington, D.C., August 1982.

Clayton, P. J. 1973. The clinical morbidity of the first year of bereavement: A review. *Compr. Psychiatry* 14: 151–157.

Clayton, P. J.; Halikas, J. A.; and Maurice, W. L. 1972. The depression of widowhood. *Br. J. Psychiatry* 120: 71–78.

Cooper, A. F.; Garside, R. F.; and Kay, D. W. K. 1976. A comparison of deaf and non-deaf patients with paranoid and affective psychoses. *Br. J. Psychiatry* 129: 532–538.

Cooper, A. F., and Porter, R. 1976. Visual acuity and ocular pathology in the paranoid and affective psychoses of later life. *J. Psychosom. Res.* 20: 107–114.

Crapper-McLachlan, D. R.; Krishnan, S. S.; and Dalton, A. J. 1973. Brain aluminum distribution in Alzheimer's disease and experimental neurofibrillary degeneration. *Science* 180: 511–513.

Crook, T. H. 1979. Psychometric assessment in the elderly. In *Psychiatric Symptoms and Cognitive Loss in the Elderly,* eds. A. Raskin and L. F. Jarvik, pp. 207–220. Washington, D.C.: John Wiley and Sons.

Crook, T. H.; Ferris, S.; McCarthy, M.; and Rae, D. 1980. Utility of digit recall tasks for assessing memory in the aged. *J. Consult. Clin. Psychol.* 48: 228–233.

Crook, T. H.; and Gershon, S. 1981. *Strategies for the Development of an Effective Treatment for Senile Dementia.* New Canaan, CT: Mark Powley Assoc.

Crookes, T. G. 1974. Indices of early dementia on WAIS. *Psychological Reports* 34: 734.

Crookes, T. G., and McDonald, K. G. 1972. Benton's visual retention test in the differentiation of depression and early dementia. *Br. J. Soc. Clin. Psychol.* 11: 66–69.

Davidson, R. J.; Schwartz, G. E.; Saron, C.; Bennett, J.; and Goleman, D. J. 1979. Frontal vs. parietal EEG asymmetry during positive and negative affect. *Psychophysiology* 16: 202–203.

Davies, P.; Katzman, R.; and Terry, R. D. 1980. Reduced somatostatic-like immunoreactivity in cerebral cortex from cases of Alzheimer disease and Alzheimer senile dementia. *Nature* 288: 279–280.

Davis, K. L.; Mohs, R. C.; Tinklenberg, J. R.; Hollister, L. E.; Pfefferbaum, A.; and Kopell, B. S. 1978. Physostigmine: Enhancement of long-term memory process in normal subjects. *Science* 201: 272–274.

de Alarcon, J. 1971. Social causes and consequences of mental illness in old age. In *Recent Development in Psychogeriatrics,* eds. D. Kay and A. Walk, pp. 75–86. London: Headley.

de Alarcon, R. 1964. Hypochondriasis and depression in the aged. *Geronto. Clin.* 6: 266–277.

de Leon, M. J.; Ferris, S. H.; George, A. E.; Reisberg, B.; Kricheff, I. I.; and Gerson, S. 1980. Computed tomography evaluations of brain–behavior relationships in senile dementia of the Alzheimer's type. *Neurobiology of Aging* 1: 69–79.

Dessonville, C.; Gallagher, D.; Thompson, L. W.; Finnell, K.; and Lewinsohn, P. M. 1982. Relation of age and health status of depression symptoms in normal and depressed older adults. *Essence* 5: 99–117.

Diagnostic and Statistical Manual of Mental Disorders (DSM-III). 1982. 3rd ed., ed. by the Committee on Nomenclature and Statistics of the American Psychiatric Association, Washington, D.C.

Dovenmuehle, R. H.; Recklass, J. B.; and Newman, G. 1970. Depressive reactions in the elderly. In *Normal Aging.* Durham, NC: Duke Univ. Press.

Drachman, D. A., and Leavitt, J. 1974. Human memory and the cholinergic system: A relationship to aging. *Arch. Neurol.,* 30: 113–121.

DuPont, R. 1976. Testimony before the subcommittee on aging and subcommittee on alcoholism and narcotics of the U.S. Senate Committee on Labor and Public Welfare, Washington, D.C. Cited in D. M. Peterson, F. I. Whittington, and E. T. Beer. 1979. Drug use and misuse among the elderly. *Journal of Drug Issues* 9(1): 5–26.

Earnest, M. P.; Heston, R. K.; Wilkinson, W. E.; and Manke, W. F. 1979. Cortical atrophy, ventricular enlargement and intellectual impairment in the aged. *Neurology* 29: 1138–1143.

Eisdorfer, C., and Cohen, D. 1978. The cognitively impaired elderly: Differential diagnosis. In *The Clinical Psychology of Aging,* eds. M. Storandt, I. Siegler, and M. Elias, pp. 7–42. New York: Plenum Press.

Eisdorfer, C.; Cohen, D.; and Buckley, C. E., III. 1978. Serum immunoglobulins and cognition in the impaired elderly. In *Alzheimer's Disease: Senile Dementia and Related Disorders,* eds. R. Katzman, R. D. Terry, K. L. Bick, pp. 401–407. New York: Raven Press.

Endicott, J., and Spitzer, R. A. 1978. A diagnostic interview: The schedule for affective disorders and schizophrenia. *Arch. Gen. Psychiatry* 35: 837–844.

Epstein, L. J. 1976. Symposium on age differentiation in depressive illness. Depression in the elderly. *J. Gerontol.* 31: 278–282.

Essen-Moller, E. 1956. Individual traits and morbidity in a Swedish rural population. *Acta Psychiatr. Neurol. Scand.* 53: 283–297.

Ferris, S. H.; Crook, T.; Clark, E.; McCarthy, M.; and Rae, D. 1980. Facial recognition memory deficits in normal aging and senile dementia. *J. Gerontol.* 35: 707–714.

Fish, F. 1960. Senile schizophrenia. *Journal of Mental Science* 106: 938–946.

Flor-Henry, P. 1979. On certain aspects of the localization of the cerebral systems, regulating and determining emotion. *Biol. Psychiatry* 14: 677–698.

Folstein, M. F.; Folstein, S. E.; and McHugh, P. R. 1975. Mini-Mental State: A practical method of grading the cognitive state of patients for the clinician. *J. Psychiatr. Res.* 12: 189–198.

Folstein, M. F., and McHugh, P. R. 1978. Dementia syndrome of depression. In *Alzheimer's Disease: Senile*

Dementia and Related Disorders, eds. R. Katzman, R. D. Terry, and K. L. Bick. *Aging,* vol. 7, pp. 87–96. New York: Raven Press.

Fox, J. H.; Kaszniak, A. W.; Huckman, M. 1979. Computerized tomographic scanning not very helpful in dementia—nor in craniopharyngioma (Letter). *New Engl. J. Med.* 300: 437.

Fox, J. H.; Topel. J. L.; and Huckman, M. S. 1975. Use of computerized tomography in senile dementia. *J. Neurol. Neurosurg. Psychiatry,* 28: 948–953.

Freeman, J. T. 1965. *Clinical Features of the Older Patient.* Springfield, Illinois: Charles C. Thomas.

Gaitz, C. M. 1977. Depression in the elderly. In *Phenomenology and Treatment of Depression,* eds. W. Fann, I. Karucan, D. Pokorny, and I. R. Williams. New York: Spectrum Publications.

Gaitz, C., and Scott, J. 1972. Age and the measurement of mental health. *J. Health Soc. Behav.* 13: 55–67.

Gallagher, D.; Breckenridge, J. N.; Thompson, L. W., Dessonville, C., and Amaral, P. 1982. Similarities and differences between normal grief and depression in older adults. *Essence* 5: 127–140.

Gatz, M.; Smyer, M.; and Lawton, M. P. 1980. The mental health system and the older adult. In *Aging in the 1980's,* ed. L. W. Poon, pp. 5–18. Washington, D.C.: American Psychological Association.

George, L. 1980. *Role Transitions in Later Life.* Monterey, CA: Brooks, Cole Pub. Co.

Gerner, R. H. 1979. Depression in the elderly. In *Psychopathology of Aging,* ed. O. J. Kaplan, pp. 97–148. New York: Academic Press.

Gerner, R.; Estabrook, W.; Steuer, J.; Waltuch, L.; Kakkar, P.; and Jarvik, L. 1980. A placebo controlled double-blind study of Imipramine and Trazedone in geriatric depression. In *Psychopathology in the Aged,* eds. J. O. Cole and J. E. Barret, pp. 167–179. New York: Raven Press.

Gerner, R., and Jarvik, L. A. In press. Antidepressant drug treatment in the elderly. In *Depression and Antidepressants: Implication for Consideration and Treatment,* eds. E. Friedman, F. Mann, and S. Gershon. New York: Raven Press.

Gianotti, G. 1975. Confabulation of denial in senile dementia. *Psychiatria Clinica* 8: 99–108.

Gianturco, D. T., and Busse, E. W. 1978. Psychiatric problems encountered during a long-term study of normal ageing volunteers. In *Studies in Geriatric Psychiatry,* eds. D. D. Isaacs and F. Post, pp. 1–16. New York: John Wiley.

Gilleard, C. J. 1980. Wechsler Memory Scale performance of elderly psychiatric patients. *J. Clin. Psychol.* 36: 958–960.

Gilleard, C. J.; Willmott, M.; and Vaddadi, K. S. 1981. Self-report measures of mood and morale in elderly depressives. *Br. J. Psychiatry* 138: 230–235.

Glantz, M. 1981. Predictions of elderly drug abuse. *J. Psychoactiv. Drugs* 13(2): 117–126.

Goldfarb, A. I. 1975. Depression in the old and aged. In *The Nature and Treatment of Depression,* ed. F. F. Flach, pp. 119–144. New York: John Wiley.

Goldfarb, A. I. 1964. The evaluation of geriatric patients

following treatment. In *The Evaluation of Psychiatric Treatment,* eds. P. Hoch and J. Zubin, pp. 271–311. New York: Grune and Stratton.

Goldstein, S. E., and Birnbom, F. 1976. Hypocondriasis and the elderly. *J. Am. Geriatr. Soc.* 24: 150–154.

Goldstein, S. F.; Filskow, S.; Weaver, L. A., and Ives, J. O. 1977. Neuropsychological effects of electroconvulsive therapy. *J. Clin. Psychol.* 33: 798–806.

Goodin, D.; Squires, K.; and Starr, A. 1978. Long latency event-related components of the auditory evoked potential in dementia. *Brain* 101: 635–649.

Gurland, B. 1981. The borderlands of dementia: The influence of sociocultural characteristics on rates of dementia occurring in the senium. In *Clinical Aspects of Alzheimer's Disease,* eds. N. Miller and G. Cohen. *Aging,* vol. 5, pp. 61–80. New York: Raven Press.

Gurland, B. J. 1976. The comparative frequency of depression in various adult age groups. *J. Gerontol.* 31: 283–292.

Gurland, B. J., and Cross, P. S. 1982. Epidemiology of psychopathology in old age. In *Psychiatric Clinics of North America,* eds. L. F. Jarvik and G. W. Small, pp. 11–26. Philadelphia: W. B. Saunders Co.

Gurland, B.; Dean, L.; Cross, P.; and Golden, R. 1980. The epidemiology of depression and dementia in the elderly: The use of multiple indicators of these conditions. In *Psychopathology in the Aged,* eds. J. O. Cole and J. E. Barrett, pp. 37–62. New York: Raven Press.

Guttman, R. 1981. Performance on the Raven progressive matrices as a function of age, education and sex. *Educational Gerontology: An International Quarterly* 7: 49–55.

Guttman, D. 1978. Patterns of legal drug use by older Americans. *Addictive Diseases: An International Journal* 3(3): 337–356.

Hachinski, V. C.; Itiff, L. D.; Zilhka, E.; DuBoulay, G. H., McAllister, V. L., Marshall, J.; Russell, R. W.; and Symon, L. 1975. Cerebral blood flow in dementia. *Arch. Neurol.* 32: 632–637.

Hall, E. H.; Savage, R. D.; Bolton, N.; Pidwell, D. M.; and Blessed, G. 1972. Intellect, mental illness and survival in the aged: A longitudinal investigation. *J. Gerontol.* 27(2): 237–244.

Harford, T. 1977. The distribution of alcohol consumption in metropolitan Boston by day and week. Unpublished.

Heller, F. J., and Wynne, R. 1975. Drug misuse by the elderly: Indications and treatment suggestions. In *Developments in the Field of Drug Abuse,* eds. E. Senay, V. Shorty, and H. Alkasne, pp. 945–955. Cambridge, Mass.: Schenkman Press.

Heston, L. L. 1976. Alzheimer's disease trisamy 21 and myeloproliferative disorders: Associations suggesting a genetic diathesis. *Science* 196: 322–323.

Hilbert, N. M.; Niederehe, G.; and Kahn, R. L. 1976. Accuracy and speed of memory in depressed and organic aged. *Educational Gerontology* 1: 131–146.

Huckman, M. S.; Fox, J.; and Topel, J. 1975. The validity of criteria for the evaluation of cerebral atrophy by computed tomography. *Radiology* 116: 85–92.

Hughes, C. P., and Gado, M. 1981. Computed tomography and aging of the brain. *Neuroradiology* 139: 391–396.

Inciardi, J.; McBride, D.; Busse, B.; and Wells, K. 1978. Acute drug reactions among the aged: A research note. *Addictive Diseases* 3: 383–388.

Inglis, J. 1959. A paired-associate learning test for use with elderly psychiatric patients. *Journal of Mental Science* 105: 440–443.

Inglis, J. 1957. An experimental study of learning and "memory function" in elderly psychiatric patients. *Journal of Mental Science* 103: 796–803.

Irving, G.; Robinson, R. A.; McAdam, W. 1970. The validity of some cognitive tests in the diagnosis of dementia. *Br. J. Psychiatry* 117: 149–156.

Jacobs, J. W.; Bernhard, M. R.; and Delgado, A. 1977. Screening for organic mental syndromes in the mentally ill. *Ann. Intern. Med.* 86: 40–46.

Jacobs, S., and Ostfeld, A. 1977. An epidemiological review of the mortality of bereavement. *Psychosom. Med.* 39: 344–357.

Jamison, K. R. 1979. Manic-depressive illness in the elderly. In *Psychopathology of Aging,* ed. O. J. Kaplan, pp. 79–95. New York: Academic Press.

Jarvik, L. F. In press. The impact of immediate life situations on depression—illnesses and losses. *Depression in the Elderly: Causes, Care Consequences,* eds. M. Hauge and L. Breslau. New York: Springer Publishing Co.

Jarvik, L. F.; Altshuler, K. Z.; Kato, T.; and Blummer, B. 1971. Organic brain syndrome and chromosome loss in aged twins. *Diseases of the Nervous System* 32: 159–170.

Jarvik, L. A., and Blum, J. E. 1971. Cognitive declines as predictors of mortality in twin pairs: A twenty-year longitudinal study of aging. In *Prediction of Life Span,* eds. E. Palmore and F. C. Jeffers, pp. 199–211. Lexington, MA: D. C. Heath and Co.

Jarvik, L. F., and La Rue, A. 1979. Prediction of the development of organic brain syndrome. Invited address presented at a meeting, "Life-Span Research on the Prediction of Psychopathology."

Jarvik, L. F.; La Rue, A.; and Liston, E. 1981–1985. Alzheimer-type dementia: A biobehavioral family study. National Institute of Mental Health, USPHS MH 36205.

Jarvik, L. F.; Matsuyama, S. S.; Kessler, J. O.; Fu, T. K.; Tsai, S. Y.; and Clark, E. O. 1982. Philothermal response of polymorphonuclear leukocytes in dementia. *Neurobiology of Aging* 3: 93–99.

Jarvik, L. F.; Mintz, J.; Steuer, J.; and Gerner, R. 1982. Treating geriatric depression: A 26-week interim analysis. *J. Am. Geriatr. Soc.* 30: 713–717.

Jarvik, L. F., and Perl, M. 1981. Overview of physiologic dysfunction and the production of psychiatric problems in the elderly. In *Psychiatric Management of Physical Disease in the Elderly,* eds. A. Levenson and R. C. W. Hall, pp. 1–15. New York: Raven Press.

Jarvik, L. F., and Perl, M. 1981. Overview of physiologic dysfunctions related to psychiatric problems in the elderly. *Aging: Neuropsychiatric Manifestations of Physical Disease in the Elderly* 14: 1–15.

Jarvik, L. F.; Ruth, V.; and Matsuyama, S. 1980. Organic brain syndrome and aging: A six-year follow-up of surviving twins. *Arch. Gen. Psychiatry* 37: 280–286.

Jarvik, L. F., and Small, G. W. 1982. Depression in the aged: A commentary. In *The Psychiatric Clinics of North America,* eds. L. F. Jarvik and G. W. Small, pp. 45–48. Philadelphia: W. B. Saunders Co.

Kahn, R. L. 1977. Excess disabilities. In *Readings in Aging and Death,* ed. S. H. Zarit, pp. 234–235. New York: Harper and Row.

Kahn, R. L.; Goldfarb, A. L.; Pollock, M.; and Peck, A. 1960. Brief objective measures for the determination of mental status in the aged. *Am. J. Psychiatry* 117: 326–328.

Kahn, R. L.; Zarit, S. H.; Hilbert, N. M.; and Niederehe, G. 1975. Memory complaint and impairment in the aged. *Arch. Gen. Psychiatry* 32: 1569–1573.

Kasl, S. V.; Ostfeld, A. M.; Brody, G. M.; Snell, L.; and Price, L. A. 1980. Effects of "involuntary" relocation on the health and behavior of the elderly. in *Proceedings of the 2nd Conference on the Epidemiology of Aging,* eds. S. Haynes and M. Feinleib, pp. 211–236. National Institute of Health. Washington, D.C.: U.S. Government Printing Office.

Kasl, S. V., and Rosenfield, S. 1980. The residential environment and its impact on the mental health of the aged. In *Handbook of Mental Health and Aging,* eds. J. E. Birren and R. B. Sloane, pp. 468–498. Englewood Cliffs, NJ: Prentice-Hall, Inc.

Kaszniak, A. W.; Fox, J.; Gandell, D. L.; Garron, D. C.; Huckman, M. S.; and Ramsey, R. G. 1978. Predictors of mortality in presenile and senile dementia. *Ann. Neurol.* 3: 246–252.

Kaszniak, A. W.; Garron, D. C.; and Fox, J. 1979. Differential effects of age and cerebral atrophy upon span of immediate recall and paired-associate learning in older patients suspected of dementia. *Cortex* 15: 285–395.

Kaszniak, A. W.; Garron, D. C.; Fox, J. H.; Bergen, D.; and Huckman, M. 1979. Cerebral atrophy, EEG slowing, age, education, and cognitive functioning in suspected dementia. *Neurology* 29: 1273–1279.045066

Kaszniak, A. W.; Garron, D. C.; Fox, J. H.; Huckman, S.; and Ramsey, R. G. 1975. Relation between dementia and cerebral atrophy as measured by computerized tomography. *Neurology* 25: 387.mography. *Neurology* 25: 387.

Kasteler, J. M.; Gray, R. M.; and Carruth, M. L. 1968. Involuntary relocation of the elderly. *Gerontologist* 8: 276–279.

Kastenbaum, R. 1978. Personality theory, therapeutic approaches, and the elderly client. In *The Clinical Psychology of Aging,* eds. M. Storandt, I. C. Siegler and M. F. Elias, pp. 199–224. New York: Plenum Press.

Katzman, R. 1978. Normal pressure hydrocephalus. In *Alzheimer's Disease: Senile Dementia and Related Disorders,* eds. R. Katzman, R. D. Terry, and K. L. Bick. *Aging,* vol. 7. New York: Raven Press.

Katzman, R. 1976. The prevalence and malignancy of Alzheimer's disease. *Arch. Neurol.* 33: 217–218.

Kay, D. 1972. Schizophrenia and schizophrenia-like states in the elderly. *Br. J. Hosp. Med.* Oct.: 369–376.

Kay, D. W. K. 1963. Late paraphrenia and its bearing on the aetiology of schizophrenia. *Acta Psychiatr. Scand.* 39: 159–169.

Kay, D. W. K. 1959. Observations on the natural history of genetics of old age psychosis: A Stockholm material. 1931–1938. *Proceedings of Royal Society of Medicine* 52: 79.

Kay, D. W. K.; Beamish, P.; and Roth, M. 1964. Old age mental disorders in Newcastle upon Tyne. *Br. J. Psychiatry* 110: 146–158.

Kay, D. W. K.; Bergmann, K.; Foster, E. M.; McKechnie, A. A.; and Roth, M. 1970. Mental illness and hospital usage in the elderly: A random sample followed up. *Compr. Psychiatry* 11: 26–35.

Kay, D. W. K.; Cooper, A. F.; Garside, R. F.; and Roth, M. 1976. The differentiation of paranoid from affective psychoses by patients' premorbid characteristics. *Br. J. Psychiatry* 129: 207–215.

Kaszniak, A. W.; Garron, D. C.; Fox, J. H.; Huckman, S.; and Ramsey, R. G. 1975. Relation between dementia and cerebral atrophy as measured by computerized tomography. *Neurology* 25: 387.

Kendrick, D. C.; Parboosingh, R. C.; and Post, F. 1965. A synonym learning test for use with elderly psychiatric subjects: A validation study. *Br. J. Soc. Clin. Psychol.* 4: 63.

Kendrick, D. C., and Post, F. 1967. Differences in cognitive status between healthy, psychiatrically ill, and diffusely brain-damaged elderly subjects. *Br. J. Psychiatry* 113: 75–81.

Kiloh, L. G. 1961. Pseudo-dementia. *Acta Psychiatr. Scand.* 37: 336–351.

Kleban, M. H.; Lawton, M. P.; Brody, E. M.; and Moss, M. 1975. Characteristics of mentally impaired aged profiting from individualized treatment. *J. Gerontol.* 30: 90–96.

Kleemeier, R. W. 1962. Intellectual changes in the senium. *Proceedings of the American Statistical Association* 1: 290.

Klisz, D. 1978. Neuropsychological evaluation in older persons. In *The Clinical Psychology of Aging,* eds. M. Storandt, I. Siegler, and M. F. Elias, pp. 71–95. New York: Plenum Press.

Kral, V. A. 1978. Benign senescent forgetfulness. In *Alzheimer's Disease: Senile Dementia and Related Disorders,* eds. R. Katzman, R. D. Terry, and K. L. Bick. pp. 47–51. New York: Raven Press.

Kramer, N., and Jarvik, L. F. 1979. Assessment of intellectual changes in the elderly. In *Psychiatric Symptoms and Cognitive Loss in the Elderly,* eds. A. Raskin and L. F. Jarvik, pp. 221–271. Washington, D.C.: Hemisphere.

Lamy, P. P. 1980. Misuse and abuse of drugs by the elderly. *Am. Pharm.* 20: 14–17.

La Rue, A. 1982. Memory loss and aging. In *The Psychiatric Clinics of North America.* eds. L. F. Jarvik and G. W. Small, Vol. 5, No. 1, pp. 89–103. Philadelphia, Pennsylvania: W. B. Saunders Co.

La Rue, A., and Jarvik, L. F. 1980. Reflections of biological changes in the psychological performance of the aged. *Age* 3: 29–32.

Lawton, P. 1972. Schizophrenia forty-five years later. *J. Genet. Psychol.* 121: 133–143.

Lawton, M. P.; Whelihan, W. M.; and Belsky, J. K. 1980. Personality and their uses with older adults. In *Handbook of Mental Health and Aging,* eds. J. E. Birren and R. B. Sloane, pp. 537–553. Englewood Cliffs, NJ: Prentice Hall, Inc.

Lehmann, H. E. 1982. Affective disorders in the aged. In *The Psychiatric Clinics of North America,* eds. L. F. Jarvik and G. W. Small, pp. 27–44. Philadelphia: W. B. Saunders.

Lemon, B. W.; Bengtson, V. L.; and Peterson, J. A. 1972. An exploration of the activity theory of aging: Activity types and life satisfaction among in-movers to a retirement community. *J. Gerontol.* 27: 511–523.

Lesse, S. 1974. Depressive equivalents and the multivariant masks of depression. In *Masked Depression,* ed. S. Lesse, pp. 3–23. New York: Jason Aronson Inc.

Levenson, A. J., ed. 1979. *Neuropsychiatric Side-Effects of Drugs in the Elderly.* New York: Raven Press.

Lipton, M. A., and Nemeroff, C. B. 1978. The biology of aging and its role in depression. In *Aging: The Process and the People,* eds. G. Usdin and C. K. Hofling, pp. 47–95. New York: Brunner/Mazel.

Liston, E. M. 1979. Clinical findings in presenile dementia: A report of 50 cases. *J. Nerv. Ment. Dis.* 167: 337–342.

Loeb, C. 1980. Clinical diagnosis of multi-infarct dementia. In *Aging of the Brain and Dementia,* eds. L. Amaducci, A. N. Davison, and P. Antuono. vol. 13, pp. 251–261. New York: Raven Press.

Loew, C. A., and Silverstone, B. M. 1971. A program of intensified stimulation and response facilitation for the senile aged. *Gerontologist* 11:341–347.

Lowenthal, M. F.; Berkman, P.; and associates. 1967. *Aging and Mental Disorders in San Francisco.* San Francisco: Jossey-Bass.

Lowenthal, M. F., and Haven, C. 1968. Interaction and adaptation: Intimacy as a critical variable. *Am. Sociol. Rev.* 33: 20–30.

Maas, J. W. 1978. Clinical and biochemical heterogeneity of depressive disorders. *Ann. Intern. Med.* 88: 556–563.

Maddox, G. L. 1964. Self assessment of health status. A longitudinal study of selected elderly subjects. *J. Chronic Dis.* 17: 449–460.

Marsden, C. D., and Harrison, M. J. G. 1972. Outcome of investigation of patients with presenile dementia. *Br. Med. J.* 29: 249–252.

Matsuyama, S. S., and Jarvik, L. F. 1980. Genetics and mental functioning in senescence. In *Handbook of Mental Health and Aging,* eds. J. E. Birren and B. Sloane, pp. 134–148. Englewood Cliffs, NJ: Prentice-Hall, Inc.

Matsuyama, S. S.; Jarvik, L. F.; Fu, T. K.; and Kessler, J. O. 1981. Leukotaxis and serum immunoglobulins in the aged. *Age* 4: 89–91.

McAllister, T. W., and Price, T. R. P. 1982. Severe depressive pseudodementia with and without dementia. *Am. J. Psychiatry* 139(5): 626–629.

McCarthy, M.; Ferris, S. H.; Clark, E.; and Crook, T.

1981. Acquisition and retention of categorized material in normal aging and senile dementia. *Exp. Aging Res.* 7: 127–135.

McGeer, E., and McGeer, P. L. 1976. Neurotransmitter metabolism in the aging brain. In *Aging,* eds. R. D. Terry and S. Gershon. Vol. 3, pp. 389–403. New York: Raven Press.

Mellinger, G. D.; Balter, M. B.; Parry, H. J.; Manheimer, D. I.; and Cisin, I. H. 1974. An overview of psychotherapeutic drug use in the United States. In *Drug Use: Epidemiological and Sociological Approaches,* eds. E. Josephson and E. E. Carroll. Washington, D.C.: Hemisphere Pub. Corp.

Miller, E. 1980. Cognitive assessment of the older adults. In *Handbook of Mental Health and Aging,* eds. J. E. Birren and R. B. Sloane, pp. 520–536. Englewood Cliffs, NJ: Prentice Hall, Inc.

Miller, E. 1975. Impaired recall and the memory disturbance in presenile dementia. *Br. J. Soc. Clin. Psychol.* 14: 73–79.

Miller, E., and Lewis, P. 1977. Recognition memory in elderly patients with depression and dementia: A signal detection analysis. *J. Abnorm. Psychol.* 86: 84–86.

Morgan, L. A. 1976. A re-examination of widowhood and morale. *J. Gerontol.* 31: 687–695.

Morris, J. N., 1975. Changes in morale experienced by elderly institutional applicants along the institutional path. *Gerontologist* 15: 345–349.

Müller, C. 1959. *Uber das Senium der Schizophrenen.* Basel, Switzerland: Karger.

Myers, M.; Sheldon, D.; and Robinson, S. S. 1963. A study of 138 elderly first admissions. *Am. J. Psychiatry* 120: 244–249.

Naeser, M. A.; Gebhardt, C.; and Levine, H. L. 1980. Decreased computerized tomography numbers in patients with presenile dementia. *Arch. Neurol.* 37: 401–409.

Neely, E., and Patrick, M. L. 1968. Problems of aged persons taking medications at home. *Nursing Research* 17: 52–55.

Naguib, M., and Levy, R. 1982. Prediction of outcome in senile dementia—A computed tomography study. *Br. J. Psychiatry* 140: 263–267.

National Institute of Mental Health. 1978. Provisional data on federally funded community mental health centers, 1976–1977. Rockville, Maryland.

Nielsen, J. 1968. Chromosomes in senile dementia. In *Senile Dementia,* eds. C. Müller and L. Ciompi, pp. 59–62. Bern Switzerland: Hans Huber.

Nielson, J. 1962. Geronto-psychiatric period—prevalence investigation in a geographically delimited population. *Acta Psychiatr. Scand.* 38: 307–330.

Nott, P. N., and Fleminger, J. J. 1975. Presenile dementia: The difficulties of early diagnosis. *Acta Psychiatr. Scand.* 51: 210–217.

Obrist, W. D.; Busse, E. W.; Eisdorfer, C., and Kleemeier, R. W. 1962. Relation of the electroencephalogram to intellectual function in senescence. *J. Gerontol.* 17: 197–207.

Ouslander, J. G. 1982. Illness and psychopathology in the elderly. In *The Psychiatric Clinics of North America,* eds. L. F. Jarvik and G. W. Small, pp. 145–158. Philadelphia: W. B. Saunders.

Overall, J. E., and Gorham, D. R. 1972. Organicity versus old age in objective and projective test performance. *J. Consult. Clin. Psychol.* 39: 98–105.

Overton, W. F., and Reese, H. W. 1973. Models of development: Methodological implications. In *Life-Span Developmental Psychology Methodological Issues,* eds. J. Nesselroade and H. Reese, pp. 65–86. New York: Academic Press.

Palmore, E.; Cleveland, W. P.; Nowlin, J. B.; Ramm, D.; and Siegler, I. C. 1979. Stress and adaptation in later life. *J. Gerontol.* 34: 841–851.

Parker, E. S., and Noble, E. P. 1977. Alcohol consumption and cognitive functioning in social drinkers. *Journal of the Study of Alcoholism* 38: 1224–1232.

Parker, C. M., and Brown, R. J. 1972. Health after bereavement: A controlled study of young Boston widowers. *Psychosom. Med.* 34: 449–461.

Parkinson, S. R.; Lindholm, J. M.; and Inman, V. W. 1982. An analysis of age differences in immediate recall. *J. Gerontol* 37: 425–431.

Parry, H. J.; Balter, M. B.; Mellinger, G. D.; Cisin, I. H.; and Manheimer, D. I. 1973. National patterns of psychotherapeutic drug use. *Arch. Gen. Psychiatry* 28: 769–783.

Parson, O. A., and Leber, W. R. 1981. The relationship between cognitive dysfunction and brain damage in alcoholics: Causal, interactive or epiphenomenal? *Alcoholism: Clinical and Experimental Research* 5: 326–343.

Pascarelli, E., and Fischer, W. 1974. Drug dependence in the elderly. *Int. J. Aging Hum. Dev.* 5: 347–356.

Perez, F. I.; Gay, J. R. A., and Taylor, R. L. 1975. WAIS performance of neurologically impaired aged. *Psychol. Rep.* 37: 1043–1047.

Perez, F. I.; Gay, J. R.; Taylor, R. L.; and Rivera, V. M. 1975. Patterns of memory performance in the neurologically impaired aged. *Can. J. Neurol. Sci.* 2: 347–355.

Perez, F. I.; Rivera, V. M.; Meyer, J. S.; Gay, J. R. A.; Taylor, R. L.; and Matthew, N. T. 1975. Analysis of intellectual and cognitive performance in patients with multi-infarct dementia, vertebrobasilar insufficiency with dementia and Alzheimer's disease. *J. Neurol. Neurosurg. Psychiatry* 38: 533–540.

Perl, D. P., and Brody, A. R. 1980. Detection of aluminum by sem-X-ray spectrometry within neurofibrillary tangle-hearing neurons of Alzheimer's disease. *Neurotoxicology* 1: 133–137.

Petersen, D. M., and Thomas C. W. 1975. Acute drug reactions among the elderly. *J. Gerontol* 30: 552–556.

Petersen, D. M.; Whittington, F. J.; and Beer, E. T. 1979. Drug use and misuse among the elderly. *Journal of Drug Issues* 9(1): 5–26.

Pfeiffer, E. 1975. A short portable mental status questionnaire for the assessment of organic brain deficit in elderly patients. *J. Am. Geriatr. Soc.* 23: 433–441.

Pfeiffer, E., and Busse, E. W. 1973. Affective disorders. In *Mental Illness in Later Life,* eds. E. W. Busse and E. Pfeiffer, pp. 107–144. Washington, D.C.: American Psychiatric Association.

Pichot, P., and Hassan, J. 1973. Masked depression and depressive equivalents—problems of definition and diagnosis. In *Masked Depression,* ed. P. Kielholz. Bern, Switzerland: Hans Huber Pub.

Post, F. 1966. *Persistent Persecutory States of the Elderly.* Oxford: Pergamon Press.

Post, F. 1972. The management and nature of depressive illnesses in late life: A follow-through study. *Br. J. Psychiatry,* 121: 393–404.

Post, F. 1975. Dementia, depression, and pseudodementia. *Psychiatric Aspects of Neurologic Disease,* eds. D. F. Benson and D. Blumer. New York: Grune and Stratton.

Post, F. 1976. Diagnosis of depression in geriatric patients and treatment modalities appropriate for the population. In *Depression: Behavioral Biochemical Diagnostic, and Treatment Concepts,* eds. D. M. Gallant and G. M. Simpson, pp. 205–231, New York: Spectrum.

Post, F. 1978. The functional psychosis. In *Studies in Geriatric Psychiatry,* eds. A. D. Isaacs and F. Post, pp. 77. Chichester: John Wiley & Sons.

Post, F. 1980. Paranoid, schizophrenia-like, and schizophrenic states in the aged. In *Handbook of Mental Health and Aging,* eds. J. E. Birren and R. B. Sloane, pp. 591–615. Englewood Cliffs, NJ: Prentice Hall.

Raskin, A. 1979. Signs and symptoms of psychopathology in the elderly. In *Psychiatric Symptoms and Cognitive Loss in the Elderly,* eds. A. Raskin and L. Jarvik, pp. 1–18. Washington, D.C.: Hemisphere.

Raskin, A., and Rae, D. S. 1980. Distinguishing depressive pseudodementia from true dementia. *Psychopharmacol. Bull.* 16: 23–25.

Raskin, A., and Rae, D. S. 1981. Psychiatric symptoms in the elderly. *Psychopharmacol. Bull.* 17: 96–99.

Raskind, M.; Peskind, E.; Rivard, M. F.; Veith, R.; and Barnes, R. 1982. Dexamethasone suppression test and cortisol circadian rhythm in primary degenerative dementia. *Am. J. Psychiatry* 139(11): 1368–1471.

Raymond, E. F.; Michals, T. J.; and Steer, R. A. 1980. Prevalence and correlates of depression in elderly persons. *Psychol. Rep.* 47: 1055–1061.

Redick, R. W.; Kramer, M.; and Taube, C. A. 1973. Epidemiology of mental illness and utilization of psychiatric facilities among older persons. In *Mental Illness in Later Life,* eds. E. W. Busse and E. Pfeiffer, pp. 94–231. New York: American Psychiatric Association.

Redick, R. W., and Taube, C. A. 1980. Demography and mental health care of the aged. In *Handbook of Mental Health and Aging,* eds. J. Birren and R. B. Sloane, pp. 57–71. Englewood Cliffs, NJ: Prentice Hall.

Reisberg, B., and Ferris, S. H., 1982. Diagnosis and assessment of the older patient. *Hosp. Community Psychiatry* 33(2): 104–109.

Retterstöl, N. 1968. Paranoid psychosis: The stability of nosological categories illustrated by a personal follow-up investigation. *Br. J. Psychiatry* 114: 553–562.

Retterstöl, N. 1966. *Paranoid and Paranoiac Psychoses.* Oslo: Universitetsforloget.

Riegel, K. F.; Riegel, R. M.; and Meyer, M. A. 1967. A study of the drop-out rate in longitudinal research

on aging, and the prediction of death. *Journal of Personality and Social Psychology* 5:342–348.

Roberts, M. A.; Caird, F. I.; Grossart, K. W., and Stevens, J. R. 1976. Computerized tomography in the diagnosis of cerebral atrophy. *J. Neurol. Neurosurg. Psychiatry* 39: 909–915.

Ron, M. A.; Toone, B. K.; Garralda, M. E.; and Lishman, W. A. 1979. Diagnostic accuracy in presenile dementia. *Br. J. Psychiatry* 124: 161–167.

Rosen, W. G.; Terry, R. D.; Fuld, P. A.; Katzman, R.; and Peck. 1980. A pathological verification of ischemic score in differentiation of dementias. *Ann. Neurol.* 7: 486–488.

Rosin, A. J., and Glatt, M. M. 1971. Alcohol excess in the elderly. *Quarterly Journal of Studies on Alcoholism* 32: 53–59.

Roth, M. 1955. The natural history of mental disorder in old age. *J. Ment. Sci.* 101: 281–301.

Roth, M., and Hopkins, B. 1953. Psychological test performance in patients over sixty. I. Senile psychosis and the affective disorders of old age. *J. Ment. Sci.* 99: 439–450.

Roth, M., and Kay, D. W. K. 1956. Affective disorder arising in the senium. II. Physical disability as an actiological factor. *J. Ment. Sci.* 102: 141–150.

Ruemke, H. C. 1963. Uber alte schizophrene. *Schweiz. Arch Neurol. Psychiatr.* 91: 201–210.

Ryan, C., and Butters, N. 1980. Further evidence for a continuum of impairment encompassing male alcoholic Korsakoff patients and chronic alcoholic men. *Alcoholism: Clinical and Experimental Research* 4: 190–198.

Salzman, C. In press. A primer on geriatric psychopharmacology. *Am. J. Psychiatry.*

Savage, R. D. 1973. Old age. In *Handbook of Abnormal Psychology* ed. H. J. Eysenck, pp. 645–688. London: Pitman.

Schaie, K. W., and Schaie, J. 1977. Clinical assessment and aging. In *Handbook of the Psychology of Aging,* eds. J. Birren and K. W. Schaie, pp. 692–723. New York: Van Nostrand Reinhold.

Schildkraut, J., and Kety, S. 1967. Biogenic amines and emotions. *Science* 156: 21–30.

Schuckit, M., and Pastor, P. 1978. The elderly as a unique population: Alcoholism. *Alcoholism: Clinical and Experimental Research* 2: 31–38.

Schwab, J. J.; Holzer, C. E.; and Warheit, G. J. 1973. Depressive symptomatology and age. *Psychosomatics* 14: 135–141.

Schwartz, D.; Wang, M.; Zeitz, L.; and Goss, M. E. W. 1962. Medication errors made by elderly chronically ill patients. *Am. J. Public Health* 52: 2018–2029.

Shulman, K., and Post, F. 1980. Bipolar affective disorder in old age. *Br. J. Psychiatry* 136(1): 26–32.

Siegler, I. C. 1975. The terminal drop hypothesis: Fact or artifact. *Experimental Aging Research* 1: 169–185.

Simon, A. 1980. The neuroses, personality disorders, alcoholism, drug use and misuse, and crime in the aged. In *Handbook of Mental Health and Aging,* eds. J. E. Birren and R. B. Sloane. pp. 653–670. Englewood Hills, NJ: Prentice Hall Inc.

Simon, A.; Epstein, L. J.; and Reynolds, L. 1968. Alcoholism in the geriatric mentally ill. *Geriatrics* 23(10): 125–131.

Sitaram, N.; Weingartner, H.; and Gillin, J. C. 1978. Human serial learning: Enhancement with arecoline and impairment with scopolamine correlated with performance on placebo. *Science* 201: 274–276.

Small, G. W., and Jarvik, L. F. 1982. The dementia syndrome. *The Lancet* 1443–1446.

Small G. W.; Liston, E. H.; and Jarvik, L. F. 1981. Diagnosis and treatment of dementia in the aged. *The Western J. Med.* 135: 469–481.

Smith, J. S., and Kiloh, I. G. 1981. The investigation of dementia: Results in 200 consecutive admissions. *The Lancet* 1: 824–827.

Spar, J. E. 1982. Dementia in the aged. In *The Psychiatric Clinics of North America,* eds. L. F. Jarvik and G. W. Small, pp. 67–86. Philadelphia: W. B. Saunders Co.

Spar, J. E., and Gerner, R. 1982. Does the dexamethasone suppression test distinguish dementia from depression? *Am. J. Psychiatry* 139(2): 238–240.

Spar, J. E., and La Rue, A. A. 1983. Major depression in the elderly: DSM III criteria and the dexamethasone suppression test as predictors of treatment response. *American Journal of Psychiatry* 140:7, 844–847.

Squires, K.; Chippendale, T.; Wrege, K.; Goodin, D.; and Starr, A. 1980. Electroplupiological assessment of mental function in aging and dementia. In *Aging in the 1980's* ed. L. Poon, pp. 125–134. Washington, D.C.: American Psychological Association.

Stenmark, D. E., and Dunn, V. K. 1982. Issues related to the training of geropsychologists. In *Psychology and the Older Adult,* eds. J. F. Santos and G. R. Vanden Bos, pp. 83–96. Washington, D.C.: American Psychological Association.

Storandt, M. 1977. Age, ability level and methods of administering and scoring the WAIS. *J. Gerontol.* 32: 175–178.

Storandt, M.; Siegler, I. C.; and Elias, M. F. 1978. *The Clinical Psychology of Aging.* New York: Plenum Press.

Straker, M. 1982. Adjustment disorders and personality disorders in the aged. In *The Psychiatric Clinics of North America,* eds. L. F. Jarvik and G. W. Small, pp. 121–129. Philadelphia: W. B. Saunders Co.

Streib, G. F. 1956. Morale of the retired. *Social Problems* 3: 270–276.

Syndulko, K.; Hansch, E.; Cohen, S.; Pearce, J.; Goldbert, Z.; Monton, B.; Tourtellotte, W.; and Potvin, A. In press. Long latency event-related potentials in normal aging and dementia. In *Clinical Applications of Evoked Potentials in Neurology,* eds. J. Courjou, F. Mauguire, and M. Revol. New York: Raven Press.

Task Force Sponsored by the National Institute on Aging. 1980. Senility reconsidered. *J. Am. Med. Assoc.* 244(3): 259–261.

Terry, R. D., and Davies, P. 1980. Dementia of the Alzheimer type. *Annual Review of Neuroscience* 3: 77–95.

Thomas, L. 1981. On the problem of dementia. *Discover,* August, 1981: 34–36.

Thompson, G. B. 1973. Work versus leisure role: An investigation of morale among employed and retired men. *J. Gerontol.* 28: 339–344.

Tomlinson, B. E.; Blessed, G.; and Roth, M. 1970. Observations on the brains of demented old people. *J. Neurol. Sci.* 11: 205–242.

Tourigny-Rivard, M. F.; Raskind, M.; and Rivard, D. 1981. The dexamethasone suppression test in an elderly population. *Biol. Psychiatry* 16: 1177–1184.

Turner, R. J., and Sternberg, M. P. 1978. Psychosocial factors in elderly patients admitted to a psychiatric hospital. *Age and Ageing* 7: 171–177.

U.S. Bureau of the Census, Statistical Abstract of the United States. 1981. 102nd ed. Washington, D.C.

U.S. Department of Health, Education and Welfare, Federal Council on Aging. 1979. Mental health and the elderly: Recommendations for action. DHEW Publication No. 80–209607. Washington, D.C.

U.S. Department of Health, Education and Welfare. 1974. Second Special Report of the U.S. Congress on Alcohol and Health from the Secretary of Health, Education and Welfare. Washington, D.C.: U.S. Government Printing Office.

Vaillant, G. E. 1979. Natural history of male psychologic health. *New England J. Med.* 301: 1249–1254.

Vaillant, G. E., and Perry, J. C. 1980. Personality disorders. In *Comprehensive Text on Psychiatry,* eds. H. Kaplan, A. Freedman, and B. Sadock. 3rd ed., pp. 1562–1590. Baltimore: Williams and Wilkins.

Varner, R. V., and Gaitz, C. M. 1982. Schizophrenic and paranoid disorders in the aged. In *The Psychiatric Clinics of North America,* eds. L. F. Jarvik and G. W. Small, Vol. 5, pp. 107–118. Philadelphia: W. B. Saunders Co.

Verwoerdt, A. 1981. *Clinical Geropsychiatry.* 2nd ed. Baltimore: Williams and Wilkins.

Verwoerdt, A. 1976. *A Clinical Geropsychiatry.* Baltimore: Williams and Wilkins.

Wang, H. S. 1973. Cerebral correlates of intellectual function in senescence. In *Intellectual Functioning in Adults,* eds. L. F. Jarvik, C. Eisdorfer, and J. E. Blum, pp. 95–106. New York: Springer.

Ward, B. E.; Cook, R. H.; Robinson, A.; and Austin, J. H. 1979. Increased aneuploidy in Alzheimer disease. *Am. J. Med. Genetics.* 3: 137–144.

Warheit, G. J. 1979. Life events, coping, stress, and depressive symptomatology. *Am. J. Psychiatry* 136(4B): 502–507.

Warheit, G. J.; Arey, S. A.; and Swanson, E. 1976. Patterns of drug use: An epidemiologic overview. *Journal of Drug Issues* 6: 223–237.

Weingartner, H.; Cohen, R. M.; Murphy, D. L.; Martello, J.; and Gerdt, C. 1981. Cognitive processes in depression. *Archives of General Psychiatry* 38: 42–47.

Weingartner, H.; Kaye, W.; Smallberg, S. A.; Ebert, M. H.; Gillin, J. C.; and Sitaram, N. 1981. Memory failures in progressive idiopathic dementia. *J. Abnorm. Psychol* 90: 187–196.

Weingartner, H., and Silberman, E. 1982. Models of cognitive impairment: Cognitive changes in depression. *Psychopharmacol. Bull.* 18: 27–42.

Weissman, M. M., and Klerman, G. L. 1977. Sex differences and the epidemiology of depression. *Arch. Gen. Psychiatry* 34: 98–111.

Weissman, M. M., and Myers, J. K. 1978. Affective disorders in a U.S. urban community. *Arch. Gen. Psychiatry* 35: 1304–1311.

Wells, C. C. 1978. Chronic brain disease: An overview. *Am. J. Psychiatry* 135: 1–12.

Wells, C. E. 1979. Pseudodementia. *Am. J. Psychiatry* 136: 895–900.

Wells, C. E. 1977. Diagnostic evaluation and treatment in dementia. In *Dementia,* ed. C. E. Wells. 2nd ed. pp. 247–276. Philadelphia: F. A. Davis.

Wells, C. E., and Buchanan, D. C. 1977. The clinical use of psychological testing in evaluation for dementia. In *Dementia,* ed. C. E. Wells, pp. 189–204. 2nd ed. Philadelphia: F. A. Davis, Co.

Wenger, P. A. 1958. A comparative study of the aging process in groups of schizophrenics and mentally well veterans. *Geriatrics* 13: 367–370.

Whanger, A. D. 1973. Paranoid syndromes of the senium. In *Psychopharmacology—Aging,* eds. E. Eisdorfer and W. E. Fann, pp. 203–211. New York: Plenum Press.

Whitehead, A. 1973. Verbal learning and memory in elderly depression. *Br. J. Psychiatry* 123: 203–208.

Whitehouse, P. J.; Price, D. L.; Clark, A. W., Coyle, J. T.; and DeLong, M. R. 1981. Alzheimer disease: Evidence for selective loss of cholinergic neurons in the nucleus basalis. *Ann. Neurol.* 10(2): 122–126.

Whittier, J. R., and Korenyi, C. 1961. Selected characteristics of aged patients: A study of mental hospital admissions. *Compr. Psychiatry* 2: 113–120.

Wigdor, B. T., and Morris, G. 1977. A comparison of twenty-year medical histories of individuals with depressive and paranoid states. *J. Gerontol.* 32: 160–163.

Wilson, W. P.; Musella, I.; and Short, M. J. 1977. The electroencephalogram in dementia. In *Dementia* ed. C. E. Wells, pp. 205–221. Philadelphia: F. A. Davis Co.

Winick, C. 1962. Maturing out of addiction. *Bull. Narcotics,* 14: 1–7.

Zarit, S. H. 1980. *Aging and Mental Disorders.* New York: The Free Press.

Zarit, S. H.; Miller, N. E., and Kahn, R. L. 1978. Brain function, intellectual impairment and education in the aged. *J. Am. Geriatrics Society* 26: 58–66.

Zimberg, S. 1978. Diagnosis and treatment of the elderly alcoholics. *Alcoholism: Clinical and Experimental Research* 2(1): 27–29.

Zimberg, S. 1974. The elderly alcoholic. *Gerontology* 14: 221–224.

Zung, W. W. K. 1967. Depression in the normal aged. *Psychosomatics* 8: 287–292.

26
ACCIDENTS AND THE AGING INDIVIDUAL

Harvey L. Sterns

Department of Psychology and Institute for Life-Span Development and Gerontology
The University of Akron

Office of Geriatric Medicine and Gerontology
Northeastern Ohio Universities College of Medicine

Gerald V. Barrett

and

Ralph A. Alexander

Department of Psychology and Institute for Life-Span Development and Gerontology
The University of Akron

An accident is that occurrence in a sequence of events that produces unintended injury, death, or property damage (National Safety Council, 1981). Individuals are subject to such events throughout the life span. As one grows older, risks of accident involvement or of disability or death as a result of such involvement may well increase.

Accident research emphasizes the dynamic relationship between the individual and the environment. Much of the literature on accidents and aging has taken a distinctly nonpsychological approach. Some conceive of accidents or injuries as being related to decisions that bring about inappropriate responses. Much of the literature deals with attempts to minimize the danger of poor decision making. Environmental modifications such as circuit breakers, smoke detectors, and anti-scald devices are clearly effective, for example, and play a major role in minimizing risk and providing greater safety to the individual (Baker and Deitz, 1979; Hogue, 1982a). Many situations do not allow for environmental modification, however, for reasons of practicality or cost. This chapter will review the major areas of accident research with an emphasis on the psychology of aging as it relates to accidents. In particular, it will discuss the capability of the older adult in terms of characteristics such as visual demand, motor response, and information processing.

There have been two major approaches to the study of accidents and injury events. One, the epidemiologic approach, has emphasized the description, classification, and incidence of injury events. This approach focuses on absolute number of injuries, exposure data, and accident rates. The other major tradition has been represented by psychological approaches that make use of ergonomics and engineering psychology and encourage the application of relevant information about human characteristics and behavior to the design of objects, machines, and environments as well as the design of selection batteries, tests, and training approaches that will minimize the risk of accidents.

Recent discussions in life-span psychology have focused on three major classes of developmental influences (Baltes, Cornelius, and Nesselroade, 1978; Baltes, Reese, and Lipsitt, 1980). Nonnormative life events are one of these classes, and accidents are one of the major examples of this type of developmental influence. Such events (i.e., accidents) may adversely affect the development of some persons but may be favorably avoided by others (Schaie, 1982). Our knowledge regarding the effects and outcomes of injury events at present is at a descriptive level and has not really received a thorough discussion in the life events literature (Hultsch and Plemons, 1979). A major emphasis of this perspective would be on antecedent patterns associated with accidents as well as the role of injury events on individual development.

In addition to treating accidents as nonnormative events, psychologically based studies of accident behavior also treat them as nonrandom. Although the occurrence of hazardous environmental circumstances may have a substantial random component, accident involvement is both reliable and predictable (Boyle, 1980; Shaw and Sichel, 1971). In a unique study, Guilford (1973) was able to show that accident involvement for women in the home environment of the kitchen was related to automobile accidents. This is one of the few empirical supports for the proposition that some individuals are accident-prone.

A psychology of accidents and aging has importance for at least three reasons:

1. Avoidance of accidents promotes independence and continued working ability or other skilled activity by older adults.
2. Improved understanding of older adult abilities and functional capacity will lead to a better understanding of the relationship between abilities and the risk of accidents.
3. Understanding system failures in older adult injury events may highlight the vulnerability of all age groups and lead to lessened risks of accidents for the total population.

MODELS OF ACCIDENT-RELATED BEHAVIOR

There are a number of different approaches to the theory and empirical investigation of human behavior as it relates to accident involvement. These approaches can usually be classified into five broad areas or models that are distinguished by their primary focus—environmental press, personality, physical energy, epidemiology, and human factors psychology.

Models of environmental press typically view the environment or any debilitating event as factors that challenge the competency of the individual (Shinar, McDonald, and Treat, 1978; Sivak, 1981). Another example of this approach is the research of Robinson and Jacobson (1978), who postulate that accidents occur as the result of normal performance variability. Many researchers view the role of alcohol and drug impairment in automobile accidents (Brewer and Sandow, 1980) and workplace accidents (Shain, 1982) in the context of environmental demands.

A substantial body of the research on accident-related behavior has taken the view that personality traits provide a useful model. Pestonjee and Singh (1980), among others, have suggested that introverts should have lower accident involvement rates than extroverts because of attentional differences in perceptually demanding situations. Svenson (1981) investigated accidents as a function of inaccuracies in the perception of one's own and others' abilities. Much research in this area focuses on various aspects of deviant personality. Clark and Prolisko (1979) see excessive risk-taking as a failure to conform to social roles. Krantz (1979) researched accidents as a function of hostility and proposed that those more likely to be involved are socially deviant. The extreme view of this personality model is represented by researchers such as Phillips (1979) who suggest that many accidents may, in fact, be the result of suicidal behavior.

Waller (1973) and Haddon and Baker (1980) represent the large number of accident researchers who suggest that the effective agent in all injuries is physical energy in one form or another (kinetic, chemical, thermal, radiant, or electric). It is excessive levels of energy exchange or excessive interference with normal patterns of energy transfer that produce tissue damage. According to this approach, the method for dealing with these sources of energy depends on the performance level of the individual and the demands of the task involved. The occurrence of an injury is seen as being dependent upon the amount of energy released, its rate of transfer, its distribution over bodily tissues, and the nature of the bodily tissue. Tissues that localize energy such as the brittle bones of older adults will be less able to spread the impact than the pliable bones of young children and will thus be subject to greater injury.

Although epidemiological approaches to accident research emphasize the typology of environmental hazard, the safety and physical well being of individuals is a major objective of engineering/human factors psychology (McCormick and Sanders, 1982). The emphasis of this perspective is on studying human error and ways to eliminate it. Although coming from a different set of assumptions, epidemiological and human factors approaches emphasize the dynamic interaction of the individual with the environment. Most discussions emphasize the use of traditional psychological constructs such as competencies, traits, and abilities and emphasize assessment approaches. No situation, however, reflects better the issue of studying concrete psychological events in their interaction with events that are internal and external to the organism than do those that involve accidents and injury events (Hultsch and Hickey, 1978; Riegel, 1976; Windley and Scheidt, 1980).

Barrett, Alexander, and Forbes (1977) identified the variables intrinsic to the individual that are important for the prediction of automobile accident involvement. These variables of perceptual style, selective attention, and perceptual motor reaction time were organized in terms of a perceptual information-processing model and were variously viewed as potential predictors of accident involvement, as a conceptual framework for driving training procedures, and as possible measures of functional age. Panek, Barrett, Sterns, and Alexander (1977) presented a detailed review of age differences in perceptual information-processing ability with regard to driving, reviewing research on perceptual style, selective attention, perceptual motor reaction time as well as vigilance and decision making.

Witkin, Lewis, Hertzman, Machover, Meissner, and Wapner (1954) and Witkin, Oltman, Raskin, and Karp (1971) developed the concept of perceptual style—the individual's ability to extract relevant information from a complex visual scene. Perceptual style has been found related to driving behavior in complex driving simulations (Barrett and Thornton, 1968; Barrett, Cabe, and Thornton, 1969) and in accident involvement (Barrett, Mihal, Panek, Sterns, and Alexander, 1977; Harano, 1963; Mihal and Barrett, 1976; Williams, 1972).

The ability to attend selectively to one message in the presence of competing messages has been a widely investigated information-processing capacity (Kahneman, 1973). Selective attention is usually measured by a dichotic listening task. The subject is presented with two simultaneous messages, one in each ear, and instructed to attend to only one message and report specified information to the experimenter. Using this type of task, aircraft flight proficiency (Gopher and Kahneman, 1971) and motor vehicle accident involvement (Barrett et al., 1977; Kahneman, Ben-Ishai, and Lotan, 1973; Mihal and Barrett, 1976) have been predicted.

Perceptual motor-reaction-time ability is measured by speed of response on single choice and complex tasks. This ability has also been found to be related to driving behavior (Babarik, 1968; Barrett et al., 1977; Fergenson, 1971; Mihal and Barrett, 1976).

This approach emphasizes the evaluation throughout the life span of individual ability levels on each of these dimensions of perceptual style, selective attention, and perceptual motor-reaction time, all of which have been found to undergo different developmental change across the life span.

THE DEMOGRAPHICS OF INJURIES

In looking at accidents or injury events at different points in the life span, we find that children have the highest injury rates for all injuries. Older adults, however, have the highest death rates and the highest dysfunction and disability rates from motor vehicle crashes, falls, fires, and burns (Baker and Deitz, 1979; Hogue, 1982a; National Safety Council, 1981).

Older adults have relatively low accident-frequency rates compared with other age groups but high disability and fatality rates. In 1978, 22.9 percent of all fatal injuries were to persons 65 years or older, yet this age group constituted only about 11 percent of the total population. Rates of days of restricted activity, disability in bed, and hospital stays are relatively high for the aged. Although adults 65 years and older have an injury rate that is only 57 percent of that for children 6 to 16 years old, they have 2.8 times the number of days of restricted activity and 2.9 times the number of days of bed-confining disability that result from injury than the 6- to 16-year-olds (Hogue, 1982a).

From the ages of 1 to 44, a person is more likely to die from an accident than from any other cause, and that accident most often is an automobile accident. Among persons of all ages, accidents are the fourth leading cause of death. For youths aged 15 to 24 years, accidents claim more lives than all other causes combined and about five times more than the next leading cause of death. Four out of five accident victims in this group are male (National Safety Council, 1981).

The magnitude of the accident problem can be illustrated by these compelling figures. In 1978, the accidental death toll in the United States was 105,561 (see Table 1). This figure was over 100,000 per year from 1966 to 1981. In 1980, almost 24,000,000 persons (approximately one-tenth of the population) suffered an injury that resulted in one or more days of restricted activity. In terms of financial loss, the cost of accidents was 83.2 billion. The breakdown was as follows: motor vehicles,

TABLE 1. Leading Causes of All Deaths.

From *Accident Facts,* 1981 Edition, National Safety Council. Deaths are for 1978 figures from National Center for Health Statistics, Public Health Service, U.S. Department of Health and Human Services.

	No. of Deaths	Death Rate*		No. of Deaths	Death Rate*
All Ages:	1,927,788	883	*25 to 44 Years:*	103,991	179
Heart disease	729,510	334	Accidents	25,024	43
Cancer	396,992	182	Motor-vehicle	14,574	25
Stroke**	175,629	80	Drowning	1,700†	3
Accidents:	105,561	48	Poison (solid, liquid)	1,210	2
Motor-vehicle	52,411	24	Falls	1,053	2
Falls	13,690	6	Fires, burns	1,044	2
Drowning	7,026	3	Other	5,443	9
Fires, burns	6,163	3	Cancer	16,866	29
Other	26,271	12	Heart disease	14,167	24
Under 1 Year:	45,945	1,434	*45 to 64 Years:*	434,246	990
Anoxia	9,556	298	Heart disease	151,564	346
Congenital anomalies	8,404	262	Cancer	134,115	306
Complications of preg-			Stroke**	21,670	49
nancy and childbirth	5,544	173	Accidents:	18,774	43
Immaturity	3,677	115	Motor-vehicle	8,048	18
Pneumonia	1,499	47	Falls	2,101	5
Accidents:	1,262	39	Fires, burns	1,400	3
Ingestion of food,			Drowning	910†	2
objects	296	9	Surg. complications	901	2
Motor-vehicle	264	8	Other	5,414	13
Mech. suffocation	242	8	Cirrhosis of liver	16,449	37
Fires, burns	154	5	Diabetes mellitus	7,790	18
Other	306	9			

TABLE 1. (continued)

	No. of Deaths	Death Rate*		No. of Deaths	Death Rate*
1 to 4 Years:	8,429	69	*65 to 74 Years:*	452,259	3,027
Accidents:	3,504	29	Heart Disease	183,880	1,231
Motor-vehicle	1,287	11	Cancer	119,623	801
Fires, burns	742	6	Stroke**	36,390	244
Drowning	630†	5	Diabetes mellitus	9,629	64
Ingestion of food,			Accidents:	9,072	61
objects	167	1	Motor-vehicle	3,217	22
Falls	121	1	Falls	1,852	13
Other	557	5	Fires, burns	789	5
Congenital anomalies	1,027	8	Surg. complications	783	5
Cancer	599	5	Ingestion of food,	483	3
			objects		
			Other	1,948	13
5 to 14 years:	12,030	34	Pneumonia	9,225	62
Accidents:	6,118	17	Cirrhosis of liver	6,209	42
Motor-vehicle	3,130	9			
Drowning	1,010†	3	*75 Years and Over*	822,388	9,012
Fires, burns	586	1	Heart disease	377,322	4,135
Firearms	297	1	Cancer	121,569	1,332
Other	1,095	3	Stroke**	113,336	1,242
Cancer	1,500	4	Pneumonia	33,777	370
Congenital anomalies	650	2	Arteriosclerosis	24,046	264
			Accidents:	15,185	166
15 to 24 Years	48,500	118	Falls	7,830	86
Accidents:	26,622	64	Motor-vehicle	2,727	30
Motor-vehicle	19,164	46	Surg. complications	963	10
Drowning	2,130†	5	Fires, burns	918	10
Firearms	561	1	Ingestion of food,	716	8
			objects		
Poison (solid, liquid)	577	1	Other	2,031	22
Other	4,120	11	Diabetes mellitus	14,748	162
Homicide	5,443	13	Emphysema	5,949	65
Suicide	5,115	12			

*Deaths per 100,000 population for each age group (rates are averages for age groups, not individual ages).
**Cerebrovascular disease
†Partly estimated

39.3 billion; work, 30.2 billion; home, 8.9 billion; and public accidents, 6.4 billion (National Safety Council, 1981).

The excellent reviews of Baker and Deitz (1979) and Hogue (1980, 1982a, and 1982b) have emphasized the following. For children under the age of five years, falls were the leading cause of nonfatal injuries, whereas the largest number of fatal injuries involved motor vehicles, drowning, and fires. Each of these categories resulted in about 800 deaths per year, with pedestrian deaths a major factor in urban areas.

Teenagers and young adults, who tend to expose themselves to such high-risk activities as contact sports, motorcycling, and high speed driving, have very high death rates from crashes, firearms, and drownings. More than one-half of the deaths in the age group of 15 to 24 result from accidents.

In the adult population of 25 to 64, motor vehicle crashes cause almost half of all deaths from unintentional injuries. Nonfatal injuries to males most often take place at work. Even among job-related injuries, motor vehicle accidents make up the largest category (approximately 4,000 annually). In addition, among occupational categories, construction workers and farmers each have relatively high accident rates (about 2,000 annually). Firefighters and miners have among the highest death rates per worker.

In the older adult group, 65 and above, high death rates reflect a generally poorer recovery and greater suceptibility to complication following an injury. In the 65-to-74 group, slightly over 35 percent of deaths from injury are due to motor vehicles, approximately 20 percent to falls, and another 8 percent to fire and other burns. In the 74-and-over age group, more than 50 percent of the injuries are due to falls and less than 20 percent to motor vehicles.

For adults 65 and over, women have higher rates of injury and death from falls than men. Men have higher injury and death rates from burns and motor vehicle and pedestrian accidents. Before the age of 75, nonwhite males have the highest rates of death from injury. For individuals 75 and older, white males have a much higher rate of death from injury than nonwhite males (Hogue, 1982a).

THE HIGHWAY ENVIRONMENT

Data has been collected on motor vehicle accidents for more than 70 years. Between 1912 and 1979, deaths per 10,000 registered vehicles were reduced 91 percent from 33 to 3. In 1912, there were 3,100 fatalities with 950,000 registered vehicles. In 1980, there were 52,600 fatalities with 165 million vehicles (National Safety Council, 1981).

Psychological approaches to driving research have been reviewed by Barrett, Alexander, and Forbes (1977); Shinar (1978); and Knapper, Leplat, and Michon (1980). Reviews on driving and age include those of DeSilva (1938); Marsh (1960); Mcfarland, Tune, and Welford (1964); Planek and Fowler (1971); and Panek, Barrett, Sterns, and Alexander (1977).

There were approximately 146 million drivers in the United States in 1980. Over 21 million (14.5 percent) were drivers 60 and over. Table 2 provides the ages of drivers and the total number of accidents in 1980. The figures in the last two columns at the right indicate the frequency of accident involvement (National Safety Council, 1981).

A State of California Department of Motor Vehicle Report (1982) indicated that 64 percent of the California population 65 and older hold a valid license (1,466,000). Almost one out of every three Californians at the age of 80 is licensed to drive. There were 3,500 valid licenses held by adults 90 years old or above as of December 1980.

The California data break down the older population into the following groups: 60–64, 65–69, 70–74, and 75 and over. Supporting much earlier research was the finding of a gradual decrease in accidents (starting below age 20) as driver age increases. When accidents were adjusted for miles driven, both older and younger drivers were found to have higher accident rates than other drivers. Accident rate per unit of mileage began to increase above age 55 for males and above age 60 for females. Older drivers involved in accidents were also more often found at fault by law enforcement agencies than those in other age groups. Drivers 70 years and older, moreover, were more often convicted of sign, right-of-way, and turning violations but less often convicted of speed, equipment, and major violations.

Fatal accident rates for older California drivers were found to be lower than for other ages. Drivers at the age of 80 did not show an over involvement in fatal accidents. These results support the earlier study of Finesilver (1969). On the other hand, a study by Lee, Glover, and Eavy (1980) of 7,581 Michigan drivers found that crashes per million miles were higher in the 65 and older group than in other age groups except those under 25. Such contradictions in the studies of older adult driving point to the need for looking more carefully at the types of driving involved and the conditions governing them.

The driving record for older adults is subject to a number of important influences. Many older adults have always had excellent driving skills and continue to perform well; others may have declining abilities but are able to compensate for this loss by driving more cautiously, at slower speeds, for fewer miles,

TABLE 2   Age of Drivers—Total Number and Number in Accidents, 1980.

From *Accident Facts*, 1981 Edition, National Safety Council. Drivers in accidents based on reports from 18 state traffic authorities. Number of drivers by age are National Safety Council estimates based on reports from state traffic authorities and research groups.

| | All Drivers | | Drivers in Accidents | | | | Per No. of Drivers | |
| | | | Fatal | | All | | | |
Age Group	Number	Percent	Number	Percent	Number	Percent	Fatal*	All*
Total	146,000,000	100.0	68,300	100.0	29,800,000	100.0	47	20
Under 20	14,300,000	9.8	10,800	15.8	5,000,000	16.8	76	35
20–24	17,400,000	11.9	14,200	20.8	5,900,000	19.8	82	34
25–29	17,500,000	12.0	9,700	14.2	4,400,000	14.8	55	25
30–34	16,800,000	11.5	8,300	12.2	3,500,000	11.7	49	21
35–39	13,900,000	9.5	4,800	7.0	2,200,000	7.3	35	16
40–44	11,700,000	8.0	4,700	6.9	1,900,000	6.4	40	16
45–49	11,400,000	7.8	3,800	5.6	1,600,000	5.3	33	14
50–54	11,700,000	8.0	2,900	4.2	1,300,000	4.4	25	11
55–59	10,100,000	6.9	2,600	3.8	1,300,000	4.4	26	13
60–64	7,500,000	5.2	2,200	3.2	900,000	3.0	29	12
65–69	6,400,000	4.4	1,700	2.5	1,000,000	3.4	27	16
70–74	4,400,000	3.0	1,200	1.8	300,000	1.0	27	7
75 and over	2,900,000	2.0	1,400	2.0	500,000	1.7	48	17

*Drivers in fatal accidents per 100,000 drivers in each age group.
**Drivers in all accidents per 100 drivers in each age group.

and over less demanding routes of travel. Still others may have declining capacities but do not recognize or compensate for them, leading to violations and/or accidents. In a Swedish study, Ysander and Herner (1976) emphasized that such factors need thorough investigation. They found that more than half of male drivers over 75 years of age and a fourth of drivers 65 to 69 had given up driving altogether. Carp (1971) reported that of 709 retired people with a mean age of 67.5, 280 owned cars and 202 had stopped driving. Some older adults may prematurely stop driving as a result of an accident, a near miss, or family pressure. The problem is that there is no opportunity for an older adult to undergo special testing and be given feedback regarding his or her driving ability. Traditional license examinations are not designed for this, nor are they extensive enough to provide such information.

More rigorous annual testing for renewal of a drivers license when some critical age has been reached has been often suggested. The use of a more extensive testing approach for older adults may be appropriate provided that the tests assess skills known to be relevant to the driving task. Age, per se, does not lead to accidents. Although correlational research indicates a relationship between age and accident rates per mile beginning with the age group of 55 to 65, the main factors predictive of motor vehicle accidents are those deficiencies in physical and psychological skills that are essential for carrying out driving tasks (Panek, Barrett, Sterns, and Alexander, 1977).

Barrett, Alexander, and Forbes (1977) identified factors that can be important in predicting driving accidents. They summarized individual differences in terms of three information-processing variables: perceptual style, selective attention, and perceptual motor-reaction time. Barrett, Mihal, Panek, Sterns, and Alexander (1977) extended the earlier research of Mihal and Barrett (1976) to determine if these information-processing variables could differentiate between drivers 25 to 41 and 43 to 64 by studying accidents over a five-year period for a group of utility company drivers. When the driver's age was correlated with the variables and accidents, it was found to have a significant effect on the measures of perceptual style, selective attention, and perceptual motor-reaction time. Results indicated that the 25-to-41 age group were more skilled at information-processing tasks and had faster reaction times and fewer accidents.

The relationship of basic skill measures and on-the-road behavior has been examined in a number of recent studies. Rackhoff and Mourant (1979) had subjects drive an instrumented vehicle. Visual search patterns, vehicle velocity, and voluntary visual occlusion times were recorded for a 60-to-70 age group and a 21-to-29 age group. Basic skill measures included a visual search test, an embedded-figures test, and a reaction-time test.

Rackhoff and Mourant found that the two groups performed equally on the least demanding task (daytime driving with eyes open). When task demands were increased, the differences between the two age groups became more pronounced. It was concluded that older drivers required more time to acquire the minimum information needed for vehicle control. Longer eye-open times for the 60-to-70 age group were seen as being related to more time being required to look for particular cues, to extract information from them, or to search for still more cues. On the basic skills tasks, the 60-to-70 age group had longer reaction and visual-search times. Some of this age group, however, performed better than the younger group. The older group took almost seven times longer on the embedded-figures test. Again, great individual differences were found. This study also revealed that both visual-search and embedded-figures scores correlated highly with eye-open times on all driving tasks. It was felt that more wide-ranging eye travels and longer eye-open durations were the result of lower capacities or greater caution and preference for more information.

Shinar, McDowell, Rackhoff, and Rockwell (1978) reported data from two studies that indicated that field-dependent subjects required more time to process the available visual information and were less effective in their on-the-road visual-search behavior.

The finding that older adults are at a disadvantage in night driving has been documented by a number of recent studies. Sivak, Olson, and Pastalan (1981) studied two groups (an under-25-year-old group and an over-61-year-old group) of equivalent high-luminance (daytime) visual acuity. The 61-and-above group exhibited legibility distances for sign reading that were only 65 to 77 percent those of the under-25 group on a nighttime sign-reading task. The author concluded that older drivers therefore have less distance and thus less time to act on information transmitted by highway signs. A follow-up study by Sivak and Olson (1982) with a 20-to-30 and a 63-to-75 age group that were matched for both high-luminance (daytime) and low-luminance (nighttime) visual acuity found no significant difference on the nighttime sign-reading task. This research indicates that visual deficits rather than information-processing deficits are probably responsible for nighttime legibility performance.

Studies of glare indicate that individuals who perform acceptably on conventional vision tests can exhibit substantial sensitivity to glare (Pulling, Wolf, Sturgis, Vaillancourt, and Dolliver, 1980). Here again we find large interpersonal variation. Sturgis, Pulling, and Vaillancourt (1981) have developed an automated technique that can be used to identify individuals who have higher glare sensitivity, sensitivity that usually increases with age. Driving restrictions based on glare sensitivity would have a major impact on older adult drivers (Sturgis and Osgood, 1982). It is apparent that some individuals have great difficulty in interpreting environmental information in the presence of low illumination and glare. It is also clear, however, that many older adults have good low-luminance acuity or are no more adversely affected by glare than younger individuals.

Both Birren (1974) and Salthouse (1982) have discussed behavioral slowing with age. To investigate this phenomenon further, Panek, Barrett, Alexander, and Sterns (1979) examined preference for pace on visual monitoring tasks. Their study focused on the relationship between intrinsic information-processing abilities and the self-selected speed of the individual in performing these tasks. Subjects in seven age groups ranging from age 17 to 72 were given an embedded-figures test, a rod-and-frame test, a complex reaction-time test, and a preference-for-pace task. Significant differences were found for the speed at which individuals choose to work, with mean speed increasing with age. It was found that poorer performance on the intrinsic information-processing tasks was significantly related to a preference for slower speeds. These results indicate that older adults may perform well when the pace of the task is congruent with their information-processing abilities. When tasks require a faster pace, however, they may have difficulty. Compensation and retraining may be helpful.

THE HOME AND COMMUNITY ENVIRONMENT

Insightful discussions of the dynamic relationship between the older individual and the environment have been presented by Lawton (1977, 1980) and Windley and Scheidt (1980). Older adults may be at considerable risk if their level of competence is low and the demands of the environment are high. They may also get into difficulty if visual demands, motor responses, physical barriers, stairs, and so forth, are beyond their capability. Older adults may not be attentive to changing capabilities and not recognize environmental hazards (Fozard and Popkin, 1978). Guidelines for the assessment of the older adult's home environment for safety hazards and for modifications providing safety and supportive features are now available. Wise, Anderson, and Jones (1979) offer one example of an interior and exterior checklist for this purpose.

Home accidents in the United States account for more than one-fifth of the accidental deaths and approximately one-third of the disabling injuries (Planek, 1982). Between 1912 and 1980, accidental home deaths per 100,000 population were reduced 64 percent, from 28 to 10. In 1912, there were 21 million homes and 26,000 to 28,000 persons killed in home accidents (National Safety Council, 1981). Since 1968, death attributed to home accidents has declined 17 percent. Mortality from falls has shown the most change, decreasing just over 30 percent. Reductions in the suffocation and fire/burn category account for the remaining decrease in home accident fatalities (Planek, 1982).

In 1980, there were 3,400,000 Americans disabled one or more days by injuries received in home accidents, or one person in 67. About 90,000 of these injuries resulted in some permanent impairment (National Safety Council, 1981). Of course, many superficial injuries— such as bruises, scratches, and burns—take place as well. Such injuries often go unreported since they do not require medical treatment or cause loss of normal activity. Accidental injuries resulting in medical treatment or disability of a day or more have been estimated to be about one-fortieth as common as these superficial injuries (Neutra and McFarland, 1972). The limitation of home-accident data estimates has been discussed by Planek (1982).

Table 3 provides information on accidental deaths of older adults for 1978 with a breakdown by age group (National Safety Council, 1981). Motor vehicle deaths are included.

The age group most affected by home accidents are those 65 and over. This group accounts for 9,900 victims, or approximately 43 percent of all home accident fatalities. Fall deaths and death rates are highest for those 75 and over. In general, death rate increases with age or falls, medical complications, fires, and burns.

The largest number of research studies on accidents and aging have been done on falls. This interest reflects the fact that falls are the leading cause of all home fatalities and the major problem area for people 65 and over. Major articles and reviews include Sheldon (1960), Waller (1978), Overstall (1978), Isaacs (1981), Gabell and Nayak (1981), and Rodstein (1982).

In the past, women have had a much higher death rate from falls than men; in recent data, however, the estimates are almost equal: a 37 percent decrease since 1969 for women as compared to a 29 percent decrease for men. The largest decrease for both sexes has been for death caused by falls on a level surface. Falls on stairs, which have also declined, continue to be the most frequent cause of fatal injuries.

Prudham and Evans (1981) studied 2,357

TABLE 3 Accidental Deaths and Death Rates for Older Adults, 1978

From *Accident Facts*, 1981 Edition, National Safety Council. Source: National Center for Health Statistics.

Age Group	All Types*	Falls	Motor Vehicle	Medical Complications†	Fires, Burns	Ingestion of Food, Objects	Drowning**	Poison (solid, liquid)	Poison by Gas
				Deaths					
65 to 69	4,602	797	1,685	407	408	244	160	117	68
70 to 74	4,470	1,055	1,532	376	381	239	140	102	42
75 to 79	4,492	1,538	1,273	353	320	245	100	80	58
80 to 84	4,464	1,277	885	311	292	211	70	47	35
85 and over	6,107	4,109	530	299	295	259	30	56	33
				Death Rates††					
65 to 69	53.7	9.3	19.6	4.7	4.8	2.8	1.9	1.4	0.8
70 to 74	70.2	16.6	24.1	5.9	6.0	3.8	2.2	1.6	0.7
75 to 79	107.7	36.9	30.5	8.5	7.7	5.9	2.4	1.9	1.4
80 to 84	162.4	79.2	32.3	11.3	10.6	7.7	2.5		1.3
85 and over	276.8	186.3	24.0	13.6	13.4	11.7	1.4	2.5	1.5

*Includes some deaths not shown separately.
†Surgical and medical complications and misadventures.
**Partially estimated.
††Per 100,000 population in each age group.

English residents aged 65 and over for a 12-month period and estimated the annual prevalence rate for falls at 28 percent. Standardized for age, the rate was found to be twice as high in women as in men at ages 65 to 74, with the sex ratio becoming equal at older ages. Fall rates increased with age for both sexes, but more steadily for men than women. Those who fell had been in more recent contact with their general practitioners, had more problems with mobility and daily living, a more frequent history of stroke and heart disease, and more episodes of vertigo, double vision, fainting, blackouts, weakness, and numbness. They also showed more evidence of cognitive impairment and were more likely to be taking diuretics or tranquilizers. In this study, 47 percent of falls took place indoors, 33 percent out-of-doors, and 20 percent had fallen in both places. Prudham and Evans found that 50.2 percent fell as a result of tripping, 21.8 percent were unable to give any reason, and 10.3 percent reported the cause to be dizziness, vertigo, or loss of consciousness.

These results are similar to those reported by Waller (1978). Acute and chronic health problems, including the misuse of alcohol, were felt to be involved in 42 percent of the falls. Identified environmental hazards contributed to 45 percent.

When older adults fall, fractures are the most common injuries. Older adults experience a high level of disability (Eddy, 1972, 1973; Hogue, 1982a). Osteoporosis is a major factor in late-life falls. As many as 190,000 older Americans suffer broken hips each year. Currently, one sixth die from the ensuing complications, and many are disabled. Osteoporosis leads to fracture by stresses that would not break normal bones. Twenty-five percent of white women have had one or more fractures by age 65.

Thus, falls are seen as very serious to the older adult because of the prevalence of acute and chronic health changes (Waller, 1978; Overstahl, 1978; Lucht, 1971). Isaacs (1981) has stated that recurrent falls in later life indicate past disease, present distress, and future disability. Both Isaacs (1981) and Rossman (1979) emphasize the importance of a thorough differential diagnosis of any patient who has sustained a fall. A number of conditions may be related to falling, including the following: gait disorders of recent origin, Parkinsonism, weak and wasted muscles, vestibular orders, epileptic seizures, drugs, alcohol, and cardiac dysrhythmias.

Institutional settings are places with extremely high risk of falls, especially in the first day or so in a hospital or long-term-care facility (Jarvinen and Jarvinen, 1968; Hogue, 1982a). Most such falls are associated with getting in and out of bed, on or off a chair, or when using the bathroom.

Waller (1978) emphasizes that the presence of ice, snow, and rough terrain represent a substantial hazard for the elderly, especially those who fall for other than health reasons. Falls precipitated by a medical problem usually do not involve an environmental factor.

Stairway falls are a major cause of fatality and injury. Almost all of these falls occur on the top step. Taking the first step involves attentive visual control of one's movements, which become less important once one has begun to descend. Adaptation to changing levels of light has been suggested as an important factor in stair falls (Fozard and Popkin, 1978; Fozard, 1981; Hughes and Neer, 1981). Archea, Collins, and Stahl (1979) also found that changing light level was a major factor. Their work demonstrates the importance of accurate perceptual cues for safe stair use, the need for good lighting, the presence of handrails, good stairway design, and absence of distractions in the stairwell.

Remedies should focus on minimizing external causes, helping older adults to walk with a normal posture and gait, and instructing them how to get up after a fall if they are able to do so. Environments should be made as free of hazards as possible and steps taken to examine the elderly on a regular basis. It is also important to restore the confidence of those who have fallen by providing family counselling and to promote independence and a supportive surrounding for daily activities.

Accidental death and death rates for fire and burns may be found in Table 3. This category does not include accidents from hot liquids, acids, steam, or other sources not involving open flames. Asphyxiation and smoke inhalation alone, or in combination with burns, account for the majority of fire-involved fatalities. Burns from nonopen flame sources usually result in injuries of a different severity.

Older adults are the group least likely to survive burns and have the highest level of injury-to-death ratio. Scalds, burns caused by flames, and contact burns are the most frequent types of injury that lead to the hospitalization of older adults. In the New York Burn Study (1979), 40 percent of the burn injuries resulting in hospitalization were from scalds. Of the hot liquid burns (793), 193 were from tap water, with approximately 95 percent of them occurring in the home. Older adults 60 and over made up 15 percent of the hospitalized individuals in this category. They experienced 27 percent of the tap water burns and 22 percent of the burns involved clothing.

Annually, there are an estimated 4.5 million residential fire incidents (U.S. Consumer Product Safety Commission, 1978). Cooking was involved in 56 percent of these incidents. Grease and food were the main ignition sources; leaving cooking unattended was another major factor. Fires caused by electric stoves that had been accidentally turned on or not turned off were frequently the culprit, pointing to the need for improvement in control and display design.

Using a kitchen as a controlled laboratory, Guilford (1973) was able to identify certain classes of behavior that are related to kitchen accidents. Paying attention to behavior such as pressing bacon with fingers in hot frying pans could serve as a foundation for a safety training program.

Abandoned cigarettes are also a frequently reported cause of fires. Cigarettes that ignite upholstered chairs or sofas, mattresses, or bedding are a major problem. Falling asleep while smoking was found to cause only a few fire incidents; however, it was associated with a high proportion of injuries and death (Planek, 1982).

Poisoning by solids and liquids include deaths from drugs, medicine, mushrooms, shellfish, and commonly recognized poisons. Such drugs as codeine, aspirin, and darvon, various sedatives and hypnotics, and alcohol account for the majority of fatal poisoning incidents. The principal sources of poisoning by gasses and vapors is the carbon monoxide that results from incomplete combustion in cooking stoves, heating equipment, and standing motor vehicles (Planek, 1982).

Pedestrian accidents have been reviewed by Smeed (1968), Haight and Olsen (1981), and Shinar (1978). In 1980, there were 800 pedestrian deaths among older adults aged 65 to 74 and 1,210 among those 75 and over. Most of the older pedestrians who are injured or killed are hit at intersections. The current time periods assigned to traffic lights and pedestrian-activated cross buttons may not be long enough for many older adults to cross safely.

THE WORKPLACE

Few studies have been able to collect uniform data about exposure to, and incidents of, injury among any homogeneous group of workers within a particular industry or occupation. Studies do show, however, that after controlling for occupation, the age-related injury patterns reported earlier for males persists, i.e., as age increases, injury frequency decreases and injury severity increases. The relationship between age and injury frequency was essentially attributable to the high injury rates for the young, as was evidenced by the aggregate and temporary injury rate. The age–injury relationship for fatal or permanently disabling injuries was U-shaped (Dillingham, 1981).

The age-injury relationship for females parallels that for males once we control for major occupational groups because of their substantial differences in occupation by age group. Of women under age 25, 78 percent were found to be in white-collar and less than 8 percent in blue-collar employment. The rest were in service jobs. The occupational distribution for women over 45 differed widely. Sixty-two percent were in white-collar employment, 19 percent in blue-collar jobs, and the others in service jobs. The employment distribution of the 25-to-44 group fell between the other two (Dillingham, 1981).

In summarizing the relationship between age and frequency of injury, we can conclude that older workers (aged 45 and over) are in-

jured much less frequently than younger workers (less than 25) and about as often as workers aged 25 to 44. With the exception of white-collar employment, older workers have the lowest incidence of temporary injuries but on the average lose more work time per injury than the younger workers. The 45-and-above group has the highest incident of fatal-injury risk. In blue-collar employment, older workers have the lowest incidence of permanently disabling injuries, but in other occupational categories they have the highest or close to the highest incidence.

One of the best studies is that of Root (1981), which was based on data collected in the Bureau of Labor Statistics Supplemental Data System (SDS). This information included more than a million workers' compensation records from 30 states, representing 40 percent of national wage and salary employment and fairly representative of the nation as a whole.

In Root's study, occupational injuries were found to occur at a lower rate to older workers than to younger ones. Their frequency declined steadily up to age 64 and then dropped even more sharply for workers over 65. More experienced workers also proved to have fewer accidents. Injuries to older workers usually reflected workplace hazards experienced by all age groups; however, some notable examples possibly involve age-related changes. Deficits in bodily coordination among older workers, for example, may contribute to increasing numbers of injuries from falls on working surfaces. Root also comments that injury to an older worker is more likely to be more severe and costly, such as a fractured bone.

Work injury ratios in Root's research were based on the percentages of work injury distribution and employment distribution within each industry or occupation. A ratio of 1.0 indicates that these percentages are equal. Ratios greater than 1.0 indicate that the percentage of injuries is greater than that of employment, and ratios less than 1.0 indicate the opposite. Work injury ratios are presented in Table 4. Work injury rates are highest for workers aged 20 to 24 and lowest for those aged 65 and over.

The pattern is similar for all industry divi-

TABLE 4   Work–Injury Ratios by Age.

Figures based on current cases in 26 states, including illnesses. From Root, 1981.

Age	Percent Employment Distribution*	Percent Work Injury Distribution	Work Injury Ratio†
16–17	3.2	1.9	0.59**
18–19	5.3	6.8	1.28
20–24	15.2	21.0	1.38
16–24	23.7	29.7	1.25
25–34	26.4	30.3	1.15
35–44	18.7	16.7	0.89
45–54	17.6	13.6	0.77**
65 and over	2.2	0.9	0.41

*Industry employment source CPS data, 1977.
†Ratio computation is column 2 divided by column 1.
**Because of the relatively small magnitudes associated with one or both components in these ratios, the relative errors for these age groups would be larger than those for the other age groups.

sions except finance, insurance, and real estate and for services. For the latter, the percentage of injury distribution is less than that of employment distribution among workers aged 25 to 34 and higher for workers aged 55 to 64. These are the only industries in which injury ratios are above 1.0 for the older age group (see Table 5).

The age of an injured worker is strongly correlated with length of service. More than 40 percent of injuries to workers under age 35 occurred among those in the first year of employment. Workers under age 35 accounted for 60 percent of the total injuries. Since this age group also accounted for the largest number of new entrants to a job in any one year, its higher injury rates would not be unexpected. Each succeeding year of service was found to account for a lower percentage of injuries. Despite the smaller likelihood of an older worker being a new employee and the smaller percentage of first-year injuries for such workers, however, the proportion of first year injuries is higher for older workers.

The more severe cases, those involving fatalities or permanent disabilities, occurred more frequently among older workers than younger ones. Fatality ratios were higher than 1.0 for the 35-to-44, 55-to-64, and 65-and-over age groups and below 1.0 for others. Permanent

TABLE 5   Ratios of Work Injury to Employment Percentages by Industry and Age, 1977.

Source of employment data: BLS, CPS Base table, 29B, December 1977. From Root, 1981.

Industry	Total All Years	Total 16–24 Years	16–17 Years	18–19 Years	20–24 Years	25–34 Years	35–44 Years	45–54 Years	55–64 Years	65+ Years
All nonfarm industries	1.0	1.25	0.59	1.28	1.38	1.15	0.89	0.77	0.77	0.41
Mining	1.0	1.53	0.50	1.65	1.53	1.14	0.94	0.57	0.56	0.45
Construction	1.0	1.14	0.39	1.03	1.27	1.24	0.88	0.77	0.73	0.40
Manufacturing	1.0	1.61	0.50	1.79	1.66	1.15	0.81	0.68	0.63	0.42
Transportation	1.0	1.15	0.38	1.13	1.21	1.20	0.99	0.84	0.67	0.40
Wholesale trade	1.0	1.58	0.93	1.79	1.59	1.14	0.82	0.67	0.65	0.33
Retail trade	1.0	1.03	0.67	1.03	1.23	1.26	0.96	0.81	0.83	0.37
Finance, et al.	1.0	1.18	1.33	1.20	1.14	0.93	0.85	0.99	1.14	0.86
Services	1.0	1.17	0.88	1.27	1.19	0.97	0.89	0.96	1.13	0.52
Public administration	1.0	1.38	1.25	1.39	1.39	1.32	0.97	0.67	0.67	0.43

disability ratios were highest for workers aged 35 to 64.

The most frequently occurring injuries to all workers were sprains and strains, cuts and lacerations, contusions, bruises, and burns, these five categories alone accounting for 75 percent of all injuries. The major difference among age groups was that fractures and hernias were markedly more frequent for older workers than for workers as a whole. Fractures among workers aged 55 and over accounted for 11 to 16 percent of their injuries, whereas fractures to all workers accounted for only 8 percent of all injuries. Conversely, cuts, lacerations, and burns occurred consistently less frequently with increasing age, perhaps reflecting the role of experience in avoiding them.

Falls, particularly falls on the same level, become an increasingly serious problem with advancing age. For workers 65 and over, falls produced nearly one-third of their injuries compared with 12.6 percent for teenagers, the lowest group. These age-specific patterns of injury characteristics were similar across industry and occupational groups.

Siskind (1982) used a ratio-index approach to estimate the injury experience of workers relative to duration of employment, linking injury and employment-duration information from the Bureau of Labor's Supplementary Data System for 1977 with work experience for the general working population from the 1977 Quality of Employment Survey and the January 1978 Current Population Survey. The results suggest that workers are subject to disproportionately high injury rates during their first few months on the job.

Overall, such findings support the need for making special training efforts to assure that new employees or employees changing jobs are given an opportunity to minimize the risk of injury.

SAFETY AND INJURY PREVENTION

Older adults continue to live and work as they always have. Unless there is compelling evidence to the contrary, they should be encouraged to maintain their life style and activities. It should be remembered, however, that age-related changes and/or declines in health caused by disease may alter the performance level of critical skills, making older adults less able to meet task demands and thus subject to an increased risk of injury.

The term "safety" may be defined as the state of being free from danger or injury, or the use of various methods and devices to reduce, control, or prevent accidents (U.S. Office of Technology Assessment, 1978). In discussing safety and risk, W. T. Singleton (1979) points out that we are often better able to specify the degree of hazard or risk than to specify the degree of "safety." Our descriptions of the danger presented by an environment are likely to be more precise than our descriptions of the lack of danger.

In carrying out their daily activities, individuals are exposed to a number of risks. Their level of skills, their exercise of these skills, and the resulting level of safety are variables in a complex cost-benefit equation. People make judgments regarding activities to determine whether the risk of injury is sufficient to be a deterrent. Since some older adults may not be aware of their changing levels of skill, they may be unrealistic in their judgments.

Theories and policies about accidents are difficult to construct because we are dealing with a heterogeneous set of events. There is a great need to deal with subgroupings having common aspects. A complex pattern of events precede an accident, and there is rarely a single identifiable cause in terms of the action of a single individual. Experience provides the opportunity to develop and maintain skills, and in many situations it may be the only way to acquire the needed knowledge and performance capability. Training should provide the needed experience in relevant skills in a compressed format.

According to Singleton (1979), the creation and maintenance of an optimally safe environment is a dynamic process involving a variety of skills performed by a number of different types of individuals. Some of the most important of these skills are possessed and practiced by the individual actually at risk. The skills of designers of hardware, training, and information are used to create situations minimizing risk. Others are responsible for the diagnosis of health problems and for their treatment; at the same time they must minimize risk by recognizing symptoms and monitoring possible negative reactions to drugs, etc. In the area of policy, managers must derive appropriate procedures that accord with national and state legislation, administrative order, company imperatives, proficiency tests, and specialized knowledge. Each of these areas require special focus and research.

Assessing the risk of accidents involving the operation of motor vehicles, aircraft, and machinery requiring skilled behaviors present a different degree of demand on the individuals concerned but are not necessarily conceptually different.

Falls and other home accidents present another important area of concern. Here too, the ability to evaluate potential risk requires a major effort. Close assessment of individual clients is a critical part of the case management of older adults. Kane and Kane (1981) have reviewed assessment approaches in geriatric practice. The physical, mental, and social well being of the aged are closely interrelated. Diagnosis and treatment must be complemented by a general perception of an individual's capabilities. Proper screening can determine those individuals who cannot cook, clean, or shop or who put themselves at risk by doing so. It usually triggers a further assessment that may broaden the diagnosis to account for, say, any negative side effects of drugs taken. Such procedures may substantially reduce the risk of unnecessary injury. The refinement and further development of assessment approaches is another important area for future research.

The screening approaches and assessment of skills developed for driving situations constitute another example. Such measures as selective attention, perceptual style, perceptual motor-reaction time, low-illumination visual acuity, dynamic visual acuity, and glare are all examples of screening tests that can be used to identify individuals at risk. The development of a voluntary diagnostic test battery could pinpoint areas of difficulty for the individual. Training in skills relevant to driving would also reduce potential risk.

Few programs are available to offer training in driving skills to older adults (Beno, 1981). Henderson and Kole (1962) investigated the effectiveness of a New Jersey driving clinic for individuals with poor driving records. This clinic did not teach any driving-related skills but did provide counseling. It appears to us that few studies have attempted to formulate a well-defined training program, although behavioral analysis of highway safety and a training approach to cautious behavior have been presented by Parsons (1976; 1979).

The Institute of Gerontology Older Driver Refresher Course (1975) offered a defensive driving approach with special emphasis on the problems that older drivers may experience. No empirical evaluation of its success has been reported.

Another approach has focused on comparing individual and group training in skills related to older adult driving and the development of a diagnostic test battery to determine areas of difficulty for older drivers (Sterns, Barrett, Alexander, Greenawalt, Gianetta, and Panek, 1976; Sterns, Barrett, Alexander, Panek, and Forbringer, 1977). The sequential training procedure used combines operant and cumulative learning hierarchy principles (Sanders, Sterns, Smith, and Sanders, 1975; Sterns and Sanders, 1980). Overall, individual training approaches were found to be most effective on the embedded-figures test, selective-attention test, and a reaction-time task and indicated that such training can lead to improved levels of performance. A number of training effects were found to hold up when retested 6 months and 18 to 24 months later. Shorter training approaches and group training approaches were found to be less effective or not effective (Sterns, Barrett, Alexander, Valasek, Forbringer, and Avolio, 1978; Sterns, Barrett, Alexander, Valasek, and McIlvried, 1984). These results support the research of Salthouse and Somberg (1982) and Salthouse (this volume) regarding improvements in skilled behavior and practice.

There is growing information on the adverse effects of alcohol and other drugs on driving skills and risk of accident. Such reviews have been presented by Linnoila (1974) and Howat and Mortimer (1978). Increased variability in driving performance under the influence of alcohol has been found (using a driving simulator) in steering against wind/road disturbances, speed control on curves, and decision making in signal-light situations (Allen and Schwartz, 1978). Moderate doses of alcohol (0.085 percent blood-alcohol concentration) were not found (using an instrumented vehicle) to affect driving skills involved in steering, car following, and passing decision making (Mortimer and Sturgis, 1979). Few studies, however, have focused on the effects of alcohol on older adult drivers, although some researchers have found that older adults are not more adversely affected than other age groups (White and Clayton, 1972; Waller, 1972). According to Baker and Deitz (1979), however, alcohol increases the likelihood of crash involvement for older adult drivers even at concentrations less than 50 mg per 100 ml. Older adults with lowered performance capability might be more adversely affected.

It is apparent that many individuals are not aware of the potential of medication to interfere with their driving. Research on the effects of secobarbital and diazepam on performance using a driving simulator was found to affect mean lane position, variability of lane position and of velocity, and control of emergency stop situations (Ziedman, Smiley, and Moskowitz, 1979). Diazepam was found to impair driving performance by producing increased lateral position variability in driving at night (O'Hanlon, Haak, Blaauw, and Riemersina, 1982). In a recent study of Finland, only 20 percent of the individuals purchasing drugs with the potential to impair driving skills had received any information concerning such effects from their physician (Maki, Linnoila, Idanpaan-Heikkila, and Isomeri, 1979). This area of research needs a great deal of attention since very little information is available to guide either the older adults or their physicians. Driving is only one aspect of a more general problem. The need of further research on effects of alcohol and drugs in the work and home environment of older adults is equally critical.

Few real criteria for screening drivers have been scientifically established since people first began driving. Most health-related criteria lack the precise, predictable cut-off points needed to indicate who can drive safely. Older adults who have demonstrated fainting, dizziness, difficulty in remembering or concentrating, and slowed thinking have shown significantly higher accident rates than middle-aged drivers whether or not they have cardiovascular disease (Waller, 1967). Drivers known to have diabetes, epilepsy, cardiovascular disease, alcoholism, and mental illness have had twice as many crashes per 1,000,000 miles of driving as did controls (Waller, 1965). A study by Crancer and McMurray (1967) found no higher level of crashes among drivers with a heart-disease license restriction but did find higher levels for drivers afflicted with epilepsy, fainting, or other health-impaired conditions. Ateriosclerotic heart disease was found by autopsy with similar frequency in drivers at fault in fatal accidents and those not at fault (Baker and Spitz, 1970).

Waller (1980) called for standards for reporting and evaluating and for the establishment of license restrictions at state level on the basis of competent consultation between medical and motor vehicle authorities. He emphasized the great need for individual evaluation. Without explicit guidelines, the issue of whether a physician should report patients who have a medical impairment likely to present a serious highway hazard has become a controversial one. Many impaired drivers go undetected unless brought to the attention of the licensing agency by a physician. A major drawback for the latter is the lack of definitive information about the relationship of medical impairment to crash causation and the even more meager data on the cut-off points at which impairment is likely to become a hazard to safe driving. Without such specific criteria, physicians have been reluctant to suggest that certain individuals might present a hazard on the highway (National Traffic Safety Administration, 1977).

A great assistance to the individuals at risk and their physicians and families would be to provide the opportunity of voluntary testing on a diagnostic driving battery, simulator, and/or road-driving test to provide additional information on the advisability of continued driving. Testing procedures in this context could be applied to other skilled behavior situations as well.

The lack of definitive medical and psychological criteria has resulted in Congressional legislation that established a mandatory hiring and termination age for certain occupations involving public safety. Airline pilots, railroad engineers, and bus drivers, for example, are responsible for the lives of others, and their sudden incapacitation could be disastrous for their passengers. The absence of reliable individualized means of prediction has similarly led the courts to uphold chronological age limitation or qualification for persons seeking employment in such positions. Bus drivers are not newly hired after 40; airline pilots may not fly commercially after 60; air traffic controllers, federal law enforcement officers, and firefighters must retire at the age of 56 unless they are granted specific exemption allowing them to serve to 61 (Edelman and Siegler, 1978).

Early recognition over forty years ago of the inadequacy of chronological age alone to evaluate skills led to major efforts to develop relevant aging research and alternative strategies (Welford, 1976), for example, to develop measurement strategies to assess the functional capacities of older adults for holding various kinds of jobs. McFarland (1943) emphasized the need to define functional age in terms of abilities to perform specific job duties efficiently, particularly whenever specific levels of ability were associated with different levels of task demand. Most research has focused on describing the status of the individual at a specific time and chronological age rather than on creating assessment devices predictive of job or task performance. The utility of the functional age approach has been carefully examined and, at present, is not seen as a useful alternative (Costa and McCrae, 1980).

At the request of Congress, the scientific evidence relevant to the age 60 rule for pilots was recently reviewed by the National Institute On Aging (1981); as part of the process, a review was also conducted by the National Academy of Sciences (1981). The N.I.A. Panel found no special medical significance to age 60, or any other specific age, as a mandatory age for the retirement of airline pilots. It nevertheless found that age-related changes in health and performance could adversely affect the ability of an increasing number of individuals to perform as pilots with the highest level of safety. The panel could not identify the existence of a medical or performance appraisal system that could single out those pilots who would pose the greatest hazard because of early or impending deterioration in health or performance. The report emphasized the lack of predictive accuracy for cardiovascular disease and the fact that risk factor concepts deal with populations rather than individuals.

Psychological tests designed to identify subtle changes in cognitive functioning have not been systematically administered to pilots, and their relevance to decision making, resource management, and vigilance under stress still needs to be established.

The N.I.A. Panel stated that graded tests of health and performance could probably be developed and applied within the present medical appraisal system if standard longitudinal risk factors were determined for all pilots. Additional screening and diagnostic procedures would be required to define health status as a guide to prognosis for those pilots with risk at some defined level. The Federal Aeronautics Administration announced just such a longitudinal study and then, in 1984, decided not to carry it out.

What emerged from the report was the need for sensitive, objective screening to reveal those decrements in cognitive and intellectual skills that are of particular concern with respect to the aging pilot. The report states that if it proves impossible to identify those individuals who will become unsafe pilots with assurance, the only recourse is for society to accept some level of risk. The design of future approaches for pilot assessment should be useful for many other situations involving complex skill behaviors.

CONCLUSIONS

A consistent picture emerges from the preceding discussion. Older adults involved in an accident have the highest death, dysfunction, and disability rates. A well-functioning older adult can be profoundly affected by an injury that results in partial or total loss of the ability to work or to maintain independent activities. Injuries at earlier points in the life span may have profound affects as well, but younger individuals usually survive and recover with lower levels of dysfunction and disability.

Environmental modification plays an important role in reducing accident risks. Installation of smoke detectors, thermostats on hot water heaters, and antiscald devices, for example, can reduce risk of injury from fire and hot substances. A careful analysis of the potential hazards in a home or work environment can lead to design changes that will lessen risk to the older person (Houge, 1982b).

Screening and assessment approaches should be developed, where appropriate, to identify those individuals who may be experiencing age-related changes that reduce their functional level and thus place them at risk of injury. A major effort must be made to develop intrinsically valid screening tests for measuring the individual characteristics that are necessary for successful performance of the task at hand. A thorough analysis of each job situation, household situation, or driving situation is essential.

Most tests involving older adults vary in terms of the demand placed on the individual. Most activities carried out by the elderly on the job, at home, or driving are only minimally demanding. Most individuals have enough reserve capacity to handle most situations even if they are experiencing an age-related decline in abilities. In situations that do place great demands on the individual (i.e., those involving some type of unusual stress or complexity), a changed level of skill may place the person at greater risk. The more familiar the situation, the more an older person can benefit from past experience and practice (Welford, 1980).

Many skills are practiced over the years for thousands of hours, and such experience leads to dramatic improvement in the efficiency and effectiveness of performance. Older adults may maintain many highly practiced activities at a constant level even though they are subject to age-related declines; in short, experience compensates for their loss of ability. The issue of greatest importance from an accident perspective is the point at which age-related decline cannot be compensated for by experience since it is here that the individual is placed at increased risk (Salthouse, 1982).

Decline, if it occurs, usually affects maximum rather than average potential and performance. Since accident avoidance behaviors often demand maximum response, tests should include demanding as well as moderate tasks. Great care must be taken to select measures that provide a good screen but do not adversely impact older adults.

Acknowledgements. We wish to acknowledge the assistance of Meg Patchett in the preparation of this chapter. Dr. Sterns was a Fellow of the Andrew Norman Institute for Advanced Study in Gerontology and Geriatrics, Andrus Gerontology Center, University of Southern California, during part of the preparation period of this chapter.

REFERENCES

Allen, R. W., and Schwartz, S. H. 1978. Alcohol effects on driver risk taking. Proceedings of the Human Factors Society, 22nd Annual Meeting, pp. 579–582.

Archea, J.; Collins, B. L.; and Stahl, F. I. May 1979. Guidelines for stair safety. NBS Building Science Series, 120. Washington, D.C.: National Bureau of Standards, Center for Building Technology, National Engineering Laboratory.

Babarik, P. 1968. Automobile accidents and driver reaction pattern. *J. Appl. Psych.* 52: 49–54.

Baker, S. P., and Deitz, P. E. 1979. Injury prevention. In *Healthy People: The Surgeon General's Report on Health Promotion and Disease Prevention Background Papers.* DHEW (PHS), Publication No. 79–55071A, pp. 53–80. Hyattsville, MD: U.S. Department of Health Education and Welfare.

Baker, S. P. and Spitz, W. 1970. Age effects and autopsy evidence of disease in fatally injured drivers. *Journal of the American Medical Assoc.* 214: 1071.

Baltes, P. B.; Cornelius, S. W.; and Nesselroade, J. R. 1978. Cohort effects in behavioral development: Theoretical and methodological perspectives. *Minnesota Symposium on Child Psychology* 11: 1–63.

Baltes, P. B.; Reese, H. W.; and Lipsitt, L. P. 1980. Life-span developmental psychology. *Annual Review of Psychology* 31: 65–110.

Barrett, G. V.; Alexander, R. A.; and Forbes, J. B. 1977. Analysis of performance measurement and training requirements for driving decision making in emergency situations. *JSAS Catalogue of Selected Documents in Psychology*, 7: 126. (MS. No. 1623.)

Barrett, G. V.; Cabe, P. A.; and Thornton, C. L. 1969. Relation between embedded figures test performance and simulator behavior. *J. Appl. Psych.* 53: 253–254.

Barrett, G. V., and Thornton, C. L. 1968. Relation between perceptual style and driver reaction to emergency situation. *J. Appl. Psych.* 52: 169–176.

Barrett, G. V.; Mihal, W. L.; Panek, P. E.; Sterns, H. L.; and Alexander, R. A. 1977. Information processing skills predictive of accident involvement for young and older commercial drivers. *Industrial Gerontology* 4: 173–182.

Beno, J. A. 1981. Driving education programs for the aged: The state of the art. *Educational Gerontology: An International Quarterly* 7: 89–96.

Birren, J. E. 1974. Translations in gerontology—from lab to life: Psychophysiology and speed of response. *American Psychologist* 29: 808–815.

Boyle, A. J. 1980. "Found experiments" accidents research: Report of a study of accident rates and implications for future research. *Journal of Occupational Psychology* 53: 53–64.

Brewer, N., and Sandow, B. 1980. Alcohol effects on driver performance under conditions of divided attention. *Ergonomics* 23: 185–190.

Carp, F. M. 1971. On becoming an exdriver: Prospect & retrospect. *Gerontologist* 11: 101–103.

Clark, A. W., and Prolisko, A. 1979. Social-role correlates of driving accidents. *Hum. Factors* 21: 655–659.

Costa, P. T., and McCrae, R. R. 1980. Functional age: A conceptual and empirical critique. *Second Conference on the Epidemiology of Aging,* eds. S. G. Haynes and M. Feinleib, pp. 23–46. Bethesda, MD: National Institute on Aging; National Institutes of Health.

Crancer, A. and McMurray, L. 1967. Accident and violation rates of Washington drivers with medical licensing and driving restrictions. Report Number 007. Olympia, WA: Washington Department of Motor Vehicles.

Crancer, A. 1969. Comprehensive vision tests and driving record. Report No. 028. Olympia, WA: Department of Motor Vehicles, Division of Research.

DeSilva, H. R. 1938. Age and highway accidents. *Scientific Monthly* 47: 536–545.

Dillingham, A. E. 1981. Age and workplace injuries. *Aging and Work* 4: 1–10.

Drury, C. G., and Brill, M. 1980. New methods of consumer product accident investigation. *Proceedings of the Symposium—Human Factors and Industrial Design in Consumer Products,* pp. 196–211. Medford, MA: Tufts University.

Eddy, T. P. 1972. Deaths from domestic falls and fractures. *Brit. J. Prev. Soc. Med.* 26: 173–179.

Eddy, T. P. 1973. Deaths from falls and fractures comparison of mortality in Scotland and the United States with that in England and Wales. *Brit. J. Prev. Soc. Med.* 27: 247–254.

Edelman, C. D., and Siegler, I. C. 1978. *Federal age discrimination in employment law.* Charlottesville, VA: The Michie Company.

Feck, G., and Baptiste, M. S. 1979. The epidemiology of burn injury in New York. *Public Health Report* 961: 312–315.

Fergensen, P. E. 1971. The relationship between information processing and driving accident and violation record. *Hum. Factors* 13: 173–176.

Finesilver, S. G. 1969. The older driver: A statistical evaluation of licensing and accident involvement in 30 states. In *Adding Life to Years, Bulletin of the Institute*

of Gerontology of the State University of Iowa 16: 3–5.

Fozard, J. L. 1981. Person-environment relationships in adulthood: Implications for human factors engineering. *Hum. Factors* 23: 7–27.

Fozard, J. L., and Popkin, S. J. 1978. Optimizing adult development: Ends and means of an applied psychology of aging. *American Psychologist* 33: 975–989.

Gabell, A., and Nayak, U.S. 1981. Balance and its measurement. *Roch. Seminars on Aging,* 6.

Gopher, D., and Kahneman, D. 1971. Individual differences in attention and the prediction of flight criteria. *Percept. Mot. Skills* 33: 1335–1342.

Guilford, J. S. 1973. Prediction of accidents in a standardized home environment. *J. Appl. Psych.* 57: 306–313.

Haddon, W., Jr., and Baker, S. P. 1980. Injury control. In *Preventive and Community Medicine,* eds. Duncan Clark and Brian MacMahon, pp. 109–140. Boston: Little Brown.

Haddon, W., Jr.; Suchman, E. A.; and Klein, D. 1964. *Accident Research Methods and Approaches.* New York: Harper and Row.

Haight, F. A., and Olsen, R. A. 1981. Pedestrian safety in the United States: Some recent trends. *Accid. Anal. & Prev.* 13: 43–55.

Harano, R. M. 1963. Relationships of field dependence and motor vehicle accident involvement. *Percept. Mot. Skills* 17: 625–626.

Henderson, H. L., and Kole, T. 1962. New Jersey driver improvement clinics: An evaluation study. *Traffic Safety Research Review* 2: 98, 100–105.

Hills, Brian L. 1980. Vision, visibility, and perception in driving. *Perception* 9: 183–216.

Hogue, C. C. 1980. Epidemiology of injury in older age. *Second Conference on the Epidemiology of Aging,* eds. S. G. Haynes and M. Feinlieb, NIH Publication No. 80–969, pp. 127–138. Hyattsville, MD: U.S. Department of Health and Human Services.

Hogue, C. C. 1982a. Injury in late life: Prevention. *J. Am. Geriat. Soc.* 30: 276–280.

Hogue, C. C. 1982b. Injury in late life: Epidemiology. *J. Am. Geriat. Soc.* 30: 183–190.

Howat, P. A., and Mortimer, R. G. 1978. Review of effects of alcohol and other licit drugs on driving-related performance. *Proceedings of the Human Factors Society,* 22nd Annual Meeting, pp. 564–572.

Hughes, P. C., and Neer, R. M. 1981. Lighting for the elderly: A psychobiological approach to lighting. *Hum. Factors* 23: 65–85.

Hultsch, D. F., and Hickey, T. 1978. External validity in the study of human development: Theoretical and methodological issues. *Hum. Develop.* 21: 76–91.

Hultsch, D. F., and Plemons, J. K. 1979. Life events and life-span development. In *Life-Span Development and Behavior,* vol. 2, eds. P. B. Baltes and O. G. Brim, Jr. New York: Academic Press.

Institute of Gerontology. 1975. *Older Driver Refresher Course Instructor Handbook.* The University of Michigan.

Isaacs, B. 1981. The clinical aspects of falling. *Roch. Seminars on Aging,* 6.

Jarvinen, K. A., and Jarvinen, P. H. 1968. Falling from

bed as a complication of hospital treatment. *J. Chronic Diseases* 21: 375–378.

Jenkins, A.; Corby, N.; Moore, J.; and Small, A. 1975. *Safety for the Elderly: A Selected Bibliography.* Los Angeles: Ethel Percy Andrus Gerontology Center, U. of Southern California.

Kahneman, D. 1973. *Attention and Effort.* Englewood Cliffs, NJ: Prentice-Hall, Inc.

Kahneman, D.; Ben-Ishai, R.; and Lotan, M. 1973. Relation of a test of attention to road accidents. *J. Appl. Psych.* 58: 113–115.

Kane, R. A., and Kane, R. L. 1981. *Assessing the Elderly: A Practical Guide to Measurement.* Lexington, MA: Lexington Books.

Kausler, D. H. 1982. *Experimental Psychology and Human Aging.* New York: John Wiley & Sons.

Knapper, C. K.; Leplat, J.; and Michon, J. A., eds. 1980. Special issue—driving behavior. *Int. Rev. of Appl. Psych.* 29.

Krantz, P. 1979. Differences between single- and multiple-automobile fatal accidents. *Accid. Anal. & Prev.* 11: 225–236.

Lawton, M. P. 1977. The impact of the environment on aging and behavior. In *Handbook of the Psychology of Aging,* eds. J. E. Birren and K. W. Schaie. New York: Van Nostrand Reinhold.

Lawton, M. P. 1980. *Environment and aging.* Monterey, CA: Brooks/Cole Publishing Co.

Lee, M. E., Glover, M. F.; and Eavy, P. W. 1980. Differences in trip attributes of drivers with high and low accident rates. *Accident Causation* 1.

Linnoila, M. 1974. Effects of drugs and alcohol on psychomotor skills related to driving. *Annals of Clinical Research* 6: 7–18.

Lucht, V. 1971. A prospective study of accidental falls and resulting injury in the home among elderly people. *Acta Socio-Medica Scandinavica* 3: 105–120.

Maki, M.; Linnoila, M.; Idanpaan-Heikkila, J.; and Isomeri, J. 1979. Information concerning drugs and driving received by customers of pharmacies. *Accid. Anal. & Prev.* 2: 117–124.

Marsh, B. W. Nov. 1960. Aging and driving. *Traffic Engineering* 3–21.

McCormick, E. J., and Sanders, M. S. 1982. *Human Factors in Engineering and Design.* 5th ed. New York: McGraw-Hill.

McFarland, R. A. 1943. The older worker in industry. *Harvard Business Review,* 510–520.

McFarland, R. A.; Tune, C. S.; and Welford, A. T. 1964. On the driving of automobiles by older people. *J. Geront.* 19: 190–197.

Mihal, W. L., and Barrett, G. V. 1976. Individual differences in perceptual-information processing and their relation to automobile accident involvement. *J. Appl. Psych.* 61: 229–233.

Mortimer, R. G., and Sturgis, S. P. 1979. Some effects of alcohol on car driving on two-lane and limited-access highways. *Proceedings of the Human Factors Society,* 23rd Annual Meeting, pp. 254–258.

National Academy of Sciences. Mar. 1981. Airline pilot age, health and performance: Scientific and medical considerations. *Report of a study by the Committee to Study Scientific Evidence Relevant to Mandatory Age Retirement for Airline Pilots.* Division of Health Sciences Policy. Institute of Medicine. Washington, D.C.: National Academy of Sciences.

National Institute on Aging. Aug. 1981. *Report of the panel on the experienced pilots study.* Department of Health and Human Services. Washington, D.C.: Public Health Service, National Institute on Aging.

National Safety Council. 1981. *Accident Facts.* Chicago, IL: National Safety Council.

National Traffic Safety Administration. Mar. 1977. *The Role of Medical Advisory Boards in Driver Licensing.* DOT HS 802 013. Washington, D.C.: NTSA.

Neutra, R., and McFarland, R. A. 1972. Accident epidemiology and the design of the residential environment. *Hum. Factors* 14: 405–420.

O'Hanlon, J. F., Haak, T. W.; Blaauw, G. J.; and Riemersina, J. B. J. 1982. Diazepam impairs lateral position control in highway driving. *Science* 217: 79–81.

Overstall, P. W. 1978. Falls in the elderly—Epidemiology, aetiology and management. In *Recent Advances In Geriatric Medicine,* ed. B. Isasas. Edinburg: Churchill Livingstone.

Panek, P. E.; Barrett, G. V.; Alexander, R. A.; and Sterns, H. L. 1979. Age and self-selected performance pace on a visual monitoring inspection task. *Aging and Work: A Journal on Age Work and Retirement* 2: 183–191.

Panek, P. E.; Barrett, G. V.; Sterns, H. L.; and Alexander, R. A. 1977. A review of age changes in perceptual information processing ability with regard to driving. *Experimental Aging Research* 3: 387–449.

Parsons, H. M. 1976. Caution behavior and its conditioning in driving. *Hum. Factors* 18(4): 397–408.

Parsons, H. M. 1979. Behavior analysis in highway safety. Invited address at the Annual Meeting of the Association for Behavior Analysis, Dearborn, Michigan, June 1979.

Pestonjee, D. M., and Singh, U. B. 1980. Neuroticism-extraversion as correlates of accident occurrence. *Accid. Anal. & Prev.* 12: 201–204.

Phillips, D. P. 1979. Suicide, motor vehicle fatalities, and the mass media: Evidence toward a theory of suggestion. *Am. J. Sociol.* 84: 1150–1174.

Planek, T. W. 1982. Home accidents: A continuing social problem. *Accid. Anal. & Prev.* 14: 107–120.

Planek, T. W., and Fowler, R. C. 1971. Traffic accident problems and exposure characteristics of the aging driver. *J. Geront.* 26: 224–230.

Prudham, D., and Evans, J. 1981. Factors associated with falls in the elderly: A community study. *Age and Ageing* 10: 141–146.

Pulling, N. H.; Wolf, E.; Sturgis, S. P.; Vaillancourt, D. R.; and Dolliver, J. J. 1980. Headlight glare resistance and driver age. *Hum. Factors* 22: 103–112.

Rackoff, N. J., and Mourant, R. R. 1979. Driving performance of the elderly. *Accid. Anal. & Prev.* 11: 247–253.

Ramsey, J. D. 1978. Ergonomic support of consumer product safety. Paper presented at the American Industrial Hygiene Association Conference, May 1978.

Riegel, K. F. 1976. The dialectics of human development. *American Psychologist* 31: 689–700.

Robinson, G. H., and Jacobson, T. R. 1978. Human performance variability in accident causation. *Proceedings of the Human Factors Society,* 22nd Annual Meeting, pp. 517–521.

Rodstein, M. 1982. Falls by the aged. In *Fundamentals of Geriatric Medicine,* eds. D. Cape, R. Coe, and Isodore Rossman. New York: Raven Press.

Root, N. 1981. Injuries at work are fewer among older employees. *Monthly Labor Review* 104: 30–34.

Rossman, I. 1979. Mortality and morbidity overview. In *Clinical Geriatrics,* 2nd ed. I. Rossman. Philadelphia: J. B. Lippincott.

Salthouse, T. A. 1982. *Adult Cognition: An Experimental Psychology of Human Aging.* New York: Springer-Verlag.

Salthouse, T. A., and Somberg, B. L. 1982. Skilled performance: Effects of adult age and experience on elementary processes. *J. Exp. Psych.: General* 111: 176–207.

Sanders, J. C.; Sterns, H. L.; Smith, M.; and Sanders, R. E. 1975. Modification of concept identification performance in older adults. *Developmental Psychology* 6: 824–829.

Schaie, K. W. 1982. Historical time and cohort effects. Paper presented at the West Virginia Conference on Life-Span Developmental Psychology: Historical and Generation Effects in Life-Span Human Development, Morgantown, West Virginia, May 1982.

Shain, M. 1982. Alcohol, drugs and safety: An updated perspective of problems and their management in the workplace. *Accid. Anal. & Prev.* 14: 239–246.

Shaw, L., and Sichel, H. S. 1971. *Accident Proneness: Research in the Occurrence, Causation and Prevention of Road Accidents.* New York: Pergamon Press.

Sheldon, J. H. 1960. On the natural history of falls in old age. *Brit. Med. J.* 2: 1685–1690.

Shinar, D. 1978. *Psychology on the Road.* New York: Wiley.

Shinar, D.; McDonald, S. T.; and Treat, J. R. 1978. The interaction between driver mental and physical conditions and errors causing traffic accidents: An analytical approach. *J. Safety Research* 10: 16–23.

Shinar, D.; McDowell, E. D.; Rackoff, N. J.; and Rockwell, T. H. 1978. Field dependence and driver visual search behavior. *Hum. Factors* 20: 553–559.

Singleton, W. T. 1979. Safety and risk. In *The Study of Real Skills,* vol. 2., *Compliance and Excellence,* ed. W. T. Singleton. Baltimore: University Park Press.

Siskind, F. 1982. Another look at the link between work injuries and job experience. *Monthly Labor Review* 105: 38–40.

Sivak, M. 1981. Human factors and highway-accident causation: Some theoretical considerations. *Accid. Anal. & Prev.* 13: 61–64.

Sivak, M. and Olson, T. L. 1982. Nighttime legibility of traffic signs: Conditions eliminating the effects of driver age and disability glare. *Accident Analysis and Prevention* 14: 87–93.

Sivak, M.; Olson, P. L.; and Pastalan, L. A. 1981. Effect of driver's age on nighttime legibility of highway signs. *Hum. Factors* 23: 59–64.

Smeed, R. J. 1968. Some aspects of pedestrian safety. *Journal of Transport Economics and Policy* 2: 255–279.

Starr, C. 1969. Social benefit versus technological risk. *Science* 165: 1232–1238.

State of California, Department of Motor Vehicles. 1982. *Senior Driver Facts,* CAL-DMV-RSS-82-82.

Sterns, H. L.; Barrett, G. V.; Alexander, R. A.; Greenawalt, J. P.; Gianetta, T.; and Panek, P. E. 1976. Improving skills of the older adult critical for effective driving performance. Final report prepared for Andrus Foundation of the NRTA/AARP, July 1976.

Sterns, H. L.; Barrett, G. V.; Alexander, R. A.; Panek, P. E.; and Forbringer, L. R. 1977. Training and evaluation of older adult skills critical for effective driving performance. Final report prepared for Andrus Foundation of the NRTA/AARP, Aug. 1977.

Sterns, H. L.; Barrett, G. V.; Alexander, R. A.; Valasek, D.; Forbringer, L. R.; and Avolio, B. J. 1978. Training and evaluation of older adult skills critical for effective driving performance. Final report prepared for Andrus Foundation of the NRTA/AARP, Aug. 1978.

Sterns, H. L.; Barrett, G. V.; Alexander, R. A.; Valasek, D.; and McIlvried, J. 1984. Research to improve diagnostic testing and training of older drivers. Interim report prepared for Andrus Foundation of the NRTA/AARP, Aug. 1984.

Sterns, H. L., and Alexander, R. 1977. Cohort, age and time of measurement: Biomorphic considerations. In *Life-Span Developmental Psychology: Dialectical Perspectives on Experimental Research,* eds. N. Datan and H. Reese, pp. 105–120. New York: Academic Press.

Sterns, H. L., and Sanders, R. E. 1980. Training and education of the elderly. In *Life-Span Developmental Psychology: Intervention,* eds. R. R. Turner and H. W. Reese, pp. 307–330. New York: Academic Press.

Sturgis, S. P., and Osgood, D. J. 1982. Effects of glare and background luminance on visual acuity and contrast sensitivity. Implication for driver night vision testing. *Hum. Factors* 24: 347–360.

Sturgis, S. P.; Pulling, N. H.; and Vaillancourt, D. R. 1981. Measuring drivers' glare sensitivity: Evaluation of an automated technique. *J. Appl. Psych.* 66: 97–101.

Svenson, O. 1981. Are we all less risk and more skillful than our fellow drivers? *Acta Psychologica* 47: 143–148.

U.S. Consumer Product Safety Commission. 1978. Special Report: Results of National Household Fire Survey (CPSC 77–68700). Directorate for Hazard Identification and Analysis-Epidemiology (HIE), Feb. 1978.

U.S. Office of Technology Assessment. 1978. *An Evaluation of Railroad Safety.* Washington, D.C.: U.S. Document Printing Office, OTA-T-61, May 1978.

Waller, J. A. 1965. Chronic medical conditions and traffic safety. *New England Journal of Medicine* 26: 1413–1420.

Waller, J. A. 1967. Cardiovascular disease, aging, and traffic accidents. *J. of Chronic Diseases* 20: 615–620.

Waller, J. A. 1972. Factors associated with alcohol and responsibility for fatal highway crashes. *Quarterly Journal of Studies of Alcohol* 33: 160–170.

Waller, J. A. 1973. Current issues in epidemiology of injury. *Am. J. Epidemiol.* 98: 72–76.

Waller, J. A. 1978. Falls among the elderly—human and environmental factors. *Accid. Anal. & Prev.* 10: 21–33.

Waller, J. A. 1980. Functional impairment in driving. *New York Journal of Medicine* 80: 1987–1991.

Welford, A. T. 1976. Thirty years of psychological research on age and work. *J. Occupational Psych.* 49: 129–138.

Welford, A. T. 1980. Sensory, perceptual and motor processes in older adults. In *Handbook of Mental Health and Aging,* eds. J. E. Birren and R. B. Sloan. Englewood Cliffs, NJ: Prentice-Hall.

White, S. B., and Clayton, C. A. 1972. Research notes: Some effects of alcohol, age of driver, and estimated speed on the likelihood of driver injury. *Accid. Anal. & Prev.* 4: 59–66.

Williams, J. R. 1972. Relationships between three-dimensional spatial relations ability and driving performance. Proceedings of the 80th Annual Convention of the American Psychological Association 7: 695–696.

Windley, P. G., and Scheidt, R. J. 1980. Person-environment dialectics: Implications for competent functioning in old age. In *Aging in the 1980s,* ed. L. W. Poon, pp. 407–423. Washington, D.C.: American Psychological Association.

Wise, J. A.; Anderson, M.; and Jones, M. 1979. Assessing the safety and supportive features of home environments for the elderly. *Proceedings of the Human Factors Society,* 22nd Annual Meeting.

Witkin, H. A.; Oltman, P. K.; Raskin, E.; and Karp, S. A. 1971. *A Manual for the Embedded Figures Test.* Palo Alto, CA: Consulting Psychologist Press.

Witkin, H. A.; Lewis, H. B.; Hertzman, M.; Machover, K.; Meissner, P. B.; and Wapner, S. 1954. *Personality Through Perception.* New York: Harper.

Ysander, L., and Herner, B. 1976. The traffic behavior of elderly male automobile drivers in Gothenburg, Sweden. *Accid. Anal. & Prev.* 8: 81–86.

Ziedman, K.; Smiley, A.; and Moskowitz, H. 1979. Effects of drugs on driving: Driving simulator tests of drazeparn and secobarbital. *Proceedings of the Human Factors Society,* 23rd Annual Meeting, pp. 259–262.

27
CLINICAL ASSESSMENT

Steven H. Zarit, John Eiler,
and Marla Hassinger
University of Southern California

Assessment is the process of gathering information about an individual or group for the purpose of answering certain clinical or research questions. Four prominent objectives of assessments can be identified. The first is to determine diagnosis, that is, to find out whether the problems presented by a given individual meet designated criteria for inclusion in a diagnostic category. The second is to assess the broad pattern of behaviors, thoughts, or emotions of the individual in order to provide more complete information about dimensions of current functioning than is encompassed by diagnosis. The third is to evaluate specific variables that can assist in treatment planning, especially in deciding among alternative forms of treatment. Finally, assessments can measure critical variables for the purpose of evaluating the outcomes of interventions. Although there is overlap in the information needed for these four objectives, there are also differences, and the choice of assessment procedures will therefore vary depending on which issues are emphasized.

Theoretical questions also underlie the decision about the assessment procedures to use and the inferences that can be drawn from them. In the clinical assessment of older persons, assumptions made about the nature and etiology of psychopathology, as well as conceptualizations of the aging process, determine what behaviors are attended to, how and under what conditions data are gathered, and how inferences are drawn from them. Because of the continuing controversies in both conceptualizations of psychopathology and the effects of aging on behavior, the examination of theoretical models is important if clinicians and researchers are to understand the basis for selection and interpretation of assessment procedures.

This review is organized into three parts. The first two address theoretical issues pertaining, respectively, to cognitive assessment and the evaluation of behavior and emotions. The third section reviews practical concerns, including special characteristics of the aging population that affect the assessment process, instruments for evaluation of mood and behavior, and assessment of senile dementia. While emphasizing a somewhat different perspective, this review builds upon several excellent reviews of assessment that have appeared in recent years, including overviews of clinical assessment by Schaie and Schaie (1977); Gallagher, Thompson, and Levy (1980); and Schaie and Stone (1982); assessment of senile dementia by Kahn and Miller (1978) and Gurland (1980); neuropsychological assessment by Albert (1981); cognitive assessment by E. Miller (1980); and personality assessment by Lawton, Whelihan, and Belsky (1980).

THEORETICAL ISSUES IN COGNITIVE ASSESSMENT OF OLDER ADULTS

Introduction: Models of Clinical Cognitive Assessment

The assessment of cognitive abilities in the aged has been and remains one of the most intensely researched areas in gerontology. Studies of normative and pathological changes in intelligence, attention, learning, and memory in older adults abound, yet considerable controversy surrounds interpretations of these data (Botwinick, 1977; 1978; Craik, 1977; Gallagher, Thompson, and Levy, 1980; Albert, 1981). These controversies arise from the series of inferential steps followed in cognitive assessment. Typically, research in cognitive assessment is structured on the model shown in Figure 1.

Test behavior refers to an individual's performance on a psychometric test or laboratory measure; it is a sample of behavior. This performance reflects an inferred level of ability on a specific psychological dimension or cognitive construct, such as intelligence or memory. Clinical assessment then typically entails an additional inferential step, namely, prediction of an individual's actual life experiences for everyday tasks that require the cognitive ability being examined.

The cognitive assessment model presented in Figure 1 has been useful in research on the level and structure of abilities. Clinicians working with younger people, for instance, are often asked questions pertaining to levels of cognitive ability, such as in assessments of school children, and these can be addressed within the framework of this model. Older people may also present problems that pertain to questions of level or structure of abilities, but they are more frequently concerned about what cognitive changes *might mean*. A primary goal of clinical cognitive assessment,

therefore, focuses on diagnosing the normalcy or pathology of the change.

In order to address this question in clinicial practice, a neuropsychological model is proposed (see Figure 2). The neuropsychological model places emphasis on a different inferential step than the cognitive assessment model does. This step involves inferences regarding brain function that may be as general as deciding whether the observed cognitive change reflects normal or pathological processes or as specific as determining the locus, etiology, course, and potential treatment of the underlying change. Inferences may be made from test performance to a cognitive construct and then to brain function, or directly from performance to brain function. As noted above, complexity and controversy accompany each inferential step in assessment, and inferences regarding brain-behavior relations are certainly no exception.

For most psychologists, the neuropsychological model does not necessitate a radical departure from existing assessment approaches. An implicit model of alterations in brain function is typically held responsible for normative age changes in cognition. Wechsler's Don't Hold tests (Wechsler, 1958; Matarazzo, 1972) and Horn and Cattell's (1967) concept of decline in fluid intelligence represent early versions of inferences from cognitive constructs to brain function. There is undeniably a neural foundation for normal cognitive changes with age (Bondareff, 1977; Brody and Vijayshankar, 1977), providing a background upon which pathological neural changes are superimposed. It is not appropriate, however, simply to diagnose "organicity," since normal changes in brain function do not usually have a significant detrimental effect on everyday competencies. The critical problem is to differ-

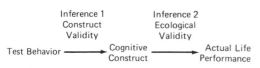

Figure 1.   The cognitive assessment model.

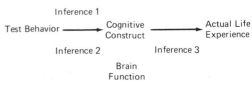

Figure 2.   The neuropsychological assessment model.

entiate pathological from normal age changes. This task requires an understanding of the brain-behavior relations underlying both normal and pathological age changes.

Brain Function Models for Normal Age-Related Changes in Cognitive Ability

The pattern of normal aging has been construed variously as similar to decrements caused by diffuse damage or lateralized right-hemisphere damage. Evidence for the first position is scant. Among the studies that have compared the test protocols of older persons with those of patients with diffuse brain damage, Botwinick and Birren's (1951) found that verbal tests from the Wechsler-Bellevue—especially Information and Comprehension—distinguished dementia patients from normal elderly, whereas differences were smaller on performance subtests thought to be age-sensitive. Similarly, Overall and Gorham (1972) reported that brain-damaged patients had decrements on verbal subtests of the WAIS —especially Information, Similarities, and Vocabulary—when compared to normal older persons. A cross-sectional comparison within their normal sample (which ranged in age between 45 and 84) revealed a different contrast, with older subjects having lower scores on Similarities, Digit Symbol, Picture Arrangement, and Object Assembly. Using the Halstead-Reitan Neuropsychological Test Battery (HRB), Goldstein and Shelly (1975) also found no resemblance between normal elderly controls and those with a diagnosis of diffuse brain damage.

Many studies have documented similarities in test performance between normal older persons and individuals with focal right-hemisphere damage. Sensitivity to left-versus-right hemisphere damage using the WAIS has been demonstrated by observing differences between Verbal IQ (VIQ) and Performance IQ (PIQ). Patients with primarily left-hemisphere damage are distinguished by lower verbal scores; those with impairment to the right hemisphere have lower performance scores (Reitan and Fitzhugh, 1971; Reitan and Davison, 1974). Patients with chronic, resolving, or static lateralized neurological disorders may not produce the expected VIQ–PIQ pattern, having compensated or recovered from acute conditions (Fitzhugh, Fitzhugh, and Reitan, 1961, 1962; Vega and Parsons, 1967). In normative aging research, scores on the performance scales have been repeatedly shown to decline with age, whereas verbal scores have not (Wechsler, 1958; Eisdorfer, Busse, and Cohen, 1959). This pattern of VIQ and PIQ differences has been referred to as the "classic aging pattern" (Botwinick, 1978).

Evidence of the similarity between right-hemisphere brain damage and aging is provided by Klisz (1978), who reanalyzed Reed and Reitan's (1963) data on the HRB and WAIS for young brain-damaged subjects, young controls, controls aged 40 to 49, and controls aged 50 and over. Subtests were categorized as sensitive to general impairment, right-hemisphere damage, and left-hemisphere damage. Although specific subtest ranks are not reported and patterns of test performance were not analyzed, the group of tests that she designated as sensitive to right-hemisphere damage were significantly better at discriminating normal middle-aged subjects from those aged 50 and over than were left-hemisphere or general impairment tests.

Schaie and Schaie (1977) also provided evidence that test performance of normal older adults suggests right-hemisphere decrements. They compared Botwinick's (1977) rank order data of WAIS scores of normal elderly with Fitzhugh, Fitzhugh, and Reitan's (1962) WAIS data from adult groups with acute and chronic diffuse and right-hemisphere damage. No similarity in subtest score patterns existed between normal elderly and those with diffuse damage. Score patterns were quite similar, however, when normal elderly were compared with both acute and chronic right-hemisphere brain-damaged patients.

The extent of decline in performance subtests has been estimated differently, depending on whether cross-sectional comparisons are used or subjects are compared with themselves in a longitudinal design. As might be expected, the cross-sectional method reflects greater decline in performance before age 70 (Botwinick,

1977). In contrast, longitudinal studies show less decline before 70, except on subtests like Digit Symbol that are heavily dependent on speed (Schaie, Labouvie, and Buech, 1973; Jarvik, Kallmann, and Falek, 1962; Honzik and Macfarlane, 1973).

Cross-sectional sampling methods exaggerate age decline because of cohort or generational differences. Since older adults tend to have had fewer years of formal schooling, this difference combined with lower socioeconomic levels and poorer nutrition and health care tends to maximize cognitive deficits when scores are compared to those of younger individuals. Longitudinal testing, however, tends to minimize age differences because of selective attrition. The poorly performing subset of the initial test sample are less likely to return for longitudinal retesting than those who initially performed well (Kleemier, 1962; Riegel, Riegel, and Meyer, 1967; Baltes, Schaie, and Nardi, 1971). Nevertheless, regardless of sampling technique, performance IQ tests do appear to be age-sensitive since they show decline with normal aging.

Should this late-life decline in PIQ be taken as an indication of selective right-hemisphere dysfunction in older adults? Although the data is still too preliminary for conclusive findings, neuroanatomic studies provide little support for this hypothesis. A review by Bondareff (1977) notes the greatest neuronal loss with age in the human frontal cortex and the superior temporal gyrus, with no mention of selective lateralized hemispheric changes in neuronal structure. Electroencephalogram (EEG) data indicate focal slowing in the left temporal anterior region, rather than in right-hemisphere function (Obrist and Busse, 1960).

Stern, Oster, and Newport (1980) looked at the relative functioning of the right and left hemispheres by examining components of reaction time in visual discrimination tasks conducive to either verbal or nonverbal processing. Subjects ranged in age from 7 to 79 years. Slowing with age was evident for each task in the transit time or motor component, whether performed with left or right hand. Among the adults in the study, faster left-hand decision time—and, by inference, more efficient right-hemisphere processing—was found

for the nonverbal task but not for the task conducive to verbal processing. Interestingly, the size of the decision time difference did not change with age. These results place limitations on the proposition that the aging process has a more detrimental effect on nonverbal and presumably right-hemisphere processing than on verbal, sequential, and presumably left-hemisphere processing. Although the verbal and nonverbal tasks in this study were considered to be equated in level of difficulty, it should be noted that these visual discrimination tasks involve less complexity than measures used in traditional cognitive assessment.

Several arguments have attempted to dismiss the performance IQ decrement, seeing it as a result of a testing artifact. One possibility is that since most performance subtests are scored for speed of response as well as for accuracy, motor slowing with age may account for the deficit. Removing the speed criterion did improve the performance of older adults on some tasks, yet even without time limits the elderly did not perform as well as younger subjects (Doppett and Wallace, 1955; Klodin, 1975; Storandt, 1977). This argument, therefore, is an insufficient explanation.

Another hypothesis is that the verbal and performance subtests differ in the demands they place on an older adult's cognitive resources. The verbal items assess stored, highly overlearned information in a very familiar, unambiguous fashion (Birren, Botwinick, Weiss, and Morrison, 1963). The performance items, on the other hand, often employ novel material that must be manipulated in an unfamiliar manner (Schonfield and Robertson, 1966). The possibility exists that, in the terms of Norman and Bobrow (1975), good performance on one task requires more "resources" of a particular neural subsystem than does another task. The VIQ–PIQ distinction may not actually represent a qualitative difference in hemispheric function but may merely derive from a quantitative difference in the resource requirements of the verbal and performance subtests.

Botwinick and Storandt (1974) provide some support for this argument in their examination of qualitative and quantitative scoring of the WAIS Vocabulary subtest. Young and old subjects were first matched on the basis of their standard quantitative scores. Then their responses were rescored on the basis of six qualitative criteria. When the more stringent qualitative scoring was employed, an age decline in vocabulary was apparent. In effect, adequate performance on the WAIS Vocabulary subtest with standard scoring can place less demand on an individual's processing resources than the qualitative scoring criteria.

An alternative strategy for balancing the resource demands of verbal and performance tests is to decrease the resource requirements of the latter by using more familiar test materials. Allowing more practice on unfamiliar tasks is easily accomplished, for example, by increasing the number of practice trials on the Digit Symbol Substitution subtest of the WAIS. Employing test materials that are familiar to older adults is another option; using playing cards in a card-sort task is an example (Krauss and Schaie, 1978).

This issue of comparisons between tests with differing resource requirements overlaps with another controversy in the neuropsychology literature—the use of narrow- versus broad-band testing. The WAIS and HRB subtests are "broad-band" assessment procedures, that is, they are complex tests, with performance dependent upon the integration of several cognitive abilities, such as motor, verbal, visual, perceptual, memory, and learning skills (Boll, 1981). In contrast, narrow-band tests assess discrete cognitive constructs, such as attention or language comprehension.

Broad-band tests may be too complex to allow for reliable inferences about brain function. As an example, adequate performance on the Digit Symbol Substitution subtest of the WAIS requires the integration of left-hemisphere verbal skills in understanding instructions, frontal-lobe planning of motor activity, primary occipital visual ability, right-parietal-lobe perceptual abilities, left-hemisphere motor performance in right-handed individuals, and memory for digit-symbol pairs after practice. The complex integration of virtually all neural areas that this test demands makes it very sensitive to brain dysfunction, and it reflects greater age decline than any

other WAIS subtest (Botwinick, 1967). Yet, although the Digit Symbol Substitution task is listed as right-hemisphere-dependent in Klisz's (1978) analysis, it is impossible to infer precisely localized brain function from it because of its multifactorial nature.

Some astute neuropsychologists, however, can make accurate inferences about brain function from the administration of a variety of broad-band tests and observations of patterns of performance. This approach involves a method of convergent validation, an ad hoc sort of factor analysis that separates common abilities from a number of overlapping cognitive tests. It demands a series of inferences to brain function from multiple, broad cognitive constructs. The level of sophistication and experience of the clinician determines the value of this method, which is not easily reduced to a "cookbook" application.

Another method of deriving precise brain function inferences from broad-band measures is process-achievement analysis (Albert and Kaplan, 1980; Ben-Yishay et al., 1971). Drawing from Werner's (1937) work, this approach recognizes that an individual may succeed or fail on a complex task for a variety of reasons, with an identical outcome achieved in multiple ways. The process-achievement model infers focal brain dysfunction from observation and qualitative analysis of the process and strategies of task performance. For example, different strategies in solving the complex Block Design subtest of the WAIS can differentiate patients with left-frontal or right-parietal pathology (Albert and Kaplan, 1980). The process-achievement approach to cognitive testing allows for the use of valuable diagnostic information that would be lost if only simple achievement-based cutoff scores were utilized.

Process achievement analysis is also used to attempt differential diagnosis of depression, dementia, and normal aging. The clinician might rule out normal aging based on test norms (see LaRue, 1982), but it is often the more qualitative aspects of tests that help differentiate depression from dementia, because test scores of these groups sometimes overlap. Application of the process-achievement approach to differential diagnosis has been successfully used by Whitehead (1973) and La-

Rue (1982). Using a paired-associates learning task, they found dementia patients to give more answers that were irrelevant to the task at hand, whereas depressed patients gave more near misses, such as errors of transposition (mispairings of specific stimulus response word pairs). On a test of recognition memory for geometric designs, Miller and Lewis (1977) and Camp and Niederehe (1978) found that depressed patients made more errors of omission and dementia patients more errors of commission. These studies suggest that depressed patients are overly cautious, having an error pattern of "don't knows" and near misses, whereas dementia patients are not cautious but tend to produce intrusions or irrelevant information.

Narrow-band measures of cognitive assessment (Boll, 1981) provide the basis of an alternative scheme of inference about brain function. A recent review of geriatric neuropsychology (Albert, 1981) presents one version of this position. Albert recommends assessment of the following five discrete cognitive constructs through relatively independent subtests: (1) Attention—separate auditory and visual tests; (2) language comprehension, repetition, reading, writing, and naming; (3) memory—verbal, nonverbal, and delayed recall; (4) visuo-spatial skills—separate perceptual and constructional tasks; and (5) cognitive flexibility—the capacity to shift and maintain performance sets and strategies. Although the functional integrity of the neural areas responsible for completing these tasks is also necessary for adequate performance on broad-band tests, inferences about brain function can be more easily reached from these more specific cognitive constructs.

Another battery of narrow-band tests that is becoming currently popular is based on A. R. Luria's (1966, 1973) "functional systems" approach. The Luria-Nebraska Neuropsychological Test Battery (Golden, Hammeke, and Purisch, 1978) offers a standardized assessment of the basic functional components of the brain. Cognitive constructs of motor, acoustico-motor, tactile, visual-spatial, receptive, and expressive speech functions, as well as reading, writing, arithmetic, memory, and the higher intellectual processes, are assessed

in a qualitative fashion at a variety of levels of difficulty. These levels begin very simply with a breakdown into the most basic components and then become increasingly complex, demanding the integration of a variety of skills, as in broad-band testing. Current age norms merely distinguish between those older or younger than age 45 (Golden and Schlutter, 1978), but studies with older clients are becoming available (Boutselis, 1982). Considerable controversy surrounds the standardized battery, and criticisms have been raised concerning reliability, validity, choice of items, and method of scoring (Adams, 1980; Golden, 1980; Golden, Ariel, McKay, Wilkening, Wolf, and MacInnes, 1982; Spiers, 1980, 1981). Luria also made a sophisticated process achievement analysis of performance which has been lost in the standardization. Nonetheless, the method of conducting cognitive assessment at incremental levels of complexity and difficulty may prove quite useful in balancing the resource demands in tests of a variety of cognitive functions.

To reiterate, although it appears clear that normal age-related changes in cognitive ability are distinct from generalized or diffuse brain damage, the pattern of cognitive change in later life and its relation to brain function has not been resolved. The classic aging pattern on intelligence tests and corroborative data from the HRB suggest stability of left-hemisphere function and decline in right-hemisphere function, but physiological and anatomical evidence for this assertion has not been established, and right-hemisphere deficits are not apparent in simple cognitive tasks such as visual discriminations. It may therefore be premature to conclude that there are major hemispheric differences in structural changes in the aging brain.

The VIQ–PIQ difference with age may be more accurately framed in terms of functional efficiency rather than structural integrity. With the currently expanding interest in hemispheric specialization of function and individual differences in preferred modes of information processing, future studies may address issues of functional efficiency and aging. For example, one might ask whether a group of older adults whose preferred mode of information processing selectively overemphasizes use of right-hemisphere functions would show the same decline as the majority of individuals whose preferred mode primarily emphasizes left-hemisphere processing. A related proposition is that there may be developmental trends in preferred cognitive style, with verbal skills more likely to be emphasized by most adults in our culture, though some individuals would manifest a different pattern.

Another hypothesis in localizing normal later-life brain change has been offered by Albert and Kaplan (1980)—a theory of alterations in frontal-lobel function in older adults. Consistent with the neuroanatomical observations cited above (Bondareff, 1977) and studies of age-related changes in arousal and attention, frontal-lobe dysfunction may account for cognitive test decrements previously attributed to right-hemisphere impairment. Although the resource-demand confound may continue to plague the complex tasks typically used in assessing integrative frontal-lobe functions, this hypothesis certainly warrants close examination.

Other Methodological Issues in Cognitive Assessment

The use of narrow-band, incremental testing in cognitive assessment can only begin to clarify inferences about normative changes in brain function. Even with the most useful psychometric tests, it is obvious that appropriate norms need to be devised before the cognitive performance of older adults can be adequately evaluated. As noted by Schaie and Schaie (1977), general adult norms simply cannot be used to assess brain damage in the elderly. In order to address the primary clinical question raised earlier, that of separating normal age-related cognitive change from pathological brain change, whatever is characteristic of brain-damaged elderly must be assessed against normal aging patterns. Establishing normative test data for older adults, although necessary, is not a simple undertaking.

As recently reviewed by Albert (1981), the health status of elderly subjects used in a normative sample may be crucial, given the influence of chronic systemic diseases on cognitive

function (Birren, Butler, Greenhouse, Sokoloff, and Yarrow, 1963; Wilkie and Eisdorfer, 1971). Using only healthy aging individuals, on the other hand, may provide unrealistically high norms for elderly clients. Eventually, normative data may be available for a variety of systemic disorders, such as hypertension or diabetes, as well as for optimally healthy older adults.

Another general problem arises from the use of normative data to establish cut-off scores for individual clinical diagnosis. Such factors as anxiety, poor motivation, unfamiliarity with testing procedures, physical illness, medication, and prior level of achievement may cause an older adult to appear impaired if only current level of performance is observed. Although these factors may be recognized by clinicians, they are not reflected in simple measures of level of performance (Boll, 1981).

Schaie and Schaie (1977) suggest another problem—that age-corrected norms may be cohort specific as a result of being developed from cross-sectional studies. Unless data from sequential studies are used to estimate expected changes in norms at given ages, norms established for a particular cohort at adulthood may be valid through late life only for that cohort, and not for succeeding generations. This question should be addressed experimentally through sequential studies of successive cohorts, because of the critical clinical implications.

Besides contributing to the development of adequate age norms, longitudinal studies can resolve important questions about differential diagnosis in another way. Perhaps the biggest challenge for clinical assessment in the next decade is to identify early cognitive changes associated with senile dementia, especially as new treatments are proposed and tested. Because early signs are relatively subtle and difficult to differentiate from fluctuations in performance resulting from mood, motivation, aging, or individual differences, longitudinal studies are necessary to validate those patterns of performance that are most likely to predict progressive decline. An example of this type of research involves clarification of the clinical significance of an older person's complaints of failing memory. Although memory complaints have sometimes been viewed as a sign of mild, early dementia, cross-sectional studies report that they are more likely to be associated with depression than with the objective cognitive deficits that are typical of dementia (Kahn, Zarit, Hilbert, and Niederehe, 1975; Gurland, Fleiss, Goldberg, Sharpe, Copeland, Kelleher, and Kellett, 1976; Zarit, 1982; Popkin, Gallagher, Thompson, and Moore, 1982). The possibility remains, however, that complaints of failing memory might reflect an ongoing process of decline that would become more pronounced over time. To address this question, a one-year follow-up was undertaken of older persons who complained of failing memory but whose initial cognitive performance did not meet the standard diagnositic criteria for dementia. Findings at one year indicated that only one of the 50 subjects now had cognitive deficits suggestive of dementia and that many persons had improved in memory performance. Rather than suggesting dementia, complaints of failing memory were associated with depression scores at both times of testing (Orr, Reever, and Zarit, 1980).

Measurement of longitudinal change in late life-disorders has not been effectively examined in the current literature, for a variety of reasons. The main difficulty in examining the course of cognitive change arises from the complexity involved in adequately equating groups of patients. As noted by Parsons and Prigatano (1978), the duration of the insult to the brain, the age at which the insult occurs, and the rate of neural change are key variables in determining the process and eventual outcome of a neurological disorder. These variables are difficult to determine conclusively, given the insidious nature of late-life degenerative disorders like Alzheimer-type dementia. Even when the onset is acute, as in cerebral vascular accidents, the eventual behavioral course will vary substantially, depending on the size and location of the lesion, as well as on the educational level and premorbid cognitive ability of each individual. Grouping brain-damaged subjects who may differ in terms of these variables introduces diverse sources of variance, causing inaccurate conclusions about brain-behavior relationships.

For example, it has been proposed that Alzheimer-type dementia progresses more rapidly when there is early onset (Feldman, Chandler, Levy, and Glaser, 1963) or when cognitive signs of parietal lobe involvement are evident (McDonald, 1969). The possibility of these or other subtypes of Alzheimer-type patients complicates the research task.

Although well-controlled group studies in this area are certainly desirable, systematic individual case studies can provide valuable reports on the patterns of neuropsychological decline or recovery following various late-life disorders. The efficacy of various treatment or rehabilitative efforts can also be addressed by the case study method. The possible experimental designs in single-case study are described in detail by Hersen and Barlow (1976), and the applications to neuropsychological research are discussed by Shallice (1979). Attention to single-case design issues making use of reliable and validated measures and repeated observations helps assure that objective data, rather than clinical impressions, are being evaluated.

Several advantages of the case study method are discussed by Parsons and Prigatano (1978), as follows: The case study method (1) provides a detailed, qualitative examination of several interacting variables, which is often impossible within the confines of group studies; (2) allows for the appraisal of the clinical as opposed to the purely "statistical" significance of a phenomenon; (3) documents theoretically important clinical case material; and (4) reminds investigators that research must eventually include some explanation of individual behavior. The disadvantages are (1) the potential unreliability of a single case, and (2) the inability to quantify accurately the effects of potentially relevant variables.

Regardless of whether group or single-case designs are used, monitoring the course of cognitive change demands special attention to the assessment measures employed. Repeated testing necessitates the development of alternative or parallel forms of measures of cognitive ability. Attention to "floor effects" is also critical in order to maximize the testability of extremely impaired clients. Albert (1981) suggests developing tasks that structure the selection and production of a simple response, using interesting and concrete situations and closely monitoring fatigue in the testing process. Extensive behavior sampling, including "testing limits" (Lezak, 1976), may be required to reduce greater variability in the response of older adults.

Summary

The current state of clinical cognitive assessment is one in which there are neither ready signs for distinguishing subtle or mild pathology from normal aging nor any possibility of constructing a cookbook that can sort out the multiple influences on test behavior. Our optimistic view of the revitalized interest in neuropsychology as both a clinical and experimental field is based on the belief that the use of narrow-band, incremental testing in a process achievement framework provides a worthwhile method for examining the connections between brain function and cognition. Even so, the problem of evaluating brain-behavior relations in normal and pathological conditions of aging is exceedingly complex and may not yield to easy solutions.

THEORETICAL ISSUES IN THE ASSESSMENT OF BEHAVIOR AND AFFECT

The clinical assessment of personality, behavior, and affect has undergone a major shift in emphasis and methods in recent years. As with cognitive assessment, inferences made from personality tests and other clinical procedures, as well as the models upon which they are based, have been questioned on both theoretical and empirical grounds. Historically, clinical assessments have relied on tests and other observations to make inferences about underlying constructs of personality or psychopathology. In contrast to neuropsychological inferences, which can ultimately be evaluated against findings of brain pathology or physiology (although the process is neither straightforward nor easy), these clinical constructs were imprecisely operationalized and unreliable and generally could not be validated with physiological evidence or by demonstrat-

ing utility in predicting current or future behavior. Because of these problems in traditional methods of psychological assessment, new approaches have been proposed from behavioral and cognitive-behavioral perspectives. These methods emphasize self-reports by patients as well as direct observations of clinical problems, rather than inferring hypothesized internal states or dynamics (Bersoff, 1973; Bem and Allen, 1974; Goldfried and Kent, 1972). The implications of these changes in the clinical assessment of older adults are far-reaching but have not been considered to any extent in prior reviews.

Critics of traditional psychological assessment methods (Ciminero, 1977; Mischel, 1968; 1975; Bersoff, 1973; Goldfried and Kent, 1972; Bem and Allen, 1974, Nelson, 1981) have emphasized four related points: (1) Psychological tests do not take into account the fact that behavior varies across situations; (2) testing procedures have been governed by nomothetic rather than idiographic assumptions; (3) the interpretation of assessment results has often required inferences that have not been supported empirically; and (4) the appropriateness of the medical model in assessment of psychopathology is questionable.

Situational Determinants of Behavior

There is ample evidence that behavior is influenced by contingencies in the environment, but most psychological tests are based on the assumption that what they measure has broad relevance for many situations. According to Bersoff (1973), many tests have their theoretical foundation in the psychoanalytic tradition, which posits that behavior is determined by underlying character structure and is relatively independent of the situation in which the person is found: "Personality is thus perceived as sets of needs, drives or transsituational traits that initiate and guide behavior" (Bersoff, 1973, pp. 892–893).

The empirical foundation of this assumption has long been considered to be weak. Predictions from measures of traits—including well-defined constructs such as introversion-extroversion, aggression, or social conformity—to behaviors that should reflect those traits are relatively low, usually falling in the 0.20 to 0.30 range (see Mischel, 1975, and Bem and Allen, 1974, for reviews).

Although these low correlations have sometimes been viewed as the result of poor measurement or conceptualization of constructs, Mischel (1975) suggests that they fall in the range one might expect, given the influence of the environment on behavior. Furthermore, he proposes that the ability to vary one's behavior in response to unique environmental demands is an important, adaptive quality.

These arguments about the limitations of inferences from tests do not contradict the neuropsychological model presented earlier. When one's primary goal is to make inferences about cognitive constructs or brain functioning, then testing under standardized conditions is an appropriate approach, but there will be more possibility for error when making inferences from test scores to everyday behavior. A different method of gathering data is needed in order to learn about the person-situation interaction.

Two straightforward assessment approaches to improve predictions to everyday behavior are possible. The first is to make observations of, or gather reports about, the situations that are of interest to the clinician, for example, those situations in which a client's problems are reported to be pronounced. The second possibility is to design a measure that assesses how people react in different situations (Goldfried and D'Zurilla, 1969). Goldfried and Kent (1972) propose a method of situational analysis in which relevant environmental events are sampled, responses for several situations are obtained, and potential responses are rated according to their degree of effectiveness. The usefulness of a measure like that depends on the ability to identify a pool of relevant situations. A taxonomy of situations, such as that proposed by Scheidt and Schaie (1978), would contribute to the construction of appropriate situational measures.

When the clinician's interest is to predict everyday behavior, a situational approach may be relevant to cognitive assessments as well. Maloney and Ward (1976), for example, will ask clients to solve problems from their every-

day life, such as: "If you had five dollars to go to the grocery store, what would you buy? How would you get there?" These types of questions may tell more about whether people can maintain themselves in the real world than the scores on a WAIS. Although these kinds of questions have long been a part of the clinical tradition, they are only now being researched in systematic ways.

NOMOTHETIC VERSUS IDIOGRAPHIC ASSUMPTIONS

Related to the issue of situational determinants of behavior is the long-standing controversy over nomothetic and idiographic models of personality. Most assessment procedures are based on a nomothetic model, that is, one positing that the relation among traits and behaviors is similar from one person to the next. According to Bem and Allen (1974, pp. 308–309), the nomothetic assumption is "that a particular trait or dimension or set of trait dimensions is universally applicable to all persons and that individual differences are to be identified with different locations on those dimensions. A more elaborate version of the same nomothetic assumption can be found in factor-analytic formulations which assume that there is a universal factor structure of personality and that individual differences are to be specified by different points in the factor n-space." As an example, two persons who score the same on a measure of honesty would be assumed to place the same value on honesty and have the same behavioral tendency to act in honest ways.

The idiographic model, which is associated with Allport (1937) and has recently been elaborated by Bem and Allen (1974), has two major features. First, behavior depends on a combination of traits and cannot be predicted consistently by scores on a single trait or personal dimension. For instance, someone might score high on the trait, honesty, but behavior will be mediated by other traits, such as the need for approval of others or the need to achieve. Furthermore, the way traits are combined varies from one person to the next.

The second feature of the model was developed by Bem and Allen (1974) to address the problem of situational determinants of behavior. Although acknowledging the influence of situational factors and the tendency of people to attribute cause to internal traits even when environmental manipulations are paramount, they argue that there are important consistencies in behavior across situations and over time. The characteristics for which consistency is manifested vary from person to person and represent a different dimension than that indicated by individual scores on measures of a trait. When a person is consistent in a trait, situational factors will have less influence on behavior, whereas individuals who are inconsistent for a particular characteristic will be more susceptible to environmental influences.

In a test of this proposition, Bem and Allen (1974) studied the relation between the ratings of subjects and informants who knew the subjects well for two traits (friendliness and conscientiousness). When subjects described themselves as consistent in the trait, there was a high degree of agreement between self-ratings and the informants' ratings and also between the ratings of different informants for the same subject. When subjects stated that they were inconsistent, however, there was little agreement between the informants among themselves or with the subjects' own ratings of how friendly or conscientious they were. Bem and Allen note that the degree of agreement between subjects and informants did not depend on how friendly or conscientious a given subject saw himself or herself; consistency was the important factor.

Idiographic approaches can be found in some early studies of the relation of personality and adaptation in aging (Reichard, Livson, and Peterson, 1962; Neugarten, Havighurst, and Tobin, 1968). These studies developed operational personality types, such as integrated, passive-dependent, and unintegrated. Although these constructs confound personality with adaptation, thereby begging the question of which types are associated with better adaptation, they represent attempts to define qualities of individuals that remain consistent across situations.

The implication of the idiographic approach for assessment is that it is necessary to evaluate both the degree of consistency in the traits of a given individual and the relation among these traits. How personal dimensions relate to behavior will depend partly on the significance of the characteristic in question to the individual and partly on the situation. As Nelson (1981) notes, even having a measure for which predictions to behavior are known to be reliable does not mean that the clinician can rely on test scores as an accurate indicator of behavior. As an example, she suggests role-playing in the clinician's office probably has a high degree of concurrent validity with observed behavior, but, for a few clients, role-playing might not be a good predictor of behavior in other situations.

This last example underscores a major difference between research and clinical methodologies. A research measure is evaluated for its ability to represent, in valid and reliable ways, the characteristics of groups of individuals. It is not crucial to most research questions if predictions from that measure are inaccurate for a small number of cases. The clinician, however, cannot assign inexactness to the error estimate in an equation. Attention needs to be paid to what is unique in a given case, and not just what is generally true.

The use of an idiographic model, however, can contribute to better research on issues of personality and aging and also creates the possibility of asking many interesting questions. For example, one might ask if traits that were consistent in youth continue to be consistent in old age and if consistency in certain characteristics is related to better or worse adaptation.

Inferred Constructs and the Question of Validity

As noted earlier, much of traditional psychological assessment has been marked by the tendency to use test responses as indicators of inferred constructs without adequate validation. The relation between the construct and the observations on which it is based tended to be supported by theory rather than empirically tested propositions.

Projective tests provide the best examples of the use of inferred constructs that lack adequate validation. Reviews of the projective test literature on older people—such as the recent, excellent one by Lawton, Whelihan, and Belsky (1980)—reveal studies that are marked by a richness of ideas but also an inattention to important methodological details.

The tendency for inferences to be made on rational-intuitive bases rather than through empirical validation can be seen both in the Rorschach literature and the TAT literature. With respect to the Rorschach, Lawton et al. (1980) summarize such studies of older people as generally finding a constriction of responses, stereotyped responses, and poor clarity (Ames, 1966; 1974; Ames, Metraux, Rodell, and Walker, 1973; Klopfer, 1946; Kuhlen and Kiel, 1951; Singer, 1963). As Lawton, Whelihan, and Belsky point out, however, many of the Rorschach studies have been conducted in institutional settings, so that factors of institutionalization, poor health, brain damage, and low education have probably all affected the findings. They also cite Klopfer (1974) on the dynamic inference concerning these patterns of tests. The records of overall constriction are interpreted as reflecting a motivation to escape from the inner tension that results from having to make discriminations beyond one's capacities. This proposition makes sense on an intuitive basis and is consistent with theoretical propositions about ego functioning.

Similar inferences have been drawn from the literature on TAT responses of older people. The TAT literature, as Lawton, Whelihan, and Belsky (1980) point out, represents a richer tradition than the Rorschach, with more careful methodology. A number of interesting propositions about personality changes with aging have been generated from samples of normal, community-living older adults (Gutmann, 1964, 1969; Cumming and Henry, 1961; Shukin and Neugarten, 1964; Lieberman, Prock, and Tobin, 1968; Britton and Britton, 1972). As an example, Rosen and Neugarten (1960) developed criteria for measuring ego energy in terms of whether nonpictured characters were introduced into the stories, of whether conflict was described, and also from the level of activity. Both cross-sectional and longitudinal differences in ego energy were reported (Rosen and Neugarten, 1960; Lubin, 1964).

The inferences about the meaning of these TAT and Rorschach responses are potentially useful for clinical assessment, but their validity and generalizability have not been demonstrated. The "projective hypothesis" holds that the characteristics revealed on these tests are central, enduring characteristics of individuals, but the generalizability of test findings across situations has not been tested empirically. It is equally plausible that the test responses are affected by properties of the test-taking situation and/or of the test. Findings may be as trivial as that older people invest less energy when confronted with ambiguous stimuli in tasks to which they ascribe little importance.

The other major problem with projective tests, as well as many constructs derived from other testing procedures, is that the observations used to define a construct actually have little or no demonstrated relation to the construct. For instance, a certain pattern of Rorschach responses may indicate motivation to escape from inner tension, or qualities of TAT stories could signify different levels of ego energy, but other plausible post-hoc explanations could be constructed. There is usually little effort to validate these constructs empirically. One might ask, for example, does a measure of ego energy relate to other variables that reflect ego energy? And, of central interest to clinical assessment, does the purported construct relate to specific clinical problems or to treatment choices, especially those that are theoretically linked to the construct, "ego energy"?

This discussion could be interpreted as a mere call for better validation of measures, but it also reflects differences in philosophy between psychodynamic and behavior orientations. At the heart of the matter is the extent to which untested and inferred propositions are appropriate in assessments. The importance of distinguishing theoretical from empirically validated propositions is that theory tends to take on a life of its own, accruing validity over time, its basic hypotheses remaining untested. A major danger of a solely rational-intuitive approach is that its interpretations are often compelling, even in the face of contradictory evidence. To illustrate this point, Goldfried and Kent (1972) cite a study by Chapman and Chapman (1969) in which they found that clinicians, on a rational-intuitive basis, identified signs of male homosexuality on Rorschach protocols, even though many of the signs had not been confirmed in prior empirical tests.

Inference, intuition, and creativity all have an important place in assessment as well as other clinical activities. They are useful for generating hypotheses to account for the apparent diversity or order in human phenomena, and it is often necessary to go beyond the data, if only because adequate explanations are lacking. At the same time, however, inferences that are supported only by other inferences can be misleading. It is important to make the relations between observations and inferences explicit and to define constructs in operational terms so as to prevent the tendencies toward making sweeping or unjustified inferences about clients and their behaviors that have hampered clinical assessment in the past.

The Medical Model: Uses and Limits

Another type of inference that has been a source of controversy is that which ascribes observed symptoms or problems to underlying disease states. The medical model has been criticized from a number of perspectives. One criticism has been the unreliability of diagnostic categories (cf. Spitzer and Fleiss, 1974; Ward, Beck, Mendelson, Mock, and Erbaugh, 1962). Another position is that many diagnostic categories have the effect of creating labels that lead to the confusion of normal and abnormal behavior. Once a label has been applied, there is a tendency to view anything a person says or does as a symptom of the disorder (Rosenhan, 1972). The vagueness of diagnostic constructs contributes to this problem.

The recent revisions in psychiatric diagnosis incorporated into the third edition of the Diagnostic and Statistical Manual of Mental Disorders of the American Psychiatric Association

(DSM III) substantially improves the reliability of diagnosis. The new approach has generally been empirical rather than theoretical. Diagnostic categories have been derived from studies of how symptoms cluster, and greater effort has been made to provide operational definitions for diagnoses (Nathan, 1981; Feighner, Robins, Guze, Woodruff, Winokur, and Munoz, 1972; Spitzer, Endicott, and Robins, 1975). Large-scale pre-testing of diagnostic categories was also undertaken as part of the development of the DSM III. As a result, diagnostic labels such as schizophrenia, which were notoriously unreliable in the past, have acceptable levels of reliability in the DSM III (Spitzer, Forman, and Nee, 1979). Further refinements in diagnostic categories and their operational definitions are found in the Research Diagnostic Criteria (RDC) for affective disorders and schizophrenia (Spitzer, Endicott, and Robins, 1978).

Reliable diagnosis has important uses. First, for some diagnostic categories, such as manic-depressive disorders; there are specific treatment implications. In other disorders for which there is no single optimal treatment, accurate diagnosis can still provide guidelines about treatment choices. A reliable diagnosis of schizophrenia, for instance, suggests that ordinary psychotherapy procedures will have limited value, and one might best proceed with a combination of medical and behavioral approaches (Nathan, 1981). Finally, accurate diagnostic procedures make comparisons across studies possible. The literature on depression, for example, is very difficult to evaluate because of the varying and sometimes unclear definitions of depression, but the development of the Research Diagnostic Criteria for affective disorders makes better comparisons possible (Endicott and Spitzer, 1978).

The limits of current diagnoses are also apparent. Many diagnostic categories have only vague treatment implications, and to view them in a concrete fashion as representing specific abnormal conditions is to go beyond their current usefulness. The example of the RDC category, Major Depressive Disorders, can illustrate this problem. It is generally assumed that Major Depressions have a biological component, an assumption bolstered by continuing research into the role of the catecholamines and other neurotransmitters in depression (Baldessarini, 1975; Blazer, 1982). Patients with major depressions are better candidates for antidepressant medications than those with less severe degrees of depression. At the same time, however, people classified as having a Major Depressive Disorder constitute a heterogeneous group. They differ in their response to drugs and other treatments and also on behavioral characteristics, such as social skills, that have implications for treatment (Lewinsohn and Lee, 1981). As Akiskal and McKinney (1973) have argued, depression may represent a spectrum of problems, rather than a single etiological entity, and biological, psychological, and social factors may contribute to the etiology in varying degrees.

These observations underscore the importance of utilizing both medical and behavioral perspectives in assessment. Even in cases where there is a well-defined illness, as with dementia, assessments of current behaviors and social resources available to the patient may reveal some aspects of the problem that can be treated with psychological interventions (Kahn, 1975; Zarit and Zarit, 1983a).

Implications for Clinical Assessment

The major implication of these criticisms of traditional psychological assessment is that direct observations of clinical problems and verbal reports made by patients about their condition should play a prominent role in assessment. Rather than evaluating overt behavior and verbalizations for signs of hypothesized internal states, the clinician can make assessments by gathering a sample of behaviors that are relevant to the presenting complaints or problems (Ciminero, 1977).

Direct observation of behavior in important situations yields very good clinical data, but there are often practical problems involved in conducting observations, including compromising the confidentiality of the patient and the amount of time required to obtain an adequate sampling of behaviors, especially since some events of interest to the clinician may

occur with low frequency (Lipinski and Nelson, 1974; Kazdin, 1974). Another problem is that the presence of an observer alters a situation.

An alternative to direct observation is to use information obtained from reports from the clients, and sometimes from family members or other informants. There are a number of strategies for gathering this information, including a clinical interview, self-report measures, or self-monitoring of targeted problems. Both overt and covert processes can be assessed. These reports can then be integrated with whatever observations of behavior are available.

Although fewer inferences have to be made from these types of observations, behavioral assessments should not be viewed as free from the constraints of assuring adequate reliability and validity (Goldfried and Linehan, 1977; Tasto, 1977). Appropriate procedures for establishing reliability and validity of behavioral assessment measures have been described by Goldfried and Linehan (1977) and by Nelson (1981).

Even when adequate psychometric properties have been determined, it would be naive to assume that all clients are accurate reporters. Denial, selective or self-serving recall, concern on the part of the client about the opinion of the clinician, reticence or suspiciousness, cognitive impairment, and inadequate skills in observing self and others can compromise self-reports. Older people may present special problems in self-reports, underreporting undesirable psychiatric symptoms on self-rating scales, on the one hand, while reporting high rates of somatic symptoms on the other (Salzman and Shader, 1972; Harmatz and Shader, 1975; Klassen, Hornstra, and Anderson, 1975). More empirical investigations are needed to determine the extent of this problem and the conditions that might minimize it. For the practicing clinician working with older clients, one implication is to base assessments upon several sources, including direct observation, rather than relying solely on a self-report inventory. Discrepancies between different assessment procedures may, in fact, represent important clinical data.

Despite these problems, self-reports may be

more consistently accurate than has usually been believed (Kazdin, 1974; Ciminero, Nelson, and Lipinski, 1977). In sleep research, for example, the use of sleep diaries may be as accurate an indicator of current functioning as other measures, including such "hard" measures as continuous monitoring of EEGs (Bootzin, Engle-Friedman, and Hazlewood, 1983). Commenting on the importance of self-reports, Tasto (1977, p. 154) observes:

> It is understandable historically how verbal reports came to be looked on as something less than the best predictor of human behavior. Yet in the realm of clinical practice, *the operational criteria for the existence of problems are self-reported verbalizations.* If a patient says there is a problem, then there is a problem. . . . With the exception of behaviors that are illegal and consequently defined as problems independently of the patient's view, it is the patient's complaint of anxiety, depression, insomnia or the like that defines whether a problem exists for clinical purposes.

One might add cognitive impairment to Tasto's exceptions, but the basic point is that patients themselves have a central role in defining clinical problems.

Procedures have been suggested for improving the accuracy of self-reports, including training patients in how to make assessments of themselves, reliability checks, and reinforcement for accurate reporting (Ciminero, Nelson, and Lipinski, 1977). With complex, and especially covert, variables, considerable training may be necessary for the patient to learn how to identify and monitor relevant responses (cf. Beck, Rush, Shaw, and Emery, 1979). Although assessment procedures that can be administered at a particular point in time may be desirable from the standpoint of convenience, it is possible that the proper assessment of complex responses depends on the development of sufficient rapport between the patient and the clinician and an increased awareness on the part of the latter of the responses being questioned. With time and training, many patients can learn to identify complex behavioral or cognitive sequences and to monitor them accurately. The criticism that self-report measures are superficial and simplistic is often justified, but reliable measurement of complex constructs is nevertheless possible if the proper assessment instruments are used after rapport has developed and the patient understands and can identify targeted responses.

PRACTICAL APPROACHES TO CLINICAL ASSESSMENT

Three practical concerns with special importance to the assessment of older persons will be considered. These concerns are (1) the differences in the assessment processes used for younger and older adults, (2) the use of clinical interviews and self-ratings measures for assessments of behavior and mood, and (3) the assessment of senile dementia.

Differences in Assessments of Younger and Older Adults

Since the older population varies more in both psychological and physiological characteristics than the younger, generalizations about them as a group can be misleading. Certain characteristics that affect assessment become more prevalent with advancing age, and the clinician needs to determine if these are present and are affecting behavior. Physical problems include becoming easily fatigued, vision and hearing decrements, and motor weaknesses or impairments. A patient's current medications and health status should always be determined because of their potential effects on mood, attention, and cognitive functioning. For instance, Salzman and Shader (1979) summarize the various illnesses and medications that can cause symptoms of depression. Psychological characteristics that can change with age and affect assessment include slowing response, increased caution, relatively poorer response to unfamiliar stimuli, and greater anxiety.

Another consideration is the need to differentiate between the age of the patient and the time of onset of the disorder. Important differences exist between individuals with chronic conditions that developed early in life and those who have functioned well most of their life but develop a problem for the first time in old age. The patient with late-life onset will usually have more resources and competencies than someone long afflicted with chronic impairments. Furthermore, problems that have existed for many years are usually resistant to change. Chronicity should not be used as a reason for withholding appropriate treatment but should rather be seen as an indicator that interventions will be more complicated and goals may need to be more modest.

Clinical Interviews

Clinical interviews have long been part of the assessment process. Although sometimes criticized for their unreliability, these interviews allow a degree of flexibility for investigating the unique problems and circumstances of a given case. Furthermore, the development of semistructured and structured interview formats diminishes a major source of unreliability—the differences in information obtained by different interviewers (Endicott and Spitzer, 1978).

Kanfer and Saslow (1965) have developed a useful format for a general clinical interview, which they call "Functional Behavioral Analysis." Similar approaches have been suggested by Goldfried and Davison (1976), Morganstern (1976), Linehan (1977), Haynes (1978), and Meyer, Liddell, and Lyons (1977). There are three major components of Functional Behavioral Analysis: (1) description of problems; (2) history; and (3) the social and cultural context. In the first step, the clinician obtains descriptions of presenting problems in operational terms and determines their frequency, intensity, duration, and whether any overt or covert antecedents or consequences of problems can be identified. This information can serve as a baseline for measuring the effects of interventions. Estimates of severity also have implications for treatment, for instance, in the differentiation between major and minor depressions or in identifying the degree of suicide risk. The assessment of antecedents or consequences serves to identify those events that control or reinforce problems. The description of presenting symptoms obtained in a clinical interview can be augmented by self-report or observational measures or by self-monitoring of targeted symptoms (see below). Self-monitoring is especially important for de-

termining possible antecedents and consequences, since patients can often report them in only a cursory fashion during an initial interview.

The second part of the interview, the history, includes obtaining information about the onset of the problems as well as a broader developmental history. The former often helps clarify the type of disorder, whereas developmental information identifies strengths and weaknesses apart from presenting problems.

The third part of the Functional Behavioral Analysis assesses the social context of current symptoms, including conflicts and resources in the person's social network. The clinician must also determine "whose problem it actually is." When the designated patient is an unwilling participant in the assessment and does not want treatment, the appropriate intervention, so long as there is no danger to self or others, may be with those persons making the original complaint.

A different approach to functional assessment that has been widely used in research and practice with older persons is the Older Americans Resources and Services Questionnaire, or OARS (Pfeiffer, 1976; Duke University, 1978). Using a structured interview format, this instrument includes evaluations of mental status, psychiatric and physical symptoms, social and economic resources, and the use of social services.

Another structured interview, the Comprehensive Assessment and Referral Evaluation (CARE), provides a similar multidisciplinary framework, including assessments of medical, psychiatric, nutritional, economic, and social problems (Gurland, Kuriansky, Sharpe, Simon, Stiller, and Birkett, 1977–78). A major feature of CARE is that indices have been derived for making reliable diagnoses of depression, dementia, and other problems (Gurland, Golden, and Challop, 1982; Gurland, Dean, Cross, and Golden, 1980).

Structured psychiatric interviews with older populations may also be useful whenever questions of diagnosis are important or equivalent populations must be identified for research. A widely used interview for diagnosing depression is the Schedule of Affect Disorders and Schizophrenia, or SADS (Endicott and

Spitzer, 1978). Although developed for younger persons, the SADS has adequate reliability and validity for identifying older persons with Major Depressive Disorders (Dessonville, Gallagher, Thompson, Finnel, and Lewinsohn, 1982). Interviews with older persons, however, have proved more lengthy than the 1 to 1½ hours typical with younger patients. Lewinsohn and Lee (1981) have described an abbreviated interview based on the SADS that may prove useful with older persons. Another psychiatric interview with possible applications for older persons is the National Institute of Mental Health Diagnostic Interview schedule (Robins, Helzer, Croughan, and Ratcliff, 1981).

Other structured measures that combine interview and observation have been used for ratings of psychiatric symptoms of older persons. Among those frequently reported in the literature are the Hamilton Depression Scale (Hamilton, 1967), the Inpatient Multidimensional Psychiatric Scale (Lorr and Klett, 1966), the Brief Psychiatric Rating Scale (Overall and Gorham, 1962), and the Global Assessment Scale (Endicott, Spitzer, Fleiss, and Cohen, 1976).

Self-ratings

A wide variety of self-report measures that assess affect and behavior have potential applications to the older population. With only a few exceptions, however, these have yet to be tested with older adults, and adequate evaluations of reliability and validity remain to be made. The most obvious problem with many self-rating scales is that some of their items may not be relevant to an older population. An important theoretical issue is whether or not particular items relate to the construct being measured (e.g., depression) in the same way as they do for a younger population. It is possible that there are age differences in the construct or its manifestations. Despite such questions, self-ratings can be used to provide a straightforward estimate of the frequency and severity of current problems.

Some of the more prominent clinical problems having self-rating measures include anxiety (Taylor, 1955; Endler, Hunt, and Rosen-stein, 1962; Spielberger, 1972; Watson and Friend, 1969; Zung, 1971), obsessive-compulsive disorders (Lavissakalian and Barlow, 1981; Cooper, 1970; Hodgson and Rachman, 1977), social skills and social inadequacy (Rathus, 1973; Gambrill and Richey, 1975; Curran and Wessberg, 1981; Youngren, Zeiss, and Lewinsohn, 1975), insomnia (Bootzin, Engle-Friedman, and Hazlewood, 1983), and marital problems (Weiss, Hops, and Patterson, 1973; Weiss and Margolin, 1977; Snyder, Wells, and Kelser, 1981; Haynes, Jensen, Wise, and Sherman, 1981). In addition, Cautela and Upper (1976) have developed a battery of self-report measures for several clinical problems, including alcohol, drug, and eating disorders.

Because of the prevalence of mood disorders in the elderly, depression scales have received considerable attention. The most widely used have been the Zung Depression Scale (Zung, 1965; 1967) and the Beck Depression Inventory (Beck, Ward, Mendelson, Mock, and Erbaugh, 1961). Short forms of the latter are also available (Beck and Beck, 1972; Reynolds and Gould, 1981). These measures, however, may confound depression and physical illness (Raskin, 1979). Blumenthal (1975), for example, found that somatic and optimism indicators on the Zung Depression Scale were correlated with indicators reflecting depressed mood in younger patients but not in older ones. In a recent study, the effects of health status and mood were compared for a sample of older persons meeting the Research Diagnostic Criteria for Major Depressive Disorder and a group of community volunteers with no significant depressive affect (Dessonville et al., 1982). Results indicated that although symptoms of poor health and of depression could usually be distinguished, there was considerable overlap for three problems: insomnia, weight loss, and lack of energy. For less severe depression, the problems of differentiating health and depressive complaints may be even greater. One strategy for handling this difficulty is to utilize self-report measures that do not include somatic items, such as the Depression Adjective Checklist (Lubin, 1964), the MMPI Depression Scale (Dahlstrom, Welsh, and Dahlstrom, 1972), or a measure developed specifically for older persons

(Brink, Yesavage, Lum, Heersema, Adey, and Rose, 1982).

In addition to measures of mood, instruments have been developed to assess behavioral and cognitive correlates of depression. These include the Pleasant Events Schedule (Lewinsohn and Libet, 1972; Lewinsohn and MacPhillamy, 1974; MacPhillamy and Lewinsohn, 1982), the Unpleasant Events Schedule (Lewinsohn and Talkington, 1979), and measures of cognitive distortions typical of depression (Hammen and Krantz, 1976; Beck, Weissman, Lester, and Trexler, 1974; Weintraub, Segal, and Beck, 1974; Munoz and Lewinsohn, 1976; Weissman and Beck, 1978). Versions of the Pleasant Events Schedule and Unpleasant Events Schedule for use with older populations have recently been developed (Teri and Lewinsohn, 1982).

In studies of treatment outcome, a broad-based assessment of symptoms is frequently desired. Reviews of available measures (Waskow, 1975) suggest that the Hopkins SCL-90 and its shorter form, the 53-item Brief Symptom Inventory, provide the best overall evaluation of symptoms (Derogatis, Lipman, Covi, Rickels, and Uhlenhuth, 1970; Williams, Lipman, Rickels, Covi, Uhlenhuth, and Mattson, 1968; Derogatis, 1977). This measure yields both an overall estimate of distress—the Global Severity Index—and scores on nine subscales: somatization, obsessive-compulsivity, interpersonal sensitivity, depression, anxiety, hostility, phobic anxiety, paranoid ideation, and psychoticism. Its reliability with older adults is comparable to a general adult sample (Pearson and Gatz, 1981). A similar omnibus mood scale for older persons is the Psychiatric Outpatient Mood Scale (POMS), developed by McNair, Lorr, and Droppleman (1971).

The most widely used symptom inventory is, of course, the MMPI (Hathaway and McKinley, 1943). Although largely used with younger patients, there has been some interest in determining its appropriateness for older persons. Much of this interest has centered around short forms of the test, which can be completed in under an hour, compared to the two to three hours needed for the standard battery (Fillenbaum and Pfeiffer, 1976). A recent comparison of four of the short versions (Hileman, 1981) suggests that the Mini-Mult (Kincannon, 1968) and Maxi-Mult (McLachlan, 1974) most accurately reflect the profiles of the long form when used with older patients.

Self-monitoring of symptoms represents a major innovation in assessment (Nelson, 1977; Kazdin, 1974; McFall, 1977). Self-monitoring procedures make it possible to assess the specific problems or symptoms presented by a given individual and the situations in which they occur. In addition to monitoring overt behaviors, such procedures can teach patients how to record fluctuations in mood and identify thought patterns (Beck et al., 1979). Self-monitoring serves to highlight situational determinants of problems that would not be easily identified by other assessment means. Furthermore, monitoring of targeted problems has, in and of itself, a mild therapeutic effect (McFall, 1970) and can encourage patients to be active in their own treatment. Applications of self-monitoring to the elderly have been limited, although examples can be found in psychotherapy for depression (Gallagher and Thompson, 1981; 1982) and treatment of sleep problems (Bootzin, Engle-Friedman, and Hazelwood, 1983).

Diagnosis and Assessment of Senile Dementia

No other assessment question has as much practical importance in work with the elderly than diagnosis of senile dementia. Because of the tendency to see elderly symptoms as "organic," senile dementia is overdiagnosed and potentially treatable conditions are overlooked (Copeland, Kelleher, Kellett, Fountain-Gourlay et al., 1974; Sabin, Vitug, and Mark, 1982). When the possibility of dementia is raised, the assessment process involves two questions: first, whether cognitive functioning is, indeed, significantly impaired, and second, whether the severity and pattern of symptoms suggest dementia or another condition. Although there are no effective medical treatments for the major forms of dementia—senile dementia of the Alzheimer type and multi-infarct dementia—many potentially treatable problems can cause dementialike symptoms or a delirium that is sometimes mistaken for dementia in older persons. These problems must be ruled out before irreversible dementia can be definitively diagnosed (NIA Task Force, 1980). Conditions that can cause either symptoms of dementia or delirium are summarized in Figure 3.

The most frequently used clinical procedures in assessment for senile dementia are mental status tests. These tests measure orientation and ability to recall overlearned information, such as the name of the current President of the United States. Calculations, figure drawings, serial subtractions, spelling backwards, and other simple tasks are sometimes included as well (Kahn, Goldfarb, Pollack, and Peck, 1960; Kahn and Miller, 1978; Pfeiffer, 1975; Katzman, Brown, Fuld, Peck, and Schechter, 1981; Folstein, Folstein and McHugh, 1975; Jacobs, Bernhard, Delgado, and Strain, 1977). Some preliminary comparisons have been made of the effectiveness of these measures for accurate diagnosis (Haglund and Schuckit, 1976; Zarit, Miller, and Kahn, 1978), but the differences between the various tests appear to be relatively small. All are useful in identifying obvious cases of dementia, but where presenting symptoms are ambiguous, test results tend to be so as well.

Because the items in mental status tests are relatively simple, errors indicate the presence of a significant degree of cognitive impairment (Zarit, Miller, and Kahn, 1978). These tests are frequently criticized, however, for their lack of sensitivity to milder degrees of cognitive impairment, such as might be manifested early in a dementia. Agreeing with this criticism, Kahn and Miller (1978) point out that mild changes caused by dementia are very difficult to differentiate from problems in cognitive function caused by depression, other mood states, or inadequate education or motivation. They believe the effects of a false positive diagnosis to be more harmful than those of a false negative diagnosis, leading to "the acceptance of a spurious organic diagnosis and the overlooking of effective treatment possibilities" (Kahn and Miller, 1978, p. 48). It is for this very reason that mental status tests and similar clinical procedures are appropriate

assessment tools because they err in the direction of under- rather than overdiagnosis.

When an elderly patient scores in the impaired range on a mental status test, further evaluation of the patient's history and symptoms can help clarify the type of disorder. Dementia usually has an insidious onset and a gradual progression of symptoms, although cases of multi-infarct dementia can start suddenly and progress in a stepwise fashion (Gurland, 1980). In contrast, delirium usually has a sudden and recent onset, whereas depression will be either episodic or chronic, but in either case, without any apparent progression of cognitive symptoms. There are also qualitative differences in responses to mental status tests that distinguish dementia from delirium. Whereas dementia patients respond to denotative aspects of questions, trying to answer the question but getting it wrong or saying that they do not know, delirium patients often have a characteristic pattern of connotative, symbolic responses (Kahn and Miller, 1978; Weinstein and Kahn, 1955). According to Kahn and Miller, "this includes misnaming and displacement. A hospital, for example, will be called by a more benign appellation or euphemism, such as a hotel, country club, 'place for rest and relaxation' or, as another patient said, 'menopause manor.' Temporal or spatial displacement can be shown, as by locating the place nearer his or her home. . . ." (Kahn and Miller, 1978, pp. 56–57). Other differences include the fact that fluctuations in awareness and hallucinations and delusions are more common with delirium (Lipowski, 1980). The possibility of delirium in a patient with a previously diagnosed dementia should also be considered and may, in fact, be more likely because of the existing brain damage (Lipowski, 1980). Medications appear to be a common cause of delirium and other reversible symptoms in dementia patients (Zarit and Zarit, 1983a). When the findings of an assessment suggest delirium, or when reversible causes of dementia have not previously been ruled out, appropriate medical evaluations should be made (NIA Task Force, 1980).

If an older person (or that person's family) complains of cognitive impairment but mental status testing falls within normal ranges and

FIGURE 3 Reversible Causes of Mental Impairment (Source: _Senility Reconsidered_, NIA Task Force).

	Dementia	Delirium	Either or Both
Therapeutic drug intoxication			Yes
Depression	Yes		
Metabolic			
a. Azolemia or renal failure (dehydration, diuretics, obstruction, hypokalemia)			Yes
b. Hyponatremia (diuretics, excess antidiuretic hormone, salt wasting, intravenous fluids)			Yes
c. Hypernatremia (dehydration, intravenous saline)		Yes	
d. Volume depletion (diuretics, bleeding, inadequate fluids)	Yes		
e. Acid-base disturbance		Yes	
f. Hypoglycemia (insulin, oral hypoglycemics, starvation)			Yes
g. Hyperglycemia (diabetic ketoacidosis, or hypersomolar coma)		Yes	
h. Hepatic failure			Yes
i. Hypothyroidism			Yes
j. Hyperthyroidism (especially apathetic)			Yes
k. Hypercalcemia			Yes
l. Cushing's syndrome	Yes		
m. Hypopituitarism			Yes
Infection, fever, or both			
a. Viral			Yes
b. Bacterial			
Pneumonia		Yes	
Pyelonephritis		Yes	
Cholecystitis		Yes	
Diverticulitis		Yes	
Tuberculosis			Yes
Endocarditis			Yes
Cardiovascular			
a. Acute myocardial infarct		Yes	
b. Congestive heart failure			Yes
c. Arrhythmia			Yes
d. Vascular occlusion			Yes
e. Pulmonary embolus		Yes	
Brain disorders			
a. Vascular insufficiency			
Transient ischemia		Yes	
Stroke			Yes

	Dementia	Delirium	Either or Both
b. Trauma			
Subdural hematoma			Yes
Concussion/contusion		Yes	
Intracerebral hemorrhage		Yes	
Epidural hematoma		Yes	
c. Infection			
Acute meningitis (pyogenic, viral)		Yes	
Chronic meningitis (tuberculous, fungal)			Yes
Neurosyphilis			Yes
Subdural empyema			Yes
Brain abscess			Yes
d. Tumors			
Metastatic to brain			Yes
Primary in brain			Yes
e. Normal pressure hydrocephalus	Yes		
Pain			
a. Fecal impaction			Yes
b. Urinary retention		Yes	
c. Fracture		Yes	
d. Surgical abdomen		Yes	
Sensory deprivation states such as blindness or deafness			Yes
Hospitalization			
a. Anesthesia or surgery			Yes
b. Environmental change and isolation			Yes
Alcohol toxic reactions			
a. Lifelong alcoholism	Yes		
b. Alcoholism new in old age			Yes
c. Decreased tolerance with age producing increasing intoxication			Yes
d. Acute hallucinosis			
e. Deliriumtremens		Yes	
Anemia			Yes
Tumor—systemic effects of nonmetastatic malignant neoplasm			Yes
Chronic lung disease with hypoxia or hypercapnia			Yes
Deficiencies of nutrients such as vitamin B_{12}, folic acid, or niacin	Yes		
Accidental hypothermia		Yes	
Chemical intoxications			
a. Heavy metals such as arsenic, lead, or mercury			Yes
b. Consciousness-altering agents[*]			Yes
c. Carbon monoxide			Yes

symptoms and history do not suggest delirium, several possibilities are raised, including: (1) early dementia that is not pronounced enough to affect mental status scores; (2) another type of brain damage; and (3) depression. More extensive neuropsychological testing can often identify patterns of performance that are typical of focal damage, such as from a head trauma, stroke, or tumor. If early dementia is suspected, this type of testing provides a baseline against which future changes can be evaluated (Zarit and Zarit, 1983b).

There are several multidimensional assessment batteries for dementia that may prove more sensitive to early changes and more useful for evaluating changes over time. The Multidimensional Assessment for Dementia Scales combines seven parameters drawn from neurological, psychometric, and observational findings (Drachman, Fleming, and Glasser, 1982). The New York University Memory Test (Randt, Brown, and Osborne, 1980; Osborne, Brown, and Randt, 1982) consists of seven modules, including general information, list learning (five items), digit span, paired associates learning, immediate and delayed recall of a short story, picture recognition, and incidental learning. Because it appears in five equivalent alternative forms, this procedure is especially useful for repeated testings. Gurland, Dean, Copeland, Gurland, and Golden (1982) propose an expanded criteria for diagnosis among community-living elderly, including mental status testing and common memory problems. The Mattis Dementia Scale (Coblentz, Mattis, Zingesser, Kasoff, Wisniewski, and Katzman, 1973) and a revision of it, the Extended Scale for Dementia (Hersch, 1979), provide a variety of simple cognitive tasks designed to provide finer distinctions of the severity of cognitive impairment.

In cases of irreversible dementia, criteria have been proposed for differentiating between senile dementia of the Alzheimer type, multi-infarct, and mixed or indeterminant types. The "ischemic" score developed by Hachinski, Lassen, and Marshall (1974) assigns points for the presence of features of multi-infarct dementia, including sudden onset, nocturnal fluctuations, focal neurological signs and symptoms, and history of stroke, hypertension, and heart disease. Hachinski and his colleagues (1974) report that cerebral blood flow is lower in patients who meet the criteria for multi-infarct dementia but normal in those judged as Alzheimer type. Findings based on biopsies and autopsies have been used to validate the ischemic score (Rosen, Terry, Fuld, Katzman, and Peck, 1980; Simard, Olesen, Paulson, Lassen, and Skinhöj, 1971), but a recent review raises important methodological problems in interpreting results from those studies (Liston and LaRue, 1983). Eisdorfer, Cohen, and Veith (1981) propose a revision of the ischemic score that adds one indicator of multi-infarct dementia (fluctuating course) and omits three other items (personality change, depression, somatic complaints).

The ischemic score has also been used to evaluate if multi-infarct and Alzheimer type dementia affect everyday behaviors of patients in different ways. Using family reports of the frequency of various memory and behavior problems typical of dementia that had occurred during the preceding week, Hassinger, Zarit, and Zarit (1982) found only a few differences between patients who were classified as the Alzheimer or multi-infarct type by the Halchinski scoring method. Among the few differences that were statistically significant, presumed Alzheimer patients asked more repetitive questions, lost things more frequently, had greater trouble completing tasks and recognizing familiar people, and experienced more auditory hallucinations, whereas presumed multi-infarct patients were more often incontinent. Type of dementia was also unrelated to the burden experienced by family members.

When a diagnosis of irreversible dementia is confirmed, assessments of current problems in functioning and the impact of the disease on family members and other supporting persons are useful for planning interventions. Determination of currently present problems in functioning is an important step, since symptoms of dementia can vary considerably from one patient to the next (Rosen and Mohs, 1982). Measures have been proposed for evaluating the current functioning of dementia patients, including the Record of Independent

Living (Weintraub, Baratz, and Mesulam, 1982), the Inventory of Psychic and Somatic Complaints (Reisberg, Ferris, Schneck, de Leon, Crook, and Gershon, 1981), and the Memory and Behavior Problems Checklist (Zarit, Reever, and Bach-Peterson, 1980; J. Zarit, 1982).

The assessment of concerns and problems experienced by family members caring for dementia patients is important, since they usually have to take on increasing responsibilities as the disease progresses. Furthermore, although interventions with the patient have only limited utility, family members can learn strategies for managing problem behaviors and thus alleviate some of their burden (Zarit and Zarit, 1983a and b). The impact of dementia on the family or other caregivers is only partly determined by the severity of symptoms or length of time in the caregiving role. Differences in the caregiver's coping style and social support as well as the relationship between the caregiver and patient all affect the burden of dementia-related changes (Zarit, Reever, and Bach-Peterson, 1980; J. Zarit, 1982). Measures of the caregivers' burden have been developed by Niederehe, Fruge, Scott, Volpendesta, Nielsen-Collins, and Woods (1982), Robinson (1983), and by Zarit, Reever, and Bach-Peterson (1980). A 20-item revised burden measure with adequate reliability and validity has been reported by Zarit (1982).

CONCLUSIONS

In conducting an assessment of an older person, the clinician poses a series of interrelated questions, and the way in which these questions are answered guides the assessment process in one direction or another. One set of questions inquires whether there is evidence of altered brain functioning and what type and severity of impairment are involved. The other set of questions has to do with current behavior and affect, as well as the social context of the clinical problem. These two directions are complementary. If there is a brain impairment, functional assessment clarifies the effect on personal and social adjustment; at the same time, it is useful to rule out brain disease and other organic causes in cases of apparent functional disorders. The choice of specific assessment methods depends on how one conceptualizes these clinical problems and the aging process as well.

The models presented in this chapter represent promising approaches that integrate clinical assessment of older persons with major trends in the neuropsychology and clinical fields. In adopting any of these procedures, however, there needs to be an adequate investigation of their reliability, validity, and appropriateness for older persons and an establishment of norms that adequately differentiate normal developmental changes from pathology.

REFERENCES

Adams, K. 1980. In search of Luria's battery: A false start. *Journal of Consulting and Clinical Psychology* 48: 511–516.

Akiskal, H. S., and McKinney, W. T. 1973. Depressive disorders: Toward a unified hypothesis. *Science* 182: 20–29.

Albert, M. S. 1981. Geriatric neuropsychology. *Journal of Clinical and Consulting Psychology* 49: 835–850.

Albert, M. S., and Kaplan, E. 1980. Organic implications of neuropsychological deficits in the elderly. In *New Directions in Memory and Aging: Proceedings of the George Talland Memorial Conference,* eds. L. W. Poon, J. L. Fozard, L. S. Cermak, D. Ehrenberg, and L. W. Thompson. Hillsdale, NJ: Erlbaum.

Allport, G. W. 1937. *Personality: A Psychological Interpretation.* New York: Holt, Rinehart & Winston.

Ames, L. B. 1966. Changes in Rorschach response throughout the human life span. *Genetic Psychology Monographs* 74: 89–125.

Ames, L. B. 1974. Calibration of aging. *Journal of Personality Assessment* 38: 507–519.

Ames, L. B.; Metraux, R.; Rodell, J.; and Walker, R. 1973. *Rorschach Responses in Old Age.* New York: Brunner/Mazel.

Baldessarini, R. J. 1975. Biogenic amine hypothesis in affective disorders. In *The Nature and Treatment of Depression,* eds. F. F. Flach and S. C. Draghi. New York: Wiley.

Baltes, P. B.; Schaie, K. W.; and Nardi, A. H. 1971. Age and experimental mortality in a seven-year longitudinal study of cognitive behavior. *Developmental Psychology* 5: 18–26.

Beck, A. T., and Beck, R. W. 1972. Screening depressed patients in family practice—A rapid technique. *Postgraduate Medicine* 52: 81–85.

Beck, A. T.; Rush, D.; Shaw, D.; and Emery, G. 1979. *Cognitive Therapy of Depression.* New York: Guilford.

Beck, A. T.; Ward, C. H.; Mendelson, M.; Mock, J. E.; and Erbaugh, J. 1961. An inventory for measuring depression. *Archives of General Psychiatry* 4: 561–571.

Beck, A. T.; Weissman, A.; Lester, D.; and Trexler, L. 1974. The measurement of pessimism: The hopelessness scale. *Journal of Consulting and Clinical Psychology* 42: 861–865.

Bem, D., & Allen, A. 1974. On predicting some of the people some of the time: The search for cross-situational consistencies in behavior. *Psychological Review* 81: 506–20.

Ben-Yishay, Y.; Diller, L.; Mandelberg, I.; Gordon, W.; and Gertsman, L. 1971. Similarities and differences in block design performance between older normal and brain injured persons: A task analysis. *Journal of Abnormal Psychology* 78: 17–25.

Bersoff, D. N. 1973. Silk purses into sow's ears: The decline of psychological testing and a suggestion for its redemption. *American Psychologist* 28: 892–899.

Birren, J. E.; Botwinick, J.; Weiss, A.; and Morrison, D. F. 1963. Interrelations of mental and perceptual tests given to healthy elderly men. In *Human Aging: A Biological and Behavioral Study*, eds. J. E. Birren, R. N. Butler, S. W. Greenhouse, L. Sokoloff, and M. R. Yarrow. Washington, D.C.: U.S. Government Printing Office.

Birren, J. E.; Butler, R. N.; Greenhouse, S. W.; Sokoloff, L., and Yarrow, M. R., eds. 1963. *Human Aging: A Biological and Behavioral Study*. Washington, D.C.: U.S. Government Printing Office.

Blazer, D. G., II. 1982. *Depression in Late Life*. St. Louis: Mosby.

Blumenthal, M. D. 1975. Measuring depressive symptomatology in a general population. *Archives of General Psychiatry* 32: 971–978.

Boll, T. J. 1981. Assessment of neuropsychological disorders. In *Behavioral Assessment of Adult Disorders*, ed. D. H. Barlow. New York: Guilford Press.

Bondareff, W. 1977. The neural basis of aging. In *Handbook of the Psychology of Aging*, eds. J. E. Birren and K. W. Schaie. New York: Van Nostrand Reinhold.

Bootzin, R. B.; Engle-Friedman, M.; and Hazlewood, L. 1983. Assessment and treatment of insomnia in the elderly. In *Coping and Adaptation in the Elderly*, eds. P. M. Lewinsohn and L. Teri. New York: Pergamon Press.

Botwinick, J., and Birren, J. E. 1951. Differential decline in the Wechsler-Bellevue subtest in the senile psychoses. *Journal of Gerontology* 6: 365–368.

Botwinick, J. 1967. *Cognitive Processes in Maturity and Old Age*. New York: Springer.

Botwinick, J. 1977. Intellectual abilities. In *Handbook of the Psychology of Aging*, eds. J. E. Birren and K. W. Schaie. New York: Van Nostrand Reinhold.

Botwinick, J. 1978. *Aging and Behavior*. 2nd ed. New York: Springer.

Botwinick, J., and Storandt, M. 1974. *Memory, Related Functions and Age*. Springfield, IL: Charles C. Thomas.

Boutselis, M. A. 1982. The use of the Luria-Nebraska memory scale in assessment of senile dementia. Paper presented at the meetings of the Western Psychological Association, Sacramento, CA.

Brink, T. L.; Yesavage, J. A.; Lum, O.; Heersema, P. H.; Adey, M., and Rose, T. L. 1982. Screening tests for geriatric depression. *Clinical Gerontologist* 1: 37–43.

Britton, J. H., and Britton, J. W. 1972. *Personality Changes in Aging*. New York: Springer.

Brody, H., and Vijayshankar, N. 1977. Anatomical changes in the nervous system. In *Handbook of the Biology of Aging*, eds. C. E. Finch and L. Hayflick. New York: Van Nostrand Reinhold.

Camp, C. J., and Niederehe, C. 1978. Signal detection analysis of recognition memory in depressed elderly. Paper presented at the 31st Annual Scientific Meeting of the Gerontological Society, Dallas, TX.

Cautela, J. R., and Upper, D. 1976. The Behavioral Inventory Battery: The use of self-reports in behavioral analysis and therapy. In *Behavioral Assessment: A Practical Handbook*, eds. M. Hersen and A. S. Bellack. Elmsford, NY: Pergamon Press.

Chapman, L. J., and Chapman, J. P. 1969. Illusory correlations as an obstacle to the use of valid psychodiagnostic signs. *Journal of Abnormal Psychology* 74: 271–280.

Ciminero, A. R. 1977. Behavioral assessment: An overview. In *Handbook of Behavioral Assessment*, eds. A. R. Ciminero, K. S. Calhoun, and H. E. Adams. New York: Wiley.

Ciminero, A. R.; Nelson, R. O.; and Lipinski, D. P. 1977. Self-monitoring procedures. In *Handbook of Behavioral Assessment*, eds. A. R. Ciminero, K. S. Calhoun, and H. E. Adams. New York: Wiley.

Coblentz, J. M.; Mattis, S.; Zingesser, L. H.; Kasoff, S. S.; Wisniewski, H. M.; & Katzman, R. 1973. Presenile dementia. *Archives of Neurology* 29: 299–308.

Cooper, J. 1970. The Leyton Obsessional Inventory. *Psychological Medicine* 1: 48–64.

Copeland, J. R. M.; Kelleher, M. J.; Kellett, J. M.; Fountain-Gourlay, A. J.; Cowan, D. W.; Barron, G.; and De Gruchy, J. (U.K.), with Gurland, B. J.; Sharpe, L.; Simon, R. J.; Kuriansky, J. B.; and Stiller, P. (U.S.). 1974. Diagnostic differences in psychogeriatric patients in New York and London. *Canadian Psychiatric Association Journal* 19: 267–271.

Craik, F. I. M. 1977. Age differences in human memory. In *Handbook of the Psychology of Aging*, eds. J. E. Birren and K. W. Schaie. New York: Van Nostrand Reinhold.

Cumming, E., and Henry W. 1961. *Growing Old*. New York: Basic Books.

Curran, J. P., and Wessberg, H. W. 1981. Assessment of social inadequacy. In *Behavioral Assessment of Adult Disorders*, ed. D. H. Barlow. New York: Guilford Press.

Dahlstrom, W. G.; Welsh, G. S.; and Dahlstrom, L. E. 1972. *An MMPI Handbook*. Minneapolis: University of Minnesota Press.

Derogatis, L. R. 1977. *SCL-90: Administration, Scoring and Procedural Manual-I for the R (revised) Version*. Baltimore: Clinical Psychometric Research Unit, John Hopkins University School of Medicine.

Derogatis, L. R.; Lipman, R. S.; Covi, L.; Rickels, K.; and Uhlenhuth, E. R. 1970. Dimensions of outpatient neurotic pathology: Comparison of a clinical versus an empirical assessment. *Journal of Consulting and Clinical Psychology* 34: 164–171.

Dessonville, C.; Gallagher, D.; Thompson, L. W.; Finnel, K.; and Lewinsohn, P. M. 1982. Relation of age and health status to depressive symptoms in normal and depressed older adults. *Essence* 5: 99–118.

Diagnostic and Statistical Manual of Mental Disorders. 3rd ed: 1980. Washington, D.C.: American Psychiatric Association.

Doppelt, J. E., and Wallace, W. L. 1955. Standardization of the Wechsler Adult Intelligence Scale for older persons. *Journal of Abnormal and Social Psychology* 51: 312–330.

Drachman, D. A.; Fleming, P.; and Glasser, G. 1982. The multidimensional assessment for dementia scales. In *Alzheimer's Disease: A Report of Research in Progress,* eds. S. Corkin, K. L. Davis, J. H. Growdon, E. Usdin, and R. J. Wurtman. New York: Raven Press.

Duke University Center for the Study of Aging and Human Development. 1978. *Multidimensional Functional Assessment: The OARS Methodology.* Durham, NC: Duke University.

Eisdorfer, C.; Busse, E. W.; and Cohen, L. D. 1959. The WAIS performance of an aged sample: The relationship between verbal and performance I. Q.'s. *Journal of Gerontology* 14: 197–201.

Eisdorfer, C.; Cohen, D.; and Veith, R. 1981. *The Psychopathology of Aging: Current Concepts.* New York: Scope Publications.

Endicott, J.; Spitzer, R. L.; Fleiss, J. L.; Cohen, J. 1976. The global assessment scale. *Archives of General Psychiatry* 33: 766–771.

Endicott, J., and Spitzer, R. L. 1978. A diagnostic interview: The Schedule for Affective Disorders and Schizophrenia. *Archives of General Psychiatry* 35: 837–844.

Endler, N. S.; Hunt, J. Mc V.; and Rosenstein, A. J. 1962. An S-R inventory of anxiousness. *Psychological Monographs* 76 (17, whole No. 536).

Feighner, J. P.; Robins, E.; Guze, S. B.; Woodruff, R. A.; Winokur, G.; and Munoz, R. 1972. Diagnostic criteria for use in psychiatric research. *Archives of General Psychiatry* 26: 57–63.

Feldman, R. G.; Chandler, K. A.; Levy, L. L.; and Glaser, G. H. 1963. Familial Alzheimer's Disease. *Neurology* 13: 811–824.

Fillenbaum, G. G., and Pfeiffer, E. 1976. The Mini-Mult: A cautionary note. *Journal of Consulting and Clinical Psychology* 44: 698–703.

Fitzhugh, K. B.; Fitzhugh, L. C.; and Reitan, R. M. 1961. Psychological deficits in relation to acuteness of brain dysfunction. *Journal of Consulting Psychology* 25: 61–66.

Fitzhugh, K. B.; Fitzhugh, L. C.; and Reitan, R. M. 1962. Wechsler-Bellevue comparisons in groups with "chronic" and "current" lateralized and diffuse brain lesions. *Journal of Consulting Psychology* 26: 306–310.

Folstein, J. F.; Folstein, S. E.; and McHugh, P. R. 1975. "Mini-mental state": A practical method for grading the cognitive state of patients for the clinician. *Journal of Psychiatric Research* 12: 189–198.

Gallagher, D., and Thompson, L. W. 1981. *Depression in the Elderly: A Behavioral Treatment Manual.* Los Angeles: University of Southern California Press.

Gallagher, D., and Thompson, L. W. 1982. Cognitive therapy for depression in the elderly: A promising model for treatment and research. In *Depression in the Elderly,* eds. L. Breslau and M. Haug. New York: Springer.

Gallagher, D.; Thompson, L.W.; and Levy, S. M. 1980. Clinical psychological assessment of older adults. In *Aging in the 1980's: Psychological Issues,* ed. L. W. Poon. Washington, D.C.: American Psychological Association.

Gambrill, E., and Richey, C. 1975. An assertion inventory for use in assessment and research. *Behavior Therapy* 6: 550–561.

Golden, C. J.; Hammeke, T. A.; and Purisch, A. D. 1978. Diagnostic validity of a standardized neuropsychological battery derived from Luria's neuropsychological test. *Journal of Consulting and Clinical Psychology* 46: 1258–1265.

Golden, C. J., and Schlutter, L. C. 1978. The interaction of age and diagnosis in neuropsychological test results. *International Journal of Neuroscience* 8: 61–63.

Golden, C. J. 1980. In reply to Adam's "In search of Luria's battery: A false start." *Journal of Consulting and Clinical Psychology* 48: 517–521.

Golden, C. J.; Ariel, R. N.; McKay, S. E.; Wilkening, G. N.; Wolf, B. A.; and MacInnes, W. D. 1982. The Luria-Nebraska Neuropsychological battery: Theoretical orientation and comment. *Journal of Consulting and Clinical Psychology* 50: 291–300.

Goldfried, M. R., and Davison, G. C. 1976. *Clinical Behavior Therapy.* New York: Holt, Rinehart, & Winston.

Goldfried, M. R., and Kent, R. N. 1972. Traditional versus behavior personality assessment: A comparison of methodological and theoretical assumptions. *Psychological Bulletin* 77: 409–420.

Goldfried, M. R., and Linehan, M. M. 1977. Basic issues in behavioral assessment. In *Handbook of Behavioral Assessment,* eds. R. Ciminero, K. S. Calhoun, and H. E. Adams. New York: Wiley.

Goldfried, M. R., and D'Zurilla, T. J. 1969. A behavioral model for assessing competence. In *Current Topics in Clinical and Community Psychology,* ed. C. D. Spielberger. New York: Academic Press.

Goldstein, G., and Shelly, C. H. 1975. Similarities and differences between psychological deficit in aging and brain damage. *Journal of Gerontology* 30: 448–455.

Gurland, B. J. 1980. The assessment of the mental status of older adults. In *Handbook of Mental Health and Aging,* eds. J. E. Birren and R. B. Sloane. Englewood-Cliffs, N.J.: Prentice-Hall.

Gurland, B. J.; Golden, R.; and Challop, J. 1982. Unidimensional and multidimensional approaches to the differentiation of depression and dementia in the elderly. In *Alzheimer's Disease: A Report of Research in Progress,* eds. S. Corkin, K. L. Davis, J. H. Growdin, E. Usdin, and R. J. Wurtman. New York: Raven.

Gurland, B. J.; Dean, L.; Cross, P.; and Golden, R. 1980.

The epidemiology of depression and dementia in the elderly: The use of multiple indicators of these conditions. In *Psychopathology in the Aged,* eds. J. O. Cole and J. E. Barrett. New York: Raven Press.

Gurland, B. J.; Fleiss, J. L.; Goldberg, K.; Sharpe, L.; Copeland, J. R. M.; Kelleher, M. J.; and Kellett, J. 1976. The geriatric mental state schedule: A factor analysis. *International Journal of Aging and Human Development* 7: 303–311.

Gurland, B. J.; Dean, L. L.; Copeland, J.; Gurland, R.; and Golden, R. 1982. Criteria for diagnosis of dementia in the community elderly. *The Gerontologist* 22: 180–186.

Gurland, B.; Kuriansky, J.; Sharpe, L.; Simon, R.; Stiller, P.; and Birkett, P. 1977–78. The comprehensive assessment and referral evaluation (CARE)—Rationale, development and reliability. *International Journal of Aging and Human Development* 8: 9–42.

Gutmann, D. L. 1964. An exploration of ego configurations in middle and later life. In *Personality in Middle and Late Life,* ed. B. L. Neugarten. New York: Atherton Press.

Gutmann, D. L. 1969. *The Country of Old Men: Cross Cultural Studies in the Psychology of Later Life.* Ann Arbor, MI: University of Michigan, Wayne State Institute of Gerontology.

Hachinski, V.; Lassen, N.; and Marshall, J. 1974. Multiinfarct dementia: A cause of mental deterioration in the elderly. *Lancet* 2: 207–210.

Haglund, R. M. J., and Shuckit, M. A. 1976. A clinical comparison of tests of organicity in elderly patients. *Journal of Gerontology* 31: 654–659.

Hamilton, M. A. 1967. Development of a rating scale for primary depressive illness. *British Journal of Social Clinical Psychology* 6: 278–296.

Hammen, C. L., and Krantz, S. 1976. Effects of success and failure on depressive cognitions. *Journal of Abnormal Psychology* 85: 577–586.

Harmatz, J., and Shader, R. 1975. Psychopharmacologic investigations in healthy elderly volunteers: MMPI depression scale. *Journal of the American Geriatric Society* 23: 350–354.

Hassinger, M. J.; Zarit, J. M.; and Zarit, S. H. 1982. A comparison of clinical characteristics of Multi-infarct and Alzheimer's dementia patients. Paper presented at the meetings of the Western Psychological Association, Sacramento, CA.

Hathaway, S. R., and McKinley, J. C. 1943. *The Minnesota Multiphasic Personality Inventory Manual.* Minneapolis: University of Minnesota Press.

Haynes, S. N. 1978. *Principles of Behavioral Assessment.* New York: Gardner Press.

Haynes, S. N.; Jensen, B. J.; Wise, E.; and Sherman, D. 1981. The marital intake interview: A multimethod criterion validity assessment. *Journal of Consulting and Clinical Psychology* 49: 379–87.

Hersch, E. L. 1979. Development and application of the Extended Scale for Dementia. *Journal of the American Geriatrics Society* 27: 348–356.

Hersen, M., and Barlow, D. H. 1976. *Single-Case Experimental Designs: Strategies for Studying Behavioral Change.* New York: Pergamon Press.

Hileman, C. 1981. The concurrent validity of four abbreviated forms of the MMPI with elderly psychiatric inpatients: A comparative investigation. Unpublished master's thesis, University of Southern California.

Hodgson, R. J., and Rachman, S. 1977. Obsessional-compulsive complaints. *Behavior Research and Therapy* 15: 389–395.

Honzik, M. P., and Macfarlane, J. W. 1973. Personality development and intellectual functioning from 21 months to 40 years. In *Intellectual Functioning in Adults: Psychological and Biological Influences,* eds. L. F. Jarvik, C. Eisdorfer, and J. E. Clum. New York: Springer.

Horn, J. L., and Cattell, R. B. 1967. Age differences in fluid and crystallized intelligence. *Acta Psychologica* 26: 107–129.

Jacobs, J. W.; Bernhard, M. R.; Delgado, A.; and Strain, J. J. 1977. Screening for organic mental syndromes in the medically ill. *Annals of Internal Medicine* 86: 40–46.

Jarvik, L. F.; Kallmann, F. J.; and Falek, A. 1962. Intellectual changes in aging twins. *Journal of Gerontology* 17: 289–294.

Kahn, R. L. 1973. The mental health system and the future aged. *Gerontologist* 15 (1, part 2): 24–31.

Kahn, R. L., and Miller, N. E. 1978. Assessment of altered brain function in the aged. In *The Clinical Psychology of Aging,* eds. M. Storandt, I. C. Siegler, and M. F. Elias. New York: Plenum.

Kahn, R. L.; Zarit, S. H.; Hilbert, N. M.; and Niederehe, G. 1975. Memory complaint and impairment in the aged. *Archives of General Psychiatry* 32: 1569–1573.

Kahn, R. L.; Goldfarb, A. I.; Pollack, M.; and Peck, R. 1960. Brief objective measures for the determination of mental status in the aged. *American Journal of Psychiatry* 117: 326–328.

Kanfer, F. H., and Saslow, G. 1965. Behavioral analysis: An alternative to diagnostic classification. *Archives of General Psychiatry* 12: 529–538.

Katzman, R.; Brown, T.; Fuld, P.; Peck, A.; and Schechter, R. 1981. A sensitive six item mental status test that correlates with histopathological changes in Alzheimer's Disease. Paper presented at the meetings of the Gerontological Society of America, Toronto.

Kazdin, A. E. 1974. Reactive self-monitoring: The effects of response desirability, goal setting, and feedback. *Journal of Consulting and Clinical Psychology* 42: 704–716.

Kincannon, J. C. 1968. Prediction of the standard MMPI scale scores from 71 items; the mini-mult. *Journal of Consulting and Clinical Psychology* 32: 319–325.

Klassen, D.; Hornstra, R. K.; and Anderson, P. B. 1975. Influence of social desirability of symptom and mood reporting in a community survey. *Journal of Consulting and Clinical Psychology* 43: 448–452.

Kleemier, R. W. 1962. *Intellectual Change in the Senium.* Proceedings of the social statistics section of the American Statistical Association.

Klisz, D. 1978. Neuropsychological evaluation in older persons. 1978. In *The Clinical Psychology of Aging,* eds. M. Storandt, I. C. Siegler, and M. F. Elias. New York: Plenum.

Klodin, U. M. 1975. Verbal facilitation of perceptual-integrative performance in relation to age. Unpublished doctoral dissertation, Washington University, St. Louis.

Klopfer, W. G. 1946. Personality patterns in old age. *Rorschach Research Exchange* 10: 145–166.

Klopfer, W. G. 1974. The Rorschach and old age. *Journal of Personality Assessment* 38: 420–422.

Krauss, E., and Schaie, K. W. 1978. Five novel tasks for the assessment of cognitive abilities in older adults. Paper presented in the XIth International Congress of Gerontology, Tokyo.

Kuhlen, R. G., and Kiel, C. 1951. The Rorschach performance of 100 elderly males. *Journal of Gerontology,* Supplement to No. 3, 6: 115.

La Rue, A. 1982. Memory loss and aging. Distinguishing dementia from benign senescent forgetfulness and depressive pseudodementia. *Psychiatric Clinics of North America* 5: 67–72.

Lavissakalian, M. R., and Barlow, D. H. 1981. Assessment of obsessive-compulsive disorders. In *Behavioral Assessment of Adult Disorders,* ed. D. H. Barlow. New York: Guilford Press.

Lawton, M. P.; Whelihan, W. M.; and Belsky, J. M. 1980. Personality tests and their uses with older adults. In *Handbook of Mental Health and Aging,* eds. J. E. Birren and R. B. Sloane. Englewood-Cliffs, NJ: Prentice-Hall.

Lewinsohn, P. M., and Lee, W. M. L. 1981. Assessment of affective disorders. In *Behavioral Assessment of Adult Disorders,* ed. D. H. Barlow. New York: Guilford Press.

Lewinsohn, P. M., and Libet, J. 1972. Pleasant events, activity schedules and depression. *Journal of Abnormal Psychology* 79: 291–95.

Lewinsohn, P. M., and MacPhillamy, D. J. 1974. The relationship between age and engagement in pleasant activities. *Journal of Gerontology* 29: 290–294.

Lewinsohn, P. M., and Talkington, J. 1979. The measurement of aversive events and relations to depression. *Applied Psychological Measurement* 3: 83–101.

Lewinsohn, P. M.; Muñoz, R. F.; Youngren, M. A.; and Zeiss, A. M. 1978. *Control Your Depression.* Englewood Cliffs, NJ: Prentice-Hall.

Lezak, M. D. 1976. *Neuropsychological Assessment.* New York: Oxford University Press.

Lieberman, M. A.; Prock, V. N.; and Tobin, S. S. 1968. Psychological effects of institutionalization. *Journal of Gerontology* 23: 343–353.

Linehan, M. M. 1977. Issues in behavioral interviewing. In *Behavioral Assessment: New Directions in Clinical Psychology,* eds. J. D. Cone and R. P. Hawkins. New York: Brunner/Mazel.

Lipinski, D. P., and Nelson, R. O. 1974. Problems in the use of naturalistic observation as a means of behavioral assessment. *Behavior Therapy* 5: 341–351.

Lipowski, Z. J. 1980. *Delirium.* Springfield, IL: Charles C. Thomas.

Liston, E. H., and LaRue, A. 1983. Clinical differentiation of primary degenerative and Multi-infarct dementia: A critical review of the evidence. Part II. Pathological studies. *Biological Psychiatry* 12: 1467–1483.

Lorr, M., and Klett, C. J. 1966. *Inpatient Multidimensional Psychiatric Scale.* Rev. ed. Palo Alto, CA: Consulting Psychologists Press.

Lubin, B. L. 1964. Adjective checklist for measurement of depression. *Archives of General Psychiatry* 12: 57–62.

Lubin, M. I. 1964. Addendum to J. L. Rosen and B. L. Neugarten. Ego functions in the middle and later years. In *Personality in Middle and Late Life,* ed. B. L. Neugarten. New York: Atherton.

Luria, A. R. 1966. *Higher Cortical Functions in Man.* (English translation by B. Haigh.) New York: Harper & Row.

Luria, A. R. 1973. *The Working Brain: An Introduction to Neuropsychology.* (English translation by B. Haigh.) New York: Basic Books.

MacPhillamy, D. J., and Lewinsohn, P. M. 1982. The Pleasant Events Schedule; Studies on reliability, validity, and scale intercorrelation. *Journal of Consulting and Clinical Psychology* 50: 363–380.

Maloney, M. P., and Ward, M. P. 1976. *Psychological Assessment: A Conceptual Approach.* New York: Oxford University Press.

Matarazzo, J. D. 1972. *Wechsler's Measurement and Appraisal of Adult Intelligence.* 5th ed. Baltimore: Williams & Wilkins.

McDonald, C. 1969. Clinical heterogeneity in senile dementia. *British Journal of Psychiatry* 115: 267–271.

McFall, R. M. 1970. Effects of self-monitoring on normal smoking behavior. *Journal of Consulting and Clinical Psychology* 35: 135–142.

McFall, R. M. 1977. Parameters of self-monitoring. In *Behavioral Self-Management: Strategies, Techniques, and Outcomes,* ed. R. B. Stuart. New York: Brunner/Mazel.

McLachlan, J. F. C. 1974. Test-retest stability of long and short form MMPI scales over two years. *Journal of Consulting Psychology* 30: 189–191.

McNair, D. M.; Lorr, M.; and Droppleman, L. F. 1971. *Profile of Mood States: Manual.* San Diego: Educational and Industrial Testing Service.

Meyer, V.; Liddell, A.; and Lyons, M. 1977. Behavioral interviews. In *Handbook of Behavioral Assessment,* eds. A. R. Ciminero, K. S. Calhoun, and H. E. Adams. New York: Wiley.

Miller, E., and Lewis, P. 1977. Recognition memory in elderly patients with depression and dementia: A signal detection analysis. *Journal of Abnormal Psychology* 86: 81–89.

Miller, E. 1980. Cognitive assessment of the older adult. In *Handbook of Mental Health and Aging,* eds. J. E. Birren and R. B. Sloane. Englewood-Cliffs, NJ: Prentice-Hall.

Mischel, W. 1968. *Personality and Assessment.* New York: Wiley.

Mischel, W. 1975. *Introduction to Personality.* 2nd ed. New York: Holt, Rinehart and Winston.

Morganstern, K. P. 1976. Behavioral interviewing: The initial stages of assessment. In *Behavioral Assessment: A Practical Handbook,* eds. M. Hersen and A. S. Bellack. New York: Pergamon Press.

Muñoz, R. F., and Lewinsohn, P. M. 1976. The Personal

Belief Inventory. Unpublished mimeo, University of Oregon.

Nathan, P. E. 1981. Symptomatic diagnosis and behavioral assessment: A synthesis. In *Behavioral Assessment of Adult Disorders*, ed. D. H. Barlow. New York: Guilford Press.

Nelson, R. O. 1977. Assessment and therapeutic functions of self-monitoring. In *Progress in Behavior Modification*, vol. 5, eds. M. Hersen, R. M. Eisler, and P. M. Miller. New York: Academic Press.

Nelson, R. O. 1981. Realistic dependent measures for clinical use. *Journal of Consulting and Clinical Psychology* 49: 168–182.

Neugarten, B. L.; Havighurst, R. J.; and Tobin, S. S. 1968. Personality and patterns of aging. In *Middle Age and Aging: A Reader in Social Psychology*, ed. B. L. Neugarten. Chicago: University of Chicago Press.

NIA Task Force. 1980. Senility reconsidered. *Journal of the American Medical Association* 244: 259–63.

Niederehe, G.; Fruge, E.; Scott, J.; Volpendesta, D.; Nielsen-Collins, K.; and Woods, A. 1982. Measuring family system characteristics in families caring for dementia patients. Paper presented at the Meetings of the Gerontological Society of America, Boston, Nov. 1982.

Norman, D. A., and Bobrow, D. G. 1975. On data-limited and resource-limited processes. *Cognitive Psychology* 7: 44–64.

Obrist, W. D., and Busse, E. W. 1960. Temporal lobe EEG abnormalities in normal senescence. *Electroencephalography and Clinical Neurophysiology* 12: 244.

Orr, N. K.; Reever, K. E.; and Zarit, S. H. 1980. Longitudinal change in performance and self-report of memory problems. Paper presented at the meetings of the Gerontological Society, San Diego, CA.

Osborne, D. P., Jr.; Brown, E. R.; and Randt, C. T. 1982. Qualitative changes in memory function: Aging and dementia. In *Alzheimer's Disease: A Report of Research in Progress*, eds. S. Corkin, K. L. Davis, J. H. Growdon, E. Usdin, and R. J. Wurtman. New York: Raven Press.

Overall, J. E., and Gorham, D. R. 1962. The Brief Psychiatric Rating Scale. *Psychological Reports* 10: 799–812.

Overall, J. E., and Gorham, D. R. 1972. Organicity versus old age in objective and projective test performance. *Journal of Consulting and Clinical Psychology* 39: 98–105.

Parsons, O. A., and Prigatano, G. P. 1978. Methodological considerations in clinical neuropsychological research. *Journal of Consulting and Clinical Psychology* 46: 608–619.

Pearson, C., and Gatz, M. 1981. Health and mental health in older adults: First steps in the study of a pedestrian complaint. *Rehabilitation Psychology* 27: 37–50.

Pfeiffer, E. 1975. A short portable mental status questionnaire for the assessment of organic brain deficit in elderly patients. *Journal of the American Geriatrics Society* 23: 433–39.

Pfeiffer, E. 1976. Multidimensional functional assessment: The OARS methodology. Durham, NC: Duke University Center for the Study of Aging and Human Development.

Popkin, S. J.; Gallagher, D.; Thompson, L. W.; and

Moore, M. 1982. Memory complaint and performance in normal and depressed older adults. *Experimental Aging Research* 8: 141–145.

Randt, C. T.; Brown, E. R.; and Osborne, D. P. 1980. A memory test for longitudinal measurement of mild to moderate deficits. *Clinical Neuropsychology* 2: 184–194.

Raskin, A. 1979. Signs and symptoms of psychopathology in the elderly. In *Psychiatric Symptoms and Cognitive Loss in the Elderly: Evaluation and Assessment Techniques*, eds. A. Raskin and L. F. Jarvik. Washington, D.C.: Hemisphere Publishing.

Rathus, S. A. 1973. A 30-item schedule for assessing assertive behavior. *Behavior Therapy* 4: 398–406.

Reed, H. B. C., Jr., and Reitan, R. M. 1963. A comparison of the effects of the normal aging process with the effects of organic brain damage on adaptive abilities. *Journal of Gerontology* 18: 177–179.

Reichard, S.; Livson, F.; and Peterson, P. G. 1962. *Aging and Personality: A Study of 87 Older Men*. New York: Wiley.

Reisberg, B.; Ferris, S. H.; Schneck, M. K.; de Leon, M. J.; Crook, T.; and Gershon, S. 1981. The relationship between psychiatric assessments and cognitive test measures in mild to moderately cognitively impaired elderly. *Psychopharmacology Bulletin* 17: 99–101.

Reitan, R. M., and Davison, L. A. 1974. *Clinical Neuropsychology: Current Status and Applications*. New York: Winston/Wiley.

Reitan, R. M., and Fitzhugh, K. B. 1971. Behavioral deficits in groups with cerebral vascular lesions. *Journal of Consulting and Clinical Psychology* 37: 215–223.

Reynolds, W. M., and Gould, J. W. 1981. A psychometric investigation of the standard and short form Beck Depression Inventory. *Journal of Consulting and Clinical Psychology* 49: 306–307.

Riegel, K. F.; Riegel, R. M.; and Meyer, G. 1967. A study of the dropout rates in longitudinal research on aging and the prediction of death. *Journal of Personality and Social Psychology* 5: 342–348.

Robins, L. N.; Helzer, J. E.; Croughan, J.; and Ratcliff, K. S. 1981. National Institute of Mental Health Diagnostic Interview Schedule. *Archives of General Psychiatry* 38: 381–387.

Robinson, B. C. 1983. Validation of a caregiver strain index. *Journal of Gerontology* 38: 344–348.

Rosen, J., and Neugarten, B. 1960. Ego functions in middle and later years. *Journal of Gerontology* 15: 62–67.

Rosen, R., and Mohs, R. C. 1982. Evolution of cognitive decline in dementia. In *Alzheimer's Disease: A Report of Research in Progress*, eds. S. Corkin, K. L. Davis, J. H. Growdon, E. Usdin, and R. J. Wurtman. New York: Raven Press.

Rosen, W. G.; Terry, R. D.; Fuld, P. A.; Katzman, R.; and Peck, A. 1980. Pathological verification of ischemic score in differentiation of dementias. *Annals of Neurology* 7: 486–488.

Rosenhan, D. L. 1972. On being sane in insane places. *Science* 179: 250–58.

Roth, M. 1980. Senile dementia and its borderlands. In *Psychopathology in the Aged*, eds. J. O. Cole and J. E. Barrett. New York: Raven Press.

Sabin, T. D.; Vitug, A. J.; and Mark, V. H. 1982. Are nursing home diagnosis and treatment adequate. *Journal of the American Medical Association* 248: 321–322.

Salzman, C., and Shader, R. I. 1972. Response to psychotropic drugs in the normal elderly. In *Psychopharmacology and Aging*, eds. C. Eisdorfer and W. E. Fann. New York: Plenum Press.

Salzman, C., and Shader, R. I. 1979. Clinical evaluation of depression in the elderly. In *Psychiatric Symptoms and Cognitive Loss in the Elderly: Evaluation and Assessment Techniques*, eds. A. Raskin and L. F. Jarvik. Washington, D.C.: Hemisphere Publishing.

Schaie, K. W., and Schaie, J. P. 1977. Clinical assessment and aging. In *Handbook of the Psychology of Aging*, eds. J. E. Birren and K. W. Schaie. New York: Van Nostrand Reinhold.

Schaie, K. W., and Stone, V. 1982. Psychological assessment. *Annual Review of Gerontology and Geriatrics* 3: 329–360.

Schaie, K. W.; Labouvie, G. V.; and Buech, V. U. 1973. Generation and cohort-specific differences in adult cognitive functioning: A fourteen year study of independent samples. *Developmental Psychology* 9: 151–166.

Scheidt, R. J., and Schaie, K. W. 1978. A taxonomy of situations for an elderly population: Generating situational criteria. *Journal of Gerontology* 33: 848–857.

Schonfield, D., and Robertson, B. 1966. Memory storage and aging. *Canadian Journal of Psychology* 20: 223–226.

Shallice, T. 1979. Case study approach in neuropsychological research. *Journal of Clinical Neuropsychology* 1: 183–212.

Shukin, A., and Neugarten, B. L. 1964. Personality and social interaction. In *Personality in Middle and Late Life*, ed. B. L. Neugarten. New York: Atherton Press.

Simard, D.; Olesen, J.; Paulson, O. B.; Lassen, N. A.; and Skinhöj, E. 1971. Regional cerebral blood flow and its regulation in dementia. *Brain* 94: 273–281.

Singer, M. T. 1963. Personality measurements in the aged. In *Human Aging: A Biological and Behavioral Study*, eds. J. E. Birren, R. N. Butler, S. W. Greenhouse, L. Sokoloff, and M. Yarrow. Washington, D.C.: U.S. Government Printing Office.

Snyder, D. K.; Wells, R. M.; and Kelser, T. W. 1981. Empirical validation of the marital satisfaction inventory: An actuarial approach. *Journal of Consulting and Clinical Psychology* 49: 262–69.

Spielberger, C. D. 1972. The State-Trait Anxiety Inventory. In *Anxiety: Current Trends in Theory and Research*, ed. C. D. Spielberger. New York: Academic Press.

Spiers, P. A. 1980. Have they come to praise Luria or to bury him?: The Luria–Nebraska battery controversy. *Journal of Consulting and Clinical Psychology* 49: 331–341.

Spiers, P. A. 1981. The Luria–Nebraska neuropsychological battery revisited: A theory in practice or just practicing? *Journal of Consulting and Clinical Psychology* 50: 301–306.

Spitzer, R. L.; Endicott, J. F.; and Robins, A. 1975. Clinical criteria for psychiatric diagnosis and DSM-III. *American Journal of Psychiatry* 132: 1187–1192.

Spitzer, R. L.; Endicott, J.; and Robins, E. 1978. Research Diagnostic Criteria: Rationale and reliability. *Archives of General Psychiatry* 35: 773–782.

Spitzer, R. L.; Forman, J. B.; and Nee, J. 1979. DSM-III field trials: Initial interrater diagnostic reliability. *American Journal of Psychiatry* 136: 815–817.

Spitzer, R. L., and Fleiss, J. L. 1974. A reanalysis of the reliability of psychiatric diagnosis. *British Journal of Psychiatry* 125: 341–347.

Stern, J. A.; Oster, P. J.; and Newport, K. 1980. Reaction time measures, hemispheric specialization, and age. In *Aging in the 1980's*, ed. L. W. Poon. Washington, D.C.: American Psychological Association.

Storandt, M. 1977. Age, ability, level, and method of administering and scoring the WAIS. *Journal of Gerontology* 32: 175–178.

Tasto, D. L. 1977. Self-report schedules and inventories. In *Handbook of Behavioral Assessment*, eds. A. R. Ciminero, L. S. Calhoun, and H. E. Adams. New York: Wiley.

Taylor, J. 1955. A personality scale of manifest anxiety. *Journal of Abnormal and Social Psychology* 48: 285–290.

Teri, L., and Lewinsohn, P. 1982. Modification of the pleasant and unpleasant events schedule for the use with the elderly. *Journal of Consulting and Clinical Psychology* 50: 444–445.

Vega, A., and Parsons, O. A. 1967. Cross validation of the Halstead Reitan tests for brain damage. *Journal of Consulting and Clinical Psychology* 31: 619–623.

Ward, C. H.; Beck, A. T.; Mendelson, M.; Mock, C. E.; and Erbaugh, J. K. 1962. The psychiatric nomenclature. *Archives of General Psychiatry* 7: 198–205.

Waskow, I. E. 1975. Selection; of a core battery. In *Psychotherapy Change Measures*, eds. I. E. Waskow and M. B. Parloff. Washington, D.C.: National Institute of Mental Health.

Watson, D., and Friend, R. 1969. Measurement of social-evaluation anxiety. *Journal of Consulting and Clinical Psychology* 33: 448–451.

Wechsler, D. 1955. *Manual for the Wechsler Adult Intelligence Scale*. New York: Psychological Corporation.

Wechsler, D. 1958. *The Measurement and Appraisal of Adult Intelligence*. Baltimore: Williams & Wilkins.

Weinstein, E. A., and Kahn, R. L. 1955. *Denial of Illness*. Springfield, IL: Charles C. Thomas.

Weintraub, M.; Segal, R. M.; and Beck, A. T. 1974. An investigation of cognition and affect in the depressive experiences of normal men. *Journal of Consulting and Clinical Psychology* 42: 911.

Weintraub, S.; Baratz, R.; and Mesulam, M. 1982. Daily living activities in the assessment of dementia. In *Alzheimer's Disease: A Report of Research in Progress*, eds. S. Corkin, K. L. Davis, J. H. Growdon, E. Usdin, and R. J. Wurtman. New York: Raven Press.

Weiss, R. L., and Margolin, G. 1977. Assessment of marital conflict and accord. In *Handbook of Behavior Assessment*, eds. A. R. Ciminero, K. D. Calhoun, and H. E. Adams. New York: John Wiley & Sons.

Weiss, R. L.; Hops, H.; and Patterson, G. R. 1973. A framework for conceptualizing marital conflict, technology for altering it, some data for evaluating it. In

Behavior Change: Methodology, Concepts, and Practice, eds. L. A. Hamerlynck, L. C. Handy, and E. J. Mash. Champaign, IL: Research Press.

Weissman, A., and Beck, A. T. 1978. Development and validation of the Dysfunctional Attitude Scale. Paper presented at the annual meeting of the Association for the Advancement of Behavior Therapy, Chicago, Dec. 1978.

Werner, H. 1937. Process and achievement: A basic problem of education and developmental psychology. *Harvard Educational Review,* May 1937.

Whitehead, A. 1973. Verbal learning and memory in elderly depressives. *British Journal of Psychiatry* 123: 203–208.

Wilkie, F., and Eisdorfer, C. 1971. Intelligence and blood pressure in the aged. *Science* 172: 959–962.

Williams, J.; Lipman, R.; Rickels, K.; Covi, L.; Uhlenhuth, E.; and Mattson, N. 1968. Replication of symptom distress factors in anxious neurotic outpatients. *Multivariate Behavioral Research* 3: 199–212.

Youngren, M. A.; Zeiss, A. M.; and Lewinsohn, P. M. 1975. The Interpersonal Events Schedule. Unpublished mimeo, University of Oregon.

Yesavage, J. A.; Brink, T. L.; Rose, T. L.; Lum, O.; Huang, V.; Adey, M.; and Leirer, V. O. 1981. Development and validation of a geriatric depression scale: A preliminary report. Unpublished paper, V.A. Medical Center, Palo Alto, CA.

Zarit, J. M. 1982. Predictors of burden and distress for caregivers of senile dementia patients. Unpublished doctoral dissertation, University of Southern California.

Zarit, S. H. 1982. Affective correlates of self-reports about memory of older people. *International Journal of Behavioral Geriatrics* 1: 25–34.

Zarit, S. H., and Zarit, J. M. 1983(a). Families under stress: Interventions for caregivers of senile dementia patients. *Psychotherapy* 19: 461–471.

Zarit, S. H., and Zarit, J. M. 1983(b). Cognitive impairment of older persons: Etiology, evaluation and intervention. In *Coping and Adaptation in the Elderly,* eds. P. M. Lewinsohn and L. Teri. New York: Pergamon Press.

Zarit, S. H.; Miller, N. E.; and Kahn, R. L. 1978. Brain function, intellectual impairment and education in the aged. *Journal of the American Geriatrics Society* 26: 58–67.

Zarit, S. H.; Reever, K. E.; and Bach-Peterson, J. 1980. Relatives of the impaired elderly: Correlates of feelings of burden. *Gerontologist* 20: 649–655.

Zung, W. W. K. 1965. A self-rating depression scale. *Archives of General Psychiatry* 12: 63–70.

Zung, W. W. K. 1967. Depression in the normal aged. *Psychosomatics* 8: 287–291.

Zung, W. W. K. 1971. A rating instrument for anxiety disorders. *Psychosomatics* 12: 371–379.

28
PSYCHOLOGICAL INTERVENTIONS WITH OLDER ADULTS

Margaret Gatz
and
Samuel J. Popkin
University of Southern California

Christopher D. Pino
Yale University

Gary R. VandenBos
University of Bergen

What is known about effective psychological treatment of older adults? What types of services are being provided in communities and institutions? What appear to be important ingredients in the therapeutic change process? What is the status of research on the efficacy of services for the older individual? The purpose of this chapter is to answer such questions by describing the range of psychological interventions with older adults and scrutinizing the empirical literature on their effectiveness.

The rubric "psychological intervention" connotes a planned interpersonal intervention that is intended to have a psychotherapeutic impact of a preventive, curative, or palliative nature. Its goals and strategies are based to varying degrees on psychological theory. Although psychotherapy is the prototypal psychological intervention, the empirical literature on clinical intervention with the aged tends to emphasize nontraditional and institutional programs. The scope of this review goes somewhat beyond a traditional view of psychotherapy but places a heavy emphasis on psychotherapeutic interventions.

Four themes emerged from our reflections on this body of literature: (1) the continuities and discontinuities between interventions with older adults and those with other age groups, (2) the process by which clinical knowledge is created for work with older adults, (3) the types of problems older individuals face, and (4) the principles of therapeutic change common to diverse approaches.

Considering the first theme, imagine a scale extending from the extreme discontinuous position that older people are clinically unique and require entirely different treatment than other age groups to the extreme continuous position that they require and benefit from the same treatment considerations and techniques. The views of various writers can be placed at differing points along this scale. We find ourselves closer to the "continuity end," believing that clinical progress may have been limited by an overemphasis on discontinuity and hence insufficient extrapolation from knowledge about psychological interventions with younger people.

The second theme concerns the evolution

of knowledge about interventions with older adults and how it mirrors the earlier evolution of research on the efficacy of psychotherapy in general. We find great similarity between these two histories. The general processes by which clinical knowledge is generated, disseminated, and implemented (cf. VandenBos and Pino, 1980) apply to the development of interventions with older adults. For example, practitioners with older adults may find some incongruity between their general theoretical beliefs and some aspect of the patient they have consistently observed. This anomaly may lead to the development of a modified technique that is then proliferated through case reports, presentations, and less formal networks. Eventually, some concepts are examined through the lens of research designs, including (1) case studies, (2) "outcome only" program evaluations, (3) studies that collect data on patients both before and after treatment, and (4) studies that use a pre–post design and include untreated control subjects. Our discussion of interventions with an elderly population will focus on work in many stages of development, from case studies with clinical commentary to formal, controlled psychotherapy outcome or process studies.

Our third theme is that interventions must be tailored to the individual; the patient's presenting problem and personality must be considered when choosing an intervention. The problems of elderly individuals fall into three general, but not mutually exclusive, categories: organic brain syndromes (the dementias and deliriums), lifelong patterns (including chronic schizophrenia, neuroses, and character disorders), and special issues of later life (including both situational stresses and existential issues). Current living situation must also be considered; it defies logic to equate an older Medicaid patient in a nursing home with a 65-year-old outpatient living in Beverly Hills. In our review, then, we attend to who was being treated as well as what the intervention was.

A fourth theme, spanning a wide variety of psychological interventions with older persons, concerns the features that have been cited to account for treatment efficacy. A few factors appeared with great regularity. These include the experience of a sense of personal effectiveness and hopefulness about change, a gratifying relationship with the practitioner, and exploring life's meaning. Finally, principles of learning theory, particularly reinforcement contingencies, have been used to account for change.

These four themes are the foundation for the sections that follow. First we will discuss the barriers that discourage older adults from entering treatment or that interfere with treatment after they are in the service setting. In the latter context, we will describe the range of interventions provided, emphasizing specific research studies. Our final section is a discussion of the substantive material from the perspective of the four themes.

BARRIERS TO OBTAINING PSYCHOLOGICAL SERVICES

It is widely believed and fairly well documented that older adults receive disproportionately few mental health services. One current estimate is that only 2.7 percent of all clinical services provided by psychologists go to older adults, although persons aged 65 and older comprise 11.3 percent of the population (VandenBos, Stapp, and Kilburg, 1981). Moreover, the proportion of community mental health center services rendered to older adults has remained relatively stable at around 4 percent over the last decade (U.S. General Accounting Office (GAO), 1982; Ozarin, Taube, and Spaner, 1972). Among persons identified by a community survey as having a psychiatric diagnosis, Myers and Weissman (1980) found that younger adults were more likely than older adults to have received treatment. Explanations that have been offered for this pattern of professional underservice can be organized into three categories: client variables, therapist variables, and mental health system variables.

Client Variables

Three factors are frequently mentioned in explaining the attitudes responsible for the failure of older clients to use mental health services: lack of "psychological-mindedness," self-reliance, and preferences with regard to the age of the helper.

Psychological-mindedness. The usual explanation is that older adults are not psychologically minded simply because of their cohort (e.g., Blum and Tallmer, 1977; Lawton, 1979). Some of the purported beliefs of older adults are that (1) people don't see a mental health professional unless they are really crazy; (2)"If there's something wrong with my head, they'll cart me straight off to the boogey house," and (3) seeing a "shrink" means lying on a couch and telling of your private feelings, which not only won't help but would also make you feel foolish or immoral.

Related to psychological-mindedness are concerns about stigma, lack of knowledge, and limited confidence in the mental health professions (Kleinman and Clemente, 1976). The belief that older adults deny their psychological problems is frequently cited as an obstacle (e.g., Kushler and Davidson, 1978). Furthermore, old people may feel skeptical or pessimistic, believing that (1) nothing can be done because the problems are due to normal aging processes (Kovar, 1980), (2) the problems have a physical basis and require physical remedies (Feigenbaum, 1973), or (3) professionals are not interested or trained in working with older adults (Patterson, 1976).

These various attributions have not been well researched; it is important to note, however, that issues such as stigma or skepticism are not unique to older patients (e.g., Fischer and Turner, 1970). If these beliefs are in fact more prevalent among older than younger adults, they may represent a historical rather than an age-related phenomenon because, to some extent, they are an accurate reflection of history. For older adults of the future, the psychotherapist will have been part of the general culture, and there will have been a broader definition of the role of mental health professionals.

Self-reliance. The value placed on self-sufficiency and independence by older adults is a frequently mentioned factor (Davis and Klopfer, 1977; Shanas and Maddox, 1976). Surveys indicate that human services are least acceptable when they imply infirmity (Bild and Havighurst, 1976) or when eligibility is based on income (Moen, 1978). Clark (1969) noted that a dilemma is created, because acceptance of help for the normal dependencies of aging is by definition not self-reliant behavior.

Both lack of psychological-mindedness and concerns about dependency are thought to contribute to an unwillingness on the part of older persons to self-refer to mental health professionals. Yet, several programs designed for older adults do not report excessive reluctance to initiate treatment (e.g., Knight, 1983; Zarit, 1980), nor is unwillingness unique to older individuals. For *all* age groups, only a fraction of those who are distressed take their problems to mental health professionals. Kulka, Veroff, and Douvan (1979) reported that individuals who saw themselves as having personal problems worthy of help sought out mental health professionals only about 35 percent of the time.

It is further believed that, once in treatment, older adults drop out. Psychotherapy studies of older outpatients have reported drop-out rates of 20 to 35 percent (Gallagher and Thompson, 1982; Ingersoll and Silverman, 1978; Sallis, Lichstein, Clarkson, Stalgaitis, and Campbell, in press; Steuer, 1982c). These figures, however, are not too discrepant with Yalom's (1970) report of drop-out rates of one-third among groups at a university outpatient clinic. More impressive was Knight's (1983) finding that drop-out for senior services was lower than that for any other unit at a community mental health center.

Age of therapist. Among their concerns about professionals, older clients are sometimes said to believe that an older counselor brings special understanding that a younger therapist cannot (Gallagher and Thompson, 1981; Pressey and Pressey, 1972). A client may think, if not exclaim, "Why, dear, you're so young to be a doctor!," or, "Oh, Lordy, how can anyone as young as you help with the kinds of problems I have?" Although there are data to suggest that older therapists are more likely to see older clients (Dörken and Webb, 1979), we cannot conclude that this is entirely a matter of patient preference.

Three studies have concerned the preferred age for service providers. Clayton and Jellison

(1975) and Furchtgott and Busemeyer (1981) surveyed individuals across a wide age range. Both studies found that the preferred age of advisors increased as the age of the respondent increased; the exception was among more highly educated older individuals, who preferred younger physicians. According to Clayton and Jellison, people do not seek advisors who are the same age as themselves; rather, they prefer advisors in the middle-age range. Lasky and Salomone (1977) showed VA inpatients slides of young and old, high and low status (furniture, attire, diploma) therapists. For older patients (over age 45), status was the salient variable. In all three studies, the most influential factor seemed to be whether the helper was perceived as competent to help.

The potential pitfalls of providing therapy for demographically dissimilar dyads are not limited to the age variable. Consider, for example, therapists who are of a different race, sex, or social class from their clients. For these other variables, the psychotherapy literature (cf. Gomes-Schwartz, Hadley, and Strupp, 1978; Parloff, Waskow, and Wolfe, 1978) suggests that professional experience with and knowledge about a given population is more important to a successful outcome than demographic similarity between the dyads. Further empirical work with age-pairings of dyads may lead to much the same conclusion.

Finally, despite concerns about a therapist's relative youth, the consensus from many accounts (e.g., Hiatt, 1971; Stern, Smith, and Frank, 1953) is that the transference with older patients is most often chronologically paradoxical, that is, the therapist becomes the parent.

To summarize, in the case of all three client variables—lack of psychological-mindedness, self-reliance, and preference for a helper one's own age—the barrier has little empirical support, the issues are not unique to older clients, and explanations other than age (e.g., period effects or secular trends) may emerge as the more powerful ones accounting for the phenomenon.

Therapist Variables

In two surveys of professional psychologists, nearly 70 percent reported never seeing older clients (Dye, 1978; VandenBos et al., 1981). The professional has been characterized as a "reluctant therapist" of the older client (Garfinkel, 1975; Kastenbaum, 1964), whose attitudes can be subsumed under four topics: unworthiness and low status, poor prognosis, misconceptions about the aged, and countertransference.

Worthiness and status. It has been suggested that professionals might believe that scarce resources should go to younger clients who have more years of life ahead of them and who are more economically productive than older ones (Cyrus-Lutz and Gaitz, 1972; Kastenbaum, 1964). To the extent that this is true, it probably reflects a general cultural bias. The cultural value of not investing resources in the unworthy and the lack of prestige attached to working with low-status groups come up in relation to all dependent populations—the aged, the chronically mentally ill, the poor, the physically handicapped, and the mentally retarded (Levine, 1981). Moreover, older adults may be poor or handicapped as well as old (Butler and Lewis, 1982). Sexism may also play a compounding role, because disproportionately more of the aged are women (Steuer, 1982b).

Actually, cultural bias is not reflected in studies measuring attitudes of service providers toward older people (Hickey, Rakowski, Hultsch, and Fatula, 1976), but, as will be discussed, it does appear to be a factor in practice.

Poor prognosis. Clinicians have been said to adopt the view that aging entails decreased flexibility or inevitable decline; hence, its conditions are seen as untreatable, or at best, as presenting limited possibilities for improvement (Butler and Lewis, 1982). Using therapists' responses to vignettes about clients of various ages, Dye (1978) found that psychologists' expectations of success were lower for older than for younger adults; similarly, Ford and Sbordonne (1980) found that psychiatrists described prognosis and suitability for psychotherapy as being poorer for older patients. Settin (1982), also using the methodology of systematically varying demographic characteristics of a stimulus client in a standard vignette, found that clinical psychologists perceived the diagnosis of older clients to be worse than that of middle-aged clients and possible interventions to be less useful. In an outpatient clinic, Karasu, Stein, and Charles (1979) compared patients who were younger, the same age, and older than their therapists. Those who were older (40 to 65 years of age) were rated by the therapists as having more severe psychopathology, less motivation for treatment, less insight, and poorer prognosis than younger patients or patients the same age as themselves. Older patients, however, were significantly more optimistic about their prognosis than were the therapists. In contrast to such beliefs by therapists, the few existing studies suggest no systematic relationship between client age and psychotherapy outcome (Garfield, 1978; Smith and Glass, 1977). At a minimum, nihilistic attitudes are unlikely to be related to a realistic appraisal of prognosis.

The supposition of poor prognosis may lead to treatment bias; for example, psychological care for the aged may be viewed as largely custodial (Kahn, 1975) or supportive (Rechtschaffen, 1959). Within community mental health centers, the aged receive disproportionately greater inpatient care (and thus, less psychotherapy, outpatient care, and consultation and education services) than younger populations (Patterson, 1976). Dye (1978) found that shorter-term behavioral approaches were favored for older clients, although diagnosis (neurotic versus psychotic) was more important than age in predicting treatment approach. Ford and Sbordonne (1980) found age differences in treatment recommendations only for depression; psychotherapy alone, without pharmacotherapy, was less often recommended for older than for younger depressives. When the service offered the older client is of lower status and less likely to have a powerful impact, the perpetuation of the myth of poor prognosis is insured.

Misconceptions of the aged. It is often stated that working with older adults requires special knowledge (e.g., Swensen, 1982). The literature on bias in clinical judgment indicates how misconceptions or lack of knowledge can influence treatment. Although the biases usually addressed are those of race, culture, and sex, Lopez (1984) elucidates four potential biases that may apply to interventions with older adults. In "overpathologizing," an older person might be seen as more disturbed or impaired than a younger person despite similar symptoms. An example might be treating signs of delirium as irreversible "senility" in older adults but as reversible in younger adults. A "minimizing" bias results in ignoring symptoms in an older adult that would be treated in a younger one. For example, a clinician who views complaints about a lowered energy level in an older person as "just old age" might be failing to recognize a treatable disorder, such as a nutritional imbalance. A third potential bias is "equalizing," in which the clinician might inappropriately equate symptoms of different age groups, for example, incorrectly viewing a suicide threat as equally predictive of a serious suicide attempt in both older and younger persons (McIntosh, Hubbard, and Santos, 1981). Fourth, the "misinterpreting" bias refers to insensitivity to age and cohort differences in the expression of a disorder; for example, depression may be manifested differently by older and younger individuals (Blazer, 1980).

The emphasis on special knowledge may also have had some unfortunate consequences. For instance, Dye (1978) reported that 64 percent of psychologists endorsed the view that older adults present different problems from younger adults. Those psychologists who did *not* see older adults were more likely to be of this opinion. Knight (1983) proposed the concept of "therapeutic inhibition" to connote therapists' reluctance to apply the skills that they have to working with older adults because of their exaggerated belief that unique training is required.

Countertransference. Countertransference as a phenomenon is certainly not unique to the therapist of older clients, although its particular content may differ. Working with older adults compels therapists to confront their own decline and finitude, current and previous problems with their own parents, fear that the patient might die during treatment, and frustration or pity brought about by dealing with loss and incapacity (Blum and Tallmer, 1977; Butler and Lewis, 1982; Hiatt, 1971; Zinberg, 1967). That therapists' anxieties are evoked is supported by the finding of Hickey et al. (1976) that, although practitioners' attitudes improved somewhat with short-term training in aging, there was also an increase in anxiety. Still another relevant countertransference issue, "respect for one's elders," may inhibit interpretation or confrontation.

Against this negative backdrop, others have commented on how gratifying it is to work with older clients, noting their appreciativeness, wisdom, maturity, and resiliency (Cyrus-Lutz and Gaitz, 1972). Butler and Lewis (1982) have noted how often chance factors first bring professionals into the field, who then find unexpected satisfactions and a tangible sense of accomplishment (Safirstein, 1972).

To summarize, therapist variables tend to reflect cultural prejudices. The empirical evidence provides some substantiation for therapist biases, but more work is needed to sort out the truth in the stereotypes and to investigate hypotheses about the ways in which biases influence therapists' practices and contribute to underservice and poor service.

Mental Health System Variables

Kahn (1975) argued that mental health system factors provide the most important explanation of why so few older adults are seen by mental health professionals. Major systems issues that hinder accessibility of services—apart from lack of sufficient personnel and services—include reimbursement, differences in perception of needs and of appropriate interventions, and patterns of coordination and referral. Lack of knowledge of where to go for services and logistical difficulties such as physical disabilities, transportation, money, "red tape," and the fragmentation of the service system are often cited as barriers (Auerbach, Gordon, Ullmann, and Weisel, 1977; Gaitz, 1974; Harris, 1975). Drop-outs from treatment often implicate transportation difficulties, health problems, schedule conflicts, and inappropriateness of the treatment modality (Frankfather, 1981; Gallagher and Thompson, 1981; Hanssen, Meima, Buckspan, Henderson, Helbig, and Zarit, 1978; Ingersoll and Silverman, 1978; Sallis et al., in press; Steuer, 1982c).

Reimbursement system. Several particular aspects of reimbursement mechanisms are thought to influence service use: (1) the bias in the nature and extent of insurance coverage (e.g., a bias toward institutional and against outpatient mental health care, as reflected in the annual Medicare limit on outpatient mental health expenditures) and (2) a less favorable copayment rate for mental health treatment than for physical health care. Another problem is that Medicare will reimburse for the cost of diagnosing Alzheimer's disease, but not for the cost of treating the patient. The justification is that the disease is not curable—this, despite the ways in which psychological intervention can maximize the patient's functioning and reduce the family's distress (Zarit and Zarit, 1982).

Two questions arise, namely, whether patients' patterns of use are influenced by the reimbursement scheme and whether professionals offer services based on whether they will be reimbursed. A tentative inference is that the ability of the patient to pay is more of an issue for the therapist (and possibly for the graduate student who will one day be a professional) than for the patient (Dye, 1978; Gaitz, 1974; Haug, 1981). Use of services is more influenced by availability than by "need," and availability is affected by reimbursement policy (Brehm, 1980; Dörken, 1981; Nardonne, 1980; Wells, Manning, Duan, Ware, and Newhouse, 1982).

Perceptions of needs. Differences among clients, families, and service providers in their perceptions of the problems of the older person can constitute an obstacle to treatment (Avant and Dressel, 1980; Reifler, Cox, and Hanley, 1981). For example, clients might be interested in services that would aid self-care and independent living, whereas families might be concerned about their relative's physical safety and service providers might be trying to establish a comprehensive system of social and health services. Literature on help-seeking (e.g., Gross, Wallston, and Piliavin, 1979) makes it clear that the manner in which aid is delivered can be an important determinant of whether people seek help and of how they feel after receiving it. The helping process can be undermined if the helper takes on responsibility for generating and implementing solutions or if the helper and the recipient have different ideas about responsibility (Brickman, Rabinowitz, Karuza, Cohn, Coates, and Kidder, 1982). One consequence of incongruent perceptions may be a service provision system that reduces the older individual's sense of self-esteem and personal control (Gatz, Smyer, and Lawton, 1980; Looft, 1973).

Referral patterns. Potential sources of referral to mental health services include informal helping agents, e.g., funeral directors (cf. Santos, Hubbard, McIntosh, and Eisner, in press), family members, the network of aging service agencies, and physicians. Weber (1977) has described the family as the chief conduit to aging services of all kinds. O'Brien and Wagner (1980) suggest the possibility that these informal social ties may block rather than facilitate appropriate access to professional services. Thus, an important area of inquiry may be to characterize the barriers to a family's seeking mental health services.

Historically speaking, there has been little cooperation between community mental health centers and Area Agencies on Aging (Griffin and Gottesman, 1983), and physicians appear to be particularly reluctant to make mental health referrals for older patients. Ginsburg and Goldstein (1974) found physicians less likely to refer patients over age 60, regardless of psychopathology. Using vignettes of hypothetical cases, Kucharski, White, and Schratz (1979) found significantly more mental health referrals for younger than for older patients, particularly on symptom pictures that captured the stereotype of inevitable decline. The consequence is that the older adult with mental health problems may not come into contact with a mental health professional. Moreover, the lack of such referrals is of particular interest insofar as some studies of younger adults have suggested that a cost-offset results from decreased use of medical services following mental health consultation (Follette and Cummings, 1967; Goldberg, Krantz, and Locke, 1970; Jones and Vischi, 1979; Rosen and Wiens, 1979).

In summary, along with client and therapist variables, there are systems-related issues that contribute to the pattern of professional underservice, such as reimbursement mecha-

nisms, discrepant perceptions of the help that is needed, and the lack of referrals from other agents in contact with older individuals who need mental health services. Again, the issues are not uniquely applicable to the aged, although there is empirical evidence supporting the negative influence of mental health system variables. How all three of these categories of barriers, whether or not empirically supported, have affected the treatments offered older adults will be apparent in the descriptions of interventions that follow.

OVERVIEW OF TYPES OF INTERVENTIONS

Individual Therapy

Clinical theory and techniques. The amenability of older individuals to psychotherapeutic strategies was questioned long ago by Freud (1924) and recently by Cross, Sheehan, and Khan (1982). Various writers have challenged such doubts and articulated modifications in technique to tailor various theories to older individuals. For example, Freud's dismissal of psychoanalysis for adults over age 50 has been challenged by those who propose modified analytic techniques (see Blum and Tross, 1980; Rechtschaffen, 1959; and Sparacino, 1978–79. Kastenbaum (1978) and Shows (1977) have advocated the applicability of Jung; Brink (1979), of Adler; Karpf (1977) and Sherman (1981), of Erikson; Schienle and Eiler (in press), of Kaiser; and Lazarus (1980), of Kohut. Behavioral and cognitive approaches have also been applied to older outpatients (Knight, 1978–79; Steuer, 1982a; Zarit, 1980). In addition, a structuralist viewpoint (Gallagher and Frankel, 1980) and rapid intervention strategies (Kovacs, 1977) have been described.

The literature abounds with suggestions for therapeutic practices that may be relevant to working with older adults. Some writers specifically argue against segregating the elderly from mainstream therapeutic thought. They urge psychotherapy to proceed, in its most basic form, as it would with anyone; attention to the problems and not the age of the patient is advised (e.g., Abraham, 1919; Gilbert, 1977;

Kastenbaum, 1978; Oberleder, 1966; Schienle & Eiler, in press). Others have emphasized differences between older and younger patients (e.g., Gallagher and Thompson, 1981; Lawton and Gottesman, 1974; Wilensky and Weiner, 1977). Suggested modifications encompass the goals and structure of therapy, the role of the therapist, techniques designed to overcome specific barriers to treatment, and particular issues that are likely to emerge in assessment and therapy with older adults.

With respect to the goals and structure of therapy, many writers agree that therapy for older adults should be short-term, although there is no consensus on the number of sessions needed, how long each session should be, or when or how termination should be brought to pass. Related to treatment length are beliefs in the value of specific and "realistic" goals (Pfeiffer, 1976; Ronch and Maizler, 1977; Zarit, 1980). Although the concern with providing shorter, more specific therapies is expressed today for *all* age-groups (Garfield and Bergin, 1978), writers representing the range of theoretical persuasions specifically emphasize the need for brevity in the treatment of older patients (cf., Brink, 1979). It has also been suggested that older patients' sense of urgency may make them desire brief treatment (e.g., Ingebretson, 1977).

Curiously juxtaposed with the time-limitation argument is the suggestion by some that it takes older adults longer to become comfortable with the role of client, longer to understand the treatment program and comply with its demands, longer to undo maladaptive patterns of living, and longer to learn new behaviors (Mintz, Steuer, and Jarvik, 1981; Storandt, 1978). Thus, it can also be argued that therapy for the older adult should be longer than that for the younger. Longer-term treatment can sometimes serve the further purpose of keeping the individual out of an institution (e.g., Safirstein, 1972). Termination is frequently described as a gradual tapering off, allowing clients to return for visits as needed (e.g., Kahn, 1982; Wayne, 1953).

A dimension of concern underlying much of the writing on the structure of treatment is that of dependence versus independence. Whereas an older individual's preference for self-reliance may constitute an initial barrier, professionals frequently complain about dependence once a client is in treatment. For example, Lipsitt (1969) observed that termination may be difficult even if no specific intervention appears to be required, and Gallagher (1981) found that 35 percent of the members of a five-week therapy group continued psychotherapy after the research was completed. Consequently, much attention is devoted to avoiding iatrogenic dependence on the therapist. In fact, many modifications can be seen, at least in part, as serving the purpose of diluting the transference (Safirstein, 1972; Wayne, 1953). Although most writers see dependency as something to minimize, Goldfarb (1969) has argued that attempting to avoid it only leads to the client experiencing more feelings of helplessness and a greater need for reassurance. Until a sense of security is present, the patient cannot learn increasingly independent ways of functioning.

The role of the therapist with older adults is most often described as more active and directive than with younger populations (e.g., Pfeiffer and Busse, 1973; Ronch and Maizler, 1977). Those who use modified psychoanalytic techniques with older patients have typically suggested that adaptive defenses be restored, not interpreted (e.g., Verwoerdt, 1976), and that coping skills be strengthened (e.g., Wolff, 1971). In addition, it is suggested that the therapist be more actively empathic with the older individual (e.g., Weinberg, 1976). The use of physical touch is also recommended (e.g., Oberleder, 1966; Burnside, 1978), although Steuer (1982a) warns that certain implications of touching, such as inadvertent patronization, be carefully considered.

The therapist's conceptualization of the later years affects choice of intervention strategy. The two most dominant views are that it is a time of losses and that it is a time for the development of ego integrity (Erikson, 1963). The more short-term, goal-oriented approaches tend to be compatible with the loss perspective as are preventive interventions focused on life transitions (Danish, Smyer, and Nowak, 1980; Lawton, 1979). Losses include both personal losses and depreciated status in the culture: retirement, diminished economic security, loss of spouse, decreased social network, physical illnesses or disabilities, decline in mental acuity, and loss of personal dignity (Brink, 1979; Burnside, 1970; Gaitz and Varner, 1980; Steuer, 1982a). Losses are often linked to lowered self-worth (cf. Kuypers and Bengtson, 1973; Lazarus, 1980), depression (Birren and Renner, 1980), or panic (Oberleder, 1970).

Two writers have presented explanations of loss and depression that bridge the alternative conceptualizations of late life. Karpf (1977) warned against diagnosing as pathological either depression that serves as a defense mechanism or feelings of sadness that should be expected to accompany reviewing one's life and coming to terms with the fact that it must end. Gutmann, Griffin, and Grunes (1982) argued that, when depression occurs for the first time in middle to late-middle life, it should be understood from a developmental rather than a loss-oriented, depletion perspective. They suggest not belaboring the losses, which are not news to the older person anyway. Instead, they focus on the transitions and transformations of later life, including those aspects of personality that make the losses potent in inducing psychopathology.

The major systematic approach that offers an alternative to goal-directed, present-focused intervention is life review therapy, which takes as its premise the need for restoring ego integrity (Lewis and Butler, 1974). As Grotjahn (1955) put it, the therapist turns retrospection into introspection. Sherman (1981) also noted ways in which reminiscence can be made to fit into a more cognitive model, e.g., enhancing self-esteem through reviewing past achievements and disputing retrospective overgeneralizations. Lewis and Butler (1974) emphasized that the therapist does not initiate life review; it is already happening. It is the therapist's role to optimize the process and make it more intentional by activities such as writing an autobiography, reunions, pilgrimages, and reviewing old photographs.

Several writers have indicated that because consequential reality problems do compound other problems (Wilensky and Weiner, 1977), active assistance in helping the older adult extends beyond the therapeutic dyad into the social system, where services may be sought out and coordinated (e.g., Lawton and Gottesman, 1974). Blum and Tross (1980) used the term "practical advocacy" to describe this expanded role of the practitioner with older adults. At the same time, because there may be such an intertwining of needs—medical, legal, psychological—McGee and Lakin (1977) warn that the practitioner must be explicit about the boundaries of his or her professional competence.

Several modifications in technique have been used to overcome various barriers to treatment. For clients confronted with transportation barriers or for whom physical mobility is problematic, telephone sessions have been used (e.g., Evans and Jaureguy, 1982) as well as home visits (e.g., Zarit, 1980). For older adults who are unfamiliar with psychotherapy, Knight (1983) developed a role-induction technique that borrows its rationale from community mental health work with poor and minority clients. Before beginning treatment, clients view a videotape of an older person and a psychologist successfully working on her problems. With *non-aged* populations, this technique has been shown to increase the congruence of therapist and client expectations about treatment and decrease dropout.

Another technique is to present programs as "psychoeducational" in nature, downplaying the stigma of seeing a psychologist. Such programs also serve a preventive purpose, as they may reach an audience not identified as having any mental disorder. As an example, workshops conducted by Petty, Moeller, and Campbell (1976) and Reinhart and Sargent (1980) included both interpersonal skills ("alternatives to depression," getting information from physicians) and information about aging (memory concerns, health and fitness, relocation decisions).

A number of issues are particularly salient, though not unique, in the ongoing assessment and treatment of older adults (Brink, 1979; Eisdorfer and Stotsky, 1977; Zarit, 1980). First, the assessment of family dynamics and the involvement of the family in treatment regimens are cited. Second, many writers urge an awareness of the contribution of drugs to psychopathology, especially the effects of polypharmacy. Third, there are the more general issues of physical health status, including the effects of physical disorders on day-to-day functioning and mood. Fourth, there is a special challenge in differentiating functional from organic symptomatology, or irreversible cognitive impairment from reversible physiological problems such as malnutrition.

Finally, as one might expect, the topic of death is prevalent in the review literature. An awareness of having less time to live is a part of the older adult's reality (cf. Kastenbaum, Barber, Wilson, Ryder, and Hathaway, 1981). Consequently, the therapist must be prepared to deal with death and its multiple meanings. It is typically suggested that the therapist invite the client to discuss mourning and dying but that the client should ultimately be allowed to control discussions of these issues (Blum and Tross, 1980; Steuer, 1982a; Zarit, 1980).

Outcome research. Paralleling research with other age groups, the bulk of controlled research with older clients has been directed toward behavioral and cognitive intervention, although the literature suggests that the use of a wide range of therapies more accurately reflects current practice (cf. Parloff, 1979). Furthermore, studies testing particular therapeutic models have often been conducted in a group format. Consequently, inferences about which approaches are suitable for older adults require a joint consideration of the studies reviewed here and in the next section.

The literature on individual psychological intervention includes both case studies and a few controlled evaluations. Case studies illustrating a behavioral approach may be found in Gallagher and Thompson (1981); psychotherapy based on self psychology, in Lazarus (1980); and an approach based on life review techniques, in Sherman (1981).

In a clear example of a controlled study, Gallagher and Thompson (1981; 1982; in press) evaluated cognitive and behavioral therapies for older individuals diagnosed as manifesting a major depressive disorder. The cognitive therapy—based on Beck, Rush, Shaw, and Emery (1969)—and the behavioral therapy—based on Lewinsohn, Muñoz, Youngren, and Zeiss (1978)—were adapted for older adults by using, for example, large print forms and more assistance with transfer of learning. Participants were randomly assigned to 16 sessions of cognitive, behavioral, or brief supportive psychotherapy. Attrition for the initial sample was just over 25 percent, with half of the group initially assigned to the behavioral condition dropping out. Analysis of the pre–post data suggested that all three therapies were effective. Four follow-ups were conducted during the year following the end of treatment. Patients who had received cognitive or behavioral therapy showed additional change after termination, presumably because they continued to use the skills learned in therapy. All three interventions were less effective for those diagnosed as having endogenous (life-long pattern) rather than exogenous (recent stress) depression.

Szapocznik, Santiseban, Hervis, Spencer, and Kurtines (1981) evaluated a therapy approach called "life enhancement counseling." This technique relies heavily on the use of reminiscence and was specifically designed to be culturally sensitive to the basic values of a Hispanic population. Average age of the counselees was 67. Pre–post evaluation by independent clinicians indicated improvement on all subscales of a multidimensional assessment of client functioning, particularly mental health, and of a psychiatric rating schedule. When individuals were grouped according to the extent to which the life enhancement technique was used in the therapy sessions, the functional assessment improved more for those with more life enhancement.

Summary. The literature cited in this section lends support to those who would refute therapeutic nihilism with respect to older adults. The research has evolved to the point of including some initial controlled studies with well-specified samples. With respect to the theme of continuity versus discontinuity, most writers present modifications of techniques developed originally for younger adults, based on their clinical experience and conceptualization of aging. Usually, a short-term, problem-centered, active approach focusing on reality problems is advocated. Although seeing merit in this position, we suggest that internal psychological issues may need attention as well. In our zeal not to induce dependency and to address the client's real-life concerns, we must beware of short-changing the client through an overemphasis on brevity and problem-focused strategies. We further suggest that the particular individual and the problem presented, not age *per se*, should be regarded as the primary determinant in establishing intervention goals and selecting therapeutic approaches.

Group Therapy

It is not known whether more older persons are treated in groups than individually, although McGee and Lakin (1977) found considerably more literature on group than on individual therapy. Groups are said to offer certain advantages: (1) They are more efficient (McGee and Lakin, 1977); (2) they multiply the positive social effects of individual therapy by promoting mutual interaction among the patients (Gilbert, 1977); and (3) they encourage participants to realize that their problems are not unique (Ingersoll and Silverman, 1978). Perhaps because of the emphasis on counteracting social isolation, a frequent feature of groups for older adults is the serving of refreshments as a way of fostering a sense of group solidarity (e.g., Petty, Moeller, and Campbell, 1976). Burnside (1978) and Hartford (1980) have reviewed various approaches to group treatment. Hartford emphasized the need for paying attention to possible negative effects of groups, such as socializing compliance in an institution or pressuring those who prefer not to take part in a group, thereby magnifying their isolation.

Life review therapy, for both groups and individuals, has been recommended as helpful to the late-life developmental task of reviewing and integrating one's life experiences. Lewis and Butler (Butler and Lewis, 1982; Lewis and Butler, 1974), the foremost proponents of the technique, informally described a series of age-integrated groups of 8 to 10 outpatients. They also reported successful use of life review therapy with organically impaired patients, provided the therapist was prepared to proceed slowly. Birren (1982) has reported on autobiography classes in which participants read sketches aloud to the group. Effects of the experience included improved insight, sense of personal integration, self-esteem, sense of control, catharsis, and group cohesion.

Therapists often refer to difficulties in engaging older patients in groups. Working with inpatients, Lesser, Lazarus, Frankel, and Havasy (1981) conducted a supportive type of group for 11 weeks but failed to stimulate any group process. They then switched to a more structured reminiscence group that met twice weekly for 45 minutes. They found it worked better, and patients began spontaneously to introduce nonreminiscence topics as well. Working in the community, Sherman (1981) discovered that group members objected to a nondirective approach but were amenable to life review and to a more structured cognitive approach. Furthermore, he felt the group useful for encouraging people to enter individual counseling.

In an especially clear case description, Wheeler and Knight (1981) reported decreased depression and memory complaints in a frail, 74-year-old man treated with behavioral and cognitive techniques in group and marital therapy. The case illustrated the interplay of behavioral and psychodynamic issues and of organic and functional disabilities.

There are two types of controlled outcome studies of group interventions. First, as mentioned previously, several studies test particular theoretical models of therapy and use the group format for convenience. Second, there are various psychoeducational workshops, holistic programs, and activity groups on which program evaluation data have been collected. In both types, group members may be either patients (outpatients or residents of an institution) or community volunteers.

To begin with the first type, Keller, Croake, and Brooking (1975) evaluated a rational-emotive therapy model. They compared a "study-discussion" group for community-residing adults aged 60 and older that met two hours a week for four weeks to a no-treatment control group. The intervention resulted in reductions in irrational thinking and anxiety.

Ingersoll and Silverman (1978) recruited anxious and depressed older individuals for "well-being" groups, assigning them to either a "Here and Now" or a "There and Then" group. Groups met for eight two-hour sessions. The "Here and Now" approach included relaxation training, disclosure of anxieties, communication training, and memory training. The "There and Then" group used structured forms of reminiscence such as genograms and autobiographical journals. Both groups had attrition problems; one-third of the "Here and Now" and one-half of the "There and Then" group members did not complete the groups. The only significant improvement was a decrease on the somatization measure for the "There and Then" group. Some members of the "Here and Now" group actually manifested increased anxiety and somatization. The authors suggested that progressive relaxation may have only gotten far enough in the time alloted to sensitize participants to tension but not to learn to relax.

Gallagher (1981) compared behavioral with supportive groups for depressed older outpatients. Groups with five to six members met biweekly for five weeks. The drop-out rate was just over 20 percent. Although there was more positive verbal interaction in the behavioral than the supportive groups, participants in both groups were significantly less depressed at post-test and at a five-week follow-up.

Sallis et al. (in press) compared two treatments—one aimed at anxiety and the other at depression—not only with each other but with a placebo control group. Groups of three to five community volunteers aged 60 and older met twice a week for five weeks. The anxiety reduction group was taught progressive relaxation and anxiety management. Behavioral and cognitive strategies were taught in the depression group. The "placebo" group was taught self-disclosure and the expression of feelings. Drop-out exceeded one-third and compliance with self-monitoring was poor for all groups. At both post-test and follow-up assessment, depression and blood pressure decreased for all three groups. Anxiety decreased only in the placebo control group.

Steuer (Jarvik, Mintz, Steuer, Gerner, Aldrich, Hammen, Linde, McCarley, Motoike, and Rosen, 1982; Steuer, 1982c) compared cognitive/behavioral groups (Beck et al., 1979) to psychodynamic groups (Grotjahn, 1955; Yalom, 1970) for outpatients, aged 55 and over, most of whom were women, and all of whom had been diagnosed as having a major depressive disorder. Groups of eight to nine members met for nine months, at first twice a week and then only once. Attrition was over one-third for each type of treatment. Patients mainly dropped out after the twelfth week, with the more depressed—and more anxiously depressed—individuals the likelier to drop out. Patients were assessed at pre-test, at four points during treatment, and at post-test. For both treatments, there was significantly reduced depression and anxiety on both self-report and observer-ratings; on one of the three depression measures (Beck Depression Inventory) there was a significant difference favoring the cognitive/behavioral group. In the cognitive/behavioral group, Steuer and Hammen (in press) found that behavioral strategies were more useful than cognitive strategies for patients whose cognitive functioning was less intact.

Assertion training has been viewed as particularly appropriate for older people as an antidote to the helplessness that accompanies what often are legitimate complaints about being put down or disregarded. Groups have been formed in various settings including nutrition sites (Wheeler, 1980), Senior Centers (Toseland, 1977), and retirement homes (Corby, 1977). Working in a nursing home, Berger and Rose (1977) compared three one-hour sessions of interpersonal skill training in difficult social situations to a discussion-control and an assessment-only control group. At post-test but not at the eight-week follow-up, the interpersonal skill training group proved to be superior on a behavior-role play test of situations in which they had received training but not in other situations or on any of the self-report measures.

Recently, other groups have been the context for psychological interventions related to memory complaints and cognitive skills. Zarit, Gallagher, and Kramer (1981) and Zarit, Cole, and Guider (1981) conducted memory training groups for participants who were not organically impaired, but for whom memory complaints indicated depression. When they compared memory training to assertion training, both programs proved effective in lessening memory complaints, enhancing some memory skills, and relieving depressive symptomatology. The memory training groups were superior to a current events discussion group in improving memory skills, but both were equally effective in reducing memory complaints. By contrast, memory complaints increased in a waiting list control group. Hughston and Merriam (1982) used structured reminiscence exercises as a memory training strategy. Gains in intelligence test performance were noted for both the reminiscence group and a group that was given learning exercises with new material, but not for a social-contact control group.

For patients with senile dementia, Zarit, Zarit, and Reever (1982) reported that both memory training making use of visual imagery and practical problem-solving training led to gains in memory performance during the training sessions but not at post-test. Family members who attended the groups with the patients showed an increase in depression. Brinkman, Smith, Meyer, Vroulis, Shaw, Gordon, and Allen (1982) found that, for suspected Alzheimer patients, an unstructured conversation control group was superior to either visual-imagery or semantic exercises.

The second type of group mentioned earlier is less problem-oriented and addresses a broader set of concerns. Examples range from workshops on aging offered in the community (Reinhart and Sargent, 1980) to self-help groups developed around a particular life transition, such as widowhood (Barrett, 1978), to activity groups in geriatric day care settings. Aronson and Graziano (1976) set up a six-week Polaroid photography group in a day care center, selecting an adult activity that would provide visible indication of the individual's success. Compared to a nonrandomly assigned control group, change was found on two of four semantic differential scales. Two weeks after the end of the program, the participants who remembered the program liked it. More holistic activity programs include stress management training, involving ele-

ments of progressive relaxation and meditation (Garrison, 1978); the Adults Health and Development Program (Leviton and Santa Maria, 1979), involving individualized exercise and health education lectures; and SAGE—Senior Actualization and Growth Exploration (Dychtwald, 1979). SAGE employs a variety of growth techniques such as relaxation training, meditation, yoga, massage, journal writing, gestalt techniques, and art and dance therapy. Lieberman and Gourash (1979) evaluated SAGE, comparing participants over age 69 to a waiting-list control group. Groups met three to four hours per week for nine months. Pre–post change in the expected direction was observed on selected measures: goal accomplishment, distress as assessed by a psychiatric symptom checklist, obsessive-compulsivity, self-esteem, and health anxiety.

The group therapy literature further demonstrates the points made in our summary of individual psychotherapy, to wit: Writers are presenting modifications of techniques developed with younger adults, controlled studies are beginning to be carried out, and group strategies have been adapted according to the patient population being served. Attrition also appears to be a significant factor, which may be an accurate reflection of the barriers described previously or perhaps a magnified one because of the inflexible structuring of treatments necessitated by experimental designs. With respect to principles of change, probably the most central observation is that comparisons among theoretical approaches or techniques with both individual and group therapies have rarely shown differential effectiveness. Although deterioration effects present an issue that is rarely considered (that is, whether there are individuals for whom a particular treatment results in negative change), on the whole, the expectation of receiving help and participation in any type of therapy program can lead to improvements on various indicators of outcome.

Other Community-based Approaches

The interventions in this section range from ones traditionally called psychotherapy or counseling to a variety of nontraditional programs intended to have a positive psychosocial effect. Like self-help and activity groups, these nontraditional community approaches extend psychological interventions to those who might not otherwise receive services. Furthermore, a wide range of populations is targeted, from those with diagnosable mental disorders to those considered "at risk" and in need of preventive interventions.

Family and marital counseling. The literature has tended to focus on unique family issues that arise when there is an older family member. Lynch and Waxenberg (1971) and LaWall (1981) described cases of conjoint therapy. Herr and Weakland (1979) presented an extension of a family systems theory approach (cf. Bateson, Jackson, Haley, and Weakland, 1956; Watzlawick, Weakland, and Fisch, 1974) to problems of aging. They included a number of case examples of family-oriented problem solving, including problems of confusion, relocation, intergenerational conflict, and dying. Most empirical work has concerned relatives of older adults with Alzheimer's disease or other disability. Fengler and Goodrich (1979) suggested that the spouses of disabled elderly should be regarded as "hidden" patients. The spouse is faced with a changed relationship at the same time as he or she must deal with managing the problematic behavior of the disabled partner (Zarit, Reever, and Bach-Peterson, 1980). The demands of the situation virtually mandate a restriction in the caregiver's social network, and both authors urged that interventions address this all-too-common experience.

Crossman, London, and Barry (1981) described a support group for wives of participants in a day care program, and Lazarus, Stafford, Cooper, Cohler, and Dysken (1981) reported on a discussion group for relatives of Alzheimer's patients. The latter evaluated the effectiveness of a series of ten weekly meetings concerning topics such as vainly seeking a cure, dealing with physicians, management issues, and questions such as whether or not one should take vacations. Post-tests showed increased sense of internal control but no increase in self-esteem or decrease in anxiety and depression.

Others have looked at the children of aged parents. Robinson and Thurnher (1979) noted that the transition to increased responsibility for one's parents usually occurs at an inopportune time in the adult child's life. Some (e.g., Hausman, 1979) have conducted groups for adult children aimed at alleviating their stress and thereby indirectly benefiting their elderly parents. Garrison and Howe (1976) describe social network interaction in which all members of the client's social network, including family, friends, and possibly service providers, are invited to meet together. Reminiscing is part of the session, along with group problem-solving.

Friendly visiting. These programs involve home visits to frail elderly with the purpose of reducing social isolation. Mulligan and Bennett (1977–78) found a reduction in psychiatric symptoms among those visited. At post-test, neither those visited nor the control group had decreased in social isolation, but at a six-month follow-up the visited group had become more social. Bogat and Jason (in press) compared two models of visiting, one which was aimed at increasing the older person's social network by encouraging participation in community activities, and the other which was relationship-oriented, emphasizing empathy and concern. The visitors were college undergraduates. Compared to a nonrandomly assigned control group, both visited groups manifested increased desire for social interaction. Stafford and Bringle (1980) compared two models of visiting and a no-contact control group. In one model, the participants were visited and given a task they could do at home, whereas in the other the visit was entirely social. A post-test two weeks after the initial visit revealed the task group to be significantly more interested than the others in increasing their involvement in other activities. Moreover, the control group was more interested than the social visit group in participating in activities such as volunteer work and bingo. The authors speculated that the social visit may have fulfilled social needs that otherwise might be met by the other activities.

Volunteer and paraprofessional programs. These programs intend to provide a meaningful role for the older helper, assist those who are being helped, and alleviate shortages of professional personnel. They enlist the developmental function of older persons as teachers, advisors, and consultants—a concept Sherman (1981) calls "androgogy." Evaluations have found benefits to both the helpers and the helped, especially the former, but with some variations according to the design of the particular program (Gatz, Barbarin, Tyler, Mitchell, Moran, Wirzbicki, Crawford, and Engelman, 1982; Gatz, Hileman, and Amaral, in press). Foster grandparent programs (Saltz, 1977; Hirschowitz, 1973) place older adults in positions to help children in various school or hospital settings. Peer counseling programs (e.g., Alpaugh and Haney, 1978; Bratter and Tuvman, 1980) involve older adults as counselors, whereas other peer programs employ older adults in community outreach roles (e.g., Toseland, Decker, and Bliesner, 1979).

Pet therapy. A final approach (which has also been seen as cost-effective) in addressing feelings of isolation, loneliness, and uselessness is pet therapy. As one woman we interviewed recently said, "I've got a cat who's black and white so I don't need the blues in between." There has been some work of this kind in institutions, where pets are seen as enhancing the treatment milieu (Brickel, 1979), and there have also been some community studies with dogs and cats (Lago, Connell, and Knight, 1983) and with birds (Mugford and M'Comisky, 1975). Pets afford companionship, demand responsibility in terms of caring for them, and provide physical contact. Effects of pet companionship have been suggested to include improved morale, increased interpersonal responsibility, and lowered blood pressure (Ory and Goldberg, 1982; Holden, 1981).

Summary. The community-based interventions reviewed in this section reveal a diversity of approaches involving a broad network of change agents, from family and friends to paraprofessionals and volunteers. Rationales for the interventions frequently cite losses, uselessness, and social isolation. Consequently, interventions are designed to foster group participation and success in some activity. Programmatic studies have demonstrated that problems of anxiety, depression, generalized loneliness, helplessness, and the behavioral and familial disruption resulting from organic brain syndrome have all been alleviated to some degree.

Other Institutional Approaches

Virtually all institutionalized older adults can be categorized in two groups. The first are psychotics (mostly chronic schizophrenics) who have grown old, and the second are elderly patients, some of them bedridden, who suffer from physical debility, senile dementia, or some combination of the two (Bockover, 1964; Kahn, 1975). Treatment considerations for old schizophrenics reflect the general evolution of state mental hospital care since the early 1960s. Still, aged mental patients were among the last to be included in the effort to replace passive (custodial) approaches with a more active (milieu) treatment. With the push to deinstitutionalization, nursing homes replaced mental hospitals as the major institutional site for the mentally ill elderly (Gopelrud, 1979; Levine, 1981; Schmidt, Reinhardt, Kane, and Olsen, 1977). Subsequently, the focus of advocacy has shifted to community-residing elderly and the prevention of institutionalization altogether, since relocation to a nursing home may itself be a stressor with major physical and psychosocial consequences (Borup and Gallego, 1981; Bourstom and Pastalan, 1981; Coffman, 1981; Kowalski, 1981; Schulz and Brenner, 1977).

Psychological interventions common in institutions include (1) individually oriented treatment, (2) behavioral programs, (3) reality orientation, and (4) milieu treatment. They are designed to address what Tobin (1969) calls "institutional dependency." Treating patients as passive recipients of care encourages helplessness and inactivity. In turn, patient demandingness increases staff care, and a vicious cycle results (Lazarus, 1976; Rodin, 1980). Kahn (1975) describes the resultant gap between a patient's observable functional level and the level one would expect from his or her degree of impairment as "excess disability." Interventions aim to decrease excess disability by interrupting the debilitating cycle and providing environmental stimulation, with the goal of facilitating successful discharge into the community as well as fostering improved morale within the institution.

Individually oriented treatment. Brody, Kleban, Lawton, and Silverman (1971) developed and evaluated a program that treated excess disability by employing various techniques to help patients achieve specific, individualized goals. At the end of one year of treatment, experimental patients showed significantly greater reductions in their targeted disabilities than controls did, but their improvement on traditional clinical indices not specifically tied to the individualized goals was no better than would be expected by chance. A follow-up nine months after the program had ended indicated deterioration on the targeted goals (Brody, Kleban, Lawton, and Moss, 1974). Social competence was predictive of which patients profited from treatment (Kleban, Lawton, Brody, and Moss, 1975) and which remained stable rather than declining (Kleban, Lawton, Brody, and Moss, 1976).

Power and McCarron (1975) and Kastenbaum, Barber, Wilson, Ryder, and Hathaway (1981) evaluated techniques for establishing personal contact with severely depressed and impaired—often bedridden—elderly patients, using physical touching and reassuring verbal interaction. Power and McCarron found that depression in the treatment group was alleviated after 15 weeks, whereas depression of the control group intensified. Both the deterioration and the improvement effects grew larger at a six-week follow-up assessment.

Behavioral programs. Behavioral programs in institutions include individually focused operant interventions, designing prosthetic environments, altering environmental contingencies (e.g., token economies), and social skills training (see Hussian, 1981, and Richards and Thorpe, 1978, for reviews of these techniques and their application). There are a number of case studies of individually focused behavioral treatment. For example, Baltes and Zerbe (1976) successfully reinstituted self-feeding, although the improved behavior declined again during post-treatment baseline and one patient died before treatment was reinstituted. Sperbeck and Whitbourne (1981) used nurses as change agents in a behavioral program. Not only did the patients improve,

but the staff also reported spending less time reinforcing dependency. Carstensen and Fremouw (1981) shaped nonparanoid conversation in a late-life paranoid individual.

Other programs target behaviors for an entire ward and set up training programs or token economies for everyone in the setting. In comparing a token economy to milieu treatment, Mishara (1978) found that both programs resulted after six months in reduction of bizarre behavior and incontinence, and neither group increased in the amount of conversing among patients. The token economy was superior in encouraging self-care. Corbin and Nelson (1980) devised a board game for residents to play with a volunteer. In the game, players drew cards that described "Angel" behaviors (e.g., personal hygiene, participation in activities) and "Devil" behaviors (e.g., hostility toward an aide). Afterwards, they discussed the ideas with a staff member. Statistical trends supported the effectiveness of the game in remedying the effects of social isolation, including noncompliance behaviors.

Finally, others have focused on social skills training, including assertion training as described previously. Using structured learning therapy, Lopez, Hoyer, Goldstein, Gershaw, and Sprafkin (1980) successfully taught interpersonal conversation skills to elderly psychiatric inpatients; the transfer effect, however, was primarily limited to similar situations. Gordon, Patterson, Eberly, and Penner (1980) developed a modular approach to building skills for older adults in a residential unit and a day treatment program and found some evidence for improvement in the functional capabilities of the participants.

Reality orientation. Reality orientation (Folsom, 1968) is perhaps the most prominent treatment approach designed particularly for hospitalized older individuals, especially those who are confused and disoriented. The treatment approach has two components, "24-hour" and "classroom." The former involves the staff, who, as part of their daily routine, remind the patients of the day of the week, the name of the institution, and the patients' own names. In the classes, a trained aide reviews such things as the date, the weather, the names of their classmates, current news events, and the rudiments of complying with a request. A bulletin board with information such as place, date, and weather on it is frequently an adjunct.

Studies of the efficacy of the approach have reported mixed results (Barnes, 1974; Citrin and Dixon, 1977; Cornbleth and Cornbleth, 1979; Harris and Ivory, 1976; Zepelin, Wolfe, and Kleinplatz, 1981). In terms of cognitive orientation, some elderly patients, given enough rehearsal and reinforcement, have demonstrated improvement at post-test on the questions practiced during classes, whereas control groups have declined on the same measures. However, change was not maintained at follow-up, and, with the exception of Cornbleth and Cornbleth, little carry-over was found with regard to improved ward behavior. In summarizing this literature, Storandt (1978) suggested that whatever positive benefits have been observed may have resulted from the opportunity for patient-staff contact afforded by the program.

It is possible that the results of some programs have suffered because the patients' realities were not adequately taken into account in the presentation of class content (Gubrium and Ksander, 1975). Hellebrandt (1978, p. 69) commented about demented residents of a home for the aged:

> Reality orientation was futile. . . . They got endless pleasure from reading and re-reading a printed table listing their birthdates and ages, yet never remembered how old they were and continued to exclaim in disbelief each time they discovered they were so old.

Milieu. Included in this section are a number of programs in which attempts have been made to normalize elderly individuals' lives in an institution, ranging from those modeled after the humanistic principles of the therapeutic community (Gottesman, Donahue, Coons, and Ciarlo, 1969) to those focused more narrowly on enriching or empowering one particular aspect of the patients' experience.

A therapeutic community stresses the responsibility inherent in normal work and social roles as well as maximum self-care. In a study of an elderly psychiatric hospital population, Steer and Boger (1975) found signifi-

cant improvement on a ward adjustment index, with the most regressed patients benefiting the most. Gatz, Siegler, and Dibner (1979–80) evaluated a state mental hospital program modeled after Gottesman et al. (1969). The program met the staff's and patients' implicit goal of providing a humane environment in which patients could live their remaining years. The explicit goal of deinstitutionalization was hindered, however, because of a lack of community placements that, in the opinions of patients and staff, substantially improved upon the living situation afforded by the new unit. Spence, Cohen, and Kowalski (1975) and Siegel and Lasker (1978) set up a 14-week therapeutic community on a university campus to which elderly state hospital patients were bused for day treatment. They found that family support was a critical element in making community placements.

Several programs have been targeted at easing the transition from the community into the nursing home. Dye and Erber (1981) met for seven sessions with groups for new residents and their families or with groups of new residents alone and compared these groups to an assessment-only control group. At post-test, the residents-only group had gained most in sense of personal control and had become less anxious. At the follow-up six months later, residents who had been in the family group gained most in cognitive functioning and were doing better in general. Friedman (1975) set up a committee of older residents to plan and implement ways of welcoming newcomers. The program benefited both the newcomers and the helpers, with the committee meetings themselves providing a therapeutic group experience for the helpers.

To evaluate the effectiveness of restoring working and helping roles, MacDonald and Settin (1978) compared sheltered workshops to reality orientation groups and an assessment-only control group. Workshop participants showed significant gains in life satisfaction and social interest. Kalson (1976) arranged for nursing home residents to meet with a group of mentally retarded adults to participate in activities with them. Both the residents in the helping group and an assessment-only control group improved in morale.

Langer and Rodin (1976) argued that the crucial problem of the nursing home environment is the loss of opportunity to exercise control and personal responsibility. They found that patients who were allowed to make several decisions, including the choice of which plant to care for, reported that they were happier and more active than control group patients who were assigned a plant. Interviewers' ratings, staff ratings, and behavioral measures also suggested more alertness and social interaction. Eighteen months after the intervention (Rodin and Langer, 1977), experimental patients remained more sociable and self-initiating, physician review indicated significant gains in their physical health, and their mortality rate was lower than that of the control group. In a related study (Rodin, 1980), each member of the experimental group was assigned a particular 15-minute period during which the nurse would be on call specifically for them, thereby increasing patients' control over their caretaking. Relative to the untreated control group, patients in the experimental group showed both improved health and sociability.

Various friendly visiting programs have been designed to enhance patients' opportunities for social interaction and for exercising personal control. Gordon and Hallauer (1976) noted that the experience was of value to the high school or college students who visited the patients. Although Wallach, Kelley, and Abrahams (1979) observed initial reluctance on the part of both students and patients, they found that a shift in the program from having students use a fairly structured remotivation technique toward more sharing of life experiences proved successful.

Schulz (1976) focused on the personal control factor in visiting programs. He compared four groups: (1) residents who chose when they would be visited, (2) residents who were told the visitor's schedule so that they could predict when the visitor would come, (3) residents who were visited randomly, and (4) residents who were not visited. Supporting the relevance of both choice and prediction, the first two groups demonstrated significant gains on self- and staff-ratings of their physical and mental well-being (e.g., zest for life, hope) and activity level, in comparison to the third and fourth groups. Two years after the friendly visiting intervention had ended (Schulz & Hanusa, 1978), the choice and prediction groups had dropped back, showing significantly more decline than the other two groups. Moreover, the only deaths were among the choice and prediction groups.

Langer, Rodin, Beck, Weinman, and Spitzer (1979) structured the environment in such a way that obtaining control over outcomes required active cognitive processing. Their study compared contingent visitation, where the patients were rewarded with gifts for remembering the answers to questions; to noncontingent visitation, where all patients were given gifts at the end of the visit; to a no-treatment control group. At post-test, the contingent group was best in memory performance and had improved in social adjustment. Based on such results, these investigators posited a connection between perceived control and restimulation of cognitive mechanisms. Reinke, Holmes, and Denney (1981) compared social and cognitive types of visitation programs—conversation-only and conversation-plus-cognitive games such as dominoes or cards—to one another and to a waiting list control group. The conversation-plus-games condition had a superior effect on memory and self-rated health; conversation-only, a superior effect on life satisfaction. The control group declined on staff ratings of morale.

Lack of mutality in interpersonal relationships in the institution has been proposed as an antecedent of helplessness (Solomon, 1982). Based on this premise, Kastenbaum (1972) set up a program of serving alcoholic beverages on the unit (excluding patients for whom alcohol was contraindicated) to facilitate social mingling among staff and patients. In a series of studies with appropriate control conditions, he found improved self-care, improved interpersonal communication, and greater staff involvement with patients. In some cases there was carry-over of group interaction into other ward activities.

Summary. A wide range of institutional interventions has been shown to have ameliorative effects for elderly residents, either by bringing about significant improvements or by stemming the decline observed in nonparticipants. Patients' improvements do not generalize well, however, and we have noted a number of instances where treatment gains failed to be sustained after a program was discontinued. In fact, there is some evidence that instituting and then dropping innovations may be detrimental.

These findings may be more reflective of the nature of institutions than of aging (Kahn and Zarit, 1974). The fact that the institution is a closed, total environment makes changing norms exceedingly difficult, yet makes *any* change potentially very powerful. Innovations, moreover, must not been seen as increasing the burden of staff, who frequently are paraprofessionals, already feeling taxed by too many demands and not enough status (Kastenbaum et al., 1981).

Across a wide variety of programs, individual attention and a personal relationship with a staff member seem to be highly therapeutic. Behavioral programs and introduction of personal control into the milieu correctly call attention to the importance of contingencies in the institutional environment. Learning principles, however, should be employed in ways that preserve the patient's dignity, and the therapeutic goals should reflect the patient's needs and desires, not merely the demands of institutional regimens. With milieu programs, difficulties may result from the establishment of unrealistic goals in an excessive burst of humanism. Finally, milieu programs may fail to address adequately the paradox of giving patients responsibility, given the power differential between patients and staff inherent in the setting.

DISCUSSION

In this section, we refer to the four themes described in the introduction—continuities and discontinuities between interventions with older adults and with other groups, the process by which clinical knowledge is created, the types of problems experienced by older individuals, and the principles of change shared by diverse approaches.

Continuities and Discontinuities

In the review of the literature on interventions, we found support for our position that ap-

proaches to psychotherapy and behavior change that were developed for other age groups are also effective with the aged. For the latter, adaptations are made; in particular, psychotherapy is shortened and more focused on immediate reality problems; life review is incorporated into therapy groups; and frequently nontraditional types of interventions such as educational workshops, activity groups, friendly visiting, and volunteer work are employed. Such changes do not represent a fundamental discontinuity of process and technique; in fact, they are conceptually similar to modifications that have been made to suit other populations. Modifications have drawn on what is known about cognition and aging, personality development, and other research literature, as well as the practitioner's direct clinical experience with older adults. As yet, there is essentially no empirical justification for adaptations of this sort such as would be obtained by assigning younger and older clients to modified and unmodified treatment groups.

Similarly, the elderly have been portrayed as particularly reluctant to engage in therapy and therapists as particularly reluctant to see older adults in treatment. The barriers that people identify are not unique to older clients, however; they pertain to many individuals and to other underserved populations. Consequently, we encourage more extrapolation from therapies developed with younger populations so long as attention is paid to the types of special considerations discussed in this chapter. We believe that such extrapolation, accompanied by evaluation of the effectiveness of the interventions, will contribute to redressing patterns of underservice to older adults in practice settings and underattention to the aged in mainstream psychotherapy literature.

Clinical Knowledge and Outcome Research

Our overview of the types of interventions included the progression of research designs, from case studies to "outcome only" and from pre-post evaluations to controlled outcome research. Based on this review, we concluded that the evidence to date warrants neither universal pessimism nor resignation to palliative measures. Rather, we noted that the aged are being treated psychotherapeutically, that they are benefiting from it, and that there exists a cadre of therapists experienced in the treatment of older adults.

Still, controlled research on psychological interventions with older adults is just beginning. Just as older adults have been excluded from various treatment regimens, so have they been omitted from outcome research. Age cutoffs have been applied on the grounds of the greater likelihood of such complications as organic brain syndrome and physical illness, of the concurrent use of prescription medications, and of logistical difficulties such as transportation to the research facility. This blanket exclusion of a population on the basis of potential methodological problems is unwarranted and unhelpful. This is not to dilute the importance of dilemmas encountered in research involving older subjects. Reviews of procedural pitfalls can be found in Kahn and Zarit's (1974) discussion of the evaluation of mental health programs for the aged in institutions and Mintz, Steuer, and Jarvik's (1981) discussion of research considerations with depressed elderly therapy subjects. In part, these pitfalls reflect the methodological issues confronted by all investigations of development in later life, but it should not be forgotten that barriers to research parallel barriers to treatment. Thus, as we see it, the task is to integrate research on psychological interventions with older adults into the domain of outcome research in general.

Types of Problems

We introduced this theme by emphasizing that interventions should be tailored to the individual. We suggested that there are three categories of problems: organic brain syndromes, lifelong patterns, and special issues of later life. Viewed as axes rather than as mutually exclusive types, these three categories can be applied to each individual case to help frame assessment questions and select a treatment strategy. We concur with Eisdorfer and Stotsky (1977) on the importance of diagnosis as the first step of intervention.

In the studies reviewed, we noted the types of patients being treated and distinguished those living in the community from those living in institutions. Nevertheless, it was not always possible to ascertain diagnoses from the reports of interventions; for example, not all studies of reality orientation were limited to patients with organic brain syndromes (unlike Zepelin et al., 1981). In therapy outcome studies, depression was far and away the predominant target complaint.

Regarding organicity, the key assessment issue is to differentiate dementia, delirium, and depression. Although organically impaired clients are often not included with other groups in outcome studies, a variety of techniques, including life review (Lewis and Butler, 1974) and behavioral group therapy (Steuer and Hammen, in press) have been successfully used to address psychological concerns, both apart from and related to the impairment. Interventions with family members of patients with dementia are also recommended (Lazarus et al., 1981; Zarit and Zarit, 1982).

With patterns that represent a continuation from earlier years, the key assessment issue is to understand the interaction of the developmental history and the current situation. Special issues of later life include both losses and existential tasks, such as life review and dealing with one's finitude, although Gutmann et al. (1982) reframe losses in *developmental* terms. As in other areas of outcome research, the literature regarding older adults mirrors the field in general insofar as more needs to be learned about matching the treatment to the diagnosis. For older adults, a tentative but provocative outcome is Gallagher and Thompson's (1982) finding that cognitive and behavioral therapies were effective with exogenous depression but less so with endogenous. Although such a conclusion demands replication, and although these diagnoses do not fully parallel the comparison between situational issues and lifelong patterns, it would appear that these briefer therapies may be particularly suited to dealing with situational issues of stress and loss.

Mechanisms of Change

An important recent development in mainstream psychotherapy literature is the revival of interest in basic therapeutic change principles that may be functioning across diverse approaches (Frank, 1976; Goldfried, 1980; Mahoney, 1982). Several types of mechanisms have been identified, including (1) nonspecifics, such as positive expectancies, hope, and a sense of personal control; (2) the therapeutic relationship; (3) catharsis; (4) meaning and insight; and (5) learning and related cognitive processes (see Pavey, in preparation). In the paragraphs below, we will briefly suggest the relevance these mechanisms have to the conceptualization of psychological intervention with older adults.

Nonspecifics. Nonspecifics are those aspects of the therapeutic process that may be curative but are not necessarily the intentional focus of the intervention. A number of writers have proposed that an important part of treatment is the kindling of positive expectancies and hope—the same factors that were once dismissed as a "placebo effect" or "Hawthorne effect." Frank (1976) believes that all persons seeking psychological aid share feelings of hopelessness and powerlessness, a phenomenon he calls "demoralization." Across all therapies, regardless of content, there are likely to be basic therapeutic functions that combat demoralization, among which Frank identifies the following: (1) All therapies increase the patient's hope, which aligns patient and therapist expectations and may be curative in itself; and (2) all therapies increase the patient's sense of control, mastery, and efficacy by providing for success experiences.

Expectancy and efficacy have emerged as issues in virtually every type of intervention with older adults. Wolff (1971) and Weinberg (1976) stressed the need to convey hope and keep life purposeful; Verwoerdt (1976) urged a realistic but optimistic approach that makes its clear that some relief is always possible; Zarit, Cole, and Guider (1981) emphasized patients' expectations of receiving help; Oberleder (1966) stressed establishing a sense of mastery; both Ingebretsen (1977) and Lazarus (1980) maintained that validation of the patient's perception of reality restores feelings of mastery; Goldfarb (1955) underscored the fact that patients' self-esteem soars specifically because they believe the success of the relationship with the therapist is due to their own

efforts; Sallis et al. (in press) and Gallagher and Thompson (1982) noted the self-efficacy that ensues from behavior change; and Wayne (1953) and Gallagher and Thompson (1981) emphasized clients' seeing themselves as playing an active role in solving problems. In more direct tests of the mechanism, both Rodin (Langer and Rodin, 1976; Rodin and Langer, 1977; Rodin, 1980) and Schulz (1976) developed interventions specifically to provide choices and thereby increase personal control; Lazarus et al. (1981) and Gatz et al. (1982) found increased sense of control among recipients of psychoeducational interventions; and there is some consensus that experiencing a stress as a normative, and therefore expected, event makes it more manageable (Danish et al., 1980). Others have highlighted the personal responsibility and sense of accomplishment inherent in task groups (MacDonald and Settin, 1978), volunteer work and other helping roles (Bratter and Tuvman, 1980; Friedman, 1975), and taking care of a pet (Lago et al., 1983). Martin and deGruchy (1930) asserted that older adults came to their Old Age Counseling Center in order to help Dr. Martin and be of some social use. "Remoralization" also parallels the idea of social reconstruction and countering negative societal stereotypes (Kuypers and Bengtson, 1973). Finally, self-efficacy is at the heart of the dilemma of the practitioner, who must provide needed help without rendering the older individual helplessly dependent.

In an earlier review of various therapies used with older adults, Levy, Derogatis, Gallagher, and Gatz (1980) observed that few studies had found a differential outcome when comparing treatments. Consequently, they suggested that the nonspecific effects of treatment may account for much of the change through psychological interventions that has been reported to date.

Therapeutic relationships. As noted in our earlier discussion of individual therapy with older adults, the therapeutic relationship seems to emerge as a central vehicle for change, if not an explicit mechanism thereof. Many cite Rogers' (1957) three conditions of genuineness, empathy, and positive regard as necessary therapist contributions to the relationship (e.g., Kastenbaum, 1978). Pfeiffer and

Busse (1973) have recognized the power of the relationship in mitigating the various losses accrued by many older adults. They coined the term "symbolic giving" to represent the deliberate use of therapy to provide solace, restore equilibrium in the patient's life, and demonstrate the possibility of developing new relationships. Lewis and Butler (1974) noted that the listener is serving an important role by bearing witness to the life of the older individual. Weinberg (1981, pp. 261–262) stated

> I would want someone who is interested in my inner life if I were to have anyone treat me . . . The ability to sit and listen to them and to really hear and to try not to dazzle them with our brilliance and advice is one of the cardinal aspects of therapy . . . We think we are here to find immediate solutions to problems. This is not quite so. We have to work very hard to provide something of ourselves.

We have seen, too, that obtaining individual attention in institutional settings and establishing a one-to-one relationship with a staff member appear to be associated with therapeutic improvement (Brody et al., 1971; Citrin and Dixon, 1977; Kastenbaum et al., 1981; Kobrynski, 1973). Some have suggested that group interventions can serve similar purposes in fostering relationships and assuring people that they are not alone. However, Kastenbaum (1972) argued that group interventions within institutions must include a changed relationship with staff, not just socialization with other patients, if they are to obtain the same results that individualized attention yields.

Catharsis. The role of emotion in the change processes of older adults is not well explored. Though inattention to catharsis in part reflects a general trend with all ages, traditional literature on catharsis exhibits a striking lack of mention of older adults. Some work with older adults does consider the emotional realm as curative. Oberleder (1966) has suggested that cathartic technique is of therapeutic value in her "crisis therapy" approach where panic is reduced by ventilating feelings. Even if it is not specifically implemented as catharsis, those employing life review techniques feel that catharsis is facilitated through reminis-

cence; the recall of events stimulates emotional release, which is experienced as therapeutic (Birren, 1982; Sherman, 1981). Thus, emotional discharge is less of an end in itself and more of a natural component of a curative mechanism.

Insight and meaning. Insight, like catharsis, has suffered a general decline in popularity. Some do not see insight as a central ingredient of change for members of any age group (Zarit, 1980). Others see it as a relevant mechanism of change for the young but less necessary for the old (Oberleder, 1966; Verwoerdt, 1976). Still others have mentioned the redevelopment of insight as one aspect of a psychodynamic approach with the aged (Ronch and Maizler, 1977; Steuer, 1982a), and Ingebretsen (1977) defines insight in a wider sense of integrating one's life experiences and accepting death.

Insight can perhaps be viewed more pertinently in terms of the reorganization of meaning. Mahoney (1982) believes that all therapy that is effective achieves a change in meaning. He sees the individual as playing an active role in constructing and reordering personal meaning. Shifting meanings requires disequilibrium, such as occurs in developmental change. Therapeutic strategies deal with the disequilibrium and contribute to the process of reordering.

Meaning is a recurrent theme across a range of rather discrepant interventions with older adults. Experiencing one's life as meaningful is the critical issue for the development of ego integrity (Erikson, 1963). Facilitating resolution of this developmental task is an issue addressed by therapists influenced by psychoanalytic formulations as well as by those explicitly engaged in life review (Butler, 1968; Szapocznik et al., 1981). Meaning is also mentioned prominently in the context of providing older persons with meaningful roles, for example, paraprofessional and volunteer work (Gatz et al., in press); with meaningful activities, for example, photography classes (Aronson and Graziano, 1976); and with meaningful cultural symbols, for example, alcoholic beverages (Kastenbaum, 1972). Given this variety of concern with issues of meaningfulness, further theorizing about meaning as a mechanism of change across interventions with older adults seems warranted.

Learning and cognition. There is consensus that learning is an important principle of change. Operant programs (Hussian, 1981), token economies (Mishara, 1978), and structured behavioral programs for outpatients (Gallagher and Thompson, 1981; Sallis et al., in press) have all been shown to be effective in changing behavior. Speculation persists, on the other hand, as to whether older adults respond to behavioral programs in the same way as younger adults, partly as a result of laboratory studies suggesting that learning processes may undergo developmental changes (cf., Botwinick, 1977). In institutional programs, generalization and maintenance of gains have been particularly problematic. Mintz et al. (1981) and Gallagher and Thompson (1981) both suggest that learning may take longer and that special effort must be devoted to providing age-specific examples, overcoming cautiousness, and enhancing generalization.

Like all of behavior therapy, behavior therapy with older adults is moving toward cognitivism. Various cognitive-behavioral methods have been seen as particularly applicable to older adults because of their susceptibility to self-defeating thoughts. Furthermore, they have proven effective in some cases (Gallagher and Thompson, in press; Sherman, 1981; Steuer and Hammen, in press; Wheeler and Knight, 1981; Zarit, 1980).

Educative activities fall under the cognitive rubric, from the provision of information about aging in workshop format to the provision of a therapeutic rationale (Gallagher and Thompson, 1981; Sallis et al., in press) and other role induction techniques (Knight, 1983). The latter preparatory activities are not necessarily linked to any one school of therapy; for example, Sallis et al. developed and provided a rationale for a self-disclosure group.

Summary. Identifying relevant mechanisms of change in psychological interventions with older adults may prove to be a heuristic application of a general trend in the psychotherapy literature. Its utility is twofold. First, such identification may assist in operationalizing

variables and testing empirical hypotheses. Second, identifying curative properties of a treatment requires more careful specification of the theoretical model of the person and of the change from which the mechanisms emerge. This second point raises another issue for exploration, namely, the extent to which these mechanisms of change also reflect processes of development. In other words, is there a model of change common to human growth and development and to psychological intervention? In our review of mainstream literature on general therapeutic factors, we were impressed by the lack of attention to age or to developmental theory in most of the writings. Conversely, few attempts have been made to use developmental theory to inform intervention. We have mentioned life review (Erikson, 1963) and the developmental approach of Gutmann et al. (1982). Additionally, Baltes and Danish (1979) have defined life-span developmental theory in terms of the dynamic interplay between the individual and the environment and have drawn parallels between primary prevention and optimizing human development. These examples illustrate ways of incorporating principles of development into decisions about how to intervene. In that sense, the integration of life-span developmental theory and models of change stands as an important challenge to the field of psychological intervention with adults of all ages.

CONCLUSION

Our review of the state of the art in psychological interventions with older adults suggests that many of them have demonstrable efficacy. Various barriers to obtaining psychological services need to be redressed or otherwise laid to rest, both to provide more psychotherapeutic services and preventive programs to older adults as well as to encourage research evaluating the effects of those interventions.

We were impressed by four themes. First, although identifying those aspects of psychological practice that are continuous or discontinuous over the life span is certainly prudent, too much attention to presumed discontinuities may have served as a barrier to careful extrapolation of knowledge from the mainstream psychotherapy literature. Second, the process by which knowledge about psychological interventions with older adults is growing reflects the same steps identified previously for mainstream research on the efficacy of psychotherapy. Moreover, all of the steps in this evolution have value as sources of information. Third, consideration of the various problems presented by older patients helps suggest how to extrapolate from knowledge of clinical psychology in general, on the one hand, and theory and research in adult development and aging, on the other. Fourth, across a striking breadth of specific types of interventions, common principles or mechanisms of change were apparent: (1) fostering a sense of control, self-efficacy, and hope; (2) establishing a relationship with the helper; (3) providing or elucidating a sense of meaning; and (4) establishing constructive contingencies in the environment.

Acknowledgements: Gratitude is extended to Stanley Pavey and Cynthia Pearson, whose criticism of earlier drafts was indispensable to the preparation of this chapter.

REFERENCES

Abraham, K. 1919. The applicability of psychoanalytic treatment to patients at an advanced age. In *Selected Papers on Psychoanalysis.* New York: Basic Books, 1959.

Alpaugh, P., and Haney, M. 1978. *Counseling the Older Adult: A Training Manual for Paraprofessionals and Beginning Counselors.* Los Angeles: University of Southern California Press.

Aronson, D. W., and Graziano, A. M. 1976. Improving elderly clients' attitudes through photography. *The Gerontologist* 16: 363–367.

Auerbach, M. I.; Gordon, D. W.; Ullman, A.; and Weisel, M. J. 1977. Health care in a selected urban elderly population: Utilization patterns and perceived needs. *The Gerontologist* 17: 341–346.

Avant, W. R., and Dressel, P. L. 1980. Perceiving needs by staff and elderly clients: The impact of training and client contact. *The Gerontologist* 20: 71–77.

Baltes, P. B., and Danish, S. J. 1979. Intervention in life-span development and aging: Issues and concepts. In *Life-Span Developmental Psychology: Intervention,* eds. R. R. Turner and H. W. Reese. New York: Academic Press.

Baltes, M., and Zerbe, M. 1976. Independence training in nursing home residents. *The Gerontologist* 16: 428–432.

Barnes, J. A. 1974. Effects of reality orientation classroom on memory loss, confusion, and disorientation in geriatric patients. *The Gerontologist* 14: 138–142.

Barrett, C. J. 1978. Effectiveness of widows' groups in facilitating change. *Journal of Consulting and Clinical Psychology* 46: 20–31.

Bateson, G.; Jackson, D.; Haley, J.; and Weakland, J. 1956. Toward a theory of schizophrenia. *Behavioral Science* 1: 251–264.

Beck, A.; Rush, J.; Shaw, B.; and Emery, G. 1979. *Cognitive Therapy of Depression.* New York: Guilford.

Berger, R. M., and Rose, S. D. 1977. Interpersonal skill training with institutionalized elderly patients. *Journal of Gerontology* 32: 346–353.

Bild, B. R., and Havighurst, R. J. 1976. Knowledge and use of services. *The Gerontologist* 16 (1, Pt. II): 76–79.

Birren, J. E. 1982. A review of the development of the self. Paper presented at the annual meeting of the Gerontological Society of America, Boston, MA.

Birren, J. E., and Renner, V. J. 1980. Concepts and issues of mental health and aging. In *Handbook of Mental Health and Aging,* eds. J. E. Birren and R. B. Sloane. Englewood Cliffs, NJ: Prentice-Hall.

Blazer, D. 1980. The epidemiology of mental illness in late life. In *Handbook of Geriatric Psychiatry,* eds. E. W. Busse and D. G. Blazer. New York: Van Nostrand Reinhold.

Blum, J. E., and Tallmer, M. 1977. The therapist vis-a-vis the older patient. *Psychotherapy: Theory, Research and Practice* 14: 361–367.

Blum, J. E., and Tross, S. 1980. Psychodynamic treatment of the elderly: A review of issues in theory and practice. In *Annual Review of Gerontology and Geriatrics,* vol. I, ed. C. Eisdorfer. N.Y.: Springer.

Bockover, J. S. 1964. Aspects of geriatric care and treatment: Moral, amoral, and immoral. In *New Thoughts on Old Age,* ed. R. Kastenbaum. N.Y.: Springer.

Bogat, G. A., and Jason, L. A. In press. An evaluation of two visiting programs for elderly community residents. *International Journal of Aging and Human Development.*

Borup, J. H., and Gallego, D. T. 1981. Mortality as affected by interinstitutional relocation: update and assessment. *The Gerontologist* 21: 8–16.

Botwinick, J. 1977. Intellectual abilities. In *Handbook of the Psychology of Aging,* eds. J. E. Birren and K. W. Schaie. New York: Van Nostrand Reinhold.

Bourstom, N., and Pastalan, L. 1981. The effect of relocation on the elderly: A reply to Borup, J. H., Gallego, D. T., and Heffernan, P. G. *The Gerontologist* 21: 4–7

Bratter, B., and Tuvman, E. 1980. A peer counseling program in action. In *Nontraditional Therapy and Counseling with the Aged,* ed. S. S. Sargent. New York: Springer.

Brehm, H. P. 1980. Organization and financing of health care for the aged: Future implications. In *Second Conference on the Epidemiology of Aging,* eds. S. G. Haynes and M. Feinleib. Bethesda, MD: National Institutes of Health.

Brickel, C. M. 1979. The therapeutic roles of cat mascots

with a hospital-based geriatric population: A staff survey. *The Gerontologist* 19: 368–372.

Brickman, P.; Rabinowitz, V. C.; Karuza, J.; Coates, D.; Cohn, E.; and Kidder, L. 1982. Models of helping and coping. *American Psychologist* 37: 368–384.

Brink, T. L. 1979. *Geriatric psychotherapy.* N.Y.: Human Sciences Press.

Brinkman, S. D.; Smith, R. C.; Meyer, J. S.; Vroulis, G.; Shaw, T.; Gordon, J. R.; and Allen, R. H. 1982. Lecithin and memory training in suspected Alzheimer's disease. *Journal of Gerontology* 37: 4–9.

Brody, E. M.; Kleban, M. H.; Lawton, M. P.; and Moss, M. 1974. A longitudinal look at excess disabilities in the mentally impaired aged. *Journal of Gerontology* 29: 79–84.

Brody, E. M.; Kleban, M. H.; Lawton, M. P.; and Silverman, H. A. 1971. Excess disabilities of mentally impaired aged: Impact of individual treatment. *The Gerontologist* 11: 124–133.

Burnside, I. M. 1970. Loss: A constant theme in group work with the aged. *Hospital & Community Psychiatry,* 21: 173–177.

Burnside, I. M. 1978. *Working with the Elderly: Group Process and Techniques.* North Scituate, MA: Duxbury Press.

Butler, R. N. 1968. Toward a psychiatry of the life-cycle: Implications of socio-psychologic studies of the aging process for the psychotherapeutic situation. *Psychiatric Research Reports* 23: 233–248.

Butler, R. N., and Lewis, M. I. 1982. *Aging and Mental Health: Positive Psychosocial Approaches.* St. Louis: C. V. Mosby Co.

Carstensen, L. L., and Fremouw, W. J. 1981. The demonstration of a behavioral intervention for late life paranoia. *The Gerontologist* 21: 329–333.

Citrin, R. S., and Dixon, D. N. 1977. Reality orientation: A milieu therapy used in an institution for the aged. *The Gerontologist* 17: 39–43.

Clark, M. 1969. Cultural values and dependency in later life. In *The Dependencies of Old People,* ed. R. A. Kalish. Ann Arbor, MI: Institute of Gerontology.

Clayton, V., and Jellison, J. M. 1975. Preferences for the age and sex of advisors: A life span approach. *Developmental Psychology* 11: 861–862.

Coffman, T. L. 1981. Relocation and survival of institutionalized aged: A reexamination of the evidence. *The Gerontologist* 21: 483–500.

Corbin, S., and Nelson, T. 1980. Using angels and devils: A board game developed for play in nursing homes. *International Journal of Aging and Human Development* 11: 243–250.

Corby, N. 1977. Assertion training with aged populations. *Counseling Psychologist* 5: 69–74.

Cornbleth, T., and Cornbleth, C. 1969. Evaluation of the effectiveness of reality orientation classes in a nursing home unit. *Journal of the American Geriatrics Society* 27: 522–524.

Cross, D. G.; Sheehan, P. W.; and Khan, J. A. 1982. Short- and long-term follow-up of clients receiving insight-oriented therapy and behavior therapy. *Journal of Consulting and Clinical Psychology* 50: 103–112.

Crossman, L.; London, C.; and Barry, C. 1981. Older women caring for disabled spouses: A model for supportive services. *The Gerontologist* 21: 464–470.

Cyrus-Lutz, C., and Gaitz, C. M. 1972. Psychiatrists' attitudes toward the aged and aging. *The Gerontologist* 12: 163–167.

Danish, S. J.; Smyer, M. A.; and Nowak, C. A. 1980. Developmental intervention: Enhancing life-event processes. In *Life-Span Development and Behavior,* vol. 3, eds. P. B. Baltes and O. G. Brim. New York: Academic Press.

Davis, R. W. M., and Klopfer, W. G. 1977. Issues in psychotherapy with the aged. *Psychotherapy: Theory, Research and Practice* 14: 343–348.

Dörken, H. 1981. The use, cost and delivery organization of mental health and psychological services in the United States. In *Does Psychotherapy Return Its Costs?,* ed. B. Christiansen. Oslo: Norwegian Council for the Sciences and Humanities.

Dörken, H., and Webb, J. T. 1979. Licensed psychologists in health care: A survey of their practices. In *Psychology and National Health Insurance,* eds. C. A. Kiesler, N. A. Cummings, and G. R. VandenBos. Washington, D.C.: American Psychological Association.

Dychtwald, K. 1979. Humanistic gerontology: Holistic approaches. *Generations* 3(4): 21–22.

Dye, C. J. 1978. Psychologists' role in the provision of mental health care for the elderly. *Professional Psychology* 9:38–49.

Dye, C. J., and Erber, J. 1981. Two group procedures for the treatment of nursing home patients. *The Gerontologist* 21: 539–544.

Eisdorfer, C., and Stotsky, B. A. 1977. Intervention, treatment, and rehabilitation of psychiatric disorders. In *Handbook of the Psychology of Aging,* eds. J. E. Birren and K. W. Schaie. New York: Van Nostrand Reinhold.

Erikson, E. H. 1963. *Childhood and Society.* New York: W. W. Norton & Co.

Evans, R. L., and Jaureguy, B. M. 1982. Phone therapy outreach for blind elderly. *The Gerontologist* 22: 32–35.

Feigenbaum, E. M. 1973. Ambulatory treatment of the elderly. In *Mental Illness in Later Life,* eds. E. W. Busse and E. Pfeiffer. Washington, DC: American Psychiatric Association.

Fengler, A., and Goodrich, N. 1979. Wives of elderly disabled men: The hidden patients. *The Gerontologist* 19: 175–183.

Fischer, E. H., and Turner, J. L. B. 1970. Orientations to seeking professional help: Development and research utility of an attitude scale. *Journal of Consulting and Clinical Psychology* 35: 79–90.

Follette, W., and Cummings, N. A. 1967. Psychiatric services and medical utilization in a prepaid health plan setting. *Medical Care* 5: 25–35.

Folsom, J. C. 1968. Reality orientation for the elderly mental patient. *Journal of Geriatric Psychiatry,* 1: 291–307.

Ford, C. V., and Sbordonne, R. J. 1980. Attitudes of psychiatrists toward elderly patients. *American Journal of Psychiatry* 137: 571–575.

Frank, J. D. 1976. Restoration of morale and behavior change. In *What Makes Behavior Change Possible?*, ed. A. Burton. New York: Brunner/Mazel.

Frankfather, D. L. 1981. Provider discretion and consumer preference in long-term care for seriously disabled elderly. *The Gerontologist* 21: 366–373.

Freud, S. 1924. On psychotherapy. In *Collected Papers*, vol. 1. London: Hogarth Press.

Friedman, S. 1975. The resident welcoming committee: Institutionalized elderly in volunteer services to their peers. *The Gerontologist* 15: 362–367.

Furchtgott, E., and Busemeyer, J. R. 1981. Age preferences for professional helpers. *Journal of Gerontology* 36: 90–92.

Gaitz, C. M. 1974. Barriers to the delivery of psychiatric services to the elderly. *The Gerontologist* 14: 210–214.

Gaitz, C. M., and Varner, R. V. 1980. Adjustment disorders of late life: Stress disorders. In *Handbook of Geriatric Psychiatry*, eds. E. W. Busse and D. G. Blazer. New York: Van Nostrand Reinhold.

Gallagher, D. 1981. Behavioral group therapy with elderly depressives: An experimental study. In *Behavioral Group Therapy*, eds. D. Upper and S. Ross. Champaign, IL: Research Press.

Gallagher, D., and Frankel, A. S. 1980. Depression in (an) older adult(s): A moderate structuralist viewpoint. *Psychotherapy: Theory, Research, and Practice* 17: 101–104.

Gallagher, D., and Thompson, L. W. 1981. *Depression in the Elderly: A Behavioral Treatment Manual*. Los Angeles, CA: University of Southern California Press.

Gallagher, D., and Thompson, L. W. 1982. Elders' maintenance of treatment benefits following individual psychotherapy for depression: Results of a pilot study and preliminary data from an ongoing replication study. Paper presented at the annual meeting of the American Psychological Association, Washington, DC.

Gallagher, D., and Thompson, L. W. In press. Cognitive therapy for depression in the elderly. A promising model for treatment and research. In *Depression in the Elderly*, eds. L. Breslau and M. Haug. New York: Springer.

Garfield, S. 1978. Research on client variables in psychotherapy. In *Handbook of Psychotherapy and Behavior Change: An Empirical Analysis*, eds. S. L. Garfield and A. E. Bergin. New York: Wiley & Sons.

Garfield, S. L., and Bergin, A. E., eds. 1978. *Handbook of Psychotherapy and Behavior Change: An Empirical Analysis*. New York: Wiley & Sons.

Garfinkel, R. 1975. The reluctant therapist. *The Gerontologist* 15: 136–137.

Garrison, J. 1978. Stress management training for the elderly: A psychoeducational approach. *Journal of the American Geriatrics Society* 26: 397–403.

Garrison, J. E., and Howe, J. 1976. Community intervention with the elderly: A social network approach. *Journal of the American Geriatrics Society* 24: 329–333.

Gatz, M.; Barbarin, O. A.; Tyler, F. B.; Mitchell, R. E.; Moran, J. A.; Wirzbicki, P. J.; Crawford, J.; and Engelman, A. 1982. Enhancement of individual and community competence: The older adult as community worker. *American Journal of Community Psychology* 10: 291–303.

Gatz, M.; Hileman, C. S.; and Amaral, P. In press. Older adult paraprofessionals: Working with and in behalf of older adults. *Journal of Counseling Psychology*.

Gatz, M.; Siegler, I. C.; and Dibner, S. S. 1979–80. Individual and community: Normative conflicts in the development of a new therapeutic community for older persons. *International Journal of Aging and Human Development* 10: 249–263.

Gatz, M.; Smyer, M. A.; and Lawton, M. P. 1980. The mental health system and the older adult. In *Aging in the 1980s: Psychological Issues*, ed. L. W. Poon. Washington, DC: American Psychological Association.

Gilbert, J. G. 1977. Psychotherapy with the aged. *Psychotherapy: Theory, Research and Practice* 14: 394–402.

Ginsburg, A. B., and Goldstein, S. G. 1974. Age bias in referral to psychological consultation. *Journal of Gerontology* 29: 410–415.

Goldberg, I. D.; Krantz, G.; and Locke, B. Z. 1970. Effect of a short-term outpatient psychiatric therapy benefit on the utilization of medical services in a prepaid group practice medical program. *Medical Care* 8: 419–428.

Goldfarb, A. I. 1955. Psychotherapy of aged persons. *Psychoanalytic Review* 42: 180–187.

Goldfarb, A. I. 1969. The psychodynamics of dependency and the search for aid. In *The Dependencies of Old People*, ed. R. A. Kalish. Ann Arbor, MI: Institute of Gerontology.

Goldfried, M. R. 1980. Toward the delineation of therapeutic change principles. *American Psychologist* 35: 991–999.

Gomes-Schwartz, B.; Hadley, S. W.; and Strupp, H. H. 1978. Individual psychotherapy and behavior therapy. In *Annual Review of Psychology*, vol. 29, eds. M. R. Rosenzweig and L. W. Porter. Palo Alto, CA: Annual Reviews, Inc.

Goplerud, E. N. 1979. Unexpected consequences of deinstitutionalization of the mentally disabled elderly. *American Journal of Community Psychology* 7: 315–328.

Gordon, S. K., and Hallauer, D. S. 1976. Impact of a friendly visiting program on attitudes of college students toward the aged: A pedagogical note. *The Gerontologist* 16: 371–376.

Gordon, R. E.; Patterson, R. L.; Eberly, D. A.; and Penner, L. A. 1980. Modular treatment of psychiatric patients. In *Current Psychiatric Therapies*, vol. 20, ed. J. H. Masserman. New York: Grune and Stratton.

Gottesman, L. E.; Donahue, W.; Coons, D.; and Ciarlo, J. 1969. Extended care of the aged: Psychosocial aspects. *Journal of Geriatrics and Psychiatry* 2: 220–237.

Griffin, L. W., and Gottesman, L. E. 1983. Training professionals in aging and mental health: It makes a difference. In *Mental Health and Aging: Programs and Evaluations*, eds. M. A. Smyer and M. Gatz. Beverly Hills, CA: Sage Publications.

Gross, A. E.; Wallston, B. S.; and Piliavin, I. M. 1979. Reactance, attribution, equity, and the help recipient. *Journal of Applied Social Psychology* 9: 297–313.

Grotjahn, M. 1955. Analytic psychotherapy in the elderly. *Psychoanalytic Review* 42: 419–427.

Gubrium, J. F., and Ksander, M. 1975. On multiple realities and reality orientation. *The Gerontologist* 15: 142–145.

Gutmann, D.; Griffith, B.; and Grunes, J. 1982. Developmental contributions to the late-onset affective disorders. In *Lifespan Development and Behavior,* vol. IV, ed. P. B. Baltes. New York: Academic Press.

Hanssen, A. M.; Meima, N. J.; Buckspan, L. M.; Henderson, B. E.; Helbig, T. L.; and Zarit, S. H. 1978. Correlates of senior center participation. *The Gerontologist* 18: 193–199.

Harris, R. 1975. Breaking the barriers to better health-care delivery for the aged. *The Gerontologist* 15: 52–56.

Harris, C. S., and Ivory, P. B. C. B. 1976. An outcome evaluation of reality orientation therapy with geriatric patients in a state mental hospital. *The Gerontologist* 16: 496–503.

Hartford, M. E. 1980. The use of group methods for work with the aged. In *Handbook of Mental Health and Aging,* eds. J. E. Birren and R. B. Sloane. Englewood Cliffs, N.J.: Prentice-Hall.

Haug, M. R. 1981. Age and medical care utilization patterns. *Journal of Gerontology* 36: 103–111.

Hausman, C. P. 1979. Short-term counseling groups for people with elderly parents. *The Gerontologist* 19: 102–107.

Hellebrandt, F. A. 1978. Comment: The senile dement in our midst: A look at the other side of the coin. *The Gerontologist* 18: 67–70.

Herr, J. J., and Weakland, J. H. 1979. *Counseling Elders and Their Families: Practical Techniques to Applied Gerontology.* New York: Springer.

Hiatt, H. 1971. Dynamic psychotherapy with the aging patient. *American Journal of Psychotherapy* 25: 591–600.

Hickey, T.; Rakowski, W.; Hultsch, D. F.; and Fatula, B. J. 1976. Attitudes toward aging as a function of in-service training and practitioner age. *Journal of Gerontology* 31: 681–686.

Hirschowitz, R. G. 1973. Foster grandparents program: Preventive intervention with the elderly poor. *Hospital Community Psychiatry* 24: 558–559.

Holden, C. 1981. Human-animal relationship under scrutiny. *Science* 214: 418–420.

Hughston, G. A., and Merriam, S. B. 1982. Reminiscence: A nonformal technique for improving cognitive functioning in the aged. *International Journal of Aging and Human Development* 15: 139–149.

Hussian, R. A. 1981. *Geriatric Psychology: A Behavioral Perspective.* N.Y.: Van Nostrand Reinhold Co.

Ingebretson, R. 1977. Psychotherapy with the elderly. *Psychotherapy: Theory, Research and Practice* 14: 319–332.

Ingersoll, B., and Silverman, A. 1978. Comparative group psychotherapy for the aged. *The Gerontologist* 18: 201–206.

Jarvik, L.; Mintz, J.; Steuer, J.; Gerner, R.; Aldrich, J.; Hammen, C.; Linde, S.; McCarley, T.; Motoike, P.;

and Rosen, R. 1982. Comparison of tricyclic antidepressants and group psychotherapies in geriatric depressed patients: An interim analysis. In *Treatment of Depression: Old Controversies and New Approaches,* eds. P. J. Clayton and J. E. Barrett. New York: Raven Press.

Jones, K. R., and Vischi, T. R. 1979. Impact of alcohol, drug abuse, and mental health treatment on medical care utilization: A review of the research literature. *Medical Care* 17 (Supplement): 1–82.

Kahn, R. L. 1975. The mental health system and the future aged. *The Gerontologist* 15(1, Part II): 24–31.

Kahn, R. L. 1982. Services and settings. In *Psychology and the Older Adult: Challenges for Training in the 1980s,* eds. J. F. Santos and G. R. VandenBos. Washington, D.C.: American Psychological Association.

Kahn, R. L., and Zarit, S. H. 1974. Evaluation of mental health programs for the aged. In *Evaluation of Behavioral Programs,* eds. P. O. Davidson, F. W. Clark, and L. A. Hamerlynch. Champaign, IL: Research Press.

Kalson, L. 1976. MASH: A program of social interaction between institutionalized aged and adult mentally retarded persons. *The Gerontologist* 16: 340–348.

Karasu, T. B.; Stein, S. P.; and Charles, E. S. 1979. Age factors in patient-therapist relationship. *Journal of Nervous and Mental Disease* 167: 100–104.

Karpf, R. J. 1977. The psychotherapy of depression. *Psychotherapy: Theory, Research and Practice* 14: 349–353.

Kastenbaum, R. 1964. The reluctant therapist. In *New Thoughts on Old Age,* ed. R. Kastenbaum. N.Y.: Springer.

Kastenbaum, R. 1972. Beer, wine, and mutual gratification in the gerontopolis. In *Research, Planning, and Action for the Elderly,* eds. D. P. Kent, R. Kastenbaum, and S. Sherwood. New York: Behavioral Publications.

Kastenbaum, R. 1978. Personality theory, therapeutic approaches, and the elderly client. In *The Clinical Psychology of Aging,* eds. M. Storandt, I. C. Siegler, and M. F. Elias. New York: Plenum.

Kastenbaum, R. J.; Barber, T. X.; Wilson, S. G.; Ryder, B. L.; and Hathaway, L. B. 1981. *Old, Sick, and Helpless: Where Therapy Begins.* Cambridge, MA: Ballinger Publishing Co.

Keller, J. F.; Croake, J. W.; and Brooking, J. Y. 1975. Effects of a program in rational thinking on anxieties in older persons. *Journal of Counseling Psychology* 22: 54–57.

Kleban, M. H.; Lawton, M. P.; Brody, E. M.; and Moss, M. 1975. Characteristics of mentally-impaired aged profiting from individualized treatment. *Journal of Gerontology* 30: 90–96.

Kleban, M. H.; Lawton, M. P.; Brody, E. M.; and Moss, M. 1976. Behavioral observations of mentally impaired aged: Those who decline and those who do not. *Journal of Gerontology* 31: 333–339.

Kleinman, M. B., and Clemente, F. 1976. Support for the medical profession among the aged. *International Journal of Health Services* 6: 295–299.

Knight, B. 1978–1979. Psychotherapy and behavior change in the non-institutionalized aged. *International*

Journal of Aging and Human Development, 9: 221–236.

Knight, B. 1983. An evaluation of a mobile geriatric outreach team. In *Mental Health and Aging: Programs and Evaluations,* eds. M. A. Smyer and M. Gatz. Beverly Hills, CA: Sage Publications.

Kobrynski, B. 1973. Innovations in programs of care for the elderly. *The Gerontologist* 13: 50–53.

Kovacs, A. L. 1977. Rapid intervention strategies in work with the aged. *Psychotherapy: Theory, Research and Practice* 14: 368–372.

Kovar, M. G. 1980. Morbidity and health care utilization. In *Second Conference on the Epidemiology of Aging,* eds. S. G. Haynes and M. Feinleib. Bethesda, MD: National Institutes of Health.

Kowalski, N. C. 1981. Institutional relocation: Current programs and applied approaches. *The Gerontologist* 21: 512–519.

Kucharski, L. T.; White, R. M.; and Schratz, M. 1979. Age bias, referral for psychological assistance and the private physician. *Journal of Gerontology,* 34: 423–428.

Kulka, R. A.; Veroff, J.; and Douvan, E. 1979. Social class and the use of professional help for personal problems: 1957 and 1976. *Journal of Health and Social Behavior* 20: 2–17.

Kushler, M. G., and Davidson, W. S. 1978. Alternative modes of outreach: An experimental comparison. *The Gerontologist* 18: 355–362.

Kuypers, J. A., and Bengtson, V. L. 1973. Social breakdown and competence. *Human Development* 16: 181–201.

Lago, D.; Connell, C. M.; and Knight, B. 1983. Initial evaluation of PACT (People and Animals Coming Together): A companion animal program for community-dwelling older persons. In *Mental Health and Aging: Programs and Evaluations,* eds. M. Smyer and M. Gatz. Beverly Hills, CA: Sage.

Langer, E. J., and Rodin, J. 1976. The effects of choice and enhanced personal responsibility for the aged: A field experiment in an institutional setting. *Journal of Personality and Social Psychology* 34: 191–198.

Langer, E.; Rodin, J.; Beck, P.; Weinman, C.; and Spitzer, L. 1979. Environmental determinants of memory improvement in late adulthood. *Journal of Personality and Social Psychology* 37: 2003–2013.

Lasky, R. G., and Salomone, P. R. 1977. Attraction to psychotherapy: Influences of therapist status and therapist-patient age similarity. *Journal of Clinical Psychology* 33: 511–516.

LaWall, J. 1981. Conjoint therapy of psychiatric problems in the elderly. *Journal of the American Geriatric Society* 29: 89–91.

Lawton, M. P. 1979. Clinical geropsychology: Problems and prospects. In *Master Lecture Series on the Psychology of Aging.* Washington, D.C.: American Psychological Association.

Lawton, M. P., and Gottesman, L. E. 1974. Psychological services to the elderly. *American Psychologist* 29: 689–693.

Lazarus, L. W. 1976. A program for the elderly at a private psychiatric hospital. *The Gerontologist* 16: 125–131.

Lazarus, L. W. 1980. Self psychology and psychotherapy with the elderly: Theory and practice. *Journal of Geriatric Psychiatry* 13: 69–88.

Lazarus, L. W.; Stafford, B.; Cooper, K.; Cohler, B.; and Dysken, M. 1981. A pilot study of an Alzheimer patient's relatives discussion group. *The Gerontologist* 21: 353–358.

Lesser, J.; Lazarus, L. W.; Frankel, R.; and Havasy, S. 1981. Reminiscence group therapy with psychotic geriatric inpatients. *The Gerontologist* 21: 291–296.

Levine, M. 1981. *The History and Politics of Community Mental Health.* New York: Oxford University Press.

Leviton, D., and Santa Maria, L. 1979. The Adults Health & Development Program: Descriptive and evaluative data. *The Gerontologist* 19: 534–543.

Levy, S. M.; Derogatis, L. R.; Gallagher, D.; and Gatz, M. 1980. Intervention with older adults and the evaluation of outcome. In *Aging in the 1980s,* ed. L. W. Poon. Washington, D.C.: American Psychological Association.

Lewinsohn, P. M.; Muñoz, R. F.; Youngren, M. A.; and Zeiss, A. M. 1978. *Control Your Depression.* Englewood Cliffs, NJ: Prentice-Hall.

Lewis, M. I., and Butler, R. N. 1974. Life-review therapy: Putting memories to work in individual and group psychotherapy. *Geriatrics* 29: 165–173.

Lieberman, M. A., and Gourash, N. 1979. Evaluating the effects of change groups on the elderly. *The International Journal of Group Pyschotherapy* 29: 283–304.

Lipsitt, D. R. 1969. A medical-psychological approach to dependency in the aged. In *The Dependencies of Old People,* ed. R. A. Kalish. Ann Arbor, MI: Institute of Gerontology.

Looft, W. R. 1973. Reflections on intervention in old age: Motives, goals and assumptions. *The Gerontologist* 13: 6–10.

Lopez, S. 1984. In search of clinical judgement bias: Some conceptual guide posts. A paper presented at the Western Psychological Association Annual Meeting, Los Angeles.

Lopez, M. A.; Hoyer, W. J.; Goldstein, A. P.; Gershaw, N. J.; and Sprafkin, R. P. 1980. Effects of overlearning and incentive on the acquisition and transfer of interpersonal skills with institutionalized elderly. *Journal of Gerontology* 35: 403–408.

Lynch, G., and Waxenberg, B. 1971. Marital therapy with the aging: A case study. *Psychotherapy: Theory, Research and Practice* 8: 59–63.

MacDonald, M. L., and Settin, J. M. 1978. Reality orientation versus sheltered workshops as treatment for the institutionalized aging. *Journal of Gerontology* 33: 416–421.

McGee, J., and Lakin, M. 1977. Social perspectives on psychotherapy with the aged. *Psychotherapy: Theory, Research and Practice* 14: 333–342.

McIntosh, J. L.; Hubbard, R. W.; and Santos, J. F. 1981. Suicide among the elderly: A review of issues with case studies. *Journal of Gerontological Social Work* 4: 63–74.

Mahoney, M. J. 1982. Psychotherapy and human change processes. In *Master Lecture Series on Psychotherapy Research and Behavior Change.* Washington, D.C.: American Psychological Association.

Martin, L. J., and deGruchy, C. 1930. *Salvaging Old Age.* New York: Macmillan.

Mintz, J.; Steuer, J.; and Jarvik, L. 1981. Psychotherapy with depressed elderly patients: Research considerations. *Journal of Consulting and Clinical Psychology* 49: 542–549.

Mishara, B. L. 1978. Geriatric patients who improve in token economy and general milieu treatment programs: A multivariate analysis. *Journal of Consulting and Clinical Psychology* 46: 1340–1348.

Moen, E. 1978. The reluctance of the elderly to accept help. *Social Problems* 25: 293–303.

Mugford, R., and M'Comisky, J. 1975. Some recent work on the psychotherapeutic value of cage birds with old people. In *Pet Animals and Society,* ed. R. S. Anderson. London: Baillière Tindall.

Mulligan, M. A., and Bennett, R. 1977–78. Assessment of mental health and social problems during multiple friendly visits: The development and evaluation of a friendly visiting program for the isolated elderly. *International Journal of Aging and Human Development* 8: 43–65.

Myers, J. K., and Weissman, M. M. 1980. Psychiatric disorders and their treatment. *Medical Care* 18: 117–123.

Nardone, M. 1980. Characteristics predicting community care for mentally impaired older persons. *The Gerontologist* 20: 661–668.

O'Brien, J. E., and Wagner, D. L. 1980. Help seeking by the frail elderly: Problems in network analysis. *The Gerontologist* 20: 78–83.

Oberleder, M. 1966. Psychotherapy with the aging: An art of the possible? *Psychotherapy: Theory, Research and Practice* 3: 139–142.

Oberleder, M. 1970. Crisis therapy in mental breakdown of the aging. *The Gerontologist* 10:111–114.

Ory, M. G., and Goldberg, E. 1982. Pet possession and life satisfaction in elderly women. In *International Conference on The Human Animal Bond,* eds. A. H. Katcher and A. M. Beck. Philadelphia, PA: University of Pennsylvania Press.

Ozarin, L. D.; Taube, C.; and Spaner, F. E. 1972. Operations indices for community mental health centers. *American Journal of Psychiatry* 128: 1511–1515.

Parloff, M. B. 1979. Can psychotherapy research guide the policymaker? *American Psychologist* 34: 296–306.

Parloff, M. B.; Waskow, I. E.; and Wolfe, B. E. 1978. Research on therapist variables in relation to process and outcome. In *Handbook of Psychotherapy and Behavior Change: An Empirical Analysis,* eds. S. L. Garfield and A. E. Bergin. New York: Wiley.

Patterson, R. D. 1976. Services for the aged in community mental health centers. *American Journal of Psychiatry* 133: 271–273.

Pavey, S. *Some Mechanisms of Change in Psychotherapy.* In preparation.

Petty, B. J.; Moeller, T. P.; and Campbell, R. Z. 1976.

Support groups for elderly persons in the community. *The Gerontologist* 16: 522–528.

Pfeiffer, E. 1976. Psychotherapy with elderly patients. In *Geriatric Psychiatry: A Handbook for Psychiatrists and Primary Care Physicians,* eds. L. Bellak and T. B. Karasu. New York: Grune and Stratton.

Pfeiffer, E., and Busse, W. E. 1973. Mental disorders in later life: Affective disorders, paranoid, neurotic, and situational reactions. In *Mental Illness in Later Life,* eds. E. W. Busse, and E. Pfeiffer. Washington, D.C.: American Psychiatric Association.

Power, C. A., and McCarron, L. T. 1975. Treatment of depression in persons residing in homes for the aged. *The Gerontologist* 15: 132–135.

Pressey, S. L., and Pressey, A. D. 1972. Major neglected need opportunity: Old-age counseling. *Journal of Counseling Psychology* 19: 362–366.

Rechtschaffen, A. 1959. Psychotherapy with geriatric patients: A review of the literature. *Journal of Gerontology* 14: 73–84.

Reifler, B. V.; Cox, G. B.; and Hanley, R. J. 1981. Problems of mentally ill elderly as perceived by patients, families, and clinicians. *The Gerontologist* 21: 165–170.

Reinhart, R. A., and Sargent, S. S. 1980. The humanistic approach: The Ventura County Creative Aging Workshops. In *Nontraditional Therapy and Counseling with the Aged,* ed. S. S. Sargent. New York: Springer.

Reinke, B. J.; Holmes, D. S.; and Denney, N. W. 1981. Influence of a "friendly visitor" program on the cognitive functioning and morale of elderly persons. *American Journal of Community Psychology* 9: 491–504.

Richards, W. S., and Thorpe, G. L. 1978. Behavioral approaches to the problems of later life. In *The Clinical Psychology of Aging,* eds. M. Storandt; I. C. Siegler, and M. F. Elias. New York: Plenum.

Robinson, B., and Thurnher, M. 1979. Taking care of aged parents: A family cycle transition. *The Gerontologist,* 19: 586–593.

Rodin, J. 1980. Managing the stress of aging: The role of control and coping. In *Coping and Health,* eds. H. Ursin and S. Levine. New York: Academic Press.

Rodin, J., and Langer, E. J. 1977. Long-term effects of a control-relevant intervention with institutionalized aged. *Journal of Personality and Social Psychology* 35: 897–902.

Rogers, C. R. 1957. The necessary and sufficient conditions of therapeutic personality change. *Journal of Consulting Psychology* 21: 95–103.

Ronch, J. L., and Maizler, J. S. 1977. Individual psychotherapy with the institutionalized aged. *American Journal of Orthopsychiatry* 47: 275–283.

Rosen, J. C., and Wiens, A. N. 1979. Changes in medical problems and use of medical services following psychological intervention. *American Psychologist* 34: 420–431.

Safirstein, S. L. 1972. Psychotherapy for geriatric patients. *New York State Journal of Medicine* 72: 2743–2748.

Sallis, J. F.; Lichstein, K. L.; Clarkson, A. D.; Stalgaitis, S.; and Campbell, M. In press. Anxiety and depression management for the elderly. *International Journal of Behavioral Geriatrics.*

Saltz, R. 1977. Fostergrandparenting: A unique child-care service. In *Looking Ahead: A Woman's Guide to the Problems and Joys of Growing Older,* eds. L. E. Troll, J. Israel, and K. Israel. Englewood Cliffs, NJ: Prentice-Hall.

Santos, J. F.; Hubbard, R. W.; McIntosh, J. L.; and Eisner, H. R. In press. Community mental health and the elderly: Serivice and training approaches. *Journal of Community Psychology.*

Schienle, D. R., and Eiler, J. M. In press. Clinical intervention with older adults. In *The Impact of Chronic Disabling Conditions on Self and Family: A Lifespan Approach,* eds. M. G. Eisenberg, M. Jansen, and L. Sutkin. New York: Springer.

Schmidt, L. J.; Reinhardt, A. M.; Kane, R. L.; and Olsen, D. M. 1977. The mentally ill in nursing homes. *Archives of General Psychiatry* 34: 687–691.

Schulz, R. 1976. Effects of control and predictability on the physical and psychological well-being of the institutionalized aged. *Journal of Personality and Social Psychology* 33: 563–573.

Schulz, R., and Brenner, G. 1977. Relocation of the aged: A review and theoretical analysis. *Journal of Gerontology* 32: 323–333.

Schulz, R., and Hanusa, B. H. 1978. Long-term effects of control and predictability-enhancing interventions: Findings and ethical issues. *Journal of Personality and Social Psychology* 11: 1194–1201.

Settin, J. M. 1982. Clinical judgment in geropsychology practice. *Psychotherapy: Theory, Research and Practice* 19: 397–404.

Shanas, E., and Maddox, G. L. 1976. Aging, health, and the organization of health resources. In *Handbook of Aging and the Social Sciences,* eds. R. H. Binstock and E. Shanas. N.Y.: Van Nostrand Reinhold.

Sherman, E. 1981. *Counseling the Aging: An Integrative Approach.* New York: The Free Press.

Shows, W. D. 1977. A psychological theory of the later years: C. G. Jung. In *Geropsychology: A Model of Training and Clinical Service,* ed. W. D. Gentry. Cambridge, MA: Ballinger Publishing Co.

Siegel, B., and Lasker, J. 1978. Deinstitutionalizing elderly patients: A program for resocialization. *The Gerontologist* 18: 293–300.

Smith, M. L., and Glass, G. V. 1977. Meta-analysis of psychotherapy outcome studies. *American Psychologist* 32: 752–760.

Solomon, K. 1982. Social antecedents of learned helplessness in the health care setting. *The Gerontologist* 22: 282–287.

Sparacino, J. 1978–1979. Individual psychotherapy with the aged: A selected review. *International Journal of Aging and Human Development* 9: 197–220.

Spence, D. L.; Cohen, S.; and Kowalski, C. 1975. Mental health, age, and community living. *The Gerontologist* 15: 77–82.

Sperbeck, D. J., and Whitbourne, S. K. 1981. Dependency in the institutional setting: A behavioral training program for geriatric staff. *The Gerontologist* 21: 268–275.

Stafford, J. L., and Bringle, R. G. 1980. The influence of task success on elderly women's interest in new activities. *The Gerontologist* 20: 642–648.

Steer, R. A., and Boger, W. P. 1975. Milieu therapy with psychiatric-medically infirm patients. *The Gerontologist* 15: 138–141.

Stern, K.; Smith, J. M.; and Frank, M. 1953. Mechanisms of transference and countertransference in psychotherapeutic and social work with the aged. *Journal of Gerontology* 8: 328–332.

Steuer, J. L. 1982a. Psychotherapy for depressed elders. In *Depression in Late Life,* ed. D. G. Blazer. St. Louis, MO: C. V. Mosby Company.

Steuer, J. L. 1982b. Psychotherapy with older women: Ageism and sexism in traditional practice. *Psychotherapy: Theory, Research and Practice* 19: 429–436.

Steuer, J. L. 1982c. Cognitive-behavioral vs. psychodynamic group psychotherapy in the treatment of geriatric depression. Paper presented at the annual meeting of the American Psychological Association, Washington, D.C.

Steuer, J. L., and Hammen, C. L. In press. Cognitive-behavioral group therapy for the depressed elderly: Issues and adaptations. *Cognitive Theory and Research.*

Storandt, M. 1978. Other approaches to therapy. In *The Clinical Psychology of Aging,* eds. M. Storandt, I. C. Siegler, and M. F. Elias. New York: Plenum.

Swensen, C. 1982. A curriculum for training psychologists for work with the aging. In *Psychology and the Older Adult: Challenges for Training in the 1980s,* eds. J. F. Santos and G. R. VandenBos. Washington, DC: American Psychological Association.

Szapocznik, J.; Santiseban, D.; Hervis, O.; Spencer, F.; and Kurtines, W. M. 1981. Treatment of depression among Cuban American elders: Some validational evidence for a life enhancement counseling approach. *Journal of Consulting and Clinical Psychology* 49:752–754.

Tobin, S. S. 1969. Institutional dependency in the aged. In *The Dependencies of Old People,* ed. R. A. Kalish. Ann Arbor, MI: Institute of Gerontology.

Toseland, R. 1977. A problem-solving group workshop for older persons. *Social Work* 22: 325–326.

Toseland, R. W.; Decker, J.; and Bliesner, J. 1979. A community outreach program for socially isolated older persons. *Journal of Gerontological Social Work* 1: 211–223.

U. S. General Accounting Office. 1982. *The Elderly Remain in Need of Mental Health Services.* Washington, D.C.: Document No. HRD-82-112, Government Printing Office.

VandenBos, G. R. and Pino, C. D. 1980. Research on the outcome of psychotherapy. In *Psychotherapy: Practice, Research, Policy,* ed. G. R. VandenBos. Beverly Hills, CA: Sage Publications.

VandenBos, G. R.; Stapp, J.; and Kilburg, R. R. 1981. Health service providers in psychology: Results of the 1978 APA Human Resources Survey. *American Psychologist* 36: 1395–1418.

Verwoerdt, A. 1976. *Clinical Geropsychiatry.* Baltimore, MD: Williams & Wilkins.

Wallach, H. F.; Kelley, F.; and Abrahams, J. P. 1979. Psychosocial rehabilitation for chronic geriatric patients: An intergenerational approach. *The Gerontologist* 19: 464–470.

Watzlawick, P.; Weakland, J.; and Fisch, R. 1974. *Change: Principles of Problem Formation and Problem Resolution.* New York: Norton.

Wayne, G. J. 1953. Modified psychoanalytic therapy in senescence. *The Psychoanalytic Review,* 40(2): 99–116.

Weber, R. E. 1977. Evaluative research: Community mental health services for the aged. In *Evaluative Research on Social Programs for the Elderly,* Administration on Aging, Department of Health, Education & Welfare. Washington, D.C.: U. S. Government Printing Office.

Weinberg, J. 1976. On adding insight to injury. *The Gerontologist* 16 (Part I): 6–10.

Weinberg, J. 1981. Comments: Needs for health care providers: Implications for training. *Gerontology and Geriatrics Education* 1: 260–262.

Wells, K. B.; Manning, W. G., Jr.; Duan, N.; Ware, J. E., Jr.; and Newhouse, J. P. 1982. *Cost-sharing and the Demand for Ambulatory Mental Health Services.* R-2960-HHS. Santa Monica, CA: The Rand Corporation.

Wheeler, E. G. 1980. Assertive training groups for the aging. In *Nontraditional Therapy and Counseling with the Aged,* ed. S. S. Sargent. New York: Springer.

Wheeler, E. G., and Knight, B. 1981. Morrie: A case study. *The Gerontologist* 21: 323–328.

Wilensky, H., and Weiner, M. B. 1977. Facing reality in psychotherapy with the aging. *Psychotherapy: Theory, Research and Practice* 14: 373–378.

Wolff, K. 1971. Rehabilitating geriatric patients. *Hospital Community Psychiatry* 22: 8–11.

Yalom, I. D. 1970. *The Theory and Practice of Group Psychotherapy.* New York: Basic Books.

Zarit, S. H. 1980. *Aging and Mental Disorders.* New York: Free Press.

Zarit, S. H.; Cole, K. D.; and Guider, R. L. 1981. Memory training strategies and subjective complaints of memory in the aged. *The Gerontologist* 21: 158–164.

Zarit, S. H.; Gallagher, D.; and Kramer, N. 1981. Memory training in the community aged: Effects on depression, memory complaint, and memory performance. *Educational Gerontology* 6: 11–27.

Zarit, S. H.; Reever, K. E.; and Bach-Peterson, S. 1980. Relatives of the impaired elderly: Correlates of feelings of burden. *The Gerontologist* 20: 649–655.

Zarit, S. H., and Zarit, J. M. 1982. Families under stress: Interventions for caregivers of senile dementia patients. *Psychotherapy: Theory, Research and Practice* 19: 461–471.

Zarit, S. H.; Zarit, J. M.; and Reever, K. E. 1982. Memory training for severe memory loss: Effects on senile dementia patients and their families. *The Gerontologist* 22: 373–377.

Zepelin, H.; Wolfe, C. S.; and Kleinplatz, F. 1981. Evaluation of a yearlong reality orientation program. *Journal of Gerontology* 36: 70–77.

Zinberg, N. E. 1967. Geriatric psychiatry: Needs and problems. *The Gerontologist* 4: 130–135.

6 PSYCHOLOGICAL APPLICATIONS TO SOCIETY

29
AGING IN INDUSTRY

Ross Stagner

Professor Emeritus of Psychology
Faculty Associate, Institute of Gerontology
Wayne State University

INTRODUCTION

Concern over the alleged inefficiency of elderly workers has been with us for many years, centuries even, but has been accentuated recently by the increasing numbers of such employees and retirees. Advances in public health have led to longer life spans and to a demand for useful, income-producing work for these older citizens. Simultaneously, concern over the increasing number of retirees, the disabled, and other nonproductive individuals has increased, focusing attention on the smaller number of productive citizens who must support the nonproducers (the "dependency ratio"). Demographic projections indicate that there will be an increase of productive workers per unit population until 1990; by 2000 A.D., however, it appears that the dependency burden will increase significantly.

Problems of the aging work force thus have become matters of concern in psychology and related fields. Glickman (1982) organized a conference in April 1981 that surveyed the available data on the abilities of aging employees and the steps by which employers could optimize the benefits of retaining older workers while minimizing the losses caused by their alleged inefficiency. It is probable that many such efforts will follow as psychologists and industrial relations experts seek to improve our data base and interpret the existing material for governments and for private industries.

THE STEREOTYPE OF THE AGING WORKER

The problem of aging in industry is peculiarly complicated by the difference between perceived reality and "objective" reality. Most discrimination against aging employees is based on an erroneous perception of older persons as less capable, less efficient, less productive than their younger counterparts. That this judgment is usually made by executives even older than the employee being discriminated against merely adds to the irony.

Pressures on employees to accept early retirement derive from an assumed decline in competence. Sheppard and Rix (1977, p. 150) sampled corporate executives' opinions on this point and concluded: "Many corporate officers maintain . . . that the costs of early retirement are returned to them in full. They believe that retirement of older workers permits the more rapid promotion of younger (and ostensibly more capable) workers who might otherwise leave the firm."

Even experienced psychologists make statements that foster, perhaps unintentionally, this stereotyped view of older individuals as incompetent. Sprott (1980, p. 160) wrote that "Most of us [researchers] agree that performance in many complex learning situations declines with advancing age." Although this may be true for populations of workers, it is false for many individuals. Similarly, Levinson

(1978, p. 213) exaggerates the decrement in ability as the years go by: "One important change [with middle age] . . . is the decline in bodily and psychological powers: In his late thirties and early forties a man falls well below his earlier peak levels of functioning." This sweeping generalization is demonstrably false for many individuals and provides unjustifiable support for the prejudicial view of older persons held by many employers.

Researchers in psychology (not to mention sociology, economics, and engineering) are in part responsible for this anomaly. Many research reports conclude with a summary sentence to the effect that "there is a significant difference in speed of cognition," or movement, or some other function "in favor of younger workers." Clearly, such research summaries provide "scientific" support for discriminatory practices. What is needed is a shift to a type of reporting that emphasizes that "30% of older workers exceeded the median performance of the younger group"—which is a typical finding—so that personnel executives would be constantly reminded that older employees are not identical to one another. In an ideal society, each individual would be evaluated on his or her own merits, as to capacities, skills, motivation, wisdom, etc. Perhaps, if each of us were treated "according to his just deserts," few would escape whipping, but more would escape punishment that is not deserved.

With this cautionary preface, we can survey some of the existing practices in industry, some of the relevant data on older workers, and some hypotheses about processes not yet validated by research. Some emphasis will also be placed on investigations still needed.

Dimensions of the Stereotype

The stereotype of the elderly worker, of course, is one including attributes such as slowed performance, decreased ability to learn new skills, more accidents, rigidity, resistance to supervision, irritability, and poor health. Craft et al. (1979) got at the dimensions of this stereotype by an ingenious method. Prospective employers were presented with resumes of hypothetical applicants for employ-

ment. All details of education, experience, marital status, etc., were held constant, but the reported chronological age was varied systematically across judges. The ages used (to fit reported work history) were 35, 50, 60, and 70 years. The judges (MBA candidates, most of whom held personnel staff jobs) indicated on an adjective check list that the older candidates were more likely to be opinionated, lower in physical strength, less serious, and less ambitious. Rosen and Jerdee (1976b) used a similar technique with persons employed fulltime in personnel departments. The results were similar to those of Craft et al. In both studies, there was a sharp drop in willingness to hire the individual after age 50.

Impact of Stereotypes

Hiring is not the only employment function in which discriminatory treatment may be a result of adverse stereotyping. The same holds true for training (many firms refuse to assign older employees to retraining programs for new technology), performance appraisal, promotions, management development programs, and early retirement policies. McAuley (1977) cites a variety of discriminatory actions reported by employees over 40.

Adverse consequences may also result from the fact that an older individual often accepts the stereotyped beliefs of those in the social environment. As a child may accept (and act on) the image of himself as a "bad boy," so the older employee may accept the definition of his abilities as declining, performance as diminishing, etc. Kogan and Wallach (1961) tested older women on motor skills tasks and also obtained responses to such questions as "How old do you feel?" The women who described themselves as "elderly" showed more caution on both the motor test and on situations described in the questionnaire. The authors suggest that "subjective age" may be as important as chronological age. The familiar "self-fulfilling prophecy" may operate here; the worker who feels "old" may start behaving accordingly.

To state that adverse treatment of the elderly is based on a stereotype is to imply that the image held of older employees is inaccurate. A considerable amount of evidence supports this assertion. The available data indicate that the loss of efficiency of older workers has been exaggerated. On the other hand, we must recognize that many industrial employees prefer to retire at age 62 (earlier, if possible). Responses of retired auto workers (Stagner, 1979) indicated that their satisfaction with life in retirement is significantly higher than their satisfaction with the last job. Early retirement, then, is not automatically a case of adverse discrimination.

Employers, it should be noted, agree that considerable age discrimination occurs. Mercer (1981) surveyed several hundred chief executives of sizeable corporations and found that 61 percent agreed with the statement that "older workers are discriminated against." At the same time, these very executives denied any discrimination within their own firms; in the absence of direct observation, we cannot judge the accuracy of this report.

JOB PERFORMANCE

The significant aspect of the stereotype, from the viewpoint of the employer, is the alleged decline in job performance. Since all of us have an economic stake in the productivity of industry, support of this allegation would be a persuasive argument for age discrimination. The research data on this point are surprisingly inadequate. In fact, the most distressing conclusion from studies of job performance changes with age is that they are ambiguous. Most investigators have used performance ratings by supervisors, which may well be lowered if the rater believes older employees are inferior. Research reports differ with respect to ages of "younger" and "older" groups, and the number in the older category is often quite small. The outcome of a survey of the literature is thus unsatisfactory, but the following paragraphs summarize some of the better investigations.

Few of the studies use objective criteria of job performance. An exception is that of Kelleher and Quirk (1973), in which U.S. Department of Labor data on 6000 clerical workers were analyzed. In this case, objective records of production were available. The findings indicate no significant difference by age in terms of total output; older workers are found to be steadier than younger ones and equal in accuracy to them. Clay (1956) stated that measured performance in two printing establishments tended to rise during the 50s, then declined slightly after age 60; however, proofreaders in the 60 and over group were better than their juniors.

A laboratory study of a task very similar to many now comprising industrial jobs is that of Panek et al. (1979), in which females were tested on a visual monitoring job analogous to the work of air traffic controllers, TV tube inspectors, and some data-processing tasks. The older workers were somewhat inferior when tested at the pace preferred by the younger group, but when allowed to slow down the rate of presentation of signals, they proved equal in accuracy. It is not clear from the report that total production by the older group would be significantly less, although it is possible. Many of the older individuals exceeded the norm of the younger group.

The literature contains a large number of studies using performance ratings by supervisors, as opposed to objective measures of output. Of five recent reports, one shows older employees to be inferior, one indicates that they are superior, one opts for equality, and two are ambiguous. It is probable that a more extensive survey would show more investigators concluding that older workers are slower or less productive. The pervasive impact of the "older worker" stereotype, however, casts doubt on the validity of these rating studies.

Horner (1980) analyzed performance ratings of 600 middle-level managers in a large midwestern public utility. She found that managers over 50, as compared with those under 50, were judged by their superiors to be less receptive to new ideas, slower to learn new things, but more technically competent. Unfortunately, it is entirely possible that these ratings, like the others cited, reflect the stereotyped beliefs held by the 200 raters rather than the attributes of those rated.

The problem arises from the fact that even experienced performance appraisers often disagree with one another. The report of Lifson (1953) is instructive. Lifson filmed the job performance of five workers doing simple factory-type jobs: twisting screws, stamping boxes with a rubber stamp, twisting bolts, packing boxes into cartons. Six "expert" raters were recruited: two professors of industrial engineering, two current time-study men for a manufacturing firm, and two former time-study men who had returned to college. All had extensive experience with performance ratings in factory situations. The important result, from the viewpoint of using ratings as criteria of declining performance, is that the six disagreed substantially on whether the worker was working at a normal pace, faster than normal, or slower than normal. Furthermore, there were differences by workers (a standard set on the basis of one worker would have been 15 percent higher than a standard set on another, even though each was working to a metronome that held work-pace constant). If expert observers cannot even tell whether an employee is working slower or faster than normal, one may suspect that ratings of overall performance may reflect the judge's bias rather than the employee's performance.

That supervisors can improve in rating performance with training is indicated by the work of Pursell, Dossett, and Latham (1980). In this study, after on-the-job supervisors were given intensive training in how to evaluate manual workers' performances, the agreement among raters increased markedly. At the beginning of the study, test scores on blueprint reading and electrical knowledge had zero correlation with rated performance on construction and electrical jobs; after the raters were trained, the test scores correlated with performance quite well.

Supporting the conclusion of Pursell et al. (1980) is the work of Cleveland and Landy (1981). In their study, several hundred middle-level managers were appraised on eight attributes; two of these (self-development and interpersonal skills) showed the older group to be judged inferior. The authors were impressed, however, by the fact that experienced appraisers showed lower correlations of age with the eight attributes than did less experienced judges. Their conclusion was that better

training of raters would minimize age bias in performance appraisals.

In a thoughtful summary of earlier research on performance and age, Meier and Kerr (1976, p. 148) concluded that "Though performance slows somewhat with age, variation among individuals increases with age. In each older age group, a substantial number of persons perform at a level at least equal to the average level of their juniors." This report is given added significance by the results of a study of engineers, a group in which age has often been considered a major variable. Price, Thompson, and Dalton (1975) compared engineers that had been rated as high, medium, and low performers and categorized by age (20–30, 31–40, 41–50, and 50+). They noted, first of all, that those on difficult jobs tended to get higher ratings than those on more routine jobs, a debatable practice. For present purposes, it is more important to note that the decline in performance rating with age was fairly slight. "The high performers in the 40-year age group and the 50+ age group have higher average ratings than do the middle and low performers in the younger age groups." That is, the older "highs" were performing better than the average of younger engineers. Finally, we may note that the sample of chief executive officers surveyed by Mercer (1981) approved this statement: "Older workers perform as well on the job as younger workers" by a margin of 90 percent to 10 percent.

Characteristics of the Rater

The stereotype of the inefficient older worker is not confined to executives. Workers are likely to see themselves as slowing down. That they do so suggested that older raters may be more severe than younger raters in their performance appraisals of their age-mates. Schwab and Heneman (1977) had personnel managers rate several descriptions of performance by hypothetical secretaries. Three descriptions were identical for all judges; the fourth systematically varied age, although performance was given as exactly the same. Although overall ratings did not show age bias, the older judges did rate the older employee more severely. The same phenomenon has been noted in nonindustrial settings; for example, Mullick (1981) found that, in descriptions of alleged accidents, older judges were more critical of an elderly driver than were the younger judges.

The question of bias in such ratings is not merely academic. Kleiman and Durham (1981) point out that discrimination on the basis of age is illegal, and review issues in performance appraisal such as these have come up in court cases. Although such cases are not yet numerous, they indicate the importance to employers of making sure that performance evaluations are made by trained observers and that attention is paid to observable aspects of performance, not to estimates of personality or attitude.

Other Aspects of Employee Performance

Accident records, turnover, absenteeism, grievances, and other job behaviors have also been considered by employers. As regards accidents, it is fairly clear that older workers have fewer mishaps (Dillingham, 1981) but will be off the job a longer time per accident. Absenteeism tends to decline with age (Spencer and Steers, 1980). Job switching (bidding for another job in the same enterprise) also declines with age (Blumberg, 1980). This statistic may be an artifact, in that the older worker may already have attained the specific assignment he or she finds most attractive.

Turnover rates are considerably lower for older workers, of course, but this should be attributed to fear of not being hired elsewhere (fear of age discrimination). These anxieties develop early (McAuley, 1977); even for workers in their 40s, a substantial number reported observations of or concern about being discriminated against.

TRAINING

A second component of the negative stereotype of the elderly worker is that he or she is incapable of, or resistant to, retraining (or initial training if hired for a job of a different

kind). In a study conducted by Rosen and Jerdee (1976b), personnel people were asked to select employees for retraining for jobs affected by technological changes in production procedures. Using descriptions of employees that differed only with respect to age, they demonstrated that assignments to a new training program would discriminate against older members of the present work force. It was apparent that the unfavorable judgment reflected a stereotype of older persons as less flexible, unwilling, or unable to change established habits.

Experimental findings from actual training programs are somewhat ambiguous. Birren (see Welford and Birren, 1965) reported that retraining of employees on telephone jobs showed no differences below age 60. It is not clear how much of a deficit occurred after that age. Chown (1972) stated that an older group proved somewhat more difficult to retrain, but a finer analysis of the data indicated that rigidity of personality was more significant than age in producing a decrement. Many older persons did as well as the mean of the younger group. Haberlandt (1973) even reported some evidence that older workers were retrained more rapidly and to a higher level than younger personnel in a large petroleum refinery. It is not clear whether any special training methods were employed.

Several authors suggest that the methods used in training programs may be important. Belbin (1965) claims that the "discovery method," in which a trainee is shown several samples of a problem and helped to "discover" the solution, helps eliminate the discrepancy between younger and older trainees. Some psychologists would argue that this method would prove superior for people of any age. Stolurow (1965) suggested that programmed instruction and teaching machines might help abolish assumed differences between age groups in training speed.

Socialization

An aspect of industrial training that is rarely discussed but clearly age-related is that of socializing the employee to the job. This implies far more than orientation sessions and a lecture on company rules. In every plant, older workers indoctrinate newcomers with regard to company rules (it is safe to break this one, but don't take a chance on that one), supervision (habits and soft spots of different supervisors, probability of discipline), and a variety of other issues. As the Hawthorne studies and many replications show, older workers may impose production norms on new employees and enforce these by a variety of sanctions (Wanous, 1980).

This aspect of informal employee training, not under managerial control, has not been well researched. Hazer and Alvares (1981) describe changes in police trainees as they make the shift from the police academy to patrols with older officers. The "intrinsic" values of police work decline rapidly, while concern for pay and perquisites goes up. Although this tendency may be especially distressing in regard to police officers (where commitment to societal values is urgently needed), it probably happens in factory work, in the U.S. Congress, and elsewhere.

A similar study by LaRocco and Jones (1980) on Navy recruits led to similar conclusions. New sailors picked up the "values, beliefs, and perspectives" of veteran Navy personnel. Many of the older men were characterized as anxious to get out of the service; this finding is somewhat contradictory to other studies (cf. McDonald and Gunderson, 1972) that show experienced personnel to be more satisfied with their jobs than the younger men.

The role of the older worker in this socialization process is obvious. Managers, however, have tended to ignore it. Constructive personnel policies calculated to involve older employees in helping new workers fit into the work environment seem to be lacking. This is true in the public domain as well as private enterprise. Planned efforts to build job involvement have only recently appeared; they will be discussed in the section on Job Redesign.

The study of work values (cf. Wollach et al., 1971) is difficult to relate to aging because of the cohort effect. Older workers show deeper job involvement, in part because of employment anxieties relating to depression years. Younger employees who lack such experiences are less concerned about "doing a good job." Since research on this issue has not made use of longitudinal designs, no firm conclusions are justified concerning individuals. It is clear, however, that the job involvement of older workers is not being transmitted in full strength to younger cohorts.

MID-CAREER CHANGE

An aspect of aging in industry that is related to performance, training, and satisfaction is the phenomenon of mid-career change. This term can be applied to two very different phenomena. In the familiar form, workers go to college and enter higher-rated occupations. In a new but more interesting form, successful professionals have abandoned their careers to take jobs as farmers, laborers, bartenders, etc. Although each change represents an effort to increase personal satisfaction, they seem to be quite different.

Sarason (1977) reported on several cases of successful professionals who abandoned careers to go into routine, poorly paid, semiskilled work. He suggested that these "burntout" individuals made this change in an attempt to forestall the onset of aging. Sarason was critical of the cultural pattern that equates one life with one career. Like monogamous marriage, he suggested, the single-career life may be on the way out. Elsewhere (Sarason et al., 1975, p. 586), we find this passage: "The process of making a career choice is the first significant confrontation with the sense of aging, involving as it does the knowledge or belief that such a decision is fateful because it determines how the rest of one's life will be 'filled in.'"

The issue of one life and one career is not relevant here. The issue of middle-aged career changes is. Certainly an individual must engage in a cost-benefit analysis, weighing the years invested in one set of skills, present income, and ego satisfactions against the present frustrations and the fantasied gains of the new career. Social costs are also involved, in that society has often invested large sums in training a physician, lawyer, or engineer, an expenditure that will be lost if the training is suddenly put on the shelf. In the Sarason (1977) study, all of those interviewed emphasized discontent with their work, and the case histories suggested that marital and family conflicts, personal neuroses, and other nonwork problems may have influenced the decision to break with the established career.

The "Burnout" Problem

Nurses and mental health counselors have also been reported to have increasing frequencies of "burnout" in middle life. This loss of interest in the job, the patient, and even in the self is variously ascribed to feelings of overwhelming magnitude of the problems to be faced or to the intolerable intensity of emotional involvement required by such work. Maslach (1978) described the conscious experience of burnout, and Maslach and Jackson (1981) offered an instrument for making comparisons between individuals to determine the extent of the problem. Jones (1981) extended the Maslach-Jackson questionnaire and demonstrated that managers as well as health workers report the burnout experience. Persons high on the burnout scale are more likely to change jobs, as would be expected from the Sarason observations. They are also more likely to be rude to patients (or customers), to ignore job responsibilities, etc.

Jones (1981) does not report age differences in burnout, but it seems probable that certain employees, perhaps those more sensitive to frustrations or more empathic with others' problems, will develop this syndrome, some early, some late. Individuals who survive 15 to 20 years in a given job may be immune; susceptible individuals leave for some other occupation.

The type of career change described by Sarason (1977) and Jones (1981) is socially alarming in that both public money and private effort have been expended to develop professional skill. Another type of career change is much more familiar and occasions no surprise. Clopton (1973) studied a small group of men who had worked for several years in manual or low-level white-collar jobs, become dissatisfied, and returned to graduate school

to qualify for professional work. Since these instances involve upward mobility, few observers feel that they require special attention. The downward-mobile cases described by Sarason are more perplexing. At present, we can only say that the valences associated with more leisure, an outdoor environment, or an escape from high-stress professional demands were more potent than the income and prestige associated with the first professional career. Similarly, we can suggest that, for Clopton's group, the positive valences of a professional career were more attractive than those of income and familiar work in a routine occupation.

The mid-career shift is important to industry because a fair number of middle-level managers have either opted for this change or seem to be on the verge of doing so. Most firms are reluctant to encourage such changes; after all, the cost of on-the-job training for such a manager may run into tens of thousands of dollars. The problem may indicate a need for more attention to the personal satisfactions of such employees, a topic that will be discussed later.

Union leaders are reported (Sheppard and Herrick, 1972) to favor employer subsidies to mid-career professional and managerial employees in an attempt to facilitate such shifts. Not surprisingly, the industrial executives interviewed showed less enthusiasm for such programs. Many individuals, of course, set aside savings to protect living standards while they obtain training for a new profession.

Another writer on mid-career change is Levinson (1978), who related the phenomenon to a "stage theory" of aging. He hypothesized that there were identifiable stages of development in adult life (entering the adult world, settling down, entering middle adulthood, etc.) His case histories, however, indicated that an abrupt career change might occur in a man's thirties, forties, or fifties. The stage theory obviously does not help us understand or predict the phenomenon.

Hall (1976) discussed mid-career changes in a context of training and counseling; that is, his attention was focused on helping the employee who has made such a change or has decided to do so. Universities and other training institutions also provide counseling and education for those who make this decision.

Career Change and Motivation

One factor probably involved in career changes is a change in dominant motivation. Of one case, Levinson (1978, p. 276) wrote: "The most striking change between 44 and 46 was [John Barnes'] greatly decreased concern for advancement and recognition, and his ability to gain intrinsic satisfaction from work and social contribution." We are not told, however, whether this individual had reached a dead-end position from which advancement was improbable. A suggestive bit of statistical evidence is provided by Reichelt (1974), who found that, among managers and staff below age 36 in an electronics manufacturing concern, measures of motivation correlated about zero with performance and promotability as rated by supervisors. On the other hand, the correlations for a group 37 and older were much higher. Older employees probably can assess their own performance and their chances of promotion fairly well; if the situation looks gloomy, motivation and performance will drop. The data cited by Heneman (1973) support this conclusion.

Most thinking about mid-life career changes has been based on the implicit assumption that people make changes only for the sake of upward mobility. Theories that stress "growth motivation" (Alderfer, 1972) or self-actualization imply that individuals move in directions calculated to provide more challenge, more decision-making opportunities, or more job involvement (as in Clopton, 1973). It is just as plausible to argue that they "actualize" by shifting to a career that is more relaxing, free of painful choices, and less demanding in terms of responsibility for others (cf. Sarason, 1977).

It is somewhat discouraging, in this connection, to note that young managers begin to lose their desire for self-actualization (in a rather broad sense) early in their careers. Bray et al. (1974, p. 104) reported that AT&T managerial trainees, over a seven-year period, lost some of their interest in higher education, "cultural activities," and self-development.

Their concern about their immediate families increased, but their involvement with their parents diminished, the latter change being much more pronounced in successful than unsuccessful trainees. It would be important to find out whether a stress on continuing education, and especially such ventures as an academic year at a university, would reverse some of these trends toward a narrow interest in the job to the exclusion of other intellectual activities.

Career counseling is appropriate for a person considering a change in either direction. Many agencies now provide services for middle-aged individuals who seek either upward mobility with more challenge or downward mobility that offers more relaxation and freedom from painful demands.

Technological Obsolescence

A possible contributor to the mid-life career crisis, as well as to pressure on professional employees to retire early, is the occurrence of technological obsolescence. It has often been alleged (cf. Dubin, 1972) that many professionals are obsolete within five to ten years after completion of their training. Cumming and Henry (1961) gave an important place to this alleged obsolescence as it relates to aging in their theory of "disengagement." Disengagement, in this context, referred to societal pressures on older individuals to withdraw from leadership roles, making way for younger, more up-to-date replacements. Many employers are concerned about technological obsolescence, although few chief executives seem to apply this concept to themselves.

Dubin's claim of obsolescence after five to ten years has been questioned by many observers. It is probable that what he identified is a loss of awareness of the very latest developments, the newest research findings or procedures. Such novel ideas may be irrelevant to 80 percent or more of an individual's activities.

McFarland (1976) criticized the hypothesis of obsolescence by pointing to the development of compensatory skills: "compensation takes place for every decline, and if certain capacities are diminished, others are enhanced" (quoted by Sheppard and Rix, 1977, p. 74). This statement is too extreme to be taken literally, but many older individuals have skills (e.g., in knowing which expert to consult, knowing how to cooperate with younger specialists) that can compensate for some modest lack of acquaintance with advanced technology.

Belief in the technological obsolescence of older employees may be a self-fulfilling prophecy. In the study by Price, Thompson, and Dalton (1975), cited earlier, it was noted that younger engineers tended to be given the more challenging assignments. Thus, if older staffers are pushed into routine jobs, they may lose interest in keeping up with new developments and so hasten the obsolescence for which they have already been convicted; they may feel that the energy cost of continuing education will not pay off.

American industry is currently evolving toward fewer traditional jobs at the manual, white-collar, professional, and technical levels. The trend is toward new jobs in high-technology occupations, a situation that threatens the older employee seriously. Regardless of the lack of support for stereotypes of rigidity, retraining difficulty, and loss of technological expertise, executives who make decisions on employment, promotion, and retirement may be disposed to discriminate against the older group.

Retraining for New Technology

When technology is changing rapidly, industry cannot simply hire a new work force composed of recent graduates from computer schools, electronics institutes, and the like. Retraining of current employees becomes necessary. Mercer (1981) found that 77 percent of his sample of executives stated that retraining was as available for older employees as for younger individuals. Evidence collected by Rosen and Jerdee (1976a), however, indicated that decision-making by personnel executives was biased against older employees. As in other studies, the investigators presented work histories that were identical except for chronological age. The probability of rejection of a hypothetical employee increased steadily with increasing age.

At the executive level a similar process of discrimination probably operates. Although

attempts to obtain age data on persons sent by their employers for a year at M.I.T., Stanford, Harvard, and similar schools (to improve their potential for promotion) have been unsuccessful, inquiries met with the comment that a preference for younger employees would not be surprising because of the large investment in the future of such employees. By implication, older middle-level managers may be bypassed because of their potentially fewer years of service after retraining.

Increased caution and anxiety at being placed in a training group with younger persons may contribute to the assumed training difficulties of the elderly. In a study of workers transferred to new jobs, Chown (1972) found that difficulty in acquiring new skills seemed to be a function of an employee's rigidity, not of chronological age; that is, younger workers with rigid personalities had more problems than older workers who were more flexible.

The experience of colleges and universities with "continuing education" for older professionals, as well as programs at the college level meant to attract older residents from the community, has convinced most educators that the elderly are capable of learning as much as younger students. There are, of course, problems of motivation (to be discussed) and presentation of materials, as suggested by Belbin (1965) and Stolurow (1965), and these must be considered by anyone designing such training programs.

The current shift in technology predicts a decided pressure for retraining. Automated controls in factory work and information-processing devices in offices are going to call for substantial changes in workplace behavior. The available evidence does not support a policy that excludes older employees from retraining to fit into the new environment. Furthermore, counseling should be made available to help older persons cope more effectively with the retraining programs.

WORK AND ABILITY

Whether society enforces antidiscriminatory legislation regarding the elderly worker or imposes penalties on employees who retire at age 62 will depend in part upon the question: Does the typical worker show a real and significant decline in ability to perform necessary duties with advancing age? It is therefore necessary to duplicate, in a small degree, the treatment of cognitive and other ability testing in another chapter of this handbook, because the implications for industry cannot be spelled out without specifying a few of the theoretical and empirical considerations that must be taken into account.

Data have been presented here to show that the stereotyped picture of elderly employees as inefficient and incompetent is not justified. It might be argued that further considerations regarding alleged ability decrement are not needed once the alleged poor performance has been disproven. This is debatable. In particular instances, an individual may indeed show declining performance, but ability testing may reveal the possibility of a transfer to another job where cognitive deficits will not be a handicap. Conversely, individuals fighting to keep their job may accept retirement more readily if tests demonstrate an important handicap that might result in injury to them or to their fellow workers. It is therefore important to draw together the scattered data on ability testing insofar as these can be related to the area of aging.

Sensory Abilities

One of the commonest forms of observable decline in psychological functioning is loss of auditory acuity. Inability to detect incoming sounds above 10,000 cps becomes much more common after the age of 55 (Dirken, 1972). Wide individual differences are found, however; in Dirken's sample of Dutch workers, all of them males, a loss of 10 to 20 percent of auditory efficiency (recognition of phonemes) was shown by 20 percent of them, ranging as high as 90 percent for 1 percent of those tested.

Such decrements can have important work implications, especially in noisy environments. Spoken instructions are likely to be misunderstood; furthermore, many alarm systems produce high-pitched sounds that might be poorly received by some older employees. In some forms of metal processing, shrill noises are indicative of malfunctions. Although a skilled worker may have learned to use other cues, there is always a possibility that the auditory loss will have a significant impact on work at a crucial moment.

Visual functions also show a statistical tendency to decline with age. Visual decrement, however, is not so closely tied to chronological age as is hearing; in Dirken's data, the "age-dependence" figure for pitch ceiling was 0.66, whereas for visual acuity it was only 0.44. It should be noted that Dirken's measure was inappropriate because he tested for distance vision, whereas numerous studies show that near vision is far more important for the typical factory or clerical job. It is obvious, moreover, that corrective devices for visual handicaps are more available and more effective than for auditory difficulties. It is thus likely that measures of visual decrement will not be important in the present context.

Information-Processing

In any analysis of abilities, it is plausible to consider the sensory problems involved in information-processing. One important variable, for example, is the signal/noise ratio, or the ability to detect a signal in the midst of background noise (auditory or visual). Regrettably, we have little information on age changes in this function, although Welford (1976) considers it a major variable. Since the older employee may compensate for any deficit by waiting for additional stimuli to arrive to make sure he has received the proper information, job performance may be slower but actually more accurate for older than for younger workers.

Short-term memory is another important factor in information-processing. Some studies suggest that older employees show a shortened immediate memory span, although this is a relatively minor problem. "Working memory" tasks, in which information must be acquired, stored, and used a few minutes later, may be more adversely affected. Some older individuals exhibit declines in the retrieval of material from long-term storage, but again compensatory strategies (note-taking, rehearsal, reminders) may reduce the deficit. When asked to recall relevant material (as opposed to nonsense or irrelevant items) the superior performance of older persons that has been reported by Baddeley and Hitch (1974) and Botwinick and Storandt (1980) suggests that apparent deficits on some tests may be a function of motivation rather than ability (see also Schaie, 1980).

Completion of figures from partial cues and shifting of set to adjust to a changing environment are other cognitive functions that have been found to decline in some older persons. A proposal for a more methodical examination of information-processing as it relates to job performance of elderly workers has been prepared by Solley (1981) but not yet implemented.

Motor Abilities

There is virtually universal agreement that motor ability deteriorates in later life, although the age of maximum performance seems to differ from different sports and probably for different jobs. In an excellent study of psychomotor development from ages 8 to 87, Noble, Baker, and Jones (1964) reported that this ability peaked early (16 for females, 20 for males) with a fairly steady decline thereafter. It must be noted that their measure was one of the speed of acquisition of a novel psychomotor skill and does not prove a decline in the performance of established skills. Welford (see Welford and Birren, 1965) reported that drill operators past age 60 were more accurate than a younger group. In performing such complex skilled jobs, it is possible that some perceptual skills (use of cues to align work properly, etc.) may compensate for any loss of motor coordination.

"General Intelligence"

Most studies on alleged declines in ability with age rely on tests of general cognitive ability or "general intelligence." The traditional view held that mental capacity peaks at about 16 years of age and declines, with some variations, thereafter. Several early studies seemed to confirm this conclusion. Regrettably, the methods employed were subject to extensive error. Cohort differences were ignored (younger subjects had more extensive education than the older persons involved); the test materials were often inappropriate for older individuals; and the scores employed were often questionable.

Longitudinal studies in which the same individuals are retested at successive ages provide a somewhat less debatable source of data. Owens (1966) found that many persons first tested as college freshmen in 1919 had, by 1950, *increased* substantially in general aptitude scores. By 1961 the overall score had declined somewhat, but at least one sub-score (reasoning) was still increasing when the mean age of the subjects was 60. Similar results were reported by Granick (1971) and Burns (1966).

Theoretical clarity was introduced to this area by Horn and Cattell (1967). They distinguished "fluid intelligence," which was assumed to be some kind of constitutional or innate capacity, from "crystallized intelligence," which represented the extent to which a person profits from experience. In operational terms, fluid intelligence was defined by such tasks as number series, figure analogies, classifications of figures, nonsense equations —all of them tasks likely to be encountered rarely and thus requiring adaptation to novel stimuli. Crystallized intelligence was defined by such measures as common information, vocabulary, simple arithmetic, etc. Thus crystallized intelligence implies a range of experience and habits of dealing efficiently with often-met problems. The hypothesis seems intuitively plausible, and the data support it. There was a clear and significant decline with age in the tests of fluid intelligence, and a generally significant increase with age as regards crystallized intelligence. This is certainly an important distinction since omnibus measures of ability may obscure such essential differences. What the authors failed to note is the need to examine individual differences within each kind of ability. Some employees decline in fluid intelligence, whereas others do not.

The utility of the fluid-crystallized distinction has been reduced somewhat by the studies of Blieszner, Willis, and Baltes (1981) and Hofland, Willis, and Baltes (1981). These demonstrated that scores on tests of "fluid intelligence" could be raised simply by practicing on similar problems for a few hours. Inductive reasoning for example, was significantly improved among adults aged 60 to 85 by five one-hour sessions of training spaced over two weeks. We may speculate that training on vocabulary, arithmetic, engineering fundamentals, or other cognitive skills would likewise lead to improved test scores. It may be the length of time out of school and away from an environment where testing is common that accounts for some of the apparent decrement in the cognitive ability of the elderly.

In a rather cautious summation of the data currently available, Schaie (1980) comments that "reliable decrement . . . cannot be found for all abilities or for all individuals" even into the 80s (p. 70). He also notes that "for most individuals there is decrement on those abilities which require speed of response, and for those . . . particularly sensitive to relatively modest impairment of the peripheral nervous system" (pp. 70–71). Schaie also emphasizes the fact that many elderly individuals continue to score at the level of middle-aged adults; in other words, for significant portions of the elderly population, intellectual decline cannot be demonstrated. Whether such research findings will ever influence stereotyped thinking in the general population is hard to predict. It is discouraging that Fritz (1978) found that public officials, industrial managers, and union leaders have similarly ignored the research data in the field of aging.

The Problem of Test Bias

Charges have been levelled against the most widely used tests of cognitive abilities (for "intelligence") that they are biased against blacks, Hispanics, and the elderly. The data are far from conclusive. It could be claimed that tests such as numerical computation are unfair to those who failed arithmetic in school. On the other hand, if safety on a job requires the ability to recognize numerical readings or to know when a critical difference has developed, a person who failed arithmetic may not be properly suited for that job.

Extensive accumulations of evidence on literally thousands of jobs (Schmidt and Hunter, 1981) indicate that job performance can be validly predicted by a number of currently available cognitive tests. Furthermore, there is no difference in their validity for majority and minority workers. Whether this finding extends to differences among age groups has not been determined since relatively little research relevant to this issue has been published. Tenopyr (1981) has suggested that abandoning tests would merely result in wider discrimination against minorities (presumably including the elderly) since greater weight would then be placed on the employment interview, notoriously subject to stereotyped judgments.

There is at least one aspect of tests that may cause older workers to be the objects of unfair treatment. This is the anxiety aroused by pencil-and-paper tests. Older people may never have been as habituated to testing as their younger colleagues, and a person who has been out of school for 40 years or more may experience considerable fear of the test itself (see AFL-CIO, 1979). Wallach and Kogan (1961) demonstrated that older persons are more cautious in their reactions to paper tests as well as to a test of motor skills. This exaggerated caution would adversely affect the applicant's performance since the typical employment test measures speed of response as well as accuracy.

Cohort Differences

Research on the effect of aging on ability is seldom simple. One important variable is that of cohort variation.

Problems introduced into aging studies by cohort differences can be well illlustrated by the data of Owens (1966). When persons tested on the Army Alpha examination in 1919 (mean age 19) were retested in 1961, they showed substantial increases in score. When a new group of 19-year-olds were tested in 1961, they scored as high as the 1961 scores of the 1919 group. Thus, the apparent improvement with age was more fundamentally a cultural change. On the other hand, the cohort variable may seem to indicate a decline, whereas longitudinal data indicates unchanged or even improved ability for specific persons. Clearly, misinterpretation may arise if data are solely based on either longitudinal or cross-sectional data. The complex design advocated by Schaie (1970) is therefore justified.

Functional Age

In his observations of aging airline pilots, McFarland (1953) coined the term "functional age" to emphasize individual differences in the rate of change in performance with age. "The important variable to consider *is not chronological age but rather functional age*" (p. 390). Perhaps he considered this distinction to be an analogue to Binet's concept of "mental age." In a later article (1973), he suggested that if two individuals are compared at 60 years of age, one may be functioning like a typical 45-year-old, the other more like a 65-year-old.

As with mental age, the use of a single index for functional age is open to criticism. Birren (1959) proposed that we examine a person's biological, social, and psychological age. Within the psychological category, one must expect variations for different skills and abilities in the same person.

The most elaborate research application of this idea is that of Dirken (1972). He applied an extensive battery of tests to 316 Dutch workers ranging in age from 30 to 69+. The tests included a group of physiological measures, sensory ability, perceptual tasks, and complex cognitive problems. After elaborate statistical manipulations, including the regression of each measure on chronological age and factor analysis to identify clusters of tests having a common variance, he developed an Index of Functional Age. This was a composite of the following: auditory pitch ceiling, visual figure comprehension, multiple-choice reaction time, accuracy in semantic categorization, maximum breathing frequency, maximum systolic tension, aerobic capacity, and expiratory one-second value. The composite index correlated highly with chronological age but not so highly as to obscure individual differences in functional aging.

Dirken's index of age-dependency for these tests reveals some interesting data. Physiological measures of physical functioning at work show a dependency index of 0.61; for sensory capacities, the age-dependency is 0.44, but for psychomotor (0.30) and psychological (0.26) measures the relationship is less. Thus CA is reflected most clearly at simple levels and only erratically at more complex abilities. Since physical work limitations (fatigue) and sensory deficits are highly visible, it may be that these findings indicate the origin of the stereotype of the older worker and that functions more closely relevant to job performance have been improperly assimilated. Thus, visual acuity correlated +0.44 with chronological age, whereas accuracy of categorization of verbal materials was only +0.14. Decline of a motor or sensory ability does not predict loss of cognitive ability.

Schaie and Parr (1981) criticized Dirken for his reliance on a single index of functional age. They suggested a profile method that would emphasize intraindividual variations. Such profiles could be prepared using the Dirken measures, since tables are provided that show the normal range of scores for workers of differing ages. The Dirken measures should probably be supplemented by scores for information-processing functions, since these are likely to be highly relevant to new jobs in "high technology" industry.

The GULHEMP Profile

One variant of the profile method has already found occasional use in the U.S. This is the so-called GULHEMP profile (Meier and Kerr, 1976). The name derives from the components measured: general physique, upper extremities, lower extremities, hearing, eyesight, mentality (intelligence), and personality. The first three are apparently measures of strength and endurance. The measures of intelligence and of personality obviously need to be broken down into more specific tests of relatively independent attributes. Each of the seven variables is rated for each applicant on a scale from 1 to 7, and these profiles are then matched to profiles of job requirements that use the same seven attributes and are likewise rated on a scale from 1 to 7. Meier and Kerr reported that many employers had used the profile to choose among elderly applicants and found many good employment prospects by doing so (1976, p. 149).

The GULHEMP profile probably places more weight on physical attributes than is appropriate for the upcoming high-technology environment. Profiles based on information-processing abilities would be more useful and place older candidates for employment in a better position. Regrettably, no suitably standardized tests for these abilities are currently available, although research in the area is active.

Measurement of abilities is generally believed to be in the best interests of the employer (workers well suited to jobs) as well as the employee (assigned to tasks for which he or she is likely to be successful.) A predicted outcome of matching worker to task is a high level of job satisfaction and mental health.

WORK OUTCOMES

Psychologists have been concerned about the impact of work upon the worker: that is, the costs and benefits associated with the job. One of the (presumed) costs is deterioration of mental health. Both are important to the individual worker and also to society.

Job Satisfaction

Employee satisfaction has both psychological and economic significance. If employees are dissatisfied, probable consequences include strikes, grievances, absenteeism, and turnover, all of which are costly to the employer. In addition, the personal life of the worker is adversely affected. These economic outcomes are well-documented in the industrial psychology literature and will not be further discussed here. Obviously, the possibility of such developments induces employers to seek to optimize job satisfaction in relation to operating costs. The data to be reviewed here relate to the age/satisfaction association, but the overall pattern of satisfaction research must be understood if the findings are to be interpreted properly.

Job satisfaction studies generally conform to one of three models: (1) studies of national samples, which ignore job duties, employer size, and geographical region; (2) studies of plant samples, involving a single employer but varied duties; and (3) studies of persons within a single job classification. The utility of each study depends on the purposes of the investigator. If the focus is on equipment, work layout, or job training, then the third model is most appropriate since frustrations related to the specific work will surface. If the focus is on company rules, supervisory practices, etc., the second is preferable. If the search is for economic or cultural variables, then the first model is most useful.

National Surveys

Weaver (1980) summarized recent findings from several national surveys, each of which asked this question: "On the whole, how satisfied are you with the work you do—would you say that you are very satisfied, moderately satisfied, a little dissatisfied, or very dissatisfied?" In each of the seven studies, the correlation of age with job satisfaction was positive. This would suggest that at least a substantial number of determinants of satisfaction relate to generalized psychological tendencies (habituation, increased tolerance for annoyances, decreased goal-seeking, and hence less anger at frustration, etc.). However, specific local processes may operate along with these; older employees get more interesting or less fatiguing jobs, for example. Weaver also noted that income correlated well with satisfaction. Although the national correlation of age with income is near zero, there is reason to expect that within a given group, such as manual workers, the older individuals may receive more income, and the same would be true for managerial and professional persons. Thus, the income variable may have contributed to the observed age/satisfaction correlation. Similarly, Opinion Research Corporation (1980) reported a steady increase in job satisfaction with advancing age. This survey included managers, clerical, and hourly employees; all three groups showed the same age trend.

There is, of course, a debate over the utility of studies that cut across many jobs and many locations. One group of experts holds that job satisfaction is unique to a particular plant and task; others seek for generalizations that cut across such variables. Andrisani and Miljus (1977) illustrate the latter view. Using two samples of about 5,000 workers each, and two age groups, 14 to 24 and 45 to 59, all employed males, they compared intrinsic and extrinsic sources of job satisfaction. The data indicated that intrinsic (job-related) satisfactions were more important than extrinsic (pay, work environment) satisfactions across both blue-collar and white-collar occupations. Interestingly enough, the older group was both more satisfied and more concerned with intrinsic job attributes.

Another finding was that the age difference for black males was relatively much greater than the age difference for white males. Obviously, cohort differences may be more important than age, since employment opportunities for young blacks are at once advertised as being greater but operationally slight, so that even employed young blacks may react with discontent; older blacks may report greater satisfaction (a contrast effect resulting from less on-the-job discrimination).

Sex differences in national samples clearly show males to be more satisfied than females; the age/satisfaction correlation is often negative for women, whereas the figure for males is almost always positive. In the absence of firm data, we can only speculate that promotion policies have adversely affected females to such an extent that older females feel more keenly frustrated than males in the same age group. Given the social pressures for equal treatment, this difference may disappear in 20 or 30 years.

Plant Studies

The commonest research model in job satisfaction is that of a plant-wide survey, usually on a carefully stratified sample to represent all job classes. This kind of survey is most likely to be useful to employers because the data permit pinpointing those jobs or departments in which discontent is most prevalent. Sometimes the data indicate a plant-wide problem—e.g., in supervisory training—but they may also point to specific areas—such as a badly managed department, skilled vs.

semiskilled pay differentials, or conflict between maintenance and production workers —as sources of dissatisfaction.

Plant-wide or industry-wide surveys run the risk of obtaining age-satisfaction correlations that are distorted by artifacts. For example, a study of several thousand persons in the U.S. Navy (McDonald and Gunderson, 1972) reported a substantial agreement of age with satisfaction. The younger group was composed mainly of young draftees anxious to leave, perhaps, whereas the older individuals were career personnel, skilled workers, noncommissioned officers, etc. The pay differential also favored the older individuals. It is possible, of course, that those persons who decided to re-enlist had already found the navy environment satisfying, but we have no information on this point.

Although the same issues arise in studies of private industry, the possibility of using statistical controls to confound variables has been explored. Several recent studies (e.g., Ronen, 1978; Hunt and Saul, 1975) have controlled for seniority, both in the plant and on the job, and still found a positive correlation of age with satisfaction; the magnitude of the relationship is reduced, however, when years of service are held constant. This suggests that some of the variables involved may be personal, even physiological, whereas others are environmental.

Facet Studies

The data cited here have involved overall responses about job satisfaction as a general attitude. It can be argued, and for practical purposes it is important, that job satisfaction should be broken into facets that can be independently studied. Thus, Muchinsky (1978) obtained responses from a group of industrial workers asking how well each was satisfied with pay, supervision, promotions, co-workers, and "the work itself." The latter variable, which reflects intrinsic or "higher order" satisfiers, includes items such as getting a feeling of accomplishment, exercising skills, making decisions, and turning out a quality product. The most interesting of Muchinsky's findings was that satisfaction with the work itself increased with age, whereas satisfaction with supervision, pay, and promotions diminished.

Another facet study is that of Smith et al. (1969), who reported that age correlated with "work itself" satisfaction (+0.27). In studies of another firm, satisfaction with promotions correlated +0.33 with age. This is less typical than the usual findings of the literature; older employees, for fairly obvious reasons, tend to feel that their firm's promotion policy is unfair whenever they have been passed over.

It is also relevant that in a national survey, Caplan et al. (1975) found older respondents less likely to report pay inequities. A possible implication is that younger workers are more competitive, or perhaps have more financial problems, and are therefore disposed to think of their pay as unfairly low; then again, it may be because older individuals at the top of the pay bracket for their jobs know that they have no one to point to as receiving preferred treatment.

Public vs. Private-Sector Employees

With the increasing importance of the public sector in our economy, more data are needed on the impact of aging on government employees. A valuable study of municipal policemen has been conducted by Fry (1982). Among 357 male police officers in a medium-sized city, Fry found a highly significant increase in job satisfaction with age. Inspection of the data indicated that this increase was due to the oldest group; young and middle-aged officers were equal in reported satisfaction.

It is worth noting that Fry (1982) also found substantially lowered work anxiety among the older officers (perhaps because of less dangerous work) and a marked increase in job commitment. Higher-order need satisfaction, on the other hand, showed a slight but nonsignificant decline with age. Since this finding contradicts some of the industrial studies, it points to a need for further research.

A comparable trend with age is reported by Toch and Klofas (1982). Although their dependent variable is labeled "job alienation," the specific items are similar to those used in satisfaction studies. The older probation and correction officers showed less alienation, and thus, presumably, more satisfaction. In-

terestingly, the tenure/alienation relationship was clearly U-shaped, but this result was not apparent when age was used as the dependent variable. As noted in some industrial studies, tenure on the job and age differ in some property not yet identified.

As with private sector workers, job satisfaction for public employees is necessarily linked with age and tenure. The reward system in public service is even more closely tied to seniority than in industry; pay, promotions, and transfers to more desirable jobs are the operative factors. Although Fry (1982) found a decrease in higher-order needs among older policemen, Toch and Klofas (1982) reported that older correction workers desired job enrichment more than the younger group.

Changes Over Time

There is little longitudinal data charting the changes of a single individual over time. Group studies suggested a U-shaped function to Herzberg et al. (1957), with satisfaction high for job entrants, a marked drop after 5 to 10 years of work, then a gradual but steady rise. Ronen (1978) offered some support for this view. On the other hand, data reported by Stagner (1975) and Sheppard and Herrick (1972) indicated that satisfaction increased in a fairly steady linear fashion. Workers in the Stagner study had remained with the same employer for long periods of time. This may not have been true in the Sheppard and Herrick survey. Whether there is a typical age-curve for individuals must await real longitudinal studies.

Objective vs. Subjective Influences

A problem with regard to all studies of job satisfaction, but of particular relevance to the aging question, is that of the relative role of objective working conditions and of perceived working conditions. Engineers and production executives assume that objectively defined machines, work loads, pace, and hours determine satisfaction. Psychologists find convincing evidence that perception of the work environment outweighs the objective factors (cf. James and Jones, 1980).

Part of the problem stems from the phenomenon of adaptation level (Helson, 1964). Workers who have complained bitterly about a working temperature of 110°F in a factory may be delighted when new ventilation equipment reduces the temperature to 95°. But ten years later, when the old conditions have long since been forgotten and the temperature is still 95°, bitter protests may be voiced about the unbearable heat. Similarly, when erratic or authoritarian supervision evokes complaints and management introduces supervisory training, the workers may be happier, but a few years later, what was then perceived as more humane supervision may now appear to be arbitrary and unfeeling.

These considerations are especially relevant when we attempt to compare younger with older workers. Younger workers, having had no experience with the "bad old days," protest more rapidly; an older group may be more likely to join in. Although older workers report relatively more job satisfaction, the specific complaints of the younger group may be echoed at all age levels.

Explanatory Variables

Several processes may account for the finding that satisfaction increases with age. Within a blue-collar group, a fairly simple one is that union contracts usually provide for job transfers based on seniority. Thus, long-service workers will have had an opportunity to move around and locate a satisfying (or minimally dissatisfying) job. One aspect of this process is that those strongly dissatisfied will quit altogether. Another hypothesis is also tenable: that unpleasant stimulation diminishes in intensity with habituation. As Helson (1964) pointed out, a person's "adaptation level" tends toward a psychological zero, which is the geometric mean of the accumulated stimuli in a particular class or category. This theory predicts that disliked stimuli will become neutral in time, and hence the "work itself" may be perceived as less annoying (or more satisfying) with increased tenure. There are other, more subtle possibilities, e.g., that a person who has spent 20 or 30 years in one job may feel embarrassed to admit that he hates it. Such an admission might imply that he was unable to get another position or was not

intelligent enough to recognize the need for a change. Ego-defense may thus be a factor in the reports of higher satisfaction among older workers.

Another relevant variable is that of retirement age. If the most discontented workers retired early, the positive correlation of age and satisfaction would be magnified. Data from blue-collar workers (Stagner, 1979) fail to support this hypothesis.

Mental Health

The impact of working conditions on the mental health of employees is another outcome measure independent of production and satisfaction. In most studies, this concept is operationally defined by reports of anxiety, worry, depression, and irritability. Kornhauser's (1965) classic study utilized judgments by psychiatrists and clinical psychologists to assess reports of good and poor mental health. While his data on age were scanty, his general conclusion was that older workers in routine repetitive jobs were somewhat better off than young ones, whereas younger skilled workers displayed better mental health scores than older skilled workers.

A more recent study by Siassi et al. (1975) reports more clear-cut results. They found that workers over 40 reported significantly *fewer* psychiatric symptoms than their younger co-workers and were also better satisfied with their jobs.

Langner and Michael (1963), using a sample of 1600 adults in New York City, related job satisfaction to mental health. "Those who are more dissatisfied [with job] have a higher mental health risk" (p. 308). Srole et al. (1962), analyzing the same data, noted that the older persons in the sample had *more* psychiatric symptoms. Regrettably, the published data provide no clues for resolving this apparent contradiction. It is particularly confusing because the data on job satisfaction so uniformly indicate more satisfaction among older workers.

A similar study on a national sample (Gurin, Veroff and Feld, 1960) fits more comfortably with the data previously cited. The older employed men in this sample were more satisfied with their jobs and also reported fewer job problems. On the other hand, they rated themselves as less happy than the younger ones did. This disparity raises the question of the relation of job satisfaction to life satisfaction. It is possible that an individual may sincerely like his job but have home and family frustrations that make him feel depressed or anxious. This would be compatible with the observation (cf. Meltzer and Stagner, 1980) that job satisfaction often shows a negative correlation with life satisfaction. The psychiatric symptoms are functions of health, family, and social adjustment problems that may increase with age.

Further ambiguity is introduced by the data of Caplan et al. (1975), who found that older workers reported more illness than younger ones only in the area of cardiovascular disease. On respiratory illnesses, the older reported only one-half as many instances as the younger group. The older subjects also reported less boredom, fewer psychosomatic symptoms, and fewer visits to plant medical facilities.

Although he did not include psychiatric symptoms, Cicirelli (1980) found that his older subjects experienced more feelings of being externally controlled (age/externality correlated +0.25), but education correlated negatively with external control (−0.35). Education, of course, would help an individual feel more internal control of his life, and hence, probably, less anxiety, but the outcome may have been a function of cohort differences, the younger group having a higher educational level.

A better controlled approach to the problem of work and mental disturbance is that of Broadbent (1978). He reported on a number of studies of British workers, both those on assembly lines and those in less repetitive jobs. He found a significant increase among the former in reports of memory lapses, daydreaming, failure to observe accurately, and other cognitive deficits. Although it is difficult in the absence of longitudinal studies to assert that the nature of a particular job is the true independent variable, the evidence seems persuasive. Premature aging or mental health problems, then, may be among the consequences of a mechanically paced job.

A related study is that of Martin et al. (1980). Studying Swiss workers on highly fragmented, repetitive jobs, they found a highly significant negative correlation (−0.55) between job tenure and verbal ability but no significant correlation of age with verbal score. The inference is that prolonged work on such tasks adversely affects cognitive skills.

The detailed analysis of job boredom, repetitive work, and fragmented tasks presented by O'Hanlon (1981) is instructive not only for clues to possible mechanisms involved in the deterimental emotional and cognitive outcomes of such jobs, but also for suggestions for improved job layouts and procedures.

We must, of course, repeat that workers are individuals and do not respond identically. Some individuals prefer repetitive jobs to changing assignments. Some do not like to take responsibility for decisions. Thus, assembly-line jobs do not automatically produce cognitive or emotional damage.

The same lesson, naturally, applies to other outcomes of work stresses. Slote (1969) described the reactions of a number of workers to the announcement that their factory would be closed permanently. For example, one 44-year-old man lost all his hair trying to cope with the threat itself, grew new hair, and then lost it again when the actual closing occurred. Such extreme manifestations of strain are rare. Every individual has a unique way of responding. Nevertheless, some generalizations can be drawn. Cobb (1974), studying this same group of workers and using personality tests and biochemical measures, found that rigidity, as measured by the California Psychological Inventory, predicted difficulty in finding new jobs and in adapting to the changed circumstances resulting from the shutdown. This personality trait, he reported, was a better predictor of difficulty in adjustment than chronological age. Cobb's finding fits the report by Chown (1972) that workers transferred to new jobs have more trouble if they fall in the upper rigidity range.

Another relevant study is that of Andrew (1973), who classified elderly persons as either "avoiders" or "sensitizers" (presumably comparable to those individuals who use either perceptual defense or perceptual vigilance as routine coping devices). Sensitizers scored higher on verbal ability in both the 50 to 61 and 62 to 78 age groups. Avoiders usually declined in verbal ability with age, whereas some sensitizers actually showed gains with age. This study and the other cited may indicate mainly that successful employees are those who have learned how to cope and at the same time maintained integrity of cognitive functioning; persons who perceive themselves as failures, on the other hand, may try to withdraw from problems and as a result deteriorate in ability.

Employers like to assume that employees who complain about working conditions are merely neurotics whose complaints can be dismissed as irrational. Clinicians dealing with such individuals, however, often conclude that the job frustrations themselves are the independent variables and that their emotional disturbance is part of the strain experienced in a stressful situation. One of the troublesome aspects of the present "Quality of Work Life" movement (to be discussed) is its tendency to identify work life with home life and to assume that a happier worker will be a happier father, husband, church member, etc. Of course, all psychologists recognize the unity of personality, but it should also be understood that many individuals prefer to keep work life and home life separate. Indeed, a major component of the wave of unionism in America in the 1930s was its demand for an end to paternalism: "Pay us decent wages and let us decide for ourselves about recreation, home, and leisure activities."

Employer Policies

Employers have not ignored the implications of job satisfaction and job motivation studies. They have introduced changes with the intention of improving job commitment, intrinsic satisfactions, and mental health. The "Quality of Work Life" movement has the avowed purpose of making workers more satisfied (with an explicit denial that increased production is expected). Such changes have included efforts to allow more worker decision-making (less rigid control over work practices), more participation (as in making suggestions about quality-control), and more socialization (as in

job teams taking over functions formerly handled by the assembly line layout). Stagner (1982) has commented extensively on some of these changes as they apply to elderly workers, finding both advantages and pitfalls in the "job enrichment" programs since they may or may not help older employees adjust to a work situation. Particularly important is the anxiety about change reported by some elderly individuals. Introduction of a new system of working, especially if it occurs suddenly, may be very stressful for older members of the work force.

Some other proposals by employers seem less threatening. Provisions for work at home by retirees (using home computer terminals, for example) can accommodate the desire of some older people for less noise, less time pressure, and more opportunities to take breaks without disturbing other workers. Union leaders express anxiety over such policies because they make monitoring of safety conditions, hourly rates of pay, and other possible avenues of exploitation very difficult.

If inflation continues to be a major problem, older workers will probably be wooed to continue to contribute to national production by measures such as these, which may lead to greater self-respect, reduced feelings of worthlessness, and thus to more self-confidence and improved functioning. An outcome that should not be expected, however, is improvement in "life satisfaction." Most workers abhor paternalism and prefer to find their own sources of satisfaction when away from work. Efforts to improve working conditions are of course valuable in themselves, but the "life satisfaction" issue should be treated as peripheral at best.

MOTIVATION

The relation of aging to motivation in general is beyond the scope of this chapter, but as far as it concerns employees, the issues can be identified fairly briefly. Western societies are characterized by the fact that the production of the goods and services needed for human survival is primarily accomplished by a relatively small number of employers directing a very large number of employees. Employees accept tasks that are often boring or unpleasant and a degree of control they often dislike in order to satisfy their own motives. Most American psychologists agree with one form or another of a hierarchical theory of motives (cf. Maslow, 1954; Alderfer, 1972) in which physiological needs such as hunger, thirst, etc., are dominant; but as these are satisfied, other motives such as love and affiliation with others, ego-enhancement and self-esteem, or altruism and self-actualization may come to control behavior. Employers emphasize pay as the primary incentive for keeping workers on the job, and pay, of course, is directly relevant to the powerful physiological drives. In the early twentieth century, employers relied almost entirely on pay as an incentive, and in recent years, industry has used it to bribe workers to tolerate supervisory control, machine-paced tasks, and other restrictive job conditions. Some observers believe that this is the root of the troubles of the automobile industry in the 1980s, i.e., that management preferred to raise pay levels rather than give up authoritarian control of the workplace.

Resistance to control from above, expressive of motives for autonomy and self-esteem, becomes salient after workers have achieved some degree of security and are not afraid of hunger or other biological threats. Baker and Hansen (1975) found this "rebellious" attitude to be characteristic of younger workers; older employees were uniformly more tolerant of managerial controls. The contrasting attitudes may be a function of cohort differences; the older workers may have recalled the depression of the 1930s, with its attendant suffering, and thus inhibited any expressions of dissatisfaction with the control system.

The history of American industry over the past century is one of increasing demands by workers for higher pay and more leisure. Leisure is often preferred to more income, as the predictable absence of workers on a Monday or Friday despite the loss of income will testify. An age difference prevails here since the absentees are preponderantly young; unworried about unemployment (at least during the 1970s), they were more motivated by sex, family affairs, group socialization, or self-expressive activities. Older employees can be as-

sumed to be more motivated by insecurity, but also by the need to build up funds for retirement, pension protection, insurance, etc.

Industrial executives show fewer age-related differences because they have fewer anxieties regarding unemployment and hardship. Desires for ego-enhancement, power, and self-expression are more readily manifested. Satisfaction of these motives may be perceived as requiring employee discipline since executive power may be threatened, say, by the power of employees organized into a union (Stagner, 1956). Thus, executives may express opinions such as "A recession is needed to shake the fat out of the economy," meaning that if their survival needs are threatened, employees will be less insistent in demanding diminished supervision and more self-expression on the job.

For elderly workers, survival needs are less likely to be urgent; they will probably have reached a maximum income for their jobs, although this may be low in absolute terms, and thus accumulated some cushion against adversity. Nevertheless, the desire for leisure to act without external control is still strong; despite the fact that full pension benefits often are delayed until age 62, the median age of retirement in major industries hovers around 58 (Stagner, 1982).

One approach to motivational analysis often accepted in industrial psychology is Vroom's (1964) adaptation of Lewinian field theory. This theory, generally referred to as VIE theory (for valence, instrumentality, and expectancy), asserts that the amount of energy channeled into a task will be a function of the valence of the work outcome, the expectancy that some performance will lead to that outcome, and the instrumental value of effort in attaining the outcome in question. Starting from this premise Heneman (1973) argued that many older workers have seen little evidence that hard work leads to promotions, salary increases, or other rewards (valences). Studying male and female mid-level managers in a retail chain, he found that goals had not changed with age, but the instrumentality of achieving these outcomes diminished. Essentially, older managers preferred that their jobs remain unchanged; they were not enthusiastic about new jobs, transfers, or enlarged responsibilities because, it appeared, they saw little likelihood that they would benefit in any way from the change. The remedy for this state of affairs, Heneman implied, lies in a change in corporate policy rather than in pep talks to try to remotivate older managers.

Anxiety about job changes is also observed in manual workers when job redesign is proposed. Whereas Chown (1972) found that rigidity was more important than age in determining such resistance, it is likely that age is relevant. If the older worker perceives himself as losing competence, he may well fear competition from younger workers. Resistance to job redesign is one result.

VIE theory requires amplification if it is to be applied to specific problems. Vroom did not say much about the origins of valences. Alderfer (1972) has suggested that survival needs (biological demands) determine the pursuit of some valences whereas relatedness needs (for social acceptance and approval) and growth needs (for self-expression, control of environment, etc.) may determine others. It seems plausible that survival valences will be most potent for entering employees, that growth needs may be at maximum during middle age, and that relatedness needs become salient as hopes of prestige and power diminish in later years.

Motivational Profiles

Reference has already been made to the utility of matching the profiles of individual applicants to job profiles that indicate the relative importance of sensory, motor, information-processing, and other abilities. The profile method can also be applied in the realm of motivation. In a study of desires for responsibility, decision-making, growth, and other intrinsic motives as compared with those for extrinsic rewards such as pay and working conditions, Phillips, Barrett, and Rush (1978) demonstrated that job satisfaction is a function of the fit between the profile of preferences and that of perceived job attributes. Since they failed to obtain any determination of job attributes that was independent of the perceiving worker, however, we do not know whether worker satisfaction led to a perception of con-

gruence or vice versa. Curiously, in opposition to most findings, their older group (47+) was not better satisfied than the younger. It preferred more responsibility, interesting work, and attention demands, whereas the younger workers preferred autonomy and social opportunities. Since these findings do not tally with some other studies, a doubt is raised about the sample studied (but not about the relevance of profile matching to satisfaction).

The importance of freedom from arbitrary controls is stressed by Baker and Hansen (1975), who found that younger workers protested most strongly against "bureaucratic structure" (operationally defined as rigid definitions of duties). Older workers in each of eight employee groups were uniformly more tolerant of such constraints. This reaction may reflect nothing more than habituation, but it is also possible that the desire for freedom of decision diminishes after years of functioning under a rigid control system. It has not been possible, as yet, to devise methods of measuring the intensity of the motive apart from the perceived expectancy of its being satisfied. This, of course, is compatible with Vroom's theory. Conceptually speaking, valence, expectancy, and effort are all independent, but if the expectancy of achieving an attractive valence (goal) declines to zero, effort also declines to zero.

Motivation and Performance

Regrettably, few studies of older workers throw light on the accuracy of VIE theory (or any other). Perhaps the most interesting observation is that measures of motivation among older workers predict performance more accurately than among younger workers (Heneman, 1973; Reichelt, 1974; Schwab and Heneman, 1977). This is a difference of considerable theoretical and practical interest. Although no clear-cut explanation is possible, it may be that older workers have assessed company policies more carefully; they would have better bases for evaluating both E and I in the Vroom terminology. Thus, in a firm where effort is rewarded, motivation and performance remain high, whereas, if promotions are perceived as political or discriminatory, motivation and performance remain low. Younger employees, lacking the knowledge necessary for such judgments, may vary at random in the energy they focus on the job, some of them channeling much of their activity into recreational or family projects. Thus, although a young worker might give answers to questions that indicate high motivation, his actual performance may be adversely affected by these competing interests.

Older workers report that job satisfaction is more closely related to intrinsic factors ("the work itself") than to pay and other extrinsic factors. Regrettably, industrial psychologists since the time of Frederick W. Taylor have tended to emphasize external rewards as the principal incentives for increased productivity. Thus, Lawler (1973) wrote that "When extrinsic rewards are related to performance, the result is higher motivation." This contradicts the observations of Deci (1975) and others that making extrinsic rewards salient tends to weaken or abolish intrinsic motivation. Thus, the policy of pay according to output may be self-defeating in the sense that it destroys interest in the work itself, which is the kind of motivation most closely related to job satisfaction in older workers.

Quality of Work Life

In direct opposition to the emphasis on pay and external incentives is the widespread movement to improve worker participation in decision-making and production processes, generally labelled "Quality of Work Life" (QWL) ventures. These innovations have included redesign of jobs to reduce machine-pacing, to allow one worker to complete one entire operation rather than being assigned to fragmented tasks, to use teams of workers instead of the assembly line format, and so on. These experiments are reported to have improved morale and job satisfaction without significant declines in productive output.

QWL experiments have not been aimed specifically at older employees, but it would seem probable that as the implementation of such procedures spreads, the problems of aging in industry could diminish. The data cited above (Kornhauser, 1965; Broadbent, 1978; Martin

et al., 1980) suggest that much apparent aging in industry is a consequence of poorly designed work. It may be that measured declines in ability and performance will disappear if QWL-type work situations became the rule rather than the exception.

Nonindustrial studies may be cited to support this speculation. Langer and Rodin (1976) and Rodin and Langer (1977) reported on an experiment with residents of an institution for the elderly. They found that allowing these residents to make some simple decisions and have some increased freedom of action led to significant improvements in morale and in physical health. Blieszner, Willis, and Baltes (1981) and Hofland, Willis, and Baltes (1981) have shown that elderly individuals can improve on so-called "fluid intelligence" tasks if allowed to practice in a nonthreatening environment and achieve success with simple problems. Such investigations point the way to further innovations in industry that may well improve employee satisfaction and mental health and avert declines in ability and performance.

AGE AND UNIONS

Since unions are also a part of the industrial environment, we may properly note that age differences within unions merit further study. The aging employee may seek additional protection from a union, whereas younger ones may assert their independence and ability to fight for themselves. In heavy industry in the U.S., the typical union contract requires all new employees to join the union; hence, the young do not have the freedom they prefer. This situation may result in intraunion conflicts.

A second source of intraunion difficulty is the difference in motivation of younger and older persons. The worker in his twenties is probably just married and may have very young children. His urgent need is for immediate income. The worker at 50 may be contemplating retirement and perhaps worried about health problems; his demands may center on pensions and insurance benefits. International union officers (who may deny such frictions publicly) will admit in private that bargaining for new contracts often becomes sticky because of this difference in preferred outcomes of the bargaining process.

Although unions do not permit breakdowns of contract ratification votes by age or seniority, the data of Martin (1981) lend support to the preceding analysis. In a survey of a large local union in a midwestern city, Martin asked about preferred policies on wage and fringe benefit bargains and correlated responses with self-reported age and tenure.

The results confirm the speculation about intergenerational conflict. The first item asked was: "Given the choice between additional fringe or the equivalent in higher wages, I would take the higher wages." Among the rank-and-file members ($N = 271$), the correlation with age was -0.18, and with tenure, -0.37 (highly significant). For stewards ($N = 185$), the agreement was less: for age, -0.13 and for tenure, -0.09.

A second item was: "If I had to choose between more fringe benefits for current employees or more fringe benefits for retirees, I would choose added benefits for retirees." On this, the members' agreement correlated with age $+0.22$ and with tenure, $+0.25$. However, the stewards' correlations were only $+0.02$ and $+0.13$.

The union was in a service industry; the data were based on a large sample from a 10,000 member local. The fact that the correlations were much higher for members than for stewards suggests that the stewards were more aware of the implications of partiality and tried to avoid a biased view. Since the average member would be less likely to consider the need for the union to take an impartial stand between older and younger members and retirees, they may have revealed their attitudes more accurately.

A second line of evidence comes from surveys of satisfaction with unions. Quinn and Shepard (1974) found that dissatisfaction with unions peaks between ages 20 and 29 and declines fairly uniformly thereafter. These figures are reasonably similar to those for job satisfaction and may imply no more than "rebellious youth" and "apathetic elders." On the other hand, observations of union elections suggest that most officers are chosen from long-time (i.e., older) members and that union policies tend to protect the interests of this group; hence, the dissatisfaction of more recent members reflects genuine conflicts of interest.

Unions and QWL Projects

Most unions have been skeptical of "Quality of Work Life" (QWL) proposals to improve job satisfaction by job redesign. This skepticism derives from fear that the job changes are designed to maximize production and profits at the expense of the workers, as in the traditional speed-up on the assembly line. It does not mean that the union leaders are indifferent to the job satisfaction of their members but that they are concerned about undermining pay rates and protective clauses in the union contract. Thus, they have resisted the "cottage industry" production plans that some older workers endorse, because hourly rates, safety, and other protective provisions earned through much effort cannot be monitored when production occurs in the worker's home.

NEEDED RESEARCH

Although the foregoing review of selected studies in industrial psychology indicates a very substantial body of data on variables associated with aging in industrial workers, there are still large gaps and ambiguities that demand clarification.

With respect to the question of alleged decline in cognitive-motor abilities, we need both more data and better insights into the conditions under which such decline occurs, or does not occur, the extent to which declines are limited to specific sensory or motor or cognitive categories, and the relevance of such changes to real job performance. The use of an information-processing framework for research on cognitive changes promises insights into whether a specific employee suffers deficiencies in short-term memory, long-term memory, decision-making, differential thresholds, etc. This kind of research should be linked with research on job requirements. It has been charged that employers establish cutting scores for specific test performances with little regard for the actual job demands (Green, 1972). Many jobs, for example, require no auditory cues, yet auditory tests are used for selection, and auditory loss may be used to justify discharge or early retirement.

Industrial psychologists must develop indicators of job performance that are less distorted by supervisory stereotypes. Such may include quantitative measures where quantity of output is relevant and qualitative evaluations of product where quality is essential. There is no reason, for example, why accounting performance or design performance should not be evaluated by judges who are unacquainted with the person who prepared the account report or the product design. Certainly, the use of appraisers who do not know the age of the employee would be helpful.

It has been argued persuasively that most employees are grossly overqualified for most of the tasks to which they are assigned. This is supported by the frequency with which the complaint, "My abilities are not utilized," is cited as justification for boredom and dissatisfaction. The problem will be accentuated as the work force becomes (as is happening today) more highly educated, healthier, and better informed and argues in favor, of course, of job enrichment programs whenever they are feasible. It also suggests, however, that entrance standards for many jobs are unrealistically high. Thus, it may be feasible to maintain productive efficiency on routine tasks by hiring people hitherto considered unemployable (because the selection standards were unrealistic) and to enhance productive efficiency in the more complex tasks by upgrading employees currently assigned to oversimplified assignments.

Proposed changes in job layout and teamwork also call for research. Consider, for example, the tendency to shift from an assembly-line fragmentation of tasks to a small-group unit-assembly layout. This change may introduce many psychological stresses. An older worker, placed with several younger employees, may find himself or herself rejected and socially isolated and hence unable to perform efficiently as part of the team. The reverse (one young person in a team of older, more skilled individuals) may also occur. We need

firm data on what happens when homogeneous or heterogeneous age-groupings are assigned to these team tasks. We may also need more information on supervisory tactics that might optimize the functioning of such groups. Although these problems spread across the age continuum, they are likely to become particularly important if the phenomenon of the "aging work force" develops.

Another controversial point calling for research is that of the ability/performance/motivation interaction. Although we know that some older workers show cognitive and/or motor deficits, there is no acceptable study showing that those developing such deficits also decline in performance. That they do not appear to do so may be a function of compensatory strategies, as proposed by McFarland (1973), or simply of the fact that most workers are overqualified to begin with (Baugher, 1978), or of the intensified motivation of the older employee. It has been fairly well established that measures of motivation correlate better with performance ratings in older than younger workers (e.g., Schwab and Heneman, 1977). So far, no research has sought to establish the factors that bring about such a change; it is possible that older workers, seeing themselves as slower and less efficient, feel impelled to "try harder" and work up to the limit of their ability; if this occurs, correlation of performance with ability or motivation may be maximized.

Most of the studies on job satisfaction and related issues have concentrated on industrial employees in lower-level jobs. In part, this may have been because there are so many of them. However, Sarason et al. (1975) make a persuasive case for more research on professionals—physicians, lawyers, engineers, etc. They allege that job satisfaction is declining among these highly skilled, well-compensated individuals, and Sarason (1977) cites numerous examples of professionals who have (more or less suddenly) abandoned their comfortable careers to go into farming, construction, bartending, and similar occupations that are both less remunerative and less intellectually complex. If we are moving toward a society with more professional-technical jobs, however, we need to know what circumstances lead to such career abandonment, why certain individuals change careers, how they differ (if at all) from those who complain of intellectually uninteresting jobs, and so on. At a time when we are trying to make low-level jobs more challenging, we must consider what to avoid, and for what kinds of personalities, and in what job contexts.

Continuing Education

Research is also needed on the kinds of continuing education that will reduce technological obsolescence and maintain the practitioner's interest in professional work. Such education is now a requirement for continued professional licensing in many states, but little is known about its quality or consequences. Similar investigation would be appropriate with respect to the weekend college programs and other educational innovations of the 1970s which have sought to facilitate either life satisfaction or upward job mobility for nonprofessionals.

Early Retirement

Although legislation has been passed to forbid mandatory retirement prior to age 70, actual retirement age in major industries continues to hover around 58 (Stagner, 1982). Not much information is available regarding the inflationary or "dependency ratio" implications of this phenomenon.

Do workers retire early because they feel pressure from younger co-workers to open up promotional possibilities? Retired auto workers deny this (Stagner, 1979), but executives polled by Mercer (1981) expressed concern that delayed retirement would have adverse effects on younger employees. Martin's (1981) data on union members suggest that there are enough younger employees endorsing the early retirement idea that older workers may indeed feel pressed to get out of the way.

Is it possible that the productive skills of these retirees can be tapped to strengthen the economy? Many manual workers have gone into the casual labor market, doing odd jobs occasionally, and thus increasing the availability of needed services, although their activities do not show up in GNP figures. Similarly, retired managers often continue working, most characteristically by setting up a consulting firm dealing with the same types of problems they handled before retirement. Public policies might well be reviewed to seek ways of encouraging such prolonged economic activity.

Private industry has begun experimenting with arrangements for partial retirement (e.g., two employees may split one job, reducing job stress somewhat). Productive work in the employee's home—the so-called "cottage industry"—is another attempt to allow older employees to work in quiet surroundings at their own pace. Union officials have expressed concern that this may be an opening to undermine wage rates, safety rules, and so on. Some new tasks, however, for example, those that involve use of home computer terminals for information-processing jobs, would not seem to be open to this criticism.

THEORETICAL CONSIDERATIONS

There is no apparent need for a new and distinctive theory of aging, either as a general phenomenon or specifically with respect to industrial workers. The laws of psychology, in so far as they merit such a label, allow of no exceptions. Thus, if a general principle is that of a differentiation from large, amorphous processes to molecular, precise processes, it should hold at all ages. On the other hand, it is recognized that under conditions of external stress, primitivation may result in dedifferentiation of the life-space (phenomenal field) and loss of precision in cognitive-motor activities. We may, therefore, ask the question: Are the data observed in studies of aging in industry compatible with the hypothesis that stress is a major explanatory concept?

Job stress is a matter of increasing concern to industrial psychologists. It may also be a major consideration with respect to industrial gerontology. A generalization that seems justified by the researches sketched in this chapter is that the cumulative effects of stress may account for many symptoms of aging and that individual differences in work history may account for the wide variation in functional age that has been documented.

External job stress (fatigue, mechanical pacing, arbitrary supervision, denial of promotions, etc.) is translated into subjective strain. Although strain usually refers to transitory experiences of anger, anxiety, or depression, it can have a cumulative effect on the self-image of the worker. If self-initiated effort and hard work fail to attain desired rewards, the individual may feel externally controlled and develop the pattern commonly called "learned helplesness." Conversely, experienced success leads to self-confidence and a feeling of control over one's own fate (internal locus of control). An aspect of external control is reduction in the amount of effort channeled into work. As Vroom (1964) would say, if the perceived instrumentality of working hard is zero, no energy is going to be mobilized.

Bamundo and Kopelman (1980) lend some support to the hypothesis that experiences of success lead to felt internal control and to a positive self-image. They found that self-esteem of workers correlated +0.27 with job satisfaction. However, Kopelman (1982) discovered no tendency for self-esteem to increase with age. It would appear, then, that self-confidence and self-esteem may account for some but not all of the increased satisfaction associated with aging.

One of the additional variables may be coping style. As noted above, Andrew (1973) found that "sensitizers" increased in verbal ability with age, whereas "avoiders" declined. The "sensitizer" is the person who is vigilant and alert for changes in the environment; the "avoider" is one who refuses to admit that problems exist or that changes must be met. It may follow that sensitizers keep cognitive abilities functional by tackling new projects, whereas avoiders stop practicing these skills.

Such an approach would suggest that aging is not built into the DNA nor inevitably tied to tissue deterioration but results from the accumulation of failures, frustrations, and the escape from challenging activities. Repeated failures to live up to aspirations, or to achieve desired goals, may result in a feeling of "learned helplessness" that in turn may trigger a withdrawal of energy from constructive efforts. "Disengagement" may be a significant phenomenon mainly for those who feel that continuing engagement is futile.

This environmentally oriented theory of aging phenomena need not be seen as opposed to studies of physiological decline. Obviously, some decrement in ability and in job performance may result from illness or from the cumulative accidents that damage the biological structure, and a convergence of job failure and physical handicap would obviously have a cumulative effect on functional age.

As regards the industrial data reviewed here, it would seem that those workers who can look back on their careers with some feeling of success will report job satisfaction and will usually show less decrement in abilities than those who assess themselves as failures. A problem for social policy is to arrange affairs so that a smaller proportion of the aging population will view life as a series of failures. This goal becomes increasingly important as the number of elderly workers in the American economy expands.

Acknowledgements: Valuable comments and suggestions were received from Drs. A. R. Bass, H. Rosen, K. W. Schaie, and C. M. Solley. Responsibility for the interpretations offered, however, is my own.

REFERENCES

AFL-CIO. 1979. The intimidation of job tests. *American Federationist,* Jan. 1979: 1–8.

Alderfer, C. P. 1972. *Existence, Relatedness, and Growth.* London: Collier-Macmillan.

Andrew, J. M. 1973. Coping style and declining verbal abilities. *Journal of Gerontology* 28: 179–183.

Andrisani, P. J., and Miljus, R. C. 1977. Individual differences in preferences for intrinsic vs. extrinsic aspects of work. *Journal of Vocational Behavior* 11: 14–30.

Baddeley, A. D., and Hitch, G. 1974. Working memory. In *The Psychology of Learning and Motivation,* vol. 8, ed. G. Bower. New York: Academic Press.

Baker, S. H., and Hansen, R. A. 1975. Job design and worker satisfaction: A challenge to assumptions. *Journal of Occupational Psychology* 48: 79–91.

Bamundo, P. J., and Kopelman, R. E. 1980. Moderating effects of occupation, age, and urbanization on the relationship between job satisfaction and life satisfaction. *Journal of Vocational Behavior* 17: 106–123.

Baugher, D. 1978. Is the older worker inherently incompetent? *Aging and Work* 1: 243–250.

Belbin, R. M. 1965. *Training Methods for Older Workers.* Paris: OECD.

Birren, J. E. 1959. Principles of research on aging. In *Handbook of Aging and the Individual,* ed. J. E. Birren. Chicago: University of Chicago Press.

Blieszner, R.; Willis, S. L.; and Baltes, P. B. 1981. Training research in aging on the fluid ability of inductive reasoning. *Journal of Applied Developmental Psychology* 2: 247–265.

Blumberg, M. 1980. Job switching in autonomous work groups: An exploratory study in a Pennsylvania coal mine. *Academy of Management Journal* 23: 287–306.

Botwinick, J., and Storandt, M. 1980. Recall and recognition of old information in relation to age and sex. *Journal of Gerontology* 35: 70–76.

Bray, D. W.; Campbell, R. J; and Grant, D. L. 1974. *Formative Years in Business: A Long-Term AT&T Study of Managerial Lives.* New York: Wiley.

Broadbent, D. E. 1978. Chronic effects from the physical nature of work. In *Man and Working Life,* ed. B. Gardell. New York: Wiley.

Burns, R. B. 1966. Age and mental ability: Re-testing with thirty-three years interval. *British Journal of Educational Psychology* 36: 116.

Caplan, R. D.; Cobb, S.; French, J. R. P., Jr.; Harrison, R. V.; and Pinneau, S. R., Jr. 1975. *Job Demands and Worker Health.* Washington, D.C.: HEW Publication (NIOSH) 75–160.

Chown, S. M. 1972. The effects of flexibility-rigidity and age on adaptability in job performance. *Industrial Gerontology* 13: 105–121.

Cicirelli, V. G. 1980. Relationship of family background variables to locus of control in the elderly. *Journal of Gerontology* 35: 108–114.

Clay, H. M. 1956. A study of performance in relation to age at two printing works. *Journal of Gerontology* 11: 417–424.

Cleveland, J. N., and Landy, F. J. 1981. Influence of rater and ratee age on two performance judgments. *Personnel Psychology* 34: 19–30.

Clopton, W. 1973. Personality and career change. *Industrial Gerontology* 17: 9–17.

Cobb, S. 1974. Physiological changes in men whose jobs were abolished. *Journal of Psychosomatic Research* 18: 245–258.

Craft, J. A.; Doctors, S. I.; Shkop, Y. M.; and Benecki, T. J. 1979. Simulated management perceptions, hiring decisions, and age. *Aging and Work* 2: 95–102.

Cumming, E., and Henry, W. E. 1961. *Growing Old: The Process of Disengagement.* New York: Basic Books.

Deci, E. L. 1975. *Intrinsic Motivation.* New York: Plenum Press.

Dillingham, A. E. 1981. Age and workplace injuries. *Aging and Work* 4: 1–10.

Dirken, J. M., ed. 1972. *Functional Age of Industrial Workers.* Groningen, The Netherlands: Wolters-Noordhoff.

Dubin, S. S., ed. 1972. *Professional Obsolescence.* Lexington, MA: D. C. Heath.

Fritz, D. 1978. Decision makers and the changing retirement scene. *Aging and Work* 1: 221–230.

Fry, L. W. 1982. Effect of age on job satisfaction of policemen. Personal communication.

Glickman, A. S., ed. 1982. *The Changing Composition of the Work Force: Implications for Research and Its Practical Application.* New York: Plenum Publishing Corporation.

Gordon, M. E.; Philpot, J. W.; Burt, R. E.; Thompson, C. A.; and Spiller, W. E. 1980. Commitment to the union: Development of a measure and an examination of the correlates. Monograph, *Journal of Applied Psychology* 65: 479–499.

Granick, S. 1971. Psychological test functioning. In *Human Aging II: An 11-Year Follow-Up Biomedical and Behavioral Study,* eds. S. Granick and R. D. Patterson. DHEW Publication [HSM] 71-9037. Rockville, MD: NIMH.

Green, R. F. 1972. Age, intelligence, and learning. *Industrial Gerontology* 12: 29–41.

Gurin, G.; Veroff, J.; and Feld, S. 1960. *Americans View Their Mental Health.* New York: Basic Books.

Haberlandt, K. F. 1973. Learning, memory, and age. *Industrial Gerontology* 19: 20–37.

Hall, D. T. 1976. *Careers in Organizations.* Pacific Palisades, CA: Goodyear Publishing Co.

Hazer, J. T., and Alvares, K. M. 1981. Police work values during organizational entry and assimilation. *Journal of Applied Psychology* 66: 12–18.

Helson, H. F. 1964. *Adaptation-Level Theory.* New York: Harper & Row.

Heneman, H. G., III. 1973. Relationship between age and motivation to perform on the job. *Industrial Gerontology* 16: 30–36.

Herzberg, F.; Mausner, B.; Peterson, R. O.; and Capwell, D. F. 1957. *Job Attitudes: Review of Research and Opinion.* Pittsburgh, PA: Psychological Service of Pittsburgh.

Hofland, B.; Willis, S.; and Baltes, P. 1981. Fluid intelligence performance in the elderly: Intraindividual variability and conditions of assessment. *Journal of Educational Psychology* 73: 573–586.

Horn, J. L., and Cattell, R. B. 1967. Age differences in fluid and crystallized intelligence. *Acta Psychologica* 26: 107–129.

Horner, P. 1980. Construction and implementation of an alternative performance rating scale and possible age group and managerial level effects on performance ratings. Unpublished M.A. thesis, Wayne State University.

Hunt, J. W., and Saul, P. N. 1975. Relationship of age, tenure, and job satisfaction in males and females. *Academy of Management Journal* 18: 690–702.

James, L. R., and Jones, A. P. 1980. Perceived job characteristics and job satisfaction: An examination of reciprocal causation. *Personnel Psychology* 33: 97–135.

Jones, J. W., ed. 1981. *The Burnout Syndrome.* Park Ridge, IL: London House press.

Kelleher, C. H., and Quirk, D. A. 1973. Age, functional capacity, and work: An annotated bibliography. *Industrial Gerontology* 19: 80–98.

Kleiman, L. S., and Durham, R. L. 1981. Performance appraisal, promotion, and the courts. *Personnel Psychology* 34: 103–121.

Kogan, N., and Wallach, M. A. 1961. The effect of anxiety on relations between subjective age and caution in an older sample. In *Psychopatholgy of Aging,* eds. P. H. Hoch and J. Zubin. New York: Grune & Stratton.

Kopelman, R. E. 1982. Personal communicaton.

Kornhauser, A. 1965. *Mental Health of the Industrial Worker.* New York: Wiley.

Langer, R. J., and Rodin, J. 1976. Effects of choice and enhanced personal responsibility for the aged: A field experiment in an institutionalized setting. *Journal of Personality and Social Psychology* 34: 191–198.

Langner, T. S., and Michael, S. T. 1963. *Life Stress and Mental Health.* New York: Free Press of Glencoe.

LaRocco, J. M., and Jones, A. P. 1980. Organizational conditions affecting withdrawal intentions and decisions as moderated by work experience. *Psychological Reports* 46: 1223–1231.

Lawler, E. E., III. 1973. *Motivation in Work Organizations.* Monterey, CA: Brooks/Cole.

Levinson, D. J. 1978. *The Seasons of a Man's Life.* New York: Knopf.

Lifson, K. A. 1953. Errors in time-study judgments of industrial work pace. *Psychological Monographs* 67: Whole No. 355.

Martin, J. E. 1981. Age and union policy preference. Personal communication.

Martin, E.; Ackerman, U.; Udris, I.; and Oergerli, K. 1980. *Monotonie in der Industrie.* Bern: Hans Huber Verlag.

Maslach, C. 1978. Job burnout: How people cope. *Public Welfare* 36: 56–58.

Maslach, C., and Jackson, S. 1981. *The Maslach Burnout Inventory.* Palo Alto, CA: Consulting Psychologists Press.

Maslow, A. H. 1954. *Motivation and Personality.* New York: Harper.

McAuley, W. J. 1977. Perceived age discrimination in hiring: Demographic and economic correlates. *Industrial Gerontology* 4: 21–28.

McDonald, B. W., and Gunderson, E. K. E. 1972. Correlates of job satisfaction in naval environments. Unpublished paper. American Psychological Association, September 1972.

McFarland, R. A. 1953. *Human Factors in Air Transportation: Occupational Health and Safety.* (See especially "Aging and efficiency in airmen," pp. 369–401.) New York: McGraw-Hill.

McFarland, R. A. 1973. The need for functional age measurements in industrial gerontology. *Industrial Gerontology* 19: 1–19.

McFarland, R. A. 1976. *The Role of Functional vs. Chronological Age Concepts in the Employment of Older Workers. (Future of Retirement Age Conference.)* Washington, D.C.: American Institutes of Research.

Meier, E. L., and Kerr, E. A. 1976. Capabilities of middle-aged and older workers. *Industrial Gerontology* 3: 147–156.

Meltzer, H. 1958. Age differences in work attitudes. *Journal of Gerontology* 13: 74–81.

Meltzer, H., and Stagner, R. 1980. Social psychology of aging in industry. *Professional Psychology* 11: 436–444.

Mercer, W. M. 1981. *Employer Attitudes: Implications of an Aging Work Force.* New York: William M. Mercer, Inc.

Muchinsky, P. M. 1978. Age and job facet satisfaction: A conceptual reconsideration. *Aging and Work* 1: 175–180.

Mullick, B. 1981. The effects of age of the perceiver, locus of control, locus of causality, and responsibility on attitudes toward the elderly. Unpublished doctoral dissertation, Wayne State University.

Noble, C. E.; Baker, B. C.; and Jones, T. A. 1964. Age and sex parameters in psychomotor learning. *Perceptual and Motor Skills* 19: 935–945.

O'Hanlon, J. F. 1981. Boredom: practical consequences and a theory. *Acta Psychologica* 49: 53–82.

Opinion Research Corporation. 1980. *Strategic Planning for Human Resources: 1981 and Beyond.* Princeton, N.J.: Opinion Research Corporation.

Owens, W. A., Jr. 1966. Age and mental abilities: A second adult follow-up. *Journal of Educational Psychology* 57: 311–325.

Panek, P. E.; Barrett, G. V.; Alexander, R. A.; and Sterns, H. L. 1979. Age and self-selected performance pace on a visual monitoring task. *Aging and Work* 2: 183–191.

Phillips, J. S.; Barrett, G. V.; and Rush, M. C. 1978. Job structure and work satisfaction. *Aging and Work* 1: 109–119.

Price, R. L.; Thompson, P. H.; and Dalton, G. W. 1975. A longitudinal study of technological obsolescence. *Research Management,* Nov. 1975: 22–28.

Pursell, E. D.; Dossett, D. L.; and Latham, G. P. 1980. Obtaining valid predictors by minimizing rating errors in the criterion. *Personnel Psychology* 33: 91–96.

Quinn, R. P., and Shepard, L. J. 1974. *The 1972–73 Quality of Employment Survey.* Ann Arbor, MI: Institute of Social Research, University of Michigan.

Quirk, D. A., and Skinner, J. H. 1973. IHCS: Physical capacity, age, and employment. *Industrial Gerontology* 19: 49–62.

Reichelt, P. A. 1974. Moderators in expectancy theory: Influence on the relationships of motivation with effort and job performance. Unpublished doctoral dissertation, Wayne State University.

Rodin, J., and Langer, E. J. 1977. Long-term effects of a control-relevant intervention with the institutionalized age. *Journal of Personality and Social Psychology* 35: 897–902.

Ronen, S. 1978. Job satisfaction and the neglected variable of job seniority. *Human Relations* 31: 297–308.

Rosen, B., and Jerdee, T. H. 1976a. Influence of age stereotypes on managerial decisions. *Journal of Applied Psychology* 61: 428–432.

Rosen, B., and Jerdee, T. H. 1976b. The nature of job-related stereotypes. *Journal of Applied Psychology* 61: 180–183.

Sarason, S. B. 1977. *Work, Aging, and Social Change.* New York: The Free Press.

Sarason, S. B.; Sarason, E. K.; and Cowden, P. 1975. Aging and the nature of work. *American Psychologist* 30: 584–592.

Schaie, K. W. 1970. A reinterpretation of age related changes in cognitive structure and functioning. In *Life-Span Developmental Psychology: Research and Theory,* eds. L. R. Goulet and P. B. Baltes. New York: Academic Press.

Schaie, K. W. 1980. Age changes in intelligence. In *Age, Learning Ability, and Intelligence,* ed. R. L. Sprott. New York: Van Nostrand Reinhold.

Schaie, K. W., and Parr, J. 1981. Concepts and criteria for functional age. In *Aging: A Challenge to Science and Social Policy,* vol, 3, ed. J. E. Birren. New York: Oxford University Press.

Schmidt, F. L., and Hunter, J. E. 1981. Employment testing: Old theories and new research findings. *American Pyschologist* 36: 1128–1137.

Schwab, D. P., and Heneman, H. G., III. 1977. Age and satisfaction with dimensions of work. *Journal of Vocational Behavior* 10: 212–222.

Sheppard, H. L., and Herrick, N. Q. 1972. *Where Have All the Robots Gone?* New York: The Free Press.

Sheppard, H. L., and Rix, S. E. 1977. *The Graying of Working America: The Coming Crisis of Retirement Age Policy.* New York: The Free Press.

Siassi, I.; Crocetti, G.; and Spiro, H. R. 1975. Emotional health, life and job satisfaction in aging workers. *Industrial Gerontology* 2: 289–296.

Slote, A. 1969. *Termination: The Closing at Baker Plant.* Indianapolis: Bobbs-Merrill.

Smith, P. C.; Kendall, L. M.; and Hulin, C. L. 1969. *The Measurement of Satisfaction in Work and Retirement.* Chicago: Rand McNally.

Solley, C. M., Jr. 1981. Information processing in elderly workers. Grant proposal, 1981.

Spencer, D. G., and Steers, R. M. 1980. The influence of personal factors and perceived work experiences on employee turnover and absenteeism. *Academy of Management Journal* 23: 567–572.

Sprott, R. L., ed. 1980. *Age, Learning Ability, and Intelligence.* New York: Van Nostrand Reinhold.

Srole, L.; Langner, T. S.; Michael, S. T.; Opler, M. K.; and Rennie, T. A. C. 1962. *Mental Health in the Metropolis: The Midtown-Manhattan Study.* Vol. 1. New York: McGraw-Hill.

Stagner, R. 1956. *Psychology of Industrial Conflict.* New York: Wiley.

Stagner, R. 1975. Boredom on the assembly line: Age and personality variables. *Industrial Gerontology* 2: 23–44.

Stagner, R. 1979. Propensity to work: An important variable in retiree behavior. *Aging and Work* 2: 161–172.

Stagner, R. 1981. Stress, strain, coping, and defense. *Research on Aging,* 3: 3–32.

Stagner, R. 1982. Postscripts and prospects. In *The Changing Composition of the Workforce: Implications for Research and Its Application,* ed. A. S. Glickman. New York: Plenum Publishing Corp.

Stolurow, L. M. 1965. Programmed instruction and teaching machines. In *The Impact of New Media on Education and Society,* eds. P. H. Rossi and B. J. Biddle. Chicago: Aldine.

Tenopyr, M. 1981. The realities of employment testing. *American Psychologist* 36: 1120–1127.

Toch, H., and Klofas, J. 1982. Alienation and desire for job enrichment among correction officers. *Federal Probation* 46: 135–144.

Vroom, V. H. 1964. *Work and Motivation.* New York: Wiley.

Wallach, M. A., and Kogan, N. 1961. Aspects of judgment and decision-making: Interrelationships and changes with age. *Behavioral Science* 6: 23–36.

Wanous, J. P. 1980. *Organizational Entry: Recruitment, Selection and Socialization of Newcomers.* Reading, MA: Addison-Wesley.

Weaver, C. N. 1980. Job satisfaction in the United States in the 1970s. *Journal of Applied Psychology* 65: 364–367.

Welford, A. T. 1976. Thirty years of psychological research on age and work. *Journal of Occupational Psychology* 49: 129–138.

Welford, A. T., and Birren, J. E., eds. 1965. *Behavior, Aging, and the Nervous System.* Springfield, IL: Charles C Thomas.

Wollach, S.; Goodale, J. G.; Wijting, J. P.; and Smith, P. C. 1971. Development of the survey of work values. *Journal of Applied Psychology* 55: 331–338.

30
TOWARDS AN EDUCATIONAL PSYCHOLOGY OF THE OLDER ADULT LEARNER: INTELLECTUAL AND COGNITIVE BASES

Sherry L. Willis
The Pennsylvania State University

INTRODUCTION

A primary purpose of this chapter is to examine theory and research within selected areas of adult developmental psychology, as they have implications for formulating an educational psychology of the adult learner. A primary focus will be on the intellectual and cognitive bases for the development of an educational psychology of later adulthood. The older adult learner brings to the learning context a long developmental history. Thus, long-term developmental change, as well as short-term behavioral change associated with learning in a specific educational context, must be considered. The first part of this chapter examines findings regarding long-term change in intellectual functioning, based on longitudinal and cohort-sequential research. The second part of the chapter considers educational implications of these research findings regarding long-term intellectual change. The third part of the chapter deals with short-term behavioral change, which is associated with cognitive training research in later adulthood, and considers some of the methodological and conceptual issues related to cognitive training research. In the final section of the chapter, potential goals of the older adult learner are

considered, and the motivational and personality factors associated with lifelong learning in later adulthood are examined.

The term *education* conjures up an image of young students in a classroom setting, receiving instruction from a teacher. The focus is on the acquisition of the academic knowledge and skills that are assumed to prepare the young person for the responsibilities of adulthood. Most of our educational efforts and resources are concentrated in the first quarter of the life span. There has been the implicit assumption that the individual can acquire in childhood sufficient knowledge and skill for effective functioning in adulthood. As a function of our rapidly changing and increasingly complex and differentiated society, the period of initial schooling has been increasing to include not only childhood but adolescence and early adulthood, and, as a result, assumption of many adult responsibilities has been delayed (Parsons and Platt, 1972). As our society continues to change and becomes ever more complex, the question arises whether further extension of the period of initial schooling is functional or desirable.

The term *education* as employed in this chapter refers to lifelong learning. Learning, as a form of adaptation, continues throughout adulthood. A primary function of lifelong education should be the facilitiation of adaptation and optimal development across the life course (Cropley, 1977; Dave, 1976; Houle, 1981; Schaie and Willis, 1978, 1982). In contrast to early schooling, much adult learning is self-determined and self-directed. Learning occurs less frequently in a formal classroom setting that has an instructor as the primary agent of knowledge dissemination. The learning context is more diverse, including the home, social functions, community organizations, and the work place. The "teacher" may now be the mass media, the printed word, friends and relatives, work colleagues, or the computer. Although acquisition may be the primary mode of learning in youth, learning in adulthood increasingly involves processes, such as application, synthesis, and integration of new learning with prior knowledge (Schaie, 1977/78) and the inhibition ("forgetting") of prior information that is irrelevant or obsolete (Goulet, 1973).

From a sociological perspective, lifelong learning is conceptualized in terms of socialization after childhood (Brim and Wheeler, 1966; Parsons and Platt, 1972). In a complex, fast changing society, socialization in childhood is not adequate for the tasks of adulthood. There may be little continuity in significant others from childhood to adulthood, and successive societal roles expected of the individual may not build upon one another. Thus, society must provide for the resocialization of individuals into roles they were not developmentally prepared for in childhood.

INTELLECTUAL AGING: AN OVERVIEW OF LONGITUDINAL AND SEQUENTIAL RESEARCH FINDINGS

A number of recent review chapters have noted the lack of integrative theories of intellectual development (Baltes and Willis, 1977; Birren, Cunningham, and Yamamoto, 1982; Labouvie-Vief and Schell, 1982). This deficiency is partly a result of the plurality of approaches (psychometric, cognitive developmental, information processing) to the study of adult intellectual development. Given the current state of the field, we will focus our

discussion on several dimensions of intellectual development that would need to be considered in such an integrative theory and that have particular relevance in deriving educational implications.

There is general consensus that two of the major aims of developmental theories of intellectual aging are the study of change occurring within a given individual (i.e., intraindividual change) and of differences between individuals in intraindividual change (i.e., interindividual differences in intraindividual change) (Hoyer, 1974; Willis and Baltes, 1980). Much of the research on adult intellectual development has presumably focused on the description and explication of changes in intellectual functioning *within* individuals (intraindividual) over time. The rate and magnitude of such change is the focus of much current debate (Botwinick, 1977; Horn and Donaldson, 1976; Schaie and Baltes, 1977). These issues focus on quantitative aspects of change. Study of qualitative aspects of change focusing on the pattern and nature of change is gaining increasing attention (Labouvie-Vief, 1977; Overton and Newman, 1981).

Developmental change has typically been construed as a *long-term* intraindividual change, that is, change occurring in the same individual over time. In contrast, there has been much less attention and research focused on *short-term* intraindividual change, that is, systematic sustained change in performance occurring over a brief time period (Baltes and Baltes, 1980; Baltes and Willis, 1979). Short-term change has typically been studied within a cognitive training paradigm, the magnitude of changes being examined as a function of training. The paucity of research on short-term change is unfortunate, since it is this type of change that is likely to have the most direct and immediate implications for an educational/instructional psychology of the adult learner.

Long-term Intraindividual Change

Intraindividual change has been studied via longitudinal and cohort-sequential research paradigms (Nesselroade and Baltes, 1979; Schaie and Hertzog, 1982). In longitudinal studies, changes in the intellectual functioning of the same individuals are examined over a number of years. Since longitudinal studies examine only one birth cohort, however, intraindividual change and cohort effects are confounded. Cohort-sequential designs involve the examination of several birth cohorts over the same chronological age period and thus permit differentiation of intraindividual change vs. birth cohort effects.

Almost all of the longitudinal and cohort-sequential studies examining intellectual functioning have been conducted within a psychometric approach to intelligence. Thus, our understanding of long-term change is largely limited to the description of changes in the individual's performance on a number of ability measures (e.g., spatial orientation, verbal ability, numerical computation, inductive reasoning, etc.). A number of review chapters have described the findings of these longitudinal and cohort-sequential studies (Botwinick, 1977; Cunningham and Owens, 1983; Eichorn et al., 1981; Schaie, 1983; Siegler, 1983; Thomae, 1976). We will only briefly summarize some of the major findings.

Peak Performance Levels. There is considerable evidence that different mental abilities exhibit different patterns of intraindividual change, both with regard to timing of peak levels of ability performance and onset of significant decline. Findings from a number of longitudinal studies (Bray and Howard, 1983; Cunningham and Owens, 1983; Schaie, 1983) suggest that contrary to the traditional assumption of maximum intellectual functioning in adolescence, there are modest increments in ability performance into the thirties and forties.

Schaie's (1983) cohort-sequential study indicates that performance on numerical computation and inductive reasoning peak in the thirties. Peak performance levels for spatial orientation occurred in the forties, and for verbal ability in the fifties. Statistically significant performance increments (from age 25) were found into the fifties for verbal ability. Figure 1 graphically summarizes the patterns of intraindividual change for four Thurstonian abilities (Verbal Meaning, Spatial Orientation,

Number, and Inductive Reasoning). Average performance at seven-year intervals (ages 32, 39, 46, 53, 60, 67, 74, 81) is shown as a proportion of performance obtained at age 25.

These data represent normative intraindividual change averaged across several cohorts. Note that even at age 81 normative performance levels are at or above 75 percent of the performance level at age 25. Given his interest in predicting academic success, Thurstone (1938) derived from ability performance an index of educational aptitude ($EA = 2$ Verbal $+$ Reasoning). Due to increments in Verbal and Reasoning ability in young and middle adulthood, this index of educational aptitude actually peaks in the forties rather than in childhood. Although such an index of educational aptitude was not developed specifically for adult learners, the index would appear to be valid, at least for adults engaged in academic pursuits in traditional instructional settings.

Decline in Intellectual Performance. There are also differential patterns of decline for various abilities. Longitudinal research, however, indicates a later onset of significant decline than stereotypic notions have assumed. When intraindividual change is assessed from young adulthood, significant normative decline is not

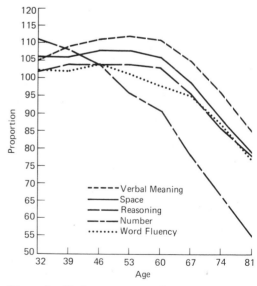

Figure 1.   Performance at various ages as a proportion of performance at age 25.

evident until the late sixties (Figure 1). This finding has been reported in a number of longitudinal studies (Cunningham and Owens, 1983; Jarvik and Banks, 1983; Schaie, 1983).

Abilities measured under speeded conditions, those involving perceptual-motor functioning or abstract reasoning, show earlier patterns of decline than abilities involving nonspeeded performance and which draw upon overlearned, culturally acquired knowledge. This differential pattern of ability change has been described as the "classical pattern of intellectual aging," given its replication across studies. Specifically, abilities assessed through speeded tests, such as the Thurstone number factor and the performance measures on the WAIS, have shown earlier decline (Jarvik and Banks, 1983; Siegler, 1983). In contrast, significant decrement in passive vocabulary does not appear until the mid to late seventies (Botwinick, 1977).

Normative data on intraindividual decline indicate a pattern of gradual, cumulative decline rather than a sudden precipitous drop in performance. The decade of the sixties appears particularly critical, since it is in this age period that significant decline is first shown for a number of abilities (number, reasoning, spatial orientation).

These differential patterns of intraindividual change bring into question the conceptualization of adult intelligence as a global, unidimensional construct (Baltes and Labouvie, 1973; Botwinick, 1977; Salthouse, 1982). Rather, a multidimensional conceptualization of intellectual functioning is required. Such differential patterns of change have led to considerable skepticism regarding a pervasive, universal pattern of decline. Smith (1980, p. 224) recently summarized this view: "A single, definitive 'deficit' hypothesis does not seem capable of surviving the weight of all the evidence . . . there is the realization that cognitive behavior is multivariate in nature."

Interindividual Differences in Intraindividual Change

In the previous section we attempted to summarize major findings regarding long-term intraindividual change. Equally important to an understanding of adult intelligence, however, is the wide range of individual differences in intraindividual change. The magnitude of these individual differences has led some (Flavell, 1970) to question whether a normative pattern of intellectual aging should be the primary focus of study. Differential patterns of aging have come to be considered by some (Thomae, 1976) as the most prominent feature of adult intellectual development. We will begin by examining the magnitude of interindividual differences in intraindividual change. Second, we will consider cohort (generational) effects as one critical source of individual differences in change. Third, we will consider several personal life style variables implicated as important sources of interindividual differences in intellectual change.

Range of Interindividual Differences in Intraindividual Change. Figure 2 provides a graphic summary of the pattern and magnitude of interindividual differences in intraindividual change for four Thurstonian abilities (Schaie, 1980, 1983). The data are expressed in standard deviations of change scores (seven-year longitudinal change scores). These data suggest that the magnitude of interindividual differences in change varies by ability and by age period. For three of the abilities (Verbal

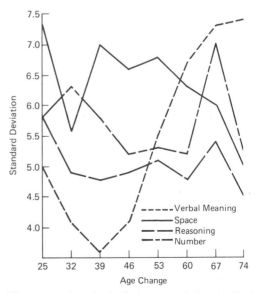

Figure 2. Standard deviations of longitudinal seven-year change scores.

Meaning, Inductive Reasoning, Number) interindividual variability in change is relatively stable during the thirties and forties and then shows an increment in the sixties. This shift in magnitude of variability is most notable for Verbal Meaning. Note that for these three abilities, interindividual differences in change peak at approximately age 67, the age period at which statistically significant decrement is first noted. For several of the abilities, there is a drop in the magnitude of interindividual variability in change in the mid seventies. For verbal ability, however, variability in change remains high. This increase in interindividual differences in intraindividual change in the sixties can have important implications for the design of instructional programs for the older adult learner.

Cohort Differences. During the last two decades there has been considerable discussion and debate within adult developmental psychology regarding cohort effects as a source of interindividual differences in intraindividual change (Botwinick and Arenberg, 1976; Horn and Donaldson, 1976; Schaie and Baltes, 1977). Although some (Botwinick, 1977; Salthouse, 1982) have sought to dismiss cohort differences as little more than variations in the "classical" pattern of intellectual aging, cohort differences do appear to have some distinctly different educational implications from age-related change. As will be elaborated on later, cohort differences may indeed be of greater practical significance than age changes in terms of social policy implications for lifelong learning.

The most comprehensive study of cohort differences in intellectual functioning has been Schaie's (1979, 1983) 21-year cohort-sequential research. Data from that study suggest that differences between cohorts in intellectual performance are equal to or may exceed the magnitude of intraindividual change when cohort effects and intraindividual change are examined over comparable time periods. Figure 3 compares performance differences between birth cohorts in terms of the proportion of performance of the cohort born in 1952; performance of the 1952 cohort is set at 100 percent.

The most common pattern indicates a positive cohort trend; that is, the performance level of earlier-born cohorts is below that of later-born cohorts when the two are compared at the same chronological age. Current elderly are significantly disadvantaged with regard to inductive reasoning ability and verbal meaning; a similar but nonsignificant trend is shown for spatial orientation. Statistically significant cohort effects occur for the 1889 to 1931 birth cohorts for inductive reasoning ability and for the 1889 to 1917 birth cohorts for verbal meaning. In contrast, word fluency shows a reverse cohort trend. Earlier-born cohorts (1889 to 1917) performed above the mean level of the 1952 cohort, whereas performance of later-birth cohorts (1924 to 1945) fell below that of the 1952 cohort. Finally, a third type of cohort trend is suggested by numerical ability. Here, a curvilinear trend is suggested, with some birth cohorts (1903 to 1924) performing at a level above that indicated for either earlier- or later-born cohorts.

Cohort effects, which reflect multidirectional patterns of change, are a dynamic form of interindividual differences, varying according to the critical life experiences of a given cohort. Most recently, there is suggestive evidence (Schaie and Hertzog, 1983) that there may be a partial reversal in the positive cohort

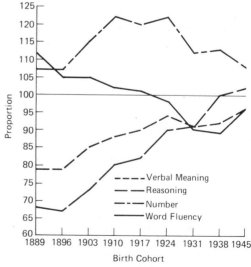

Figure 3. Performance of various cohorts as a proportion of the performance of cohort born in 1952.

trend for verbal ability in current young adult cohorts, a trend also suggested by recent reports on a decline in scores in college entrance examinations.

Health. With increasing age, the incidence of cumulative chronic disease also increases. Thus, there is a likelihood of an increasing association between health status and cognitive change. Longitudinal research indicates a very complex pattern of relationships between psychological functioning and health status (Hertzog, Schaie, and Gribbin, 1978; Siegler, 1983; Siegler, Nowlin, and Blumenthal, 1980). The health variable that has been the most thoroughly examined is circulatory disorders. Heart disease is correlated with other sources of individual differences, such as cohort and socioeconomic status. When these variables have been controlled for, circulatory disorders are found to be related to seven-year declines in intellectual functioning (Hertzog, Schaie, and Gribbin, 1978); however, heart disease accounts for only a small amount of the variance associated with cognitive change. Although heart disease has been associated with cognitive change on a composite measure of intellectual ability, it has been difficult to identify the particular cognitive abilities that are most susceptible to the effects of heart problems.

Life Style. In terms of concurrent individual difference variables associated with intellectual change, life style variables present some intriguing findings. Decline in intellectual functioning over a seven-year period in mid- to later adulthood has been significantly associated with a life style of personal disengagement and of family dissolution (Gribbin, Schaie, and Parham, 1980). In particular, older women who reported a less actively engaged life style, who had experienced some form of family dissolution (loss of spouse), and who lived in relatively inaccessible environments showed the most dramatic drop in cognitive functioning over a seven-year period.

Given their longer life expectancies and the likelihood of a lengthy period of widowhood, educational intervention programs targeted at older women appear to have particular prom-

ise. The adult education literature (Burgess, 1971; Carp, Peterson, and Roelfs, 1974) indicates that one major motivation for participation in educational programs is the desire for social interaction (to meet new people, feel a sense of belonging). Data relating life styles to cognitive change suggest that women seeking social interactions within the context of educational activities may also be particularly in need of intellectual stimulation.

Education and Socioeconomic Status. In considering the association between education and intellectual functioning, it is important to distinguish between the relation of education to current level of intellectual performance and the relation of education and long-term changes in intellectual functioning. Educational level has frequently been associated with current level of functioning on a number of cognitive measures such as problem solving, mental abilities, and learning (Birren and Morrison, 1961; Kessler, Denney, and Whitely, 1976). A significant relation has not been found, however, between education level and change (decline) in cognitive functioning (Stone and Schaie, 1980).

Education appears to play an interactive role, then, in the maintenance of intellectual functioning. In early stages in the life span, those of higher ability may seek out or be given greater educational opportunities; education serves to foster the development of skills and a knowledge base for future learning. Second, educational level is associated with certain types of life styles that foster the maintenance or decline of intellectual abilities. For example, prior level of educational attainment is the most significant predictor of participation in adult education activities in midlife (Cross, 1981; Johnstone and Riviera, 1965).

Longitudinal Research: Its Relevance and Limitations

Some may question our utilization of longitudinal-research findings for deriving educational implications, given the recent debate regarding the potential limitations of this type of research (Botwinick, 1977). The aim of education is the facilitation of certain dimensions of *intraindividual* change via educational intervention. The central thesis of most educational theories of learning and instruction is the description and explication of variables associated with intraindividual change in the instructional context. In the assessment and evaluation of educational endeavors, the focus is on intraindividual change, occurring as a function of educational programs, and on interindividual differences in intraindividual change (e.g., comparison of the relative effectiveness of various programs).

Longitudinal research provides the only direct information on long-term intraindividual change and thus, in spite of some limitations, would appear to be the data base of choice in deriving educational implications. Likewise, cohort-sequential research is the only paradigm for deriving estimates of cohort differences; findings of such research are essential to developing a knowledge base for intervention into cohort-related obsolescence.

As longitudinal studies progress over a number of years, subjects drop out of these studies in a nonrandom order. The remaining subjects have usually been found to be more highly educated, to exhibit higher levels of intellectual performance, and to be in better health than the subjects dropping out of the study (Schaie, Labouvie, and Barrett, 1973). Thus, findings from longitudinal research are somewhat positively biased. What might this mean in terms of educational implications? Consideration of the subject sample is an important issue in deriving generalizations or implications from any research study. Since longitudinal studies typically involve much larger sample sizes—with greater care given to subject selection at the inception of the study—findings should be more reliable than those obtained from single-shot studies involving small sample sizes. Replication is the *sine qua non* of scientific research; in this regard, the consistency of findings across a number of longitudinal studies regarding the timing of significant age-related decline is noteworthy.

The positive sample bias in longitudinal research may in fact increase the relevance of the findings for adult education. Currently, only 4.5 percent of adults over age 55 partici-

pate in formal adult education activities (National Center for Education Statistics, 1980). Educational attainment is the most powerful predictor of participation in adult education. Thus, current older participants in adult education are clearly a positively biased subgroup of the elderly and appear to be biased, moreover, along the same dimensions as are longitudinal samples. Findings from longitudinal research may therefore be particularly relevant to the group of current older learners engaged in formal educational pursuits.

Some have questioned the unique contribution of longitudinal findings, suggesting that there is little qualitative difference in the findings of longitudinal and cross-sectional research (Botwinick, 1977; Salthouse, 1982). The question of whether onset of significant age-related decline begins at age 47, as suggested by cross-sectional research, or at age 67, as found in longitudinal research, appears to have been dismissed by some as a mere quantitative difference. Nevertheless, important *qualitative* differences in terms of the educational and social policy implications do exist (Riley, Abeles, and Teitelbaum, 1982). Qualitatively different educational procedures are likely to be needed in the remediation of age-related decline vs. the alleviation of cohort disadvantage. For example, very different types of educational programming might be developed for returning middle-aged women students, depending on whether those in higher education consult cross-sectional or longitudinal findings. Likewise, qualitative differences in decision making on social policy issues such as mandatory retirement, social security, and health insurance would occur if based on cross-sectional vs. longitudinal data (Riley, 1983).

EDUCATIONAL IMPLICATIONS FROM LONGITUDINAL AND SEQUENTIAL RESEARCH

Peaks and Decline in Intellectual Functioning

The allocation of educational resources to the first quarter of the life span has been partially based on the assumption that educational intervention is likely to be most beneficial during maximal levels of intellectual functioning (Cropley, 1977). Since intellectual development has long been assumed to peak in adolescence and young adulthood, secondary and higher education has been targeted on those age periods. Findings of longitudinal research, however, indicate that intellectual functioning actually peaks in midlife, and thus the thirties and forties should be considered as prime periods for learning. If development of complex problem-solving skills, such as those involved in career or family responsibilities, is assumed to profit from a maximal level of functioning on a number of requisite abilities (verbal, reasoning, etc.), then the thirties even more than the twenties appear particularly suited to higher educational pursuits (Schaie, 1977/78). When long-term data on intellectual development are considered, society's allocation of major roles and responsibilities to persons in midlife appears eminently reasonable.

These data also suggest the important role of early work experience in the continued growth of abilities. A stimulating work environment has been found to be associated with continued intellectual development, so much so that the workplace for many persons provides an important mechanism for continued learning. In fact, the largest provider of adult education in middle adulthood is industry, not higher education (Cross, 1981; see Stagner, this volume, for a more detailed discussion). The longitudinal research of Bray and Howard (1983) within an industrial setting indicates that both college and high school graduates assigned to beginning management positions showed increases in intellectual functioning through midlife. The interaction between ability functioning and complexity of the work environment has also been supported by the work of Kohn and Schooler (1979).

The differential pattern of stability and change found for specific abilities also has educational relevance. For example, most instructional procedures in adult education are primarily verbal in nature. The considerable stability, into at least the mid seventies, of verbal ability (passive vocabulary) supports both the popularity and effectiveness of printed material as an instructional medium.

Studies of adult learning indicate printed material to be one of the most important and frequently used sources of information (Penland, 1979). Such printed materials are particularly relevant in self-directed learning because of their accessibility. Verbal ability has been shown to be a significant predictor of text comprehension (Taub and Long, 1976).

A cautionary statement regarding the relation of verbal ability and verbal instruction is also needed, however. Although there is considerable intraindividual stability in verbal meaning, this ability also shows the strongest negative cohort effects for current older cohorts (Schaie, 1983). Thus, older adults today may exhibit a relatively lower level of verbal proficiency (when compared with today's younger adults), although little if any age-related decline has occurred (Walmsley and Allington, 1982). These cohort effects may become most evident in verbal material involving technical terminology or involving societal shifts in language pattern usage. In assessing the readability of patient education materials for older adults, Holcomb (1979) found educational level but not age to be a significant predictor.

The timing of educational intervention has focused primarily on *optimal* developmental periods for knowledge and skill acquisition. Until the last two decades, remedial or compensatory education, even in mainstream education, has been a secondary concern. Somewhat ironically, when considered within a life-span perspective, the terms *remedial* or *compensatory education* have typically been used to describe intervention in the first quarter of the life span (Lazar, Darlington, Murray, Royce, and Snipper, 1982). Given the limited interest in adult education, relatively little consideration has been given to remedial or compensatory educational efforts associated with age-related decline or cultural change (Hesburgh, Miller, and Wharton, 1974).

Longitudinal findings suggest that the timing of remedial efforts in later adulthood should vary by ability. The decade of the sixties appears particularly salient, since it is during this decade that significant decline first becomes apparent for several abilities. The cognitive training research, to be reviewed in the next section, strongly suggests that intervention efforts can produce significant improvement. The data in Figure 1 suggest that even in the early eighties older adults are functioning, on average, at 75 to 80 percent of the performance level of a 25-year-old, clearly indicating a capacity to learn and profit from instruction even in late old age.

Patterns of Quantitative Change

Our brief review of longitudinal research suggests that long-term intraindividual changes in intellectual functioning involve three major change patterns: stability, modest increment, and gradual decline (Willis and Baltes, 1980). In this section, we attempt to delineate further these types of change with regard to educational concerns. Although these change patterns have typically been studied separately from one another, it is important to note that two or more of them are likely to be exhibited simultaneously in the complex behavior of a given individual in later adulthood.

Irreversible Decrement. In earlier research on intelligence, there was the implicit, if not explicit, assumption that most quantitative change in intellectual performance with age was irreversible (Schaie, 1973). Irreversible decline involves significant decrement that cannot be reversed and for which adequate compensatory mechanisms do not exist. Irreversible decline of sufficient magnitude to substantially impair behavior functioning is associated primarily with advanced biological aging, pathologies, or catastrophic illnesses or accidents. There is growing recognition that whether or not a decline is irreversible cannot be determined solely from longitudinal research on age changes but must be examined empirically through medical and/or behavioral intervention research (Smith, 1980).

Decrement with Compensation. This form of decline involves behavioral change for which compensatory mechanisms can be employed to maintain an adequate level of functioning although reversal of the deficit is not currently feasible (Schaie, 1973). Prosthetics

such as eye glasses and hearing aids, even if incapable of reversing the deficit, enable an individual to function effectively. Recent advances in high technology must be considered in the further development of such mechanical prosthetics. The utility of home computers, voice synthesizers, digital alarms, or memory phones as mechanical prosthetics for the elderly suffering from sensory or cognitive loss needs to be explored (Hardiman, Holbrook, and Hedrick, 1979; Weisman, 1983).

The increasingly rich descriptive research base in cognitive aging should begin to yield important implications for the development of cognitive-behavioral as well as mechanical prosthetics. Considerable research within mainstream cognitive psychology, as well as within cognitive aging, has focused on adults' understanding and use of "compensatory" strategies that compensate for capacity limitations, for example, in memory (Perlmutter, 1978). A hallmark of cognitively sophisticated learners appears to be their facility in usage of such aids (Charness, 1981; Chi, Glaser, and Rees, 1982). Extension of this research holds promise for the identification of useful cognitive-behavioral prosthetics in cases of age-related decline in capacity, or possibly a decline in energy level that makes it more difficult to sustain high levels of performance (Robertson-Tchabo, 1980).

Disuse. A third form of performance decline may be that associated with disuse (Salthouse, 1982). Negative changes in cognitive performance may occur, not because of changes in competence or capacity, but as a result of the individual's having little opportunity or need to exercise a particular skill or knowledge area (Gardner and Monge, 1977; Murrell and Humphries, 1978). Performance declines associated with disuse are evident not only in advanced age but throughout adulthood, as any teacher can attest. It might be expected, however, that the probability of performance decline associated with disuse will increase in later adulthood, since the extent of knowledge and skill increases cumulatively across the life course and the portion that can be kept (or should be kept) in active use declines. In cases of performance decline as a function of disuse, minimal intervention efforts should suffice to reactivate the knowledge or skill.

Continued Increment. One of the most positive findings from longitudinal research is the fact that modest increments in intellectual performance continue into midlife for a number of abilities (Cunningham and Owens, 1983; Jarvik and Bank, 1983). For the ability of verbal meaning, these increments are statistically significant until the fifties. It has been suggested that those abilities that are most actively used in the tasks and responsibilities of adult living (e.g. verbal) should be the ones most likely to show continued growth (Ferguson, 1954, 1956). It is likely that from midlife onward there will be increasing individual differences in the particular abilities that show continued growth. Increasingly, such increment patterns may become a reflection of unique life styles and nonnormative life events.

Baltes, Dittman-Kohli, and Dixon (1982) have chosen to discuss the issue of continued intellectual development and old age under the term "selective optimization." Their position is that the individual comes to focus selectively on certain types of intellectual skills and pursuits with increasing age, and it is within these limited areas that continued intellectual development is most likely to occur. Facilitation of such selective optimization pursuits would appear to be a major responsibility for continuing education and adult education programming.

Interindividual Differences in Intraindividual Change: Educational Implications

Descriptive research in cognitive aging has focused on chronological age as the major variable for examining interindividual differences in intraindividual change. In spite of their limitations, cross-sectional age comparative studies predominate in the intellectual aging literature (Giambra and Arenberg, 1980; Krauss, 1980). With regard to applied concerns, however, cohort differences appear to be of greater interest and relevance. In terms of educational implications, cohort differences appear to be of equal, if not greater, concern than age-related change for three reasons: (1) In contrast to age-related change, cohort differences are of educational concern across the entire adult life course. (2) Since cohort effects are generally considered to be a function of environmental/experiential differences, it is assumed that they should be susceptible to educational intervention. (3) There is considerable suggestive evidence that early educational experiences are themselves significant contributors to such cohort effects.

Differential cohort effects are evident by age 25 in the longitudinal research literature (Schaie, 1983). If we assume that recent reports of drops in scholastic aptitude tests reflect similar cohort effects, then such generational differences are already evident by age 17, and such effects thus appear to have their origin during the early portion of the life span during which schooling plays a major socialization role (Parsons and Platt, 1968, 1972). Although these effects probably originate in childhood, their consequences are probably most debilitating in old age.

Obsolescence and Cohort Effects. One form of cohort difference of particular educational interest is that more commonly described as *obsolescence*. This term has been used to refer to job-related obsolescence, particularly with regard to professional obsolescence in high-technology industries such as engineering (Ferdinand, 1966; Shearer and Stegar, 1975). Obsolescence has typically been defined as a form of interindividual differences in intraindividual change. For example, in discussing obsolescence in the engineering profession, Siefert (1964) defines it as the difference between the knowledge and skills possessed by a new graduate of a modern engineering curriculum and the knowledge and skills possessed by the practicing engineer who may have completed his formal education a number of years before. In this context, obsolescence is not viewed primarily as reflecting individual decline but rather differences in the early educational experiences of different cohorts of professionals (i.e. interindividual differences in intraindividual change).

The sources of professional cohort differences are to be found in the rapid growth of knowledge and change in a particular area of specialization. The term "professional half-life" has been coined to refer to the length of time from the completion of a person's professional training until at least half of the acquired professional knowledge has become obsolete (Dubin, 1972). In a sense, the half-life concept is a measure of when professional cohort differences reach a level of practical significance. Continuous professional updating, either through self-directed learning or formal educational procedures, is seen as the major mechanism for the prevention or at least remediation of professional cohort differences (Dubin, 1977; Houle, 1981). Dubin (1972) has derived estimates of the amount of time different professionals would need to spend in professional updating activities, based on rate of knowledge growth within a given discipline. Dubin's calculations suggest that, given the relatively rapid knowledge growth in our own discipline, psychologists would need to spend approximately 20 percent of their work time in professional updating!

The study of professional obsolescence has been used to illustrate the more practical implications of cohort effects as a form of interindividual differences in intraindividual change. To the extent that such cohort differences impact the effective functioning of the individual, educational intervention is strongly implicated. Longitudinal research suggests both that the magnitude of cohort effects varies by ability and that the pattern of cohort effects is dynamic and may differ across cohorts, given different life experiences.

The implications for the field of education are twofold. First, given the dynamic nature of cohort effects, it is necessary to monitor continually the course of these effects for successive cohorts. Educational programming, responding to these effects, will need to be flexible and attentive to changing patterns of cohort trends. Fortunately, there is suggestive evidence that at least some forms of cohort effects become evident early in the life span; in the case of negative cohort trends, it should thus be possible to engage in educational intervention in young adulthood so as to minimize consequences for middle and later adulthood. Unfortunately, our society's current educa-

tional response to evidence of negative cohort trends is to focus primarily on attempts to prevent their recurrence in future cohorts but to do little toward remediation of the effects in current adult cohorts who have suffered from previous negligence. A second implication for education is that the field must continue to engage in serious reflection on the historical trends within its own subdisciplines of teacher education, curriculum development, and instructional psychology so as to gain a better understanding of how changes in socialization and educational practice are reflected in the observed cohort differences.

Socio-cultural Change and the Role of Education. From a sociological perspective, Parsons has suggested that cohort differences result from changes in the structure of socialization systems (Parsons and Platt, 1972). As a society becomes increasingly complex and differentiated, the socialization process is temporally extended. As a result of the extension of the socialization process and its movement outside the home, education has become an increasingly important agent of socialization in our society. This expansion of the educational system has changed the relations among cohorts; they differ from one another because they have been socialized to different extents within the educational context. The role of education as an agent of socialization takes on particular significance, since socialization, within Parsonian theory, involves acquisition of basic values, not only acquisition of knowledge and skills. Parsons has recently suggested that a new and important stage of socialization (college education) is evolving in which higher education will be the primary agent of socialization.

COGNITIVE TRAINING RESEARCH: SHORT-TERM CHANGE

We turn now from a discussion of long-term intraindividual change to short-term change. Most research on long-term change has been descriptive, examining normative developmental change across adulthood. In contrast, study of short-term changes has primarily been experimental-manipulative, examining modifiability or plasticity in intellectual performance as a function of some brief experimental treatment (Baltes and Willis, 1979). Just as with long-term change, study of short-term change is concerned with intraindividual change and interindividual differences in intraindividual change.

Three major questions need to be considered: (1) What intellectual abilities and/or cognitive processes are subject to modification via experimental treatments? (2) What is the range or magnitude of change in performance? (3) Under what experimental conditions does intraindividual change occur?

Abilities and Cognitive Tasks as Targets of Training

Examination of the first question is, of course, strongly influenced by the researcher's particular theoretical orientation to intellectual development (Baltes and Willis, 1982). For example, if one adopts the traditionally held view of an early peak and precipitous global decline in intellectual functioning, then experimental intervention with regard to almost any intellectual ability or process may be of interest. In contrast, if research is guided by a particular theory of intellectual development, then the target of intervention should be dictated by the theory. For example, the differential pattern of developmental change specified by the theory of fluid and crystallized intelligence (Cattell, 1971) should lead to a focus on fluid abilities as the target of intervention. A more pragmatic approach is to identify those abilities showing earliest decline within longitudinal and cohort-sequential data sets.

Magnitude (Range) of Training Effects

We now turn to the second question, that of the magnitude or range of training effects. Discussion of the range and magnitude of intraindividual improvement as a function of training involves a number of issues. In many cognitive training studies, there has been the implicit, if not explicit, assumption that training improvement primarily reflects the remediation of age-related decline. Since no training study to date has had available longitudinal data

on the training subjects, however, it has not been possible to examine directly the extent to which training primarily involves the remediation of decline. Figure 1 indicates that a substantial number of elderly have not experienced significant decline, and thus training for these persons would involve acquisition of new skill levels rather than remediation. The more cautious researchers in this area have then assessed training effects by examining the range of intraindividual variability or plasticity in intellectual aging, without focusing on the specific nature of the change effected (i.e., whether the change involves remediation or acquisition of new skills).

Nature of Training Effects. Consideration of the practical implications of such training endeavors would seem to require a more detailed understanding of the specific nature of intraindividual change effected through training. Figures 1 and 3 suggest that both age-related decline and cohort effects must be considered in the assessment of intraindividual change associated with training. The matrix in Figure 4 presents in a simplified manner some of the types of intraindividual change that might occur as a function of training.

The left side of the matrix depicts forms of intraindividual change that would occur if the target of training is an ability or skill exhibiting differential cohort effects for the current elderly population. Figure 3 suggests that a given cohort may experience both positive and negative cohort effects with regard to different abilities. Both types of effects must be considered in educational programming, particularly in multicohort learning contexts. Negative cohort differences will be focused on in the discussion below.

For adults with no significant age-related decline, training improvement may be largely a function of initial lower levels of functioning associated with cohort effects (upper left-hand cell). Given that normative age-related decline does not become substantial until age 67 or older, training improvement for adults in their early sixties may primarily reflect the modifiability of negative cohort effects. If we assume that older adults who participate in adult education or in training studies are selectively biased along the same dimensions as subjects who remain in longitudinal studies, it then follows that a disproportionate number of subjects in our studies may fall into this cell of the matrix. The lower left-hand cell represents that portion of the adult population who are disadvantaged not only with regard to cohort differences but who also have experienced age-related decline. This portion of the elderly may be the most in need of educational intervention.

The middle and right-hand cells of the matrix depict forms of intraindividual change that might be exhibited if the target of intervention is an ability showing few significant cohort differences or on which there is a positive cohort effect in favor of earlier-born cohorts. This would be the case with an ability such as word fluency. Training improvement for subjects falling within the lower middle or right-hand cells should then primarily reflect remediation of age-related decline. In contrast, training improvement for subjects within the upper middle or right-hand cell of the matrix should reflect performance levels increased beyond those previously exhibited by the subject, since neither cohort differences nor age-related decline are significant for these persons. It should be noted that the matrix oversimplifies the forms of intraindividual change, particularly with regard to cohort effects. There is, of course, considerable variability regarding the extent to which specific individuals within a given age/cohort have experienced the effects associated with their birth cohort.

Empirical examination of the effectiveness of training programs in remediating age-related decline vs. cohort effects would, of course, require a subject population with prior longitudinal data on the relevant ability dimensions. To date, no cognitive training study has employed such a subject sample. Thus, at present, we can only speculate about different types of performance (learning) curves that might be associated with training for different cells of the matrix shown in Figure 4. If we assume that cohort effects originate fairly early in the life course and that the magnitude of such effects remains relatively stable across

adulthood, then we might expect training improvement that is associated primarily with cohort differences to be represented by the traditional learning curve. The performance level of the subject would be relatively low (compared to more advantaged cohorts) prior to training, and steady, gradual improvement would be expected across training sessions. Indeed, findings from several training studies involving multiple practice or training sessions (Beres and Baron, 1981; Hofland, Willis, and Baltes, 1981; Taub, 1973) do reflect performance improvement approximating the traditional learning curve.

In terms of educational implications, intervention in cohort deficiencies would most likely require more lengthy, intensive training procedures than would be the case if previously acquired skills were simply being reactivated. Likewise, it would be expected that the pattern of training improvement associated with the upper right-hand cell of the matrix would also approximate the traditional learning curve. Again, training would involve increasing the subject's performance level, rather than providing remediation.

In contrast, the case illustrated in the lower

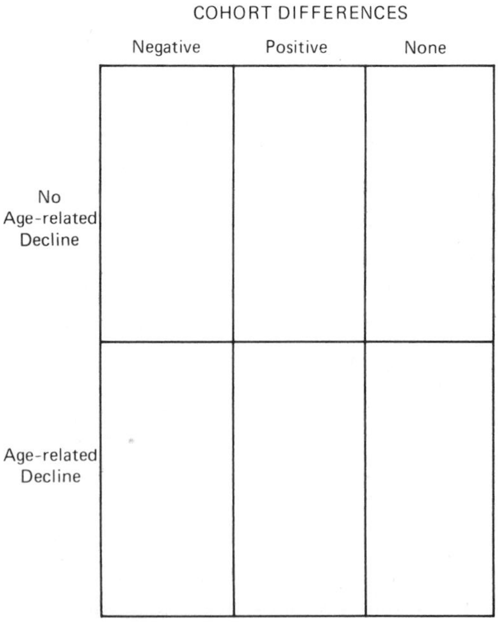

Figure 4.   Types of intraindividual change as a function of training.

right-hand cell represents the purest instance of age-related decline per se. If decline is primarily a function of disuse, then training improvement might exhibit a strong linear curve, at least until the individual's prior level of functioning is approximated. If such age-related decline is largely irreversible, then little training improvement would be shown. Estimation of the performance curve associated with the lower left-hand cell is the most difficult, since remediation of age-related decline and intervention into cohort differences are both involved. Again, if age-related decline is associated with disuse, the performance curve ought to be somewhat more linear than the traditional learning curve.

Although discussion regarding the pattern and magnitude of differential forms of training improvement can only be conjectural at this time, it appears important to engage in such speculations since we believe that future research on these issues is critical to advancing our understanding of intraindividual plasticity in intellectual aging.

Earlier in this chapter we suggested that while change patterns for different abilities (i.e., stability, decrement, increment, cohort effects) have typically been discussed and examined separately from one another, two or more change patterns may be involved in complex problem solving. Consider the following hypothetical situation. Mrs. Jones, aged 65 years, has been diagnosed as diabetic. The prescribed medical treatment involves self-administered medication and compliance with some dietary restrictions, the latter requiring somewhat complex menu planning. Mrs. Jones, although sufficiently motivated to comply, is having difficulty following the prescribed treatment routine. Further discussion indicates that Mrs. Jones had misinterpreted label instructions on one medication and was having difficulty planning a daily menu, given her dietary restrictions.

What cognitive abilities and patterns of change might be implicated in designing appropriate patient education? Recent structural analyses of the primary abilities associated with reading comprehension tasks, such as interpretation of medicine bottle labels and dietary charts, suggest that inductive reasoning and, secondarily, verbal ability may be important for adequate performance on such tasks (Willis and Schaie, 1983). Recall that inductive reasoning and vocabulary are two abilities showing the strongest negative cohort effects for current elderly cohorts. Since normative decline on inductive reasoning begins in the late sixties, Mrs. Jones may also have begun to experience some decline in this ability. In contrast, normative data on vocabulary ability would suggest no significant decline. Moreover, recent research indicates that knowledge of disease processes and the purposes of medication are significantly lower for elderly patients than for younger ones, suggestive of cohort differences (Klein et al., 1982). If Mrs. Jones has significant visual impairment, frequently associated with diabetes, she may also have difficulty in seeing the print or numerals on medication labels or treatment apparatus (e.g., syringes).

Patient education efforts may then involve consideration of at least three patterns of change (stability, decrement with compensation, cohort differences). Sensory deficits may be compensated for with enlarged print and use of magnifying equipment (decrement with compensation). Improvement in menu planning skill and in the comprehension of treatment instructions may need to focus on cognitive reasoning strategies, as well as on factual knowledge of medical terms and procedures (remediation of negative cohort effects and decrement with compensation, if decline on reasoning ability has occurrred). On the other hand, Mrs. Jones' general verbal ability has probably remained quite stable and should facilitate educational efforts.

We now turn to a brief review of the empirical findings on the magnitude of intraindividual short-term change as a function of experimental-manipulative research. Three criteria can be employed in the examination of the range of short-term intraindividual change as a function of training (Willis and Baltes, 1980; Willis, Blieszner, and Baltes, 1981). First, what is the size or magnitude of the effect? Second, is there evidence of a differential pattern of training transfer across near and far transfer tasks? Third, are training effects maintained over time? Unfortunately, the design of many training studies has not permitted a careful examination of these issues.

Limitations of Age Comparative Studies. Consideration of the first question requires that the magnitude of training effects be compared against some criterion. The criterion of comparison that is chosen, of course, depends on the question being asked. It is with regard to the criterion for assessing the magnitude of training effects that some researchers go awry, in that performance of a younger age/cohort is chosen as the criterion for examining the magnitude of training effects in an older sample. It has been argued that if age differences are due largely to environmental/experiential deficits, then the elderly should be expected to benefit more from training than a younger sample. Such a conclusion appears to reflect on the part of some of our colleagues (Birren et al., 1982; Denney, 1982; Donaldson, 1981; Salthouse, 1982) a difference of opinion or misunderstanding regarding cohort effects as they relate to the interpretation of training research.

Given the sizeable differences in performance level between current adult cohorts, there is strong evidence (see Figure 3) that many older adults functioned at a significantly lower performance level as young adults than do current young adult cohorts. This initial cohort difference is compounded both by the cumulative effects of functioning at a relatively lower performance level across young and middle adulthood, plus the possible onset of age-related decline. To demand greater training improvement for the elderly than for the young adult comparison sample is to expect that a very brief training program can remediate a significant initial cohort difference, plus the cumulative effects of this early disadvantage, plus possible aging decline. Furthermore, longitudinal data suggest that young adult samples in their twenties would be expected to exhibit considerable plasticity in their intellectual functioning, since intellectual performance on many abilities peaks, not in the twenties, but in the thirties or forties.

If age comparative training research is examined in the light of cohort effects and their potential cumulative effects on intellectual functioning, then the results of comparative training studies appear quite favorable to the older adults. The lack of a significant age × treatment interaction, which has been interpreted typically as a negative finding, provides important information regarding the considerable plasticity of intellectual functioning in later adulthood. Absence of a significant age × treatment interaction (assuming a significant main effect for training) suggests that the training gain for the older group is as great as the training gain for the younger group. A main effect for age is to be expected, given cohort differences. In such age comparative research, training improvement (magnitude of intraindividual change for the older group compared with magnitude of intraindividual change for the younger group) is the most defensible unit of comparison, given the strong cohort effects that are reflected in performance level (see Nunnally, 1982, and Schaie and Hertzog, this volume, for discussion of gain scores).

Age comparative training research has typically violated critical assumptions of quasi-experimental designs (Campbell and Stanley, 1963; Krauss, 1980). Comparisons of treatment effects are based on the assumption that the effect of all variables expected to be related to the treatment effects, except for the variable of interest (i.e., age), have been eliminated either through random assignment or statistical control procedures. Of course, age cannot be randomly assigned. Rarely have training studies focusing on age comparisons given careful consideration to comparability of subject variables such as educational level, testing experience, health and sensory impairment, all of which have been shown to be related to intellectual performance.

Some have suggested that the utility of a younger age/cohort comparison group lies not in evaluating the magnitude of training effects, but in facilitating understanding of age-related changes in cognitive processes. For example, it is well documented in learning and memory studies that younger adults more frequently employ cognitive strategies and memory mnemonics than do older adults. What does this age difference in usage of cognitive strategies suggest regarding age-related change? Have current older adult cohorts *declined* in their usage of cognitive strategies? Or, are there cohort differences in strategy usage, even when cohorts are compared at the same chronological age? Unfortunately, current longitudinal and sequential studies have been conducted within psychometric, rather than cognitive or information processing, approaches to intelligence, and there is thus only limited longitudinal data on cognitive strategy usage.

Higher intellectual performance levels, however, have been found to be strongly associated with frequency and facility of strategy usage (Chi et al., 1982; Schmitt, Murphy, and Sanders, 1981). The significantly lower intellectual performance of earlier cohorts in longitudinal research when compared to later cohorts at the same chronological age suggests, then, that earlier cohorts may have been less adept in strategy usage, even in young adulthood. Thus age differences reported for some types of cognitive processing may reflect cohort differences. Examination of the cognitive behavior of younger comparison groups in cross-sectional research can provide important information on the most efficient strategies for performing many cognitive tasks, similar to the current research on experts within mainstream psychology (Chi et al., 1982). The question of whether age differences in strategy usage reflects age-related change, however, must be addressed longitudinally.

Empirical Findings on Magnitude of Training Gain. If intraindividual change is the major concern, as we argue it should be, then training improvement needs to be compared with the individual's performance at some earlier time in development (e.g., peak performance level) or with the individual's level of performance immediately prior to training (e.g., pretest score). Since lack of longitudinal data has precluded comparison of training gain with earlier level of performance, the individual's pretest score becomes the most obvious criterion for comparison. Unfortunately, some training studies have not even included a pretest. Given the test naivete of many el-

derly subjects, significant improvement can occur merely as a function of pre- and posttesting. To assess the portion of improvement that can be reliably attributed to training alone, it is necessary to compare post-training performance of the treatment group with a control group randomly drawn from the same subject population that receives only pre- and posttesting.

When the magnitude of training improvement (treatment vs. control) is examined in terms of standard deviation units, several studies report effect magnitudes on the order of 0.75 to 1.00 standard deviations (Hornblum and Overton, 1976; Labouvie-Vief and Gonda, 1976; Schultz and Hoyer, 1976; Willis, Blieszner, and Baltes, 1981). Since none of the training studies have been conducted within a longitudinal design, it is not possible to make a direct comparison of the magnitude of training effects with the size of cohort differences or the magnitude of normative age-related decline. Examination of relevant data from Schaie's (1983) cohort-sequential study, however, provides some estimates. Cohort differences between the cohorts born in 1917 and 1952 for the abilities of verbal meaning and inductive reasoning showed significant effects on the order of 0.33 and 0.50 standard deviation units, respectively. Likewise, age-related decline from peak level of performance to age 67 (verbal meaning = 53 years; inductive reasoning = 46 years) was on the order of 0.23 and 0.22 standard deviation units for these two abilities. Thus, the magnitude of training improvement reported in several studies is comparable to, or greater than, the size of the cohort effect *or* to the magnitude of age-related decline as estimated from cohort-sequential data. For individuals suffering from the combined effects of a cohort disadvantage and age-related decline, however, more intensive intervention efforts than those described in current training studies may well be required.

Assessment of Training Transfer. In a number of studies, the posttest assessment battery has been limited to one or two measures of near transfer. In some cases, the same task stimuli were even used in training and posttests (Denney, Jones, and Krigel, 1979). Assessment of the nature and the range of training effects requires a broad transfer battery, however, one that involves not only measures predicted to show training effects (*near transfer*) but also measures hypothesized to demonstrate no training effects (*far transfer*). A *priori* predictions regarding the pattern of training transfer expected across near- and far-transfer measures should be derived either from a well-established measurement theory or on the basis of an empirical examination of the structural relationships among the measures. Unfortunately, too many studies have neglected this step, and thus assessment of training effects becomes a fishing expedition across a sea of *ad hoc* measures.

Why should both near- and far-transfer measures be included? In a well-conceived study, the researcher has formulated a priori hypotheses regarding the specific cognitive skills, strategies, or environmental conditions that underlie performance on the target ability or skill. The training program is then designed to foster these specific strategies or processes in the expectation of ability-specific or skill-specific treatment effects. The training should result in improvement on the target ability or skill, not just any cognitive variable.

If the researcher hypothesized *a priori* that the lower performance level of the elderly is associated with certain environmental conditions (e.g., lack of reinforcement or feedback) rather than a deficit in cognitive skills, then the treatment should focus on the optimization of such environmental conditions. Whether the treatment focuses on cognitive skill or environmental conditions, the critical issue is for the researcher to formulate *a priori* hypotheses regarding a relationship between the treatment (involving certain cognitive strategies and/or environmental conditions) and performance on a target ability/skill. The training effects may then be predicted to be specific to that target ability/skill.

Comparison of training improvement on near-transfer measures vs. far-transfer measures provides a test of the hypothesized relationships between the treatment and performance on the target ability-skill (near transfer). For the predicted relationship between treatment conditions and target ability to be confirmed, training transfer must be shown to the target-ability tasks (near-transfer), but *not* to nontargeted (far-transfer) measures. If general improvement occurs for both target-specific (near-transfer) *and* nontargeted ability tasks (far-transfer), then interpretation of the relationship between treatment condition and targeted ability becomes equivocal. General, rather than target-specific, improvement may have resulted from any number of unspecified factors (e.g., test naivete, motivation) that might influence performance on both near- and far-transfer measures, not solely the targeted (near-transfer) tasks.

Several recent reviews of training research (Birren et al., 1982; Denney, 1982; Donaldson, 1981) have suggested that the reported training effects are quite limited, since training improvement was shown only for the targeted ability tasks and no transfer was shown to far-transfer ability measures. However, findings of target-specific (near) transfer are actually in line with the author's predictions that training effects would occur *only* for the target ability to be trained (Baltes and Willis, 1982).

In our program of training research (Baltes and Willis, 1982; Blieszner, Willis, and Baltes, 1981; Willis, Blieszner, and Baltes, 1981; Willis, Cornelius, and Baltes, 1983), we have repeatedly demonstrated significant training effects for several measures of the target ability (near transfer), as predicted; far-transfer effects have always been minimal. This pattern of differential transfer effects has also been demonstrated in those other training studies that have included a broad transfer battery (e.g., Baltes and Dittman-Kohli, 1983; Hornblum and Overton, 1976; Schultz and Hoyer, 1976).

The third criterion for examining the magnitude of treatment effects focuses on the maintenance of training improvement over time. Temporal durability of effects is important both for theoretical and practical reasons. From a theoretical perspective, if it is argued that training impacts the target ability/skill rather than some nonability performance factors (e.g., anxiety, test sophistication), then maintenance of the improved level of performance over time is critical.

From a more applied educational perspective, the utility of training is greatly diminished unless proficiency is maintained over time. Relatively few training studies to date have examined the maintenance issue. If future training research is to have practical implications for adult education and lifelong learning, this will be a critical issue to examine. Of the few studies that have examined maintenance effects (Blieszner, Willis, and Baltes, 1981: Hornblum and Overton, 1976; Labouvie-Vief and Gonda, 1976; Willis, Blieszner, and Baltes, 1981), most have reported significant near-transfer effects from two weeks to six months following training. Sanders and Sanders (1978) report significant maintenance one year after training.

Experimental Conditions and Training Effects

We turn now to the third question raised with regard to the study of short-term intraindividual change: Under what experimental conditions can significant short-term intraindividual change be observed? It may be useful to organize our discussion with regard to the model of learning, adapted from Jenkins (1979) and Smith (1980), that is shown in Figure 5. At first glance, the model appears quite simple, but it becomes more complex upon further consideration (Brown, 1982). The diagram represents the learner-in-context; in this case, the training context. A minimum of four factors need to be considered. We will begin by considering each factor independently. Then we will speculate on some two- or possibly three-way interactions.

Learner Characteristics. Older adult learners vary tremendously in the factual knowledge and repertory of relevant skills/strategies they bring to the training context; these learner characteristics, of course, influence their performance during training. Prior training research, following in the tradition of descriptive studies (see Krauss, 1980), has tended to treat within-age/cohort interindividual differences as error variance to be statistically controlled or has restricted the examination of learner characteristics to demographic variables, such as age or educational level. Examination of the full range of possible intraindividual change, however, will necessitate consideration of the potential interactions between learner characteristics and various forms of training.

At least three types of learner characteristics need to be examined: (1) *a priori* cognitive knowledge, abilities, and strategies that are

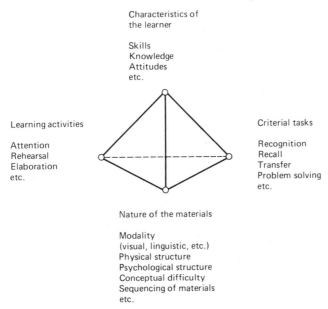

Characteristics of
the learner

Skills
Knowledge
Attitudes
etc.

Learning activities

Attention
Rehearsal
Elaboration
etc.

Criterial tasks

Recognition
Recall
Transfer
Problem solving
etc.

Nature of the materials

Modality
(visual, linguistic, etc.)
Physical structure
Psychological structure
Conceptual difficulty
Sequencing of materials
etc.

Figure 5.   Model of learner-in-context.

directly related to the training task; (2) meta-cognition, or self-knowledge of ability and relevant skills; and (3) noncognitive variables such as attitudes, beliefs, or cognitive styles. The subject's *a priori* familiarity with the criterion task or factual knowledge about that type of problem is a learner characteristic that has frequently been associated with performance proficiency. For example, Hoyer and Plude (1980) suggest that the degree of the learner's *a priori* familiarity with the target task may be related to utilization of automatic vs. effortful processes. Likewise, *a priori* knowledge has been related to the depth of semantic processing and to the complexity of the organizational strategies utilized. The range of interindividual differences in *a priori* knowledge regarding the criterion task is likely to be greater in adulthood than at any other age period. Such a learner characteristic is highly salient in applied educational endeavors (Robertson-Tchabo, 1980).

One noteworthy attempt to incorporate learner characteristics into the design of training research was undertaken by Gonda (1981). This study examined the interaction between locus of control and the degree of directiveness in the instruction given. It was hypothesized and confirmed that subjects exhibiting an external locus of control would profit more from a highly structured instructional setting than would learners with a higher internal locus of control. Unfortunately, the study is flawed, since locus of control is correlated with level of performance on the target cognitive task. Nevertheless, the study provides a useful example of including learner characteristics in the design of training research.

Learning Activities. This factor in the model deals with the cognitive activities or behaviors the learner is expected to engage in during training. Such activities are assumed to be related to, or to underlie, proficiency on criterion tasks. It is with respect to this factor that the descriptive research within cognitive aging is most relevant. A major thrust of experimental research during the last decade has been the examination of the strategies and processes that are related to successful performance on a number of cognitive tasks as well as of the older adult's limitations in employing these

strategies (Giambra and Arenberg, 1980; Hartley, Harker, and Walsh, 1980; Hoyer and Plude, 1980; Salthouse, 1982).

An important next step in educational research will be the incorporation of this knowledge regarding salient strategies into the design of educational programs. A number of studies suggest that the older adult has knowledge of such strategies as mnemonic aids (Perlmutter, 1978, 1980) and also can often successfully employ such strategies when instructed to do so in a specific context (Robertson-Tchabo, Hausman, and Arenberg, 1976). Many older adults, however, exhibit only a limited spontaneous usage of such strategies. Thus, future training efforts may increasingly need to focus on executive processes that train the older adult to determine the suitable contexts for using such skills.

Training studies have differed widely in the degree to which the treatment focuses on specific learning activities. In one group of training studies, specific skills or strategies were identified as being critical to performance on the criterion task, and training activities focused directly on increasing subjects' strategy usage. In a number of studies, Denney (1982) has successfully trained subjects' usage of constraint-seeking questions via modeling procedures. Several studies (Robertson-Tchabo et al., 1976; Schmitt et al., 1981) have demonstrated significant improvement in free recall tasks by training older adults in categorical rehearsal or imagery strategies. Likewise, training on various types of rule eduction strategies has been shown to significantly improve older adults' performance on a variety of concept-formation and complex problem-solving tasks (Labouvie-Vief and Gonda, 1976; Sterns and Sanders, 1980; Willis, Blieszner, and Baltes, 1981).

Yet another group of studies is of interest because of their focus on the subjects' activation of their *own* learning activities rather than strategies determined by the researcher (Beres and Baron, 1981; Grant, Storandt, and Botwinick, 1978; Hofland, Willis, and Baltes, 1981; Hornblum and Overton, 1976; Labouvie-Vief and Gonda, 1976). These studies have typically provided the subject with the opportunity to practice on a number of instances of a particular type of task or problem, with or without feedback regarding the correctness of their responses.

Most of these studies have reported significant improvement, suggesting that if given a number of practice trials, older adults are spontaneously able to activate learning strategies related to performance improvement. Significant improvement associated with practice has been reported for tasks as varied as memory digit span (Taub and Long, 1976), digit symbol substitution (Beres and Baron, 1981; Grant, Storandt, and Botwinick, 1978), area conservation (Hornblum and Overton, 1976), inductive reasoning (Blieszner, Willis, and Baltes, 1981; Labouvie-Vief and Gonda, 1976), concept formation (Sanders et al., 1975), and forward visual masking (Coyne, 1981). The few studies that have included near- and far-transfer measures have shown improvement only on near-transfer tasks, suggesting that ability-specific rather than non-ability-specific performance factors accounted for the improvement (Hofland, Willis, and Baltes, 1981; Hornblum and Overton, 1976).

There is a somewhat confusing discrepancy between these practice studies that suggest that older adults are capable of spontaneously generating strategies resulting in improved performance and studies in the experimental literature that frequently report the absence of strategy usage. Research by Hultsch (1974) on the "learning to learn" phenomenon, which examined free recall over multitrials, suggests one possible interpretation. In contrast to younger adults who exhibited positive transfer at all stages of learning, older adults exhibited a pattern of negative transfer in the early stages of learning, followed by positive transfer during the later stages of learning.

It is possible that multiple practice trials are particularly conducive to facilitating older adults' spontaneous generation of appropriate learning activities and that experimental studies, which usually provide less opportunity for practice, thus present a restrictive picture of older adults' capabilities. Hartley, Harker, and Walsh (1980, p. 249) have recently echoed this concern:

> Most of our accumulated knowledge about the adult development of learning and memory grows out of investigations that collect small samples of behavior from large samples of subjects. The differences these investigations report may be statistically reliable, but their generality across larger samples of behavior (e.g. extended practice on the same task) may be questionable. An intuition shared by many of us is that it is easier to learn new information about a topic and retain it longer as our knowledge about the topic increases.

Materials and Environmental Conditions. The third factor in the model to be considered focuses on the nature of the training materials and other features of the training context. Experimental studies suggest that acquisition and retrieval can be influenced by a number of features of the task stimuli, including the organization and structure of the material, the utilization of examples, the abstract vs. concrete nature of the content, and the redundancy of information. Thus far, it is unclear to what extent training studies have taken into account these findings in the design of training materials. Descriptions of training procedures and stimuli used in training materials are currently quite abbreviated in the literature.

Another aspect of the materials and conditions factor focuses on those nonability-specific features of the learning environment that may affect performance. A number of variables have been examined, including monetary and social reinforcement (Denney, 1980; Sanders et al., 1975), anxiety reduction (Labouvie-Vief and Gonda, 1976), and prior performance success (Denney, 1980). Likewise, Storandt and associates have examined the effect of a number of noncognitive variables on cognitive task performance (Storandt, 1977; Storandt and Futterman, 1982). In general, these studies have not reported the significant improvement on cognitive tasks that has been shown when cognitive strategy training or practice was the focus of treatment. It cannot be concluded on the basis of these studies that noncognitive factors play no role in older adults' performance on cognitive tasks. Several of these variables, when combined with cognitive training, have led to improved performance (Willis and Schaie, 1981).

Criterion Task. The final factor in the model deals with the types of cognitive behaviors the learner will be expected to exhibit as a result of training. These behaviors are assessed at posttest by means of one or more outcome measures. We have suggested that criterion tasks should include both near- and far-transfer measures in order to examine adequately what specific changes in the learner's behavior can be attributed to training. Note that the criterion task in Figure 5 is defined not by test name, but by the cognitive behaviors that the criterion task is expected to assess. The learner's performance on a particular criterion task reflects not only the cognitive behaviors of interest but also indicates task-specific measurement variance. Given that any one criterion task reflects multiple sources of variance, the reliability of assessing the desired cognitive behaviors is increased if multiple measures assumed to tap those behaviors are included at posttest.

Interactions among Model Factors. It is the interaction among the model factors that will provide the most useful information regarding the range of intraindividual plasticity in aging and the conditions under which such plasticity can be achieved. Unfortunately, most training research to date has not focused on such interactions. We will briefly illustrate two types of interactions that could provide important information. Given the increasing range of interindividual differences in later adulthood, the learner characteristics × learning activities interaction should be of particular interest. For example, different forms of learning activities should be more useful for the older adult suffering from a cohort disadvantage than for the older adult whose performance has dropped as a function of disuse. As we have suggested previously, more intensive training intervention may be required in the alleviation of cohort disadvantage than in the remediation of decline associated with disuse.

A second example illustrates a triple interaction (learner characteristics × learning activities × criterion task). It is probable that the breadth of training transfer (criterion task) achieved may be a function of the learner's prior knowledge level and the intensity of the learning activities (e.g., self-directed practice vs. strategy instruction). The more able learner should achieve considerable transfer with less intensive learning activities, whereas strategy instruction may be required for the less able learner to demonstrate training transfer.

THE ADULT LEARNER

We turn now to the final section of this chapter. We will begin by considering the personal and motivational factors that may be associated with a lifelong learning orientation. Although achievement motivation theory has traditionally been closely associated with research on learning and academic success in childhood, recent extensions of the theory focus more specifically on achievement-related concerns in adulthood. We will therefore discuss those studies in the survey literature that evaluate self-reported reasons for participation in adult education activities. Finally, we will consider the question of the potential goals of the adult learner.

Personal and Motivational Factors

There is suggestive evidence that adults in our society are less satisfied with the quality of their intellectual functioning than with some other aspects of their lives. In 1975 Flanagan and Russ-Eft (1976) followed up a representative sample of Project TALENT subjects first studied as high school students in 1960. These subjects were now in their early thirties. Subjects were interviewed on the quality of their life in 15 areas. They were asked both how important a given area was to them and how satisfied they were with their current status. On the issue of physical and mental health, 98 percent considered it an important area to them, and 86 percent were satisfied with their status. However, for the area of "development and use of your mind through learning, attending school, improving your understanding or acquiring additional knowledge," 83 percent considered the area important, but only 54 percent were satisfied with their status. The disparity between value and satisfaction was greater here than for any other area.

Personal Characteristics. What are the personal characteristics of those who engage in adult learning activities and why do they seek out those pursuits? We will focus our survey of the adult education literature primarily on education in formal, organized learning contexts, since this form of education has been better documented. Some consideration will also be given to learning activities described as "self-directed" (Tough, 1971), since this form of learning may be of particular relevance in later adulthood. Organized adult learning activities may be conducted for credit, but usually are not; they are offered by continuing education and extension divisions, industry, community agencies, and so on. They often involve class-like formats with groups of learners but can also include tutorials and correspondence study. Estimates of participation rates in this form of adult education vary from 12 to 30 percent of the adult population. Self-directed learning pursuits are typically self-planned, sustained efforts to learn knowledge or skills (Tough, 1971). It is estimated that 79 to 98 percent of the adult population engage in such activities (Penland, 1979).

Adults involved in organized adult education activities are more likely to be in young or middle adulthood and to be above average in educational level and family income. Those employed or seeking employment are more likely to be involved than those staying at home. A college graduate is more than twice as likely to be engaged in adult education as a high-school graduate. A high-school graduate is more than twice as likely to be involved as a nongraduate (Carp et al., 1974). The participation rate of adults 55 years of age and older is 4.5 percent, compared with 12 percent for all adults (Boaz, 1978). Interest and participation in education begin to decline from the early 30's through the 40's and drop significantly after age 55.

The lower participation rate of current older cohorts is particularly associated with educational level. These cohorts have a median educational level of 9 years, compared with a median of 12 years for the total adult population. High-school graduation appears to be a particularly significant benchmark for participation in adult education. The participation rate for those completing two years of high school is 4.1 percent (comparable to the elderly's participation rate); for high-school graduates, participation increases to 10.9 percent (Anderson and Darkenwald, 1979). The low participation rate of the current elderly may reflect in part a cohort effect. If prior educational attainment continues to be the most significant predictor of continuing education participation, then as the educational level of future elder cohorts rises, their participation in adult education should increase dramatically (Birren and Woodruff, 1973; Hiemstra, 1976).

In contrast to the low participation rates of older cohorts in formal adult education, there is some suggestive evidence that older adults are engaging in self-directed learning. Hiemstra (1976) studied the learning activities of 200 persons over age 55 and found that the average person reported spending approximately 325 hours each year in some form of learning activity; over 50 percent of these activities were self-directed. Penland's (1979) study of self-directed learning indicated that most learners focused on practical, problem-centered topics (e.g. health, home repairs, hobbies/crafts).

Self-Reports and Adult Education Participation. Numerous surveys have examined the self-reports of adults on their reasons for participation in adult education. Most of these studies have yielded descriptive data, but attempts to utilize this data for hypothesis testing or to extend psychological theories of motivation have been meager. Burgess (1971) factor analyzed the responses of a large number of adults regarding their reasons for participation in adult education. He found that seven factors could be described as basic learning orientations: (1) desire to know (knowing for the sake of knowing), (2) desire to reach a personal goal (often career-oriented), (3) desire to reach a social goal, (4) desire to reach a religious goal, (5) desire to take part in social activity, (6) desire to escape an unpleasant/tedious task, and (7) desire to comply with formal requirements of an employer or social organization. Burgess then attempted to categorize the original protocols according to these orientations. Over half of the sample had two or more dominant orientations. One-third of the sample could be classified according to a single orientation.

Burgess' learning orientations were employed in one of the more recent comprehensive national surveys of participation in organized adult learning conducted in 1972 by the Educational Testing Service (Carp et al., 1974). Seventy-seven percent of the sample indicated a desire to know more about some topic (would-be learners) whereas only 31 percent indicated that they had participated in an educational activity during the past 12 months (learners). One-third or more of the learners gave reasons for educational participation focusing on knowledge, personal goals (primarily career-related goals), and complying with a formal request of an employer. Would-be learners reported similar reasons for wanting to participate (Carp et al., 1974).

Relatively little research has been conducted on older adults' reasons for participation in formal education. One study by Daniel, Templin, and Shearon (1977) examined the self-reported reasons of two groups of older adults enrolled in community colleges, either for credit or noncredit. The three top-ranked reasons given by those enrolled for credit were (1) to contribute to society, (2) to become more cultured, and (3) to earn more money. Younger students in credit courses emphasized getting a job, obtaining a general education, and earning money. Older adults enrolled in noncredit courses gave as reasons the learning of interesting things, meeting interesting people, and contributing to society. The reasons of younger students enrolled in noncredit courses also cited learning interesting things but were concerned with earning money and getting a job. One of the major findings of this type of survey research is that learners have multiple reasons for participating in educational activities. For example, "would-be learners" gave an average of 4.6 reasons in the ETS study. Such citations of multiple reasons for participating in adult education call into question the utility of learner typologies that emphasize only one motive for a given individual. Moreover, one cannot assume that all individuals reporting an interest in the same content area have similar motivational reasons for studying it. The ETS study (Carp et al., 1974) examined desired content areas for study and motivational reasons separately. A great diversity of motivational reasons were cited with regard to each content area.

Consideration of motivation and adult learning from a sociological perspective is also instructive (Brim and Wheeler, 1966; Parsons and Platt, 1972). As we discussed earlier, sociologists have suggested that socialization in childhood is not adequate for the tasks of adulthood and that further socialization in adulthood is thus required. Adult socialization, however, is conceived to be qualitatively different from earlier socialization. Brim and Wheeler (1966) suggest that the purposes of socialization are to provide the individual with knowledge of what is expected of him, with the ability to meet role requirements, and with motivation (the desire to practice the behavior and pursue the appropriate means). The most important change in the content of socialization from childhood to adulthood is the shift from concern with values and motives to a concern with ability, knowledge, and overt behavior. Socialization after childhood is less concerned with attempts to influence motivation of a fundamental kind or to influence basic values.

Rosow (Brim and Wheeler, 1966) questions whether adult socialization should try to reshape motivation for certain types of performance or, the limitations on the control of conditions for learning in adulthood being what they are, should be content to deal with overt behavior only. Society may need to accept conforming behavior as evidence of satisfactory adult socialization, foregoing any concern with value systems. An issue, then, for adult education is whether to work within the adult's existing motivational system—the most commonly accepted approach—or to consider resocialization of motives *per se*. There is considerable discussion in sociology about the possible extension of the initial period of socialization that is concerned with establishment of values and motives into young adulthood (Parsons and Platt, 1972). Can socialization with regard to basic motives be extended across the total life course?

Achievement Motivation and the Adult Learner. Recent extensions of achievement motivation theory by Raynor (Atkinson and Raynor, 1974; Raynor and Rubin, 1971) suggest interesting applications of it to issues related to mid and late career striving and to motivation for continued professional updating as opposed to obsolescence. A critical addition to the theory focuses on the relation of future orientation and motivation. Raynor suggests that individual differences in future orientation interact with individual differences in achievement motivation to determine the strength of motivation sustaining the immediate activity. Career paths are distinguished insofar as they involve either contingent or noncontingent future orientation. Within a contingent career path, success in the immediate activity (or career stage) guarantees opportunity to strive for future success, whereas failure in the immediate activity guarantees future failure because of a loss of opportunity to continue on the career path. The anticipation that success in a contingent career path involves movement to higher levels of knowledge and skill, with concomitant extrinsic rewards, is viewed as the single greatest motivational impetus for career striving.

Another important distinction in the theory is between closed and open contingent career paths. A closed contingent career path involves a finite number of steps along the way, with a final or ultimate career goal in view. If retirement is viewed as a final career goal, then most persons in late career stages may function on a closed career path. As Raynor notes, however, the individual's *view* of the path (contingent vs. noncontingent, closed vs. open) is the important psychological variable, not the objective description by an outsider.

The number of remaining steps to the final goal in a closed contingent career path should influence the strength of motivation for the immediate activity. Raynor suggests that there are two independent gradients of motivation (achievement and extrinsic), which operate in opposite directions across career stages. In later stages of a closed contingent career path, achievement motivation should decrease and extrinsic motivation should increase. In con-

trast, within an open contingent career path, achievement motivation is not predicted to decrease, since additional possibilities for continued career striving become apparent as one moves along the career path. Since learning has traditionally been associated with high levels of achievement motivation, continued professional updating would appear most likely when one perceives one's career as following an open contingent career path. There should be a net rise in motivation since both its achievement and extrinsic components are expected to increase. This theory suggests that simple predictions of an increment or decrement in motivation across career stages is not adequate since multiple types of motivation with different gradients across career stages must be considered. Also critical to the theory are the individual's perceptions of the qualitative dimensions of the career path.

The concepts of contingency and openness may also be applicable to lifelong learning in a broader sense. Willingness or interest in engaging in continued learning activities may be related to the individual's perception of the degree to which attainment of desired goals are contingent on further learning. Furthermore, when the focus of study is a narrow, restricted area of content or skills, motivation for learning may best be conceptualized as reflecting a closed contingent path. In contrast, if the focus is on "learning for the sake of learning" or on a topic (e.g., hobby) that has no ultimate goal, then motivation for learning may reflect an open path and achievement motivation may remain high.

Goals of the Adult Learner

There has been comparatively little empirical research on the learning or educational goals of the older adult. Daniel, Templin, and Shearon (1977) found that older adults enrolled in a community college program cited both the desire to learn and engage in self-improvement and the desire to satisfy sociocultural needs (to meet people and to contribute to society) as primary motivational factors. Two other studies (Knowlton, 1977; Romaniuk and Romaniuk, 1982) were conducted with *elderhostel* participants and support the previous findings that older adults are interested in learning for the sake of learning and for seeking new challenges.

The limited research suggests five possible goals for the older adult learner (Schaie and Quayhagen, 1979; Willis and Schaie, 1981). Education may first be sought by adult learners to help them comprehend changes in their body and behavior that reflect maturation and aging. Second, the mature learner may need help in understanding the rapid technological and cultural change characteristic of contemporary societies. A third objective may be the development of skills for combatting the personal consequences of socio-cultural change and obsolescence. Fourth, the adult learner may seek to acquire new vocational skills, possibly an education for a second career. Finally, the older adult may find education to be a means of developing satisfactory and meaningful retirement roles.

Education as a Means of Comprehending One's Own Aging. Beginning with middle age, there is a substantial need to seek information on what is known about biological and psychological changes in adulthood (Klein, German, McPhee, Smith, and Levine, 1982), particularly those changes that relate to memory, learning, and problem solving. The human aging process is frequently taken for granted as something that one learns to live with and that does not require special attention until there are significant physiological or psychological problems. The cognitive aging literature suggests that many older adults, whether as a result of cohort differences, low levels of education, or age-related decline, do not spontaneously employ cognitive strategies effective in problem solving or memory tasks; they can nevertheless be trained to employ such strategies with minimal intervention efforts.

Education as a Means of Comprehending Socio-cultural Change. Rapid technological and socio-cultural change has rendered older cohorts particularly vulnerable to the threat of obsolescence. The first step in combatting such threats is to provide them with educational opportunities for improving their understanding of the social and technological upheavals they are forced to confront. Rapid change can be very threatening, particularly when it suggests a loss of personal control. A traditional objective of adult education dedicated to continuing or lifelong education has been to interpret to adults past the stage of formal education those aspects of social and technological transitions that are likely to affect both their personal behavior and the course of societies.

A Means of Combatting Technological and Socio-cultural Obsolescence. It is quite evident that the educational level attained by most older persons in their youth often no longer suffices to enable them to cope many decades later. Adult education can be instrumental in overcoming generational differences in both knowledge and relevant skills. Whether or not there will be a need for another period of "compulsory" education in the adult years may be of concern to future social policy planners. At present, it is advantageous not only for the individual but also for society to provide educational opportunities that can help its older members maintain an independent life style and cope successfully as community dwellers with a changing environment.

Second Career Education. Past traditions have required that individuals make their career choice quite early, prepare for that choice, and then maintain their career throughout life. This pattern has changed drastically, partially as a function of technological change. Technological specialization increases the number of different occupations and reduces the life expectancy of any one occupation. Most workers today are engaged in specialized jobs that did not exist a generation ago. Therefore, the older adult who wishes to remain in the work force is increasingly likely to require retraining for a second or third career (Lieberman and Lieberman, 1983).

Education as a Source of Generating Satisfactory Retirement Roles. A final objective of the adult learner may be to cope with the problems posed by giving up a work-oriented life pattern for one that is predominantly directed towards leisure activities. Education with this in mind, as in second-career education, must focus on the development or honing of relevant skills, but with the difference that personal satisfaction rather than economic gain is the primary learning incentive. As part of this process, educational programs should be developed that focus on self-discovery and the detailed examination of individual expectations, potentials, and resources.

Leisure-oriented skills, however, need not be solely directed to the satisfaction of personal needs. Many societal roles are not filled adequately by professionals, and one of the most promising retirement roles may well be the greater involvement of the older person in significant volunteer roles of a quasi-professional nature. Opportunities for such roles exist particularly in the human services fields and often in service to other less advantaged older persons. Effective and satisfying involvement in such roles, however, usually requires the acquisition of new skills and information, as well as the help of appropriate placement services (Seguin and O'Brien, 1976).

A particular problem during the retirement years is the imbalance of life expectancy between men and women, resulting in the high probability of widowhood for most elderly women. Special educational opportunities should therefore be provided for widows to help them develop or redevelop skills for independent living outside the traditional family unit, for the adequate management of personal economic resources, and for the development of new interpersonal relationships.

larly disadvantaged intellectually as a function of negative cohort trends. Intergenerational differences in level of intellectual functioning become particularly salient in periods of rapid cultural and technological change. The combination of significant cohort differences, occurring early in the life span, and the possible onset of age-related change in later adulthood may put many elderly at double risk with regard to effective cognitive functioning. We have therefore suggested that education targeted at the alleviation of cohort effects may be particularly relevant with increasing age.

The growing literature on cognitive training research in later adulthood suggests that the elderly can profit from a variety of instructional procedures. The applicability of training research to the design of gerontological educational programming requires that such research focus on intraindividual change and interindividual differences in change. Of particular importance in future experimental manipulative research will be a greater concern with interindividual differences in learner characteristics and the inclusion of individual difference variables in the design of training procedures.

The research literature in adult developmental psychology demonstrates that older adults have a substantial learning potential and presents evidence of a special need for continuing educational opportunities in later life. It is our hope that this chapter has provided a convincing rationale for the establishment of an educational psychology applicable to the adult learner.

SUMMARY

In this chapter we have attempted to review a portion of the relevant literature on adult intellectual development for the purpose of deriving educational implications that apply to the older adult learner. Longitudinal research on intraindividual change in intellectual functioning presents a fairly positive picture of the continued learning potential of the adult throughout most of the life span.

Research on cohort differences indicates, however, that the older adult may be particu-

REFERENCES

Anderson, R., and Darkenwald, G. 1979. *Participation and Persistence in American Adult Education.* New York: College Board.

Atkinson, J. W., and Raynor, J. O. 1974. *Motivation and Achievement.* Washington, D.C.: Winston.

Baltes, P. B., and Baltes, M. M. 1980. Plasticity and variability in psychological aging: Methodological and theoretical issues. In *Determining the Effects of Aging on the Central Nervous System,* ed. G. Gurski. Berlin: Schering.

Baltes, P. B., and Danish, S. J. 1980. Intervention in life-span development and aging: Issues and concepts. In *Life-Span Developmental Psychology: Intervention,* eds. R. E. Turner and H. W. Reese. New York: Academic Press.

Baltes, P. B., and Dittmann-Kohli, F. 1983. *Cross-Cultural Replication and Multiple-Ability Extension of Cognitive Training Research in Aging.* Unpublished manuscript, Max Planck Institute for Human Development and Education, Berlin, Germany.

Baltes, P. B.; Dittmann-Kohli, F.; and Dixon, R. A. 1982. *Intellectual Development During Adulthood: General Propositions Towards Theory and a Dual-Process Conception.* Paper given at the SSRC Conference on Life-course Human Development, Berlin, Germany.

Baltes, P. B., and Labouvie, G. V. 1973. Adult development in intellectual performance: Description, explanation, and modification. In *The Psychology of Adult Development and Aging,* eds. C. Eisdorfer and M. P. Lawton. Washington, D.C.: American Psychological Association.

Baltes, P. B., and Willis, S. L. 1977. Toward psychological theories of aging and development. In *Handbook of the Psychology of Aging,* eds. J. E. Birren and K. W. Schaie. New York: Van Nostrand Reinhold.

Baltes, P. B., and Willis, S. L. 1979. Life-span developmental psychology, cognitive functioning, and social policy. In *Aging from Birth to Death,* ed. M. W. Riley. Boulder, CO: Westview Press.

Baltes, P. B., and Willis, S. L. 1982. Enhancement (plasticity) of intellectual functioning in old age: Penn State's Adult Development and Enrichment Project (ADEPT). In *Aging and Cognitive Process,* eds. F. I. M. Craik and S. E. Trehub. New York: Plenum Press.

Beres, C., and Baron, A. 1981. Improved digit substitution by older women as a result of extended practice. *Journal of Gerontology* 36: 591–597.

Birren, J. E.; Cunningham, W. R.; and Yamamoto, K. 1982. Psychology of adult development and aging. *Annual Review of Psychology* 34: 543–575.

Birren, J. E., and Morrison, D. 1961. Analysis of the WAIS subtests in relation to age and education. *Journal of Gerontology* 16: 363–369.

Birren, J. E., and Woodruff, D. W. 1973. Human development over the life span through education. In *Life-span Developmental Psychology: Personality and Socialization,* eds. P. B. Baltes and K. W. Schaie. New York: Academic Press.

Blieszner, R.; Willis, S. L.; and Baltes, P. B. 1981. Training research in aging on the fluid ability of inductive reasoning. *Journal of Applied Developmental Psychology* 2: 247–265.

Boaz, R. 1978. *Participation in Adult Education. Final Report 1975.* Washington, D.C.: National Center for Educational Statistics.

Botwinick, J. 1977. Intellectual abilities. In *Handbook of the Psychology of Aging,* eds. J. E. Birren and K. W. Schaie. New York: Van Nostrand Reinhold.

Botwinick, J., and Arenberg, D. 1976. Disparate time spans in sequential studies of aging. *Experimental Aging Research* 2: 55–61.

Bray, D. W., and Howard, A. 1983. The AT&T longitudinal studies of managers. In *Longitudinal Studies of Adult Psychological Development,* ed. K. W. Schaie. New York: Guilford Press.

Brim, O., and Wheeler, S. 1966. *Socialization After Childhood: Two Essays.* New York: Wiley.

Brown, A. L. 1982. Learning and development: The problems of compatibility, access, and induction. *Human Development* 25: 89–115.

Burgess, P. 1971. Reasons for adult participation in group educational activities. *Adult Education* 22: 3–29.

Campbell, D. T., and Stanley, J. C. 1963. *Experimental and Quasi-Experimental Designs for Research.* Chicago: Rand McNally.

Carp, A.; Peterson, R.; and Roelfs, P. 1974. Adult learning interests and experiences. In *Planning Non-Traditional Programs: An Analysis of the Issues of Postsecondary Education,* eds. K. P. Cross and J. R. Valley. San Francisco: Jossey-Bass.

Cattell, R. B. 1971. *Abilities: Structure, Growth and Action.* New York: Houghton-Mifflin.

Charness, N. 1981. Visual short-term memory and aging in chess players. *Journal of Gerontology* 36: 615–619.

Chi, M; Glaser, R.; and Rees, E. 1982. Expertise in problem solving. In *Advances in the Psychology of Human Intelligence,* vol. 1, ed. R. Sternberg. Hillsdale, NJ: Erlbaum.

Coyne, A. C. 1981. Age differences and practice in forward visual masking. *Journal of Gerontology* 36: 730–732.

Cropley, A. J. 1977. *Lifelong Education: A Psychological Analysis.* New York: Pergamon.

Cross, K. P. 1981. *Adults as Learners.* San Francisco: Jossey-Bass.

Cunningham, W. R., and Owens, W. A. Jr. 1983. The Iowa State study of the adult development of intellectual abilities. In *Longitudinal Studies of Adult Psychological Development,* ed. K. W. Schaie. New York: Guilford Press.

Daniel, D. E.; Templin, R. G.; and Shearon, R. W. 1977. The value orientation of older adults towards education. *Educational Gerontology* 2: 33–42.

Dave, R. H., ed. 1976. *Foundations of Lifelong Education.* Oxford: Pergamon Press.

Denney, N. W. 1980. The effect of manipulation of peripheral, noncognitive variables on the problem-solving performance of the elderly. *Human Development* 23: 268–277.

Denney, N. W. 1982. Aging and cognitive changes. In *Handbook of Developmental Psychology,* ed. B. B. Wolman. Englewood Cliffs, NJ: Prentice-Hall.

Denney, N. W., and Denney, D. 1974. Modeling effects on the questioning strategies of the elderly. *Developmental Psychology* 10: 400–404.

Denney, N. W.; Jones, F.; and Krigel, S. 1979. Modifying the questioning strategies of young children and elderly adults. *Human Development* 22: 23–36.

Donaldson, G. 1981. Letter to the editor. *Journal of Gerontology* 36: 634–636.

Dubin, S. 1972. Obsolescence or lifelong education: A choice for the professional. *American Psychologist* 17: 486–498.

Dubin, S. 1977. *A Learning Model for Updating Older*

Technical and Professional Persons. Paper presented at meeting of the American Psychological Association, San Francisco.

Eichorn, D. H.; Clausen, J. A.; Haan, N.; Honzik, M. P.; and Mussen, P., eds. 1981. *Present and Past in Middle Life.* New York: Academic Press.

Ferdinand, F. 1966. On the obsolescence of scientists and engineers. *American Scientist* 54: 45–56.

Ferguson, G. A. 1954. On learning and human ability. *Canadian Journal of Psychology* 8: 95–112.

Ferguson, G. A. 1956. On transfer and the abilities of man. *Canadian Journal of Psychology* 10: 121–131.

Flanagan, J. C., and Russ-Eft, D. 1976. *An Empirical Study Aid in Formulating Educational Goals.* Palo Alto, CA: American Institutes for Research.

Flavell, J. 1970. Cognitive changes in adulthood. In *Life-Span Developmental Psychology: Research and Theory,* eds. L. R. Goulet and P. B. Baltes. New York: Academic Press.

Gardner, E. F., and Monge, R. H. 1977. Adult age differences in cognitive abilities and educational background. *Experimental Aging Research* 3: 337–383.

Giambra, L., and Arenberg, D. 1980. Problem solving, concept learning and aging. In *Aging in the 1980s,* ed. L. Poon. Washington, D.C.: American Psychological Association.

Goulet, L. R. 1973. The interfaces of acquisition: Models and methods for studying the active, developing organism. In *Life-Span Developmental Psychology: Methodological Issues,* eds. J. R. Nesselroade and H. W. Reese. New York: Academic Press.

Grant, E.; Storandt, M.; and Botwinick, J. 1978. Incentive and practice in the psychomotor performance of the elderly. *Journal of Gerontology* 33: 413–415.

Gribbin, K.; Schaie, K. W.; and Parham, I. A. 1980. Complexity of lifestyle and maintenance of intellectual abilities. *Journal of Social Issues* 36: 47–61.

Hardiman, C.; Holbrook, A.; and Hedrick, D. 1979. Nonverbal communication systems for the severely handicapped geriatric patients. *Gerontologist* 19: 96–101.

Hartley, J.; Harker, J.; and Walsh, D. 1980. Contemporary issues and new directions in adult development of learning and memory. In *Aging in the 1980s,* ed. L. W. Poon. Washington, D.C.: American Psychological Association.

Hertzog, C.; Schaie, K. W.; and Gribbin, K. 1978. Cardiovascular disease and changes in intellectual functioning from middle to old age. *Journal of Gerontology* 33: 872–883.

Hesburgh, T.; Miller, P.; and Wharton, C. 1974. *Patterns for Lifelong Learning.* San Francisco: Jossey-Bass.

Hiemstra, R. 1976. *Lifelong Learning.* Lincoln, NE: Professional Educators Publications.

Hofland, B. F.; Willis, S. L.; and Baltes, P. B. 1981. Fluid intelligence performance in the elderly: Intraindividual variability and conditions of assessment. *Journal of Educational Psychology* 73: 573–586.

Holcomb, C. A. 1979. The Cloze Procedure and older adults: Effects of age and schooling. *Educational Gerontology* 4: 279–295.

Horn, J. L., and Donaldson, G. 1976. On the myth of intellectual decline in adulthood. *American Psychologist* 31: 701–719.

Hornblum, J. N., and Overton, W. F. 1976. Area and volume conservation among the elderly: Assessment and training. *Developmental Psychology* 12: 68–74.

Houle, C. O. 1981. *Continuing Learning in the Professions.* San Francisco: Jossey-Bass.

Hoyer, W. J. 1974. Aging as intraindividual change. *Developmental Psychology* 10: 821–826.

Hoyer, W. J., and Plude, D. J. 1980. Attentional and perceptual processes in the study of cognitive aging. In *Aging in the 1980s,* ed. L. W. Poon. Washington, D.C.: American Psychological Association.

Hultsch, D. F. 1974. Learning to learn in adulthood. *Journal of Gerontology* 29: 302–308.

Jarvik, L. F., and Banks, L. 1983. Aging twins: Longitudinal psychometric data. In *Longitudinal Studies of Adult Psychological Development,* ed. K. W. Schaie. New York: Guilford Press.

Jenkins, J. 1979. Four points to remember: A tetrahedral model of memory experiments. In *Levels of Processing in Human Memory,* eds. L. Cermak and F. I. M. Craik. Hillsdale, NJ: Lawrence Erlbaum.

Johnstone, J., and Riviera, R. 1965. *Volunteers for Learning.* Chicago: Aldine.

Kessler, M. S.; Denney, N. W.; and Whitely, S. 1976. Factors influencing problem solving in middle-aged and elderly adults. *Human Development* 19: 310–320.

Klein, L.; German, P.; McPhee, S.; Smith, C.; and Levine, D. 1982. Aging and its relationship to health knowledge and medication compliance. *Gerontologist* 22: 384–387.

Knowlton, M. P. 1977. Liberal arts: The Edlerhostel plan for survival. *Educational Gerontology* 2: 87–93.

Kohn, M. L., and Schooler, C. 1979. The reciprocal effects of the substantive complexity of work and intellectual flexibility: A longitudinal assessment. In *Aging from Birth to Death,* ed. M. W. Riley. Boulder, CO: Westview Press.

Krauss, I. 1980. Between and within-group comparisons in aging research. In *Aging in the 1980s,* ed. L. W. Poon. Washington, D.C.: American Psychological Association.

Labouvie-Vief, G. 1977. Adult cognitive development: In search of alternative interpretations. *Merrill Palmer Quarterly* 23: 227–263.

Labouvie-Vief, G., and Gonda, J. N. 1976. Cognitive strategy training and intellectual performance in the elderly. *Journal of Gerontology* 31: 327–332.

Labouvie-Vief, G., and Schell, D. 1982. Learning and memory in later life. In *Handbook of Developmental Psychology,* ed. B. B. Wolman. Englewood Cliffs, NJ: Prentice-Hall.

Lazar, I.; Darlington, R.; Murray, H.; Royce, J.; and Snipper, A. 1982. Lasting effects of early education. *Monographs of the Society for Research in Child Development,* Serial No. 195.

Lieberman, L., and Lieberman, L. 1983. Second careers in art and craft fairs. *Gerontologist* 23: 266–272.

Murrell, K. F. H., and Humphries, S. 1978. Age, experience, and short-term memory. In *Practical Aspects of*

Memory, eds. M. M. Gruneberg, P. E. Morris, and R. N. Sykes. London: Academic Press.

National Center for Education Statistics. 1980. *Preliminary Data, Participation in Adult Education, 1978.* Washington, D.C.: Office of Education, U.S. Department of Health, Education and Welfare.

Nesselroade, J. R., and Baltes, P. B., eds. 1979. *Longitudinal Research in the Study of Behavior and Development.* New York: Academic Press.

Nunnally, J. 1982. The study of human change: Measurement, research strategies, and methods of analysis. In *Handbook of Developmental Psychology,* ed. B. B. Wolman. Englewood Cliffs, NJ: Prentice-Hall.

Overton, W. F., and Newman, J. 1981. *Life-Span Cognitive Intervention Research: A Competence-Activation/Utilization Approach.* Paper presented at the meeting of the International Society for the Study of Behavioral Development, Toronto, Canada.

Parsons, T., and Platt, G. 1968. Considerations on the American academic system. *Minerva* 497–523.

Parsons, T., and Platt, G. 1972. Higher education and changing socialization. In *Aging and Society: A Sociology of Age Stratification,* eds. M. W. Riley, A. Foner et al. New York: Russell Sage Foundation.

Penland, P. 1979. Self initiated learning. *Adult Education* 29: 170–179.

Perlmutter, M. 1978. What is memory aging the aging of? *Developmental Psychology* 14: 330–345.

Perlmutter, M. 1980. An apparent paradox about memory aging. In *New Directions in Memory and Aging,* eds. L. Poon, J. Fozard, L. Cermak, D. Arenberg, and L. Thompson. Hillsdale, NJ: Erlbaum.

Raynor, J. O., and Rubin, I. S. 1971. Effects of achievement motivation and future orientation on level of performance. *Journal of Personality and Social Psychology* 17: 36–41.

Riley, M. W. 1983. Aging, health and social change, an overview. In *Perspectives on Behavioral Medicine Vol. 4: Behavioral and Psychosocial Dimensions of Aging,* eds. M. W. Riley, A. S. Baum, and J. D. Matarazzo. New York: Academic Press.

Riley, M. W.; Abeles, R. P.; and Teitelbaum, M. S., eds. 1982. *Aging from Birth to Death: Sociotemporal Perspectives.* Boulder, CO: Westview Press.

Robertson-Tchabo, E. A. 1980. Cognitive skill and training for the elderly: Why should "old dogs" acquire new tricks. In *New Directions in Memory and Aging,* eds. L. Poon, J. Fozard, L. Cermak, D. Arenberg, and L. Thompson. Hillsdale, NJ: Erlbaum.

Robertson-Tchabo, E. A.; Hausman, C. P.; and Arenberg, D. 1976. A classical mnemonic for older learners: A trip that works! *Educational Gerontology* 1: 215–226.

Romaniuk, J., and Romaniuk, M. 1982. Participation motives of older adults in higher education: The Elderhostel experience. *Gerontologist* 22: 364–368.

Salthouse, T. A. 1982. *Adult Cognition.* New York: Springer-Verlag.

Sanders, J. C.; Sterns, H. L.; Smith, M.; and Sanders, R. E. 1975. Modification of concept identification performance in older adults. *Developmental Psychology* 11: 824–829.

Sanders, R. E., and Sanders, J. C. 1978. Long-term dura-

bility and transfer of enhanced conceptual performance in the elderly. *Journal of Gerontology* 33: 408–412.

Schaie, K. W. 1973. Methodological problems in descriptive developmental research on adulthood and aging. In *Life-Span Developmental Psychology: Methodological Issues,* eds. J. R. Nesselroade and H. W. Reese. New York: Academic Press.

Schaie, K. W. 1977/78. Toward a stage theory of adult cognitive development. *Journal of Aging and Human Development* 8: 129–138.

Schaie, K. W. 1979. The primary mental abilities in adulthood: An exploration in the development of psychometric intelligence. In *Life-Span Development and Behavior,* vol. 2, eds. P. B. Baltes and O. G. Brim, Jr. New York: Academic Press.

Schaie, K. W. 1980. *Intraindividual Change in Intellectual Abilities: Normative Considerations.* Paper presented at annual meeting of the Gerontological Society, San Diego.

Schaie, K. W. 1983. The Seattle Longitudinal Study: A twenty-one year investigation of psychometric intelligence. In *Longitudinal Studies of Adult Psychological Development,* ed. K. W. Schaie. New York: Guilford Press.

Schaie, K. W., and Baltes, P. B. 1977. Some faith helps to see the forest: A final comment on the Horn and Donaldson myth of the Baltes-Schaie position on adult intelligence. *American Psychologist* 32: 1118–1120.

Schaie, K. W., and Hertzog, C. 1982. Longitudinal methods. In *Handbook of Developmental Psychology,* ed. B. B. Wolman. Englewood Cliffs, NJ: Prentice-Hall.

Schaie, K. W., and Hertzog, C. 1983. Fourteen-year cohort-sequential studies of adult intelligence. *Developmental Psychology* 19: 531–543.

Schaie, K. W.; Labouvie, G. V.; and Barrett, T. J. 1973. Selective attrition effects in a fourteen-year study of adult intelligence. *Journal of Gerontology* 28: 328–334.

Schaie, K. W., and Quayhagen, M. 1979. Life-span educational psychology: Adulthood and old age. In *Probleme und Perpektiven der Pädagogischen Psychologie,* eds. J. Brandstätter, G., Reinert, and K. A. Schneewind. Stuttgart: Klett.

Schaie, K. W., and Willis, S. L. 1978. Life-span development: Implications for education. *Review of Research in Education* 6: 120–156.

Schaie, K. W., and Willis, S. L. 1982. Life-span development. In *Encyclopedia of Educational Research,* ed. H. E. Mitzel. 5th ed. New York: MacMillan.

Schmitt, F.; Murphy, M.; and Sanders, R. E. 1981. Training older adult free recall rehearsal strategies. *Journal of Gerontology* 36: 329–337.

Schultz, N. R., and Hoyer, W. J. 1976. Feedback effects on spatial egocentrism in old age. *Journal of Gerontology* 31: 72–75.

Seguin, M. M., and O'Brien, B. 1976. *Releasing the Potential of the Older Volunteer.* Los Angeles: University of Southern California Press.

Shearer, R., and Stegar, J. 1975. Manpower obsolescence: A new definition and empirical investigation of personal variables. *Academy of Management Journal* 18(2): 263–275.

Siefert, W. W. 1964. The prevention and cure of obsolescence in scientific and technical personnel. *Research Management* 7: 143–154.

Siegler, I. C. 1983. Psychological aspects of the Duke Longitudinal Studies. In *Longitudinal Studies of Adult Psychological Development,* ed. K. W. Schaie. New York: Guilford Press.

Siegler, I. C.; Nowlin, J. B.; and Blumenthal, J. A. 1980. Health and bahavior: Methodological considerations for adult development and aging. In *Aging in the 1980s,* ed. L. W. Poon. Washington, D.C.: American Psychological Association.

Smith, A. 1980. Cognitive issues: Advances in the cognitive psychology of aging. In *Aging in the 1980s,* ed. L. W. Poon. Washington, D.C.: American Psychological Association.

Sterns, H. L., and Sanders, R. E. 1980. Training and education in the elderly. In *Life-Span Developmental Psychology: Intervention,* eds. R. E. Turner and H. W. Reese. New York: Academic Press.

Stone, V., and Schaie, K. W. 1980. *Intelligence, Life Stress and Health: A LISREL Analysis.* Paper presented at annual meeting of the Gerontological Society, San Diego.

Storandt, M. 1977. Age, ability level, and method of administering and scoring the WAIS. *Journal of Gerontology* 32: 175–178.

Storandt, M., and Futterman, A. 1982. Stimulus size and performance on two subtests of the Wechsler Adult Intelligence Scale by younger and older adults. *Journal of Gerontology* 37: 602–603.

Taub, H. A. 1973. Memory span, practice and aging. *Journal of Gerontology* 28: 335–358.

Taub, H. A., and Long, M. K. 1976. The effects of practice on short-term memory of young and old subjects. *Journal of Gerontology* 27: 494–499.

Thomae, H., ed. 1976. *Patterns of Aging: Findings from the Bonn Longitudinal Study of Aging.* Basel: Karger.

Thurstone, L. L. 1938. *Primary Mental Abilities.* Chicago: University of Chicago Press.

Tough, A. 1971. *The Adult's Learning Projects.* Toronto: Ontario Institute for Studies in Education.

Walmsley, S., and Allington, R. 1982. Reading abilities of elderly persons in relation to the difficulty of essential documents. *Gerontologist* 22: 36–38.

Weisman, S. 1983. Computer games for the frail elderly. *Gerontologist* 23: 361–363.

Willis, S. L., and Baltes, P. B. 1980. Intelligence in adulthood and aging: Contemporary issues. In *Aging in the 1980s,* ed. L. W. Poon. Washington, D.C.: American Psychological Association.

Willis, S. L.; Blieszner, R.; and Baltes, P. B. 1981. Intellectual training research in aging: Modification of performance on the fluid ability of figural relations. *Journal of Educational Psychology* 73: 41–50.

Willis, S. L.; Cornelius, S. W.; and Baltes, P. B. 1983. Training research in aging: Attentional processes. *Journal of Educational Psychology* 75: 257–270.

Willis, S. L., and Schaie, K. W. 1981. Maintenance and decline of adult mental abilities: II. Susceptibility to experimental manipulation. In *Adult Learning and Development,* eds. F. Grote and R. Feringer. Bellingham, WA: Western Washington University.

Willis, S. L., and Schaie, K. W. 1983. *Ability Correlates of Real Life Tasks in Young and Later Adulthood.* Paper presented at the biennial meeting of the Society for Research in Child Development, Detroit.

31
LEISURE AND RECREATION

Lei Lane Burrus-Bammel
and
Gene Bammel
West Virginia University

INTRODUCTION

In everyday language, the words leisure and recreation mean different things to different people. The words have significantly different connotations today from the earliest uses found in ancient Greek literature (Bammel and Bammel, 1982). Kraus (1978) identified four widely found meanings of "leisure": (1) the "classical" or traditional view, (2) leisure as a function of social class, (3) leisure as a form of activity, and (4) leisure as free time. The classical or normative notion of leisure prescribed a norm or pattern of leisure as an end in itself, "a state of mind." Leisure represented the cultivation of mind and spirit. Veblen (1899) contended that leisure was the prerogative of an elite class that was characterized by conspicuous consumption and deliberate pursuit of matters of no consequence. Leisure has more recently been defined as nonwork activity in which people engage during their free time for the purpose of relaxation, entertainment, or personal development (Dumazedier, 1967). Kraus (1978) believed the most frequently used definition to be leisure as unobligated time, often referred to as the "residual definition." In this sense, the time left over when existence and subsistence necessities of life have been taken care of is classified as "leisure."

Murphy (1975) discussed leisure as contemplative and as discretionary time, but he addi-tionally expressed a social instrument concept, an antiutilitarian concept, and a holistic or multidimensional concept. Simplistically, leisure can be defined either objectively or subjectively (Neulinger, 1974). Objectively, leisure is considered as time left over after work; subjectively, it refers to a state of mind (Iso-Ahola, 1980). Forty-five percent of the men and 37 percent of the women in the Pfeiffer and Davis (1971) study defined leisure as "anything that is relaxing," while 32 percent of the men and 33 percent of the women chose "anything that is fun." "Free time" and "other" definitions received less than 10 percent each.

Definitions, concepts, or notions of leisure center around the three variables of activity, time, and frame of mind. No one definition of leisure quite nails down the term, for like the Hindu god Shiva, it has many faces, many different ways of being realized. "In leisure occur most of the important events of one's life: insights, personal relationships, choices of careers, and delights in ourselves, our friends, and the natural world" (Bammel and Bammel, 1982, p. 32). Leisure can provide (1) rest, respite, and restoration; (2) self-realization; (3) "spiritual renewal" in contemplation, and (4) entertainment (Meyersohn, 1972).

Generally speaking, leisure has the connotation of the attitude, time or activities that enable personal growth or development. Recreation connotes activities that can be specified, such as walking or TV watching. All leisure activities are presumed to be recreational, for they re-create the person so engaged, but all recreation activities are not necessarily leisure. More complete reviews on leisure definitions and conceptualizations can be found in Bammel and Bammel (1982), Neulinger (1981), Kaplan (1975), and Kando (1975).

LEISURE THEORIES

A number of attempts have been made to explain why people take their leisure as they do as well as to predict future leisure behavior. The first known theory of leisure behavior was partially outlined by Aristotle in the Nichomachean Ethics. For Aristotle, everything in life was related to leisure since leisure was "the goal of all activity." Leisure is only for those who passionately pursue it. This Aristotelian version inspired Sebastian de Grazia (1962) and was updated by Cox (1969) and Joseph Pieper (1963), who professed that leisure was the basis of culture.

Two theories concentrate on the relationship between work and leisure. The compensatory theory is the one most frequently voiced (Roberts, 1970). Mills (1951) suggests that "whenever the individual is given the opportunity to avoid his regular routine he will seek a directly opposite activity" (Burch, 1969, p. 127). Work is viewed as the dominant force in life, and leisure offers the individual the freedom to compensate for constraints, tensions, limitations, etc., of a job by engaging in a radically different experience (Wilensky, 1960). The opposite theory states that leisure is a "spillover" from work and that the experiences sought in leisure parallel work activity and complement it. Those who have dull jobs seem either to compensate radically or to have drab leisure routines (Parker, 1971). Wilensky (1960) noted that alienation from work becomes alienation from life, that mental stultification produced by one's labor will permeate one's leisure. Workers with routine jobs were found by Kornhauser (1965) to be less sociable and to have less satisfactory family relations than white collar or highly skilled factory workers.

The important role of the peer group is the premise of the personal community theory. It assumes that "gross social issues and psychological drives are significantly filtered and redirected by the social circles of workmates, family, and friends" (Burch, 1969, p. 138). Peer groups are perceived to be influential in determining leisure behavior. Psychiatric counselors have noted that people return repeatedly to places where special events occurred in their lives (Hunt, 1969). Burch (1969) hypothesized that "familiarity" might be an important variable. This familiarity hypothesis explains leisure in terms of what one has learned to be comfortable with (Bammel and Bammel, 1982). If leisure is a time at which people feel their personal best, there are likely to be factors in the environment that condition their responses.

Dumazedier (1967) explained leisure as an activity to which individuals turn at will for either relaxation, diversion, or broadening of knowledge; it is activity that is frequently social and that makes some demand on the individual's creative capacity. This is the most comprehensive theory. A meaningful leisure theory should relate other aspects of human behavior to the central concern and offer some basis for predicting future leisure behavior. The function of leisure, like play, could be viewed as the striving of an individual to maintain an optimal state of arousal and as a form of self-expression (Alderman, 1974). DeCarlo's (1974) data supports the notion that the psychological role of leisure participation changes over the life span but that its importance increases during periods of transitional crisis, particularly after the age of 60 (Iso-Ahola, 1980). Five major leisure needs were isolated by McAvoy (1979), as follows: 89.9 percent of his sample mentioned socializing; 76.6 percent, self-fulfillment; 73.3 percent, closeness to nature; 61 percent, physical exercise; whereas 51.6 percent explained their leisure participation and motivation in terms of learning.

VARIABLES THAT AFFECT LEISURE BEHAVIOR

Work Orientation and Occupation

Americans have been classified as work-oriented. Cohn (1979) mentioned Veblen (1899) and McDougall (1913) as two writers who considered the need to work a basic human instinct. The importance of work in the process of "self-actualization" and the development of self-esteem was emphasized by Maslow (1970). Ninety percent of the 261 men interviewed by Pfeiffer and Davis (1971) indicated that they would still work for a living even if they did not actually have to. Ninety-seven percent of those in the 66 to 71 age group also elected for the work response. The figures were slightly lower for the 241 women interviewed. These same 502 subjects, aged 47 to 71, were asked, "What is more satisfying to you, your work or leisure activities?" Only 13 percent of the men and 16 percent of the women indicated that they derived greater satisfaction from leisure activities.

Not only are Americans work-oriented, but the satisfaction associated with work is reported to increase with age (Melzer, 1965). Older respondents have identified themselves more with work than leisure, perceive themselves as having less leisure, desire shorter vacations than their younger counterparts, and have a lower affinity for leisure (Neulinger and Breit, 1971). The higher one's income and educational level, the more likely one is to identify with work rather than leisure (Neulinger and Breit, 1971). Married individuals tend to be more work-oriented than singles, those divorced, or those separated (Neulinger and Breit, 1971).

Low morale upon retirement has been documented for work-oriented men (Lowenthal and Robinson, 1976). The analyses of Palmore et al. (1979, p. 847) showed that "retirement was followed by more negative changes than any other life event." It was pointed out by Parker (1976) that work is so enjoyed by some American executives that they see no distinction between work and leisure. Men, it is believed, view work as being essential to their personal and social identity; thus, it influences the structuring of other aspects of their lives (Lowenthal and Robinson, 1976). Occupational and educational status were the only status factors that had a significant effect on life satisfaction in the Hurst and Guldin study (1982).

Work activities tend to spill over into retirement. Simpson, Back, and McKinney (1966) pointed out that middle-status jobs are oriented around people, upper white collar jobs around symbols, and semiskilled jobs around things. The greatest amount of spill-over occurred among those with jobs oriented around people. Individuals in the highest or professional occupations exhibit a greater variety of activities and participate more frequently in activities requiring a certain expense of energy (Burdge, 1969; White, 1975). Workers with undemanding employment do not participate in leisure activities that require "planning, coordination, and purposeful action" (Godbey and Parker, 1976). People employed at more creative jobs have been found to prefer wilderness camping, whereas those with routine jobs more often prefer public campgrounds (Etzhorn, 1964). Life achievement patterns (homemakers, career workers, job holders) and retirement status of gifted aged women affect the relationship of activities to happiness and life satisfaction (Holahan, 1981).

Finances

An association between socioeconomic variables and leisure activity has been documented by Cheek (1971). Markides and Martin (1979, p. 90–91) reported that "the strongest indirect effects via Activity are those of Income." Retirement can mean a drop in income of 50 percent or more. The median income in 1979 for families headed by persons under 65 was $21,201; the median income for families headed by a person 65 and over was $11,316 (Allan and Brotman, 1981). The same pattern holds true for individuals living alone or with nonrelatives. Poverty rates for the elderly are higher than for the total population. In 1979, the poverty level was $3,472 for individuals and $4,364 for couples. Fifteen and one-tenth percent of the elderly were at or below the poverty level, while another 10 percent were classified as "near poor" (125 percent of poverty level). The ranks of the elderly poor are disproportionately represented by older females, particularly those who live alone. Forty-two percent of black women and 16 percent of white women aged 65 and older were technically living in "poverty" in 1979 (Allan and Brotman, 1981). A reported 3.84 million senior citizens are living in poverty, with an additional 2.5 million in the "near poor" category (Sanoff and Cole, 1982). In the 1975 Harris poll (NCOA), 15 percent of the respondents over 65 indicated that they did not have enough money to live on. The lowest income group (under $3,000 in 1975) suffers more seriously from every problem than the more affluent (NCOA, 1975).

Only half of the private work force in 1979 was covered by a company- or union-sponsored pension plan (Tuhy, 1979). The buying power of a $10,000 pension, given a 7 percent yearly cost of living increase, would be $2,584 twenty years later, meaning that three-fourths of the buying power had been lost. A couple that could live on $25,000 a year in 1979 would need $144,000 a year in 2009 (Tuhy, 1979).

Income has been related to both activity patterns and life satisfaction. A negative correlation between income and constriction of leisure activities of older adults who have entered an age-segregated environment was found by Morgan and Godbey (1978). As current income increases, the number of activities dropped by the subjects decreases. In the Edwards and Klemmack study (1973), family income had the highest correlation with life satisfaction. Economic sufficiency and self-assessed health were the strongest predictors of life satisfaction for groups over and under the age of 65 (Spreitzer and Snyder, 1974). Annual income also occurred in the Chatfield (1977) investigation as a significant variable in life satisfaction. Leisure time has greater appeal to those with higher incomes (NCOA, 1975). People who live in houses engage in hobbies more frequently than those living in apartments (Rapoport and Rapoport, 1975).

Time

In 1961, Kleemeier commented that a major problem of the elderly was having too much free time. Riley and Foner (1968) noted that the proportion of elderly who say that they do not know what to do with their time increases with age and "few complain about not having enough time, nor do they want more of it" (Lowenthal and Robinson, 1976, p. 443). Yet, nationwide, people indicated that the best thing about being over 65 was "having more leisure" (NCOA, 1975). Sixteen percent of the men and eight percent of the women aged 66 to 71 in the Pfeiffer and Davis (1971) study complained of "too much free time," whereas 15 percent of the males and 17 percent of the females felt that there was too little of it. Lack of time has been mentioned by the elderly as their third most prevalent problem when trying to participate in preferred activities (McAvoy, 1979). Only 6 percent of the elderly in the NCOA (1975) survey reported "not enough to do to keep busy" as a very serious personal problem.

Health and Mobility

The elderly have not been a highly mobile group. On the average, they have "lived in their communities thirty-two years and in their homes sixteen years" (Birren, 1970). Between 1975 and 1979, 44.8 percent of the population under 65 changed residence, whereas only 17 percent of the elderly moved, and only 3.6 percent of these moved out of state (Allan and Brotman, 1981). Nevertheless, interstate movement of the elderly has come to dominate migration patterns over the past two decades (Longino, 1982). Retirees migrating to Arizona often base their decision on health considerations, whereas those selecting Florida tend to seek a more leisure-oriented life-style (Bultena and Wood, 1970).

Lack of transportation was the fourth most prevalent problem encountered by the elderly when they tried to participate in preferred activities (McAvoy, 1979). A GAO (General Accounting Office) study found that 68 percent of the sampled elderly were dependent in some degree on others for transportation (Allan and Brotman, 1981). Twenty-two percent of the elderly listed difficulty in walking and climbing stairs as a very serious problem (NCOA, 1975); 2.6 percent needed help to get around the neighborhood; and 8.4 percent needed assistance to travel outside the neighborhood (Allan and Brotman, 1981). Other places in general (except for houses of religious worship, places to shop, and homes of relatives or friends) are viewed as considerably less convenient by the elderly. The recorded inconvenience seems to be more a function of economics, fear of crime, education, and physical mobility than it is of actual geographic location (NCOA, 1975).

In 1979, the National Center for Health Statistics reported that 80 percent of the population that was 65 and over had at least one chronic condition; multiple conditions were common. Forty-four percent suffered from arthritis, 39 percent from hypertension, 28 percent from a hearing impairment, 27 percent from heart conditions, 12 percent from visual limitations, and 12 percent from diabetes. One-fifth were aware that some limitation had been imposed on their activity (Allan and Brotman, 1981).

Lack of ability was mentioned by the elderly as their most important problem in trying to participate in preferred activities. It was mentioned three times as frequently as any other problem (McAvoy, 1979). Individuals who perceived their health to be average or better were more likely to expand their leisure activity participation patterns (Morgan and Godbey, 1978).

Research investigations commissioned by the President's Council on Physical Fitness and Sports indicated that older adults are basically unfit (Clarke, 1977) and that those who attempt to stay healthy and fit through physical exercise programs are in the minority (Crase and Rosato, 1979). The 39 percent who report pursuing a systematic program of exercise list walking as "the favorite form of exercise," followed by calisthenics, swimming, bicycling, jogging, and some weight training (men only).

Thompson (1973) summarized that morale declines as perceptions of one's health become more negative. Health has a greater effect on morale than subjective integration, financial satisfaction, objective integration, or socioeconomic status (Liang, Dvorkin, Kahana, and Mazian, 1980). Although all age groups are provided high levels of satisfaction from marriage, family, and friends, health is another matter. It "provides one of the highest areas of satisfaction range for the younger re-

spondents, but is the lower end of the relative satisfaction range for the older respondents" (Cutler, 1979, p. 576). Health is significantly correlated to psychological well being, morale, and life satisfaction as well as being a strong predictor of the latter (Beckman and Houser, 1982). Thirty years of research on the subjective well-being of older Americans has indicated that health has the strongest influence on it (Larson, 1978).

Family and Friends

People travel to work alone but recreate together, and the family is the most common recreation unit (Cheek, Field, and Burdge, 1976). Lowenthal and Haven (1968) suggested that "the presence of a stable, intimate relationship with a single 'confidante' is the strategic correlate of high morale." Lack of companionship was recorded as the second most prevalent problem encountered by the elderly in relation to participating in their preferred leisure activity (McAvoy, 1979). In the McAvoy study, about 25 percent of the sample pursued leisure activities by themselves, 8.2 percent with their children or grandchildren, 24.8 percent with a younger age group, and the majority, 56.3 percent, with their own age group (McAvoy, 1979). An earlier study, however, reported that over half of the leisure activities were individual pursuits, a third with family members, one-tenth with friends, and less than 2 percent in formal groups (Cowgill and Baulch, 1962). Maddox (1963) separated activities that involved contact with other persons from noninterpersonal activities. His data indicated that noninterpersonal activity scores held constant over time whereas interpersonal activity scores tended to decline. Such studies suggest that activities for a living alone lifestyle or an at home life-style should be recreational goals (Nystrom, 1974). As much as 85 percent of leisure activities have been reported to take place in a home environment (Cowgill and Baulch, 1962). Programs that stress socializing activities alone are too limited and unrealistic. A direct relationship between morale and the number of solitary activities an individual engages in was found by Sauer (1977).

Most older males are married whereas most older females are widows. Only twenty-two percent of women over 75 are married compared to 69 percent of men in that age group. Less than 48 percent of the females aged 65 to 74 are married compared to 81 percent of the men (Allan and Brotman, 1981). A greater percentage of elderly men have access to a spouse or live-in companionship (see Table 1).

Marital status has been found to be a strong predictor of both morale and psychological well-being (Sauer, 1977; Spreitzer and Snyder, 1974). Holahan (1981) found that divorced subjects have less total lifetime satisfaction than either widowed or married subjects. Widowed, childless women have lower psychological well-being than widowed mothers (Beckman and Houser, 1982). Sixty percent of recently divorced (nine months or less) men over 50 years of age and 50 percent of recently divorced women in that age group responded that they were "not too happy" (Chiriboga, 1982). Payne and Pittard (1969) concluded that divorce among the long-time married may be disruptive because of their greater entrenchment in an established social order. In the Chiriboga (1982) study of divorced individuals, more psychological distress was exhibited by the older respondents.

Three-quarters of the population aged 65 and over have children that live within a 30-minute travel radius. Seventy-five percent of a sampled population reported having seen at least one of their children during the previous week (Allan and Brotman, 1981). Sauer (1977) reported a direct relationship between morale and the frequency of interaction with family. Satisfaction with family was found by Medley (1976) to make the "greatest single impact on life satisfaction" for individuals aged 65 and older. The family is the major tie of the elderly to the community (Shanas, 1979).

Age as a Predictive Variable

Participation rates in some activities decline as users become older. Gordon, Gaitz, and Scott (1976) registered a -0.49 correlation of age and the level of general leisure activity. Older individuals are said to increase the amount of time devoted to leisure and recreation but decrease the range of activities by placing a greater emphasis on sedentary and home-bound forms (Gordon et. al., 1976). Zborowski (1962, p. 308), however, concluded that "aging has a rather insignificant influence upon people's recreational patterns and preferences." In past activity studies, age and other socioeconomic-demographic variables have accounted for only a small percentage of variance (ORRRC, 1962). Variance values have been as low as 2 percent when nonusers have been eliminated from the sample population (Field and O'Leary, 1973). Over 75 percent of the variance was unaccounted for when Morgan and Godbey (1978) investigated the effect of entering an age-segregated environment upon the leisure activity patterns of older adults. Low product-moment correlations were found between participation of men living in selected Arizona retirement communities and age (-0.14), income (0.10), education (0.15), and health status (0.15) (Bultena and Wood, 1970). More specifically, Romsa and Girling (1976) demonstrated that socioeconomic-demographic factors do not differenti-

TABLE 1   Percent of Noninstitutionalized Elderly in Various Living Arrangements.*

		Living arrangements		
Age group	Gender	With spouse	Other relative	Alone or nonrelative
65–74	Male	78	7	15
65–74	Female	47	15	38
75+	Male	67	10	23
75+	Female	21	27	52

*Data adopted from Allan and Brotman (1981), *Chart Book on Aging in America.*

ate between participation typology groups within an activity nor do they significantly differ between various recreational activity groups. When attempting to assess and understand recreation populations, aggregate variables are helpful, but "they do not provide a measure of individual behavior" (Cheek, Field, and Burdge, 1976, p. 4).

"Age alone is insufficient to predict an individual's level of activity . . . The best estimate of how active an older person is at any particular age is how active he was at an earlier date" (Videbeck and Knox, 1965, pp. 43–44). Nystrom (1974), like Morgan and Godbey (1978), found that the age variable had no predictive effect, and no differences were found for either activity frequency or activity variety. Palmore (1968), taking four repeated measurements over 10 years, reported relatively unchanged patterns of behavior and attitudes for 127 ambulatory, noninstitutionalized elderly (70 to 93 years of age). Such findings have not been restricted to the United States. Two hundred and twenty-four (224) lower-middle-class Germans (28 to 60 years of age) were interviewed about 55 leisure-time activity characteristics. Age, once again, was found not to be a key variable (Schmitz-Scherzer and Strödell, 1971). Activity frequency and variety has not been shown to be age dependent, nor has "self-image" or life satisfaction (National Council on the Aging, 1975, pp. 54, 151, 161).

Other Key Variables

Key demographics such as income, race, gender, and education are more important indicators than age. Education, more often than any other single variable, is identified as being the most crucial when it comes to recreation and leisure (White, 1975). The National Council on the Aging (1975) found that both the appeal and value of leisure time increases as a function of higher education (college). Surveys have reflected that "interest and participation in many activities, particularly the arts and other cultural pursuits, are closely related to the amount of full time education that people have received" (Godbey and Parker, 1976).

Place of residence can determine the availa-

bility of certain activities (Bammel and Bammel, 1982). Hunting and camping participation can vary over 10 percent from one region of the country to another (Hendee and Potter, 1975). Findings of different recreation participation patterns for rural and urban residents is common (ORRRC, 1962). Eighty-six propositions, in 20 articles, suggesting the importance of rural-urban differences in recreation behavior were identified by Nielsen (as cited in Hendee, 1969). Residence in a metropolitan area increases the probability of discontinuing fishing and hunting when other factors are held constant (Charbonneau and Lyons, 1980). Preferences have varied when place of residence was considered. Walking for pleasure, attending meetings, and enjoying a pleasant public park were significantly preferred by Metropolitan Area subjects, whereas fishing, hunting, and gardening were favored by Resource Rich Area subjects (McAvoy, 1979).

A debate has been in progress over the importance of place of residence as a meaningful variable. One school of thought believes that acculturation is reducing (Palen, 1979) and eventually will eliminate rural-urban differences (van Es and Brown, 1974). Others contend that these differences are not only still present (Weisner, 1979) but critical (Lowe and Peek, 1974) at two levels of analysis—that of the community and that of the individual (Schnore, 1966).

Race and ethnic background account for some differences in recreation and leisure patterns (Murphy, 1974; Neulinger, 1974; Washburn, 1978). Blacks, in comparison to whites, comprise the more closely knit group. The same people repeatedly get together, and the activities in which they participate are less diverse. The cohesion, more limited life space (territory), and constricted activities of blacks may be the result of discrimination (Cheek, Field and Burdge, 1976). Nonwhite urban minorities are especially dependent on public recreation services. A series of articles in the *Chicago Sun-Times* analyzed recreation programs at parks located in white and black neighborhoods. The opportunities found in predominantly black areas were reported to be distinctly lower in both quantity and quality

(Wendling, 1980). Two explanations of black/ white recreational differences have been offered, one labelled "marginality" and the other "ethnicity" (Washburn, 1978). Each has received limited support (Cheek, Field, and Burdge, 1976).

Race "could be a major factor in shaping leisure behavior, attitudes, and policies, if not now, then in the near future" (Neulinger, 1974). A number of major American cities are expecting their populations to be at least 50 percent black by the year 2000 (Kahn and Wiener, 1970).

The importance of understanding culturally predetermined expectations of ethnic groups when planning meaningful activities for the elderly was pointed out by Guttman (1973). A number of people have stressed individualizing senior center activities by including cultural programs (Guttman, 1973; Solender, 1969). Cultural programs designed to attract older adults born in Eastern Europe failed to meet the needs of American born and educated Jewish aged (Guttman, 1973).

Current Leisure Patterns

Drawing valid conclusions from activity inventory studies is difficult since the subjects' attitudes or motivations are unknown. Gardening might be a recreational activity or work done for financial reasons. Between-study comparisons are often impossible because of differences in operationalizing the activity variable through various measurement techniques. Time diary studies can reveal an average of two hours per day of unaccounted time (Pfeiffer and Davis, 1971). Accurate responses are not always attained because of limited recall ability, psychological weighting of certain items, serial positioning effect, the possible desire to please the researcher, and/or the possible need to maintain a personal image. Intervening variables of accessibility, knowledge of existing opportunities, transportation, family status, life style, etc., are seldom controlled or considered.

Havighurst (1977) identified patterns of free-time activity based upon open-ended interviews with retired workers in eight countries. Free time was primarily occupied by (1)

challenging new experiences, (2) instrumental service, (3) expressive pleasure, (4) mildly active time-filling routines, and (5) expanding ordinary routines to fill the day and week.

In their Houston study of leisure across the life span, Gordon, Gaitz, and Scott (1976) classified 17 activities into the following five categories: (1) relaxation, (2) diversion, (3) developmental, (4) creativity, and (5) sensual transcendence. Relaxation was the only category that increased over the life span for both genders. TV viewing, discussion, spectator sports, cultural consumption, entertaining, club and organization participation, and home embellishment stayed about the same. Decreases were noted for dancing and drinking, movies, sports and exercise, guns, outdoor activities, travel, reading, and cultural production. Analysis of related pleasure scores produced four patterns associated with specific activities: (1) continuously reduced leisure involvement, (2) pleasure peaking in middle age, (3) little difference over the life span, and (4) increases with age.

An individual's repertoire of leisure activity might be viewed as an elongated diamond with its two narrow ends representing childhood and old age. Iso-Ahola (1980) emphasized that the relationship between age and leisure cannot adequately be examined by analyzing only one dimension. The number of activities is not important. The fact that a person's leisure repertoire can continue to be broad during retirement so long as substitutions or alterations can be made "within" activities is important. Activities can be altered, when needed or desired, by changing

(1) intensity of participation, (2) the locus of participation (e.g. outside vs. inside home), (3) social company of participation, both quantitatively (few vs. many partners) and qualitatively (males vs. females; old vs. young; close vs. distant friends, etc.), (4) psychological reasons of participation (social interaction vs. physical exercise, etc.) and (5) time (morning vs. evening, etc.) (Iso-Ahola, 1980, pp. 171–172).

Being able to substitute or make alterations "within" activities is crucial since few older people show a tendency to adopt completely new forms of leisure (Schmitz-Scherzer, 1976).

By combining two variables Breen produced

the following four activity categories (Peppers, 1976):

1. Active-social: Activities that require considerable physical effort and normally take place in a group (e.g., team sports);
2. Active-isolate: Activities that require considerable physical effort and are normally performed by one person (e.g., jogging);
3. Sedentary-social: Activities that require little physical effort and are normally performed in groups (e.g., Bingo);
4. Sedentary-isolate: Activities that require little physical effort and are normally performed by one person (e.g., reading).

Variety and type of activity have been found to correlate with life satisfaction. Higher life-satisfaction scores were recorded for individuals who engaged in a larger number of activities and for those who participated in the active-social category. Individuals in both active categories scored higher than those classified as sedentary. Social people exceeded isolates on the overall life-satisfaction score (Peppers, 1976). No major changes occurred in the nature of activities after retirement, but a significant increase in the absolute number of activities was recorded (Peppers, 1976).

Popular Activities

Reports on the most popular activities among the elderly (see Table 2) are not in complete agreement. Peppers (1976), like McAvoy (1979), listed visiting friends first and watching TV second. Watching TV, however, is more commonly reported as the most popular (Kubey, 1980; Moss and Lawton, 1982). Actual viewing time ranges from a high of 30 hours a week (Peppers, 1976) to a low of 5 hours or less per week (Davis, 1971). In the most recent study, Moss and Lawton (1982) reported 3.3 hours a day. In the Davis sample, 60.3 percent recognized the "companionship service" of television. Television viewing also allows for "simultaneous consumption," that is, engaging in two or more activities at the same time. One shortcoming of devoting so much time to television is the paucity of role identity provided; 48.7 percent believed that the elderly were negatively portrayed (Davis, 1971).

Time devoted to animal care offers a number of advantages. Pets, or mascots, have been

TABLE 2   Rankings of the Most Popular Activities.

Activity	Pepper, 1976			McAvoy, 1979*		
	Percentage of Sample Participating	Post-Retirement Ranking	Pre-Retirement Ranking	Percentage of Sample Participating	Rank	Preference
Visiting friends	77.6	1	3	74.6	1	1
Watching TV	76.2	2	2	68.5	2	6
Odd jobs at home	71.8	3	1			
Travel (group)	66.0	4	5			
Reading	65.5	5	4	66.9	3	2
Sitting and thinking	71.6	6	—			
Fishing	59.2	7	8			
Walking	58.2	8	8	30.7	7	9
Gardening	56.7	9	6	49.4	4	4
Travel (alone)	47.0	10	17			
Hobbies				45.6	5	3
Driving for pleasure				32.4	6	8
Indoor games				29.4	8	5
Attending organizations and club meetings				29.4	9	7
Caring for animals				10.6	10	10

*Subjects were asked their top five; percentage of sample relates to number including that activity in their top five.

observed to stimulate responsiveness, provide pleasure, enhance treatment milieu, and act as a form of reality therapy (Brickel, 1979). Other popular activities mentioned in various studies, but not listed in Table 2, include listening to music, listening to the radio, dining out, and writing letters. Pfeiffer and Davis (1971) reported that "active participation in hobbies or sports accounted for only a small number of hours per week"—2.9 hours for men and 3.4 hours for women. Forty-four percent of the men and 52 percent of the women reported that they did not spend any time on either a hobby or sport.

Cowgill and Baulch (1962) found that 85 percent of leisure activities take place in the home; Moss and Lawton (1982) reported this figure as 75 percent. Only 6.5 percent of an older person's leisure has been reported to take place in commercial facilities (Cowgill and Baulch (1962). Cowgill and Baulch also found that the majority of leisure pursuits are individual. The needs most frequently used to explain leisure participation are socializing, self-fulfillment, closeness to nature, physical exercise, and learning (McAvoy, 1979).

Physical Exercise

The percentage of individuals engaging in vigorous physical activity appears to decline with increasing age (Ostrow, 1980) even though McAvoy's (1979) elderly subjects identified physical exercise as one of the five needs satisfied by leisure participation. Only 5 percent of the male sample in Cowgill and Baulch's survey (1962) had participated in an active sport on the previous day. This decline in participation appears to occur earlier and more frequently among women (Ostrow, 1980).

The elderly represent about 11.2 percent of the U.S. population (Allan and Brotman, 1981) but occupy 40 to 50 percent of the beds in large urban hospitals (Leaf, 1973). An inverse relationship between mortality rates and frequency of participation in physical activity was found by Belloc (1973). Clarke (1973) reported that 39 percent of Americans aged 60 or older participate in systematic exercise. Other studies suggest that senior citizens give a low priority to their need for physical activ-

ity and that their attitudes toward it are more negative than for the other age groups studied (Ostrow, 1980). Kenyon (1968a, 1968b) developed a model that attributes six values to physical activity: social experience, health and fitness, pursuit of vertigo, catharsis, aesthetic experience, and ascetic experience.

The inherent values of participation in lifetime sports have been well documented (Alderman, 1974). Individuals do not make radical adjustments in their participation upon retirement. Highly physically active elderly have a background of active participation in vigorous sports (Harris, 1970). "Innumerable reports attest the benefits of exercise in human disease states" (Bortz, 1980). Clarke (1977), commissioned by the Presidents Council on Physical Fitness and Sports, found that over 60 percent of adults aged 60 to 70 were basically unfit.

A sedentary life style accelerates the aging process as it relates to flexibility, muscular strength, endurance, neuromuscular coordination, cardiac output, and respiratory efficiency (Crase and Rosato, 1979; Clarke, 1977; deVries, 1976). Results of a previously inactive life style can be improved by an exercise training program (Crase and Rosato, 1979). The percentage of improvement or relative gains are roughly the same for the elderly as for the young. Aerobic capacity, the most important determinant of vigor for the elderly, can be improved from 10 to 30 percent (deVries, 1976). Leg strength, an important factor in remaining ambulatory, was increased 50 percent in elderly subjects by isometric and isotonic exercises during a six-week period (Perkins and Kaiser, 1961). Exercise can add 15 or more years to an inactive 70-year old's life (Bortz, 1980).

LEISURE AND THEORIES OF AGING

Disengagement Theory

In the disengagement theory, aging is viewed as a mutual withdrawal by both the aging individual and society at large, with either party being the initiator (Cumming and Henry, 1961). This process of withdrawal replaces the equilibrium that had existed between the individual and society in middle life with a new balance characterized by greater distance. The disengagement theory resulted from observations and research studies indicating that as people age there is (1) a change from active to passive modes of mastery, (2) increased introversion, (3) decline in intellectual efficiency, plus (4) reduction in activities and interest (Birren, 1964). Disengagement was believed to begin sometime during middle life when certain changes in perception, like heightened awareness of the inevitability of death, occur (Cumming, 1963).

Support for the disengagement theory has been mixed, depending on the variables selected to measure the interaction. Involvement in physical activity has been reported to decline with increasing age in some studies (Ostrow, 1980; Gordon et. al., 1976). Others found little support for this premise (Videbeck and Knox, 1965; Palmore, 1968). Decreases have also been recorded for interpersonal but not for noninterpersonal activities (Maddox, 1963). Maddox (1966) suggested that the disengaged state was most likely "to be observed primarily among the very old whose declining health reduces their capacity to play any social roles successfully and among those for whom disengagement is a life style antedating old age." Data from cross-cultural studies indicate that disengagement is not inevitable (Palmore, 1975). Sill (1980) concluded that factors other than age were more significantly related to activity. Kleiber and Kelly (1980) commented that limiting factors such as poor health, reduced income, and inadequate transportation are more responsible for disengagement than the aging process itself.

Disengagement theory, which has been a major paradigm in social gerontology (Streib and Schneider, 1971), receives less support over time (Sill, 1980) as well as increased criticism (Rose, 1964) with respect to its factual (Palmore, 1975) and methodological basis (Hochschild, 1975). Its potential danger when used to formulate social policy has been expounded on by Blau (1973).

Activity Theory

Diametrically opposed to the disengagement theory of aging is the activity theory. The ac-

tivity theory evolved out of the early work of Havighurst (Havighurst and Albrecht, 1953) concerned with the importance of social role participation in adjustment to old age. The theory's premise is that there "is a positive relationship between activity and life satisfaction and that the greater the role loss, the lower the life satisfaction" (Lemon, Bengtson, and Peterson, 1972, p. 511). Therefore, successful or optimal aging would be characterized by activity and resistance to any diminution of the social world (Bell, 1978). The maintenance of middle-age activity levels is viewed as a means of inhibiting deteriorative trends in functional potential and of increasing life satisfaction.

Secondary group activities and physical activities may be two of the strongest contributors to successful aging (Palmore, 1979). DeCarlo (1974) found that activity levels correlate with successful aging. The criteria for successful aging include physical health, mental health, and intellectual performance. A significant positive relationship was also found between cognitive recreation activities and intellectual performance. Activities of a cognitive, affective, and sensory-motor nature, separately and combined, showed significant relationships to mental health. Contrary to popular contention, cognitive, not motor, activities showed the highest relationship to general health and longevity. Individuals who engaged regularly in activities were more successful in aging than those who engaged only sporadically. Activity emerged in the Markides and Martin (1979) study as a strong predictor of life satisfaction for both sexes. Regular participants in an age-segregated leisure program had higher morale and life-satisfaction scores than intermittent participants (Bley, Goodman, Dye, and Harel, 1972). No one in the Bultena (1969) sample whose activity increased after retirement ranked low in life satisfaction. Subjects with high activity scores tended to have high morale scores (Maddox, 1963).

Social participation has long been considered an important factor in determining the happiness, morale, well-being, and/or life satisfaction of elderly individuals (Mutran and Reitzes, 1981). Four significant social activities mentioned were radio listening, visiting with friends, membership in voluntary associations, and attendance at meetings of voluntary associations (Graney, 1975). Active social participation has been identified as the best guarantee of successful aging (Iso-Ahola, 1980). Active recreation has been shown to correlate with the overall quality of life (Flanagan, 1978). Brooks and Elliott (1971) concluded that "those who learned to derive satisfaction from active forms of leisure in early years were psychologically better adjusted 30 years later than those who had learned to derive their leisure from passive forms like TV-watching" (as cited in Iso-Ahola, 1980, p. 384).

As in the case of disengagement theory, some methodological issues arise in connection with the activity theory (Graney, 1975). One criticism relates to the making of inferences about the process of aging from cross-sectional analysis of data. Operationalizing concepts such as activity, life satisfaction, and successful aging have raised questions of validity. Cross references are questionable when different studies use happiness, morale, self-esteem, or life satisfaction as the measure of successful aging. Perhaps quality or type of interaction should be a more important consideration than quantity or frequency (Cutler, 1979; Lowenthal and Haven, 1968). Other intervening variables like personality and work orientation (career vs. noncareer) should perhaps be included (Lemon et al., 1972; Holahan, 1981). Considerable overlap has also existed in the sets of predictors; when these have been controlled, previously reported relationships have been greatly reduced or eliminated (Palmore, 1979). There have been "few instances in which explicit hypotheses are systematically specified and tested" (Hoyt, Kaiser, Peters, and Babchuk, 1980).

Identity Crisis Theory

Aging was viewed by Miller (1965) as a time of social dilemma. Retirement causes the loss of occupational identity and a functional role in society. Inherent assumptions are that people want to remain working because of the all-pervasive nature of occupational identity and that the "implied inability to perform" associated with retirement creates "the portent of embarrassment" that in turn causes an individual to change behavior patterns.

Research has tended to contradict Miller's contention. Chatfield (1977, p. 593) concluded that the lowered satisfactions of recently retired subjects resulted from their loss of income and "not from the loss of a worker-producer role." Spreitzer and Snyder (1974) reported that life satisfaction tended to increase, not decrease, for men after age 65.

Continuity Theory

Retirement can result in a loss of the sense of involvement, but this has not been shown to produce identity crises. The role loss seems unrelated to other variables of self-image or self-concept (Atchley, 1977). Findings more consistently support the concept of continuity in activities, personality, and behavioral patterns in general over time (Zborowski, 1962; Gordon, Gaitz, and Scott, 1976; Ostrow, 1980). Participation in youth is related to current levels of activity (Sofranko and Nolan, 1972; Burch, 1969; Hendee, 1969). All age groups derive high levels of satisfaction from marriage, family, and friends (Cutler, 1979). "Successful aging is marked by autonomy and stability throughout time while the converse is true for unsuccessful aging" (Kuypers, 1972, p. 339).

Theory of the Aged as a Subculture

Arnold Rose (1965) theorized that social identities and self-concepts of the elderly are maintained neither by holding on to middle-aged standards nor by making substitutions sanctioned by middle-aged people but rather by forming a subculture. Membership in this subculture and not the continuation of middle-age activities maintains older persons' social identities and self-concepts (Williamson, Evans, and Munley, 1972). Interactionists view the subculture as being based on shared histories and interest, whereas the conflict perspective views the elderly as banning together in defense against intergenerational conflict and discord (Williamson et al., 1972).

Rose (1965) identified several trends to support the subculture notion. Integenerational dwelling-together is decreasing. The number of self-segregation retirement communities is increasing, as is the proportion of the population that is over 65. Common grievances such as high medical costs are emerging, and the elderly have become a dominant force in some rural areas.

The elderly, Rose (1974, p. 76) pointed out, "do not identify themselves with the aged and they are most reluctant to do so." A Harris poll (NCOA, 1975) revealed similar findings. If an aged subculture exists, then it does so for only a minority of the elderly (Rosow, 1974). In investigating social integration, gerontophilia, and self-conception, Longino, Kent, McClelland, and Peterson (1980) failed to find evidence for a politically oriented group consciousness among the aged.

Theories of Aging in Review

Ryff (1982) has pointed out that a more responsive conceptualization of successful aging is needed. The current theories appear inadequate, insufficiently complex to explain research findings (Havighurst et al., 1968), and neglectful of individual differences (Ryff, 1982) or life style (Maddox, 1966). Larson (1978) concluded that the commonly selected independent variables (activity, health, SES, etc.) left the greatest proportion of variance in subjective well-being unexplained. Linear models, which many social psychological investigations are based upon, are too simplistic. A model employing the features of systems theory might be more realistic (Lemon et al., 1972) and might help to support and justify future research.

SUMMARY

The provision of leisure and recreation services has not kept pace with the demand in either quantity or quality of programming. More "meaningful" experiences are necessary, with increased emphasis on both cognitive and physical activities. Americans have long been known for their work orientation, although not-yet-retired populations have indicated a greater affinity for leisure than their predecessors. The latter will represent higher levels of health, education, financial planning, and political astuteness. Leisure services will need to respond to these changes while paying special attention to those hard-to-reach subgroups (minorities, officially classified poor, etc.) that have traditionally been underrepresented.

In one sense, the field of leisure studies is just beginning to be recognized for its contributions to life satisfaction and general well-being. The expressed needs for socializing, self-fulfillment, closeness to nature, physical exercise, learning, and creativity can and have been met through various leisure experiences. Leisure has mutlidimensional effects.

Future leisure research will require an interdisciplinary approach. The plethora of cross-sectional studies will be complemented by more longitudinal data. Likewise, the traditional socio-economic demographic variables will be complemented by variables with greater predictive ability. Selected variables will be better operationalized. And finally, retrieval, distribution, and utilization of data will occur as the accumulating knowledge begins to indicate a strategy for action.

REFERENCES

Alderman, R. B. 1974. *Psychological Behavior in Sport.* Philadelphia: W. B. Saunders.

Allan, C., and Brotman. (compilers). 1981. *Chartbook on Aging in America.* 1981 White House Conference on Aging. Government Document.

Atchley, R. C. 1977. *The Social Forces in Later Life.* Belmont, CA: Wadsworth Publishing Company, Inc.

Bammel, G., and Bammel, L. 1982. *Leisure and Human Behavior.* Dubuque, IA: Wm. C. Brown Co.

Beckman, L. J., and Houser, B. B. 1982. The consequences of childlessness on the social-psychological well-being of older women. *J. Geront.* 37: 243–250.

Bell, J. Z. 1978. Disengagement versus engagement—a need for greater expectation. *J. Am. Geriat. Soc.* 26 (No. 2): 89–95.

Belloc, N. B. 1973. Relationship of health practices and mortality. *Prev. Med.* 2: 67.

Birren, J. 1964. *Relations of Development and Aging.* Springfield, IL: Charles C. Thomas.

Birren, J. 1970. The abuse of the urban aged. *Psychology Today,* March 1970: 37–38, 76.

Blau, Z. S. 1973. *Old Age in a Changing Society.* New York: New Viewpoints.

Bley, N.; Goodman, M.; Dye, D.; and Harel, B. 1972. Characteristics of aged participants in an age-segregated leisure program. *Gerontologist* 12: 368–370.

Bortz, W. M. 1980. Effects of exercise on aging—effect of aging on exercise. *J. Am. Geriat. Soc.* 28 (No. 2): 49–51.

Brickel, C. M. 1979. The therapeutic roles of cat mascots with a hospital-based geriatric population: A staff survey. *Gerontologist* 19: 368–372.

Brooks, J. B., and Elliott, D. M. 1971. Predictions of psychological adjustment at age thirty from leisure time activities and satisfactions in childhood. *Hum. Develop.* 14: 51–61.

Bultena, G. 1969. Life, continuity and morale in old age. *Gerontologist* 9(4): 251–253.

Bultena, G., and Wood, V. 1970. Leisure orientation and recreational activities of retirement community residents. *J. Leisure Research* 2: 3–15.

Burch, W. R., 1969. The social circles of leisure: Competing explanations. *J. Leisure Research* 1: 125–147.

Burdge, R. J. 1969. Levels of occupational prestige and leisure activity. *J. Leisure Research* 1: 262–274.

Chatfield, W. F. 1977. Economic and sociological factors influencing life satisfaction of the aged. *J. Geront.* 32: 593–599.

Charbonneau, J. J., and Lyons, J. R. 1980. Hunting and fishing trends in the U.S. In *Proceedings, 1980 National Outdoor Recreation Trends Symposium*, vol. 1. USDA, Forest Service, General Technical Report NE-57, pp. 121–126.

Cheek, N. H. 1971. Toward a theory of not-work. *Pacific Sociological Review* 14: 245–258.

Cheek, N. H.; Field, D. R.; and Burdge, R. J. 1976. *Leisure and Recreation Places.* Ann Arbor, MI: Ann Arbor Science Publishers Inc.

Chiriboga, D. A. 1982. Adaptation to marital separation in later and earlier life. *J. Geront.* 37: 109–114.

Clarke, H. H., ed. 1973. National adult physical fitness survey. In *Presidents Council on Physical Fitness and Sports Newsletter*, pp. 1–27.

Clarke, H. H. 1977. Exercise and aging. In *Physical Fitness Research Digest.* Washington, D.C.: Presidents Council on Physical Fitness and Sports, April 1977.

Cohn, R. M. 1979. Age and the satisfactions from work. *J. Geront.* 24: 264–272.

Cowgill, O., and Baulch, N. 1962. The use of leisure time by older people. *Gerontologist* 2: 47–50.

Cox, H. 1969. *The Feast of Fools.* Cambridge: Harvard University Press.

Crase, D., and Rosato, F. D. 1979. Exercise and aging: New perspectives and educational approaches. *Educational Gerontology* 4: 367–376.

Cumming, E. 1963. Further thoughts on the theory of disengagement. *Int. Soc. Sci. J.* 15: 377–393.

Cumming, E., and Henry, E. E. 1961. *Growing Old: The Process of Disengagement.* New York: Basic Books.

Cutler, N. E. 1979. Age variations in the dimensionality of life satisfaction. *J. Geront.* 34: 573–578.

Davis, R. H. 1971. Television and the older adult. *J. Broadcasting* 15 (No. 2): 153–159.

DeCarlo, T. J. 1974. Recreation participation patterns and successful aging. *J. Geront.* 29: 416–422.

de Grazia, S. 1962. *Of Time, Work, and Leisure.* Garden City, New York: Doubleday and Company, Inc.

deVries, H. A. 1976. Fitness after fifty. *J. Physical Education and Recreation* 47 (No. 4): 47–49.

Dumazedier, J. 1967. *Toward a Society of Leisure.* London: Collier.

Edwards, J. N., and Klemmack, D. L. 1973. Correlates of life satisfaction: A re-examination. *J. Geront.* 28: 497–502.

Etzhorn, K. P. 1964. Leisure and camping: The social meaning of a form of public recreation. *Sociology and Social Research* 49 (No. 1): 76–90.

Field, D., and O'Leary, J. 1973. Social groups as a basis for assessing participation in selected water activities. *J. Leisure Research* 5: 16–25.

Flanagan, J. C. 1978. A research approach to improving our quality of life. *American Psychologist* 33: 138–147.

Godbey, G., and Parker, S. 1976. *Leisure Studies and Services: An Overview.* Philadelphia: Saunders.

Gordon, C.; Gaitz, C. M.; and Scott, J. 1976. Leisure and lives. In *Handbook of Aging and the Social Sciences*, eds. R. H. Binstock and E. Shanas. New York: D. Van Nostrand.

Graney, M. J. 1975. Happiness and social participation in aging. *J. Geront.* 30: 701–706.

Guttman, D. 1973. Leisure-time activity interests of Jewish aged. *Gerontologist* 13: 219–223.

Harris, D. V. 1970. Physical activity attitudes of middle-aged males. In *Contemporary Psychology of Sport*, ed. G. S. Kenyon. Chicago: The Athletic Institute.

Havighurst, R. J. 1977. Life-style and leisure patterns. In *The Later Years*, ed. R. A. Kalish. Monterey, CA: Brooks/Cole.

Havighurst, R. J., and Albrecht, R. 1953. *Older People.* New York: Longmans, Green and Co.

Havighurst, R. J.; Neugarten, B. L.; and Tobin, S. S. 1968. Disengagement and patterns of aging. In *Middle Age and Aging*, ed. B. L. Neugarten. Chicago: The University of Chicago Press.

Hendee, J. C. 1969. Rural-urban differences reflected in outdoor recreation participation. *J. Leisure Research* 1: 333–340.

Hendee, J. C., and Potter, D. R. 1975. Hunters and hunting: Management implications of research. In *Proceedings of the Recreation Research Application Workshop.* Asheville, N.C.: September 15–18, 1975.

Hochschild, A. R. 1975. Disengagement theory: A critique and proposal. *Am. Sociol. R.* 40: 553–569.

Holahan, C. K. 1981. Lifetime achievement patterns, retirement and life satisfaction of gifted aged women. *J. Geront.* 36: 741–749.

Hoyt, D. R.; Kaiser, M. A.; Peters, G. R.; and Babchuk, N. 1980. Life satisfaction and activity theory: A multidimentional approach. *J. Geront.* 35: 935–941.

Hunt, M. 1969. *The Affair.* New York: Signet.

Hurst, C. E., and Guldin, D. A. 1982. The effects of intra-individual and inter-spouse status inconsistency on life satisfaction among older persons. *J. Geront.* 36: 112–121.

Iso-Ahola, S. E. 1980. *The Social Psychology of Leisure and Recreation.* Dubuque, IA: Wm. C. Brown Co.

Kahn, H., and Wiener, A. J. 1970. Black population in major cities. In *Leisure Service for the Disadvantaged,* eds. J. A. Nesbitt, P. D. Brown, and J. Murphy. Philadelphia: Lea and Febiger.

Kando, T. M. 1975. *Leisure and Popular Culture in Transition.* Saint Louis: The C. V. Mosby Company.

Kaplan, M. 1975. *Leisure: Theory and Policy.* New York: Wiley.

Kenyon, G. S. 1968a. A conceptual model for characterizing physical activity. *Research Quarterly* 39: 96–105.

Kenyon, G. S. 1968b. Six scales for assessing attitude toward physical activity. *Research Quarterly* 39: 566–574.

Kleemeier, R. W. 1961. *Aging and Leisure.* New York: Oxford University Press.

Kleiber, D. A., and Kelly, J. R. 1980. Leisure, socialization and the life cycle. In *Social Psychological Perspectives in Leisure and Recreation,* ed. S. E. Iso-Ahola. Springfield, IL: Charles C Thomas.

Kornhauser, A. 1965. *Mental Health of the Industrial Worker.* New York: John Wiley.

Kraus, R. 1978. *Recreation and Leisure in Modern Society.* 2nd ed. Santa Montica, CA: Goodyear.

Kubey, R. W. 1980. Television and aging: Past, present, and future. *Gerontologist* 20 (No. 1): 16–33.

Kuypers, J. A. 1972. Changeability of life-style and personality in old age. *Gerontologist* 12: 336–341.

Larson, R. 1978. Thirty years of research on the subjective well-being of older Americans. *J. Geront.* 33: 109–125.

Leaf, A. 1973. Unusual longevity: The common denominators. *Hospital Practice* 8 (No. 10): 74–86.

Lemon, W. B.; Bengtson, V. L.; and Peterson, J. A. 1972. An exploration of the activity theory of aging: Activity types and life satisfaction among in-movers to a retirement community. *J. Geront.* 27: 511–523.

Liang, J.; Dvorkin, L.; Kahana, E.; and Mazian, R. 1980. Social integration and morale: A re-examination. *J. Geront.* 35: 746–757.

Longino, C. F. 1982. Changing aged nonmetropolitan migration patterns, 1955 to 1960 and 1965 to 1970. *J. Geront.* 37: 228–234.

Longino, C. F.; Kent, A.; McClelland, K. A.; and Peterson, W. A. 1980. The aged subculture hypothesis: Social integration, gerontophilia and self-conception. *J. Geront.* 35: 758–767.

Lowe, G. D., and Peek, C. 1974. Location and lifestyle: The comparative explanatory ability of urbanism and rurality. *Rural Sociology* 39(3): 392–420.

Lowenthal, M. F., and Haven, C. 1968. Interaction and adaptation: Intimacy as a critical variable. *Am. Sociol. R.* 33: 20–30.

Lowenthal, M. F., and Robinson, B. 1976. Social networks and isolation. In *Handbook of Aging and the Social Sciences,* eds. R. H. Binstock and E. Shanas. New York: P. Van Nostrand.

McAvoy, L. 1979. The leisure preferences, problems, and needs of the elderly. *J. Leisure Research* 11: 40–47.

McDougall, W. 1913. *An Introduction to Social Psychology.* London: Methien and Co.

Maddox, G. L. 1963. Activity and morale: A longitudinal study of selected elderly subjects. *Social Forces* 42: 195–204.

Maddox, G. L. 1966. Persistence of life style among the elderly: A longitudinal study of patterns of social activity in relation to life satisfaction. In *Middle Age and Aging,* ed. B. L. Neugarten. Chicago: The University Press, 1968.

Markides, K. S., and Martin, H. W. 1979. A causal model of life satisfaction among the elderly. *J. Geront.* 34: 86–93.

Maslow, A. 1970. *Motivation and Personality.* Evanston, IL: Harper & Row.

Medley, M. L. 1976. Satisfaction with life among persons sixty-five and older. *J. Geront.* 31: 448–455.

Melzer, H. 1965. Mental health implications of aging in industry. *J. Genet. Psychol.* 107: 193–203.

Meyersohn, R. 1972. Leisure. In *The Human Meaning of Social Change,* eds. A. Campbell and P. E. Converse. New York: Russell Sage Foundation.

Miller, S. J. 1965. The social dilemma of the aging leisure participant. In *Older People and Their Social World,* eds. A. M. Rose and W. A. Peterson. Philadelphia: F. A. Davis.

Mills, C. W. 1951. *White Collar.* Oxford: Oxford University Press.

Morgan, A., and Godbey, G. 1978. The effect of entering an age segregated environment upon the leisure activity patterns of older adults. *J. Leisure Research* 10: 177–190.

Moss, M., and Lawton, M. P. 1982. Time budgets of older people: A window on four lifestyles. *J. Geront.* 37: 115–123.

Murphy, J. F. 1974. *Concepts of Leisure.* Englewood Cliffs, NJ: Prentice-Hall.

Murphy, J. F. 1975. *Recreation and Leisure Service.* Dubuque, IA: Brown.

Mutran, E., and Reitzes, D. 1981. Retirement, identity and well-being: Realignment of role relationships. *J. Geront.* 36: 733–740.

National Council on the Aging, Inc. 1975. *The Myth and Realty of Aging in America.* Washington, D.C.: Louis Harris and Associates, Inc.

Neulinger, J. 1974. *The Psychology of Leisure.* Springfield, IL: Charles C Thomas.

Neulinger, J. 1981. *To Leisure: An Introduction.* Boston: Allyn and Bacon.

Neulinger, J., and Breit, M. 1971. Attitude dimensions of leisure: A replication study. *J. Leisure Research* 3: 108–115.

Nystrom, E. P. 1974. Activity patterns and leisure concepts among the elderly. *American Journal of Occupational Therapy* 28: 337–345.

Ostrow, A. C. 1980. Physical activity as it relates to the health of the aged. In *Transitions of Aging,* eds. N. Datan and N. Lohmann. New York: Academic Press.

Outdoor Recreation Resources Review Commission. 1962. *Report 20, Outdoor Recreation for America.* Washington, D.C.: Government Printing Office.

Palen, J. J. 1979. *Social Problems.* New York: McGraw-Hill.

Palmore, E. B. 1968. The effects of aging on activities and attitudes. *Gerontologist* 8: 259–263.

Palmore, E. 1975. *The Honorable Elders: A Cross-Cultural Analysis of Aging in Japan.* Durham, NC: Duke University Press.

Palmore, E. 1979. Predictors of successful aging. *Gerontologist* 19: 427–431.

Palmore, E.; Cleveland, W. P.; Nowlin, J. B.; Ramm, D.; and Siegler, I. C. 1979. Stress and adaption in later life. *J. Geront.* 34: 841–851.

Parker, S. 1971. *The Future of Work and Leisure.* New York: Praeger.

Parker, S. 1976. *The Sociology of Leisure.* New York: International Publications Service.

Payne, R., and Pittard, B. 1969. Divorce in the middle years. *Sociological Symposium* 1: 115–124.

Peppers, L. G. 1976. Patterns of leisure and adjustment to retirement. *Gerontologist* 16: 441–446.

Perkins, L. C., and Kaiser, H. L. 1961. Results of short term isotonic and isometric exercise programs in people over sixty, *Physical Therapy Review,* 41: 633–635.

Pfeiffer, E., and Davis, G. C. 1971. The use of leisure time in middle life. *Gerontologist* 11: 187–195.

Pieper, J. 1963. *Leisure, the Basis of Culture.* London: Paladin Press.

Rapoport, R., and Rapoport, R. N. 1975. *Leisure and the Family Life Cycle.* London: Routledge and Kegan Paul.

Riley, M. W., and Foner, A. 1968. *Aging and Society.* Volume One: *An Inventory of Research Findings.* New York: Russell Sage Foundation.

Roberts, K. 1970. *Leisure.* London: Longman.

Romsa, G. H., and Girling, S. 1976. The identification of outdoor recreation market segments on the basis of frequency of participation. *J. Leisure Research* 8: 259–263.

Rose, A. M. 1964. A current theoretical issue in social gerontology. *Gerontologist* 4: 46–50.

Rose, A. M. 1965. The subculture of aging: A framework in social gerontology. In *Older People and Their Social World,* eds. A. M. Rose and W. A. Peterson. Philadelphia: Davis.

Rosow, I. 1974. *Socialization to Old Age.* Berkely: University of California Press.

Ryff, C. D. 1982. Successful aging: A developmental approach. *J. Geront.* 22: 209–214.

Sanoff, A., and Cole, B. M. 1982. Funds for the aged: Ticklish dilemma. *U.S. News & World Report,* Oct. 18, 1982: 55–58.

Sauer, W. 1977. Morale of the urban aged: A regression analysis by race. *J. Geront.* 32: 600–608.

Schmitz-Scherzer, R. 1976. Longitudinal change in leisure behavior of the elderly. *Contributions to Human Development* 3: 127–136.

Schmitz-Scherzer, R., and Strödell, I. 1971. Age-dependence of leisure-time activities. *Hum. Develop.* 14: 47–50.

Schnore, L. F. 1966. The rural-urban variable: An urbanite's perspective. *Rural Sociology* 31(2): 131–143.

Shanas, E. 1979. The family as a social support system in old age. *Gerontologist* 19: 169–174.

Sill, J. S. 1980. Disengagement reconsidered: Awareness of finitude. *Gerontologist* 20: 457–462.

Simpson, I. H.; Back, K. W.; and McKinney, J. C. 1966. Continuity of work and retirement activities, and self-evaluation. In *Social Aspects of Aging,* eds. I. H. Simpson, K. W. Back, and J. C. McKinney. Durham, NC: Duke University Press.

Sofranko, A. J., and Nolan, M. F. 1972. Early life experiences and adult sports participation. *J. Leisure Research* 4: 6–18.

Solender, S. 1969. Contemporary issues affecting Jewish community center planning. *J. Jewish Communal Service* 46: 123–133.

Spreitzer, E., and Snyder, E. E. 1974. Correlates of life satisfaction among the aged. *J. Geront.* 29: 454–458.

Streib, G. F., and Schneider, C. J. 1971. *Retirement in American Society: Impact and Process:* Ithaca and London: Cornell University Press.

Thompson, G. B. 1973. Work versus leisure roles: An investigation of morale among employed and retired men. *J. Geront.* 28: 339–344.

Tuhy, C. 1979. A tuner and a tutor look toward the twenty-first century. *Money,* July, 1979: 49–50.

van Es, J. C., and Brown, J. E. 1974. The rural-urban variable once more: Some individual level observations. *Rural Sociology* 39(3): 373–391.

Veblen, T. 1899. *Theory of the Leisure Class.* New York: Macmillian.

Videbeck, R., and Knox, A. B. 1965. Alternative participatory responses to aging. In *Older People and Their Social World,* eds. A. M. Rose and W. A. Peterson. Philadelphia: F. A. Davis.

Washburn, R. F. 1978. Black under-participation in wildland recreation: Alternative explanations. *Leisure Sciences* 1: 175–189.

Wendling, R. C. 1980. Black/white differences in outdoor recreation behavior: State of the art and suggestions for management and research. A paper presented at the Conference on Social Research in National Parks and Wildland Area. Great Smoky Mountains National Park, Gatlinburg, TN, March 21–22, 1980.

Weisner, T. S. 1979. Urban-rural differences in sociable and disruptive behavior of Kenya children. *Ethnology* 18(2): 153–172.

White, T. H. 1975. The relative importance of education and income as predictors in outdoor recreation participation. *J. Leisure Research* 7: 191–199.

Wilensky, H. R. 1960. Work, careers, and social integration. *Int. Social Science Journal* 12: 543–560.

Williamson, J. B.; Evans, L.; and Munley, A. 1972. *Aging and Society.* New York: Rinehart and Winston.

Zborowski, M. 1962. Aging and recreation. *J. Geront.* 7: 302–309.

32
SPECIALIZED LIVING ENVIRONMENTS FOR OLDER PEOPLE

Rudolf H. Moos
and
Sonne Lemke
Social Ecology Laboratory
Geriatric Research, Educational, and Clinical Center
Veterans Administration and
Stanford University Medical Center

The present state of specialized housing for older people results from an interplay of demographic, economic, and social factors. These include the sheer number of older people and the prevalence of poverty, mental illness, and physical disabilities that define the extent and characteristics of the potential users. The demand for specialized housing is also related to the relative access of the elderly to resources accruing from their position in the family, society, and the economy. In turn, society's response to their unmet needs is determined in part by the prevailing ethos with respect to poverty and dependence.

Despite these complex factors, a body of research pertaining to specialized housing and its impact on the older person has gradually evolved. Some of this research focuses on taxonomic and descriptive concerns, such as defining the types and characteristics of specialized housing. Other research considers the relationship between specialized housing and resident characteristics. What conditions impel older people to choose such housing? What effects do these settings have on the people who live in them? Who benefits from a particular housing program?

In order to structure our review of this research, we will first provide a guide to the pertinent terminology and a brief history of the development of residential settings for older people. We will then present a conceptual framework highlighting the themes that will recur throughout, including the value of conceptualizing and measuring environmental factors and their relationships, the value of examining person-environment interactions, and the value of considering different types of group residences within a common framework. In general, our review indicates that specialized residential settings can make an important difference in the quality of older people's lives. Moreover, information about the design and impact of group residences can guide researchers and practitioners to create more positive residential contexts for aging individuals.

CATEGORIES OF SPECIALIZED LIVING ENVIRONMENTS

We use a number of terms interchangeably to delimit the range of settings in which the elderly reside with nonrelatives and thereby gain access to various services. These terms include "specialized residences," "supportive residences," "residential programs," and "sheltered care settings." At one end of this continuum, we include hospitals for the chronically ill, skilled nursing facilities, and other long-term care settings. At the other end are settings that provide minimal services, such as a meal program and weekly housecleaning. We exclude from this category settings where sojourns are short-term (acute care hospitals, hotels), where residents are related (single-family homes), or where no services beyond shelter are provided (most apartments and single-room occupancy hotels, mobile home parks, and retirement communities).

The decision to group these disparate forms of housing is a self-conscious one, reflecting our view that they can be usefully compared on a number of common dimensions. By bringing unrelated individuals together in a residential setting and providing them access to services, these settings create a stage for distinctive social processes. Individuals in these settings must deal with an additional layer of social organization. As Markson (1982, p. 52) puts it, "While monasteries obviously differ from college campuses, and a residential congregate-complex for those sixty-five and over is distinctly different from a skilled-nursing facility, all have more common facilities, rules and regulations, social norms, and encourage closer contact with other residents than does traditional community living."

For certain purposes, however, it is useful to distinguish subgroups of specialized residences, and we have opted to do so in terms of three levels of care: nursing homes, residential care facilities, and congregate apartments. For our purposes, nursing homes are settings in which a majority of residents regularly receive professional nursing services. Housekeeping, meals, and personal care are also routinely provided. Residential care facilities provide routine housekeeping and meals and supervision or assistance with activities of daily living for the majority of residents but offer only limited medical services. Congregate apartments typically provide at least a meal program but do not give routine care to the majority of residents. These subgroups have evolved gradually as society has sought to respond to the needs of the elderly who are frail, indigent, or otherwise less able to maintain an independent household.

HISTORICAL AND CONTEMPORARY TRENDS

Because of the prevalence of infectious disease and the hard conditions of life, few individuals in preindustrial Western societies survived to old age. Among those who did, the sick or impoverished were expected to rely on their families, or, where the family failed in its duty, to turn to the church or one of the handful of benevolent associations that provided care for socially marginal individuals. Although society compensated for the social changes accompanying industrialization by assuming some responsibility for the elderly, it did so grudgingly. In England, for example, the Elizabethan poor laws gave local governments responsibility for administering almshouses, but conditions in these almshouses were deliberately unpleasant in order to discourage all but the most destitute from using them.

The American colonies followed the example of the Elizabethan poor laws, although the most prevalent form of assistance was payment to the family or boarding-out with nonrelatives. In the decades following the Revolutionary War, localities began to establish almshouses in order to reduce the cost of care by centralizing it. In addition to saving money by their economy of scale, these institutions were supposed to be financially self-sufficient by relying on the residents' labor (Sherwood and Mor, 1980).

During the second half of the nineteenth century, the large, centralized institution became the model of specialized housing for the older person. As the century progressed, provision for certain groups of the elderly, including widows and soldiers, was given more willingly. For example, in 1827, the Navy opened the U.S. Naval Home. Following the Civil War, Congress established the National Asylum for Disabled Volunteer Soldiers, which evolved into the National Homes and later into the VA domiciliaries. States, too, began to establish homes for veterans who were no longer able to maintain themselves in the community. Private philanthropy also grew during the nineteenth century, until, by the 1920s, nonprofit homes for the aged had become the common model of care for the elderly, supplemented by psychiatric hospitals and county homes.

A growing distrust of large institutions manifested itself in the Social Security Act of 1933. Under this Act, payments were made directly to indigent older persons to purchase housing and other services; "public institutions" were barred from receiving these monies. During the 1930s and 1940s, increasing numbers of older people assumed the role of boarder in private homes or entered small, family-run rest homes or sanitaria. As these residents aged and became more disabled, "nursing care" was often added to the services. In part because of the availability of public money, the number of such facilities increased markedly. In the 1950s, the Social Security Act was amended to allow federal assistance for care in "institutions" and to require state agencies to supervise all "medical" settings receiving Federal funds (for more detailed histories, see Achenbaum, 1978; Brody, 1977).

A striking change since the 1950s is the growth in the nursing home sector resulting from increases both in the number of facilities and in their capacity. These increases have been traced to the aging of the population, the introduction of programs of Federal support and their accompanying regulations, and the movement to "de-institutionalize" mental hospital patients (Dunlop, 1979). There have also been qualitative changes in the nursing home sector as nursing has achieved stature as a profession, and both Federal and state regulations have been imposed. At the time of the National Nursing Home Survey in 1977, there were 1.1 million persons living in facilities that provided professional nursing services to the majority of residents (National Center for Health Statistics, 1979).

Nursing homes and residential care facilities evolved from a common source but now comprise distinctive subgroups. Regulation of residential care settings is not uniform and is altogether absent in some states. As a consequence, settings in this category are more varied, and statistics on their utilization are more difficult to establish. With the advent of more direct financial assistance to older people with limited economic resources, there has been a reduction in the number of well but indigent people in institutions (Brody, 1977). In addition, more emphasis is being placed on assisting those with some physical impairment to maintain individual households and on placing those with severe impairments in settings with professional nursing care. Together, these factors help account for the relatively stable numbers in residential care homes. The impact of these policies can be illustrated with figures on the population of VA domiciliaries. In 1953, there were 17,000 veterans in such facilities. By 1966, the figure had dropped to 14,000, and by 1980, it was down to about 8,000. In contrast, VA nursing home units have served ever increasing numbers: 4,500 in 1971 and 7,900 in 1980 (U.S. Veterans Administration, 1981). In the 1977 National Nursing Home Survey, one-third of the facilities (housing about 190,000 residents) were personal care and domiciliary care settings (National Center for Health Statistics, 1979).

Another type of residential setting received additional impetus when the first program of low-rent public housing for the elderly was authorized in 1956. A number of programs of federal assistance for housing for the elderly have been instituted over the years and now serve about 4 percent of the older population. These settings vary in the services available; some are indistinguishable from independent apartments except for age concentration, whereas others are associated with programs offering extensive support services. Similar housing programs were developed without Federal assistance.

Estimates indicate that about 10 percent of the 25 million people in the United States who are over 65 currently reside in one of these types of specialized residential settings. But these cross-sectional statistics underestimate the impact of such settings on older people's lives. For example, in one urban sample, a full 15 percent had stays of six months or more in a nursing home (Vicente, Wiley and Carrington, 1979). Demographic and social trends suggest that specialized residential programs will play an increasingly salient role during the next few decades (Dunlop, 1979).

The growth and cost of such programs highlight the need for controlled evaluation research. Planners and program managers need guidelines to help them make informed choices on how to alter existing settings and design new ones.

CONCEPTUAL PERSPECTIVES

Several assumptions guide our approach to understanding specialized living environments and their impacts. First, although there is diversity in group residences for older people, we believe that they can be evaluated within a common conceptual framework and that doing so has several advantages. It allows us, for example, to identify similar processes occurring in different types of settings and to specify the extent of environmental change experienced by an individual moving from one type of setting to another.

Second, in order to explore the influence of residential settings on health and adaptation, we need better conceptualizations and measures of environmental factors. Although most program evaluators would endorse the idea that behavior is determined by both personal and environmental factors, the paradigm typically used in evaluation research conceptualizes the residential program as a "black box" intervening between resident inputs and outcomes. The housing program is the sole environmental determinant of resident functioning that is actually examined, and it is usually assessed in terms of broad categories (such as whether the setting is age-segregated). Better methods of measuring environmental factors will enable us to identify specific aspects of residential programs that are related to variations in outcome criteria.

A third assumption here is that more emphasis should be placed on the process intervening between personal and environmental factors and resident outcomes. To understand the influence of group-living settings more fully, it is necessary to examine the social and coping resources people use to adapt to the stress of relocation or living in inadequate housing. Although the complexity of person-environment transactions has been generally recognized, empirical work has not adequately reflected the multicausal, interrelated nature of the process.

An Integrative Framework

The model shown in Fig. 1 follows these guidelines and provides a conceptual framework for examining specialized residential settings and their influences on older people. In this model, the link between an environmental system (Panel I) and a personal system (Panel II) and subsequent adaptation (Panel V) is mediated by cognitive appraisal (Panel III) and coping responses (Panel IV). The model specifies domains that should be included in a comprehensive evaluation. The model can also guide more focused evaluations and serve

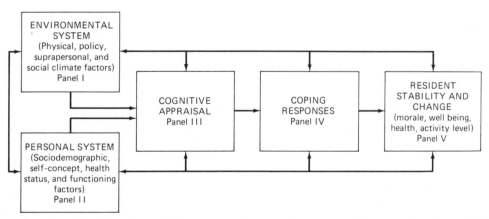

Figure 1.   A model of the relationship between environmental and personal factors and resident stability and change.

as a framework for integrating research results.

The environmental system includes such factors as the physical design and organizational structure of the setting, the aggregate characteristics of the individuals involved, and the quality of their interpersonal relationships. The personal system includes an individual's socio-demographic characteristics and such personal resources as health status, cognitive and functional ability, and self-esteem. The environmental and personal systems can influence each other through selection and allocation. For instance, most environments admit new members selectively, and people usually have some voice in choosing the environments they wish to enter.

An individual's appraisal and coping responses are affected by both personal and environmental factors. For example, aspects of the environmental system may contribute to the perception that residents are active and involved with one another, including such physical features as the availability of special activity areas and such policies as offering many organized social activities. Personal characteristics such as age, functional health, and present activity level may also influence the appraisal of activity level and group cohesion in a setting, as well as an individual's actual level of social engagement. An individual's use of a coping skill can in turn effect a change in either system. Residents who make more social contacts or who participate in planning activities may experience improved self-esteem (a change in the personal system). Residents who complain about the lack of activities may help effect a change in the environmental system, such as the hiring of an activity director.

Efforts at adaptation ultimately influence such outcome indices as the resident's health, well-being, and level of functioning. These outcome criteria also are more directly affected by personal factors. For example, individuals whose health is better when they enter a facility are likely to be in better health a year later. Environments may have some direct effects as well, as when an individual experiences better health because of the good health care provided in a setting. Finally, the model acknowledges the continuing, reciprocal interplay between individuals and their environment. Outcomes at a given point in time are inputs to future adaptation in the form of aspects of the personal system. Individual outcomes also contribute to defining the environmental system. For example, when the health outcomes for all individuals in a setting are considered together, they constitute one aspect of the suprapersonal environment.

Person-Environment Congruence

Our framework notes that people and settings exert mutual influences. A given environmental feature can vary in the way it affects different residents. High expectations for independent behavior may enhance functioning for one resident but elicit anxiety in another. The provision of supportive services may be beneficial for some residents but prematurely erode independent functioning among others. Several theorists have formulated models of person-environment congruence that include predictions about outcome criteria.

Lawton (1975, 1982) has developed a transactional perspective relating personal competence and environmental press to affective responses and adaptive behavior. Personal competence is a diverse collection of characteristics that define the individual's functional capacity, including physical health and cognitive ability. The environment is characterized in terms of its "objective" press or its potential for activating behavior. The model assumes that for each individual there is a level of environmental press or demand that permits maximum performance. In general, demands that deviate only slightly from an individual's adaptation level elicit positive affect and adaptive behavior, whereas those that deviate substantially in either direction elicit negative affect and maladaptive behavior.

Several predictions have been developed from this model. For example, competent people are thought to have greater latitude for person-environment congruence and to be able to function effectively in a wider range of environments. Conversely, less competent individuals can function adequately in only a relatively narrow range of settings. This idea is embodied in the environmental docility hypothesis, which proposes that variation in the behavior of less competent individuals is more subject to environmental factors than that of more competent individuals. The model further assumes that environmental stimulation or demand can be either too high or too low and that person-environment congruence can be enhanced by either changing the person or the environment.

Lawton's model has been criticized for focusing primarily on environmental demands (rather than opportunities), personal competencies to respond to demands (rather than preferences for opportunities), an understanding of pathology (rather than of adaptability), and assessment of people's responses in evaluative (rather than value-free) terms (Carp, 1978–79). Individual capacities may be important determinants of the outcome of person-environment transactions among older persons who are below some competence threshold. However, when older people are sufficiently competent to deal with their environments, personal preferences and needs and the degree of need satisfaction assume increased importance. According to Carp, a comprehensive model of person-environment transaction must consider the relationship of environmental resources to human needs, as well as of human capacities to environmental demands.

In this vein, Kahana (1982) has formulated a person-environment congruence model that emphasizes residents' needs and preferences. The framework includes seven dimensions of congruence, three of which are based on setting characteristics (segregate, congregate, and institutional control) formulated by Kleemeier (1961), whereas the other four are related to individual factors that show characteristic changes with age (need for activity, open expression of affect, tolerance of ambiguity, and ability to control impulses). Persons and settings can show varying degrees of congruence along these seven dimensions. For example, environments differ in their provision of activities, tolerance for affective expression, and acceptance of impulsivity. Similarly, indi-

viduals differ in their need for activity, emotional expressiveness, and impulse control. In theory, incongruence can vary in its impact, depending upon the personal need.

Applications of the Model

These efforts to specify the relationship between person-environment congruence and outcomes illustrate how the general model can be elaborated in terms of specific hypotheses. It can also help to organize the approach to a number of traditional issues in gerontology. For example, early work on the impact of institutionalization tended to focus on the personal attributes that characterize older people in some supportive group settings. These attributes, such as apathy, withdrawal, and dependency, were treated as outcomes (Panel V) and traced to the features of these settings (Panel I) that distinguish them from independent living. In their review of this research, Tobin and Lieberman (1976) point out that such studies are inconclusive because they do not take into account possible selection bias or the effects of events preceding institutionalization. Similarly, early work on relocation focused on the stressful event of moving from one setting to another and on the subsequent functioning of the individual. Only later did researchers begin to examine the extent of change in the environmental system (Panel I) that was experienced during relocation or the individual characteristics (Panel II) that predisposed the individual to particular outcomes.

Research on the quality of care further illustrates applications of the model. Quality of care has been defined in terms of structural, process, or outcome measures. In studies using structural or process measures, certain aspects of the environment are taken to indicate good or poor quality of care. Thus, physical therapy might be defined as a beneficial element in a nursing home environment. Other indices of the structure of care include measures of staffing levels, the presence of in-service programs, and various architectural features of the facility. Process indices focus primarily on the interactions between residents and staff and on such psychosocial factors as how policies are made, how social activities are planned and executed, and how the daily routine of life is organized. In contrast, outcome measures focus on the individual and include the mood, behavior, functioning, and satisfaction of the consumers of care.

Occasional attempts are made to link outcomes (Panel V) to structural or process measures (Panel I). By expanding the inquiry to include two panels of the model, these efforts can shed light on the validity of the quality of care measures. For example, does a higher staffing level result in better health outcomes, higher morale, or higher activity level? Can better than expected outcomes be linked to factors such as low staff turnover, more social activities, or greater flexibility of routine? Clearly, a more comprehensive examination of quality of care would also take into account the individual system (who benefits from what care?).

In the following sections, we shall pursue some of these issues by organizing our discussion of the literature along the lines of the model. After focusing on ways of conceptualizing environmental domains and their interconnections, we examine how these domains are related to personal factors and criterion indices.

THE ENVIRONMENTAL SYSTEM

Knowledge about the environmental system serves as a foundation for exploring the interrelationships depicted in the model. Yet, aside from some valuable naturalistic descriptions of specific residential facilities (for examples, see Hochschild, 1973, and Ross, 1977), the task of describing and measuring the environmental system has been generally neglected. One factor contributing to this neglect is the difficulty of selecting a measurement strategy. For example, a person's milieu can be described by cataloging specific features, by describing the arrangement or structure of these elements, or by specifying their function. Descriptive terms can range from those that are relatively close to the raw data to higher order variables. Staff members, residents, or outside observers can report on the environment. Finally, measurement can focus on one or several distinct domains of environmental variables, ranging from physical features to social relations.

These domains of environmental variables roughly correspond to disciplinary boundaries. In the search for useful sets of environmental indices, four such research traditions can be distinguished. Architects and designers have considered such factors as the quality of the physical milieu, safety, accessibility to the handicapped, and site selection for security and community involvement (Bednar, 1977; Howell, 1976; Lawton, 1975). Specific architectural criteria have been formulated to guide the development of open nursing homes intended to maximize resident independence (Koncelik, 1976).

Sociologists and social psychologists have focused on the policy and program aspects of specialized living settings. Some researchers have considered such indices as size and staffing levels, whereas others have examined complex organizational characteristics. For instance, Goffman (1961) described "total institutions" as those that combine ordinarily separate spheres of an individual's life (such as places of work, residence, and recreation), that require residents to organize their life in terms of a fixed daily schedule, and that limit social interchange with the outside world. Similarly, Kleemeier (1961) characterized specialized housing in terms of a congregate dimension (enforced closeness of individuals and absence of privacy) and a control dimension (extent to which individuals are subject to social control through restrictive rules and policies).

A third tradition involves the use of aggregated personal characteristics as measures of environmental factors. This approach is based on the belief that the aggregate of the members' attributes (the suprapersonal environment) helps to define the subculture that develops in a group. This subculture is thought to influence the behavior of individual members (Lawton, 1975). For example, Messer (1967) suggests that an age homogeneous setting is less stressful because it presents less role conflict and the group norms are more likely to be age appropriate.

The social climate perspective represents a fourth research tradition. In this view, discrete events are manifestations of underlying characteristics of the setting or its "environmental press." For example, if older people in a residential program have a say in making the rules, if their suggestions are acted upon, and if they can try out new and different ideas, then it is likely that the program emphasizes resident influence. Research in a variety of settings has led to the identification of three sets of social climate dimensions. Relationship dimensions assess the quality of interpersonal relations. Personal growth or goal orientation dimensions measure the directions in which personal development tends to occur in the setting. System maintenance and change dimensions deal with the degree to which the environment is orderly, clear in expectations, and responsive to change (Moos, 1974).

Measuring the Environmental Domains

Considering all these matters, a researcher who wishes to assess the residential environment is faced with numerous choices and an absence of clarifying conceptual models. Early environmental measures tended to use raters to focus on either specific aspects or the overall quality of care in a setting. For example, Bennett and Nahemow (1965) used Goffman's concept of totality to formulate a 10-item index that covers information such as the disposition of personal property, provisions for dissemination of normative information, and type of sanction system. The index discriminated predictably between a public housing project, supervised apartment residence, nursing home, and geriatric inpatient ward.

The Nursing Home Rating Scale developed by Linn (1966) was designed to incorporate criteria utilized in licensing and accreditation and to differentiate between nursing homes in the areas of patient care, administration, staffing, and physical features. Trained observers showed good agreement in rating nursing homes on these indices, which can be combined to obtain a measure of the overall quality

of their care. In addition, there was agreement between ratings based on these explicit criteria and global ratings made by social workers using implicit criteria.

Another approach to assessing the environmental system is exemplified by the Home for the Aged Description Questionnaire (HDQ) developed by Pincus (Pincus, 1968; Pincus and Wood, 1970). The HDQ taps five aspects of the milieu: privacy, freedom, provision of activities and meaningful social roles, opportunities for involvement in the outside community, and the closeness of relationships between staff and residents. Each dimension is composed of items describing either the physical features or policies of the institution or staff and resident behavior. For example, items in the privacy dimension include the proportion of single and double rooms (physical features), whether the rules allow residents to close the doors to their rooms (policy), and whether the staff knock on doors before entering residents' rooms (staff behavior). Although the HDQ dimensions thus combine physical, policy, and behavioral aspects, the information itself is obtained from residents' and staff members' judgments. Very little research has been done with the HDQ, but the conceptual approach it embodies has been applied in the development of newer measures.

The Quality Evaluation System

A recent, systematic attempt to assess long-term care settings has resulted in the Quality Evaluation System (QES), which focuses on facility resources and resident needs (Dennis, Burke, and Garber, 1977). The QES was developed on a large sample of facilities in Illinois. Items were selected for their ability to discriminate between facilities and were grouped using cluster analysis techniques. The QES involves an inspection of a facility by two members of an assessment team, interviews with two randomly selected staff members, a questionnaire completed by the facility administrator, and interviews with and a review of the medical records of a sample of residents.

This instrument measures three components of facility resources. The institutional services component taps factors related to maintaining a resident's room and board and providing basic personal care, such as the provision of environmental prostheses and staff levels in nursing service. The professional services component assesses the health care services, the rehabilitative and restorative care, as well as the administrative services (such as inservice programs). The psychosocial environment component is composed of measures of resident involvement in activities, the quality of resident-staff relationships, and the extent to which the environment is enriched and personalized. Data on residents' needs for nursing, personal, and psychosocial care are obtained for a sample of residents and can be summarized as profiles of individual residents or aggregated into a single profile of the facility's residents. This information can be used in a matching process to determine how well a facility meets the needs of its residents. The QES shows promise as a measure to be used in lieu of (or as a supplement to) existing licensing and certification procedures. It has been proposed as a basis for developing a reimbursement system in which financial incentives are given for providing high quality care (Dennis, Burke, and Garber, 1977).

The Multiphasic Environmental Assessment Procedure

The Multiphasic Environmental Assessment Procedure (MEAP) incorporates many features of earlier efforts to assess supportive residential settings for older people (Moos and Lemke, 1984). It can be applied to a range of settings, from skilled nursing facilities to semi-independent apartments. However, it is also designed to measure fine enough detail to discriminate among facilities of a given type. The MEAP was developed on the basis of data obtained from a representative sample of 93 residential settings in California and has been applied to a group of over 200 additional settings across the United States.

The MEAP assesses four aspects of the facility environment: physical features, policies and program, resident and staff characteristics, and social climate. Each dimension is conceptually unified by a common functional implication for residents. The items represent opportunities or environmental resources for a given area of functioning. For example, flexible meal hours provide residents with a choice about when to eat. Other items on the policy choice dimension similarly tap the flexibility of the daily routine and the options available to residents to structure their own lives.

The first part of the MEAP, the Physical and Architectural Features Checklist (PAF), relies on direct observation to obtain information about the physical setting (Moos and Lemke, 1980). The dimensions tap such issues as the availability of amenities and features that foster social and recreational activities, features that promote safety, orientational aids, space allowances, and facilities for the staff. The second part of the MEAP, the Policy and Program Information Form (POLIF), assesses ten dimensions of the policy and programmatic resources of a setting as reported by the administrator or other responsible staff members (Lemke and Moos, 1980). It measures the behavioral requirements imposed on residents, opportunities for resident input in decision making, provisions for privacy, and the availability of services and activities. The MEAP also includes the Resident and Staff Information Form (RESIF), which taps nine aspects of the suprapersonal environment (Lemke and Moos, 1981), as well as the Sheltered Care Environment Scale (SCES), which assesses residents' and staff members' perceptions of seven characteristics of a facility's social environment (Moos, Gauvain, Lemke, Max, and Mehren, 1979).

The MEAP subscales have moderate to high internal consistencies and test-retest reliabilities and discriminate between facilities that offer different levels of care and between facilities that offer the same level of care. The procedure has been used to explore the interrelationships among the four domains of environmental factors (Moos and Igra, 1980) as well as their impacts (Moos, 1981; David, Moos, and Kahn, 1981). In order to provide information for designing new facilities and addressing person-environment congruence issues, the portions of the MEAP that assess physical features, policies, and social climate have been adapted to tap individual preferences (Moos, Lemke, and David, in press).

Existing measures of environmental factors in specialized residential settings are at an early stage of development. The MEAP, for example, has several limitations that point to the need for further development. These limitations include the dichotomous-item scoring criteria and a scoring system that gives equal weight to highly salient and less salient environmental features. Nevertheless, such measures can be used to specify the current conditions of group residences, to provide feedback about these conditions to program managers and staff, to guide and monitor facility change, to examine the interrelationships among setting characteristics, and to explore the impact of group residences.

Conceptualizing the Environment as a System

A facility's environment is a system of interrelated factors. Economic constraints may underlie such disparate aspects of a facility as its physical resources, the characteristics of the resident population, and the available services. Size may also be related to the available services, as well as to the functioning of the organization. It is thus reasonable to ask how environmental factors relate to one another. Do larger facilities offer a richer array of services but develop more bureaucratic, controlling social environments? Do nonproprietary facilities offer better quality care because humanitarian motives predominate over economic ones? (For recent studies of these issues, see Fottler, Smith, and James, 1981; Ullmann, 1981; and Weihl, 1981.)

The complexities of identifying the effects of specific environmental factors, such as size and ownership, indicate the need for a general framework that can be used to examine the environment as an interrelated system. One approach is to develop taxonomies to identify groups of similar settings. Empirical typologies can reflect the relationships among individual dimensions and thereby help capture the overall impression created by a setting. Little work of this kind has been done on residential settings for older people, but the utility of such an approach can be illustrated by the work of Gottesman (1974), who distinguished three types of nursing homes in terms of their ownership, source of payment, and resident characteristics. Nonprofit church-related facilities tended to cater to older white women who have had children and maintained contacts in the community. Proprietary, private-pay nursing homes were patronized by a somewhat younger group composed mainly of white women who were more likely to have entered the facility from a hospital and to require skilled nursing care. Proprietary, public-paid nursing homes also housed younger patients, but more of these were men, who were likely, moreover, to have disturbed marital histories and a history of psychiatric hospitalization. A typology such as this could be extended to a broader range of facilities as well as a more varied set of program characteristics.

Another approach is to view the environment as a dynamic system. One such model (see Fig. 2) posits that the institutional context (factors such as level of care and type of ownership) can affect physical design, program, suprapersonal factors, and the type of social environment that emerges in a setting. In addition, each of these factors can have reciprocal effects. For instance, settings with more social-recreational aids and available space (physical features) may facilitate group activities (program factors) and thereby increase resident cohesion (social climate). Physical features can also influence the types of residents who decide to enter a setting (suprapersonal factors). The type of setting, facility policies, and aggregate resident and staff characteristics may influence the social environment and one another through similar processes.

In a study that examined a portion of this framework, Moos and Igra (1980) found that social environments high in cohesion, resident influence, and physical comfort were most likely to emerge in facilities with more physical amenities, better social-recreational aids, and more space and architectural choice. Such settings tended to be highly selective, to have more socially competent and functionally able residents, and to provide their residents with broader personal choice, more opportunity to

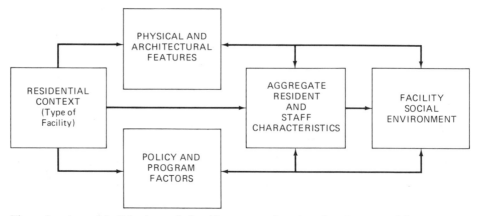

Figure 2.   A model of the interrelationships among domains of environmental factors.

participate in facility decision making, and a richer array of social and recreational activities.

This kind of framework can guide the formulation of hypotheses about the effects of such facility characteristics as size and type of ownership. Since these facility factors do not impinge directly on residents, their effects can be understood only by tracing the processes by which they influence intervening environmental factors, such as policies and social climate, that do affect residents directly. Knowledge about such processes may help to specify the conditions within which larger size and profit-oriented ownership can have benefits for residents. By considering the sets of environmental factors in conjunction with one another, such a framework can guide the planning of integrated programmatic change in residential settings and make it possible to identify settings that are amenable to change and to indicate the directions in which change is likely to occur.

THE EFFECTS OF RESIDENTIAL PROGRAMS

Using the available techniques for characterizing specialized housing environments, a number of researchers have proceeded to explore how particular settings influence the lives of their older residents. To illustrate, we provide a selective overview of longitudinal studies that have focused on the ways in which environmental and/or personal factors (Panels I and II in our framework) affect outcome criteria (Panel V).

Evaluations of Retirement Housing

The Victoria Plaza Study

In one of the first evaluations of congregate apartment housing for older people, Carp (1966) studied individuals who were selected to reside in Victoria Plaza (VP), a high-rise building with a community center. Almost 80 percent of the applicants were women, all of them healthy individuals, with an average age of 72. Compared to applicants who were not selected to be tenants (N = 148), those who were accepted (N = 204) were more sociable, cooperative, and cheerful, saw themselves as less dissatisfied and moody, and were rated more positively by interviewers on indices such as alertness and ability to remember and to learn new things.

Information was obtained on the status of the residents and the comparison group (applicants who were not accepted) after both one year and eight years. At the end of a year, those who had moved into VP were more satisfied with their housing and living arrangements than the comparison group and showed less desire for social and medical services but were somewhat more worried about their financial security. They also reported having more close friends, participating in more leisure and social activities, being more involved in active pursuits, and experiencing higher morale and self-esteem. Although contacts with family members constituted a reduced portion of all social contacts, they nevertheless reported greater satisfaction with family relationships.

In a series of reports on the eight-year follow-up, Carp (1976b, 1977, 1978–79) documented that VP tenants continued to be happier and better satisfied than individuals in the comparison group. The VP residents were more active and sociable and had higher morale, better health, and somewhat lower mortality. Although there was considerable attrition in the number of respondents (127 of the residents and 62 of the nonresidents were reassessed after eight years), the results suggest that the social and health benefits of an enriched living situation may be sustained over time. Since the processes of selection (of VP by applicants and of residents by VP management) probably resulted in high person-environment congruence, these conclusions may not apply to situations in which all applicants are accepted or in which older people lack the autonomy and opportunity to judge the suitability of the new living situation (Carp, 1976a).

Congregate Versus Traditional Housing

Although Carp's research has highlighted the potentially positive effects of freely selected congregate housing, the generality of such effects remains an issue. Lawton and Cohen (1974) used a longitudinal design to examine the impact of rehousing on the well-being of older people selected to move into five new senior housing sites. Tenants were interviewed before and one year after entering and compared to elderly community residents. Those who were and were not rehoused were compared for change over time on nine indices of well-being by means of multiple regression analyses that controlled for demographic factors and initial state of health and morale. The rehoused were better off than the community residents on indices of satisfaction with the status quo, perceived change for the better, housing satisfaction, morale, and involvement in activities; however, their state of functional health was poorer. Tenants may have been more willing to admit physical limitations after moving into the new site than they were

as applicants, but it is also possible that the more "protected" environment discouraged independent striving and led to a decline in health (Lawton and Cohen, 1974).

A subsequent study compared the relative impact of congregate and traditional housing by focusing on tenants immediately before and one year after moving into one of the two types of sites. Congregate housing tenants showed relative improvements in housing satisfaction, morale, and available social networks but relative decrements in involvement in off-site activities. These findings are consistent with the idea that service-rich congregate settings may encourage "passive contentment" (decreased activity and enhanced satisfaction), whereas traditional housing is associated with "active strain" (Lawton, 1976).

Retirement Versus Conventional Dispersed Housing

One of the most extensive studies of housing environments for the well elderly involved interviews with 100 residents at each of six retirement housing sites. The 600 residents were compared to 600 sociodemographically matched individuals living in conventional dispersed housing. Nearly 80 percent of the respondents were reinterviewed two years later (Sherman, 1973). Between 55 and 70 percent of all respondents were satisfied with their housing, and there was no overall difference between retirement housing residents and their controls. In four of the six sites, residents in retirement housing participated in more leisure activities and were more involved in clubs and social pursuits than were their community controls. Moreover, social life among residents declined less, or even increased, over the two-year period as compared to the controls. There was some evidence that the provision of facility-based activities was more important for those older, less functionally able residents who had a predisposition for high activity participation. Although residents in the retirement facilities had more new friends and visited more with neighbors and age-peer friends, they interacted less with their relatives and fewer of them had friends younger than forty. Sherman (1974) concluded that by providing an age-homogeneous milieu and facility-based activities, retirement housing can contribute toward maintaining a high activity level for those residents who wish to be involved in social and recreational pursuits (Sherman, 1975a, 1975b).

There were essentially no differences between retirement site residents and community controls in the frequency of health problems or in their perceived health. The reported need for health and community services varied extensively among the six sites. Residents at the most isolated site expressed the strongest need for more on-site health and counseling services, presumably because of their remote location and the lack of convenient transportation. There was no evidence of erosion of independence at the sites at which services were provided, and, in fact, the availability of services seemed to enhance residents' feelings of security and to enable them to enjoy independence by maintaining themselves at optimal levels (Sherman 1975c).

Multilevel Housing

A number of advantages have been attributed to multilevel housing, including reduction in relocation stress, proximity for couples in which one member needs more services, and appropriate services to accommodate short-term fluctuations in health. Nevertheless, critics suggest that an older person's morale may decline in the presence of those with low functioning and that the availability of services may undermine feelings of independence. In addition, some research suggests that on-site services might lead residents to withdraw from community contacts.

Gutman (1978) addressed these issues in an evaluation of a new multilevel facility that offered apartments, board-residence, and light and heavy personal care units. Five groups of respondents were interviewed prior to the opening of the new building and followed up a year and a half later. These groups consisted of applicants who moved into the multilevel facility, applicants who did not, applicants who moved into a facility offering apartments only, applicants to the apartment facility who did not move in, and community controls. There was some evidence that those who entered multilevel housing had more contacts

with neighbors, more new friends, higher morale, and were getting out more than they had before the move. There was no evidence of negative impact of the multilevel housing on health status, interaction with family and friends, or activity level.

Evaluations of Service-Supported Community Housing

The pressure to develop a greater range of residential options for older people has fostered a diversity of service-supported community housing programs. The two programs we describe here have addressed such issues as the level of health and social services needed in such settings, the selection of residents, and the impact of the housing service package on resident functioning.

The Philadelphia Geriatric Center Community Housing Project

The Philadelphia Geriatric Center's (PGC) Community Housing (CH) consists of efficiency apartments in remodeled single-family homes located in an area that includes high-rise, age-segregated apartment housing and a hospital and long-term care facility. Special physical features were installed in order to make the physical environment as barrier-free as possible. The program provides building maintenance and janitorial services, access to a telephone "hot line" and to social services, and optional extras such as meal delivery and housekeeping and linen service. In order to evaluate the program, individuals who moved into CH (N = 24) were compared with two control groups. All groups consisted of people aged 62 or over who were living in unsatisfactory arrangements in the community and who requested help in relocating. One control group (N = 22) was composed of those who moved to other living arrangements within six months, whereas the other (N = 41) consisted of those who remained in their original housing.

By moving, both the CH and control movers apparently resolved the problems of dissatisfaction with their housing, but these problems remained for the nonmovers. In fact, at the six-month follow-up, the nonmover group had lower morale, lived in more deteriorated housing, and still had a desire to move. In contrast, the CH tenants liked their living arrangement, felt they were enjoying life more and had more close friends, and perceived themselves to be in better health. At the two-year follow-up, the CH tenants and the control movers were both satisfied with their overall living arrangements, though the CH group was still more satisfied with their apartments. The control nonmovers fared as poorly at the two-year as they had at the six-month evaluation. The sponsors of CH felt that the 24-hour maintenance service, the protection afforded by the surroundings, and the numerous religious and social activities contributed to the tenants' security and well-being (Brody, 1979; Brody, Kleban, and Liebowitz, 1975).

The Highland Heights Project

The Fall River Highland Heights Apartments (HH) are a federally sponsored apartment building designed for physically impaired, low-income adults. The building is located on the grounds of a hospital and includes a fully equipped outpatient clinic. Nighttime emergency services and some social case work services are provided, as are on-site activities and a limited meal plan. More than 200 applicants who obtained apartments at HH (the experimental group) were individually matched on a set of socio-demographic variables with other elderly and physically impaired persons who had applied for residency but had not yet become residents (the controls). These two groups were followed for up to five years.

As hoped, residency in HH reduced the likelihood and length of time spent in a long-term care facility. Among those who were institutionalized, for example, HH residents averaged 261 days, whereas the matched nonresidents averaged 586 days, in long-term care facilities during the five-year period. For the first four years of the impact period, HH residents were less likely to die than were the controls. However, HH residents were more likely to be admitted and to spend more days in an acute care hospital. There were no differences between the two groups on other health outcomes (such as functional health and perception of health) or on indices of cognitive and emotional state, but HH residents were more likely to prefer their current living situation.

Of particular interest is the experience of 51 persons who moved to HH from a long-term care setting. A total of 43 of these individuals (84 percent) were able to maintain themselves in HH for 12 months or more, whereas 25 (49 percent) lived in HH for over 36 months. Comparisons showed that living in a long-term care setting was over four times as expensive, even when service utilization costs at HH were considered along with basic living costs. These results indicate that housing that includes specialized architecture in conjunction with health and social services can help maintain some elderly and physically impaired persons in a community setting (Sherwood, Greer, Morris, and Mor, 1981).

Evaluations of Nursing Care Settings

Some studies have compared outcomes in different types of nursing care programs, whereas others have examined differential outcomes among facilities of one type (such as community nursing homes). In an example of the former kind of study, Mitchell (1978) compared health status outcomes in three programs affiliated with the Veterans Administration: (1) home care, (2) VA-approved community nursing homes, and (3) VA hospital-based nursing home care. Patients were assessed on an index of functional health status when they were transferred from an acute care hospital to one of the three treatment programs and three months later. Although patients placed in the home care program showed the greatest overall improvement in health status, there was some evidence that patients who varied in initial health status and prognosis showed different rates of improvement in the three programs. The home care program was superior for patients with good or guarded prognoses, regardless of their initial levels of physical functioning. Very disabled patients with guarded prognoses seemed to do as well in the hospital-based as in the home care program, whereas patients who were expected to deteriorate over time were most successful when placed in community nursing homes.

The findings also suggested that a hospital with multiple treatment options placed its long-term care patients more appropriately and more successfully. Specifically, patients from one hospital that offered all three treatment programs showed more improvement in physical functioning than did patients from three hospitals that each offered only one of the three programs. The treatment and interaction effects just described accounted for an increment of only 5 percent of the outcome variance. Since the patient outcomes were based upon a relatively short time in treatment (three months) and the variables involved could be manipulated by policymakers, Mitchell concluded that this represents a meaningful treatment effect.

Linn and her colleagues (1977) examined the differential outcomes in VA-approved community nursing homes by focusing on a sample of 1,000 men placed from a VA hospital into one of 40 such settings. The men were evaluated on their functional status and classified by their physicians on the basis of their expected outcome given optimal nursing home care. They were followed up six months later, retested on functional status, and classified in regard to their location (discharged from the nursing home, still in the home, readmitted to the hospital) and functional status (improved, the same, deteriorated, or dead). The nursing homes were assessed on several structural variables and rated on the Nursing Home Rating Scale (NHRS) described earlier.

Patient outcomes were related to nursing home characteristics by multivariate analyses controlling for expected outcome and some demographic and health variables. Homes with more RN hours per patient and better meal services were more likely to have patients who were alive and improved. More RN hours per patient and a higher professional staff-to-patient ratio, better medical records, and better meal services were related to being discharged from the nursing home. The authors noted that RN hours per patient might reflect the organization and philosophy of the home in addition to the provision of direct nursing care, and that higher discharge rates might

be the result of the attention staff paid to patient evaluations. They also suggest that an emphasis on various aspects of meal services can have a positive impact on outcome by providing an opportunity for communication and social interaction.

By focusing on the process of institutionalization and adaptation to a home for the aged, Tobin and Lieberman (1976) attempted to identify the extent to which such settings contribute to resident dysfunction. Prospective residents were interviewed while they were on a waiting list to enter one of three sectarian homes, and about half of those who were admitted were reinterviewed one year later. The two comparison groups were older people residing in the community and people who had lived in one of the homes between one and three years. The psychological status of the persons awaiting admission was poorer than that of community residents but similar to that shown by the current residents. Tobin and Lieberman (1976) concluded that the adverse psychological effects attributed to entering and living in an old age home were already present in individuals on the waiting list and thus were not due to relocation or characteristics of the homes themselves. Krantz and Schulz (1980) question the legitimacy of using long-term residents as a comparison group since they are a biased sample composed of survivors of the institutionalization process. Nevertheless, the findings sensitize us to the many possible sources of decrement in the functioning of older people in institutional settings.

Lieberman (1974) has also conducted several studies of older state hospital patients who were relocated into a variety of community-based long-term care settings. He found that "facilitative" environments provided residents with more interpersonal contact and stimulation, warmth, autonomy, control, and privacy. These settings did not offer more resources; they were low in care giving and did not tolerate deviant behavior. Such findings suggest that positive challenges may be present in facilities that have relatively high expectational sets, treat older people as responsible adults, and are not indulgent or permissive about deviant behavior. As the sample was largely comprised of people who had grown old in state hospitals, Lieberman cautions against generalizing these results to community elderly moving into group settings for the first time.

Integrating the Evaluation Results

The foregoing studies indicate that residential programs can offer a positive environment for older people. Naturally, the exact nature and extent of impact depends upon the characteristics of the environments and persons being compared. Whenever existing housing options are limited and judged to be of poor quality, benefits from specialized programs may be most striking. For example, in the case of Victoria Plaza or PGC Community Housing, the housing of the residents prior to their move and of the comparison group was generally substandard. On the other hand, the development of Highland Heights was accompanied by a number of other housing programs and services for older people in the community, thus reducing its distinctiveness as a residential environment and its potential for differential impact. The results of program evaluations must therefore be interpreted within a changing economic and social context.

In general, older people who choose to reside in congregate apartments tend to be more satisfied with their living situation, to report higher morale, to have more age-peer friends, and to engage in more activities than their nonresident counterparts. The finding of less involvement in off-site activities and lower functional health led Lawton (1976) to speculate that service-rich settings may foster passive contentment. This hypothesis is consistent with Lieberman's (1974) results on the positive effects of low care giving and high expectations, but it is at variance with Sherman's (1975c) conclusion that the provision of services in retirement housing does not erode independence (see also Gutman, 1978). The danger of premature dependency must be recognized, but we believe that the availability of physical and service "supports" enhances residents' feelings of security and independence.

In community nursing homes, facilities that foster environmental stimulation and interpersonal interaction, as well as autonomy and personal choice, seem to have beneficial effects on functional status (Lieberman, 1974). Higher professional and nursing staff ratios and the maintenance of better meal services and medical records are also related to better than expected outcome (Linn et al., 1977). Although these findings are preliminary, they are consistent with conclusions about the effects of environmental factors in psychiatric programs. Therapeutic environments appear to facilitate interpersonal relationships, emphasize autonomy and personal control within the limits of an orderly, well-structured setting, and inhibit the open expression of anger and aggression. Consistent with a congruence perspective, patients who are functioning marginally need a more supportive and structured setting that protects them from experiencing too much anxiety, whereas patients who are functioning more adequately are more likely to benefit from a program that emphasizes independence and individual choice (Finney and Moos, 1984).

These conclusions must be tempered by the fact that the evaluation studies we have reviewed have focused either on new resource-rich programs (such as HH or PGC) or on previously existing programs that provide high quality services (such as the VA-approved nursing homes studied by Mitchell and Linn et al. and the sectarian nursing homes studied by Tobin and Lieberman). The findings thus estimate the potential benefits that can accrue from well managed, high-quality residential programs but do not provide an accurate index of the impact of ordinary programs. Moreover, none of the studies made use of random assignment, although an unusually careful individual matching procedure was employed in the HH project. Other methodological issues arise from the differential attrition in comparison groups, the lack of comparability among studies in measures of environmental and personal characteristics, and the problem of pinpointing the specific environmental factors that are linked to differential outcomes.

The difference in outcomes between programs or between specialized and traditional housing is relatively small. The proportion of variance in outcome criteria that is statistically accounted for by program factors typically varies between 1 and 10 percent. In fact, a recent review of the literature produced little evidence that mental health benefits accrue from the physical features of housing (Kasl and Rosenfield, 1980). On the other hand, it is important to select outcome criteria that are maximally sensitive to environmental factors. Improved residential settings may lead to higher satisfaction with housing but perhaps not to fewer symptoms of anxiety or depression. In addition, we have seen that a package of service-supported housing can help prevent institutionalization without necessarily leading to higher morale or activity level (Sherwood et al., 1981).

Although we agree with Lawton and Cohen (1974) that we cannot expect environmental effects to be large in comparison to the effects of personal attributes reflecting life-long patterns of functioning, we believe that the differential effects of residential and service programs are often underestimated. Because studies have not tapped the full range of existing residential settings, they probably underestimate the influence of environmental conditions. In addition, multivariate statistical procedures are typically used in such a way as to credit environments only with the variance added after the "effects" of personal characteristics have been considered. Since selection and allocation processes operate to foster person-environment congruence (that is, statistical overlap in the characteristics of residents and programs), it is likely that such procedures systematically underestimate the importance of environmental factors.

The Effects of Choice and Control

To exemplify research on the impact of particular environmental features, we turn now to the extensive body of work on the relationships between internal-external control orientation (Panel I in our framework), environmental opportunities for autonomy (Panel II), and resident health and morale (Panel V). Both the expectancy of and desire for control are related to life satisfaction, self-esteem, and

health among older people (Reid and Ziegler, 1980; Wolk and Kurtz, 1975). The individual's control orientation and the relationship between control orientation and adjustment, however, seem to be influenced by the degree of constraint imposed by the environment. Individuals in higher constraint environments are likely to report less latitude of choice in specific situations (Hulicka, Morganti, and Cataldo, 1975) and to score higher on external control (Wolk, 1976). This congruence between the control orientation of residents and the opportunities for choice available in their setting may come about as a result of initial self-selection or of the reduction in expectancy of control in higher constraint settings.

Although research usually reveals a positive relationship between internal locus of control and adaptation, the strength and direction of the relationship may depend on the nature of the setting and the method for assessing control orientation. For example, one measure of perceived latitude of choice consisted of asking respondents about the availability and importance of choice in daily activities. Perceived latitude of choice was found to be related to self-esteem and life satisfaction, but this relationship proved to be stronger for women in a long-term care setting than for similar women in traditional housing (Hulicka, Morganti, and Cataldo, 1975). The results suggest that above a certain threshold, additional opportunities for exercising autonomy have less impact on adaptation. In contrast, Wolk (1976) found a relationship between adaptation and control orientation in a less constraining setting but no such relationship in a more restrictive retirement home.

Instead of assuming locus of control to be a global trait, Felton and Kahana (1974) asked residents of old age homes how they would solve specific problems likely to arise there (a measure of coping responses, or Panel IV in the framework). The solutions were coded according to who constituted the locus of control: self, significant others, or staff. In general, residents who saw staff and others as the locus of control showed higher life satisfaction and morale and were rated as better adjusted and more satisfied by staff than the residents who did not. Since viewing others as the locus of control reflects the reality of institutional life, an orientation toward external control may be considered an adaptive trait in such settings.

In our own work, we have assumed that personal control can be fostered by allowing residents to determine their daily routine (policy choice) and to take responsibility for some aspects of facility programs and policies (resident control). We studied a group of 93 residential settings and found that higher levels of policy choice and resident control were associated with more cohesive, organized, independence-oriented social environments and higher resident activity levels. Women residents reacted more positively than men to the provision of choice over daily activities, and the more functionally able residents reacted more positively to the provision of some control over facility policies. These findings indicate that both personal history factors and current personal resources affect residents' reactions to environmental opportunities and demands (Moos, 1981).

Enhancing Adjustment by Increasing Choice and Control

By emphasizing the importance of autonomy and choice, the foregoing studies have led investigators to explore the value of control-enhancing interventions in nursing homes. Schulz (1976) noted that the experimental introduction of predictable and controllable positive events had a beneficial influence on the morale and well-being of nursing home residents but that these benefits lasted only as long as did the intervention itself (Schulz and Hanusa, 1978). Schulz and Hanusa (1979) subsequently found that increasing environmental predictability for new residents of a long-term care facility enhanced adaptation. New residents who obtained relevant information about the facility engaged in more active pursuits, reported an improvement in emotional health, and were rated higher on health status than those given irrelevant information or no treatment.

Consistent with a congruence perspective, however, the enhancement of personal competencies or coping skills without adequate

provision of new opportunities to utilize these skills has been found to introduce problems. Schulz and Hanusa (1979) noted that a group of institutionalized older people exposed to both competence- and control-enhancing interventions was relatively worse off on indicators of health and psychological status than groups exposed to only one of these interventions. They concluded that environmental press or demand needs to keep pace with increasing levels of perceived competence and that the nursing home setting may not have enabled the individuals exposed to both interventions to exercise their newly found abilities.

Rodin (1980) and her colleagues have manipulated actual and perceived control by offering nursing home residents meaningful responsibility. Participants in these studies were randomly assigned to different floors of a nursing home. In one project, the administrator told the experimental group about the choices and possibilities for decision making that existed in the home, whereas the control group was given a "benign and caring" communication that emphasized staff's responsibility to provide care. Residents in the experimental group reported feeling happier, became more active and alert, and increased their involvement in activities. There were also striking differences in the death rates of the two groups; in the subsequent 18 months only 15 percent of the individuals in the experimental group died, as compared to 30 percent in the comparison group. Residents given a responsibility-enhancing communication may alter their interactions with staff and other residents, and this may trigger a reciprocal set of changes that are maintained for a relatively long period (Langer and Rodin, 1976; Rodin and Langer, 1977).

In another project, residents in an experimental group were assigned a 15-minute interval in which they could have a nurse's attention. The intervention grew from observations of tensions between residents and nurses, with nurses apparently making residents feel helpless and then punishing them for their dependence. Although residents initially exercised their control by calling nurses for trivial as well as important reasons, they summoned nurses less as the study progressed. General health and sociability improved in the experimental group relative to the untreated group, indicating that control does not need to be exercised continuously in order to produce benefits. Rodin (1980) concludes that the individual's internal equilibrium and stress resistance can be improved either by altering the environment or by helping individuals to cope more effectively (improving the equilibrium between person and environment).

Choice and Control and the Effects of Relocation

A considerable body of research has examined the ways in which relocation can affect older people. Some studies have identified pervasive negative effects of relocation, including increased mortality rates, whereas others have not only failed to show such effects but have noted some positive impacts. In the light of several recent reviews of this literature (Coffman, 1981; Kasl and Rosenfield, 1980; Krantz and Schulz, 1980), we confine ourselves to a selective overview of the hypothesis that the stress of relocation is moderated when an individual appraises it as a controllable or predictable event (Schulz and Brenner, 1977).

Relocation has fewer negative effects on people who move voluntarily and thereby experience control over the move or who find their environment more predictable because of pre-move counseling. Since predictability decreases with environmental discontinuity, negative effects are more likely when pre- and post-relocation environments are dissimilar. Consistent with this hypothesis, the largest negative effects of relocation are shown by individuals who move involuntarily from their home to an institution, whereas those who move involuntarily from one institution to another show a somewhat less negative outcome. Relocation seems to have particularly strong negative effects when environmental change is accompanied by a deterioration in the social support system, as when an individual moves to a new facility populated by an unfamiliar group of residents and staff (Coffman, 1981). Finally, there is some evidence that individuals who are oriented toward internal control are more adversely affected by forced relocation, particularly when they move to a less controllable environment (Borup, 1981; Gutman and Herbert, 1976; Kasl and Rosenfield, 1980; Schulz and Hanusa, 1980).

Recent critical reviews of this literature have raised questions about the extent to which elevated morbidity or mortality rates actually occur and whether they reflect the stressful consequences of environmental change per se. Alternative explanations involve the lack of comparability of transferred and nontransferred individuals, the effects of self-selection and the anticipation of institutionalization, and the influence of exposure to noxious aspects of an institutional environment, such as poor diet and lack of adequate care (Kasl and Rosenfield, 1980; Tobin and Lieberman, 1976).

This brief review highlights the approaches used to understand the role of one particular environmental factor in determining outcomes for older people in specialized housing. Other such issues, which cannot be covered here, include the effects of age integration (Carp, 1976a; Lawton, 1977), the impact of particular spatial arrangements and physical features (Howell, 1980), and security and fear of crime (Kasl and Rosenfield, 1980). The strategy of focusing on specific environmental factors works best in experimental designs such as Rodin's. In more naturalistic studies, a major hazard of this approach is that settings that differ in the dimension under study may also differ in other respects.

MATCHING RESIDENT CHARACTERISTICS AND FACILITY RESOURCES

Throughout this discussion, we have mentioned results illustrating the differential effects of a given environmental factor on different individuals. For example, depending upon initial health status and prognosis, patients may do better in home care or community nursing homes (Mitchell, 1978). A rich activity program may not affect the activity level of older people who are relatively healthy, but it may have a significant impact on the lives of more impaired persons (Sherman, 1974). Two questions emerge from these findings: (1)

To what extent are residents' characteristics typically matched with facility resources? (2) What resident characteristics related to adequate functioning and morale in group residential settings?

Self-Selection and Social Allocation

The inhabitants of residential settings do not constitute a simple cross section of the older population, and they are not randomly distributed into available programs. A variety of personal and social forces help determine who seeks such residential options and where they live. Among these forces are the individual's functional abilities and needs, the availability of alternative sources of support, economic constraints, attractiveness and availability of housing, and life style preferences.

Functional ability is a major selection criterion, particularly in determining nursing home utilization. As a group, applicants for nursing homes are more impaired than community samples (Tobin and Lieberman, 1976). Moreover, selection among settings that vary in level of care is related largely to an individual's functional abilities. Through self-selection and screening, individuals with greater need tend to be matched with facilities offering more services or higher staffing (Lawton, 1976; Manard, Woehle and Heilman, 1977). Within a particular level of care, however, residents with lower functioning may be in facilities offering fewer services or lower staffing (Lemke and Moos, 1981), or there may be no relationship between resident functioning and such resources (Kahn, Hines, Woodson, and Burkham-Armstrong, 1977). This situation occurs in part because functioning undergoes many short-term changes not accompanied by residential relocation and because people differ in the economic and social resources available to compensate for disabilities.

Functional ability and need for services are the major bases for selection of an appropriate level of care, but such factors as socioeconomic status, referral source, geographic location, and cost of care and reimbursement procedures increase the probability of placement in a particular setting. These selective mechanisms operate to increase the relative suprapersonal homogeneity of settings, particularly for those who have more personal resources. For instance, residents who are white, well educated, married, and of higher socioeconomic status are likely to be in homogeneous living groups with others of similar background (Lemke and Moos, 1981). Such sociodemographic and cultural homogeneity is related to enhanced resident social interaction and satisfaction (Bergman and Cibulski, 1981; Rosow, 1967).

By maximizing person-environment fit, however, homogeneous settings may provide too little stimulation and fail to maintain maximum levels of functioning. Selection policies that increase the heterogeneity of individuals in a setting can create a more therapeutic environment. Kahana and Kahana (1970) randomly assigned elderly psychiatric patients to an age-integrated custodial ward, an age-segregated custodial ward, and an intensive therapy ward. The patients in the age-heterogeneous unit showed significant increases on measures of cognitive functioning over a three-week period (increases equal to those found in the intensive therapy ward), whereas the individuals assigned to the age-homogeneous ward exhibited no improvement. The heterogeneous suprapersonal environment in the age-integrated unit apparently provided a more cognitively complex and involving milieu for the older patients. Sherwood and her colleagues (1981) have also noted that a mix of high- and low-need individuals can foster higher staff morale and the development of networks of mutual assistance among residents.

Predictors of Morale and Adjustment

Most of the research that has tried to identify personal characteristics predictive of differential outcomes of institutionalization has not explicitly considered environmental factors. There is evidence that a vigorous, assertive personality style may predict successful adaptation to an institutional setting, whereas passivity seems to increase the risk of deterioration (Kasl and Rosenfield, 1980). Other investigators have noted that persons who are depressed and engage in little social activity, or who are isolates prior to relocation, subsequently develop fewer social contacts and have a more difficult time learning about and adapting to life in the new setting (Bennett, 1980).

In addressing these issues among VP residents, Carp (1968) found that persons who were extroverted and sociable and who were involved in leisure pursuits or community service work before entering VP tended to participate in more activities, to be happier, to be more popular with other residents, and to be perceived by administrators as better adjusted. The VP environment led to a decline in social activity among a small minority of the initially least social residents. Since high activity was encouraged by the staff, these findings seem to support the idea that satisfaction and adjustment depend in part upon person-environment congruence (Carp, 1978–79; Carp and Carp, 1981).

Kahana (1982) operationalized the seven dimensions included in her person-environment congruence model by developing an Individual Preference Questionnaire (IPQ) to tap residents' preferences or needs and an Environmental Questionnaire (EQ) to tap environmental opportunities as perceived by staff members. Residents who were functioning relatively well in nursing home settings were tested to find out whether congruence between preferences and opportunities was related to resident morale. Individual preferences for affective expression and freedom from institutional control were related to morale, as was the degree of stimulation afforded by the environment. Person-environment congruence was not important in these three areas, but it was important in the areas of segregation, congregation, and impulse control (Kahana, Liang, and Felton, 1980).

Harel (1981) measured seven somewhat different dimensions and found that congruence in the areas of ties with other people and privacy and personal space was related to higher resident morale. Congruence in the areas of personal responsibility and options for the gratification of basic and social needs was less important. Such comparisons of needs and resources are complicated by the difficulty of measuring each and of determining what level of need is congruent with what level of resources.

Some recent studies have developed selection procedures to help maximize the match between resident and facility characteristics (Haddad, 1981). Sherwood and her colleagues constructed a screening instrument to identify individuals clinically judged to be well-suited to residency in a long-term care facility. These individuals were of lower socioeconomic status, in poor functional health, had more friends and belonged to more social groups, and were more likely to be living with someone other than a spouse and sharing a bath with a nonfamily member. Follow-up of those persons who were eventually admitted to long-term care showed that life satisfaction increased for the "suited" group, whereas it stayed the same or decreased for those rated less suited. Members of the better suited group may have experienced less environmental change in the move into a long-term care setting (Sherwood, Glassman, Sherwood, and Morris, 1974; Sherwood, Morris, and Barnhart, 1975). In additional work along these lines, a mathematical model was constructed to replicate clinical team judgments concerning the appropriateness of service-rich sheltered housing such as HH. In general, persons who had more physical and cognitive limitations, who participated less frequently in religious activities, reported fewer social activities, and rarely did their own shopping were judged to be more suitable for HH (Sherwood, Greer, Morris and Mor, 1981).

Although these studies are important, the complexity of this issue is illustrated by the fact that somewhat different predictors were related to different adjustment criteria in Carp's study of VP. A further illustration is provided by selection models; individuals judged "suited" to a long-term care setting were more active in social activities, whereas those judged suited to settings like HH reported fewer social activities. Thus, different settings may require different adaptive strategies of their residents. Finally, the generality of the factors identified must await longitudinal research that relates these factors to criterion indices.

FUTURE DIRECTIONS

In this section we consider the value of an expanded paradigm for evaluating specialized residential settings. We also describe ways to apply the knowledge gained from evaluation procedures to the design and improvement of residential facilities. Gurland, Bennett, and Wilder (1981, p. 67) caution against expecting dramatic contrasts between programs directed toward meeting the older person's needs for long-term care but suggest that evaluation research can "improve the information available to consumers on what they can personally expect from specific alternatives, to providers on what they can do for specific clients, and to policy makers on ways and costs of improving the system."

Expanding the Traditional Evaluation Paradigm

As we noted earlier, the traditional evaluation paradigm, in which the residential program is thought of as a "black box" between resident inputs and outcomes, reveals little about the program or the causal paths for its impact. The design and evaluation of specialized residential settings can be improved by expanding the paradigm to include information about the program environment and extraprogram factors. The assessment of program implementation has been labeled the "third face of evaluation," complementing as it does both outcome assessment and research design. Without this check, there is a risk of evaluating a program that has been only partially implemented or operationalized in a form different from that intended. Furthermore, decision makers need to know about external validity, or the extent to which the results of a particular evaluation can be expected to generalize to new situations in which the program may be implemented. Such extrapolations can be made more readily if the evaluation has provided information on the causal mechanisms through which the treatment exerts its effect (for further discussion of these issues, see Finney and Moos, 1984).

The conceptual framework we have used here is a first step in this direction in that it involves a systematic examination of the environmental system and considers cognitive appraisal and coping factors as two related sets of determinants of the process of resident selection and reaction to group living situations. Several other considerations should be kept in mind in designing evaluations.

The paradigm typically employed in evaluations of group residential settings implicitly assumes a "closed system" in which older people are exposed only to a residential program. In reality, the residential setting is but one of the multiple environmental "microsystems" in which the person functions. The influences emanating from other enduring microsystems, such as extended family and peer networks, may have a stronger effect on an individual's morale and well-being than the characteristics of the residential setting (Kasl and Rosenfield, 1980). On the other hand, the residential program can influence the nature of these other microsystems. As programs are developed that allow older people to enter and leave residential settings more readily (such as respite care), there will be a growing need to include information about extraprogram factors in evaluation projects.

Individuals not only participate in numerous microsystems, but a given microsystem may perform different functions for different individuals. Thus, supportive residential and health care settings provide a work environment for staff as well as a treatment or living environment for residents. Although these two facets of the environment serve different functions, they are closely related. For instance, the press of required activities may lead staff to use less time-consuming methods of care, and these, in turn, are likely to reinforce passive dependent behavior on the part of residents. Such behavior may in turn lead to negative stereotyping of older persons and to additional dependency-producing staff behavior, to more rapid functional deterioration among residents, and ultimately to lower staff morale. On the other hand, staff attention and positive expectations are powerful resources that facilitate resident functioning by enhancing cognitive and social stimulation and setting standards for acceptable behavior (Barton, Baltes, and Orzech, 1980). It is important, therefore, to clarify how the organizational design of residential programs affects service delivery as a result of its impact on work stress and staff motivation. Available evidence indicates that staff vacancy and turnover rates are partly a function of the organization of care, the degree of difficulty involved in providing services, and the amount of autonomy and support afforded staff (Cherniss, 1980; Knapp and Harissis, 1981).

In this way, an expanded framework can help us to formulate alternative ways of thinking about the links between institutional structures and resident outcomes. For instance, a recent model developed in facilities for long-term mental patients suggests that better resident functioning at intake is related to greater staff and resident participation in treatment decisions and higher staff morale, which in turn foster more individualized resident management practices and ultimately better resident functioning (Holland, Konick, Buffum, Smith, and Petchers, 1981).

Designing and Changing Residential Programs

We have emphasized the use of measures of environmental factors in summative evaluation directed toward documenting the impacts of residential programs. We should note, however, that such measures have an equally important role to play in planning and changing residential programs. Our perspective underscores the need for designers and program evaluators to cooperate in long-term evaluations. We see a collaborative role for program designers and evaluators in each phase of the history of a residential setting.

In the planning phase, more attention should be directed toward the expected behavioral implications of program factors. The input from potential building users should focus on the probable behavioral impacts of design decisions as much as on user preferences. In the selection phase, prospective residents are identified and recruited, and designers can use their knowledge about individual preferences and probable design impacts to help identify a congruent but somewhat varied resident group. Participation in the orientation of po-

tential and prospective residents will provide designers with useful information about how individuals initially evaluate and adapt to physical design features.

In the post-occupancy phase, designers and evaluators can assess changes in preferences and sources of satisfaction over time, as well as problems of adaptation that occur in regard to specific design features (Carp, 1976b). Staff and residents can be involved in ongoing data-based feedback. This process involves (1) program assessment, (2) feedback of the results of the assessment, (3) planning and instituting change, and (4) reassessment (Moos, Lemke, and Clayton, 1983). This approach allows participants to analyze the multiple dimensions of a setting's functioning and brings into awareness important characteristics of the environment that are often overlooked. The history of changes in facility design and programming factors should be recorded, together with the reasons for these changes and their impacts on residents (for an example, see Sherwood, et al., 1981). A national information registry of practices and preferences in specialized residential settings, their stability and variation over time, and their influence on residents and staff could help formulate data-based design guidelines. Such a plan could be implemented by allocating a fraction of 1 percent of the cost of program operation for program evaluation.

Our overview indicates that high-quality residential settings can facilitate morale and effective functioning among older people who choose to live in them. Since current findings are a function of available residential options, they can provide only limited information about the potential influence of environmental factors (Carp, 1976a). By encouraging a variety of innovative residential programs, we can create new opportunities to broaden our knowledge and to provide better living situations for both healthy and impaired older people.

Acknowledgments: Preparation of the manuscript was supported by NIMH Grants MH16744 and MH28177 and also by Veterans Administration Health Services Research and Development funds. We wish to thank Ruth

Bennett, Powell Lawton, and Margaret Linn for their helpful comments on an earlier draft.

REFERENCES

Achenbaum, W. A. 1978. *Old Age in the New Land.* Baltimore: Johns Hopkins University Press.

Barton, E. M.; Baltes, M. M.; and Orzech, M. 1980. Etiology of dependence in older nursing home residents during morning care: The role of staff behavior. *J. Pers. Soc. Psychol.* 38:423–431.

Bednar, M. J. 1977. *Barrier-Free Environments.* Stroudsburg, PA: Dowden, Hutchinson, and Ross.

Bennett, R., ed. 1980. *Aging, Isolation, and Resocialization.* New York: Van Nostrand Reinhold.

Bennett, R., and Nahemow, L. 1965. Institutional totality and criteria of social adjustment in residences for the aged. *J. Soc. Issues* 21:44–78.

Bergman, S., and Cibulski, I. 1981. Environment, culture and adaptation in congregate facilities: Perspectives from Israel. *Gerontologist* 21:240–246.

Borup, J. H. 1981. Relocation: Attitudes, information network, and problems encountered. *Gerontologist* 21:501–511.

Brody, E. M. 1977. *Long-Term Care of Older People.* New York: Human Sciences Press.

Brody, E. M. 1979. Service-supported independent living in an urban setting: The Philadelphia Geriatric Center's community housing for the elderly. In *Environmental Context of Aging*, eds. T. O. Byerts, S. C. Howell, and L. A. Pastalan. New York: Garland.

Brody, E. M.; Kleban, M. H.; and Liebowitz, B. 1975. Intermediate housing for the elderly: Satisfaction of those who moved in and those who did not. *Gerontologist* 15:350–356.

Carp, F. M. 1966. *A Future for the Aged.* Austin: University of Texas Press.

Carp, F. M. 1968. Person-situation congruence in engagement. *Gerontologist* 8:184–188.

Carp, F. M. 1976a. Housing and living environments of older people. In *Handbook of Aging and the Social Sciences*, eds. R. H. Binstock and E. Shanas. New York: Van Nostrand Reinhold.

Carp, F. M. 1976b. User evaluation of housing for the elderly. *Gerontologist* 16:102–111.

Carp, F. M. 1977. Impact of improved living environment on health and life expectancy. *Gerontologist* 17:242–249.

Carp, F. M. 1978–79. Effects of the living environment on activity and use of time. *Int. J. Aging Hum. Devel.* 9:75–91.

Carp, F., and Carp, A. 1981. Mental health characteristics and acceptance/rejection of old age. *Am. J. Orthopsychiatry* 51:230–241.

Cherniss, C. 1980. *Professional Burnout in Human Service Organizations.* New York: Praeger.

Coffman, T. L. 1981. Relocation and survival of institutionalized aged: A re-examination of the evidence. *Gerontologist* 21:483–500.

David, T. G.; Moos, R. H.; and Kahn, J. R. 1981. Community integration among elderly residents of sheltered care settings. *Am. J. Community Psychol.* 9:513–526.

Dennis, L. C., Burke, R. E., and Garber, K. G. 1977. Quality Evaluation System: An approach for patient assessment. *J. Long-Term Care Administration* 5:28–51.

Dunlop, B. D. 1979. *The Growth of Nursing Home Care.* Lexington, MA: D. C. Heath & Co.

Felton, B., and Kahana, E. 1974. Adjustment and situationally-bound locus of control among institutionalized aged. *J. Gerontol.* 29:295–301.

Finney, J., and Moos, R. H. 1984. Environmental assessment and evaluation research: Examples from mental health and substance abuse programs. *Evaluation and Program Planning* 7:151–176.

Fottler, M. D.; Smith, H. L.; and James, W. L. 1981. Profits and patient care quality in nursing homes: Are they compatible? *Gerontologist* 21:532–538.

Goffman, E. 1961. Asylums: *Essays on the Social Situation of Mental Patients and Other Inmates.* Garden City, NY: Doubleday.

Gottesman, L. E. 1974. Nursing home performance as related to resident traits, ownership, size and source of payment. *Am. J. Public Health* 64:269–276.

Gurland, B.; Bennett, R.; and Wilder, D. 1981. Reevaluating the place of evaluation in planning for alternatives to institutional care for the elderly. *J. Soc. Issues* 37(3):51–70.

Gutman, G. 1978. Issues and findings relating to multilevel accommodation for seniors. *J. Gerontol* 33:592–600.

Gutman, G. M., and Herbert, C. P. 1976. Mortality rates among relocated extended-care patients. *J. Gerontol.* 31:352–357.

Haddad, L. B. 1981. Utilizing rating instruments for evaluating behavioral characteristics differentiating elderly patients selected for skilled nursing, intermediate, and psychiatric care. *J. Gerontol.* 36:583–585.

Harel, Z. 1981. Quality of care, congruence and well-being among institutionalized aged. *Gerontologist* 21:523–531.

Hochschild, A. R. 1973. *The Unexpected Community.* Englewood Cliffs, NJ: Prentice-Hall.

Holland, T. P.; Konick, A.; Buffum, W.; Smith, M. K.; and Petchers, M. 1981. Institutional structure and resident outcomes. *J. Health Social Behavior* 22:433–444.

Howell, S. C. 1976. Site selection and the elderly. In *Community Planning for an Aging Society*, eds. M. P. Lawton, R. J. Newcomer, and T. O. Byerts. Stroudsburg, PA: Dowden, Hutchinson, and Ross.

Howell, S. C. 1980. Environments as hypotheses in human aging research. In *Aging in the 1980s: Psychological Issues*, ed. L. W. Poon. Washington, D.C.: American Psychological Association.

Hulicka, I. M.; Morganti, J. B.; and Cataldo, J. F. 1975. Perceived latitude of choice of institutionalized and noninstitutionalized elderly women. *Exp. Aging Res.* 1:27–39.

Kahana, E. 1982. A congruence model of person-environment interaction. In *Aging and the Environment: Theo-*

retical Approaches, eds. M. P. Lawton, P. G. Windley, and T. O. Byerts. New York: Springer Publishing Co.

Kahana, E., and Kahana, B. 1970. Therapeutic potential of age integration. *Arch. Gen. Psychiat.* 23:20–29.

Kahana, E.; Liang, J.; and Felton, B. J. 1980. Alternative models of person-environment fit: Prediction of morale in three homes for the aged. *J. Gerontol.* 35:584–595.

Kahn, K. A.; Hines, W.; Woodson, A. S., and Burkham-Armstrong, G. 1977. A multi-disciplinary approach to assessing the quality of care in long-term care facilities. *Gerontologist* 17:61–65.

Kasl, S. V., and Rosenfield, S. 1980. The residential environment and its impact on the mental health of the aged. In *Handbook of Mental Health and Aging,* eds. J. E. Birren and R. B. Sloane. Englewood Cliffs, NJ: Prentice-Hall.

Kleemeier, R. W. ed. 1961. *Aging and Leisure.* New York: Oxford University Press.

Knapp, M., and Harissis, K. 1981. Staff vacancies and turnover in British old peoples' homes. *Gerontologist* 21:76–84.

Koncelik, J. A. 1976. *Designing the Open Nursing Home.* Stroudsburg, PA: Dowden, Hutchinson, & Ross.

Krantz, D. S., and Schulz, R. 1980. Life crisis, control, and health outcomes: A model applied to cardiac rehabilitation and relocation of the elderly. In *Advances in Environmental Psychology,* vol. 2, eds. A. Baum and J. E. Singer. Hillsdale, NJ: Lawrence Erlbaum.

Langer, E. J., and Rodin, J. 1976. The effects of choice and enhanced personal responsibility for the aged: A field experiment in an institutional setting. *J. Pers. Soc. Psychol.* 34:191–198.

Lawton, M. P. 1975. *Planning and Managing Housing for the Elderly.* New York: Wiley.

Lawton, M. P. 1976. The relative impact of congregate and traditional housing on elderly tenants. *Gerontologist* 16:237–242.

Lawton, M. P. 1977. The impact of the environment on aging and behavior. In *Handbook of the Psychology of Aging,* eds. J. E. Birren and K. W. Schaie. New York: Van Nostrand Reinhold.

Lawton, M. P. 1982. Competence, environmental press, and the adaptation of older people. In *Aging and the Environment: Theoretical approaches,* eds. M. P. Lawton, P. G. Windley, and T. O. Byerts. New York: Springer Publishing Co.

Lawton, M. P., and Cohen, J. 1974. The generality of housing impact on the well-being of older people. *J. Gerontol.* 29:194–204.

Lemke, S., and Moos, R. H. 1980. Assessing the institutional policies of sheltered care settings. *J. Gerontol.* 35:96–107.

Lemke, S., and Moos, R. H. 1981. The suprapersonal environments of sheltered care settings. *J. Gerontol.* 36:233–243.

Lieberman, M. A. 1974. Relocation research and social policy. *Gerontologist* 14:494–501.

Linn, M. W. 1966. A nursing home rating scale. *Geriatrics* 21:188–192.

Linn, M. W.; Gurel, L.; and Linn, B. S. 1977. Patient outcome as a measure of quality of nursing home care. *Am. J. Public Health* 67:337–344.

Manard, B. B.; Woehle, R. E.; and Heilman, J. M. 1977. *Better Homes for the Old.* Lexington, MA: D. C. Heath & Co.

Markson, E. W. 1982. Placement and location: The elderly and congregate care. In *Congregate Housing for Older People,* eds. R. D. Chellis, J. F. Seagle, and B. M. Seagle. Lexington, MA: D. C. Heath & Co.

Messer, M. 1967. The possibility of an age-concentrated environment becoming a normative system. *Gerontologist* 7:247–251.

Mitchell, J. B. 1978. Patient outcomes in alternative long-term care settings. *Medical Care* 16:439–452.

Moos, R. H. 1974. *The Social Climate Scales: An Overview.* Palo Alto, CA: Consulting Psychologists Press.

Moos, R. H. 1981. Environmental choice and control in community care settings for older people. *J. Appl. Soc. Psychol.* 11:23–43.

Moos, R. H.; Guavain, M.; Lemke, S.; Max, W.; and Mehren, B. 1979. Assessing the social environments of sheltered care settings. *Gerontologist* 19:74–82.

Moos, R. H., and Igra, A. 1980. Determinants of the social environments of sheltered care settings. *J. Health Soc. Behavior* 21:88–98.

Moos, R. H., and Lemke, S. 1980. Assessing the physical and architectural features of sheltered care settings. *J. Gerontol.* 35:571–583.

Moos, R. H. and Lemke, S. 1984. *Multiphasic Environmental Assessment Procedure: Manual.* Palo Alto, CA: Social Ecology Laboratory, Stanford University and Veterans Administration Medical Center.

Moos, R. H., Lemke, S.; and Clayton, J. 1983. Comprehensive assessment of residential programs: A means of facilitating evaluation and change. *Interdisciplinary Topics in Gerontology* 17:69–83.

Moos, R. H.; Lemke, S.; and David, T. G. In press. Environmental design and programming in residential settings for the elderly: Practices and preferences. In *Housing for the Elderly: Satisfactions and Preferences,* eds. V. Regnier and J. Pynoos. New York: Garland.

National Center for Health Statistics. 1979. *The National Nursing Home Survey: 1977 Summary for the United States.* Washington, D.C.: Government Printing Office.

Pincus, A. 1968. The definition and measurement of the institutional environment in homes for the aged. *Gerontologist* 8:207–210.

Pincus, A., and Wood, V. 1970. Methodological issues in measuring the environment in institutions for the aged and its impact on residents. *Aging and Human Development* 1:117–126.

Reid, D. W., and Ziegler, M. 1980. Validity and stability of a new desired control measure pertaining to psychological adjustment of the elderly. *J. Gerontol.* 35:395–402.

Rodin, J. 1980. Managing the stress of aging: The role of control and coping. In *Coping and Health,* eds. S. Levine and H. Ursin. New York: Plenum.

Rodin, J., and Langer, E. J. 1977. Long-term effects of a control-relevant intervention with the institutionalized aged. *J. Pers. Soc. Psychol.* 35:897–902.

Rosow, I. 1967. *Social Integration of the Aged.* New York: Free Press.

Ross, J. 1977. *Old People, New Lives: Community Creation in a Retirement Residence.* Chicago: University of Chicago Press.

Schulz, R. 1976. Effects of control and predictability on the physical and psychological well-being of the institutionalized aged. *J. Pers. Soc. Psychol.* 33:563–573.

Schulz, R., and Brenner, G. 1977. Relocation of the aged: A review and theoretical analysis. *J. Gerontol.* 32:323–333.

Schulz, R., and Hanusa, B. H. 1978. Long-term effects of control and predictability-enhancing interventions: Findings and ethical issues. *J. Pers. Soc. Psychol.* 36:1194–1201.

Schulz, R., and Hanusa, B. H. 1979. Environmental influences on the effectiveness of control and competence enhancing interventions. In *Choice and Perceived Control,* eds. L. C. Perlmutter and R. A. Monty. New York: Lawrence Erlbaum.

Schulz, R., and Hanusa, B. H. 1980. Experimental social gerontology: A social psychological perspective. *J. Soc. Issues* 36:30–46.

Sherman, S. R. 1973. Methodology in a study of residents of retirement housing. *J. Gerontol.* 28:351–358.

Sherman, S. R. 1974. Leisure activities in retirement housing. *J. Gerontol.* 29:325–335.

Sherman, S. R. 1975a. Mutual assistance and support in retirement housing. *J. Gerontol.* 30:479–483.

Sherman, S. R. 1975b. Patterns of contacts for residents of age-segregated and age-integrated housing. *J. Gerontol.* 30:103–107.

Sherman, S. R. 1975c. Provision of on-site services in retirement housing. *Int. J. Aging Hum. Devel.* 6:229–247.

Sherwood, S.; Glassman, J.; Sherwood, C.; and Morris, J. N. 1974. Pre-institutionalization factors as predictors of adjustment to a long-term care facility. *Int. J. Aging Hum. Devel.* 5:95–105.

Sherwood, S.; Greer, D. S.; Morris, J. N.; and Mor, V. 1981. *An Alternative to Institutionalization: The Highland Heights Experiment.* Cambridge, MA: Ballinger.

Sherwood, S., and Mor, V. 1980. Mental health institutions and the elderly. In *Handbook of Mental Health and Aging,* eds. J. E. Birren and R. B. Sloane. Englewood Cliffs, NJ: Prentice-Hall.

Sherwood, S.; Morris, J. N.; and Barnhart, E. 1975. Developing a system for assigning individuals into an appropriate residential setting. *J. Gerontol.* 30:331–342.

Tobin, S. S., and Lieberman, M. A. 1976. *Last Home for the Aged.* San Francisco: Jossey-Bass.

Ullmann, S. G. 1981. Assessment of facility quality and its relationship to facility size in the long-term care industry. *Gerontologist* 21:91–97.

U. S. Veterans Administration. 1981. *1980 Annual Report.* Washington, D.C.: Government Printing Office.

Vicente, L.; Wiley, J. A.; and Carrington, R. A. 1979. The risk of institutionalization before death. *Gerontologist* 19:361–367.

Weihl, H. 1981. On the relationship between the size of residential institutions and the well-being of residents. *Gerontologist* 21:247–250.

Wolk, S. 1976. Situational constraint as a moderator of the locus of control-adjustment relationship. *J. Consult. Clin. Psychol.* 44:420–427.

Wolk, S., and Kurtz, J. 1975. Positive adjustment and involvement during aging and expectancy for internal control. *J. Consult. Clin. Psychol.* 43:173–178.

Name Index

Subject Index

Abstract thought, 486

Accidents: age of drivers and, 709; behavioral models of, 704–705; behavioral slowing with age, 710–711; burns, 713; death from, 705–708; definition of, 703–704; effects of drugs on, 717–718; elderly and, 703–724; fire, 713; highway-environment, 708–711; home-environment, 711–714; as nonnormative life events, 704; older workers and, 793; personality traits and, 704; poisoning, 713–714; predictive factors of, 709–711; prevention of, 716–719; work-environment, 714–716
See also Falls; Injury

Accident theory, 15

Accuracy-emphasis hypothesis, 411

Acidic glycosaminoglycans, 98

Action naming test, 465

Activity, 130–131

Activity theory, 858–859

Adaptation: adaptive maturity, 521; cognitive appraisal model of, 594, 601–605; cognitive-phenomenological, 601; competence, 248–249; definition of, 597; ecology of aging and, 246; ecology of perceived neighborhood and, 252–253; environmental press, 248–249; intelligence and, 506; intrapsychic component of, 251; Lawton and Nahemow's adaptation mode, 248–249; life-course perspective, 594–595; life-events model of, 594, 597–601; life-span construct, 609–615; models of, 594–609; psychological age and, 8–9; subjective well-being model of, 594, 605–609; tasks for the elderly, 225–226; theoretical framework, 525
See also Adjustment; Coping

Adjustment: to disability, 656–657; as reaction of late life, 539; in specialized housing, 883–885
See also Adaptation; Coping

Affect: affective states, 532–533; duration of, 533, 541; elicitors, instigators of, 533–534, 541; frequency of, 533, 541; intensity of, 533, 540; loss of, 537; structure of expression of, 533–534, 540–541; quality of, 533, 541
See also Emotion

Age: adolescent, 197–198; criteria, 223–224; norms, 202, 731–732; roles, 202–203; alcoholism and, 154–155; assessment and, 739–740; biological, 8; changes in the nervous system, 388–392; chronological, 222; cohort variance, 505; comparative perspective, 218–223; compliance, 159; cultural values and, 225–227; definitions of, 8, 14; drivers and, 708–711; estimation of, 221; functional, 63; hair-cell loss, 342; as independent variable, 63–64; as index, 12–14; intelligence and, 512–513; language and, 463–473; leisure and, 853–854; measurement of, 51–53; measurement equivalence and, 69; mental, 63; nature of, 62–64; problem solving and, 479–496; psychological, 8–9; retirement, 197–198; sensory-motor ability and, 409–411; sex, personality, and, 224–

228; social, 8; social boundaries and, 233–235; speed of behavior and, 400–426; subjective, 790; types of, 8–9

Aged: *See* Elderly

Age-related slowing: *See* Slowing with age phenomenon

Age-status: age roles and, 202–203; in the American tradition, 195–197; basis for, 201; cumulative deprivation, 204–206; devaluation of, 193–197; educational level and, 204–205; eldership complex, 192–193; "grey" movement and, 201; historico-sociological dynamics and, 203–204; industrialization and, 231–235; love and, 201; meaning and, 199; modernization and, 229–231; poverty personality and, 204–206; resources and, 200–204; self-fulfillment and, 200–202; socio-economic forces, 193–200; symbolic interpretation, 197

Aging: accident theory of, 15; active, 198; activity theory of, 858–859; ageism, 17; arousal and, 261–295; atrophic changes in neurons, 103–106; behavior and, 216–244; brain function and, 727–731; cascade model of, 22–23; comparative approach to, 14–15; compression of senescence, 507; continuity theory of, 859; counterpart theory of, 15–17; cross-cultural research on, 218–219; culture and, 17, 192–193, 216–244; decreased inhibition, 282–287; definition of, 4–6; disease processes and, 507; disengagement theory of, 857–858; electroencephalogram frequencies, 268–269; eldering, 8; endogenous view of, 5, 19; environment and, 5–6, 13, 513–514; ethnicity and, 216–244; evolution of, 14–17; exogenous view of, 5, 19; extraneuronal structures and, 96–99; fixed cells and, 11–12; general concepts of, 501; genetics of, 13, 15–16, 129–138; geronting, 8; holocultural research, 218; human society and, 16–18; identity crisis theory of, 859; immune system and, 11; industrialization and, 231–235; in nonindustrial societies, 227–228; intellectual aging, 500, 515–519, 819–824; legends about, 6; leisure theories of, 857–860; mass aging, 198–200; maturity, 509–511; memory and, 427–462, 503; mental disorders and, 664–702; modernization and, 229–231; negative age, 21–22; neural basis of, 95–108; operational issues in studying, 18–23; personality and, 538–539; primary, 19–23; research design, 23–25, 35–60; secondary, 19, 21, 23; sleep and, 261–295; spiritual renewal and, 194–195; values and positions of, 190–215; in Western culture, 190–215
See also Age-status; Behavioral aging; Chronological age; Ecology of aging; Functional age; Longevity; Psychology of aging; Senescence; Slowing with age phenomenon

Alpha rhythms, 271–272

Alpha wave hypothesis, 415

921